THE EXPOSITOR'S BIBLE COMMENTARY

THE EXPOSITOR'S BIBLE COMMENTARY

in Thirteen Volumes

When complete, the Expositor's Bible Commentary will include the following volumes:

Volume 1: Genesis–Leviticus
Volume 2: Numbers–Ruth
Volume 3: 1 Samuel–2 Kings
Volume 4: 1 Chronicles–Job
Volume 5: Psalms
Volume 6: Proverbs–Isaiah
Volume 7: Jeremiah–Ezekiel
Volume 8: Daniel–Malachi
Volume 9: Matthew–Mark
Volume 10: Luke–Acts
Volume 11: Romans–Galatians
Volume 12: Ephesians–Philemon
Volume 13: Hebrews–Revelation

To see which titles are available, visit www.zondervan.com.

THE

EXPOSITOR'S BIBLE COMMENTARY

REVISED EDITION

Matthew ~ Mark

Tremper Longman III & David E. Garland

General Editors

ZONDERVAN ACADEMIC

Matthew and Mark

Published in Grand Rapids, Michigan, by Zondervan. Zondervan is a registered trademark of The Zondervan Corporation, L.L.C., a wholly owned subsidiary of HarperCollins Christian Publishing, Inc.

Requests for information should be addressed to customercare@harpercollins.com.

Zondervan titles may be purchased in bulk for educational, business, fundraising, or sales promotional use. For information, please email SpecialMarkets@Zondervan.com.

Library of Congress Cataloging-in-Publication Data

The expositor's Bible commentary / [general editors], Tremper Longman III and David E. Garland. – Rev.
p. cm.
Includes bibliographical references.
ISBN 978-0-310-26892-5
1. Bible. N.T. – Commentaries. I. Longman, Tremper. II. Garland, David E.
BS2341.53.E96 2005
220.7 – dc22 2005006281

Interior design: Tracey Walker

Printed in the United States of America

---

26 27 28 29 30 31 32 33 34 35 36 37 38 39 40 /TRM/ 32 31 30 29 28 27 26 25 24 23 22 21 20 19 18 17 16 15

CONTENTS

CONTRIBUTORS TO VOLUME NINE

Matthew: **D. A. Carson** (Ph.D., Cambridge University) is research professor of New Testament at Trinity Evangelical Divinity School in Deerfield, Illinois.

Mark: **Walter W. Wessel** (Ph.D., University of Edinburgh) was professor of New Testament and Greek studies at Bethel Seminary in San Diego, California.

Mark: **Mark L. Strauss** (Ph.D., University of Aberdeen) is professor of New Testament at Bethel Seminary in San Diego, California.

General editor: **Tremper Longman III** (Ph.D., Yale University) is Robert H. Gundry professor of biblical studies at Westmont College in Santa Barbara, California.

General editor: **David E. Garland** (Ph.D., Southern Baptist Theological Seminary) is dean and William M. Hinson professor of Christian Scriptures at George W. Truett Seminary, Baylor University, in Waco, Texas.

PREFACE

Frank Gaebelein wrote the following in the preface to the original Expositor's Bible Commentary (which first appeared in 1979): "The title of this work defines its purpose. Written primarily by expositors for expositors, it aims to provide preachers, teachers, and students of the Bible with a new and comprehensive commentary on the books of the Old and New Testaments." Those volumes achieved that purpose admirably. The original EBC was exceptionally well received and had an enormous impact on the life of the church. It has served as the mainstay of countless pastors and students who could not afford an extensive library on each book of the Bible but who wanted solid guidance from scholars committed to the authority of the Holy Scriptures.

Gaebelein also wrote, "A commentary that will continue to be useful through the years should handle contemporary trends in biblical studies in such a way as to avoid becoming outdated when critical fashions change." This revision continues the EBC's exalted purpose and stands on the shoulders of the expositors of the first edition, but it seeks to maintain the usefulness of the commentary by interacting with new discoveries and academic discussions. While the primary goal of this commentary is to elucidate the text and not to provide a guide to the scholarly literature about the text, the commentators critically engage recent academic discussion and provide updated bibliographies so that pastors, teachers, and students can keep abreast of modern scholarship.

Some of the commentaries in the EBC have been revised by the original author or in conjunction with a younger colleague. In other cases, scholars have been commissioned to offer fresh commentaries because the original author had passed on or wanted to pass on the baton to the next generation of evangelical scholars. Today, with commentaries on a single book of the Old and New Testaments often extending into multiple volumes, the need for a comprehensive yet succinct commentary that guides one to the gist of the text's meaning is even more pressing. The new EBC seeks to fill this need.

The theological stance of this commentary series remains unchanged: the authors are committed to the divine inspiration, complete trustworthiness, and full authority of the Bible. The commentators have demonstrated proficiency in the biblical book that is their specialty, as well as commitment to the church and the pastoral dimension of biblical interpretation. They also represent the geographical and confessional diversity that characterized the first contributors.

The commentaries adhere to the same chief principle of grammatico-historical interpretation that drove the first edition. In the foreword to the inaugural issue of the journal *New Testament Studies* in 1954, Matthew Black warned that "the danger in the present is that theology, with its head too high in the clouds, may end by falling into the pit of an unhistorical and uncritical dogmatism. Into any new theological undertaking must be brought all that was best in the old ideal of sound learning, scrupulous attention to philology, text and history." The dangers that Black warned against over fifty years ago have not vanished. Indeed, new dangers arise in a secular, consumerist culture that finds it more acceptable to use God's name in exclamations than in prayer and that encourages insipid theologies that hang in the wind and shift to tickle the ears and to meet the latest fancy. Only a solid biblical foundation can fend off these fads.

The Bible was not written for our information but for our transformation. It is not a quarry to find stones with which to batter others but to find the rock on which to build the church. It does not invite us simply to speak of God but to hear God and to confess that his Son, Jesus Christ, is Lord to the glory of God the Father (Php 2:10). It also calls us to obey his commandments (Mt 28:20). It is not a self-interpreting text, however. Interpretation of the Holy Scriptures requires sound learning and regard for history, language, and text. Exegetes must interpret not only the primary documents but all that has a bearing, direct or indirect, on the grammar and syntax, historical context, transmission, and translation of these writings.

The translation used in this commentary remains the New International Version (North American edition), but all of the commentators work from the original languages (Hebrew and Greek) and draw on other translations when deemed useful. The format is also very similar to the original EBC, while the design is extensively updated with a view to enhanced ease of use for the reader. Each commentary section begins with an introduction (printed in a single-column format) that provides the reader with the background necessary to understand the Bible book. Almost all introductions include a short bibliography and an outline. The Bible text is divided into primary units that are often explained in an "Overview" section that precedes commentary on specific verses. The complete text of the New International Version is provided for quick reference, and an extensive "Commentary" section (printed in a double-column format) follows the reproducing of the text. When the Hebrew or Greek text is cited in the commentary section, a phonetic system of transliteration and translation is used. The "Notes" section (printed in a single-column format) provides a specialized discussion of key words or concepts, as well as helpful resource information. The original languages and their transliterations will appear in this section. Finally, on occasion, expanded thoughts can be found in a "Reflections" section (printed in a double-column format) that follows the Notes section.

One additional feature is worth mentioning. Throughout this volume, wherever specific biblical words are discussed, the Goodrick-Kohlenberger (GK) numbers have been added. These numbers, which appear in the *Strongest NIV Exhaustive Concordance* and other reference tools, are based on the numbering system developed by Edward Goodrick and John Kohlenberger III and provide a system similar but superior to the Strong's numbering system.

The editors wish to thank all of the contributors for their hard work and commitment to this project. We also deeply appreciate the labor and skill of the staff at Zondervan. It is a joy to work with them—in particular Jack Kuhatschek, Stan Gundry, Katya Covrett, and Dirk Buursma. In addition, we acknowledge with thanks the work of Connie Gundry Tappy as copy editor.

We all fervently desire that these commentaries will result not only in a deeper intellectual grasp of the Word of God but also in hearts that more profoundly love and obey the God who reveals himself to us in its pages.

David E. Garland, associate dean for academic affairs and William M. Hinson professor of Christian Scriptures, George W. Truett Theological Seminary at Baylor University

Tremper Longman III, Robert H. Gundry professor of biblical studies, Westmont College

ABBREVIATIONS

Bible Texts, Versions, Etc.

ASV	American Standard Version
AT	*The Complete Bible: An American Translation* (NT: E. J. Goodspeed)
Barclay	*The New Testament, A New Translation*
Beck	*New Testament in Language of Today*
BHK	*Biblia Hebraica Kittel*
BHS	*Biblia Hebraica Stuttgartensia*
CEV	Contemporary English Version
CSB	Christian Standard Bible
ESV	English Standard Version
GNB	Good News Bible (see also TEV)
GWT	God's Word Translation
JB	Jerusalem Bible
KJV	King James Version
Knox	*Holy Bible: A Translation from the Latin Vulgate*
MLB	Modern Language Bible
Moffatt	*A New Translation of the Bible*, James Moffatt
Montgomery	*Centenary Translation of the New Testament in Modern English*
NA^{27}	*Novum Testamentum Graece*, Nestle-Aland, 27th ed.
NAB	New American Bible
NASB	New American Standard Bible
NCV	New Century Version
NEB	New English Bible
NET	New English Translation (www.netbible.com)
NIV	New International Version
NJB	New Jerusalem Bible
NJPS	New Jewish Publication Society
NKJV	New King James Version
NLT	New Living Translation
Norlie	*New Testament in Modern English*
NRSV	New Revised Standard Version
Phillips	*New Testament in Modern English*, J. B. Phillips
REB	Revised English Bible
Rieu	*Penguin Bible*
RSV	Revised Standard Version
RV	Revised Version
Tanakh	Tanakh, a Jewish translation of the Hebrew Bible
TCNT	Twentieth Century New Testament
TEV	Today's English Version
TNIV	Today's New International Version
UBS^4	*The Greek New Testament*, United Bible Societies, 4th ed.
Weymouth	*New Testament in Modern Speech*, R. F. Weymouth
Williams	*The New Testament in the Language of the People*, C. B. Williams

Old Testament, New Testament, Apocrypha

Ge	Genesis	Mt	Matthew
Ex	Exodus	Mk	Mark
Lev	Leviticus	Lk	Luke
Nu	Numbers	Jn	John
Dt	Deuteronomy	Ac	Acts
Jos	Joshua	Ro	Romans
Jdg	Judges	1–2Co	1–2 Corinthians
Ru	Ruth	Gal	Galatians
1–2Sa	1–2 Samuel	Eph	Ephesians
1–2 Kgdms	1–2 Kingdoms (LXX)	Php	Philippians
1–2Ki	1–2 Kings	Col	Colossians
3–4 Kgdms	3–4 Kingdoms (LXX)	1–2Th	1–2 Thessalonians
1–2Ch	1–2 Chronicles	1–2Ti	1–2 Timothy
Ezr	Ezra	Tit	Titus
Ne	Nehemiah	Phm	Philemon
Est	Esther	Heb	Hebrews
Job	Job	Jas	James
Ps/Pss	Psalm/Psalms	1–2Pe	1–2 Peter
Pr	Proverbs	1–2–3Jn	1–2–3 John
Ecc	Ecclesiastes	Jude	Jude
SS	Song of Songs	Rev	Revelation
Isa	Isaiah	Add Esth	Additions to Esther
Jer	Jeremiah	Add Dan	Additions to Daniel
La	Lamentations	Bar	Baruch
Eze	Ezekiel	Bel	Bel and the Dragon
Da	Daniel	Ep Jer	Epistle of Jeremiah
Hos	Hosea	1–2 Esd	1–2 Esdras
Joel	Joel	1–2 Macc	1–2 Maccabees
Am	Amos	3–4 Macc	3–4 Maccabees
Ob	Obadiah	Jdt	Judith
Jnh	Jonah	Pr Azar	Prayer of Azariah
Mic	Micah	Pr Man	Prayer of Manasseh
Na	Nahum	Ps 151	Psalm 151
Hab	Habakkuk	Sir	Sirach/Ecclesiasticus
Zep	Zephaniah	Sus	Susanna
Hag	Haggai	Tob	Tobit
Zec	Zechariah	Wis	Wisdom of Solomon
Mal	Malachi		

Dead Sea Scrolls and Related Texts

CD	Cairo Genizah copy of the *Damascus Document*
DSS	Dead Sea Scrolls
1QapGen	*Genesis Apocryphon* (texts from Qumran)
1QH	*Hôdāyōt* or *Thanksgiving Hymns* (texts from Qumran)
1QIsa	Isaiah (texts from Qumran)
1QM	*Milḥâmâh* or *War Scroll* (texts from Qumran)
1QpHab	Pesher Habakkuk (texts from Qumran)
1QS	*Serek hayyaḥad* or *Rule of the Community* (texts from Qumran)
1QSa	*Rule of the Congregation* (texts from Qumran)
1QpMic	*Pesher Micah* (text from Qumran)
4QpNa	*Pesher Nahum* (texts from Qumran)
4QpPs	*Pesher Psalms* (texts from Qumran)
4Q44 (4QDt^{q})	Deuteronomy (texts from Qumran)
4Q174	*Florilegium* (texts from Qumran)
4Q252	*Commentary on Genesis A*, formerly *Patriarchal Blessings* (texts from Qumran)
4Q394	*Miqṣat Maʿáśê ha-Torah^{a}* (texts from Qumran)
4Q400	*Songs of the Sabbath Sacrifice* (texts from Qumran)
4Q502	*Ritual of Marriage* (texts from Qumran)
4Q521	*Messianic Apocalypse* (texts from Qumran)
4Q525	*Beatitudes* (texts from Qumran)
11QPs^{a}	*Psalms Scroll^{a}*
11Q13	*Melchizedek* (texts from Qumran)
11QT^{a}	Temple Scroll^{a}

Other Ancient Texts

ʾAbot R. Nat.	*ʾAbot of Rabbi Nathan*
Abraham	*On the Life of Abraham* (Philo)
Ad.	*Adelphi* (Terence)
Aeth.	*Aethiopica* (Heliodorus)
Ag.	*Agamemnon* (Aeschylus)
Ag. Ap.	*Against Apion* (Josephus)
Agr.	*De Lege agraria* (Cicero)
Alc.	*Alcibiades* (Plutarch)
Alex.	*Alexander the False Prophet* (Lucian)
Amic.	*De amicitia* (Cicero)
An.	*De anima* (Tertullian)
Anab.	*Anabasis* (Xenophon)
Ann.	*Annales* (Tacitus)
Ant.	*Antigone* (Sophocles)
Ant.	*Jewish Antiquities* (Josephus)
Ant. rom.	*Antiquitates romanae* (Dionysius of Halicarnassus)
1 Apol.	*First Apology* (Justin Martyr)
Apol.	*Apologia* (Plato, Tertullian)
Apos. Con.	*Apostolic Constitutions*
Ascen. Isa.	*Ascension of Isaiah*
As. Mos.	*Assumption of Moses*
Att.	*Epistulae ad Atticum* (Cicero)
Aug.	*Divus Augustus* (Suetonius)
b. ʿAbod. Zar.	*ʿAbodah Zarah* (Babylonian Talmud)
2–4 Bar.	*2–4 Baruch*
b. ʿAbod. Zar.	*ʿAbodah Zarah* (Babylonian Talmud)
b. ʿArak	*ʿArakin* (Babylonian Talmud)
b. B. Bat.	*Bava Batra* (Babylonian Talmud)

b. B. Meṣ. — *Baba Meṣ'a* (Babylonian Talmud)
b. B. Qam. — *Baba Qamma* (Babylonian Talmud)
b. Ber. — *Berakhot* (Babylonian Talmud)
b. Ḥag. — *Ḥagigah* (Babylonian Talmud)
b. Hor. — *Horayot* (Babylonian Talmud)
b. Ker. — *Kerithot* (Babylonian Talmud)
b. Ketub. — *Ketubbot* (Babylonian Talmud)
b. Meg. — *Megillah* (Babylonian Talmud)
b. Menaḥ. — *Menaḥot* (Babylonian Talmud)
b. Mo'ed Qat. — *Mo'ed Qatan* (Babylonian Talmud)
b. Ned. — *Nedarim* (Babylonian Talmud)
b. Pesaḥ. — *Pesaḥim* (Babylonian Talmud)
b. Roš Haš. — *b. Roš Haššanah* (Babylonian Talmud)
b. Šabb. — *Šabbat* (Babylonian Talmud)
b. Sanh. — *Sanhedrin* (Babylonian Talmud)
b. Šebu. — *Shevu'ot* (Babylonian Talmud)
b. Soṭah — *Soṭah* (Babylonian Talmud)
b. Ta'an. — *Ta'anit* (Babylonian Talmud)
b. Yebam. — *Yebamot* (Babylonian Talmud)
b. Yoma — *Yoma* (Babylonian Talmud)
Bapt. — *De baptismo* (Tertullian)
Barn. — *Barnabas*
Ben. — *De beneficiis* (Seneca)
Bibl. — *Bibliotheca* (Photius)
Bibl. hist. — *Bibliotheca historica* (Diodorus Siculus)
Brev. coll. — *Breviculus Collationis cum Donatistis* (Augustine)
Bride — *Advice to the Bride and Groom* (Plutarch)
Cant. Rab. — *Canticles* (Song of Solomon) *Rabbah*
Cels. — *Contra Celsum* (Origen)
Cic. — *Cicero* (Plutarch)
Claud. — *Divus Claudius* (Suetonius)
1–2 Clem. — *1–2 Clement*
Comm. Dan. — *Commentarium in Danielem* (Hippolytus)
Comm. Jo. — *Commentarii in evangelium Joannis* (Origen)
Comm. Matt. — *Commentarium in evangelium Matthaei* (Origen)
Corrept. — *De correptione et gratia* (Augustine)
Cyr. — *Cyropaedia* (Xenophon)
Decal. — *De decalogo* (Philo)
Decl. — *Declamationes* (Quintilian)
Def. orac. — *De defectu oraculorum* (Plutarch)
Deipn. — *Deipnosophistae* (Athenaeus)
Deut. Rab. — *Deuteronomy Rabbah*
Dial. — *Dialogus cum Tryphone* (Justin Martyr)
Diatr. — *Diatribai* (Epictetus)
Did. — *Didache*
Disc. — *Discourses* (Epictetus)
Doctr. chr. — *De doctrina christiana* (Augustine)
Dom. — *Domitianus* (Suetonius)
Don. — *Post collationem adversus Donatistas* (Augustine)
Ebr. — *De ebrietate* (Philo)
Ecl. — *Eclogae* (Virgil)
E Delph. — *De E apud Delphos* (Plutarch)
1–2 En. — *1–2 Enoch*
Ench. — *Enchiridion* (Epictetus)
Ep. — *Epistulae morales* (Seneca)
Eph. — *To the Ephesians* (Ignatius)
Epist. — *Epistulae* (Jerome, Pliny, Hippocrates)
Ep. Tra. — *Epistulae ad Trajanum* (Pliny)
Eth. nic. — *Ethica nichomachea* (Aristotle)
Exod. Rab. — *Exodus Rabbah*
Fam. — *Epistulae ad familiares* (Cicero)
Fast. — *Fasti* (Ovid)
Fid. Grat. — *De fide ad Gratianum* (Ambrose)
Flacc. — *In Flaccum* (Philo)
Flight — *On Flight and Finding* (Philo)
Fr. Prov. — *Fragmenta in Proverbia* (Hippolytus)
Gen. Rab. — *Genesis Rabbah*
Geogr. — *Geographica* (Strabo)

Gorg.	*Gorgias* (Plato)
Haer.	*Adversus Haereses* (Irenaeus)
Hec.	*Hecuba* (Euripides)
Heir	*Who Is the Heir?* (Philo)
Hell.	*Hellenica* (Xenophon)
Hist.	*Historicus* (Polybius, Cassius Dio, Thucydides)
Hist.	*Historiae* (Herodotus, Tacitus)
Hist. eccl.	*History of the Church* (Eusebius)
Hist. Rome	*The History of Rome* (Livy)
Hom. Acts	*Homilies on Acts* (John Chrysostom)
Hom. Col.	*Homilies on Colossians* (John Chrysostom)
Hom. Jo.	*Homilies on John* (John Chrysostom)
Hom. Josh.	*Homilies on Joshua* (Origen)
Hom. Phil.	*Homilies on Philippians* (John Chrysostom)
Hom. Rom.	*Homilies on Romans* (John Chrysostom)
Hom. 1 Tim.	*Homilies on 1 Timothy* (John Chrysostom)
Hom. 2 Tim.	*Homilies on 2 Timothy* (John Chrysostom)
Hom. Tit.	*Homilies on Titus* (John Chrysostom)
Hypoth.	*Hypothetica* (Philo)
Il.	*Iliad* (Homer)
Inst.	*Institutio oratoria* (Quintilian)
Jos. Asen.	*Joseph and Aseneth*
Joseph	*On the Life of Joseph* (Philo)
Jub.	*Jubilees*
J.W.	*Jewish War* (Josephus)
Lam. Rab.	*Lamentations Rabbah*
L.A.E.	*Life of Adam and Eve*
Leg.	*Legum allegoriae* (Philo)
Legat.	*Legatio ad Gaium* (Philo)
Let. Aris.	*Letter of Aristeas*
Lev. Rab.	*Leviticus Rabbah*

Life	*The Life of Flavius Josephus* (Josephus)
Liv. Pro.	*Lives of the Prophets*
m. Bek.	*Bekhorot* (Mishnah)
m. Ber.	*Berakot* (Mishnah).
m. Beṣah	*Beṣah* (Mishnah)
m. Bik.	*Bikkurim* (Mishnah)
m. B. Meṣ.	*Baba Meṣʿa* (Mishnah)
m. B. Qam.	*Baba Qamma* (Mishnah)
m. ʿEd.	*ʿEduyyot* (Mishnah)
m. Giṭ.	*Giṭṭin* (Mishnah)
m. Ḥag.	*Ḥagigah* (Mishnah)
m. Ketub.	*Ketubbot* (Mishnah)
m. Maʿaś. Š.	*Maʿaśer Šeni* (Mishnah)
m. Mak.	*Makkot* (Mishnah)
m. Mid.	*Middot* (Mishnah)
m. Moʿed Qaṭ.	*Moʿed Qaṭan* (Mishnah)
m. Naz.	*Nazir* (Mishnah)
m. Ned.	*Nedarim* (Mishnah)
m. Nid.	*Niddah* (Mishnah)
m. Pesaḥ.	*Pesaḥim* (Mishnah)
m. Qidd.	*Qiddušin* (Mishnah)
m. Roš Haš.	*Roš Haššanah* (Mishnah)
m. Šabb.	*Šabbat* (Mishnah)
m. Sanh.	*Sanhedrin* (Mishnah)
m. Šebu.	*Šebuʿot* (Mishnah)
m. Šeqal.	*Šeqalim* (Mishnah)
m. Taʿan.	*Taʿanit* (Mishnah)
m. Ṭehar.	*Ṭeharot* (Mishnah)
m. Yad.	*Yadayim* (Mishnah)
m. Yebam.	*Yebamot* (Mishnah)
m. Zebaḥ.	*Zebaḥim* (Mishnah)
Magn.	*To the Magnesians* (Ignatius)
Mand.	*Mandate* (Shepherd of Hermas)
Marc.	*Adversus Marcionem* (Tertullian)
Mek.	*Mekilta*
Mem.	*Memorabilia* (Xenophon)
Midr. Ps.	*Midrash on Psalms*
Migr.	*De migratione Abrahami* (Philo)
Mor.	*Moralia* (Plutarch)

Moses	*On the Life of Moses* (Philo)	*Rhet.*	*Volumina rhetorica* (Philodemus)
Nat.	*Naturalis historia* (Pliny)	*Rom.*	*To the Romans* (Ignatius)
Num. Rab.	*Numbers Rabbah*	*Rosc. com.*	*Pro Roscio comoedo* (Cicero)
Od.	*Odyssey* (Homer)	*Sacrifices*	*On the Sacrifices of Cain and Abel* (Philo)
Onir.	*Onirocritica* (Artemidorus)		
Or.	*Orationes* (Demosthenes)	*Sat.*	*Satirae* (Horace, Juvenal)
Or.	*Orationes* (Dio Chrysostom)	*Sera*	*De sera numinis vindicta* (Plutarch)
Paed.	*Paedagogus* (Clement of Alexandria)	*Serm.*	*Sermones* (Augustine)
		Sib. Or.	*Sibylline Oracles*
Peregr.	*The Passing of Peregrinus* (Lucian)	*Sim.*	*Similitudes* (Shepherd of Hermas)
Pesiq. Rab.	*Pesiqta Rabbati*	*Smyrn.*	*To the Smyrnaeans* (Ignatius)
Pesiq. Rab Kah.	*Pesiqta of Rab Kahana*	*S. ᶜOlam Rab.*	*Seder ᶜOlam Rabbah*
Phaed.	*Phaedo* (Plato)	*Somn.*	*De somniis* (Philo)
Phil.	*To the Philippians* (Polycarp)	*Spec.*	*De specialibus legibus* (Philo)
Phld.	*To the Philadelphians* (Ignatius)	*Stat.*	*Ad populum Antiochenum de statuis* (John Chrysostom)
Phorm.	*Phormio* (Terence)		
Planc.	*Pro Plancio* (Cicero)	*Strom.*	*Stromata* (Clement of Alexandria)
Plant.	*De plantatione* (Philo)	*T. Ash.*	*Testament of Asher*
Pol.	*Politica* (Aristotle)	*T. Benj.*	*Testament of Benjamin*
Pol.	*To Polycarp* (Ignatius)	*T. Dan*	*Testament of Dan*
Posterity	*On the Posterity of Cain* (Origen)	*T. Gad*	*Testament of Gad*
Praescr.	*De praescriptione haereticorum* (Tertullian)	*T. Iss.*	*Testament of Issachar*
		T. Naph.	*Testament of Naphtali*
Princ.	*De principiis* (Origen)	*Tg. Neof.*	*Targum Neofiti*
Prom.	*Prometheus vinctus* (Aeschylus)	*Tg. Onq.*	*Targum Onqelos*
Prot. Jas.	*Protevangelium of James*	*Tg. Ps.-J.*	*Targum Pseudo-Jonathan*
Pss. Sol.	*Psalms of Solomon*	*Tg. Yer. I*	*Targum Yerušalmi I*
Pud.	*De pudicitia* (Tertullian)	*Tg. Zec.*	*Targum Zechariah*
Pyth.	*Pythionikai* (Pindar)	*Theaet.*	*Theaetetus* (Plato)
Pyth. orac.	*De Pythiae oraculis* (Plutarch)	*t. Ḥul.*	*Ḥullin* (Tosefta)
Quaest. conv.	*Quaestionum convivialum libri IX* (Plutarch)	*T. Jos.*	*Testament of Joseph*
		T. Jud.	*Testament of Judah*
Quint. fratr.	*Epistulae ad Quintum fratrem* (Cicero)	*T. Levi*	*Testament of Levi*
		T. Mos.	*Testament of Moses*
Rab. Perd.	*Pro Rabirio Perduellionis Reo* (Cicero)	*T. Naph.*	*Testament of Naphtali*
		t. Ned.	*Nedarim* (Tosefta)
Resp.	*Respublica* (Plato)	*Trall.*	*To the Trallians* (Ignatius)
Rewards	*On Rewards and Punishments* (Philo)	*T. Reu.*	*Testament of Reuben*
		t. Sanh.	*Sanhedrin* (Tosefta)
Rhet.	*Rhetorica* (Aristotle)	*Tusc.*	*Tusculanae disputationes* (Cicero)

Verr.	*In Verrem* (Cicero)	*Vit. soph.*	*Vitae sophistarum* (Philostratus)
Vesp.	*Vespasianus* (Suetonius)	*y. ʿAbod. Zar.*	*ʿAbodah Zarah* (Jerusalem Talmud)
Virt.	*De virtutibus* (Philo)	*y. Ber.*	*Berakot* (Jerusalem Talmud)
Vis.	*Visions* (Shepherd of Hermas)	*y. Ḥag.*	*Ḥagigah* (Jerusalem Talmud)
Vit. Apoll.	*Vita Apollonii* (Philostratus)	*y. Pesaḥ.*	*Pesaḥim* (Jerusalem Talmud)
Vit. beat.	*De vita beata* (Seneca)	*y. Šabb.*	*Šabbat* (Jerusalem Talmud)

Journals, Periodicals, Reference Works, Series

AASOR	Annual of the American Schools of Oriental Research
AB	Anchor Bible
ABD	*Anchor Bible Dictionary*
ABR	*Australian Biblical Review*
AbrN	*Abr-Nahrain*
ABRL	Anchor Bible Reference Library
ABW	*Archaeology in the Biblical World*
ACCS	Ancient Christian Commentary on Scripture
ACNT	Augsburg Commentaries on the New Testament
AcT	*Acta theological*
AGAJU	Arbeiten zur Geschichte des antiken Judentums und des Urchristentums
AIs	*Ancient Israel, by Roland de Vaux*
AJBI	*Annual of the Japanese Biblical Institute*
AJSL	*American Journal of Semitic Languages and Literature*
AnBib	Analecta biblica
ANEP	*The Ancient Near East in Pictures Relating to the Old Testament*
ANET	*Ancient Near Eastern Texts Relating to the Old Testament*
ANF	*Ante-Nicene Fathers*
AnOr	Analecta orientalia
ANRW	*Aufstieg und Niedergang der römischen Welt*
AOAT	Alter Orient und Altes Testament
AR	*Archiv für Religionssissenschaft*
ASORMS	American Schools of Oriental Research Monograph Series
ASTI	*Annual of the Swedish Theological Institute*
AThR	*Anglican Theological Review*
ATLA	American Theological Library Association
AuOr	Aula orientalis
AUSDDS	Andrews University Seminary Doctoral Dissertation Series
AUSS	*Andrews University Seminary Studies*
BA	*Biblical Archaeologist*
BAGD	Bauer, Arndt, Gingrich, and Danker (2d ed.). *Greek-English Lexicon of the New Testament and Other Early Christian Literature*
BAR	*Biblical Archaeology Review*
BASOR	*Bulletin of the American Schools of Oriental Research*
BBB	Bonner biblische Beiträge
BBR	*Bulletin for Biblical Research*
BCPE	*Bulletin du Centre protestant d'études*
BDAG	Bauer, Danker, Arndt, and Gingrich (3d ed.). *Greek-English Lexicon of the New Testament and Other Early Christian Literature*
BDB	Brown, Driver, and Briggs. *A Hebrew and English Lexicon of the Old Testament*

BDF	Blass, Debrunner, and Funk. *A Greek Grammar of the New Testament and Other Early Christian Literature*
BEB	*Baker Encyclopedia of the Bible*
BECNT	Baker Exegetical Commentary on the New Testament
Ber	*Berytus*
BETL	Bibliotheca ephemeridum theologicarum lovaniensium
BGU	*Aegyptische Urkunden aus den Königlichen Staatlichen Museen zu Berlin, Griechische Urkunden*
BI	*Biblical Illustrator*
Bib	*Biblica*
BibInt	*Biblical Interpretation*
BibOr	Biblica et orientalia
BibS(N)	Biblische Studien (Neukirchen)
Bijdr	*Bijdragen: Tijdschrit voor filosofie en theologie*
BJRL	*Bulletin of the John Rylands University Library of Manchester*
BJS	Brown Judaic Studies
BKAT	Biblischer Kommentar, Altes Testament
BN	*Biblische Notizen*
BR	*Biblical Research*
BRev	*Bible Review*
BSac	*Bibliotheca sacra*
BST	The Bible Speaks Today
BT	*The Bible Translator*
BTB	*Biblical Theology Bulletin*
BTh	*Bibliotheca theological*
BWANT	Beiträge zur Wissenschaft zum Alter und Neuen Testament
BZ	*Biblische Zeitschrift*
BZAW	Beihefte zur Zeitschrift für die alttestamentliche Wissenschaft
BZNW	Beihefte zur Zeitschrift für die neutestamentliche Wissenschaft
CAD	*Assyrian Dictionary of the Oriental Institute of the University of Chicago*
CAH	Cambridge Ancient History
CahRB	Cahiers de la Revue biblique
Case	*Centre for Apologetic Scholarship and Education*
CBC	Cambridge Bible Commentary
CBQ	*Catholic Biblical Quarterly*
CBQMS	Catholic Biblical Quarterly Monograph Series
CGTC	Cambridge Greek Testament Commentary
CH	*Church History*
ChrT	*Christianity Today*
CHS	Johann Peter Lange, *Commentary on the Holy Scriptures*
CIG	*Corpus inscriptionum graecarum*
CIL	*Corpus inscriptionum latinarum*
CJT	*Canadian Journal of Theology*
CNTUOT	*Commentary on the New Testament Use of the Old Testament*
ConBNT	Coniectanea biblica: New Testament Series
ConBOT	Coniectanea biblica: Old Testament Series
COS	*The Context of Scripture*
CTJ	*Calvin Theological Journal*
CTM	*Concordia Theological Monthly*
CTQ	*Concordia Theological Quarterly*
CTR	*Criswell Theological Review*
DDD	*Dictionary of Deities and Demons in the Bible*
DJD	Discoveries in the Judean Desert
DRev	*Downside Review*
DukeDivR	*Duke Divinity Review*
EA	El-Amarna tablets
EBC	Expositor's Bible Commentary
EBib	*Études bibliques*
EBr	*Encyclopedia Britannica*

ECC	Eerdmans Critical Commentary
EcR	*Ecumenical Review*
EDNT	*Exegetical Dictionary of the New Testament*
EgT	*Eglise et théologie*
EGT	Expositor's Greek Testament
EncJud	*Encyclopedia Judaica*
ErIsr	*Eretz-Israel*
ERT	*Evangelical Review of Theology*
ESCJ	Etudes sur le christianisme et le judaisme (Studies in Christianity and Judaism)
EstBib	*Estudios bíblicos*
ETL	*Ephemerides theologicae Lovanienses*
ETR	*Études théologiques et religieuses*
ETS	Evangelical Theological Society
EuroJTh	*European Journal of Theology*
EvJ	*Evangelical Journal*
EvQ	*Evangelical Quarterly*
EvT	*Evangelische Theologie*
ExAud	*Ex auditu*
Exeg	*Exegetica*
ExpTim	*Expository Times*
FF	Foundations and Facets
FRLANT	Forschungen zur Religion und Literatur des Alten und Neuen Testaments
GBS	Guides to Biblical Scholarship
GKC	*Genesius' Hebrew Grammar*
GNS	*Good News Studies*
GR	*Greece and Rome*
Grammar	*A Grammar of the Greek New Testament; in the Light of Historical Research* (A. T. Robertson)
GRBS	*Greek, Roman, and Byzantine Studies*
HALOT	Koehler, Baumgartner, and Stamm. *The Hebrew and Aramaic Lexicon of the Old Testament*
HAR	*Hebrew Annual Review*
HAT	handbuch zum Alten Testament
HBD	*HarperCollins Bible Dictionary*
HBT	*Horizons in Biblical Theology*
Herm	Hermeneia commentary series
HeyJ	*Heythrop Journal*
HNT	Handbuch zum Neuen Testament
HNTC	Harper's New Testament Commentaries
Hor	*Horizons*
HS	*Hebrew Studies*
HSM	Harvard Semitic Monographs
HSS	Harvard Semitic Studies
HTKNT	Herders theologischer Kommentar zum Neuen Testament
HTR	*Harvard Theological Review*
HTS	Harvard Theological Studies
HUBP	Hebrew Union Bible Project
HUCA	*Hebrew Union College Annual*
IB	*Interpreter's Bible*
IBC	Interpretation: A Bible Commentary for Teaching and Preaching
IBHS	*An Introduction to Biblical Hebrew Syntax*
IBS	*Irish Biblical Studies*
ICC	International Critical Commentary
IDB	*Interpreter's Dictionary of the Bible*
IDBSup	*Interpreter's Dictionary of the Bible: Supplement*
IEJ	*Israel Exploration Journal*
IJT	*Indian Journal of Theology*
Imm	*Immanuel*
Int	*Interpretation*
ISBE	*International Standard Bible Encyclopedia*, 2d ed.
IVPBBC	IVP Bible Background Commentary
IVPNTC	IVP New Testament Commentary

JAAR	*Journal of the American Academy of Religion*
JAARSup	JAAR Supplement Series
JANESCU	*Journal of the Ancient Near Eastern Society of Columbia University*
JAOS	*Journal of the American Oriental Society*
JAOSSup	Journal of the American Oriental Society Supplement Series
JBL	*Journal of Biblical Literature*
JBMW	*Journal for Biblical Manhood and Womanhood*
JBQ	*Jewish Biblical Quaterly*
JBR	*Journal of Bible and Religion*
JCS	*Journal of Cuneiform Studies*
Jeev	*Jeevadhara*
JE	*Jewish Encyclopedia*
JETS	*Journal of the Evangelical Theological Society*
JJS	*Journal of Jewish Studies*
JNES	*Journal of Near Eastern Studies*
JNSL	*Journal of Northwest Semitic Languages*
JPOS	*Journal of the Palestine Oriental Society*
JQR	*Jewish Quarterly Review*
JRS	*Journal of Roman Studies*
JSHJ	*Journal for the Study of the Historical Jesus*
JSNT	*Journal for the Study of the New Testament*
JSNTSup	JSNT Supplement Series
JSOT	*Journal for the Study of the Old Testament*
JSOTSup	JSOT Supplement Series
JSP	*Journal for the Study of the Pseudepigrapha*
JSS	*Journal of Semitic Studies*
JSSEA	*Journal of the Society for the Study of Egyptian Antiquities*
JTC	*Journal for Theology and the Church*
JTS	*Journal of Theological Studies*
K&D	Keil and Delitzsch, *Biblical Commentary on the Old Testament*
KB	Koehler-Baumgartner, *Hebräisches und Aramäisches Lexicon zum Alten Testament* (first or second edition; third edition is *HALOT*)
KEK	Kritisch-exegetischer Kommentar über das Neue Testament
KTU	*Die keilalphabetischen Texte aus Ugarit*
L&N	Louw and Nida. *Greek-English Lexicon of the New Testament: Based on Semantic Domains*
LCC	Library of Christian Classics
LCL	Loeb Classical Library
LEC	Library of Early Christianity
LNTS	Library of New Testament Studies
LS	*Louvain Studies*
LSJ	Liddell, Scott, and Jones. *A Greek-English Lexicon*
LTP	*Laval théologique et philosophique*
MM	Moulton and Milligan. *The Vocabulary of the Greek Testament*
MSJ	*The Master's Seminary Journal*
NAC	New American Commentary
NBC	*New Bible Commentary*, rev. ed.
NBD	*New Bible Dictionary*, 2d ed.
NCBC	New Century Bible Commentary
Neot	*Neotestamentica*
NewDocs	*New Documents Illustrating Early Christianity*
NIBC	New International Biblical Commentary
NICNT	New International Commentary on the New Testament
NICOT	New International Commentary on the Old Testament

NIDNTT	*New International Dictionary of New Testament Theology*
NIDOTTE	*New International Dictionary of Old Testament Theology and Exegesis*
NIGTC	New International Greek Testament Commentary
NIVAC	NIV Application Commentary
NIVSB	Zondervan NIV Study Bible
Notes	*Notes on Translation*
NovT	*Novum Testamentum*
NovTSup	Novum Testamentum Supplements
NPNF	*Nicene and Post-Nicene Fathers*
NRTh	*La nouvelle revue théologique*
NSBT	New Testament Studies in Biblical Theology
NTC	New Testament Commentary (Baker)
NTD	Das Neue Testament Deutsch
NTG	New Testament Guides
NTOA	Novum Testamentum et orbis antiquus
NTS	*New Testament Studies*
NTT	New Testament Theology
NTTS	New Testament Tools and Studies
OBO	Orbis biblicus et orientalis
OJRS	*Ohio Journal of Religious Studies*
OLA	Orientalia lovaniensia analecta
Or	*Orientalia* (NS)
OTE	Old Testament Essays
OTG	Old Testament Guides
OTL	Old Testament Library
OTS	Old Testament Studies
OtSt	*Oudtestamentische Studien*
PEGLMBS	*Proceedings, Eastern Great Lakes and Midwest Bible Societies*
PEQ	*Palestine Exploration Quarterly*
PG	Patrologia graeca
PL	Patrologia latina
PNTC	Pillar New Testament Commentary
Presb	*Presbyterion*
PresR	*Presbyterian Review*
PRSt	*Perspectives in Religious Studies*
PTMS	Pittsburgh Theological Monograph Series
PTR	*Princeton Theological Review*
RB	*Revue biblique*
RBibLit	*Review of Biblical Literature*
RefJ	*Reformed Journal*
RelSRev	*Religious Studies Review*
ResQ	*Restoration Quarterly*
RevExp	*Review and Expositor*
RevQ	*Revue de Qumran*
RevScRel	*Revue des sciences religieuses*
RHPR	*Revue d'histoire et de philosophie religieuses*
RTR	*Reformed Theological Review*
SAOC	Studies in Ancient Oriental Civilizations
SBB	Stuttgarter biblische Beiträge
SBG	Studies in Biblical Greek
SBJT	*Southern Baptist Journal of Theology*
SBLDS	Society of Biblical Literature Dissertation Series
SBLSP	*Society of Biblical Literature Seminar Papers*
SBLWAW	Society of Biblical Literature Writings from the Ancient World
SBT	*Studies in Biblical Theology*
ScEccl	*Sciences ecclésiastiques*
ScEs	*Science et esprit*
ScrHier	Scripta hierosolymitana
SE	*Studia evangelica*
SEG	Supplementum epigraphicum graecum
Sem	*Semitica*
SJLA	Studies in Judaism of Late Antiquity

SJT — *Scottish Journal of Theology*
SNT — Studien zum Neuen Testament
SNTSMS — Society for New Testament Studies Monograph Series
SNTSU — Studien zum Neuen Testament und seiner Umwelt
SP — Sacra Pagina
SR — *Studies in Religion*
ST — *Studia theologica*
Str-B — Strack, H. L., and P. Billerbeck, *Kommentar zum Neuen Testament aus Talmud und Midrasch*
StudBT — *Studia biblica et theologica*
SUNT — Studien zur Umwelt des Neuen Testaments
SVF — *Stoicorum veterum fragmenta*
SVT — Studia in Veteris Testamenti
SwJT — *Southwestern Journal of Theology*
TA — *Tel Aviv*
TBl — *Theologische Blätter*
TBT — *The Bible Today*
TDNT — Kittel and Friedrich. *Theological Dictionary of the New Testament*
TDOT — Botterweck and Ringgren. *Theological Dictionary of the Old Testament*
TF — *Theologische Forschung*
THAT — *Theologisches Handwörterbuch zum Alten Testament*
Them — *Themelios*
ThEv — *Theologia Evangelica*
THKNT — Theologischer Handkommentar zum Neuen Testament
ThR — *Theologische Rundschau*
ThTo — *Theology Today*
TJ — *Trinity Journal*
TLNT — *Theological Lexicon of the New Testament*
TLOT — *Theological Lexicon of the Old Testament*
TLZ — *Theologische Literaturzeitung*
TNTC — Tyndale New Testament Commentaries
TOTC — Tyndale Old Testament Commentaries
TQ — *Theologische Quartalschrift*
TS — *Theological Studies*
TSAJ — Texte und Studien zum antiken Judentum
TWOT — *Theological Wordbook of the Old Testament*
TynBul — *Tyndale Bulletin*
TZ — *Theologische Zeitschrift*
UBD — *Unger's Bible Dictionary*
UF — *Ugarit-Forschungen*
UT — *Ugaritic Textbook*
VE — *Vox evangelica*
VT — *Vetus Testamentum*
VTSup — Supplements to Vetus Testamentum
WBC — Word Biblical Commentary
WBE — *Wycliffe Bible Encyclopedia*
WMANT — Wissenschaftliche Monographien zum Alten und Neuen Testament
WTJ — *Westminster Theological Journal*
WUNT — Wissenschaftliche Untersuchungen zum Neuen Testament
YCS — *Yale Classical Studies*
ZAH — *Zeitschrift für Althebräistik*
ZAW — *Zeitschrift für die alttestamentliche Wissenschaft*
ZKT — *Zeitschrift für katholische Theologie*
ZNW — *Zeitschrift für die neutestamentliche Wissenschaft und die Kunde der älterern Kirche*
ZPEB — *Zondervan Pictorial Encyclopedia of the Bible*
ZTK — *Zeitschrift für Theologie und Kirche*
ZWT — *Zeitschrift für wissenschaftliche Theologie*

General

AD	*anno Domini* (in the year of [our] Lord)
Akkad.	Akkadian
Arab.	Arabic
Aram.	Aramaic
AUC	from the year of the founding of Rome
BC	before Christ
Byz	The reading of the *Byzantine* witnesses
ca.	*circa* (around, about, approximately)
cf.	*confer*, compare
ch(s).	chapter(s)
d.	died
diss.	dissertation
ed(s).	editor(s), edited by, edition
e.g.	*exempli gratia*, for example
esp.	especially
et al.	*et alii*, and others
EV	English versions of the Bible
f(f).	and the following one(s)
fig.	figuratively
frg.	fragment
FS	Festschrift
Gk.	Greek
GK	Goodrick & Kohlenberger numbering system
Heb.	Hebrew
ibid.	*ibidem*, in the same place
idem	that which was mentioned before, same, as in same author
i.e.	*id est*, that is
JPS	Jewish Publication Society
Lat.	Latin
lit.	literally
LXX	Septuagint (the Greek OT)
MS(S)	manuscript(s)
MT	Masoretic Text of the OT
n(n).	note(s)
n.d.	no date
NS	New Series
NT	New Testament
OL	Old Latin
OT	Old Testament
p(p).	page(s)
par.	parallel (indicates textual parallels)
para.	Paragraph
repr.	reprinted
rev.	revised
Samar.	Samaritan Pentateuch
s.v.	*sub verbo*, under the word
Syr.	Syriac
Tg.	Targum
TR	Textus Receptus (Greek text of the KJV translation)
trans.	translator, translated by
v(v).	verse(s)
vs.	versus
Vul.	Vulgate

MATTHEW

D. A. CARSON

Introduction

1. **The Criticism of Matthew**
2. **History and Theology**
3. **The Synoptic Problem**
4. **Unity**
5. **Authorship**
6. **Date**
7. **Place of Composition and Destination**
8. **Occasion and Purpose**
9. **Canonicity**
10. **Text**
11. **Themes and Special Problems**
12. **Literary Genre**
13. **Bibliography**
14. **Structure and Outline**

1. THE CRITICISM OF MATTHEW

The earliest church fathers to mention this gospel concur that the author was the apostle Matthew. Papias's famous statement (cf. section 3) was interpreted to mean, "Matthew composed the *Logia* [gospel?] in the Hebrew [Aramaic?] dialect and everyone interpreted them as he was able." In other words, the apostle first wrote his gospel in Hebrew or Aramaic, and it was subsequently translated into Greek. Matthean priority was almost universally upheld; Mark was considered an abbreviation and therefore somewhat inferior. These factors—apostolic authorship (unlike Mark and Luke) and Matthean priority—along with the fact that Matthew preserves much of Jesus' teaching not found elsewhere, combined to give this first gospel enormous influence and prestige in the church. With few exceptions, these perspectives dominated gospel study till after the Reformation.

The consensus could not last. An indication of its intrinsic frailty came in 1776 and 1778 when, in two posthumously published essays, A. E. Lessing insisted that the only way to account for the parallels and seeming discrepancies among the Synoptic Gospels was to assume that they all derived independently from an Aramaic "Gospel of the Nazarenes." Others (J. A. Eichorn, J. G. Herder) developed this idea; and the supposition of a "primal gospel," whether oral or literary, began to gain influence. Meanwhile J. J. Griesbach (1745–1812) laid the foundations of the modern debate over the "synoptic problem" (see section 3) by arguing with some care for the priority of both Matthew and Luke over Mark, which was taken to be a condensation of the other two. In the middle of the nineteenth century, many in the Tübingen school adopted this view. As a result, Matthew as an historical and theological source was elevated above the other Synoptics.

By the end of the nineteenth century, a new tide was running. Owing largely to the meticulous work of H. J. Holtzmann (1834–1910), the "two-source hypothesis" gained substantial acceptance. By the beginning of the twentieth century, this theory was almost universally adopted, and subsequent developments were in reality mere modifications of this theory. B. H. Streeter, advocating a "four-source hypothesis" that was essentially a detailed refinement of the two-source theory, argued that Luke's gospel is made-up of a "Proto-Luke" that was filled out with Mark and Q.[1] This raised the historical reliability of Proto-Luke to the same level as Mark. Streeter's hypothesis still has some followers, and today most scholars adopt some form of the two-source theory or the four-source theory. This consensus has recently been challenged (see section 3).

These predominantly literary questions combined with the substantial antisupernaturalism of some critics toward the beginning of the twentieth century to produce various reconstructions of Jesus' life and teaching. During the 1920s and 1930s, the source criticism implicit in these efforts was largely passed by in favor of form criticism. Philologists first applied this method to the "folk literature" of primitive civilizations, especially the Maoris. H. Gunkel and H. Gressmann then used it to classify OT materials according to their "form." New Testament scholars, especially K. L. Schmidt, M. Dibelius, and R. Bultmann, applied the method to the Gospels in an effort to explore the so-called tunnel period between Jesus and the earliest written sources.[2] They began by isolating small sections of the Gospels that they took to be units of oral tradition, classifying them according to form. Only the passion narrative was taken as a connected account from the beginning. Oral transmission was thought to effect regular modifications common to all such literature—e.g., repetition engenders brevity in pronouncement stories and provides names in legends, rhythm and balance in didactic sayings, and multiple details in miracle stories. The form critics then assigned these forms to various *Sitze im Leben* ("life settings") in the church.

The historical value of any pericope was then assessed against a number of criteria. For instance, the "criterion of dissimilarity" was used to weed out statements attributed to Jesus that were similar to what Palestinian Judaism or early Christianity might have said. Only if a statement was "dissimilar" could it be ascribed with reasonable confidence to Jesus. The net result was a stifling historical skepticism with respect to the canonical gospels. Many scholars used the same literary methods in a more conservative fashion (e.g., V. Taylor's great commentary on Mark);[3] but the effect of form criticism was to increase the distance between our canonical gospels and the historical Jesus, a distance increased further in Matthew's case because of the continued dominance of the two-source hypothesis. Few any longer believed that Matthew the apostle was the first evangelist.[4]

1. B. H. Streeter, *The Four Gospels* (London: Macmillan, 1924).
2. See, e.g., Rudolf Bultmann, *The History of the Synoptic Tradition*, trans. J. Marsh (Oxford: Blackwell, 1963).
3. Vincent Taylor, *The Gospel according to St. Mark* (2nd ed.; London: Macmillan, 1966).
4. For a convenient history of the criticism of Matthew up to this point, see, in addition to some of the major introductions, W. G. Kümmel, *The New Testament: The History of the Investigation of Its Problems* (trans. S. McL. Gilmour and H. C. Kee; Nashville: Abingdon, 1972); Stephen Neill, *The Interpretation of the New Testament, 1861–1986* (2nd ed.; Oxford: Oxford Univ. Press, 1988).

Following World War II a major change took place. Anticipated by George D. Kilpatrick's study, which focused on the distinctives in Matthew's theology,[5] the age of redaction criticism as applied to Matthew began with a 1948 essay by Günther Bornkamm.[6] He presupposed Mark's priority and then in one pericope sought to explain every change between the two gospels as a reflection of Matthew's theological interests and biases. Redaction criticism offered one great advantage over form criticism: it saw the evangelists not as mere compilers of the church's oral traditions and organizers of stories preserved or created in various forms but as theologians in their own right, shaping and adapting the material in order to make their own points.

It became important to distinguish between "traditional" material and "redactional" material, i.e., between what came to the evangelist already formed and the changes and additions he made. In other words, while tradition may preserve authentic historical material, redactional material does not do so. It rather serves as the best way of discerning an evangelist's distinctive ideas. In his meticulous study of one pericope, Bornkamm sought to demonstrate a better method of understanding Matthew's theology—a method that could best be discerned by trying to understand how and why Matthew changed his sources (esp. Mark and Q).

Countless studies poured forth in Bornkamm's wake, applying the same methods to virtually every pericope in Matthew. The translation of redaction-critical studies by G. Bornkamm, G. Barth, and H. J. Held exercised profound influence in the world of New Testament scholarship.[7] In 1963, the first full-scale redaction-critical commentary on Matthew appeared, in which Pierre Bonnard handles his tools fairly conservatively, frequently refusing to comment on historical questions and focusing on Matthew's theology and the reasons (based on reconstructed "life settings") for it.[8] His work, which is immensely valuable, became the forerunner of several later English commentaries (notably David Hill's).[9]

Nevertheless, a rather naive optimism regarding historical reconstruction developed that influenced many writers, who tended to think they could read off from Matthew's redaction the theological beliefs either of Matthew's community or of the evangelist himself as he sought to correct or defend some part of his community. The last four or five decades displayed a wide variety of such reconstructions. Kilpatrick argues that the book is catechetical, designed for the church of Matthew's time. Stendahl thinks the handling of the OT quotations reflects a "school" that stands behind the writing of this gospel, a disciplined milieu of instruction.[10] The major redaction-critical studies attempt to define the historical context in which the evangelist writes—the community circumstances that call this gospel into being (it is thought) between AD 80 and AD 100—and pay little useful attention to the historical context of Jesus. One need

5. G. D. Kilpatrick, *The Origins of the Gospel according to St. Matthew* (Oxford: Clarendon, 1946).

6. Günther Bornkamm, "The Stilling of the Storm in Matthew," in *Tradition and Interpretation in Matthew* (ed. G. Bornkamm, G. Barth, and H. J. Held; Philadelphia: Westminster, 1963), 52–57.

7. Bornkamm, Barth, and Held, *Tradition and Interpretation in Matthew.*

8. Pierre Bonnard, *L'Évangile selon Saint Matthieu* (2nd ed.; Neuchatel: Delachaux et Niestlé, 1970).

9. David Hill, *The Gospel of Matthew* (Grand Rapids: Eerdmans, 1972).

10. Krister Stendahl, *The School of St. Matthew and Its Use of the Old Testament* (2nd ed.; Lund: C. W. K. Gleerup, 1954).

only think of such works as those of Trilling, Strecker, Cope, Hare, Frankemölle, and Kunzel, to name a few.[11]

Not all redaction critics interpret Matthew's reconstructed community the same way; indeed, the differences among them are often great. Moreover, some critics have argued that much more material in the Gospels (including Matthew's) is authentic than others have thought.[12] Yet the wide diversity of opinion suggests at least some methodological and presuppositional disarray.

Today arguments that depend almost exclusively on redaction-critical judgments are no longer in vogue. In line with developments that have been taking place across the field of New Testament studies, Matthean scholars reflect the enormous diversity of competing special interests. Redaction criticism competes with numerous other foci of interest, including narrative criticism (with its interest in plot development and characterization), close analysis of this book's literary genre, the nature of oral witness, postfoundational epistemology, an emphasis on the theology of Matthew without bothering to try to sort out historical claims, attempts at delineating the social structures reflected in this gospel (and perhaps calling forth this gospel), and much else. The diversity of approaches is then matched by a diversity of conclusions. Two fairly recent general introductions to Matthew make the point tellingly. They both competently survey the field, but Carter holds that Matthew contains some historically reliable information even though the focus of his work is elsewhere, while Westerholm insists that Matthew is drawing theological and pastoral lessons but sees a much higher place for historical fidelity.[13] Similarly, the most recent commentaries are sharply divided. The major work by Ulrich Luz, reflected also in his brief *Studies in Matthew*, argues that Matthew is not biography but fictional narrative, while the commentary by R. T. France holds the opposite view.[14]

---

11. Wolfgang Trilling, *Das wahre Israel: Studien zur Theologie des Matthäus-Evangeliums* (München: Kosel, 1964); Georg Strecker, *Der Weg der Gerechtigkeit* (FRLANT 82; Göttingen: Vandenhoeck & Ruprecht, 1962); O. Lamar Cope, *Matthew: A Scribe Trained for the Kingdom of Heaven* (Washington, D.C.: Catholic Biblical Association, 1976); D. R. A. Hare, *The Theme of Jewish Persecution of Christians in the Gospel according to St. Matthew* (Cambridge: Cambridge Univ. Press, 1967); Hubert Frankemölle, *Jahwebund und Kirche Christi: Studien zur Form und Traditionsgeschichte des "Evangeliums" nach Matthäus* (Munster: Aschendorff, 1974); G. Kunzel, *Studien zum Gemeindeverständnis des Matthaus-Evangeliums* (Stuttgart: Calwer, 1978); for a survey of Matthean studies, see R. P. Martin, *New Testament Foundations* (Grand Rapids: Eerdmans, 1975–78), 1:224–43, and esp. the careful essay by Graham N. Stanton, "The Origin and Purpose of Matthew's Gospel: Matthean Scholarship from 1945 to 1980," in *Aufstieg und Niedergang der römischen Welt* (New York: de Gruyter, 1982), 2:25.
12. See, e.g., B. F. Meyer, *The Aims of Jesus* (London: SCM Press, 1979); R. Latourelle, *Finding Jesus through the Gospels* (trans. A. Owen; New York: Alba, 1979); and the writings of such scholars as M. Hengel and H. Schürmann.
13. Warren Carter, *Matthew and the Margins: A Sociopolitical and Religious Reading* (Bible and Liberation 204; Sheffield: Sheffield Academic, 2001) and *Matthew: Storyteller, Interpreter, Evangelist* (Peabody, Mass.: Hendrickson, 2004); Stephen Westerholm, *Understanding Matthew: The Early Christian Worldview of the First Gospel* (Grand Rapids: Baker, 2006).
14. Ulrich Luz, *Studies in Matthew* (Grand Rapids: Eerdmans, 2005); R. T. France, *The Gospel of Matthew* (NICNT; Grand Rapids: Eerdmans, 2007); for further survey of the direction of Matthean studies, see Donald Senior, "Directions in Matthean Studies," in *The Gospel of Matthew in Current Study* (ed. David E. Aune; Grand Rapids: Eerdmans, 2001), 5–21.

A modern commentary that aims primarily to explain the text must to some extent respond to current questions, the more so if it adopts a fairly independent stance, for many of these questions significantly affect our understanding of what the text says.[15]

2. HISTORY AND THEOLOGY

Few problems are philosophically and theologically more complex than the possible relationships between history and theology. The broader issues in the tension between these two cannot be discussed here: e.g., How does a transcendent God manifest himself in space-time history? Can the study of history allow, in its reconstructions of the past, for authority and influence outside the space-time continuum? To what extent is the supernatural an essential part of Christianity, and what does it mean to approach such matters "historically"? What are the epistemological bases for a system professing to be revealed religion?[16] Even the titles of recent books about Jesus show the chasm that separates scholar from scholar on these points.[17]

This section will therefore ask some preliminary methodological questions.[18] How appropriate and reliable are the various methods of studying the Gospels if we are to determine not only the theological distinctives of each evangelist but also something of the teaching and life of the historical Jesus? We must begin by avoiding many of the historical and theological disjunctions notoriously common among NT

---

15. The various periods described are not completely sealed off from the other ones, and some scholars did run against the tide of their age. From rather different perspectives, Adolf Schlatter (*Der Evangelist Matthäus* [6th ed.; Stuttgart: Calwer, 1963]) and Ned B. Stonehouse (*The Witness of Matthew and Mark to Christ* [Grand Rapids: Eerdmans, 1944]) anticipated the more useful and reliable elements of redaction criticism, pointing out distinctive themes in Matthew's gospel with deliberate caution and precision. On the other hand, when William Hendriksen produced his large commentary (*The Gospel of Matthew* [Grand Rapids: Baker, 1973]), he took relatively little note of recent developments; yet his work is doubtless of considerable help to pastors. Compare also the independent stances of Gerhard Maier (*Matthäus-Evangelium* [2 vols.; Neuhausen: Hanssler, 1979–80]) and of W. F. Albright and C. S. Mann (*Matthew* [Garden City, N.J.: Doubleday, 1971]).

16. On these and similar questions, see E. E. Cairns, *God and Man in Time: A Christian Approach to Historiography* (Grand Rapids: Baker, 1979); G. H. Clark, *Historiography: Secular and Religious* (Nutley, N.J.: Craig Press, 1971); C. T. McIntyre, ed., *God, History and Historians: An Anthology of Modern Christian Views of History* (New York: Oxford Univ. Press, 1977); J. A. Passmore, "The Objectivity of History," in *Philosophical Analysis and History* (ed. W. H. Doty; New York: Harper, 1966), 75–94; A. C. Thiselton, *The Two Horizons* (Grand Rapids: Eerdmans, 1980); Paul Barnett, *Is the New Testament History?* (London: Hodder & Stoughton, 1986); and esp. Kevin J. Vanhoozer, *Is There a Meaning in This Text?* (Grand Rapids: Zondervan, 1998).

17. Contrast G. Vos, *The Self-Disclosure of Jesus: The Modern Debate about the Messianic Consciousness* (Grand Rapids: Eerdmans, 1954), and G. Vermes, *Jesus the Jew: A Historian's Reading of the Gospels* (London: Collins, 1973); or, again, contrast N. T. Wright, *Jesus and the Victory of God* (London: SPCK, 1996), and many of the writings of John Dominic Crossan (e.g., *The Historical Jesus: The Life of a Mediterranean Jewish Peasant* [San Francisco: HarperSanFrancisco, 1991]).

18. Cf. H. Palmer, *The Logic of Gospel Criticism* (London: Macmillan, 1968); Meyer, *Aims of Jesus*, esp. 76–110; Robert H. Gundry, *The Use of the Old Testament in St. Matthew's Gospel, with Special Reference to the Messianic Hope* (NovTSup 18; Leiden: Brill, 1975), 189ff.; Birger Gerhardsson, *The Reliability of the Gospel Tradition* (Peabody, Mass.: Hendrickson, 2001); Barry D. Smith, "The Historical-Critical Method, Jesus Research, and the Christian Scholar," *TJ* 15 (1994): 201–20; and many essays in E. Earle Ellis, *History and Interpretation in New Testament Perspective* (Leiden: Brill, 2001).

scholars.[19] Consider, for example, the essay by K. Tagama, who arrives at his conclusion that the central theme of Matthew is "people and community" by insisting that all other important themes are mutually contradictory and therefore cancel one another out.[20] But contradiction is a slippery category. As most commonly used in NT scholarship, it does not refer to logical contradiction but to situations, ideas, beliefs that on the basis of the modern scholar's reconstruction of early church history are judged to be mutually incompatible.[21]

Such judgments are only as convincing as the historical and theological reconstructions undergirding them; and too often, historical reconstructions that in many cases have no other sources than the NT documents depend on illicit disjunctions. Did Jesus preach the nearness of the end of history and of the consummated kingdom? Then he could not have preached that the kingdom had already been inaugurated, and elements apparently denying this conclusion obviously spring from the church. Or did Jesus preach that the kingdom had already dawned? Then the apocalyptic element in the Gospels must be largely assigned to the later church. (On this particular problem, see comments at 3:2; 10:23; ch. 24.) Was Jesus a proto-rabbi, steeped in OT law and Jewish tradition? Then Paul's emphasis on grace is entirely innovative. Or did Jesus break Jewish halakah (rules of conduct based on traditional interpretations of the law)? Then clearly Matthew's emphasis on the law (e.g., 5:17–20; 23:1–26) reflects the stance of Matthew's church, or suggests that Matthew wishes to legislate for his church, without helping us come to grips with the historical Jesus. Better yet, Matthew's gospel may even be considered a Jewish-Christian reaction against "Paulinism."

All such disjunctive reconstructions are suspect. Historical "contradictions," as David Fischer has shown, too often reside in the eye of the historian.[22] Strange combinations of ideas may coexist side by side in one generation, even though a later generation cannot tolerate them and therefore breaks them up. So we need to be cautious about pronouncing what ideas can be "historically" incompatible. Acts and the early Pauline epistles show us considerable diversity in the fast-growing infant church, as a number of NT studies attempt to explain.[23]

Reconstruction is a necessary part of historical inquiry. Sometimes meticulous reconstruction from a number of reliable documents shows that some further document is not what it purports to be. But as far as the gospel of Matthew (or any of the canonical gospels) is concerned, we must frankly confess we have no access to the alleged "Matthean [or Markan, Lukan, etc.] community" apart from the individual gospel itself. The numerous studies describing and analyzing Matthew's theology against the background

---

19. See David Fischer, *Historians' Fallacies: Toward a Logic of Historical Thought* (New York: Harper & Row, 1970). A fine example is Eduard Schweizer's statement (*The Good News according to Matthew* [Atlanta: John Knox, 1975], 11) that "the evangelist's intent ... was theological rather than historical."

20. K. Tagama, "People and Community in the Gospel of Matthew," *NTS* 16 (1969–70): 149–62.

21. This is dealt with at some length in Martin Hengel, *Acts and the History of Earliest Christianity* (London: SCM Press, 1979), 35–68; D. A. Carson, "Historical Tradition in the Fourth Gospel—After Dodd, What?" in *Gospel Perspectives* (ed. R. T. France and D. Wenham; Sheffield: JSOT Press, 1980–81), 2:115–21.

22. Fischer, *Historians' Fallacies*.

23. See D. A. Carson, "Unity and Diversity: On the Possibility of Systematic Theology," in *Scripture and Truth* (ed. D. A. Carson and J. D. Woodbridge; Grand Rapids: Zondervan, 1983), 65–95.

of Christianity and Judaism contemporary with Matthew's "community" in AD 80–100 (e.g., Allison, Carter, Stanton)[24] beg a host of methodological questions. This is not to deny that Matthew's gospel may have been written within a community about AD 80 or may have addressed some such community; rather, is it to argue the following points.

1. What Matthew aims to write is a gospel telling us about Jesus, not a church circular addressing an independently known problem.[25]

2. There is substantial evidence that the early church was interested in the historical Jesus and wanted to know what he taught and why. Equally there is strong evidence that the Gospels constitute, at least in part, an essential element of the church's kerygmatic ministry, its evangelistic proclamation—each gospel having been shaped for particular audiences.[26]

3. It is therefore methodologically wrong to read off some theme attributed by the evangelist to Jesus and conclude that what is actually being discussed is not the teaching of Jesus but an issue of AD 80, unless the theme or saying can be shown to be anachronistic.[27]

4. Matthew's reasons for including or excluding this or that tradition or for shaping his sources must owe something to the circumstances he found himself in and the concerns of his own theology. But it is notoriously difficult to reconstruct such circumstances and commitments from a gospel about Jesus of Nazareth.

5. Moreover, virtually all the themes isolated as reflections of AD 80 could in fact reflect interests of any decade from AD 30 to 100. In the early thirties, for instance, Stephen was martyred because he spoke against the law and the temple. Similar concerns dominated the Jerusalem Council (AD 49) and demanded thought both before and after the Jewish War (AD 66–70). The truth is that such themes as law and temple and even many christological formulations (see section 11) offer very little help in identifying a "life setting" for the church in Matthew's day. Although Matthean scholarship may advance by trying out new theories, no advance that forces a Procrustean synthesis based on methodologically dubious deductions constitutes genuine progress.

For those who are strongly influenced by the rather extreme voices of the "Jesus Seminar," whose members still rely heavily on source criticism and redaction criticism, a few things must be said. This approach to the Gospels has been scrutinized elsewhere (e.g., Carson and the literature cited there);[28] and only a few points need be made here.

---

24. Carter, *Matthew and the Margins* and *Matthew*; Stanton, "Origin and Purpose," ch. 3; Dale C. Allison Jr., *Studies in Matthew: Interpretation Past and Present* (Grand Rapids: Baker, 2005).

25. See Richard Bauckham, *Jesus and the Eyewitnesses: The Gospels as Eyewitness Testimony* (Grand Rapids: Eerdmans, 2006).

26. Graham N. Stanton, *Jesus of Nazareth in New Testament Preaching* (Cambridge: Cambridge Univ. Press, 1974).

27. See Craig L. Blomberg, *Jesus and the Gospels* (2nd ed.; Nashville: Broadman, 2009); Paul Barnett, *Jesus and the Rise of Early Christianity: A History of New Testament Times* (Downers Grove, Ill.: InterVarsity, 1999); and esp. Bauckham, *Jesus and the Eyewitnesses*.

28. D. A. Carson, "Redaction Criticism: On the Legitimacy and Illegitimacy of a Literary Tool," in *Scripture and Truth* (ed. Carson and Woodbridge), 119–42.

1. The "criteria of authenticity," as has often been pointed out, are hopelessly inadequate.[29] For instance, the "criterion of dissimilarity," namely, that only if a statement was "dissimilar" from what Palestinian Judaism or early Christianity might have said could it be ascribed with reasonable confidence to Jesus, can only cull out the distinctive or the eccentric while leaving the characteristic untouched—unless one is prepared to argue that Jesus' teaching characteristically never resembled contemporary Judaism and was never adopted by the church.

2. The analysis of the descent of the tradition, though useful in itself, is marred by four major flaws. First, comparative studies in oral transmission have dealt largely with periods of hundreds of years, not decades. On any dating of the Gospels, some eyewitnesses were still alive when the evangelists published their books. Second, the work of several Scandinavian scholars has drawn attention to the role of memory in Jewish education.[30] Their work has been seriously criticized, but even their most perceptive critics recognize that too little attention has been paid to the power of human memory before Gutenberg—a phenomenon attested in many Third-World students today.[31] More impressive yet, the detailed attack on form criticism by Erhardt Guttgemanns is so compelling that one wonders whether form criticism is of any value as a historical (as opposed to literary) tool.[32] Oral traditions, especially religious oral traditions, are not conducive to tampering and falsification but are remarkably stable. Third, convincing reasons have been advanced for concluding that some written notes were taken even during Jesus' public ministry.[33] Written material, of course, necessarily fits into various forms or genres; but such genres must be considered quite separately from the forms of oral transmission and the shaping that takes place by this means. If traditions of Jesus' words and deeds were passed on by both oral and written forms, many of the historical conclusions of the form-critical model collapse. Fourth, classic form criticism is intrinsically incapable of dealing historically with several similar sayings of Jesus, since they all tend toward the same form.

3. More broadly, the fact that Jesus was an itinerant preacher (see comments at 4:23–25; 9:35–38; 11:21) is passed over too lightly. To attempt a tradition history of somewhat similar sayings, which the evangelists

---

29. See R. T. France, "The Authenticity of the Sayings of Jesus," in *History, Criticism and Faith* (ed. C. Brown; Downers Grove, Ill.: InterVarsity, 1976), 101–43; R. H. Stein, "The 'Criteria' for Authenticity," in *Gospel Perspectives* (ed. France and Wenham), 1:225–63; Hengel, *Acts and the History of Earliest Christianity*, esp. 3–34; Stanley E. Porter, *The Criteria for Authenticity in Historical-Jesus Research: Previous Discussion and New Proposals* (JSNTSup 191; Sheffield: Sheffield Academic, 2000); Simon J. Gathercole, "Redaction Criticism, Tradition-History and Myth in New Testament Theology: In Response to Georg Strecker," *Them* 28/3 (2003): 40–48.

30. See H. Riesenfeld, "The Gospel Tradition and Its Beginnings," *SE* 1 (1959): 43–65; B. Gerhardsson, *Memory and Manuscript: Oral Tradition and Written Transmission in Rabbinic Judaism and Early Christianity* (Lund: Gleerup, 1961); and esp. Samuel Byrskog, *Jesus the Only Teacher: Didactic Authority and Transmission in Ancient Israel, Ancient Judaism and the Matthean Community* (ConBNT 24; Uppsala: Almqvist & Wiksell, 1994); Samuel Byrskog, *Story as History—History as Story: The Gospel Tradition in the Context of Ancient Oral History* (Tübingen: Mohr, 2000).

31. See W. D. Davies, *The Setting of the Sermon on the Mount* (Cambridge: Cambridge Univ. Press, 1963), 464ff.; Peter H. Davids, "The Gospels and Jewish Tradition," in *Gospel Perspectives* (ed. France and Wenham), 1:75–99; Peter Head, "The Role of Eyewitnesses in the Formation of the Gospel Tradition," *TynBul* 52 (2001): 275–94.

32. E. Guttgemanns, *Candid Questions Concerning Gospel Form Criticism* (trans. W. H. Doty; Pittsburgh: Pickwick, 1979).

33. See E. E. Ellis, "New Directions in Form Criticism," in *Jesus Christus in Historie und Theologie* (ed. G. Strecker; Tübingen: Mohr, 1975), 299–315.

place in quite different contexts, overlooks the repetitive nature of itinerant ministry. Of course, each case must be examined on its own merits and depends in some instances on source-critical considerations; but we shall observe how frequently this basic observation is ignored. See especially the introductory discussion on parables at 13:3a.

4. To deduce that all changes in Mark and Q (however Q may be defined), including omissions and additions, are the result of exclusively theological motives fails to reckon with the extreme likelihood of a multiplicity both of reasons for introducing changes and of sources, oral and written, within the first few decades (cf. Lk 1:1–4) and with the possibility that the author was an apostle (see section 5). While apostolic authorship would not give the text more authority than nonapostolic authorship, it must affect our judgment of the role of oral and written sources in the making of this gospel. These factors—multiplicity of sources and possible apostolic authorship—suggest that in most instances there is no compelling reason for thinking that material judged redactional is for that reason unhistorical.

5. Modern redaction criticism also suffers from dependency on a particular solution to the Synoptic Problem (see section 3).

6. Also, redaction criticism fails to consider how many changes from Mark to Matthew (assuming Mark's priority) might owe something to stylistic predilections rather than theology. For example, Frans Neirynck has clearly shown that Matthew's account of the feeding of the five thousand, often said to reflect more clearly than Mark the institution of the Eucharist, in reality turns out to be entirely consistent with the stylistic changes he introduces elsewhere.[34]

7. Too many redaction-critical studies develop an understanding of the theology of Matthew's gospel solely on the basis of the changes instead of giving adequate thought to the document as a whole. Surely what Matthew retains is as important to him as what he modifies. The possibility of distortion becomes acute when, on the basis of changes, Matthew's distinctive theology is outlined and then anything conflicting with this model is reckoned to be "unassimilated tradition" or the like. It is far wiser to check the "changes" again and determine whether they have been rightly understood and, avoiding a priori disjunctions, to seek to integrate them into all that Matthew writes down.

Such considerations do not eliminate the need for redaction criticism. In God's providence we are able to compare the Synoptic Gospels with one another, and such study helps us better understand each of them. Matthew's topical treatment of miracles (Mt 8–9), his chiastic arrangement of parables (Mt 13), the differences he exhibits when closely compared with Mark—these all help us identify his distinctives more precisely than would otherwise be possible. Thus no responsible modern commentary on the Synoptic Gospels can avoid using redaction criticism. But redaction criticism, trimmed of its excesses and weaned from its radical heritage, throws only a little light on historical questions; and one must always guard against its dethroning what is essential by focusing on what is distinctive and idiosyncratic. It is best deployed when one is simultaneously utilizing an array of other approaches that together commit the student to attentive listening to the entire text.

34. F. Neirynck, "La rédaction Matthéenne et la structure du premier évangile," in *De Jésus aux evangiles* (ed. I. de la Potterie; Gembloux: Duculot, 1967), 41–73, esp. 51.

It is possible to approach the question of how much history is found in Matthew by examining the genre of literature—either of the gospel as a whole or of some section of it. Perhaps a "gospel" is not meant to convey historical information; perhaps certain stories in Matthew are midrash and, like parables, make theological points without pretending to be historical. Anticipating later discussion (section 12), we conclude that the evangelists, including Matthew, intended that their gospels convey historical information. This does not mean they intended to write dispassionate, modern biographies. But advocacy does not necessarily affect truth telling. A Jewish writer on the Holocaust is not necessarily either more or less accurate because his family perished at Auschwitz. Nor is it proper in the study of any document professedly dealing with history to approach it with a neutral stance that demands proof of authenticity as well as proof of inauthenticity.[35]

Stewart Goetz and Craig Blomberg, in an adaptation of a Kantian argument, write:

> If the assumption was that no one ever wrote history for the sake of accuracy, then no fraudulent history could ever be written with the expectation that it would be believed. The process of deception is parasitic on the assumption that people normally write history with the intent of historical accuracy. People must (a) acknowledge the a priori truth that truth telling is the logical backdrop to lying, and (b) *actually* assume that people tell the truth in order for a lie to be told with the expectation that it will be believed.[36]

So with any particular historian, including Matthew, the writer of history must be assumed reliable until shown to be otherwise. "The reader must make this a priori commitment if the practice of writing history is to be viable."[37] In other words, other things being equal, the burden of proof rests with the skeptic.

From this perspective, harmonization, which currently has a bad name in NT scholarship, retains a twofold importance: negatively, it is nothing more than one way of applying the coherence test for authenticity; and, positively, once we no longer insist that every gospel distinctive is the result of theological commitment or that the only possible sources are Mark, Q, and a little undefined oral tradition, harmonization carefully handled may permit the illumination of one source by another, provided legitimate redaction-critical distinctions are not thereby obliterated.

This commentary endeavors to apply these observations and assessments to the gospel of Matthew. Rigorous application would have trebled the length. Therefore, certain sections and pericopes were singled out for more extensive treatment (see, e.g., comments at 5:1; 6:9–13; 8:16–17; 13:3; 26:6, 17), in the hope that the positions outlined in this introduction could be grounded in the hard realities of the text. The aim must be to understand as closely as possible the gospel of Matthew.

3. THE SYNOPTIC PROBLEM

The return of the Synoptic Problem to center stage as the focus of much debate (see section 1) during the last several decades necessitates some assessment of the developments that impinge on questions of authorship, date, and interpretation of Matthew. One contributing factor to the debate is the quotation

35. See Morna D. Hooker, "Christology and Methodology," *NTS* 17 (1970–71): 480–87.

36. Stewart C. Goetz and Craig L. Blomberg, "The Burden of Proof," *JSNT* 11 (1981): 39–63, esp. 52, emphasis theirs.

37. Ibid.

from Papias (ca. AD 135) recorded by Eusebius.[38] Several of Papias's expressions are ambiguous: "Matthew *synetaxato* [composed? compiled? arranged?] the *logia* [sayings? gospel?] in *Hebraidi dialektō* [in the Hebrew (Aramaic?) language? in the Hebrew (Aramaic?) style?]; and everyone *hērmēneusen* [interpreted? translated? transmitted?] them as he was able [contextually, who is 'interpreting' what?]." The early church understood the sentence to mean that the apostle Matthew first wrote his gospel in Hebrew or Aramaic and then it was translated. But few today accept this.[39] Although Matthew has Semitisms, much evidence suggests it was first composed in Greek.

The most important attempts to understand this sentence from Papias include the following.[40]

1. T. W. Manson made popular the view that identifies the *logia* with sayings of Jesus found in Q.[41] That would make Matthew the author of Q (a source or sources including approximately 250 verses common to Matthew and Luke) but not of this gospel. Papias confused the two. This view falters on two facts. First, it cannot explain how an important apostolic source such as the Q that this theory requires could have so completely disappeared that there is no other mention of it, let alone a copy. Indeed, the entire Q hypothesis, however reasonable, is still only a hypothesis. Second, Papias's two other instances of *logia* (recorded by Eusebius) suggest the word refers to both sayings and deeds of Jesus, while Q is made up almost exclusively of the former. From this perspective, *logia* better fits the gospel of Matthew than a source such as Q.

2. This last criticism can also be leveled against the view that *logia* refers to OT "testimonia," a book of OT "proof texts" compiled by Matthew from the Hebrew canon and now incorporated into the gospel.[42] Furthermore, it is not certain that such "testimonia" ever existed as separate books; and in any case it would have been unnecessary to compile them in Hebrew and then translate them, since the LXX was already well established. Matthew demonstrably follows the LXX in passages where Mark has parallels (see section 11).

3. If by *logia* Papias meant our canonical Matthew,[43] then in the opinion of many scholars convinced that canonical Matthew was set down in Greek (e.g., David Hill), Papias was plainly wrong. Either his testimony must be ignored as valueless or we must suppose that Papias was right as to the language but confused the gospel with some other Semitic work, perhaps the apocryphal gospel according to the Hebrews.

4. Josef Kürzinger offers a possible way out of the dilemma.[44] He thinks *logia* refers to canonical Matthew but that *Hebraidi dialektō* refers not to Hebrew or Aramaic language but to Semitic style or literary

38. Eusebius, *Hist.eccl.*, 3.39.16.

39. For general discussion of this difficult question, see the NT introductions and the literature cited below. For arguments against the view that canonical Matthew uses translation Greek, see Nigel Turner, *Style* (vol. 4 of *A Grammar of New Testament Greek*, ed. J. H. Moulton; Edinburgh: T&T Clark, 1976), 4:37–38.

40. For more discussion, see Donald Guthrie, *New Testament Introduction* (3rd ed.; Downers Grove, Ill.: InterVarsity, 1970), 34–37.

41. T. W. Manson, *The Sayings of Jesus* (London: SCM Press, 1949), 18ff.

42. Cf. J. R. Harris, *Testimonies* (2 vols.; rev. ed.; Cambridge: Cambridge Univ. Press, 1920); F. C. Grant, *The Gospels: Their Origin and Their Growth* (New York: Harper, 1957), 65, 144.

43. So, among others, C. S. Petrie, "The Authorship of 'The Gospel According to Matthew': A Reconsideration of the External Evidence," *NTS* 14 (1967): 15–32.

44. J. Kürzinger, "Das Papiaszeugnis und die Erstgestalt des Matthäusevangeliums," *BZ* 4 (1960): 19–38. The argument above diverges from Kürzinger at one or two minor points.

form. Matthew arranged his gospel in Semitic (i.e., Jewish-Christian) literary form dominated by Semitic themes and devices. In this view, the last clause of Papias's statement cannot refer to translation, since language is no longer in view. Kürzinger points out that immediately before Papias's sentence about Matthew, he describes how Mark composed his gospel by putting down Peter's testimony; and there Mark is called the *hermēneutēs* of Peter. This cannot mean Mark was Peter's translator. It means he "interpreted" or "transmitted" (neither English word is ideal) what Peter said. If the same meaning is applied to the cognate verb in Papias's statement about Matthew, then it could be that everyone "passed on" or "interpreted" Matthew's gospel to the world, as he was able.

It is difficult to decide which interpretation is correct. A few still argue that Matthew's entire gospel was first written in Aramaic.[45] That view best explains the language of Papias, but it is not easy to reconcile with Matthew's Greek. Why, for instance, does he sometimes use a Greek source such as the LXX? It cannot be argued that the alleged translator decided to use the LXX for all OT quotations in order to save himself some work, for only some of them are from the LXX. If this interpretation of Papias's statement does not stand, then Papias offers no support for Matthean priority.

The other two plausible interpretations of Papias are problematic. The view that Papias was referring to Q or some part of it offers the easiest rendering of *Hebraidi dialektō* ("in the Hebrew [Aramaic] language") but provides an implausible rendering for *logia*. Kürzinger's solution provides the most believable rendering of *logia* (namely, canonical Matthew) but a less likely interpretation of *Hebraidi dialektō* ("in the Semitic literary form"). Yet this rendering is possible and makes sense of the whole,[46] even though Kürzinger's view has not been well received. The important point is that either of these last two views fits easily with a theory of Markan priority, which may also be hinted at in the fact that, as Eusebius preserves him, Papias discusses Mark at length before turning rather briefly to Matthew.[47]

Quite apart from the testimony of Papias, the NT evidence itself demands some decisions, however tentative, regarding the Synoptic Problem. Its boundaries are well-known. About 90 percent of Mark is found in Matthew, and very frequently Matthew agrees with Mark's ordering of pericopes as well as his wording (see esp. chs. 3–4; 12–28). Matthew's pericopes are often more condensed than Mark's but have a great deal of other material, much of it discourses. Of this material, about 250 verses are common to Luke, and again the order is frequently (though by no means always) the same. In both instances the wording is often so similar throughout such lengthy passages that it is difficult to see oral fixation of the tradition as an adequate explanation. Some literary dependence seems self-evident. It is easier to support the view that Matthew and Luke both depend on Mark than vice versa, largely because Matthew and Mark frequently agree against Luke, and Mark and Luke frequently agree against Matthew, but Matthew and Luke seldom agree against Mark.

---

45. See Schlatter, *Matthäus*; P. Gaechter, *Das Matthäus Evangelium* (Innsbruck: Tyrolia-Verlag, 1963); J. W. Wenham, "Gospel Origins," *TJ* 7 (1978): 112–34; see also n. 59 below.

46. LSJ, 401.

47. See the full discussion of the problem in W. D. Davies and D. C. Allison. *A Critical and Exegetical Commentary on the Gospel according to Saint Matthew* (ICC; Edinburgh: T&T Clark, 1988–97), 1:7–17.

It is not the argument from order itself that is convincing, for all that proves is that Mark stands in the middle between the other two. What is more impressive is that close study finds it easier to explain changes from Mark to Matthew and Luke than the other way around.[48] The two-source hypothesis, despite its weaknesses—what, for instance, is the best explanation for the so-called minor agreements of Matthew and Luke against Mark if both Matthew and Luke depend on Mark?—is still more defensible than any of its competitors.[49]

Before pointing out a few of the historical and interpretive implications of this view, notice must be taken of the main alternatives.

1. By far the most common alternative is some form of the Griesbach hypothesis. This argues for Matthean priority, dependence of Luke on Matthew (according to some), and Mark as an abbreviation of Matthew and Luke. Despite increasingly sophisticated defenses of this position, it remains implausible. It appears highly unlikely that any writer, let alone a first-century writer such as Mark, would take two documents (in this case Matthew and Luke) and analyze them so carefully as to write a condensation virtually every word of which is in the sources—a condensation that is graphic, forceful, and not artificial.[50] The impressive list of literary analogies compiled by Roland Frye,[51] who argues that Mark must be secondary because it is much shorter than Matthew and Luke and that literary parallels confirm that writers deeply dependent on written sources condense their sources, actually confounds his conclusion; for where he follows Mark, Matthew's account is almost always shorter. His greater total length—and even the occasional longer Matthean pericope—always comes from new material added to that from the Markan source. Frye therefore inadvertently supports the two-source hypothesis. Moreover, the Griesbach hypothesis flies in the face of other evidence from Papias, who insists that Mark wrote his gospel on the basis of material from Peter, not by condensing Matthew and Luke.[52]

2. Antonio Gaboury and Xavier-Léon Dufour argue that the pericopes preserving the same order in the triple tradition (i.e., in Matthew, Mark, and Luke) constitute a primary source on which all three Synoptic Gospels have been built.[53] But it is demonstrable that sometimes the evangelists chose topical arrangements quite different from their parallels (e.g., see comments at chs. 8–9). So why should it be assumed

48. See Christopher M. Tuckett, "The Argument from Order and the Synoptic Problem," *TZ* 36 (1980): 338–54.

49. In addition to the standard NT introductions, see esp. Ned Stonehouse, *Origins of the Synoptic Gospels: Some Basic Questions* (Grand Rapids: Eerdmans, 1963), 48–77; G. M. Styler, "The Priority of Mark," in *The Birth of the New Testament* (C. F. D. Moule; 3rd ed.; London: Black, 1981), 285–316. For a convenient summary and recent bibliography, see D. A. Carson and Douglas J. Moo, *An Introduction to the New Testament* (2nd ed.; Grand Rapids: Zondervan, 2005), 77–133.

50. See Hill, *Matthew*, 28.

51. Roland Mushat Frye, "The Synoptic Problems and Analogies in Other Literatures," in *The Relationships among the Gospels: An Interdisciplinary Dialogue* (ed. W. O. Walker Jr.; San Antonio, Tex.: Trinity Univ. Press, 1978), 261–302.

52. Eusebius, *History of the Church*, 3.39.15.

53. A. Gaboury, *La structure des évangiles synoptiques* (NovTSup 22; Leiden: Brill, 1970); X.-Léon Dufour, "Redaktionsgeschichte of Matthew and Literary Criticism," in *Jesus and Man's Hope* (ed. D. Miller; Pittsburgh: Pittsburgh Theological Seminary, 1970), 9–35.

that all three synoptists conveniently chose to take over this alleged source without any change in topical arrangements?

3. Several scholars adopt Markan priority but deny the existence of Q.[54] Parallels between Matthew and Luke are explained by saying that Luke read Matthew before composing his own gospel. That is possible; but if so, he has hidden the fact extraordinarily well (cf., e.g., Mt 1–2 and Lk 1–2). Gundry holds to the existence of a somewhat expanded Q but argues as well that Luke used Matthew—and this explains the "minor agreements" between Matthew and Luke.[55] But this view, though possible, is linked in Gundry's mind with his theory that sources shared by Matthew and Luke include even such matters as the nativity story—and this is very doubtful.[56]

4. John Rist and one or two contemporary commentators (e.g., Jeffrey Gibbs) reject both the two-source hypothesis and the Griesbach hypothesis and argue for the independence of Matthew and Mark.[57] As many others have done, Rist focuses attention on 4:12–13:58, where there are numerous divergences in order between Matthew and Mark. He examines a short list of passages in the triple tradition where there is not only close verbal similarity but identical order and argues that in each case the order is either logical or the result of memory, not literary dependence. But Rist does not adequately weigh the impressive list of instances where Matthew agrees with Mark's order without close verbal similarity. Such order argues strongly for some kind of literary dependence, no matter how the verbal dissimilarities are explained.

5. Others, in the hope of keeping Matthean priority alive, argue that his gospel was first written in Aramaic; and this became a source for Mark, which in turn influenced the Greek rendering of Matthew.[58]

---

54. So H. Benedict Green, *The Gospel according to Matthew* (Oxford: Oxford Univ. Press, 1975); A. M. Farrer, "On Dispensing with Q," in *Studies in the Gospels* (ed. D. E. Nineham; Oxford: Blackwell, 1955), 55–88; M. D. Goulder, *Midrash and Lection in Matthew* (London: SPCK, 1974); Mark Goodacre and Nicholas Perrin, eds., *Questioning Q* (London: SPCK, 2004). This is quite different from B. C. Butler (*The Originality of St Matthew* [Cambridge: Cambridge Univ. Press, 1951]), who argued that Matthew was prior, Mark abridged Matthew, and Luke was dependent on Matthew for what we call Q material and on Mark for what Matthew and Mark had in common.

55. Robert H. Gundry, *Matthew: A Commentary on His Literary and Theological Art* (Grand Rapids: Eerdmans, 1981); 2nd ed. titled *Matthew: A Commentary on His Handbook for a Mixed Church under Persecution* (Grand Rapids: Eerdmans, 1994).

56. See comments at chs. 1–2; D. A. Carson, "Gundry on Matthew: A Critical Review," *TJ* 3:1 (1982): 71–91.

57. J. M. Rist, *On the Independence of Matthew and Mark* (Cambridge: Cambridge Univ. Press, 1978); Jeffrey A. Gibbs, *Matthew 1:1–11:1* (Concordia Commentary; St. Louis, Mo.: Concordia, 2006).

58. See J. W. Wenham, "Gospel Origins," 112 n. 45; Pierson Parker, *The Gospel before Mark* (Chicago: Univ. of Chicago Press, 1953); L. Vaganay, *Le problème synoptique—une hypothèse de travail* (Tournai: Desclée, 1954). Somewhat similar is the view of J. A. T. Robinson (*Redating the New Testament* [Philadelphia: Westminster, 1976], 97–98). Others think the alleged Semitic original was written in Hebrew rather than Aramaic (e.g., Gaechter, *Matthäus*; Jean Carmignac, *Recherches sur le "Notre Père"* [Paris: Letouzey et Ané, 1969], 33ff.). Johannes Munck ("Die Tradition über das Matthäusevangelium bei Papias," in *Neotestamentica et Semitica* [NovTSup 6; Leiden: Brill, 1962], 249ff.) disposes of the entire problem by supposing Papias was in error and that the early assumption of a Semitic source for Matthew developed in connection with the formation of the canon as a way to resolve the Synoptic Problem. Munck's proposal confuses content and purpose. Even if Papias and others were interested in explaining synoptic differences (a doubtful point), it does not follow that their "facts" are historically incorrect. It would be necessary to show they invented their "facts" in order to offer an explanation.

This is possible, but we have already seen that Papias's testimony may not support a Semitic Matthew at all. And it remains linguistically improbable that the whole of Matthew was originally in Aramaic.

There are other proposed solutions to the Synoptic Problem, generally of much greater complexity. But not only do they suffer from the improbability of some of their details; the theories as a whole are so complex as to be unprovable.

The two-source hypothesis remains the most attractive general solution. This does not mean that it can be proved with mathematical certainty or that all arguments advanced in its favor are convincing.[59] But some small details are very weighty. Robert Gundry has shown that the OT quotations and allusions Matthew and Mark have in common are consistently from the LXX, whereas those found in Matthew alone are drawn from a variety of versions and textual traditions.[60] It is singularly unlikely that Mark was condensing Matthew, for so consistent a collection of Matthew's OT quotations—only those from the LXX—seems too coincidental to be believed. The pattern is easy enough to understand if Matthew depended on Mark.[61]

Yet in itself the two-source hypothesis is almost certainly too simple. Source-critical questions are enormously complex;[62] many facets of the question demand tighter controls.[63] Moreover, close study has convinced some careful scholars that the evidence does not warrant the degree of certainty with which many hold the two-source hypothesis.[64] Such uncertainty is unpopular, but it is scarcely more scientific to go beyond the evidence than to admit uncertainty where the evidence does not provide an adequate basis for anything more. Such hesitations are especially anathema to radical redaction critics, for every major redaction-critical study of Matthew rests on the two-source hypothesis. Their aim is to find out how Matthew changed Mark.

---

59. David Wenham ("The Synoptic Problem Revisited: Some New Suggestions about the Composition of Mark 4:1–34," *TynBul* 23 [1972]: 8–17) exposes some of the weaker arguments—though not all of his criticisms are equally telling.

60. Gundry, *Use of the Old Testament*.

61. Occasionally Gundry's judgment regarding textual affinities may be called into question, especially when he deals with brief allusions to the OT rather than explicit quotations, though the thrust of his argument is not lessened by these few points. D. Wenham ("Synoptic Problem") unsuccessfully attempts to reduce the cogency of Gundry's argument. Wenham points out that Mark almost always cites the OT on the lips of participants in his narrative, not in his own descriptions, and that Matthew normally uses the LXX when his participants cite the OT, even though his own use of the OT betrays a much broader array of textual affinities. Therefore it is possible, Wenham reasons, that Mark depended on Matthew; and Mark's consistent appeal to the LXX is explained by his decision to use OT (and therefore LXX) quotations primarily when they are on the lips of participants in his narratives. Wenham's critique, though clever, is not convincing. Not only are there exceptions to his observations, but more importantly, Wenham deals only with explicit OT quotations, not with OT allusions that, though harder to handle, are more widely distributed.

62. See Palmer, *Logic of Gospel Criticism*, 112–74.

63. For instance, we speak of Q with little consensus of what is meant (cf. S. Schulz, *Q: Die Spruchquelle der Evangelisten* [Zurich: Theologischer Verlag, 1972]; M. Devisch, "Le document Q source de Matthieu. Problematique actuelle," in *L'Évangile selon Matthieu: Rédaction et Théologie* (ed. M. Didier; BETL 29; Gembloux: Duculot, 1972), 71–97. Joseph A. Fitzmyer (*A Wandering Aramean: Collected Aramaic Essays* [Missoula, Mont.: Scholars Press, 1978], 1ff., 85ff.) offers wise counsel on method in the search for Aramaic substrata underlying sayings of Jesus in the NT.

64. See esp. E. P. Sanders, *The Tendencies of the Synoptic Tradition* (SNTSMS 9; Cambridge: Cambridge Univ. Press, 1969).

In view of the weaknesses inherent in a radical use of redaction criticism and the uncertainties surrounding the two-source hypothesis, this commentary adopts a cautious stance. The two-source hypothesis is sufficiently credible that we do not hesitate to speak of Matthew's changes of, additions to, and omissions from Mark. But such statements say little about historicity or about the relative antiquity of competing traditions.[65] In some instances it is apparent that Matthew used not only Mark but Q (however Q is conceived), probably other sources, and perhaps his own memory as well. In some instances an excellent case can be made for Matthew's use of a source earlier than Mark. Any theory of literary dependence must also face subsidiary problems, such as the perplexing features of Luke's "central section" (see comments at 19:1–2). Changes Matthew has introduced may sometimes be motivated by other than theological concerns; but in any case the total content of any pericope in Matthew's gospel as a whole is a more reliable guide to determine distinct theological bent than the isolated change.

As for diversity (see comments at 16:13–20; 19:16–30), the detailed differences must be treated and plausible reasons for the changes suggested. Rarely, however, are the solutions offered in this commentary so dependent on the two-source hypothesis that a shift in scholarly opinion on the Synoptic Problem would irreparably damage them. The aim throughout has been to let Matthew speak as a theologian and historian independent of Mark, even if Mark has been one of his most important sources.[66]

4. UNITY

The question of the unity of Matthew's gospel has little to do with source-critical questions. Instead it deals with how well the evangelist has integrated his material to form cohesive pericopes and a coherent whole. In sections very difficult to interpret (e.g., ch. 24), it is sometimes argued that the evangelist has sewn together diverse traditions that by nature are incapable of genuine coherence. Failing to understand the material, he simply passed it on without recognizing that some of his sources were mutually incompatible.

There are so many signs of high literary craftsmanship in this gospel that such skepticism is unjustified. It is more likely, not to say more humble, to suppose that in some instances we may not understand enough of the first-century setting to be able to grasp exactly what the text says.

5. AUTHORSHIP

Nowhere does the first gospel name its author. The universal testimony of the early church is that the apostle Matthew wrote it, and our earliest textual witnesses attribute it to him (*kata Matthaion*). How much of that testimony depends on Papias is uncertain. We have already noted that many today think Papias is referring to some source of canonical Matthew rather than to the finished work or, alternatively, that Papias was wrong (see section 3). If Papias is right, the theory of Matthew's authorship may receive gentle support from passages like 10:3, where on this theory the apostle refers to himself in a self-deprecating way not found in Mark or Luke.

65. See Meyer, *Aims of Jesus*, 71–72.

66. See the restrained summary in John Nolland, *The Gospel of Matthew: A Commentary on the Greek Text* (Grand Rapids: Eerdmans, 2005), 4–9.

Modern literary criticism offers many reasons for rejecting Matthew's authorship. If the two-source hypothesis is correct, then (it is argued) it is unlikely that the eyewitness and apostle Matthew would depend so heavily on a document written by Mark, who was neither an apostle nor (for most events) an eyewitness. Moreover, the reconstructions of canonical Matthew's life setting, fostered by redaction criticism, converge on AD 80–100 in some kind of savage Jewish-Christian conflict. This is probably a trifle late to assume Matthew's authorship (though cf. traditions that say the apostle John composed his gospel ca. AD 90); and the details of the reconstructed settings discourage the notion. Werner Kümmel argues that "the systematic and therefore nonbiographical form of the structure of Matthew, the late-apostolic theological position and the Greek language of Matthew make this proposal completely impossible."[67] He concludes that the identity of the first evangelist is unknown to us but that he must have been a Greek-speaking Jewish Christian with some rabbinic knowledge, who depended on "a form of the Jesus tradition which potently accommodated the sayings of Jesus to Jewish viewpoints."[68]

These reasons for rejecting Matthew's authorship are widely accepted today. Thus alternate proposals have sprung up. George Kilpatrick suggests that the early patristic tradition connecting the first gospel with Matthew arose as a conscious community pseudonym by the church that wrote the gospel, in order to gain acceptance and authority for it.[69] Ernest Abel argues that Matthew's extra material is so confused and contradictory that we must assume it represents the efforts of two separate individuals working independently of each other.[70] Several redaction-critical studies have denied that the author was a Jew, feeling that the antipathy exhibited toward Jesus in this gospel and the ignorance of Jewish life are so deep that the writer must have been a Gentile Christian.[71] Those who think Papias was referring to Q or to some other source used by Matthew are often prepared to say that the apostle composed the source if not the gospel.[72] There are several other theories.

The objections are not as weighty as they at first seem. If what the modern world calls "plagiarism" (the wholesale takeover, without acknowledgment, of another document) was an acceptable literary practice in the ancient world, it is difficult to see why an apostle might not find it congenial. If Matthew thought Mark's account to be reliable and generally suited to his purposes (and he may also have known that Peter stood behind it), there can be no objection to the view that an apostle depended on a nonapostolic document. Kümmel's rejection of Matthew's authorship on the grounds that this gospel is "systematic and therefore nonbiographical"[73] is a non sequitur because (1) a topically ordered account can yield biographical facts as easily as a strictly chronological account,[74] and (2) Kümmel wrongly supposes that apostolicity

67. Werner Georg Kümmel, *Introduction to the New Testament* (trans. Howard Clark Kee; Nashville: Abingdon, 1975), 121.

68. Ibid.

69. Kilpatrick, *Origins of the Gospel according to Matthew*, 138–39.

70. Ernest L. Abel, "Who Wrote Matthew?" *NTS* 17 (1970–71): 138–52.

71. See John P. Meier, *The Vision of Matthew: Christ, Church, and Morality in the First Gospel* (New York: Paulist, 1979), 17–23; Strecker, *Weg der Gerechtigkeit*, 34; Sjef van Tilborg, *The Jewish Leaders in Matthew* (Leiden: Brill, 1972), 171.

72. See, e.g., Hill, *Matthew.*

73. Kümmel, *Introduction to the New Testament*, 121.

74. Not a few contemporary biographies treat certain parts of their subject's life in topical arrangements (e.g., A. Fraser, *Cromwell: Our Chief of Men* [St. Albans: Panther, 1975], esp. 455ff.).

is for some reason incapable of choosing anything other than a chronological form. The alleged lateness of the theological position may be disputed at every point (see section 6).

Those who argue that the author could not have been a Jew, let alone an apostle, allege serious ignorance of Jewish life, including inability to distinguish between the doctrines of the Pharisees and the Sadducees (16:12) or, worse, thinking that the Sadducees were still an active force after AD 70 (22:23). But the second of these two passages has synoptic parallels (Mk 12:18; Lk 20:27; here Matthew has interpreted Mark's verb as a historical present); and neither Matthean passage denies that there are differences separating Pharisees and Sadducees—differences Matthew elsewhere highlights (22:23–33)—but merely insists that on some things the Pharisees and Sadducees could cooperate. This is scarcely surprising. After all, both groups sat in the same Sanhedrin. Politics and theology make strange bedfellows (see section 11.f). Other "glaring errors"[75] prove equally ephemeral (e.g., Matthew's use of Zec 9:9; see comments at 21:4–5). Also Kilpatrick's suggestion of a conscious community pseudonym cannot offer any parallel.[76]

The charge that the Greek of the first gospel is too good to have come from a Galilean Jew overlooks the trilingual character of Galilee, the possibility that Matthew greatly improved his Greek as the church reached out to more and more Greek speakers (both Jews and Gentiles), and the discussion of Robert Gundry, who argues that Matthew's training and vocation as a tax gatherer (9:9–13; 10:3) would have uniquely equipped him not only with the languages of Galilee but with an orderly mind and the habit of jotting down notes, which may have played a large part in the transmission of the apostolic gospel tradition.[77] C. F. D. Moule wonders whether 13:52, which many take as an oblique self-reference by the evangelist, hides a use of *grammateus* (GK *1208*) that does not mean "teacher of the law" (NIV) but "clerk," or "secular scribe." "Is it not conceivable that the Lord really did say to that tax collector Matthew, 'You have been a "writer" ...; you have had plenty to do with the commercial side of just the topics alluded to in the parables—farmer's stock, fields, treasure-trove, fishing revenues; now that you have become a disciple, you can bring all this out again—but with a difference.'"[78]

Moule proposes an apostle who was a secular scribe and note taker and who wrote primarily in a Semitic language, leaving behind material that was arranged by another scribe, a Greek writer unknown to us. One may wonder if *grammateus*, used so often in the Jewish sense of "teacher of the law," can so easily be assigned a secular sense. But whatever its other merits or demerits, Moule's argument suggests that the link between this first gospel and the apostle Matthew cannot be dismissed as easily as some have thought.

Richard Bauckham has recently introduced a fresh argument against Matthean authorship. On the basis of his study of equivalent names in the first century, Bauckham does not think that the "Levi" of Mark 2:14–17 can be identified with the "Matthew" of Matthew 9:9–13 (see comments at 9:9). He suggests that the writer *knew* Matthew.[79] That is possible, but Bauckham seems to be hanging much on very little.[80]

---

75. So Meier, *Vision of Matthew*, 17–23.
76. Kilpatrick, *Origins of the Gospel according to Matthew*.
77. Gundry, *Use of the Old Testament*, 178–85.
78. C. F. D. Moule, "St. Matthew's Gospel: Some Neglected Features," *SE* 2 (1964): 98.
79. Bauckham, *Jesus and the Eyewitnesses*, 108–12.
80. See Michael J. Kruger, review of Richard Bauckham, *Jesus and the Eyewitnesses*, *WTJ* 69 (2007): 413–17.

None of the arguments for Matthew's authorship are conclusive. Thus we cannot be entirely certain who the author of the first gospel is. But there are solid reasons in support of the early church's unanimous ascription of this book to the apostle Matthew, and on close inspection the objections do not appear substantial. Though Matthew's authorship remains the most defensible position,[81] very little in this commentary depends on it. Where it may have a bearing on the discussion, a cautionary notice is inserted.

6. DATE

During the first three centuries of the church, Matthew was the most highly revered and frequently quoted canonical gospel.[82] The earliest extant documents referring to Matthew are the epistles of Ignatius (esp. *To the Smyrnaeans* 1.1 [cf. Mt 3:15], ca. AD 110–15). So the end of the first century or thereabouts is the latest date for the gospel of Matthew to have been written.

The earliest possible date is much more difficult to nail down because it depends on so many other disputed points. If Luke depends on Matthew (which seems unlikely), then the date of Luke would establish a new terminus ad quem for Matthew; and the date of Luke is bound up with the date of Acts.[83] If the Griesbach hypothesis (see sections 1 and 3) is correct, then Matthew would have to be earlier than Mark. Conversely, if the two-source hypothesis is adopted, Matthew is later than Mark; and a terminus a quo is theoretically established. Even so there are two difficulties. First, we do not know when Mark was written, but most estimates fall between AD 50 and 65. Second, on this basis most critics think Matthew could not have been written until 75 or 80. But even if Mark is as late as 65, there is no reason based on literary dependence why Matthew could not be dated AD 66. As soon as a written source is circulated, it is available for copying.

Two other arguments are commonly advanced to support the view now in the ascendancy that Matthew was written between 80 and 100 (between which dates there is great diversity of opinion). First, many scholars detect numerous anachronistic details. Though many of these are discussed in the commentary, one frequently cited instance will serve as an example. It is often argued that Matthew transforms the parable of the great banquet (Lk 14:15–24) into the parable of the wedding banquet (Mt 22:1–14); and the process of transformation includes an explicit reference to the destruction of Jerusalem in AD 70 (22:7). Therefore this gospel must have been written after that. But the conclusion is much too hasty. Those who deny that Jesus could foretell the future concede that Mark predicts the fall of Jerusalem (Mk 13:14; Mt 24:15), arguing that if Mark wrote about AD 65, he was so close to the events that he could see how political circumstances were shaping up. But on this reasoning Matthew could have done the same thing in 66.

More fundamentally, it is at least doubtful that Matthew's parable (22:1–10) is a mere rewriting of Luke 14:15–24; more likely they are separate parables.[84] And on what ground must we insist that Jesus could

81. See E. J. Goodspeed, *Matthew, Apostle and Evangelist* (Philadelphia: Winston, 1959); Guthrie, *New Testament Introduction*, 33–44; Maier, *Matthäus-Evangelium*; very cautiously, E. F. Harrison, *Introduction to the New Testament* (2nd ed.; Grand Rapids: Eerdmans, 1971), 176–77, and esp. Gundry, *Matthew*, 609–22; Stonehouse, *Origins of the Synoptic Gospels*, 1–47.

82. See E. Masseaux, *Influence de l'Évangile de Saint Matthieu sur la littérature chrétienne avant Saint Irenée* (Louvain: Publications Universitaires de Louvain, 1950).

83. Cf. esp. A. J. Mattill Jr., "The Date and Purpose of Luke-Acts: Rackham Reconsidered," *CBQ* 40 (1978): 335–50.

84. See Stonehouse, *Origins of the Synoptic Gospels*, 35–42.

not foretell the future? That conclusion derives, not from the evidence, but from an antisupernatural presuppositionalism. Moreover, the language of 22:7 derives from OT categories of judgment,[85] not from the description of an observer. One could almost say that the lack of more detailed description of the events of AD 70 argues for an earlier date. In any event, if it is legitimate to deduce from 22:7 a post–70 date, it must surely be no less legitimate to deduce from 5:23–24, 12:5–7; 23:16–22; and 26:60–61 a pre–70 date, when the temple was still standing. The absurdity of this contradictory conclusion must warn us against the dangers of basing the date of composition on passages that permit other interpretations.

Second, recent studies have tended to argue that the life setting presupposed by the theological stance of the gospel best fits the conditions of AD 80–100. It is more difficult to reconstruct a life setting than is commonly recognized (see section 2). Many of the criteria for doing so are doubtful. Explicit references to "church" (16:18; 18:17–18) are taken to reflect an interest in later church order. But the authenticity of 16:18 has been ably defended by B. F. Meyer and others (see comments at 16:17–20). Moreover 18:17–18 says nothing about the details of order (e.g., elders or deacons are not mentioned) but only of broad principles appropriate to the earliest stages of Christianity. Persecution (24:9) and false prophets (24:11) are often taken to reflect circumstances of 80–100. Yet these circumstances appear as prophecies in Matthew and did not need to wait for 80, as Acts and the early Pauline epistles make clear.

Though Matthew's gospel seems to presuppose uneasy relations between church and synagogue, the gospel is less anti-Jewish than anti-Jewish leaders and their position on Jesus (see section 11.f); and such a stance stretches all the way back to the days of Jesus' ministry. Significantly, Matthew records more warnings against the Sadducees than all other NT writers combined; and after AD 70 the Sadducees no longer existed as a center of authority. Other small touches seem to show that a definite break with Judaism had not yet occurred;[86] and these agree with Bo Reicke, who says, "The situation presupposed by Matthew corresponds to what is known about Christianity in Palestine between AD 50 and ca. 64."[87]

We must face the awkward fact that criteria such as Matthew's Christology are not very reliable indices of Matthew's date (see section 11.a). They might easily allow a range from 40 to 100. Gundry believes Luke depends on Matthew and that Luke-Acts was completed not later than 63, so he concludes that Matthew must be still earlier.[88] Clearly this conclusion is only as valid as the hypothesis of Luke's dependence on

---

85. See Bo Reicke, "Synoptic Prophecies on the Destruction of Jerusalem," in *Studies in New Testament and Early Christian Literature* (ed. D. E. Aune; Leiden: Brill, 1972), 123.

86. See Robinson, *Redating the New Testament*, 103–5, esp. 103: "Matthew's gospel shows all the signs of being produced for a community (and by a community) that needed to formulate, over against the main body of Pharisaic and Sadducaic Judaism, its own line on such issues as the interpretation of scripture and the place of the law, its attitude to the temple and its sacrifices, the Sabbath, fasting, prayer, food laws and purification rites, its rules for admission to the community and the discipline of offenders, for marriage, divorce and celibacy, its policy toward Samaritans and Gentiles in a predominantly Jewish milieu, and so on. These problems reflect a period when the needs of co-existence force a clarification of what is the distinctively Christian line on a number of practical issues which previously could be taken for granted." (See further section 8.) This view differs from that of Douglas Hare and others who think a decisive break had already come about by the time this gospel was written.

87. Reicke, "Synoptic Prophecies," 133.

88. Gundry, *Matthew*, 599ff.

Matthew, a hypothesis that does not seem well grounded. While surprisingly little in the gospel conclusively points to a firm date, perhaps the sixties are the most likely decade for its composition.[89]

7. PLACE OF COMPOSITION AND DESTINATION

Most scholars take Antioch as the place of composition. Antioch was a Greek-speaking city with a substantial Jewish population; and the first clear evidence of anyone using the gospel of Matthew comes from Ignatius, bishop of Antioch at the beginning of the second century. This is as good a guess as any. Yet we must remember that Ignatius depends more on John's gospel and the Pauline epistles than on Matthew. But this does not mean they were all written in Antioch.

Other centers proposed in recent years include Alexandria,[90] Edessa,[91] the province of Syria,[92] and perhaps Tyre[93] or Caesarea Maritima.[94] In each instance the grounds are inadequate.[95] More plausible is H. Dixon Slingerland's proposal that Matthew 4:15 and 19:1 show that the gospel was written somewhere east of the Jordan (he specifies Pella, but this is an unnecessary and unprovable refinement).[96] If he is right, then Antioch is ruled out.

We cannot be sure of the first gospel's place of composition. Still more uncertain is its destination. The usual assumption is that the evangelist wrote it to meet the needs of his own center—a not implausible view. But the evangelist may have been more itinerant than usually assumed; and out of such a ministry he may have written his gospel to strengthen and inform a large number of followers and to give them an evangelistic and apologetic tool. We do not know. The only reasonably certain conclusion is that this gospel was written somewhere in the Roman province of Syria, and many others (for the area covered by the designation "Syria," see comments at 4:25).[97]

8. OCCASION AND PURPOSE

Unlike many of Paul's epistles or even John's gospel (20:30–31), Matthew tells his readers nothing about his purpose in writing or its occasion. To some extent, the gospel shows Matthew's purpose in the way it presents certain information about Jesus. But to go much beyond this and specify the kind of group(s) Matthew was addressing, the kind of problems they faced, and his own deep psychological and theological motivations may verge on speculation. Three restraints are necessary.

---

89. Similarly France, *Matthew*, 18–19.
90. Van Tilborg, *Jewish Leaders in Matthew*, 172.
91. Benjamin W. Bacon, *Studies in Matthew* (London: Constable, 1930), 15, 36, 51; R. E. Osborne, "The Provenance of Matthew's Gospel," *SR* 3 (1973): 22–25.
92. E. Schweizer, *Matthäus und seine Gemeinde* (Stuttgart: KBW, 1974), 138–39f.
93. Kilpatrick, *Origins of the Gospel according to Matthew*, 130ff.
94. B. T. Viviano, "Where Was the Gospel According to Matthew Written?" *CBQ* 41 (1979): 533–46.
95. See Stanton, "Origin and Purpose," ch. 5; Hill, *Matthew*.
96. H. Dixon Slingerland, "The Transjordanian Origin of St. Matthew's Gospel," *JSNT* 3 (1979): 18–28.
97. So Filson, *Gospel according to St. Matthew*; Kümmel, *Introduction to the New Testament*, 119–20; France, *Gospel of Matthew* [NICNT]; Hill, *Gospel of Matthew*.

1. It is unwise to specify too precise an occasion and purpose because the possibility of error and distortion increases as one leaves hard evidence behind for supposition.

2. It is unwise to specify only one purpose; reductionism cannot do justice to the diversity of Matthew's themes.

3. Great caution is needed in reconstructing the situation in the church of Matthew's time from material that speaks of the historical Jesus (see sections 1–3). In one sense, this may be legitimate, for in all probability Matthew did not compose his gospel simply out of a dispassionate curiosity about history. He intended to address his contemporaries. But it does not necessarily follow that what he alleges occurred in Jesus' day is immediately transferable to his own day.

Nowhere are these restraints more important than in weighing recent discussion about the diverse emphases on evangelism in this gospel. On the one hand, the disciples are forbidden to preach to others than Jews (10:5–6); on the other, they are commanded to preach to all nations (28:18–20). Because of this bifurcation, some scholars have suggested that Matthew is preserving the traditions of two distinct communities—one that remained narrowly Jewish and the other that was more outward looking. Others think Matthew had to walk a tightrope between conflicting perspectives within his own community, and therefore he preserves both viewpoints—a sort of committee report that satisfied neither side. Still others erect a more specific "occasion" for this tension, a conflict between the church and the synagogue over the place of Gentile mission, with Matthew taking a mediating (not to say compromised) position whose aim was to avoid cleavage between the two groups.[98] Though such reconstructions cannot be ruled out, they suffer from a serious flaw. They fail to recognize that Matthew himself makes distinctions between what Jesus expects and demands during his earthly ministry and what he expects and demands after his resurrection.

Matthew 10:5–6 tells us what Jesus required of his disciples in their first-recorded major assignment; it does not necessarily tell us anything about what was going on in Matthew's day. The reason Matthew includes 10:6 as well as 28:18–20, and all the texts akin to one passage or the other, may be to explain how Jesus began with his own people and moved outward from there. One might argue that Jesus' own example is the foundation of Paul's "first for the Jew, then for the Gentile" (Ro 1:14–17). This change develops not merely on pragmatic grounds but as the outworking of a particular understanding of the OT (see comments at 1:1; 4:12–17; 8:5–13; 12:21; 13:11–17) and of the distinctive role of Jesus the Messiah in salvation history (see comments at 2:1–12; 3:2; 4:12–17; 5:17–20; 8:16–17; 10:16–20; 11:7–15, 20–24; 12:41–42; 13:36–43; 15:21–39; 21:1–11, 42–44; 24:14; 26:26–29, 64; 28:18–20). Matthew thus shows how from the nascent community during Jesus' ministry the present commission of the church developed.

If this is a responsible approach to the evidence, then we are not justified in postulating conflicting strands of tradition within the Matthean community. It may be that by this retelling of the changed perspective effected by Jesus' resurrection Matthew is encouraging Jewish Christians to evangelize beyond

98. There are many other reconstructions. For example, K. W. Clark ("The Gentile Bias in Matthew," *JBL* 66 [1947]: 165–72) argues that the evangelist or final redactor must have been a Gentile addressing a Gentile Christian church. Schuyler Brown ("The Matthean Community and the Gentile Mission," *NovT* 22 [1980]: 193–221) locates the Matthean church in a Greek-speaking area of Syria, after AD 70, when much Jewish Christianity was forced to move to Syria and therefore new crises in evangelism and conflicts with the Pharisees arose.

their own race. Or it may be that he is justifying before non-Christian Jews what he and his fellow Christian Jews are doing. Or it may be that he is explaining the origins of Christian mission to zealous Jewish-Christian personal evangelists who after the warmth of their initial experience want to learn about the historical developments and teaching of Jesus that made the Jewish remnant of his day the church of their own day. Or it may be that, though such questions have not yet arisen, Matthew foresees that they cannot be long delayed and, like a good pastor, decides to forestall the problem by clear teaching. Or it may be that Matthew has Gentile readers in mind. Or it may be that all these factors were at work because Matthew envisages an extensive and varied readership. Several other possibilities come to mind. But such precise reconstructions outstrip the evidence, fail to consider what other purposes Matthew may have had in mind, and frequently ignore the fact that he purports to talk about Jesus, not a Christian community in the sixth, eighth, or tenth decade of the first century.

Particularly unfortunate are several recent works that define the purpose of Matthew's gospel in categories, both reductionistic and improbable. Rolf Walker argues that Matthew does not reflect specific church problems but that it was written as a piece of theological combat, designed to show that Israel has been totally rejected in the history of salvation and had been displaced by the church so completely that the Great Commission must be understood as a command to evangelize Gentiles only (see comments at 28:18–20).[99] The Jewish leaders are nothing but representative figures, and Matthew's gospel as a whole has no interest in and little accurate information about the historical Jesus. Only rarely is Walker exegetically convincing; nowhere does he adequately struggle with the fact that all the disciples and early converts are Jews.

Hubert Frankemölle in his final chapter argues that Matthew's work is so different from Mark's—long discourses, careful structure, prologue, epilogue—that it is meaningless to say it is a "gospel" in the same sense as Mark (see section 12).[100] Instead, Matthew belongs to the literary *Gattung* (form or genre) to which Deuteronomy and Chronicles belong. Frankemölle cites several phrases (e.g., cf. Dt 31:1, 24; 32:44–45) used by Matthew to round off his own discourses, and from such evidence he concludes that Matthew's "gospel" is in reality a "book of history," not of "salvation history" as normally understood but of the community as it summarized its beliefs.[101] Matthew, Frankemölle maintains, does not distinguish between the life and teaching of the historical Jesus and that of the present exalted Lord. In his "literary fiction," Matthew fuses the two.[102] Thus Jesus becomes the idealized authority behind Matthew the theologian, who here addresses his community. But Frankemölle overemphasizes formal differences between Mark and Matthew and neglects the substantial differences between Matthew and Deuteronomy or Chronicles. His investigation is far from evenhanded.

Frankemölle's insistence that Matthew is a unified book is surely right. Yet a book may be theologically unified by appealing to prophecy-fulfillment and other salvation-historical categories. Theological unity does not entail ignoring historical data. Moreover, neither Walker nor Frankemölle adequately recognizes

99. Rolf Walker, *Die Heilsgeschichte im ersten Evangelium* (Göttingen: Vandenhoeck & Ruprecht, 1967).

100. Frankemölle, *Jahwebund und Kirche Christi.*

101. Ibid., 394.

102. Ibid., 351.

that for most of his gospel Matthew depends heavily on Mark and Q (however Q may be understood). Matthew was creative, but not as creative as Walker and Frankemölle think.

Michael Goulder offers a lectionary theory.[103] Arguing somewhat along the lines of Carrington and Kilpatrick,[104] Goulder maintains that Matthew's purpose was to provide a liturgical book. He argues that the evangelist has taken the pattern of lections of the Jewish festal year as his base and developed a series of readings to be used in liturgical worship week by week. Mark, a lectionary book for a half-year cycle, has been expanded by Matthew (not the apostle) to a yearlong lectionary; and Mark is Matthew's only source. Luke, dependent on Matthew, has also written a lectionary for a full year but has displaced the festal cycle followed by Matthew with the annual Sabbath cycle of readings. Q does not exist.

Despite Goulder's immense erudition, there is little to commend his thesis. We know very little of the patterns of worship in first-century Judaism.[105] At the end of the second century AD, triennial cycles were used in some Jewish worship. But the annual cycles Goulder discerns behind Luke are almost certainly later than their triennial counterparts. As for Matthew, we have no evidence of a fixed "festal lectionary" in the first century; and even if it existed, it would have been connected with temple worship, with no evidence that it was ever connected with the synagogue worship Goulder's thesis requires.[106]

Not only is our knowledge of first-century *Jewish* liturgical custom very slender, our knowledge of *Christian* worship in the first century is even more slender. Thus we do not know whether Christian lectionary cycles—if they existed—developed out of Jewish lectionary cycles—if those cycles existed! Certainly by the time of Justin Martyr, the churches of which he had knowledge read the "memoirs of the apostles" (i.e., the Gospels) for "as long as time allowed,"[107] not according to some lectionary specification. Moreover, to make his pattern fit, Goulder must postulate lections in Matthew that vary enormously in length. Goulder's thesis is unlikely to convince many.[108]

In recent years, a number of scholars have emphasized the "anti-Gentile" passages in Matthew (5:46–47; 6:7–8, 31–32; 18:17) and downplayed the Great Commission (28:19) to conclude that Matthew's church is essentially still deeply Jewish, such that the Gentiles are at best a peripheral interest.[109] This seems as lop-sided, but in the opposite direction, as the view that insists Matthew's church is entirely separate from the Jewish world.[110] Moreover, we have already seen that it is precarious to build more than vague suggestions about Matthew's "church" when (1) the document itself purports to give us information about Jesus in the

103. Goulder, *Midrash and Lection*.

104. P. Carrington, *The Primitive Christian Calendar* (Cambridge: Cambridge Univ. Press, 1952); Kilpatrick, *Origins of the Gospel according to Matthew*, 100.

105. See Leon Morris, *The New Testament and the Jewish Lectionaries* (London: Tyndale, 1964).

106. See Stanton, "Origin and Purpose," ch. 4.

107. Justin Martyr, *1 Apol.* 1.67.

108. See critical reviews of Goulder's *Midrash and Lection in Matthew* in *Int* 30 (1976): 91–94; in *JBL* (1977), 453–55; and in J. D. G. Dunn, *Unity and Diversity in the New Testament* (London: SCM Press, 1977), 141–48.

109. See esp. David C. Sim, *The Gospel of Matthew and Christian Judaism: The History and Social Setting of the Matthean Community* (Edinburgh: T&T Clark, 1998).

110. See France, *Gospel of Matthew* [NICNT], 17.

days of his flesh, and (2) it is increasingly viewed as at least possible, and perhaps probable, that Matthew's intended readership was not a well-defined "Matthean church" but Christians everywhere.[111]

Numerous studies characterized by more sober judgment have contributed to our understanding of Matthew's purposes. Many of these are referred to in the commentary. At the broadest level, we may say that Matthew's purpose is to demonstrate that (1) Jesus is the promised Messiah, the Son of David, the Son of God, the Son of Man, Immanuel; (2) many Jews, and especially the leaders, sinfully failed to perceive this during his ministry; (3) the messianic kingdom has already dawned, inaugurated by the life, ministry, death, resurrection, and exaltation of Jesus; (4) this messianic reign, characterized by obedience to Jesus and consummated by his return, is the fulfillment of OT prophetic hopes; (5) the church, the community of those, both Jew and Gentile, who bow unqualifiedly to Jesus' authority, constitutes the true locus of the people of God and the witness to the world of the "gospel of the kingdom"; and (6) throughout this age Jesus' true disciples must overcome temptation, endure persecution from a hostile world, witness to the truth of the gospel, and live in deeply rooted submission to Jesus' ethical demands, even as they enjoy the new covenant, which is simultaneously the fulfillment of old covenant anticipation and the experience of forgiveness bestowed by the Messiah who came to save his people from their sins and who came to give his life as a ransom for many.

Such a complex array of themes was doubtless designed to meet many needs: (1) to instruct and perhaps catechize (something facilitated by the careful arrangement of some topical sections);[112] (2) to provide apologetic and evangelistic material, especially in winning Jews; (3) to encourage believers in their witness before a hostile world; and (4) to inspire deeper faith in Jesus the Messiah, along with a maturing understanding of his person, work, and unique place in the unfolding history of redemption.

9. CANONICITY

As far as our sources go, the gospel of Matthew was promptly and universally received as soon as it was published.[113] It never suffered the debates that divided the Eastern church and the Western church over, for example, the epistle to the Hebrews but was everywhere regarded as Scripture, at least from Ignatius (d. 110) onward.

10. TEXT

Compared with that of Acts, the text of Matthew is fairly stable. Important variants do occur, however, and some of these are discussed. The most difficult textual questions in Matthew arise because it is a Synoptic Gospel. This provides many opportunities for harmonization or disharmonization in the textual tradition (see comments at 12:47; 16:2–3; 18:10–11). Although harmonization is a secondary feature, this does not necessarily mean that every instance of possible harmonization must be understood as being secondary (see comments at 12:4, 47; 13:35). Certainly harmonization is more common in the sayings of Jesus than

111. See Richard Bauckham, ed., *The Gospels for All Christians: Rethinking the Gospel Audiences* (Grand Rapids: Eerdmans, 1998).

112. See Moule, *Birth of the New Testament*, 91.

113. This does not rule out debate over whether some documents are actually dependent on Matthew. See, esp., Huub van de Sandt, ed., *Matthew and the Didache: Two Documents from the Same Jewish-Christian Milieu?* (Assen: Van Gorcum, 2005).

elsewhere. But much work remains to be done in this area, especially in examining the phenomenon of harmonization in conjunction with the Synoptic Problem (cf. section 3).[114]

11. THEMES AND SPECIAL PROBLEMS

We may consider Matthew's principal themes along with the special problems of this gospel, because so many of Matthew's themes have turned into foci for strenuous debate. To avoid needless repetition, the following paragraphs do not so much summarize the nine themes selected as sketch in the debate and then provide references to the places in the commentary where these things are discussed.

a. Christology

Approaches to the distinctive elements of Matthew's Christology usually run along one of three lines, and these are not mutually exclusive.

The first compares Matthew with Mark to detect what differences lie between the two wherever they run parallel. Perhaps the first important study along these lines was an essay by G. M. Styler.[115] He argues that Matthew's Christology is frequently more explicit than Mark's (he compares, for instance, the two accounts of the triumphal entry [21:1–11]). This is surely right, at least in some instances. But it is much less certain that Matthew focuses more attention than Mark on ontology (see comments at 9:1–8; 19:16–17), at least in those pericopes treated by both evangelists.[116]

The second approach examines the christological titles used in Matthew's gospel. These are rich and diverse. "Son of David" appears in the first verse, identifying Jesus as the promised Davidic Messiah, and then the title recurs, often on the lips of the needy and the ill, who anticipate relief from him who will bring in the messianic age (see comments at 9:27). Matthew uses *kyrios* ("Lord," GK *3261*) more often than Mark, and some have taken this to indicate an anachronistic ascription of divinity to Jesus. But *kyrios* is a word with a broad semantic range. It often means no more than "sir" (e.g., 13:27). It seems fairer to say that Matthew frequently uses the word because it is vague. During Jesus' ministry before the cross, it is very doubtful whether it was used as an unqualified confession of deity. But because it is the most common LXX term for referring to God, the greater insight into Jesus' person and work afforded by the postresurrection perspective made the disciples see a deeper significance to their own use of *kyrios* than they could have intended at first. A somewhat similar but more complex ambiguity surrounds "Son of Man," which is discussed in the Reflections (p. 247). Other titles receive comment where they are used by the evangelist.

The third approach to Matthew's Christology is the examination of broad themes, either in exclusively Matthean material (e.g., Brian Nolan's study on Mt 1–2, which focuses on a Christology shaped by the

114. See Gordon D. Fee, "Modern Text Criticism and the Synoptic Problem," in *J. J. Griesbach: Synoptic and Text-Critical Studies, 1776–1976* (ed. Bernard Orchard and Thomas R. W. Longstaff; Cambridge: Cambridge Univ. Press, 1978), 154–69; more broadly, cf. C. M. Martini, "La problématique générale du texte de Matthieu," in Didier, *L'Évangile selon Matthieu*, 21–36. See Matthew C. Williams, *Two Gospels from One: A Comprehensive Text-Critical Analysis of the Synoptic Gospels* (Grand Rapids: Kregel, 2006).

115. G. M. Styler, "Stages in Christology in the Synoptic Gospels," *NTS* 10 (1963–64): 398–409.

116. See Hill, *Matthew*, 64–66.

Davidic covenant)[117] or throughout the gospel. Some reference is made to these throughout the commentary. Doubtless it is best for these christological titles and themes to emerge from an inductive study of the text, for narrower approaches often issue in substantial distortion. For example, though Jack Dean Kingsbury ably demonstrates how important "Son of God" is in Matthew (see comments at 2:15; 3:17; 4:3; 8:29; 16:16; 17:5; 26:63),[118] his insistence that it is the christological category under which, for Matthew's community, all the others are subsumed cannot be sustained.[119] Matthew offers his readers vignettes linked together in diverse ways. The resulting colorful mosaic is reduced to dull gray when we elevate one theme (a christological title or something else) to a preeminent place that suppresses others.

b. Prophecy and fulfillment

Untutored Christians are prone to think of prophecy and fulfillment as something not very different from straightforward propositional prediction and fulfillment. A close reading of the NT reveals that prophecy is more complex than that. The epistle to the Hebrews, for instance, understands the Levitical sacrificial system to be prophetic of Christ's sacrifice, Melchizedek to point to Jesus as High Priest, and so on. In Matthew we are told that Jesus' return from Egypt fulfills the OT text that refers to the Exodus (2:15); the weeping of the mothers of Bethlehem fulfills Jeremiah's reference to Rachel's weeping for her children in Ramah; the priests' purchase of a field for thirty pieces of silver fulfills Scriptures describing actions performed by Jeremiah and Zechariah (27:9); and, in one remarkable instance, Jesus' move to Nazareth fulfills "what was said through the prophets" even though no specific text appears to be in mind (2:23). Add to this one other major peculiarity. A number (variously estimated between ten and fourteen) of Matthew's OT quotations are introduced by a fulfillment formula characterized by a passive form of *plēroō* ("fulfill," GK *4444*) and a text form rather more removed from the LXX than other OT quotations. These "formula quotations" are all asides of the evangelist, his own reflections (hence the widely used German word for them, *Reflexionszitate*). What explains these phenomena?

Such problems have been extensively studied with very little agreement.[120] When Matthew cites the OT, this commentary deals with many of these issues. In anticipation of these discussions, four observations may be helpful.

---

117. See Brian M. Nolan, *The Royal Son of God: The Christology of Matthew 1–2 in the Setting of the Gospel* (Göttingen: Vandenhoeck & Ruprecht, 1979).

118. See Jack Dean Kingsbury, *Matthew* (Philadelphia: Fortress, 1977).

119. See the telling critique by David Hill, "Son and Servant: An Essay on Matthean Christology," *JSNT* 6 (1980): 2–16. Kingsbury maintains, for instance, that "Son of God" dominates the thought of one section of six chapters where the title does not once appear.

120. See the bibliography in J. W. Doeve, *Jewish Hermeneutics in the Synoptic Gospels and Acts* (Assen: Van Gorcum, 1954), and in Craig Blomberg, "Matthew," in *Commentary on the New Testament Use of the Old Testament* (ed. G. K. Beale and D. A. Carson; Grand Rapids: Baker, 2007), 1–109; Gundry, *Use of the Old Testament*; Richard S. McConnell, *Law and Prophecy in Matthew's Gospel* (Basel: Friedrich Reinhardt, 1969); Wilhelm Rothfuchs, *Die Erfüllungszitate des Matthäus-Evangeliums* (Stuttgart: Kohlhammer, 1969); George M. Soares-Prabhu, *The Formula Quotations in the Infancy Narrative of Matthew* (Rome: Biblical Institute Press, 1976); Stendahl, *School of St. Matthew*; Strecker, *Weg der Gerechtigkeit* .

1. From very different perspectives, Robert Gundry and George Soares-Prabhu argue that Matthew is responsible for the formula quotations (the difference between them is that Gundry thinks the evangelist was the apostle Matthew and Soares-Prabhu does not). Wherever he follows Mark, Matthew uses the LXX; but he in no case clearly demonstrates a personal preference for the LXX by introducing closer assimilation. The most recent major study cautiously argues that what Matthew uses is an already-existing revised form of the LXX,[121] but it still seems difficult to distinguish that stance from one that holds that Matthew selected and sometimes translated the non-LXX formula quotations. Doubtless both Hebrew and Greek OT textual traditions were somewhat fluid during the first century (as the Dead Sea Scrolls attest); and so it is not always possible to tell where the evangelist is using a text form known in his day and where he is providing his own rendering. What does seem certain, however, is that there is no good reason to support the view that the fulfillment quotations arose from a Matthean "school"[122] or were taken over by the evangelist from a collection of testimonia.[123]

2. Though often affirmed, it does not seem very likely that the evangelists, Matthew included, invented their "history" in order to have stories corresponding to their favorite OT proof texts. The question is most acute in Matthew 1–2 and 27:9 and is raised there. Several points, however, argue against a wholesale creation of traditions. The NT writers do not exploit much of the rich OT potential for messianic prediction. The very difficulty of the links between story and OT text argues against the creation of the stories, because created stories would have eliminated the most embarrassing strains. The parallel of the Dead Sea Scrolls cannot be overlooked. Even when they treat the OT most tortuously, the Qumran covenanters do not invent "history."[124]

3. The ways the events surrounding Jesus are said to fulfill the OT vary enormously and cannot be reduced to a single label. Even the Jewish categories commonly applied need certain qualification (on "Midrash," see section 12).

Some of Matthew's fulfillment quotations are said to be examples of pesher exegesis.[125] Such rabbinical exegesis stresses revelation and authoritatively declares, "This event is the fulfillment of that prophecy" (e.g., Ac 2:16). But even here we must be careful. The clearest examples of pesher exegesis are found in 1QpHab. What is striking about its authoritative pronouncements is that the OT prophecy it refers to, Habakkuk, is interpreted exclusively in terms of the "fulfillments" it is related to, making its original context meaningless.[126] Even the most difficult passages in Matthew, such as 2:15, do not hint that the original OT meaning is void—in this case that the people of Israel were not called by God out of Egypt at the exodus.

4. We must now face a difficult question. Even if Matthew does not deny the OT setting of the texts he insists are being fulfilled in Jesus, on what basis does he detect any relationship of prophecy to fulfillment? The verb *plēroō* ("fulfill") is discussed in the commentary (see comments at 2:15 and esp. 5:17); but when it

---

121. See M. J. J. Menken, *Matthew's Bible: The Old Testament Text of the Evangelist* (BETL 173; Leuven: Leuven Univ. Press, 2004).

122. See Stendahl, *School of St. Matthew.*

123. See Strecker, *Weg der Gerechtigkeit.*

124. See Gundry, *Use of the Old Testament*, 193–204.

125. See, e.g., Stendahl, *School of St. Matthew*, 203; Richard N. Longenecker, *Biblical Exegesis in the Apostolic Period* (Grand Rapids: Eerdmans, 1975), 143.

126. See F. F. Bruce, *Biblical Exegesis in the Qumran Texts* (Grand Rapids: Eerdmans, 1960), 16–17.

refers to fulfilling Scripture, it does not lose all teleological force except in rare and well-defined situations. Opinion varies as to exactly how these OT Scriptures point forward. Sometimes the OT passages cited are plainly or at least plausibly messianic. Often the relation between prophecy and fulfillment is typological: Jesus, it is understood, must in some ways recapitulate the experience of Israel or of David. Jesus must undergo wilderness testing and call out twelve sons of Israel as apostles. Even the kind of typology varies considerably. Yet the perception remains constant that the OT was preparing the way for Christ, anticipating him, pointing to him, leading up to him. When we ask how much of this forward-looking or "prophetic" aspect in what the OT writers wrote was recognized by them, the answer must vary with the particular text. But tentative, nuanced judgments are possible, even in the most difficult cases (see comments at 1:23; 2:15, 17–18, 23; 4:15–16; 5:17; 8:16–17; 11:10–11; 12:18–21; 13:13–15; 21:4–5, 16, 42; 22:44; 26:31; 27:9). Care in such formulations will help us perceive the deep ties that bind together the OT and NT.

c. Law

Few topics in the study of Matthew's gospel are more difficult than his attitude to the law. The major studies are discussed elsewhere (see comments at 5:17–48);[127] but we may summarize some aspects of the problem here.

The difficulties stem from several factors. First, several passages can be understood as staunch defenses of the law (e.g., 5:18–19; 8:4; 19:17–18) and even of the authority of the Pharisees and teachers of the law in interpreting it (23:2–3). Jesus' disciples are expected to fast, give alms (6:2–4), and pay the temple tax (17:24–27). Second, some passages can be seen as a softening of Mark's dismissal of certain parts of the law. The addition of the "except" clause in 19:9 and the omission of Mark 7:19b ("In saying this, Jesus declared all foods 'clean'") in Matthew's corresponding pericope (Mt 15:1–20) have convinced many that Matthew does not abrogate any OT command. Third, there are some passages where, formally at least, the letter of OT law is superseded (e.g., 5:33–37) or a revered OT institution appears to be depreciated and potentially superseded (e.g., 12:6). Fourth, there is one passage, 5:17–20, that is widely recognized to be programmatic of Matthew's view of the law. However, it embraces interpretive problems of extraordinary difficulty.

In light of these things, various theories have been proposed. Benjamin Bacon, followed by Kilpatrick, argues that the gospel of Matthew presents a "new law" that is to the church what the Torah is to Judaism.[128] The five discourses of Matthew (see section 14) became the new Pentateuch. Today few follow this theory; its thematic and formal links are just too tenuous. Some suggest that this gospel reflects a Matthean church that has not yet broken away from Judaism, while others argue that the church has just broken free and now finds it necessary to define itself over against Judaism (cf. expressions such as "their teachers of the law," "their synagogues," or "your synagogues," when addressing certain Jews [e.g., 7:29; 9:35; 23:34]).

But such arguments are rather finespun. Does "their synagogue" imply a break with Judaism or distinctions within Judaism? The Qumran covenanters used the pronoun "their" of the Pharisees and mainline Judaism. Therefore, could not Jesus himself have used such language to distinguish his position from that

127. See Stanton, "Origin and Purpose," ch. 4.4.

128. Bacon, *Studies in Matthew*; Kilpatrick, *Origins of the Gospel according to Matthew*, 107–9.

of his Jewish opponents without implying he was not a Jew? A liberal or high churchman in the Church of England may refer to their colleges, referring to Church of England training colleges reflecting evangelical tradition, without suggesting that any of the three principal groups does not belong to the Anglican communion. And if Jesus spoke in such terms and if Matthew reports this, then Matthew may also be consciously reflecting the circumstances of his own church. But if so, it still remains unclear whether his church (if it is in his mind at all) has actually broken free from Judaism (see comments at 4:23; 7:29; 9:35; 10:17; 11:1; 12:9–10; 13:35).

Another example (8:4) is commonly taken to mean that the writer believes Jesus upholds even the ceremonial details of OT law, and that this reflects a conservative view of the continuing validity of the law in Matthew's community. This interpretation, though hard to prove, is logically possible. Alternatively, one might also argue that 8:4 reflects a pre–AD 70 community since after that, offering temple sacrifices was impossible. Again, if Jesus said something like this, then Matthew's including it may not have been because of his community's conservatism but because it shows how Jesus used even ceremonial law to point to himself (see comments at 8:4).

It is difficult to narrow down these various possibilities. Clearly they are related to how one uses redaction criticism (see sections 1–3, 5, 7–8). Too frequently these methodological questions are not so much as raised, even when the most astounding conclusions are confidently put forward as established fact. Some argue that Matthew's church had so conservative a view of the OT law that the "evildoers" (lit., "workers of lawlessness") denounced in 7:23 are Pauline Christians.[129] Quite apart from the authenticity of Jesus' saying and the danger of anachronism, this view misunderstands both Matthew and Paul. Matthew's attacks are primarily directed against Jewish leaders, especially the Pharisees, whose legal maneuvers blunt the power of the law and who fail to see the true direction in which the law pointed. They are, as the Qumran covenanters bitterly said, "expounders of smooth things" (CD 1:18).[130] As for Paul, doubtless many saw him as being antinomian. But he, too, spoke strongly about the kind of behavior necessary to enter the kingdom (Ro 8:14; 13:10; Gal 5:14).

Yet if Matthew attacks Pharisees, does this mean the Pharisees of Jesus' day, of Matthew's day, or of both? The least we can say is that Matthew chose to write a gospel, not a letter. Since he chose to write about Jesus as the Messiah, the presumption must be that he intended to say something about Jesus' life and relationships. This leads us to ask whether some differences between Matthew and Paul are to be explained by the distinctive places in salvation history of their subject matter. Though he writes after Paul wrote Romans, Matthew writes about an earlier period. Undoubtedly he had certain readers and their needs in mind. Yet it is no help in understanding Matthew's treatment of the law to view the needs of his first readers from the viewpoint of his modern readers without first weighing the historical background of his book—the life and teaching of Jesus.

Jesus' teaching about the law, whether gathered from Matthew or from all four gospels, is not easy to define precisely. The tendency in the last two or three decades has been to tighten the connections

129. See, e.g., Barth, "Matthew's Understanding of the Law," in *Tradition and Interpretation in Matthew* (ed. Bornkamm, Barth, and Held), 74–75.

130. Several have pointed out the pun between *ḥ^{a}lāqōt* ("smooth things") and *h^{a}lākōt* ("legal decisions affecting conduct"), the latter the aim of the Pharisees.

between Jesus and Judaism.[131] Phillip Sigal has recently set forth an iconoclastic theory.[132] He argues that the Pharisees of Jesus' day are not to be linked with the rabbis of the Mishnah (see section 11.f) but were a group of extremists wiped out by the events of AD 70. These extremists were opposed both by Jesus and by other teachers who occupied roles similar to his own. After all, ordination was unknown in Jesus' day, so there was no distinction between Jesus and other teachers. Jesus was himself a "proto-rabbi"—Sigal's term for the group that gave rise to the ordained rabbis of the post-Jamnian period (AD 85 on). All Jesus' legal decisions, Sigal says, fall within the range of what other proto-rabbis might say. Sigal tests this theory in Matthew's reports of Jesus' handling of the Sabbath (12:1–14) and divorce (19:1–12).

Sigal makes many telling points. His exegesis of 5:17–20 and other test passages is not convincing, however, because he eliminates all christological claims (e.g., 12:8) as the church's interpolations into the narrative (see comments at 5:17–20). He nowhere discusses, on literary or historical grounds, the authenticity of Jesus' christological claims but writes them off merely by referring to similar dismissals by other scholars. Yet the issue is crucial. If Jesus offered judgments concerning the law by making claims, implicit or explicit, concerning his messiahship, the function of the law in Jesus' teaching will certainly be presented differently from the way it would be if Jesus saw himself as no more than a "proto-rabbi." The commentary deals at length with this question (see comments at 5:17–20; 8:1–4, 16–17; 11:2–13; 12:1–14; 21; 13:35, 52; 15:1–20; 17:5–8; 19:3–12; 22:34–40; 27:51).

Doubtless we may link Matthew's treatment of the law with his handling of the OT (see section 11.b). Matthew holds that Jesus taught that the law had a prophetic function pointing to himself. Its valid continuity lies in Jesus' own ministry, teaching, death, and resurrection. The unifying factor is Jesus himself, whose ministry and teaching stand with respect to the OT (including law) as fulfillment does to prophecy. To approach the problem of continuity and discontinuity—what remains unchanged from the Mosaic code—in any other terms is to import categories alien to Matthew's thought and his distinctive witness to Jesus (see esp. comments at 5:17–20; 11:7–15). Within this unifying framework, the problem passages mentioned at the beginning of this discussion can be most fairly explained; by it we may avoid the thesis that makes the double love commandment the sole hermeneutical key to Jesus' understanding of the OT (see comments at 22:34–40).

d. Church

The word *ekklēsia* ("church," GK *1711*) occurs twice in Matthew (16:18; 18:17). Partly because it appears in no other gospel, the "ecclesiasticism" of Matthew has often been overstressed.[133]

Certain things stand out. First, Matthew insists that Jesus predicted the continuation of his small group of disciples in a distinct community, a holy and messianic people, a "church" (see comments at 16:18).

131. See, e.g., E. P. Sanders, *Jesus and Judaism* (Philadelphia: Fortress, 1985).

132. Phillip Sigal, *The Halakhah of Jesus of Nazareth according to the Gospel of Matthew* (rev. ed.; Studies in Biblical Literature 18; Atlanta: SBL Press, 2007).

133. For a convenient summary of recent literature, see Stanton, "Origin and Purpose," ch. 4, section 2. Stanton neglects to mention the extraordinarily important work by B. F. Meyer, *The Aims of Jesus* (see comments at 16:17–19).

This motif rests on numerous passages, not just one or two texts of disputed authenticity. Second, Jesus insists that obeying the ethical demands of the kingdom, far from being optional to those who make up the church, must characterize their lives. Their allegiance proves false wherever they do not do what Jesus teaches (e.g., 7:21–23). Third, a certain discipline must be imposed on the community (see comments at 16:18–19; 18:15–18). But Matthew describes this discipline in principles rather than in details (there is no mention of deacons, elders, presbyteries, or the like), and therefore this discipline is not anachronistic provided we can accept the fact that Jesus foresaw the continuation of his community.

This third theme is much stronger in Matthew than in Mark or Luke. One might speculate on the pressures that prompted Matthew to include this material—apathy in the church, return to a kind of casuistical righteousness, infiltration by those not wholly committed to Jesus the Messiah, the failure to discipline lax members. But this is speculation. The essential factor is that Matthew insists that the demand for a disciplined church goes back to Jesus himself.

e. Eschatology

Matthew consistently distinguishes among four time periods: (1) the period of revelation and history previous to Jesus; (2) the inauguration of something new in his coming and ministry; (3) the period beginning with his exaltation, from which point forward all of God's sovereignty is mediated through him and his followers proclaim the gospel of the kingdom to all nations; and (4) the consummation and beyond.

Many features of Matthew's eschatology are still being studied. The seven most important of these (the number may be eschatologically significant!) and the places where they are principally discussed in this commentary are (1) the meaning of peculiarly difficult verses (e.g., 10:23; 16:28); (2) the distinctive flavor of Matthew's dominant "kingdom of heaven" over against "kingdom of God" preferred by the rest of the NT writers (see comments at 3:2); (3) the extent to which the kingdom has already been inaugurated and the extent to which it is wholly future, awaiting the consummation (a recurring theme; cf. esp. ch. 13); (4) the bearing of the parables on eschatology (ch. 13, 25); (5) the relation between the kingdom and the church (another recurring theme; cf. esp. 13:37–39); (6) the sense in which Jesus saw the kingdom as imminent (see comments at ch. 24); and (7) the Olivet Discourse (chs. 24–25).

f. The Jewish leaders

Two areas need clarification for understanding Matthew's treatment of the Jewish leaders. The first is the identification of the Pharisees at the time of Jesus. A generation ago the patterns for the debate were already set. We may distinguish four viewpoints, each represented by able Jewish scholars.

1. The traditional approach is well defended by Alexander Guttmann, who argues that the Pharisees were more effective leaders than the OT prophets.[134] The prophets were uncompromising idealists; the Pharisees, whose views are largely reflected by their successors, the rabbis behind the Mishnah, were

---

134. Alexander Guttmann, *Rabbinic Judaism in the Making: A Chapter in the History of the Halakah from Ezra to Judah I* (Detroit: Wayne State Univ. Press, 1970).

adaptable, adjusting the demands of Torah by a finely tuned exegetical procedure issuing in legal enactments designed to make life easier and clarify right conduct.

2. By contrast, Jacob Neusner insists that a chasm yawns between the rabbinic views reflected in Mishnah and pre–AD 70 Pharisaism.[135] The Pharisees shaped the life of pre–AD 70 Judaism by extending the purity rituals of the temple to the daily experience of every Jew.

3. Ellis Rivkin argues that the Pharisees—a post-Maccabean and theologically revolutionary group—were men of considerable learning and persuasiveness.[136] They developed the oral law, now largely codified in the Mishnah, and unwittingly departed radically from their OT roots. Rivkin denies that they had separatistic or ritualistic tendencies; their influence was broad and pervasive.

4. Phillip Sigal argues for a complete disjunction between the Pharisees, whom he identifies as the *perushim* ("separatists"), and the rabbis behind Mishnah.[137] In Jesus' day the rabbis were not officially ordained; ordination had not yet been invented. That is why Jesus himself is addressed as "rabbi" in the Gospels (e.g., 26:49; Mk 9:5; 10:51; 11:21; Jn 1:38, 49; 3:2). He belonged to a class of "proto-rabbis," the forerunners of the ordained rabbis of the Mishnaic period. His opponents, the Pharisees, were extremists who died out after AD 70 and left virtually no literary trace.

The tentative assessment adopted in this commentary is that these competing interpretations of the evidence are largely right in what they affirm and wrong in what they deny. Sigal is almost certainly right in arguing that ordination was unknown in Jesus' day, though there may have been informal procedures for recognizing a teacher of Scripture.[138] There can be no simple equation of Pharisee and Mishnaic rabbi. But against Sigal, it is unlikely that the Pharisees were so separatistic that they did not embrace most if not all "proto-rabbis." The Gospels refer to every other major religious grouping—Sadducees, priests, scribes—and it is almost inconceivable that the evangelists should say almost nothing about the "proto-rabbis," the dominant group after AD 70, and vent so much criticism on a group (the Pharisees) so insignificant in Jesus' day that they disappeared from view after AD 70. The fairly rapid disappearance of the Sadducees after AD 70 is no parallel because much of their life and influence depended on the temple destroyed by the Romans; and in any case the evangelists do give us some description of their theological position.

As for Jesus, he cannot be reduced to a "proto-rabbi," training his followers to repeat his legal decisions. His messianic claims cannot so easily be dismissed. To onlookers he appeared as a prophet (21:11, 46).[139] Guttmann is right in saying that the Pharisees adapted the laws to the times and were effective leaders (see point 1 above). The problem is that their minute regulations made ritual distinctions too difficult and morality too easy. The radical holiness demanded by the OT prophets became domesticated,

---

135. Jacob Neusner, *The Rabbinic Traditions of the Pharisees* (3 vols.; Leiden: Brill, 1971). For a simplified treatment, see his *From Politics to Piety: The Emergence of Pharisaic Judaism* (Englewood Cliffs, N.J.: Prentice-Hall, 1973).

136. Ellis Rivkin, *A Hidden Revolution: The Pharisee's Search for the Kingdom Within* (Nashville: Abingdon, 1978).

137. Sigal, *Halakhah of Jesus*; see also his *The Emergence of Contemporary Judaism, Part I and II: The Foundations of Judaism from Biblical Origins to the Sixth Century AD* (Pittsburgh: Pickwick, 1980). A somewhat similar dichotomy is adopted by John Bowker, *Jesus and the Pharisees* (Cambridge: Cambridge Univ. Press, 1973).

138. See Stephen Westerholm, *Jesus and Scribal Authority* (CBNTS 10; Lund: Gleerup, 1978), 26–39.

139. See B. Lindars, "Jesus and the Pharisees," in *Donum Gentilicium* (ed. E. Bammel, C. K. Barrett, and W. D. Davies; Oxford: Clarendon, 1978), 51–63, esp. 62–63.

preparing the way for Jesus' preaching that demanded a righteousness greater than that of the Pharisees (5:20). Though Neusner correctly detects the Pharisees' concern with ceremonial purity (cf. 15:1–12), his skepticism concerning the fixity of many oral traditions and the possibility of knowing more about the Pharisees is unwarranted. The evidence from Josephus cannot be so easily dismissed as Neusner would have us think. Even allowing for Josephus's own bias toward the Pharisees, his evidence so consistently demonstrates their wide influence in the nation, not to say their centrality during the Jewish War, that it is very difficult to think of them as a minor separatistic group (so Sigal) or as concerned exclusively with ritual purity.

The Mishnah (ca. AD 200) cannot be read back into AD 30 as if Judaism had not faced the growth of Christianity and the shattering destruction of temple and cultus. Nevertheless, it preserves more traditional material than is sometimes thought. One suspects that the Pharisees of Jesus' day include the proto-rabbis, ideological forebears of the Mishnaic *Tannaim* (lit., "repeaters," i.e., the "rabbis" from roughly AD 70 to 200). In this view, they included men every bit as learned and creative as the second-century rabbis. But they also included many lesser men, morally and intellectually, who were largely purged by the twin effects of the growth of Christianity and the devastation of AD 70. These events called forth a "counterreformation" whose legacy is Mishnah. Rivkin is undoubtedly right in seeing the Pharisees as learned scholars whose meticulous application and development of OT law massively influenced Judaism (see point 3 above), though his identification of Pharisees with scribes and his handling of the development of oral law are simplistic. More recent work has produced a plethora of studies aimed at helping contemporary readers to discern, along quite different lines, which material in the Mishnah probably dates from the time of Jesus.[140]

I hold that the Pharisees were a nonpriestly group of uncertain origin, generally learned, committed to the oral law, and concerned with developing halakah (rules of conduct based on deductions from the law). Most teachers of the law were Pharisees; and the Sanhedrin included men from their number as well (see comments at 21:23), though the leadership of the Sanhedrin belonged to the priestly Sadducees.

The second area needing clarification is the way Matthew refers to Jewish leaders. It is universally agreed that Matthew is quite strongly anti-Pharisaic. Recently, however, more and more scholars have argued that Matthew's picture of the Pharisees reflects the rabbis of the period AD 80–100, not the situation around AD 30. His grasp of the other Jewish parties, which largely fell away after AD 70, is shallow and sometimes wrong. Lloyd Gaston thinks the depth of Matthew's ignorance, especially of the Sadducees, is "astonishing."[141]

The question is complex.[142] Certain observations, however, will qualify the charge of Matthew's ignorance.

140. The most seminal of these works is that of David Instone-Brewer, *Techniques and Assumptions in Jewish Exegesis before 70 CE* (TSAJ 30; Tübingen: Mohr, 1992).

141. L. Gaston, "The Messiah of Israel as Teacher of the Gentiles," *Int* 29 (1975): 34.

142. Cf. D. A. Carson, "Jewish Leaders in Matthew's Gospel: A Reappraisal," *JETS* 25 (1982): 161–74. For a concise presentation of the data, see David E. Garland, *The Intention of Matthew 23* (Leiden: Brill, 1979), 218–21.

1. If Matthew's sole target had been the rabbis of AD 80–100, designated "Pharisees," it is astonishing that they are virtually unmentioned during the Passion Week and the Passion Narrative when feeling against Jesus reached its height. What we discover is that the chief opponents are priests and elders, who were members of the Sanhedrin, which is just what we would expect in the vicinity of Jerusalem before AD 70. This demonstrates that Matthew is not entirely ignorant of historical distinctions regarding Jewish leaders; it calls into question the thesis that his opponents are exclusively Pharisees and urges caution in making similar judgments.

2. Matthew mentions the Sadducees more often than all the other evangelists combined. If Matthew was so ignorant of them, and if they were irrelevant to his alleged circumstances in AD 80–100, why did he multiply references to them?

3. Matthew demonstrates that he was aware of some of the Sadducees' doctrinal distinctives (see comments at 22:23–33). This should make us cautious in evaluating the most difficult point—namely, that in five places Matthew uses the phrase "Pharisees and Sadducees" in a way that links them closely (3:7; 16:1, 6, 11, 12). This linking is peculiar to Matthew. The known antipathy between the two groups was sufficiently robust that many modern commentators have concluded this gospel was written late enough and by someone far enough removed from the setting of AD 30 for this incongruity to slip into the text. But in addition to Matthew's historical awareness, two complementary explanations largely remove the difficulty.

First, the linking of Pharisees and Sadducees under one article in Matthew 3:7 may reflect, not their theological agreement, but their common mission. Just as the Sanhedrin raised questions about Jesus' authority, it is intrinsically likely they sent delegates to sound out John the Baptist. The Sanhedrin included both Pharisees and Sadducees (Ac 23:6); and their mutual distrust makes it likely that the delegation was made up of representatives from both parties. The fourth gospel suggests this. The "Jews of Jerusalem" (who else but the Sanhedrin?) sent "priests and Levites" (Jn 1:19)—certainly Sadducees—to ask John who he was; but Pharisees were also sent (Jn 1:24). Matthew's language may therefore preserve accurate historical reminiscence. Something similar may be presupposed in 16:1. We must always remember that though the Pharisees and Sadducees could fight each other fiercely on certain issues, their political circumstances required that they work together at many levels.

Second, though the linking of the Pharisees and Sadducees in the remaining references (16:6, 11, 12) appears to make their teaching common, the context demands restraint. In certain circumstances, a Baptist may warn against "the teaching of the Presbyterians and Anglicans," not because he is unaware of fundamental differences between them (or even among them!), but because he wishes to set their paedobaptism against his own views. Quite clearly in 16:5–12, Jesus cannot be denouncing everything the Pharisees and Sadducees teach, for some of what they teach he holds in common with them. The particular point of teaching in this context is their attitude toward Jesus and their desire to domesticate revelation and authenticate it—an attitude so blind it cannot recognize true revelation when it appears (see comments at 16:1–4). It is against this "yeast of the Pharisees and Sadducees" that Jesus warns his disciples. In his view both parties were guilty of the same error.

4. Categories for the Jewish leaders overlap in the Gospels, Matthew included. As far as we know, the Sanhedrin, for instance, was made up of Sadducees, Pharisees, and elders. The Sadducees were mostly

priests. The elders were mostly lay nobility and probably primarily Pharisees. Thus "Pharisees" in the Sanhedrin were "laymen" in the sense that they were not priests; but many of them were scribes ("teachers of the law") and thus different from the elders. When 21:23 speaks of the chief priests and elders of the people coming to Jesus, it is probably referring to members of the Sanhedrin described in terms of their clerical status rather than their theological position. The ambiguities are considerable, but we must avoid indefensible disjunctions.

5. Our own ignorance of who the Pharisees were and of the distinctive beliefs of the Sadducees (we know them almost entirely through the writings of their opponents—"almost" because some scholars think that Sirach, for instance, is a proto-Sadducean document) should make us hesitate before ascribing "astonishing" ignorance to the evangelist. The astonishing ignorance may be our own. One suspects that in some instances Matthew's treatment of Jewish leaders is being pressed into a mold to suit a date of AD 80–100. The truth is that our knowledge of both Judaism and Christianity during that period has formidable gaps. Though Matthew may have been written then—though in my view this is unlikely—his treatment of Jewish leaders cannot be used to defend the late date view.

But is Matthew's polemic so harsh that he must be considered anti-Semitic (see comments at 23:1–36; 26:57–59)? The judgment of Simon Legasse is sound: Matthew's sternest denunciations are not racially motivated; they are prompted by the response of people to Jesus.[143] These denunciations extend to professing believers whose lives betray the falseness of their profession (7:21–23; 22:11–14) as well as to Jews; the governing motives are concern for the perseverance of the Christian community and for the authoritative proclamation of the "gospel of the kingdom" to "all nations," Jew and Gentile alike (see comments at 28:18–20), to bring all to submission to Jesus the Messiah. As for the charge of anti-Judaism (which, of course, is predominantly theological rather than racial), the conclusion of Ulrich Luz is right: the root of the perceived problem is in the absolute claims that Jesus made for himself.[144]

g. Mission

Many have long recognized that the closing pericope (28:16–20) is fully intended to be the climax toward which all of Matthew moves. By tying together some of Matthew's most dominant themes, these verses give them a new depth that reaches back and sheds light on his entire gospel. For instance, the Great Commission is perceived to be the result of God's providential ordering of history (1:1–17) to bring to a fallen world a Messiah who would save his people from their sins (1:21); but the universal significance of Jesus' birth, hinted at in 1:1 and repeatedly raised in the flow of the narrative (see comments at 2:1–12; 4:14–16, 25; 8:5–13; 10:18–13:52; 15:21–28; 24:9, 14) is now confirmed by the concluding lines.[145]

We have already observed that the extent of the Great Commission has been limited by some—though on inadequate grounds—to Gentiles only (section 8; see comments at 28:18–20). Matthew does not trace the context of the people of God from a Jewish one to an exclusively Gentile one but from a Jewish context

143. S. Legasse, "L''antijudaisme' dans l'Évangile selon Matthieu," in Didier, *L'Évangile selon Matthieu*, 417–28.

144. Luz, *Studies in Matthew*, 260–61.

145. See Paul Foster, *Community, Law and Mission in Matthew's Gospel* (Tübingen: Mohr, 2004).

to a racially inclusive one. Unlike Luke (Lk 21:24) and Paul (Ro 11:25–27), Matthew raises no questions about Israel's future as a distinct people.

h. Miracles

The biblical writers do not see miracles as divine interventions in an ordered and closed universe. Rather, God as Lord of the universe and of history sustains everything that takes place under his sovereignty. Sometimes, however, he does extraordinary things; and then we in the modern world call them "miracles." Biblical writers preferred terms like "sign," "wonder," or "power." Parallels between Jesus and Hellenistic miracle workers are not as close as some form critics have thought.[146] On the other hand, the value of miracles as proof of Jesus' deity is not as conclusive as some conservative expositors have thought.

Miracles in Matthew share certain characteristics with those in the other Synoptics, and these characteristics must be understood before Matthew's distinctives can be explored. Jesus' miracles are bound up with the inbreaking of the promised kingdom (8:16–17; 12:22–30; cf. Lk 11:14–23). They are part of his messianic work (Mt 4:23; 11:4–6) and therefore the dual evidence of the dawning of the kingdom and of the status of Jesus the King, the Messiah. This does not mean that Jesus did miracles on demand as a kind of spectacular attestation (see comments at 12:38–42; cf. Jn 4:48). Faith and obedience are not guaranteed by great miracles, though faith and God's mighty power working through Jesus are linked in several ways. Lack of faith may be an impediment to this power (e.g., Mt 17:19–20), not because God's power is curtailed, but because real trust in him submits to his powerful reign and expects mercies from him (e.g., 15:28; cf. Mk 9:24).

"Nature miracles" (the stilling of the storm or the multiplication of loaves and fish) not only attest the universal sweep of God's power but may in some cases (calming the storm) provide the creation rebelling against God with a foretaste of restored order—an order to be climaxed by the consummation of the kingdom. In some cases (the multiplication of loaves and fish, the withered fig tree), miracles constitute a "prophetic symbolism" that promises unqualified fruition (the messianic banquets, the certainty of judgment) at the end.

Matthew's miracles are distinctive for the brevity with which they are reported. He condenses introductions and conclusions, omits secondary characters, and the like (see comments at 8:14). Nevertheless, it is too much to say, as Held does, "The miracles are not important for their own sakes, but by reason of the message they contain."[147] This might almost suggest that the facticity of the miracles is of no consequence to Matthew provided their message is preserved. Matthew himself specifically disallows this (11:3–6). All the evangelists hold that miracles point beyond the mere factuality of wonderful events. In this, Matthew is no different from the others. He simply shifts the balance of event and implication a little in order to stress the latter.

The particular themes most flavored by Matthew in connection with Jesus' miracles are worked out in the commentary.

---

146. See Albright and Mann, *Matthew*, cxxiv–cxxxi.

147. Heinz Joachim Held, "Matthew as Interpreter of the Miracle Stories," in Bornkamm, Barth, and Held, 210.

i. The disciples' understanding and faith

Ever since the work of Gerhard Barth, many scholars have held that whereas in Mark the disciples do not understand what Jesus says till he explains it to them in secret, Matthew attributes large and instant understanding to the disciples.[148] Indeed, what sets them apart from the crowd is that the disciples understand; the outsiders do not. Where the disciples falter and must improve is not in their understanding but in their faith.

The thesis can be defended by a careful selection of the data, but it will not withstand close scrutiny. Apart from depending too much on the "messianic secret" in Mark (see comments in this vol. at Mk 9:9), it does not adequately treat the disciples' request for private instruction (Mt 13:36), their failure to understand Jesus' teaching about his passion even after his explanations (e.g., 16:21–26; 17:23; 26:51–56), and the passages that deal with "stumbling" or "falling away." These are not peripheral matters; they are integral to what Jesus and Matthew say about discipleship.

The thesis also errs, not only for the two reasons mentioned above, but also for a third. Adopting a doctrinaire form of redaction criticism, it so stresses what the relevant passages reveal about Matthew's church that it blunts their real thrust. In particular, the failure of the disciples to understand the significance of Jesus' passion and resurrection predictions is largely a function of the disciples' unique place in salvation history. They were unprepared before the events to accept the notion of a crucified and resurrected Messiah; not a few of Jesus' christological claims are sufficiently vague that their full import could be grasped by those with a traditional Jewish mind-set only after Calvary and the empty tomb.[149] To this extent, the disciples' experience of coming to deeper understanding and faith was unique because it was locked into a phase of salvation history rendered forever obsolete by the triumph of Jesus' resurrection.

Matthew's readers, whether in the first century or today, may profit from studying the disciples' experience as he records it. But to try subjectively to imitate the disciples' coming to full faith and understanding following Jesus' resurrection is futile. Rather we should look back on this witness to the divine self-disclosure, observing God's wisdom and care as through his Son he progressively revealed himself and his purposes to redeem a fallen and rebellious race. Feeding our faith and understanding on the combined testimony of the earliest witnesses who tell how they arrived by a unique historical sequence at their faith and understanding, we shall learn to focus our attention not on the disciples but on their Lord. This is not to say that the disciples have nothing to teach us about personal growth; rather, it is to insist that we will basically misunderstand this gospel if we do not see that it deals with a unique coming to faith and understanding. This topic is so important that the commentary refers to it repeatedly (e.g., 13:10–13, 23, 36, 43, 51–52; 14:15–17; 15:15–16; 16:21–28; 17:13, 23; 20:17–19, 22; 23:13–36; 24:1; 28:17). Elsewhere it has been comprehensively treated by Andrew Trotter.[150]

---

148. Barth, "Matthew's Understanding of the Law," in *Tradition and Interpretation in Matthew* (ed. Bornkamm, Barth, and Held), 105ff.

149. See D. A. Carson, "Christological Ambiguities in the Gospel of Matthew," in *Christ the Lord: Studies in Christology Presented to Donald Guthrie* (ed. Harold Rowdon; Downers Grove, Ill.: InterVarsity, 1982), 97–114.

150. Andrew H. Trotter, "Understanding and Stumbling: A Study of the Disciples' Understanding of Jesus and His Teaching in the Gospel of Matthew" (PhD diss.; Cambridge: Cambridge University, 1986).

12. LITERARY GENRE

The interpretation of any piece of literature is affected by an understanding of its genre. A sonnet, novel, parable, history, fable, free verse, or an aphorism must be read according to its literary form.

a. Gospel

What, then, is a gospel? Many theories have been proposed and affinities discovered in other writings (e.g., apocalyptic literature, OT books, Graeco-Roman biographies, etc.). Some time ago, Charles Talbert argued that the gospel belongs to the genre of Graeco-Roman biography.[151] In a convincing rejoinder, David Aune showed that Talbert has misunderstood not a few ancient sources and has arrived at his conclusions by adopting ambiguous categories that hide essential differences.[152] Aune, followed by many, insists that the gospels belong in a class of their own. This does not mean that the gospels have no relation to other genres. The truth is that "'new' genres were constantly emerging during the Graeco-Roman period, if by 'new' we mean a recombination of earlier forms and genres into novel configurations."[153] Today the pendulum is swinging back toward carefully nuanced discussions that demonstrate the closest literary genre to the canonical gospels is the ancient biographies of the Hellenistic world, regardless of the unavoidable differences.[154]

Thus our gospels are made up of many pericopes, some belonging to recognized genres, others with close affinities to recognized genres. Each must be weighed, but the result is a flexible form that aims to give a selective account of Jesus, including his teaching and miracles and culminating in his death by crucifixion and his burial and resurrection. The selection includes certain key points in his career (his baptism, ministry, passion, and resurrection) and aims at a credible account of these historical events. At the same time, the material is organized so as to stress certain subjects and motifs. The writing is not dispassionate but confessional—something the evangelists considered an advantage. Some of the material is organized along thematic lines, some according to a loose chronology; still other pericopes are linked by some combination of catchwords, themes, OT attestation, genre, and logical coherence. The result is not exactly a history, biography, theology, confession, catechism, tract, homage, or letter—though it is in some respects all of these. It is a "gospel," a presentation of the "good news" of Jesus the Messiah.

b. Midrash

Scholars have increasingly recognized the Jewishness of the NT and have therefore cultivated Jewish literary categories for understanding these documents. Among the most important of these categories is *midrash.*

151. C. H. Talbert, *What Is a Gospel? The Genre of the Canonical Gospels* (Philadelphia: Fortress, 1977).

152. D. E. Aune, "The Problem of the Genre of the Gospels," in *Gospel Perspectives* (ed. France and Wenham), 9–60; cf. R. H. Gundry, "Recent Investigations into the Literary Genre 'Gospel,'" in *New Dimensions in New Testament Study* (ed. Richard N. Longenecker and Merrill C. Tenney; Grand Rapids: Zondervan, 1974), 97–114.

153. Aune, "Problem of Genre," 48.

154. Perhaps the most important work is that of Richard A. Burridge, *What Are the Gospels? A Comparison with Graeco-Roman Biography* (2nd ed.; Cambridge: Cambridge Univ. Press, 2004).

One application of this work, the lectionary theory of Michael Goulder, has already been discussed (section 8).[155] The major commentary on Matthew by Robert Gundry is another. He argues that Q is larger than is customarily recognized, embracing material normally designated "M" (see section 3), including the birth narratives in Matthew 1–2. What Matthew does according to Gundry, is apply "midrashic techniques" to the tradition he takes over, adding nonhistorical touches to historical material, sometimes creating stories, designated *midrashim*, to make theological points, even though the stories, like parables, have no historical referent.

Everything depends on definition. Etymologically, *midrash* simply means "interpretation." But in this sense, every comment on another text is midrash—including this commentary. Such a definition provides no basis for saying that because Matthew relates midrashic stories in Matthew 1–2, they are not historically true. Most other definitions, however accurate, are not sufficient to yield Gundry's conclusion. J. Duncan M. Derrett, for instance, defines midrashic method in terms of its allusiveness to many sources, not in terms of historicity at all.[156] Klyne Snodgrass defines midrash, not as a genre, but "as a process in which forms of tradition develop and enrich or intensify later adaptation of Old Testament texts."[157] Jacob Neusner tends to look for patterns across time.[158] Many other definitions have been offered.[159]

To compound the difficulty, the term seems to undergo a semantic shift within Jewish literature. By the time of the Babylonian Talmud (fourth century AD), midrash had developed a more specialized meaning akin to what Gundry clearly wants. Other Jewish commentaries, mainly the Qumran Pesharim,[160] were characterized by three things: (1) they attempted to deal systematically with every point in the text; (2) they limited themselves almost exclusively to the text; and (3) they adopted a revelatory stance toward the text that identified virtually every point in the text with a point of fulfillment in the interpreter's day or later, without any sense of historical context. By contrast, the midrashim worked through the text of Scripture more haphazardly, using Scripture as a sort of peg on which to hang discourse, stories, and other pieces to illuminate the theological meaning of the text. This was in conscious distinction from "peshat," the more "literal" meaning of the text. But in the first two centuries, it is very doubtful whether midrash had a meaning even this specialized. It referred rather to "an interpretive exposition however derived and irrespective of the type of material under consideration."[161]

In a wide-ranging work, Douglas Moo discusses the various ways in which literature that treats the OT text may be analyzed.[162] He distinguishes literary genre (form and general content), citation procedures

---

155. Goulder, *Midrash and Lection*.
156. J. D. M. Derrett, *Studies in the New Testament* (2 vols.; Leiden: Brill, 1977–78).
157. Klyne R. Snodgrass, "Streams of Tradition Emerging from Isaiah 40:1–5 and Their Adaptation in the New Testament," *JSNT* 8 (1980): 40.
158. See Jacob Neusner, *Judaism and the Interpretation of Scripture: Introduction to Rabbinic Midrash* (Peabody, Mass.: Hendrickson, 2004).
159. See Jacob Neusner and Alan J. Avery Peck, eds., *Encyclopedia of Midrash: Biblical Interpretation in Formative Judaism* (2 vols.; Leiden: Brill, 2005).
160. See Maurya P. Horgan, *Pesharim: Qumran Interpretation of Biblical Books* (Washington, D.C.: Catholic Biblical Association, 1979).
161. Longenecker, *Biblical Exegesis*, 32.
162. Douglas J. Moo, *The Old Testament in the Gospel Passion Narratives* (Sheffield: Almond, 1983).

(e.g., explicit quotation, allusion, conceptual influence, and the like), appropriation technique (the ways the OT text is applied to the contemporary setting), and the hermeneutical axioms implicitly adopted by the interpreter (e.g., that the Scripture was a closed entity needing to be ingeniously interpreted to elicit answers to questions about conduct not specifically treated in the text).

Now if midrash refers to genre, in the first century it is too wide a term to bear the weight Gundry places on it and is inadequate on other grounds.[163] Attempts to define midrash in terms of appropriation techniques have not proved successful, because none of the techniques are restricted to midrash. Moo tentatively suggests that midrash be characterized "in terms of the hermeneutical axioms which guide the approach."[164] There is considerable merit in this; but of course this results in largely limiting midrash to rabbinic Judaism, since the operative hermeneutical axioms of this approach include a largely noneschatological perception and a deep preoccupation with enunciating its identity and directing its conduct (corresponding roughly to the two forms haggadic midrash and halakic midrash).[165] By contrast, the stories of Matthew 1–2 are fundamentally eschatological. They are said to fulfill Scripture in the context of a book in which messianic fulfillment and the dawning of the eschatological kingdom constitute fundamental themes. Matthew 1–2 is little concerned with rules of conduct or the identity of the people of God. It bursts with christological concern and a teleological perspective.

When distinctions such as these are borne in mind, the modern category "midrash pesher," which some wish to apply to Matthew's treatment of the OT, is seen as an inadequate label for the Qumran commentaries. Midrash and pesher are alike in many of their techniques, but the hermeneutical axioms are profoundly different. But if the makeshift midrash pesher is inappropriate for the commentaries of Qumran, it is usually inappropriate for Matthew. And in any case, it is definitely not a genre recognized by Jewish readers of the first century.

These conclusions are inevitable:

1. Gundry cannot legitimately appeal to midrash as a well-defined and recognized genre of literature in the first century.

2. In particular, if midrash reflects genre, as opposed to hermeneutical axioms irrelevant to Matthew, it is being given a sense more or less well-defined only from the fourth century on. This raises the question of what we could expect Matthew's readers to have thought. Gundry argues that the reason the church has failed to recognize the midrashic (and therefore nonhistorical) nature of Matthew 1–2 is that this gospel was quickly taken over by the Gentiles, who had little appreciation for Jewish literary genres. This plausible argument is weakened by strong evidence that midrash in any specialized sense relevant to Gundry's thesis is too late in Jewish circles to be useful.

3. Even if we adopt this late narrowing of the term *midrash*, it is still inappropriate as a description of Matthew's "M" material. Although the Jewish midrashim are often only loosely connected with the texts they "expound," yet a line of continuity runs through those OT texts. By contrast, Matthew's continuity

163. See Gundry, *Matthew*, 63ff.

164. Moo, *Old Testament in the Gospel Passion Narratives*, 66.

165. See Daniel Patte, *Early Jewish Hermeneutic in Palestine* (Missoula, Mont.: SBL, 1975), 49ff.

in chs. 1–2, for instance, is established by the story line, not the OT texts, all of which could be removed without affecting the passages' cohesion.

4. Much of the force of Gundry's argument depends on his assessment of the tendencies in Matthew's editing of sources. Gundry feels that demonstrable tendencies in Matthew require appeal to midrashic technique as the only adequate explanation of material that diverges so radically from the sources. But another assessment of the same evidence is often possible. Few will be convinced by his postulation of a common source behind Matthew 1–2 and Luke 1–2. Moreover some of the "tendencies" he detects in Matthew—e.g., he follows the now popular line on the disciples' understanding (see section 11.i)—are better interpreted in other ways. These points depend on details of exegesis and emerge in this commentary.[166]

An important element in Gundry's argument is that the stories cannot be taken as history because, read that way, they include some demonstrable errors. On some of these matters, I will say more in the commentary. Here it is sufficient to say that whoever uses *midrash* of any part of Matthew's gospel should tell their readers precisely what the term means.

c. Miscellaneous

Several other important forms of literature make up the constituent parts of our canonical gospels: wisdom sayings, genealogies, discourses, parables, and so forth. The most important receive brief treatment in the commentary, with the most extensive note being devoted to parables (see comments at 13:3).

13. BIBLIOGRAPHY

The following is a selective list of resources on Matthew, confined for the most part to those referred to in the commentary. Commentaries will be referred to simply by the author's name [and initials only when necessary to distinguish two authors of the same surname]). General works and other resources will be referred to by the author's name and short title. In instances where the same author has written a commentary as well as (a) book(s) and/or (an) article(s), the commentary will be referred to by the author's name, and the book(s)/article(s) by the author's name and short title. When a commentary is cited without a page number, it is assumed that the reference points the reader to the appropriate section from the specific verse or verses under consideration.

References to resources that do not appear in the bibliography will carry full bibliographic details at the first mention and thereafter a short title.

Commentaries

Albright, W. F., and C. S. Mann. *Matthew*. Garden City, N.J.: Doubleday, 1971.
Alexander, J. A. *The Gospel according to Matthew*. New York: Scribner, 1860.
Allen, Willoughby C. *A Critical and Exegetical Commentary on the Gospel according to S. Matthew*. Edinburgh: T&T Clark, 1912.
Benoit, P. *L'Évangile selon Saint Matthieu*. 4th ed. Paris: Cerf, 1972.

166. See D. A. Carson, "Gundry on Matthew: A Critical Review," *TJ* 3 n.s. (1982): 71–91.

Blomberg, Craig L. *Matthew*. New American Commentary. Nashville: Broadman, 1992.

______. "Matthew." Pages 1–109 in *Commentary on the New Testament Use of the Old Testament*. Edited by G. K. Beale and D. A. Carson. Grand Rapids: Baker, 2007.

Bonnard, Pierre. *L'Évangile selon Saint Matthieu*. 2nd ed. Neuchatel: Delachaux et Niestlé, 1970.

Broadus, John. *Commentary on the Gospel of Matthew*. Valley Forge, Pa.: American Baptist Publication Society, 1886.

Calvin, John. *Calvin's New Testament Commentaries: Matthew, Mark, and Luke*. Edited by D. W. Torrance and T. F. Torrance. Translated by A. W. Morrison and T. H. L. Parker. 3 vols. Grand Rapids: Eerdmans, 1972.

Davies, W. D., and D. C. Allison. *A Critical and Exegetical Commentary on the Gospel according to Saint Matthew*. 3 vols. International Critical Commentary. Edinburgh: T&T Clark, 1988–97.

Fenton, J. C. *Saint Matthew*. Harmondsworth: Penguin, 1963.

Filson, Floyd V. *A Commentary on the Gospel according to St. Matthew*. New York: Harper, 1960.

France, R. T. *The Gospel according to Matthew: An Introduction and Commentary*. Tyndale New Testament Commentaries. Leicester: InterVarsity, 1985.

______. *The Gospel of Matthew*. New International Commentary on the New Testament. Grand Rapids: Eerdmans, 2007.

Gaebelein, Arno C. *The Gospel of Matthew: An Exposition*. 2 vols. New York: Our Hope Publications, 1910.

Gaechter, Paul. *Das Matthäus Evangelium*. Innsbruck: Tyrolia-Verlag, 1963.

Garland, David E. *Reading Matthew: A Literary and Theological Commentary on the First Gospel*. New York: Crossroad, 1993.

Gibbs, Jeffrey A. *Matthew 1:1–11:1*. Concordia Commentary. St. Louis, Mo.: Concordia, 2006.

Green, H. Benedict. *The Gospel according to Matthew*. Oxford: Oxford Univ. Press, 1975.

Grosheide, F. W. *Het heilig evangelie volgens Mattheus*. Kampen: Kok, 1954.

Grundmann, Walter. *Das Evangelium nach Matthäus*. 4th ed. Berlin: Evangelische Verlagsanstalt, 1975.

Gundry, Robert H. *Matthew: A Commentary on His Literary and Theological Art*. Grand Rapids: Eerdmans, 1981. 2nd ed. titled *Matthew: A Commentary on His Handbook for a Mixed Church under Persecution*. Grand Rapids: Eerdmans, 1994 [pagination unchanged; additional preface and endnotes].

Hagner, Donald A. *Matthew*. 2 vols. Word Biblical Commentary 33A and 33B. Dallas: Word, 1993.

Harrington, Daniel J. *The Gospel of Matthew*. Sacra Pagina 1. Collegeville, Minn.: Liturgical Press, 1991.

Hendriksen, William. *The Gospel of Matthew*. Grand Rapids: Baker, 1973.

Henry, Matthew. *A Commentary on the Holy Bible*. London: Marshall Bros., n.d.

Hill, David. *The Gospel of Matthew*. Grand Rapids: Eerdmans, 1972.

Keener, Craig S. *A Commentary on the Gospel of Matthew*. Grand Rapids: Eerdmans, 1999.

Kingsbury, Jack Dean. *Matthew*. Philadelphia: Fortress, 1977.

Klostermann, Erich. *Das Matthäus-Evangelium*. 2nd ed. Tübingen: Mohr, 1927.

Lagrange, M.-J. *Évangile selon Saint Matthieu*. Paris: Lecoffre, 1948.

Lenski, R. C. H. *Interpretation of St. Matthew's Gospel*. Columbus, Ohio: Lutheran Book Concern, 1932.

Lohmeyer, Ernst. *Das Evangelium des Matthäus*. Edited by W. Schmauch. Göttingen: Vandenhoeck & Ruprecht, 1956.

Loisy, A. *Les évangiles synoptiques*. 2 vols. Ceffonds: Loisy, 1907–08.

Luther, Martin. *Luther's Works*. 55 vols. Edited by Jaroslav Pelikan and Helmut T. Lehman. Philadelphia: Muehlenberg and Fortress, and St. Louis, Mo.: Concordia, 1955–86.

Luz, Ulrich. *Matthew: A Commentary*. 3 vols. Hermeneia. Minneapolis: Fortress, 2001.

Maier, Gerhard. *Matthäus-Evangelium*. 2 vols. Neuhausen: Hanssler, 1979–80.

McNeile, Alan Hugh. *The Gospel according to St. Matthew: The Greek Text with Introduction, Notes, and Indices*. London: Macmillan, 1915.

Meyer, Heinrich August Wilhelm. *Critical and Exegetical Commentary on the New Testament*. Part I. *The Gospel of Matthew*. Translated by W. P. Dickson and W. Stewart. 2 vols. Edinburgh: T&T Clark, 1877–79.

Morison, James. *A Practical Commentary on the Gospel according to St. Matthew*. London: Hodder and Stoughton, 1892.

Nolland, John. *The Gospel of Matthew: A Commentary on the Greek Text*. Grand Rapids: Eerdmans, 2005.

Plummer, Alfred. *An Exegetical Commentary on the Gospel according to S. Matthew*. London: Robert Scott, 1915.

Plumptre, E. H. *The Gospel according to Matthew*. Repr., Grand Rapids: Zondervan, 1957.

Ridderbos, H. N. *Het evangelie naar Mattheus*. Kampen: Kok, 1952.

Sabourin, Leopold. *L'Évangile selon Saint Matthieu et ses principaux paralleles*. Rome: Biblical Institute Press, 1978.

Schlatter, Adolf. *Der Evangelist Matthäus: Seine Sprache, sein Ziel, seine Selbstandigkeit.* 6th ed. Stuttgart: Calwer, 1963.
Schniewind, Julius. *Das Evangelium nach Matthäus.* Göttingen: Vandenhoeck & Ruprecht, 1956.
Schweizer, Eduard. *The Good News according to Matthew.* Atlanta: Knox, 1975.
Stendahl, Krister. "Matthew." Pages 769–98 in *Peake's Commentary on the Bible.* London: Nelson, 1962.
Tasker, R. V. G. *The Gospel according to St. Matthew: An Introduction and Commentary.* London: InterVarsity, 1961.
Turner, David L. *Matthew.* Baker Exegetical Commentary on the New Testament. Grand Rapids: Baker, 2008.
Walvoord, John F. *Matthew: Thy Kingdom Come.* Chicago: Moody, 1974.
Witherington, Ben, III. *Matthew.* Smyth & Helwys Bible Commentary. Macon, Ga.: Smyth & Helwys, 2006.
Zahn, Theodor. *Das Evangelium des Matthäus.* Leipzig: Deichert, 1903.

General Works

Alford, Henry. *The New Testament for English Readers.* 3 vols. Cambridge, U.K.: Rivingtons, 1868.
Allison, Dale C., Jr. *Studies in Matthew: Interpretation Past and Present.* Grand Rapids: Baker, 2005.
Arens, Eduardo. *The Ἦλθον-sayings in the Synoptic Tradition: A Historico-Critical Investigation.* Göttingen: Vandenhoeck & Ruprecht, 1976.
Bacon, Benjamin W. *Studies in Matthew.* London: Constable, 1930.
Bailey, Kenneth E. *Jesus through Middle Eastern Eyes: Cultural Studies in the Gospels.* Downers Grove, Ill.: InterVarsity, 2008.
Banks, Robert. *Jesus and the Law in the Synoptic Tradition.* Cambridge: Cambridge Univ. Press, 1975.
Bauckham, Richard J. *Jesus and the Eyewitnesses: The Gospels as Eyewitness Testimony.* Grand Rapids: Eerdmans, 2006.
Beasley-Murray, G. R. *Baptism in the New Testament.* London: Macmillan, 1954.
Bengel, Johann Albrecht. *Gnomon of the New Testament.* 4th ed. Translated by James Bandinel et al. Edinburgh: T&T Clark, 1860.
Benoit, P. *Jesus and the Gospel.* New York: Herder and Herder, 1973.
Best, Ernest. *The Temptation and the Passion: The Markan Soteriology.* Cambridge: Cambridge Univ. Press, 1965.
Best, Ernest, and Robert McL. Wilson, eds. *Text and Interpretation.* Cambridge: Cambridge Univ. Press, 1979.
Betz, Hans Dieter. *The Sermon on the Mount: A Commentary on the Sermon on the Mount, including the Sermon on the Plain (Matthew 5:3–7:27 and Luke 6:20–49).* Hermeneia. Minneapolis: Augsburg, 1995.
Beyer, Klaus. *Semitische Syntax im Neuen Testament.* Göttingen: Vandenhoeck & Ruprecht, 1968.
Black, Matthew. *An Aramaic Approach to the Gospels and Acts.* 3rd ed. Oxford: Clarendon, 1967.
Blair, Edward P. *Jesus in the Gospel of Matthew.* New York: Abingdon, 1960.
Blickenstaff, Marianne. *"While the Bridegroom Is with Them": Marriage, Family, Gender and Violence in the Gospel of Matthew.* Journal for the Study of the New Testament Supplement Series 292. London: T&T Clark, 2005.
Blinzler, Josef. *The Trial of Jesus.* Translated by F. McHugh. Cork: Mercier, 1959.
Blomberg, Craig L. *Contagious Holiness: Jesus' Meals with Sinners.* New Testament Studies in Biblical Theology 19. Downers Grove, Ill.: InterVarsity, 2005.
Bock, Darrell L. *Blasphemy and Exaltation in Judaism and the Final Examination of Jesus.* Wissenschaftliche Untersuchungen zum Neuen Testament 106. Tübingen: Mohr, 1998.
Bolt, Peter G. *The Cross from a Distance: Atonement in Mark's Gospel.* New Testament Studies in Biblical Theology 18. Downers Grove, Ill.: InterVarsity, 2004.
Bonhoeffer, Dietrich. *The Cost of Discipleship.* 2nd ed. London: SCM Press, 1959.
Bornkamm, Günther. *Jesus of Nazareth.* London: Hodder and Stoughton, 1960.
______. *Geschichte und Glaube I.* Munich: Chr. Kaiser, 1968.
Bornkamm, Günther, Gerhard Barth, and Heinz Joachim Held, eds. *Tradition and Interpretation in Matthew.* Translated by Percy Scott. Philadelphia: Westminster, 1963.
Boucher, Madeleine. *The Mysterious Parable: A Literary Study.* Washington, D.C.: Catholic Biblical Association, 1977.
Brown, Raymond E. *The Birth of the Messiah: A Commentary on the Infancy Narratives in Matthew and Luke.* 2nd ed. Garden City, N.J.: Doubleday, 1993.
______. *The Death of the Messiah: From Gethsemane to the Grave; A Commentary on the Passion Narratives in the Four Gospels.* New York: Doubleday, 1994.

Brown, Raymond E., Karl P. Donfried, and John Reumann, eds. *Peter in the New Testament*. Minneapolis: Augsburg, 1973.

Bultmann, Rudolf. *Theology of the New Testament*. 2 vols. Translated by K. Grobel. London: SCM Press, 1952–55.

______. *The History of the Synoptic Tradition*. Translated by J. Marsh. Oxford: Blackwell, 1963.

Burger, Christoph. *Jesus als Davidssohn: Eine traditionsgeschichtliche Untersuchung*. Göttingen: Vandenhoeck & Ruprecht, 1970.

Carmignac, Jean. *Recherches sur le "Notre Père."* Paris: Letouzey et Ané, 1969.

Carson, D. A. *The Sermon on the Mount*. Grand Rapids: Baker, 1978.

______. *Divine Sovereignty and Human Responsibility*. Atlanta: Knox, 1981.

Carson, D. A., ed. *From Sabbath to Lord's Day*. Grand Rapids: Zondervan, 1982.

Carson, D. A., and J. D. Woodbridge, eds. *Scripture and Truth*. Grand Rapids: Zondervan, 1983.

Carter, Warren. *Matthew and the Margins: A Sociopolitical and Religious Reading*. Bible and Liberation 204. Sheffield: Sheffield Academic, 2001.

Carter, Warren, and John Paul Heil. *Matthew's Parables: Audience-Oriented Perspectives*. Catholic Biblical Quarterly Monograph Series 30. Washington, D.C.: Catholic Biblical Association, 1998.

Casey, Maurice. *Son of Man: The Interpretation and Influence of Daniel 7*. London: SPCK, 1980.

______. *The Solution to the "Son of Man" Problem*. London: Continuum, 2007.

Catchpole, David R. *The Trial of Jesus: A Study in the Gospels and Jewish Historiography from 1770 to the Present Day*. Leiden: Brill, 1971.

Chae, Young S. *Jesus as the Eschatological Davidic Shepherd*. Wissenschaftliche Untersuchungen zum Neuen Testament 216. Tübingen: Mohr, 2006.

Charette, Blaine. *The Theme of Recompense in Matthew's Gospel*. Journal for the Study of the New Testament Supplement Series 79. Sheffield: Sheffield Academic, 1992.

Chilton, Bruce D. *God in Strength: Jesus' Announcement of the Kingdom*. Freistadt: Plochl, 1977.

Clarke, Howard. *The Gospel of Matthew and Its Readers: A Historical Introduction to the First Gospel*. Bloomington: Indiana Univ. Press, 2003.

Cope, O. Lamar. *Matthew: A Scribe Trained for the Kingdom of Heaven*. Washington, D.C.: Catholic Biblical Association, 1976.

Cranfield, C. E. B. *The Gospel according to St. Mark*. Cambridge: Cambridge University Press, 1972.

Cullmann, O. *Baptism in the New Testament*. Studies in Biblical Theology 1. London: SCM Press, 1950. Translated by Shirley C. Guthrie and Charles A. M. Hall. 2nd ed. Philadelphia: Westminster, 1963.

Dahl, N. A. *Jesus in the Memory of the Early Church*. Minneapolis: Augsburg, 1976.

Dalman, A. *Jesus-Jeshua: Studies in the Gospels*. London: SPCK, 1929.

Daube, David. *The New Testament and Rabbinic Judaism*. London: Athlone, 1956.

Davies, W. D. *Christian Origins and Judaism*. London: Darton, Longman, 1962.

______. *The Setting of the Sermon on the Mount*. Cambridge: Cambridge Univ. Press, 1963.

Deissmann, Gustav Adolph. *Light from the Ancient East*. Translated by L. R. M. Strachan. Grand Rapids: Baker, 1978.

______. *Bible Studies*. Edinburgh: T&T Clark, 1923. Repr., Winona Lake, Ind.: Alpha, 1979 .

Derrett, J. D. M. *Law in the New Testament*. London: Darton, Longman, 1970.

______. *Studies in the New Testament*. 2 vols. Leiden: Brill, 1977–78.

Didier, M., ed. *L'Évangile selon Matthieu: Rédaction et Théologie*. Bibliotheca ephemeridum theologicarum lovaniensium 29. Gembloux: Duculot, 1972.

Dodd, C. H. *The Parables of the Kingdom*. London: Nisbet, 1936.

Douglas, J. D., ed. *Illustrated Bible Dictionary*. 3 vols. Rev. ed. Wheaton, Ill.: Tyndale, 1980.

Dunn, J. D. G. *Jesus and the Spirit: A Study of the Religious and Charismatic Experience of Jesus and the First Christians as Reflected in the New Testament*. London: SCM Press, 1975.

______. *Christology in the Making: An Inquiry into the Origins of the Doctrine of the Incarnation*. London: SCM Press, 1980.

Dupont, Jacques. *Mariage et divorce dans l'évangile: Matthieu 19, 3–12 et paralleles*. Bruges: Desclée de Brouwer, 1959.

Edersheim, Alfred. *The Life and Times of Jesus the Messiah*. London: Longmans, Green, 1912.

Elliott, J. K., ed. *Studies in New Testament Language and Text*. Novum Testamentum Supplements 44. Leiden: Brill, 1976.

Ellis, E. Earle, and Max Wilcox, eds. *Neotestamentica et Semitica*. Edinburgh: T&T Clark, 1969.

Ellis, E. Earle, and E. Grässer, eds. *Jesus und Paulus*. Göttingen: Vandenhoeck & Ruprecht, 1975.
Fischer, David. *Historians' Fallacies: Toward a Logic of Historical Thought*. New York: Harper, 1970.
Fitzmyer, Joseph A. *Essays on the Semitic Background of the New Testament*. London: Chapman, 1971.
______. *A Wandering Aramean: Collected Aramaic Essays*. Missoula, Mont.: Scholars Press, 1978.
Flender, Helmut. *Die Botschaft Jesu von der Herrschaft Gottes*. Munich: Chr. Kaiser, 1968.
France, R. T. *Jesus and the Old Testament: His Application of Old Testament Passages to Himself and His Mission*. London: Tyndale, 1971.
France, R. T., and D. Wenham, eds. *Gospel Perspectives*. 2 vols. Sheffield: JSOT Press, 1980–81.
Frankemölle, Hubert. *Jahwebund und Kirche Christi: Studien zur Form und Traditionsgeschichte des "Evangeliums" nach Matthäus*. Munster: Aschendorff, 1974.
Garland, David E. *The Intention of Matthew 23*. Leiden: Brill, 1979.
Gaston, Lloyd. *No Stone on Another: Studies in the Significance of the Fall of Jerusalem in the Synoptic Gospels*. Leiden: Brill, 1970.
Gerhardsson, Birger. *The Mighty Acts of Jesus according to Matthew*. Lund: Gleerup, 1979.
Gnilka, J., ed. *Neues Testament und Kirche*. Freiburg: Herder, 1974.
Goppelt, Leonhard. *Theologie des Neuen Testaments*. Edited by Jürgen Roloff. Göttingen: Vandenhoeck & Ruprecht, 1976.
Goulder, M. D. *Midrash and Lection in Matthew*. London: SPCK, 1974.
Gundry, Robert H. *The Use of the Old Testament in St. Matthew's Gospel, with Special Reference to the Messianic Hope*. Novum Testamentum Supplements 18. Leiden: Brill, 1975.
Guthrie, Donald. *New Testament Theology*. Downers Grove, Ill.: InterVarsity, 1981.
Ham, Clay Alan. *The Coming King and the Rejected Shepherd: Matthew's Reading of Zechariah's Messianic Hope*. New Testament Monographs 4. Sheffield: Sheffield Phoenix, 2005.
Hannan, Margaret. *The Nature and Demands of the Sovereign Rule of God in the Gospel of Matthew*. London: T&T Clark, 2006.
Hare, Douglas R. A. *The Theme of Jewish Persecution of Christians in the Gospel according to St. Matthew*. Cambridge: Cambridge Univ. Press, 1967.
Hawthorne, G. F., ed. *Current Issues in Biblical and Patristic Interpretation*. Grand Rapids: Eerdmans, 1975.
Hengstenberg, E. W. *Christology of the Old Testament*. 2 vols. Repr., McLean, Va.: MacDonald, 1972.
Hennecke, E. *New Testament Apocrypha*. 2 vols. London: Lutterworth, 1965.
Hill, David. *Greek Words with Hebrew Meanings*. Society for New Testament Studies Monograph Series 5. Cambridge: Cambridge Univ. Press, 1967.
Hoehner, Harold W. *Herod Antipas*. Society for New Testament Studies Monograph Series 17. Cambridge: Cambridge Univ. Press, 1972.
______. *Chronological Aspects of the Life of Christ*. Grand Rapids: Zondervan, 1977.
Hoekema, A. A. *The Bible and the Future*. Grand Rapids: Eerdmans, 1979.
Hoffmann, Paul, et al., eds. *Orientierung an Jesus*. Freiburg: Herder, 1973.
Hooker, Morna D. *Jesus and the Servant*. London: SPCK, 1959.
______. *The Son of Man in Mark*. London: SPCK, 1967.
Hubbard, B. J. *The Matthean Redaction of a Primitive Apostolic Commissioning: An Exegesis of Matthew 28:16–20*. Society of Biblical Literature Dissertation Series 19. Missoula, Mont.: Scholars Press, 1974.
Hull, John M. *Hellenistic Magic and the Synoptic Tradition*. London: SCM Press, 1974.
Hummel, Reinhardt. *Die Auseinandersetzung zwischen Kirche und Judentum im Matthäusevangelium*. Munich: Chr. Kaiser, 1966.
Jeremias, J. *Jesus' Promise to the Nations*. Translated by John Bowden. London: SCM Press, 1958.
______. *Jerusalem in the Time of Jesus*. Translated by F. H. Cave and C. H. Cave. London: SCM Press, 1962.
______. *The Parables of Jesus*. Translated by S. H. Hooke. London: SCM Press, 1963.
______. *The Eucharistic Words of Jesus*. Translated by N. Perrin. 3rd ed. London: SCM Press, 1966.
______. *The Prayers of Jesus*. Translated by John Bowden and Christoph Burchard. London: SCM Press, 1967.
______. *New Testament Theology*. Part 1. *The Proclamation of Jesus*. Translated by John Bowden. London: SCM Press, 1971.
Johnson, Marshall D. *The Purpose of the Biblical Genealogies*. Cambridge: Cambridge Univ. Press, 1969.
Kilpatrick, G. D. *The Origins of the Gospel according to St. Matthew*. Oxford: Clarendon, 1946.

Kingsbury, Jack Dean. *The Parables of Jesus in Matthew 13: A Study in Redaction-Criticism*. London: SPCK, 1969.
______. *Matthew: Structure, Christology, Kingdom*. Philadelphia: Fortress, 1975.
Kistemaker, Simon J. *The Parables of Jesus*. Grand Rapids: Baker, 1980.
Knowles, Michael. *Jeremiah in Matthew's Gospel: The Rejected Prophet Motif in Matthaean Redaction*. Journal for the Study of the New Testament Supplement Series 68. Sheffield: Sheffield Academic, 1993.
Kümmel, W. G. *Promise and Fulfillment*. Translated by Dorothea M. Barton. 2nd ed. Studies in Biblical Theology 23. London: SCM Press, 1961.
______. *Introduction to the New Testament*. Translated by Howard Clark Kee. Nashville: Abingdon, 1975.
Kupp, David D. *Matthew's Emmanuel: Divine Presence and God's People in the First Gospel*. Society for New Testament Studies Monograph Series 90. Cambridge: Cambridge Univ. Press, 1996.
Ladd, G. E. *The Presence of the Future: The Eschatology of Biblical Realism*. Grand Rapids: Eerdmans, 1974.
______. *A Theology of the New Testament*. Grand Rapids: Eerdmans, 1974.
Lane, William L. *The Gospel according to Mark*. Grand Rapids: Eerdmans, 1974.
Lindars, Barnabas. *New Testament Apologetic*. London: SCM Press, 1961.
Livingstone, E. A., ed. *Studia Biblica 1978*. 2 vols. Sheffield: JSOT Press, 1980.
Longenecker, Richard N. *The Christology of Early Jewish Christianity*. London: SCM Press, 1970.
______. *Biblical Exegesis in the Apostolic Period*. Grand Rapids: Eerdmans, 1975.
Longenecker, Richard N., and Merrill C. Tenney, eds. *New Dimensions in New Testament Study*. Grand Rapids: Zondervan, 1974.
Luz, Ulrich. *Studies in Matthew*. Grand Rapids: Eerdmans, 2005.
Machen, J. Gresham. *The Virgin Birth of Christ*. New York: Harper, 1930.
Manson, T. W. *The Sayings of Jesus*. London: SCM Press, 1949.
Marshall, I. Howard. *The Gospel of Luke: A Commentary on the Greek Text*. Grand Rapids: Eerdmans, 1978.
______. *Last Supper and Lord's Supper.* Exeter: Paternoster, 1980.
Marshall, I. Howard, ed. *New Testament Interpretation*. Exeter: Paternoster, 1977.
McConnell, Richard S. *Law and Prophecy in Matthew's Gospel*. Basel: Friedrich Reinhardt, 1969.
McHugh, John. *The Mother of Jesus in the New Testament*. Garden City, N.J.: Doubleday, 1975.
McKnight, Scot. *Jesus and His Death: Historiography, the Historical Jesus, and Atonement Theory*. Waco, Tex.: Baylor Univ. Press, 2005.
Meier, John P. *Law and History in Matthew's Gospel: A Redactional Study of Mt. 5:17–48*. Analecta biblica 71. Rome: Biblical Institute Press, 1976.
______. *The Vision of Matthew: Christ, Church, and Morality in the First Gospel*. New York: Paulist, 1979.
Menken, M. J. J. *Matthew's Bible: The Old Testament Text of the Evangelist*. Bibliotheca ephemeridum theologicarum lovaniensium 173. Leuven: Leuven Univ. Press, 2004.
Metzger, Bruce M. *A Textual Commentary on the Greek New Testament*. London: UBS, 1971.
______. *New Testament Studies: Philological, Versional, and Patristic*. Leiden: Brill, 1980.
Meyer, Ben F. *The Aims of Jesus*. London: SCM Press, 1979.
Mohrlang, R. *Matthew and Paul: A Comparison of Ethical Perspectives*. Society for New Testament Studies Monograph Series 48. Cambridge: Cambridge Univ. Press, 1984.
Moo, Douglas J. *The Old Testament in the Gospel Passion Narratives*. Sheffield: Almond, 1983.
Moore, G. F. *Judaism in the First Centuries of the Christian Era*. 3 vols. Cambridge, Mass.: Harvard Univ. Press, 1927–30.
Morris, Leon. *The Apostolic Preaching of the Cross*. Grand Rapids: Eerdmans, 1955.
______. *The Gospel according to John*. Grand Rapids: Eerdmans, 1971.
Moule, C. F. D. *An Idiom Book of New Testament Greek*. 2nd ed. London: Cambridge Univ. Press, 1959.
______. *The Origin of Christology*. Cambridge: Cambridge Univ. Press, 1977.
______. *The Birth of the New Testament*. 3rd. ed. London: A. & C. Black, 1981.
Moulton, James Hope. *A Grammar of New Testament Greek*. Vol. 1, *Prolegomena*. Edinburgh: T&T Clark, 1908.
______. *A Grammar of New Testament Greek*. Vol. 2, *Accidence and Word Formation*. Edited by W. F. Howard. Edinburgh: T&T Clark, 1920.
Nolan, Brian M. *The Royal Son of God: The Christology of Matthew 1–2 in the Setting of the Gospel*. Göttingen: Vandenhoeck & Ruprecht, 1979.

Orton, David E. *The Understanding Scribe: Matthew and the Apocalyptic Ideal.* Journal for the Study of the New Testament Supplement Series 25. Sheffield: Sheffield Academic, 1989.

Parrot, André. *Golgotha and the Church of the Holy Sepulchre.* Translated by E. Hudson. London: SCM Press, 1957.

Pennington, Jonathan T. *Heaven and Earth in the Gospel of Matthew.* Novum Testamentum Supplements 126. Leiden: Brill, 2007.

Piper, John. *"Love Your Enemies": Jesus' Love Command in the Synoptic Gospels and Early Christian Paraenesis: A History of the Tradition and Interpretation of Its Uses.* Society for New Testament Studies Monograph Series 38. Cambridge: Cambridge Univ. Press, 1979.

Przybylski, Benno. *Righteousness in Matthew and His World of Thought.* Society for New Testament Studies Monograph Series 41. Cambridge: Cambridge University Press, 1980.

Ridderbos, Herman. *The Coming of the Kingdom.* Translated by R. Zorn. Philadelphia: Presbyterian and Reformed, 1962.

Robertson, A. T. *Word Pictures in the New Testament.* 6 vols. New York: Harper, 1930.

Robinson, John A. T. *Twelve New Testament Studies.* London: SCM Press, 1962.

Rothfuchs, Wilhelm. *Die Erfüllungszitate des Matthäus-Evangeliums.* Stuttgart: Kohlhammer, 1969.

Sand, Alexander. *Das Gesetz und die Propheten: Untersuchungen zur Theologie des Evangeliums nach Matthäus.* Regensburg: Pustet, 1976.

Schottroff, Luise, et al. *Essays on the Love Commandment.* Philadelphia: Fortress, 1978.

Schürer, Emil. *A History of the Jewish People in the Time of Christ.* Translated by Sophia Taylor and Peter Christie. 2 vols. 2nd ed. Edinburgh: T&T Clark, 1901.

Schweitzer, Albert. *The Quest of the Historical Jesus.* 2nd ed. Translated by W. Montgomery. London: A. & C. Black, 1911.

Senior, Donald. *The Passion Narrative according to Matthew: A Redactional Study.* Bibliotheca ephemeridum theologicarum lovaniensium 39. Leuven: Leuven Univ. Press, 1975.

Sherwin-White, A. N. *Roman Society and Roman Law in the New Testament.* Oxford: Clarendon, 1963.

Sigal, Phillip. *The Halakhah of Jesus of Nazareth according to the Gospel of Matthew.* Rev. ed. Studies in Biblical Literature 18. Atlanta: SBL Press, 2007 [1986].

Sim, David C. *The Gospel of Matthew and Christian Judaism: The History and Social Setting of the Matthean Community.* Edinburgh: T&T Clark, 1998.

Soares-Prabhu, George M. *The Formula Quotations in the Infancy Narrative of Matthew.* Rome: Biblical Institute Press, 1976.

Stanton, Graham N. *Jesus of Nazareth in New Testament Preaching.* Cambridge: Cambridge Univ. Press, 1974.

______. *A Gospel for a New People: Studies in Matthew.* Edinburgh: T&T Clark, 1992.

Stendahl, Krister. *The School of St. Matthew and Its Use of the Old Testament.* 2nd ed. Lund: Gleerup, 1954.

Stier, Rudolf. *The Words of the Lord Jesus.* Translated by W. B. Pope. 2 vols. Edinburgh: T&T Clark, 1874.

Stonehouse, Ned B. *The Witness of Matthew and Mark to Christ.* Grand Rapids: Eerdmans, 1944.

______. *Origins of the Synoptic Gospels: Some Basic Questions.* Grand Rapids: Eerdmans, 1963.

Stott, John R. W. *The Message of the Sermon on the Mount.* Downers Grove, Ill.: InterVarsity, 1985.

Strecker, Georg, ed. *Der Weg der Gerechtigkeit.* 3rd ed. Forschungen zur Religion und Literatur des Alten und Neuen Testaments 82. Göttingen: Vandenhoeck & Ruprecht, 1962.

______. *Jesus Christus in Historie und Theologie.* Tübingen: Mohr, 1975.

Suggs, M. Jack. *Wisdom, Christology, and Law in Matthew's Gospel.* Cambridge, Mass.: Harvard Univ. Press, 1970.

Taylor, Vincent. *The Gospel according to St. Mark.* 2nd ed. London: Macmillan, 1966.

Thompson, William G. *Matthew's Advice to a Divided Community: Mt. 17, 22–18, 35.* Rome: Biblical Institute Press, 1970.

Thrall, Margaret E. *Greek Particles in the New Testament.* Leiden: Brill, 1962.

Trench, R. C. *Studies in the Gospels.* London: Macmillan, 1878.

Trilling, Wolfgang. *Das wahre Israel: Studien zur Theologie des Matthäus-Evangeliums.* München: Kosel, 1964.

Turner, Nigel. *Syntax.* Vol. 3 of J. H. Moulton. *A Grammar of New Testament Greek.* Edinburgh: T&T Clark, 1963.

______. *Grammatical Insights into the New Testament.* Edinburgh: T&T Clark, 1965.

______. *Christian Words.* Edinburgh: T&T Clark, 1980.

Urbach, E. E. *The Sages: Their Concepts and Beliefs*. Translated by I. Abrahams. 2 vols. Jerusalem: Magnes, 1975.
van der Loos, Hendrik. *The Miracles of Jesus*. Leiden: Brill, 1965.
van Tilborg, Sjef. *The Jewish Leaders in Matthew*. Leiden: Brill, 1972.
Verseput, Donald J. *The Rejection of the Humble Messianic King: A Study of the Composition of Matthew 11–12*. Frankfurt: Lang, 1986.
Via, Dan O. *The Parables*. Philadelphia: Fortress, 1967.
Walker, Rolf. *Die Heilsgeschichte im ersten Evangelium*. Göttingen: Vandenhoeck & Ruprecht, 1967.
Warfield, Benjamin B. *Selected Shorter Writings*. 2 vols. Edited by John E. Meeter. Nutley, N.J.: Presbyterian and Reformed, 1970.
Wenham, David, ed. *The Rediscovery of Jesus' Eschatological Discourse*. Gospel Perspectives 4. Sheffield: JSOT Press, 1984.
Westerholm, Stephen. *Jesus and Scribal Authority*. Coniectanea biblica: New Testament Series 10. Lund: Gleerup, 1978.
Wilson, Alistair I. *When Will These Things Happen? A Study of Jesus as Judge in Matthew 21–25*. Bletchley, U.K.: Paternoster, 2004.
Wright, N. T. *Jesus and the Victory of God*. Christian Origins and the Question of God 2. London: SPCK, 1996.
______. *The Resurrection of the Son of God*. Christian Origins and the Question of God 3. London: SPCK, 2003.
Zerwick, M. *Biblical Greek*. Rome: Scripta Pontificii Instituti Biblici, 1963.
Zumstein, Jean. *La condition du croyant dans l'Évangile selon Matthieu*. Göttingen: Vandenhoeck & Ruprecht, 1977.

Articles

Bacon, Benjamin W. "The 'Five Books' of Moses Against the Jews." *The Expositor* 15 (1918): 56–66.
Barth, Gerhard. "Matthew's Understanding of the Law." Pages 58–164 in *Tradition and Interpretation in Matthew*. Edited by Günther Bornkamm, Gerhard Barth, and Heinz Joachim Held. Philadelphia: Westminster, 1963.
Berger, Klaus. "Die königlichen Messiastraditionen des Neuen Testaments." *New Testament Studies* 20 (1974): 1–44.
Blaising, Craig A. "Gethsemane: A Prayer of Faith." *Journal of the Evangelical Theological Society* 22 (1979): 333–43.
Bornkamm, Günther. "End-Expectation and the Church in Matthew." Pages 15–51 in *Tradition and Interpretation in Matthew*. Edited by Günther Bornkamm, Gerhard Barth, and Heinz Joachim Held. Philadelphia: Westminster, 1963.
______. "The Stilling of the Storm in Matthew." Pages 52–57 in *Tradition and Interpretation in Matthew*. Edited by Günther Bornkamm, Gerhard Barth, and Heinz Joachim Held. Philadelphia: Westminster, 1963.
Carson, D. A. "Historical Tradition in the Fourth Gospel—After Dodd, What?" Pages 83–145 in *Gospel Perspectives*. Edited by R. T. France and D. Wenham. Vol. 2. Sheffield: JSOT Press, 1980–81.
______. "Jesus and the Sabbath in the Four Gospels." Pages 57–97 in *From Sabbath to Lord's Day*. Edited by D. A. Carson. Grand Rapids: Zondervan, 1982.
______. "Jewish Leaders in Matthew's Gospel: A Reappraisal." *Journal of the Evangelical Theological Society* 25 (1982): 161–74.
______. "Christological Ambiguities in the Gospel of Matthew." Pages 97–114 in *Christ the Lord: Studies in Christology Presented to Donald Guthrie*. Edited by Harold Rowdon. Downers Grove, Ill.: InterVarsity, 1982.
______. "Redaction Criticism: On the Legitimacy and Illegitimacy of a Literary Tool." Pages 119–42 in *Scripture and Truth*. Edited by D. A. Carson and J. D. Woodbridge. Grand Rapids: Zondervan, 1983.
______. "The ὅμοιος Word-Group as Introduction to Some Matthean Parables." *New Testament Studies* 31 (1985): 277–82.
Dodd, C. H. "New Testament Translation Problems I." *Bible Translator* 27 (1976): 301–11.
Dupont, J. "Le point de vue de Matthieu dans le chapitre des paraboles." Pages 221–59 in *L'Évangile selon Matthieu: Rédaction et Théologie*. Bibliotheca ephemeridum theologicarum lovaniensium 29. Edited by M. Didier. Gembloux: Duculot, 1972.
Ellis, E. E. "New Directions in Form Criticism." Pages 299–315 in *Jesus Christus in Historie und Theologie*. Edited by Georg Strecker. Tübingen: Mohr, 1975.
Fee, G. D. "Modern Text Criticism and the Synoptic Problem." Pages 154–69 in *J. J. Griesbach: Synoptic and Text-Critical Studies, 1776–1976*. Edited by Bernard Orchard and Thomas R. W. Longstaff. Cambridge: Cambridge Univ. Press, 1978.

France, R. T. "The Servant of the Lord in the Teaching of Jesus." *Tyndale Bulletin* 19 (1966): 26–52.

______. "God and Mammon." *Evangelical Quarterly* 51 (1979): 3–21.

______. "Exegesis in Practice: Two Samples." Pages 252–81 in *New Testament Interpretation*. Edited by I. Howard Marshall. Exeter: Paternoster, 1977.

Gooding, D.W. "Structure littéraire de Matthieu, XIII, 53 à XVIII, 35." *Revue Biblique* 85 (1978): 227–52.

Heil, John Paul. "Significant Aspects of the Healing Miracles in Matthew." *Catholic Biblical Quarterly* 41 (1979): 274–87.

Held, Heinz Joachim. "Matthew as Interpreter of the Miracle Stories." Pages 165–299 in *Tradition and Interpretation in Matthew*. Edited by Günther Bornkamm, Gerhard Barth, and Heinz Joachim Held. Philadelphia: Westminster, 1963.

Hill, David. "Son and Servant: An Essay on Matthean Christology." *Journal for the Study of the New Testament* 6 (1980): 2–16.

Huffmann, Norman A. "Atypical Features in the Parables of Jesus." *Journal of Biblical Literature* 97 (1978): 207–20.

Kaiser, W. C. "The Weightier and Lighter Matters of the Law." Pages 176–92 in *Current Issues in Biblical and Patristic Interpretation*. Edited by G. F. Hawthorne. Grand Rapids: Eerdmans, 1975.

Lachs, S. T. "Some Textual Observations on the Sermon on the Mount." *Jewish Quarterly Review* 69 (1978): 98–111.

Liefeld, Walter L. "Theological Motifs in the Transfiguration Narrative." Pages 162–79 in *New Dimensions in New Testament Study*. Edited by Richard N. Longenecker and Merrill C. Tenney. Grand Rapids: Zondervan, 1974.

Moo, Douglas J. "Jesus and the Authority of the Mosaic Law." *Journal for the Study of the New Testament* 20 (1984): 3–49.

Neil, William. "Five Hard Sayings of Jesus." Pages 157–71 in *Biblical Studies*. Edited by J. R. McKay and J. F. Miller. London: Collins, 1976.

O'Brien, P. T. "The Great Commission of Matthew 28:18–20." *Evangelical Review of Theology* 2 (1978): 254–67.

Ogawa, Akira. "Paraboles de l'Israël véritable? Reconsidération critique de Mt. xxi.28 xxii.14." *Novum Testamentum* 21 (1979): 121–49.

Pamment, Margaret. "The Kingdom of Heaven according to the First Gospel." *New Testament Studies* 27 (1980–81): 211–32.

Payne, Philip Barton. "The Authenticity of the Parable of the Sower and Its Interpretation." Pages 163–207 in *Gospel Perspectives*. Edited by R. T. France and D. Wenham. Vol. 2. Sheffield: JSOT Press, 1980–81.

Reicke, Bo. "Synoptic Prophecies on the Destruction of Jerusalem." Pages 121–34 in *Studies in New Testament and Early Christian Literature*. Edited by D. E. Aune. Leiden: Brill, 1972.

Slingerland, H. Dixon. "The Transjordanian Origin of St. Matthew's Gospel." *Journal for the Study of the New Testament* 3 (1979): 18–28.

Stanton, Graham N. "The Origin and Purpose of Matthew's Gospel: Matthean Scholarship from 1945 to 1980." Page 25 in *Aufstieg und Niedergang der römischen Welt*. Vol. 2. New York: de Gruyter, 1982.

Wenham, David. "The Synoptic Problem Revisited: Some New Suggestions About the Composition of Mark 4:1–34." *Tyndale Bulletin* 23 (1972): 3–38.

______. "The Resurrection Narratives in Matthew's Gospel." *Tyndale Bulletin* 24 (1973): 21–54.

______. "The Interpretation of the Parable of the Sower." *New Testament Studies* 20 (1974): 299–319.

______. "The Structure of Matthew XIII," *New Testament Studies* 25 (1978–79): 516–22.

Unpublished Material

Blomberg, Craig. "The Tendencies of the Tradition in the Parables of the Gospel of Thomas." Master's thesis, Trinity Evangelical Divinity School, 1979.

Trotter, Andrew H. "Understanding and Stumbling: A Study of the Disciples' Understanding of Jesus and His Teaching in the Gospel of Matthew." PhD diss., Cambridge University, 1986.

Wood, Thomas R. "The Regathering of the People of God: An Investigation into the New Testament's Appropriation of the Old Testament Prophecies Concerning the Regathering of Israel." PhD diss., Trinity Evangelical Divinity School, 2005.

14. STRUCTURE AND OUTLINE

Structure

As a skilled literary craftsman, Matthew gave his gospel structure, form, and rhythm. Two of his larger chiasms are indicated in the outline below. But the structure of the gospel as a whole is still disputed. With minor variations, there are three main views.

First, some have detected a geographical framework.[167] Matthew 1:1–2:23 is the prologue; 3:1–4:11 is Jesus' preparation for ministry; 4:12–13:58 finds Jesus in Galilee; 14:1–20:34 pictures him around Galilee and heading toward Jerusalem; and 21:1–28:20 finds him at Jerusalem. The divisions are neither precise nor helpful, for the result tells us nothing of Matthew's purposes.

Second, Jack Dean Kingsbury, taking a hint from Lohmeyer and Stonehouse,[168] argues for three sections.[169] The first he titles "The Person of Jesus Messiah" (1:1–4:16), the second "The Proclamation of Jesus Messiah" (4:17–16:20), and the third "The Suffering, Death, and Resurrection of Jesus Messiah" (16:21–28:20). Immediately after the two breaks comes the phrase *apo tote* ("from that time on"). Kingsbury further notes that the last two sections each contain three "summary" passages—4:23–25; 9:35; 11:1 and 16:21; 17:22–23; 20:17–19 respectively—and he suggests that this outline does justice to the centrality of Matthew's Christology.

Though this outline has gained adherents, it has serious weaknesses. It is not at all clear that *apo tote* is so redactionally important for Matthew. He also uses it in 26:16 without any suggestion of a break in his outline. One could argue that there are four passion summaries in the third section, not three (add 26:2). Kingsbury's outline not only breaks up the prime Peter passage in an unacceptable way (see comments at 16:13–16), but at both transitions Matthew may have been more influenced by the order of Mark than by "structural" considerations. The most important weakness, however, is the artificiality of the topical headings. The person of Jesus (section 1) is still a focal point in sections 2 and 3 (e.g., 16:13–16; 22:41–46). Why the proclamation of Jesus should be restricted to section 2 when two of the discourses (chs. 18; 24–25) and several important exchanges (chs. 21–23) await the third section is not clear. The last heading, "The Suffering, Death, and Resurrection of Jesus Messiah," though it accurately summarizes the increasingly dominant theme of 16:21–28:20, seems an inadequate designation of much in those chapters (e.g., most of 18; 21–25). Considerably more sophisticated variations of this narrative outline have been advanced, each with its own strengths and weaknesses.[170] For example, the one by Ulrich Luz finally depends heavily on the assumption that the narrative flow is analyzable on the assumption that Matthew depends *only* on Mark and Q.

---

167. See, e.g., Alan Hugh McNeile, *The Gospel according to St. Matthew* (London: Macmillan, 1915).

168. Lohmeyer, *Das Evangelium des Matthäus*; Stonehouse, *Witness of Matthew*, 129–31.

169. Jack Dean Kingsbury, *Matthew: Structure, Christology, Kingdom* (Philadelphia: Fortress, 1975).

170. See, e.g., Ulrich Luz, both in his commentary, *Matthew*, and in his *Studies*. See also Wim J. C. Weren, "The Macrostructure of Matthew's Gospel: A New Proposal," *Bib* 87 (2006): 171–99, who argues for a large structure grounded in topographical data, and then refined by various "kernels" and "satellites."

The third scheme makes the book center on the five main discourses (see outline below). Each begins by placing Jesus in a specific context and ends with a formula found nowhere else in the gospel (see comments at 7:28–29) and a transitional pericope with links pointing forward and backward. Benjamin Bacon believed the five discourses correspond to the five books of the Pentateuch;[171] but there is little in favor of this refinement, since Moses typology is very weak in this gospel and the links between the five discourses and the five books of Moses minimal.

Two frequently raised difficulties must be overcome.

1. Why restrict oneself to *five* discourses when ch. 11 could fall into that category? This objection misses the mark. The fivefold sequence of discourses does not assume that Jesus is not portrayed as speaking in the narrative sections. He may do so, even extensively (see comments at ch. 21). The point is that the five discourses are sufficiently well defined that it is hard to believe Matthew did not plan them as such.

2. Does this not relegate the birth narrative (chs. 1–2) and the passion and resurrection (chs. 26–28) to a sort of secondary status outside the central outline? There is little difficulty in seeing chs. 1–2 as a prologue anticipating the opening of the gospel, a formal opening common to all the canonical gospels (see comments at 1:1). But certainly Matthew 26–28 must not be dismissed as an epilogue; this section is too much the point toward which the gospel moves for that to be true. On the other hand, chs. 26–28 do not constitute an ordinary "conclusion," for the final verses are purposely open-ended and anticipatory. It seems best to take 26:6–28:20 as constituting an exceptional sixth narrative section, with the corresponding teaching section being laid on the shoulders of the disciples (28:18–20).

But no outline should be taken too seriously. The Gospels use vignettes—organized ones, doubtless, but vignettes nonetheless. The following outline organizes Matthew's gospel and reflects some demonstrable structure—a structure, however, that provides a guide to its contents, not a comprehensive explanation.

171. Benjamin Bacon, "The 'Five Books' of Moses Against the Jews," *Expositor* 15 (1918): 56–66.

Outline
(References in outline are tied to commentary)

I. Prologue: The Origin and Birth of Jesus the Christ (1:1–2:23)
  A. The Genealogy of Jesus (1:1–17)
  B. The Birth of Jesus (1:18–25)
  C. The Visit of the Magi (2:1–12)
  D. The Escape to Egypt (2:13–15)
  E. The Massacre of Bethlehem's Boys (2:16–18)
  F. The Return to Nazareth (2:19–23)
II. The Gospel of the Kingdom (3:1–7:29)
  A. Narrative (3:1–4:25)
    1. Foundational steps (3:1–4:11)
      a. The ministry of John the Baptist (3:1–12)
      b. The baptism of Jesus (3:13–17)
      c. The temptation of Jesus (4:1–11)
    2. Jesus' early Galilean ministry (4:12–25)
      a. The beginning (4:12–17)
      b. Calling the first disciples (4:18–22)
      c. Spreading the news of the kingdom (4:23–25)
  B. First Discourse: The Sermon on the Mount (5:1–7:29)
    1. Setting (5:1–2)
    2. The kingdom of heaven: its norms and witness (5:3–16)
      a. The norms of the kingdom (5:3–12)
        (1) The Beatitudes (5:3–10)
        (2) Expansion (5:11–12)
      b. The witness of the kingdom (5:13–16)
        (1) Salt (5:13)
        (2) Light (5:14–16)
    3. The kingdom of heaven: its demands in relation to the OT (5:17–48)
      a. Jesus and the kingdom as fulfillment of the OT (5:17–20)
      b. Application: the antitheses (5:21–48)
        (1) Vilifying anger and reconciliation (5:21–26)
        (2) Adultery and purity (5:27–30)
        (3) Divorce and remarriage (5:31–32)
        (4) Oaths and truthfulness (5:33–37)
        (5) Personal injury and self-sacrifice (5:38–42)
        (6) Hatred and love (5:43–47)
      c. Conclusion: the demand for perfection (5:48)
    4. Religious hypocrisy: its description and overthrow (6:1–18)
      a. The principle (6:1)

b. Three examples (6:2–18)
(1) Alms (6:2–4)
(2) Prayer (6:5–15)
(a) Ostentatious prayer (6:5–6)
(b) Repetitious prayer (6:7–8)
(c) Model prayer (6:9–13)
(d) Forgiveness and prayer (6:14–15)
(3) Fasting (6:16–18)
5. Kingdom perspectives (6:19–34)
a. Metaphors for unswerving loyalty to kingdom values (6:19–24)
(1) Treasure (6:19–21)
(2) Light (6:22–23)
(3) Slavery (6:24)
b. Uncompromised trust (6:25–34)
(1) The principle (6:25)
(2) The examples (6:26–30)
(a) Life and food (6:26–27)
(b) Body and clothes (6:28–30)
(3) Distinctive living (6:31–32)
(4) The heart of the matter (6:33)
(5) Abolishing worry (6:34)
6. Balance and perfection (7:1–12)
a. The danger of being judgmental (7:1–5)
(1) The principle (7:1)
(2) The theological justification (7:2)
(3) An example (7:3–5)
b. The danger of being undiscerning (7:6)
c. Source and means of power (7:7–11)
d. Balance and perfection (7:12)
7. Conclusion: call to decision and commitment (7:13–27)
a. Two ways (7:13–14)
b. Two trees (7:15–20)
c. Two claims (7:21–23)
d. Two builders (7:24–27)
8. Transitional conclusion: Jesus' authority (7:28–29)
III. The Kingdom Extended under Jesus' Authority (8:1–11:1)
A. Narrative (8:1–10:4)
1. Healing miracles (8:1–17)
a. A leper (8:1–4)
b. The centurion's servant (8:5–13)

c. Peter's mother-in-law (8:14–15)
d. Many at evening (8:16–17)
2. The cost of following Jesus (8:18–22)
Reflections: "The Son of Man" as a Christological Title
3. Calming a storm (8:23–27)
4. Further demonstration of Jesus' authority (8:28–9:8)
a. Exorcising two men (8:28–34)
b. Healing a paralytic and forgiving his sins (9:1–8)
5. Calling Matthew (9:9)
6. Eating with sinners (9:10–13)
7. Fasting and the dawning of the messianic joy (9:14–17)
8. A resurrection and more healings (9:18–34)
a. Raising a girl and healing a woman (9:18–26)
b. Healing two blind men (9:27–31)
c. Exorcising a dumb man (9:32–34)
9. Spreading the news of the kingdom (9:35–10:4)
a. Praying for workers (9:35–38)
b. Commissioning the Twelve (10:1–4)
B. Second Discourse: Mission and Martyrdom (10:5–11:1)
1. Setting (10:5a)
2. The commission (10:5b–16)
3. Warnings of future sufferings (10:17–25)
a. The Spirit's help (10:17–20)
b. Endurance (10:21–23)
c. Inspiration (10:24–25)
4. Prohibition of fear (10:26–31)
a. The emergence of truth (10:26–27)
b. The nonfinality of death (10:28)
c. Continuing providence (10:29–31)
5. Characteristics of discipleship (10:32–39)
a. Acknowledging Jesus (10:32–33)
b. Recognizing the gospel (10:34–36)
c. Preferring Jesus (10:37–39)
6. Encouragement: response to the disciples and to Jesus (10:40–42)
7. Transitional conclusion: expanding ministry (11:1)
IV. Teaching and Preaching the Gospel of the Kingdom: Rising Opposition (11:2–13:53)
A. Narrative (11:2–12:50)
1. Jesus and John the Baptist (11:2–19)
a. John's question and Jesus' response (11:2–6)
b. Jesus' testimony to John (11:7–19)

(1) John in redemptive history (11:7–15)
(2) The unsatisfied generation (11:16–19)
2. The condemned and the accepted (11:20–30)
a. The condemned: woes on unrepentant cities (11:20–24)
b. The accepted (11:25–30)
(1) Because of the revelation of the Father (11:25–26)
(2) Because of the agency of the Son (11:27)
(3) Because of the Son's gentle invitation (11:28–30)
3. Sabbath conflicts (12:1–14)
a. Picking heads of grain (12:1–8)
b. Healing a man with a shriveled hand (12:9–14)
4. Jesus as the prophesied Servant (12:15–21)
5. Confrontation with the Pharisees (12:22–45)
a. The setting and accusation (12:22–24)
b. Jesus' reply (12:25–37)
(1) The divided kingdom (12:25–28)
(2) The strong man's house (12:29)
(3) Blasphemy against the Spirit (12:30–32)
(4) Nature and fruit (12:33–37)
c. Continued confrontation (12:38–42)
(1) Request for a sign (12:38)
(2) The sign of Jonah (12:39–42)
d. The return of the evil spirit (12:43–45)
6. Doing the Father's will (12:46–50)
B. Third Discourse: The Parables of the Kingdom (13:1–53)
1. The setting (13:1–3a)
2. To the crowds (13:3b–33)
a. The parable of the soils (13:3b–9)
b. Interlude (13:10–23)
(1) On understanding parables (13:10–17)
(2) Interpretation of the parable of the soils (13:18–23)
c. The parable of the weeds (13:24–30)
d. The parable of the mustard seed (13:31–32)
e. The parable of the yeast (13:33)
3. Pause (13:34–43)
a. Parables as fulfillment of prophecy (13:34–35)
b. Interpretation of the parable of the weeds (13:36–43)
4. To the disciples (13:44–52)
a. The parable of the hidden treasure (13:44)
b. The parable of the expensive pearl (13:45–46)

c. The parable of the net (13:47–48)
d. Interlude (13:49–51)
(1) Interpretation of the parable of the net (13:49–50)
(2) On understanding parables (13:51)
e. The parable of the teacher of the law (13:52)
5. Transitional conclusion: movement toward further opposition (13:53)
V. The Glory and the Shadow: Progressive Polarization (13:54–19:2)
A. Narrative (13:54–17:27)
1. Rejected at Nazareth (13:54–58)
2. Herod and Jesus (14:1–12)
a. Herod's understanding of Jesus (14:1–2)
b. Background: Herod's execution of John the Baptist (14:3–12)
3. The feeding of the five thousand (14:13–21)
4. The walk on the water (14:22–33)
5. Transitional summary of constant and unavoidable ministry (14:34–36)
6. Jesus and the tradition of the elders (15:1–20)
7. More healings (15:21–31)
a. The Canaanite woman (15:21–28)
b. The many (15:29–31)
8. The feeding of the four thousand (15:32–39)
9. Another demand for a sign (16:1–4)
10. The yeast of the Pharisees and Sadducees (16:5–12)
11. Peter's confession of Jesus and its aftermath (16:13–23)
a. The confession (16:13–20)
b. The first passion prediction (16:21–23)
12. The way of discipleship (16:24–28)
13. The Transfiguration (17:1–13)
a. Jesus transfigured (17:1–8)
b. The place of Elijah (17:9–13)
14. The healing of an epileptic boy (17:14–20 [21])
15. The second major passion prediction (17:22–23)
16. The temple tax (17:24–27)
B. Fourth Discourse: Life under Kingdom Authority (18:1–19:2)
1. Setting (18:1–2)
2. Humility and greatness (18:3–4)
3. The heinousness of causing believers to sin (18:5–9)
4. The parable of the lost sheep (18:10–14)
5. Treatment of a sinning brother (18:15–20)
6. Forgiveness (18:21–35)
a. Repeated forgiveness (18:21–22)

b. The parable of the unmerciful servant (18:23–35)

7. Transitional conclusion: introduction to the Judean ministry (19:1–2)

VI. Opposition and Eschatology: The Triumph of Grace (19:3–26:5)

A. Narrative (19:3–23:39)

1. Marriage and divorce (19:3–12)

2. Blessing little children (19:13–15)

3. Wealth and the kingdom (19:16–30)

a. The rich young man (19:16–22)

b. Grace and reward in the kingdom (19:23–30)

4. The parable of the workers (20:1–16)

5. Third major passion prediction (20:17–19)

6. Suffering and service (20:20–28)

7. Healing two blind men (20:29–34)

8. Opening events of Passion Week (21:1–23:39)

a. The Triumphal Entry (21:1–11)

b. Jesus at the temple (21:12–17)

c. The fig tree (21:18–22)

d. Controversies in the temple court (21:23–22:46)

(1) The question of authority (21:23–27)

(2) The parable of the two sons (21:28–32)

(3) The parable of the tenants (21:33–46)

(4) The parable of the wedding banquet (22:1–14)

(5) Paying taxes to Caesar (22:15–22)

(6) Marriage at the resurrection (22:23–33)

(7) The greatest commandments (22:34–40)

(8) The son of David (22:41–46)

e. Seven woes on the teachers of the law and the Pharisees (23:1–36)

(1) Warning the crowds and the disciples (23:1–12)

(2) The seven woes (23:13–32)

(a) First woe (23:13 [14])

(b) Second woe (23:15)

(c) Third woe (23:16–22)

(d) Fourth woe (23:23–24)

(e) Fifth woe (23:25–26)

(f) Sixth woe (23:27–28)

(g) Seventh woe (23:29–32)

(3) Conclusion (23:33–36)

f. Lament over Jerusalem (23:37–39)

B. Fifth Discourse: The Olivet Discourse (24:1–26:5)

1. Setting (24:1–3)

2. The birth pains (24:4–28)
 a. General description of the birth pains (24:4–14)
 b. The sharp pain: the fall of Jerusalem (24:15–21)
 c. Warnings against false messiahs during the birth pains (24:22–28)
3. The coming of the Son of Man (24:29–31)
4. The significance of the birth pains (24:32–35)
5. The day and hour unknown: the need to be prepared (24:36–41)
 a. The principle (24:36)
 b. Analogy of the days of Noah (24:37–39)
 c. Two in the field; two with a mill (24:40–41)
6. Parabolic teaching: variations on watchfulness (24:42–25:46)
 a. The homeowner and the thief (24:42–44)
 b. The two servants (24:45–51)
 c. The ten virgins (25:1–13)
 d. The talents (25:14–30)
 e. The sheep and the goats (25:31–46)
7. Transitional conclusion: fourth major passion prediction and the plot against Jesus (26:1–5)

VII. The Passion and Resurrection of Jesus (26:6–28:20)
 A. The Passion (26:6–27:66)
 1. Anointed at Bethany (26:6–13)
 2. Judas's betrayal agreement (26:14–16)
  Reflections: Chronological Considerations
 3. The Lord's Supper (26:17–30)
  a. Preparations for the Passover (26:17–19)
  b. Prediction of the betrayal (26:20–25)
  c. The words of institution (26:26–30)
 4. Prediction of abandonment and denial (26:31–35)
 5. Gethsemane (26:36–46)
 6. The arrest (26:47–56)
 7. Jesus before the Sanhedrin (26:57–68)
 8. Peter's denial of Jesus (26:69–75)
 9. Formal decision of the Sanhedrin (27:1–2)
 10. The death of Judas (27:3–10)
 11. Jesus before Pilate (27:11–26)
 12. The soldiers' treatment of Jesus (27:27–31)
 13. The crucifixion and mocking (27:32–44)
 14. The death of Jesus (27:45–50)
 15. Immediate impact of the death (27:51–56)
 16. The burial of Jesus (27:57–61)
 17. The guard at the tomb (27:62–66)

- B. The Resurrection (28:1–15)
  - 1. The empty tomb (28:1–7)
  - 2. First encounter with the risen Christ (28:8–10)
  - 3. First fraudulent denials of Jesus' resurrection (28:11–15)
- C. The Risen Messiah and His Disciples (28:16–20)
  - 1. Jesus in Galilee (28:16–17)
  - 2. The Great Commission (28:18–20)

Text and Exposition

I. PROLOGUE: THE ORIGIN AND BIRTH OF JESUS THE CHRIST (1:1–2:23)

In each gospel, Jesus' earthly ministry is preceded by an account of John the Baptist's ministry. This formal similarity does not extend to the introductions to the Gospels. Mark 1:1 opens with a simple statement. Luke begins with a first-person preface in which he explains his purpose and methods, followed by a detailed and often poetic account of the miraculous births of John and Jesus (Lk 1:5–2:20) and a brief mention of Jesus' boyhood trip to the temple (2:21–52). Luke reserves Jesus' genealogy for ch. 3. John's prologue (Jn 1:1–18) traces Jesus' beginnings to eternity and presents the incarnation without referring to his conception and birth.

In each gospel, the introduction anticipates major themes and emphases. In Matthew, the prologue (Mt 1:1–2:23) introduces such themes as the son of David, the fulfillment of prophecy, the supernatural origin of Jesus the Messiah, and the Father's sovereign protection of his Son in order to bring him to Nazareth and accomplish the divine plan of salvation from sin (see Stonehouse, *Witness of Matthew*, 123–28).

A. The Genealogy of Jesus (1:1–17)

1 A record of the genealogy of Jesus Christ the son of David, the son of Abraham:

2 Abraham was the father of Isaac,
Isaac the father of Jacob,
Jacob the father of Judah and his brothers,
3 Judah the father of Perez and Zerah, whose mother was Tamar,
Perez the father of Hezron,
Hezron the father of Ram,
4 Ram the father of Amminadab,
Amminadab the father of Nahshon,
Nahshon the father of Salmon,
5 Salmon the father of Boaz, whose mother was Rahab,
Boaz the father of Obed, whose mother was Ruth,
Obed the father of Jesse,
6 and Jesse the father of King David.

David was the father of Solomon, whose mother had been Uriah's wife,
7 Solomon the father of Rehoboam,
Rehoboam the father of Abijah,
Abijah the father of Asa,

8Asa the father of Jehoshaphat,
Jehoshaphat the father of Jehoram,
Jehoram the father of Uzziah,
9Uzziah the father of Jotham,
Jotham the father of Ahaz,
Ahaz the father of Hezekiah,
10Hezekiah the father of Manasseh,
Manasseh the father of Amon,
Amon the father of Josiah,
11and Josiah the father of Jeconiah and his brothers at the time of the exile to Babylon.

12After the exile to Babylon:
Jeconiah was the father of Shealtiel,
Shealtiel the father of Zerubbabel,
13Zerubbabel the father of Abiud,
Abiud the father of Eliakim,
Eliakim the father of Azor,
14Azor the father of Zadok,
Zadok the father of Akim,
Akim the father of Eliud,
15Eliud the father of Eleazar,
Eleazar the father of Matthan,
Matthan the father of Jacob,
16and Jacob the father of Joseph, the husband of Mary, of whom was born Jesus, who is called Christ.

17Thus there were fourteen generations in all from Abraham to David, fourteen from David to the exile to Babylon, and fourteen from the exile to the Christ.

COMMENTARY

1 The first two words of Matthew, *biblos geneseōs*, may be translated "record of the genealogy" (NIV), "record of the origins," or "record of the history." The NIV limits this title to the genealogy (1:1–17), the second could serve as a heading for the prologue (1:1–2:23), and the third as a heading for the entire gospel. The expression is found only twice in the LXX. In Genesis 2:4 it refers to the creation account (Ge 2:4–25), and in Genesis 5:1 to the ensuing genealogy. From the latter, it appears possible to follow the NIV (so also Hendriksen; McNeile; France [NICNT]), but because the noun *genesis* (NIV, "birth") reappears in Matthew 1:18 (one of only five NT occurrences), it seems likely that the heading in 1:1 extends beyond the genealogy. No occurrence of the expression as a heading for a book-length document has come to light. Therefore we must discount the increasingly popular view (Davies, *Setting*; Gaechter; Hill; Maier) that Matthew means to refer to his entire gospel, "A record of the history of Jesus Christ." Matthew rather intends his first two chapters to be a coherent and unified "record of the origins of Jesus Christ" (rightly, Blomberg [NAC]).

The designation "Jesus Christ the son of David, the son of Abraham" resonates with biblical nuances. (For "Jesus," see comments at 1:21.) "Christ" is roughly the Greek equivalent to "Messiah" or "Anointed." In the OT, the term could refer to a variety of people anointed for some special function: priests (Lev 4:3; 6:22), kings (1Sa 16:13; 24:10; 2Sa 19:21; La 4:20), and, metaphorically, the patriarchs (Ps 105:15) and the pagan king Cyrus (Isa 45:1). Already in Hannah's prayer, "Messiah" parallels "king": the Lord "will give strength to his king and exalt the horn of his anointed" (1Sa 2:10). With the rising number of OT prophecies concerning King David's line (e.g., 2Sa 7:12–16; cf. Ps 2:2), "Messiah, or "Christ," became the designation of a figure representing the people of God and bringing in the promised eschatological reign.

In Jesus' day, Palestine was rife with messianic expectation. Not all of it was coherent, and many Jews expected two different "Messiahs." But Matthew's linking of "Christ" and "son of David" leaves no doubt about what he is claiming for Jesus.

In the Gospels, "Christ" is relatively rare (as compared with Paul's epistles). More important, it almost always appears as a title, strictly equivalent to "the Messiah" (see esp. 16:16). But it was natural for Christians after the resurrection to use "Christ" as a name not less than as a title; increasingly they spoke of "Jesus Christ" or "Christ Jesus" or simply "Christ." Paul normally treats "Christ," at least in part, as a name, but it is doubtful whether the titular force ever entirely disappears. Of Matthew's approximately eighteen occurrences, all are exclusively titular except this one (1:1), probably 1:16, certainly 1:18, and possibly the variant at 16:21. The three uses of "Christ" in the prologue reflect the confessional stance from which Matthew writes. He is a committed Christian who has long since become familiar with the common way of using the word as both title and name. At the same time, it is a mark of Matthew's concern for historical accuracy that Jesus is not so designated by his contemporaries.

"Son of David" is an important designation in Matthew. Not only does David become a turning point in the genealogy (1:6, 17), but the title recurs throughout the gospel (9:27; 12:23; 15:22; 20:30–31; 21:9, 15; 22:42, 45). God swore covenant love to David (Ps 89:28) and promised that one of his immediate descendants would establish the kingdom — even more, that David's kingdom and throne would endure forever (2Sa 7:12–16). Isaiah foresaw that a "son" would be given, a son with the most extravagant titles:

> Wonderful Counselor, Mighty God,
> Everlasting Father, Prince of Peace:
> Of the increase of his government and peace
> there will be no end.
> He will reign on David's throne
> and over his kingdom,
> establishing and upholding it
> with justice and righteousness
> from that time on and forever.
> The zeal of the LORD Almighty
> will accomplish this.
>
> *Isaiah 9:6–7*

In Jesus' day, at least some branches of popular Judaism understood "son of David" to be messianic (cf. *Ps. Sol.* 17:21; for a summary of the complex intertestamental evidence, see Berger, "Die königlichen Messiastraditionen," esp. 3–9). The theme was important in early Christianity (cf. Lk 1:32, 69; Jn 7:42; Ac 13:23; Ro 1:3; Rev 22:16). God's promises, though long delayed, had not been forgotten; Jesus and his ministry were perceived as God's fulfillment of covenantal promises now centuries old. The tree of David, hacked off so that only a stump remained, was sprouting a new branch (Isa 11:1).

Jesus is also "son of Abraham." It could not be otherwise, given that he is son of David. Yet Abraham is mentioned for several important reasons. "Son of Abraham" may have been a recognized messianic title in some branches of Judaism (cf. *T. Levi* 8:15). The covenant with the Jewish people had first been made with Abraham (Ge 12:1–3; 17:7; 22:18), a connection Paul sees as basic to Christianity (Gal 3:16). More important, Genesis 22:18 had promised that through Abraham's offspring "all nations" (*panta ta ethnē*, LXX) would be blessed; so with this allusion to Abraham, Matthew is preparing his readers for the final words of this offspring from Abraham—the commission to make disciples of "all nations" (Mt 28:19, *panta ta ethnē*). Jesus the Messiah came in fulfillment of the kingdom promises to David and of the Gentile-blessings promised to Abraham (see Mt 3:9; 8:11).

2–17 Study has shown that genealogies in the Ancient Near East could serve widely diverse functions: economic, tribal, political, domestic (to show family or geographical relationships), and others (see Johnson, *Purpose of the Biblical Genealogies*; Robert R. Wilson, *Genealogy and History in the Biblical World* [New Haven, Conn.: Yale Univ. Press, 1977]; Brown, *Birth of the Messiah*, 64–66). The danger in such study is that Matthew's intentions may be overridden by colorful backgrounds of doubtful relevance to the text itself. Johnson sees Matthew's genealogy as a response to Jewish slander. H. V. Winkings ("The Nativity Stories and Docetism," *NTS* 23 [1977]: 457–60) sees it as an answer to late first-century Docetism that denied the essential humanity of Jesus. One wonders whether a virgin birth would have been the best way to go about correcting the Docetists.

D. E. Nineham ("The Genealogy in St. Matthew's Gospel and Its Significance for the Study of the Gospels," *BJRL* 58 [1976]: 491–544) finds in this genealogy the assurance that God is in sovereign control. Yet it is unclear how he reconciles this assurance with his conviction that the genealogy is of little historical worth. If Matthew made much of it up, then we may admire his faith that God was in control. But since Matthew's basis was (according to Nineham) faulty, it gives the reader little incentive to share the same faith.

Actually, Matthew's chief aims in including the genealogy are hinted at in the first verse—namely, to show that Jesus Messiah is truly in the kingly line of David, heir to the messianic promises, the one who brings divine blessings to all nations. Therefore the genealogy focuses on King David (1:6) on the one hand, yet on the other hand includes Gentile women (see comments at v.6). Many entries would touch the hearts and stir the memories of biblically literate readers, though the principal thrust of the genealogy ties together promise and fulfillment. F. F. Bruce (*NBD*, 459) writes, "Christ and the new covenant are securely linked to the age of the old covenant. Marcion, who wished to sever all the links binding Christianity to the Old Testament, knew what he was about when he cut the genealogy out of his edition of Luke."

For many, whatever its aims, the historical value of Matthew's genealogy is nil. R. E. Brown (*Birth of the Messiah*, 505–12) bucks the tide when he cautiously affirms that Jesus sprang from the house of David. Many ancient genealogies are discounted as being of little historical value because they evidently intend to impart more than historical information (cf. esp. Wilson, *Genealogy and History*). To do this, however, is to fall into a false historical disjunction, for many genealogies intend to make more than historical points by referring to historical lines.

Part of the historical evaluation of vv.2–17 rests on the reliability of Matthew's sources. The names in the first two-thirds of the genealogy are taken from the LXX (1Ch 1–3, esp. 2:1–15; 3:5–24; Ru 4:12–22). After Zerubbabel, Matthew relies on extrabiblical sources of which we know nothing. But there is good evidence that records were kept at least till the end of the first century. Josephus (*Life* 6 [1]) refers to the "public registers" from which he extracts his genealogical information (see also Josephus, *Ag. Ap.* 1.28–56 [6–10]). According to Genesis Rabbah 98:8, Rabbi Hillel was proved to be a descendant of David because a genealogical scroll was found in Jerusalem. Eusebius (*Hist. eccl.* 3.19–20) cites Hegesippus to the effect that Emperor Domitian (AD 81–96) ordered all descendants of David slain. Nevertheless, two of them, when summoned, though admitting their Davidic descent, showed their calloused hands to prove they were but poor farmers. So they were let go. But the account shows that genealogical information was still available.

While no twentieth-century Jew could prove he was from the tribe of Judah, let alone from the house of David, this does not appear to have been a problem in the first century, when lineage was important in gaining access to temple worship. Whether Matthew had access to the records himself or gleaned his information from intermediate sources, we cannot know from this distance; but in any case, we "have no good reason to doubt that this genealogy was transmitted in good faith" (Albright and Mann).

More difficult is the question of the relation of Matthew's genealogy to Luke's, in particular the part from David on (cf. Lk 3:23–31). There are basic differences between the two: Matthew begins with Abraham and moves forward; Luke begins with Jesus and moves backward to Adam. Matthew traces the line through Jeconiah, Shealtiel, and Zerubbabel; Luke through Neri, Shealtiel, and Zerubbabel. More important, Luke 3:31 traces the line through David's son Nathan (cf. 2Sa 5:14), and Matthew through the kingly line of Solomon. It is often said that no reconciliation between the two genealogies is possible (so E. L. Abel, "The Genealogies of Jesus *ho Christos*" *NTS* 20 [1974]: 203–10). Nevertheless two theories are worth weighing:

1. Some have argued that Luke gives Mary's genealogy but substitutes Joseph's name (Lk 3:23) to avoid mentioning a woman. And there is some evidence to support the notion that Mary herself was a descendant of David (cf. Lk 1:32). That Mary was related to Elizabeth, who was married to the Levite Zechariah (Lk 1:5–36), is no problem, since intermarriage between tribes was not uncommon. Indeed, Aaron's wife may well have sprung from Judah (cf. Ex 6:23; Nu 2:3) (so *CHS*; Bengel, *Gnomon*; Luther). H. A. W. Meyer rearranges the punctuation in Luke 3:23 to read "being the son (of Joseph as was supposed) of Heli [i.e., Mary's father], of Matthat." But this is painfully artificial and could not easily be deduced by a reader with a text without punctuation marks or brackets, which is how the NT Greek manuscripts were first written. Few would guess simply by reading Luke that he is giving Mary's genealogy. The theory stems, not from the text of Luke, but from the need to harmonize the two genealogies. On the face of it, both Matthew and Luke aim to give Joseph's genealogy.

2. Others have argued, more plausibly, that Luke provides Joseph's real genealogy and Matthew the throne succession—a succession that finally jumps to Joseph's line by default. In his commentary, David Hill offers independent Jewish evidence for a possible double line (*Tg. Zec.* 12:12). This hypothesis has various forms. The oldest goes back to Julius Africanus (ca. AD 225; cf. Eusebius, *Hist. eccl.* 1. 7), who argued that Matthew provides the natural genealogy and Luke the royal—the reverse of the modern theory (so Hill). In its modern form, the theory seems reasonable enough: where the purpose is to provide Joseph's actual descent back to David, this could best

be done by tracing the family tradition through his real father Heli, to his father Matthat, and thus back to Nathan and David (so Luke); and where the purpose is to provide the throne succession, it is natural to begin with David and work down.

As most frequently presented, this theory has a serious problem (cf. Brown, *Birth of the Messiah*, 503–4). It is normally argued that Joseph's father in Matthew 1:16, Jacob, was a full brother of Joseph's father mentioned in Luke 3:23, Heli; that Jacob, the royal heir, died without offspring; and that Heli married Jacob's widow according to the laws of levirate marriage (Dt 25:5–10). (Though levirate marriages may not have been common in the first century, it is unlikely that they were completely unknown. Otherwise the question of the Sadducees [Mt 22:24–28] was phrased in irrelevant terms.) But if Jacob and Heli are to be reckoned as full brothers, then Matthan (Matthew) and Matthat (Luke) must be the same man—even though their fathers, Eleazar (Matthew) and Levi (Luke) respectively, are different. It seems artificial to appeal to a second levirate marriage. Some have therefore argued that Jacob and Heli were only half brothers, which entails a further coincidence, namely, that their mother married two men, Matthan and Matthat, with remarkably similar names. We do not know whether levirate marriage was practiced in the case of half brothers. Moreover, since the whole purpose of levirate marriage was to raise up a child in the deceased father's name, why does Luke provide the name of the actual father?

R. E. Brown judges the problems insurmountable but fails to consider the elegant solution suggested by J. Gresham Machen (*Virgin Birth*, 207–9) fifty years ago. If we assume that Matthat and Matthan are *not* the same person, there is no need to appeal to levirate marriage. The difficulty regarding the father of Matthat and the father of Matthan disappears; yet their respective sons Heli and Jacob may have been so closely related (e.g., if Heli was an heirless only son whose sister married Jacob son of Matthan) that if Heli died, Jacob's son Joseph became his heir. Alternatively, if Matthan and Matthat *are* the same person (presupposing a levirate marriage one generation earlier), we "need only to suppose that Jacob [Joseph's father according to Matthew] died without issue, so that his nephew, the son of his brother Heli [Joseph's father according to Luke], would become his heir" (p. 208).

Other differences between Matthew and Luke are more amenable to obvious solutions. As for the omissions from Matthew's genealogy and the structure of the three series of fourteen, see comments at v.17.

2 Of the twelve sons of Jacob, Judah is singled out, as his tribe bears the scepter (Ge 49:10; cf. Heb 7:14). The words "and his brothers" are not "an addition which indicates that of the several possible ancestors of the royal line Judah alone was chosen" (Hill), since that restriction was already achieved by stipulating Judah; and in no other entry (except v.11; see comments there) are the words "and his brothers" added. The point is that, though he comes from the royal line of Judah and David, Messiah emerges within the matrix of the covenant people (cf. the reference to Judah's brothers). Neither the half siblings of Isaac nor the descendants of Jacob's brother, Esau, qualify as the covenant people in the OT. This allusive mention of the twelve tribes as the locus of the people of God becomes important later (cf. 8:11 with 19:28). Even the fact that there were twelve apostles is relevant.

3–5 Probably Perez and Zerah (v.3) are both mentioned because they are twins (Ge 38:27; cf. 1Ch 2:4); Judah's other sons receive no mention. Ruth 4:12, 18–22 trace the messianic line from Perez to David. There is some evidence that "son of Perez" was a rabbinic designation of Messiah (Str-B, 1:18), but the dating of the sources is uncertain.

Tamar, wife of Judah's son Er, is the first of four women mentioned in the genealogy (see comments at 1:6). Little is known of Hezron (Ge 46:12; 1Ch

2:5), Ram (1Ch 2:9), Amminadab (Mt 1:4; Ex 6:23; Nu 1:7; 1Ch 2:10), Nahshon (Nu 2:3; 7:12; "the leader of the people of Judah," 1Ch 2:10), and Salmon (Mt 1:5; Ru 4:20–21; 1Ch 2:11). Amminadab is associated with the desert wanderings in the time of Moses (Nu 1:7). Therefore, approximately four hundred years (Ge 15:13; Ex 12:40) are covered by the four generations from Perez to Amminadab. Doubtless several names have been omitted—the Greek verb translated "was the father of" (*gennaō*, GK *1164*) does not require immediate relationship but often means something like "was the ancestor of" or "became the progenitor of."

Similarly, the line between Amminadab and David is short. More names may have been omitted. Whether such names properly fit before Boaz, so that Rahab was not the immediate mother of Boaz (just as Eve was not immediately "the mother of all the living," Ge 3:20), or after Boaz, or both, one cannot be sure. It is almost certain, however, that the Rahab mentioned is the prostitute of Joshua 2 and 6 (see comments at 1:6). Boaz (1Ch 2:11–12), who figures so prominently in the book of Ruth, married the Moabitess (see comments at 1:6) and sired Obed, who became the father of Jesse (Ru 4:22; 1Ch 2:12).

6 The word "King" with "David" would evoke profound nostalgia and arouse eschatological hope in first-century Jews. Matthew thus makes the royal theme explicit: King Messiah has appeared. David's royal authority, lost at the exile, has now been regained and surpassed by "great David's greater son" (so James Montgomery's hymn "Hail to the Lord's Anointed"; cf. Hill; see 2Sa 7:12–16; Pss 89:19–29, 35–37; 132:11). David became the father of Solomon; but Solomon's mother "had been Uriah's wife" (cf. 2Sa 11:27; 12:4). Bathsheba thus becomes the fourth woman to be mentioned in this genealogy.

Inclusion of these four women in the Messiah's genealogy instead of an all-male listing (which was customary)—or at least the names of such great matriarchs as Sarah, Rebekah, and Leah—shows that Matthew is conveying more than merely genealogical data. Tamar enticed her father-in-law into an incestuous relationship (Ge 38). The prostitute Rahab saved the spies and joined the Israelites (Jos 2; 6). Hebrews 11:31 and James 2:25 encourage us to think she abandoned her former way of life. She is certainly prominent in Jewish tradition, some of it fantastic (see A. T. Hanson, "Rahab the Harlot in Early Christian Tradition," *JSNT* 1 [1978]: 53–60). Ruth, Tamar, and Rahab were aliens. Bathsheba was taken into an adulterous union with David, who committed murder to cover it up. Matthew's peculiar way of referring to her, "Uriah's wife," may be an attempt to focus on the fact that Uriah was not an Israelite but a Hittite (2Sa 11:3; 23:39). Bathsheba herself was apparently the daughter of an Israelite (1Ch 3:5 [variant reading]), but her marriage to Uriah probably led to her being regarded as a Hittite.

Several reasons have been suggested to explain the inclusion of these women. Some have pointed out that three were Gentiles and the fourth probably regarded as such (Lohmeyer; Maier; Schweizer). This goes well with the reference to Abraham (see comments at v.1); the Jewish Messiah extends his blessings beyond Israel, even as Gentiles are included in his line. Others have noted that three of the four were involved in gross sexual sin; but it is highly doubtful that this charge can be legitimately applied to Ruth. As a Moabitess, however, she had her origins in incest (Ge 19:30–37); and Deuteronomy 23:3 banned the offspring of Moabites from the assembly of the Lord to the tenth generation. R. E. Brown (*Birth of the Messiah*, 71–72) discounts this interpretation of the role of the four women because in first-century Jewish piety they were largely whitewashed and revered. Yet it is not at all certain that Matthew follows his contemporaries in all this. It is important that in this same chapter Matthew introduces Jesus as the one who "will save his people from their sins" (v.21), and this verse may imply a backward glance at some of the better-known sins of his own progenitors.

A third interpretation (favored by Allen; Fenton; Filson; Green; Hill; Lohmeyer; Brown, *Birth of the Messiah*) holds that all four reveal something of the strange and unexpected workings of providence in preparation for the Messiah and that as such they point to Mary's unexpected but providential conception of Jesus.

There is no reason to rule out any of the above interpretations. Matthew, Jew that he is, knows how to write with an allusive touch; and readers steeped in the OT would naturally call to mind a plethora of images associated with many names in this selective genealogy.

7–10 The names in these verses seem to have been taken from 1 Chronicles 3:10–14. Behind "Asa" (v.7) lurks a difficult textual decision (see Notes). There is no obvious pattern. Wicked Rehoboam was the father of wicked Abijah, the father of the good king Asa. Asa was the father of the good king Jehoshaphat (v.8), who sired the wicked king Joram. Good or evil, they were part of Messiah's line; for though grace does not run in the blood, God's providence cannot be deceived or outmaneuvered.

Three names have been omitted between Joram and Uzziah: Ahaziah, Joash, and Amaziah (2Ki 8:24; 1Ch 3:11; 2Ch 22:1, 11; 24:27). "Uzziah" (vv.8–9) is equivalent to Azariah (1Ch 3:11; cf. 2Ki 15:13, 30 with 2Ki 15:1). The three omissions not only secure fourteen generations in this part of the genealogy (see comments at v.17) but are dropped because of their connection with Ahab and Jezebel, renowned for wickedness (2Ki 8:27), and because of their connection with wicked Athaliah (2Ki 8:26), the usurper (2Ki 11:1–20). Two of the three were notoriously evil; all three died violently.

R. E. Brown (*Birth of the Messiah*, 82) points out that Manasseh was even more wicked, and he is included. Therefore (with Schweizer), Brown proffers an explanation of the omissions based on a text-critical confusion between "Azariah" and "Uzziah." This conjecture is plausible; but if it is correct, it would have to be pre-Matthean, because Matthew's "fourteens" (see comments at 1:17) would require this omission or an equivalent. But there is no textual evidence to support the conjecture. Also, Manasseh (v.10), though notoriously evil, repented (2Ch 33:12–13), unlike the other three.

11 Another name has been dropped. Josiah was the father of Jehoiakim (609–597 BC), who was deposed in favor of his son Jehoiachin (some manuscripts in both OT and NT have "Jeconiah" for the latter). He was deposed after a reign of only three months, and his brother Zedekiah reigned in his stead till the final deportation and destruction of the city in 587 BC (cf. 2Ki 23:34; 24:6, 14–15; 1Ch 3:16; Jer 27:20; 28:1). The words "and his brothers" are probably added in this instance because one of them, Zedekiah, maintained a caretaker reign until the tragedy of 587 BC; but Zedekiah is not mentioned because the royal line does not flow through him but through Jeconiah. The exile to Babylon marked the end of the reign of David's line—a momentous event in OT history. Alternatively, "and his brothers" may refer, not to the royal brothers, but to all the Jews who went into captivity with Jeconiah (so Gundry). The locus of the people of God is thus traced from the patriarchs ("and his brothers," Mt 1:2) to the shame of the exile, a theme to be developed later (see comments at 2:16–18).

12 The final list of "fourteen" (see comments at 1:17) begins with a further mention of the exile. First Chronicles 3:17 records that Jeconiah (Jehoiachin) was the father of Shealtiel. Matthew goes on to present Shealtiel as the father of Zerubbabel, in accord with Ezra 3:2; 5:2; Nehemiah 12:1; Haggai 1:1; 2:2, 23. The difficulty lies in 1 Chronicles 3:19, which presents Zerubbabel as the son of Pedaiah, a brother of Shealtiel.

Several solutions have been offered, most not very convincing (cf. Machen, *Virgin Birth*, 206–7). Some Greek manuscripts omit Pedaiah in 1 Chronicles 3:19. But the best suggestion is a levirate marriage (Dt 25:5–10; cf. Ge 38:8–9), scarcely an embarrassment to those who have adopted the explanation above (see comments at 1:2–17) and find no other levirate marriage in the genealogy. If Shealtiel were the older brother and died childless, Pedaiah might well have married the widow to "build up his brother's family line" (Dt 25:9). In any case, Zerubbabel himself becomes a messianic model (cf. Hag 2:20–23).

13–15 The nine names from Abiud to Jacob are not otherwise known to us today. Possibly names have been omitted from this genealogical section also, but then one wonders why this third section of the genealogy appears to lack one entry (see comments at v.17). Robert Gundry's explanations of these names are tortured: certain names from Luke's list "catch the evangelist's [Matthew's] eye," as do names from the priestly (nonroyal) list in 1 Chronicles 6:3–14—names that then need abbreviating or changing to mask their priestly connection.

16 The wording in the best reading (see Notes), reflected in the NIV, is precise. Joseph's royal line has been traced; Joseph is the husband of Mary; Mary is the mother of Jesus. The relation between Joseph and Jesus is so far unstated. But this peculiar form of expression cries out for the explanation provided in the ensuing verses. Legally, Jesus stands in line to the throne of David; physically, he is born of a woman "found to be with child through the Holy Spirit" (v.18). Her son is Jesus, "who is called Christ." The Greek does not make it clear whether "Christ" is titular or not; but name or title, Jesus' messiahship is affirmed.

17 It was customary among Jewish writers to arrange genealogies according to some convenient scheme, possibly for mnemonic reasons. Strictly speaking, the Greek text speaks of "all the generations from Abraham to David ... to Christ" (cf. KJV, NASB); but since the omissions are obvious to both Matthew and his readers, the expression must mean "all the generations ... included in this table." So it becomes a hint that the fourteens, here so strongly brought to the reader's attention, are symbolic.

Various arrangements of the three fourteens have been proposed. In one the first set of fourteen runs from Abraham to David, the second from Solomon to Jeconiah, and the third attains fourteen by repeating Jeconiah and running to Jesus. Hendriksen, 125–26, suggests Matthew purposely counts Jeconiah twice: first he presents Jeconiah as cursed, childless, deported (2Ki 24:8–12; Jer 22:30), and the second time he reminds the reader that Jeconiah was subsequently released from prison and restored and became the father of many (2Ki 25:27–30; 1Ch 3:17–18; Jer 52:31–34)—a new man as it were. But Matthew does not mention these themes, which do not clearly fit into the main concerns of this chapter. Schweizer prefers to count from Abraham to David. Then, because David is mentioned twice, he passes from David to Josiah, the last free king; and then Jeconiah to Jesus provides a third set of fourteen, at the expense of making the central set one member short and of ignoring the small but distinct literary pause at the end of v.11. McNeile postulates a possible loss of one name between Jeconiah and Shealtiel owing to homoeoteleuton (identical endings), but there is no textual evidence for it. Gundry thinks that Mary as well as Joseph counts for one, pointing to the two kinds of generation, legal (Joseph's) and physical (Mary's). No solution so far proposed seems entirely convincing, and it is difficult to rule any out.

The symbolic value of the fourteens is of more significance than their precise breakdown. Herman C. Waetjen ("The Genealogy as the Key to the Gospel according to Matthew," *JBL* 95 [1976]:

205–30; cf. Johnson, *Purpose of the Biblical Genealogies*, 193–94) tries to solve both problems by appealing to 2 Baruch 53–74 (usually dated ca. AD 50–70). This apocalyptic book divides history into a scheme of 12 + 2 = 14 units. Matthew, Waetjen argues, holds that just as David and Jeconiah are transitional figures in the genealogy, so also is Jesus. He is the end of the third period and simultaneously the beginning of the fourth, the inaugurated kingdom. Jesus is therefore the thirteenth and the fourteenth entries, the former a period of gloom in 2 Baruch (corresponding to the passion in Matthew) and the fourteenth opening into the new age.

But this analysis will not do. Two objections are crucial: (1) It is not at all clear that one may legitimately jump from schematized time periods in apocalyptic literature to names in a genealogy (Is anything less apocalyptic than a genealogy?) just because of a common number. (2) Waetjen has "corrected" the omission in the third set of fourteen by listing Jesus twice, even though the second reference to Jesus, in his scheme, properly belongs to the inaugurated kingdom and not to the third set, which remains deficient.

Schemes like those of Hendriksen that reduce the 3 × 14 pattern to 6 × 7 and then picture Jesus' coming to inaugurate the seventh seven—the sign of perfection, the dawning of the Messianic Age (cf. *1 En.* 91:12–17; 93:1–10)—stumble over the fact that Matthew has not presented his genealogy as six sevens but as three fourteens (cf. Brown, *Birth of the Messiah*, 75). Other suggestions include those of Johnson (*Purpose of the Biblical Genealogies*, 189–208) and Goulder (*Midrash and Lection*, 228–33).

The simplest explanation—the one that best fits the context—observes that the numerical value of "David" in Hebrew is fourteen (see Notes). By this symbolism, Matthew points out that the promised "son of David" (1:1), the Messiah, has come. And if the third set of fourteen is short one member, perhaps it will suggest to some readers that just as God cuts short the time of distress for the sake of his elect (24:22), so also he mercifully shortens the period from the exile to Jesus the Messiah.

NOTES

1 For a broader grasp of the place of the Messiah in the OT, cf. Ladd, *Theology of the New Testament*, 136ff.; *Illustrated Bible Dictionary* [ed. Douglas], 2:987–95.

3 Older EV (e.g., KJV) have the names Tamar and Hezron in the OT and Thamar and Esrom in the NT. Because English OT names are roughly transliterated from the Hebrew and English NT names are roughly transliterated from the Greek, which for many names transliterates from the Hebrew, we have these variations. The NIV rightly smoothes them out.

7–8 In these verses, the best textual evidence supports Ἀσάφ (*Asaph*), not Ἀσά (*Asa*). It is transcriptionally more probable that *Asaph* would be changed to *Asa* than vice versa (for the opposite view, see Lagrange). Robert Gundry suggests that *Asaph* is a deliberate change by Matthew to call up images of the psalmist (Pss 50, 73–83), as "Amos" (see Notes, v.10) calls to mind the prophet. This is too cryptic to be believable. Orthography was not as consistent in the ancient world as it is today. Josephus (*Ant.* 8.290–315 [12.1–6]), for instance, uses Ἄσανος (*Asanos*), but in the ancient Latin translation, *Asaph* is presupposed. "Mary" varies in the NT between Μαρία (*Maria*) and Μαριάμ (*Mariam*). In 1 Chronicles 3:10 (LXX), most MSS read Ἀσά (*Asa*), but one offers Ἀσάβ (*Asab*; see Metzger, *Textual Commentary*,

1 n. 1). In short, Matthew could well be following a MS with *Asaph* even though *Asa* is quite clearly the person meant.

10 The textual evidence for Ἀμώς (*Amōs*) and Ἀμών (*Amōn*) breaks down much as in vv.7–8. In this case, however, there is greater diversity in the readings of LXX MSS for 1 Chronicles 3:14, on which Matthew 1:10 depends.

11 The term μετοικεσία (*metoikesia*, "exile," GK *3578*) occurs but four times in the NT, all in this chapter (vv.11–12, 17); but it refers (in LXX) to the Babylonian exile in 2 Kings 24:16; 1 Chronicles 5:22; Ezekiel 12:11. Βαβυλῶνος (*Babylōnos*, "Babylon") is a genitive "of direction and purpose" (cf. BDF, para. 166).

Eduard Schweizer's suggestion that Jehoiakim and his son Jehoiachin have been fused into a single figure because in 2 Kings 24:6 (LXX) they are both called "Jehoiakim" explains little, since Matthew betrays a deep knowledge of the OT not likely to be confused by one versional mistransliteration; and in any case, Matthew's term is "Jeconiah."

16 The best textual variant, supported by a spread of text types in Greek and versional witnesses and by all but one uncial, stands behind the NIV. Several Caesarean and OT witnesses prefer "Joseph, to whom was betrothed the virgin Mary who begot Jesus who is called Christ." This is transcriptionally less likely than the first alternative, in which "the husband" of Mary might well have been thought misleading. No Greek MS supports syr[s] in its reading: "Joseph, to whom was betrothed Mary the virgin, begot Jesus who is called the Christ." At first glance it seems to deny the virgin birth by ascribing paternity to Joseph; but the "begot" may have merely legal significance, since Mary is still referred to as "the virgin." In any case, this last reading is not well attested. Peter J. Williams (*Early Syriac Translation Technique and the Textual Criticism of the Greek Gospels* [Piscataway, N.J.: Gorgias, 2004], 240–44) shows convincingly that this Syriac version may itself be dependent on a misreading of an early Greek recension. The enormously complex problems of textual criticism in this verse are competently treated by Metzger, *New Testament Studies*, 105–13; Machen, *Virgin Birth*, 176–87; Brown, *Birth of the Messiah*, 62–64, 139; and A. Globe, "Some Doctrinal Variants in Matthew 1 and Luke 2, and the Authority of the Neutral Text," *CBQ* 42 (1980): 55–72, esp. 63–65.

17 In the ancient world, letters served not only as the building blocks of words but also as symbols of numbers. Hence any word had a numerical value. The use of such symbolism is known as gematria. In Hebrew, "David" is דָּוִד : (*dāwid*); and d = 4, w = 6 (the vowels, a later addition to the text, don't count). Therefore "David" = *dwd* = 4 + 6 + 4 = 14. (This would not work in the Dead Sea Scrolls, where, with one exception [CD 7:16], the consonantal spelling of "David" is *dwyd* = דָּוִיד.)

B. The Birth of Jesus (1:18–25)

OVERVIEW

Two matters call for brief remarks: the historicity of the virgin birth (more properly, virginal conception), and the theological emphases surrounding this theme in Matthew 1–2 and its relation to the NT.

First, the historicity of the virgin birth is questioned for many reasons.

1. The accounts in Matthew and Luke are apparently independent and highly divergent. This argues for creative forces in the church making up all or parts of the stories in order to explain the person of Jesus. But the stories have long been shown to be compatible (Machen, *Virgin Birth*), even mutually complementary. Moreover, literary independence of Matthew and Luke at this point does not demand the conclusion that the two evangelists were ignorant of each other's content. Yet if they were, their differences suggest to some the strength of mutual compatibility without collusion. Matthew focuses largely on Joseph, Luke on Mary. R. E. Brown (*Birth of the Messiah*, 35) does not accept this because he finds it inconceivable that Joseph could have told his story without mentioning the annunciation or that Mary could have passed on her story without mentioning the flight to Egypt. True enough, though it does not follow that the evangelists were bound to include all they knew. It is hard to imagine how the annunciation would have fit in very well with Matthew's themes. Moreover, we have already observed that Matthew was prepared to omit things he knew in order to present his chosen themes coherently and concisely.

2. Some simply discount the supernatural. Goulder (*Midrash and Lection*, 33) says Matthew made the stories up; Schweizer contrasts the ancient world in which virgin birth was (allegedly) an accepted notion with modern scientific limitations on what is possible (similarly Robert J. Miller, *Born Divine: The Births of Jesus and Other Sons of God* [Santa Rosa, Calif.: Polebridge, 2003]). But the antithesis is greatly exaggerated. Thoroughgoing rationalists were not uncommon in the first century (e.g., Lucretius); and millions of modern Christians, scientifically aware, find little difficulty in believing in the virgin birth or in a God who is capable of intervening miraculously in what is, after all, his own creation. (On Miller, see the rather scathing review by Kim Paffenroth in *CBQ* 68 [2006]: 341–42.)

More important, Matthew's point in these chapters is surely that the virgin birth and attendant circumstances were most extraordinary. Only here does he mention Magi; and dreams and visions as a means of guidance are by no means common in the NT (though even here one wonders whether Western Christianity could learn something from Third-World Christianity). Certainly Matthew's account is infinitely more sober than the wildly speculative stories preserved in the apocryphal gospels (e.g., *Prot. Jas.* 12:3–20:4; cf. Hennecke, *New Testament Apocrypha*, 1:381–85). R. E. Brown (*Birth of the Messiah*) accepts the historicity of the virgin birth but discounts the historicity of the visit of the Magi and related events. But if he can swallow the virgin birth, it is difficult to see why he strains out the Magi. (See the useful book of Manuel Miguens, *The Virgin Birth: An Evaluation of Scriptural Evidence* [Westminster, Md.: Christian Classics, 1975].)

3. Many point to artificialities in the narrative: e.g., the structure of the genealogy or the delay in mentioning Bethlehem as the place of birth (e.g., Hill). We have noted, however, that though Matthew's arrangement of the genealogy gives us more than a mere table of names and dates, it does not tell us less. More than any of the synoptists, Matthew delights in topical arrangements. But that does not make his accounts less than historical. We are not shut up to the extreme choice—historical chronicles or theological invention! Matthew does not mention Bethlehem in 1:18–25 because it does not suit any of his themes. In ch. 2, however, as Tatum has shown (W. B. Tatum Jr., "The Matthean Infancy Narratives: Their Form, Structure, and Relation to the Theology of the First Evangelist" [PhD diss., Duke University, 1967]), one of the themes unifying

Matthew's narrative is Jesus' "geographical origins"; and therefore Bethlehem is introduced.

4. It has become increasingly common to identify the literary genre in Mt 1–2 as "midrash" or "midrashic haggadah" and to conclude that these stories are not intended to be taken literally (e.g., with widely differing perspectives, Gundry; Goulder, *Midrash and Lection*; Davies, *Setting*, 66–67). There is nothing fundamentally objectionable in the suggestion that some stories in the Bible are not meant to be taken as fact; parables are such stories. The problem is the slipperiness of the categories (see Introduction, section 12.b; comments at 2:16–18). If the genre has unambiguous formal characteristics, there should be little problem in recognizing them. But this is far from being so. The frequently cited parallels boast as many formal differences (compared with Mt 1–2) as similarities. To cite one obvious example—Jewish midrashim (in the technical, fourth-century sense) present stories as illustrative material by way of comment on a running OT text. By contrast, chs. 1–2 offers no running OT text. The continuity of the text depends on the story line; and the OT quotations, taken from a variety of OT books, could be removed without affecting that continuity (cf. M. J. Down, "The Matthean Birth Narratives," *ExpTim* 90 [1978–79]: 51–52; France, *Jesus and the Old Testament*; see comments at 2:16–18).

R. E. Brown (*Birth of the Messiah*, 557–63) argues convincingly that Matthew 1–2 is not midrash. Yet he thinks the sort of person who could invent stories to explain OT texts (midrash) could also invent stories to explain Jesus. Matthew 1–2, though not itself midrash, is at least midrashic. That may be so. Unfortunately, not only does the statement fall short of proof, but the appeal to a known and recognizable literary genre is thus lost. So we have no objective basis for arguing that Matthew's first readers would readily detect his midrashic methods. Of course, if "midrashic" means that Matthew intends to present a panorama of OT allusions and themes, these chapters are certainly midrashic. In that sense, the studies of Goulder, Gundry, Davies, and others have served us well by warning us against a too rigid pattern of linear thought. But used in this sense, it is not at all clear that "midrashic material" is necessarily unhistorical.

5. A related objection insists that these stories "are not primarily didactic" but "kerygmatic" (Davies, *Setting*, 67), that they are intended as proclamations about the truth of the person of Jesus but not as factual information. The rigid dichotomy between proclamation and teaching is not as defensible as when C. H. Dodd first proposed it (see comments at 3:1). More important, we may ask just what the proclamation intended to proclaim. If the stories express the appreciation of the first Christians for Jesus, precisely what did they appreciate? On the face of it, Matthew in chs. 1–2 is not saying something vague, such as, "Jesus was so wonderful there must be a touch of the divine about him," but rather, "Jesus is the promised Messiah of the line of David, and he is 'Immanuel,' 'God with us,' because his birth was the result of God's supernatural intervention, making Jesus God's very Son; and his early months were stamped with strange occurrences which, in the light of subsequent events, weave a coherent pattern of theological truths and historical attestation to divine providence in the matter."

6. Some argue that the (to us) artificial way these chapters cite the OT shows small concern for historicity. The reverse argument is surely more impressive: If the events of chs. 1–2 do not relate easily to the OT texts, this attests their historical credibility; for no one in his right mind would invent "fulfillment" episodes problematic to the texts being fulfilled. The fulfillment texts, though difficult, do fit into a coherent pattern (see Introduction, section 11.b; comments at vv.22–23). More important,

their presence shows that Matthew sees Jesus as one who fulfills the OT. This not only sets the stage for some of Matthew's most important themes; it also means Matthew is working from a perspective on salvation history that depends on before and after, prophecy and fulfillment, type and antitype, relative ignorance and progressive revelation. This has an important bearing on our discussion of midrash, because whatever else Jewish midrash may be, it is not related to salvation history or fulfillment schemes. Add to the foregoing considerations the fact that, wherever in chs. 1–2 he can be tested against the known background of Herod the Great, Matthew proves reliable (some details below). There is a good case for treating chs. 1–2 as both history and theology.

Second, the following theological considerations require mention.

1. Often it is argued or even assumed (e.g., Dunn, *Christology*, 49–50) that the concepts "virginal" conception and "preexistence" applied to the one person Jesus are mutually exclusive. Certainly it is difficult to see how a divine being could become genuinely human by means of an ordinary birth. Nevertheless, there is no logical or theological reason to think that virginal conception and preexistence preclude each other.

2. Related to this is the theory of R. E. Brown (*Birth of the Messiah*, 140–41), who proposes a retrojected Christology. The early Christians, he argues, first focused attention on Jesus' resurrection, which they perceived as the moment of his installation into his messianic role. Then with further reflection they pushed back the time of his installation to his baptism, then to his birth, and finally to a theory regarding his preexistence. There may be some truth to the scheme. Just as the first Christians did not come to an instant grasp of the relationship between law and gospel (as the book of Acts amply demonstrates), so their understanding of Jesus doubtless matured and deepened with time and further revelation. But the theory often depends on a rigid and false reconstruction of early church history (see Introduction, section 2) and dates the documents, against other evidence, on the basis of this reconstruction. Worse, in the hands of some it transforms the understanding of the disciples into historical reality—i.e., Jesus had no preexistence and was not virgin born, but these things were progressively predicated of him by his followers. Gospel evidence for Jesus' self-perception as preexistent is then facilely dismissed as late and inauthentic. The method is of doubtful worth.

Matthew, despite his strong insistence on Jesus' virginal conception, includes several veiled allusions to Jesus' preexistence, and there is no reason to think he found the two concepts incompatible. Moreover R. H. Fuller ("The Conception/Birth of Jesus as a Christological Moment," *JSNT* 1 [1978]: 37–52) has shown that the virginal conception-birth motif in the NT is not infrequently connected with the "sending of the Son" motif, which (contra Fuller) in many places already presupposes the preexistence of the Son.

3. We are dealing in these chapters with King Messiah, who comes to his people in covenant relationship. The point is well established, if occasionally exaggerated, by Brian Nolan (*Royal Son of God*), who speaks of the "Royal Covenant Christology."

4. It is remarkable that the title "Son of God," important later in Matthew, is not found in chs. 1–2. It may lurk behind 2:15. Still it would be false to argue that Matthew does not connect the virgin birth with the title "Son of God" (though more commonly Matthew connects the title with Davidic royal messianism). Matthew 1–2 serve as a finely wrought prologue for every major theme in the gospel. We must therefore understand Matthew to be telling us that if Jesus is physically Mary's son and legally Joseph's son, at an even more fundamental level he is

God's Son; and in this, Matthew agrees with Luke's statement (Lk 1:35). The dual paternity, one legal and one divine, is unambiguous (see Cyrus H. Gordon, "Paternity at Two Levels," *JBL* 96 [1977]: 101).

18This is how the birth of Jesus Christ came about: His mother Mary was pledged to be married to Joseph, but before they came together, she was found to be with child through the Holy Spirit. 19Because Joseph her husband was a righteous man and did not want to expose her to public disgrace, he had in mind to divorce her quietly.

20But after he had considered this, an angel of the Lord appeared to him in a dream and said, "Joseph son of David, do not be afraid to take Mary home as your wife, because what is conceived in her is from the Holy Spirit. 21She will give birth to a son, and you are to give him the name Jesus, because he will save his people from their sins."

22All this took place to fulfill what the Lord had said through the prophet: 23"The virgin will be with child and will give birth to a son, and they will call him Immanuel"—which means, "God with us."

24When Joseph woke up, he did what the angel of the Lord had commanded him and took Mary home as his wife. 25But he had no union with her until she gave birth to a son. And he gave him the name Jesus.

COMMENTARY

18 The word translated "birth" is, in the best MSS (see Notes), the word translated "genealogy" in 1:1. Maier prefers "history" of Jesus Christ, taking the phrase to refer to the rest of Matthew's gospel. Yet it is best to take the word to mean "birth" or "origins" in the sense of the beginnings of Jesus Messiah. Even a well-developed Christology would not want to read the man "Jesus" and his name back into a preexistent state (see comments at 1:1). The pledge to be married was legally binding. Only a divorce writ could break it, and infidelity at that stage was considered adultery (cf. Dt 22:23–24; Moore, *Judaism*, 2:121–22). The marriage itself took place when the groom (already called "husband," Mt 1:19) ceremoniously took the bride home (see comments at 25:1–13). Mary is here introduced unobtrusively. Though comparing the gospel accounts gives us a picture of her, she does not figure largely in Matthew.

"Before they came together" (*prin ē synelthein autous*) occasionally refers in classical Greek to sexual intercourse (LSJ, 1712); in the other thirty instances of *synerchomai* (GK *5302*) in the NT, there is, however, no sexual overtone. But here sexual union is included, occurring at the formal marriage when the "wife" moved in with her "husband." Only then was sexual intercourse proper. The phrase affirms that Mary's pregnancy was discovered while she was still betrothed, and the context presupposes that both Mary and Joseph had been chaste (cf. McHugh, *Mother of Jesus*, 157–63; and for the customs of the day, *m. Qidd.* ["Betrothals"] and *m. Ketub.* ["Marriage Deeds"]).

That Mary was "found" to be with child does not suggest a surreptitious attempt at concealment ("found out") but only that her pregnancy became obvious. This pregnancy came about through the Holy Spirit (even more prominent in Luke's birth narratives). There is no hint of pagan deity-human coupling in crassly physical terms. Instead, the power of the Lord, manifest in the Holy Spirit who was expected to be active in the messianic age, miraculously brought about the conception.

19 The peculiar Greek expression in this verse allows several interpretations. There are three important ones.

1. Because Joseph, knowing about the virginal conception, was a just man and had no desire to bring the matter out in the open (i.e., to divulge this miraculous conception), he felt unworthy to continue his plans to marry one so highly favored and planned to withdraw (so Gundry; Schlatter; McHugh, *Mother of Jesus*, 164–72). This assumes that Mary told Joseph about the conception. Nevertheless, the natural way to read vv.18–19 is that Joseph learned of his betrothed's condition when it became unmistakable, not when she told him. Moreover, the angel's reason for Joseph to proceed with the marriage (v.20) assumes (contra Zerwick, *Biblical Greek*, para. 477) that Joseph did not know about the virginal conception.

2. Because Joseph was a just man and because he did not want to expose Mary to public disgrace, he proposed a quiet divorce. The problem with this is that "just" (NIV, "righteous," GK *1465*) is not defined according to OT law but is taken in the sense of merciful, not given to passionate vengeance, or even nice (cf. 1Sa 24:17). But this is not its normal sense. Strictly speaking, justice conceived in Mosaic prescriptions demanded some sort of action.

3. Because he was a righteous man, Joseph therefore could not in conscience marry Mary, who was now thought to be unfaithful. And because such a marriage would have been a tacit admission of his own guilt and also because he was unwilling to expose her to the disgrace of public divorce, Joseph therefore chose a quieter way, permitted by the law itself. The full rigor of the law might have led to Mary's stoning, though that was rarely carried out in the first century. Still, a public divorce was possible, though Joseph was apparently unwilling to expose Mary to such shame. The law also allowed for private divorce before two witnesses (Nu 5:11–31 interpreted as in *m. Soṭah* 1:1–5; cf. David Hill, "A Note on Matthew i.19," *ExpTim* 76 [1964–65]: 133–34; A. Tosato, "Joseph, Being a Just Man (Mt 1:19)," *CBQ* 41 [1979]: 547–51). That was what Joseph purposed. It would leave both his righteousness (his conformity to the law) and his compassion intact.

20 Joseph tried to solve his dilemma in what seemed to him the best way possible. Only then did God intervene with a dream. Dreams as means of divine communication in the NT are concentrated in Matthew's prologue (1:20; 2:2, 13, 19, 22; elsewhere, possibly 27:19; Ac 2:17). An "angel of the Lord" (four times in the prologue: Mt 1:20, 24; 2:13, 19) calls to mind divine messengers in past ages (e.g., Ge 16:7–14; 22:11–18; Ex 3:2–4:16), in which it was not always clear whether the heavenly "messenger" (the meaning of *angelos*, GK *34*) was a manifestation of Yahweh. They most commonly appeared as men. We must not read medieval paintings into the word "angel" or the stylized cherubim of Revelation 4:6–8. The focus is on God's gracious intervention and the messenger's private communication, not on the details of angelology and their panoramic sweeps of history common in Jewish apocalyptic literature (cf. Bonnard).

The angel's opening words, "Joseph son of David," tie this pericope to the preceding genealogy, maintain interest in the theme of the Davidic Messiah, and, from Joseph's perspective, alert him to the significance of the role he is to play. The prohibition "do not be afraid" confirms that Joseph had already decided on his course when God intervened. He was to "take" Mary home as his wife—an expression primarily reflecting marriage customs of the day but not excluding sexual intercourse (cf. *TDNT*, 4:11–14, for other uses of the verb)—because Mary's pregnancy was the direct action of the Holy Spirit (a reason that makes nonsense of the attempt by James LaGrand ["How Was the Virgin Mary 'Like a Man' ...? A Note on Mt 1:18b and Related Syriac Christian Texts," *NovT* 22 (1980): 97–107] to make the reference to the Holy Spirit in v.18, *ek pneumatos hagiou* ["through the Holy Spirit"], mean that Mary brought forth, "as a man, by will").

21 It was no doubt divine grace that solicited Mary's cooperation before the conception and Joseph's cooperation only after it. Here Joseph is drawn into the mystery of the incarnation. In patriarchal times, either a mother (Ge 4:25) or a father (Ge 4:26; 5:3; cf. Brown, *Birth of the Messiah*, 130) could name a child. According to Luke 1:31, Mary was told Jesus' name, but Joseph was told both the name and the reason for it. The Greek is literally "you will call his name Jesus," strange in both English and Greek. Not only is this a Semitism (BDF, para. 157 [2]—the expression recurs in Mt 1:23, 25; Lk 1:13, 31); it uses the future indicative (*kaleseis*, lit., "you will call," GK *2813*) with imperatival force—hence the NIV, "You are to give him the name Jesus." This construction is very rare in the NT, except where the LXX is being cited, and the effect is to give the verse a strong OT nuance.

"Jesus" (*Iēsous*, GK *2652*) is the Greek form of "Joshua" (cf. Gk. of Ac 7:45; Heb 4:8), which, whether in the long form *yᵉhôšûaʿ* (GK 3397, "Yahweh is salvation," Ex 24:13) or in one of the short forms, e.g., *yēšûaʿ* ("Yahweh saves," Ne 7:7), identifies Mary's son as the one who brings Yahweh's promised eschatological salvation. There are several Joshuas in the OT, at least two of them not very significant (1Sa 6:14; 2Ki 23:8). Two others, however, are used in the NT as types of Christ: Joshua, successor to Moses and the one who led the people into the promised land (and a type of Christ in Heb 4), and Joshua the high priest, contemporary of Zerubbabel (Ezr 2:2; 3:2–9; Ne 7:7), "the Branch" who builds the temple of the Lord (Zec 6:11–13). But instead of referring to either of these, the angel explains the significance of the name by referring to Psalm 130:8: "He [Yahweh] himself will redeem Israel from all their sins" (cf. Gundry, *Use of the Old Testament*, 127–28).

There was much Jewish expectation of a Messiah who would "redeem" Israel from Roman tyranny and even purify his people, whether by fiat or appeal to law (e.g., *Ps. Sol.* 17). But there was no expectation that the Davidic Messiah would give his own life as a ransom (Mt 20:28) to save his people from their sins. The verb "save" (*sōzō*, GK *5392*) can refer to deliverance from physical danger (8:25), disease (9:21–22), or even death (24:22); in the NT it commonly refers to the comprehensive salvation inaugurated by Jesus that will be consummated at his return. Here it focuses on what is central, namely, salvation from sins; for in the biblical perspective, sin is the basic (if not always the immediate) cause of all other calamities. This verse therefore orients the reader to the fundamental purpose of Jesus' coming and the essential nature of the reign he inaugurates as King Messiah, heir of David's throne (cf. Ridderbos, *Coming of the Kingdom*, 193, 201).

Though to Joseph "his people" would be the Jews, even Joseph would understand from the OT that some Jews fell under God's judgment, while others became a godly remnant. In any event, it is not long until Matthew says that both John the Baptist (3:9) and Jesus (8:11) picture Gentiles joining with the godly remnant to become disciples of the Messiah and members of "his people" (see comments at 16:18; cf. Ge 49:10; Tit 2:13–14; Rev 14:4). The words "his people" are therefore full of meaning that is progressively unpacked as Matthew's gospel unfolds. They refer to "Messiah's people."

22 Although most EV conclude the angel's remarks at the end of v.21, there is good reason to think they continue to the end of v.23, or at least to the end of the word "Immanuel." This particular fulfillment formula occurs only three times in Matthew—here; 21:4; 26:56. In the last, it is natural to take it as part of Jesus' reported speech (cf. 26:55), and this is possible, though less likely, in 21:4. Matthew's patterns are fairly consistent. So it is not unnatural to extend the quotation to the end of 1:23 as well. (The JB recognizes Matthew's consistency by ending Jesus' words in 26:55, making 26:56 Matthew's remark!) This is more convincing when we recall that only these three fulfillment formulas use the perfect *gegonen* (NIV, "took place") instead of the expected aorist. Some take the verb as an instance of a perfect standing for an aorist (so BDF, para. 343, but this is a disputed classification). Others think it means the event "stands recorded" in the abiding Christian tradition (McNeile; Moule, *Idiom Book*, 15); still others take it as a stylistic indicator that Matthew himself introduced the fulfillment passage (Rothfuchs, *Erfüllungszitate*, 33–36). But if we hold that Matthew presents the angel as saying the words, then the perfect may enjoy its normal force: "all this has taken place" (cf. Fenton; Stendahl, "Matthew," in *Peake's Commentary*).

R. E. Brown (*Birth of the Messiah*, 144 n. 31) objects that nowhere in Scripture does an angel cite Scripture in this fashion; but, equally, nowhere in Scripture is there a virgin birth in this fashion. Matthew knew that Satan can cite Scripture (4:6–7); he may not have thought it strange if an angel does. Broadus's objection, that the angel would in that case be anticipating an event that has not yet occurred, and this is strange when cast in fulfillment language, lacks weight, for the conception has occurred and the pregnancy has become well advanced, even if the birth has not yet taken place. Joseph needs to know at this stage that "all this took place" to fulfill what the Lord had said through the prophet. The weightiest argument is the perfect tense.

The last clause is phrased with exquisite care, literally, "the word spoken by [*hypo*] the Lord through [*dia*] the prophet." The prepositions make a distinction between the mediate and the intermediate agent (*Grammar*, 636), presupposing a view of Scripture like that in 2 Peter 1:21. Matthew uses the verb "fulfill" (*plēroō*, GK *4444*) primarily in his own fulfillment formulas (1:22; 2:15, 17, 23; 4:14; 8:17; 12:17; 13:35; 21:4; 26:56; 27:9; cf. 26:54) but also in a few other contexts (3:15; 5:17; 13:48; 23:32). (On Matthew's understanding of fulfillment and on the origins of his fulfillment texts, see comments at 5:17; Introduction, section 11.b.)

Here two observations are in order. First, most of Matthew's OT quotations are easy enough to understand, but the difficult exceptions have sometimes tended to increase the difficulty of the easier ones. Hard cases make bad theology as well as bad law. Second, Matthew is not simply ripping texts out of OT contexts because he needs to find a prophecy in order to generate a fulfillment. Discernible principles govern his choices, the most important being that he finds in the OT not only isolated predictions regarding the Messiah but also OT history and people as paradigms that, to those with eyes to see, point forward to the Messiah (see comments at 2:15).

23 This verse, on which the literature is legion, is reasonably clear in its context here in Matthew. Mary is the virgin; Jesus is her son, Immanuel. But because it is a quotation from Isaiah 7:14, complex issues are raised concerning Matthew's use of the OT.

The linguistic evidence is not as determinative as some think. The Hebrew word *ʿalmâ* (GK 6625) is not precisely equivalent to the English word "virgin" (NIV), in which all the focus is on the lack of sexual experience; nor is it precisely equivalent to "young woman," in which the focus is on age without reference to sexual experience. Many prefer the translation "young woman of marriageable age." Yet most of the few OT occurrences refer to a young woman of marriageable age who is also a virgin. The most disputed passage is Proverbs 30:19: "The way of a man with a *maiden*" (italics added). Here the focus of the word is certainly not on virginity. Some claim that here the maiden cannot possibly be a virgin; others (see esp. E. J. Young, *Studies in Isaiah* [London: Tyndale, 1954], 143–98; Richard Niessen, "The Virginity of the עַלְמָה in Isaiah 7:14," *BSac* 137 [1980]: 133–50) insist that Proverbs 30:19 refers to a young man wooing and winning a maiden still a virgin.

Although it is fair to say that most OT occurrences presuppose that the *ʿalmâ* is a virgin, because of Proverbs 30:19, one cannot be certain the word necessarily means that. Linguistics has shown that the etymological arguments (reviewed by Richard Niessen) have little force. Young argues that *ʿalmâ* is chosen by Isaiah because the most likely alternative (*b^etûlâ*, GK 1435) can refer to a married woman (Joel 1:8 is commonly cited; Young is supported by Gordon J. Wenham, "*Bethulah*, 'A Girl of Marriageable Age,'" *VT* 22 [1972]: 326–29). Again, however, the linguistic argument is not as clear-cut as we might like. Tom Wadsworth ("Is There a Hebrew Word for Virgin? *Bethulah* in the Old Testament," *ResQ* 23 [1980]: 161–71) insists that every occurrence of *b^etûlâ* in the OT does refer to a virgin—the woman in Joel 1:8, for instance, is betrothed. Again the evidence is a trifle ambiguous. For the most recent bibliography, see the notes in R. Bruce Compton, "The Immanuel Prophecy in Isaiah 7:14–16," *Detroit Baptist Seminary Journal* 12 (2007): 3–15. In short, there is a presumption in favor of rendering *ʿalmâ* by "young virgin" or the like in Isaiah 7:14. Nevertheless, other evidence must be given a hearing.

The LXX renders the word by *parthenos* (GK *4221*), which almost always means "virgin." Yet even with this word there are exceptions. Genesis 34:3 refers to Dinah as a *parthenos*, even though the previous verse makes it clear she is no longer a virgin. This sort of datum prompts Dodd ("New Testament Translation Problems I," 301–5) to suggest that *parthenos* means "young woman" even in Matthew 1:23 and Luke 1:27. This will not do; the overwhelming majority of the occurrences of *parthenos* in both biblical and profane Greek require the rendering "virgin"; and the unambiguous context of Matthew 1 (cf. vv.16, 18, 20, 25) puts Matthew's intent beyond dispute, as Jean Carmignac ("The Meaning of *parthenos* in Luke 1.27: A reply to C. H. Dodd," *BT* 28 [1977]: 327–30) was quick to point out. If, unlike the LXX, the later (second century AD) Greek renderings of the Hebrew text of Isaiah 7:14 prefer *neanis* ("young woman") to *parthenos* (so Aq., Symm., Theod.), we may legitimately suspect a conscious effort by the Jewish translators to avoid the Christian interpretation of Isaiah 7:14.

The crucial question is how we are to understand Isaiah 7:14 in its relationship to Matthew 1:23. Of the many suggestions, six deserve mention.

1. David Hill, J. B. Taylor (*Illustrated Bible Dictionary* [ed. Douglas], 3:1625), and others support the argument of W. C. van Unnik ("Dominus Vobiscum," in *New Testament Essays* [ed. A. J. B. Higgins; Manchester: Manchester Univ. Press, 1959], 270–305), who claimed Isaiah meant that a young woman named her child Immanuel as a tribute to God's presence and deliverance and that the passage applies to Jesus because Immanuel fits his mission. This does not take the "sign" (Isa 7:11, 14) seriously; v.11 expects something spectacular. Nor does it adequately consider the time lapse (vv.15–17). Moreover, it assumes a casual link between Isaiah and Matthew.

2. Many others take Isaiah as saying that a young woman—a virgin at the time of the prophecy (Broadus; Blomberg, "Matthew," in *CNTUOT*)—will bear a son and that before he reaches the age

of discretion (perhaps less than two years from the time of the prophecy), Ahaz will be delivered from his enemies. Matthew, being an inspired writer, sees a later fulfillment in Jesus; and we must accept it on Matthew's authority. W. S. LaSor thinks this provides canonical support for a *sensus plenior* ("fuller sense") approach to Scripture ("The *Sensus Plenior* and Biblical Interpretation," in *Scripture, Tradition, and Interpretation* [ed. W. W. Gasque and W. S. LaSor; Grand Rapids: Eerdmans, 1978], 271–72). In addition to several deficiencies in interpreting Isaiah 7:14–17 (e.g., the supernaturalness of the sign in 7:11 is not continued in 7:14), this position is intrinsically unstable, seeking either a deeper connection between Isaiah and Matthew or less reliance on Matthew's authority. Hendriksen, 140, holds that the destruction of Pekah and Rezin was a clear sign that the line of the Messiah was being protected. But this is to postulate, without textual warrant, two signs—the sign of the child and the sign of the deliverance—and it presupposes that Ahaz possessed remarkable theological acumen in recognizing the latter sign.

3. Many (esp. older) commentators (e.g., Alexander; E. J. Young; Hengstenberg, *Christology of the Old Testament*) reject any notion of double fulfillment and say that Isaiah 7:14 refers exclusively to Jesus Christ. This does justice to the expectation of a miraculous sign, the significance of "Immanuel," and the most likely meaning of *ʿalmâ* and *parthenos*. But it puts more strain on the relation of a sign to Ahaz. It seems weak to say that before a period of time equivalent to the length of time between Jesus' (Immanuel's) conception and his reaching an age of discretion, Ahaz's enemies will be destroyed. Most commentators in this group insist on a miraculous element in "sign" (v.11). But though Immanuel's birth is miraculous, how is the "sign" given Ahaz miraculous?

4. A few have argued (e.g., Gene Rice, "A Neglected Interpretation of the Immanuel Prophecy," *ZAW* 90 [1978]: 220–27) that in Isaiah 7:14–17 Immanuel represents the righteous remnant—God is "with them"—and that the mother is Zion. This may be fairly applied to Jesus and Mary in Matthew 1:23, since Jesus' personal history seems to recapitulate something of the Jews' national history (cf. 2:15; 4:1–4). Yet this sounds contrived. Would Ahaz have understood the words so metaphorically? And though Jesus sometimes appears to recapitulate Israel, it is doubtful that NT writers ever thought that Mary recapitulates Zion.

5. R. Bruce Compton (cited above) has recently argued that Isaiah 7:13–14, with its collection of plural "you" expressions, is addressed not to Ahaz but to the entire nation, giving them reassurance that the Davidic line will prevail. By contrast, Isaiah 7:15, with its singular "you," is addressed to Ahaz. It is not only the threat to the Davidic line that is at issue, but the threat to this specific Davidic king. To him the assurance is given that before the short period of time specified, Rezin and Pekah will be threats no more. In short, Compton envisages a prophecy in two parts. That may be, but it sounds like a way out of a difficulty rather than an obvious reading of the text.

6. The most plausible view is that of J. A. Motyer ("Context and Content in the Interpretation of Isaiah 7:14," *TynBul* 21 [1970]: 118–25). It is a modified form of the third interpretation and depends in part on recognizing a crucial feature in Isaiah. Signs in the OT may function as a present persuader (e.g., Ex 4:8–9) or as future confirmation (e.g., Ex 3:12). Isaiah 7:14 falls in the latter case because Immanuel's birth comes too late to be a "present persuader." The "sign" (v.11) points primarily to threat and foreboding. Ahaz has rejected the Lord's gracious offer (vv.10–12), and Isaiah responds in wrath (v.13). The "curds and honey" Immanuel will eat (v.15) represent the only food left in the land on the day of wrath (vv.18–22). Even the promise of Ephraim's destruction (v.8) must be understood to embrace a warning (v.9b; Motyer, "Context and

Content," 121–22). Isaiah sees a threat, not simply to Ahaz, but to the "house of David" (vv.2, 13), which is caught up in faithlessness. To this faithless house Isaiah utters his prophecy. Therefore, Immanuel's birth follows the coming events (it is a "future confirmation") and will take place when the Davidic dynasty has lost the throne.

Motyer shows the close parallels between the prophetic word to Judah (Isa 7:1–9:7) and the prophetic word to Ephraim (9:8–11:16). To both comes the moment of decision as the Lord's word threatens wrath (7:1–17; 9:8–10:4), the time of judgment mediated by the Assyrian invasion (7:18–8:8; 10:5–15), the destruction of God's foes but the salvation of a remnant (8:9–22; 10:16–34), and the promise of a glorious hope as the Davidic monarch reigns and brings prosperity to his people (9:1–7; 11:1–16). The twofold structure argues for the cohesive unity between the prophecy of Judah and that to Ephraim. If this is correct, Isaiah 7:1–9:7 must be read as a unit—i.e., 7:14 must not be treated in isolation. The promised Immanuel (7:14) will thwart all opponents (8:10) and appear in Galilee of the Gentiles (9:1) as a great light to those in the land of the shadow of death (9:2). He is the Child and Son called "Wonderful Counselor, Mighty God, Everlasting Father, Prince of Peace" in 9:6, whose government and peace will never end as he reigns on David's throne forever (9:7).

Much of Motyer's work is confirmed by an article by Joseph Jensen ("The Age of Immanuel," *CBQ* 41 [1979]: 220–39; he does not refer to Motyer), who extends the plausibility of this structure by showing that Isaiah 7:15 should be taken in a final sense; i.e., Immanuel will eat the bread of affliction in order to learn (unlike Ahaz!) the lesson of obedience. There is no reference to "age of discretion." Further, Jensen believes that Isaiah 7:16–25 points to Immanuel's coming only after the destruction of the land (6:9–13 suggests the destruction extends to Judah as well as to Israel); that Immanuel and Maher-Shalal-Hash-Baz, Isaiah's son (8:1), are not the same; and that only Isaiah's son sets a time limit relevant to Ahaz.

If Motyer's view fairly represents Isaiah's thought, and if Matthew understood him in this way, then much light is shed on the first gospel. The Immanuel figure of Isaiah 7:14 is a messianic figure, a point Matthew has rightly grasped. Moreover this interpretation turns on an understanding of the place of the exile in Isaiah 6–12, and Matthew has divided up his genealogy (1:11–12, 17) precisely in order to draw attention to the exile. In 2:17–18 the theme of the exile returns. A little later, as Jesus begins his ministry (4:12–16), Matthew quotes Isaiah 9:1–2, which, if the interpretation adopted here is correct, properly belongs to the Immanuel prophecies of Isaiah 7:14; 9:6. Small wonder that after such comments by Matthew, Jesus' next words announced the kingdom (4:17; cf. Isa 9:7). Isaiah's reference to Immanuel's affliction for the sake of learning obedience anticipates Jesus' humiliation, suffering, and obedient sonship, a recurring theme in this gospel.

This interpretation also partially explains Matthew's interest in the Davidic lineage, and it strengthens a strong interpretation of "Immanuel." Most scholars (e.g., Bonnard) suppose that this name in Isaiah reflects a hope that God would make himself present with his people ("Immanuel" derives from *ʿimmānû ʾēl*, "God with us"), and they apply the name to Jesus in a similar way, to mean that God is with us, and for us, because of Jesus. But if Immanuel in Isaiah is a messianic figure whose titles include "Mighty God," there is reason to think that "Immanuel" refers to Jesus himself, that he is "God with us." Matthew's use of the preposition "with" at the end of 1:23 favors this (see J. C. Fenton, "Matthew and the Divinity of Jesus: Three Questions Concerning Matthew 1:20–23," in *Studia Biblica 1978* [ed. Livingstone], 2:81). Though

"Immanuel" is not a name in the sense that "Jesus" is Messiah's name (1:21), in the OT Solomon was named "Jedidiah" ("Beloved of Yahweh," 2Sa 12:25), even though he apparently was not called that. Similarly Immanuel is a "name" in the sense of title or description.

No greater blessing can be conceived than for God to dwell with his people (Isa 60:18–20; Eze 48:35; Rev 21:23). Jesus is the one called "God with us" (the designation evokes Jn 1:14, 18). As if that were not enough, Jesus promises just before his ascension to be with us to the end of the age (28:20; cf. 18:20), when he will return to share his messianic banquet with his people (25:10).

If "Immanuel" is rightly interpreted in this sense, then the question must be raised whether "Jesus" (1:21) should receive the same treatment. Does "Jesus" ("Yahweh saves") mean Mary's son merely brings Yahweh's salvation, or is he himself in some sense the Yahweh who saves? If "Immanuel" entails the higher Christology, it is not implausible that Matthew sees the same in "Jesus." The least we can say is that Matthew does not hesitate to apply OT passages descriptive of Yahweh directly to Jesus (see comments at 3:3).

Matthew's quotation of Isaiah 7:14 is very close to the LXX, but he changes "you will call" to "they will call." This may reflect a rendering of the original Hebrew, if 1QIsa[a] is pointed appropriately (cf. Gundry, *Use of the Old Testament*, 90). But there is more here. The people whose sins Jesus forgives (1:21) are the ones who will gladly call him "God with us."

24–25 When Joseph woke up, he "took Mary home as his wife" (v.24; same expression as in 1:20). Throughout chs. 1–2, the pattern of God's sovereign intervention followed by Joseph's or the Magi's response is repeated. While the story is told simply, Joseph's obedience and submission under these circumstances is scarcely less remarkable than Mary's (Lk 1:38).

Matthew wants to make Jesus' virginal conception quite unambiguous, for he adds that Joseph had no sexual union with Mary (lit., he did not "know" her, an OT euphemism) until she gave birth to Jesus (v.25). The "until" clause most naturally means that Mary and Joseph enjoyed normal conjugal relations after Jesus' birth (see comments at 12:46; 13:55). Contrary to McHugh (*Mother of Jesus*, 204), the imperfect *eginōsken* ("did not know [her]," GK *1182*) does not hint at continued celibacy after Jesus' birth but stresses the faithfulness of the celibacy until Jesus' birth.

So the virgin-conceived Immanuel was born. And eight days later, when the time came for him to be circumcised (Lk 2:21), Joseph named him "Jesus."

NOTES

18 Some MSS have γέννησις (*gennēsis*, "birth," GK *1167*) instead of γένεσις (*genesis*, "birth," "origin," or "history," GK *1161*). The two words are easily confused both orthographically and, in early pronunciation systems, phonetically. The former word is common in the Fathers to refer to the Nativity and is cognate with γεννάω (*gennaō*, "I beget"); so it is transcriptionally less likely to be original.

The δέ (*de*, "but") beginning the verse is doubtless a mild adversative. All the preceding generations have been listed, "but" the birth of Jesus comes into a class of its own.

Οὕτως (*houtōs*, "thus") with the verb ἦν (*ēn*, "was") is rare and is here equivalent to τοιαύτη (*toiautē*, "in this way"; cf. BDF, para. 434 [2]).

"Holy Spirit" is anarthrous, which is not uncommon in the Gospels; and in that case the word order is always πνεῦμα ἅγιον (*pneuma hagion*). When the article is used, there is an approximately even distribution between τὸ ἅγιον πνεῦμα (*to hagion pneuma*, "the Holy Spirit") and τὸ πνεῦμα τὸ ἅγιον (*to pneuma to hagion*, "the Spirit the Holy"); cf. Moule, *Idiom Book*, 113.

19 In δίκαιος ὢν καὶ μὴ θέλων (*dikaios ōn kai mē thelōn*, lit., "being just and not willing"; NIV, "a righteous man and did not want"), it does not seem possible to take the first participle concessively (i.e., "although a righteous man") because of the *kai*. The two participles should be taken as coordinate.

20 Ἰδού (*idou*, "behold") appears for the first of sixty-two times in Matthew. It often introduces surprising action (Schlatter) or serves to arouse interest (Hendriksen), but it is so common it seems sometimes to have no force at all (cf. Moulton, *Grammar: Prolegomena*, 11; E. J. Pryke, "ΙΔΕ and ΙΔΟΥ," *NTS* 14 [1968]: 418–24).

21 The noun ἁμαρτία (*hamartia*, "sin," GK *281*) occurs at 3:6; 9:2, 5–6; 12:31; 26:38; ἁμαρτάνω (*hamartanō*, "I sin," GK *279*) is found at 18:15, 21; 27:4; and ἁμαρτωλός (*hamartōlos*, "sinner," GK *283*) at 9:10–11, 13; 11:19; 26:45.

22 Contrary to Moule (*Idiom Book*, 142), the ἵνα (*hina*, "in order to" or "with the result that") clause is not ecbatic (consecutive). Although in NT Greek, ἵνα, *hina*, is not always telic, the very idea of fulfillment presupposes an overarching plan; and if there be such a plan, it is difficult to imagine Matthew saying no more than that such and such took place with the result that the Scriptures were fulfilled, unless the Mind behind the plan has no power to effect it—which is clearly contrary to Matthew's thought. See comments at 5:17.

C. The Visit of the Magi (2:1–12)

OVERVIEW

Few passages have received more diverse interpretations than this one (cf. W. A. Schulze, "Zur Geschichte der Auslegung von Matth. 2:1–12," *TZ* 31 [1975]: 150–60; M. Hengel and H. Merkel, "Die Magier aus dem Osten und die Flucht nach Ägypten (Mt 2) im Rahmen der antiken Religionsgeschichte und der Theologie des Matthäus," in *Orientierung an Jesus* [ed. Hoffmann et al.], 139–69). During the last hundred years or so, such diversity has sometimes sprung from a reluctance to accept either the supernatural details or the entire story as historically true. Thus it becomes necessary to find a theological motive for creating the pericope. E. Nellessen (*Das Kind und seine Mutter* [Stuttgart: KBW, 1969]), though acute in his theological observations, maintains the evangelist has fused and improved two Palestinian (and probably Galilean) legends (similarly Soares-Prabhu, *Formula Quotations*, 261–93).

Many (e.g., Gundry, Hill, Schweizer) suppose that the OT quotations constituted a collection of testimonia to Jesus in their own right before Matthew (or the church from which he sprang) embellished them with midrashic stories to produce our Matthew 2. The stories have doubtful ties with history. For many, the historicity of these accounts must simply remain an open question (e.g., Harrington), but in any case their real point is theological—to show that the Messiah was born in Bethlehem as predicted and that his appearance provoked Jewish hostility but won Gentile acceptance (the Magi), and, above all, to set up a contrast between Moses and Jesus.

Jewish tradition is steeped in stories about Pharaoh's astrologers knowing that the mother of Israel's future deliverer was pregnant, that there was a slaughter (by drowning) of all Jewish and Egyptian infants for the next nine months, that the entire house in which Moses was born was filled with great light, etc. Matthew, therefore, may have been trying to show Jesus' significance by ascribing to his birth similar and perhaps greater effects. Full-blown, these stories about Moses are preserved in Midrash Rabbah on Exodus 1, an eighth-century AD compilation. Their roots, however, stretch at least as far back as the first century (Josephus, *Ant.* 2.205–7, 15–16 [9.2–3]; cf. *Tg.Yer. I* on Ex 1:15; see Davies, *Setting*, for other veiled hints to Moses in Mt 1–2).

This reconstruction has numerous weaknesses. The independent existence of collected testimonia is not certain. There is no evidence of Midrashim written on such a diverse collection of texts (if the collection itself ever existed). The presupposed antithesis between theology and history is false; on the face of it, Matthew records history so as to bring out its theological significance and its relation to Scripture. Matthew writes at so early a time that if Jesus had not been born in Bethlehem this claim would have been challenged. We are dealing with decades, not the millennium and a half separating Moses from Josephus.

First-century stories about astrological deductions connected with Augustus Caesar's birth (Suetonius, *Aug.* 2.94) or about Moses' birth (above) may suggest to some that Matthew 2:1–12 was fabricated; but they may equally attest the prevalence of astrology and the fact that some such visits undoubtedly occurred in the ancient world. Thus they would establish the verisimilitude of the passage. More important, the stories about Moses' birth (e.g., in Josephus) were almost certainly regarded by most readers as factually true; and there can be little doubt (contra Gundry) that Matthew intends his stories about Jesus to be read the same way. If so, we may conceivably argue that Matthew was himself deceived or else wished to deceive. What we cannot do is argue that he wrote in a fashion recognized by its form to be divorced from historical reality. In any case, the suggested backdrop—stories about Moses' birth—is not very apt. Close study shows the theological matrix of the prologue centering on Jesus as the Davidic King and Son of God (cf. Kingsbury; Nolan, *Royal Son of God*), not on him as the new Moses, to whom the allusions are few and inexplicit.

Of course, Matthew did not just chronicle meaningless events. He wrote to develop his theme of fulfillment of Scripture (Had not God promised that nations would be drawn to Messiah's light [Isa 60:3]?); to establish God's providential and supernatural care of this virgin-born Son; to anticipate the hostilities, resentment, and suffering he would face; and to hint at the fact that Gentiles would be drawn into his reign (cf. Isa 60:3; Nellessen, *Das Kind*, 120, acutely compares Mt 8:11–12; cf. 28:16–20). The Magi will be like the men of Nineveh who will rise up in judgment and condemn those who, despite their privilege of much greater light, did not receive the promised Messiah and bow to his reign (12:41–42).

[1]After Jesus was born in Bethlehem in Judea, during the time of King Herod, Magi from the east came to Jerusalem [2]and asked, "Where is the one who has been born king of the Jews? We saw his star in the east and have come to worship him."

[3]When King Herod heard this he was disturbed, and all Jerusalem with him. [4]When he had called together all the people's chief priests and teachers of the law, he asked them where the Christ was to be born. [5]"In Bethlehem in Judea," they replied, "for this is what the prophet has written:

[6]"'But you, Bethlehem, in the land of Judah,
are by no means least among the rulers of Judah;
for out of you will come a ruler
who will be the shepherd of my people Israel.'"

[7]Then Herod called the Magi secretly and found out from them the exact time the star had appeared. [8]He sent them to Bethlehem and said, "Go and make a careful search for the child. As soon as you find him, report to me, so that I too may go and worship him."

[9]After they had heard the king, they went on their way, and the star they had seen in the east went ahead of them until it stopped over the place where the child was. [10]When they saw the star, they were overjoyed. [11]On coming to the house, they saw the child with his mother Mary, and they bowed down and worshiped him. Then they opened their treasures and presented him with gifts of gold and of incense and of myrrh. [12]And having been warned in a dream not to go back to Herod, they returned to their country by another route.

COMMENTARY

1 Bethlehem, the place near where Jacob buried his Rachel (Ge 35:19) and Ruth met Boaz (Ru 1:22–2:6), was preeminently the town where David was born and reared. For Christians, it has become the place where angel hosts broke the silence and announced Messiah's birth (Lk 2). It is distinguished from the Bethlehem in Zebulun (Jos 19:15) by the words "in Judea." Scholars have seen in these two words a preparation for v.6—"Bethlehem, in the land of Judah" (though there the Hebrew form "Judah" is used rather than the Greek "Judea")—or for v.2, "king of the Jews." But "Bethlehem in Judea" may not be much more than a stereotyped phrase (cf. Jdg 17:7, 9; 19:1–20; Ru 1:1–2; 1Sa 17:12; Mt 2:5). Luke 2:39 makes no mention of an extended stay in Bethlehem and a trip to Egypt before the return to Nazareth; if he knew of these events, Luke found them irrelevant to his purpose.

Unlike Luke, Matthew offers no description of Jesus' birth or the shepherds' visit. He specifies the time of Jesus' birth as having occurred during King Herod's reign (so also Lk 1:5). Herod the Great, as he is now called, was born in 73 BC and was named king of Judea by the Roman senate in 40 BC. By 37 BC, he had crushed, with the help of Roman forces, all opposition to his rule. Son of the Idumean Antipater, he was wealthy, politically gifted, intensely loyal, an excellent administrator, and clever enough to remain in the good graces of successive Roman emperors. His famine relief was superb and his building projects (including the temple, begun in 20 BC) admired even by his foes.

But he loved power, inflicted incredibly heavy taxes on the people, and resented the fact that many Jews considered him a usurper. In his last years, suffering an illness that compounded his paranoia, he turned to cruelty and in fits of rage and jealousy killed close associates, his wife Mariamne (of Jewish descent from the Maccabeans), and at least two of his sons (see Josephus, *Ant.* 14–18; S. Perowne, *The Life and Times of Herod the Great* [London: Hodder & Stoughton, 1956]; and esp. Abraham Schalit, *König Herodes: Der Mann und sein Werk* [Berlin: de Gruyter, 1969]).

Traditionally, some have argued that Herod died in 4 BC; so Jesus must have been born before that. Josephus (*Ant.* 17.167 [6.4]) mentions an eclipse of the moon shortly before Herod's death, and this has normally been identified as having occurred on 12–13 March 4 BC. After Herod's death there was a Passover celebration (Josephus, *J.W.* 2.10 [1.3]; *Ant.* 17.213 [9.3]), presumably 11 April 4 BC; so the date of his death at first glance seems secure. However, Ernest L. Martin (*The Birth of Christ Recalculated!* [Pasadena, Calif.: FBR, 1978], 22–49) has advanced solid reasons for thinking the eclipse occurred 10 January 1 BC, and, integrating this information with his interpretation of other relevant data, Martin proposes a birth date for Jesus in September, 2 BC. (His detailed pinpointing of 1 Sept., based on his understanding of Rev 12:1–5, is too speculative to be considered.) Several lines of evidence stand against this thesis: Josephus (*Ant.* 17.191 [8.1]; *J.W.* 1.665 [33.8]) dates the length of Herod's reign as thirty-seven years from his accession or thirty-four from the time of his effective reign, and these favor a death date in 4 BC. Coins dated at the time of 4 BC, minted under the reign of Herod's sons, support the traditional date.

Martin answers these objections by supposing that Herod's successors antedated their reigns to 4 BC in honor of Herod's sons Alexander and Aristobulus, whom he had killed in that year, and by arguing that between 4 BC and 1 BC there was some form of joint rule shared by Herod and his son Antipater. In that case, Josephus's figures relating to the length of Herod's rule refer to his unshared reign. This is psychologically unconvincing. The man who murdered two of his sons out of paranoia and jealousy and arranged to have hundreds of Jewish leaders executed on the day of his death was not likely to share his authority, even in a merely formal way. The question remains unresolved. For a more traditional dating of Jesus' birth in late 5 BC or early 4 BC, see Hoehner, *Chronological Aspects*, 11–27 (written before Martin's work).

The "Magi" (*magoi*, GK *3407*) are not easily identified with precision. Several centuries earlier, the term was used for a priestly caste of Medes who enjoyed special power to interpret dreams. Daniel (Da 1:20; 2:2; 4:7; 5:7) refers to *magoi* in the Babylonian Empire. In later centuries down to NT times, the term loosely covered a wide variety of men interested in dreams, astrology, magic, books thought to contain mysterious references to the future, and the like. Some Magi honestly inquired after truth; many were rogues and charlatans (e.g., Ac 8:9; 13:6, 8; cf. Brown, *Birth of the Messiah*, 167–68, 197–200; *TDNT*, 4:356–59). Apparently these men came to Bethlehem spurred on by astrological calculations. But they had probably built up their expectation of a kingly figure by working through assorted Jewish books (cf. W. M. Ramsey, *The Bearing of Recent Discovery on the Trustworthiness of the New Testament* [4th ed.; London: Hodder & Stoughton, 1920], 140–49).

The tradition that the Magi were kings can be traced as far back as Tertullian (d. ca. 225). It probably developed under the influence of OT passages that say kings will come and worship Messiah (cf. Pss 68:29, 31; 72:10–11; Isa 49:7; 60:1–6). The theory that there were *three* "wise men" is probably a deduction from the *three* gifts (2:11). By the end of the sixth century, the wise men were named: Melkon (later Melchior), Balthasar, and Gasper. Matthew gives no names. His *magoi* come to Jerusalem (which, like Bethlehem, has strong Davidic connections [2Sa 5:5–9]), arriving, apparently (see Notes), from the east—possibly from Babylon, where a sizable Jewish settlement wielded considerable influence, but possibly from Persia or from the Arabian desert. The more distant Babylon may be supported by the travel time apparently required (see comments at 2:16).

2 The Magi saw a star "when it rose" (NIV text note; see Notes, vv.1–2). What they saw remains uncertain.

1. The German astronomer Johannes Kepler (d. 1630) pointed out that in the Roman year AUC 747 (7 BC), there occurred a conjunction of the planets Jupiter and Saturn in the zodiacal constellation of Pisces, a sign sometimes connected in ancient astrology with the Hebrews. Many details can be fitted to this suggestion (cf. Brown, *Birth of the Messiah*, 172–73; *NIDNTT*, 3:735), not least that medieval Jews saw messianic significance in the same planetary conjunction. Moreover, the conjunction occurred in May, October, and November of 7 BC, and one of the latter two appearances could account for 2:9. But there is no solid evidence that the ancients referred to such conjunctions as "stars"; and even at their closest proximity, Jupiter and Saturn would have been about one degree apart—a perceived distance about twice the diameter of the moon—and therefore never fused into one image.

2. Michael Molnar (*The Star of Bethlehem: The Legacy of the Magi* [Piscataway, N.J.: Rutgers Univ. Press, 1999]) suggests that twice in 6 BC the moon comes in front of Jupiter, totally obscuring it (a lunar "occultation" of Jupiter), and that astrologically this indicates a royal birth. He then makes other connections to tie this to the birth to Judah. The problem is that these occultations were not visible in Babylon (the most likely provenance of the Magi) since Jupiter at that time of year was below the horizon. Molnar acknowledges the point, but thinks the Magi might nevertheless have calculated the occultation without witnessing it. Matthew, however, stipulates that the Magi "saw" the star (v.2). Moreover, Molnar's theory does not align well with v.9 (see below).

3. Kepler himself preferred the suggestion that this was a supernova—a faint star that violently explodes and gives off enormous amounts of light for a few weeks or months. A recent defense of this view is that of Mark Kidger (*The Star of Bethlehem: An Astronomer's View* [Princeton, N.J.: Princeton Univ. Press, 1999]), who argues for a nova in 5 BC, preceded by three precursors (e.g., a triple conduction of Saturn and Jupiter in Pisces in 7 BC). There is little confirming evidence, and it is difficult on this theory to account for 2:9.

4. Others have suggested comets, what some older writers refer to as "variable stars." The most likely is Halley's Comet (cf. Lagrange), which passed overhead in 12 BC; but this seems impossibly early.

5. Ernest L. Martin opts for a number of planetary conjunctions and massings in 3/2 BC. This suggestion depends on his entire reconstruction and late date for Herod's death (see comments at v.1), which is no more than a possibility. The theory also shares some of the difficulties of point 1.

6. In the light of 2:9, many commentators insist that astronomical considerations are a waste of time: Matthew presents the "star" as strictly supernatural. This, too, is possible and obviously impossible to falsify, but v.9 is not as determinative as is often suggested (see comments at v.9).

7. Because it is difficult to imagine a "star" of any conceivable astronomical variety guiding the Magi along the road to Bethlehem, Allison (*Studies in Matthew*, 17–41) suggests that the "star" is actually

a guiding angel. It is easy to list many texts in which stars and angels are linked; it is more difficult to find convincing parallels in which a star simply represents an angel. Moreover, the difficulty many find with v.9 is not nearly as great as some have thought (see comments at vv.9–10).

The evidence is insufficient to come down firmly on one particular astronomical theory.

Matthew uses language almost certainly alluding to Numbers 24:17: "A star will come out of Jacob; a scepter will rise out of Israel." This oracle, spoken by Balaam, who came "from the eastern mountains" (Nu 23:7), was widely regarded as messianic (*Tg. Ps.-J.*; *Tg. Onq.*; CD 7:19–20; 1QM 11:6; 1QSb 5:27; 4QTest 12–13; *T. Jud.* 24:1). Both Matthew and Numbers deal with the king of Israel (Nu 24:7), though Matthew does not resort to the uncontrolled allegorizing on "star" frequently found in early postapostolic Christian writings (cf. Jean Danielou, *The Theology of Jewish Christianity* [London: Darton, Longman, 1964], 214–24).

Granting Matthew's informed devotion to the OT, he surely knew that the OT mocks astrologers (Isa 47:13–15; Da 1:20; 2:27; 4:7; 5:7) and forbids astrology (Jer 10:1–2). Nevertheless, it was widely practiced in the first century, even among Jews (cf. Albright and Mann). Matthew neither condemns nor sanctions it; instead, he contrasts the eagerness of the Magi to worship Jesus, despite their limited knowledge, with the apathy of the Jewish leaders and the hostility of Herod's court—all of whom had the Scriptures to inform them. Formal knowledge of the Scriptures, Matthew implies, does not in itself lead to knowing who Jesus is. Just as God sovereignly worked through Caesar's decree that a census be taken (Lk 2:1) to ensure that Jesus' birth in Bethlehem would fulfill prophecy, so God sovereignly used the Magi's calculations to bring about the situation this pericope describes.

The question the Magi asked does not tell how their astrology led them to seek a "king of the Jews" and what made them think this particular star was "his." The widely held idea that the ancient world was looking for a Jewish leader of renown (based largely on Josephus, *J.W.* 6.312–13 [5.4]; Suetonius, *Vesp.* 4; Tacitus, *Hist.* v.13; Virgil, *Ecl.* 4) cannot stand close scrutiny. The Josephus passage refers to Jewish expectations of Messiah, and the others probably borrowed from Josephus. The Magi may have linked the star to "the king of the Jews" through studying the OT and other Jewish writings—a possibility made plausible by the presence of the large Jewish community in Babylon.

We must not think that the Magi's question meant, Where is the one born to become king of the Jews? but, Where is the one born king of the Jews? (see Notes). His kingly status was not conferred on him later on; it was his from birth. Jesus' participation in the Davidic dynasty has already been established by the genealogy. The same title the Magi gave him found its place over the cross (27:37).

"Worship" (see Notes) need not imply that the Magi recognized Jesus' divinity; it may simply mean "do homage" (Broadus). Their own statement suggests homage paid royalty rather than the worship of Deity. But Matthew, having already told of the virginal conception, doubtless expected his readers to discern something more—namely, that the Magi "worshiped" better than they knew.

3 In contrast with (*de*, a mild adversative; NIV, "when") the Magi's desire to worship the King of the Jews, Herod is deeply troubled. In this, "all Jerusalem" joins him, not because most of the people would have been sorry to see Herod replaced or because they were reluctant to see the coming of King Messiah, but because they well knew that any question, such as the Magi's, would result in more cruelty from the ailing Herod, whose paranoia had led him to murder his favorite wife and two sons.

4 Here "all" modifies "chief priests and teachers of the law," not "the people," and refers to those who were living in Jerusalem and could be quickly consulted. "Chief priests" refers to the hierarchy, made up of the current high priest and any who had formerly occupied this post (since Herod, contrary to the law, made fairly frequent changes in the high priesthood), and a substantial number of other

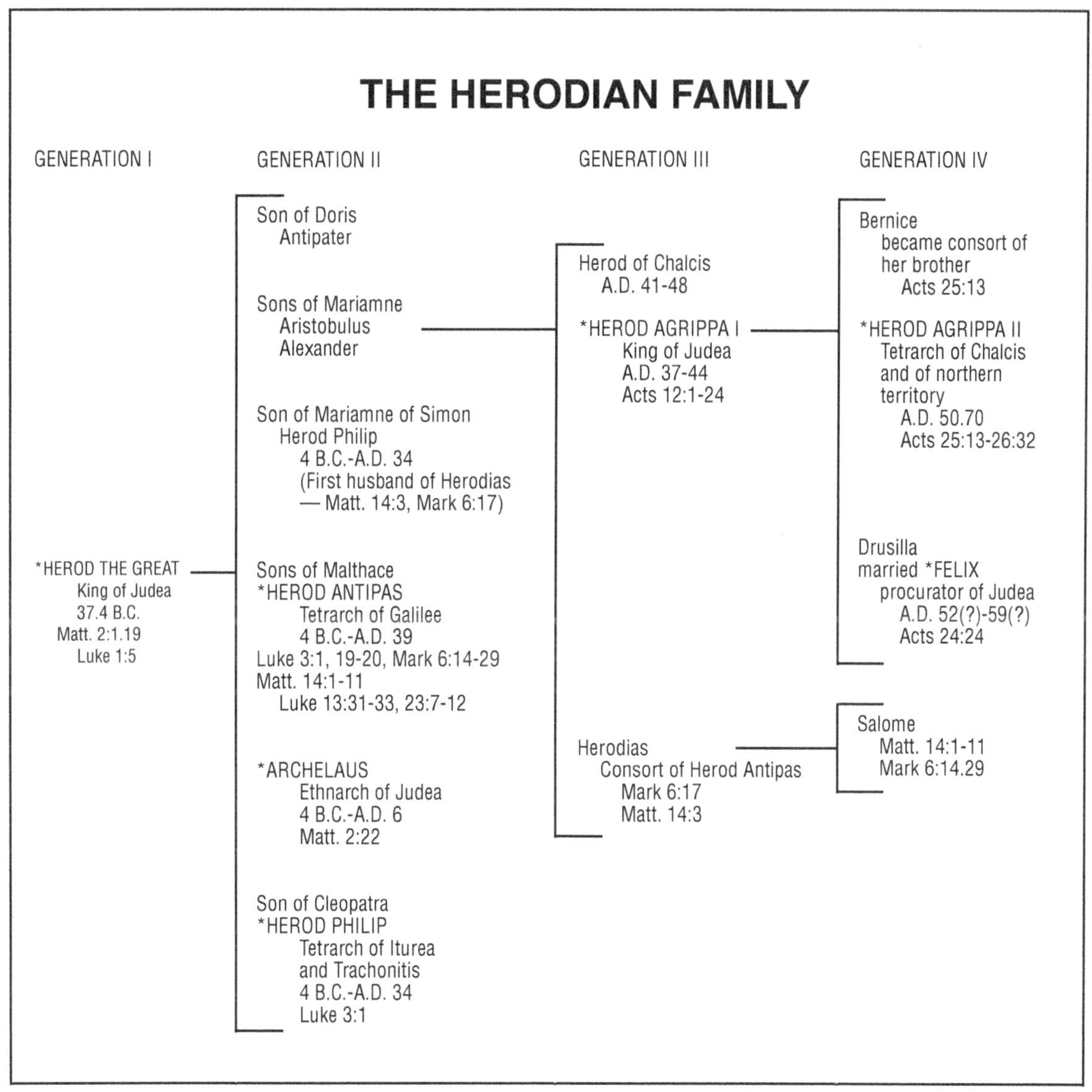

Several generations that descended from Herod the Great walk across the pages of the New Testament. Those mentioned are in capital letters, together with the relevant passages in Scripture. Used by permission of Zondervan.

leading priests (cf. Josephus, *Ant.* 20.180 [8.8]; *J.W.* 4.159–60 [3.9]; the same Greek word (*archiereus*) is used for "high priests" and "chief priests"). The "teachers of the law," or "scribes" as other EV call them, were experts in the OT and in its copious oral tradition. Their work was not so much copying out OT manuscripts (as the word "scribes" suggests) as teaching the OT. Because much civil law was based on the OT and the interpretations of the OT fostered by the leaders, the "scribes" were also "lawyers" (cf. 22:35: "expert in the law").

The vast majority of the scribes were Pharisees; the priests were Sadducees. The two groups barely got along, and therefore Schweizer judges this verse "historically almost inconceivable." But Matthew does not say the two groups came together at the same time; Herod, unloved by either group, may well have called both to guard against being tricked. If the Pharisees and Sadducees barely spoke to one another, there was less likelihood of collusion. "He asked them" (*epynthaneto*, GK *4785*; the imperfect tense sometimes connotes tentative requests [Herod may have expected the rebuff of silence]; cf. Turner, *Grammatical Insights*, 27) where the Christ (here a title; see comments at 1:1) would be born, understanding that "the Christ" and "the king of the Jews" (2:2) were titles of the same expected person. (See 26:63; 27:37 for the same equivalence.)

5 The Jewish leaders answered the question by referring to what stands written, which is the force of the perfect passive verb *gegraptai* (NIV, "has written," GK *1211*), suggesting the authoritative and regulative force of the document referred to (cf. Deissmann, *Bible Studies*, 112–14, 249–50). The NIV misses the preposition *dia* (lit., "what stands written *through* the prophet"), which implies that the prophet is not the ultimate source of what stands written (see comments at 1:22). Both in 1:22 and here, some textual witnesses insert the name of the prophet (e.g., Micah or even Isaiah). "Bethlehem in Judea" was introduced into the narrative in 2:1.

6 While expectation that the Messiah must come from Bethlehem occurs elsewhere (e.g., Jn 7:42; cf. Targum on Mic 5:1: "Out of you shall come forth before me the Messiah"), here it rests on Micah 5:2 (1 MT), to which are appended some words from 2 Samuel 5:2 (1Ch 11:2). Matthew follows neither the MT nor LXX, and his changes have provoked considerable speculation.

1. "Bethlehem Ephrathah" (LXX, "house of Ephrathah") becomes "Bethlehem, in the land of Judah." Hill says this change was made to exclude "any other Judean city like Jerusalem." But this reads too much into what is a normal LXX way of referring to Bethlehem (cf. Gundry, *Use of the Old Testament*, 91). "Ephrathah" is archaic and even in the MT primarily restricted to poetical sections like Micah 5:2.

2. The strong negative "by no means" (*oudamōs*) is added in Matthew and formally contradicts Micah 5:2. It is often argued that this change has been made to highlight Bethlehem as the birthplace of the Messiah. Indeed, Gundry's commentary uses this change as an example of Matthew's midrashic use of the OT, a use so free that he does not fear outright contradiction. There are better explanations. Even the MT of Micah implies Bethlehem's greatness: "though you are small among the clans [or rulers, who personify the cities; the KJV's "thousands" is pedantically correct, but "thousands" was a way of referring to the great clans into which the tribes were subdivided; cf. Jdg 6:15; 1Sa 10:19; 23:23; Isa 60:22] of Judah" sets the stage for the greatness that follows. Equally, Matthew's formulation assumes that, apart from being Messiah's birthplace, Bethlehem is indeed of little importance (cf. Hengstenberg, *Christology of the Old Testament*, 1:475–76, noted by Gundry, *Use of the Old Testament*, 91–92). To put it another way, though the second line of

Micah 5:2 formally contradicts the second line of Matthew 2:6, a holistic reading of the verses shows the contradiction to be merely formal. Matthew 2:6 has perhaps slightly greater emphasis on the one factor that makes Bethlehem great.

3. Matthew adds the shepherd language of 2 Samuel 5:2, making it plain that the ruler in Micah 5:2 is none other than the one who fulfills the promises to David.

It is tempting to think that Matthew sees a pair of contrasts (1) between the false shepherds of Israel who have provided sound answers but no leadership (cf. 23:2–7) and Jesus, who is the true Shepherd of his people Israel, and (2) between a ruler like Herod and the one born to rule. The words "my people Israel" are included, not simply because they are found in 2 Samuel 5:2, but because Matthew, like Paul, faithfully records both the essential Jewish focus of the OT promises and the OT expectation of broader application to the Gentiles (see comments at 1:1, 5, 21). Jesus is not only the promised Davidic king but also the promised hope of blessing to all the nations, the one who will claim their obeisance (cf. Ps 68:28–35; Isa 18:1–3, 7; 45:14; 60:6; Zep 3:10). That same duality makes the desires of the Gentile Magi to worship the Messiah stand out against the apathy of the leaders, who did not, apparently, take the trouble to go to Bethlehem. Of course, the Jewish leaders may have seen the arrival of the Magi in Jerusalem as one more false alarm.

As far as we can tell, the Sadducees (and therefore the chief priests) had no interest in the question of when the Messiah would come; the Pharisees (and therefore most teachers of the law) expected him to come only somewhat later. The Essenes alone, who were not consulted by Herod, expected the Messiah imminently (cf. R. T. Beckwith, "The Significance of the Calendar for Interpreting Essene Chronology and Eschatology," *RevQ* 38 [1980]: 167–202). But Matthew plainly says that, though Jesus was the Messiah, born in David's line and certain to be Shepherd and Ruler of Israel, it was the Gentiles who came to worship him.

7–10 The reason Herod wanted to learn, at his secret meeting with the Magi (v.7), the exact time the star appeared was that he had already schemed to kill the small boys of Bethlehem (see v.16). The entire story hangs together (see comments at v.16). Herod's hypocritical humility—"so that I too may go and worship him" (v.8)—deceived the Magi. Conscious of his success, Herod sent no escort with them. This was not "absurdly trusting" (Schweizer), since the deception depended on winning the Magi's confidence. Herod could scarcely have been expected to foresee God's intervention (v.12).

Matthew does not say that the rising star the Magi had seen (see comments at v.2) led them to Jerusalem. They went first to the capital city because they thought it the natural place for the King of the Jews to be born. But now the star reappeared ahead of them (v.9) as they made their way to Bethlehem (it was not uncommon to travel at night). Taking this as confirming their purposes, the Magi were overjoyed (v.10). The Greek text does not imply that the star pointed out the house where Jesus was or that it led the travelers through twisty streets; it may simply have hovered over Bethlehem as the Magi approached it. They would then have found the exact house through discreet inquiry since, according to Luke 2:17–18, the shepherds who came to worship the newborn Jesus did not keep silent about what they saw.

11 This verse plainly alludes to Psalm 72:10–11 and Isaiah 60:6, passages that reinforce the emphasis on the Gentiles (see comments at v.6). Nolan's suggestion (*Royal Son of God*, 206–9) that the closest parallel is Isaiah 39:1–2 is linguistically attractive but contextually weak. The evidence that Hezekiah served as an eschatological figure is poor and fails to explain why he should be opening up his treasure store to his visitors. Some time had elapsed since Jesus' birth (Mt 2:7, 16), and the family was settled in a house. While the Magi saw both the child and his mother, their worship (see comments at v.2) was for him alone.

Bringing gifts was particularly important in the ancient East when approaching a superior (cf. Ge 43:11; 1Sa 9:7–8; 1Ki 10:2). Usually such gifts were reciprocated (Derrett, *Studies in the New Testament*, 2:28). That is not mentioned here, but a first-century reader might have assumed it and seen the Great Commission (28:18–20) as leading to its abundant fruition. Frankincense is a glittering, odorous gum obtained by making incisions in the bark of several trees; myrrh exudes from a tree found in Arabia and a few other places and was a much-valued spice and perfume (Ps 45:8; SS 3:6) used in embalming (Jn 19:39). Commentators, ancient (Origen, *Cels.* 1.60) and modern (Hendriksen), have found symbolic value in the three gifts—gold suggesting royalty, incense divinity, and myrrh the passion and burial. This interpretation demands too much insight from the Magi. The three gifts were simply expensive and not uncommon presents and may have helped finance the trip to Egypt. The word "treasures" probably means "coffers" or "treasure boxes" in this context.

12 This second dream (cf. 1:20) mentions no angel. Perhaps Joseph and the Magi compared notes and saw their danger (cf. P. Gaechter, "Die Magierperikope," *ZKT* 90 [1968]: 257–95). Amid their fear and uncertainty, the dreams led them (vv.12–13) to flee. Which way the Magi went is unclear; they might have gone around the north end of the Dead Sea, avoiding Jerusalem, or they might have gone around the south end of the sea.

NOTES

1–2 The word ἀνατολή (*anatolē*, GK *424*) can mean "rising" or "east." In v.1, ἀπὸ ἀνατολῶν (*apo anatolōn*, "from the east") is rightly translated by the NIV, since the noun normally indicates the point of the compass when it is plural and anarthrous (cf. BDF, 253 [5]). By the same token ἐν τῇ ἀνατολῇ (*en tē anatolē*) in vv.2, 9 is less likely to be "in the East" than "at its rising" (the article can have mild possessive force). Other suggestions—e.g., that the expression refers to a particular land in the east or to Anatolia in the west—seem less convincing; but the question is extraordinarily complex (see Turner, *Grammatical Insights*, 25–26; Brown, *Birth of the Messiah*, 173).

2 The participle in the construction ὁ τεχθεὶς βασιλεύς (*ho techtheis basileus*, lit., "the born king") is adjectival, not substantival, and is used attributively. Moreover, there is no suggestion of "newborn" (cf. C. Burchard, "Fussnoten zum neutestamentlichen Griechisch II," *ZNW* 29 [1978]: 143–57), which is already ruled out by chronological notes (vv.7, 16).

The verb προσκυνέω (*proskyneō*, "worship," GK *4686*) occurs three times in this pericope (cf. vv.8, 11) and ten other times in Matthew. In the NT, the object of this "worship" is almost always God or Jesus, except where someone is acting ignorantly and is rebuked (Ac 10:25–26; Rev 19:10; 22:8–9). But Revelation 3:9 is an important exception (NIV, "fall down at your feet"). Secular Greek used the verb for a wide variety of levels of obeisance, and it is precarious to build too much Christology on the use of the term in the Gospels.

3 The words πᾶσα Ἱεροσόλυμα (*pasa Hierosolyma*, "all Jerusalem") betray breach of concord, since *pasa* is feminine, but this form of "Jerusalem," unlike the alternative Ἰερουσαλήμ (*Ierousalēm*), is not feminine but neuter plural. Possibly πᾶσα, *pasa*, is a precursor of modern Greek's indeclinable πᾶσα, *pasa* (so BDF, para. 56 [4]); but it is marginally more likely that the noun is being treated as feminine singular since there are other instances where it is construed as feminine singular even though no πᾶσα, *pasa*, is present.

5–6 Matthew uses the singular προφήτου (*prophētou*, "prophet," GK *4737*) even though two different passages, from the Latter and Former Prophets respectively, are cited. Yet it seems a common practice to refer to one author, perhaps the principal one, when citing two or three (cf. 27:9–10; Mk 1:2–3).

7 Τότε (*tote*, "then") is very common in Matthew, occurring ninety times as compared with Mark's six and Luke's fourteen; but in Matthean usage only occasionally does it have temporal force (as here), serving more frequently as a loose connective.

10 The words "they were overjoyed" render a cognate accusative, ἐχάρησαν χαράν (*echarēsan charan*, lit., "they rejoiced with joy"), probably under Semitic influence (cf. Moule, *Idiom Book*, 32; BDF, para. 153 [1]).

D. The Escape to Egypt (2:13–15)

OVERVIEW

Many commentators think this account has been created to flesh out the OT text said to be "fulfilled" (v.15). On the broader critical questions, see Overviews, 1:18–25; 2:1–12. Given what we know of Herod's final years, there is nothing historically improbable about this account, and precisely because the fulfillment text is difficult, one may assume that the story called forth reflection on the OT text rather than vice versa.

13When they had gone, an angel of the Lord appeared to Joseph in a dream. "Get up,"
he said, "take the child and his mother and escape to Egypt. Stay there until I tell you, for
Herod is going to search for the child to kill him."
14So he got up, took the child and his mother during the night and left for Egypt,
15where he stayed until the death of Herod. And so was fulfilled what the Lord had said
through the prophet: "Out of Egypt I called my son."

COMMENTARY

13–14 The verb "had gone" (*anachōrēsantōn*) is the same as "returned" in the preceding verse, tying the two accounts together. This is the third dream in these two chapters, and for the second time an angel of the Lord is mentioned (cf. 1:20; 2:12). The point is that God took sovereign action to preserve his Messiah, his Son—something well understood by Jesus himself, and a major theme in the gospel of John. Egypt was a natural place to which to flee. It was nearby, a well-ordered Roman province outside Herod's jurisdiction, and, according to Philo (writing ca. AD 40), its population included about a million Jews. Earlier generations of Israelites fleeing their homeland (1Ki 11:40; Jer 26:21–23; 43:7) had sought refuge in Egypt. But if Matthew was thinking of any particular OT parallel, probably Jacob and his family (Ge 46) fleeing the famine in Canaan was in his mind, since that is the trip that set the stage for the exodus (cf. v.15).

The angel's command was explicit. Joseph, Mary, and the child must remain in Egypt not only until Herod's death but until given leave to return (cf. vv.19–20). The command was also urgent. Joseph left at once, setting out by night to begin the seventy-five-mile journey to the border. The focus on God's protection of "the child" is unmistakable. Herod was going to try to kill him (v.13), and Joseph took "the child and his mother" (v.14—not the normal order) to Egypt.

15 The death of Herod brought relief to many. Only then, for instance, did the Qumran covenanters return to their center, destroyed in 31 BC, and rebuild it. In Egypt, Herod's death made possible the return of the child, Mary, and Joseph, who awaited a word from the Lord. The Greek could be rendered "And so was fulfilled" (NIV) or "[This came about] in order that the word of the Lord ... might be fulfilled." Either way, the notion of fulfillment preserves some telic force in the sentence: Jesus' exodus from Egypt fulfilled Scripture written long before.

The OT quotation almost certainly (see Notes) comes from Hosea 11:1 and exactly renders the Hebrew, not the LXX, which has "his children," not "my son." (In this Matthew agrees with Aq., Symm., and Theod., but only because all four rely on the Hebrew.) Some commentators (e.g., Bengel, *Gnomon*; Gundry, *Use of the Old Testament*, 93–94) argue that the preposition *ek* (NIV, "out of") should be taken temporally, i.e., "since Egypt" or, better, "from the time [he dwelt] in Egypt." The preposition can have that force; and it is argued that Matthew 2:15 means God "called" Jesus, in the sense that he specially acknowledged and preserved him from the time of his Egyptian sojourn on, protecting him against Herod. After all, the exodus itself is not mentioned until vv.21–22.

Some commentators interpret the calling of Israel in Hosea 11:1 in a similar way. But there are convincing arguments against this. The context of Hosea 11:1 mentions Israel's *return* to Egypt (11:5), which presupposes that 11:1 refers to the exodus. To preserve the temporal force of *ek* in Matthew 2:15, Gundry is reduced to the unconvincing assertion that the preposition in Hosea is both temporal and locative. In support of this view, it is pointed out that Jesus' actual departure *out of* Egypt is not mentioned until v.21. But, although this is so, it is nevertheless implied by vv.13–14. The reason Matthew has introduced the Hosea quotation at this point, instead of after v.21, is probably that he wishes to use the return journey itself to set up the reference to the destination, Nazareth (v.23), rather than the starting point, Egypt (cf. Brown, *Birth of the Messiah*, 220).

If Hosea 11:1 refers to Israel's exodus from Egypt, in what sense can Matthew mean that Jesus' return to the land of Israel "fulfilled" this text? Four observations clarify the issue.

1. Many have noticed that Jesus is often presented in the NT as the antitype of Israel or, better, the typological recapitulation of Israel. Jesus' temptation after forty days of fasting recapitulated the forty years' trial of Israel (see comments at 4:1–11). Elsewhere, if Israel is the vine that does not bring forth the expected fruit, Jesus, by contrast, is the

True Vine (Isa 5; Jn 15). The reason Pharaoh must let the people of Israel go is that Israel is the Lord's son (Ex 4:22–23), a theme picked up by Jeremiah (31:9) as well as Hosea (11:1, 3; cf. Ps 2:6–7, 12). The "son" theme (cf. T. de Kruijf, *Der Sohn des lebendigen Gottes: Ein Beitrag zur Christologie des Matthäusevangeliums* [Rome: Biblical Institute Press, 1962], 56–58, 109)—already present since Jesus is messianic "son of David" and, by the virginal conception, Son of God—becomes extraordinarily prominent in Matthew (see comments at 3:17): "This is my Son, whom I love."

2. The verb "fulfill" has broader significance than mere one-to-one prediction (see Introduction, section 11.b; comments at 5:17). Not only in Matthew but elsewhere in the NT, the history and laws of the OT are perceived to have prophetic significance (see comments at 5:17–20). The letter to the Hebrews argues that the laws regarding the tabernacle and the sacrificial system were from the beginning designed to point toward the only Sacrifice that could really remove sin and the only Priest who could serve once and for all as the effective Mediator between God and man. Likewise, Paul insists that the Messiah sums up his people in himself. When David was anointed king, the tribes acknowledged him as their bone and flesh (2Sa 5:1); i.e., David as anointed king summed up Israel, with the result that his sin brought disaster on the people (2Sa 12, 24). Just as Israel is God's son, so the promised Davidic son is also Son of God (2Sa 7:13–14; cf. N. T. Wright, "The Paul of History," *TynBul* 29 [1978]: esp. 66–67). "Fulfillment" must be understood against the background of these interlocking themes and their typological connections.

3. It follows, therefore, that the NT writers do not think they are reading back into the OT things that are not already there germinally. This does not mean that Hosea had the Messiah in mind when he penned Hosea 11:1. This admission prompts W. L. LaSor ("Prophecy, Inspiration, and *Sensus Plenior*," *TynBul* 29 [1978]: 49–60) to see in Matthew's use of Hosea 11:1 an example of *sensus plenior*, by which he means a "fuller sense" than what was in Hosea's mind but something nevertheless in the mind of God. But so blunt an appeal to what God has absolutely hidden seems a strange background for Matthew's insisting that Jesus' exodus from Egypt in any sense fulfills the Hosea passage. This observation is not trivial. Matthew is reasoning with Jews who could say, "You are not playing fair with the text!" A mediating position is therefore necessary.

Hosea 11 pictures God's love for Israel. Although God threatens judgment and disaster, yet because he is God and not man (11:9), he looks to a time when in compassion he will roar like a lion and his children will return to him (11:10–11). In short Hosea himself looks forward to a saving visitation by the Lord. Therefore his prophecy fits into the larger pattern of OT revelation up to that point, revelation that both explicitly and implicitly points to the Seed of the woman, the Elect Son of Abraham, the Prophet like Moses, the Davidic King, the Messiah.

The "son" language is part of this messianic matrix (cf. Willis J. Beecher, *The Prophets and the Promise* [New York: Crowell, 1905], 331–35); insofar as that matrix points to Jesus the Messiah and insofar as Israel's history looks forward to one who sums it up, then so far also does Hosea 11:1 look forward. To ask whether Hosea thought of Messiah is to ask the wrong question, akin to using a hacksaw when a scalpel is needed. It is better to say that Hosea, building on existing revelation, grasped the messianic nuances of the "son" language already applied to Israel and David's promised heir in previous revelation so that had he been able to see Matthew's use of 11:1, he would not have disapproved, even if messianic nuances were not in his mind when he wrote that verse. He provided one small part of the revelation unfolded during salvation history; but that part he himself understood to be a pictorial representative of divine, redeeming love.

The NT writers insist that the OT can be rightly interpreted only if the entire revelation is kept in perspective as it is historically unfolded (e.g., Gal 3:6–14). Hermeneutically, this is not an innovation. OT writers drew lessons out of earlier salvation history, lessons difficult to perceive while that history was being lived, but lessons that retrospect would clarify (e.g., Asaph in Ps 78; see comments at 13:35). Matthew does the same in the context of the fulfillment of OT hopes in Jesus Christ. We may therefore legitimately speak of a "fuller meaning" than any one text provides. But the appeal should be made, not to some hidden divine knowledge, but to the pattern of revelation up to that time—a pattern not yet adequately discerned. The new revelation may therefore be truly new, yet at the same time capable of being checked against the old.

4. If this interpretation of v.15 is correct, it follows that for Matthew, Jesus himself is the locus of true Israel. This does not necessarily mean that God has no further purpose for racial Israel; but it does mean that the position of God's people in the messianic age is determined by reference to Jesus, not race.

NOTES

13 The historical present φαίνεται (*phainetai*, lit., "appears") adds a vivid touch.

15 Because "out of Egypt" occurs in Numbers 23:22; 24:8, some have suggested a connection between v.15 and Numbers 24:7–8 (e.g., Hill, Schweizer). In its strongest form, this argument depends on the LXX, which reads, "A man shall come forth from his seed," instead of, "Water will flow from their buckets" (Nu 24:7), and "him" instead of "them" (Nu 24:8). This transforms Numbers 24:8 into a reference to God bringing Messiah out of Egypt. Apart from the textual question, it must be noted that (1) v.15 corresponds exactly with MT Hosea 11:1 but only approximately with LXX Numbers 24:8; (2) the LXX rendering makes Numbers 24 rather incoherent.

E. The Massacre of Bethlehem's Boys (2:16–18)

OVERVIEW

Few sections of Matthew 1–2 have been as widely criticized as this one. Most modern scholars think Matthew made the story up (e.g., Goulder, *Midrash and Lection*, 33; E. M. Smallwood, *The Jews under Roman Rule* [Leiden: Brill, 1976], 103–4), spinning it out of Jeremiah 31:15, cited in Matthew 2:18 (so C. T. Davis, "Tradition and Redaction in Matthew 1:18–2:23," *JBL* 90 [1971]: 419). In this view, perhaps Matthew invented the tale to draw an analogy between Jesus and Moses or between Jesus and late Jewish traditions about Abraham or Jacob or out of an apologetic need to construct an initial sign of the impending judgment on Israel for rejecting her Messiah (Kingsbury, *Structure*, 48). But v.16 cannot be excised from the chapter without rewriting it all.

The OT citation in v.18, like other such citations in chs. 1–2, is itself not strictly necessary to the narrative. These citations illumine the narrative and show its relation to OT Scripture, but they do not create it (see Overviews, 1:18–25; 2:1–12). It is difficult to see a real parallel with Moses, since Pharaoh's edict was general and before Moses' birth, whereas Herod's edict was specifically for Bethlehem and came after Jesus' birth. At best, the parallel is tenuous. Furthermore vv.16–18 offer a poor sign of the destruction to befall Israel—not least because Jesus escapes rather than suffers, and the children have done Jesus no harm.

Actually, the story is in perfect harmony with what we know of Herod's character in his last years (cf. Abraham Schalit, *König Herodes* [Berlin: de Gruyter, 1969], 648). That there is no extra-Christian confirmation is not surprising; the same can be said of Jesus' crucifixion. The death of a few children (perhaps a dozen or so; Bethlehem's total population was not large) would hardly have been recorded in such violent times. (See the excellent treatment by R. T. France, "Herod and the Children of Bethlehem," *NovT* 21 [1979]: 98–120.) "Matthew is not simply meditating on Old Testament texts, but claiming that in what has happened they find fulfillment. If the events are legendary, the argument is futile" (p. 120).

16 When Herod realized that he had been outwitted by the Magi, he was furious, and he
gave orders to kill all the boys in Bethlehem and its vicinity who were two years old and
under, in accordance with the time he had learned from the Magi. 17 Then what was said
through the prophet Jeremiah was fulfilled:

18 "A voice is heard in Ramah,
weeping and great mourning,
Rachel weeping for her children
and refusing to be comforted,
because they are no more."

COMMENTARY

16 It probably did not take long to carry out Herod's barbarous order. Bethlehem is only five miles from Jerusalem. The Magi set out in the same evening (v.9) and may have left that same night after their dream (v.12); the same would be true of Joseph with Jesus and Mary (vv.13–15). By the next evening Herod's patience would have been exhausted. The two-years-age limit was to prevent Jesus' escape; at the time he was between six and twenty months old. Herod, aiming to eliminate a potential king, restricted the massacre to boys. Furious at being deceived (a better translation than "outwitted"), he raged against the Lord and his Anointed One (Ps 2:2). Yet this was no narrow escape. The One enthroned in heaven laughs and scoffs at the Herods of this world (Ps 2:4).

17–18 Jeremiah is named three times in Matthew (here; 16:14; 27:9) and nowhere else in the NT. The text form of this OT citation in these verses is complex but is probably Matthew's rendering of the Hebrew (cf. Gundry, *Use of the Old Testament*, 94–97; Brown, *Birth of the Messiah*, 221–23).

It is uncertain whether Jeremiah 31:15 refers to the deportation of the northern tribes by Assyria in 722–721 BC or to the deportation of Judah and Benjamin in 587–586 BC (cf. Brown, *Birth of the Messiah*, 205–6). The latter is more likely. Nebuzaradan, commander of Nebuchadnezzar's imperial guard, gathered the captives at Ramah before taking them into exile in Babylon (Jer 40:1–2). Ramah lay north of Jerusalem on the way to Bethel; Rachel's tomb was at Zelzah in the same vicinity (1Sa 10:2). Jeremiah 31:15 depicts mourning at the prospect of exile; Rachel is seen as crying out from her tomb because her "children," her descendants (Rachel is the idealized mother of the Jews, though Leah gave birth to more tribes than Rachel), "are no more"—i.e., they are being removed from the land and are no longer a nation. But elsewhere we are told that Rachel was buried on the way to Ephrathah, identified as Bethlehem (Ge 35:19; 48:7). Some see a confusion of traditions here and assume that the clan of Ephrathah later settled in Bethlehem and gave it its name, thus starting a false connection Matthew follows. The problem, however, is artificial. Genesis 35:16 makes it clear that Jacob was some distance from Bethlehem-Ephrathah when Rachel died—somewhere between Bethel and Bethlehem (only 1Sa 10:2 says more exactly where he was). Moreover, Matthew does not say Rachel was buried at Bethlehem; the connection between the prophecy and its "fulfillment" is more subtle than that.

Why does Matthew refer to this OT passage? Some think the connection results from word association: the children were killed at Bethlehem, Bethlehem = Ephrathah, Ephrathah is connected with Rachel's death, and Rachel figures in the oracle. Rothfuchs (*Erfüllungszitate*, 64) sees a parallel between the condemnation to exile as a result of sin (Jeremiah) and the judgment on Israel as a result of rejecting the Messiah (an interpretation that sees the slaughter at Bethlehem as a sign of the latter). More believable is the observation (Gundry, *Use of the Old Testament*, 210; Tasker) that Jeremiah 31:15 occurs in a setting of hope. Despite the tears, God says, the exiles will return; and now Matthew, referring to Jeremiah 31:15, likewise says that, despite the tears of the Bethlehem mothers, there is hope because Messiah has escaped Herod and will ultimately reign. The further suggestion that the deep grief in Bethlehem reflected the belief that the Messiah had been massacred and news of his escape should assuage that grief (so Broadus) is fanciful.

There may be a further reason why Matthew quotes this OT passage, a reason discernible once the differences between Matthew and the OT are spelled out. Here Jesus does not, as in v.15, recapitulate an event from Israel's history. The exile sent Israel into captivity and thereby called forth tears. But here the tears are not for him who goes into "exile" but because of the children who stay behind and are slaughtered. Why, then, refer to the exile at all? Help comes from observing the broader context of both Jeremiah and Matthew. Jeremiah 31:9, 20 refer to Israel = Ephraim as God's dear son and also introduce the new covenant (31:31–34) the Lord will make with his people. Therefore the tears associated with exile (31:15) will end. Matthew has already made the exile a turning point in his thought (1:11–12), for at that time the Davidic line was dethroned. The tears of the exile are now being "fulfilled"—i.e., the tears begun in Jeremiah's day are climaxed and ended by the tears of the mothers of Bethlehem. The heir to David's throne has come, the exile is over, the true Son of God has arrived—and he will introduce the new covenant (26:28) promised by Jeremiah.

NOTES

16 "He gave orders to kill" is an excellent rendering of the "graphic participle" in ἀποστείλας ἀνεῖλεν (*aposteilas aneilen*, lit., "having sent, he killed"; cf. Zerwick, *Biblical Greek*, para. 363).

17 Only here and in 27:9 is the fulfillment formula devoid of a ἵνα (*hina*) or a ὅπως (*hopōs*), both of which normally have telic force ("in order that"), though consecutive force is not uncommon in NT Greek (see comments at v.15). This is probably because in these two passages the action that is fulfilling Scripture is so horrible that there is an instinctive reluctance to use phraseology that might be (mis)understood to ascribe enormous wickedness to God (cf. Broadus).

18 The longer reading, reflected in the KJV ("lamentation and weeping and great mourning"), is most likely an assimilation to some LXX witnesses.

F. The Return to Nazareth (2:19–23)

19 After Herod died, an angel of the Lord appeared in a dream to Joseph in Egypt 20 and
said, "Get up, take the child and his mother and go to the land of Israel, for those who were
trying to take the child's life are dead."
21 So he got up, took the child and his mother and went to the land of Israel. 22 But when
he heard that Archelaus was reigning in Judea in place of his father Herod, he was afraid
to go there. Having been warned in a dream, he withdrew to the district of Galilee, 23 and
he went and lived in a town called Nazareth. So was fulfilled what was said through the
prophets: "He will be called a Nazarene."

COMMENTARY

19–21 This fourth dream and third mention of the angel of the Lord continues the divine initiative in preserving and guiding the child, who is again made prominent ("the child and his mother," v.20). On the date of Herod's death, see comments at 2:1. (Josephus, *Ant.* 17.168–69 [6.5], gives a shocking account of Herod's final illness.) The plural ("those who were trying to take the child's life") may owe something to Exodus 4:19 (so Hill, following Davies, *Setting*). If so, Jesus is being compared with Moses. But that motif is weak in Matthew 1–2, and the plural may be accounted for in other ways. H. A. W. Meyer suggests that Herod's father, Antipater, who died a few days before him, may have been associated with Herod in the massacre. More probably, the plural is a generalizing or categorical plural (cf. Turner, *Syntax*, 25–26; BDF, para. 141). "Land of Israel" occurs only in vv.20–21 (cf. "cities of Israel," 10:23). Although the whole land was before him and he apparently hoped to settle in Judea (perhaps in Bethlehem, the city of David), Joseph was forced to retire to despised Galilee.

22 Probably Joseph had expected Herod Antipas to reign over the entire kingdom, but Herod the Great made a late change in his will, dividing his kingdom into three parts. Archelaus, known for his ruthlessness, was given Judea, Samaria, and Idumea (see map on p. 125). Augustus Caesar agreed and gave him the title "ethnarch" (more honorable than "tetrarch") and promised the title "king" if it was earned. But Archelaus proved to be a poor ruler and was banished for misgovernment in AD 6. Rome ruled the south through a procurator. But by that time, Joseph had settled the family in Galilee. Herod Antipas, who reappears in 14:1–10, was given the title "tetrarch" and ruled in Galilee and in Perea. Herod Philip (not to be confused with Herodias's first husband, who was not a king) became tetrarch of Iturea, Trachonitis, and some other territories. He was the best of Herod the Great's children. Jesus frequently retired into his territory (14:13; 15:29; 16:13), away from the weak but cruel Antipas. Joseph, guided by the fifth and final dream, settled the family in Galilee.

23 The town Joseph chose was Nazareth, which, according to Luke 1:26–27; 2:39, was his former home and that of Mary (cf. 13:53–58). This final quotation formula, like that of v.15, should probably be construed as telic: this took place "in order to fulfill." But the formula is unique in two respects: only here does Matthew use the plural "prophets," and only here does he omit the Greek equivalent of "saying" and replace it with the conjunction *hoti*, which can introduce a direct quotation (NIV) but more probably should be rendered "that," making the quotation indirect: "in order to fulfill what was said through the prophets, that he would be called a Nazarene" (cf. W. Barnes Tatum Jr., "Matthew 2:23," *BT* 27 [1976]: 135–37). This suggests that Matthew had no specific OT quotation in mind; indeed, these words are found nowhere in the OT.

The interpretation of this verse has such a long history (for older works, cf. Broadus; for recent studies, cf. Gundry, *Use of the Old Testament*, 97–104; Brown, *Birth of the Messiah*, 207–13) that it is not possible to list here all the major options. We may exclude those that see some wordplay connection with an OT Hebrew word but have no obvious connection with Nazareth. This eliminates the popular interpretation that makes Jesus a Nazirite or second Samson (cf. esp. Jdg 13:5, 7; 16:17, where LXX has *Naziraios* as opposed to Matthew's *Nazōraios*; cf. Lk 1:15). Defenders include Calvin, Loisy, Schweizer, and Ernst Zuckschwerdt ("*Nazōraios* in Matth. 2:23," *TZ* 31 [1975]: 65–77). Also to be eliminated are interpretations that try to find in Matthew's term a reference to some kind of pre-Christian sect. The evidence for this is feeble (cf. Soares-Prabhu, *Formula Quotations*, 197–201) and the connection with Nazareth merely verbal. E. Earle Ellis ("How the New Testament Uses the Old," in *New Testament Interpretation* [ed. Marshall], 202) sees a pun here as an "implicit midrash," but significantly he then has to put the word "fulfillment" in quotation marks.

Matthew certainly used *Nazōraios* as an adjectival form of *apo Nazaret* ("from Nazareth" or "Nazarene"), even though the more acceptable adjective is *Nazarēnos* (cf. Bonnard; Albright and Mann; Soares-Prabhu). Possibly *Nazōraios* derives from a Galilean Aramaic form. Nazareth was a despised place (Jn 7:42, 52), even to other Galileans (cf. Jn 1:46). Here Jesus grew up, not as "Jesus the Bethlehemite," with its Davidic overtones, but as "Jesus the Nazarene," with all the opprobrium of the sneer. When Christians were referred to in Acts as the "Nazarene sect" (24:5), the expression was meant to hurt. First-century Christian readers of Matthew, who had tasted their share of scorn, would have quickly caught Matthew's point. He is not saying that a particular OT prophet foretold that the Messiah would live in Nazareth; he is saying that the OT prophets foretold that the Messiah would be despised (cf. Pss 22:6–8, 13; 69:8, 20–21; Isa 11:1; 49:7; 53:2–3, 8; Da 9:26). The theme is repeatedly picked up by Matthew (e.g., 8:20; 11:16–19;

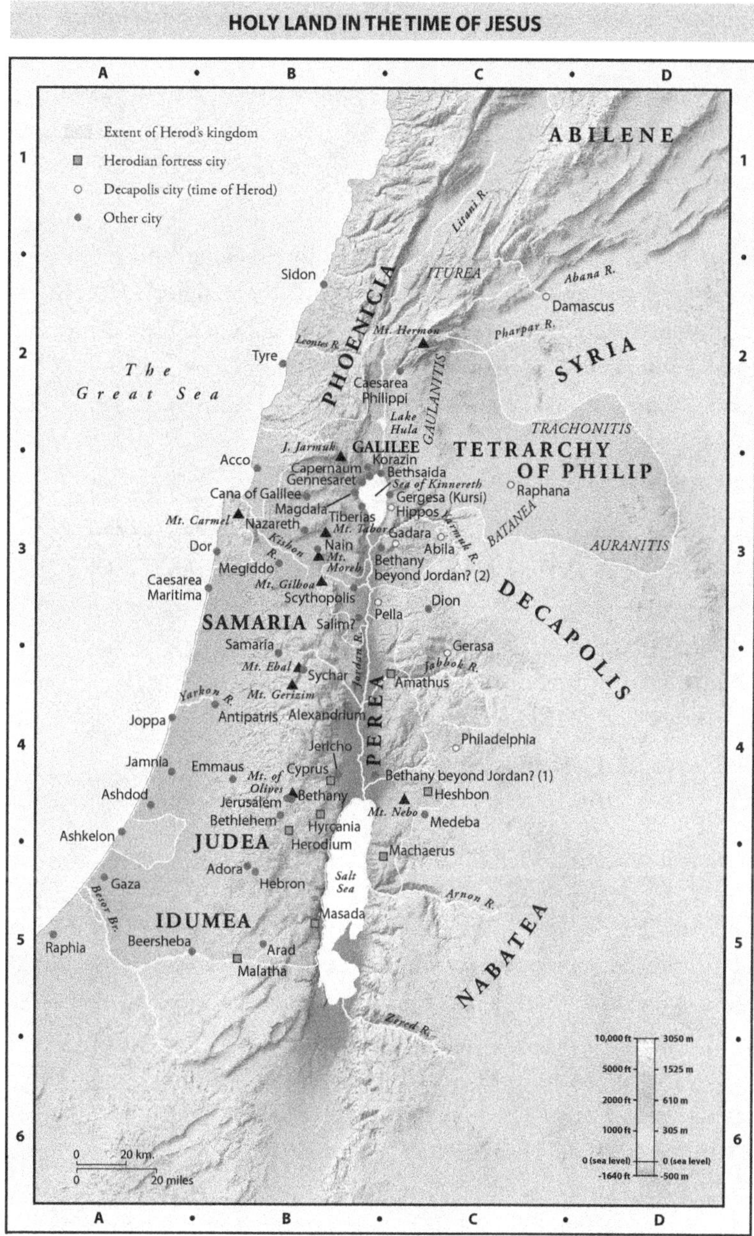

HOLY LAND IN THE TIME OF JESUS

15:7–8; see Turner). In other words Matthew gives us the substance of several OT passages, not a direct quotation (so also Ezr 9:10–12; cf. Str-B, 1:92–93).

It is possible that at the same time there is a discreet allusion to the *nēṣer* ("branch") of Isaiah 11:1, which received a messianic interpretation in the Targums, rabbinic literature, and Dead Sea Scrolls (cf. Gundry, *Use of the Old Testament*, 104), for here, too, it is affirmed that David's son would emerge from humble obscurity and low state. Jesus is King Messiah, Son of God, Son of David; but he was a branch from a royal line hacked down to a stump and reared in surroundings guaranteed to win him scorn. Jesus the Messiah, Matthew is telling us, did not introduce his kingdom with outward show or present himself with the pomp of an earthly monarch. In accord with prophecy, he came as the despised Servant of the Lord.

NOTES

20 The participle of οἱ ζητοῦντες (*hoi zētountes*, lit., "those seeking"; NIV, "those who were trying"), quite apart from its being plural, does not, though a present tense, signify antecedent action but rather continued, persistent action; the context determines that temporally it is virtually an imperfect (cf. Turner, *Syntax*, 80–81; Moule, *Idiom Book*, 206; rightly, NIV).

22 It is uncertain whether the verb χρηματίζω (*chrēmatizō*, "warn," GK *5976*) includes the specification of Nazareth as Joseph's proper destination, or whether he was merely "warned" not to remain in Judea, leaving to him the choice of town.

II. THE GOSPEL OF THE KINGDOM (3:1–7:29)

A. Narrative (3:1–4:25)

1. Foundational steps (3:1–4:11)

a. The ministry of John the Baptist (3:1–12)

OVERVIEW

For the first time, Matthew parallels Mark (Mk 1:1–11), Luke (Lk 3:1–22), and, more loosely, John (Jn 1:19–34). Whatever diversity there is among prologues, the four gospels unanimously preface the ministry of Jesus with that of John the Baptist. Matthew omits any mention of Jesus' youth (Lk 2:41–52) or of John's birth and background (Lk 1:5–25, 39–45, 57–80). This may imply that Matthew's readers were already familiar with that background (so Tasker) or that Matthew wants to plunge dramatically into his account. After four hundred silent years, God was speaking through a new prophet, who called people to repentance and promised someone greater to come.

In addition to the implications of this commentary's outline of Matthew, the gospel has many substructures pointing to a writer of great literary skill. Gooding ("Structure littéraire," 234) points out interesting parallels between chs. 1–2 and 3–4, too lengthy to be detailed here.

1In those days John the Baptist came, preaching in the Desert of Judea 2and saying,
"Repent, for the kingdom of heaven is near." 3This is he who was spoken of through the
prophet Isaiah:

"A voice of one calling in the desert,
'Prepare the way for the Lord,
make straight paths for him.'"

4John's clothes were made of camel's hair, and he had a leather belt around his waist.
His food was locusts and wild honey. 5People went out to him from Jerusalem and all
Judea and the whole region of the Jordan. 6Confessing their sins, they were baptized by
him in the Jordan River.

7But when he saw many of the Pharisees and Sadducees coming to where he was
baptizing, he said to them: "You brood of vipers! Who warned you to flee from the coming
wrath? 8Produce fruit in keeping with repentance. 9And do not think you can say to yourselves, 'We have Abraham as our father.' I tell you that out of these stones God can raise up
children for Abraham. 10The ax is already at the root of the trees, and every tree that does
not produce good fruit will be cut down and thrown into the fire.

11"I baptize you with water for repentance. But after me will come one who is more
powerful than I, whose sandals I am not fit to carry. He will baptize you with the Holy Spirit
and with fire. 12His winnowing fork is in his hand, and he will clear his threshing floor,
gathering his wheat into the barn and burning up the chaff with unquenchable fire."

COMMENTARY

1 Matthew's temporal note, "In those days," is vague and reflects a similarly loose expression in the OT (e.g., Ge 38:1; Ex 2:11, 23; Isa 38:1). His phrase may mean "in those crucial days" (Hill) or even "in the days in which Jesus and his family lived at Nazareth" (Broadus; cf. 4:13). More likely, however, it is a general term that reveals little chronologically but insists that the account is historical (Bonnard). Luke 3:1 offers more chronological help, but its significance is disputed (cf. Hoehner, *Chronological Aspects*, 29–44). The year was AD 27, 28, or 29 (less likely 26).

"John," or "Johanan," had been a popular name among the Jews from the time of John Hyrcanus (d. 106 BC). Four or five "Johns" are mentioned in the NT. The John in Matthew 3:1 was soon designated "the Baptist" (see Notes) because baptism was so prominent in his ministry. He began his preaching in the "Desert of Judea," a vaguely defined area including the lower Jordan Valley north of the Dead Sea and the country immediately west of the Dead Sea. It is hot and, apart from the Jordan itself, largely arid, though not unpopulated. It was used for pasturage (Ps 65:12; Joel 2:22; Lk 15:4) and had Essene communities. "Desert" had long had prophetic overtones (the Law was given in the "wilderness"). The Zealots used the desert as a hiding place (cf. Mt 24:26; Ac 21:38; see Josephus, *Ant.* 20.97–98 [5.1]). Therefore some commentators see more theological than geographical force in Matthew 3:1 (e.g., Bonnard, Maier). The modifying phrase "of Judea" makes the antithesis between geography and theology false. The desert was a particular area (cf. R. Funk, "The Wilderness," *JBL* 78 [1959]: 205–14) but may also have had prophetic implications for first-century readers.

2 John's preaching had two elements. The first was a call to repent. Though the verb *metanoeō* (GK *3566*) is often explained etymologically as "to change one's mind," or popularly as "to be sorry for something," neither rendering is adequate. In classical Greek, the verb could refer to a purely intellectual change of mind. But the NT usage has been influenced by the Hebrew verbs *nāḥam* ("to be sorry for one's actions," GK 5714) and *šûb* ("to turn around to new actions," GK 8740). The latter is common in the prophets' call to the people to return to the covenant with Yahweh (cf. *NIDNTT* 1:357–59; Turner, *Christian Words*, 374–77). What is meant is not a merely intellectual change of mind or mere grief, still less doing penance (see Notes), but a radical transformation of the entire person, a fundamental turnaround involving mind and action and including overtones of grief, which results in "fruit in keeping with repentance" (v.8). Of course, all this assumes that human actions are fundamentally off course and need radical change. John applies this repentance to the religious leaders of his day (3:7–8) with particular vehemence. (On the differences between biblical and rabbinic emphases on repentance, see Lane, *Mark*, 593–600.)

The second element in John's preaching was the nearness of the kingdom of heaven, and this is given as the ground for repentance. Throughout the OT, there was a rising expectation of a divine visitation that would establish justice, crush opposition, and renew the very universe. This hope was couched in many categories. It was presented as the fulfillment of promises to David's heir, as the Day of the Lord (which often had dark overtones of judgment, though there were bright exceptions, e.g., Zep 3:14–20), as a new heaven and a new earth, and as a time of regathering Israel, as the inauguration of a new and transforming covenant (2Sa 7:13–14; Isa 1:24–28; 9:6–7; 11:1–10; 64–66; Jer 23:5–6; 31:31–34; Eze 37:24; Da 2:44; 7:13–14; cf. Ridderbos, *Coming of the Kingdom*, 3–15; Ladd, *Presence of the Future*, 45–75).

The predominant meaning of "kingdom" in the OT (Heb. *malkût*, GK 4895; Aram. *malkûta*, see GK 10424) is "reign"; the term has dynamic force. Similarly in the NT, though *basileia* ("kingdom," GK *993*) can refer to a territory (4:8), the overwhelming majority of instances use the term with dynamic force. This stands over against the prevailing rabbinic terminology, in which "kingdom" was increasingly spiritualized or planted in men's hearts (e.g., *b. Ber.* 4a). In the first century, there was little agreement among Jews as to what the messianic kingdom would be like (cf. Joseph A. Fitzmyer, *The One Who Is to Come* (Grand Rapids: Eerdmans, 2007]). One popular assumption was that the Roman yoke would be shattered and there would be political peace and mounting prosperity. For excellent surveys of this history of interpretation of "kingdom of God/heaven" from the OT documents through to Matthew, see Christian Grappe, *Le Royaume de Dieu: Avant, avec et après Jésus* (Geneva: Labor et Fides, 2001); Rick Brown, "A Brief History of Interpretations of 'The Kingdom of God' and Some Consequences for Translation," *Notes* 15 (2001): 3–23; Hannan, *Nature and Demands*.

Except at 12:28; 19:24; 21:31, 43, and in some MSS of 6:33, Matthew always uses "kingdom of heaven" instead of "kingdom of God" (this reckoning excludes references to "my kingdom" and the like), whereas Mark and Luke prefer "kingdom of God." Matthew's preferred expression certainly does not restrict God's reign to the heavens. The biblical goal is the manifest exercise of God's sovereignty, his "reign" on earth and among men. There are enough parallels among the Synoptics to imply that "kingdom of God" and "kingdom of heaven" denote the same thing (e.g., Mt 19:23–24 = Mk 10:23–25); the connotative distinction is less certain.

Classic dispensationalists (e.g., A. C. Gaebelein, John Walvoord) hold that "kingdom of God" is a distinctively spiritual kingdom, a narrower category embracing only true believers, whereas "kingdom of heaven" is the kingdom of millennial splendor, a broader category including (as in the parable, 13:47–50) both good and bad fish. The distinction is unfortunate. It comes perilously close to confusing kingdom and church (see comments at 16:17–19), fails to account for passages where the Matthean category is no less restrictive than "kingdom of God" in the other evangelists, and fundamentally misapprehends the dynamic nature of the kingdom. Equally unconvincing is the suggestion of Margaret Pamment ("Kingdom of Heaven") that "kingdom of heaven" always refers to the future reign following the consummation, whereas in Matthew "kingdom of God" refers to the present manifestation. To arrive at this absolute dichotomy, Pamment must resort to very unlikely interpretations of numerous passages (e.g., 11:12; parables in ch. 13). Many other proposals are stated firmly but cannot withstand close scrutiny.

The most common explanation is that Matthew avoided "kingdom of God" to remove unnecessary offense to Jews who often used circumlocutions like "heaven" to refer to God (e.g., Da 4:26; 1 Macc 3:50, 60; 4:55; Lk 15:18, 21). The suggestion cannot be ruled out entirely but cannot be given much weight in the light of the fact that Matthew is often happy to refer to "God" directly.

Matthew is a subtle and allusive writer, and other factors appear to be involved: (1) "Kingdom of heaven" may anticipate the extent of Christ's postresurrection authority. God's sovereignty *in heaven* and on earth is now mediated through him (Mt 28:18). (2) "Kingdom of God" makes God the King, and though this does not prevent the other Synoptics from ascribing the kingship to Jesus (cf. Lk 22:16, 18, 29–30), there is less room to maneuver. Matthew's "kingdom of heaven" assumes it is God's kingdom and occasionally assigns it specifically to the Father (Mt 26:29), though leaving room to ascribe it frequently to Jesus (16:28; 25:31, 34, 40; 27:42; probably 5:35); for Jesus is King Messiah. This inevitably has christological implications. The kingdom of heaven is simultaneously the kingdom of the Father and the kingdom of the Son of Man. (3) Jonathan Pennington (*Heaven and Earth*) has shown that Matthew contrasts "heaven" and "earth" as two spheres, two kingdoms—one that embraces all that is God-centered and good, the other all that is in rebellion and characterized by corruption. By preferring "kingdom of heaven" to "kingdom of God," Matthew is sustaining this powerful antithesis and drawing attention to the quality of the kingdom that both the Baptist and Jesus announce.

This kingdom, John preached, "is near" (*ēngiken*, lit., "has drawn near," GK *1581*). Jews spoke of the Messiah as "the coming one" (11:3) and the messianic age as "the coming age" (Heb 6:5): John says it has now drawn "near," the same message preached by Jesus (Mt 4:17) and his disciples (10:7). It is possible, but not certain, that the verb has the same force as *ephthasen* (GK *5777*) in 12:28. There Jesus unambiguously affirms that the kingdom "has come." That passage makes it clear that it is the exercise of God's saving sovereignty or reign that has dawned. The ambiguous "is near" (3:2; 4:17), coupled with the dynamic sense of "kingdom," prepares us for a constant theme: The kingdom came with Jesus and his preaching and miracles, it came with his death and resurrection, and it will come at the end of the age.

Matthew has already established that Jesus was born King (2:2). Later Jesus declared that his work testified the kingdom had come (12:28), even though he frequently spoke of the kingdom as something to be inherited when the Son of Man comes in his glory. It is false to say that "kingdom" undergoes a radical shift with the mention of mystery (NIV, "secrets"; see comments at 13:11). Already in the Sermon on the Mount, entering the kingdom (5:3, 10; 7:21) is equivalent to entering into life (7:13–14; cf. 19:14, 16; see Mk 9:45, 47).

These and related themes become clearer as Matthew's gospel progresses (cf. Ladd, *Theology of the New Testament*, 57–90). But two observations cannot be delayed. First, the Baptist's terminology, though veiled, necessarily roused enormous excitement (v.5). But assorted apocalyptic and political expectations would have brought about a profound misunderstanding of the kingdom being preached. Therefore Jesus himself purposely used veiled terminology when treating themes like this. This becomes increasingly obvious in Matthew. The second observation relates to the first. Just as the angel's announcement to Joseph declared Jesus' primary purpose to be to save his people from their sins (1:21), so the first announcement of the kingdom is associated with repentance and confession of sin (v.6). These themes are constantly intertwined in Matthew (cf. Goppelt, *Theologie des Neuen Testaments*, 128–88).

3 If the *gar* ("for") has its full force, then the NIV should read, "For this is he"; and v.3 becomes the ground for the Baptist's preaching in v.2. This is the one OT citation of Matthew's own eleven direct OT quotations that is not introduced by a fulfillment formula (see Introduction, section 11.b). It goes too far, however (contra Gundry), to say that the omission of fulfillment language means that for Matthew, John the Baptist does not fulfill Scripture but serves merely as a "prototypical Christian preacher." If Matthew had wanted to say so little, he would have been better off eliminating the OT passage. Instead, he introduces it with a pesher formula (e.g., Ac 2:16; see Introduction, section 11.b) that can only be understood as identifying the Baptist in an eschatological, prophecy-and-fulfillment framework with the one of whom Isaiah (Isa 40:3) spoke.

The Baptist's role is minimally exemplary. According to John 1:23, the Baptist once applied this passage to himself. Here Matthew does it for him. In the MT, the words "in the desert" modify "prepare": "In the desert prepare the way of the LORD." But all three Synoptics here follow the LXX. The immediate effect is to locate in the desert the one who is calling. Some have thought this a deliberate attempt to make the fulfillment extend to geographical details. But Mark consistently follows the LXX, and Matthew often follows Mark. So we must not read too much into the change. There may be an error in the Hebrew accents, which associate "in the desert" with "prepare" (Gundry, *Use of the Old Testament*, 10). In any case, if one shouts a command in the desert, his intent is that it be spread everywhere; so there is little difference in meaning (Alexander).

In Isaiah 40:3, the way of Yahweh is being "made straight" (a metaphor using road building to refer to repentance); in Matthew 3:3 it is the way of Jesus. This sort of identification of Jesus with Yahweh is common in the NT (e.g., Ex 13:21 and 1Co 10:1; Ex 17:6 and 1Co 10:4; Isa 6:1 and Jn 12:41; Ps 68:18 and Eph 4:8; Ps 102:25–27 and Heb 1:10–12) and confirms the kingdom as being equally the kingdom of God and the kingdom of Jesus. While the deity of Christ is only implicit in such texts, it certainly goes beyond Jesus' being merely a royal envoy. The Qumran covenanters cited the same passage to foster study of the law in preparation for the eschaton (1QS 8:12ff.; 9:19; cf. Fitzmyer, *Essays on the Semitic Background*, 34–36); but Matthew identifies the Baptist as the voice and the eschatological age as already dawning in Jesus' coming.

4–5 Clothes of camel's hair and a leather belt (the latter to bind up the loose outer garment) not only were the clothes of poor people, but they establish links with Elijah (2Ki 1:8; cf. Mal 4:5).

"Locusts" (*akrides*) are large grasshoppers, still eaten in the East, not the fruit of the "locust tree" (cf. BDAG, 39). Wild honey is what it purports to be, not gum from a tree (cf. Jdg 14:8–9; 1Sa 14:25–29; Ps 81:16). Both suggest a poor man used to wilderness living, and this suggests a connection with the prophets (cf. Mt 3:1; 11:8–9)—so much so that in Zechariah's day (13:4) some false prophets dressed like prophets to deceive people. Both Elijah and John had stern ministries in which austere garb and diet confirmed their message and condemned the idolatry of physical and spiritual softness. "Even the food and dress of John preached" (Bengel, *Gnomon*). See James Kelhoffer, *The Diet of John the Baptist: 'Locusts and Wild Honey' in Synoptic and Patristic Interpretation* (Tübingen: Mohr, 2005). John's impact was enormous (v.5), and his crowds came from a wide area. In Greek, the places are personified (as in 2:3).

6 Confession of sin was commanded in the law, not only as part of a priest's duties (Lev 16:21), but as an individual responsibility for wrongs done (Lev 5:5; 26:40; Nu 5:6–7; Pr 28:13). In Israel's better days, this was carried out (Ne 9:2–3; Ps 32:5). In the NT (cf. Ac 19:18; 1Jn 1:9), confession is scarcely less important. Because Matthew does not include "for the forgiveness of sins" (Mk 1:4), some have deduced that he wants to avoid suggesting any possibility of forgiveness until Jesus' death (Mt 26:28). This is too subtle. A first-century reader would hardly hold that sins were not forgiven after being honestly confessed. And since Matthew regularly abbreviates Mark where he uses him, we must be cautious in drawing theological conclusions from such omissions.

The Greek does not make clear whether the confession was individual or corporate, simultaneous with baptism or antecedent to it. Josephus (*Ant.* 18.116–17 [5.2]) says that John, "surnamed the Baptist," required righteous conduct as a "necessary preliminary if baptism was to be acceptable to God." Since John was urging people to prepare for the Messiah's coming by repenting and being baptized, we may surmise that open renunciation of sin was a precondition of his baptism, which was, therefore, both a confirmation of confession and an eschatological sign.

Since the discovery of the Dead Sea Scrolls, many have tried to link John's baptism with that of the Qumran covenanters. But their washings, though related to confession, were probably regarded as purifying and were repeated (cf. 1QS 1:24ff.; 5:13–25) to remove ritual uncleanness. John's baptism, probably a once-only rite (contra Albright and Mann), was unrelated to ceremonial impurity. The rabbis used baptism to induct proselytes but never Jews (Str-B, 1:102–12). It is best to read John's baptism against the complex background of OT rituals, Jewish proselyte baptism, and the washing practices of sectarians like those at Qumran rather than against the background of a specific group (so, rightly, Turner). As far as we know, though baptism itself was not uncommon, the pointed but limited associations placed on John's baptism stem from the Baptist himself—not unlike circumcision, which predates Abraham but lacked covenantal significance before his time.

The Jordan River is fast flowing. No doubt John stationed himself at one of the fords and prepared the way for the Lord.

7 Many have raised the question of the probability of individuals from groups so mutually hostile as Pharisees and Sadducees (see Introduction, section 11.f) presenting themselves together (one article governs both nouns) for baptism. But the Greek text need not be taken to mean they came to be baptized. It may only mean they were "coming to where John was baptizing" (see Notes). If so, it might suggest that representatives of the Sanhedrin (composed of both parties with elders) came to examine what he was doing (cf. Jn 1:19, 24, which mentions not only priests and Levites

[Sadducees] but also Pharisees). Or many Pharisees and Sadducees may have come for baptism with the ostentation that characterized their other religious activities (e.g., Mt 6:2, 5, 16)—i.e., they were showing the world how ready they were for Messiah, though they had not truly repented. Matthew lumps them together because they were leaders; elsewhere he distinguishes them (22:34).

The question with which the Baptist confronted them has this sense: "Who suggested to you that you would escape the coming wrath?" Thus John's rhetorical question takes on a sarcastic nuance: "Who warned you to flee the coming wrath and come for baptism—when, in fact, you show no signs of repentance?" Though the question is the same in Luke 3:7, there Luke relates it to the crowd, whereas Matthew relates it to the Jewish leaders.

John the Baptist stands squarely in the prophetic tradition—a tradition in which the Day of the Lord points much more to darkness than to light for those who think they have no sin (Am 2:4–8; 6:1–7). "You brood of vipers!" also belongs to the prophetic tradition (cf. Isa 14:29; 30:6; cf. CD 19:22); in Mt 12:34, Jesus uses these terms to excoriate the Pharisees.

8–9 The coming of God's reign either demands repentance (v.2) or brings judgment. Repentance must be genuine. If we wish to escape the coming wrath (v.7), then our entire lifestyle must be in harmony with our oral repentance (v.8). Mere descent from Abraham is not enough (v.9). In the OT, God repeatedly cut off many Israelites and saved a remnant. Yet in the intertestamental period, the general use of descent from Abraham, in the context of a rising merit theology, supported the notion that Israel was chosen because it was choice and that the merits of the patriarchs would suffice for their descendants (cf. Carson, *Divine Sovereignty*, 39ff.). But not only may God narrow Israel down to a remnant; he may also raise up authentic children of Israel from "these stones" (perhaps stones lying in the riverbed—both Hebrew and Aramaic have a pun on "children" and "stones"). Ordinary stones will suffice; there is no need for the "rocks" of the patriarchs and their merits (cf. S. Schechter, *Some Aspects of Rabbinic Theology* [London: A. & C. Black, 1903], 173; see Ro 4). This and the not dissimilar thought in Matthew 8:11–12 prepare the way for Paul's repeated emphasis on the fact that the true "sons of Abraham" are those who share Abraham's faith, not necessarily his genes (Ro 4; Gal 3). Matthew 3:9 not only rebukes the self-righteousness of the leaders but implies that participation in the kingdom results from grace and extends the borders of God's people beyond racial frontiers (cf. 8:11).

10 The ax is "already" (emphatic) at the root of the trees (for the idiom, see Isa 10:33–34; Jer 46:22). "Not only is there a coming messianic wrath, but already there is a beginning messianic discrimination among the descendants of Abraham" (Broadus). Just as the kingdom is dawning already (v.2), so also is the judgment; the two are inseparable. To preach the kingdom is to preach repentance; any tree (not "every tree," NIV; cf. Turner, *Syntax*, 199), regardless of its roots, that does not bring forth good fruit will be destroyed.

11 Compare vv.11–12 with Luke 3:15–18 (Q?). Because only Matthew says, "I baptize you with *water for repentance*" (emphasis mine), Hill detects a conscious effort to subordinate John to Jesus. John baptizes as preparation "for repentance"; Jesus baptizes for fulfillment "with the Holy Spirit and fire." But both Mark (1:4) and Luke (3:3) have spoken of John's baptism as one of repentance. And when Jesus begins to preach, he too demands repentance (Mt 4:17). If there is an antithesis here between John and Jesus, it is in all three Synoptic Gospels. Matthew may be stressing the difference between the baptisms of John and Jesus in order to make a point about eschatology (see below and comments at 11:7–13).

The phrase "for repentance" (*eis metanoian*) is difficult. *Eis* plus the accusative frequently suggests purpose ("I baptize you in order that you will repent"). Contextually (v.6), this is unlikely, even in the peculiar telic sense suggested by Broadus: "I baptize you with a view to continued repentance." But causal *eis*, or something very close to it, is not unknown in the NT (cf. Turner, *Syntax*, 266–67): "I baptize you because of your repentance." The force may, however, be weaker—i.e., "I baptize you with reference to or in connection with repentance" (so Blomberg [NAC]; Murray Harris, *NIDNTT* 3:1208–9). In any case, John wants to contrast his baptism with that of the one who comes after him (any allusion here to the messianic title "the one who comes" is doubtful; cf. Arens, Ἦλθον-*sayings*, 288–90). That one is "more powerful" than John: the same term (*ischyros*, GK *2708*) is applied to God in the OT (LXX Jer 32:18; Da 9:4; cf. also Isa 40:10), and the cognate noun to the Messiah in *Psalms of Solomon* 17. This is not the normal order. Usually the one who follows is the disciple, the lesser one (cf. 16:24; Jn 13:16; 15:20). But because John's particular ministry is to announce the eschatological figure, he cannot do other than precede him.

Though John was the most sought-after preacher in Israel to appear in centuries, he protested that he was not fit to "carry" (Mark and Luke have "untie") the sandals of the Coming One. Many scholars have argued that this saying must be a late invention of Christians determined to keep the Baptist in his place and exalt Jesus. In fact, such humility as John's is in Christian ethics a virtue, not a weakness. Moreover, if he saw his role as that of forerunner to the Messiah, John could not well have set himself on a par with the one to whom he pointed (cf. Jn 3:28–31). No doubt the church readily used John's self-depreciation in later conflicts with his followers. But there is no evidence they invented it.

It follows that just as John's purpose was to prepare a way for the Lord by calling people to repentance, so his baptism pointed to the one who would bring the eschatological baptism in spirit and fire. John's baptism was "essentially preparatory" (cf. J. D. G. Dunn, *Baptism in the Holy Spirit* [London: SCM Press, 1970], 14–17; Bonnard); Jesus' baptism inaugurated the messianic age.

"Baptism in the Holy Spirit" is not a specialized term in the NT. Its OT background includes Ezekiel 36:25–27; 39:29; Joel 2:28. We need not think that John the Baptist could not have mentioned the Holy Spirit, not least because of somewhat similar references in the literature at Qumran (1QS 3:7–9; 4:21; 1QH 16:12; cf. Dunn, *Baptism in the Holy Spirit*, 8–10). But Matthew and Luke add "and fire." Many see this as a double baptism, one in the Holy Spirit for the righteous and one in fire for the unrepentant (cf. the wheat and chaff in Mt 3:12). Fire (Mal 4:1) destroys and consumes.

There are good reasons, however, for taking "fire" as a purifying agent along with the Holy Spirit. The people John is addressing are being baptized by him; presumably they have repented. More important, the preposition *en* ("with") is not repeated before fire. The one preposition governs both "Holy Spirit" and "fire," and this normally suggests a unified concept, Spirit-fire or the like (see *NIDNTT*, 3:1178; Dunn, *Baptism in the Holy Spirit*, 10–13). Fire often has a purifying, not destructive, connotation in the OT (e.g., Isa 1:25; Zec 13:9; Mal 3:2–3). John's water baptism relates to repentance, but the one whose way he is preparing will administer a Spirit-fire baptism that will purify and refine. In a time when many Jews felt the Holy Spirit had been withdrawn until the messianic age, this announcement could only have been greeted with excited anticipation.

12 Messiah's coming will separate grain from chaff. A winnowing fork tossed both into the air.

The wind blew the chaff away, and the heavier grain fell to be gathered up from the ground. The scattered chaff was swept up and burned and the threshing floor cleared (cf. Ps 1:4; Isa 5:24; Da 2:35; Hos 13:3). The "unquenchable fire" signifies eschatological judgment (cf. Isa 34:10; 66:24; Jer 7:20)—hell (cf. 5:29). "Unquenchable fire" is not just metaphor. Fearful reality underlies Messiah's separation of grain from chaff. The "nearness" of the kingdom therefore calls for repentance (v.2).

NOTES

1 Matthew has ὁ βαπτιστής (*ho baptistēs*, "the baptist"); Mark (1:4) uses the participle [ὁ] βαπτίζων ([*ho*] *baptizōn*, lit., "the baptizer"). It is doubtful whether any distinction is intended, since "Baptist" has no sectarian or denominational flavor. It is too much to say with Gundry that Matthew consistently uses "the Baptist" instead of "the baptizer" to divert attention from John's practice of baptism to his role as preacher, for the latter is not stressed, and Matthew includes the specific statement of 3:6, "they were baptized by" John.

"Preaching" (verb κηρύσσω [*kēryssō*, GK *3062*], noun κήρυγμα [*kērygma*, GK *3060*]) has often been distinguished from "teaching" (διδαχή [*didachē*, GK *1439*]) in such a way that the so-called kerygmatic elements were often robbed of content, and virtually everything in the NT was confidently assigned to one category or the other. Studies over the past few decades have demonstrated how grossly oversimplified such an antithesis is (cf. J. I. H. McDonald, *Kerygma and Didache* [Cambridge: Cambridge Univ. Press, 1980]) and have suggested other equally important and sometimes overlapping categories (e.g., A.A. Trites, *The New Testament Concept of Witness* [Cambridge: Cambridge Univ. Press, 1977]).

2 The verb μετανοέω (*metanoeō*, "repent," GK *3567*) was rendered in Latin *poenitentiam agere* ("exercise penitence"), the word "penitence" suggesting grief, distress, pain, but not necessarily change. Eventually, *poenitentiam agite* ("do penitence") became preferred, and the contraction to "do penance" completed the slide to a pernicious concept quite alien to the NT.

7 The expression ἐπὶ τὸ βάπτισμα αὐτοῦ (*epi to baptisma autou*) is peculiar (lit., coming "to his baptism"); it could either mean "coming to be baptized" or "coming to the place where he was baptizing" (so NIV).

10 Moule (*Idiom Book*, 53) sees πρός (*pros*) plus the accusative here as combining linear motion with punctiliar rest on arrival. The ax has taken its first chop, as it were. But it is possible that the verb κεῖται (*keitai*, lit., "lies"; NIV, "is") suggests the ax is merely lying at the root of the tree, ready for action.

b. The baptism of Jesus (3:13–17)

OVERVIEW

Comparing the three synoptic accounts of Jesus' baptism (cf. Mk 1:9–11; Lk 3:21–22) reveals distinctive features (e.g., only Mt has 3:14–15). But it is easy to exaggerate differences. As is often pointed out, Luke does not say John baptized Jesus; but in view of Luke 3:1–21, there is no doubt of this. As will be shown, some alleged distinctions among the evangelists are artificial; others highlight valuable theological emphases.

[13]Then Jesus came from Galilee to the Jordan to be baptized by John. [14]But John tried to deter him, saying, "I need to be baptized by you, and do you come to me?"

[15]Jesus replied, "Let it be so now; it is proper for us to do this to fulfill all righteousness." Then John consented.

[16]As soon as Jesus was baptized, he went up out of the water. At that moment heaven was opened, and he saw the Spirit of God descending like a dove and lighting on him. [17]And a voice from heaven said, "This is my Son, whom I love; with him I am well pleased."

COMMENTARY

13 "Then" (*tote*) is vague in Matthew (see comments at 2:7); each use needs separate handling. Here *tote* implies that during the time John the Baptist was preaching to the crowds and baptizing them, "then" Jesus came—i.e., it is equivalent to Luke's "When all the people were being baptized, Jesus was baptized too" (3:21). If so, to say that in Luke baptism is a public testimony to Jesus but a private one in Matthew is artificial. This conclusion is especially important to Kingsbury (*Structure*, 13–15) because he wants to avoid any public recognition of Jesus until 4:17. Jeremias (*New Testament Theology*, 51) thinks Luke is closer to historical reality and supposes that Jesus immersed himself along with others in John's presence. Both refinements are too fine-spun. Any interpretation demanding either privacy or crowds at Jesus' baptism as Matthew or Luke report it reads too much into the texts and probably misses the evangelists' chief points. Jesus came from Galilee (Mark specifies Nazareth) to be baptized by John (Matthew makes this aim explicit; in Mark and Luke it is implicit), and as a result the Father testified to his Son. This much is common to all three accounts, and it matters little whether only John heard this heavenly witness or whether the crowds heard it as well.

14 Matthew 3:14–15 is peculiar to this gospel. John tried to deter Jesus (imperfect of attempted action) from his baptism, insisting (the pronouns are emphatic) that he stood in need of baptism by Jesus. Earlier John had difficulty baptizing the Pharisees and Sadducees because they were not worthy of his baptism. Now he has trouble baptizing Jesus because his baptism is not worthy of Jesus.

There are two possible ways of understanding John's reluctance:

1. John recognizes Jesus as the Messiah and wants to receive Jesus' Spirit-and-fire baptism. Despite the rising popularity of this view, it entails serious difficulties. The Spirit theme is not important in Matthew; righteousness is, and it is central to Jesus' response (v.15). Matthew does not present Jesus as bestowing his Spirit-and-fire baptism on anyone. The cross and resurrection are focal for him; and writing after Pentecost (Ac 2), Matthew doubtless believes Jesus' baptism was bestowed on his people later than the time he is writing about. In view of the Baptist's statements about his relation

to the Messiah (v.11), if he had recognized Jesus as the Messiah it is doubtful whether Jesus' rebuttal would have convinced him (v.15). Moreover, this view brings Matthew into needless conflict with the fourth gospel (Jn 1:31–34), which says the Baptist did not "know" Jesus—i.e., recognize him as the Messiah—until after his baptism.

2. John's baptism did not have purely eschatological significance. It also signified repentance and confession of sin. Whether John knew Jesus well, we do not know. It is, however, inconceivable that his parents had not told him of Mary's visit to Elizabeth some three decades earlier (Lk 1:39–45). At the very least, John must have recognized that Jesus, to whom he was related, whose birth was more marvelous than his own and whose knowledge of Scripture was prodigious even as a child (Lk 2:41–52), outstripped him. John the Baptist was a humble man; conscious of his own sin, he could detect no sin Jesus needed to repent of and confess. So John thought that Jesus should baptize him. Matthew does not tell us when John also perceived that Jesus was the Messiah (though that may be implied by vv.16–17); Matthew focuses on Jesus' sinlessness and the Father's testimony, not on John's testimony (unlike the fourth gospel, where the Baptist's witness to Jesus is very important).

15 John's consent was won because Jesus told him, "It is proper for us to do this to fulfill all righteousness." Here interpretations are legion. They may be summed up as follows:

1. By undergoing baptism, Jesus anticipates his own baptism of death, by which he secures "righteousness" for all. This reads in the Suffering Servant of Isaiah 53:11 ("by his knowledge my righteous servant will justify many"). This view, espoused by many, is well defended by Cullmann (*Baptism in the New Testament*, 15ff.). It presupposes that the significance of Christian baptism should be read back into John's baptism and takes no account of its salvation-historical location. Worse, Cullmann reads Paul's use of "righteousness" back into Matthew, who in fact never uses the term that way but always as meaning "conformity to God's will" or the like (see Przybylski, *Righteousness in Matthew*, 91–94). Moreover, the "us" is not a royal "us"; *both* Jesus *and* John must "fulfill all righteousness," which renders doubtful any theory that ties the righteousness too closely to Jesus' death. Gerhard Barth ("Matthew's Understanding of the Law," 140ff.) rejects Cullmann's view but falls into the same weaknesses, holding that Jesus fulfills all righteousness by humbly entering the ranks of sinners and acting for them. The same objections apply. It is claiming too much, however, to say with Geerhardus Vos (*Biblical Theology* [Grand Rapids: Eerdmans, 1948], 320) that Jesus here "repented for the people vicariously."

2. Others suggest that Jesus must obey ("fulfill") every divine command ("all righteousness"), and baptism is one such command. Put so crassly, this view forgets that the baptism relates to repentance and confession of sins, not to righteousness itself. A slight modification of it says that by being baptized Jesus is acknowledging as valid the righteous life preached by John and demanded of those who accept John's baptism, for Jesus acknowledges (21:32) that John came to show the way of righteousness. But this view forces "fulfill" to become "acknowledge" and neglects the fact that John's baptism relates not to the standards of righteousness John preached but to repentance.

3. The strengths of the alternative views may be integrated in a better synthesis. John's baptism had two foci—repentance and its eschatological significance. Jesus affirms, in effect, that it is God's will ("all righteousness") that John baptize him; and *both* John *and* Jesus "fulfill" that will, that righteousness, by going through with it ("it is proper for us"). The aftermath, as Matthew immediately notes (vv.16–17), shows that this baptism really did point

to Jesus. Within this framework we may recognize other themes. In particular, Jesus is indeed seen as the Suffering Servant (Isa 42:1; see comments at v.17). But the Servant's first mark is obeying God: he "fulfills all righteousness" since he suffers and dies to accomplish redemption in obedience to the will of God. By his baptism, Jesus affirms his determination to do his assigned work. Thus the "now" may be significant. Jesus is saying that John's objection (v.14) is in principle valid. Yet he must "now," at this point in salvation history, baptize Jesus, for at this point Jesus must demonstrate his willingness to take on his servant role, entailing his identification with the people. Contrary to Gundry, "now" does not serve to tell Christian converts they must not delay "this first step on the way of righteousness."

This interpretation assumes that Jesus knew of his Suffering-Servant role from the beginning of his ministry (see comments at v.17). This role was hinted at in 2:23; here it makes its first veiled appearance in Jesus' actions. The immediately following temptation narrative confirms it (4:1–11). There Jesus rejects the devil's temptation to pursue messianic glory and power, choosing instead the servant role of obeying every word that comes from the mouth of God.

16 "As soon as" suggests not only that Jesus left the water immediately after his baptism but that the Spirit's witness was equally prompt. Jesus' baptism and its attestation are of a piece and must be interpreted together. "He saw" most naturally refers to Jesus (cf. Mk 1:10), not John, not so much because Matthew excludes John as because he is not the focus of interest. The presence of John (and possibly others) is probably implied by the third-person address "This is my Son" (v.17), displacing Mark's "You are my Son" (Mk 1:11).

"Heaven ... opened" calls to mind OT visions (e.g., Isa 64:1; Eze 1:1; cf. Ac 7:56; Rev 4:1; 19:11). The simile "the Spirit of God descending like a dove" could mean either that the manner of the Spirit's descent was like a dove's or that the Spirit appeared in a dove's form. Whether or not the latter is visionary, Luke 3:22 specifies it. Because no clear pre-Christian reference links dove and Holy Spirit, some have advanced complex theories: e.g., Mark collected two stories, one mentioning the Holy Spirit's descent and the other the dove's descent, and fused them together (cf. S. Gero, "The Spirit as a Dove at the Baptism of Jesus," *NovT* 18 [1976]: 17–35). But to exclude any new metaphor from the Christian revelation is surely rash. (For a fine discussion of possible dove symbolism, see Davies and Allison.) The Spirit's descent cannot be adequately considered apart from v.17, and so resolution of its meaning awaits comment there.

17 Some see in the "voice from heaven" the *bat-qôl* (lit., "daughter of a voice"), the category used by rabbinic and other writers to refer to divine communication echoing the Spirit of God after the Spirit and the prophets through whom he spoke had been withdrawn. The point, however, is stronger than that. This voice is God's ("from heaven") and testifies that God himself has broken silence and is again revealing himself to human beings—a clear sign of the dawning of the messianic age (cf. 17:5; Jn 12:28). What heaven says in Mark and Luke is "You are my Son"; here it is "This is my Son." The change not only shows Matthew's concern only for the *ipsissima vox* (not generally the *ipsissima verba*; see Notes) but also assumes someone besides Jesus heard heaven's witness. There may have been a crowd; if so, that does not interest Matthew. But John needed to hear the Voice confirm his decision (v.15).

Despite arguments to the contrary (e.g., Hooker, *Jesus and the Servant*, 70ff.), the utterance reflects Isaiah 42:1: "Here is my servant, whom I uphold, my chosen one in whom I delight; I will put my Spirit upon him"; and this has been modified by Psalm 2:7: "You are my Son" (cf. Gundry, *Use of the Old Testament*, 29–32; esp. Moo, *Old Testament in the Gospel Passion Narratives*, 112ff.). The results are extraordinarily important.

1. These words from heaven link Jesus with the Suffering Servant at the very beginning of his ministry and confirm our interpretation of v.15.

2. God here refers to Jesus as "my Son"; implicitly the title "Son of God" is introduced and picked up immediately in the next chapter (4:3, 6). Psalm 2 is Davidic. Though it was not regarded in the first century as messianic, the link with David recalls other "son" passages where David or his heir is seen as God's son (e.g., 2Sa 7:13–14; Ps 89:26–29).

3. Jesus has already been set forth as the true Israel to which actual Israel was pointing and as such God's Son (see comments at 2:15); now the heavenly witness confirms the link.

4. At the same time, the virginal conception suggests a more than titular or functional sonship: in this context there is the hint of an ontological sonship, made most explicit in the gospel of John.

5. These things are linked in the one utterance. At the very beginning of Jesus' public ministry, his Father presented him, in a veiled way, as at once Davidic Messiah, very Son of God, representative of the people, and Suffering Servant. Matthew has already introduced all these themes and will develop them further. Indeed, he definitely cites Isaiah 42:1–4 in Matthew 12:18–21, which ends with the assertion (already made clear) that the nations will trust in this Servant.

"Son of God" has particularly rich associations. Therefore it is hard to nail down its precise force at every occurrence. As it is wrong to see ontological sonship in every use, so is it wrong to exclude it prematurely. (For more adequate discussion, see, in addition to the standard dictionaries, Blair, *Jesus in the Gospel of Matthew*, 60ff.; Cullman, *Christology*, 270–305; Kingsbury, *Structure*, 40–83 [though he exaggerates the importance of the theme in Matthew: cf. Hill, "Son and Servant," 2–16]; Ladd, *Theology of the New Testament*, 159–72; Moule, *Origin of Christology*, 22ff.)

The Spirit's descent in v.16 needs to be understood in the light of v.17. The Spirit is poured out on the servant in Isaiah 42:1, to which v.17 alludes. This outpouring does not change Jesus' status (he was the Son before this) or assign him new rights. Rather it identifies him as the promised Servant and Son and marks the beginning of his public ministry and direct confrontation with Satan (4:1), the dawning of the messianic age (12:28).

NOTES

14 The καί (*kai*, "and") has adversative force—"and yet" (cf. Zerwick, *Biblical Greek*, para. 455; Turner, *Syntax*, 334). This may reflect the beginning of an Aramaic apodosis (Lagrange, xci).

16 If αὐτῷ (*autō*) is the correct reading, the text says the heavens opened "to him," i.e., to Jesus. But this need not mean no one else experienced anything (see comments on "This is" at v.17) but only that, in addition to the more public voice, Jesus alone perceived heaven opening. In the NT period, the preposition ἀπό (*apo*, "out of") cannot always be distinguished in meaning from ἐκ (*ek*), used in Mark 1:10 (cf. Zerwick, *Biblical Greek*, para. 87; Turner, *Syntax*, 259).

17 The Latin *vox* means "voice," and *verba* "words." *Ipsissima*, from the Latin *ipse* ("self"), basically means "all by oneself" or the like. *Ipsissima vox* and *ipsissima verba* in NT study usually refer to "[Jesus'] own voice" and "[Jesus'] own words" respectively. The first implies that Jesus' teaching is accurately preserved but in the evangelist's own words, style, etc., whereas the latter refers to those places where Jesus' actual words are preserved. In the narrowest sense, however, *ipsissima verba*, since Jesus spoke primarily Aramaic, would be restricted to words such as *abba, talitha koum*, etc. Others understand the term to include words of Jesus that are given in precise translation into Greek; but this, too, would be a destructive category to use as the only acceptable reflection of what Jesus taught. In this verse, of course, the words are not those of Jesus but of the Voice from heaven. Even so, Matthew preserves only the general sense, the *ipsissima vox*.

c. The temptation of Jesus (4:1–11)

OVERVIEW

In the past, many scholars took this pericope and its parallel (Lk 4:1–13) as imaginative embellishments of Mark's much briefer account. But J. Dupont ("L'arrière-fond biblique du récit des tentations de Jésus," *NTS* 3 [1956–57]: 287–304) has argued persuasively that Mark's brevity and the ambiguity of such statements as "he was with the wild animals" (Mk 1:13) imply that Mark's readers were familiar with a larger account to which Mark makes brief reference. The account could only have come from Jesus, given to his disciples perhaps after Caesarea Philippi (so Dupont). Therefore it gives an important glimpse into Jesus' self-perception as the Son of God (Mt 3:17; 4:3, 6) and, judging by the Scripture he quotes, the way he perceived his own relation to Israel (cf. France, *Jesus and the Old Testament*, 50–53).

Both Matthew and Mark tie the temptations to Jesus' baptism (see comments at v.1). Luke, however, inserts his genealogy between the two, suggesting a contrast between Adam, who though tested in the bliss of Eden yet fell, and Jesus, who was tested in the hardships of the wilderness yet triumphed. Jesus' responses to Satan (all taken from Dt 6–8; i.e., 6:13, 16; 8:3) have led some to argue that this account is a haggadic midrash—i.e., explanatory but minimally historical stories—on the OT text (cf. esp. Birger Gerhardsson, *The Testing of God's Son (Matt 4:1–11 and par.)* [Lund: Gleerup, 1966]). But the story line stands independent of the OT background. There are more themes allusively hidden in Matthew's account than first meet the eye (e.g., possible "new Moses" motifs: Davies, *Setting*, 45–48; cf. Bonnard; Petr Pokorny, "The Temptation Stories and Their Intention," *NTS* 20 [1974]: 115–27), and the repeated reference to Deuteronomy 6–8 is better explained in terms of Israel-Christ typology.

Luke reverses the order of the last two temptations for topographical reasons. Matthew's order is almost certainly original (cf. Schweizer; Walvoord).

It is difficult to be certain exactly what happened or in what form Satan came to Jesus. Standing on a high mountain (v.8) would not itself provide a glimpse of "all the kingdoms of the world"; some supernatural vision is presupposed. Moreover, a forty-day fast is scarcely the ideal background for a trek to three separate and rugged sites. When we remember that Paul was not always sure whether his visions were "in the body or out of the body" (2Co 12:2), we may be cautious about dogmatizing here. But there is no reason to think the framework of the story is purely symbolic as opposed to visionary, representing Jesus' inward struggles. If the demons could address him directly (e.g., Mt 8:29, 31), it is difficult to say Satan wouldn't or couldn't do this.

[1]Then Jesus was led by the Spirit into the desert to be tempted by the devil. [2]After
fasting forty days and forty nights, he was hungry. [3]The tempter came to him and said, "If
you are the Son of God, tell these stones to become bread."
[4]Jesus answered, "It is written: 'Man does not live on bread alone, but on every word
that comes from the mouth of God.'"
[5]Then the devil took him to the holy city and had him stand on the highest point of the
temple. [6]"If you are the Son of God," he said, "throw yourself down. For it is written:

"'He will command his angels concerning you,
and they will lift you up in their hands,
so that you will not strike your foot against a stone.'"

[7]Jesus answered him, "It is also written: 'Do not put the Lord your God to the test.'"
[8]Again, the devil took him to a very high mountain and showed him all the kingdoms of
the world and their splendor. [9]"All this I will give you," he said, "if you will bow down and
worship me."
[10]Jesus said to him, "Away from me, Satan! For it is written: 'Worship the Lord your God,
and serve him only.'"
[11]Then the devil left him, and angels came and attended him.

COMMENTARY

1 Jesus' three temptations tie into his baptism, not only by the references to sonship and the Spirit, but by the opening "Then" (*tote*). Jesus' attestation as the Son (3:17) furnishes "the natural occasion for such special temptations as are here depicted" (Broadus). The same Spirit who engendered Jesus (1:20) and attested the Father's acknowledgment of his sonship (3:16–17) now leads him into the desert to be tempted by the devil. The "desert" (see comments at 3:1) is not only the place associated with demonic activity (Isa 13:21; 34:14; Mt 12:43; Rev 18:2; cf. Trench, *Studies in the Gospels*, 7–8) but, in a context abounding with references to Deuteronomy 6–8, the place where Israel experienced her greatest early testings.

The devil must not be reduced to impersonal "forces" behind racism and pogroms (Schweizer). The Greek word *diabolos* (GK *1333*) strictly means "slanderer," but the term is the regular LXX rendering of "Satan" (e.g., 1Ch 21:1; Job 1:6–12; 2:1–7; Zec 3:1–2), the chief opposer of God, the archenemy who leads all the spiritual hosts of darkness (cf. Ge 3; Jn 8:37–44; 2Co 11:3; 12:7; Rev 12:3–9; 20:1–4, 7–10).

That Jesus should be led "by the Spirit" to be tempted "by the devil" is no stranger than Job 1:6–2:7 or 2 Samuel 24:1 (1Ch 21:1). Recognizing that "to tempt" (*peirazō*, GK *4279*) also means "to test" in a good or bad sense somewhat eases the problem. In Scripture, "tempting" or "testing" can reveal or develop character (Ge 22:1; Ex 20:20; Jn 6:6; 2Co 13:5; Rev 2:2) as well as solicit to evil (1Co 7:5; 1Th 3:5). For us to "tempt" or "test" God is wrong because it reflects unbelief or attempted bribery (Ex

17:2, 7 [Ps 95:9]; Dt 6:16 [Mt 4:7]; Isa 7:12; Ac 5:9; 15:10). Moreover God uses means and may bring good out of his agents' evil motives—see Joseph's experience (Ge 50:19–20). In Jesus' "temptations" God clearly purposed to test him just as Israel was tested, and Jesus' responses prove that he understood. Each of the temptations is replete with allusions to OT events and to a variety of themes within Matthew (cf. Clarke, *Gospel of Matthew and Its Readers*, 44–48; Blomberg, "Matthew," in *CNTUOT*).

2 The parallels with historic Israel continue. Jesus' fast (doubtless total abstention from food but not from drink; cf. Lk 4:2) of forty days and nights reflected Israel's forty-year wandering (Dt 8:2). Both Israel's and Jesus' hunger taught a lesson (Dt 8:3); both spent time in the desert preparatory to their respective tasks. The main point is that both "sons" were tested by God's design (Dt 8:3, 5; cf. Ex 4:22; Gerhardsson, *Testing of God's Son*, 19–35), the one after being redeemed from Egypt and the other after his baptism, to prove their obedience and loyalty in preparation for their appointed work. The one "son" failed but pointed to the "Son" who would never fail (see comments at 2:15). In this sense, the temptations legitimized Jesus as God's true Son (see Berger, "Die königlichen Messiastraditionen," 15–18).

At the same time, Jesus' hunger introduces us to a number of ironies to which Matthew more or less explicitly alludes: Jesus is hungry (v.2) but feeds others (14:13–21; 15:29–39); he grows weary (8:24) but offers others rest (11:28); he is the King Messiah but pays tribute (17:24–27); he is called the devil but casts out demons (12:22–32); he dies the death of a sinner but comes to save his people from their sins (1:21); he is sold for thirty pieces of silver but gives his life as a ransom for many (20:28); he will not turn stones to bread for himself (4:3–4) but gives his own body as bread for people (26:26).

3–4 The tempter came to Jesus—we cannot say in what form—and referred to Jesus' sonship. The form of the "if" clause in Greek (*ei* + indicative) does not so much challenge his sonship as assume it to build a doubtful imperative. Satan is not inviting Jesus to doubt his sonship but to reflect on its meaning. Sonship of the living God, he suggests, surely means Jesus has the power and right to satisfy his own needs.

Jesus' response is based solely on Scripture: "It is written" (v.4). The Scripture is Deuteronomy 8:3, following the LXX, which reads "every word" instead of a more ambiguous Hebrew expression (unless the non-LXX reading of D is adopted: cf. Gundry, *Use of the Old Testament*, 67), and it applies initially to Israel. But the statement itself is an aphorism. Even though "man" (*ho anthrōpos*) can specify old Israel (e.g., Ps 80:17), yet it is always true that everyone must recognize his utter dependence on God's word. Jesus' food is to do the will of his Father who sent him (Jn 4:34).

The point of each temptation must be determined by closely examining both the temptation and Jesus' response. This clearly shows that this first temptation was no simple incitement to use improper means of making bread (Morison), nor an attempt to use a miracle to prove to himself that he was really God's Son (Robinson, *Twelve New Testament Studies*, 55–56), nor to act alone without thought of others (H. Riesenfeld, *The Gospel Tradition* [Philadelphia: Fortress, 1970], 87–88); it was a temptation to use his sonship in a way inconsistent with his God-ordained mission. The same taunt, "If you are the Son of God," is hurled at him in 27:40, when for him to have left the cross would have annulled the purpose of his coming. Similarly, though Jesus could have gained the aid of legions of angels, how then could the Scriptures that say Jesus had to suffer and die have been fulfilled (26:53–54)? Israel's hunger had been intended to show them that hearing and obeying the word of God is the most important thing in life (Dt 8:2–3). Likewise, Jesus learned obedience through suffering as a son in God's house (Heb 3:5–6; 5:7–8). More necessary than bread for Jesus was obedience to God's word.

In the light of these parallels, we must conclude that Satan's aim was to entice Jesus to use powers that were rightly his but which he had voluntarily abandoned to carry out the Father's mission. Reclaiming them for himself would deny the self-abasement implicit in his mission and in the Father's will. Israel demanded its bread but died in the wilderness; Jesus denied himself bread, retained his righteousness, and lived by faithful submission to God's word. (There may be an allusion to Hab 2:4; cf. J. Andrew Kirk, "The Messianic Role of Jesus and the Temptation Narrative," *EvQ* 44 [1972]: 11–29, 91–102.)

5–7 The second temptation (Luke's third) is set in the "holy city," Jerusalem (cf. Ne 11:1; Isa 48:2; Da 9:24; Mt 27:53), on the highest point of the temple complex (*hieron* probably refers to the entire complex, not the sanctuary itself, which Jesus, not being a Levite, would not have approached; but see comments at 27:5). Josephus (*Ant.* 15.412 [11.5]) testifies to the enormous height from the structure's top to the ravine's bottom. Late Jewish midrash says that Messiah would prove himself by leaping from the temple pinnacle; but apart from its lateness, it mentions no spectators. So it is unlikely that this was a temptation for Jesus to prove himself to the people as a new "David" who will again rid Jerusalem of the "Jebusites" (i.e., Romans—contra Kirk, "Messianic Role," 91–95).

Satan quoted Psalm 91:11–12 (v.6) from the LXX, omitting the words "to guard you in all your ways." The omission itself does not prove he handled the Scriptures deceitfully (contra Walvoord), since the quotation is well within the range of common NT citation patterns. Satan's deceit lay in misapplying his quotation into a temptation that easily traps the devout mind by apparently warranting what might otherwise be thought sinful. Psalm 91:11–12 refers to anyone who trusts God and thus preeminently to Jesus. The angels will lift such a person up in their hands like a nurse a baby (cf. Nu 11:12; Dt 1:31; Isa 49:22; Heb 1:14). At the temple, the place where God has particularly manifested himself, Jesus is tempted to test his sonship ("If you are the Son of God") against God's pledge to protect his own. Deuteronomy 6:16 was Jesus' reply.

Jesus' hesitation came not from wondering whether he or his Father could command the normal forces of nature (cf. 8:26; 14:31) but because Scripture forbids putting God to the test (v.7). The reference alludes to Exodus 17:2–7 (cf. Nu 20:1–13), where the Israelites "put the Lord to the test" by demanding water. So Jesus was tempted by Satan to test God, but Jesus recognized Satan's testing as a sort of manipulative bribery expressly forbidden in the Scriptures (cf. Robinson, *Twelve New Testament Studies*, 54–56). For both Israel and Jesus, demanding miraculous protection as proof of God's care was wrong; the appropriate attitude is trust and obedience (Dt 6:17). We see, then, something of Jesus' handling of Scripture. His "also" shows he would not allow any interpretation that generates what he knew would contradict another passage.

8–10 The "very high mountain" (v.8) does not seem much more than a prop for the vision of the world's kingdoms (see Overview). It is doubtful there is a conscious reference to Moses' looking at the Promised Land (Dt 34:1–4; contra Hill); the parallels are not close. No condition Moses could have met at that point would have let him enter the land.

Satan offers the kingdoms of the world and their "splendor" without showing their sin. Jesus, however, came to remove sin. Here was a temptation "to achieve power by worship of God's rival" (France, *Jesus and the Old Testament*, 52), a shortcut to fullest messianic authority. Satan was offering an interpretation of the theocratic ideal that sidestepped the cross and introduced idolatry. At Jesus' baptism, the Voice spoke words that united Davidic messiahship and suffering servanthood (see comments at 3:17); here was enticement to enjoy the former without the latter. Small wonder Jesus would later turn on Peter so sharply when the apostle made a similar suggestion (16:23).

Jesus recognized that Satan's suggestion entailed depriving God of his exclusive claim to worship. Neither God's "son" Israel nor God's "Son" Jesus may swerve from undivided allegiance to God himself (v.10; cf. Ex 23:20–33; Dt 6:13; see McNeile, Bonnard). So Jesus responded with a third "it is written" and banished Satan from his presence. The time would come when Jesus' expanding kingdom would progressively destroy the kingdom Satan had to offer (12:25–28; cf. Lk 10:18). The day still lies ahead when King Messiah's last enemy is destroyed (1Co 15:25–26). But Jesus achieves it all without compromising his filial submission to the Father.

In other words, Jesus had in mind from the very beginning of his earthly ministry the combination of royal kingship and suffering servanthood attested at his baptism and essential to his mission. Moreover, the twin themes of kingly authority and filial submission, developed so clearly in the fourth gospel (cf. Carson, *Divine Sovereignty*, 146–62), are already present as the complementary poles of the life and self-revelation of Immanuel: "God with us."

11 The devil left Jesus "until an opportune time" (Lk 4:13). Though the conflict has barely begun, the pattern of obedience and trust has been established. He has learned to resist the devil (cf. Jas 4:7). The angelic help is not some passing blessing but a sustained one (the imperfect tense is probably significant). Jesus had refused to relieve his hunger by miraculously turning stones to bread; now he is fed supernaturally (*diēkonoun*, "attended," GK *1354*, is often used in connection with food; e.g., Mt 8:15; 25:44; 27:55; Ac 6:2; cf. Elijah in 1Ki 19:6–7). He had refused to throw himself off the temple heights in the hope of angelic help; now angels feed him. He had refused to take a shortcut to inherit the kingdom of the world; now he fulfills Scripture by beginning his ministry and announcing the kingdom in Galilee of the Gentiles (vv.12–17).

NOTES

1–11 The question of the impeccability of Christ is much discussed in older literature but is of doubtful concern to Matthew in this pericope. The problem is partly definitional. To say Christ could not sin does not resolve the nature of the impossibility, and many writers have said he could not sin because he would not (cf. Trench, *Studies in the Gospels*, 25–30). But at a deeper level, the problem concerns the truth of the incarnation and how to formulate it. The NT documents affirm both Jesus' deity and his humanity, and neither of these affirmations may be permitted to deny the complementary truth. One might argue that Christ's impeccability is a function of his deity but must not be taken to mitigate his humanity, and Christ's temptability is a function of his humanity but must not be taken to mitigate his deity.

2 The aorist participle νηστεύσας (*nēsteusas*, "after fasting") does not prove the hunger began only after the forty days were over, since an aorist participle sometimes indicates action coordinate with the main verb. Luke's more explicit statement has been pushed too hard by some scholars. Luke is saying that Jesus' hunger was caused by the forty-day fast, not that the hunger began then. There is little exegetical warrant for appealing to the supernatural here.

2. Jesus' early Galilean ministry (4:12–25)

a. The beginning (4:12–17)

[12]When Jesus heard that John had been put in prison, he returned to Galilee. [13]Leaving Nazareth, he went and lived in Capernaum, which was by the lake in the area of Zebulun and Naphtali — [14]to fulfill what was said through the prophet Isaiah:

15 "Land of Zebulun and land of Naphtali,
the way to the sea, along the Jordan,
Galilee of the Gentiles —
16 the people living in darkness
have seen a great light;
on those living in the land of the shadow of death
a light has dawned."

[17]From that time on Jesus began to preach, "Repent, for the kingdom of heaven is near."

COMMENTARY

12 John the Baptist's imprisonment appears to have prompted Jesus to return (see Notes) to Galilee. Though Mark 1:14–15 likewise links the two events, it is saying too much to conclude that Matthew has so strengthened the language to make John's imprisonment the cause of Jesus' withdrawal (*akousas* more likely means "when he heard" than "because he heard"). Equally important is the fact that the language suggests that Jesus remained for some time in Judea—unless we suppose the Baptist's arrest immediately followed Jesus' baptism. The Synoptics make no mention of Jesus' early Judean ministry but imply that his ministry began in Galilee. By contrast, the fourth gospel seems to presuppose an earlier Galilean ministry (Jn 1:19–2:12), a Judean ministry that overlapped with that of the Baptist (Jn 2:13–3:21), and then a return to the north via Samaria (Jn 3:22–4:42). The Johannine chronology has often been dismissed as of little historical worth. Yet there are hints even in the Synoptic Gospels that presuppose an early Judean ministry (e.g., Lk 10:38), one such hint being the delay implicit in this verse.

If this approach is valid, we must ask why the synoptists eliminate Jesus' earliest months of ministry. Several reasons are possible.

1. With the Baptist's removal from the scene, Jesus' ministry entered a new phase. The function of the forerunner was over; the one to whom he pointed had come. This transfer might be neatly indicated by beginning the account of Jesus' ministry from the time of John's imprisonment. (Compare years of intercalation among OT kings and their varied treatment by OT writers.)

2. By contrast, when the fourth gospel was written, the explicit connection between the Baptist and Jesus may have been of more urgent interest if the writer was responding to organized groups of

the Baptist's followers (cf. Ac 19:1–4). The synoptists do not seem to be under such pressure.

3. In Matthew, Galilee is of profound significance because it heralds the fulfillment of prophecy (vv.14–16) and points to the gospel's extension to "all nations" (28:19).

According to 1 Maccabees 5:23, the Jewish population in Galilee in 164 BC was so small it could be transported to Judea for protection. By Jesus' day, however, though the large population was mixed, owing to both the proximity of Gentile peoples in surrounding areas and the importation of colonists during the Maccabean conquest, the Jewish population was substantial. The many theories concerning the influence of this region on Jesus and thence on Christianity have been neatly summarized and criticized by L. Goppelt (*Christentum und Judentum* [Gütersloh: Bertelsmann, 1954] 32–41); debates continue today (e.g., Mark A. Chancey, *The Myth of a Gentile Galilee* [Cambridge: Cambridge Univ. Press, 2002]). "Galilee" as referring to some part of the northern district has long roots (cf. Jos 20:7; 1Ki 9:11; 2Ki 15:29).

13 In Luke, Jesus' move from Nazareth to Capernaum (Lk 4:31) follows the violent reaction of the Nazareth townspeople (vv.16–30), and it is uncertain whether Matthew's account (13:54–58) reports the same incident or another one. Capernaum ("village of Nahum"?) lay a little north of the plain of Gennesaret (14:34), on the northwest shore of Lake Galilee. Tell Hum marks the site today, its synagogue ruins dating from the second century. The village enjoyed a fishing industry that probably demanded the presence of a tax collector's booth (9:9). Here, too, was Peter's house (8:14; cf. Mk 1:29; 2:1). But Matthew is interested in pointing out Capernaum's location with reference to the ancient tribal allotments of Zebulun and Naphtali as showing the minute correspondence with the prophecy cited in vv.15–16.

14–16 Jesus' move fulfilled (v.14; see Notes) Isaiah 9:1–2. This prophecy is part of a large structure looking to Immanuel's coming (see comments at 1:23). It is extraordinarily difficult to identify the text form. This either is an independent translation of the Hebrew (Gundry, *Use of the Old Testament*, 105–8) or a modification of divergent LXX manuscripts (Chilton, *God in Strength*, 111). The NIV's "the way to the sea" (v.15) is better translated "seawards," i.e., lying by the Sea of Galilee, and "along the Jordan," though convenient, has little lexical warrant and should be replaced by "beyond the Jordan" (see Notes).

The point of the quotation is clear enough. In despised Galilee, the place where people live in darkness (i.e., without the religious and cultic advantages of Jerusalem and Judea), the land of the shadow of death (i.e., where the darkness is most dense; cf. Job 10:21; Ps 107:10; Jer 13:16; Am 5:8), here the light has dawned (v.16). "Dawned" (*aneteilen*, GK *422*) suggests that the light first shone brilliantly here, not that it was shining brightly elsewhere and then moved here (Lindars, *New Testament Apologetic*, 198). This was God's prophesied plan. Matthew is not interested in the mere fact that some prophecy was fulfilled in Galilee but in this particular prophecy: from of old the Messiah was promised to "Galilee of the Gentiles" (*Galilaia tōn ethnōn*), a foreshadowing of the commission to "all nations" (*panta ta ethnē*, 28:19). Moreover, if the messianic light dawns on the darkest places, then Messiah's salvation can only be a bestowal of grace—namely, that Jesus came to call not the righteous but sinners (9:13).

17 Several have argued that the words "from that time on" (*apo tote*), found only here and in 16:21; 26:16, mark major turning points in this gospel (Stonehouse, *Witness of Matthew*, 129–31; Kingsbury, *Structure*). In its strong form, this theory divides Matthew into three sections (1:1–4:16; 4:17–16:20; 16:21–28:20) with important interpretive implications. Though there are good reasons for rejecting this structure (see Introduction, section 14), the phrase "from that time on" nevertheless marks an important turning point because it ties something new to what has just preceded it.

We best see this when we examine the content of Jesus' preaching. Assuming the soundness of the text preserved in the NIV (see Notes), the burden of Jesus' preaching so far is, in itself, identical to that of John the Baptist: "Repent, for the kingdom of heaven is near" (v.17; cf. 3:2). Matthew often shows ties between Jesus and John the Baptist (Klostermann; Chilton, *God in Strength*, 117; Dale C. Allison Jr., "The Continuity between Jesus and John," *JSHJ* 1 [2003]: 6–27). But when John the Baptist says these words, they are placed in an OT context that highlights his function as the forerunner who looks forward to the Messiah and his kingdom (3:2–12); when Jesus says the same words, they are linked by "from that time" with an OT context that insists Jesus fulfills the promises of a light rising to shine on the Gentiles (Schweizer; cf. Wood, "Regathering of the People of God").

The longstanding debate that largely discounted C. H. Dodd's theory (that "is near" [3:2; 4:17] equals "has come" [12:28]) rather misses the mark. Neither Dodd nor his critics are subtle enough. The kingdom (see comments at 3:2) is still future. But the separate contexts of the announcements made by John and by Jesus (3:2; 4:17) show that with Jesus the kingdom has drawn so near that it has actually dawned. Therefore, Jesus' hearers must repent—a demand made not only by the Baptist but by Jesus. The structure of the book thus sets up an implicit parallelism. Jesus is not so much a new Moses as a new Joshua (on their names, see 1:21); for as Moses did not enter the Promised Land but was succeeded by Joshua who did, so John the Baptist announces the kingdom and is followed by Jesus (Joshua), who leads his people into it (cf. Albright and Mann).

NOTES

12 The verb ἀνεχώρησεν (*anechōrēsen*, "returned," GK *432*) is characteristic of Matthew (2:12, 13, 14, 22; 4:12; 12:15; 14:13; 15:21; 27:5). Only in 9:24 does Jesus use it; elsewhere in the NT it occurs only in Mark 3:7; Jn 6:15; Ac 23:19; 26:31. On the basis of Matthew's usage, Hill, following Fenton, suggests the verb means Jesus withdrew strategically—i.e., that the rejection of God's word in one place (here in John's ministry) leads to its proclamation in another place (in Jesus' ministry). But this meaning is possible only in 12:15; 14:13; 15:21; it is impossible in most of the other occurrences in Matthew. More commonly Jesus "withdraws" because of threats or plots. That he then preaches elsewhere is a consequence of his withdrawal for safety's sake, not a sign of judgment on a people who will not hear.

14 The dash separating vv.13 and 14 (NIV) rightly interprets the ἵνα (*hina*, "in order to") as referring to Jesus' move rather than Jesus' motive. In other words, judging by his usage elsewhere (e.g., 1:22; 2:15), Matthew is not saying that Jesus moved in order to fulfill Scripture but that his move fulfilled Scripture.

15 The words ὁδὸν θαλάσσης (*hodon thalassēs*, "the way to the sea") are in LXX Isaiah 8:23 and may well be a literal rendering of the Hebrew דֶּרֶךְ הַיָּם (*derek hayyām*), "seawards"; i.e., "by the sea" (cf. NIV, "by the way of the sea," Isa 9:1) rather than the "way to the sea" (cf. Turner, *Syntax*, 247). The translation "along the Jordan" for πέραν τοῦ Ἰορδάνου (*peran tou Iordanou*) reflects the fact that Zebulun and Naphtali do not extend east of the Jordan. But linguistically the phrase must mean "beyond the Jordan."

Normally "beyond the Jordan" refers to the east bank, but the vantage of the speaker must be borne in mind, and sometimes it refers to the west bank (e.g., Nu 32:19; Dt 11:30; Jos 5:1; 22:7). The Hebrew is more naturally translated "beyond Jordan." Most likely, Isaiah sees the Assyrians coming from the northeast; as they progressively inflict judgment on the nation, they proceed "beyond the Jordan" to the west bank. So Matthew's rendering may simply preserve the same stance—in which case, is there a further reference to the "exile" now ended by Messiah's coming (see comments at 2:17–18)? The LXX inserts a καί (*kai*, "and") before "beyond the Jordan," eliminating the problem by making two regions. Yet if Matthew is reflecting his own stance, it is possible he is writing from the east bank (so Slingerland, "Transjordanian Origin"), perhaps from the Decapolis. It is hard to be sure because of uncertainties in the text form of the quotation and in the meaning of the Hebrew. See comments at 19:1.

16 Αὐτοῖς (*autois*, "on them") is redundant after τοῖς καθημένοις (*tois kathēmenois*, lit., "on those sitting [NIV, 'living']"); but, though not unknown in classical Greek, this technique is common in Hebrew (cf. BDF, para. 466 [4]).

17 The reading omitting μετανοεῖτε (*metanoeite*, "repent") and γάρ (*gar*, "for") is not well attested but is treated seriously because of the possibility of assimilation to 3:2. Nevertheless, the longer text stands (cf. Chilton, *God in Strength*, 302–10; Fee, "Modern Text Criticism," 164–65).

b. Calling the first disciples (4:18–22)

OVERVIEW

Since no temporal expression links this pericope with the last one, there may have been some time lapse. Bultmann's skepticism (*History of the Synoptic Tradition*, 28) about the historical worth of these verses is unwarranted (cf. Hill).

The relation of the various "callings" of the disciples in the gospel records is obscure. If we take John 1:35–51 as historical, Simon, Andrew, Philip, and Nathanael first followed Jesus at an earlier date. On returning to Galilee, they again took up their normal work. This is inherently plausible. The disciples' commitment and understanding advanced by degrees. Even after the resurrection, they returned once more to their fishing (Jn 21). Here (Mt 4:20) an earlier commitment may explain their haste in following Jesus. If the miracle of Luke 5:1–11 occurred the night before Matthew 4:18–22 (Mk 1:16–20), that would be another reason for their immediate response to Jesus. In this connection, the meaning of *katartizontas* ("preparing," v.21, GK *2936*; see comments at v.21) is significant.

18 As Jesus was walking beside the Sea of Galilee, he saw two brothers, Simon called
Peter and his brother Andrew. They were casting a net into the lake, for they were
fishermen. 19 "Come, follow me," Jesus said, "and I will make you fishers of men." 20 At once
they left their nets and followed him.

[21]Going on from there, he saw two other brothers, James son of Zebedee and his brother John. They were in a boat with their father Zebedee, preparing their nets. Jesus called them, [22]and immediately they left the boat and their father and followed him.

COMMENTARY

18 In Hebrew, "sea," like the German *See*, can refer to lakes. Classical Greek prefers not to use *thalassa* (GK *2498* or *thalatta*—"sea") for lakes, and Luke follows the same pattern by using *limnē* ("lake"), though Matthew, Mark, and John prefer "sea." The Sea of Galilee (named from the district), otherwise known as the "Lake of Gennesaret" (the name "Kinnereth" [Nu 34:11; Jos 12:3] comes from a plain on its northwest shore; cf. Mt 14:34), or the "Sea of Tiberias" (a city Herod built on the southwest shore: Jn 6:1; 21:1), is 12¼ by 8¾ miles at the longest and broadest points respectively. Its surface is 682 feet below sea level. It is subject to violent squalls. In Jesus' day, it supported flourishing fisheries. On its west shore were nine towns, and "Bethsaida" may be freely translated "Fishtown." Simon and his brother Andrew came from Bethsaida (Jn 1:44), though Capernaum was now their home (Mk 1:21, 29).

Simon, Matthew says, was "called Peter"; but he does not tell us how Peter received this name (cf. 10:2; 16:18; Mk 3:16; Lk 6:14). While uncertainties remain, what is quite certain is that *kêpā*ʾ ("rock," "stone"), the Aramaic equivalent of "Peter," was already an accepted name in Jesus' day (cf. Joseph A. Fitzmyer, "Aramaic *Kepha'* and Peter's Name in the New Testament," in *Text and Interpretation* [ed. Best and Wilson], 121–32)—a fact that has an important bearing on the interpretation of Matthew 16:17–18.

Simon and Andrew were casting a "net" (*amphiblēstron*, a NT hapax legomenon [found only once], with a cognate at Mk 1:16). It refers to a circular "casting net" and is not to be confused with the more generic term *diktua* in v.20.

19–20 Greek has several expressions for "follow me" (cf. 10:38; Lk 9:23; 14:27), but they all presuppose a physical "following" during Jesus' ministry. His "followers" were not just "hearers"; they actually followed their Master around (as students then did) and became, as it were, trainees. The metaphor "fishers of men" glances back to the work of the two being called. It may also be reminiscent of Jeremiah 16:16. There Yahweh sends "fishermen" to gather his people for the exile; here Jesus sends "fishermen" to announce the end of the exile (see comments at 1:11–12; 2:17–18) and the beginning of the messianic reign. But this allusion is uncertain. The danger of "parallelomania" (coined by S. Sandmel, "Parallelomania," *JBL* 81 [1962]: 2–13) is evident when E. C. B. MacLaurin ("The Divine Fishermen," *St. Mark's Review* 94 [1978]: 26–28) works out many parallels and then opts for Ugaritic mythology a millennium-and-a-half old. In any case, there is a straight line from this commission to the Great Commission (Mt 28:18–20). Jesus' followers are indeed to catch men.

On the prompt obedience of Simon and Andrew (v.20), see Overview. Peter later used this obedience almost as a bartering point (19:27).

21–22 This second pair of brothers were "preparing their nets" (v.21), which sounds as if they were just setting out. The verb *katartizō* (GK *2936*), however, connotes "mend" or "restore to a former condition." So James and John may have been making repairs after a night's fishing (cf. Lk 5:1–11 and its possible place in the chronology). Fenton notes that Paul uses *katartizō* for perfecting the church (1Co 1:10; 2Co 13:11) and sees here an allusion to pastoral ministry. But this is fanciful because the verb is not a technical term. The boat (*ploion* [GK *4450*] was used of all kinds of boats) was big enough for several men (Mk 1:20). Mark's remark that hired men were left with Zebedee when his sons followed Jesus reminds us that we must not exaggerate the ignorance and poverty of Jesus' first followers. While they were not trained scribes or rabbis, they were not illiterate, stupid, or destitute. Indeed, Peter's protest in 19:27 implies that many or all of the Twelve had given up much to follow Jesus.

Jesus took the initiative and "called" James and John. In the Synoptics, unlike Paul's epistles, Jesus' call is not necessarily effectual. But in this instance it was immediately obeyed.

c. Spreading the news of the kingdom (4:23–25)

OVERVIEW

Summaries are common to narrative literature; but the one before us, with its parallel in 9:35–38, has distinctive features.

1. It does not just summarize what has gone before but shows the geographical extent and varied activity of Jesus' ministry.

2. It therefore sets the stage for the particular discourses and stories that follow and implies that the material presented is but a representative sampling of what was available.

3. It is not a mere chronicle but conveys theological substance. Thus it is easy to detect different emphases between this summary and 9:35–38 (see comments there).

Older commentators see in vv.23–25 a first circuit of Galilee and in 9:35–38 a second one. This is possible, but both pericopes may refer to the constant ministry of Jesus rather than to tightly defined circuits.

**23 Jesus went throughout Galilee, teaching in their synagogues, preaching the good
news of the kingdom, and healing every disease and sickness among the people. 24 News
about him spread all over Syria, and people brought to him all who were ill with various
diseases, those suffering severe pain, the demon-possessed, those having seizures, and
the paralyzed, and he healed them. 25 Large crowds from Galilee, the Decapolis, Jerusalem,
Judea and the region across the Jordan followed him.**

COMMENTARY

23 Jesus' ministry included teaching, preaching, and healing. Galilee, the district covered, is small (approximately seventy by forty miles), but according to Josephus (*Life* 235 [45]; *J.W.* 3.41–43 [3.2]), writing one generation later, Galilee had 204 cities and villages, each with no fewer than fifteen thousand persons. Even if this figure refers only to the walled cities and not to the villages (which is not what Josephus says), a most conservative estimate points to a large population, even if less than Josephus's three million. At the rate of two villages or towns per day, three months would be required to visit all of them, with no time off for the Sabbath. Jesus "went around doing good" (Ac 10:38; cf. Mk 1:39; 6:6). The sheer physical drain must have been enormous. Above all, we must recognize that Jesus was an itinerant preacher and teacher, who necessarily repeated approximately the same material again and again and faced the same problems, illnesses, and needs again and again.

The connection between "teaching" and "synagogue" recurs at 9:35; 13:54. A visiting Jew might well be asked to teach in the local synagogue (cf. Moore, *Judaism*, 1:281–307; *Illustrated Bible Dictionary* [ed. Douglas], 3:1499–1503) as part of regular worship (e.g., Lk 4:16). The word "their" may indicate a time when the synagogue and the church had divided. On the other hand, it may simply indicate that the author and his readers viewed these events from outside Galilee (see comments at 7:29; 9:35).

The message Jesus preaches is the "good news [*euangelion*, "gospel," GK *2295*] of the kingdom." The term recurs in 9:35; 24:14, and becomes "this gospel" in 26:13. "Of the kingdom" is an objective genitive. The "good news" concerns the kingdom (see Notes), whose "nearness" has already been announced (3:2; 4:17) and which is the central subject of the Sermon on the Mount (chs. 5–7). Mark prefers "the gospel" or "the gospel of Christ" or "the gospel of God" (Mk 1:1, 14; 8:35; 10:29; 13:10); but the difference between these expressions and "gospel of the kingdom" is one of connotation, not denotation, since the "good news" concerns God and the inbreaking of his saving reign in the person of his Son the Messiah.

The healings of various diseases among the people further attest the kingdom's presence and advance (cf. 11:2–6; Isa 35:5–6). Walvoord, 39, relegates these "kingdom blessings ... due for fulfillment in the future kingdom" to the status of mere "credentials of the King"; but if the kingdom blessings are present, then the kingdom too must have broken in, even if not yet in the splendor of its consummation (cf. Rev 21:3–5).

24 The geographical extent of "Syria" is uncertain. From the perspective of Jesus in Galilee, Syria was to the north. From the Roman viewpoint, Syria was a Roman province embracing all of Palestine (cf. Lk 2:2; Ac 15:23, 41; Gal 1:21), Galilee excepted, since it was under the independent administration of Herod Antipas at this time. The term "Syria" reflects the extent of the excitement aroused by Jesus' ministry. If the Roman use of the term is here presumed, it shows his effect on people far beyond the borders of Israel. Those "ill with various diseases" and "those suffering severe pain" are divided into three overlapping categories: (1) the demon-possessed (cf. Mt 8:28–34; 12:22–29); (2) those having seizures—namely, any kind of insanity or irrational behavior whether or not related to demon-possession (17:14–18; on *selēniazomenous* ["epileptics," GK *4944*], which etymologically refers to the "moonstruck" [i.e., "lunatic"], cf. *NIDNTT*, 3:734; J. M. Ross, "Epileptic or Moonstruck?" *BT* 29 [1978]: 126–28); and (3) the paralyzed, whose condition also had various causes.

In the NT, sickness may result directly from a particular sin (e.g., Jn 5:14; 1Co 11:30) or may not (e.g., Jn 9:2–3). But both Scripture and Jewish tradition take sickness as resulting directly or indirectly from living in a fallen world (see comments at 8:17). The messianic age would end such grief (Isa 11:1–5; 35:5–6). Therefore Jesus' miracles, dealing with every kind of ailment, not only herald the kingdom but show that God has pledged himself to deal with sin at a basic level (cf. 1:21; 8:17).

25 Jesus' reputation at this point extended far beyond Galilee, even though that is where the light "dawned" (v.16). Two of the named areas, the region across the Jordan (east bank? see comments at v.15) and the Decapolis, were mostly made up of Gentiles, a fact already emphasized (see comments at 1:3–5; 2:1–12, 22–23; 3:9; 4:8, 15–16). The Decapolis (lit., "Ten Cities") is a region east of Galilee extending from Damascus in the north to Philadelphia in the south, ten cities (under varied reckonings) making up the count (cf. S. Thomas Parker, "The Decapolis Reviewed," *JBL* 94 [1975]: 437–41). People from all these areas "followed" Jesus. Despite contrary arguments, "follow" does not necessarily indicate solid discipleship. It may, as here, refer to those who at some particular time followed Jesus around in his itinerant ministry and thus were loosely considered his disciples.

NOTES

23 Further evidence that "preaching the good news of the kingdom" requires taking "of the kingdom" as an objective genitive is suggested by comparing the Greek κηρύσσων τὸ εὐαγγέλιον τῆς βασιλείας (*kēryssōn to euangelion tēs basileias*, "preaching the good news of the kingdom") with the expression found in Luke 8:1: εὐαγγελιζόμενος τὴν βασιλείαν (*euangelizomenos tēn basileian*, "proclaiming the good news of the kingdom"), in which "kingdom" is the direct object.

24 The strange expression τοὺς κακῶς ἔχοντας (*tous kakōs echontas*; NIV, "[those] ill") is idiomatic (found elsewhere in the NT at 8:16; 9:12; 14:35; Mk 1:32; 2:17; 6:55; Lk 5:31). The only other strictly comparable constructions in the NT are in Acts 24:25; 1 Timothy 5:25; 1 Peter 4:5.

B. First Discourse: The Sermon on the Mount (5:1–7:29)

OVERVIEW

The Sermon on the Mount is the first of five major discourses in the gospel of Matthew. All five follow blocks of narrative material; all five end with the same formula (see comments at 7:28–29; Introduction, section 14). Not only because it is first and longest of the five, and therefore helps determine the critical approach toward all of them, but also because it deals with ethical issues of fundamental importance in every age, this "sermon" has called forth thousands of books and articles. Some orientation is necessary.

A useful starting point is Warren S. Kissinger's *The Sermon on the Mount: A History of Interpretation and Bibliography* (Metuchen, N.J.: Scarecrow, 1975). The bibliographies in the major recent commentaries on Matthew (esp. France [NICNT], Keener, Luz, Nolland, Turner) offer a surfeit of literature. To this must be added the Hermeneia commentary devoted exclusively to the Sermon on the Mount (Betz). K. Beyschlag ("Zur Geschichte der Bergpredigt in der Alten Kirche," *ZTK* 74 [1977]: 291–322) and Robert M. Grant ("The Sermon on the Mount in Early Christianity," *Semeia* 12 [1978]: 215–31) unfold the treatment of these chapters in the earliest centuries of Christianity. For clarification of the varied treatment of the sermon during the twentieth century, we are indebted to Ursula Berner (*Die Bergpredigt: Rezeption und Auslegung im 20. Jahrhundert* [Göttingen: Vandenhoeck & Ruprecht, 1979]). Popular expositions of use to the working preacher include Carson, *Sermon on the Mount*; D. Martyn Lloyd-Jones, *Studies in the Sermon on the Mount* (2 vols.; London: InterVarsity, 1959–60); F. B. Meyer, *The Sermon on the Mount* (repr., Grand Rapids: Baker, 1959); Stott, *Message of the Sermon on the Mount*.

Four introductory matters demand comment:

1. *Unity and authenticity of the discourse*. Since the work of Hans Windisch (*The Meaning of the Sermon on the Mount* [repr., Philadelphia: Fortress, 1951]), few have regarded Matthew 5–7 as thoroughly authentic. The most common proposal today is that these chapters preserve some authentic teaching of Jesus, originally presented at various occasions and collected and shaped by oral tradition. To this the evangelist has added church teaching, taught, perhaps, by an inspired prophet speaking for the exalted Christ; and the discourse has then been further molded by catechetical and liturgical considerations (so, e.g., J. Jeremias, *The Sermon on the Mount* [Philadelphia: Fortress, 1963]; see the magisterial study by Davies, *Setting*). According to these critics, at best the so-called Sermon on the Mount preserves no more than isolated sayings of Jesus.

Much of one's judgment in these matters depends on conclusions as to source, form, and redaction criticism (see Introduction, sections 1–3). For instance, if one insists that every saying elsewhere in the Gospels similar to any saying in Matthew 5–7 must be traced back to one utterance only (thus ignoring Jesus' role as an itinerant preacher), one may develop a more or less plausible theory of the growth of oral tradition in each case (so, e.g., H. T. Wrege, *Die Überlieferungsgeschichte der Bergpredigt* [WUNT 9; Tübingen: Mohr, 1968]). This can be done precisely because so many sayings in these chapters do occur elsewhere, either in roughly similar or in identical language (see comments at 5:13, 15, 18, 25, 29, 32; 6:9, 22, 24–25; 7:2, 7, 17, 23). Moreover, where parallels exist, Matthew's forms are often more stylized or structured.

There is no need to repeat introductory remarks about authenticity. Several observations will, however, focus the approach adopted here.

a. We cannot make much out of Matthew's clear tendency to treat his material topically. Nor can we conclude from his grouping of miracles that he has composed his discourses out of grouped but independent sayings. In the former case, Matthew does not pretend to do otherwise, whereas in all his discourses he gives the impression, especially in his concluding formulas (7:28–29; 11:1; 13:53; 19:1; 26:1), that the material is not only authentic but delivered on one occasion.

b. We dare not claim too much on the basis of the unity or its lack in the discourses. Even if the Sermon on the Mount represents material Jesus delivered on one occasion, perhaps over several days, its extreme compression, necessary selection, and problems of translation from Aramaic to Greek (assuming Jesus preached in Aramaic) might all unite to break the flow. If the unity of the discourse is defended (e.g., by Austin Farrer, *St. Matthew and St. Mark* [2nd ed.; London: Dacre, 1966], but cf. Davies, *Setting*, 9–13), that unity might be nothing more than the evangelist's editing. He must have seen some coherence in these chapters to leave them in this form. Thus neither unity nor disunity is a sufficient criterion for the authenticity of a brief account of extensive discourse.

c. We must suppose that Jesus preached the same thing repeatedly (see comments at 4:23–25); he was an extremely busy itinerant preacher. The pithier the saying, the more likely it was to be repeated word-perfect. The more common the natural phenomenon behind a metaphor or aphorism, the more likely Jesus repeated it in new situations. Any experienced itinerant preacher will confirm the inescapability of these tendencies. More important, if one distances oneself from the more radical presuppositions of form and tradition criticism, the NT documents themselves confirm this approach (cf. 11:15 with 13:9; 18:3 with 19:14; Mt 10:32 with Lk 9:26 and 12:8; Mt 10:24 with Lk 6:40 and Jn 13:16 and 15:20; Mt 10:38–39 with 16:24–25 and Lk 17:33 and Jn 12:25). Even longer sections, such as Jesus' model prayer (Mt 6:9–13; see discussion below), are susceptible to such treatment, if for different reasons.

d. Jesus himself was a master teacher. In his sayings, whose authenticity is not greatly disputed, there is evidence of structure, contrast, and assonance. So when some scholars tell us that Matthew's account has more structure (perhaps from catechetical influence) than the other Synoptics, is this a sign of greater nearness to or distance from Jesus? What criteria are there for distinguishing the two possibilities? Surely if we do not pretend to be able to retrieve all the *ipsissima verba* of Jesus but only his *ipsissima vox* (see Notes, 3:17), most of the common criteria for testing authenticity evaporate.

e. The assumptions of some form critics make their work more questionable than they think. For if a certain kind of saying tends to take on a certain form in oral tradition and if the period of oral transmission is long enough to develop that form, then the repetition of the saying on half a dozen different occasions in slightly different words would ultimately lead to one common form of the saying. Thus, far from enabling the critic to trace a precise development, form criticism obliterates the richness of the tradition attested by the evangelists themselves.

f. As Matthew's gospel stands, we must weigh two disparate pieces of evidence: (1) that all five of Matthew's discourses are bracketed by introductory and concluding remarks that cannot fail to give the impression that he presents his discourses as not only authentic but delivered by Jesus on the specified occasions and (2) that many individual bits of each discourse find synoptic parallels in other settings. Many think the second point to be so strong that they conclude that Matthew himself composed the discourses. Conservative writers in this camp say that all of Jesus' sayings are authentic but that Matthew brought them together in their present form. Therefore the first piece of evidence has to be reinterpreted—i.e., the introductory and concluding notes framing each of Matthew's discourses are seen as artistic compositional devices.

A more subtle approach is to say that Jesus actually did deliver a discourse on each of the five occasions specified but that not all of the material Matthew records is from that occasion. In other words, the evangelist has added certain "footnotes" of his own, at a time when orthography was much more flexible and there were no convenient ways to indicate what he was doing. While either of these reconstructions is possible, each faces two steep hurdles: (1) the introductory and concluding brackets around the five discourses do not belong to any clear first-century pattern or genre that would show the reader they are merely artistic devices and not the real settings they manifestly claim to be; and (2) it is remarkable that each conclusion sweeps together all the sayings of the preceding discourse under some such rubric as "when Jesus had finished saying these things" (a possible exception is 11:1). That the introductory and concluding formulas were not recognizable as artistic devices is confirmed by the fact that for the first millennium and a half or so of its existence, the church recognized them as concrete settings. (This is not a surreptitious appeal to return to precritical thinking but a note on the recognizability of a literary genre.)

In view of the above, it seems the wiser course to believe Matthew intended to present real, historical settings for his discourses; and the parallels found elsewhere, though they must be considered individually, do not seem to present insurmountable problems. While many sayings in the Gospels appear in "loose" or "floating" settings, where an evangelist ostensibly specifies the context, the authenticity of that context must be assumed. This is particularly easy to maintain in Matthew if the date and authorship are as stated in the Introduction (sections 5–6). Thus this commentary takes Matthew's settings seriously. Not that it takes all the discourses as verbatim accounts or unedited reports of Jesus' teaching; it rather assumes they are condensed notes, largely in Matthew's idiom, selected and presented in accord with his own concerns. But behind them stand the voice and authority of Jesus.

2. *Relation to the Sermon on the Plain (Lk 6:20–49).* Augustine claimed that Matthew 5–7 and the passage in Luke are two separate discourses, and almost all writers agreed with him until the Reformation. Even after it, some scholars followed Augustine (e.g., Alexander, Plumptre), and today some are returning to Augustine's view.

Origen, Chrysostom, Calvin, and the majority of recent scholars, however, defend the view (often with appropriate theorizing about Q) that the two accounts represent the same discourse. This has much to commend it. The two sermons begin with beatitudes and end with the same simile. Nearly everything in the Sermon on the Plain is in some form in the Sermon on the Mount and often in identical order. Both are immediately followed by the same events—namely, entrance into Capernaum and healing the centurion's servant. (The point is valid even if it indicates nothing more than a common link in the tradition.) Luke's sermon is much shorter and has its own thematic emphases (e.g., humility); and much of the extra material in Matthew is scattered elsewhere in Luke, especially in his "travel narrative" (Lk 9:51–18:14; discussed at Mt 19:1–2). Moreover, Matthew speaks of a mountain, Luke a plain; and Luke's discourse follows the choosing of the Twelve, which does not take place in Matthew until ch. 10.

But these problems can be readily solved.

a. Much of what Luke omits, mostly in Matthew 5:17–37; 6:1–18, is exactly the sort of material that would interest Matthew's Jewish readers more than Luke's readers. Luke has also omitted some material from his "Sermon on the Plain" that he has placed elsewhere (Mt 6:25–34; Lk 12:22–31). It is possible that Jesus gave the sermon more than once. Alternatively, Luke's context is so loose that he may have been responsible for the topical rearrangement. In any case, to insist that a writer must include everything he knows or everything in his sources is poor methodology. In the other Matthean discourses, Matthew includes much, and Luke includes less; in the Sermon on the Mount, though Matthew's account is much longer than Luke's, in certain places Luke preserves a little more than Matthew (cf. Mt 5:12 with Lk 6:23–26; Mt 5:47 with Lk 6:33–35).

b. Of the several solutions to the mountain or plain, the most convincing one takes Matthew's "on a mountainside" to mean "up in the hills" and Luke's "plain" as being some kind of plateau. The linguistic evidence is convincing (see Notes, 5:1).

c. Luke's order, placing the sermon after the choosing of the Twelve, is historically believable. But Matthew is clearly topical in his order. Connectives at 5:1; 8:1; 9:35; 11:2; 12:1; 14:1 et al. are loose; his favorite word "then" is general in meaning (see Notes, 2:7). It is unlikely that Matthew intends his readers to think that the Sermon on the Mount succeeded Jesus' circuit (4:23–25). Rather, this sermon was preached during that circuit.

Moreover, some of Matthew's reasons for placing it here instead of after 10:1–4 are apparent (see below under 4). It seems best, then, to take Matthew 5–7 and Luke 6:20–49 as separate reports of the same occasion, each dependent on some shared tradition (Q?), but not exclusively so. Space limitations prevent tracing all the likely connections; but some attention will be given selected critical problems within this overall approach.

d. Judgment about the relationship between the Sermon on the Mount and Luke's Sermon on the Plain is inevitably tied to a number of complex issues surrounding the Synoptic Problem. Hans Dieter Betz's magisterial commentary on the Sermon on the Mount is extraordinarily valuable for the richness of its material on the history of interpretation and for many possible links with the Greco-Roman world. Nevertheless, Betz's hypothesis that Matthew has simply taken over the entire sermon from Q without adapting it, which accounts not only for differences between this sermon and Luke's Sermon on the Plain but also for ostensible differences between the Sermon on the Mount and the rest of Matthew, has been repeatedly criticized (see Gundry, *The Old Is Better* [WUNT 178; Tübingen: Mohr, 2005], ch. 3). The Jesus Betz finds in the Sermon on the Mount aligns nicely with universalizing tendencies in the ill-defined phenomenon of religion—or, as Gundry puts it, Jesus becomes "something of a Jewish liberal" (p. 148).

3. *Theological structure and affinities.* Whatever its sources and manner of compilation, the inclusion of the Sermon on the Mount in Matthew must be significant. Some have noted its similarities to Jewish thought. G. Friedlander's classic work, *The Jewish Sources of the Sermon on the Mount* (New York: Ktav, 1911), shows that virtually all the statements in Matthew 5–7 can be paralleled in the Talmud or other Jewish sources. Of course this is right, but it is a little like saying that the parts of a fine automobile can be found in a vast warehouse. Read any fifty pages of the Babylonian Talmud and compare them with Matthew 5–7, and it becomes obvious they are not saying the same things. Sigal (*Halakhah of Jesus*) argues that the forms of argument in Matthew 5–7 fit into well-accepted patterns of the early rabbis ("proto-rabbis"); Gary A. Tuttle ("The Sermon on the Mount: Its Wisdom Affinities and Their Relation to Its Structure," *JETS* 20 [1977]: 213–30) draws attention to connections with the forms of argument in wisdom literature. Both are too restrictive. Rabbinic and wisdom argumentation overlap much more than is commonly acknowledged, and Jesus and Matthew echo both. Even more, they must be interpreted first of all in their own right. Far more impressive is Martin Hengel's demonstration of a primarily Jewish background to the Sermon on the Mount, without attempting to determine too narrowly the precise profile of that background ("Zur matthäischen Bergpredigt und ihrem jüdischen Hintergrund," *ThR* 52 [1987]: 327–400).

The attempt to understand the Sermon on the Mount within a unified theological grid has not produced consistent results. Schweizer lists seven major interpretive approaches; Harvey K. McArthur (*Understanding the Sermon on the Mount* [New York: Harper, 1960], 105–48) lists twelve. Some of the most important are as follows:

a. Lutheran orthodoxy often understands the Sermon on the Mount as an exposition of law designed to drive people to cry for grace. This is Pauline (Ro 3–4; Gal 3), and grace is certainly presupposed in the sermon (e.g., see comments at 5:3). But though one of Jesus' purposes may have been to puncture self-righteous approaches to God, the sermon cannot be reduced to this. The righteousness envisaged (see comments at 5:20) is not imputed righteousness. Moreover, Paul himself insists that personal righteousness must characterize one who inherits the kingdom (Gal 5:19–24). Above all, this view fails to grasp the flow of salvation history (see below).

b. Some have argued that Jesus' eschatology is so "realized" that the ethic of the Sermon on the Mount is a sort of moral road map toward social progress. Fewer scholars adopt this stance today than once was the case, though on the street it is still remarkably powerful. Many who have never read these chapters, still less Matthew's gospel, identify the Sermon on the Mount with turning the other cheek and not judging others, but they have no idea how to integrate such themes with, say, 7:21–23. Nor can the classic liberal vision be integrated with apocalyptic elements in Jesus' teaching (e.g., ch. 24) or with the vision of a suffering and witnessing community (ch. 10).

c. The sermon is often interpreted as a set of moral standards used catechetically within Matthew's community. While that may be so if there was a Matthean community (though increasingly today, people are coming round to the view that Matthew's gospel was written for all Christians, not for a closed community), this view is reductionistic. It fails to wrestle adequately with Matthew's location in salvation history. The entire book of Matthew presents itself as Jesus' teaching and ministry before the church was called into existence in the full, post-Pentecost sense. This gospel does not present itself as the catechesis of a church but as a theological portrayal of the one who fulfilled Scripture and introduced the end times.

d. The Anabaptist-Mennonite tradition interprets the ethical demands to apply to all believers in every age and every circumstance (see Stanley Hauerwas, *Matthew* [Brazos Theological Commentary on the Bible; Grand Rapids: Brazos, 2006], 61). The resulting philosophy of pacifism in the context of a power-loving world demands the conclusion that Christians should not seek to be involved in affairs of state. This tradition rightly perceives the separate status of the believing community, which must not be confused with the world (e.g., 7:13–14, 21–23). But it is insensitive to the place of this sermon in the progress of redemption and absolutizes some of its teaching in a way incompatible with its context and with other Scripture (see comments at 5:38–42; 6:5–8; more broadly, cf. D. A. Carson, *Christ and Culture Revisited* [Grand Rapids: Eerdmans, 2008]). It is remarkably selective about the parallels it adduces.

e. Existential interpretation finds in these chapters a summons to personal decision and authentic faith but jettisons the personal and infinite God who makes the summons. Also, by denying the uniqueness of the Jesus who delivers the sermon, it fails to cope with its fulfillment theme and its implications.

f. Still others claim that Jesus is advocating an "interim ethic" to remain in force until the soon-expected consummation. But Jesus, they assume, erred as to the timing of this event, so the "interim ethic" must be toned down accordingly. All this rests on a view of Jesus derived from other passages (not least chs. 24–25 and parallels).

g. It is common among evangelicals and others to interpret the Sermon on the Mount as an intensifying or radicalizing of OT moral law (e.g., Stott, *Messsage of the Sermon on the Mount*). But this depends largely on a doubtful interpretation of 5:17–20 (see below).

h. Classic dispensationalism interprets the Sermon on the Mount as law for the millennial kingdom first offered by Jesus to the Jews. This has faced so many objections (e.g., Can any age be justly described as "millennial" that requires "laws" to govern face slapping?) that the approach has been qualified. J. Dwight Pentecost ("The Purpose of the Sermon on the Mount," *BSac* 115 [1958]: 128ff., 212ff., 313ff.) and John Walvoord take the ethical content of the sermon to be binding on any age but continue to drive a wedge between these chapters and the Christian gospel by pointing out that they do not mention the cross, justification by faith, new birth, etc. On that basis, the epistle of James is also non-Christian! Moreover, they misinterpret Matthew's fulfillment motif and impose a theological structure on this gospel demanding improbable exegesis of numerous passages (occasionally identified in this commentary). The disjunction between Matthew 5–7 and the Christian gospel is theologically and historically artificial.

This sketch overlooks many variations of the principal interpretations of the Sermon on the Mount. Several scholars have narrowed the focus: C. Burchard ("The Theme of the Sermon on the Mount," in *Essays on the Love Commandment* [ed. Schottroff et al.], 57–75) understands chs. 5–7 to provide rules of conduct for the Matthean church in the light of opposition to its witness; G. Bornkamm ("Der Aufbau der Bergpredigt," *NTS* 24 [1977–78]: 419–32) interprets the sermon around the Lord's Prayer (6:9–13). A debate that is sometimes tied to one or another of the theological approaches just listed concerns possible affinities between Jesus and Moses (see discussion in Keener). Some see the tightest possible affinities; others remain unconvinced, preferring a nuanced judgment like that of Garland: "While Matthew presents Jesus as Moses-like, he does not depict him as a new Moses, but as the Lord, the son of God." Though these and other interpretive grids highlight neglected themes, they overlook the thrust of the sermon as a whole and its place in Matthew.

The unifying theme of the sermon is the kingdom of heaven (see comments at 3:2, 12; 4:17). This is established, not by counting how many times the expression occurs, but by noting where it occurs. It envelops the beatitudes (5:3, 10) and appears in 5:17–20, which details the relation between the OT and the kingdom, a subject that leads to another literary envelope around the body of the sermon (5:17; 7:12). It returns at the heart of the Lord's Prayer (6:10), climaxes the section on kingdom perspectives (6:33), and is presented as what must finally be entered (7:21–23). Matthew places the sermon immediately after two verses insisting that the primary content of Jesus' preaching was the gospel of the kingdom (4:17, 23). It provides ethical guidelines for life in the kingdom, but does so within an explanation of the place of the contemporary setting within redemption history and Jesus' relation to the OT (5:17–20). The community forming around him, his "disciples," is not yet so cohesive and committed a group that exhortations to "enter" (7:13–14) are irrelevant. The glimpse of kingdom life (horizontally and vertically) in these chapters anticipates not only the love commandments (22:34–40) but also grace (5:3; 6:12; 7:7–11; cf. 21:28–46).

4. Location in Matthew. Unlike Luke, Matthew does not place the sermon after the calling of the Twelve (10:1–4); there he puts a second discourse, one concerning mission. This links the call with the commission, a theme of great importance to Matthew (see comments at 11:11–12; 28:16–20). No less important is the location of the Sermon on the Mount so early in the gospel, before any sign of controversies between Jesus and the Jewish leaders as to the law's meaning. This means that, despite the antitheses in 5:17–48 ("You have heard ... but I tell"), these should not be read as tokens of confrontation but in the light of the fulfillment themes richly set out in chs. 1–4 and made again explicit in 5:17–20: Jesus comes "to fulfill" the Law and the Prophets (i.e., the OT Scriptures). Therefore, his announcements concerning the kingdom must be read against that background, not with reference to debates over halakic details. This framework is Matthew's; by it he tells us that whatever controversies occupied Jesus' attention, the burden of his kingdom proclamation always made the kingdom the goal of the Scriptures, the long-expected messianic reign foretold by the Law and the Prophets alike.

1. Setting (5:1–2)

[1]Now when he saw the crowds, he went up on a mountainside and sat down. His disciples came to him, [2]and he began to teach them, saying:

COMMENTARY

1 The "crowds" are those referred to in 4:23–25. Here Jesus stands at the height of his popularity. Although his ministry touched the masses, he saw the need to teach his "disciples" (*mathētai*, GK *3412*) closely. The word "disciple" must not be restricted to the Twelve, whom Matthew has yet to mention (10:1–4). Nor is it a special word for full-fledged believers, since it can also describe John the Baptist's followers (11:2). In the Lukan parallel, we are told of a "large crowd of his disciples" as well as "a great number of people" (6:17). This goes well with Matthew 4:25, which says large crowds "followed" Jesus. Those who especially want to attach themselves to him, Jesus takes aside to instruct; but it is anachronistic to suppose that all are fully committed in the later "Christian" sense of Acts 11:26 (cf. Mt 7:13–14, 21–23). Matthew sees the disciples as paradigms for believers in his own day but never loses sight, as we shall repeatedly notice, of the unique historical place of the first followers (contra U. Luz, "Die Jünger im Matthäusevangelium," *ZNW* 62 [1971]: 141–71—though Luz wisely avoids reducing Matthew's disciples to the Twelve). On the importance of the theme of discipleship in this gospel, see Martin H. Franzmann, *Follow Me: Discipleship according to Saint Matthew* [St. Louis, Mo.: Concordia, 1961]).

At this point in his ministry, Jesus could not escape the mounting crowds; and by the end of his sermon (7:28–29), he was surrounded by even larger crowds. This suggests that his teaching covered several days, not just an hour or two (cf. the three-day meeting, 15:29–39). The place of retreat Jesus chose was in the hill country (see Notes, v.1), not "on a mountainside." He "sat down" to teach. Sitting was the accepted posture of synagogue or school teachers (Lk 4:20; cf. Mt 13:2; 23:2; 24:3; see *NIDNTT*, 3:588–89). The attempt of Lachs ("Textual Observations," 99–101) to find an anachronism here fails because his sources refer to the position of one who is *learning* Torah, not teaching it. Luke has Jesus standing (6:17) but ministering to the larger crowd from which he could not escape (6:17–19).

2 The NIV masks the idiom "he opened his mouth and taught them," found elsewhere in the NT (13:35; Ac 10:34; 18:14) and reflecting OT roots (Job 3:1; 33:2; Da 10:16). It is used in solemn or revelatory contexts. The verb "teach" (*edidasken*) is imperfect and inceptive: "He began to teach them." Contrary to Davies (*Setting*, 7–8), one must not draw too sharp a distinction between preaching (*kēryssō*, GK *3062*, Mt 4:17) and teaching (*didaskō*, GK *1438*: see comments at 3:1 and the linking of these categories in 4:23; 9:35). Str-B, 1:189, notes that teaching was not uncommonly done outdoors as well as in synagogues.

NOTES

1 The NIV's "on a mountainside" renders εἰς τὸ ὄρος (*eis to oros*). The article does not suggest some well-known mountain (contra Hendriksen; Turner, *Syntax*, 173), still less the mountain where Moses received the law (contra Loisy). Even Davies (*Setting*, 93), after exploring all possibilities, concedes Matthew could have more explicitly delineated a "new Moses" theme. In fact, τὸ ὄρος, *to oros* (lit., "the mountain," GK *4001*) and the corresponding Hebrew and Aramaic may mean nothing more than "the mountain region" or "the hill country." Jesus withdrew to the hill country west of Lake Galilee—the text requires nothing more. Attempts to discern profound symbolic significance (e.g., Gundry) are misguided. Moreover πεδινός (*pedinos*, "plain" or "a level place") in Luke 6:17, a NT hapax legomenon, should not conjure up images of American prairie but a relatively flat place in rough, rocky, or hilly terrain—perhaps "plateau" (cf. usage in Jer 21:13 LXX ["rocky plateau" in the NIV], or in Isa 13:2 LXX—ἐπ' ὄρους πεδινοῦ [*ep' orous pedinou*, lit., "on a level (flat) mountain"; NIV, "on a bare hilltop"]). There is little difference between Matthew's "mountain" and Luke's "plain."

2. The kingdom of heaven: its norms and witness (5:3–16)

a. The norms of the kingdom (5:3–12)

(1) The Beatitudes (5:3–10)

OVERVIEW

The beatitudes (Lat. *beatus*, "blessed"), otherwise called macarisms (from Gr. *makarios*, "blessed," GK *3421*), have been the subject of many valuable studies, the most detailed being J. Dupont's *Les Béatitudes* (3 vols.; 2nd ed.; Paris: Gabalda, 1969). As to form, beatitudes find their roots in Wisdom literature and especially the psalms (for the best discussion of the OT background, see W. Zimmerli, "Die Seligpreisungen der Bergpredigt und das Alte Testament," in *Donum Gentilicium* [ed. E. Bammel et al.; Oxford: Clarendon, 1978], 8–26; cf. Pss 1:1; 31:1–2; 144:15; Pr 3:13; Da 12:12). OT beatitudes never bunch more than two together (e.g., Ps 84:4–5; elsewhere, cf. Sir 25:7–9).

Comparison of 5:3–12 with Luke 6:20–26 shows that, along with smaller differences, the four Lukan beatitudes stand beside four woes—all in the second person. But Matthew mentions no woes, and his eight beatitudes (Mt 5:3–10) are in the third person, followed by an expansion of the last one in the second person (vv.11–12). Pre-NT beatitudes are only rarely in the second person (e.g., *1 En.* 58:2) and occur with woes only in the Greek text of Ecclesiastes 10:16–17; so on formal grounds there is no reason to see Matthew's beatitudes as late adaptations.

No doubt both Matthew and Luke selected and shaped their material. But though this results in differences in the thrust of the two sets of beatitudes, such differences are often overstated (e.g., C. H. Dodd, *More New Testament Studies* [Manchester: Manchester Univ. Press, 1968], 7–8). Dupont (*Les

Béatitudes) and Marshall (*Gospel of Luke*) argue that Luke describes what disciples actually are, Matthew what they ought to be; Luke, the social implications of Jesus' teaching and reversals at the consummation, Matthew, the standards of Christian righteousness to be pursued now for entrance into the kingdom. Similarly, G. Strecker ("Les macarismes du discours sur la montagne," in *L'Évangile selon Matthieu* [ed. Didier], 185–208) insists that in Matthew's beatitudes ethics has displaced eschatology: the beatitudes become ethical entrance requirements rather than eschatological blessings associated with the messianic age.

A more nuanced interpretation is presented by R. A. Guelich ("The Matthean Beatitudes: 'Entrance-Requirements' or Eschatological Blessings?" *JBL* 95 [1973]: 415–34). He notes that Matthew 5:3–5 contains planned echoes of Isaiah 61:1–3, which is certainly eschatological in orientation. Moreover, both Isaiah 61:1–3 and the Matthean beatitudes are formally declarative but implicitly hortatory: one must not overlook function for form. The beatitudes "are but an expression of the fulfillment of Isaiah 61, the OT promise of the *Heilszeit* ['time of salvation'], in the person and proclamation of Jesus. This handling of the beatitudes is certainly in keeping with Matthew's emphasis throughout the gospel that Jesus comes in light of the OT promise" (p. 433). The implicit demands of the beatitudes are therefore comprehensible only because of the new state of affairs the proclamation of the kingdom initiates (4:17, 23), the insistence that Jesus has come to fulfill the Law and the Prophets (5:17). Gibbs insightfully remarks that these beatitudes constitute "a sort of 'doorway' through which Matthew's readers/hearers must pass if they are to grasp aright the Lord's great teaching in the Sermon."

3 "Blessed are the poor in spirit,
for theirs is the kingdom of heaven.
4 Blessed are those who mourn,
for they will be comforted.
5 Blessed are the meek,
for they will inherit the earth.
6 Blessed are those who hunger and thirst for righteousness,
for they will be filled.
7 Blessed are the merciful,
for they will be shown mercy.
8 Blessed are the pure in heart,
for they will see God.
9 Blessed are the peacemakers,
for they will be called sons of God.
10 Blessed are those who are persecuted because of righteousness,
for theirs is the kingdom of heaven.

COMMENTARY

3 Two words and their cognates stand behind "blessed" and "blessing" in the NT. The word used in vv.3–11 is *makarios* (GK *3421*), which usually corresponds in the LXX to *ʾašrê* (GK 897), a Hebrew term used almost as an interjection: "Oh the blessednesses [pl.] of." Usually *makarios* describes the person who is singularly favored by God and therefore in some sense "happy"; but the word can apply to God (1Ti 1:11; 6:15). The other word is *eulogētos* (GK *2329*), found in the LXX primarily for Hebrew *b*^{e}*rākâ* (GK 1388) and used chiefly in connection with God in both OT and NT (e.g., Mk 14:61; Lk 1:68; Ro 1:25; 2Co 1:3). *Eulogētos* does not occur in Matthew; but the cognate verb appears five times (Mt 14:19; 21:9; 23:39; 25:34; 26:26), in one of which it applies to man (25:34), not God or Christ. Attempts to make *makarios* mean "happy" and *eulogētos* "blessed" (Broadus) are therefore futile. Though both appear many times, both can apply to either God or man. It is difficult not to conclude that their common factor is approval: man "blesses" God, approving and praising him; God "blesses" man, approving him in gracious condescension. Applied to man, the OT words are certainly synonymous (cf. *THAT*, 1:356).

As for "happy" (TEV), it will not do for the beatitudes, having been devalued in modern usage. The Greek "describes a state not of inner feeling on the part of those to whom it is applied, but of blessedness from an ideal point of view in the judgment of others" (Allen). In the eschatological setting of Matthew, "blessed" can only promise eschatological blessing (cf. *NIDNTT*, 1:216–17; *TDNT*, 4:367–70); and each particular blessing is specified by the second clause of each beatitude.

The "poor in spirit" are the ones who are "blessed." Since Luke speaks simply of "the poor," many have concluded that he preserves the true teaching of the historical Jesus—concern for the economically destitute—while Matthew has "spiritualized" it by adding "in spirit." The issue is not so simple. Already in the OT, "the poor" has religious overtones. The word *ptōchos* ("poor"—in classical Gr., "beggar," GK *4777*) has a different force in the LXX and NT. It translates several Hebrew words, most important (in the plural) *ʿ*^{a}*nāwîm* ("the poor," the plural of GK 6705; see also GK 6714), i.e., those who because of sustained economic privation and social distress have confidence only in God (e.g., Pss 37:14; 40:17; 69:28–29, 32–33; Pr 16:19 [NIV, "the oppressed"; NASB, "the lowly"]; 29:23; Isa 61:1; cf. *Pss. Sol.* 5:2, 11; 10:7). Thus it joins with passages affirming God's favor on the lowly and contrite in spirit (e.g., Isa 57:15; 66:2). This does not mean there is lack of concern for the materially poor but that poverty itself is not the chief thing (cf. the prodigal son's "self-made" poverty). Far from conferring spiritual advantage, wealth and privilege entail great spiritual peril (see comments at 6:24; 19:23–24). Yet, though poverty is neither a blessing nor a guarantee of spiritual rewards, it can be turned to advantage if it fosters humility before God.

That this is the way to interpret v.3 is confirmed by similar expressions in the Dead Sea Scrolls (esp. 1QM 11:9; 14:6–7; 1QS 4:3; 1QH 5:22). "Poor" and "righteous" become almost equivalent in Sirach 13:17–21; CD 19:9; 4QpPs (37) 2:8–11 (cf. Schweizer; Bonnard; Dodd, "New Testament Translation Problems I," 307–10). These parallels do not prove literary dependence, but they do show that Matthew's "poor in spirit" rightly interprets Luke's "poor" (cf. Gundry, *Use of the Old Testament*,

69–71). In rabbinic circles, too, meekness and poverty of spirit were highly praised (cf. Felix Böhl, "Die Demut als höchste der Tugenden," *BZ* 20 [1976]: 217–23).

Yet biblical balance is easy to prostitute. The emperor Julian the Apostate (AD 332–63) is reputed to have said with vicious irony that he wanted to confiscate Christians' property so that they might all become poor and enter the kingdom of heaven. On the other hand, the wealthy too easily dismiss Jesus' teaching about poverty here and elsewhere (see comments at 6:24) as merely attitudinal and confuse their hoarding with good stewardship. R. T. France ("God and Mammon," 3–21) presents a fine balance in these matters.

To be poor in spirit is not to lack courage but to acknowledge spiritual bankruptcy. It confesses one's unworthiness before God and utter dependence on him. Therefore those who interpret the Sermon on the Mount as law and not gospel—whether by H. Windisch's historical reconstructions (*The Meaning of the Sermon on the Mount* [Philadelphia: Westminster, 1951] or by classical dispensationalism (cf. Carson, *Sermon on the Mount*, 155–57), which calls the sermon "pure law" (though it concedes that its principles have a "beautiful moral application" for the Christian)—stumble at the first sentence (cf. Stott, *Message of the Sermon on the Mount*, 36–38). The kingdom of heaven is not given on the basis of race (cf. 3:9), earned merits, the military zeal and prowess of Zealots, or the wealth of a Zacchaeus. It is given to the poor, the despised publicans, the prostitutes, those who are so "poor" they know they can offer nothing and do not try. They cry for mercy, and they alone are heard.

These themes recur repeatedly in Matthew and present the sermon's ethical demands in a setting that does not treat the resulting conduct as conditions for entrance to the kingdom that people themselves can achieve. All must begin by confessing that by themselves they can achieve nothing. Fuller disclosures of the gospel in the years beyond Jesus' earthly ministry do not change this; in the last book of the canon, an established church must likewise recognize its precarious position when it claims to be rich and fails to see its own poverty (Rev 3:14–22).

The kingdom of heaven (see comments at 3:2; 4:17) belongs to the poor in spirit. It is they who enjoy Messiah's reign and the blessings he brings. They joyfully accept his rule and participate in the life of the kingdom (7:14). The reward in the last beatitude is the same as in the first. The literary structure, an "inclusio" or envelope, establishes that everything included within it concerns the kingdom: i.e., the blessings of the intervening beatitudes are kingdom blessings, and the beatitudes themselves are kingdom norms.

While the rewards of vv.4–9 are future ("will be comforted," "will inherit," etc.), the first and last are present ("for theirs is the kingdom of heaven"). Yet one must not make too much of this, for the present tense can function as a future, and the future tense emphasizes expectation, not mere futurity. There is little doubt that here the kingdom sense is primarily future, postconsummation, made explicit in v.12. But the present tense "envelope" (vv.3, 10) should not be written off as insignificant or as masking an Aramaic original that did not specify present or future, for Matthew must have meant something when he chose *estin* ("is") instead of *estai* ("will be"). The natural conclusion is that, though the full blessedness of those described in these beatitudes awaits the consummated kingdom, they already share in the kingdom's blessedness so far as it has been inaugurated (see comments at 4:17; 8:29; 12:28; 19:29).

4 Black (*Aramaic Approach*, 157) notes how the Matthean and Lukan (6:21b, 25b) forms of this beatitude could each have been part of a larger parallelism—an observation that goes nicely with the hypothesis that the Sermon on the Mount and the Sermon on the Plain are reports of one discourse, relying somewhat on common sources (see Overview, 5:1–7:29).

Some commentators deny that this mourning is for sin (e.g., Bonnard). Others (e.g., Schweizer) understand it to be mourning for any kind of misery. The reality is subtler. The godly remnant of Jesus' day weeps because of the humiliation of Israel, but they understand that it comes from personal and corporate sins. The psalmist testified, "Streams of tears flow from my eyes, for your law is not obeyed" (Ps 119:136; cf. Eze 9:4). When Jesus preached, "The kingdom of heaven is near," he, like John the Baptist before him, expected not jubilation but contrite tears. It is not enough to acknowledge personal spiritual bankruptcy (Mt 5:3) with a cold heart. Weeping for sins can be deeply poignant (Ezr 10:6; Ps 51:4; Da 9:19–20) and can cover a global as well as personal view of sin and our participation in it. Paul understands these matters well (cf. Ro 7:24; 1Co 5:2; 2Co 12:21; Php 3:18).

"Comfort, comfort my people" (Isa 40:1) is God's response. These first two beatitudes deliberately allude to the messianic blessing of Isaiah 61:1–3 (see Lk 4:16–19; cf. France, *Jesus and the Old Testament*, 134–35), confirming them as eschatological and messianic. The Messiah comes to bestow "the oil of gladness instead of mourning, and a garment of praise instead of a spirit of despair" (Isa 61:3). But these blessings, already realized partially but fully only at the consummation (Rev 7:17), depend on a Messiah who comes to save his people from their sins (1:21; cf. 11:28–30). Those who claim to experience all its joys without tears mistake the nature of the kingdom. In Charles Wesley's words:

He speaks, and listening to his voice,
New life the dead receive;
The mournful, broken hearts rejoice,
The humble poor believe.

5 This beatitude and those in vv.7–10 have no parallel in Luke. It would be wrong to suppose that Matthew's beatitudes are for different groups of people or that we have the right to half the blessings if we determine to pursue four out of the eight. They are a unity and describe the norm for Messiah's people.

The word "meek" (*praus*, GK *4558*) is hard to define. It can signify absence of pretension (1Pe 3:4, 14–15) but generally suggests gentleness (cf. 11:29; Jas 3:13) and the self-control it entails. The attempt to understand a "meek" person to be nonviolent and law-observant (Michel Talbot, *Heureux les doux, car ils hériteront la terre: (Mt 5:4 [5])* [Paris: Gabalda, 2002]) is unconvincing in its methods and doctrinaire in its conclusions. The Greeks extolled humility in wise men and rulers, but such humility smacked of condescension. In general, the Greeks considered meekness a vice because they failed to distinguish it from servility. To be meek toward others implies freedom from malice and a vengeful spirit. Jesus best exemplifies it (11:29; 21:5). Lloyd-Jones (*Sermon on the Mount*, 1:65–69) rightly applies meekness to our attitudes toward others. We may acknowledge our own bankruptcy (v.3) and mourn (v.4). But to respond with meekness when others tell us of our bankruptcy is far harder (cf. Stott, *Message of the Sermon on the Mount*, 43–44). Meekness, therefore, requires such a true view about ourselves as will express itself even in our attitude toward others.

And the meek—not the strong, aggressive, harsh, tyrannical—will inherit the earth. The verb "inherit" often relates to entrance into the promised land (e.g., Dt 4:1; 16:20; cf. Isa 57:13; 60:21). But the specific OT allusion here is Psalm 37:9, 11,

29, a psalm recognized as messianic in Jesus' day (4QpPs 37). There is no need to interpret the land metaphorically, as having no reference to geography or space; nor is there need to restrict the meaning to "land of Israel" (see Notes). Entrance into the promised land ultimately became a pointer toward entrance into the new heaven and *the new earth* ("earth" is the same word as "land"; cf. Isa 66:22; Rev 21:1), the consummation of the messianic kingdom. While in Pauline terms, believers may now possess all things in principle (1Co 3:21–23; 2Co 6:10) since they belong to Christ, Matthew directs our attention yet further to the "renewal of all things" (19:28).

6 "Hunger and thirst" vividly express desire. The sons of Korah cried, "My soul thirsts for God, for the living God" (Ps 42:2; cf. 63:1). The deepest spiritual famine is hunger for the word of God (Am 8:11–14).

The precise nature of the righteousness for which the blessed hunger and thirst is disputed. Some argue that it is the imputed righteousness of God—eschatological salvation or, more narrowly, justification: the blessed hunger for it and receive it (e.g., Grundmann; McNeile; Zahn; Barth ["Matthew's Understanding of the Law," 123–24]; Bultmann [*Theology of the New Testament*, 1:273]; Schrenk [*TDNT*, 2:198]). This is certainly plausible, since the immediate context does arouse hopes for God's eschatological action, and hungering suggests that the righteousness that satisfies will be given as a gift.

The chief objection is that *dikaiosynē* ("righteousness," GK *1466*) in Matthew does not have that sense anywhere else (cf. Przybylski, *Righteousness in Matthew*, 96–98). So it is better to take this righteousness as simultaneously personal righteousness (cf. Hill, *Greek Words*, 127–28.; Strecker, *Weg der Gerechtigkeit*, 156–58) and justice in the broadest sense (cf. Ridderbos, *Coming of the Kingdom*, 190–91; Turner). These people hunger and thirst, not only that they may be righteous (i.e., that they may wholly do God's will from the heart), but that justice may be done everywhere. All unrighteousness grieves them and makes them homesick for the new heaven and new earth—the home of righteousness (2Pe 3:13). Satisfied with neither personal righteousness alone nor social justice alone, they cry for both. In short, they long for the advent of the messianic kingdom. What they taste now whets their appetites for more. Ultimately they will be satisfied (same verb as in 14:20; Php 4:12; Rev 19:21) without qualification only when the kingdom is consummated (see discussion in Gundry).

7 This beatitude is akin to Psalm 18:25 (reading "merciful" [ASV] instead of "faithful" [NIV]; following MT [v.26], not LXX [17:26]; cf. Pr 14:21). Mercy embraces both forgiveness for the guilty and compassion for the suffering and needy. No particular object of the demanded mercy is specified, because mercy is to be a function of Jesus' disciples, not of the particular situation that calls it forth. The theme is common in Matthew (6:12–15; 9:13; 12:7; 18:33–34). The reward is not mercy shown by others but by God (cf. the saying preserved in *1 Clem.* 13:2). This does not mean our mercy is the causal ground of God's mercy but its occasional ground (see comments at 6:14–15). This beatitude, too, is tied to the context. "It is 'the meek' who are also 'the merciful'. For to be meek is to acknowledge to others that *we* are sinners; to be merciful is to have compassion on others, for they are sinners too" (Stott, *Message of the Sermon on the Mount*, 48, emphasis his).

8 Commentators are divided on "pure in heart."

1. Some take it to mean inner moral purity as opposed to merely external piety or ceremonial cleanness. This is an important theme in Matthew and elsewhere in the Scriptures (e.g., Dt 10:16; 30:6; 1Sa 15:22; Pss 24:3–4 [to which there is

direct allusion here]; 51:6, 10; Isa 1:10–17; Jer 4:4; 7:3–7; 9:25–26; Ro 2:9; 1Ti 1:5; 2Ti 2:22, cf. Mt 23:25–28).

2. Others take it to mean single-mindedness, a heart "free from the tyranny of a divided self" (Tasker; cf. Bonnard). Several of the passages just cited focus on freedom from deceit (Pss 24:4; 51:4–17; cf. Ge 50:5–6; Pr 22:11). This interpretation also prepares the way for Matthew 6:22. The "pure in heart" are thus "the utterly sincere."

The dichotomy between these two options is a false one; it is impossible to have one without the other. The one who is single-minded in commitment to the kingdom and its righteousness (6:33) will also be inwardly pure. Inward sham, deceit, and moral filth cannot coexist with sincere devotion to Christ. Either way, this beatitude excoriates hypocrisy (see comments at 6:1–18). The pure in heart will see God—now with the eyes of faith and finally in the dazzling brilliance of the beatific vision in whose light no deceit can exist (cf. Heb 12:14; 1Jn 3:1–3; Rev 21:22–27).

9 Jesus' concern in this beatitude is not with the peaceful but with the peacemakers. Peace is of constant concern in both Testaments (e.g., Pr 15:1; Isa 52:7; Lk 24:36; Ro 10:15; 12:18; 1Co 7:15; Eph 2:11–22; Heb 12:14; 1Pe 3:11). But as some of these and other passages show, the making of peace can itself have messianic overtones. The Promised Son is called the "Prince of Peace" (Isa 9:6); and Isaiah 52:7—"How beautiful on the mountains are the feet of those who bring good news, who proclaim peace, who bring good tidings, who proclaim salvation, who say to Zion, 'Your God reigns!'"—linking as it does peace, salvation, and God's reign, was interpreted messianically in the Judaism of Jesus' day.

Jesus does not limit the peacemaking to only one kind, and neither will his disciples. In the light of the gospel, Jesus himself is the supreme peacemaker, making peace between God and man, and man and man. Our peacemaking will include the promulgation of that gospel. It must also extend to seeking all kinds of reconciliation. Instead of delighting in division, bitterness, strife, or some petty "divide and conquer" mentality, disciples of Jesus delight to make peace wherever possible. Making peace is not appeasement. The true model is God's costly peacemaking (Eph 2:15–17; Col 1:20). Those who undertake this work are acknowledged as God's sons. In the OT, Israel has the title "sons" (Dt 14:1; Hos 1:10; cf. *Pss. Sol.* 17:30; Wis 2:13–18). Now it belongs to the heirs of the kingdom, who, meek and poor in spirit, loving righteousness yet merciful, are especially equipped for peacemaking and so reflect something of their heavenly Father's character. "There is no more godlike work to be done in this world than peacemaking" (Broadus). This beatitude must have been shocking to Zealots when Jesus preached it, when political passions were inflamed (Morison).

10 It is no accident that Jesus should pass from peacemaking to persecution, for the world enjoys its cherished hates and prejudices so much that the peacemaker is not always welcome. Opposition is a normal mark of being a disciple of Jesus, as normal as hungering for righteousness or being merciful (see Jn 15:18–25; Ac 14:22; 2Ti 3:12; 1Pe 4:13–14; cf. the woe in Lk 6:26). Lachs ("Textual Observations," 101–3) cannot believe Christians were ever persecuted because of righteousness; so he repoints an alleged underlying Hebrew text to read "because of the Righteous One"—a reference to Jesus. But he underestimates how offensive genuine righteousness, "proper conduct before God" (Przybylski, *Righteousness in Matthew*, 99), really is (cf. Isa 51:7). The reward of these persecuted people is the same as the reward of the poor in spirit—namely, the kingdom of heaven, which terminates the inclusio (see comments at v.3).

NOTES

3 Most scholars interpret τῷ πνεύματι (*tō pneumati*, "spirit") as a dative of respect (e.g., Zerwick, *Biblical Greek*, para. 53), so that the phrase πτωχοὶ τῷ πνεύματι (*ptōchoi tō pneumati*) means, literally, "poor with respect to the spirit." Moule (*Idiom Book*, 46) wonders whether it might not border on an instrumental usage, which can often best be rendered by an English adverb, i.e., οἱ πτωχοὶ τῷ πνεύματι (*hoi ptōchoi tō pneumati*) = "the poor used in its spiritual [i.e., religious] sense," over against "the literally [i.e., materially] poor" of James 2:5. But he acknowledges that Psalm 34:18 points in another direction.

5 The word γῆ (*gē*, "land," GK *1178*) occurs forty-three times in Matthew—once for the land of Judah (2:6); twice for the land of Israel (2:20–21); several times for some region (e.g., 4:15; 9:26, 31; 11:24; and possibly 27:45); several times in the expression "heaven and earth" or something similar (5:18, 35; 11:25; 24:35; 28:18); several times to distinguish earth from heaven (6:10; 9:6; 16:19; 18:18 [2x], 19; 23:9); once to refer to the place where sinful people live (5:13); several times to refer to "ground" (e.g., 10:29; 15:35; 25:18, 25; 27:51), "soil" (13:5, 8, 23), or "shore" (14:24); and several times to refer to the whole earth without any of the above connotations (12:40, 42; 17:25; 23:35; 24:30). In Matthew, therefore, γῆ, *gē*, is used to refer to a specified region or nation (Israel, Judah, Zebulon, Naphtali, et al.) only if that region's name is given. The possible exception is 27:45. The most natural way to render this notice in v.5 is therefore "earth," not "land [of Israel]."

9 Although "son of" can have ontological force, it often means "one who reflects the character of" or the like. Hence a "son of Belial" (= "son of worthlessness") refers to a worthless person, someone of worthless conduct. Similarly "son of God" may have ontological or purely functional force, depending on the context.

10 The perfect passive participle οἱ δεδιωγμένοι (*hoi dediōgmenoi*, "those who are persecuted," GK *1503*) is rather awkward if the traditional perfect force is retained: "those who have been persecuted." Many see this as a sign of anachronism—persecution had broken out by the time Matthew wrote (e.g., Hill). Some older commentators treat it as a more or less Hebraizing "prophetic" perfect; and Broadus adds that the perfect accords "with the fact that the chief rewards of such sufferers do not so much attend on the persecution as follow it." But then we may ask why a future perfect isn't used, or why the same rule isn't applied to those who mourn (v.4). It is better, under verbal aspect theory, to recognize that the semantic force of the perfect is stative.

(2) Expansion (5:11–12)

11"Blessed are you when people insult you, persecute you and falsely say all kinds of evil against you because of me. 12Rejoice and be glad, because great is your reward in heaven, for in the same way they persecuted the prophets who were before you."

COMMENTARY

11–12 These two verses (cf. Lk 6:22–23, 26), switching from third person to second, apply the force of the last beatitude (v.10), not to the church (which would be anachronistic), but to Jesus' disciples. Doubtless Matthew and his contemporaries also applied it to themselves. Verse 11 extends the persecution of v.10 to include insult and slander (Lk 6:22–23 adds hate). The reason for the persecution in v.10 is "because of righteousness"; now, Jesus says, it is "because of me." "This confirms that the righteousness of life that is in view is in imitation of Jesus. Simultaneously, it so identifies the disciple of Jesus with the practice of Jesus' righteousness that there is no place for professed allegiance to Jesus that is not full of righteousness" (Carson, *Sermon on the Mount*, 28). Moreover, it is an implicit christological claim, for the prophets to whom the disciples are likened were persecuted for their faithfulness to God and the disciples for faithfulness to Jesus. Not Jesus but the disciples are likened to the prophets. Jesus places himself on a par with God. The change from "the Son of Man" (Luke) to "me" is probably Matthew's clarification (see Reflections, p. 000).

The appropriate response of the disciple is rejoicing. The second verb, *agalliasthe* ("be glad," GK *22*), Hill takes to be "something of a technical term for joy in persecution and martyrdom" (cf. 1Pe 1:6, 8; 4:13; Rev 19:7). Yet its range of associations seems broader (Lk 1:47; 10:21; Jn 5:35; 8:56; Ac 2:26; 16:34). The disciples of Jesus are to rejoice under persecution because their heavenly reward (see Notes, v.12) will be great at the consummation of the kingdom (v.12). Opposition is sure, for the disciples are aligning themselves with the OT prophets who were persecuted before them (e.g., 2Ch 24:21; Ne 9:26; Jer 20:2; cf. Mt 21:35; 23:32–37; Ac 7:52; 1Th2:15). This biblical perspective was doubtless part of the historical basis on which Jesus built his own implied prediction that his followers would be persecuted. Treated seriously, it makes ineffective the ground on which some treat the prediction as anachronistic (e.g., Hare, *Theme of Jewish Persecution*, 114–21). Stendahl's suggestion ("Matthew," in *Peake's Commentary*) that Matthew here refers to Christian prophets is not only needlessly anachronistic but out of step with both Matthew's use of "prophet" and his link between the murder of "prophets" and the sin of the "forefathers" (23:30–32), which shows that the prophets belong to the OT period.

These verses neither encourage seeking persecution nor permit retreating from it, sulking, or retaliation. From the perspective of both redemptive history ("the prophets") and eternity ("reward in heaven"), these verses constitute the reasonable response of faith, one which the early Christians readily understood (cf. Ac 5:41; 2Co 4:17; 1Pe 1:6–9; cf. Da 3:24–25). "Discipleship means allegiance to the suffering Christ, and it is therefore not at all surprising that Christians should be called on to suffer. In fact it is a joy and a token of his grace" (Bonhoeffer, *Cost of Discipleship*, 80–81). But in reassuring his disciples that their sufferings are "neither new, nor accidental, nor absurd" (Bonnard), Jesus spoke of principles that will appear again (esp. Mt 10, 24).

NOTES

11 Matthew's "falsely say all kinds of evil against you" (cf. Ac 28:21) is an explanation of a Hebrew or Aramaic idiom still preserved in Luke's "reject your name as evil" (Lk 6:22; cf. Dt 22:14, 19). The word ψευδόμενοι (*pseudomenoi*, "falsely," GK *6017*), given a C in UBS[4], is implied, whether original or not. External evidence strongly favors inclusion; the internal evidence is equivocal.

12 Morton Smith, *Tannaitic Parallels to the Gospels* (Philadelphia: SBL, 1951), 46–77, 161–84, represents those who hold that the concept of reward in the Synoptic Gospels does not differ materially from the concept of reward in early rabbinic literature. His work is essentially a word study and overlooks the substantial conceptual differences; nor does he mention the balanced treatment of A. Marmorstein, *The Doctrine of Merits in the Old Rabbinical Literature* (London: Jesus' College, 1920). The book by E. P. Sanders (*Paul and Palestinian Judaism* [London: SCM Press, 1977]) rightly warns against reading late Jewish traditions, steeped in merit theology, back into the NT period; but he seriously oversteps the evidence when he sees no difference at all, on the grace-merit front, between Paul and the "covenantal nomism" of Judaism (cf. Carson, *Divine Sovereignty*, ch. 8). C. S. Lewis (*They Asked for a Paper* [London: Geoffrey Bles, 1962], 198) rightly distinguishes various kinds of rewards. A man who marries a woman for her money is "rewarded" by her money, but he is rightly judged mercenary because the reward is not naturally linked with love. On the other hand, marriage is the proper reward of an honest and true lover; and he is not mercenary for desiring it because love and marriage are naturally linked. "The proper rewards are not simply tacked on to the activity for which they are given, but are the activity itself in consummation" (p. 198). The rewards of the NT belong largely to this second category. Life lived under kingdom norms is naturally linked with the bliss of life in the consummated kingdom. Talk of "merit" or of "earning" the reward betrays lack of understanding of Jesus' meaning (see comments at 11:25; 19:16–26; 20:1–16; 25:31–46).

b. The witness of the kingdom (5:13–16)

(1) Salt (5:13)

13"You are the salt of the earth. But if the salt loses its saltiness, how can it be made salty again? It is no longer good for anything, except to be thrown out and trampled by men."

COMMENTARY

13 Salt and light are such common substances (cf. Pliny, *Nat.* 31.102: "Nothing is more useful than salt and sunshine") that they doubtless generated many sayings. Therefore it is improper to attempt a tradition history of all gospel references as if one original stood behind the lot (cf. Mk 4:21; 9:50; Lk 8:16; 11:33; 14:34–35). Equally, the suggestion that Jesus is referring to the "covenant of salt" (Lev 2:13; Nu 18:19; 2Ch 13:5) seems unlikely. Where that expression shows up in the OT, it seems to be connected with the permanence or stability of God's covenant with his people. Here, however, Jesus says that *his disciples* are "salt." There is no mention of covenant, and, far from symbolizing stability, the salt of which Jesus speaks loses its effectiveness.

The reality is that "salt" is not a technical word with only one set of associations. It can even be connected with judgment (Lot's wife is turned into a pillar of salt, Ge 19:26; one might ruin an enemy's field by sowing it with salt, Jdg 9:45). Salt was used in the ancient world to flavor foods and even in small doses as a fertilizer (cf. Eugene P. Deatrick, "Salt, Soil, Savor," *BA* 25 [1962]: 44–45, who wants *tēs gēs* to read "for the soil," not "of the earth"; but notice the parallel "of the world" in v.14). Sometimes the word is simply referring to a commodity (Ezr 6:9) or identifies a place (2Sa 8:13). Above all, salt was used as a preservative. Rubbed into meat, a little salt would slow decay. Strictly speaking, salt cannot lose its saltiness; sodium chloride is a stable compound. But most salt in the ancient world derived from salt marshes or the like rather than by evaporation of salt water, and therefore contained many impurities. The actual salt, being more soluble than the impurities, could be leached out, leaving a residue so dilute it was of little worth.

In modern Israel, savorless salt is still said to be scattered on the soil of flat roofs. This helps harden the soil and prevent leaks; and since the roofs serve as playgrounds and places for public gathering, the salt is still being trodden under foot (Deatrick, "Salt, Soil, Savor," 47). This explanation negates the attempt by some (e.g., Lenski, Schniewind) to suppose that, precisely because pure salt cannot lose its savor, Jesus is saying that true disciples cannot lose their effectiveness. The question "How can it be made salty again?" is not meant to have an answer, as Schweizer rightly says. The rabbinic remark that what makes salt salty is "the afterbirth of a mule" (mules are sterile) rather misses the point (cf. Schweizer). The point is that if Jesus' disciples are to act as a preservative in the world by conforming to kingdom norms, if they are "called to be a moral disinfectant in a world where moral standards are low, constantly changing, or nonexistent ..., they can discharge this function only if they themselves retain their virtue" (Tasker).

NOTES

13 The verb μωρανθῇ (*mōranthē*, "loses its saltiness," GK *3701*) is used four times in the NT. In Luke 14:34, it again relates to salt, but in Romans 1:22 and 1 Corinthians 1:20, it has its more common meaning "to make or become foolish" (cf. cognate μωρέ [*mōre*, "fool"] in v.22). It is hard not to conclude that disciples who lose their savor are in fact making fools of themselves. The Greek may hide an Aramaic תפל (*tpl*, "foolish") and תבל (*tbl*, "salted"; see Black, *Aramaic Approach*, 166–67).

(2) Light (5:14–16)

[14]"You are the light of the world. A city on a hill cannot be hidden. [15]Neither do people light a lamp and put it under a bowl. Instead they put it on its stand, and it gives light to everyone in the house. [16]In the same way, let your light shine before men, that they may see your good deeds and praise your Father in heaven."

COMMENTARY

14–15 As in v.13, "you" is emphatic—namely, You, my followers and none others, are the light of the world. Though the Jews saw themselves as the light of the world (Ro 2:19), the true light is the Suffering Servant (Isa 42:6; 49:6), fulfilled in Jesus himself (Mt 4:16; cf. Jn 8:12; 9:5; 12:35; 1 Jn 1:7). Derivatively, his disciples constitute the new light (cf. Eph 5:8–9; Php 2:15). Light is a universal religious symbol. In the OT as in the NT, it most frequently symbolizes purity as opposed to filth, truth or knowledge as opposed to error or ignorance, and divine revelation and presence as opposed to reprobation and abandonment by God.

The reference to the "city on a hill" is at one level fairly obvious. Often built of white limestone, ancient towns gleamed in the sun and could not easily be hidden. At night the inhabitants' oil lamps would shed some glow over the surrounding area (cf. Bonnard). As such cities could not be hidden, so also it is unthinkable to light a lamp and hide it under a peck measure (v.15, NIV, "bowl"). A lamp is put on a lampstand to illuminate all. Attempts to identify "everyone in the house" as a reference to all Jews in contrast with Luke 11:33, referring to Gentiles (so Manson, *Sayings of Jesus*, 93), are probably guilty of making the metaphor run on all fours, especially in view of the Gentile theme so strongly present in Matthew.

But the "city on a hill" saying may also refer to OT prophecies about the time when Jerusalem or the mountain of the Lord's house, or Zion, would be lifted up before the world, the nations streaming to it (e.g., Isa 2:2–5; cf. chs. 42, 49, 54, 60). This allusion has been defended by Grundmann, Trilling (*Das wahre Israel*, 142), and especially K. M. Campbell ("The New Jerusalem in Matthew 5.14," *SJT* 31 [1978]: 335–63). It is not a certain allusion, and the absence of definite articles tells against it; if valid, it insists that Jesus' disciples constitute the true locus of the people of God, the outpost of the consummated kingdom, and the means of witness to the world—all themes central to Matthew's thought.

16 Jesus drives the metaphor home. What his disciples must show is their "good works," i.e., all righteousness, everything they are and do that reflects the mind and will of God. And people must see this light. It may provoke persecution (vv.10–12), but that is no reason for hiding the light others may see and by which they may come to glorify the Father—the disciples' only motive (cf. 2Co 4:6; 1Pe 2:12). Witness includes not just words but deeds; as Stier (*Words of the Lord Jesus*) remarks, "The good word without the good walk is of no avail."

Thus the kingdom norms (vv.3–12) so work out in the lives of the kingdom's heirs as to produce the kingdom witness (vv.13–16). If salt (v.13) exercises the negative function of delaying decay and warns disciples of the danger of compromise and conformity to the world, then light (vv.14–16) speaks positively of illuminating a sin-darkened world and warns against a withdrawal from the world that does not lead others to glorify the Father in heaven. "Flight into the invisible is a denial of the call. A community of Jesus which seeks to hide itself has ceased to follow him" (Bonhoeffer, *Cost of Discipleship*, 106).

NOTES

15 There are several probable Semitisms in this verse (cf. Hill). The μόδιος (*modios*, "bowl," GK *3654*) is a wooden grain measure, usually given as 8¾ liters, i.e., almost exactly one peck (see comments at 13:33). It is doubtful whether the vessel was used for hiding light, despite various suggestions. A different word is used in Josephus (*Ant.* 5.223 [6.5]). In any case, Jesus' point turns on what is *not* done.

3. The kingdom of heaven: its demands in relation to the OT (5:17–48)

a. Jesus and the kingdom as fulfillment of the OT (5:17–20)

OVERVIEW

Three important debates bear on the interpretation of these complex yet programmatic verses.

1. Apart from parallels to v.18 in Mark 13:31 and Luke 16:17, these verses have no synoptic parallel. Partly because of this, many have argued that these four verses represent four separate sayings from different and even conflicting churches or strata, heavily edited by Matthew (for discussion and examples, see R. G. Hamerton-Kelly, "Attitudes to the Law in Matthew's Gospel," *BR* 17 [1972]: 19–32; Arens, Ἦλθον-*sayings*, 91–116). G. Barth, for instance, insists that the leap from v.19 to v.20 is so great that both could not have come from Matthew ("Matthew's Understanding of the Law," 66). A better synthesis is possible. Yet even if the leap between these verses were as great as Barth imagines, what possessed Matthew (or the "final redactor") to put them together? He must have thought they meant something. And then how does one distinguish methodologically between weak links discerned by a redactor and weak links written up by an author? We will focus primary attention on the meaning of the text as it stands.

2. The theological and canonical ramifications of one's exegetical conclusions on this pericope are so numerous that discussion becomes freighted with the intricacies of biblical theology. At stake are the relation between the Testaments, the place of law in the context of gospel, and the relation of this pericope to other NT passages that unambiguously affirm that certain parts of the law have been abrogated as obsolete (e.g., Mk 7:19; Ac 10–11; Heb 7:1–9:10). Only glancing attention may be given to these issues here.

3. It is often argued that the setting of the pericope is debate in the church, especially among Palestinian Jewish Christians, about the continuation of law. There is no inherent implausibility in this hypothesis if by setting we refer to the circle in which these teachings were preserved because of their immediate relevance. But we must remember that Matthew presents these sayings as the teaching of the historical Jesus, not the creation of the church; and we detect no implausibility in his claim. More important, this view is often tied to the assumption that Matthew's community is essentially law

observing in a comprehensive way, but that Matthew's understanding of what this means is filtered through the love commandment and the Golden Rule (7:12) at the center (e.g., Wolfgang Reinbold, "Das Matthäusevangelium, die Pharisäer und die Tora," *BZ* 50 [2006]: 51–73). This approach fails to wrestle adequately with the ways in which Jesus is himself the eschatological *fulfillment* of hopes and anticipations established by the antecedent revelation of the Old Testament.

17"Do not think that I have come to abolish the Law or the Prophets; I have not come to abolish them but to fulfill them. 18I tell you the truth, until heaven and earth disappear, not the smallest letter, not the least stroke of a pen, will by any means disappear from the Law until everything is accomplished. 19Anyone who breaks one of the least of these commandments and teaches others to do the same will be called least in the kingdom of heaven, but whoever practices and teaches these commands will be called great in the kingdom of heaven. 20For I tell you that unless your righteousness surpasses that of the Pharisees and the teachers of the law, you will certainly not enter the kingdom of heaven."

COMMENTARY

17 The formula "Do not think that" (or "Never think that," Turner, *Syntax*, 77) is repeated by Jesus in 10:34 (cf. 3:9). Jesus' two sayings were designed to set aside potential misunderstandings as to the nature of the kingdom, but neither demonstrably flows out of open confrontation on the issue at stake. Matthew has not yet recorded any charge that Jesus was breaking the law. (On the relation between these verses and the preceding pericopes, see W. J. Dumbull, "The Logic of the Role of the Law in Matthew 5:1–20," *NovT* 23 [1981]: 1–21.)

Some have argued that many Jews in Jesus' day believed that law would be set aside and a new law introduced at Messiah's coming (cf. Davies, *Setting*, 109ff., 446ff.). But this view has been decisively qualified by R. Banks ("The Eschatological Role of Law," in *Pre- and Post-Christian Jewish Thought* [ed. R. Banks; Exeter: Paternoster, 1982], 173–85; *Jesus and the Law*, 65ff.), who presents a more nuanced treatment.

The upshot of the debate is that the introductory words "Do not think that" must be understood, not as the refutation of some well-entrenched and clearly defined position, but as a teaching device Jesus used to clarify certain aspects of the kingdom and of his own mission and to remove potential misunderstandings. Moreover, comparison with 10:34 shows that the antithesis may not be absolute. Few would want to argue that there is *no* sense in which Jesus came to bring peace (see comments at v.9). Why then argue that there is no sense in which Jesus abolishes the law?

The words "I have come" do not necessarily prove Jesus' consciousness of his preexistence, for "coming" language can be used of prophets and indeed is used of the Baptist (11:18–19). But it can also speak of coming into the world (common in John; cf. 1Ti 1:15) and, in light of Matthew's prologue, is probably meant to attest Jesus' divine origins. At very least, it shows Jesus was sent on a mission (cf. Maier).

Jesus' mission was not to "abolish" (a term more frequently connected with the destruction of buildings [24:2; 26:61; 27:40], but not exclusively so [e.g., 2 Macc 2:22]) "the Law or the Prophets." By these words Matthew forms a new inclusio (5:17–7:12), which marks out the body of the sermon and shows that Jesus is taking pains to relate his teaching and place in the history of redemption to the OT Scriptures. For that is what "the Law or the Prophets" here means — the Scriptures. The disjunctive "or" makes it clear that neither is to be abolished. The Jews of Jesus' day could refer to the Scriptures as "the Law and the Prophets" (7:12; 11:13; 22:40; Lk 16:16; Jn 1:45; Ac 13:15; 28:23; Ro 3:21); "the Law ..., the Prophets and the Psalms" (Lk 24:44); or just "the Law" (v.18; Jn 10:34; 12:34; 15:25; 1Co 14:21); the divisions were not yet stereotyped. Thus even if "or the Prophets" is redactional (Dalman, *Jesus-Jeshua*, 62, and many after him), the referent does not change when only law is mentioned in v.18, but it may be a small hint that law also has a prophetic function (cf. 11:13, and comments there). Yet it is certainly illegitimate to see in "the Law or the Prophets" some vague reference to the will of God (so G. S. Sloyan, *Is Christ the End of the Law?* [Philadelphia: Westminster, 1978], 49–50; Sand, *Gesetz und die Propheten*, 186) and not to Scripture, especially in the light of v.18.

The nub of the problem lies in the verb "fulfill" (*plēroō*, GK *4444*). N. J. McEleney ("The Principles of the Sermon on the Mount," *JBL* 41 [1979]: 552–70) finds the verb so difficult in a context (vv.17–48) dealing with law that he judges it a late addition to the tradition. Not a few writers, especially Jewish scholars and some in the Reformed tradition, take the verb to reflect the Aramaic verb *qûm* ("establish," "validate," or "confirm" the law; GK 10624). Jesus did not come to abolish the law but to confirm it and establish it (e.g., Dalman, *Jesus-Jeshua*, 56–58; Daube, *New Testament and Rabbinic Judaism*, 60–61; Schlatter, 153–54.; and esp. Sigal, *Halakhah of Jesus*, 23ff.; Greg Bahnsen, *Theonomy in Christian Ethics* [Nutley, N.J.: Craig Press, 1979], 90ff.).

There are several objections.

1. The focus of Matthew 5 is the relation between the OT and Jesus' teaching, not his actions. So any interpretation that says Jesus fulfills the law by doing it misses the point of this passage.

2. If it is argued that Jesus confirms the law, even its jot and tittle, by both his life and his teaching (e.g., Hill; Maier; Mark E. Ross, *Let's Study Matthew* [Edinburgh: Banner of Truth, 2009]); Ridderbos, *Coming of the Kingdom*, 292–321) — the latter understood as setting out his own halakah (rules of conduct) within the framework of the law (Sigal) — one marvels that the early church, as the other NT documents testify, misunderstood Jesus so badly on this point; and even the first gospel, as we shall see, is rendered inconsistent.

3. The LXX never uses *plēroō* ("fulfill") to render *qûm* or cognates (which prefer *histēmi* [GK *2705*] or *bebaioō* ["establish" or "confirm," GK *1011*]). The verb *plēroō* renders *mālē*ʾ (GK 4848) and means "to fulfill." In OT usage, this characteristically refers to the "filling up" of volume or time, meanings that also appear in the NT (e.g., Ac 24:27; Ro 15:19). But though the NT uses *plēroō* in a number of ways, we are primarily concerned with what is meant by "fulfilling" the Scriptures. Included under this head are specific predictions, typological fulfillments, and even the entire eschatological hope epitomized in the OT by God's covenant with his people (cf. C. F. D. Moule, "Fulfillment Words in the New Testament: Use and Abuse," *NTS* 14 [1967–68]: 293–320; see comments at 2:15).

The lack of background for *plēroō* as far as it applies to Scripture requires cautious induction from the NT evidence. In a very few cases, notably James 2:23, the NT writers detect no demonstrable predictive force in the OT passage introduced. Rather, the

OT text (in this case Ge 15:6) in some sense remains "empty" until Abraham's action "fulfills" it. But Genesis 15:6 does not predict the action. Most NT uses of *plēroō* in connection with Scripture, however, require some teleological force (see Notes, 1:22); and even the ambiguous uses presuppose a typology that in its broadest dimensions is teleological, even if not in every detail (see comments at 2:15). In any case, the interchange of *mālēʾ* ("fulfill") and *qûm* ("establish") in the Targumim is not of sufficient importance to overturn the LXX evidence, not least owing to problems of dating the Targumim (cf. Meier, *Law and History*, 74; Banks, *Jesus and the Law*, 208–9).

Other views are not much more convincing. Many argue that Jesus is here referring only to moral law: the civil and ceremonial law are indeed abolished, but Jesus confirms the moral law (e.g., Hendriksen; D. Wenham, "Jesus and the Law: An Exegesis on Matthew 5:17–20," *Them* 4 [1979]: 92–96). Although this tripartite distinction is old, its use as a basis for explaining the relationship between the Testaments is not demonstrably derived from the NT and probably does not antedate Aquinas (cf. R. J. Bauckham's chapters in Carson, *From Sabbath to Lord's Day*; Carson, "Jesus and the Sabbath"). Also, the interpretation is invalidated by the all-inclusive "not the smallest letter, not the least stroke of a pen" (v.18).

Others understand the verb *plēroō* to mean that Jesus "fills up" the law by providing its full, intended meaning (so Lenski), understood perhaps in terms of the double command to love (so O. Hanssen, "Zum Verständnis der Bergpredigt," in *Der Ruf Jesu und die Antwort der Gemeinde* [ed. Edward Lohse; Göttingen: Vandenhoeck & Ruprecht, 1970], 94–111). This, however, requires an extraordinary meaning for *plēroō*, ignores the "jot and tittle" of v.18, and misinterprets 22:34–40.

Still others, in various ways, argue that Jesus "fills up" the OT law by extending its demands to some better or transcendent righteousness (v.20), again possibly understood in terms of the command to love (e.g., Lagrange; Grundmann; A. Feuillet, "Morale ancienne et morale chrétienne d'après Mt 5:17–20; Comparaison avec la doctrine de l'épître aux Romains," *NTS* 17 [1970–71]: 123–37, esp. 124; Trilling, *Das wahre Israel*, 174–79). Thus the reference to prophets (v.17) becomes obscure, and the entire structure is shaky in view of the fact that mere extension of law will not abolish any of its stringencies—yet in both Matthew and other NT documents some abolition is everywhere assumed. H. Ljungman (*Das Gesetz erfüllen* [Lund: Gleerup, 1954]) takes the "fulfillment" to refer to the fulfillment of Scripture in the self-surrender of the Messiah, which in turn brings forgiveness of sins and the new righteousness the disciples are both to receive and to do. But in addition to weaknesses of detail, it is hard to see how all this can be derived from vv.17–20.

The best interpretation of these difficult verses says that Jesus fulfills the Law and the Prophets in that they point to him, and he is their fulfillment. The antithesis is not between "abolish" and "keep" but between "abolish" and "fulfill." "For Matthew, then, it is not the question of Jesus' relation to the law that is in doubt but rather its relation to him!" (R. Banks, "Matthew's Understanding of the Law: Authenticity and Interpretation in Matthew 5:17–20," *JBL* 93 [1974]: 226–42). Therefore, we see in *plēroō* ("fulfill") exactly the same meaning as in the formula quotations, which in the prologue (Mt 1–2) have already laid great stress on the prophetic nature of the OT and the way it points to Jesus (see Davies and Allison; France [TNTC]; Gibbs; Turner; Roland Deines, *Die Gerechtigkeit der Tora im Reich des Messias: Mt 5:13–20 als Schlüsseltext der mattäischen Theologie* [WUNT 177; Tübingen: Mohr, 2004]). Even OT events have this prophetic significance (see comments at 2:15).

"It is eschatological actualization that is in view" (Tom Wells and Fred Zaspel, *New Covenant Theology* [Frederick, Md.: New Covenant Media, 2002], 115). A little later Jesus insists that "all the Prophets and the Law prophesied" (11:13).

The manner of the prophetic foreshadowing varies. The exodus, Matthew argues (2:15), foreshadows the calling out of Egypt of God's "son." The writer to the Hebrews argues that many cultic regulations of the OT pointed to Jesus and are now obsolete. In the light of the antitheses (vv.21–48), the passage before us insists that just as Jesus fulfilled OT prophecies by his person and actions, so he fulfilled OT law by his teaching. In no case does this "abolish" the OT as canon, any more than the obsolescence of the Levitical sacrificial system abolishes tabernacle ritual as canon. Instead, the OT's real and abiding authority must be understood through the person and teaching of him to whom it points and who so richly fulfills it.

As in Luke 16:16–17, Jesus is not announcing the termination of the OT's relevance and authority (else Lk 16:17 would be incomprehensible), but that "the period during which men were related to God under its terms ceased with John" (Moo, "Jesus and the Authority of the Mosaic Law," esp. 23); and the nature of its valid continuity is established only with reference to Jesus and the kingdom. The general structure of this interpretation has been well set forth by Banks (*Jesus and the Law*), Meier (*Law and History*), Moo ("Jesus and the Authority of the Mosaic Law"; see also his "The Law of Christ as the Fulfillment of the Law of Moses: A Modified Lutheran View," in *The Law, the Gospel, and the Modern Christian* [ed. Wayne G. Strickland; Grand Rapids: Zondervan, 1993], 319–76), Wells and Zaspel (*New Covenant Theology*), and, at a popular level, Carson (*Sermon on the Mount*, 33–40). For a somewhat similar approach, see McConnell (*Law and Prophecy*, 96–97), who points out that Jesus' implicit authority is also found in the closing verses of the sermon (7:21–23) where as eschatological Judge he exercises the authority of God alone. Of course, if Jesus *fulfills* the law and the prophets in this eschatological sense, such fulfillment brings with it both continuity and discontinuity. The authority of the older revelation is not called into question, but its continuing power lies not in unchanging legal prescription but in that to which it points, its fulfillment.

Several objections to this view have been raised. One is that the use of "to fulfill" in the fulfillment quotations is in the passive voice, whereas here the voice is active. But it is doubtful whether much can be made out of this distinction (cf. Meier, *Law and History*, 80–81). Perhaps one of the weightiest objections has come from Greg Welty ("Eschatological Fulfilment and the Confirmation of Mosaic Law: A Response to D. A. Carson and Fred Zaspel on Matthew 5:17–48" [*www.the-highway.com/mosaic-law_Welty.html*], last revised on March 28, 2002). Welty's lengthy discussion depends almost entirely on his claim that what is being argued here is that OT *prophecies* are fulfilled in Jesus' person and actions, while OT *law* is fulfilled in the teaching of Jesus. But that means the former category cannot be used as a reliable analogy of the latter—and the latter Welty finds incoherent for a number of reasons. But it is very doubtful that such a sharp antithesis can legitimately be introduced:

(a) Matthew 11:13 insists that both the Law and the Prophets *prophesy*. Similarly here: Jesus comes to *fulfill* both the Law and the Prophets.

(b) It is not only OT *prophecies* (understood as verbal predictions) that "prophesy" and are "fulfilled," but very frequently the "prophecies" are in fact legal structures and institutions that "prophesy" and are "fulfilled." They are, in short, typologies that establish patterns that point forward. That is presupposed by Paul, for instance, when he tells us that Christ our

Passover has been sacrificed (1Co 5:7): the legally established Passover of the Mosaic covenant is a prophecy that anticipates the ultimate "Passover." It is presupposed again when texts that describe David or some other early Davidic king are said to be "fulfilled" in King Jesus, the ultimate Davidide.

(c) When one speaks of "prophecy" and "fulfillment" in this larger eschatological sense, inevitably there is both continuity and discontinuity between the prophecy and the fulfillment. If X in some sense prophesies Y, and Y in some sense fulfills X, it is impossible to think of continuity alone. Equally, however, it is impossible to think of discontinuity alone, for all links between X and Y would disappear. If the ancient Passover celebration anticipates Christ our Passover, the discontinuities are plain: Jesus is not a literal lamb, his blood was never put on the two doorposts and the lintel, he is not eaten by a family, and so forth. Yet the fundamental continuity is equally plain: Just as the death of the Passover lamb and the sprinkling of its blood ensured that the angel of death "passed over" the house, so the death of Christ our Passover and the shedding of his blood ensure that those protected by Christ escape the certainty of death and judgment. The Passover ritual simultaneously looked back to the Passover night in Egypt, and looked forward to the ultimate Passover sacrifice.

(d) One must not forget the commonplace observation that *tôrâ* (GK 9368), "law," fundamentally means "instruction" rather than "legal demand" (Lat. *lex*). The "instructions" or "laws" related to the observation of Passover celebrations clearly (from the perspective of NT writers) point forward to the ultimate Passover. It is difficult to imagine why "laws" such as "Do not commit murder" might not also point forward to something deeper—not merely the prohibition of murder but the promised transformation of God's image bearers such that they will love. The orientation, in other words, is eschatological. In other words, the bifurcations that Welty detects simply are not there.

(e) It appears that the fundamental reason why Welty cannot allow something called "law" to foreshadow the teaching of Jesus is that he is operating with an a priori definition of moral law. Thus in the antitheses (vv.21–48), when Jesus says, for instance, that under his authority the prohibition of adultery includes the prohibition of lust, Welty says this is merely unpacking moral dimensions that are implicit in the OT commandment; there is no discontinuity. But it is better to say that the "fulfillment" terminology suggests that all the moral dimensions Jesus delineates are not *already* in the legal antecedent but are precisely that to which the legal antecedent points. In other words, both Welty and this exposition usually come out at the same place when it comes to understanding what Jesus is teaching and demanding, but Welty claims such material was already present in the OT law—and thus he loses the eschatological framework, the sense that the new *fulfills* the old.

(f) The approach adopted here does not render useless the category of "moral law." The difference is this: Welty and many others promote an a priori definition of moral law as that law which never changes, unlike civil and ceremonial law, both of which pass away as the locus of the people of God escapes the national boundaries of the OT and becomes an international community, and the ceremonies give way to the realities. This a priori understanding of moral law then becomes the criterion by which to establish patterns of continuity and discontinuity between the Testaments, without first taking on board the categories used by the biblical writers themselves. By contrast, one might usefully come up with an a posteriori ("after the fact") definition of moral law. One might attempt to delineate the patterns of continuity and discontinuity between the Testament *on their own terms* and then label "moral" those instructions and laws that change the least across time (contra Richard Barcellos, *In Defense of the Decalogue: A Critique of New Covenant Theology* [Enumclaw, Wash.: Winepress, 2001]).

(g) Finally, we should reflect on 7:12, where, we are told, the Golden Rule "sums up" the Law and the Prophets. The verb used is *estin* ("is," GK *1639*)—but transparently this verb takes on various emphases from its context. It cannot in 7:12 be making an *ontological* claim (that would be silly); the NIV attempts to catch the idea by rendering it "sums up." One might as easily supply "fulfills," as in Acts 2:16 and elsewhere. This is all the more attractive when one observes that 7:12 closes the body of the Sermon on the Mount as the paragraph vv.17–20 opens it.

Three theological conclusions are inevitable. First, if the antitheses (vv.21–48) are understood in the light of this interpretation of vv.17–20, then Jesus is not engaged there primarily in extending, annulling, or intensifying OT law but in showing the direction in which it points, on the basis of his own authority (to which, again, the OT points). This may work out in any particular case to have the same practical effect as "intensifying" the law or "annulling" some element; but the reasons for that conclusion are quite different. On the ethical implications of this interpretation, see the essay by Moo ("Jesus and the Authority of the Mosaic Law").

Second, if vv.17–20 are essentially authentic (cf. Davies, *Christian Origins*, 31–66) and the above interpretation is sound, the christological implications are important. Here Jesus presents himself as the eschatological goal of the OT and thereby its sole authoritative interpreter, the one through whom alone the OT finds its valid continuity and significance.

Third, this approach eliminates the need to pit Matthew against Paul, or Palestinian Jewish Christians against Pauline Gentile believers, the first lot adhering to Mosaic stipulations and the second abandoning them. Nor do we need the solution of Brice Martin ("Matthew and Paul on Christ and the Law: Compatible or Incompatible Theologies?" [PhD diss., McMaster Univ., 1976]), who argues that Matthew's and Paul's approaches to law are noncomplementary but noncontradictory; they simply employ different categories. This fails to wrestle with Matthew's positioning of Jesus within the history of redemption; and Paul well understood that the Law and the Prophets pointed beyond themselves (e.g., Ro 3:21; Gal 3–4; cf. Ro 8:4). The focus returns to Jesus, which is where, on the face of it, both Paul and Matthew intend it to be. The groundwork is laid out in the Gospels for an understanding of Jesus as the one who established the essentially christological and eschatological approach to the OT employed by Paul. But this is made clearer in v.18.

18 "I tell you the truth" signals that the statement to follow is of the utmost importance (see Notes). In Greek it is connected to the preceding verse by an explanatory "for" (*gar*): v.18 further explains and confirms the truth of v.17. The "jot" (KJV) has become "the smallest letter" (NIV). This is almost certainly correct, for it refers to the letter י (*yôd*), the smallest letter of the Hebrew alphabet. The "tittle" (NIV, "least stroke of a pen," *keraia*, GK *3037*) has been variously interpreted: it is the Hebrew letter ו (*wāw*) (so G. Schwarz, "ἰῶτα ἓν ἢ μία κεραία [Matthäus 5:18]," *ZNW* 66 [1975]: 268–69) or the small stroke that distinguishes several pairs of Hebrew letters (e.g., כ/ב; ר/ד; ך/ד) (so Filson, Lenski, Allen) or a purely ornamental stroke, a "crown" (Tasker, Schniewind, Schweizer; but cf. *NIDNTT*, 3:182); or it forms a hendiadys with "jot," referring to the smallest part of the smallest letter (Lachs, "Textual Observations," 106–8). In any event, Jesus here upholds the authority of the

OT Scriptures right down to the "least stroke of a pen." His is the highest possible view of the OT.

Verses 17–18 do not wrestle abstractly with OT authority but with the nature, extent, and duration of its validity and continuity. The nature of these has been set forth in v.17. The reference to "jot and tittle" establishes its extent. It will not do to reduce the reference to moral law, or to the law as a whole but not necessarily its parts, or to God's will in some general sense. "Law" almost certainly refers to the entire OT Scriptures, not just the Pentateuch or moral law (note the parallel in v.17).

That leaves the duration of the OT's authority. The two "until" clauses answer this. The first—"until heaven and earth disappear"—simply means "until the end of the age": i.e., not quite "never" (contra Meier, *Law and History*, 61), but "never, as long as the present world order persists." The second—"until everything is accomplished"—is more difficult. Some take it to be equivalent to the first (cf. Sand, *Gesetz und die Propheten*, 36–39). But it is more subtle than that. The word *panta* ("all things" or "everything") has no antecedent. Contrary to Sand (p. 38), Hill, Bultmann (*History of the Synoptic Tradition*, 138, 405), and Grundmann, the word cannot very easily refer to all the demands of the Law that must be "accomplished," because (1) "Law" almost certainly refers here to all Scripture and not just its commands—but even if that were not so, v.17 has shown that even imperatival law is prophetic; (2) the word *genētai* ("is accomplished," GK *1181*) must here be rendered "happens," "comes to pass" (i.e., "is accomplished" in that sense, not in the sense of obeying a law; cf. Meier, *Law and History*, 53–54; Banks, *Jesus and the Law*, 215ff.).

Hence *panta* ("everything") is best understood to refer to everything in the Law considered under the Law's prophetic function—namely, until all these things have taken place as prophesied. This is not simply pointing to the cross (Davies, *Christian Origins*, 60ff.), nor simply to the end of the age (Schniewind). The parallel with 24:34–35 is not that close, since in the latter case, the events are specified. Verse 18d simply means the entire divine purpose prophesied in Scripture must take place; not one jot or tittle will fail of its fulfillment. A similar point is made in 11:13. Thus the first "until" clause focuses strictly on the duration of OT authority, but the second returns to considering its nature. It reveals God's redemptive purposes and points to their fulfillment, their "accomplishment," in Jesus and the eschatological kingdom he is now introducing and will one day consummate (cf. Gibbs).

Meier (*Law and History*) ably establishes the centrality of the death and resurrection of Jesus as the pivotal event in Matthew's presentation of salvation history. Before it Jesus' disciples are restricted to Israel (10:5–6); after it they are to go everywhere. Similarly, the precise form of the Mosaic law may change with the crucial redemptive events to which it points. For that which prophesies is in some sense taken up in and transcended by the fulfillment of the prophecy. Meier has grasped and explained this redemptive-historical structure better than most commentators. He may, however, have gone too far in interpreting v.18d too narrowly as a reference to the cross and the resurrection.

19 The contrast between the least and the greatest in the kingdom probably supports gradation within kingdom ranks (as in 11:11, though the word for "least" is different there; cf. 18:1–4). It is probably not a Semitic way of referring to the exclusion-inclusion duality (contra Bonnard). The one who breaks "one of the least of these commandments" is not excluded from the kingdom—the linguistic usage is against this interpretation (see Meier, *Law and History*, 92–95)—but is very small or unimportant in the kingdom (taking *elachistos* [GK *1788*] in the elative sense). The idea of gradations of privilege or dishonor in the kingdom occurs elsewhere in the Synoptic Gospels (20:20–28; cf. Lk 12:47–48). Distinctions are made not only according to the measure by which one keeps "the least of these commandments" but also according to the faithfulness with which one teaches them.

But what are "these commandments"? It is hard to justify restriction of these words to Jesus' teachings (so Banks, *Jesus and the Law*, 221–23), even though the verb cognate to "commands" (*entolōn*, GK *1953*) is used of Jesus' teachings in 28:20 (*entellomai*); the noun in Matthew never refers to Jesus' words, and the context argues against it. Restriction to the Ten Commandments (*TDNT*, 2:548) is alien to the concerns of the context. Nor can we say "these commandments" refers to the antitheses that follow, for in Matthew *houtos* ("this," plural "these") never points forward. It appears, then, that the expression must refer to the commandments of the OT Scriptures. The entire Law and the Prophets are not scrapped by Jesus' coming but fulfilled. Therefore the commandments of these Scriptures—even the least of them (on distinctions in the law, see comments at 22:36; 23:23)—must be practiced. But the nature of the practicing has already been affected by vv.17–18. The law pointed forward to Jesus—his activity and his teaching—so it is properly obeyed by conforming to his word. As it points to him, so he, in fulfilling it, establishes what continuity it has, the true direction to which it points and the way it is to be obeyed. Thus ranking in the kingdom turns on the degree of conformity to Jesus' teaching as that teaching fulfills OT revelation. His teaching, toward which the OT pointed, must be obeyed.

20 And that teaching, far from being more lenient, is nothing less than perfection (see comments at v.48). The Pharisees and teachers of the law (see comments at 2:4; 3:7; Introduction, section 11.f) were among the most punctilious in the land. Jesus' criticism is "not that they were not good, but that they were not good enough" (Hill). While their multiplicity of regulations could engender a "good" society, it domesticated the law and lost the radical demand for absolute holiness demanded by the Scriptures.

What Jesus demanded is the righteousness to which the law truly points, exemplified in the antitheses that follow (vv.21–48). The law, for instance, forbids adultery. Someone might truthfully say that he has kept that law. But if that law points forward to such righteousness as prohibits adultery in one's heart, the stakes are higher than can be met by even the most law-abiding Pharisee. Contrary to Helmut Flender (*Die Botschaft Jesu*, 45f.), v.3 (poverty of spirit) and v.20 (demand for radical righteousness) do not stand opposite each other in flat contradiction. Verse 20 does not establish how the righteousness is to be gained, developed, or empowered; it simply lays out the demand. Messiah will develop a people who will be called "oaks of righteousness ... for the display of [Yahweh's] splendor" (Isa 61:3). The verb "surpasses" suggests that the new righteousness outstrips the old both qualitatively and quantitatively (Bonnard; see comments at 25:31–46). Anything less does not enter the kingdom.

NOTES

18 "I tell you the truth" is the NIV's rendering of two expressions merged together: (1) ἀμήν (*amēn*, GK *297*)—a Greek transliteration of a Hebrew word meaning "faithful" or "reliable" and often used in the OT as an adverb ("surely," "truly"), often at the end of a sentence endorsing or wishing that the sentence is true or may prove true (cf. "Amen" in English at the end of prayers); it also begins some sentences (Jer 28:6; Rev 7:12; 19:4; 22:20) or develops into a response (1Co 14:16; Rev 5:14; cf. Dt 27:15–26; cf. Daube, *New Testament and Rabbinic Judaism*, 388–93; Jeremias, *Prayers of Jesus*, 112–15)—and (2) γὰρ λέγω ὑμῖν (*gar legō hymin*, "for I tell you"), which, of course, would take the order λέγω γὰρ ὑμῖν (*legō gar hymin*) if it stood on its own.

b. Application: the antitheses (5:21–48)

OVERVIEW

Verses 21–48 are often called the six antitheses because all six sections begin with some variation of "You have heard it said,... but I say." David Daube (*New Testament and Rabbinic Judaism*, 55–62) offers a number of much-cited rabbinic parallels, some of which, in the first part, raise an interpretation as a theoretical possibility only to reject it, and others of which raise a literal interpretation only to circumscribe it with broader considerations. Daube rightly points out that the first part of Matthew's formulas means something like "you have understood" or "you have literally understood." That is, Jesus is not criticizing the OT but the understanding of the OT many of his hearers adopted. This is especially true of vv.22, 43, where part of what was "heard" certainly does not come from the OT.

Beginning with this point, many (e.g., Stendahl, "Matthew," in *Peake's Commentary*; Hill) hold that Jesus nowhere abrogates the law but merely intensifies it or shows its ultimate meaning. Others (e.g., McConnell, *Law and Prophecy*) point out that, formally speaking, some OT laws are indeed contravened (e.g., laws on oaths, vv.33–37). R. A. Guelich ("The Antitheses of Matthew 5:21–48: Traditional or Redactional?" *NTS* 22 [1975–76]: 444–57), in the course of arguing that the first, second, and fourth are traditional and the third, fifth, and sixth redactional, suggests that the former transcend the law's demands, whereas the latter annul the law—a point contested by G. Strecker ("Die Antithesen der Bergpredigt," *ZNW* 69 [1978]: 36–72). Apart from the fact that the traditional-redactional bifurcation is not an entirely happy one (see Introduction, sections 1–3), a unifying approach to the antitheses is possible in the light of our exegesis of vv.17–20.

The contrast between what the people had heard and what Jesus taught is not based on distinctions like casuistry versus love, outer legalism versus inner commitment, or even false interpretation versus true interpretation, though all of them impinge collaterally on the text. Rather, in every case, Jesus contrasts the people's misunderstanding of the law with the true direction in which the law points, according to his own authority as the law's "fulfiller" (in the sense established in v.17). He makes no attempt to fence in the law (contra Przybylski, *Righteousness in Matthew*, 80–87) but declares unambiguously the true direction to which it points. Thus if certain antitheses revoke at least the letter of the law (and they do; cf. Meier, *Law and History*, 125ff.), they do so, not because they are thereby affirming the law's true spirit, but because Jesus insists that his teaching on these matters is the direction in which the laws actually point.

Likewise Jesus' "you have heard ..., but I say" is not quite analogous to corresponding rabbinic formulas; Jesus is not simply a proto-rabbi (contra Daube; Sigal, *Halakhah of Jesus*). The Sermon on the Mount is not set in a context of scholarly dispute over halakic details but in a context of messianic and eschatological fulfillment. Jesus' authority bursts the borders of the relatively "narrow context of legal interpretation and innovation which the rabbis circumscribed for themselves" (Banks, *Jesus and the Law*, 85). It is for this reason that the crowds were amazed at his authority (7:28–29).

(1) Vilifying anger and reconciliation (5:21–26)

21"You have heard that it was said to the people long ago, 'Do not murder, and anyone who murders will be subject to judgment.' 22But I tell you that anyone who is angry with his brother will be subject to judgment. Again, anyone who says to his brother, 'Raca,' is answerable to the Sanhedrin. But anyone who says, 'You fool!' will be in danger of the fire of hell.

23"Therefore, if you are offering your gift at the altar and there remember that your brother has something against you, 24leave your gift there in front of the altar. First go and be reconciled to your brother; then come and offer your gift.

25"Settle matters quickly with your adversary who is taking you to court. Do it while you are still with him on the way, or he may hand you over to the judge, and the judge may hand you over to the officer, and you may be thrown into prison. 26I tell you the truth, you will not get out until you have paid the last penny."

COMMENTARY

21–22 Jesus' contemporaries had heard that the law given their forefathers (see Notes) forbade murder (not the taking of all life, which could, for instance, be a judicial mandate: cf. Ge 9:6) and that the murderer must be brought to "judgment" (*krisis* [GK *3213*], which here refers to legal proceedings, perhaps the court set up in every town [Dt 16:18; 2Ch 19:5; cf. Josephus, *Ant.* 4.214 (7.14); *J.W.* 2.570–71 (20.5)]; or the council of twenty-three persons set up to deal with criminal matters, Str-B, 1:275). But Jesus insists—the "I" is emphatic in each of the six antitheses—that the law really points to his own teaching: the root of murder is anger, and anger is murderous in principle (Mt 5:22). One has not conformed to the better righteousness of the kingdom simply by refraining from homicide. The angry person will be subject to *krisis* ("judgment"), but it is presupposed this is God's judgment, "since no human court is competent to try a case of inward anger" (Stott, *Message of the Sermon on the Mount*). To stoop to insult exposes one not merely to (God's) council (*synedrion* [GK *5284*] can mean either "Sanhedrin" [NIV] or simply "council") but to the "fire of hell."

The expression "fire of hell" (*geenna tou pyros*, lit., "gehenna [GK *1147*] of fire") comes from the Hebrew *gêᵓ-hinnōm* ("Valley of Hinnom," a ravine south of Jerusalem once associated with the pagan god Moloch and his disgusting rites [2Ki 23:10; 2Ch 28:3; 33:6; Jer 7:31; Eze 16:20; 23:37] prohibited by God [Lev 18:21; 20:2–5]). When Josiah abolished the practices, he defiled the valley by making it a dumping ground for filth and the corpses of criminals (2Ki 23:10). Late traditions suggest that in the first century it may still have been used as a rubbish pit, complete with smoldering fires. The valley came to symbolize the place of eschatological punishment (cf. *1 En.* 54:12; *2 Bar.* 85:13; cf. Mt 10:28; 23:15, 33 [18:9 for the longer expression "gehenna of fire"]). Gehenna and Hades (11:23 [NIV text note]; 16:18) are often thought to refer, respectively, to eternal hell and the abode of the dead in the intermediate state. But the distinction can be maintained in few passages. More commonly, the two terms are synonymous and mean "hell" (cf. W. J. P. Boyd, "Gehenna—According to J. Jeremias," in *Studia Biblica 1978* [ed. Livingstone], 2:9–12).

"Brother" (*adelphos*, GK *81*) cannot in this case be limited to male siblings. Matthew's gospel uses the word extensively. Whenever it clearly refers to people beyond physical brothers, it is on the lips of Jesus, and its narrow usage is almost always Matthean. This suggests that the Christian habit of calling one another "brother" goes back to Jesus' instruction, possibly part and parcel of his training them to address God as Father (6:9). Among Christian brothers, anger is to be eliminated. On the other hand, it is possible that Allison (*Studies in Matthew*, 65–78) is right in detecting (along with some church fathers) an allusion to Genesis 4, where Cain slays *his brother* Abel.

The passage does not suggest a gradation and climax of punishments (so Hendriksen, 297–99), for this would require a similar gradation of offense. There is no clear distinction between the person with seething anger, the one who insultingly calls his brother a fool, and the one who prefers, as his term of abuse, "Raca" (transliteration for Aram. *rēkâ*ʾ, "imbecile," "fool," "blockhead"). To a Greek, *mōros* (GK *3704*) would suggest foolishness or senselessness; but to a speaker of Hebrew, the Greek word might call to mind the Hebrew *mōreh* (from the verb GK 5286), which has overtones of moral apostasy, rebellion, and wickedness (cf. Ps 78:8 [77:8 LXX]; Jer 5:23).

Many Jewish maxims warn against anger (examples in Bonnard), but this is not just another maxim. Here Jesus does not merely offer advice; he insists that the sixth commandment points prophetically to the kingdom's condemnation of hate.

Jesus' anger, expressed in diverse circumstances (21:12–19; 23:17; Mk 3:1–5), is no personal inconsistency.

1. Jesus is a preacher who gets down to essentials on every point he makes. Thus for a clear understanding of his thought on a particular issue, one must examine the balance of his teaching (cf., e.g., 6:2–4 with Luke 18:1–8). Similarly, to learn all Jesus says about anger, it is necessary to integrate this passage with others such as 21:12–13 without absolutizing any one text.

2. When suffering, Jesus is proverbial for his gentleness and forbearance (Lk 23:34; 1Pe 2:23). But if he comes as Suffering Servant, he comes equally as Judge and King. His anger erupts not out of personal pique but out of outrage at injustice, sin, unbelief, and exploitation of others. Unfortunately, his followers are more likely to be angered at personal affronts (cf. Carson, *Sermon on the Mount*, 41–42).

3. In the context of the balance of themes in Scripture, the handling of hatred is not exactly like the handling of, say, lust or greed. Lust and greed must be suppressed; better, we must triumph over them. But there is a certain sense in which *righteous* hatred is to be encouraged (cf. Ps 139), "an indignation wholly directed to wickedness and evil, purged of moodiness, petulance, inflamed irritability, unreasonable suspicion" (Oliver O'Donovan, "Scripture and Christian Ethics," *Case* 12 [2007]: 22). Merely to suppress all anger fails to recognize

that Scripture also mandates, not least by the example of Jesus, righteous anger—and still love for our enemies. O'Donovan further comments:

> When I learn so to hate that I long for the justice of God, then I recognize that that *same* justice is precisely what my enemy needs. The injustice in the relation is to be put right not only *for me*, but *for him* too, because it is God's justice, which is like the sun which he makes to rise on the evil and the good, and the rain which he sends on the just and the unjust. So I begin to love my enemy as myself, by discovering that what I want for myself I want most profoundly for him too.

23–24 Jesus gives two illustrations exposing the seriousness of anger, the first in a setting of temple worship (vv.23–24, which implies a pre–70 setting), and the second in a judicial setting (vv.25–26). The first concerns a brother (see comments at v.22); the second an adversary. Remarkably, neither illustration deals with "your" anger but with "your" offense that has prompted the brother's or the adversary's rancor. Some take this as a sign that vv.23–26 represent displaced, independent logia. Yet the connection with vv.21–22 is powerful. We are more likely to remember when we have something against others than when we have done something to offend others. And if we are truly concerned about our anger and hate, we shall be no less concerned when we engender them in others.

The "altar" (v.23) is the one in the inner court. There amid solemn worship, recollection of a brother with something against one (on the expression, see Mk 11:25) should in Christ's disciples prompt immediate efforts to be reconciled (v.24). Only then is formal worship acceptable.

25–26 Compare Luke 12:57–59, where the contextual application warns impenitent Israel to be reconciled to God before it is too late. Many conclude that Matthew has "ethicized" an originally eschatological saying. But the language of the two pericopes is not close, and it is more realistic to postulate two stories from one itinerant preacher. Explanations for one or two of the changes (e.g., McNeile) are not convincing unless they fit a pattern that justifies all the changes.

Jesus again urges haste (v.25). Settle matters with the offended adversary while still "with him on the way" to court, not on "the road to life" (Bonnard). In the ancient world, debtors were jailed until the debts were paid. Thus v.26 is part of the narrative fabric and gives no justification for purgatory, universal restoration, or urgent reconciliation to God. It simply insists on immediate action. Malicious anger is so evil—and God's judgment so certain (v.22)—that we must do all in our power to end it (cf. Eph 4:26–27).

NOTES

21 The word ἀρχαίοις (*archaiois*, "to the people long ago") is translated as an instrumental dative in KJV: "by them of old time," following Beza. The reading is also found in some OL copies: *ab antiquis* (it$^{a.b.c.}$) instead of *antiquis* (it$^{d.f.ff.}$), which is as ambiguous as the Greek (similarly in v.33). The NIV is almost certainly right: (1) the normal way of expressing agency in Greek is with ὑπό (*hypo*, "by") plus the genitive (though there are exceptional datives, e.g., 6:1; 23:5); and (2) Jesus' point is not to correct "the people long ago" but the misunderstandings of his contemporaries, for which the NIV rendering is more suitable.

In the command οὐ φονεύσεις (*ou phoneuseis*, "Do not murder"), the verb is future, a not uncommon way for the LXX to express an imperative. Most examples in the NT are in quotations from the LXX (e.g.,

5:33, 43, 48). But the construction is not unknown in secular Greek, and some non-LXX instances occur in the NT (e.g., 6:5; 20:26; 21:3, 13; cf. Turner, *Syntax*, 86).

22 The words "without cause" (NIV text note) probably reflect an early and widespread softening of Jesus' strong teaching. Their absence does not itself prove there is no exception (see comments at v.22).

23 The change from plural to singular occurs again at 5:29, 36, 39; 6:5, and may reflect the style of a preacher who knows how to bring his lesson home by making it personal.

(2) Adultery and purity (5:27–30)

[27]"You have heard that it was said,'Do not commit adultery.' [28]But I tell you that anyone who looks at a woman lustfully has already committed adultery with her in his heart. [29]If your right eye causes you to sin, gouge it out and throw it away. It is better for you to lose one part of your body than for your whole body to be thrown into hell. [30]And if your right hand causes you to sin, cut it off and throw it away. It is better for you to lose one part of your body than for your whole body to go into hell."

COMMENTARY

27–28 The OT command not to commit adultery (Ex 20:14; Dt 5:18) is often treated in Jewish sources not so much as a function of purity as of theft: it was to steal another's wife (references in Bonnard). Jesus insisted that the seventh commandment points in another direction—toward purity that refuses to lust (v.28). The tenth commandment had already explicitly made the point; and *gynē* (GK *1222*) here more likely means "woman" than "wife." "To interpret the law on the side of stringency is not to annul the Law but to change it in accordance with its own intention" (Davies, *Setting*, 102; cf. Job 31:1; Pr 6:25; 2Pe 2:14).

Klaus Haacker ("Der Rechtsatz Jesu zum Thema Ehebruch," *BZ* 21 [1977]: 113–16) has convincingly argued that the second *autēn* ("[committed adultery] with her") is contrary to the common interpretation of this verse. In Greek it is unnecessary, especially if the sin is entirely the man's. But it is explainable if *pros to epithymēsai autēn*, commonly understood to mean "with a view to lusting for her," is translated "so as to get her to lust." The evidence for this interpretation is strong (see Notes). The man is therefore looking at the woman with a view to enticing her to lust. Thus, so far as his intention goes, he is committing adultery *with her*, and he makes her an adulteress. This does not weaken the force of Jesus' teaching. The heart of the matter is still lust and intent.

29–30 The radical treatment of parts of the body that cause one to sin (see Notes) has led some (notoriously Origen) to castrate themselves. But that is not radical enough, since lust is not thereby removed. The "eye" (v.29) is the member of the body most commonly blamed for leading us astray, especially in sexual sins (cf. Nu 15:39; Pr 21:4; Eze 6:9; 18:12; 20:8; cf. Ecc 11:9); the "right eye" refers to one's best eye. But why the "right hand" (v.30) in a context dealing with lust? This may be merely illustrative or a way of saying that even lust is a kind of theft. More likely, it is a euphemism for the male sexual organ (cf. *yād*, "hand" [GK 3338], most likely used in this way in Isaiah 57:8 [cf. BDB, 4.g]; see Lachs, "Textual Observations," 108–9).

Cutting off or gouging out the offending part is a way of saying that Jesus' disciples must deal radically with sin. Imagination is a God-given gift; but if it is fed dirt by the eye, it will be dirty. All sin, not least sexual sin, begins with the imagination. Therefore, what feeds the imagination is of maximum importance in the pursuit of kingdom righteousness (cf. Php 4:8). Not everyone reacts the same way to all objects. But if your eye is causing you to sin, gouge it out, or at very least, don't look (cf. the sane exposition of Stott, *Message of the Sermon on the Mount*, 88–91)! The alternative is sin and hell—sin's reward. The point is so fundamental that Jesus doubtless repeated it on numerous occasions (cf. 18:8–9).

NOTES

28 The verb ἐπιθυμέω (*epithymeō*, "lust," GK *2121*) can have positive force ("desire"), but more commonly it has a bad sense. It is used explicitly in connection with sexual lust in Romans 1:24.

If Haacker (see above) is right in his contention that the second αὐτήν, *autēn*, is unnecessary on the customary reading of this verse, the problem is resolved if the first αὐτήν, *autēn*, within the expression πρὸς τὸ ἐπιθυμῆσαι αὐτήν (*pros to epithymēsai autēn*), functions as the accusative of reference (i.e., the quasisubject) of the infinitive (as in the equivalent construction in Lk 18:1) to generate the translation "so that she lusts."

29 The verb σκανδαλίζω (*skandalizō*, GK *4997*) can mean (1) "cause to stumble," "cause to sin" (as here; 18:6–9; Lk 17:2; Ro 14:21; 1Co 8:13; 2Co 11:29); (2) "obstruct another's path," and, hence, "cause [someone] to disbelieve, reject, forsake" (11:6; 13:21, 57; 15:12; 24:10; 26:31, 33; Jn 16:1); or (3) "offend" (17:27; Jn 6:61). The cognate noun σκάνδαλον (*skandalon*), originally referring to the trigger of a trap (cf. Ro 11:9), comes to mean, in a similar breakdown, (1) "stumbling block," i.e., "causing another to fall into sin" (13:41; 18:7; Lk 17:1; Ro 14:13; 1Jn 2:10; Rev 2:14); (2) "an obstruction," and, hence, "an occasion of disbelief" (Ro 9:32–33; 16:17; 1Co 1:23; 1Pe 2:8); or (3) an object one strikes and that hurts or repels one; hence, "an offense" (16:23; Gal 5:11). Some texts may appeal to more than one meaning (cf. Broadus; *NIDNTT*, 2:707–10).

(3) Divorce and remarriage (5:31–32)

31"It has been said, 'Anyone who divorces his wife must give her a certificate of divorce.'
32But I tell you that anyone who divorces his wife, except for marital unfaithfulness, causes her to become an adulteress, and anyone who marries the divorced woman commits adultery."

COMMENTARY

31–32 The introductory formula "It has been said" is shorter than all the others in this chapter and is linked to the preceding by a connective *de* ("and"). Therefore, though these two verses are innately antithetical, they carry further the argument of the preceding pericope. The OT points toward insisting not only that lust is the moral equivalent of adultery (vv.27–30) but that divorce is as well. This arises out of the fact that the divorced woman will in most circumstances remarry (esp. in first-century Palestine, where this would probably be her means of support). That new marriage, whether from the perspective of the divorcée or the one marrying her, is adulterous.

The OT passage to which Jesus refers (v.31) is Deuteronomy 24:1–4, whose thrust is that if a man divorces his wife because of "something indecent" (not further defined) in her, he must give her a certificate of divorce, and if she then becomes another man's wife and is divorced again, the first man cannot remarry her. This double restriction—the certificate and the prohibition of remarriage—discouraged hasty divorces. Here Jesus does not go into the force of "something indecent." Instead he insists that the law was pointing to the sanctity of marriage.

The natural way to take the "except" clause is that divorce is wrong because it generates adultery *except* in the case of fornication. In that case, where sexual sin has already been committed, nothing is laid down, though it appears that divorce is then implicitly permitted, even if not mandated (see the paraphrase in Stonehouse, *Witness of Matthew*, 203).

The numerous points for exegetical dispute (e.g., the meaning of *porneia* ["fornication," or, in the NIV, "marital unfaithfulness," GK *4518*], the force of the "except" clause, and the tradition history behind these verses and their relationship to 19:3–9; Mk 10:11–12; Lk 16:18) are treated more fully at 19:3–12. The one theory that must be rejected here (because it has no counterpart in 19:3–12) is that which takes the words "makes her an adulteress" to mean "stigmatizes her as an adulteress (even though it is not so)" (B. Ward Powers, "Divorce and the Bible," *Interchange* 23 [1938]: 159). The Greek uses the verb, not the noun (cf. NIV, "causes her to become an adulteress"). The verbal construction disallows Powers's paraphrase.

(4) Oaths and truthfulness (5:33–37)

33"Again, you have heard that it was said to the people long ago, 'Do not break your
oath, but keep the oaths you have made to the Lord.' 34But I tell you, Do not swear at
all: either by heaven, for it is God's throne; 35or by the earth, for it is his footstool; or by
Jerusalem, for it is the city of the Great King. 36And do not swear by your head, for you
cannot make even one hair white or black. 37Simply let your 'Yes' be 'Yes,' and your 'No,'
'No'; anything beyond this comes from the evil one."

COMMENTARY

33 "Again" probably confirms 5:31–32 as an excursus to the preceding antithesis rather than a new one. Matthew now reports an antithesis on a new theme. What the people have heard is not given as direct OT quotation but as a summary statement accurately condensing the burden of Exodus 20:7; Leviticus 19:12; Numbers 30:2; and Deuteronomy 5:11; 6:13; 23:21–23. The Mosaic law forbade irreverent oaths, light use of the Lord's name, broken vows. Once Yahweh's name was invoked, the vow to which it was attached became a debt that had to be paid to the Lord.

A sophisticated casuistry judged how binding an oath really was by examining how closely it was related to Yahweh's name. Incredible distinctions proliferate under such an approach. Swearing by heaven and earth was not binding, nor was swearing by Jerusalem, though swearing *toward* Jerusalem was. That an entire Mishnaic tract (*m. Šebu.*) is given over to the subject (cf. also *m. Sanh.* 3.2; *t. Ned.* 1; Str-B, 1:321–36) shows that such distinctions became important and were widely discussed. Matthew returns to the topic with marvelous examples in the polemical setting of 23:16–22. The context is not overtly polemical here but simply explains how Jesus relates the kingdom and its righteousness to the OT.

34–36 If oaths designed to encourage truthfulness become occasions for clever lies and casuistical deceit, Jesus will abolish oaths, for the direction in which the OT points is the fundamental importance of thorough and consistent truthfulness. If one does not swear at all, one does not swear falsely. Not dissimilar reasoning was found among the Essenes, who avoided taking oaths, "regarding it as worse than perjury for they say that one who is not believed without an appeal to God stands condemned already" (Josephus, *J.W.* 2.135 [8.6])—though they did require "tremendous oaths" of neophytes joining the community (ibid., 2.139 [8.7]; cf. 1QS 5:7–11; CD 15:5).

Jesus insists that whatever a man swears by is related to God in some way, and therefore every oath is implicitly in God's name; heaven, earth, Jerusalem, even the hairs of the head are all under God's sway and ownership (v.36). (There may be allusions here to Ps 48:2; Isa 66:1.) Significantly, Matthew breaks the flow to say (in Gr.) "toward Jerusalem" rather than "by Jerusalem" (on the distinction, see comments at v.33). The "Great King" (v.35) may well be God, but see comments at 25:34.

37 The Greek might more plausibly be translated "But let your word be, 'Yes, Yes; No, No.'" The doubling has raised questions. According to some rabbinic opinion, a doubled "yes" or "no" constitutes an oath; Broadus suggests this is an appropriate way to strengthen an assertion. This sounds like casuistry every bit as tortuous as that which Jesus condemns. The doubling is probably no more than preacher's rhetoric, the point made clear by the NIV (cf. Jas 5:12). *Tou ponērou* could be rendered either "of evil" or "of the evil one" ("the father of lies," Jn 8:44). The same ambiguity recurs at 5:39; 6:13; 13:38.

Many groups (e.g., Anabaptists, Jehovah's Witnesses) have understood these verses absolutely literally and have therefore refused even to take court oaths. Their zeal to conform to Scripture is commendable, but they have probably not interpreted the text very well.

1. The contextual purpose of this passage is to stress the true direction in which the OT points—namely, the importance of truthfulness. Where oaths are not being used evasively and truthfulness is not being threatened, it is not immediately obvious they require such unqualified abolition.

2. In the Scriptures God himself "swears" (e.g., Ge 9:9–11; Lk 1:72–75; cf. Ps 16:10 and Ac 2:27–31), not because he sometimes lies, but in order to help people believe (Heb 6:17). The earliest Christians still took oaths, if we may judge from Paul's example (Ro 1:9; 2Co 1:23; 1Th 2:5, 10; cf. Php 1:8), for much the same reason. Jesus himself testified under oath (26:63–64).

3. Again we need to remember the antithetical nature of Jesus' preaching (see comments at vv.27–30; 6:5–8).

It must be frankly admitted that here Jesus formally contravenes OT law. What it permits or commands (Dt 6:13), he forbids. But if his interpretation of the direction in which the law points is authoritative, then his teaching fulfills it.

NOTES

34 **Ὀμοσαι ἐν** or **εἰς** (*omosai en* or *eis*, "to swear by" or "by-toward" [Gr. is not entirely unambiguous]) is Hebraic (cf. Moulton, *Grammar: Accidence*, 463–64); only with "Jerusalem" is **εἰς**, *eis*, used in the NT. Turner (*Insights*, 31) argues that the present prohibition in James 5:12 means "stop swearing," whereas the aorist prohibition here presupposes that the disciples have stopped and now forbids them from starting. This classic distinction based on tenses in prohibitions usually holds but can be too finely spun (cf. Moule, *Idiom Book*, 21). In the strictest sense, the aorist is timeless; and linked in v.34 with μὴ ... ὅλως (*mē ... holōs*, "not ... at all"), it probably simply generates an unconditional negative: "Do not swear at all" (NIV; cf. Schlatter).

(5) Personal injury and self-sacrifice (5:38–42)

OVERVIEW

The order of the last two antitheses (vv.38–48) is reversed in Luke 6:27–36. While the reasons for this are debatable, if both evangelists are recording the same sermon, the reversal shows that rearranging the order of the materials (preserved in Q and/or other notes) was thought acceptable. Parallels repudiating vengeance and vindictiveness are not unknown (*T. Benj.* 4:1–5:5; 1QS 10:18; CD 8:5–6). The distinctive element in Jesus' teaching is the way he sets it over against the *lex talionis* (the principle of retribution) and the reasons he does this.

38"You have heard that it was said, 'Eye for eye, and tooth for tooth.' 39But I tell you, Do
not resist an evil person. If someone strikes you on the right cheek, turn to him the other
also. 40And if someone wants to sue you and take your tunic, let him have your cloak as
well. 41If someone forces you to go one mile, go with him two miles. 42Give to the one who
asks you, and do not turn away from the one who wants to borrow from you."

COMMENTARY

38 The OT prescription (Ex 21:24; Lev 24:19–20; Dt 19:21) was not given to foster vengeance; the law explicitly forbade that (Lev 19:18). Rather, it was given, as the OT context shows, to provide the nation's judicial system with a ready formula of punishment, not least because it would decisively terminate vendettas. On occasion, payment in money or some other commodity was exacted instead (e.g., Ex 21:26–27), and in Jesus' day the courts seldom imposed *lex talionis*. The trouble is that a law designed to limit retaliation and punish fairly could be appealed to as justification for vindictiveness. But it will not do to argue that Jesus is doing nothing more than combating a personal as opposed to a judicial use of the *lex talionis*, since in that case the examples would necessarily run differently: e.g., if someone strikes you, don't strike back but let the judiciary administer the just return slap. The argument runs in deeper channels.

39 Jesus' disciple is not to resist "an evil person" (*tō ponērō* [GK *4505*] could not easily be taken to refer here to the devil or to evil in the abstract). In the context of the *lex talionis*, the most natural way of understanding the resistance is "do not resist in a court of law." This interpretation is required in the second example (v.40). As in vv.33–37, therefore, Jesus' teaching formally contradicts the OT law. But in the context of vv.17–20, what Jesus is saying is reasonably clear: the OT, including the *lex talionis*, points forward to Jesus and his teaching. But like the OT laws permitting divorce, enacted because of the hardness of men's hearts (19:3–12), the *lex talionis* was instituted to curb evil because of the hardness of men's hearts. "God gives by concession a legal regulation as a dam against the river of violence which flows from man's evil heart" (Piper, *"Love Your Enemies,"* 90).

As this legal principle is overtaken by that toward which it points, so also is this hardness of heart. The OT prophets foretold a time when there would be a change of heart among God's people, living under a new covenant (Jer 31:31–34; 32:37–41; Eze 36:26). Not only would the sins of the people be forgiven (Jer 31:34; Eze 36:25); obedience to God would spring from the heart as well (Jer 31:33; Eze 36:27) as the eschatological age dawned. Thus Jesus' instruction on these matters is grounded in eschatology. In Jesus and the kingdom, fulfillment (even if partial) of the OT promises takes place. The eschatological age that the Law and Prophets had prophesied (11:13) arrives. The prophecies that curbed evil while pointing forward to the eschaton are now superseded by the new age and the new hearts it brings (cf. Piper, *"Love Your Enemies,"* 89–91).

Four illustrations clarify Jesus' point and drive it home. In the first, a man strikes another on the cheek—not only a painful blow but also a gross insult (cf. 2Co 11:20). If a right-handed person strikes someone's right cheek, presumably it is a slap by the back of the hand, probably considered more insulting than a slap by the open palm (cf. *m. B. Qam.* 8:6). The verb "strikes" (*rhapizei*, GK *4824*) probably refers to a sharp slap. Many commentators contrast Luke's *typtō* ("strikes," GK *5597*; Lk 6:29), arguing the latter refers to blows with a rod—i.e., Luke deals not with insult but with pain and damage. The contrast is false; the semantic overlap between the two verbs is substantial, and *typtō* can refer to a slap (e.g., Ac 23:3). But instead of seeking recompense at law under the *lex talionis*, Jesus' disciples will gladly endure the insult again. (There are overtones of Isa 50:6 here, applied in 26:67 to Jesus; cf. Gundry, *Use of the Old Testament*, 72–73.)

40 Although under Mosaic law the outer cloak was an inalienable possession (Ex 22:26; Dt 24:13), Jesus' disciples, if sued for their tunics (not equivalent to our underwear but to clothes worn under the "tunic" but customarily worn next to the skin), far from seeking satisfaction, will gladly part with what they may legally keep. Luke 6:29 says nothing about legal action but mentions the garments in reverse order. This has led some to think that Luke had violent robbery in mind because then the outer garment would be snatched off first. But perhaps the order is simply that in which the garments would normally be removed.

41 The third example refers to the Roman practice of commandeering civilians to carry the luggage of military personnel a prescribed distance, one Roman "mile." (On the verb *angareuō* ("commandeer," GK *30*; NIV, "force"), see W. Hatch, *Essays in Biblical Greek* [Oxford: Clarendon, 1889], 37–38.) Impressment, like a lawsuit, evokes outrage, but the attitude of Jesus' disciples under such circumstances must not be spiteful or vengeful but helpful—willing to go a second mile (exemplars of the Western text say "two more [miles]," making a total of three!). This illustration is also implicitly anti-Zealot.

42 The final illustration requires not only interest-free loans (Ex 22:25; Lev 25:37; Dt 23:19) but a generous spirit (cf. Dt 15:7–11; Pss 37:26; 112:5). The parallel form of this verse (Lk 6:30) does not imply two requests but only one; the repetition reinforces the point. These last two illustrations confirm our interpretation of vv.38–39. The entire pericope deals with the heart's attitude, the better righteousness. For there is actually no legal recourse to the oppression in the third illustration, and in the fourth no harm that might lead to retaliation has been done.

REFLECTIONS

While these four vignettes have powerful shock value, they were not meant to be new legal prescriptions. Verse 42 does not commit Jesus' disciples to giving endless amounts of money to everyone who seeks a "soft touch" (cf. Pr 11:15; 17:18; 22:26). Verse 40 is clearly hyperbolic. No first-century Jew would go home wearing only a loincloth. Nor does this pericope deal with the validity of a state police force. Yet the illustrations must not be diluted by endless equivocations. The only limit to the believer's response in these situations is what love and the Scriptures impose. Paul could "resist" (same Gr. word [*anthistēmi*, GK *468*] as "resist" in v.38) Peter to his face (Gal 2:11) because love demanded it in light of the damage being done to the gospel and to fellow believers. (On the practical outworking of this antithesis, see Neil, "Five Hard Sayings," 160–63; Piper, *"Love Your Enemies,"* 92–99; Stott, *Message of the Sermon on the Mount*, 104–14.)

(6) Hatred and love (5:43–47)

43"You have heard that it was said, 'Love your neighbor and hate your enemy.' **44**But I tell you: Love your enemies and pray for those who persecute you, **45**that you may be sons of your Father in heaven. He causes his sun to rise on the evil and the good, and sends rain on the righteous and the unrighteous. [46]If you love those who love you, what reward will you get? Are not even the tax collectors doing that? [47]And if you greet only your brothers, what are you doing more than others? Do not even pagans do that?"

COMMENTARY

43 The command "Love your neighbor" is found in Leviticus 19:18, but no OT Scripture adds "and hate your enemies." Rabbinic literature as it was later preserved does not usually leap to so bold and negative a conclusion. Thus some commentators have taken this passage as a later Christian mockery of Jewish values. But other considerations question this.

1. The Qumran covenanters explicitly commanded love for those within the community ("those whom God has elected") and hatred for the outsider (cf. 1QS 1:4, 10; 2:4–9; 1QM 4:1–2; 15:6; 1QH 5:4), and they doubtless represent other groups with similar positions. This love-hate antithesis may be mitigated by the covenanters' conviction that they alone were the faithful remnant; at least some of the language anticipates divine eschatological language. But not all of it can be dismissed so easily (cf. Davies, *Setting*, 245ff.).

2. Quite apart from the problems in dating rabbinic literature, we must remember that such literature represents scholarly debate, not common thought. For example, Carl F. H. Henry wrote learned tomes read by a few thousand; Joel Osteen writes popular material read by millions. In a hundred years, if the world lasts that long, some of Henry's work may still be in print, but few will remember Osteen. Yet today Osteen is read by far more church people than Henry, and the wise preacher will not forget it. Likewise the popular perversion of Leviticus 19:18 presupposed by Matthew 5:43 was doubtless far more widespread than the rabbinic literature intimates.

The quotation also omits "as yourself," words included in 19:19; 22:39; and the attitude reflected ignores the fact that Leviticus 19:33–34 also commands love of the same depth for the sojourner, the resident alien in the land. The popular reasoning seems to have been that if God commands love for "neighbor," then hatred for "enemies" is implicitly conceded and perhaps even authorized. Luke 10:25–37 shows how far the "neighbor" category extends.

44–45 Jesus allowed no casuistry. The real direction indicated by the law is love, rich and costly and extended even to enemies. Many take the verb "love" (*agapaō*, GK *26*) and the noun (*agapē*, GK *27*) as always signifying self-giving regardless of emotion. For instance, Hill comments on this passage: "The love which is inculcated is not a matter of sentiment and emotion, but, as always in the OT and NT, of concrete action." If this were so, 1 Corinthians 13:3 could not disavow "love" that gives everything to the poor and suffers even to martyrdom; for these are "concrete actions." The same verb is used when Amnon incestuously loves his half sister Tamar (2Sa 13:1 LXX); when Demas, because he loves this world (2Ti 4:10), forsakes Paul; and when tax collectors love those who love them (v.46).

The rise of this word group in Greek is well traced by Robert Joly, Ἀγαπᾶν *et* Φιλεῖν*: Le vocabulaire chrétien de l'amour, est-il original?* (Brussels: Presses

Universitaires, 1968). Christians doubtless took over the word group and largely filled it with their own content, but the content of that love is not based on a presupposed definition but on Jesus' teaching and example. To love one's enemies, though it must result in doing them good (Lk 6:32–33) and praying for them (v.44), cannot justly be restricted to activities devoid of any concern, sentiment, or emotion. Like the English verb "to love," *agapaō* ranges widely from debased and selfish actions to generous, warm, costly self-sacrifice for another's good. There is no reason to think the verb here in Matthew does not include emotion as well as action.

Much recent scholarship identifies the "enemies" with the persecutors of Matthew's church. Verses 44–47 are then seen as Matthew's transformation of Luke's more general exhortation (6:32–35) into encouragement for believers in Matthew's day to submit graciously to their persecutors. If Matthew's first readers were being persecuted for their faith, that was doubtless one application they made, though it is unlikely that Matthew himself intends to be quite so restrictive and anachronistic. The words "those who persecute you" introduce one important kind of "enemy" but do not exclude other kinds. Jesus himself repeatedly warns his disciples of impending persecution (e.g., vv.10–12; 10:16–23; 24:9–13), so there is little need to doubt the authenticity of the warning here.

One manifestation of love for enemies will be in prayer; praying for an enemy and loving him will prove mutually reinforcing. The more love, the more prayer; the more prayer, the more love. John Stott (*Message of the Sermon on the Mount*, 119) writes, "Jesus seems to have prayed for his tormentors actually while the iron spikes were being driven through his hands and feet; ... 'Father, forgive them; for they know not what they do' (Luke 23:34). If the cruel torture of crucifixion could not silence our Lord's prayer for his enemies, what pain, pride, prejudice, or sloth could justify the silencing of ours?"

Jesus' disciples have as their example God himself, who loves so indiscriminately that he sends sun and rain (they are his to bestow) on both the righteous and the unrighteous (cf. Seneca, *Ben.* 4.26; *b. Ta'an.* 7b). Yet we must not conclude that God's love toward men is in all respects without distinction and that therefore all must be saved in the end. The same Jesus teaches otherwise (e.g., in 25:31–46), and the NT shows that some aspects of God's love are indeed related to his moral character and demands for obedience (e.g., Jn 15:9–11; Jude 21).

Theologians since Calvin have related God's love in vv.44–45 to his "common grace" (i.e., the gracious favor God bestows "commonly," without distinction, on all men). He could with justice condemn all; instead he shows repeated and prolonged favor on all. That is the point here established for our emulation, not that God's love is amoral or without any distinctions whatsoever. See D.A. Carson, *The Difficult Doctrine of the Love of God* (Wheaton, Ill.: Crossway, 2000).

It is equally unsound to conclude that the OT requires harsh terms for an enemy but that the NT overcomes this dark portrait with new demands for unqualified love. Counterevidence refutes this notion: the OT often mandates love for others (e.g., Ex 23:4–5; Lev 19:18, 33–34; 1Sa 24:5; Job 31:29; Ps 7:4; Pr 24:17, 29; 25:21–22 [cf. Ro 12:20], and the NT speaks against the reprobate (e.g., Lk 18:7; 1Co 16:22; 2Th 1:6–10; 2Ti 4:18; Rev 6:10). Rather, vv.44–45 insist that the OT law cited (v.43) points to the wealth of love exercised by the heirs of the kingdom, a love qualitatively different from that experienced by other people (see comments at vv.46–47).

45 God's example provides the incentive for Jesus' disciples to be (*genēsthe*, more likely "become") sons of their Father. Ultimately this clause does not mean that the disciples act in a loving way to show what they already are (contra Schniewind, Zahn) but to become what they not yet are (Bonnard, Lagrange)—sons of the Father, in the sense established in v.9. The point of the passage is not to state the means of becoming sons but the necessity of pursuing a certain kind of sonship patterned after the Father's character. "To be persecuted because of righteousness is to align oneself with the prophets (5:12); but to bless and pray for those who persecute us is to align oneself with the character of God" (Carson, *Sermon on the Mount*, 53). "To return evil for good is devilish; to return good for good is human; to return good for evil is divine" (Plummer). Both vv. 44 and 45 show that Jesus' disciples must live and love in a way superior to the patterns around them.

46 Luke 6:32 uses *charis* ("grace," GK *5921*; NIV, "credit") rather than *misthos* ("reward," GK *3635*), a distinction that has fostered various complex theories concerning the relationship between the two passages. But in the same context, Luke also speaks of *misthos* ("reward," 6:35), and his use of *charis* means no more than thanks or gratitude: "What thanks have you?" (cf. BDAG, 1080; hence "credit" in the NIV). The two passages are therefore very close, and neither construes "reward" in purely meritorious categories (see comments at v.12). But the Scriptures do appeal to the hopes and fears of men (e.g., Heb 11:2, 26; cf. Mt 5:12; 6:1) and to greater and lesser felicity in heaven and punishment in hell (Lk 12:47–48; cf. 1Co 9:16–18). The verb *echete* ("you have"; NIV, "you get") may be a literal present; but more likely it is future along the line of 6:19–21: i.e., a man "stores up" and therefore "has" various treasure awaiting him in heaven.

The tax collectors (*telōnēs*) in the Synoptics are not the senior holders of the tax-farming contracts (Lat. *publicani*), usually foreigners, but local subordinate collectors (Lat. *portitores*) working under them (BDAG, 999). The latter were despised, not only because the tax-farming scheme encouraged corruption on a massive scale, but also because strict Jews would perceive them as both traitorous (raising taxes for the enslaving power) and potentially unclean (owing to possible contamination from association with Gentiles—a danger for at least the senior ranks of *portitores*, who necessarily had dealings with their Gentile overlords). They are often associated with harlots and other public sinners (see Notes). But even these people love those who love them—at least their mothers and other tax collectors!

47 Proper salutation was a mark of courtesy and respect; but if Jesus' disciples tender such greeting only to their "brothers"—i.e., other like-minded disciples (see comments at vv.23–24)—they do not rise above the standards of *ethnikoi* (strictly speaking, "Gentiles," but since most Gentiles were pagans, the word came to have more than racial overtones). "In loving his friends a man may in a certain sense be loving only himself—a kind of expanded selfishness" (Broadus). Jesus will not condone this. "The life of the old (fallen) humanity is based on rough justice, avenging injuries and returning favors. The life of the new (redeemed) humanity is based on divine love, refusing to take revenge but overcoming evil with good" (Stott, *Message of the Sermon on the Mount*, 123).

NOTES

43 Zerwick (*Biblical Greek*, para. 279) argues that the future μισήσεις (*misēseis*, GK *3631*) may here be used modally: "You shall love your neighbor but you may hate your enemy." This is unlikely because

(1) the only parallel, 7:4, renders a question; and (2) the command to love in the same sentence is also in the future form (ἀγαπήσεις [*agapēseis*, GK *26*; "you shall love"—see comments at v.21]). It is therefore best to see the second verb as imperatival, as in the NIV.

44 The extra words in KJV are assimilations to Luke 6:27–28. Not only are they absent from some early representatives of Alexandrian, Western, and Caesarean texts; "the divergence of reading among the added clauses likewise speaks against their originality" (Metzger, *Textual Commentary*, 14).

46 William O. Walker Jr. ("Jesus and the Tax Collectors," *JBL* 97 [1978]: 221–38) has argued that passages like this and others unflattering to tax collectors suggest that Jesus did not have so warm a relationship with such men as has generally been supposed and that therefore passages supporting the latter (esp. 9:10–13; 11:19; and par.) must not be accepted as authentic too readily. But Walker creates a false historical disjunction—either this or that, when all the evidence demands both/and. Jesus denounces all sin but befriends both tax collectors and Pharisees (see comments at 9:9–13).

c. Conclusion: the demand for perfection (5:48)

48"Be perfect, therefore, as your heavenly Father is perfect."

COMMENTARY

48 Some interpret this verse as the conclusion of the last antithesis (vv.43–47; e.g., Allen, Hendriksen). In that case the perfection advocated is perfection in love. But "perfection" has far broader associations, and it is better to understand v.48 as the conclusion to the antitheses.

The word *teleios* ("perfect," GK *5455*) usually reflects *tāmîm* ("perfect," GK 9459) in the OT. It can refer to the soundness of sacrificial animals (Ex 12:5) or to thorough commitment to the Lord and therefore uprightness (Ge 6:9; Dt 18:13; 2Sa 22:26). The Greek word can be rendered "mature" or "full-grown" (1Co 14:20; Eph 4:13; Heb 5:14; 6:1). Many judge its force to be nonmoral here in v.48, which becomes an exhortation to total commitment to God (e.g., Bonnard). But this makes for a fairly flat conclusion of the antitheses.

A better understanding of the verse does justice to the word *teleios* but also notes that the form of the verse is exactly like Leviticus 19:2, with "holy" displaced by "perfect," possibly due to the influence of Deuteronomy 18:13 (where the NIV renders LXX *teleios* by "blameless"; cf. Gundry, *Use of the Old Testament*, 73–74). Nowhere is God directly and absolutely called "perfect" in the OT: he is perfect in knowledge (Job 37:16) or in his way (Ps 18:30), and a man's name may be "Yahweh is perfect" (so *yôtām* [Jotham], Jdg 9:5; 2Ki 15:32). But here for the first time perfection is predicated of God (cf. L. Sabourin, "Why Is God Called 'Perfect' in Matthew 5:48?" *BZ* 24 [1980]: 266–68).

In the light of the preceding verses (vv.17–47), Jesus is saying that the true direction in which the law has always pointed is not toward mere judicial restraints, concessions arising out of the hardness of human hearts, still less casuistical perversions, nor even to the law of love (contra C. Dietzfelbinger, "Die Antithesen der Bergpredigt im Verständnis des Matthäus," *ZNW* 70 [1979]: 1–15; see comments at 22:34–35). No, it pointed rather to all the perfection of God, exemplified by the authoritative interpretation of the law bound up in the preceding antitheses. This perfection Jesus' disciples must emulate if they are truly followers of him who fulfills the Law and the Prophets (v.17).

The Qumran community understood perfection in terms of perfect obedience, as measured exclusively by the teachings of their community (1QS 1:8–9, 13; 2:1–2; 4:22–23; 8:9–10). Jesus has transposed this to a higher key, not by reducing the obedience, but by making the standard the perfect heavenly Father. Ronald A. Ward (*Royal Theology* [London: MMS, 1964], 117–20) points out that in classical and Hellenistic usage *teleios* can have a static and a dynamic force, "the one appropriate to One Who does not develop, and the other suitable for men who can *grow* in grace" (p. 119, emphasis his): "Be perfect, therefore, as your heavenly Father is perfect."

The gospel writers refer to God as Father only in contexts pertaining to the Messiah or to believers. He is not the Father of all men but the Father of Jesus and the Father of Jesus' disciples (cf. H. F. D. Sparks, "The Doctrine of the Fatherhood of God in the Gospels," in *Studies in the Gospels* [ed. D. E. Nineham; Oxford: Blackwell, 1955], 241–62). Just as in the OT it was the distinctive mark of Israel that they were set apart for God to reflect his character (Lev 19:2; cf. 11:44–45; 20:7, 26), so the messianic community carries on this distinctiveness (cf. 1Pe 1:16) as the true locus of the people of God (cf. France, *Jesus and the Old Testament*, 61–62). This must not encourage us to conclude that Jesus teaches that unqualified perfection is already possible for his disciples. He teaches them to acknowledge spiritual bankruptcy (v.3) and to pray "Forgive us our debts" (6:12). But the perfection of the Father, the true eschatological goal of the law, is what all disciples of Jesus pursue.

NOTES

48 The future ἔσεσθε (*esesthe*, lit., "you will be") is imperatival, as in LXX Leviticus 19:2 (see comments at v.21).

Many commentators compare Luke 6:36 ("Be merciful, just as your Father is merciful") and discuss which form of the saying is closer to the original. For instance, Hill notes (1) that "merciful" eminently suits Luke's context and (2) that Matthew's τέλειοι (*teleioi*, "perfect") may render the Aramaic שְׁלִים (*šᵉlîm*, "perfect"), which could have been part of a pun with שְׁלָם (*šᵉlām*, "greetings") in the greetings of 5:47; (3) he concludes that Matthew's version is probably more original. But a good case could be made for the position that there were two sayings:

1. Not only does Matthew have "perfect" and Luke "merciful," the verb is different in the two cases: ἔσεσθε (*esesthe*, "Be," GK *1639*) and γίνεσθε (*ginesthe*, "Be," GK *1181*) respectively. Luke also omits "heavenly." In other words, the two sayings have little in common except the comparison between the believer and the Father.

2. Luke's verse indeed fits its context admirably, but so does Matthew's.

3. Matthew may have omitted any reference to mercy in his sixth beatitude because he has already dealt with the theme in 5:7 (absent from Luke; and there the word for "mercy" is different).

4. The Aramaic pun is possible (though another Semitic term more commonly stands behind τέλειος [*teleios*, "perfect"]). Strictly speaking, however, such evidence supports the authenticity of 5:48 but does not render Luke 6:36 secondary unless it is already assumed they came from the same source—which is the very point in dispute.

4. Religious hypocrisy: its description and overthrow (6:1–18)

a. The principle (6:1)

[1]"Be careful not to do your 'acts of righteousness' before men, to be seen by them. If you do, you will have no reward from your Father in heaven."

COMMENTARY

1 If the text behind the NIV is correct (see Notes), Jesus, having told his disciples of the superior righteousness expected of them, now warns them of the danger of religious hypocrisy. "Your righteousness," first occurring in 5:20, recurs here, though the focus has changed from "righteousness" in a purely positive sense to "righteousness" in a formal, external sense. Modern translations try to show the distinction by various means. The NIV renders the word "acts of righteousness" (in quotation marks), the RSV offers "Beware of practicing your piety before men," and the NEB, "Be careful not to make a show of your religion before men." Unfortunately, they are overstepping the evidence.

"To do righteousness" is an expression found elsewhere (Ps 106:3; Isa 58:2; 1Jn 2:29; 3:7, 10). In 1 John 2:29, for instance, it is rendered by the NIV "to do what is right," and that could suffice here in v.1 as well. Jesus is not so much dealing with a different kind of righteousness or with mere acts of righteousness as with the motives behind righteous living. To attempt to live in accord with the righteousness spelled out in the preceding verses but out of motives eager for human applause is to prostitute that righteousness. For this there will be no reward (see comments at 5:12) from the heavenly Father. There is no contradiction with 5:14–16, where disciples are told to let their light shine before men so that they may see their good deeds; there the motive is for men to praise the heavenly Father. Righteous conduct under kingdom norms must be visible so that God may be glorified. Yet it must never be visible in order to win human acclaim. Better by far is to hide any righteous deed that may lead to ostentation. To trade the goal of pleasing the Father for the trivial and idolatrous goal of pleasing man will never do.

This verse introduces the three chief acts of Jewish piety (cf. vv.2–18)—almsgiving, prayer, fasting (C. G. Montefiore and H. Loewe, *A Rabbinic Anthology* [London: Macmillan, 1938], 412–39; Moore, *Judaism*, 2:162–79). In each act the logical structure is the same: (1) a warning not to do the act to be praised by men, (2) a guarantee that those who ignore this warning will get what they want but no more, (3) instruction on how to perform the act of piety secretly, and (4) the assurance that the Father who sees in secret will reward openly (for details of the logical structure, see H. D. Betz, "Eine juden-christliche Kult-Didache in Matthäus 6:1–18," in *Jesus Christus* [ed. Strecker], 445–57).

NOTES

1 Two variants are of interest.

Ἐλεημοσύνην (*eleēmosynēn*, "alms") was probably an early marginal gloss on δικαιοσύνην (*dikaiosynēn*, "righteousness"), since in the LXX "righteousness" in Hebrew was often rendered "alms." The gloss was then inserted into the text by a copyist. If "alms" were in fact original, then v.1 should be read with vv.2–4, not as the introduction to vv.2–18; and this would break the carefully wrought structure (discussed above). Moreover, the external evidence strongly supports δικαιοσύνην, *dikaiosynēn*.

The evidence in favor of the connective δέ (*de*, "but") is evenly divided (brackets in UBS[4]; untranslated in NIV). An adversative δέ, *de*, fits the context very well and therefore may have been inserted.

On εἰ δέ μή γε (*ei de mē ge*, "otherwise," or "If you do" [NIV]), cf. Thrall, *Greek Particles*, 9–10.

b. Three examples (6:2–18)

(1) Alms (6:2–4)

OVERVIEW

Although 6:1–6 has no parallel in the Synoptic Gospels, its authenticity is supported by the numerous wordplays in Aramaic reconstructions (cf. Black, *Aramaic Approach*, 176–78).

2"So when you give to the needy, do not announce it with trumpets, as the hypocrites do in the synagogues and on the streets, to be honored by men. I tell you the truth, they have received their reward in full. 3But when you give to the needy, do not let your left hand know what your right hand is doing, 4so that your giving may be in secret. Then your Father, who sees what is done in secret, will reward you."

COMMENTARY

2 The "you" is singular (see comments at 5:28). While some in Jesus' day believed almsgiving earned merit (e.g., Tob 12:8–9; Sir 3:30; 29:11–12), ostentation, not merit theology, is the point here. Jesus assumes his disciples will give alms: "When you give to the needy," he says, not "If you give to the needy" (cf. 10:42; 25:35–45; 2Co 9:6–7; Php 4:18–19; 1Ti 6:18–19; Jas 1:27). Rabbinic writers also warn against ostentation in almsgiving (cf. Str-B, 1:391ff.). The frequency of the warnings attests the commonness of the practice.

The reference to trumpet announcements is difficult. Many commentators say this refers to "the practice of blowing trumpets at the time of collecting alms in the Temple for the relief of some signal need" (Hill, following Bonnard), but no Jewish sources confirm this, and the idea seems to stem only from early Christian expositors who assumed its correctness. Likewise there is no evidence (contra Calvin) that the almsgivers themselves really blew trumpets on their way to the temple. Alfred Edersheim (*The Temple: Its Ministry and Services* [London: Religious Tract Society, n.d.], 26), followed by Jeremias (*Jerusalem*, 170 n.73), suggests this is a reference to horn-shaped collection boxes used at the temple to discourage pilfering. Lachs ("Textual Observations," 103–5), without mentioning Edersheim, has followed up on that idea by postulating a mistranslation from an underlying Semitic source. But unless the trumpet is a metaphorical caricature (like "tooting your own horn")—a poorly attested suggestion—the solution of A. Buchler ("St. Matthew 6:1–6 and Other Allied Passages," *JTS* 10 [1909]: 266–70) still seems best: public fasts were proclaimed by the sounding of trumpets. At such times, prayers for rain were recited in the streets (cf. v.5), and it was widely thought that almsgiving ensured the efficacy of the fasts and prayers (e.g., *b. Sanh.* 35a; *m. Taʿan* 2:6; *Lev. Rab.* 34:14). But these occasions afforded golden opportunities for ostentation.

Lachs objects that this interpretation makes the givers pompous but not hypocrites. In older Greek a *hypokritēs* ("hypocrite," GK *5695*) was an actor, but by the first century the term came to be used for those who play roles and see the world as their stage. What Lachs overlooks is that there are different kinds of hypocrisy. In one the hypocrite feigns goodness but is actually evil and knows he is being deceptive (e.g., 22:15–18). In another the hypocrite is carried away by his own acting and deceives himself. Such pious hypocrites (as in 7:1–5), though unaware of their own deceit, do not fool most onlookers, and this *may* be the meaning here. A third kind of hypocrite deceives himself into thinking he is acting for the best interests of God and man and also deceives onlookers. The needy are unlikely to complain when they receive large gifts, and their gratitude may flatter and thus bolster the giver's self-delusion (cf. D.A. Spieler, "Hypocrisy: An Exploration of a Third Type," *AUSS* 13 [1975]: 273–79). Perhaps it is best to identify the hypocrisy in v.2 with this third type.

The Pharisees' great weakness was that they loved human praise more than God's praise (cf. Jn 5:44; 12:43). Those who give out of this attitude receive their reward in full (such is the force of *apechousin* [GK *600*]; cf. Deissmann, *Light from the Ancient East*, 110–11). They win human plaudits, and that is all they get (cf. Ps 17:14).

3–4 The way to avoid hypocrisy is not to cease giving but to do so with such secrecy that we scarcely know what we have given. Jesus' disciples must themselves be so given to God (cf. 2Co 8:5) that their giving is prompted by obeying God and having compassion on others. Then their Father, who sees what is done in secret (Heb 4:13), will reward them. The verb "to reward" (*apodidomai*, GK *625*), with God as subject, here and in vv.6, 18, is different from that used in v.2. Bonnard rightly notes it has a sense of "pay back," and this is compatible with "reward" (see comments at 5:12). "Openly" (KJV), here and in vv.6, 18, is a late gloss designed to complete the antithetic parallelism with "secretly" or "in secret." Jesus does not discuss the locale and nature of the reward, but we will not be far from the NT evidence if we understand it to be "both in time and in eternity, both in character and in felicity" (Broadus).

(2) *Prayer (6:5–15)*

(a) Ostentatious prayer (6:5–6)

[5]"And when you pray, do not be like the hypocrites, for they love to pray standing in the synagogues and on the street corners to be seen by men. I tell you the truth, they have received their reward in full. [6]But when you pray, go into your room, close the door and pray to your Father, who is unseen. Then your Father, who sees what is done in secret, will reward you."

COMMENTARY

5 Again Jesus assumes that his disciples will pray, but he forbids the prayers of "hypocrites" (see comments at v.2). Prayer had a prominent place in Jewish life and led to countless rabbinic decisions (cf. *m. Ber.*). In synagogue worship, someone from the congregation might be asked to pray publicly, standing in front of the ark. And at certain times prayers could be offered in the streets (*m. Taʿan.* 2:1–2; see comments at v.2). But the location was not the critical factor. Neither is the "standing" posture in itself significant. In the Bible people pray prostrate (Nu 16:22; Jos 5:14; Da 8:17; Mt 26:39; Rev 11:16), kneeling (2Ch 6:13; Da 6:10; Lk 22:41, Ac 7:60; 9:40; 20:36; 21:5), sitting (2Sa 7:18), and standing (1Sa 1:26; Mk 11:25; Lk 18:11, 13). Again it is the motive that is crucial—"to be seen by men." And again there is the same reward (cf. Mt 6:2 and 5).

6 If Jesus were forbidding all public prayer, then clearly the early church did not understand him (e.g., 18:19–20; Ac 1:24; 3:1; 4:24–30). The public versus private antithesis is a good test of one's motives. The person who prays more in public than in private reveals that he is less interested in God's approval than in human praise. Not piety but a reputation for piety is his concern. Far better to deal radically with this hypocrisy (cf. 5:29–30) and pray in a private "room"; the word *tameion* (GK *5421*) can refer to a storeroom (Lk 12:24), some other inner room (Mt 12:26; 24:26; Lk 12:3, 24), or even a bedroom (Isa 26:20 LXX, with which this verse has several common elements; see also 2Ki 4:33). The Father, who sees in secret, will reward the disciple who prays in secret (see comments at v.4).

NOTES

5 UBS[4] and Nestle[27] follow the plural reading, Nestle-Kilpatrick (Η ΚΑΙΝΗ ΔΙΑΘΗΚΗ [ed. E. Nestle and G. D. Kilpatrick; London: British and Foreign Bible Society, 1958]) the singular. The former is marginally more probable on external grounds, and many argue that corruption to the singular occurred because of assimilation to the singular in v.4 and v.6. But copyists might equally have noted the recurring pattern of plural to singular changes in these verses (v.1—vv.2–4; v.16—vv.17–18). See comments at 5:23.

The use of the future οὐκ ἔσεσθε (*ouk esesthe*, "do not be") with imperatival force usually reflects legal language from the OT (BDF, para. 362). But here and in 20:26 it is found in words ascribed to Jesus with no unambiguous OT precedent (Zerwick, *Biblical Greek*, para. 443).

On the idiom φιλοῦσιν ... προσεύχεσθαι (*philousin* ... *proseuchesthai*, "they love ... to pray"), see Turner, *Syntax*, 226.

(b) Repetitious prayer (6:7–8)

[7]"And when you pray, do not keep on babbling like pagans, for they think they will be heard because of their many words. [8]Do not be like them, for your Father knows what you need before you ask him."

COMMENTARY

7–8 Verses 7–15 focus on the second of the three chief acts of Jewish piety, namely prayer. Prayer is central to a believer's life. So Jesus gives further warnings and a positive example.

Many argue that whereas vv.5–6 warn against the prayer practices of Jews, vv.7–8 warn against those of Gentiles ("pagans"; see comments at 5:47). But the distinction is not quite so cut-and-dried. Every religious group harbors some who pray repetitiously. So with the Jews of Jesus' day. He labeled all such praying—even that of his own people—as pagan! "Pagans" (cf. 1Ki 18:26) are not so much the target as the negative example of all who pray repetitiously.

The verb *battalogeō* ("keep on babbling") is very rare, apart from writings dependent on the NT (BDAG, 172). It may derive from the Aramaic *battal* ("idle," "useless") or some other Semitic word; or it may be onomatopoetic. If so, "babble" is a fine English equivalent. Jesus is not condemning prayer any more than he is condemning almsgiving (v.2) or fasting (v.16). Nor is he forbidding all long prayers or all repetition. He himself prayed at length (Lk 6:12), repeated himself in prayer (Mt 26:44; unlike Sir 7:14!), and told a parable to show his disciples that "they should always pray and not give up" (Lk 18:1). His point is that his disciples should avoid meaningless, repetitive prayers offered under the misconception that mere length will make prayers efficacious. Such thoughtless babble can occur in liturgical and extemporaneous prayers alike. Essentially it is thoroughly pagan, for pagan gods allegedly thrive on incantation and repetition. But the personal Father God to whom believers pray does not require information about our needs (v.8). "As a father knows the needs of his family, yet teaches them to ask in confidence and trust, so does God treat his children" (Hill).

(c) Model prayer (6:9–13)

OVERVIEW

"The Lord's Prayer," as it is commonly called, is not so much his own prayer (Jn 17 is just that) as the model he gave his disciples. Much of the literature has focused on the complex question of the relation between vv.9–13 and Luke 11:2–4. The newer EV reveal the many differences. KJV does not show the differences so clearly because it preserves the numerous assimilations to Matthew in late MSS of Luke (cf. Metzger, *Textual Commentary*, 154–56). Various theories attempt to account for the differences.

1. Formerly some argued that Matthew's form is the original and Luke's a simplified version of it. This view is no longer popular, largely because of the difficulty of believing that Luke, who was highly interested in Jesus' prayer life, would omit words and clauses from one of his prayers if they were already in a source.

2. Others have argued strongly that Luke's account is original and that Matthew has added to it according to his own theology and linguistic habit (so Jeremias, *Prayers of Jesus*, 85ff.; Hill). Several reasons for this theory follow.

a. All Luke's content is found in Matthew 6:9–13. But this could support condensation by Luke as easily as expansion by Matthew. More important, mere expansion-condensation theories do not account for the linguistic differences (e.g., tense in the fourth petition, vocabulary and tense in the fifth), and the theory is further weakened when it is argued (e.g., by Hill) that in the fourth petition the priorities are reversed and Matthew's form is probably more original than Luke's.

b. Matthew's more rhythmical, liturgical formulation may reflect the desire to construct an ecclesiastical equivalent for Jewish Christians of the synagogue's main prayer, the *Eighteen Benedictions* (Davies, *Setting*, 310ff.), to which the Lord's Prayer structurally and formally corresponds. But these correspondences have been greatly exaggerated. They are no closer than those found in fine extemporaneous prayers prayed in evangelical churches every Wednesday night (on the differences, see Günther Bornkamm, *Jesus of Nazareth* [London: Hodder & Stoughton, 1960], 136–37). Moreover, Jesus was far removed from innovation for its own sake. Why should he not have expressed himself in current forms of piety?

c. Many argue that the Matthean introduction (v.9) suggests that the prayer is a standardized liturgical form. On the contrary, the text reads, "This is how (*houtōs*) you should pray," not, "This is what you should pray." The emphasis is on paradigm or model, not liturgical form.

d. It has been argued that the emphatic "you" (v.9) "sets off the new Christian community from the synagogue (and Gentile usage) whose piety is being contrasted with Christian worship in the surrounding context." Not only is this needlessly anachronistic, but it also ignores the constant stress on "you," designating Jesus' disciples as the exclusive messianic community in Jesus' day (see comments at v.2).

3. Ernst Lohmeyer (*The Lord's Prayer* [London: Collins, 1965], 293) argues that the two prayers do not spring from one source (Q?) but from two separate traditions. In Matthew the prayer reflects the liturgical tradition of the Galilean Christian community and emphasizes a certain eschatological outlook, whereas in Luke the prayer reflects the liturgical tradition of the Jerusalem church and focuses more on daily life. He refuses to be drawn out on what stands behind these two traditions. Lohmeyer's geographical speculations are not convincing, but his emphasis on two separate traditions of the Lord's Prayer is worth careful consideration. Evidence from the *Didache* and the demonstrable tendency for local churches to think of themselves as Christian synagogues (e.g., in the letters of Ignatius) and to adopt some synagogal liturgical patterns combine to suggest that the Lord's Prayer was used in corporate worship from a very early date. If (and this is a big "if") such church liturgies stretch back to the time when Matthew and Luke were written,

it seems unlikely that the evangelists would disregard the liturgical habits of their own communities, unless for overwhelming historical or theological reasons (e.g., correction of heresy within the accepted liturgy). But none such is evident. This reinforces the theory of two separate liturgical traditions. On the other hand, if fixed liturgical patterns had not yet included any form of the Lord's Prayer by the time the evangelists wrote, the differences between the two are not easily explained by a common source.

4. These complexities have generated several mediating theories. To give but one, Marshall (*Gospel of Luke*, 455) suggests that Luke drew his form of the prayer either from Q or from a recension of Q different from that of Matthew, whereas Matthew drew his either from separate tradition and substituted it for what he found in Q (if his recension of Q was the same as Luke's) or else from a separate recension. This is little more than an elegant way of saying that Lohmeyer's two-traditions theory is basically correct. It may be too elegant. Many suspect that Q is not a single document (see Introduction, section 3), and to speak thus of recensions of Q when our knowledge of Q is so uncertain makes one wonder how to distinguish methodologically between recensions of Q and entirely separate accounts of two historical occasions within Jesus' ministry. Resolving the unknown by appealing to the more unknown is of dubious merit.

5. Though the evidence for two traditions is strong, equally significant is the fact that there are two entirely different historical settings of the prayer. Unless one is prepared to say that one or the other is made up, the reasonable explanation is that Jesus taught this sort of prayer often during his itinerant ministry and that Matthew records one occasion and Luke another. Matthew's setting is not as historically specific as that of Luke only if one interprets the introduction and the conclusion of the entire discourse loosely or if one postulates Matthew's freedom to add "footnotes" to the material he provides (see Overview, 5:1–7:29). The former is exegetically doubtful, the latter without convincing literary controls, and even in these instances the evidence for two separate traditions for the Lord's Prayer is so strong that the simplest comprehensive explanation is that Jesus himself taught this form of prayer on more than one occasion.

Few have doubted that the prayer is in some form authentic. Goulder (*Midrash and Lection*, 296–301) argues that Matthew composed it from fragments, most of which were authentic but uttered on other and separate occasions, and that Luke copied and adapted Matthew's work. His theory is unconvincing because it does no more than show parallels between elements of this prayer and other things Jesus said or prayed. The same evidence could equally be read as supporting the prayer's authenticity. It is well worth noting that there is no anachronism in the prayer—no mention of Jesus as high priestly Mediator, no allusion to themes developed only after the resurrection.

There are signs of Semitic background, whether Aramaic (e.g., Black, *Aramaic Approach*, 203–8) or Hebrew (Carmignac, *Recherches sur le "Notre Père,"* 29–52). Scholars debate whether Matthew's version has six petitions (Chrysostom, Calvin, and Reformed theologians) or seven, interpreting v.13 as two (Augustine, Luther, most Lutheran theologians). The issue affects the meaning but little. More important, as Bengel (*Gnomon*) remarks, is the division of the petitions. The first three are cast in terms of God's glory ("your ... your ... your"); the others in terms of our good ("us ... us ... us"). For recent theological meditations on this prayer, see Gerald Bray, *Yours Is the Kingdom* (Leicester: Inter-Varsity, 2006), and Philip Graham Ryken, *The Prayer of Our Lord* (Wheaton, Ill.: Crossway, 2007).

9"This, then, is how you should pray:

"'Our Father in heaven,
hallowed be your name,
10 your kingdom come,
your will be done
on earth as it is in heaven.
11 Give us today our daily bread.
12 Forgive us our debts,
as we also have forgiven our debtors.
13 And lead us not into temptation,
but deliver us from the evil one.'"

COMMENTARY

9 By contrast with ostentatious prayer (vv.5–6) or thoughtless prayer (vv.7–8), Jesus gives his disciples a model. But it is only a model: "This is how [not what] you should pray."

The fatherhood of God is not a central theme in the OT. Where "father" does occur with respect to God, it is commonly by way of analogy, not direct address (Dt 32:6; Ps 103:13; Isa 63:16; Mal 2:10). One can also find occasional references to God as father in the Apocrypha and Pseudepigrapha (Tob 13:4; Sir 23:1; 51:10; Wis 2:16; 14:3; *Jub.* 1:24–25, 28; *T. Levi* 18:6; *T. Jud.* 24:2—though some of these may be Christian interpolations). There is but one instance in the Dead Sea Scrolls (1QS 9:35); the assorted rabbinic references are relatively rare and few unambiguously antedate Jesus (*b. Taʿan.* 25b; the fifth and sixth petitions of the *Eighteen Benedictions*). Pagans likewise on occasion addressed their gods as father, e.g., *Zeu pater* ("Zeus, Father"; Lat. *Jupiter*). But not until Jesus is it characteristic to address God as "Father" (Jeremias, *Prayers of Jesus*, 11ff.). This can be understood only against the background of customary patterns for addressing God.

The tendency in Jewish circles was to multiply titles ascribing sovereignty, lordship, glory, grace, and the like to God (cf. Carson, *Divine Sovereignty*, 45ff.). Against such a background, Jesus' habit of addressing God as his own Father (Mk 14:36) and teaching his disciples to do the same could appear only familiar and presumptuous to opponents, personal and gracious to followers. Unfortunately, many modern Christians find it difficult to delight in the privilege of addressing the Sovereign of the universe as "Father" because they have lost the heritage that emphasizes God's transcendence.

Jesus' use of *Abba* ("Father" or "my Father"; GK *5*, but see also GK 10003; Mk 14:36; cf. Mt 11:25; 26:39, 42; Lk 23:34; Jn 11:41; 12:27; 17:1–26) was adopted by early Christians (Ro 8:15; Gal 4:6), and there is no evidence of anyone before Jesus using this term to address God (cf. *NIDNTT*, 1:614–15). Throughout the prayer the reference is plural: "Our Father" (which in Aram. would have been *ʾabînû*, not *ʾabba*). In other words, this is an example of a prayer to be prayed in fellowship with other disciples (cf. 18:19), not in isolation (cf. Jn 20:17).

Striking is Jesus' use of pronouns with "Father." When forgiveness of sins is discussed, Jesus speaks of "your Father" (6:14–15) and excludes himself. When he speaks of his unique sonship and authority, he speaks of "my Father" (e.g., 11:27) and excludes others. The "our Father" at the beginning of this model prayer is plural but does not include Jesus, since it is part of his instruction regarding what his disciples should pray.

This opening designation establishes the kind of God to whom prayer is offered: He is personal (no mere "ground of being") and caring (a Father, not a tyrant or an ogre, but the one who establishes the real nature of fatherhood; cf. Eph 3:14–15). That he is "our Father" establishes the relationship that exists between Jesus' disciples and God. In this sense he is not the Father of all people indiscriminately (see comments at 5:43–47). The early church was right to forbid non-Christians from reciting this prayer as vigorously as they forbade them from joining with believers at the Lord's Table. But that he is "our Father in heaven" (the designation occurs twenty times in Matthew, once in Mark [Mk 11:25], never in Luke, and in some instances may be a Matthean formulation) reminds us of his transcendence and sovereignty, while preparing us for v.10b. The entire formula is less concerned with the proper protocol in approaching Deity than with the truth of who he is, to establish within the believer the right frame of mind (Stott, *Message of the Sermon on the Mount*, 146).

God's "name" is a reflection of who he is (cf. *NIDNTT*, 2:648–56). God's "name" is God himself as he is and has revealed himself, and so his name is already holy. Holiness, often thought of as "separateness," is less an attribute than what he is. It has to do with the very godhood of God. Therefore to pray that God's "name" be "hallowed" (the verbal form of "holy," recurring in Matthew only at 23:17, 19 [NIV, "makes sacred"]) is not to pray that God may become holy but that he may be treated as holy (cf. Ex 20:8; Lev 19:2, 32; Eze 36:23; 1Pe 1:15), that his name should not be despised (Mal 1:6) by the thoughts and conduct of those who have been created in his image.

10 As God is eternally holy, so he eternally reigns in absolute sovereignty. Yet it is appropriate to pray not only "hallowed be your name" but also "your kingdom come." God's "kingdom" or "reign" (see comments at 3:2; 4:17, 23) can refer to that aspect of God's sovereignty under which there is life—eternal life. That kingdom is breaking in under Christ's ministry, but it is not consummated until the end of the age (28:20). To pray "your kingdom come" is therefore simultaneously to ask that God's saving, royal rule be extended now as people bow in submission to him and already taste the eschatological blessing of salvation and to cry for the consummation of the kingdom (cf. 1Co 16:22; Rev 11:17; 22:20). Godly Jews were waiting for the kingdom (Mk 15:43), "the consolation of Israel" (Lk 2:25). They recited "Kaddish" ("Sanctification"), an ancient Aramaic prayer, at the close of each synagogue service. In its oldest extant form, it runs, "Exalted and *hallowed* be his great name in the world which he created according to his will. *May he let his kingdom rule* in your lifetime and in your days and in the lifetime of the whole house of Israel, speedily and soon. And to this, say, Amen" (Jeremias, *Prayers of Jesus*, 98, emphasis his). But the Jew looked forward to the kingdom, whereas the reader of Matthew's gospel, while looking forward to its consummation, perceives that the kingdom has already broken in and prays for its extension as well as its unqualified manifestation.

To pray that God's will, which is "good, pleasing and perfect" (Ro 12:2), be done on earth as in heaven is to use language broad enough to embrace three requests.

1. The first request is that God's will be done now on earth as it is now accomplished in heaven.

The word *thelēma* ("will," GK *2525*) includes both God's righteous demands (7:21; 12:50; cf. Ps 40:8) and his determination to bring about certain events in salvation history (18:14; 26:42; cf. Ac 21:14). So for that will to be "done" includes both moral obedience and the bringing to pass of certain events, such as the cross. This prayer corresponds to asking for the present extension of the messianic kingdom.

2. The second request is that God's will may ultimately be as *fully accomplished* on earth as it is now accomplished in heaven. "Will" has the same range of meanings as before, and this prayer corresponds to asking for the consummation of the messianic kingdom.

3. The third request is that God's will may ultimately be done on the earth *in the same way* as it is now accomplished in heaven. In the consummated kingdom, it will not be necessary to discuss superior righteousness (5:20–48) as antithetical to lust, hate, retaliatory face slapping, divorce, and the like; for then God's will, construed now as his demands for righteousness, will be done as it is now done in heaven: freely, openly, spontaneously, and without the need to set it over against evil (Carson, *Sermon on the Mount*, 66–67).

These first three petitions, though they focus on God's name, God's kingdom, and God's will, are nevertheless prayers that he may act in such a way that his people will hallow his name, submit to his reign, and do his will. It is therefore impossible to pray this prayer in sincerity without humbly committing oneself to such a course.

11 The last petitions explicitly request things for ourselves. The first is "bread," a term used to cover all food (cf. Pr 30:8; Mk 3:20; Ac 6:1; 2Th 3:12; Jas 2:15). Many early fathers thought it inappropriate to talk about physical food here and interpreted "bread" as a reference to the Lord's Supper or to the Word of God. This depended in part on Jerome's Latin rendering of *epiousios* (NIV, "daily," GK *2157*) as *superstantialem*: Give us today our "supersubstantial" bread—a rendering that may have depended in part on the influence of Marius Victorinus (cf. F. F. Bruce, "The Gospel Text of Marius Victorinus," in *Text and Interpretation* [ed. Best and Wilson], 70). There is no linguistic justification for this translation. The bread is real food, and it may further suggest all that we need in the physical realm (Luther).

That does not mean that *epiousios* is easy to translate. The term appears only here and in Luke's prayer (Lk 11:3); and the two possible extrabiblical references, which could support "daily," have had grave doubt cast on them by Bruce M. Metzger ("How Many Times Does ἐπιούσιος Occur Outside the Lord's Prayer?" *ExpTim* 69 [1957–58]: 52–54). P. Grelot ("La quatrième demande du 'Pater' et son arrièreplan sémitique," *NTS* 25 [1978–79]: 299–314) has attempted to support the same translation ("daily") by reconstructing an Aramaic original, but his article deals inadequately with the Greek text, and other Aramaic reconstructions are possible (e.g., Black, *Aramaic Approach*, 203–7).

The prayer is for our needs, not our greeds. It is for one day at a time ("today"), reflecting the precarious lifestyle of many first-century workers who were paid one day at a time and for whom a few days' illness could spell tragedy. Many have suggested a derivation from *epi tēn ousan* [namely, *hēmeran*] ("for today") or *hē epiousa hēmera* ("for the coming day"), referring in the morning to the same day and at night to the next (for *hēmera[n]*, see GK *2465*). This meaning is almost certainly right, but it is better supported by deriving the word from the feminine participle *epiousa*, already well established with the sense of "immediately following" by the time the NT was written. Whatever the etymological problems, this makes sense of Luke 11:3, where "each day" is part of the text: "Give us each day our bread for the coming day." Equally it makes sense in Matthew, where "today" displaces "each day": "Give us today our bread for the coming day." This may sound redundant to Western readers, but it is a precious and urgent petition to those who live from hand to mouth.

Some derive *epiousios* ("daily") from the verb *epienai*, referring not to the future, still less to the food of the messianic banquet (contra Jeremias, *Prayers of Jesus*, 100–102), but to the bread that belongs to it, i.e., that is necessary and sufficient for it (cf. R. Ten Kate, "Geef ons heden ons 'dagelijks' brood," *Nederlands Theologisch Tijdschrift* 32 [1978]: 125–39; with similar conclusions but by a different route, H. Bourgoin, "Ἐπιούσιος expliqué par la notion de préfixe vide," *Bib* 60 [1979]: 91–96; and for literature, BDAG, 376–77; Gundry, *Use of the Old Testament*, 74–75). This has the considerable merit of meshing well with both "today" and "each day" (Matthew and Luke respectively), and in Matthew's case it may be loosely rendered "Give us today the food we need." But the derivation is linguistically artificial (cf. Colin Hemer, "Ἐπιούσιος, *JSNT* 22 [1984]: 81–94).

The idea of God "giving" the food in no way diminishes responsibility to work (see comments at vv.25–34) but presupposes not only that Jesus' disciples live one day at a time (cf. v.34) but that all good things, even our ability to work and earn our food, come from God's hand (cf. Dt 8:18; 1Co 4:7; Jas 1:17). It is a lesson easily forgotten when wealth multiplies and absolute self-sufficiency is portrayed as a virtue.

12 The first three petitions stand independently from one another. The last three, however, are linked in Greek by "ands," almost as if to say that life sustained by food is not enough. We also need forgiveness of sin and deliverance from temptation.

In Matthew, what we ask to be forgiven for is *ta opheilēmata hēmōn* ("our debts," GK *4052*); in Luke, it is our "sins." Hill notes that the crucial word *to opheilēma* ("debt") "means a literal 'debt' in the LXX and NT, except at this point." And on this basis, S. T. Lachs ("On Matthew 6.12," *NovT* 17 [1975]: 6–8) argues that in Matthew this petition of the Lord's Prayer is not really dealing with sins but with loans in the sixth year, one year before the Jubilee. But the linguistic evidence can be read differently. The word *opheilēma* is rather rare in biblical Greek. It occurs only four times in the LXX (Dt 24:10 [2x]; 1 Esd 3:20; 1 Macc 15:8); and in Deuteronomy 24:10, where it occurs twice, it renders two different Hebrew words. In the NT, it appears only here and in Romans 4:4. On this basis it would be as accurate to say the word always means "sin" in the NT except at Romans 4:4 as to say it always means "debt" except at Matthew 6:12.

More important, the Aramaic word *ḥôbā* ("debt") is often used (e.g., in the Targums) to mean "sin" or "transgression." Deissmann (*Bible Studies*, 225) notes an instance of the cognate verb *hamartian opheilō* (lit., "I owe sin"). Probably Matthew has provided a literal rendering of the Aramaic Jesus most commonly used in preaching; and even Luke (Lk 11:4) uses the cognate participle in the second line, *panti opheilonti hēmin* ("everyone who sins against us"). There is therefore no reason to take "debts" to mean anything other than "sins," here conceived as something owed God (whether sins of commission or omission).

Some have taken the second clause to mean that our forgiveness is the real cause of God's forgiveness, i.e., that God's forgiveness must be earned by our own. The problem is often judged more serious in Matthew than Luke, because the latter has the present "we forgive," the former the aorist (not perfect, as many commentators assume) *aphēkamen* ("we have forgiven"; GK *918*). Many follow the suggestion of Jeremias (*Prayers of Jesus*, 92–93), who says that Matthew has awkwardly rendered an Aramaic *perfectum praesens* (a "present perfect"): he renders the clause "as we also herewith forgive our debtors."

The real solution is best expounded by C. F. D. Moule ("'... As we forgive ...': a Note on the Distinction between Deserts and Capacity in the Understanding of Forgiveness," in *Donum Gentilicium* [ed. E. Bammel et al.; Oxford: Clarendon 1978], 68–77), who, in addition to detailing the most important relevant Jewish literature, rightly insists on distinguishing "between, on the one hand, earning or meriting forgiveness, and, on the other hand, adopting an attitude which makes forgiveness possible—the distinction, that is, between deserts and capacity.... Real repentance, as contrasted with a merely self-regarding remorse, is certainly a *sine qua non* of receiving forgiveness—an indispensable condition" (pp. 71–72). "Once our eyes have been opened to see the enormity of our offense against God, the injuries which others have done to us appear by comparison extremely trifling. If, on the other hand, we have an exaggerated view of the offenses of others, it proves that we have minimized our own" (Stott, *Message of the Sermon on the Mount*, 149–50; see comments at 5:5, 7; 18:23–35).

13 The word *peirasmos* ("temptation," GK *4280*) and its cognate verb rarely if ever before the NT mean "temptation" in the sense of "enticement to sin" (whether from inward lust or outward circumstances) but rather "testing" (see comments at 4:1–12). But testing can have various purposes (e.g., refinement, ascertaining the strength of character, enticement to sin) and diverse results (greater purity, self-confidence, growth in faith, sin); as a result, the word can slide over into the entirely negative sense of "temptation." See comments on the cognate verb in 4:1. The word sustains the unambiguous meaning in James 1:13–14, which assures us that "God cannot be tempted by evil, nor does he tempt anyone [i.e., with evil]" (cf. Mt 4:1, 3; 1Co 7:5; 1Th 3:5; Rev 2:10). In this light, *peirasmos* cannot easily mean "temptation" here in v.13, for that would be to pray that God would not do what in fact he cannot do, akin to praying that God would not sin.

But if *peirasmos* here means testing, we face another problem. The NT everywhere insists that believers will face testings or trials of many kinds but that these should be faced with joy (Jas 1:2; cf. 1Co 10:13). If this is so, to pray for grace and endurance in trial is understandable; but to pray not to be brought to testings is strange. For detailed probing of the problem and interaction with the sources, see C. F. D. Moule, "An Unsolved Problem in the Temptation-Clause in the Lord's Prayer," *RTR* 33 (1974): 65–75.

Some have argued that the testing is the eschatological tribulation, the period of messianic woes (e.g., Jeremias, *Prayers of Jesus*, 104–7) characterized by apostasy. The petition becomes a plea to be secured from that final apostasy and is reflected in the NEB's "do not bring us to the test." But not only is *peirasmos* never used for this tribulation unless carefully qualified (and therefore Rev 3:10 is no exception, regardless of its interpretation), but one would at least expect to find the article in the Matthean clause. Carmignac (*Recherches sur le "Notre Père,"* 396, 445) so reconstructs the alleged Hebrew original that he distinguishes "to testing" from "into testing," interpreting the latter to mean actually succumbing. The prayer then asks to be spared, not from testing, but from failing. Unfortunately, his linguistic arguments are not convincing.

Many cite *b. Ber.* 60b as a parallel: "Bring me not into sin, or into iniquity, or into temptation, or into contempt." It is possible that the causative form of the Lord's Prayer is, similarly, not meant to be unmediated but has a permissive nuance: "Let us not be brought into temptation [i.e., by the devil]." This interpretation is greatly strengthened if the word "temptation" can be taken to mean "trial or temptation that results in fall"; this appears to be required in two NT passages (Mk 14:38; Gal 6:1; cf.

J.V. Dahms, "Lead Us Not into Temptation," *JETS* 17 [1974]: 229).

It also may be that we are forcing this sixth petition into too rigid a mold. The NT tells us that this age will be characterized by wars and rumors of wars (see comments at 24:6) but does not find it incongruous to urge us to pray for those in authority so "that we may live peaceful and quiet lives" (1Ti 2:2). While Jesus told his disciples to rejoice when persecuted (Mt 5:10–12), he nevertheless exhorted them to flee from it (10:23) and even to pray that their flight should not be too severe (24:20). Similarly, a prayer requesting to be spared testings may not be incongruous when placed beside exhortations to consider such testings, when they come, as pure joy.

"Deliver us" (*rhyomai*, GK *4861*) could mean either, on the one hand, "spare us from," "preserve us against," or, on the other hand, "deliver us out of," "save us from" (BDAG, 907–8). Both are spiritually relevant, and which way the verb is taken depends largely on how the preceding clause is understood. The words *tou ponērou* ("the evil one," GK *4505*) could be either neuter ("evil"; cf. Lk 6:45; Ro 12:9; 1Th 5:22) or masculine ("the evil one," referring to Satan; Mt 13:19, 38; Eph 6:16; 1 Jn 2:13–14; 3:12; 5:19). In some cases, the Greek does not distinguish the gender (see comments at 5:37). However, a reference to Satan is far more likely here for two reasons: (1) "deliver us" can take either the preposition *ek* ("from") or *apo* ("from"), the former always introducing things from which to be delivered, the latter being used predominantly of persons (cf. J. B. Bauer, "Liberanos a malo," *Verbum Domini* 34 [1965]: 12–15; Zerwick, *Biblical Greek*, para. 89); and (2) Matthew's first mention of temptation (4:1–11) is unambiguously connected with the devil. Thus the Lord's model prayer ends with a petition that, while implicitly recognizing our own helplessness before the devil, whom Jesus alone could vanquish (4:1–11), delights to trust the heavenly Father for deliverance from the devil's strength and wiles.

The doxology—"for yours is the kingdom and the power and the glory forever. Amen"—is found in various forms in many MSS. The diversity of what parts are attested is itself suspicious (for full discussion, see Metzger, *Textual Commentary*, 16–17; cf. Hendriksen, 337–38). The MS evidence is overwhelmingly in favor of omission—a point conceded by Davies (*Setting*, 451–53), whose liturgical arguments for inclusion are not convincing.

The doxology itself is theologically profound and contextually suitable and was no doubt judged especially suitable by those who saw in the last three petitions a veiled allusion to the Trinity: the Father's creation and providence provides our bread, the Son's atonement secures our forgiveness, and the Spirit's indwelling power assures our safety and triumph. But "surely it is more important to know what the Bible really contains and really means than to cling to something not really in the Bible, merely because it gratifies our taste, or even because it has for us some precious associations" (Broadus).

NOTES

12 The KJV has the present "we forgive" in both Matthew and Luke and is widely supported. The aorist is attested by א* B Z 1 22 124^{mg} 1365 1582, five MSS of the Latin Vulgate, and several MSS of the Syriac and Coptic versions. This represents a fair spread of text type. But the convincing arguments are the likelihood of assimilation to Luke and the converse implausibility of a copyist changing the present to an aorist.

(d) Forgiveness and prayer (6:14–15)

[14]"For if you forgive men when they sin against you, your heavenly Father will also forgive you. [15]But if you do not forgive men their sins, your Father will not forgive your sins."

COMMENTARY

14–15 These verses reinforce the thought of the fifth petition (see comments at v.12). The repetition serves to stress the deep importance for the community of disciples to be a forgiving community if its prayers are to be effective (cf. Ps 66:18). The thought is repeated elsewhere (18:23–35; Mk 11:25). (On the possible literary relation with Mk 11:25, see Lane, *Mark*, 410–11.)

(3) Fasting (6:16–18)

[16]"When you fast, do not look somber as the hypocrites do, for they disfigure their faces to show men they are fasting. I tell you the truth, they have received their reward in full. [17]But when you fast, put oil on your head and wash your face, [18]so that it will not be obvious to men that you are fasting, but only to your Father, who is unseen; and your Father, who sees what is done in secret, will reward you."

COMMENTARY

16 Under Mosaic legislation, fasting was commanded only on the Day of Atonement (Lev 16:29–31; 23:27–32; Nu 29:7); during the exile regular fasts of remembrance were instituted (Zec 7:3–5; 8:19). In addition to these national fasts, both OT and NT describe personal or group fasts with a variety of purposes, especially to indicate and foster self-humiliation before God, often in connection with the confession of sins (e.g., Ne 9:1–2; Ps 35:13; Isa 58:3, 5; Da 9:2–20; 10:2–3; Jnh 3:5; Ac 9:9) or to lay some special petition before the Lord, sometimes out of anguish, danger, or desperation (Ex 24:18; Jdg 20:26; 2Sa 1:12; 2Ch 20:3; Ezr 8:21–23; Est 4:16; Mt 4:1–2; Ac 13:1–3; 14:23). It may belong to the realm of normal Christian self-discipline (1Co 9:24–27; cf. Php 3:19; 1Pe 4:3), but already in the OT, it is bitterly excoriated when it is purely formal and largely hypocritical (Isa 58:3–7; Jer 14:12; Zec 7:5–6)—when, for instance, men fasted but did not share their food with the hungry (Isa 58:1–7).

In Jesus' day, the Pharisees fasted twice a week (Lk 18:12; cf. Str-B, 2:242ff.), probably Monday and Thursday (*m. Taʿan.* 1:4–7). Some devout people (e.g., Anna) fasted often (Lk 2:37). But such voluntary fasts provided marvelous opportunities for religious showmanship to gain a reputation for piety. One could adopt an air that was "somber" (or "downcast," Lk 24:17, the only other place in the NT where the word *skythrōpos* is used) and disfigure oneself, perhaps by not washing and shaving, by sprinkling ashes on one's head to signify deep contrition or self-abnegation, or by omitting normal use of oil to signify deep distress (cf. 2Sa 14:2; Da 10:3). The point is not that there was no genuine contrition but that these hypocrites were purposely drawing attention to themselves. They wanted the plaudits of men and got them. And that's all they got.

17–18 Yet Jesus, far from banning fasting, assumes his disciples will fast, even as he assumes they will give alms and pray (vv.3, 6). His disciples may not fast at the moment, for the messianic bridegroom is with them and it is the time for joy (9:14–17). But the time will come when they will fast (9:15). (Observe in passing that here Jesus assumes the continued existence of his disciples after his departure.) What he condemns is ostentation in fasting. Moreover, he forbids any sign at all that a fast has been undertaken, because the human heart is so mixed in its motives that the desire to seek God will be diluted by the desire for human praise, thus vitiating the fast.

Washing and anointing with oil (v.17) were merely normal steps in hygiene. Oil does not here symbolize extravagant joy but normal body care (cf. Ru 3:3; 2Sa 12:20; Pss 23:5; 104:15; 133:2; Ecc 9:8; Lk 7:46; cf. *NIDNTT*, 1:120). The point of v.18 is not to draw attention to oneself, whether by somber mien or extravagant joy. Jesus desires reticence, not deception. And the Father, who sees in secret, will provide the reward (see comments at v.4).

REFLECTIONS

The three principal acts of Jewish piety (vv.1–18) are only examples of many practices susceptible of religious hypocrisy. Early in the second century, the Christian document *Didache* (8:1), while polemicizing against the Monday and Thursday "fasts of the hypocrites," enjoins Christians to fast on Wednesday and Friday. Christian copyists added "fasting" glosses at several points in the NT (17:21; Mk 9:29; Ac 10:30; 1Co 7:5). Hypocrisy is not the sole preserve of Pharisees. The solution is not to abolish fasting (cf. Alexander's remark that mortification of the flesh "can be better attained by habitual temperance than by occasional abstinence") but to set it within a biblical framework (see references at v.16) and sincerely to covet God's blessing. For if the form of vv.1–18 is negative, the point is positive—namely, to seek first God's kingdom and righteousness (cf. v.33).

5. Kingdom perspectives (6:19–34)

OVERVIEW

Many argue that these verses are made up of four blocks of material that originally had independent settings: (1) Mt 6:19–21 = Lk 12:33–34; (2) Mt 6:22–23 = Lk 11:34–36; (3) Mt 6:24 = Lk 16:13; (4) Mt 6:25–34 = Lk 12:22–31. But the first pair are very different and should be treated as separate traditions of separate sayings; the third pair are very close (only a one-word difference), and both Matthew and Luke assign it to the same sermon; the second and fourth pairs are fairly close, but exegesis of Luke suggests his settings are topical. The context Matthew establishes should be accepted at face value. Certainly the flow is coherent. Having excoriated religious piety that is little more than ostentation, Jesus warns against the opposite sins of greed, materialism, and worry that stem from misplaced and worldly priorities. Instead, he demands unswerving loyalty to kingdom values (vv.19–24) and uncompromised trust (vv.25–34).

a. Metaphors for unswerving loyalty to kingdom values (6:19–24)

(1) Treasure (6:19–21)

OVERVIEW

Black (*Aramaic Approach*, 178–79) shows the poetical character of vv.19–21, v.19 warning against the wrong way, v.20 prescribing the right way, and v.21 rounding it off with a memorable aphorism. Hill comments, "Such rhythm and balance suggest that these verses contain original dominical teaching." The assessment is fair. One wonders, however, why similar structure and rhythm should elsewhere be judged liturgical, catechetical, and inauthentic (see comments at 5:1–12).

19"Do not store up for yourselves treasures on earth, where moth and rust destroy, and
where thieves break in and steal. 20But store up for yourselves treasures in heaven, where
moth and rust do not destroy, and where thieves do not break in and steal. 21For where
your treasure is, there your heart will be also."

COMMENTARY

19 The present tense prohibition *mē thēsaurizete* (GK *2564*) conceives of the "storing up" as a process, a practice that must be stopped (similarly at v.25).

The love of wealth is a great evil (1Ti 6:10), calling forth frequent warnings. For heirs of the kingdom to hoard riches in the last days (Jas 5:2–3) is particularly shortsighted. Yet, as with many of Jesus' prohibitions in this sermon, it would be foolhardy so to absolutize this one that wealth itself becomes an evil (see Lk 14:12; Jn 4:21; 1Pe 3:3–4 for other statements that cannot properly be absolutized). Elsewhere the Scriptures require a man to provide for his relatives (1Ti 5:8), commend work and provision for the future (Pr 6:6–8), and encourage us to enjoy the good things the Creator has given us (1Ti 4:3–4; 6:17). Jesus is concerned about selfishness in misplaced values. His disciples must not lay up treasure *for themselves*; they must honestly ask where their heart is (vv.20–21).

This verse does not prohibit "being provident (making sensible provision for the future) but being covetous (like misers who hoard and materialists who always want more)" (Stott, *Message of the Sermon on the Mount*, 155). But it is folly to put oneself in the former category while acting and thinking in the latter (cf. France, "God and Mammon").

The "treasures on earth" might be clothing that could be attacked by moths. Fashions changed little, and garments could be passed on. They could also deteriorate. "Rust" (*brōsis*, GK *1111*) refers not only to the corrosion of metals but to the destruction effected by rats, mildew, and the like. Older commentaries often picture a farm being devoured by mice and other vermin. Less corruptible treasures could be stolen. Thieves could "break in [*diorys-sousin*, "dig through," referring to the mud brick walls of most first-century Palestinian homes] and steal."

20–21 By contrast, the treasures in heaven are forever exempt from decay and theft (cf. Lk 12:33). The words "treasures in heaven" go back to Jewish literature (*m. Pe'ah* 1:1; *T. Levi* 13:5; *Pss. Sol.* 9:9). Here it refers to whatever is of good and eternal significance that comes out of what is done on earth. Doing righteous deeds, suffering for Christ's sake, forgiving one another—all these have the promise of "reward" (see comments at 5:12; cf. 5:30, 46; 6:6, 15; 2Co 4:17). Other deeds of kindness also store up treasure in heaven (10:42; 25:40), including willingness to share (1Ti 6:13–19).

In the best MSS, the final aphorism (v.21) reverts to second person singular (cf. vv.2, 6, 17; see comments at 5:23). The point is that the things most highly treasured occupy the "heart," the center of the personality, embracing mind, emotions, and will (cf. *NIDNTT*, 2:180–84), and thus the most cherished treasure subtly but infallibly controls the whole person's direction and values. "If honor is rated the highest good, then ambition must take complete charge of a man; if money, then forthwith greed takes over the kingdom; if pleasure, then men will certainly degenerate into sheer self-indulgence" (Calvin). Conversely, those who set their minds on things above (Col 3:1–2), determining to live under kingdom norms, discover at last that their deeds follow them (Rev 14:13).

(2) Light (6:22–23)

[22]"The eye is the lamp of the body. If your eyes are good, your whole body will be full of light. [23]But if your eyes are bad, your whole body will be full of darkness. If then the light within you is darkness, how great is that darkness!"

COMMENTARY

22–23 "The eye is the lamp of the body" in the sense that through the eye the body finds its way. The eye lets in light, and so the whole body is illuminated. But bad eyes let in no light, and the body is in darkness (v.23). The "light within you" seems ironic. Those with bad eyes, who walk in darkness, think they have light, but this light is in reality darkness. The darkness is all the more terrible for failure to recognize it for what it is (cf. Jn 9:41).

This fairly straightforward description has metaphorical implications. The "eye" can be equivalent to the "heart." The heart set on God so as to hold to his commands (Ps 119:10) is equivalent to the eye fastened on God's law (Ps 119:18, 148; cf. 119:36–37). Similarly Jesus moves from "heart" (v.21) to "eye" (vv.22–23). Moreover, the text moves between physical description and metaphor by the words chosen for "good" and "bad." *Haplous* ("good," v.22, GK *606*) and its cognates can mean either "single" (vs. *diplous*, "double," 1Ti 5:17, GK *1487*) in the sense of "single, undivided loyalty" (cf. 1Ch 29:17) or in cognate forms "generous," "liberal" (cf. Ro 12:8; Jas 1:5). Likewise, *ponēros* ("bad," v.23, GK *4505*) can mean "evil" (e.g., Ro 12:9) or in the Jewish idiomatic expression "the evil eye" can refer to miserliness and selfishness (cf. Pr 28:22; see Hagner). Jesus is therefore saying either (1) that the man who "divides his interest and tries to focus on both God and possessions ... has no clear vision, and will live without clear orientation or direction" (Filson)—an interpretation nicely compatible with v.24; or (2) that the man who is stingy and selfish cannot really see where he is going; he is morally and spiritually blind—an interpretation compatible with vv.19–21. Either way, the early crossover to metaphor may account for the difficult language of v.22.

At the physical level, the "whole body" is just that, a body, of which the eye is the part that provides "light" (cf. R. Gundry, *Soma* [Cambridge: Cambridge Univ. Press, 1976], 24–25). At the metaphorical level, it represents the entire person who is plunged into moral darkness. The "light within you" is therefore the vision that the eye with divided loyalties provides, or the attitude characterized by selfishness; in both cases it is darkness indeed. This approach, which depends on the OT and Jewish usage, is much to be preferred to the one that goes to Hellenistic literature and interprets "the light within you" in a Neoplatonic sense (e.g., H. D. Betz, "Matthew 6.22–23 and Ancient Greek Theories of Vision," in *Text and Interpretation* [ed. Best and Wilson], 43–56).

(3) Slavery (6:24)

24"No one can serve two masters. Either he will hate the one and love the other, or he
will be devoted to the one and despise the other. You cannot serve both God and Money."

COMMENTARY

24 John Stott (*Message of the Sermon on the Mount*, 158) comments, "Jesus now explains that behind the choice between two treasures (where we lay them up) and two visions (where we fix our eyes) there lies the still more basic choice between two masters (whom we are going to serve)." "Money" renders Greek *mamōna* ("mammon," GK *3440*), itself a transliteration of Aramaic *māmônā* (in the emphatic state; "wealth," "property"). The root in both Aramaic and Hebrew (*mn*) indicates that in which one has confidence, and the connection with money and wealth, well attested in Jewish literature (e.g., *m. Peʾah* 1:1; *b. Ber.* 61b; *m. ʾAbot* 2:7; and not always in a negative sense), is painfully obvious. Here it is personified. Both God and Money are portrayed, not as employers, but as slave owners. A man may work for two employers; but since "single ownership and full-time service are of the essence of slavery" (Tasker), he cannot serve two slave owners. Either God is served with a single-eyed devotion, or he is not served at all. Attempts at divided loyalty betray not partial commitment to discipleship but deep-seated commitment to idolatry.

b. Uncompromised trust (6:25–34)

(1) The principle (6:25)

[25]"Therefore I tell you, do not worry about your life, what you will eat or drink; or about your body, what you will wear. Is not life more important than food, and the body more important than clothes?"

COMMENTARY

25 "Therefore," in the light of the alternatives set out (vv.19–24) and assuming his disciples will make the right choices, Jesus goes on to prohibit worry. The KJV's "Take no thought" is deceptive in modern English, for Jesus himself demands that we think even about birds and flowers (vv.26–30). "Do not worry" can be falsely absolutized by neglecting the limitations the context imposes and the curses on carelessness, apathy, indifference, laziness, and self-indulgence expressed elsewhere (cf. Carson, *Sermon on the Mount*, 82–86; Stott, *Message of the Sermon on the Mount*, 165–68). The point is not to worry about the physical necessities, let alone the luxuries implied in the preceding verses, because such fretting suggests that our entire existence focuses on and is limited to such things. The argument is *a fortiori* ("how much more") and not (contra Hill) *a minori ad maius* ("from the lesser to the greater") but the reverse: if God has given us life and a body, both admittedly more important than food and clothing, will he not also give us the latter? Therefore fretting about such things betrays the loss of faith and the perversion of more valuable commitments (cf. Lk 10:41–42; Heb 13:5–6).

NOTES

25 Because the subjunctives τί φάγητε ἢ τί πίητε (*ti phagēte ē ti piēte*, "what you will eat or drink") are in indirect discourse, they should be taken as deliberative subjunctives retained with the shift in discourse (cf. the subjunctives in v.31).

(2) The examples (6:26–30)

(a) Life and food (6:26–27)

[26]"Look at the birds of the air; they do not sow or reap or store away in barns, and yet your heavenly Father feeds them. Are you not much more valuable than they? [27]Who of you by worrying can add a single hour to his life?"

COMMENTARY

26 To worry about food and drink is to have learned nothing from the natural creation. If the created order testifies to God's "eternal power and divine nature" (Ro 1:20), it testifies equally to his providence. The point is not that disciples need not work—birds do not simply wait for God to drop food into their beaks—but that they need not fret. Disciples may further strengthen their faith when they remember that God is in a special sense their Father (not the birds' Father), and that they are worth far more than birds ("you" is emphatic). Here the argument is from the lesser to the greater.

This argument presupposes a biblical cosmology without which faith makes no sense. God is so sovereign over the universe that even the feeding of a wren falls within his concern. Because he normally does things in regular ways, there are "scientific laws" to be discovered. But the believer with eyes to see simultaneously discovers something about God and his activity (cf. Carson, *Sermon on the Mount*, 87–90).

27 The word *hēlikia* ("life," GK *2461*) can also be rendered "stature" (cf. Lk 19:3) or "age" (Heb 11:11); *pēchys* (NIV, "hour," GK *4388*) also means "cubit" (about eighteen inches; see NIV text note). No combination fits easily. No one would be tempted to think worrying could add eighteen inches to his stature (KJV), and a linear measure (eighteen inches) does not fit easily with "life." This disparity accounts for the diversity of translations. Most likely, the linear measure is being used in a metaphorical sense (cf. RSV, "add one cubit to his span of life"), akin to "passing a milepost" at one's birthday (cf. Betz, *Sermon on the Mount*, 475; Davies and Allison). Worry is more likely to shorten life than prolong it, and ultimately such matters are in God's hands (cf. Lk 12:13–21). To trust him is enough.

NOTES

26 Τὰ πετεινὰ τοῦ οὐρανοῦ (*ta pateina tou ouranou*, lit., "the birds of the heaven") is rightly rendered "birds of the air" (NIV) because "heaven" can refer to the atmosphere around us (cf. Ge 1:26; Mt 8:20; 13:32).

(b) Body and clothes (6:28–30)

28"And why do you worry about clothes? See how the lilies of the field grow. They do not labor or spin. 29Yet I tell you that not even Solomon in all his splendor was dressed like one of these. 30If that is how God clothes the grass of the field, which is here today and tomorrow is thrown into the fire, will he not much more clothe you, O you of little faith?"

COMMENTARY

28–30 "Lilies of the field" may be any of the wild flowers so abundant in Galilee, and these "flowers of the field" correspond to "birds of the air." The point is a little different from the first illustration, where birds work but do not worry. The flowers neither toil nor spin (see Notes). The point is not that Jesus' disciples may opt for laziness but that God's providence and care are so rich that he clothes the grass with wild flowers that are neither productive nor enduring (v.30). Even Solomon, the richest and most extravagant of Israel's monarchs, "in all his splendor" (v.29) was not arrayed like one of these fields. Small wonder that Jesus gently chastises his disciples as *oligopistoi* ("people of little faith," GK *3899*; cf. 8:26; 14:31; 16:8; and the abstract noun at 17:20). The root of anxiety is unbelief.

NOTES

28 On the nest of variants, see Metzger (*Textual Commentary*, 18) and the literature he cites, to which may be added K. Brunner, "Textkritisches zu Mt 6.28: *ou xainousin* statt *auxanousin* vorgeschlagen," *ZKT* 100 (1978): 251–56.

30 The κλίβανος (*klibanos*, "oven," GK *3106*) was a pottery oven often fired by burning grass inside, the ashes falling through a hole and the flat cakes distributed both inside and on top. The term was used metaphorically to refer to the day of judgment as early as Hosea 7:4 LXX.

(3) Distinctive living (6:31–32)

31"So do not worry, saying, 'What shall we eat?' or 'What shall we drink?' or 'What shall we wear?' 32For the pagans run after all these things, and your heavenly Father knows that you need them."

COMMENTARY

31–32 In the light of God's bountiful care ("So"), the questions posed in v.31 (cf. v.25) are unanswerable and the underlying attitudes are thoughtless and an affront to God, who knows the needs of his people (cf. v.8). Worse, they are essentially pagan (v.32), for pagans "run after" (*epizētousin*, a strengthened form of "seek") these things, not God's kingdom and righteousness (v.33). Jesus' disciples must live lives qualitatively different from those of people who have no trust in God's fatherly care and no fundamental goals beyond material things.

(4) The heart of the matter (6:33)

33"But seek first his kingdom and his righteousness, and all these things will be given to you as well."

COMMENTARY

33 In view of vv.31–32, this verse makes it clear that Jesus' disciples are not simply to *refrain* from the pursuit of temporal things as their primary goal in order to differentiate themselves from pagans; instead, they are to *replace* such pursuits with goals of far greater significance. To seek first the kingdom ("of God" in some MSS) is to desire above all to enter into, submit to, and participate in spreading the news of the saving reign of God, the messianic kingdom already inaugurated by Jesus, and to live so as to store up treasures in heaven in the prospect of the kingdom's consummation. It is to pursue the things already prayed for in the first three petitions of the Lord's Prayer (vv.9–10).

To seek God's righteousness is not, in this context, to seek justification (contra Filson, McNeile). "Righteousness" must be interpreted as in 5:6, 10, 20; 6:1. It is to pursue righteousness of life in full submission to the will of God, as prescribed by Jesus throughout this discourse (cf. Przybylski, *Righteousness in Matthew*, 89–91). Such righteousness will lead to persecution by some (5:10), but others will themselves become disciples and praise the Father in heaven (5:16). Such goals alone are worthy of one's wholehearted allegiance. For any other concern to dominate one's mind is to stoop to pagan fretting. "In the end, just as there are only two kinds of piety, the self-centered and the God-centered, so there are only two kinds of ambition: one can be ambitious either for oneself or for God. There is no third alternative" (Stott, *Message of the Sermon on the Mount*, 172). Within such a framework of commitment, Jesus' disciples are assured that all the necessary things will be given to them by their heavenly Father (see comments at 5:45; 6:9), who demonstrates his faithfulness by his care even for the birds and his concern even for the grass.

(5) Abolishing worry (6:34)

34"Therefore do not worry about tomorrow, for tomorrow will worry about itself. Each day has enough trouble of its own."

COMMENTARY

34 In view of God's solemn promise to meet the needs of those committed to his kingdom and righteousness (v.33), "therefore" do not worry about tomorrow. Today has enough *kakia* (NIV, "trouble," GK *2798*; what is evil from man's point of view, and once applied to crop damage caused by hail [MM]; frequently translates Heb. *rāʿâ* ["evil," "misfortune," "trouble," GK 8288] in LXX: Ecc 7:14; 12:1; Am 3:6) of its own.

Worry over tomorrow's misfortunes is nonsensical, because today has enough to occupy our attention and because tomorrow's feared misfortunes may never happen (cf. *b. Sanh.* 100b; *b. Ber.* 9a). It is almost as if Jesus, aware that his disciples are still unsettled and immature, ends his argument by setting the highest ideals and motives aside for a moment and, in a whimsical sally, appeals to common sense. At the same time, he is implicitly teaching that, even for his disciples, today's grace is sufficient only for today and should not be wasted on tomorrow. If tomorrow does bring new trouble, there will be new grace to meet it.

6. Balance and perfection (7:1–12)

OVERVIEW

Many argue that these verses (1) have no connection with what precedes, (2) have little internal cohesion, and (3) probably find their original context in Luke 6:37–38, 41–42. Only the third assertion is believable.

1. The lack of Greek connectives at vv.1, 7 is not inherently problematic. Similar omissions (e.g., 6:19, 24) do not disturb the flow of thought so much as indicate a new "paragraph" or set off an aphorism. The connection with what precedes is internal. The demand for the superior righteousness of the kingdom, in fulfillment of the OT (5:17–20), has called forth warnings against hypocrisy (6:1–18) and the formulation of kingdom perspectives (6:19–34). But there are other dangers. Demands for perfection can breed judgmentalism (7:1–5), while demands for love can cause chronic shortage of discernment (v.6).

2. Thus the internal connection is in part established by dealing with opposing evils. But such great demands on Jesus' followers must force them to recognize their personal inadequacy and so drive them to prayer (vv.7–11). The Golden Rule (v.12) summarizes the body of the sermon (5:17–7:12).

3. The relationship between 7:1–12 and Luke 6:37–38, 41–42 (part of Luke's "sermon") is difficult to assess. After his beatitudes and woes (Lk 6:20–26), Luke adds material (6:27–30) akin to Matthew 5:38–48. He then adds the Golden Rule (Lk 6:31), some material akin to Matthew 5, and then the parallel to Matthew 7:1–5. Thus he omits all of Matthew 6, while Matthew 7:1–5 omits part of what Luke keeps in Luke 6:37–42. One or both of the evangelists have rearranged the order of the material. Both make such good sense in their own context that it seems impossible to decide in favor of either. Though a saying as aphoristic as the Golden Rule may well have been repeated during the course of several days' teaching, there is no sure way of demonstrating this was or was not the case.

a. The danger of being judgmental (7:1–5)

(1) The principle (7:1)

1"Do not judge, or you too will be judged."

COMMENTARY

1 The verb *krinō* ("judge," GK *3212*) has a wide semantic range: "judge" (judicially), "condemn," "discern." It cannot here refer to the law courts, any more than 5:33–37 forbids judicial oaths. Still less does this verse forbid all judging of any kind, for the moral distinctions drawn in the Sermon on the Mount require that decisive judgments be made. Jesus himself goes on to speak of some people as dogs and pigs (v.6) and to warn against false prophets (vv.15–20). Elsewhere he demands that people "make a right judgment" (Jn 7:24; cf. 1Co 5:5; Gal 1:8–9; Php 3:2; 1 Jn 4:1). All this presupposes that some kinds of judging are not only legitimate but mandated.

Jesus' demand here is for his disciples not to be judgmental and censorious. The verb *krinō* has the same force in Romans 14:10–13 (cf. Jas 4:11–12). The rigor of the disciples' commitment to God's kingdom and the righteousness demanded of them do not authorize them to adopt a judgmental attitude. Those who "judge" like this will in turn be "judged," not by men (which would be of little consequence) but by God (which fits the solemn tone of the discourse). The disciple who takes it on himself to be the judge of what another does usurps the place of God (Ro 14:10) and therefore becomes answerable to him. The *hina mē* ("in order that ... not"; NIV, "or") should therefore be given full telic force: "Do not assume the place of God by deciding you have the right to stand in judgment over all—do not do it, I say, in order to avoid being called to account by the God whose place you usurp" (cf. *b. Šabb.* 127b; *m. Soṭah* 1:7; *b. B. Meṣ.* 59b).

(2) The theological justification (7:2)

2"For in the same way you judge others, you will be judged, and with the measure you use, it will be measured to you."

COMMENTARY

2 The strong play on words in Greek suggests that this is a proverbial saying. Formally it is very close to *m. Soṭah* 1:7, but the use made of it is in each case rather distinctive (cf. Dalman, *Jesus-Jeshua*, 223–24). Indeed, precisely because it is a proverb, Jesus himself elsewhere turns it to another use (cf. Mk 4:24). The point is akin to that already established (Mt 5:7; 6:12, 14–15): the judgmental person by not being forgiving and loving testifies to his own arrogance and impenitence, by which he shuts himself out from God's forgiveness (cf. Manson, *Sayings of Jesus*, 56).

According to some rabbis, God has two "measures"—mercy and justice (*Lev. Rab.* 29.3). Possibly Jesus used this language, adapting it to his own ends. He who poses as a judge cannot plead ignorance of the law (Ro 2:1; cf. Jas 3:1); he who insists on unalloyed justice for others is scarcely open to mercy himself (Jas 2:13; 4:12). The problem returns in 18:23–35; here "the command to *judge not* is not a requirement to be blind but rather a plea to be generous. Jesus does not tell us to cease to be men (by suspending our critical powers which help to distinguish us from animals) but to renounce the presumptuous ambition to be God (by setting ourselves up as judges)" (Stott, *Message of the Sermon on the Mount*, 177, emphasis his).

(3) An example (7:3–5)

[3]"Why do you look at the speck of sawdust in your brother's eye and pay no attention to the plank in your own eye? [4]How can you say to your brother, 'Let me take the speck out of your eye,' when all the time there is a plank in your own eye? [5]You hypocrite, first take the plank out of your own eye, and then you will see clearly to remove the speck from your brother's eye."

COMMENTARY

3–5 The *karphos* ("speck of sawdust," GK *2847*) could be any bit of foreign matter. The *dokos* ("plank" or "log," GK *1512*) is obviously colorful hyperbole. Jesus does not say it is wrong to help your brother (for "brother," see comments at 5:22; Jesus is apparently referring to the community of his disciples) remove the speck of dust in his eye, but it is wrong for a person with a "plank" in his eye to offer help. That is sheer hypocrisy of the second sort (see comments at 6:2). Second Samuel 12:1–12 is a dramatic OT example (cf. Lk 18:9). It will not do to say that Jesus' words in this pericope are "meant to exclude all condemnation of others" (Hill), for to do that requires not taking v.5 seriously and excluding what v.6 says. In the brotherhood of Jesus' disciples, censorious critics are unhelpful. But when a brother in a meek and self-judging spirit (cf. 1Co 11:31; Gal 6:1) removes the log from his own eye, he still has the responsibility of helping his brother remove his speck (cf. 18:15–20).

NOTES

4 The future πῶς ἐρεῖς (*pōs ereis*, lit., "How will you say") is an instance in which, under Semitic influence, this tense is sometimes used modally to describe what may be (cf. Zerwick, *Biblical Greek*, para. 279). See Luke 6:42: πῶς δύνασαι λέγειν (*pōs dynasai legein*, "How can you say").

b. The danger of being undiscerning (7:6)

[6]"Do not give dogs what is sacred; do not throw your pearls to pigs. If you do, they may trample them under their feet, and then turn and tear you to pieces."

COMMENTARY

6 Though used later to exclude unbaptized persons from the Eucharist (*Did.* 9.5), that is not the purpose of this saying. Nor is it connected with the previous verses by dealing now with persons who, though properly confronted about their "specks," refuse to deal with them, as in 18:12–20 (so Schlatter). Rather, it warns against the converse danger. Disciples exhorted to love their enemies (5:43–47) and not to judge (7:1) might fail to consider the subtleties of the argument and become undiscerning simpletons. This verse guards against such a possibility.

The "pigs" are not only unclean animals but wild and vicious, capable of savage action against a person. "Dogs" must not be thought of as household pets. In the Scriptures they are normally wild, associated with what is unclean, despised (e.g., 1Sa 17:43; 24:14; 1Ki 14:11; 21:19; 2Ki 8:13; Job 30:1; Pr 26:11; Ecc 9:4; Isa 66:3; Mt 15:27; Php 3:2; Rev 22:15). The two animals serve together as a picture of what is vicious, unclean, and abominable (cf. 2Pe 2:22). The four lines of v.6 are an ABBA chiasmus (cf. Turner, *Syntax*, 346–47). The pigs trample the pearls under foot (perhaps out of animal disappointment that they are not morsels of food), and the dogs are so disgusted with "what is sacred" that they turn on the giver.

The problem lies in *to hagion* ("what is sacred," GK *41*). How is this parallel to "pearls," and what reality is envisaged to make the saying "work"?

1. Some suggest *to hagion* refers to "holy food" offered in connection with the temple services (cf. Ex 22:31; Lev 22:14; Jer 11:15; Hag 2:12). But this is a strange way to refer to it, and it is not obvious why the dogs would spurn it.

2. Another suggestion is that *to hagion* is a mistranslation of the Aramaic *qᵉdaša* (Heb. *nezem*, "ring," GK 5690), referring to Proverbs 11:22 (cf. Black, *Aramaic Approach*, 200ff.). But appeals to mistranslation should not be the first line of approach; and here the parallelism of pearls and pigs, pearls obviously being mistaken for food, is destroyed.

3. P. G. Maxwell-Stuart ("'Do not give what is holy to the dogs' [Matthew 7:6]," *ExpTim* 90 [1978–79]: 341) offers a textual emendation.

4. However, it seems wiser to recognize that, as in 6:22–23, the interpretation of the metaphor is already hinted at in the metaphor itself. "What is sacred" in Matthew is the gospel of the kingdom. So the aphorism forbids proclaiming the gospel to certain persons designated as dogs and pigs. Instead of trampling the gospel under foot, everything must be "sold" in pursuit of it (13:45–46).

Verse 6 is not a directive against evangelizing the Gentiles, especially in a book full of various supports for this, not least 28:18–20 (10:5, properly understood, is no exception). "Dogs" and "pigs" cannot refer to all Gentiles but, as Calvin rightly perceived, only to persons of any race who have given clear evidences of rejecting the gospel with vicious scorn and hardened contempt. The disciples are later given a similar lesson (10:14; 15:14), and the postresurrection Christians learned it well (cf. Ac 13:44–51; 18:5–6; 28:17–28; Tit 3:10–11). So when taken together vv.1–5 and v.6 become something of a gospel analogue to the proverb "Do not rebuke a mocker or he will hate you; rebuke a wise man and he will love you" (Pr 9:8). "If genuine introspection does not occur, a disciple may blunder on the side of judgmental hypocrisy or naive gullibility" (Turner).

c. Source and means of power (7:7–11)

7"Ask and it will be given to you; seek and you will find; knock and the door will be opened to you. 8For everyone who asks receives; he who seeks finds; and to him who knocks, the door will be opened.

[9]"Which of you, if his son asks for bread, will give him a stone? [10]Or if he asks for a fish, will give him a snake? [11]If you, then, though you are evil, know how to give good gifts to your children, how much more will your Father in heaven give good gifts to those who ask him!"

COMMENTARY

7–8 Zahn tries to establish a connection between these verses and the preceding ones by saying that Jesus now teaches that it is best to ask God to remove the speck in the other person's eye. Stott (*Message of the Sermon on the Mount*, 174–75) understands vv.1–11 in terms of relationships: to believers (vv.1–5), to "pigs" and "dogs" (v.6), and to God (vv.7–11). Bonnard best exemplifies those who say there is no connection at all between vv.7–11 and the preceding verses. Yet there are, in fact, deep thematic connections. Schlatter perceives one of them when he remarks that Jesus, having told his disciples the difficulties, now exhorts them to prayer. Moreover, one of the most pervasive features of Jesus' teaching on prayer is the assurance it will be heard. But such praying is not for selfish ends but always for the glory of God according to kingdom concerns. So here: the Sermon on the Mount lays down the righteousness, sincerity, humility, purity, and love expected of Jesus' followers, and now it assures them such gifts are theirs if sought through prayer.

The sermon has begun with acknowledgment of personal bankruptcy (5:3) and has already provided a model prayer (6:9–13). Now (v.7) in three imperatives (ask, seek, knock) symmetrically repeated (v.8) and in the present tense to stress the persistence and sincerity required (cf. Jer 29:13), Jesus assures his followers that, far from demanding the impossible, he is providing the means for the otherwise impossible. "One may be a truly industrious man, and yet poor in temporal things; but one cannot be a truly praying man, and yet poor in spiritual things" (Broadus). Far too often, Christians do not have the marks of richly textured discipleship because they do not ask, or they ask with selfish motives (Jas 4:2–3). But the best gifts, those advocated by the Sermon on the Mount, are available to "everyone" (v.8) who persistently asks, seeks, and knocks.

Jesus' disciples will pray ("ask") with earnest sincerity ("seek") and active, diligent pursuit of God's way ("knock"). Like a human father, the heavenly Father uses these means to teach his children courtesy, persistence, and diligence. If the child prevails with a thoughtful father, it is because the father has molded the child to his way. If Jacob prevails with God, it is Jacob who is wounded (Ge 32:22–32).

9–11 Another *a fortiori* argument (see comments at 6:25) is introduced. In Greek both v.9 and v.10 begin with *ē* ("or"), probably meaning "or to put the matter another way, which of you, etc." No parent would deceive a child asking for bread or fish by giving him a similar-looking but inedible stone or a dangerous snake. The point at issue is not merely the parents' willingness to give but their willingness to give good gifts—even though they themselves are evil. Jesus presupposes the sinfulness (v.11) of human nature (himself exempted; "you," he says, not "we") but implicitly acknowledges this does not mean all human beings are as bad as they could be or utterly evil in all they do. People are evil; they are self-centered, not God-centered. This taints all they do. Nevertheless, they can give good gifts to their children. How much more, then, will the heavenly Father, who is pure goodness without alloy, give good gifts to those who ask?

Four observations will tie up some loose ends.

1. Lachs ("Textual Observations," 109–10) insists that the "concept that man is evil from birth, born in sin, and similar pronouncements, is a later theological development" and therefore proposes to emend the text of an alleged Semitic original. While it is true that rabbinic literature does not normally portray man as inherently evil, it is false to say that the idea arose only after Jesus, presumably with Paul (cf. Pss 14:1–3; 51; 53:1–3; Ecc 7:20). Jesus regularly assumes the sinfulness of humanity (cf. *TDNT*, 6:554–55). Therefore, the rabbinic parallels to vv.7–11 are of limited value. They stress the analogy of the caring parent, but not on the supposition that the human parent is evil.

2. The fatherhood-of-God language is reserved for God's relationship with Jesus' disciples (see comments at 5:45). The blessings promised as a result of these prayers are not the blessings of common grace (cf. 5:45) but of the kingdom. And though we must ask for them, it is not because God must be informed (6:8) but because this is the Father's way of training his family.

3. What is fundamentally at stake is a person's picture of God. God must not be thought of as a reluctant stranger who can be cajoled or bullied into bestowing his gifts (6:7–8), as a malicious tyrant who takes vicious glee in the tricks he plays (7:9–10), or even as an indulgent grandfather who provides everything requested of him. He is the heavenly Father, the God of the kingdom, who graciously and willingly bestows the good gifts of the kingdom in answer to prayer. See Jayhoon Yang, "Ask, Seek and Knock? A Reconsideration of Matthew 7:7–12," *ExpTim* 119 (2008): 170–75.

4. On the "good gifts" as spiritual gifts (cf. Ro 3:8; 10:15; Heb 9:11; 10:1) and the parallel reference to the Holy Spirit (Lk 11:13), see Marshall, *Gospel of Luke*, 469–70.

d. Balance and perfection (7:12)

12"So in everything, do to others what you would have them do to you, for this sums up the Law and the Prophets."

COMMENTARY

12 The Golden Rule was not invented by Jesus; it is found in many forms in highly diverse settings. About AD 20, Rabbi Hillel, challenged by a Gentile to summarize the law in the short time the Gentile could stand on one leg, reportedly responded, "What is hateful to you, do not do to anyone else. This is the whole law; all the rest is commentary. Go and learn it" (*b. Šabb.* 31a). Apparently only Jesus phrased the rule positively. Thus stated, it is certainly more telling than its negative counterpart, for it speaks against sins of omission as well as sins of commission. The goats in 25:31–46 would be acquitted under the negative form of the rule but not under the form attributed to Jesus.

The *oun* ("therefore"; NIV, "so") might refer to vv.7–11 (i.e., because God gives good gifts, therefore Jesus' disciples should live by this rule as a function of gratitude) or to vv.1–6 (i.e., instead of judging others, we should treat them as we ourselves would want to be treated). But more probably it refers to the entire body of the sermon (5:17–7:12), for here there is a second reference to "the Law and the Prophets"; and this appears to form an envelope with 5:17–20. "Therefore," in the light of all I have taught about the true direction in which the OT law points, obey the Golden Rule, for this is (*estin*; NIV, "sums up") the Law and the Prophets (cf. Ro 13:9).

This way of putting it provides a powerful yet flexible maxim that helps us decide moral issues in a thousand cases without the need for multiplied case law. The rule is not arbitrary, without rational support, as in radical humanism; in Jesus' mind its rationale ("for") lies in its connection with revealed truth recorded in "the Law and the Prophets." The rule embraces quantity ("in everything") and quality (*houtōs kai*, "[do] even so"). And in the context of fulfilling the Scriptures, the rule provides a handy summary of the righteousness to be displayed in the kingdom.

Above all, this verse is not to be understood as a utilitarian maxim such as "Honesty pays." We are to do to others what we would have them do to us, not just because we expect the same in return, but because such conduct is the goal of the Law and the Prophets. The verb *estin* (NIV, "sums up") might properly be translated "fulfill," as in Acts 2:16. In the deepest sense, therefore, the rule is the Law and the Prophets in the same way the kingdom is the fulfillment of all that the Law and the Prophets foretold.

7. Conclusion: call to decision and commitment (7:13–27)

a. Two ways (7:13–14)

OVERVIEW

The Sermon on the Mount ends with four warnings, each offering paired contrasts: two ways (vv.13–14), two trees (vv.15–20), two claims (vv.21–23), and two builders (vv.24–27): see the useful chart of David Turner. Such pairs reflect preaching in the Wisdom tradition (note, for instance, how people in Proverbs are following either Lady Wisdom or Dame Folly). Here the pairs focus on eschatological judgment and so make it plain that the theme is still the kingdom of heaven. But if some will not enter it (vv.13–14, 21–23), the sole basis for such a tragedy is present response to Jesus' words. At the close of the sermon, the messianic claim is implicit and only thinly veiled.

[13]"Enter through the narrow gate. For wide is the gate and broad is the road that leads to destruction, and many enter through it. [14]But small is the gate and narrow the road that leads to life, and only a few find it."

COMMENTARY

13–14 "Two ways" language is common in Jewish literature, both canonical and extracanonical (e.g., Dt 30:19; Ps 1; Jer 21:8; Sir 21:11–14; 2 Esd 7:6–14; *T. Ash.* 1:3, 5; 1QS 3:20ff.). The general picture is clear enough. There are two gates, two roads, two crowds, two destinations. The "narrow" gate (KJV's "strait" is from Lat. *strictum*, "narrow"; nothing is said about this gate or road being "straight," despite the modern phrase "straight and narrow") is clearly restrictive and does not permit entrance to what Jesus prohibits. The "wide" gate seems far more inviting. The "broad" road (not "easy," NRSV) is spacious and accommodates the crowd and their baggage; the other road is "narrow"—but two different words are used: *stenē̆s* ("narrow," v.13, GK *5101*) and *tethlimmenē* (v.14, GK *2567*), the latter being cognate with *thlipsis* ("tribulation," GK *2568*), which almost always refers to persecution. So this text says that the way of discipleship is "narrow," restricting, because it is the way of persecution and opposition—a major theme in Matthew (see comments at 5:10–12, 44; 10:16–39; 11:11–12; 24:4–13; cf. A. J. Mattill Jr., "The Way of Tribulation," *JBL* 98 [1979]: 531–46). Compare Acts 14:22: "We must go through many hardships [*dia pollōn thlipseōn*, 'through much persecution'] to enter the kingdom of God."

But the two roads are not ends in themselves. The narrow road leads to life, i.e., to the consummated kingdom (cf. vv.21–23; John's gospel), but the broad road leads to *apōleia* ("destruction," GK *724*)—"definitive destruction, not merely in the sense of the extinction of physical existence, but rather of an eternal plunge into Hades and a hopeless destiny of death" (*TDNT*, 1:396); cf. 25:34, 46; Jn 17:12; Ro 9:22; Php 1:28; 3:19; 1Ti 6:9; Heb 10:39; 2Pe 2:1, 3; 3:16; Rev 17:8, 11). (On the relative numbers ["many ... few"], see 22:14; Lk 13:22–30; Rev 7:9.)

Democratic decisions do not determine truth and righteousness in the kingdom. That there are only two ways is the inevitable result of the fact that the one that leads to life is exclusively by revelation. But if truth in such matters must not be sought by appealing to majority opinion (Ex 23:2), neither can it be found by each person doing what is right in his own eyes (Pr 14:12; cf. Jdg 21:25). God must be true and every man a liar (Ro 3:4).

There remains an important metaphorical difficulty. Granted the correctness of the text (cf. Metzger, *Textual Commentary*, 19), are we to think of roads heading up to the gate, so that once through the gate the traveler has arrived at his destination, whether destruction or the consummated kingdom? Or is the gate something entered *in this life*, with the roads, broad and narrow, stretching out before the pilgrim? Tasker as well as Jeremias (*TDNT*, 6:922–23) adopt the former alternative. Jeremias appeals to Luke 13:23–24, where a door, not a road, is mentioned, and argues that Jesus originally said something about entering a door or gate and that Matthew's form is a popular *hysteron-proteron* ("later-earlier") way of saying things with the real order reversed (like "thunder and lightning").

Not only is Luke 13:23–24 so far removed from the language of Matthew 7:13–14 (even "door," not "gate") that one may question whether the two spring from the same saying, but even in Luke, entrance through the door is not merely eschatological since there comes a time when the door is shut and no more may enter. This suggests that it is the shutting of the door that eliminates further opportunity for entrance, while the entrance itself takes place now—a form of realized eschatology. This conceptual parallel with Matthew, plus the order of gate-road, suggests, not that the gate marks entrance into the consummated kingdom, nor that the gate and road are a hendiadys (Ridderbos), but that entrance through the gate into the narrow way of persecution begins now but issues in the consummated kingdom at the other end of that way (Grosheide, Hendriksen). The narrow gate is not thereby rendered superfluous; instead, it confirms that even the beginning of this path to life is restrictive. Here is no funnel that progressively narrows down but a decisive break.

This exegesis entails two conclusions.

1. Jesus is not encouraging committed disciples, "Christians," to press on along the narrow way and be rewarded in the end. He is rather commanding his disciples to enter the way marked by persecution and rewarded in the end. Jesus' "disciples" (see comments at 5:1) are therefore not full-fledged Christians in the post-Pentecost sense. Jesus is dealing with people more or less committed to him but who have not yet really entered on the "Christian" way. How could they have entered on it? Only now was it being introduced into the stream of redemptive history as the fulfillment of what had come before. That Matthew should preserve such fine distinctions speaks well of his ability to follow the development of salvation history and thus avoid historical anachronism. Theologian though he is, Matthew is a responsible historian.

2. Implicitly, entrance into the kingdom—or, to preserve the language Matthew uses here but not always elsewhere (e.g., 12:28), entrance into the way to the kingdom—begins here and now in coming through the small gate, onto the narrow way of persecution, and under the authority of Jesus Christ (cf. vv.21, 26).

NOTES

13 The phrase δι' αὐτῆς (*di' autēs*, "through it") could in Greek refer to either the gate or the road (cf. 8:28); but the main lines of exegesis (see above) are not affected.

14 Probably τί (*ti*, normally "what?" or "why?"; KJV, "for"; NIV, "but") is the correct reading, carrying the same force as מָה (*mâ*, "how"—e.g., Ps 139:17) in Hebrew (cf. Black, *Aramaic Approach*, 123; BDF, para. 299 [4]; Metzger, *Textual Commentary*, 19).

b. Two trees (7:15–20)

OVERVIEW

Much recent debate has focused attention on the identity of these false prophets in the Matthean church. The argument turns in large part on identifying v.15 as Matthew's creation and on attempting to discuss the tradition history of vv.16–20; 12:33–35; Luke 6:43–45. The same evidence is better interpreted to support the thesis that Jesus in his itinerant preaching uses similar metaphors in a wide variety of ways.

Verse 15 has no synoptic parallel, but the thought is certainly not foreign to Jesus' other warnings (e.g., 24:4–5, 11, 23–24; Mk 13:22), and Matthew's language is small evidence for inauthenticity (see Introduction, section 2). The very diversity of the identifications—the false prophets are Zealots, Gnostics, scribes, antinomians, anti-Paulinists (for a recent survey, see David Hill, "False Prophets and Charismatics: Structure and Interpretation in Matthew

7:15–23," *Bib* 57 [1976]: 327–48)—argues that Jesus gave a warning with rather broad limits susceptible to diverse applications. Hill himself sees Pharisees of the AD 80 period in vv.15–20 and Charismatics in vv.21–23. E. Cothenet ("Les prophètes chrétiens dans l'Évangile selon Saint Matthieu," in *L'Évangile selon Matthieu* [ed. Didier], 281–308) thinks Jesus in vv.15–23 is condemning Zealots, but Matthew applies his words to condemn antinomians. And Paul Minear ("False Prophecy and Hypocrisy in the Gospel of Matthew," in *Neues Testament und Kirche* [ed. Gnilka], 76–93) criticizes theories that center on antinomians and Pharisees and understands the pericope to warn against hypocrisy and false prophecy entirely within the Christian community.

There is nothing intrinsically unlikely about the notion that Jesus warned against false prophets, provided he foresaw the continued existence of his newly formed community for a sustained period. He was doubtless steeped in the OT reports of earlier false prophets (Jer 6:13–15; 8:8–12; Eze 13; 22:27; Zep 3:4). Certainly the first Christians faced the false prophets (cf. v.15) Jesus had predicted (Ac 20:29; 2Co 11:11–15; 2Pe 2:1–3, 17–22; cf. 1Jn 2:18, 22; 4:1–6). In view of Matthew's care in preserving historical distinctions (see comments at vv.13–14), there is little reason to doubt that he is here dealing with the teaching of the historical Jesus. Of course, this presupposes that Jesus saw himself as true prophet (cf. 21:11, 46).

15"Watch out for false prophets. They come to you in sheep's clothing, but inwardly
they are ferocious wolves. 16By their fruit you will recognize them. Do people pick grapes
from thornbushes, or figs from thistles? 17Likewise every good tree bears good fruit, but a
bad tree bears bad fruit. 18A good tree cannot bear bad fruit, and a bad tree cannot bear
good fruit. 19Every tree that does not bear good fruit is cut down and thrown into the fire.
20Thus, by their fruit you will recognize them."

COMMENTARY

15 Warnings against false prophets are necessarily based on the conviction that not all prophets are true, that truth can be violated, and that the gospel's enemies usually conceal their hostility and try to pass themselves off as fellow believers. At first glance, they use orthodox language, show biblical piety, and are indistinguishable from true prophets (cf. 10:41). Thus it is vital to know how to distinguish sheep from wolves in sheep's clothing. Jesus does not explicitly say who will have the discernment to protect the community but implies that the community itself, by whatever agency, must somehow protect itself from the wolves.

Neither the damage these false prophets do nor their brand of false teaching is stated, but the flow of the Sermon on the Mount and its OT background suggest they neither acknowledge nor teach the narrow way to life subject to persecution (vv.13–14; cf. Jer 8:11; Eze 13, where prophets cry "Peace!" when there is no peace). They have never really come under kingdom authority (vv.21–23); and since the only alternative to life is destruction (vv.13–14), they imperil their followers.

16–20 From a distance the little blackberries on the buckthorn could be mistaken for grapes, and the flowers on certain thistles might deceive one into thinking figs were growing (v.16). But no one would be long deceived. So with people! One's "fruit"—not just what one does but all one says and does—will ultimately reveal what one is (cf. Jas 3:12). The Semitic way of expression (i.e., both positive and negative—namely, every good tree bears good fruit; no good tree bears bad fruit, etc.) makes the test certain but not necessarily easy or quick. Living according to kingdom norms can be feigned for a time, but what one is will eventually reveal itself in what one does. However guarded one's words, they will finally betray him (cf. 12:33–37; Lk 6:45). Ultimately false prophets tear down faith (2Ti 2:18) and promote divisiveness, bitterness (e.g., 1Ti 6:4–5; 2Ti 2:23), and various kinds of ungodliness (2Ti 2:16). Meek discernment and understanding the dire consequences of the false prophets' teachings are needed. But at the same time, censoriousness over minutiae must be avoided.

The common wording between 3:10 (spoken by the Baptist) and 7:19 may suggest that v.19 was proverbial or that during the time Jesus and the Baptist were both ministering, various expressions became standard (cf. 3:2; 4:17). Verse 19 is an important example of this, for here we have independent evidence that Jesus preached in this vein (cf. Mk 1:15) so that there is no need to suppose Matthew has transferred a saying of the Baptist to the lips of Jesus.

c. Two claims (7:21–23)

[21]"Not everyone who says to me, 'Lord, Lord,' will enter the kingdom of heaven, but only he who does the will of my Father who is in heaven. [22]Many will say to me on that day, 'Lord, Lord, did we not prophesy in your name, and in your name drive out demons and perform many miracles?' [23]Then I will tell them plainly, 'I never knew you. Away from me, you evildoers!'"

COMMENTARY

21–23 If vv.15–20 deal with false prophets, vv.21–23 deal with false followers. Perhaps some became false because of the false prophets. Their cry of "Lord, Lord" reflects fervency. In Jesus' day, it is doubtful whether "Lord" when used to address him meant more than "teacher" or "sir." But in the postresurrection period, it becomes an appellation of worship and a confession of Jesus' deity. Therefore some suspect an anachronism here. Two factors support authenticity: (1) the parallel in Luke 6:46 (cf. Jn 13:12–16), and (2) the fact that throughout Jesus' ministry he referred to himself in relatively veiled categories whose full significance could be grasped only after the resurrection. The latter point is central to understanding the "Son of Man" title (see comments at 8:20), recurs in various forms throughout all the Gospels, and is especially focal in John (cf. Carson, "Christological Ambiguities"; also his "Understanding Misunderstandings in the Fourth Gospel," *TynBul* [1982]: 59–91).

On the background of *kyrios* ("Lord," GK *3261*) as a christological title, see Fitzmyer, *Wandering Aramean*, 115–32. Here Jesus' point is made during his ministry, if at that time his disciples understood

"Lord" to mean "teacher." But implicitly Jesus is claiming more, since his "name" becomes the focus of kingdom activity; and he alone decrees who does or does not enter the kingdom (vv.22–23). Thus the warning and rebuke would take on added force when early Christians read the passage from their postresurrection perspective.

Indeed, the tables may be turned. Far from providing evidence that virtually every use of *kyrios* in this gospel is anachronistic because it presupposes a high Christology (e.g., Kingsbury), these verses suggest that Matthew is painfully aware that the title may mean nothing. This explains, for instance, the deep irony of Peter's "Never, Lord" (16:22). Jesus himself is preparing his followers to put the deepest content in the title, for finally obedience, not titles, is decisive.

The determinative factor regarding who enters the kingdom is obedience to the Father's will (v.19; cf. 12:50). This is the first use of "my Father" in Matthew (cf. Lk 2:49; Jn 2:16); as such it may support the truth, taught throughout the sermon, that Jesus alone claims to be the authoritative revealer of his Father's will (Mt 7:21). It quite misses the point to say that the Father's will is simply the OT law mildly touched up by Jesus, and that therefore the Matthean church "seems to have been unaware of or uninfluenced by Pauline Christianity" (Hill).

1. If the preceding exegesis of the Sermon on the Mount is correct, Matthew is not saying that Jesus is simply taking over the law but that Jesus *fulfills* the law and thus determines the nature of its continuity.

2. Within this framework, Matthew presents Jesus as standing at a different (i.e., earlier) point in salvation history than any church in Matthew's day, for Jesus is the one who brings about the new dispensation.

3. Paul's alleged antinomian tendencies are implicitly exaggerated by Hill's reconstruction, for it is difficult to think of one thing in the sermon Paul does not say in other words. The differences between Matthew and Paul—and there are major ones—have more to do with differences in interest and in their relative place in the stream of redemptive history. Moreover, Matthew, as we shall see, strongly stresses grace; therefore, it is legitimate to wonder whether he is presenting obedience to the will of the Father as the ground or as the requirement for entrance to the kingdom. Paul would deny only the former and insist on the latter no less than Matthew would.

"That day" is the day of judgment (cf. Mal 3:17–18; *1 En.* 45:3; cf. Mt 25:31–46; Lk 10:12; 2Th 1:7–10; 2Ti 1:12; 4:8; Rev 16:14). The false claimants have prophesied in Jesus' name and by that name exorcised demons and performed miracles. There is no reason to judge their claims false; their claims are not false but insufficient. Significantly, the miracles Jesus specifies were all done by his disciples during his ministry (cf. 10:1–4). He does not mention a later gift, such as tongues. The argument of David C. Sim ("Matthew 7:21–23: Further Evidence of its Anti-Pauline Perspective," *NTS* 53 [2007]: 325–43) that these verses betray an anti-Pauline bias depends on an arbitrary alignment of material. Sim argues that according to these verses Jesus as final judge condemns the very sort of people who belong to Paul and his circle—people who are lawless and defend themselves by saying they prophesy, work miracles, and perform exorcisms in the name of Jesus; i.e., they engage in charismatic activities. But the same Paul insists that those who continue in their pre-conversion sins will never inherit the kingdom (e.g., 1Co 6:9–11), which is much in line with what Jesus here underscores.

Verse 23 presupposes an implicit Christology of the highest order. Jesus himself decides not only who enters the kingdom on the last day but also who will be banished from his presence. That he never knew these false claimants strikes a common biblical note, namely, how close to spiritual reality one may come while knowing nothing of its fundamental reality (e.g., Balaam; Judas Iscariot; cf. Mk 9:38–39; 1Co 13:2; Heb 3:14; 1Jn 2:19). "But not everyone who speaks in a spirit is a prophet, except he have the behavior of the Lord" (*Did.* 11.8).

Two final observations: (1) Although "I have nothing to do with you" is the mildest of rabbinic bans (Str-B, 4:293), the words used here are clearly final and eschatological in a solemn context of "that day" and entrance into the kingdom; and (2) "Away from me, you evildoers" is quoted from Psalm 6:8 (cf. Lk 13:27). In the psalm, the sufferer, vindicated by Yahweh, tells the evildoers to depart. Again it is difficult to avoid the conclusion that Jesus himself links the authority of the messianic King with the righteous Sufferer, however veiled the allusion may be (see comments at 3:17).

d. Two builders (7:24–27)

[24]"Therefore everyone who hears these words of mine and puts them into practice
is like a wise man who built his house on the rock. [25]The rain came down, the streams
rose, and the winds blew and beat against that house; yet it did not fall, because it had its
foundation on the rock. [26]But everyone who hears these words of mine and does not put
them into practice is like a foolish man who built his house on sand. [27]The rain came
down, the streams rose, and the winds blew and beat against that house, and it fell with a
great crash."

COMMENTARY

24–27 Luke's sermon ends on the same note (Lk 6:47–49). Probably the evangelists adapted the parable to the situation of their readers. Verses 21–23 contrast "saying" and "doing"; these verses contrast "hearing" and "doing" (Stott, *Message of the Sermon on the Mount*, 208), not unlike James 1:22–25; 2:14–20 (cf. Eze 33:31–32). Moreover, the will of the Father (v.21) becomes definitive in what Jesus calls "these words of mine" (v.24). *His* teaching is definitive (see comments at 5:17–20; 28:18–20).

In the light of the radical choice of vv.21–23, "therefore" (v.24) the two positions can be likened to two builders and their houses. Each house looks secure in good weather. But Palestine is known for torrential rains that can turn dry wadis into raging torrents. Only storms reveal the quality of the work of the two builders. The thought reminds us of the parable of the sower, in which the seed sown on rocky ground lasts only a short time, until "trouble or persecution comes because of the word" (13:21). The greatest storm is eschatological (cf. Isa 28:16–17; Eze 13:10–13; see also Pr 12:7). But Jesus' words about the two houses need not be thus restricted. The point is that the wise man (a repeated term in Matthew; cf. 10:16; 24:45; 25:2, 4, 8–9) builds to withstand anything.

What wisdom (*phronimos*, GK *5861*; the term is absent from Mark and occurs twice in Luke [12:42; 16:8]) consists of is clear. A wise person represents those who put Jesus' words into practice; they too are building to withstand anything. Those who pretend to have faith, who have a merely intellectual commitment, or who enjoy Jesus in small doses are foolish builders. When the storms of life come, their structures fool no one, above all not God (cf. Eze 13:10–16).

The sermon ends with what has been implicit throughout it—the demand for radical submission to the exclusive lordship of Jesus, who fulfills the Law and the Prophets and warns the disobedient that the alternative to total obedience, true righteousness, and life in the kingdom is rebellion, self-centeredness, and eternal damnation.

NOTES

24 The future passive reading ὁμοιωθήσεται (*homoiōthēsetai*, lit., "will become like," GK *3929*) is more probable than the active ὁμοιώσω αὐτόν (*homoiōsō auton*, lit., "I will liken him to"), not only on textual grounds, but also because of the possibility of assimilation to the active in Luke 6:47–48: ὑποδείξω ὑμῖν ... ὅμοιος (*hypodeixō hymin ... homoios*, "I will show you what he is like"). The future tense is significant: the one who puts Jesus' words into practice will become like the man who ...; i.e., on Judgment Day, when the great storm comes, he will stand fast because of his good foundation (see comments at 13:24).

24–26 The words ἀκούει μου τοὺς λόγους τούτους (*akouei mou tous logous toutous*, "hears these words of mine") could be rendered "hears me, in respect of these sayings"; Davies (*Setting*, 94) argues that "in this sense, the ethical teaching is not detached from the life of him who uttered it and with whom it is congruous." But the verb ἀκούω (*akouō*, "hear," GK *201*) only once takes the genitive in Matthew, and then it is not a pronoun. The emphatic μου (*mou* "of mine") is best understood as a way of forcefully identifying Jesus' teaching with the will of his Father (v.21), an important point in light of the exegesis of 5:17–20.

8. Transitional conclusion: Jesus' authority (7:28–29)

28When Jesus had finished saying these things, the crowds were amazed at his teaching,
29because he taught as one who had authority, and not as their teachers of the law.

COMMENTARY

28–29 This is the first of the five formulaic conclusions that terminate the discourses in this gospel. All five begin with *kai egeneto* (lit., "and it happened") plus a finite verb (v.28; 11:1; 13:53; 19:1; 26:1), a construction common in the LXX (classical Greek preferred *egeneto* plus the infinitive; cf. Zerwick, *Biblical Greek*, para. 388; Beyer, *Semitische Syntax*, 41–60). The only other occurrence in

Matthew is of the rather different "Hebrew" construction *kai egeneto ... kai* (lit., "and it happened ... and") plus a finite verb, which appears once (9:10). Matthew's formula is therefore a self-conscious stylistic device that establishes a structural turning point. (It is not necessary to adopt Benjamin Bacon's theory of parallelism to the Five Books of Moses; see Introduction, section 14.) Moreover, in each case the conclusion is transitional and prepares for the next section. Here (as we shall see below) mention of Jesus' authority leads into his authority in other spheres (8:1–17). In 11:1, Jesus' activity sets the scene for John the Baptist's question (11:2–3). And 13:53 anticipates rejection of Jesus in his hometown, while 19:1–2 points forward to his Judean ministry with new crowds and renewed controversies. Finally, 26:1–5 looks to the cross, now looming very near.

The crowds—probably a larger group than his disciples—again pressing in on him (see comments at 5:1–2) are amazed. Because this is the only conclusion to a discourse that mentions the crowds' amazement, Hill suggests that Matthew is returning to Mark 1:22 (Lk 4:32) as his source. This is very tenuous: (1) a closer Matthean parallel is 13:54, and (2) the next pericope in Matthew (8:1–4) is paralleled in Mark by Mark 1:40–45, too far on for us to believe Matthew has "returned to his source" at 1:22.

The word *didachē* ("teaching," GK *1439*) can refer to both content and manner, and no doubt the crowds were astonished at both. Their astonishment says nothing about their own heart commitment. The cause of their astonishment was Jesus' *exousia* ("authority," GK *2026*). The term embraces power as well as authority, and the theme becomes central (cf. 8:9; 9:6, 8; 10:1; 21:23–24, 27; 28:18). In his authority, Jesus differs from the "teachers of the law" (see comments at 2:4). Many of them limited their teaching to the authorities they cited, and a great part of their training centered on memorizing the received traditions. They spoke by the authority of others; Jesus spoke with his own authority. Yet many teachers of the law did indeed offer new rulings and interpretations, so some have tried to interpret vv.28–29 along other lines.

Daube (*New Testament and Rabbinic Judaism*, 205–16), in arguing that Jesus' lack of official rabbinic authority was an early issue in his ministry, says that some of the crowds' response in Galilee was because they did not often hear ordained rabbis so far north. Sigal (*Halakhah of Jesus*), dating the sources a little differently, insists (probably rightly) that there was no official ordination of rabbis until after Jesus' death. He argues that Jesus himself was not essentially different in his authority from other proto-rabbis. Both these instructions miss the central point, which transcends halakic applications of the law, the formulas used, and the latitude of interpretation permitted.

The central point is this: Jesus' entire approach in the Sermon on the Mount is not only ethical but messianic—i.e., christological and eschatological. Jesus is not an ordinary prophet who says, "Thus says the Lord!" Rather, he speaks in the first person and claims that his teaching fulfills the OT, that he determines who enters the messianic kingdom, that as the Divine Judge he pronounces banishment, that the true heirs of the kingdom will be persecuted for their allegiance to him, and that he alone fully knows the will of his Father. It is methodologically indefensible for Sigal to complain that all such themes are later Christian additions and therefore to focus exclusively on points of halakic interpretation. Jesus' authority is unique (see comments at 5:21–48), and the crowds recognized it, even if they did not always understand it. This same authority is now to be revealed in powerful, liberating miracles, signs of the kingdom's advance (chs. 8–9; cf. 11:2–5).

NOTES

29 The word "their" may indicate a distinction between "Christian" teachers and those of the synagogues. Hummel (*Auseinandersetzung*, 28ff.) and others, following Kilpatrick (*Origins*, 40), make much of Matthew's "their" (4:23; 9:35; 10:17; 12:9; 13:54; 23:34) to support a theory that Matthew's life setting is *just before* the division between church and synagogue (since 6:2, 5; 23:6 make no allusion to Christian synagogues). But "their" may be quite innocuous. It may reflect the geographical stance of a writer not in Galilee (see comments at 4:23). Better yet, where Jesus' authority is emphasized, "their" may subtly remind the reader that Jesus himself, though a Jew of the line of David (1:1), has his ultimate origin beyond the Jewish race (1:19–25) and so cannot be classed with *their* teachers of the law. Moreover, in one place Matthew is merely following Mark (Mk 1:23) and seems to use "their" in still other, highly unusual places (e.g., 11:1; NIV text note, "in their towns"), which caution the reader against reading too much into the word. And some of the preceding debate (e.g., as to the relevance of 6:2, 5; 23:6) is relevant only if anachronism is already assumed, since these references make perfectly good sense under the obvious assumption that Matthew's gospel really is about Jesus. Yet there may well be theological significance in some of the "their" passages (see comments at 10:17), which gets transferred by association to other occurrences of the pronoun.

III. THE KINGDOM EXTENDED UNDER JESUS' AUTHORITY (8:1–11:1)

A. Narrative (8:1–10:4)

OVERVIEW

Matthew's arrangement of the pericopes in chs. 8–9 is demonstrably topical, not chronological. All these pericopes except 8:5–13, 18–22; 9:32–34 are paralleled in Mark, but not in the same order, and these three are paralleled in Luke. Mark 1:40–2:22 appears to provide the basic framework with numerous exceptions. The events in Matthew 8:18–22 originally occurred not only after the Sermon on the Mount but apparently after the "day of parables" (ch. 13; cf. Lk 8:22–56). On the other hand, Matthew 8:2–4; 8:14–17; 9:2–13 almost certainly took place before the Sermon on the Mount (cf. Mk 1:29–34, 40–45; Lk 4:38–41; see Hendriksen). Matthew does not purport to follow anything other than a topical arrangement, and most of his "time" indicators are very loose.

This does not mean that Matthew's arrangement is entirely haphazard but that it is governed by themes. Linkage from pericope to pericope is provided by ideas, catchwords, and dominant motifs (cf. K. Gatzweiler, "Les récits de miracles dans l'évangile selon saint Matthieu," in *L'Évangile selon Matthieu* [ed. Didier], 209–20). However, it does not follow that all the outlines suggested by various scholars to explain this topical design are equally convincing. Klostermann, for instance, notes the central place of the ten plagues in Jewish thought (e.g., *Pirke Avot* 5:5, 8) and suggests that the ten miracles in these chapters are planned to picture Jesus as the new Moses or the church as a new exodus (cf. Grundmann; Davies, *Setting*, 86–93). But this is not convincing: Matthew lays no stress on the number ten, his miracles are not individually parallel to the plagues, and his main themes run on other lines.

J. D. Kingsbury ("Observations on the Miracle Chapters of Matthew 8–9," *CBQ* 40 [1978]: 559–73) ably discusses and rejects outlines proposed by Christoph Burger (*Jesus als Davidssohn*), William Thompson (*Matthew's Advice*), and others, and he opts for a modification of Burger's fourfold division: (1) 8:1–17 treats Christology; (2) 8:18–34 concerns discipleship; (3) 9:1–17 focuses on questions pertaining to the separation of Jesus and his followers from Israel; (4) 9:18–34 centers on faith; and over all the "Son of God" Christology predominates.

But it is hard to avoid the feeling that this outline, like the others, is too simplistic. Christology extends beyond 8:1–17; a new title appears in 8:20 and reappears in 9:6; and Jesus' godlike authority to forgive sins does not appear until ch. 9. Why discipleship should be restricted to 8:18–34 when Matthew is called in 9:9–13 and the distinctive habits of Jesus' disciples are discussed in 9:14–17 is unclear. The distinctions between Jesus' followers and racial Israel can scarcely be said to await 9:1–17 in the light of 8:10, 28–34. Faith, far from awaiting the fourth division, is already central in 8:5–13. And we have already seen that Kingsbury tends to emphasize the "Son of God" theme while minimizing other equally strong christological emphases (see comments at 3:17). Luz (*Studies in Matthew*, 221–40) argues that the arrangement is designed to draw the readers into the accounts, so that the miracle stories not only speak of what happened but are presented so that readers make analogous connections with their own historical situation. That is the sort of theory that is reasonable enough when painted with broad strokes, but when it is defended in excruciating detail, these details become speculative and frankly unbelievable.

Certainly these chapters cannot legitimately be broken down in some simplistic fashion. Though Matthew's pericopes cohere nicely, he intertwines his themes, keeping several going at once like a literary juggler. Thus these chapters are best approached inductively; and one can trace emphases on faith, discipleship, the Gentile mission, a diverse christological pattern, and more. At the same time, these chapters prove that Jesus, whose mission in part was to preach, teach, and heal (4:23; 9:35), fulfilled the whole of it.

1. Healing miracles (8:1–17)

a. A leper (8:1–4)

OVERVIEW

Matthew has shown Jesus preaching the gospel of the kingdom (4:17, 23) and teaching (chs. 5–7). Now he records some examples of his healing ministry.

The first miracle, the healing of a leper, is much shorter in Matthew (8:1–4) than in Mark (Mk 1:40–45). The omission of Mark 1:41a, 45 and several other bits prompts some to think Matthew is here independent of Mark (Lohmeyer, Schlatter), others to think oral tradition is still having its influence (Bonnard, Hill), still others to offer some theological explanation, e.g., that Matthew suppressed any reference to Jesus' compassion because it did not fit the image the Matthean church members had formed of Christ (Sabourin; cf. Hull, *Hellenistic Magic*, 133–34). But when Matthew follows Mark, he condenses controversy stories by about 20 percent, stories that prove Jesus is the Christ by about 10 percent, actual sayings of Jesus scarcely at all, and miracle stories by about 50 percent (cf. Schweizer). Matthew, though allusive, is a highly disciplined writer, rigorously eliminating everything unrelated to his immediate concerns. So we must take it as a rule of thumb that Matthew's theology cannot be accurately discovered by studying what he omits—which cannot show more than what is not his immediate concern, and even then some of his omissions are purely stylistic—but primarily by what he includes. This is especially significant in the miracles, where Matthew leaves out so much. In the leper's healing, Sabourin's suggestion is especially implausible since Matthew stresses elsewhere Jesus' compassion and draws theological meaning from it (9:35–38).

[1]When he came down from the mountainside, large crowds followed him. [2]A man with
leprosy came and knelt before him and said, "Lord, if you are willing, you can make me clean."
[3]Jesus reached out his hand and touched the man. "I am willing," he said. "Be clean!"
Immediately he was cured of his leprosy. [4]Then Jesus said to him, "See that you don't tell
anyone. But go, show yourself to the priest and offer the gift Moses commanded, as a
testimony to them."

COMMENTARY

1 Jesus came down out of the hills (see comments at 5:1), where the Sermon on the Mount had been delivered, and still the great crowds (4:23–25; 7:28–29) pursued him.

2–3 The introductory *kai idou* (lit., "and behold"; also in Luke, absent from Mark, untranslated in NIV) does not require that this healing immediately follow the sermon. In Matthew, *kai idou* has a broad range, sometimes serving as a loose connective, sometimes introducing a startling thought or event, and sometimes, as here, marking the beginning of a new pericope.

Whether NT leprosy was actual leprosy (Hansen's disease; cf. *NIDNTT*, 2:463–66) or a broader category of skin ailments including leprosy is uncertain. But the Jews abhorred it, not only because of the illness itself, but because it rendered the sufferer and all with whom he came in direct contact ceremonially unclean. To be a leper was interpreted as being cursed by God (cf. Nu 12:10, 12; Job 18:13). Healings were rare (cf. Nu 12:10–15; 2Ki 5:9–14) and considered as difficult as raising the dead (2Ki 5:7, 14; cf. Str-B, 4:745ff.). In the messianic age there would be no leprosy (cf. 11:5).

The man *prosekynei* ("knelt," GK *4686*) before Jesus, but the verb can also mean "worshiped." Clearly the former is meant in this historical setting. Yet, as with the title "Lord" (see comments at 7:22–23), Christian readers of Matthew could not help concluding that this leper spoke and acted better than he knew.

"If you are willing" reflects the leper's great faith, prompted by Jesus' healing activity throughout the district (4:24). He had no question about Jesus' healing power but feared only that he would be passed by. In affirming his willingness to heal, Jesus proved that his will is decisive. He already had the authority and power and only needed to decide and act. J. D. Kingsbury ("Retelling the 'Old, Old Story,'" *Currents in Theology and Missions* 4 [1976]: 346) suggests that "reached out his hand" symbolizes the exercise of authority (cf. Ex 7:5; 14:21; 15:6; 1Ki 8:42), but Matthew's use of the same Greek expression elsewhere (Mt 12:13 [2x], 49; 14:31; 26:51) shows that Kingsbury's interpretation is fanciful. More probably, Jesus had to reach to touch the leper because the leper did not dare come close to him.

By touching an unclean leper, Jesus would become ceremonially defiled himself (cf. Lev 13–14). But at Jesus' touch nothing remains defiled. Far from becoming unclean, Jesus makes the unclean clean. Both Jesus' word and touch (8:15; 9:20–21, 29; 14:36) are effective, possibly implying that authority is vested in his message as well as his person.

4 Despite Heinz Joachim Held's view ("Matthew as Interpreter of the Miracle Stories," 256), this verse is not the "entire goal of this story." That is reductionistic and ignores the intertwined themes (see Overview, 8:1–10:4; Heil, "Significant Aspects of the Healing Miracles," 280 n. 25). While prohibitions against telling of cures and exorcisms are more common in Mark than Matthew, they are not unknown in the latter (8:4; 9:30; 12:16; cf. 16:20; 17:9). They have nothing to do with the so-called messianic secret proposed by William Wrede (*The Messianic Secret* [Greenwood, S.C.: Attic, 1971; German ed., 1901]; see Introduction in Mark, p. 674), as Hill rightly holds. Nor does this particular prohibition enjoin silence only until the cured leper has been to Jerusalem to be cleared by the priest (so Lenski). The synoptic parallels (Mk 1:45; Lk 5:15) as well as other similar occurrences in Matthew demonstrate that these commands to be silent have other functions—to show that Jesus is not presenting himself as a mere wonder worker (Stonehouse, *Witness of Matthew*, 62; Maier) who can be pressured into messiahship by crowds whose messianic views are materialistic and political. Jesus' authority derives from God alone, not the acclaim of men (Bonnard); he came to die, not to trounce the Romans. The people who disobeyed Jesus' injunctions to silence only made his mission more difficult.

Jesus commanded the cured man to follow the Mosaic prescriptions for lepers who claimed healing (cf. Lev 14). This, he said, was *eis martyrion autois* ("as a testimony to them"). Much debate surrounds *autois*. Is the testimony positive, "for them" (Trilling, *Das wahre Israel*, 128–29), as proof of the healing, or negative, "against them" (Hummel, *Auseinandersetzung*, 81–82), as a sort of denunciation of their unbelief? Such conflicting categories are not helpful and leave some commentators undecided (e.g., Nolland). Of the other places where the Synoptics use *eis martyrion* ("for a witness"; 10:18; 24:14; Mk 1:44; 6:11; 13:9; Lk 5:14; 9:5; 21:13), only two require "witness against" (contra Frankemölle, *Jahwebund und Kirche Christi*, 120 n. 193, who insists 10:18 and 24:14 are also negative). Most of the rest are "neutral" and imply division around the "witness" presented.

Better progress can be made by asking why, in this setting, Jesus commands obedience. It cannot be simply to prove that Jesus remains faithful to the law (Calvin) and so encourages Matthew's Jewish Christians to be similarly faithful (Hill, Schniewind, Schweizer). Formally speaking, Jesus has already transcended the law by touching the leper without being defiled, a confirmation of our exegesis of 5:17–20. Furthermore, if around AD 85 (when Hill thinks the first gospel was written) Matthew were simply trying to get his community to adhere (unlike Pauline communities) to the details of OT law, he chose a singularly ill-suited story to make his point, because by that date the destruction of the temple had effectively abolished priests and offerings. It is far easier to deduce from the setting that this material is authentic.

In one sense, Jesus does submit to the law. He puts himself under its ordinances. But the result is startling. The law achieves new relevance by pointing to Jesus. In conforming to the law, the cured leper becomes the occasion for the law to confirm Jesus' authority as the healer who needs but to will the deed for it to be done. Thus the supreme function of the "gift" Moses commanded is not as a guilt offering (Lev 14:10–18) but as a witness to men concerning Jesus. In this context, "to them" is relatively incidental. It might refer to the priests or the people, but in either case it points to Jesus Christ (see comments at 5:17–20).

b. The centurion's servant (8:5–13)

OVERVIEW

If this story (cf. Lk 7:1–10) comes from Q, then at least in this instance Q contains more than short sayings of Jesus; or, better, this is evidence against a unitary Q. It is uncertain whether this account is the same as the one in John 4:46–53. The many differences argue against this, though admittedly some of these are overemphasized. In John, Jesus rebukes the centurion and the onlookers for their love of signs. Though there is no mention of that here, Matthew treats that theme elsewhere (12:38–39; 16:1–4). Most modern scholars, unlike those of earlier generations, simply assume there is but one incident. However, the matter is ably discussed by Edward F. Siegman, "St. John's Use of Synoptic Material," *CBQ* 30 (1968): 182–98. (On the distinctive theological emphases of Matthew and Luke, cf. R. P. Martin, "The Pericope of the Healing of the 'Centurion's' Servant/Son [Mt 8:5–13 par. Lk 7:1–10]: Some Exegetical Notes," in *Unity and Diversity in the New Testament* [ed. R.A. Guelich; Grand Rapids: Eerdmans, 1978], 14–22.)

Form critics find the purpose of the story in the dialogue to which the miracle leads and call it a "pronouncement story" or "apophthegm" rather than a "miracle story." One wonders why it can't be both (cf. Stephen H. Travis, "Form Criticism," in *New Testament Interpretation* [ed. Marshall], esp. 157–60). The chief difference, apart from theological emphases, between vv.5–13 and Luke 7:1–10 is the use of intermediaries in the latter. Probably Matthew, following his tendency to condense, makes no mention of the servants in order to lay the greater emphasis on faith according to the principle *qui facit per alium facit per se* ("he who acts by another acts himself")—a principle the centurion's argument implies (vv.8–9).

5When Jesus had entered Capernaum, a centurion came to him, asking for help. 6"Lord,"
he said, "my servant lies at home paralyzed and in terrible suffering."
7Jesus said to him, "I will go and heal him."

8The centurion replied, "Lord, I do not deserve to have you come under my roof. But just
say the word, and my servant will be healed. 9For I myself am a man under authority, with
soldiers under me. I tell this one, 'Go,' and he goes; and that one, 'Come,' and he comes. I
say to my servant, 'Do this,' and he does it."
10When Jesus heard this, he was astonished and said to those following him, "I tell you
the truth, I have not found anyone in Israel with such great faith. 11I say to you that many
will come from the east and the west, and will take their places at the feast with Abraham, Isaac and Jacob in the kingdom of heaven. 12But the subjects of the kingdom will be
thrown outside, into the darkness, where there will be weeping and gnashing of teeth."
13Then Jesus said to the centurion, "Go! It will be done just as you believed it would."
And his servant was healed at that very hour.

COMMENTARY

5 This is Matthew's second mention of Capernaum (cf. 4:13). In Jesus' day it was an important garrison town. No Roman legions were posted in Palestine, but there were auxiliaries under Herod Antipas, who had the right to levy troops. These were non-Jews, probably recruited from outside Galilee, perhaps from Lebanon and Syria. Centurions were the military backbone throughout the empire, maintaining discipline and executing orders. Luke stresses this centurion's Jewish sympathies and his humility, Matthew his faith and race (vv.10–11). Indeed, one reason Matthew says nothing of the intermediaries may be that they were Jews, and he does not want to blur the racial distinction.

6–7 On "Lord," see comments at 7:21–23. The word *pais* (GK *4090*) can mean "servant" or "son." Luke's word (*doulos*, GK *1528*) means "servant," and many (e.g., Bultmann, *History of the Synoptic Tradition*, 38 n. 4) insist Matthew's *pais* means "son." But fair examination of NT usage (cf. France, "Exegesis in Practice," 256) reveals that only one of twenty-four NT occurrences requires "son," namely, John 4:51. This further supports the view that John 4 records a different healing on a separate occasion. Conceivably it was the earlier healing of an official's son (Jn 4) that strengthened the centurion's faith in this instance. Though paralysis coupled with severe pain is attested elsewhere (e.g., 1 Macc 9:55–56), the nature of the servant's malady is unknown. Derrett's psychosomatic speculations (*Studies in the New Testament*, 1:156–57, 166–68) are fanciful.

Jewish rabbis, like ministers today, were often invited to pray for the sick (cf. Str-B, 1:475); but the parallels are not close, for the centurion is implicitly asking for healing, not prayers. Many (Zahn; Klostermann; Turner [*Grammatical Insights*, 50–51]; Held ["Matthew as Interpreter of the Miracle Stories," 194]) interpret Jesus' response (v.7) as a question: "Shall I [*ego*, emphatic; i.e., I, a Jew] come and heal him?" This is probably right. The parallel with the Canaanite woman (15:21–28) is compelling, and otherwise it is difficult to explain the emphatic "I." Jesus' response was not based on fears of ritual defilement—vv.1–4 set that to rest—or even on his general restriction of his ministry to Israel (see comments at 10:5–6; 15:24; but even in Matthew there are significant exceptions, e.g., 8:28–34). It was based on a desire to find out exactly what the centurion was after and what degree of faith stood behind his ambiguous request (v.6).

8–9 Both here and in the story of the Canaanite woman (15:21–28), faith triumphs over the obstacle Jesus erects. Luke records neither Jesus' question nor the story of the Canaanite woman; his treatment of faith is not quite so pointed. The centurion's reply opens with "Lord," implying tenacity and deference (cf. v.6; 7:21–23). As John the Baptist felt unworthy to baptize Jesus, so this centurion felt unworthy to entertain him in his home. The feeling of unworthiness did not arise from an awareness that the centurion might render Jesus ceremonially defiled (contra Bonnard); race had nothing to do with it. *Hikanos* ("sufficient," "worthy," GK *2653*) here as elsewhere (3:11; 1Co 15:9; 2Co 2:16) reveals the man's sense of unworthiness (NIV, "do not deserve") in the face of Jesus' authority (cf. *TDNT*, 3:294; France, "Exegesis in Practice," 258). "Here was one who was in the state described in the first clauses of the 'Beatitudes,' and to whom came the promise of the second clauses; because Christ *is* the connecting link between the two" (Edersheim, *Life and Times*, 1:549; emphasis his).

The centurion believed that Jesus' word was sufficient to heal his servant. It is significant that we have no recorded evidence that up to this point Jesus had performed a healing miracle at a distance and by word alone (unless Jn 4:46–53 is an exception). The centurion's thinking here is profound. There is no need to take the first clause in v.9 as implying that the *only* parallel between his authority and that of Jesus was in their ability to order things to be done: "I, although I am a man under orders, can effect things by my word" (Hill). That is a barely possible rendering of the opening *kai gar ego*; the more natural translation is that of the NIV ("for I myself"), which applies the words to the entire verse. This means that the centurion's words presuppose an understanding of the Roman military system. All "authority" (*exousia*, as in 7:29) belonged to the emperor and was delegated. Therefore, because he was under the emperor's authority, when the centurion spoke, he spoke with the emperor's authority, and so his command was obeyed. A foot soldier who disobeyed would not be defying a mere centurion but the emperor, Rome itself, with all its imperial majesty and might (cf. Derrett, *Studies in the New Testament*, 1:159–60). This self-understanding the centurion applied to Jesus. Precisely because Jesus was under God's authority, he was vested with God's authority, so that when Jesus spoke, God spoke. To defy Jesus was to defy God; and Jesus' word must therefore be vested with God's authority that is able to heal sickness. This analogy, though not perfect, reveals an astonishing faith that recognizes that Jesus needed neither ritual, magic, nor any other help; his authority was God's authority, and his word was effective because it was God's word.

10 In Mark 6:6, Jesus is astonished at deeply rooted unbelief. Here he is astonished (same verb) at the faith of the centurion. "Though amazement is not appropriate for God, seeing it must arise from new and unexpected happenings, yet it could occur in Christ, inasmuch as he had taken on our human emotions, along with our flesh" (Calvin). Jesus spoke to those following him (not necessarily his disciples; cf. 4:25; 8:1) with the prefatory notice ("I tell you"; see comments at 5:22) that warns of the solemn remark to follow.

Jesus commended the man's faith (cf. v.13). The greatness of his faith did not rest in the mere fact that he believed Jesus could heal from a distance but in the degree to which he had penetrated the secret of Jesus' authority. That faith was the more surprising since the centurion was a Gentile and lacked the heritage of OT revelation to help him understand Jesus. But this Gentile penetrated more deeply into the nature of Jesus' person and authority than any Jew of his time. Matthew's words stress even more than Luke's the uniqueness of the centurion's faith and underline the movement of the gospel from the Jews to the Gentiles, or rather from the Jews to all people regardless of race—a movement prophesied in the OT, developed in Jesus' ministry (see comments at 1:1, 3–5; 2:1–12; 3:9–10; 4:15–16), and commanded by the Great Commission (28:18–20). "This incident is a preview of the great insight which came later through another centurion's faith, 'Then to the Gentiles God has granted repentance unto life' (Acts 11:18)" (France, "Exegesis in Practice," 260).

11–12 Again "I say to you" solemnizes what follows (cf. v.10). Most interpreters assume that Matthew has added these two verses (not in Luke) to the narrative, taking them from an entirely different setting (namely, Lk 13:28–29; e.g., Chilton, *God in Strength*, 179–201). But this is problematic apart from clear criteria distinguishing it from the obvious alternative—that Jesus said similar things more than once. The words of the saying are not very close in the two passages, but the imagery is so colorful that an itinerant preacher could have used it repeatedly, especially if warnings to the Jews and the prospect of Gentile admission to the fellowship of God's people were two of his major themes.

The picture is that of the "messianic banquet," derived from such OT passages as Isaiah 25:6–9 (cf. 65:13–14) and embellished in later Judaism (cf. *TDNT*, 2:34–35). These embellishments did not usually anticipate the presence of Gentiles at the banquet, which symbolized the consummation of the messianic kingdom (cf. 22:1–14; 25:10; 26:29). But Jesus here insists that many will come from the four points of the compass and join the patriarchs at the banquet. These "many" can only be Gentiles, contrasted as they are with "subjects of the kingdom" (*hoi huioi tēs basileias*, lit., "the sons of the kingdom," v.12).

"Son of" or "sons of" can mean "belonging to" or "destined for" (cf. "sons of the bridal chamber" [9:15; NIV, "guests of the bridegroom"] and "son of hell" [23:15; cf. Str-B, 1:476–78; 1QS 17:3; see comments at 5:9]). So the "subjects of the kingdom" are the Jews, who see themselves as sons of Abraham (cf. 3:9–10), belonging to the kingdom by right. Some Jews (e.g., those at Qumran) restricted the elect to a smaller group of the pious within Israel. But Jesus reverses roles (cf. 21:43), and the sons of the kingdom are thrown aside, left out of the future messianic banquet, consigned to darkness where there are tears and gnashing of teeth—elements common to descriptions of gehenna, hell (cf. *4 Ezra* 7:93; *1 En.* 63:10; *Pss. Sol.* 14:9; 15:10; Wis 17:21; cf. Mt 22:13; see comments at 5:29). Yet although this reversal theme cannot be overlooked and is stressed by many commentators (e.g., Hagner; France [NICNT]; Luz) who rightly see in these verses an anticipation of the Great Commission (28:18–20), others are right to remind us (e.g., Turner; Witherington) that the "reversal" is not absolute. The patriarchs in these verses are Jews, as are Jesus and his apostles (who will rule the twelve tribes of Israel in the world to come, 19:28), and even after the resurrection most of the earliest disciples were Jews (Ro 11:1–5).

The crucial point for both Jews and Gentiles is their relation to Jesus. Certainly Jesus' words could only shock his hearers. The attempt of Davies and Allison to argue that these "many ... from the east and the west" are not Gentiles but underprivileged Jews is unconvincing since the central figure in this account, apart from Jesus, is a Gentile centurion whose faith Jesus contrasts with that of Jews. If these verses do not quite authorize the Gentile mission, they open the door to it and prepare for the Great Commission (28:18–20) and Ephesians 3.

The definite articles with "weeping" (*klauthmos*, GK *3088*) and "gnashing" (*brygmos*, GK *1106*) emphasize the horror of the scene: *the* weeping and *the* gnashing (Turner, *Syntax*, 173). Weeping suggests suffering and gnashing of teeth despair (McNeile).

There may be a still deeper implication in these words of Jesus. OT passages that may be reflected in vv.11–12 can be divided into three groups: (1) those that describe a gathering of Israel from all quarters of the earth (Ps 107:3; Isa 43:5–6; 49:12); (2) those that predict the worship of God by Gentiles in all parts of the earth (Isa 45:6; 59:19; Mal 1:11); (3) those that predict the coming of Gentiles to Jerusalem (Isa 2:2–3; 60:3–4; Mic 4:1–2; Zec 8:20–23). The closest literary parallels lie between vv.11–12 and the first group (cf. Gundry, *Use of the Old Testament*, 76–77). On this basis France ("Exegesis in Practice," 261–63) proposes that a typology is assumed—the true "Israel" is now being gathered from the four corners of the earth, i.e., from the Gentiles. This is possible, for we have already seen several ways Matthew treats OT history as prophetic. But because he is not using fulfillment language here, Jesus may be using OT language without affirming that the relationship between OT and NT at this point is typological.

13 The *hōs* (NIV, "just as") must be rightly understood. Jesus performed a miracle, not in *proportion to* the centurion's faith, nor *because of* the centurion's faith, but in content what was *expected by* the centurion's faith (cf. 15:28, where the emphasis is also on faith).

NOTES

9 The three commands are aorist, present, and aorist respectively. Sometimes "the tense appears to be determined more by the meaning of the verb or by some obscure habit than by the 'rules' of *Aktionsart*" (Moule, *Idiom Book*, 135).

11 The verb ἀνακλιθήσονται (*anaklithēsontai*, lit., "will recline," GK *369*) describes the normal posture when eating: people lay on low couches or pallets (cf. Jn 13:23; 21:20). In the NT, reclining is not restricted to banquets (e.g., Mk 6:39; Lk 7:36), and there is no theological or symbolic significance in the act itself (contra Schlatter; Lohmeyer). Hence the NIV's paraphrastic "take their places."

12 Stonehouse (*Witness of Matthew*, 231–32), to avoid saying that the "subjects of the kingdom" are such only in appearance and self-estimation, understands βασιλείας ("kingdom," GK *993*) to refer to the "theocratic kingdom" as opposed to the "kingdom of heaven." But strictly speaking, the theocratic kingdom was no longer in existence, and it is difficult to see how "kingdom" in the phrase "subjects of the kingdom" may properly be taken as anything other than the kingdom just mentioned (v.11).

c. Peter's mother-in-law (8:14–15)

14When Jesus came into Peter's house, he saw Peter's mother-in-law lying in bed with
a fever. 15He touched her hand and the fever left her, and she got up and began to wait
on him.

COMMENTARY

14–15 In Mark 1:29–31 and Luke 4:38–39, this incident follows the driving out of a demon on a Sabbath from a man in the synagogue at Capernaum. Presumably this healing takes place on that same Sabbath. Matthew, however, condenses the account by omitting what does not bear on his immediate theme—Jesus' authority.

Peter was married (1Co 9:5) and had moved with his brother Andrew from their home in Bethsaida (Jn 1:44) to Capernaum, possibly to remain near Jesus (Mt 4:13). His mother-in-law's fever (v.14) may have been malarial; fever itself was considered a disease, not a symptom, at that time (cf. Jn 4:52; Ac 28:8). Jewish halakah forbade touching persons with many kinds of fever (Str-B, 1:479–80). But Jesus healed with a touch (v.15). As in v.3, the touch did not defile the healer but healed the defiled.

The imperfect *diēkonei* (GK *1354*) is best taken as conative: "began to serve," almost certainly a reference to waiting on him. Matthew mentions her service, not to tell his readers that those touched by Jesus become his servants (contra P. Lamarche, "La guérison de la belle-mère de Pierre et le genre littéraire des évangiles," *NRTh* 87 [1965]: 515–26), but to make it clear that the miracle was effective and instantaneous (cf. v.26, where the result of Jesus' stilling the storm is complete calm). Jesus' authority instantly accomplishes what he wills.

d. Many at evening (8:16–17)

[16]When evening came, many who were demon-possessed were brought to him, and he drove out the spirits with a word and healed all the sick. [17]This was to fulfill what was spoken through the prophet Isaiah:

"He took up our infirmities
and carried our diseases."

COMMENTARY

16 Because the context is still the Sabbath in Mark 1:32–34 and Luke 4:40–41, mention of the evening there suggests that the people waited until Sabbath was over at sundown before again flocking to Jesus with their sick. Here in Matthew, where there is no indication this is a Sabbath, mention of the evening simply shows the pace of Jesus' ministry (cf. other summaries—4:23–24; 9:35; 11:4–5; 12:15; 14:35; 15:30; 19:2).

With the exception of the quotation from Isaiah 53 in v.17, most of Matthew's other changes are not very significant. The addition of "a word" is neither typical (vv.3, 8) nor atypical (v.15) of Matthew's healing reports. The change from "many" (Mark) to "all" (Matthew) is less significant than is often claimed, for Mark does not say Jesus healed many but not all the sick; rather, when "the whole town gathered at the door," he healed "many" of the people (Mk 1:33–34). Matthew does not say that Jesus forbade the demons to tell who he was; he prefers to focus attention on Jesus' power and on the Scripture witness to his person and ministry. Other differences are even more minor. (Omission of Lk 4:41 may tell against Kingsbury's view of the centrality of the "Son of God" theme.)

Jesus drives out *ta pneumata* ("the spirits" ["demons" in Mark and Luke]), often recognized in intertestamental literature as agents of disease. They are normally qualified by the adjective "evil" in the NT. On the idiom for "the sick," see comments at 4:24.

17 On the fulfillment formulas, see comments at 1:23; 2:5, 15, 23; 4:14; Introduction, section 11.b.

This quotation is Isaiah 53:4. Matthew's rendering does not follow LXX or Targum, both of which spiritualize the Hebrew. Most likely, v.17 is Matthew's own translation of the Hebrew (Stendahl, *School of St. Matthew*, 106–7). Because Isaiah 52:13–53:12, the fourth "Servant Song," pictures the Servant suffering vicariously for others, whereas, on the face of it, Matthew renders the Hebrew in such a way as to speak of "taking" and "carrying" physical infirmities and physical diseases but not in terms of suffering vicariously for sin, many detect in this passage strong evidence that Matthew cites the OT in an indefensible and idiosyncratic fashion. McConnell (*Law and Prophecy*, 120) sees this as another instance of Matthew's using an OT passage out of context for his own ends (cf. Rothfuchs, *Erfüllungszitate*, 70–72). McNeile suggests Isaiah 53:4 had already become detached from its context when Matthew used it.

There are, however, better ways of interpreting this passage:

1. It is generally understood since the work of C. H. Dodd (*According to the Scriptures* [London: Nisbet, 1952]) that when the NT quotes a brief OT passage, it often refers implicitly to the entire context of the quotation. This is very likely here, for Matthew has a profound understanding of the OT. Moreover, Isaiah 53:7 is probably alluded to in Matthew 27:12, Isaiah 53:9 in 27:57, and Isaiah 53:10–12 in 20:28, the last in a context affirming vicarious atonement theology. Any interpretation of v.17 that does not take into account the thrust of the entire Servant Song is therefore dubious.

2. Both Scripture and Jewish tradition understand that all sickness is caused, directly or indirectly, by sin (see comments at 4:24; cf. Gundry, *Use of the Old Testament*, 230–31). This encourages us to look for a deeper connection between v.17 and Isaiah 53:4.

3. Isaiah is thinking of the servant's "taking the diseases of others upon himself through his suffering and death for their sin" (Gundry, *Use of the Old Testament*, 230). The two verbs he uses are *nāśāʾ* ("took up [our infirmities]") and *s*[e]*bālām* ("carried [our sorrows]"), which do not themselves necessarily have the force of substitution, though they can be interpreted that way. The LXX spiritualizes "infirmities" to "sins"; and in this sense the verse is referred to in 1 Peter 2:24 in defense of substitutionary atonement. That interpretation of the verse is legitimate because the flow of the Servant Song supports it. But strictly speaking, Isaiah 53:4 simply speaks of the Servant's bearing infirmities and carrying sicknesses; and it is only the context, plus the connection between sickness and sin, which shows that the way he bears the sickness of others is through his suffering and death.

4. Isaiah 53, as we have seen, is important among NT writers for understanding the significance of Jesus' death (e.g., Ac 8:32–33; 1Pe 2:24); but when Matthew here cites Isaiah 53:4, at first glance he applies it only to Jesus' healing ministry, not to his death. But in the light of the three preceding points, the discrepancy is resolved if Matthew holds that *Jesus' healing ministry is itself a function of his substitutionary death*, by which he lays the foundation for

destroying sickness. Matthew's two verbs, contrary to some opinion, exactly render the Hebrew: the Servant "took up" (*elaben*, GK *3284*) our infirmities and "carried" (*ebastasen*, GK *1002*) our diseases (Gundry, *Use of the Old Testament*, 109, 111). Matthew could not have used the LXX and still referred to physical disease. Yet his own rendering of the Hebrew, far from wrenching Isaiah 53:4 out of context, indicates his profound grasp of the theological connection between Jesus' healing ministry and the cross.

5. That connection is supported by various collateral arguments. The prologue insists Jesus came to save his people from their sin, and this within the context of the coming of the kingdom. When Jesus began his ministry, he not only proclaimed the kingdom but healed the sick (see comments at 4:24). Healing and forgiveness are tied together, not only in a pericope such as 9:1–8, but by the fact that the consummated kingdom, in which there is no sickness, is made possible by Jesus' death and the new covenant that his death enacted (26:27–29). Thus the healings during Jesus' ministry can be understood not only as the foretaste of the kingdom but also as the fruit of Jesus' death. It could be that Matthew also judges Isaiah 53:4 appropriate because it seems to form a transition from the Servant's being despised to his suffering and death. Certainly at least some rabbinic tradition understood Isaiah 53:4 to refer to physical disease (cf. Str-B, 1:481–82).

6. This means that for Matthew, Jesus' healing miracles pointed beyond themselves to the cross. In this, he is like the evangelist John, whose "signs" similarly point beyond themselves.

7. But even here there is a deeper connection than first meets the eye. These miracles (ch. 8) have been framed to emphasize Jesus' authority. This authority was never used to satisfy himself (cf. 4:1–10). He healed the despised leper (8:1–4), a Gentile centurion's servant who was hopelessly ill (vv.5–13), and other sick people (vv.14–15), no matter how many (vv.16–17). Thus when he gave his life as a ransom for many (20:28), it was nothing less than an extension of the same authority directed toward the good of others (cf. Hill, "Son and Servant," 9, 11, who also points out how reductionistic Kingsbury's "Son of God" Christology is in light of such intertwining themes). Jesus' death reflected the intermingling of authority and servanthood already noted (e.g., 3:17) and now progressively developed. After all, following the momentous miracles of vv.1–17, the Son of Man had nowhere to lay his head (v.20).

Despite the stupendous signs of kingdom advance, the royal King and Suffering Servant faced increasingly bitter opposition. The Father had committed everything to him, but he was gentle and humble in heart (11:27, 29). This moving theme needs to be traced out inductively (cf. B. Gerhardsson, "Gottes Sohn als Diener Gottes: Messias, *Agape* und Himmelherrschaft nach dem Matthäus-evangelium," *ST* 27 [1973]: 73–106). If the Davidic Messiah of Jewish expectation (*Pss. Sol.* 17:6) purifies his people by annihilating sinners, Matthew's Davidic Messiah–Suffering Servant purifies his people with his death, takes on himself their diseases, and opens fellowship to sinners (cf. Hummel, *Auseinandersetzung*, 124–25).

8. One cannot fail to observe that of the many healing miracles Matthew could have related in the first half of this chapter, he has focused on a leper, a Gentile, and a woman. The leper was ceremonially unclean and therefore an outcast; the Roman centurion, though a man of status within Roman legions, was a Gentile and therefore without religious status in this Jewish context; as a woman, Peter's mother-in-law would have been excluded from some privileges and responsibilities open only to males. But they are the ones whose healing Matthew reports.

This discussion does not resolve two related questions.

1. Did Jews in Jesus' day understand Isaiah 53 messianically? Most scholars say no. Joachim Jeremias answers more cautiously—namely, many Jews did so interpret Isaiah's "Servant" but ignored references to his suffering (cf. J. Jeremias and W. Zimmerli, *The Servant of the Lord* [London: SCM Press, 1965]).

2. Did Jesus interpret his own ministry in terms of the Suffering Servant? Verse 17 does not help us because it gives us no more than Matthew's understanding of the significance of Jesus' healing miracles. (See comments at 20:28; cf. Hooker, *Jesus and the Servant*; T. W. Manson, *The Servant Messiah* [Cambridge: Cambridge Univ. Press, 1953], 57–58, 73.)

This discussion cannot be used to justify healing on demand. This text and others clearly teach that there is healing in the atonement; but similarly there is the promise of a resurrection body in the atonement, even if believers do not inherit it until the Parousia. From the perspective of the NT writers, the cross is the basis for all the benefits that accrue to believers, but this does not mean that all such benefits can be secured at the present time on demand, any more than we have the right and power to demand our resurrection bodies. The availability of any specific blessing can be determined only by appealing to the overall teaching of Scripture.

2. The cost of following Jesus (8:18–22)

OVERVIEW

Compare Luke 9:57–62, in a later but detached setting, with three inquirers, not two. The stilling-of-the-storm incident (vv.23–27; Mk 4:35–41), following the "day of parables," shows that v.18 parallels Mark 4:35. Matthew does not specify the time of this pericope (vv.18–22) beyond saying that it was one of many occasions when crowds pressed Jesus. Apparently Matthew chose to insert these two vignettes here because they help show the nature of Jesus' ministry and the disciples he was seeking. M. Hengel's attempt (*Nachfolge und Charisma* [Berlin: Topelmann, 1968], 68–70) to limit to a few selected individuals Jesus' call to discipleship is insensitive to Jesus' place in the history of redemption and the ambiguity of what it meant at that time to be his disciple (see comments below).

18When Jesus saw the crowd around him, he gave orders to cross to the other side
of the lake. 19Then a teacher of the law came to him and said, "Teacher, I will follow you
wherever you go."
20Jesus replied, "Foxes have holes and birds of the air have nests, but the Son of Man
has no place to lay his head."
21Another disciple said to him, "Lord, first let me go and bury my father."
22But Jesus told him, "Follow me, and let the dead bury their own dead."

COMMENTARY

18–19 Perhaps Jesus' imminent departure to the east side of the lake prompted certain people to beg him to include them in the circle of disciples going with him. Discipleship in the strict sense required close attachment to the master's person. The fact that the first candidate was "a [*heis*, "one," can have the force of *tis*, "a certain," in NT Greek: cf. Zerwick, *Biblical Greek*, para. 155; Moule, *Idiom Book*, 125] teacher of the law" (see comments at 2:4) has led to no little controversy; for it is often argued that the opponents in Matthew are Pharisees and scribes ("teachers of the law"), yet here a scribe appears as a candidate for discipleship. Rolf Walker (*Heilsgeschichte*, 26–27) and others say Jesus rejected this teacher of the law (v.19). By comparison with the next inquirer, he is neither called a disciple nor told to follow Jesus (vv.21–22). But this reasoning will not stand up.

1. "Disciple" (*mathētēs*, GK *3412*) does not necessarily refer to a fully committed follower and cannot have that force in v.21 (see comments at 5:1). Albright and Mann dislike this fact so much that they are reduced to emending the text. It is difficult to see why a wedge should be drawn between the two inquirers, both "disciples" in this loose sense.

2. Verse 21 reads "Another disciple," implying that the teacher of the law was also a disciple in this loose sense. Moreover, *heteros* ("another," sometimes "another of a different kind") cannot normally be distinguished in the NT from *allos* ("another," sometimes "another of the same kind"), and certainly not in Matthew (cf. BDAG, 399).

3. Judged by their respective approaches to Jesus, if either of the two people approaches Jesus with no hesitation, it is the teacher of the law, not the "other disciple." Significantly, the scribe, a teacher of the law, addressed Jesus as "teacher" and simply promised to follow him anywhere.

4. In this light, Jesus' response to the second man—"Follow me"—does not mean he is preferred but is necessary precisely because the inquirer is not at this time planning to follow Jesus.

Scholars who reject the reconstruction of Walker and others argue that Matthew, far from being opposed to teachers of the law, has positive things to say about them (v.19; 13:52; 23:8–10, 34), some of which even suggest that Matthew's church had leaders who called themselves "teachers of the law" (cf. Grundmann; Hummel, *Auseinandersetzung*, 27; Kilpatrick, *Origins*, 110ff.).

But this reverse argument is too strong. What other categories could Jesus have used for his church's future leaders than those already established (13:52; 23:34)? A great deal of the reconstructed Matthean church hangs by the thread of overdrawn exegesis. But these scholars have correctly pointed out that vv.19–20 and similar passages show that Matthew is not in principle anti-scribe or anti-anyone else. Rather, in Matthew's view, all people, scribes or not, divide around the absolute claims of Jesus and must be weighed according to their response to him (cf. van Tilborg, *Jewish Leaders*, 128–31). This is the fruit, not of anti-Semitism (see comments at 26:57–68), but of claims to truth and, like other matters judged offensive by both Jews and Gentiles (1Co 1:21–23), cannot be eliminated without relativizing truth and him who is the truth.

20 Jesus' response shows that he identifies the scribe's request as less the commitment of an Ittai (2Sa 15:21) than the overconfidence of a Peter (Lk 22:33). "Nothing has done more harm to Christianity than the practice of filling the ranks of Christ's army with every volunteer who is willing to make a little profession, and talk fluently of experience" (J. C. Ryle, *Matthew*, in *Expository Thoughts on the Gospels* [repr., Grand Rapids: Baker, 1977], 1:78). "Nothing was less aimed at by our Lord than to have *followers*, unless they were genuine and sound; he is as far from desiring this as it would have been easy to attain it" (Stier, *Words of the Lord Jesus*, 1:354, emphasis his). Jesus' reply says nothing about the inquirer's response. Strictly speaking, it was neither invitation nor rebuke but a pointed way of saying that true discipleship to the "Son of Man" (see Reflections, below) is not comfortable and should not be undertaken without counting the cost (cf. Lk 14:25–33). In the immediate context of Jesus' ministry, the saying does not mean that Jesus was penniless but homeless; the nature of his mission kept him on the move (cf. 4:23–25; 9:35–38) and would keep his followers on the move.

21–22 For the significance of the reference to "disciples," see comments at vv.19–20. If the scribe was too quick in promising, this "disciple" was too slow in performing (v.21). Palestinian piety, basing itself on the fifth commandment (Ex 20:12; cf. Dt 27:16), expected sons to attend to the burial of their parents (cf. Tob 4:3; 14:10–11; *m. Ber.* 3:1; see Ge 25:9; 35:29; 50:13). Jesus' reply used paradoxical language (as in 16:25): Let the (spiritually) dead bury the (physically) dead (see Notes). Yet the response seems harsh to many interpreters; thus they understand the inquirer to be requesting a delay to wait for an aged parent to die rather than a delay to bury a father who has died. Hebrew or Aramaic could mean that, Greek only with difficulty, and it is difficult to see how it makes Jesus' answer (v.22) more compassionate. Though in the OT, certain people were not permitted to come into contact with corpses (Lev 21:1–12; Nu 6:7), it is doubtful that Jesus saw his followers as priests or Nazirites needing special ceremonial safeguards (contra Trench, *Studies in the Gospels*, 169). More likely, vv.21–22 provide a powerful way of expressing the thought in 10:37—even closest family ties must not be set above allegiance to Jesus and the proclamation of the kingdom (Lk 9:60).

In actuality, we may well question whether Jesus was really forbidding attendance at the father's funeral, any more than he was really advocating self-castration in 5:27–30. In this inquirer he detected insincerity, a qualified acceptance of Jesus' lordship. And that was not good enough. Commitment to Jesus must be without reservation. Such is the importance Jesus himself attached to his own person and mission.

NOTES

22 Black (*Aramaic Approach*, 207–8) suggests that the original Aramaic may have read "Let the מְתִּנִיִּין [*m*e*tinîyn*, 'waverers'] bury their מִיתִיהוֹן [*mîtîhûn*, 'dead']"—and the first of the two Aramaic words has been mistakenly translated as if it were from מִיתִין (*mîtîn*, "corpses"). But like many of Black's suggestions, though philologically plausible, these hardly help explain the text and are hampered by the implausible thesis that Matthew (or some unknown person in the process of the oral tradition) was rather incompetent in Hebrew and Aramaic.

REFLECTIONS: "THE SON OF MAN" AS A CHRISTOLOGICAL TITLE

During the last fifty years, dozens of books and scores of important articles on the Son of Man have appeared. My reflections here on the Son of Man as a christological title will provide some of the evidence and its interpretation in this debate and will sketch in the approach adopted for the commentary. Good summaries of earlier treatments are found in the works of A. J. B. Higgins, *Jesus and the Son of Man* [London: Lutterworth, 1964]), J. Neville Birdsall ("Who Is This Son of Man?" *EvQ* 42 [1970]: 7–17), and I. H. Marshall ("The Son of Man in Contemporary Debate," *EvQ* 42 [1970]: 67–87).

Treatments of the term and its major theological implications may be found in the works and bibliographies of C. Colpe (*TDNT*, 8:400–477), C. F. D. Moule (*Origin of Christology*, 11–22), I. H. Marshall (*The Origins of Christology* [Downers Grove, Ill.: InterVarsity, 1976], 63–82), the essays edited by R. Pesch and R. Schnackenburg (*Jesus und der Menschensohn* [Freiburg: Herder, 1975]), L. Goppelt (*Theologie des Neuen Testaments*, 226–53), G. E. Ladd (*Theology of the New Testament*, 145–58), J. D. G. Dunn (*Christology*, 65–97), D. Guthrie (*New Testament Theology*, 270–82), Matthew Black ("Jesus and the Son of Man," *JSNT* 1 [1978]: 4–18), G. N. Stanton (*Jesus of Nazareth*, 156ff.), and A. J. B. Higgins (*The Son of Man in the Teaching of Jesus* (Cambridge: Cambridge Univ. Press, 1980).

To this can be added works by Maurice Casey (see his 1980 and 2007 volumes). The best recent summary of the debate is in the commentary by Davies and Allison. The comprehensive volume by Delbert Burkett (*The Son of Man Debate: A History and Evaluation* [Cambridge: Cambridge Univ. Press, 2000]) is less reliable.

The expression "Son of Man" occurs eighty-one times in the Gospels, sixty-nine in the Synoptics. In every instance it is found either on Jesus' lips or, in two instances, on the lips of those quoting Jesus (Lk 24:7; Jn 12:34). Outside the Gospels it is found in the NT as a christological title only in Acts 7:56; Revelation 1:13; 14:14 (Heb 2:6–8 is not relevant). The gospel occurrences are usually classified according to the themes associated with the title: (1) the apocalyptic Son of Man who comes at the end of the age, (2) the suffering and dying Son of Man, and (3) the earthly Son of Man, engaged in a number of present ministries (in this context the title may serve as a circumlocution for "I"). Ladd (*Theology of the New Testament*, 149–51) offers a typical breakdown of all the passages. There is some overlap of these categories and room for differences of interpretation. But of the thirty occurrences of "Son of Man" in Matthew, approximately thirteen belong to the first category (13:41; 16:27; 19:28; 24:27, 30 [2x], 37, 44; 25:31; 26:64; probably 24:39; and possibly 10:23; 16:28), ten to the second (12:40; 17:9, 12, 22; 20:18, 28; 26:2, 24 [2x], 45), and seven to the third (8:20; 9:6; 11:19; 12:8, 32; 13:37; probably 16:13; cf. the variant at 18:11).

The meaning of any term or title depends at least in part on the way it has been used before. Much of the debate surrounding the precise significance of "Son of Man" in the Gospels turns on the influence ascribed to one or the other of the following backgrounds.

1. Daniel 7:13–14 pictures "one like a son of man" who approaches the Ancient of Days and is given "authority, glory and sovereign power" and "an everlasting dominion that will not pass away" in which "all peoples, nations and men of every language" worship him.

2. In Psalm 8:4, it is used generically for human beings.

3. In Ezekiel, it appears repeatedly in the vocative as God's favorite way of addressing the prophet.

4. Psalm 80:17 places "son of man" in the context of vine imagery in such a way that it clearly refers to the nation Israel.

5. In 1QapGen 21:13 it appears as a Semitism for humankind generically ("I will make your descendants as the dust of the earth, which no son of man can number"). According to G. Vermès ("The Use of רב אשׁנ רב שׁנ in Jewish Aramaic," appendix E, in Black, *Aramaic Approach*), "son of man" or "the

son of man" in Aramaic was used in Jesus' day to refer generically to man or as a circumlocution by which a speaker might refer to himself (cf. G. Vermès, "The 'Son of Man' Debate," *JSNT* 1 [1978]: 19–32). But some of his claims must be tempered by the more sober dating and philology of Joseph A. Fitzmyer ("Another View of the 'Son of Man' Debate," *JSNT* 4 [1979]: 58–68).

6. Many detect a background in the Similitudes of Enoch (*1 En.* 37–71) or other apocalyptic literature. Some have raised grave doubts that such literature is pre-Christian, based largely on the fact that the Similitudes are not found in the Dead Sea Scrolls copy of *1 Enoch*; and if they are right, clearly the use of "Son of Man" in *1 Enoch* 37–71 cannot have influenced Jesus' use of the term (cf. Longenecker, *Christology of Early Jewish Christianity*, 82–88; Dunn, *Christology*, 67–82). The consensus among specialists of *1 Enoch*, however, is that the Similitudes were in fact written before Jesus' ministry, but that the "Son of Man" in these writings unambiguously refers to Enoch. The famous but unsupported emendation by R. H. Charles ("This is the Son of Man who was born unto Righteousness," *1 En.* 71:14) is without warrant. The text reads "Thou, O Enoch, art the Son of Man" (cf. James H. Charlesworth, *The Old Testament Pseudepigrapha and the New Testament* [Cambridge: Cambridge Univ. Press, 1985]). We thus reach an ironic conclusion: the Similitudes are pre-Christian and therefore must be considered a possible influence on Jesus' usage of "the Son of Man," but they narrowly identify the figure with Enoch, and so whatever influence they exercised cannot be more than that of model or pattern, if that.

Against such diverse backgrounds, then, how are we to understand "the Son of Man" in the NT? Numerous proposals have been made, many of which fail to explain the evidence. The following are the most important.

1. Bultmann (*Theology of the New Testament*, 1:29–31, 49) made popular the view that Jesus never used the title "Son of Man" of himself but only of another figure coming in the future; this future figure was based in Jesus' mind on the apocalyptic redeemer figure in *1 Enoch*. This idea has been developed by other scholars, who say that Jesus originally justified his authority by referring to a future apocalyptic figure who would come and vindicate him but that the church connected that figure with Jesus himself. This will not do, for even if the Similitudes are not a late addition to *1 Enoch*, the "Son of Man" figure there *may* not be an apocalyptic figure (cf. Casey, *Son of Man*, 99–112) and in any case refers primarily to Enoch. Moreover, the NT evidence connects Jesus with the Son of Man (e.g., Mk 14:62 and par.), and more important yet, any interpretation is called in question that flies in the face of the fact that the gospel writers never use the term to describe Jesus but always report it as being on Jesus' lips. On the face of it, this shows that it was Jesus' favorite self-designation and that the early church respected this, even when it did not always know what to make of it (cf. Jeremias, *New Testament Theology*, 267–68).

2. Jeremias (pp. 257–76) has argued that some of the Son of Man sayings in all three classifications are authentic; but where in synoptic parallels one gospel includes the reference to the Son of Man and another omits it (e.g., 24:39—Lk 17:27; Mt 10:32—Lk 12:8), the latter is authentic. On the last point, some have argued just the reverse (e.g., F. H. Borsch, *The Son of Man in Myth and History* [London: SCM Press, 1967]). The weakness of Jeremias's view lies primarily in the consistency with which the expression occurs on Jesus' lips alone. If evangelists were adding the title to displace "I," it is at least strange they never use the title to refer to Jesus in contexts where there is no synoptic parallel. Here it seems best to side with Borsch, though we

cannot be sure. Moreover, Jeremias's chosen background runs from Daniel 7:13–14 in a straight line through the Similitudes of Enoch to the NT. Thus he depends on an established apocalyptic Son of Man figure that the sources do not support.

3. By appealing to Aramaic background, G. Vermès (appendix E, in Black, *Aramaic Approach*) argues that only those passages are authentic in which "Son of Man" is no more than a circumlocution for "I," by which the speaker refers to himself obliquely out of modesty or humility; the other uses in the Gospels are the creation of an apocalyptically minded church. Somewhat similar stances are adopted by Casey and Lindars. Casey holds that Jesus himself used first-century Aramaic idiom, in which "son of man" was a way of referring to human beings, and that Jesus used this expression to refer to himself. Only eleven such expressions in the NT are authentic; all others are the creation of the church. Similarly Barnabas Lindars ("Jesus as Advocate: A Contribution to the Christology Debate," *BJRL* 62 [1980]: 476–97; "The New Look on the Son of Man," *BJRL* 63 [1981]: 437–62) argues that the use of the article (*ho*) in Greek, making the expression "*that* Son of Man" or "the [known] Son of Man" or "the [expected] Son of Man," shows that it was the translation of the tradition from Aramaic to Greek that gave messianic or Danielic meaning to the term. Therefore, usages reflecting such meaning cannot be authentic. Quite apart from problems surrounding the dating of the linguistic evidence (cf. Fitzmyer, "Another View"), this theory postulates a creative church and a comparatively dull Jesus even though the evangelists consistently restrict the creative use of "Son of Man" to Jesus. The more it is argued that the church exercised a creative role in the theological development of this title, the stranger it is that the evangelists themselves do not apply the term to Jesus. Moreover, however insightful this or that back-translation (from Greek to Aramaic), we cannot avoid the reality that theories that depend entirely on the credibility of back-translations are intrinsically speculative.

4. In his book *The Son of Man in the Teaching of Jesus*, A. J. B. Higgins reiterates and polishes his thesis that the "kernel" (i.e., authentic) sayings are all from Q and refer without exception to some of the future activities of the Son of Man but not to his "coming" or "coming in glory," based on the "reasonable assumption of the existence of a Son of man concept in Judaism" (p. 124), and on a strange appeal to multiple attestation even though all his "kernel" sayings originally spring from Q (p. 125). Higgins says Jesus does not so much identify himself as the Son of Man (counterevidence, such as Mk 14:62, he ascribes to the church) as confine the term "to Jesus' clothing of his message of his anticipated judicial function in the judgment in symbolic imagery" (p. 125). The theory thus falls under the strictures raised against 1 and 2.

5. C. F. D. Moule ("Neglected Features in the Problem of 'the Son of Man,'" in *Neues Testament und Kirche* [ed. Gnilka], 413ff.), in contrast to Vermès, insists that the definite article (used everywhere except Jn 5:27) proves the designation to be titular, and thus whatever Semitic construction lay behind it, it must have referred to a particular, known "Son of Man." The only candidate is the figure in Daniel 7:13–14, possibly expounded in Judaism. This figure was understood to refer in a corporate way to "the saints of the Most High" (Da 7:18); applied to Jesus, the title simultaneously affirms that he represents those saints and is a part of them. "Son of Man" is less a title than "a symbol of a vocation to be utterly loyal, even to death, in the confidence of ultimate vindication in the heavenly court.... Jesus is thus referring to the authority (whether in heaven or on earth) of true Israel, and so, of authentic Man, obedient, through thick and thin, to God's design" (Moule, *Origin of Christology*,

14). This theory has been updated by Thomas Kazen ("The Coming Son of Man Revisited," *JSHJ* 5 [2007]: 155–74).

Despite attractive features of this reconstruction, some reservations must be voiced. There appears to be more titular (indeed, messianic) force in some passages than Moule allows (e.g., Mt 16:13–20; 26:63–64); yet ironically, he may be overemphasizing the significance of the definite article, since there is evidence in the Gospels that the people of Jesus' day did not always understand the designation to refer to the "well-known" Son of Man (e.g., 16:13–30; Jn 12:34).

The best explanation attempts to avoid the reductionism that is implicit in most of the previous approaches, which too quickly rules out certain kinds of evidence or takes them as late creations of the church. Apart from the fact that in the Gospels "Son of Man" is always found on Jesus' lips, the authenticity of the Son of Man sayings stands up well under the criteria of redaction criticism (cf. R. N. Longenecker, "'Son of Man' Imagery," *JETS* 18 [1975]: 8–9; Davies and Allison).

But what did Jesus mean by the expressions? The simplest answer is that he used the term precisely because it was ambiguous; it could conceal as well as reveal (cf. E. Schweizer, "The Son of Man," *JBL* 79 [1960]: 128; Longenecker, "'Son of Man' Imagery," 10–12; Hendriksen; Marshall, *Origins of Christology*, 76–78). When Jesus vested the term with its full messianic significance, it could refer only to Daniel 7:13–14. He did this most often toward the end of his ministry when alone with his disciples and talking about eschatological events (esp. Mt 24:27, 30 and par.), or when under oath at his trial (26:63–64).

Despite the fact that the Danielic figure is often said to be a symbol for the saints of the Most High (Da 7:18), this is not certain. A good case can be made for the hypothesis that "one like a son of man" is not a symbol for the saints (7:18, 27). *He* is in the presence of the Ancient of Days; *they* are on earth during the time of the "little horn" (7:8, 21). Perhaps "one like a son of man" secures the everlasting kingdom for the saints of the Most High (cf. W. J. Dumbrell, "Daniel 7 and the Function of Old Testament Apocalyptic," *RTR* 34 [1975]: 16ff.; esp. Christopher Rowland, "The Influence of the First Chapter of Ezekiel on Jewish and Early Christian Literature" [PhD diss., Cambridge University, 1974], 95). One "like a son of man" is a representative figure, not a corporate one; and the use of the symbol of the cloud rider favors a personal rather than a corporate interpretation.

Be that as it may, the messianic import of the title in some NT passages can scarcely be doubted. But Daniel 7:13–14 did not wield such large influence on first-century Judaism that simple reference to "the Son of Man," even with the article, would be instantly taken to refer to the Messiah. John Bowker ("The Son of Man," *JTS* 28 [1977]: 19–48) has decisively shown how many Semitic passages—in Ezekiel, Psalm 8, the Targums—use the term to contrast the chasm between frail mortal man and God himself. This admirably suits a host of NT references, not only the suffering and passion texts, but others, such as Matthew 8:20. Jesus combined the two, Danielic Messiah and frail mortal, precisely because his own understanding of messiahship was laced with both themes.

We have already detected in Matthew the intermingling of Davidic Messiah and Suffering Servant. While "Son of Man" captures both authority and suffering, it is ambiguous enough that people who did not think of the Messiah in this dual way would have been mystified until after the cross. It may well have been an acceptable way for a speaker to refer to himself, in which case the titular usage could only have been discerned from the context. Moreover, it would have been extremely difficult for Jews expecting a purely political and glorious Messiah to know what the title meant, because just when they thought they had discerned its messianic significance, Jesus inserted something about the Son of Man's sufferings. This explains the perplexed question, "Who is this 'Son of Man'?" (Jn 12:34; cf. Lk 22:69–70). Even the disciples, who had at some level begun to recognize Jesus the Son of Man as Messiah (Mt 16:13–16), could not accept or comprehend Jesus' repeated assertions that the Son of Man was destined to suffer and die (16:21–23; 17:9–12, 22, and par.). Only when under oath and when it no longer mattered whether his enemies heard his clear claim to messiahship did Jesus reveal without any ambiguity at all that he, the Son of Man, was the messianic figure of Daniel 7:13–14 (Mt 26:63–64 and par.); and then his opponents did not realize that an essential part of his messiahship was suffering and death. In Jesus' ministry, "Son of Man" both reveals and conceals. Therefore, he chose it as the ideal expression for, progressively and to some extent retrospectively, revealing the nature of his person and work.

After the passion, Jesus' disciples could not help but find in his frequent earlier use of the term a messianic claim. Indeed, it is a mark of their fidelity to the separate historical stages of the unfolding history of redemption that in describing Jesus' prepassion ministry they confine the designation to the lips of Jesus alone. Thus no reader of Matthew who through the prologue knows that Jesus, though a man, is more than a man and through 16:13–20; 26:63–64 knows that the Son of Man is the Messiah could fail to see irony in 9:1–8. Jesus forgives sins and performs a miracle so that the onlookers may know that the "Son of Man" has authority on earth to forgive sins; but the people praise God because he has given such authority "to men." They are right (Jesus, the Son of Man, is mortal, a man born of woman, and heading for suffering and death), and they are wrong (they do not yet recognize him as more than a man, virgin born, and the messianic figure who appeared "as a son of man"—i.e., in human form—in one of Daniel's visions). So the interpretation that prevailed from the second century on—that "Son of Man" designates Jesus' humanity and "Son of God" his divinity—is not so much wrong as simplistic.

In 8:20, "the Son of Man" could easily be replaced by "I." Moreover, it occurs in a setting that stresses Jesus' humanity and may foreshadow his sufferings. For postpassion Christian readers, it could only speak of the Messiah's wonderful self-humiliation. For the teacher of the law (vv.18–19), Jesus' words constituted a great challenge—just how great a one could only be known after the resurrection.

3. Calming a storm (8:23–27)

OVERVIEW

Jesus' authority over nature is now displayed. He may have less shelter than the beasts and birds of nature (v.20); yet he is nature's master (cf. parallels in Mk 4:35–41; Lk 8:22–25). O. Lamar Cope's attempt (*Matthew*, 96–98) to argue that the pericope, at a pre-Matthean level, has been structured on Jonah is far from convincing. His parallels are either painfully forced ("a miraculous stilling related to the main character") or so general that it is difficult to conceive of any miraculous "stilling of the sea" story that would not fit in his list of parallels.

[23]Then he got into the boat and his disciples followed him. [24]Without warning, a furious storm came up on the lake, so that the waves swept over the boat. But Jesus was sleeping. [25]The disciples went and woke him, saying, "Lord, save us! We're going to drown!"

[26]He replied, "You of little faith, why are you so afraid?" Then he got up and rebuked the winds and the waves, and it was completely calm.

[27]The men were amazed and asked, "What kind of man is this? Even the winds and the waves obey him!"

COMMENTARY

23–25 The narrative moves forward from v.18. The order to cross the lake to escape the crowd is now carried out. A *ploion* ("boat," GK *4450*) was a vessel of almost any size and description. Here it is doubtless a fishing boat, big enough for a dozen or more men and a good catch of fish, but not large, and without sails.

Bornkamm's insight—namely, that this pericope faces Matthew's readers with the demand for greater faith (v.26) in a setting requiring total discipleship (vv.18–22; cf. Bornkamm, "Stilling of the Storm," 52–57)—has been distorted to make discipleship the exclusive concern. Because the disciples "followed" Jesus into the boat, Matthew, it is alleged (e.g., Bonnard, Hill), is using a characteristic theme, almost a technical term, to describe discipleship: those who follow Jesus need not fear, for they will be safe in any storm. But in Matthew *akoloutheō* ("follow," GK *199*), though it can refer to true followers (e.g., 4:20, 22; 9:9), often describes the action of the crowd as opposed to the disciples (e.g., 4:25; 8:1, 10; 12:15). When someone is physically following another, it is risky to invest the term with deep notions of discipleship; in 9:19 Jesus and his disciples "followed" (NIV, "went with") the ruler but were certainly not his disciples! And if "follow" is so crucial a category for Matthew, why in 8:28–34 does he omit the parallel reference to following Jesus (Mk 5:18–20)?

Tertullian (*Bapt.* 12) saw in the boat a picture of the church. Therefore, some conclude that the storm "is a threat to the boat, rather than to the disciples" because it stands for the church, "and, in particular, the church facing the upheaval of persecution (perhaps under Domitian, AD 81–96)" (Hill). But aside from the anachronistic nature of this appeal to Domitian, it is historically very doubtful whether there was widespread persecution under his reign (cf. John Sweet, *Revelation* [London: SCM Press, 1979], esp. 25–27). And is Matthew's story greatly helped by seeing danger for the boat but not the disciples? One wonders what would happen to them if the boat were destroyed.

While Matthew may have seen some kind of valid application of the principles in this pericope to his own situation, the story was for him primarily a miracle story with christological implications (see comments at vv.26–27). Some redaction critics, in their desire to interpret the gospels exclusively in terms of reconstructed church life settings instead of hearing the church's thoughtful witness to the historical Jesus, come close to undisciplined allegorizing.

It is well-known that violent squalls (the term *seismos* can refer to an earthquake or a sea storm, GK *4939*) develop quickly on Lake Galilee (v.24). The surface is more than six hundred feet below sea level, and the rapidly rising hot air draws from the southeastern tablelands violent winds whose cold air churns up the water. Those among Jesus' contemporaries who really knew the OT would remember that in it God is presented as the one who controls and stills the seas (cf. Job 38:8–11; Pss 29:3–4, 10–11; 65:5–7; 89:9; 107:23–32).

The form of the cry *Kyrie, sōson* (lit., "Lord, save!" v.25) is often thought to reflect liturgical influence (cf. Mk 4:38; Lk 8:24). But it is doubtful that the disciples all used the same words, and the verbal differences among the Synoptics may reflect not theological motivation but historical recollection of various cries (esp. if Matthew was present). This event almost certainly occurs later chronologically than Matthew's call (9:9–13; cf. Lk 5:27–32). The words of later liturgy took on this form. Yet we know almost nothing about first-century liturgy, and it is more likely that the Bible influenced the shape of liturgy than vice versa. Significantly, later textual tradition adds "us" (cf. Metzger, *Textual Commentary*, 22). The verb *sōzō* ("save") does not require a direct object, though it is difficult to see why "us" should have been eliminated if it had been there originally. The later liturgical form prefers to abandon the "us." If that form was not strong enough to control the textual tradition, is it likely that it was strong enough (let alone early enough) to control the shape of the cry in the transfer from Mark to Matthew?

26–27 "He does not chide them for disturbing him with their prayers, but for disturbing themselves with their fears" (Matthew Henry). The word *oligopistoi* ("you of little faith," v.26, GK *3899*) occurs five times in the NT (6:30; here; 14:31; 16:8; Lk 12:28; cf. the cognate noun at 17:20) and always with reference to disciples. Lack of faith among those for whom faith must be central is especially disappointing. Mark (4:40) has "Do you still have no faith?" and Matthew's "little faith" is therefore taken by many as a conscious toning down of the rebuke, perhaps because he cannot envisage discipleship apart from some faith (Gundry). But there are reasons for thinking this conclusion is somewhat hasty.

1. It may be pushing Mark's question too hard to understand it as meaning that the disciples were utterly without faith. An exasperated preacher might well berate those he regards as believing disciples with words like those in Mark precisely because he believes their conduct in the face of some crisis belies their profession of faith. The large change in meaning ascribed to Matthew may therefore rest on too pedantic an understanding of Mark. This is confirmed by Mark's not developing the notion of "disciples" who have no faith.

2. *Both* Matthew (17:17) *and* Mark (9:19) preserve sayings about the unbelieving generation that must in context be applied to Jesus' disciples.

3. The word *oligopistoi* ("you of little faith") probably does not refer merely to quantity of faith but to its poor quality (see comments at 17:20). If so, Matthew may be credited with a little more theological precision than Mark but scarcely a radically new meaning. The change from a question (Mark) to the one-word epithet *oligopistoi* (Matthew) is quite within the range of reportage in the Gospels. What Jesus' exact words were we cannot know; nor can we be certain that Matthew's only access to the event was Mark's report.

4. If Matthew were so eager to insist that true discipleship involves *some* faith and changes Mark's expression for this reason, it is strange that he would insert a verse such as 17:20 (contrast Mk 9:29). It is more likely that Matthew favors *oligopistoi* as part of his working vocabulary, but without heavy,

theological implications the demonstrable redactional tendencies of an author do not necessarily bear on questions of authenticity (see Introduction, section 2).

5. What is clear is that both Mark and Matthew set faith over against fear. Faith chases out fear, or fear chases out faith.

That the disciples could cry to Jesus for help reveals that they believed, or hoped, he could do something. More than others, they had witnessed his miracles and apparently believed he could rescue them. Jesus' rebuke is therefore not against skepticism of his ability, nor against the fear that the disciples, like others, might drown. Rather, they failed to see that the one so obviously raised up by God to accomplish the messianic work could not possibly have died in a storm while that work remained undone. They lacked faith not so much in his ability to save them as in Jesus as Messiah, whose life could not be lost in a storm, as if the elements were out of control and Jesus himself the pawn of chance. This aspect of their unbelief is hinted at in Mark and Luke; in Matthew it is rendered more explicit with the disciples' cry to save them, for here they cannot be thought to be awakening Jesus because of pique at his still being asleep. Jesus' sleep stems not only from his exhaustion (see comments at v.16) or from the Son of Man having nowhere to lay his head (v.20) but from his confidence that, to use John's language, his hour had not yet come.

The disciples' response to the miracle (v.27) does not weaken this interpretation, as if their surprise shows they were not expecting Jesus to intervene. Just as a crowd expects a magician to do his trick, yet marvels when it is done, so the disciples turn to Jesus for help, yet are amazed when he stills the storm so that there is complete calm. What kind of man is this? Readers of this gospel know the answer—he is the virgin-born Messiah who has come to redeem his people from their sins and whose mission is to fulfill God's redemptive purposes. But the disciples did not yet understand these things. They saw that his authority extended over nature and were thus helped in their faith. Yet they did not grasp the profundity of his rebuke. Indeed, wherever *oligopistos* is used in Matthew, a root cause of the "little faith" is the failure to see beyond the mere surface of things. Thus the pericope is deeply christological. Themes of faith and discipleship are of secondary importance and point to the "kind of man" (cf. BDF, para. 298 [3]) Jesus is.

It may also be that Matthew is again juxtaposing Jesus with human limitations and Jesus with God's authority, a device he so effectively uses in this gospel. As Jesus is tempted but rebukes Satan (4:1–11), as he is called the devil but drives out demons (12:22–32), so he sleeps from weariness but muzzles nature.

4. Further demonstration of Jesus' authority (8:28–9:8)

a. Exorcising two men (8:28–34)

OVERVIEW

All three synoptists (cf. Mk 5:1–20; Lk 8:26–39) place this event after the boat landed, after the storm had been stilled. Matthew's account is much shorter than the other two, and he does not refer to "Legion" or to the desire of the liberated men to follow Jesus. The central motif, Jesus' authority over the evil spirits, is accented and only lightly interwoven with other themes.

[28]When he arrived at the other side in the region of the Gadarenes, two demon-
possessed men coming from the tombs met him. They were so violent that no one could
pass that way. [29]"What do you want with us, Son of God?" they shouted. "Have you come
here to torture us before the appointed time?"
[30]Some distance from them a large herd of pigs was feeding. [31]The demons begged
Jesus, "If you drive us out, send us into the herd of pigs."
[32]He said to them, "Go!" So they came out and went into the pigs, and the whole herd
rushed down the steep bank into the lake and died in the water. [33]Those tending the pigs
ran off, went into the town and reported all this, including what had happened to the
demon-possessed men. [34]Then the whole town went out to meet Jesus. And when they
saw him, they pleaded with him to leave their region.

COMMENTARY

28 The locale seems to have been in the district controlled by the town of Gadara, near the village of Gerasa (see Notes), which lay about midpoint on the lake's eastern shore. On the adjacent hillside are ancient tombs. Probably small antechambers or caves provided some protection from the weather, and a graveyard would, apparently, prove a congenial environment for demons and render the man ceremonially defiled. This region lay in the predominantly Gentile territory of the Decapolis (see comments at 4:25). The presence of the pigs (v.30), inconceivable in a Jewish milieu, points to its Gentile background. Jesus has withdrawn here, not for ministry, but to avoid the crowds (v.18). Yet there can be no rest as long as the hosts of darkness oppose him.

On differences between Jewish and NT views of demon-possession, see Edersheim (*Life and Times*, appendix 16; cf. Str-B, 1:491–92). Matthew mentions two men; Mark and Luke only one. This pattern occurs elsewhere (20:30), making it very unlikely that Matthew changed the number because he saw an implication of more than one man in Mark's "Legion" (applied to the demons). It is even less likely that Matthew introduced the extra person to make up the legally acceptable minimum of two witnesses, since not only is the witness theme not found in either of the two Matthean pericopes (vv.28–34; 20:29–34), but here Matthew has eliminated the witness theme (cf. Mk 5:18–20). While the disciples could have served as witnesses, the best explanation is that Matthew had independent knowledge of the second man. Mention of only one by the other gospel writers is not problematic. Not only was one sufficient for the purpose at hand, but where one person is more remarkable or prominent, it is not uncommon for the Gospels to mention only that one (cf. "I saw John Smith in town today. I hadn't seen him in years"—even though both John and Mary Smith were actually seen).

The violence of these demoniacs is more fully described by Mark and Luke.

29 "While the men in the boat are doubting what manner of man this is, that even the winds and the sea obey him, the demons come to tell them" (Theophylact, cited in Broadus). They knew who Jesus was and yet remained demons; to know

Jesus yet hate him is demonic. The question the demoniacs hurled at Jesus could be either harsh or gentle, depending on context (2Sa 16:10; Mk 1:24; Jn 2:4). Here it is hateful and tinged with fear. Despite the assertions of some that the title "Son of God" had no messianic overtone before it was applied to Jesus, the title seems to have been connected with the promised Davidic Messiah (see Adela Yarbro Collins, "Mark and His Readers: The Son of God among the Jews," *HTR* 92 [1999]: 393–408; cf. 4Q246; see comments at 3:17). Here, however, the title "Son of God" is probably to be taken in its richest sense: he has authority even over the demonic world. Even if Jesus had already begun to confront them when they reacted so venomously (cf. Mk 5:7–8), there was nothing in Jesus' command in itself to betray his identity. We must suppose that the demons enjoyed some independent knowledge of Jesus' identity (cf. Ac 19:15; Ladd, *Theology of the New Testament*, 165).

The second question shows there will be a time for demonic hosts to be tortured and rejected forever (cf. Jude 6; Rev 20:10; cf. *1 En.* 16:1; *Jub.* 10:8–9; *T. Levi* 18:12, 1QS 3:24–25; 4:18–20). As the question is phrased, it recognizes that Jesus is the one who will discharge that judicial function at the "appointed time"; therefore it confirms the fullest meaning of "Son of God." That Jesus was in any sense circumscribing their activity before the appointed time (Matthew only) already shows that Jesus' driving out of demons was an eschatological function, a sign that the kingdom was dawning (cf. 12:28).

The significance of "here" is disputed. It can mean either (1) "here in this Gentile territory," reflecting "the difficulty of the church's mission in those regions of Palestine" (Hill)—but surely demon-possession was not restricted to Gentile territory (cf. 10:5, 8; 12:22–24), and "the appointed time" makes little sense in such an interpretation—or (2) "here on earth, here where we have been given some freedom to trouble men before the end." This obvious sense of the text presupposes that Jesus has come to the earth before the end. It is difficult to avoid the conclusion that Jesus' preexistence is presupposed. See Simon J. Gathercole, *The Preexistent Son: Recovering the Christologies of Matthew, Mark, and Luke* (Grand Rapids: Eerdmans, 2006).

30–31 Mark (5:13) puts the number of the herd at two thousand and says it was "there." Matthew says it was "some distance from them" (v.30), the sort of detail an eyewitness might well remember. This detail also weakens the suggestion that the pigs stampeded because of the men's convulsions. J. D. M. Derrett's proposed reconstruction ("Legend and Event: The Gerasene Demoniac: An Inquest into History and Liturgical Projection," in *Studia Biblica 1978* [ed. Livingstone], 2:63–73), based on the Romans' sacrificing of pigs and on Jewish myths connecting Gentiles with bestiality, has no textual support. There are other reasons why the demons may have pled (v.31) to be sent into the herd of pigs: (1) desire for a bodily "home"; (2) hatred of God's creatures; (3) desire to stir up animosity against Jesus. The first does not seem likely because the first thing the demons do is precipitate the death of their new "home." The second and third are more plausible, because the Gospels elsewhere show that exorcised evil spirits sometimes expressed their rage by visible acts of violence or mischief (e.g., 17:14–20 = Mk 9:14–32; cf. Josephus, *Ant.* 8.48 [2.5], often cited, but of doubtful relevance because the exorcist there commands the demon to manifest himself).

Gundry observes that the herd rushes down the slope but that in Matthew "they" (plural) die; i.e., Matthew has transformed Mark to make the demons die. Thus Jesus "tortures" the demons "before the appointed time" by sending them to the torments of hell, and Matthew thus "deals in a bit of realized eschatology." This reconstruction is far from convincing for these reasons: (1) There is no hint that the drowning of the pigs sends the demons to hell. (2) Mark also shifts from the singular—the herd rushing down the slope—to the plural—"were drowning"; the only difference is that Matthew has omitted reference to the number "two thousand." (3) But if Matthew's plural verb cannot refer back to "two thousand," its most natural subject is the word "pigs," found in this same verse (v.32). The reason Matthew does not use a singular verb for died is that it would be awkward to speak of a herd's dying. Matthew has therefore preserved Mark's pattern—single verb followed by plural verb.

32–34 The question as to why Jesus would grant the demons their desire and let them destroy the herd of pigs (v.32), the livelihood of their owners, is part of larger questions as to why human beings are possessed or why disease, misfortune, or calamity overtake us—questions only to be answered within the context of a broad theodicy outside the scope of this commentary (cf. D. A. Carson, *How Long, O Lord? Reflections on Suffering and Evil* [2nd ed.; Grand Rapids: Baker, 2006]). But the context offers some hints. He who is master of nature (vv.23–27) is also its ultimate owner (vv.28–34; cf. Ps 50:10). The "appointed time" (v.29) for full destruction of the demons' power has not yet arrived. The pigs' stampede dramatically proved that the former demoniacs had indeed been freed (v.33). But in the light of vv.33–34, the loss of the herd became a way of exposing the real values of the people in the vicinity. They preferred pigs to persons, swine to the Savior.

This ending of the pericope bears significantly on its total meaning. If the story shows once more that Jesus' ministry was not restricted to the Jews but foreshadowed the mission to the Gentiles, it likewise shows that opposition to Jesus is not exclusively Jewish. To this extent it confirms earlier exegesis (see comments at vv.11–12) that showed that opponents in Matthew are not selected on the basis of race but according to their response to Jesus.

NOTES

28 The textual evidence in all three Synoptic Gospels, though highly complex, has been well summarized by Metzger (*Textual Commentary*, 23–24). The three options are Gadara, Gerasa, and Gergesa. In Mark and Luke the textual evidence is strongest for Gerasa, probably in reference to a little village (modern Kersa or Koursi) on the eastern shore. However, there was a city of the Decapolis named Gerasa (modern Jerash) some thirty miles southeast of Galilee. Clearly that is geographically incompatible with v.32, so early copyists made emendations.

Gadara (modern Um Qeis), also a Decapolis city, was five miles southeast. Origen (*Comm. Jo* 6.41) objected to both Gerasa (as commonly understood to refer to the city thirty miles off) and Gadara for similar reasons of distance. But Josephus (*Life* 42.9) says Gadara had territory and villages on the border of the lake, and probably this included the little village of Gerasa. Indeed, coins of Gadara sometimes display a ship (cf. Schürer, *History of the Jewish People*, 2:132–36). Gadara was thus the regional or toparchic capital (cf. Sherwin-White, *Roman Society*, 128 n. 3). The external evidence in Matthew favors Gadara. For some reason, the name of the toparchic capital was preferred to Gerasa (which in Matthew enjoys only versional support).

Origen, rejecting Gerasa and Gadara, proposed Gergesa, but on entirely inadequate grounds, including doubtful etymology (see Metzger, above; Tj. Baarda, "Gadarenes, Gerasenes, Gergesenes, and the 'Diatessaron' Traditions," in *Neotestamentica et Semitica* [ed. Ellis and Wilcox, 181–97). Gergesa could also be suggested by a very guttural *r* in Gerasa. Other variants doubtless resulted from later attempts at "correction" and from mutual assimilation (cf. Lane, *Mark*, 181 n. 6; Franz Annen, *Heil für die Heiden* [Frankfurt: Knecht, 1976], 201–4).

32 The phrase κατὰ τοῦ κρημνοῦ (*kata tou krēmnou*, "down the steep bank") is a very rare instance of this preposition plus genitive in a local sense and here means "down and over" (BDF, para. 225) or "down along" (Moule, *Idiom Book*, 60).

b. Healing a paralytic and forgiving his sins (9:1–8)

OVERVIEW

Again Matthew's account is shortened (cf. Mk 2:2–12; Lk 5:17–26), the entrance through the roof having been eliminated. The interrelationships among the Synoptics in this pericope are complex. It has been shown, as Bo Reicke says, that the various narrative elements "cannot be derived from any source that did not include the essentials of the quotation elements represented by three gospels together" ("The Synoptic Reports on the Healing of the Paralytic: Matt. 9:1–8 with Parallels," in *Studies in New Testament Language* [ed. Elliott], 325; though it is doubtful that Reicke has disproved the two-source hypothesis, as he seems to think).

The shortened opening does not change this from a "miracle story" to a "controversial story" (contra Held, "Matthew as Interpreter of the Miracle Stories," 176–77). John Paul Heil ("Significant Aspects of the Healing Miracles," 276–78) has shown that the form-critical marks of a miracle story are retained. Still less is this a miracle story into which a controversy about forgiving sin has been inserted, sparked by the church's attempt to tie its own forgiving function to Jesus' ministry (so Bultmann, *History of the Synoptic Tradition*, 14–16). The pericope is exclusively christological and has nothing to do with the disciples. Form-critical categories are handled mechanically if taken a priori to require that no controversy triggered by the way Jesus performed a healing could have been passed on! Moreover, the close connections between sin and sickness (see comments at v.17) and this extension of Jesus' authority beyond healing, nature, and the demonic realm to the forgiveness of sins make the narrative internally coherent and contextually suitable.

1 Jesus stepped into a boat, crossed over and came to his own town.
2 Some men brought to him a paralytic, lying on a mat. When Jesus saw their faith, he said to the paralytic, "Take heart, son; your sins are forgiven."

3 At this, some of the teachers of the law said to themselves, "This fellow is blaspheming!"

[4]Knowing their thoughts, Jesus said, "Why do you entertain evil thoughts in your
hearts? [5]Which is easier: to say, 'Your sins are forgiven,' or to say, 'Get up and walk'? [6]But so
that you may know that the Son of Man has authority on earth to forgive sins ..." Then he
said to the paralytic, "Get up, take your mat and go home." [7]And the man got up and went
home. [8]When the crowd saw this, they were filled with awe; and they praised God, who
had given such authority to men.

COMMENTARY

1 It is unclear whether this verse ties in more closely with 8:28–34 or with 9:2–8. The problem is not just academic, for the preceding pericope is almost certainly chronologically later (cf. Mk 5:1–20) than this one (cf. Mk 2:2–12); and a break more easily fits between 9:1 and 9:2 than between 8:34 and 9:1. Begged to leave (8:34), Jesus embarked in the boat he had so recently left and returned to "his own town," namely, Capernaum (4:13), on the western shore of the lake.

A larger problem concerning synoptic interrelationships now faces us. Matthew 9:14 and Luke 5:33 show that the questions about fasting sprang from the dinner Matthew sponsored. And 9:18 shows that the healing of Jairus's daughter and of the hemorrhaging woman immediately followed. Mark 5:21–23 and Luke 8:40–44 place the raising of Jairus's daughter after Jesus returned from Gadara (as in Matthew) but the healing of the paralytic (Mk 2:2–12; Lk 5:17–26) much earlier—even though Matthew places it after Gadara and seems to tie it to the pericopes that follow in his account.

Harmonization should be avoided where details are obscure, but refusal to attempt harmonization of documents treating the same events is methodologically irresponsible. Here a fairly straightforward solution is possible. There is a significant time lapse between Matthew's calling and the dinner he gives his friends. All three synoptists put these two personally related events side by side. But significantly no synoptist makes a temporal connection between the two. The following shows the arrangement.

Time A: before Gadara	healing of a paralytic; calling of Matthew
	[TIME LAPSE: Gadara incident and others]
Time B: after Gadara	dinner given by Matthew; raising of Jairus's daughter

All Synoptics put these two events together.	Mark and Luke place these three together at Time A.	Matthew places all four together at Time B.

Thus all the Synoptics put the raising of Jairus's daughter in the correct chronological order. Mark and Luke report the healing of the paralytic and the calling of Matthew at the earlier time, when they occurred, but then link to them Matthew's dinner—a topical arrangement. Matthew connects all four together, placing them later, though there is a chronological break at vv.1–2 (see above) and again between Matthew's call and Matthew's dinner. The first evangelist has introduced the first chronological break in order to preserve the topical arrangement of his presentation of Jesus' authority, and the second break (vv.9–10), along with Mark and Luke, because of the personal connection

(Matthew's call and Matthew's dinner). This rather obvious solution is invalid only if Matthew's (and Luke's) sole source of information in this pericope is Mark. But despite some critics, this is most unlikely (see Introduction, sections 1–5).

2 Many (e.g., Hill) insist that though in Mark and Luke the paralytic is lowered through a roof, here the imperfect *prosepheron* (NASB, "they were bringing") means the paralytic and his bearers met Jesus in the street. But the imperfect tense often adds color to action (cf. the imperfect even in Luke), and little is gained by manufacturing discrepancies.

Jesus "saw" *their* faith—presumably that of the paralytic and those carrying him—exemplified in their coming. But he spoke only to the paralytic. "Son" (*teknon*) is no more than an affectionate term from one's senior (see, e.g., 1Jn 2:1, 28). What Jesus went on to say implies a close link between sin and sickness (see comments at 8:17)—perhaps in this case a direct one (cf. Jn 5:14; 1Co 11:29–30). It implies that of the two, paralysis and sin, sin is the more basic problem. The best MSS read *aphientai* ("Your sins are forgiven," GK *918*), not the perfect *apheōntai* ("Your sins have been forgiven"; see Notes). The latter might imply that the man's sins were forgiven at some time in the past and now remain forgiven.

3 Some teachers of the law (see comments at 2:4; 8:18–22) muttered among themselves that Jesus was blaspheming. It is God alone who forgives sin (Isa 43:25; 44:22), since it is against him only that men commit sin (Ps 51:4). The verb *blasphēmeō* (GK *1059*) often means "slander"; and when something is said that slanders God, the modern meaning of "blaspheme" is not far away. Though among Jews in Jesus' day the precise definition of blasphemy was hotly disputed (cf. Str-B, 1:1019–20), the consensus seemed to be that using the divine name was an essential element. Here the teachers of the law, in their whispered consultation, expanded blasphemy to include Jesus' claim to do something only God could do.

4 Jesus had seen the faith of the paralytic and his friends; now he saw the evil thoughts of some of the teachers of the law (see Notes). Such discernment may have been supernatural, though not necessarily so. In this situation, it would not have been difficult to surmise what the teachers of the law were whispering about. Jesus' charge probed beyond their talk of blasphemy to what they were thinking in their hearts. And what they were thinking was untrue, unbelieving, and blind to what was being revealed before their eyes.

5–7 Jesus did not respond to his opponents' thoughts according to the skeptical view—namely, that to say "Your sins are forgiven" is easier to say than "Get up and walk." On the contrary, he responded according to the perspective of the teachers of the law—namely, that to say "Get up and walk" is easier since only God can forgive sins. Jesus claimed to do the more difficult thing. Thus v.6 is ironical—"All right, I'll also do the lesser deed." Yet if Jesus had blasphemed in pronouncing forgiveness, how could he now perform a miracle (cf. Jn 9:31)? But so that they might know that he had authority to forgive sin, he proceeded to the easier task. The healing therefore showed that Jesus truly had authority to forgive sins. To do this is the prerogative of the "Son of Man." This expression goes beyond self-reference and, seen in the light of the postresurrection period, surely indicates that the eschatological Judge had already come "on earth" (cf. "here" in 8:29) with the authority to forgive sin (cf. Hooker, *Son of Man*, 81–93). This is the authority of Immanuel, "God with us" (1:23), sent to "save his people from their sins" (1:21). Jesus did not finish the sentence. The broken syntax (BDF, para. 483) is followed by Jesus' word of power and his command to the paralytic to go home (*hypage*, "go," is here gentle as in 8:13, not rough as in 4:10). To sum up, the healing not only cured the paralytic (v.7); it also assured him that his sins were forgiven and refuted the charge of blasphemy.

8 The external evidence for "were afraid" is early and in three text types (Alexandrian, Western, Caesarean). Copyists, failing to see the profundity of the verb, softened it to "were amazed." The NIV's "were filled with awe" implies fear but is too paraphrastic. Men *should* fear the one who has the authority to forgive sins. Indeed, they should fear whenever they are confronted by an open manifestation of God (cf. 17:6; 28:5, 10). Such fear breeds praise.

Matthew alone adds the clause "who had given such authority to men." Many argue that "to men" refers to the church and cite 16:19; 18:18 in support (e.g., Benoit; Hill). But this is unlikely. If "Son of Man" (9:6) refers to the eschatological Judge, then it is unlikely this function is to be shared with the church, at least in the same way (cf. *TDNT*, 8:405). The pericope has christological, not ecclesiastical, concerns, compatible with the prologue (1:21, 23; see comments at vv.5–7). The onlookers simply saw a man exercising the authority of God, but readers recognize him as "God with us" and eschatological "Son of Man." God's gracious reign has come "on earth" (v.6); the kingdom of David's Son, who came to save his people from their sins, has dawned.

NOTES

2 The reasons the perfect displaced the present in many MSS are clear enough: the present in Greek is often durative, which here makes little sense ("your sins are being forgiven"), and there is assimilation to Luke 5:20, where the text is firm (Mk 2:5 has a similar difficulty).

4 "Seeing their thoughts," not "knowing their thoughts," is almost certainly the correct reading, not least because the change from the former to the latter is comprehensible, but the reverse is highly unlikely. But "seeing" is obviously metaphorical, a point recognized by the KJV and NIV in their periphrastic rendering "knowing."

5. Calling Matthew (9:9)

9As Jesus went on from there, he saw a man named Matthew sitting at the tax collector's booth. "Follow me," he told him, and Matthew got up and followed him.

COMMENTARY

9 The locale is probably the outskirts of Capernaum. Matthew was sitting "at the tax collector's booth," a customs and excise booth at the border between the territories of Philip and Herod Antipas. On attitudes toward tax collectors, see comments at 5:46 (cf. Str-B, 1:377–80). Having demonstrated his authority to forgive sins (vv.1–8), Jesus now called to himself a man whose occupation made him a pariah—a sinner and an associate of sinners (cf. 1Ti 1:15).

The name "Matthew" may derive from the Hebrew behind "Mattaniah" (1Ch 9:15), meaning "gift of God," or, in another etymology, from a word meaning "the faithful" (Heb. *ʾĕmet*, GK

622). In Mark the name is "Levi" (though in Mark there are difficult textual variants), and the change to "Matthew" in the first gospel has prompted much speculation. The most radical theory is that of R. Pesch ("Levi-Matthäus," *ZNW* 59 [1968]: 40–56), who says that the first evangelist purposely substituted a name from the apostolic band because he habitually uses "disciple" for the Twelve and therefore could not allow an outsider to stand. The evangelist then made a "sinner" out of him to represent the "sinners" among the apostles. "Matthew" in the first gospel is thus reduced entirely to a redactional product. But Pesch's understanding of "disciple" is questionable (see comments at 5:1–2; 8:18–22), and his skepticism is vast.

Across the centuries, the simple equation of Levi and Matthew has been the most obvious course to take. Matthew may have been a Levite. Such a heritage would have assumed an intimate acquaintance with Jewish tradition. Mark and Luke have "Matthew" in their lists of apostles (Mk 3:18; Lk 6:15; Pesch has to say Mk 3:18 is also redactional). On the ground of the formidable onomastic evidence gathered by Tal Ilan (*Lexicon of Jewish Names in Late Antiquity: Part I: Palestine 330 BCE–200 CE* [TSAJ 91; Tübingen: Mohr, 2002]), Bauckham has argued (*Jesus and the Eyewitnesses*, 108–12) that it is unlikely that one man had two common Jewish names. Bauckham himself works through possible exceptions, judging they are either not convincing or rather rare. The better-known instances where one Jewish man has two Jewish names (e.g., 27:16–17; Ac 4:36; Josephus, *Ant.* 12.285; 18.35, 95; 20.196), commonly adduced by commentators (e.g., Gundry; Davies and Allison; Turner), Bauckham rules out of court because in each instance the second name is likely either a nickname (like "Barnabas") or a family name. Yet whatever the onomastic improbability, the identification of Levi (Mark's gospel) with Matthew (here) seems less implausible than Bauckham's explanation: the unknown evangelist knew that Matthew was a tax collector (like Levi), and knew he was one of the Twelve, and so simply transferred the story across (on the assumption that the conversion of one tax collector would be very much like the conversion of another?).

Gundry (*Use of the Old Testament*, 181–83) suggests that Matthew's work as a tax collector assured his fluency in Aramaic and Greek and that his accuracy in keeping records fitted him for note taking and later writing his gospel. Hill, following Stendahl ("Matthew," in *Peake's Commentary*), thinks it unlikely that a person living on "the despised outskirts of Jewish life" could be responsible for this gospel. But does it not also seem unlikely that "a son of thunder" should become the apostle of love, or that the archpersecutor of the church should become its greatest missionary and theologian? If Matthew wrote 9:9 regarding his own call, it is significant that it is more self-deprecating than Luke's account, which says that Matthew "left everything" and followed Jesus.

6. Eating with sinners (9:10–13)

OVERVIEW

On the chronological relation between v.9 and vv.10–13, see comments at v.1. Matthew abbreviates the account of Jesus' eating with tax collectors and sinners, excluding descriptive elements that do not contribute to the confrontation but adding an OT quotation (v.13).

[10]While Jesus was having dinner at Matthew's house, many tax collectors and "sinners" came and ate with him and his disciples. [11]When the Pharisees saw this, they asked his disciples, "Why does your teacher eat with tax collectors and 'sinners'?"

[12]On hearing this, Jesus said, "It is not the healthy who need a doctor, but the sick. [13]But go and learn what this means: 'I desire mercy, not sacrifice.' For I have not come to call the righteous, but sinners."

COMMENTARY

10–11 For more on the opening words *kai egeneto* ("and it came to pass"; NIV, "while"), see comments at 7:28–29. The Greek text does not mention "Matthew's" house, though v.9 implies it is Matthew's, and both Mark and Luke specify it (so NIV). Jesus himself had said that even a tax collector has his friends (5:46), and Matthew's dinner substantiates this. "Sinners" may include common folk who did not share all the scruples of the Pharisees (cf. *TDNT*, 1:324–25); hence the quotation marks in the NIV. But almost certainly it groups together those who broke Pharisaic halakoth (rules of conduct)—harlots, tax collectors, and other disreputable people (cf. Hummel, *Auseinandersetzung*, 22ff.). Though eating with them entailed dangers of ceremonial defilement, Jesus and his disciples did so. The Pharisees' question, put not to Jesus but to his disciples, was less a request for information than a charge, and contemptuously it lumped together tax collectors and "sinners" under one article (cf. 11:19; Lk 15:1–2 for the same attitude).

There can be little doubt that Jesus was known as a friend to tax collectors and sinners (11:19; cf. M. Volkel, "'Freund der Zöllner und Sünder,'" *ZNW* 69 [1978]: 1–10; Blomberg, *Contagious Holiness*; see Notes, 5:46).

12–13 These verses again connect Jesus' healing ministry with his "healing" of sinners (see comments at 8:17). The sick need a doctor, and Jesus healed them; likewise the sinful need mercy, forgiveness, restoration, and Jesus healed them (v.13). The Pharisees were not as healthy as they thought (cf. 7:1–5); more important, they did not understand the purpose of Jesus' mission. Expecting a Messiah who would crush the sinful and support the righteous, they had little place for one who accepted and transformed the sinner and dismissed the "righteous" as hypocrites. Jesus explained his mission in terms reminiscent of 1:21. There is no suggestion here that he went to sinners because they gladly received him; rather, he went to them because they were sinners, just as a doctor goes to the sick because they are sick.

The quotation (v.13) is from Hosea 6:6 and is introduced by the rabbinic formula "go and learn," used of those who needed to study the text further. Use of the formula may be slightly sardonic: those who prided themselves in their knowledge of and conformity to Scripture needed to "go and learn" what it means. The quotation, possibly translated from the Hebrew by Matthew himself, is cast in Semitic antithesis: "not A but B" often means "B is of more basic importance than A."

The Hebrew word for "mercy" (*ḥesed*, GK 2876) is close in meaning to "covenant love," which, according to Hosea, is more important than "sacrifice." Through Hosea, God said that the apostates of Hosea's day, though continuing the formal ritual of temple worship, had lost its center. As applied to the Pharisees by Jesus, therefore, the Hosea quotation was not simply telling them that they should be more sympathetic to outcasts and less concerned about ceremonial purity, but that they were aligned with the apostates of ancient Israel in that they too preserved the shell while losing the heart of the matter, as exemplified by their attitude to tax collectors and sinners (cf. France, *Jesus and the Old Testament*, 70). Jesus' final statement (v.13b) therefore cannot mean that he viewed the Pharisees as righteous people who did not need him, who were already perfectly acceptable to God by virtue of their obedience to his laws so that their only fault was the exclusion of others (contra Hill, *Greek Words*, 130–31). If the Pharisees were so righteous, the demand for righteousness surpassing that of the Pharisees and teachers of the law (5:20) would be incoherent.

On the other hand, it may not be exactly right to say that "righteous" is ironic here. The saying simply defines the essential nature of Jesus' messianic mission as he himself saw it. If pushed, he would doubtless have affirmed the universal sinfulness of man (cf. 7:11). Therefore, he is not dividing men into two groups but is disavowing one image of what Messiah should be and do, replacing it with the correct one. His mission was characterized by grace, a pursuit of the lost, of sinners. The verb *kalesai* ("to call," GK *2813*) means "to invite" (unlike Paul's usage, where the call is always efficacious). By implication, those who do not see themselves in the light of Jesus' mission not only fail to grasp the purpose of his coming but exclude themselves from the kingdom's blessings.

If Matthew does not add "to repentance" after "sinners" (as Lk 5:32), it is not because he is disinterested in repentance (cf. 3:2; 4:17). Rather, the words are not in his principal source (Mark) and do not contribute to his present theme.

Hosea 6:6 is also quoted in 12:7, again in a context challenging the Pharisees' legal scruples. Cope (*Matthew*, 68–70) suggests that the verse reveals a contrast between the substantial demands of mercy and merely legal and ceremonial piety, a contrast traceable in the following pericopes (vv.14–17, 18–26, 27–34, 35–38). But his evidence is slightly overdrawn. In vv.27–34, for instance, vv.27–31 raise no overt hints of ceremonial defilement.

7. Fasting and the dawning of the messianic joy (9:14–17)

14Then John's disciples came and asked him, "How is it that we and the Pharisees fast,
but your disciples do not fast?"
15Jesus answered, "How can the guests of the bridegroom mourn while he is with
them? The time will come when the bridegroom will be taken from them; then they will
fast.
16"No one sews a patch of unshrunk cloth on an old garment, for the patch will pull
away from the garment, making the tear worse. 17Neither do men pour new wine into old
wineskins. If they do, the skins will burst, the wine will run out and the wineskins will be
ruined. No, they pour new wine into new wineskins, and both are preserved."

COMMENTARY

14 Mark (2:18–22; cf. Lk 5:33–39) says that both the Pharisees and the disciples of John were fasting—probably on one of the regularly observed but voluntary fast days (see comments at 4:2; 6:16–18)—and that "some people" asked this question. Luke makes it the Pharisees, Matthew the disciples of John. On the face of it (see Luke), the setting is the same as for the previous pericope, and regarding fasting, the disciples of John are in accord with the Pharisees. The Baptist himself showed a noble freedom from jealousy when Jesus' ministry began to supersede his own (cf. esp. Jn 3:26–31). But some of John's disciples felt differently now that he was in prison (4:12), and because they kept up their leader's asceticism (11:18), not heeding his strong witness to Jesus, they saw an occasion for criticism.

Most modern commentators believe that here Matthew is referring to the Baptist's followers who never accepted Jesus' supremacy and who by the end of the first century had developed their own sect. Doubtless Matthew would have cheerfully applied Jesus' response to them also. But there is no reason to deny that this incident happened during Jesus' ministry. Moreover, after the bridegroom was taken away (v.15), Jesus' disciples often fasted (e.g., Ac 13:3; 14:23; 27:9), making it less likely that these Baptist sectarians would have leveled their charge after the passion and resurrection than before it. Just as the "questioners" (accusers?) had approached Jesus' disciples about his conduct (v.11), so now questioners approached Jesus about his disciples' conduct.

15 In his response, Jesus used three illustrations (Lk 5:39 adds a fourth), all given in the same order by the Synoptics. There seems little to be gained by supposing that the sayings were at one time separate.

The first illustration about the "guests of the bridegroom" (lit., "the sons of the bridal chamber"; see comments at 5:9; 8:12) picks up a metaphor from the Baptist, who saw himself as the "best man" and Jesus as the groom (Jn 3:29). This similar metaphor would therefore be the more effective to this audience—Jesus is the groom and the disciples his "guests" who are so overjoyed at being with him that for them to fast is inappropriate.

In exonerating his disciples' eating, Jesus used messianic-eschatological terms. In the OT, the bridegroom metaphor was repeatedly applied to God (Isa 54:5–6; 62:4–5; Hos 2:16–20); and Jews sometimes used it of marriage in connection with Messiah's coming or with the messianic banquet (cf. Str-B, 1:500–518; in the NT, cf. Mt 22:2; 25:1; 2Co 11:2; Eph 5:23–32; Rev 19:7, 9; 21:2). Thus Jesus' answer was implicitly christological: he himself is the messianic bridegroom, and the messianic age has dawned.

The objection is often made that the second part of Jesus' answer, regarding the disciples' mourning once the groom is "taken" (*aparthē* may bear overtones of Isa 53:8 LXX) from them, is not authentic on two chief grounds.

1. Such an obvious reference to the passion (and ascension?) comes too early in Jesus' ministry. Some try to avoid this objection by supposing that Jesus was saying no more than that he, like other men, must die sometime. Neither the objection nor its proposed solution is relevant to one who has already revealed so formidable a messianic self-consciousness.

2. Matthew has allegorized the original parable—a sign of late accretion or adaptation. Yet this simplistic view of "parable" will not withstand scrutiny (see comments at 13:3a). Above all, the language is so cryptic that it is doubtful whether even Jesus' disciples grasped the messianic implications of these words until the early weeks of the postresurrection church.

16–17 Luke 5:36 labels these illustrations a "parable." In general terms, the first of this pair is clear enough: a piece of unshrunk cloth tightly sewed to old and well-shrunk cloth in order to repair a tear will cause a bigger tear (v.16). Admittedly, the grammar is difficult (see Notes). The second (v.17) is also a "slice of life" in the ancient world. Skin bottles for carrying various fluids were made by killing the chosen animal, cutting off its head and feet, skinning the carcass, and sewing up the skin, fur side out, to seal off all orifices but one (usually the neck). The skin was tanned with special care to minimize disagreeable taste. In time, the skin became hard and brittle. If new wine, still fermenting, were put into such an old skin, the buildup of fermenting gases would split the brittle container and ruin both bottle and wine. New wine was placed only in new wineskins still pliable and elastic enough to accommodate the pressure.

These illustrations show that the new situation introduced by Jesus could not simply be patched onto old Judaism or poured into the old wineskins of Judaism. New forms would have to accompany the kingdom Jesus was now inaugurating; to try to domesticate him and incorporate him into the matrix of established Jewish religion would succeed only in ruining both Judaism and Jesus' teaching.

Two extreme interpretations must be avoided.

1. Some, noticing that the words "and both are preserved" (v.17) are found only in Matthew, conclude that this first gospel, unlike Mark, envisages the renewal and preservation of Judaism, not its abolition. This will not do. The "both" that are preserved refers to the new wine and the new wineskins, not the old wineskins. Jesus' teaching and the kingdom now dawning must be poured into new forms. Matthew makes it at least as clear as does Mark that the new wine can be preserved only in new forms. Is it any surprise that Matthew includes explicit mention of the church (16:18; 18:17)?

2. Some dispensationalists are inclined to make this wine so new that there is no connection whatsoever with what has come before. Walvoord (70) cites Ironside: "[Jesus] had not come to add something to the legal dispensation but to supersede it with that which was entirely new.... The new wine of grace was not to be poured into the skin-bottles of legality." So sharp an antithesis is suspect on three grounds: (1) the grace-legality disjunction is greatly exaggerated; (2) it is not very obviously a set of Matthean categories; and (3) Matthew, as we have seen, repeatedly connects the OT with his own message in terms of prophecy and fulfillment.

The two parables of vv.16–17 are frequently said to be independent sayings tacked on here, since they go beyond the question of fasting. That may be, but all three synoptists put them in the same place. Moreover, they go beyond the question of fasting only to lay the groundwork for the coherence of Jesus' answer about fasting. The newness Jesus brings cannot be reduced to or contained by traditions of Jewish piety. The messianic bridegroom has come. These parables bring unavoidable and radical implications for the entire structure of Jewish religion as its leaders then conceived it. Scholars who understand the first gospel to reflect a Jewish Christian community that preserves all the old forms of piety not only misinterpret 5:17–20 but do not adequately weigh this pericope.

NOTES

16 The verb αἴρει (*airei*, "takes," "draws," "pulls," GK *149*) is consistently transitive in the active voice (BDAG, 28–29), and therefore τὸ πλήρωμα αὐτοῦ (*to plērōma autou*, lit., "its fullness"; NIV, "patch,"

GK *4445*) must be construed as the direct object, perhaps referring to the overlapping section of the patch. See the rendering of Michael G. Steinhauser ("The Patch of Unshrunk Cloth [Mt 9:16]," *ExpTim* 87 [1975–76]: 312–13): "No one puts a patch of unshrunk cloth to an old cloak, because the patch of unshrunk cloth draws the overlapping section of the unshrunk cloth from the cloak and the tear becomes worse."

8. A resurrection and more healings (9:18–34)

a. Raising a girl and healing a woman (9:18–26)

OVERVIEW

For the chronology, see comments at v.1. Matthew abbreviates Mark (Mk 5:21–43; cf. Lk 8:40–46) by almost one-third. Again, the three synoptists are very close in reporting the words of Jesus.

Gérard Rochais (*Les récits de résurrection des morts dans le Nouveau Testament* [Cambridge: Cambridge Univ. Press, 1980], 88–99) reduces the point of Matthew's account to the importance of faith. Faith is indeed an important theme (v.22) but scarcely exclusive of others. While these are best discovered inductively, we may note that in vv.18–34, Jesus performs three new kinds of miracles: raising the dead (the healing of the hemorrhaging woman is already an integral part of this account in the Markan source) and healing the blind and the dumb. The latter two appear in Matthew much earlier than in the closest parallels in Mark and Luke (see comments at vv.27–31), because his topical concerns demand it. He includes at this point these final examples of spheres over which Jesus has authority because they figure in his defense to the disciples of John the Baptist (11:2–5): the blind receive sight; the lame walk; those who have leprosy are cured; the deaf hear (deafness is usually associated with muteness); the dead are raised. Jesus' messianic credentials are thus being grouped together.

18While he was saying this, a ruler came and knelt before him and said, "My daughter
has just died. But come and put your hand on her, and she will live." 19Jesus got up and
went with him, and so did his disciples.
20Just then a woman who had been subject to bleeding for twelve years came up
behind him and touched the edge of his cloak. 21She said to herself, "If I only touch his
cloak, I will be healed."
22Jesus turned and saw her. "Take heart, daughter," he said, "your faith has healed you."
And the woman was healed from that moment.
23When Jesus entered the ruler's house and saw the flute players and the noisy crowd,
24he said, "Go away. The girl is not dead but asleep." But they laughed at him. 25After the
crowd had been put outside, he went in and took the girl by the hand, and she got up.
26News of this spread through all that region.

COMMENTARY

18–19 Matthew tightly links this narrative to the dinner in his house. Mark 5:21 provides another setting: while Jesus was by the lake, etc. This anomaly has called forth numerous explanations, mostly unsatisfactory. Some have postulated that Matthew follows another source (a desperate expedient that does not explain why he chooses to contradict Mark); others that Matthew simplifies Mark in the interests of catechesis (How is catechesis helped by a different setting almost as long as the first?); others have supposed that the dinner party in v.10 took place in a house by the lake (barely possible but artificial); still others believe that vv.14–17 should be detached from the dinner (barely possible, but artificial in light of Lk 5:33).

The best solution accepts the connection between Matthew's dinner (vv.9–13), the discussion about fasting (vv.14–17), and this miracle (vv.18–26). But the NIV rendering of Mark 5:21–22 links Jesus by the lake with the approach of the synagogue ruler ("While he was by the lake, one of the synagogue rulers ..."). The Greek does not suggest this. Syntactically, Jesus' presence by the lake terminates the thought of Mark 5:21: Jesus crossed back after the Gadara episode, a large crowd again gathered, and he was by the lake. Verse 22 then begins a new pericope without a necessary transition—which is exactly what Mark does elsewhere (e.g., 3:20, 31; 8:22; 10:46; 14:66). In some instances, such as this one (Mk 5:22; cf. 1:40), the precise division is ambiguous. But Mark's practice elsewhere encourages us to think this interpretation is right and the NIV translation wrong.

"A ruler" (see Notes), in the context of Capernaum, almost certainly refers to a synagogue ruler (v.18), a point made explicit by Mark 5:22, which also tells us his name was Jairus. He must therefore have been a Jew and a man of considerable influence in the lives of the people. He "knelt before" Jesus. The verb here does not suggest "worship" (contra KJV) but deep courtesy, a pleading homage before someone in a position to grant a favor (see comments at 2:2; 8:2).

The daughter "has just died." Mark (5:22) has "is dying"; Luke (8:42) has "was dying." Matthew, having eliminated the messengers as extraneous to his purposes, condenses "so as to present at the outset what was actually true before Jesus reached the house" (Broadus). Such is Matthew's condensed style elsewhere (see comments at 8:5).

The synagogue ruler felt Jesus' touch had special efficacy, but his faith was not as great as that of the centurion, who believed that Jesus could heal by his word (8:5–13). Jesus did not refuse this man but responded to faith, small or great. He "got up" (v.19; the word *egeirō* [GK *1586*] most likely means, in this context, "rose from reclining at table" [of v.10]; see comments on harmonization above) and "went with [*akoloutheō*, GK *199*; evidence that this verb does not necessarily imply discipleship; see comments at 8:23] him."

20–21 The nature of the woman's hemorrhage is uncertain; if, as seems probable, it was chronic bleeding from the womb, then she was perpetually unclean (cf. Lev 15:25–33). The regulation of such a woman's life was considered so important that the Mishnah devotes an entire tractate to the subject (*Zabim*) and gives some of the "remedies" for stanching the flow. Having heard of others who had been healed at Jesus' touch, this woman decided to touch even a tassel of Jesus' cloak (v.21). Moved in part by a superstitious view of Jesus, she struggled through the crowd, which, because of her "unclean" condition, she should have avoided.

The word *kraspedon* (GK *3192*) can mean either "edge" or "tassel." The former may be the meaning here (so NIV), but the latter is certainly the meaning in 23:5. Tassels (Heb. *ṣîṣit*, GK 7492) were sewn on the four corners of every Israelite's cloak (Nu 15:37–41; Dt 22:12) as reminders to obey God's commands. While the tassels could easily become mere showpieces (23:5), Jesus himself, like any male Jew, doubtless wore them.

22 Though Matthew's account is again abbreviated, various explanations—e.g., short accounts are easier to memorize (Hill) or Matthew eliminates magical elements (Hull, *Hellenistic Magic*, 136–37)—are less convincing than the obvious one: Matthew keeps only what is of most interest to him. The account is so short that it is not entirely clear whether Jesus turned and saw the woman before or after she touched him. The parallel accounts say the latter, and this may well be reflected in the perfect tense "your faith has healed you." The woman was healed after touching Jesus' cloak. He said that it was her faith that was effective, not the superstition mingled with it.

This seems better than the view that holds that Jesus first encouraged the woman ("Take heart, daughter") and then healed her without any reference to touching. Matthew 9:2; 14:27 are cited as parallels for this order. In fact, the three incidents differ somewhat; 9:2 according to the best variant says, in effect, "Take heart, for I now forgive you"; 9:22 says, "Take heart, for you have now been healed"; and 14:27 is quite different, since "Take heart" logically relates to "It is I," and the miracle of the calming of the wind is yet future. The final clauses of v.22 should therefore be interpreted to mean, not that the woman was healed from the "moment" Jesus spoke, but that she was healed from the *hōra* (lit., "hour," GK *6052*) of this encounter with Jesus.

23–26 Flute players were employed both on festive occasions (Rev 18:22) and at funerals. Matthew alone mentions them, not so much because he had special knowledge of Jewish funeral customs (cf. *m. Ketub.* 4:4, which required even a poor family to hire two flute players and one professional wailing woman), but out of personal recollection. Jesus was about to reverse funeral symbolism of the finality of death. The "noisy crowd" was made up of friends mourning, not in the hushed whispers characteristic of our Western funerals, but in loud outbursts of grief and wailing augmented by cries of hired mourners. Jesus' miracle not only brought a corpse to life (v.24) but hope to despair.

"Laughed" (*katagelaō*, GK *2860*) occurs only here (v.24) and in the synoptic parallels. The crowd mocked Jesus, not just because he had said, "The girl is not dead but asleep," but even more because they thought this great healer had arrived too late. Now he was going too far. Carried away by his own success, he would try his skill on a corpse and make a fool of himself. In such a situation, Jesus' words became, in retrospect, all the more profound. They not only denied that death—confronted by his power—was final; they also assumed that, contrary to the Sadducean view (22:23), "sleep" better described the girl's condition. In the Bible, "sleep" often denotes "death" but never "nonexistence" (cf. Da 12:2; Jn 11:11; Ac 7:60; 1Co 15:6, 18; 1Th 4:13–15; 2Pe 3:4).

The mocking crowd was ejected from the house (v.25). Matthew does not tell us, as Mark does, that the five witnesses remained; nor does he give us Jesus' words. But Matthew says that Jesus touched the corpse, and the body, far from defiling him, came to life. By itself, the miracle did not prove Jesus to be more than a prophet or an apostle (cf. 1Ki 17:17–24; 2Ki 4:17–37; Ac 9:36–42). But prophets and apostles never claimed to be more than their office indicated. Jesus made vastly greater claims; so for Matthew the miracle showed that Jesus' authority as the Christ extended even over the dead.

NOTES

18 Ἄρχων εἷς (*archōn heis*) is a relatively rare but not unknown way of saying "a ruler" or "a certain ruler," *heis* (lit., "one") functioning more or less like the enclitic τις (*tis*, "a certain"). Interpretation is compounded by complex variants, probably generated not only by the rarity of the construction but the ambiguity of Uncial texts: ΕΙΣΕΛΘΩΝ could be read εἷς ἐλθών (*heis elthōn*, lit., "one having come") or εἰςελθών (*eiselthōn*, lit., "having entered"), the latter presupposing the house of v.10. For a defense of the text behind the NIV, cf. J. O. Callaghan, "La variante εις/ελθων en Mt 9:18," *Bib* 62 (1981): 104–6.

20 "Tassel" or "edge" in Matthew and Luke makes this one of the most important "minor agreements" of Matthew and Luke against Mark, one that has generated many theories. Some take it with other "minor agreements" as sufficient evidence to defend the Griesbach hypothesis (see Introduction, section 3); others postulate a shared source, a coincidence, a textual emendation, or (most recently) the influence of Mark 6:56 (J.T. Cummings, "The Tassel of His Cloak: Mark, Luke, Matthew—and Zechariah," in *Studia Biblica 1978* [ed. Livingstone], 2:47–61). However explained—and perhaps some theory of common information is best—it is scarcely enough to threaten the two-source hypothesis. Why Matthew should include such a descriptive detail when he eliminates so much is hard to say. Yet Matthew's narrative is not unpolished. He includes the piquant touch and occasional small detail while eliminating characters and scenes not germane to his purpose.

b. Healing two blind men (9:27–31)

OVERVIEW

This pericope is usually taken as a doublet of the Bartimaeus miracle (20:29–34; Mk 10:46–52; Lk 18:35–43). But close examination shows little verbal correspondence between the Synoptics, and such correspondence as exists is considerably less than that between two pericopes in Matthew telling of entirely different miracles (cf. Held, "Matthew as Interpreter of the Miracle Stories," 219–20).

Blindness was and still is common in the Mideast. Jesus performed many such miracles (see comments at 4:23; 8:16–17; 9:35). The most striking parallel is the cry "Have mercy on us, Son of David" (v.27). But this also occurs in 15:22 in a story having nothing to do with blindness; so the title "Son of David" may well have another explanation (see below). Certainly the point of 20:29–34 is quite different from that of this pericope. Here the focus is on Jesus' authority and the blind men's faith; there it is on the compassion of Jesus the King as he interrupts his journey to Jerusalem to respond to their cries. Moreover, Matthew, as we have repeatedly observed, condenses his narratives. Proposals that similar stories are doublets (a form of lengthening) must therefore be treated with suspicion. Likewise the supposition that Matthew has two blind men because Mark (his source) has two stories (Mk 8:22–26; 10:46–52), each describing the healing of one blind man, and that Matthew has simply added the number of the men and put them into one story is fanciful. Mark does have two stories of separate healings, one of which Matthew takes over (Mk 10:46–52; Mt 20:29–34). And Matthew and

Mark each add another healing-of-the-blind miracle (Mt 9:27–31; Mk 8:22–26). This is scarcely surprising in view of the prevalence of blindness and the extent of Jesus' healing ministry.

[27]As Jesus went on from there, two blind men followed him, calling out, "Have mercy on us, Son of David!"

[28]When he had gone indoors, the blind men came to him, and he asked them, "Do you believe that I am able to do this?"

"Yes, Lord," they replied.

[29]Then he touched their eyes and said, "According to your faith will it be done to you";
[30]and their sight was restored. Jesus warned them sternly, "See that no one knows about
this." [31]But they went out and spread the news about him all over that region.

COMMENTARY

27–28 Apparently Jesus was returning from the ruler's house (v.23) either to his own house (4:13) or to that of Matthew (vv.10, 28—the article in Greek implies it was either his own dwelling or the one previously mentioned). We should probably envisage a large crowd after the dramatic raising of the ruler's daughter. Attached to the crowd were two blind men who had faith enough to follow him indoors.

This is the first time Jesus is called "Son of David," and there can be no doubt that the blind men were confessing Jesus as Messiah (see comments at 1:1). They may have been physically blind, but they really "saw" better than many others—further evidence that Jesus came to those who needed a doctor (vv.12–13; see comments at 15:22). "The use of the Davidic title [cf. 15:22; 20:30; 21:9, 15; 22:42] in address to Jesus is less extraordinary than some think: in Palestine, in the time of Jesus, there was an intense Messianic expectation" (Hill).

The messianic age was to be characterized as a time when "the eyes of the blind [would] be opened and the ears of the deaf unstopped," when "the lame [would] leap like a deer, and the mute tongue shout for joy" (Isa 35:5–6). If Jesus was really the Messiah, the blind reasoned, then he would have mercy on them; and they would have their sight. So their need drove them to faith. Perhaps this is what lies behind the fact that in the Synoptics "Son of David" is so often associated with the needy—those possessed by demons or, as here, in need of healing (cf. Burger, *Jesus als Davidssohn*; Dennis C. Duling, "The Therapeutic Son of David: An Element in Matthew's Christological Apologetic," *NTS* 24 [1978]: 392–410; K. Paffenroth, "Jesus as Anointed and Healing Son of David in the Gospel of Matthew," *Bib* 80 [1999]: 547–54; Lidija Novakovic, *Messiah, the Healer of the Sick: A Study of Jesus as the Son of David in the Gospel of Matthew* [WUNT 170; Tübingen: Mohr, 2003]). See especially the magisterial study of Young S. Chae (*Jesus as the Eschatological Davidic Shepherd*).

Jesus did not deal with the blind men until they were indoors (v.28). This may have been to dampen messianic expectations (see comments at v.30) on a day marked by two highly public and dramatic miracles (v.26). It may also have been a device to increase their faith. The latter is suggested by his question (v.28), which accomplished two other things: (1) it revealed that their cries were not merely those of desperation only but of faith, and (2) it showed that their faith was directed not to God alone but to Jesus' person and to his power and authority. Their title for Jesus was therefore right; he is truly the messianic Son of David. Thus we return to the first reason for delaying the healing—its being done within the house prevented the excited crowd from witnessing an implicit christological claim.

29–31 Jesus' touching the blind men's eyes—perhaps no more than a compassionate gesture to encourage faith—was not the sole means of this healing; it also depended on Jesus' authoritative word. "According to your faith" does not mean "in proportion to your faith" (so much faith, so much sight) but rather "since you believe, your request is granted"—cf. "your faith has healed you" (v.22). The miracle accomplished (v.30), Jesus "warned them sternly" to tell no one. *Embrimaomai* ("sternly warn") occurs only five times in the NT and always in connection with deep emotion (cf. Mk 1:43; 14:5; Jn 11:33, 38). This rather violent verb reveals Jesus' intense desire to avoid a falsely based and ill-conceived acclaim that would not only impede but also endanger his true mission (see comments at 8:4). But the men whose faith brought them to Christ for healing did not stay with him to learn obedience. So the news spread like wildfire throughout the region (cf. v.26).

NOTES

27 Instead of the vocative υἱέ (*huie*, "son," GK *5626*), the text offers the nominative υἱός Δαυίδ (*huios Dauid*, "son of David"). It is surprising that the nominative noun in such a construction is anarthrous. This may well reflect Hebrew construction (cf. BDF, para. 147 [3]).

c. Exorcising a dumb man (9:32–34)

OVERVIEW

Again many see in these verses a "partial doublet," this time with 12:22–24; and again the verbal parallels are minimal. Hill says that 9:32–34 has been formed out of 12:22–24 "in order to complete the cases of miraculous healing presupposed in 11:5 and 10:1." But Matthew 4:24 shows that Jesus performed many exorcisms. Was Matthew so pressed for another example that he had to tell the same story twice? If so, why is the demon-possessed man in ch. 12 both blind and mute and this one only mute? Moreover, if v.34 is genuine (see below), it is surely not surprising that the charge of being in league with Beelzebub (12:24) should begin on a private scale and take some time to explode into the open (12:24). In any case, the charge is presupposed by 10:25.

32While they were going out, a man who was demon-possessed and could not talk was
brought to Jesus. 33And when the demon was driven out, the man who had been mute
spoke. The crowd was amazed and said, "Nothing like this has ever been seen in Israel."
34But the Pharisees said, "It is by the prince of demons that he drives out demons."

COMMENTARY

32–33 The word *kōphos* ("who could not talk," GK *3273*) in classical, Hellenistic, and biblical Greek means "deaf" or "dumb" or "deaf mute"; the two ailments are commonly linked, especially if deafness is congenital. Perhaps the man here was not only mute but a deaf mute. (On demon-possession, see comments at 4:24; 8:28, 31.) The NT frequently attributes various diseases to demonic activity; but since the same ailment appears elsewhere without any suggestion of demonic activity (e.g., Mk 7:32–33), the frequent connection between the two is not based on primitive superstition but presupposes a real ability to distinguish between natural and demonic causes. The crowd's amazement (v.33) climaxes the earlier excitement (vv.26, 31). Nothing has ever been seen like this in Israel—and, by implication, if not among God's chosen people, then nowhere. But the same amazement ominously sets the stage for the Pharisees' cynical response (v.34).

34 This verse is missing from the Western textual tradition. Allen, Klostermann, Zahn, and others follow suit, detecting an intrusion from 12:24. But the external evidence is strong; and the verse seems presupposed in 10:25. This is not the first intimation of direct opposition to Jesus in Matthew (9:3, 11, 14, 24; cf. 5:10–12, 44), and even here the imperfect *elegon* (lit., "they were saying"; NIV, "said") may imply that the ferment was constantly in the background. But the tide of opposition, which later brought Jesus to the cross, now becomes an essential part of the background to the next discourse (cf. 10:16–28).

9. Spreading the news of the kingdom (9:35–10:4)

a. Praying for workers (9:35–38)

OVERVIEW

As 4:23–25 prepares for the first discourse (chs. 5–7), so 9:35–38 provides a report and summary that prepares for the second (10:5–11:1). A new note is added; not only are we told again of the extensiveness of Jesus' labors, but we now learn that the work was so great that many workers were needed. This leads to the commissioning of 10:1–4 and to the related discourse of 10:5–11:1.

Mark 6:6b has few affinities with this passage. Verse 35 is close to Matthew 4:23. Verse 36 is akin to Mark 6:34, and vv.37–38 to Luke 10:2 (cf. Jn 4:35).

35Jesus went through all the towns and villages, teaching in their synagogues,
preaching the good news of the kingdom and healing every disease and sickness. 36When
he saw the crowds, he had compassion on them, because they were harassed and
helpless, like sheep without a shepherd. 37Then he said to his disciples, "The harvest is
plentiful but the workers are few. 38Ask the Lord of the harvest, therefore, to send out
workers into his harvest field."

COMMENTARY

35 The setting is the same as in Mark 6:6b. For the exegesis, see comments at 4:23. The principal difference is the omission of any mention of Galilee, though doubtless that is the region in view. It is possible, as older commentaries suggest, that this represents a second circuit through Galilee, but in view of Matthew's highly topical arrangement, it is precarious to deduce so much from it. Verse 35 summarizes the heart of Jesus' Galilean ministry and prepares us for the new phase of mission via the Twelve. (On "their" synagogues, see comments at 7:29; 10:17.)

36 Like Yahweh in the OT (cf. Eze 34), Jesus showed compassion on the shepherdless crowds and judgment on the false leaders. The "sheep" Jesus sees are "harassed" (not "fainted" [KJV], which has poor attestation), i.e., bullied, oppressed. In the face of such problems, they are "helpless," unable to rescue themselves or escape their tormentors. The language here is close to Numbers 27:17 (which could almost make Joshua a "type" of Jesus); but other parallels (e.g., 1Ki 22:17; 2Ch 18:16; Isa 53:6; Eze 34:23–24; 37:24) remind us not only of the theme's rich background but also that the shepherd can refer either to God or to the Davidic Messiah God will send (cf. 2:6; 10:6, 16; 15:24; 25:31–46; 26:31).

37–38 The metaphor changed from sheep farming to harvest, as Jesus sought to awaken similar compassion in his disciples. Later on, the harvest is the end of the age (13:39) and the judgment it brings—a common symbol (cf. Isa 17:11; Joel 3:13). Many commentators see this verse as a warning to Israel that judgment time is near. The word "plentiful" stands in the way of this interpretation; it makes sense only if here *therismos* (GK *2546*) does not mean "harvest time" but "harvest crop" (cf. BDAG, 453), as in Luke 10:2 and John 4:35b. In that case, the crop will be plentiful. Many people will be ready to be "reaped" into the kingdom.

Jesus is speaking here to "his disciples," which many take to refer to the Twelve. More likely, "his disciples" designates a larger group exhorted to ask (v.38) that the Lord of the harvest (possibly "Lord who is harvesting," if this is a verbal genitive, cf. G. H. Waterman, "The Greek 'Verbal Genitive,'" in *Current Issues* [ed. Hawthorne], 292) will thrust laborers into his *therismou* (here in the sense "harvest field"). By contrast, the Twelve are immediately commissioned as workers (10:1–4). This interpretation best fits 10:1: Jesus "called his twelve disciples to him." The clause is clumsy if they are the same as the "disciples" of vv.37–38 and natural only if they are part of the larger group.

b. Commissioning the Twelve (10:1–4)

[1]He called his twelve disciples to him and gave them authority to drive out evil spirits and to heal every disease and sickness.

[2]These are the names of the twelve apostles: first, Simon (who is called Peter) and his brother Andrew; James son of Zebedee, and his brother John; [3]Philip and Bartholomew; Thomas and Matthew the tax collector; James son of Alphaeus, and Thaddaeus; [4]Simon the Zealot and Judas Iscariot, who betrayed him.

COMMENTARY

1 He whose word (chs. 5–7) and deed (chs. 8–9) were characterized by authority now delegates something of that authority to twelve men. This is the first time Matthew has explicitly mentioned the Twelve (cf. v.2; 11:1; 20:17; 26:14, 20, 47), who are introduced a little earlier in Mark (3:16–19). This commission appears to be the culmination of several previous steps (Jn 1:35–51; see comments at 4:18–22). Indeed, Matthew's language suggests that the Twelve became a recognized group somewhat earlier. At the same time, this commission was a stage in the training and preparation of those who, after Pentecost, would lead the earliest thrust of the fledgling church. Twelve were chosen, probably on an analogy to the twelve tribes of Israel (cf. the council of twelve at Qumran, 1QS 8:1ff.), and they point to the eschatological renewal of the people of God (see comments at 19:28–30).

The authority the Twelve received enabled them to heal and drive out "evil [*akathartos*, lit., 'unclean,' GK *176*] spirits"—spirits in rebellion against God, hostile to man, and capable of inflicting mental, moral, and physical harm, directly or indirectly. This is the first time in Matthew that demons are so described, and only again at 12:43 (but see comments at 8:16). "Every kind of disease and sickness" is exactly the expression in 4:23; 9:35. The authority granted the Twelve is in sharp contrast to the charismatic "gifts [plural] of healing" at Corinth (1Co 12:9, 28), which apparently were individually more restricted in what diseases each could cure.

2–4 For the first and only time in Matthew, the Twelve are called "apostles." *Apostolos* ("apostle," GK *693*), cognate with *apostellō* ("send," GK *690*), is not a technical term in the background literature. This largely accounts for the fact that as used in NT documents it has narrower and wider meanings (cf. *NIDNTT*, 1:126–37). Luke 6:13 explicitly affirms that Jesus himself called the Twelve "apostles"; certainly Luke shows more interest in this question than the other three, partly in preparation for his work on the Acts of the Apostles. But in the NT, the term can mean merely "messenger" (Jn 13:16) or refer to Jesus ("the apostle and high priest whom we confess," Heb 3:1) or elsewhere (esp. in Paul) denote "missionaries" or "representatives"—i.e., a group larger than the Twelve and Paul (Ro 16:7; 2Co 8:23). Nevertheless, the most natural reading of 1 Corinthians 9:1–5; 15:7; Galatians 1:17, 19 et al. is that even Paul could use the term in a narrow sense to refer to the Twelve plus himself (by special dispensation, 1Co 15:8–10).

Lists of the Twelve are found here and in three other places in the NT:

	Matthew 10:2–4	**Mark 3:16–19**	**Luke 6:13–16**	**Acts 1:13**
1.	Simon Peter	Simon Peter	Simon Peter	Peter
2.	Andrew	James	Andrew	John
3.	James	John	James	James
4.	John	Andrew	John	Andrew
5.	Philip	Philip	Philip	Philip
6.	Bartholomew	Bartholomew	Bartholomew	Thomas

7. Thomas	Matthew	Matthew	Bartholomew
8. Matthew	Thomas	Thomas	Matthew
9. James son of Alphaeus	James son of Alphaeus	James son of Alphaeus	James son of Alphaeus
10. Thaddaeus	Thaddaeus	Simon the Zealot	Simon the Zealot
11. Simon the Cananaean (NRSV)	Simon the Cananaean (NRSV)	Judas brother of (or son of) James	Judas brother of (or son of) James
12. Judas Iscariot	Judas Iscariot	Judas Iscariot	[vacant]

Many significant things arise from comparing these lists.

1. Peter is always first, Judas Iscariot always last. Matthew uses "first" in connection with Peter. The word cannot mean he was the first convert (Andrew or perhaps John was) and probably does not simply mean "first on the list," which would be a trifling comment (cf. 1Co 12:28). More likely it means *primus inter pares* ("first among equals"; see comments at 16:13–20).

2. The first four names of all four lists are those of two pairs of brothers whose call is mentioned first (cf. 4:18–22).

3. In each list, there are three groups of four, each group headed by Peter, Philip (not to be confused with the evangelist), and James son of Alphaeus respectively. But within each group the order varies (even from Luke to Acts!) except that Judas is always last. This suggests, if it does not prove, that the Twelve were organizationally divided into smaller groups, each with a leader.

4. The commission in Mark 6:7 sent the men out two by two; perhaps this accounts for the pairing in the Greek text of Matthew 10:2–4.

5. Some variations in order can be accounted for with a high degree of probability. For the first four names, Mark lists Peter, James, John, and appends Andrew, doubtless because the first three were an inner core privileged to witness the raising of Jairus's daughter and the transfiguration and invited to be close to Jesus in his Gethsemane agony. Matthew preserves the order suggested by sibling relationships. He not only puts himself last in his group but mentions his less-than-savory past. Is this a sign of Christian humility?

6. Apparently Simon the Cananaean (Matthew, Mark) is the same person as Simon the Zealot (Luke, Acts). If so, then apparently Thaddaeus is another name for Judas the brother of (or son of) James (see comments below).

Not much is known concerning most of these men (see Reflections below). For interesting but mostly incredible legends about them, see Hennecke (*New Testament Apocrypha*, 2:167–531).

NOTES

1 The construction ὥστε (*hōste*, "so that") plus an infinitive to indicate purpose is extraordinary (cf. BDF, para. 391 [3]; Zerwick, *Biblical Greek*, para. 352) but cannot easily be taken any other way.

REFLECTIONS

Simon Peter. Simon is probably a contraction of *Simeon* (cf. Ge 29:33). Natives of Bethsaida on Galilee (Jn 1:44), he and his brother Andrew were fishermen (Mt 4:18–20) and possibly disciples of John the Baptist before they became disciples of Jesus (Jn 1:35–42). Jesus gave Simon the name *Cephas* (in Aram.; "Peter" in Gk. [Jn 1:42]; see comments at 4:18). Impulsive and ardent, Peter's great strengths were his great weaknesses. NT evidence about him is abundant. Tracing Peter's movements after the Jerusalem Council (Ac 15) is very difficult.

Andrew. Peter's brother is not nearly so prominent in the NT. He appears again only in Mark 13:3; John 1:35–44; 6:8; 12:22, and in late and unreliable traditions. The Johannine evidence shows him to have been quietly committed to bringing others to Jesus.

James and John. James was probably the older (he almost always appears first). But as he became the first apostolic martyr (Ac 12:2), he never achieved his brother's prominence. The brothers were sons of Zebedee the fisherman, whose business was successful enough to employ others (Mk 1:20) while his wife was able to support Jesus' ministry (Mt 27:55–56). His wealth may help account for the family's link with the house of the high priest (Jn 18:15–16), as well as for the fact that he alone of the Twelve stood by the cross. The brothers' mother was probably Salome (cf. Mt 27:56; Mk 15:40; 16:1), and her motives were not unmixed (see comments at 20:20–21). Perhaps the sons inherited something of her aggressive nature; whatever its source, the nickname "sons of thunder" (Mk 3:17; cf. also Mk 9:38–41, Lk 9:54–56) reveals something of their temperament. John may have been a disciple of John the Baptist (Jn 1:35–41). Of James we know nothing until Matthew 4:21–22. John was undoubtedly a special friend of Peter (Lk 22:8; Jn 18:15; 20:2–8; Ac 3:1–4:21; 8:14; Gal 2:9). Reasonably reliable tradition places him after the fall of Jerusalem in Ephesus, where he ministered long and usefully into old age, taking a hand in the nurture of leaders like Polycarp, Papias, and Ignatius. Broadus's summary does not seem too fanciful: "[The] vaulting ambition which once aspired to be next to royalty in a worldly kingdom [Mt 20:20–23] now seeks to overcome the world, to bear testimony to the truth, to purify the churches, and glorify God."

Philip. Like Peter and Andrew, Philip's home was Bethsaida (Jn 1:44). He too left the Baptist to follow Jesus. For incidents about him, see John 6:5–7; 12:21–22; 14:8–14. In the lists he invariably appears first in the second group of four. Polycrates, a second-century bishop, says Philip ministered in the Roman province of Asia and was buried at Hierapolis.

Bartholomew. The name means "son of Tolmai" or "son of Tholami" (cf. Jos 15:14 LXX) or "son of Tholomaeus" (cf. Josephus, *Ant.* 20.5 [1.1]). Many have identified him with Nathanael on the grounds that (1) the latter is apparently associated with the Twelve (Jn 21:2; cf. 1:43–51), (2) Philip brought Nathanael to Jesus (Jn 1:43–46), and (3) Philip and Bartholomew are always associated in the lists of apostles. The evidence is not strong, but if it is solid, we also know he came from Cana (Jn 21:2). He is remembered for Jesus' tribute to him (Jn 1:47).

Thomas. Also named "Didymus" (Jn 11:16; 21:2), which in Aramaic means "Twin," Thomas appears in gospel narratives only in John 11:16; 14:5; 20:24–29. Known for his doubt, he should also be known for his courage (Jn 11:16) and his profound confession (Jn 20:28). Some traditions claim he went to India as a missionary and was martyred there; others place his later ministry in Persia.

Matthew. See comments at 9:9; Introduction, section 5.

James son of Alphaeus. The extra phrase distinguishes him from James son of Zebedee. If we assume (and this is highly likely) that this James is not the same as "James the brother" of Jesus (see comments at 13:55), we know almost nothing about him. Assuming Matthew = Levi (see comments at 9:9), Matthew's father was also called Alphaeus (Mk 2:14); and if this is the same Alphaeus, then James and Matthew are another pair of brothers among the Twelve. Some have argued that Alphaeus is an alternative form of Cleophas (Clopas), which would mean that "James son of Alphaeus" is the same person as "James the younger" (Mk 15:40) and that his mother's name was Mary (Mt 27:56; Mk 15:40; 16:1; Jn 19:25). But such connections are by no means certain.

Thaddaeus. The textual variants are difficult. The longer ones (e.g., KJV, "Lebbaeus, whose surname was Thaddaeus") are almost certainly conflations. "Thaddaeus" has the support of early representatives from Alexandrian, Western, and Caesarean witnesses (cf. Metzger, *Textual Commentary*, 26). Through elimination he appears to be identified with (lit.) "Judas of James"—which could mean either "Judas son of James" or "Judas brother of James." The former is perhaps the more normal meaning; but the author of the epistle of Jude designates himself as "Jude [Gk. *Ioudas*],... a brother of James" (Jude 1, where *adelphos* ["brother"] is actually used). If Jude is the apostolic "Judas of James," then the meaning of the latter expression is fixed. On the other hand, if canonical Jude is the half brother of Jesus and full brother of Jesus' half brother James (see comments at 13:55), then "Judas of James" most likely means "Judas son of James." "Thaddaeus" comes from a root roughly signifying "the beloved." Perhaps this apostle was called "Judas the beloved" = "Judas Thaddaeus," and "Thaddaeus" was progressively used to distinguish him from the other Judas in the apostolic band. Only John 14:22 provides us with information about him. Later traditions are worthless.

Simon the Zealot. Matthew and Mark have "Simon the Cananaean" (NRSV; *Kananaios*, GK *2831*; not "Canaanite," which would suggest a pagan Gentile; cf. the different Gk. word in 15:22: *Chananaios*). "Cananaean" (*qan'ân*) is the Aramaic form of "Zealot" specified in Luke–Acts. The Zealots were nationalists, strong upholders of Jewish traditions and religion. Some decades later, they became a principal cause of the Jewish War in which Rome sacked Jerusalem. The Zealots were probably not so influential in Jesus' time. The nickname may reveal Simon's past political and religious associations; it also distinguishes him from Simon Peter.

Judas Iscariot. Judas's father is called "Simon Iscariot" in John 6:71; 13:26. Scholarly interest has spent enormous energy and much ingenuity on the name "Iscariot." Explanations include (1) "man of Kerioth" (there are two eligible villages of that name [cf. *ZPEB*, 3:785; *IDB*, 2:830]); (2) transliteration of Latin *sicarius*, used to refer to a Zealot-like movement; (3) "man of Jericho," an explanation depending on a Greek corruption; (4) a transliteration of the Aramaic *š^eqāryā'* ("falsehood," "betrayal"; cf. C. C. Torrey, "The Name Iscariot," *HTR* 36 [1943]: 51–62), which could therefore become a nickname for Judas only after his ignominy and not at this point in his life; cf. S. Morschauser, "A Note on *Iskariot*: 'The Pariah,'" *Journal of Higher Criticism* 10 (2003): 66–74; (5) "Judas the dyer," reflecting his occupation (cf. A. Ehrman, "Judas Iscariot and Abba Saqqara," *JBL* 97 [1978]: 572–73; Y. Arbeitman, "The Suffix of Iscariot," *JBL* 99 [1980]: 122–24); (6) as an adaptation of the last, "Judas the redhead" (Albright and Mann). The first and fifth seem most likely; the second is perhaps most popular. Judas was treasurer for the Twelve but not an honest one (Jn 12:6, 13:29; see comments at 26:14–16; 27:3–10). Matthew and Mark add the damning indictment—"who betrayed him." Luke 6:16 labels him a traitor.

B. Second Discourse: Mission and Martyrdom (10:5–11:1)

OVERVIEW

For a general introduction to the discourses and their problems, see comments at 5:1.

On the face of it, this discourse is as tightly bracketed as the others (v.5a; 11:1), giving at least the impression that all the material of vv.5b–42 was delivered on one occasion. It is also peculiarly difficult. Two separate but related questions need careful attention before a judgment is formed.

The literary question. Roughly speaking, vv.5–15 have some parallels with Mark 6:8–11; Luke 9:3–5; 10:5–15. The last of these references, however, concerns the mission of the seventy-two, not found in Matthew or Mark. Matthew 10:16a resembles Luke 10:3. But Matthew 10:17–25, concerning the disciples' persecution and their arraignment before tribunals, finds its closest parallel in the Olivet Discourse (Mk 13:9–13; Lk 21:12–19; cf. Mt 24:9–14). The final section (vv.26–42), setting out conditions for discipleship in more general terms, resembles material in Mark 9 and Luke 12:2–12. With the exception of only a few places (vv.5–6, 8, 16b), little in vv.5–42 is peculiar to the first gospel, though admittedly some parallels are not as close as others.

The most common literary theory is that Matthew composed this address from segments of his two principal sources, Mark and Q. Those who reject Mark's priority and insist on Matthew's priority do not need Q and have an easier time defending the unity of this chapter. But Mark's priority still has the best credentials (see Introduction, section 3), and so the problems remain. David Wenham (*Rediscovery of Jesus' Eschatological Discourse*, 231–51) has argued that almost this entire discourse comes from various strands of the Q tradition (this does not necessarily mean Q is a single, written document). Mark's parallels are thereby judged secondary and condensations of earlier sources.

The historical and theological question. How do such source theories affect the context Matthew establishes? Here there is little agreement. F. W. Beare ("The Mission of the Disciples and the Mission Charge: Matthew 10 and Parallels," *JBL* 89 [1970]: 1–13) does not think there ever was a mission of the Twelve. The setting is a fabrication designed to enhance the discourse, itself an edited collection of sayings, few of them authentic. Many scholars, including conservative ones, suppose the discourse to be an amalgam of authentic material given on at least two separate occasions (e.g., Allen, Grosheide). Tasker leaves the question open. R. Morosco ("Redaction Criticism and the Evangelical: Matthew 10 a Test Case," *JETS* 22 [1979]: 323–31) resurrects the old theory of Benjamin Bacon ("'Five Books' of Moses"), assuming not only five discourses in Matthew but also their having been modeled on the five books of the Pentateuch (see Introduction, section 14). Morosco does not make clear, however, whether he thinks (1) that there is some historical commissioning of the Twelve to which a collage of material has been attached, (2) that a discourse was delivered on that occasion, and this is an expanded adaptation of it, or (3) that the setting itself is fictitious.

Related to the historical question are several observations about the content of Matthew 10. In vv.5–16, all Jesus' instructions neatly fit the situation of the Twelve during Jesus' public ministry. This includes Jesus' prohibition of ministry to anyone other than Jews (vv.5–6). But vv.17–22 clearly envisage a far more extensive ministry—even to kings and Gentiles. The persecution described does not fit the period of the first apostolic ministry but looks beyond it to times of major conflict long after Pentecost. As a result the great majority of modern commentators take this to be what Schuyler Brown describes as a literary means for Jesus to instruct "the Matthean community through the transparency of the twelve missionary disciples" ("The Mission to Israel in Matthew's Central Section," *ZNW* 69 [1978]: 73–90)—though, of course, many of the sayings are not thought to be dominical.

The historical and especially the literary issues are complex and intertwined, as is clear from the diversity of proposed solutions. The evidence can be weighed variously. Most solutions mask some unproved presuppositions and embrace a succession of judgments that could go another way.

Since Luke records both the commission of the Twelve and that of the seventy-two (9:1–6; 10:1–16), we must assume that these were separate events. But probably the Twelve were part of the seventy-two; instructions given the latter were therefore given the former. Although v.5a is historically specific about the fact of Jesus' instructing the Twelve and commissioning them, it does not pinpoint the exact time in his ministry when this took place. We have already found that Matthew, in condensing the account of the raising of Jairus's daughter and omitting the messengers, effectively collapses the first approach of Jairus and the news from the messengers, with the result that the daughter is presented as dead a little earlier than in the synoptic parallels (see comments at 9:18–26). Similarly, if Jesus instructed the Twelve both at their own first commissioning and later as part of the commissioning of the seventy-two, the omission of the latter might well be motive enough to combine elements of the two sets of instructions. Both 10:5a and 11:1 would still be strictly true.

David Wenham (*Rediscovery of Jesus' Eschatological Discourse*, 251 n. 1) would go further. He notes that 11:1 is the only ending to a Matthean discourse that omits "these words" or "these parables" or the like and wonders whether the omission might be a hint that this second discourse, unlike the others, is meant to be taken as a Matthean collection of Jesus' sayings. Such an argument from silence seems a slender thread on which to hang so much, not least because, apart from the opening words *kai egeneto* (lit., "and it happened"—see comments at 7:28–29), the fivefold formula at the end of each discourse varies considerably. But it is difficult simply to discount the possibility; and the suggestion that Matthew has collapsed the two commissionings is not implausible, even if not demonstrable.

Careful study of vv.5–42 suggests that the discourse is more unified than often recognized. Many of the alleged discrepancies are artificial. There is no conflict, for instance, between the ready harvest of 9:37–38 and the resistance in 10:16–22 (contra Morosco, "Redaction Criticism," 325). "The blood of the martyrs is the seed of the church" is a valid principle, and many great awakenings, including the Whitefield and Wesleyan revivals, have shown afresh that the harvest is most plentiful when the workers reap in the teeth of opposition. If Matthew omits the account of the Twelve's actual departure and return (kept in Mk 6:12–13; Lk 9:6, 10), it cannot mean that he does not know of the event or does not believe it happened; otherwise Matthew 10:1, 5; 11:1 are incoherent. Matthew is less interested in the details of many events he relates than in Jesus' words; but "less interested" does not mean "not interested," which seems to be the favorite disjunction of many redaction critics.

Certainly vv.17–23 go beyond the immediate mission of the Twelve, and in at least two ways the latter verses envisage a mission to the Gentiles, unlike vv.5b–6, and one with far severer opposition than anything the Twelve faced during Jesus' ministry. Yet these are not new themes. We have already found Jesus predicting severe persecution (e.g., 5:10–12), seeing a time of prolonged witness to the "world" (5:13–14; 7:13–14) after his departure (9:15), and many Gentiles participating in the messianic banquet (8:11–12). Therefore it is surely not unnatural for Jesus to treat this commission of the Twelve as both an explicit short-term itinerary and a paradigm of the longer mission stretching into the years ahead. For the latter, the Twelve need further instruction beyond those needed for the immediate tour, which they must see as, in part, an exercise anticipating something more. In this sense, the Twelve become a paradigm for other disciples in their post-Pentecost witness, a point Matthew understands (cf. 28:18–20); in this sense he intends that Matthew 10 should also speak to his readers.

The very fact that Matthew includes both what is historically specific in the first, short-term commission (e.g., restriction to Jews, certain clothing) and what is historically relevant only to the post-Pentecost church strongly supports his material's authenticity. If he were simply addressing his own community, much of ch. 10 would be irrelevant. Attempts to get around this by envisaging a divided Matthean community of people for and against a Gentile mission (e.g., S. Brown, "The Two-fold Representation of the Mission in Matthew's Gospel," *ST* 31 [1977]: 21–32) are extremely speculative. Such a theory depends not only on a selective reading of the Gospels that judges inauthentic all evidence that refutes it but also on an evangelist abysmally incapable of editing his sources into a coherent whole. Yet Brown ("The Matthean Community and the Gentile Mission," *NovT* 22 (1980): 194) writes, "The fact that contradictory missionary mandates are placed on Jesus' lips is evidence enough that he himself took no position on this matter, one way or the other, and this is not surprising. Jesus took for granted that he and his disciples were sent to Israel."

The presuppositions here are (1) that Jesus did not envisage a racially mixed church and (2) that the Gospels must be read as church documents that do not distinguish between Jesus' day and the time of writing. The first point is repeatedly denied by all four gospels; the second is called into question by explicit "before/after" passages (e.g., Jn 2:20–22) and themes or titles. Jesus says and does many things in the Gospels before the cross and resurrection that are fully comprehensible only after these events. The real contrast between vv.5–16 and vv.17–42 is salvation-historical. There is implicit recognition that the two situations are not the same, but the first prepares for the second. This distinction is ascribed to Jesus and thus confirms that he saw a continuing community that would grow under fire. Moreover, there is evidence elsewhere that Jesus was prepared to discuss widely separate events within the same framework if those separate events were internally connected in some way (see comments at chs. 24–25).

If this second discourse is coherent, some account must be given of parallels scattered elsewhere in the Synoptics. Earlier discussion (see comments at chs. 5–7) is still relevant: Jesus was an itinerant preacher who said the same things many times in similar words; the evangelists rarely claim to present *ipsissima verba* but almost always claim to present *ipsissima vox* (see comments at 3:17); their discourses are very substantial condensations in line with their own interests; and they do not hesitate to rearrange the order of presentation of some material within a discourse in order to highlight topical interests. But the sad fact is that there are few methodologically reliable tools for distinguishing between, say, two forms of one aphoristic saying, two reports of the same saying uttered on two occasions, or one report of one such a saying often repeated in various forms but preserved in the tradition in one form (surely not problematic if only the *ipsissima vox* is usually what is at stake).

Suppose, for instance, that David Wenham is essentially right, and most of vv.5–42 comes from Q, conceived as a variety of sources, oral and written, of Jesus' words. What historical conclusions does such a theory entail? The surprising answer is "Not much." For it is possible that some sayings of Jesus, repeated by him often and on diverse occasions, were jotted down in a sort of amalgam form encapsulating their substance and then used by the evangelists in different contexts and adapted accordingly. Those contexts may well include the historical settings in which the teaching was first uttered. That would be easy to believe if the apostle Matthew really did compose the first gospel (see Introduction, section 5). Authorship does not necessarily affect the authority of any NT book. But it does affect the way the tradition descended and thereby limits the wildest form-critical speculation (see Introduction, section 2).

Although Wenham's Q hypothesis may be challenged at many points on the ground that his argument turns on debatable judgments, yet the chief point is that the notion of Q sources behind vv.5–42 does not itself preclude the authenticity or unity of this discourse. A dozen variations could be shown to produce the same equivocal result. Problems arise only when theories regarding the contributing factors (authors, sources, context, redaction, historical reconstruction of Jesus' life and of the early church) are so aligned as to produce a synthesis that quite unnecessarily contradicts the text or some part of it. This is extremely unfortunate when in fact the text is the only hard evidence we have.

It is not possible in small compass to demonstrate the many factors contributing to scholars' diverse decisions in each passage of the mission discourse and how such factors may, taking full account of the hard evidence, come together in a way justifying Matthew's presentation of this material as a discourse to the Twelve. While the following exposition focuses on the meaning of the text as it stands, a few hints are given as to how difficult source-critical and historical problems may be most profitably probed.

1. Setting (10:5a)

5a These twelve Jesus sent out with the following instructions:

COMMENTARY

5a The setting Matthew gives must be accepted. Although he arranges much of his material topically, uses loose time connectives, and condenses his sources and sometimes paraphrases them, there is no convincing evidence that Matthew *invents* settings. Nor will appeal to some elusive genre suffice.

If Matthew is a coherent writer, such nonhistorical material must be reasonably and readily separable from his historical material, if the alleged "genre" was recognizable to the first readers. Verse 5a could scarcely be clearer: "These twelve Jesus sent out with the following instructions."

2. The commission (10:5b–16)

5b"Do not go among the Gentiles or enter any town of the Samaritans. 6Go rather to the
lost sheep of Israel. 7As you go, preach this message: 'The kingdom of heaven is near.' 8Heal
the sick, raise the dead, cleanse those who have leprosy, drive out demons. Freely you have
received, freely give. 9Do not take along any gold or silver or copper in your belts; 10take
no bag for the journey, or extra tunic, or sandals or a staff; for the worker is worth his keep.
11"Whatever town or village you enter, search for some worthy person there and stay at
his house until you leave. 12As you enter the home, give it your greeting. 13If the home is
deserving, let your peace rest on it; if it is not, let your peace return to you. 14If anyone will
not welcome you or listen to your words, shake the dust off your feet when you leave that
home or town. 15I tell you the truth, it will be more bearable for Sodom and Gomorrah on
the day of judgment than for that town. 16I am sending you out like sheep among wolves.
Therefore be as shrewd as snakes and as innocent as doves."

COMMENTARY

5b–6 Jesus forbade the Twelve from taking the road to the Gentiles (see Notes)—presumably toward Tyre and Sidon in the north or the Decapolis in the east—and from visiting Samaritan towns in the south. They were to remain in Galilee, ministering to the people of Israel (v.6). Jews despised Samaritans, not only because they preserved a separate cult (cf. Jn 4:20), but also because they were a mixed race, made up partly of the poorest Jews who had been left in the land at the time of the exile and partly of Gentile peoples transported into the territory and with whom the remaining Jews had intermingled, thereby succumbing to some syncretism (cf. 2Ki 17:24–28; cf. *ISBE*, 4:2673–74). The Twelve were to restrict themselves to "the lost sheep of Israel." This designation does not refer to a certain segment of the Jews (so Stendahl, "Matthew," in *Peake's Commentary*), since in the OT background (esp. Eze 34; see comments at 9:36; cf. Isa 53:6; Jer 50:6) the term refers to all the people (Hill).

Why this restriction? In part it was probably because of pragmatic considerations. That Jesus felt it necessary to mention the Samaritans at all presupposes John 4. The disciples, happy in the exercise of their ability to perform miracles, might have been tempted to evangelize the Samaritans because they remembered Jesus' success there. Judging by Luke 9:52–56, however, the Twelve were still temperamentally ill-equipped to minister to Samaritans. And even after Pentecost, despite an explicit command from the risen Lord (Ac 1:8), the church moved only hesitantly toward the Samaritans (Ac 8).

The most important consideration, however, was not pragmatic but theological. Jesus stood at the nexus in salvation history where as a Jew and the Son of David he came in fulfillment of his people's history as their King and Redeemer. Yet his personal claims would offend so many of his own people that he would be rejected by all but a faithful remnant. Why increase their opposition by devoting time to Gentile ministry? His mission, as predicted, was worldwide in its ultimate aims (see comments at 1:1; 2:1; 3:9–10; 4:15–16; 5:13–16; 8:1–13; 10:18; 21:43; 24:14; 28:16–20), and all along he had warned that being a Jew was not enough. But his own people must not be excluded because premature offense could be taken at such broad perspectives. Therefore, Jesus restricted his own ministry primarily (15:24), though not exclusively (8:1–13; 15:21–39), to Jews. He himself was sent as their Messiah. The messianic people of God developed out of the Jewish remnant and expanded to include Gentiles. The restriction of vv.5–6, therefore, depends on a particular understanding of salvation history (cf. Meier, *Law and History*, 27–30) that ultimately goes back to Jesus. Paul well understood that both salvation and judgment were for the Jew first, then for the Gentile (Ro 1:16), and this conviction governed his own early missionary efforts (e.g., Ac 13:5, 44–48; 14:1).

On modern theories of the significance of vv.5–6, see Overview, 10:5–11:1.

7–8 The content of the disciples' message was very much like that in 3:2; 4:17. "Repent" is not mentioned but is presupposed. The long-awaited kingdom was now "near" enough (see comments at 4:17) to be attested by miracles directed at demonism and malady. The "authority" in v.1 cannot be limited to the list of powers mentioned there, for here (v.8) two more are added—raising the dead (textually well attested, if not quite certain) and cleansing lepers (see comments at 9:18–26; 8:1–4).

Jesus expected the Twelve to be supported by those to whom they were to minister (cf. vv.9–13; 1Co 9:14), but they needed to understand that what they had received—the good news of the kingdom, Jesus' authority, and this commission—they had received "freely" (not "in large bounty"—though that was true—but gratis). Therefore it would have been mercenary to charge others (NEB: "You have received without cost; give without charge"; cf. *Did.* 11–13; *Pirke Avot* 1:13). The danger of profiteering is still among us (cf. Mic 3:11).

9–10 The imperative *mē ktēsēsthe* ("Do not take along") more likely means "Do not procure" (as in Ac 1:18; 8:20; 22:28). Even then, the longer expression *mē ktēsēsthe* ... *eis* ("Do not procure ... with a view to [filling your belts]") could mean either "Do not accept money [i.e., fill your money belt] for your ministry" or "Do not provide your belt with money when you start out." The parallel in Mark 6:8 obviously means the latter. Gold, silver, and copper refer either to money or to a supply of the metals that could be exchanged for goods or money.

Mark permits "taking" (*airō*, GK *149*) sandals and a staff (a walking stick) and forbids everything else (Mk 6:8–9); Matthew's account forbids "procuring" (*ktaomai*, GK *3227*) even sandals or a walking stick (10:10). It may be that Mark's account clarifies what the disciples are permitted to bring, whereas Matthew's assumes that the disciples already have certain things (one cloak, sandals, a walking stick) and forbids them from "procuring" anything more. Two cloaks (see comments at 5:40) might seem too much but would be comforting if one were sleeping out. The disciples needed to learn the principle that "the worker is worth his keep" (cf. 1Co 9:14; 1Ti 5:17–18) and to shun luxury while learning to rely on God's providence through the hospitality of those who would take them in overnight, thus obviating the need for a second cloak. See discussion in the Notes.

What is clear is that the Twelve must travel unencumbered, relying on hospitality and God's providence. The details ensure that the instructions were for that mission alone (cf. Lk 22:35–38) and confirm Matthew's consciousness of the historicity of this part of the discourse.

11–13 To settle into the house of a "worthy" person implies that the disciples were not to shop around for the most comfortable quarters. Here "worthy" probably does not refer to a morally upright, honorable, or religious person but to one willing and able to receive an apostle of Jesus and the gospel of the kingdom (cf. Bonnard)—the opposite of "dogs" and "pigs" (7:6). As the disciples entered the house, they were to give it their "greeting." Luke (10:5) gives us the actual words: "Peace to this house." Neither Matthew nor Luke is introducing postresurrection notions of *šālôm* ("peace," GK 8934), even though later Christians would be reminded of the peace Jesus achieved for them (Lk 24:36; Jn 14:27). Instead, the greeting prepares for v.13: "As you enter the home," you are to give the normal greeting; but if the home turns out to be "unworthy" (as defined above), contrary to what you had been led to believe, then let your greeting of peace return to you (v.13); i.e., don't stay. The Twelve were emissaries of Jesus. Those who received them received him (cf. v.40). Their greeting was of real value because of their relationship to him. Loss of their greeting was loss of their presence and therefore loss of Jesus. Potiphar's household was blessed because of Joseph's presence (Ge 39:3–5). How much more those homes that harbored the apostles of the Messiah!

14–15 What was true for the home applied equally to the town. A pious Jew, on leaving Gentile territory, might remove from his feet and clothes all the dust of the pagan land now being left behind (Str-B, 1:571), thus dissociating himself from the pollution of those lands and the judgment in store for them. For the disciples to do this to Jewish homes and towns would be a symbolic way of saying that the emissaries of Messiah now view those places as pagan, polluted, and liable to judgment (cf. Ac 13:51; 18:6). The actions, while outrageously shocking, accord with 8:11–12; 11:20–24.

Sodom and Gomorrah (v.15) faced catastrophic destruction because of their sin (Ge 19) and became bywords of loathsome corruption (Isa 1:9; Mt 11:22–24; Lk 17:29; Ro 9:29; 2Pe 2:6; Jude 7; cf. *Jub.* 36:10). Although there is still worse to come for them on the day of judgment, there is yet more awful judgment for those who reject the word and the messengers of the Messiah (cf. Heb 2:1–3).

16 The first part of v.16 has a close parallel in Luke 10:3, part of the commission to the seventy-two. Because it is short and aphoristic, it is impossible to be certain how many times Jesus said it. Here it links the preceding pericope with the following warnings about persecution. The verse goes as well with what succeeds as what precedes.

Jesus pictured his disciples, defenseless in themselves, located in a dangerous environment. This is where he himself was sending them. The shepherd in this metaphor sends his sheep into the wolf pack (cf. 7:15; Jn 10:12; Ac 20:29). Therefore they must be *phronimoi* ("shrewd," GK *5861*) as serpents, which in several ancient Near Eastern cultures were proverbial for prudence. But prudence can easily degenerate into cheap cunning unless it goes with simplicity. The disciples must prove not only "shrewd" but *akeraioi* ("innocent"; used elsewhere only in Ro 16:19; Php 2:15). Yet innocence becomes ignorance, even naïveté, unless combined with prudence.

The dove was not an established symbol. In Hosea 7:11, a dove is pictured as "easily deceived and senseless." In a late midrash the serpent-dove contrast appears ("God saith to the Israelites: 'Towards me they are sincere as doves, but toward the Gentiles they are cunning as serpents'" [*Cant. Rab.* 2:14]). Yet not only is this midrash late; the contrast is not at all what Jesus had in mind. His followers were to be not prudent toward outsiders and innocent toward God, but both prudent and innocent in their mission to outsiders. In this light the dove image becomes clear. Doves are retiring but not astute; they are easily ensnared by the fowler. So Jesus' disciples, in their mission as sheep among wolves, must be "shrewd," avoiding conflicts and attacks where possible, but they must also be "innocent," i.e., not so cautious, suspicious, and cunning that circumspection degenerates into fear or elusiveness. The balance is difficult, but not a little of Jesus' teaching combines such poles of meaning (see comments at 7:1–6).

NOTES

5 The prohibition εἰς ὁδὸν ἐθνῶν μὴ ἀπέλθητε (*eis hodon ethnōn mē apelthēte*) means literally "Do not go away on the road of the Gentiles"—i.e., Do not go in the direction of (Aram. לֶאֱרַח *leʾōraḥ*) the Gentiles; "Do not take the road to Gentile lands" (NEB).

9–10 Though the distinction between κτάομαι (*ktaomai*, "procure") and αἴρω (*airō*, "take") may work in Matthew and Mark, it fails in Luke, who uses αἴρω, *airō* (as in Mark), but forbids a staff in 9:3 and sandals in 10:4. This suggests to Marshall (*Gospel of Luke*, 352–53) that Matthew and Luke depend on Q as opposed to Mark. That is possible. But the fact that Luke's verb (*airō*) is the same as Mark's calls it in question. Many solutions have been proposed, none altogether convincing (cf. E. Power, "The Staff of the Apostles: A Problem in Gospel Harmony," *Bib* 4 [1923]: 241–66; Lagrange; Schniewind; Lane, *Mark*, 207–8). Perhaps the simplest is that Luke has not changed Mark but in both passages (Lk 9:3; 10:4) draws from Q, like Matthew; but in 9:3 Luke changes κτάομαι, *ktaomai* ("procure"), to αἴρω, *airō* ("take"), which has a semantic range large enough to mean the former, and in 10:4 changes κτάομαι, *ktaomai*, to βαστάζω (*bastazō*, "bear," "carry," GK *1002*), the latter perhaps suggesting carrying some luggage: no "purse" (no "money"), no "bag" (no "luggage"), and no "sandals" (none carried). This suggestion is supported by the fact that the two verbs in Luke and the one in Matthew are all imperatives, unlike Mark's subordinate construction and subjunctive mood. In other words, Matthew and Luke agree not only on what is permitted but on the grammatical construction. Luke's only agreement with Mark is in one of his two verbs.

16 The pronoun ἐγώ (*egō*, "I") is probably not emphatic, as ἰδοὺ ἐγώ (*idou egō*, lit., "behold I") reflects a Semitic parallel that is not emphatic (cf. Turner, *Syntax*, 38).

REFLECTIONS

Once again the christological claim, though implicit, is unambiguous here. As in 7:21–23, Jesus insists that one's eternal destiny turns on relationship to him or even to his emissaries. At the same time, even in their early ministry, Jesus' apostles were to face the certainty of opposition—as did Jesus himself, rejected at Nazareth (13:53–58) and in Samaria (Lk 9:52–53), and not believed in the towns of Galilee (Mt 11:20–24). That early opposition pointed to the greater suffering still to come (vv.17–23) and also aligned the disciples of Jesus with the prophets of old (5:10–12) and with Jesus himself (10:24–25). Thus the disciples began to learn that the advance of the kingdom was divisive (vv.34–35; cf. 2Co 2:15–16) and would meet with violent opposition (see comments at 11:11–12).

3. Warnings of future sufferings (10:17–25)

OVERVIEW

There are parallels in vv.17–25 both to 24:9, 13 and to Luke 6:40; 12:11–12; 21:12. Although it has often been affirmed, it is doubtful that Matthew has simply pulled back some material from the Olivet Discourse (see Overview, 10:5–11:1). But there may be substantial reliance on Q (cf. D. Wenham, *Rediscovery of Jesus' Eschatological Discourse*). The language is demonstrably Palestinian. Even if Matthew applies some of these things to his own readers (cf. Hare, *Theme of Jewish Persecution*, 96–114), there is no reason to doubt the authenticity of these warnings. What this means is that Jesus envisaged an extended time of witness in the midst of persecution—in short, a witnessing and suffering church.

a. The Spirit's help (10:17–20)

17"Be on your guard against men; they will hand you over to the local councils and flog
you in their synagogues. 18On my account you will be brought before governors and kings
as witnesses to them and to the Gentiles. 19But when they arrest you, do not worry about
what to say or how to say it. At that time you will be given what to say, 20for it will not be
you speaking, but the Spirit of your Father speaking through you."

COMMENTARY

17 The *de* (untranslated in NIV) does not have adversative force. It merely connects this warning with the aphorism in v.16, showing how it is to be applied. The men who will hand over the disciples must be Jews, as the context is the synagogue; and so the persecution envisaged is Jewish persecution of Christians (unlike v.18). The *synedria* ("local councils," plural only here in the NT), which could be civic or synagogal, were charged with preserving the peace. That flogging is used for punishment, rather than the broader term "beating," implies that the opposition is not mob violence but the result of judicial action (Hare, *Theme of Jewish Persecution*, 104). Moreover, Jesus is envisaging a time before the absolute separation of church and synagogue has taken place, for synagogue floggings (cf. 23:34; Mk 13:9; Ac 22:19; cf. 2Co 11:24–25) were most easily inflicted on synagogue members. At a later period, the worshipers would sometimes sing a psalm while the flogging took place. But there is no evidence this was practiced in NT times. In any case, we are reminded of the slowness with which Jewish Christians withdrew from broader Jewish worship in the post-Pentecost period.

The reference to "their" synagogues is often interpreted as an anachronism, reflecting the church-synagogue polarity (see comments at 4:23; 7:29; 9:35; 11:1; 12:9; 13:54). Normally the word "their" is explicitly Matthean, but here Jesus uses it. This may suggest redactional phrasing. Significantly, however, the OT prophets in speaking for God commonly used "their" and "them" language when referring to apostate Israel. Here it is very likely that the OT background explains the usage. And because Matthew makes much of the failure of most Jews to receive their own Messiah, it is likely that the OT has affected his phrasing elsewhere. Certainly Christian readers, understanding themselves to be recipients of the revelation most Jews had refused, would see the "their" within this polarized context. Nevertheless, the term itself is no proof of anachronism unless it was similarly anachronistic in its OT setting, which is absurd. Indeed, if this OT background is determinative, then both Jesus and Matthew self-consciously spoke of Israel from the perspective of a divine revelatory stance that warned Israel afresh against apostasy, a theme made explicit elsewhere (e.g., 8:11–12).

18 As the witness would extend at some future time beyond Galilee and the Jewish race, so also the opposition. "Governors" (*hēgemonas*, rulers and magistrates at various levels) and "kings" make this clear. As in 8:4 and 24:14, the "witness" is not against people but to them; it becomes either the means by which they accept the truth or, when they reject it, a condemnation. The disciples would be harassed and persecuted, not on account of who they are but on account of who Christ is (see comments at 5:10–12). For his sake, their witness would extend "to them and to the Gentiles"—probably not a reference "to Jews [or Jewish magistrates] and to the Gentiles," but "to governors and kings and to [other] Gentiles." Overlapping between the paired elements is not uncommon in such constructions (e.g., Mk 16:7; Gr. of Ac 5:29; 9:16; cf. Hare, *Theme of Jewish Persecution*, 108–9).

19–20 The translation of *paradidōmi* (lit., "hand over," as in v.17, GK *4140*) as "arrest" is doubtful. The subject is ambiguous. "People," "opponents," or "Jewish leaders" could be "handing over" the disciples to the Gentile authorities. Later on, this happened to Paul and other Christians, who at first witnessed to their faith with relative impunity under the Roman laws granting exemptions from emperor worship to Jews, but fell victim to increasing Roman wrath as the Jews progressively denied any link between themselves and Christians.

Confronting a high Roman official would be far more terrifying to Jewish believers than confronting a synagogue council. High officials, even when hated, were accorded far greater respect than in modern democracies; and they used professional orator-lawyers in legal matters (e.g., Tertullus, Ac 24:1). But if Jesus warned his disciples of dangers, he also promised them help. The Spirit would speak through them when the time came; so they should not fret about their response. This promise is neither a sop for lazy preachers nor equivalent to the promises given the Twelve in the farewell discourse (Jn 14–16) that the Spirit would recall to their memory all they had heard from Jesus (Jn 14:16, 26). It is a pledge to believers who have been brought before tribunals because of their witness. The promised assistance does not assume an absolute disjunction between "you" and the "Spirit" (10:20), for the underlying Semitic disjunction is rarely absolute (e.g., Ge 45:8; Ex 16:8; cf. Zerwick, *Biblical Greek*, para. 445). The history of Christian martyrs is studded with examples of the fulfillment of this promise.

Unlike Luke, Matthew does not often mention the Spirit. But from other passages in his gospel, it is clear that he associates the Spirit with the kingdom's dramatic coming (3:11; 12:28, 31) and the church's witness (28:18–20). That same Spirit, "the Spirit of your Father," would provide Jesus' followers with the help they needed under persecution when facing hostile officials.

b. Endurance (10:21–23)

[21]"Brother will betray brother to death, and a father his child; children will rebel against their parents and have them put to death. [22]All men will hate you because of me, but he who stands firm to the end will be saved. [23]When you are persecuted in one place, flee to another. I tell you the truth, you will not finish going through the cities of Israel before the Son of Man comes."

COMMENTARY

21–22 It is not enough for Jesus' disciples to be opposed by Jewish and Gentile officialdom. They will be hounded and betrayed by their own family members (see vv.34–39). The theme of division between persons as a sign of the end is not unknown in Jewish apocalyptic literature (*4 Ezra* 5:9; *Jub.* 23:19; *2 Bar.* 70:3—though none of these refer explicitly to family divisions). Here the allusion is to Micah 7:6, quoted in Matthew 10:35–36. "All men" (v.22) does not mean "all men without exception," for then there would be no converts, but "all men without distinction"—all men irrespective of race, color, or creed. That the good news of the kingdom of God and his righteousness should elicit such intense and widespread hostility is a sad commentary on "all men." The hatred erupts, Jesus says, *dia to onoma mou* (lit., "on account of my name")—either because one bears the name "Christian" (cf. 1Pe 4:14) or, less anachronistically and more likely, "on account of me" (see comments at 5:10–12).

The one who "stands firm"—the verb *hypomenō* (GK *5702*) does not signify active resistance so much as patient endurance (cf. Da 12:12 LXX; Mk 13:13; Ro 12:12; 1Pe 2:20)—will be saved; but he must stand firm *eis telos* ("to the end"). Though this anarthrous expression could be taken adverbially to mean "without breaking down," it is far more likely purposely ambiguous to mean either "to the end of one's life" or, because of the frequent association of *telos* ("end," GK *5465*) and cognates with the eschatological end, "to the end of the age." This is not to say that only martyrs will be saved; but if the opposition one of Jesus' disciples faces calls for the sacrifice of life itself, commitment to him must be so strong that the sacrifice is willingly made. Otherwise there is no salvation. Thus from earliest times Christians have been crucified, burned, impaled, drowned, starved, racked—for no other reason than that they belonged to him. As with martyrs among God's people before the coming of Jesus, so now: the world was not worthy of them (Heb 11:38).

23 This verse is among the most difficult in the NT canon. The textual variants (cf. Metzger, *Textual Commentary*, 28) are complex but affect the main interpretive questions little. Ulrich Luz includes an admirable survey of major options.

1. Some have understood the coming of the Son of Man to refer to a coming of the historical Jesus in the wake of the mission of the Twelve as in the mission of the seventy-two (Lk 10:1). The focus of attention has thus reverted back to the immediate commission (Mt 10:5b–16). Jesus is telling the Twelve to "get a move on," because they will not have visited the cities of Israel before he "comes" to them—i.e., catches up with them. This view has been elegantly defended by J. Dupont ("'Vous n'aurez pas achevé les villes d'Israël ...' [Matt. 10:23]," *NovT* 2 [1958]: 228–44), who points out that elsewhere Matthew can bring the title "Son of Man" back (from 16:21 to 16:13) to a new location where it is equivalent to no more than a sonorous "I" (assuming his source is Mk 8:27, 31). Dupont suggests that in Matthew's source, 10:23 was read after 10:5–6, which would confirm his interpretation. This view, therefore, turns in part on finding a source common to Matthew 10:23 and Luke 10:1—presumably a Q tradition—and this possibility has been strengthened somewhat by the source-critical arguments of H. Schürmann ("Zur Traditions- und Redaktionsgeschichte von Mt 10:23," *BZ* 3 [1959]: 82–88) and David Wenham (*Rediscovery of Jesus' Eschatological Traditions*), who try to show that Matthew 10:23 springs from Q. The arguments are unconvincing. In Wenham's case, they hinge on the assertion that v.23 is awkward because the literary parallel with vv.19–20 is inexact (v.23 uses the verb "persecute" instead of the verb "hand over"). But it is not at all clear why Matthew should use the same verb. Most Semitic parallelism depends on small verbal changes.

Wenham argues that v.23 "seems something of an afterthought in its present position following the climactic 'he who endures to the end shall be saved.'" But v.23 is anticlimactic only if the coming of the Son of Man refers exclusively to Jesus' follow-up ministry. If, instead, Jesus in v.22 is enjoining perseverance amid suffering witness, in clear reference to a post-Pentecost setting, then the persecution in v.23 should be similarly interpreted. The disciples' perseverance to the end does not mean withdrawal but moving on from city to city until the Son of Man comes. In this light, v.23 is still difficult but certainly not anticlimactic.

Indeed, this first interpretation fails to come to grips with two major hurdles. It fails to explain adequately why Matthew should move a comprehensible saying from a location following vv.5–6 (or even v.14) and place it here, where (we must implausibly suppose) the verse has nothing to do with its immediate context. Moreover, the geographical territory to be covered (see comments at 4:23–25) embraces enough towns and villages that, under this interpretation, the urgent call for haste seems inept. And Luke 10:1, the alleged parallel, does not speak of ministry to all the cities of Israel but only to the towns to which Jesus was about to go. Above all, there is no evidence in any gospel that the Twelve were actively persecuted during their first mission but only on occasion rebuffed (as in 10:11–15).

2. Some take "the Son of Man's coming" to refer to the public identification of Jesus as the Messiah, presumably at the resurrection (Sabourin) or shortly after. Not only would this be an odd use of the expression, but the interpretation fails to show how the disciples were actually persecuted up to that time, or how there could be any urgency in such a deadline. Older commentators follow a similar line, exchanging the coming of the Spirit (Jn 14:16, 23–26) for the resurrection (e.g., Chrysostom, Calvin, Beza). But we have noted that the Spirit is not a major theme in Matthew (see comments at vv.19–20); and in any case never in the NT is the Son of Man completely identified with

him. A better modification of this view is offered by Stonehouse (*Witness of Matthew*, 139–40), who argues that this is the lesser inbreaking of the kingdom in the events succeeding Pentecost, the most probable meaning of 16:28 (below). But in v.23, this interpretation fails to account for the note of urgency. One might almost make a case for delaying witness until such an inbreaking. A modification of this view is found in the commentary by France (NICNT), who has altered his earlier view. France now thinks the language is evocative of the vindication of the Son of Man, most probably with 28:18 in view. After Jesus' resurrection and in the light of his ascension and session, the restriction to the villages of Israel is removed as the gospel goes to all the nations. Yet the phrase "before the Son of Man *comes*" is not naturally heard as the Son of Man *going* to his heavenly throne, thoroughly vindicated and commissioning a universal mission.

3. Others take the verse to refer to the second coming, equivalent to 24:30; 25:31; 26:64 (Turner). Although some would argue the point (see Overview, 24:1–25:46), the language of the Son of Man's coming most easily fits that interpretation. The problem then is the words "of Israel," so difficult in this interpretation that they are wrongly omitted by B (Alexandrian) and D (Western). Various expedients are appealed to in order to mitigate the problem: "Israel" is a symbol for the world or for the church, or there is some kind of double fulfillment (on the latter, see Hendriksen, who speaks of "prophetic foreshortening"; A. Feuillet, "Les origines et la signification de Mt 10, 23b," *CBQ* 23 (1961): 197–98—though the article as a whole, 182–98, supports 7 below). That "Israel" represents church or world is almost impossible in the context of Matthew's theology, and that there is some kind of double fulfillment is not much more than a surreptitious appeal for double incoherence; in the first fulfillment, the difficulties of 1 remain, while in the second, the problem words "of Israel" are still not explained. Whatever one thinks of multiple fulfillment in the Scriptures, this is not a clear instance of it. Bonnard sees a reference to Jesus' second coming in v.23b but sees no urgency. The verse simply insists on all the possibilities of witness given in Israel until the end and closely ties together Israel with that end (as in Ro 11:25). This view has its attractions. Nevertheless, the note of urgency linking v.23a and v.23b cannot be disposed of so easily. Gundry has a similar view and also argues that the verse is redactional and therefore not authentic.

4. At the turn of the century, Schweitzer (*Quest of the Historical Jesus*, 358ff.) used this text to develop his "thoroughgoing eschatology." He argued that v.23b shows that Jesus believed the end of time would take place so soon that he did not expect to see the disciples return before the end arrived. Jesus was wrong, of course, and therefore had to adjust his own theology. This was the first "delay of the Parousia." Unfortunately, Jesus was also wrong in expecting God to exonerate him before he died. Therefore, the church was forced to adjust its theology to accommodate these errors; and only a few traces of Jesus' earliest teachings, such as this passage, still peep unambiguously through the text. This view is well criticized by Kümmel (*Promise and Fulfillment*, 61ff.).

5. A combination of the last two views is now espoused by several scholars (e.g., Fenton, Hill) who think v.23b refers to the second coming and that Jesus expected it within one generation or so (see comments at 24:34; Hill specifies forty or fifty years). But there are so many hints of a much longer delay before the second coming (e.g., 13:24–33; 18:15–35; 19:28; 21:43; 23:32, 39) that there seems little to be gained by this interpretation and much to be lost.

6. Dispensationalists are inclined to see v.23b as a reference to the second coming that "views

the entire present church age as a parenthesis not taken into account in this prophecy" (Walvoord). Quite apart from the correctness or otherwise of the entire theological structure presupposed by this interpretation, it detaches v.23 from its context (if vv.16–22 refer to post-Pentecost *Christian* experience—so Walvoord) or else detaches vv.16–23 from their context (if the verses do not apply to any of Jesus' disciples but to believers living during the tribulation after the church has been raptured away). There is no exegetical warrant for either detachment, and both would be incomprehensible, not only to Jesus' hearers, but also to the first readers of Matthew's gospel.

7. The "coming of the Son of Man" here refers to his coming in judgment against the Jews, culminating in the sack of Jerusalem and the destruction of the temple (so France, *Jesus and the Old Testament*, 140; Feuillet, "Les origines," 182–98; Moule, *Birth of the New Testament*, 90; J. A. T. Robinson, *Jesus and His Coming* [London: SCM Press, 1957], 80, 91–92). Calvin thinks this interpretation farfetched, Hill that it is improbable. A powerful case, though, can be made for it. The coming of the Son of Man refers to the same event as the coming of the kingdom, even though the two expressions are conceptually complementary. Thus *the* coming of the Son of Man brings in the consummated kingdom (see comments at 24:30–31; 25:31). But the kingdom, as we have seen, comes in stages (see comments at 4:17; 12:28). In one sense, Jesus was born a king (see comments at 2:2); in another, he has all authority as a result of his passion and resurrection (28:18); and in yet another, his kingdom awaits the end. Mingled with this theme of the coming of the kingdom are Jesus' repeated warnings to the Jews concerning the disaster they are courting by failing to recognize and receive him (cf. Feuillet). In this he stands on the shoulders of the OT prophets, but his warnings are unique because he himself is the eschatological judge and because the messianic reign is now dawning in both blessing and wrath (8:11–12; 21:31–32).

Against this background the coming of the Son of Man in v.23 marks that stage in the coming of the kingdom in which the judgment repeatedly foretold falls on the Jews. With it the temple cultus disappears, and the new wine necessarily takes to new wineskins (see comments at 9:16–17). The age of the kingdom comes into its own, precisely because so many of the structured foreshadowings of the OT, bound up with the cultus and nation, now disappear (see comments at 5:17–48). The Son of Man comes.

Above all, this interpretation makes contextual sense of v.23. The connection is not with v.22 alone but with vv.17–22, which picture the suffering witness of the church in the post-Pentecost period *during a time when many of Jesus' disciples are still bound up with the synagogue.* During that period, Jesus says in v.23, his disciples must not use the opposition to justify quitting or bravado. Far from it. When they face persecution, they must take it as no more than a signal for strategic withdrawal to the next city (W. Barclay, *The Gospel of Matthew* [Philadelphia: Westminster, 1975], 1:378–80), where witness must continue, for the time is short. They will not have finished evangelizing the cities of Israel before the Son of Man comes in judgment on Israel.

Interpreted in this way the "Son of Man" saying of v.23 belongs to the eschatological category (see Reflections, p. 247), but the eschatology is somewhat realized. The strength of this interpretation is sometimes diluted by applying it unchanged to 16:28; 24:31. There are, in fact, important differences disallowing the view that all these texts refer to the fall of Jerusalem in AD 70. Nevertheless, they confirm the view that "the coming of the Son of Man" bears in Matthew the same rich semantic field as "the coming of the kingdom" (see comments at 6:10; 12:28).

c. Inspiration (10:24–25)

24 “A student is not above his teacher, nor a servant above his master. 25 It is enough for the student to be like his teacher, and the servant like his master. If the head of the house has been called Beelzebub, how much more the members of his household!”

COMMENTARY

24–25 The two brief analogies in vv.24–25a occur in various forms elsewhere in the NT (Lk 6:40; Jn 13:16; 15:20) and in Jewish literature (*b. Ber.* 58b). Like many good proverbs, they could be applied variously by capable preachers. Here Jesus forbids the disciples from being surprised when they suffer persecution. If they follow him, they should expect no less. The statement reveals something of Jesus' perception of the nature of his own ministry and of the way the "gospel of the kingdom" will advance in the world.

Those who deny the authenticity of vv.24–25a and other passages in which Jesus speaks implicitly of his sufferings do so not on literary evidence but on the basis of a priori decisions about what Jesus could and could not have known.

The insult "Beelzebub" (or, to preserve the best orthography, *Beelzeboul*) has an uncertain derivation. In the NT, the term occurs only here and at 12:24, 27; Mk 3:22, Lk 11:15, 18–19. It may have come from OT Hebrew *baʿalzᵉbûb* ("lord of flies"), a mocking takeoff of *baʿal zebûl* ("Prince Baal"), a pagan deity (2Ki 1:2–3, 16). But in that case, one wonders why the final syllable has been changed in NT Greek to *boul*. Other derivations include a mocking "lord of dung" and "lord of the heights" (heaven). One of the best suggestions is that of E. C. B. MacLaurin ("Beelzeboul," *NovT* 20 [1978]: 156–60), who shows it may well be a straightforward translation of *oikodespotēs* (NIV, "head of the house"). Beelzeboul is recognized in the NT as the prince of the demons and identified with Satan (12:24–27; Mk 3:22–26, Lk 11:18–19). Thus the real head of the house, Jesus, who heads the household of God, is being willfully confused with the head of the house of demons. The charge is shockingly vile—the Messiah himself rejected as Satan! If so, why should his disciples expect less?

This verse has not been constructed by the evangelist out of bits from 12:22–32, as if the charge were leveled at Jesus only the once. On the contrary, 9:34 suggests that it was a frequent slur.

4. Prohibition of fear (10:26–31)

OVERVIEW

Probably vv.26–27 are also transitional, like v.16. Consideration of how disciples must expect to face persecution and opprobrium makes it necessary to say something about how to handle fear (vv.26–31) and about the high standards of discipleship such a perspective presupposes. There are similar sayings elsewhere (cf. Lk 12:2–9; see also Mk 4:22; 8:38; Lk 9:26; 21:18). Yet there is no easy source pattern (cf. Hill), and most of the individual sayings are brief, easily memorized, and usable again and again.

a. The emergence of truth (10:26–27)

[26]"So do not be afraid of them. There is nothing concealed that will not be disclosed, or hidden that will not be made known. [27]What I tell you in the dark, speak in the daylight; what is whispered in your ear, proclaim from the roofs."

COMMENTARY

26–27 "Them" refers to the persecutors (v.23). The connective *oun* ("so") may simply begin a new exhortation based on the preceding (Bonnard), or it may offer a tighter connection: in view of a master who suffers ahead of his disciples, *therefore* do not fear, etc. The truth must emerge. The gospel and its outworkings in the disciples may not now be visible to all, but nothing will remain hidden forever. And if the truth will emerge at the end, how wise to declare it fully and boldly now. Flat rooftops of Palestinian houses provided excellent places for speakers (cf. Josephus, *J.W.* 2.611 [21.5]). In a sense, the apostles were to have more of a public ministry than Jesus himself. He told them things in private, some of which they did not even understand until after the resurrection (see Reflections, p. 252; cf. Jn 14:26; 16:12–15). But they were to teach them fully and publicly.

b. The nonfinality of death (10:28)

[28]"Do not be afraid of those who kill the body but cannot kill the soul. Rather, be afraid of the One who can destroy both soul and body in hell."

COMMENTARY

28 The second reason for learning not to fear men emerges from the fact that the worst they can do does not match the worst God can do. Though Satan may have great power (6:13; 24:22), only God can destroy soul and body in hell. "The fear of the Lord is" therefore "the beginning of wisdom" (Pr 9:10), for if God be truly feared, none other need be. Fear of men proves to be a snare (Pr 29:25). The same thought is found in extracanonical Jewish literature (e.g., Wis 16:13–14; 2 Macc 6:26; 4 Macc 13:14–15).

On "hell," see comments at 5:22. The force of *psychē* ("soul," GK *6034*) in the NT is closely related to *nepeš* ("soul," GK 5883) and *lēb* ("heart," "inner man," GK 4213) in the OT (for full discussion, see *NIDNTT*, 3:676–89). The thought is not so much of an ontological part utterly distinct from body as of the inner man destined for salvation or damnation (cf. 1Pe 1:9; 2:11, 25; 4:19). Unavoidable in this context is the thought that hell is a place of torment for the whole person; there will be a resurrection of the unjust as well as of the just.

c. Continuing providence (10:29–31)

29"Are not two sparrows sold for a penny? Yet not one of them will fall to the ground apart from the will of your Father. 30And even the very hairs of your head are all numbered. 31So don't be afraid; you are worth more than many sparrows."

COMMENTARY

29–31 The third reason for not being afraid is an a fortiori argument: If God's providence is so all-embracing that not even a sparrow drops from the sky apart from the will of God, cannot that same God be trusted to extend his providence over Jesus' disciples? The sparrow was used for food by very poor people. Two might be sold for "a penny" (one-sixteenth of a denarius, which was about a day's wage; cf. Deissmann, *Light from the Ancient East*, 272–75). "Your Father" adds a piquant touch: this God of all providence is the disciples' Father. God's sovereignty is not limited only to life-and-death issues; even the hairs of our heads are counted. Jesus' third argument against fear is thus the very opposite of what is commonly advanced. People say that God cares about the big things but not about little details. But Jesus says that God's sovereignty over the tiniest detail should give us confidence that he also superintends the larger matters.

5. Characteristics of discipleship (10:32–39)

a. Acknowledging Jesus (10:32–33)

32"Whoever acknowledges me before men, I will also acknowledge him before my Father in heaven. 33But whoever disowns me before men, I will disown him before my Father in heaven."

COMMENTARY

32–33 Many assume that Matthew here edits Mark 8:38, which was addressed to a crowd (cf. Lk 12:8–9). But Mark's words have a structure that has led to much of the debate over the "Son of Man" question.

Whoever confesses me ...
the Son of Man will confess ...
Whoever disowns (or is ashamed of) me ...
the Son of Man will disown (or be ashamed of) ...

This ABAB parallelism has induced many, especially since Bultmann (*History of the Synoptic Tradition*, 112, 128), to argue that the historical Jesus distinguished the Son of Man from himself (see Reflections, p. 247), and that Matthew's editing, by eliminating the "Son of Man" elements and substituting the first person personal pronoun, has identified Jesus with the Son of Man. The explanation of Hooker (*Son of Man*, 120–21, 189) is generally satisfying. The "I" clauses in Mark picture Jesus speaking to those thinking of following him in his earthly life; the "Son of Man" clauses picture Jesus in the future, and at this point some of his claims are still veiled. It is difficult to see how Jesus could have proclaimed another Son of Man and still have left room for himself. Elsewhere he explicitly identifies the two (Mk 14:61–62). But we may take Hooker's argument one step further. Obviously vv.32–33 are not addressed to indiscriminate crowds but to the Twelve. The reason for the clarity of Matthew's form of the saying may therefore turn, not on a development in the church's theology, but on the distinction in the audience. This was one of the things Jesus said clearly to his disciples in secret and which they would one day shout from the housetops (v.27).

Though addressed to the Twelve (vv.1–5), like much of vv.17–42, this saying looks beyond the apostles to disciples at large. The point is made clear by "whoever" (v.32). A necessary criterion for being a disciple of Jesus is to acknowledge him publicly (cf. Ro 1:16; 10:9). This will vary in boldness, fluency, wisdom, sensitivity, and frequency from believer to believer (cf. Calvin); but consistently to disown Christ (same verb as in 26:69–75) is to be disowned by Christ. Jesus now speaks not of "your Father" (as in v.29) but of "my Father." In view is his special filial relationship with the Father, by which the final destiny of all humanity depends solely on his word (see comments at 7:21–23; cf. 25:12). The christological implications of Jesus' words are unavoidable. "Jesus makes the entire position of men in the world to come, whether for weal or woe, to depend upon their relationship to and attitude toward him in this present world. Is this a claim which any mere man might have made? Do we not encounter here essentially the exclusiveness of Acts 4:12?" (Stonehouse, *Origins*, 190).

NOTES

32 The rather strange Greek ὁμολογήσει ἐν ἐμοί (*homologēsei en emoi*, "acknowledge me," GK *3933*) is perfectly natural Aramaic (but not Heb.); cf. Moulton, *Grammar: Accidence*, 463; Moule, *Idiom Book*, 183.

b. Recognizing the gospel (10:34–36)

34"Do not suppose that I have come to bring peace to the earth. I did not come to bring peace, but a sword. 35For I have come to turn

"'a man against his father,
a daughter against her mother,
a daughter-in-law against her mother-in-law—
36 a man's enemies will be the members of his own household.'"

COMMENTARY

34–36 As many Jews in Jesus' day thought the coming of Messiah would bring them political peace and material prosperity, so today many in the church think that Jesus' presence will bring them a kind of tranquility. But Jesus insisted that his mission entailed strife and division. Prince of Peace though he is (see comments at 5:9), the world will so violently reject him and his reign that men and women will divide over him (vv.35–36; cf. Lk 12:49–53; Neil, "Five Hard Sayings of Jesus," 157–60). Before the consummation of the kingdom, even the peace Jesus bequeaths his disciples will have its setting in the midst of a hostile world (Jn 14:27; 16:33; cf. Jas 4:4). Blickenstaff (*While the Bridegroom*, ch. 4) finds these verses so repellant—Jesus did not come to bring peace, but a sword—that she insists we must give them a "resistant reading."

The repeated statement "I have come" shows Jesus' christological and eschatological awareness (contra Arens, Ἦλθον-*sayings*, 63–90, who uses the same evidence to argue that such elements must be church creations). Earlier he warned his disciples of the world's hatred of his followers, a hatred extending even to close relatives (vv.21–22); now he ties this perspective to an OT analogy (Mic 7:6; on the text form, see Stendahl, *School of St. Matthew*, 90–91; Blomberg, "Matthew," in *CNTUOT*, 35–37). Micah describes the sinfulness and rebellion in the days of King Ahaz, but insofar as Jesus' disciples by following him align themselves with the prophets (5:10–12), the situation in Micah's time points to the greater division at Messiah's coming. Many critics think these verses apply solely to Christians in Matthew's day, and doubtless they caused Matthew's readers to think of their own sufferings. But some older commentators (e.g., Plumptre) wonder whether the Twelve, even during Jesus' earthly ministry, did not face some opposition from family and friends—as did Jesus himself (13:53–58; Jn 7:3–5). In any case, the context suggests Jesus is focusing on the future. Even today the situation has not greatly eased. In the "liberal" West, people who have become Christians have occasionally been disowned and disinherited by their families and have lost their jobs. And under totalitarian regimes of the right or the left there has been and still is untold suffering for Christ—witness Christians in southern Sudan and in some islands of Indonesia.

c. Preferring Jesus (10:37–39)

[37]"Anyone who loves his father or mother more than me is not worthy of me; anyone who loves his son or daughter more than me is not worthy of me; [38]and anyone who does

not take his cross and follow me is not worthy of me. [39]Whoever finds his life will lose it, and whoever loses his life for my sake will find it."

COMMENTARY

37–39 The absolutism of the Semitic idiom (Lk 14:26) is rightly interpreted by Matthew: a man must love his wife, family, friends, and even his enemies (see comments at 5:44–47), but he must love Jesus supremely. Again the saying is either that of the Messiah or a maniac. The rabbinic parallels of the master-disciple relationship (cf. *b. B. Meṣ.* 2:11) are not very close. Though they place the master above the father, they allow the disciple's personal interest to stand above his allegiance to his master. Jesus demanded death to self (vv.38–39). "Taking one's cross" does not mean putting up with some awkward or tragic situation in one's life, but painfully dying to self. In that sense, every disciple of Jesus bears the same cross. After Jesus' death and resurrection, the emotional impact of these sayings must have been greatly heightened, but even before those events, the reference to crucifixion would vividly call to mind the shame and pain of such a sacrifice. For "worthy," see comments at v.11.

The appeal is not to gloom but to discipleship. There is a strong paradox here. Those who lose their *psychē* ("soul," "life"—see comments at v.28), whether in actual martyrdom or disciplined self-denial, will "find" it in the age to come. Those who "find" it now (the expression in classical Greek means "to win or preserve" life) by living for themselves and refusing to submit to the demands of Christian discipleship lose it in the age to come (cf. 16:25; Mk 8:35; Lk 9:24; 17:33).

6. Encouragement: response to the disciples and to Jesus (10:40–42)

OVERVIEW

The foregoing teaching about what it means to be a disciple of Jesus has its darker side. This final section of the discourse is more encouraging. It reverts again to the ultimate tie between the treatment of Jesus and that of his followers (see comments at vv.24–25); it turns our eyes to the future (see comments at v.28) and shows us that God is indebted to no one.

[40]"He who receives you receives me, and he who receives me receives the one who sent
me. [41]Anyone who receives a prophet because he is a prophet will receive a prophet's
reward, and anyone who receives a righteous man because he is a righteous man will
receive a righteous man's reward. [42]And if anyone gives even a cup of cold water to one of

these little ones because he is my disciple, I tell you the truth, he will certainly not lose his reward."

COMMENTARY

40–42 It is commonly understood in the NT that a man's agent must be received as the man himself (cf. Lk 10:16; Jn 12:44–45; 13:20; Ac 9:4). And as this section closes the discourse that opens with instructions to the Twelve, many interpret "prophet" and "righteous man" (v.41) as alternative designations of the apostles in v.40, and v.42 as an extension to all disciples (e.g., Bonnard; Allen; Manson, *Sayings of Jesus*, 183). By contrast, David Hill ("Δίκαιοι as a Quasi-Technical Term," *NTS* 11 [1964–65]: 296–303) has advanced another interpretation. He suggests that both "prophets" and "righteous men" refer to distinguishable classes within Christianity. "Prophets" are distinguishable from "apostles," and "righteous men" refers to some other distinguishable group of teachers (cf. 13:17; 23:29; see comments at 7:15–23). In his commentary, Hill further suggests that v.42, derived from Mark 9:41, is given this setting "to suggest that traveling and persecuted missionaries [the "little ones"] are dependent on the hospitality and help of non-Christians." E. Schweizer ("Observance of the Law and Charismatic Activity in Matthew," *NTS* 16 [1969–70]: 213–30) says the coloration of "prophet" and "righteous man" in v.41 means that Matthew urges his community to imitate the ideal of a charismatic ("prophet") still bound by the law as interpreted by Jesus ("righteous man"). E. Käsemann (*New Testament Questions of Today* [London: SCM Press, 1969], 90–91) sees in "prophets" the leaders of Matthew's community and in "righteous men" the general body of believers.

A better synthesis is possible. As the discourse, viewed as a whole, moves from the Twelve to all believers, so also does its conclusion. Verse 40 probably refers primarily to the apostles, and vv.41–42 move through "prophets" and "righteous men" down to "these little ones"—namely, the least in the kingdom, seen as persecuted witnesses in the latter part of the discourse. The order "descends" only according to prominence. But the classes mentioned are not mutually exclusive, since "these little ones" surely includes the apostles, prophets, and righteous men; they are all "little ones" because they are all targets of the world's enmity. To give a cup of cold freshly drawn water, the least courtesy demands, to the least disciple just because he is a disciple does not go unrewarded. Thus the "little ones" are not portrayed as a special class of "traveling missionaries" (contra Hill) but as disciples. "Prophets" are referred to, not because Christian prophets are in view, but because this is an already accepted category for God's spokesmen and for those with whom Jesus' followers are aligned (5:10–12).

"Righteous men" is more difficult. But in two of the three passages where the term occurs in connection with "prophets" (13:17; 23:29), it must refer to righteous men of earlier generations—OT and perhaps Maccabean figures, not Christian contemporaries of Matthew, and not traveling teachers. It seems best to take the term here from the same perspective. None of Hill's evidence points unambiguously to a class of teachers known as "righteous men." Most of his Dead Sea Scrolls evidence (1QS 3:20, 22; 5:2, 9; 9:14; 1QSa 1:2, 24; 2:3) clearly demonstrates that the sectarians perceived themselves as "the righteous" over against other men. Moreover, it is far from certain that Daniel 12:3 refers to a part of the people of God with a special assignment to teach righteousness. Even there it is easy to detect a reference to all of God's people. After all, "righteousness" is a category already used in Matthew to describe all of Jesus' disciples (5:20).

Some scholars have been too eager to read anachronisms into the text and detect special groups on the basis of slender evidence. In reality, v.40, though very general, applies in the first instance to the Twelve; v.41 repeats the aphorism twice more using OT categories familiar to Jesus but extending the application from prophets to all of God's righteous people. Verse 42 groups the previous aphorisms together to make it quite clear that the sole reason for rewarding those who treat Jesus' disciples well is not that they are prophets or righteous people—they are in fact but "little ones"—but that they are Jesus' disciples. The prophet's reward and the righteous man's reward are therefore not disparate but kingdom rewards (see comments at 5:12) that are the fruit of discipleship. To receive a prophet because he is a prophet (as in 1Ki 17:9–24; 2Ki 4:8–37) presupposes, in the context of v.40, that he is Christ's prophet—so also for the "righteous man." Thus the person who receives a prophet receives Christ, his word, his ways, and his gospel and expresses solidarity with the people of God, these little ones, by receiving them for Jesus' sake (cf. 2Jn 10–11; 3Jn 8). No such person will lose his reward. While the applications to Matthew's churches, as to our own, are many, the text itself does not venture so far.

NOTES

41–42 The expression εἰς ὄνομα προφήτου (*eis onoma prophētou*, "because he is a prophet"), with its parallels, is an instance of the causal use of εἰς, *eis* (cf. Zerwick, *Biblical Greek*, para. 98, 106; contra M. J. Harris, *NIDNTT*, 3:1187). Some hold this is important in understanding Matthew's baptismal formula, but see comments at 28:18–20.

7. Transitional conclusion: expanding ministry (11:1)

1 After Jesus had finished instructing his twelve disciples, he went on from there to teach and preach in the towns of Galilee.

COMMENTARY

1 For the significance of the formulas that end Jesus' discourses, see comments at 7:28–29. This one omits "these things" or the like (see comments at 10:5a). Unlike Mark 6:30; Luke 9:10, there is no mention of the return of the Twelve, since their early successes are of less concern to Matthew than is Jesus' teaching. Attention returns to Jesus' ministry, for he did not send out the apostles in order to relieve himself of work but in order to expand the proclamation of the kingdom (9:35–10:4).

NOTES

1 The pronoun αὐτῶν (*autōn*; NIV text note, "their") is exceptionally awkward here. It cannot refer to the apostles but to the Galileans, not mentioned in the context. Nor can this easily be taken as an anachronistic distinction between church and synagogue. Most likely it is an instance of pronominal sense construction not uncommon in then contemporary secular Greek and found throughout the NT (cf. Turner, *Insights*, 149–50). If so, it is especially important not to be hasty in reading church/synagogue anachronisms into other similar passages (see comments at 4:23; 7:29; 9:35; 10:17).

IV. TEACHING AND PREACHING THE GOSPEL OF THE KINGDOM: RISING OPPOSITION (11:2–13:53)

OVERVIEW

Matthew 12–13 depend in large part on Mark 2:23–3:12; 3:20–4:34. Before this comes 11:2–30, most of which is paralleled in various parts of Luke. Daniel Boerman ("The Chiastic Structure of Matthew 11–12," *CTJ* 40 [2005]: 313–25) discerns a chiastic structure in Matthew 11–12, but it is not altogether convincing. Thematically, the three chapters (chs. 11–13) are held together by the rising tide of disappointment in and opposition to the kingdom of God that was resulting from Jesus' ministry. He was not turning out to be the kind of Messiah the people had expected. Even John the Baptist had doubts (11:2–19), and the Galilean cities that were sites of most of Jesus' miracles hardened themselves in unbelief (vv.20–24). The nature of Jesus' person and ministry was "hidden" (an important word) from the wise, despite the most open and compassionate of invitations (vv.28–30). Conflicts with Jewish leaders began to intensify (12:1–45), while people still misunderstood the most basic elements of Jesus' teaching and authority (12:46–50). But does this mean he had been checkmated or that the kingdom had not come after all? Matthew 13 is the answer—the kingdom of God was continuing its advance, even though it was often contested and ignored.

A. Narrative (11:2–12:50)

1. Jesus and John the Baptist (11:2–19)

OVERVIEW

Matthew 11:2–19 is closely paralleled by Luke 7:18–35. Occasional divergences are noted below (see esp. comments at v.19).

a. John's question and Jesus' response (11:2–6)

[2]When John heard in prison what Christ was doing, he sent his disciples [3]to ask him, "Are you the one who was to come, or should we expect someone else?"

[4]Jesus replied, "Go back and report to John what you hear and see: [5]The blind receive sight, the lame walk, those who have leprosy are cured, the deaf hear, the dead are raised, and the good news is preached to the poor. [6]Blessed is the man who does not fall away on account of me."

COMMENTARY

2–3 According to Josephus (*Ant.* 18.119 [5.2]), Herod imprisoned John the Baptist in the fortress of Machaerus, east of the Dead Sea. The bare fact is recorded in Matthew 4:12, the circumstances in 14:3–5. Apparently John had been in prison during Jesus' extensive Galilean ministry, perhaps as long as a year. The one to whom he had pointed, the one who would come in blessing and judgment (3:11–12), had brought healing to many but, it would seem, judgment to none—not even to those who had immorally and unlawfully confined the Baptist in a cruel prison, doubtless made the more unbearable for its contrast with his accustomed freedom (cf. Lk 1:80).

John heard "what Christ was doing" (v.2). The clause hides two subtle points. First, the use of (lit.) "the Christ" is peculiar, for at this stage in Jesus' ministry there was but little thoughtful ascription of this title to Jesus; and Matthew normally avoids it. Some have thought that at this point Matthew was somewhat careless about consistency in his narrative. Precisely the opposite is the case. His entire gospel is written from the perspective of faith. The very first verse affirms Jesus as the Messiah, and the prologue (chs. 1–2) seeks to prove it. So at this point Matthew somewhat unusually refers to Jesus as "the Christ" in order to remind his readers who it was that John the Baptist was doubting. Though John doubted, from Matthew's perspective the time for doubt had passed. Far from being an anachronism, this use of "the Christ" is Matthew's own designation of Jesus. Indeed, Matthew's fidelity is attested by the way he distinguishes between his own understanding and insight, drawn from his postresurrection perspective, and the gradual development of that understanding historically, including the Baptist's doubts.

The second point is that *ta erga tou Christou* (lit., "the works of Christ"; NIV, "what Christ was doing") is suitably vague to embrace a triple allusion, not only to Jesus' miracles (chs. 8–9), but also to his teaching (chs. 5–7) and growing mission (ch. 10).

As a result of these reports, John sent a pointed question "by" (reading *dia* as in the NRSV, not *duo* ["two"] as in the KJV) his disciples. This use of "disciples" shows that the term is a nontechnical one for "Christians" or "the Twelve" in Matthew (see comments at 5:1–6; 9:37). The objection, probably first raised by D. F. Strauss (*The Life of Jesus Critically Examined* [1846; repr. London: SCM Press,

1973], 219–30, esp. 229), that John was in no position to send messengers presumes to know more about security arrangements at Machaerus than we do—the more so since the Gospels show that Herod himself was ambivalent toward the prophet (Mk 6:17–26). John's question was whether Jesus was *ho erchomenos* ("the coming one," v.3, GK *2262*), exactly the same expression ascribed to John at 3:11 (cf. also 21:9; 23:39; Jn 6:14; 11:27; Heb 10:37). The expression is not a common messianic title in intertestamental literature. It probably was drawn from such passages as Psalm 118:26; Isaiah 59:20. The description of the actions of "the coming one" in 3:11 nullifies the old theory (Schweitzer, *Quest of the Historical Jesus*) that the Baptist merely expected Elijah *redivivus* ("come to life again") to follow him. John was asking Jesus whether he was the Messiah.

The question at first glance seems so out of character for what we know of the Baptist that many of the Fathers and Reformers suggest that John asked it, not for his own sake, but for the sake of his followers. Not a shred of exegetical evidence supports this view. Not only may the Baptist have become demoralized, like his namesake Elijah (cf. Keener), but the Baptist had preached in terms of imminent blessing and judgment (3:12; cf. G. R. Beasley-Murray, *Jesus and the Kingdom of God* [Grand Rapids: Eerdmans, 1986], 81). By contrast, Jesus was preaching in veiled fulfillment terms and bringing much blessing but no real judgment (cf. Dunn, *Jesus and the Spirit*, 55–62), and as a result the Baptist was having second thoughts. Wood ("Regathering of the People of God," 513) convincingly argues that in addition to the link between Israel's promised restoration and Messiah's concern for the relief of certain physical ailments—a link established by Jesus' use of the Isaiah texts—three other OT themes are called to mind: (1) the Deuteronomic curses result in diseases as a part of God's judgment, so Jesus' ministry is ending those curses; (2) the prophets regularly tie diseases to the harsh conditions of the exile, so Jesus' ministry is ending the (spiritual) exile; and (3) Ezekiel suggests that much of the suffering of the people has come on them because of the wicked shepherds that have ruled over them, and now the ideal Davidic Shepherd-King has arrived.

4–6 Jesus' answer briefly summarized his own miracles and preaching, but in the language of Isaiah 35:5–6; 61:1 (with possible allusions to 26:19; 29:18–19). At one level the answer was straightforward: Isaiah 61:1 is an explicit messianic passage, and Isaiah 35:5–6, though it has no messianic figure, describes the return of God's people to Zion with accompanying blessings (e.g., restoration of sight). Jesus definitely claimed that these messianic visions were being fulfilled in the miracles he was performing and that his preaching the Good News to the poor (see comments at 5:3) was as explicit a fulfillment of the messianic promises of Isaiah 61:1–2 as Luke 4:17–21. The powers of darkness were being undermined; the kingdom was advancing (cf. v.12).

But there is a second, more subtle level to Jesus' response. All four of the Isaiah passages refer to judgment in their immediate context: e.g., "your God will come ... with vengeance; with divine retribution" (35:4); "the day of vengeance of our God" (61:2). Thus Jesus was allusively responding to the Baptist's question: the blessings promised for the end time have broken out and prove it is here, even though the judgments are delayed (cf. Jeremias, *Jesus' Promise*, 46; Dunn, *Jesus and the Spirit*, 60). Matthew 11:6, which may include an allusion to Isaiah 8:13–14 (in which case Jesus is set in the place of Yahweh; see comments at vv.9–11), is then a gentle warning, applicable both to John and his disciples: Blessed (see comments at 5:3) is the "man who does not fall away" (for this verb, see comments at 5:29) on account of Jesus, i.e., who does not find in him and his ministry an obstacle to belief and therefore reject him. The miracles themselves were not irrefutable proof of who Jesus was (cf. Mk 8:11–12 and par.); faith was still required to read the evidence against the background of Scripture and to hear in Jesus' claim the ring of truth. But the beatitude in this form assumes the questioner has begun well and now must avoid stumbling. It is therefore an implicit challenge to reexamine one's presuppositions about what the Messiah should be and do in the light of Jesus and his fulfillment of Scripture and to bring one's understanding and faith into line with him.

b. Jesus' testimony to John (11:7–19)

(1) John in redemptive history (11:7–15)

OVERVIEW

John had often borne witness to Jesus; now Jesus bears witness to John. But the effect is to point back to himself as the sole figure who brings in the kingdom. Historically it was almost inevitable for Jesus to define the position of John the Baptist with respect to himself. Most scholars doubt he did so consecutively, as set forth here. Nevertheless, the passage holds together well, and there is little literary or historical evidence to suggest this is a composite of words spoken on other occasions. The parallel in Luke 7:24–35 preserves the same themes and movement. It omits Matthew 11:12–13 and adds Luke 7:29–30. The extra verses in Matthew are usually said to derive from Mark 9:11–13. But the two passages are linguistically and thematically rather distinct, and it is easy to imagine that Jesus had to take some position on John more than once and very definitely so for his disciples. Moreover, the tone of this passage reflects no personal conflict between John and Jesus. And this is typical of the NT witness of the relationship between the two men (cf. esp. J. A. T. Robinson, *Twelve New Testament Studies*, 28–52).

7As John's disciples were leaving, Jesus began to speak to the crowd about John: "What
did you go out into the desert to see? A reed swayed by the wind? 8If not, what did you
go out to see? A man dressed in fine clothes? No, those who wear fine clothes are in kings'
palaces. 9Then what did you go out to see? A prophet? Yes, I tell you, and more than a
prophet. 10This is the one about whom it is written:

"'I will send my messenger ahead of you,
who will prepare your way before you.'

11I tell you the truth: Among those born of women there has not risen anyone greater
than John the Baptist; yet he who is least in the kingdom of heaven is greater than he.
12From the days of John the Baptist until now, the kingdom of heaven has been forcefully

advancing, and forceful men lay hold of it. 13For all the Prophets and the Law prophesied until John. 14And if you are willing to accept it, he is the Elijah who was to come. 15He who has ears, let him hear."

COMMENTARY

7–8 "Began" does not imply that Jesus commenced his remarks while the Baptist's disciples were leaving and completed them only after they had gone (Broadus); as in v.20, it means that he took the opportunity to speak to the crowd. The rhetorical questions about John are a gently ironic way of eliminating obviously false answers in order to give the truth in vv.10–11. "A reed [probably a collective singular referring to cane grass, found in abundance along the Jordan] swayed by the wind" suggests a fickle person, tossed about in his judgment by the winds of public opinion or private misfortune (Lucian uses a similar metaphor, BDAG, 502). Certainly the people did not go out to witness such an ordinary spectacle. Nor did they go out into the desert to find a man dressed "in fine clothes" (v.8). "Fine" (*malakos*), used elsewhere in the NT only at Luke 7:25 and 1 Corinthians 6:9, connotes "softness" or even "effeminacy" and may be ironic. Contrast the rugged garb the prophet actually wore (see comments at 3:4–6). Those who are "in kings' palaces" is a sly dig at the man who was keeping John in prison.

It appears, then, that Jesus spoke in this way to disarm suspicion among the people that John's question (v.3) might betray signs of fickleness (v.7) or undisciplined weakness (v.8). Not so, responds Jesus; the man the people went out to see was neither unstable nor faithless. His question arose not from personal weakness or failure but from misunderstanding about the nature of the Messiah, owing to John's place in salvation history (see comments below). Hence Jesus addressed the crowd, not to defend himself following the Baptist's question, but to defend the Baptist.

9–11 What the people had flocked to the desert to see was a prophet, since it was commonly agreed that a true prophet had not appeared for centuries but only the *bat-qôl* (lit., "daughter of a voice"; see comments at 3:17). Small wonder there was such excitement. Jesus confirms the crowd's judgment but goes beyond it—John was not only a prophet but more than a prophet. In what respect? In this: Not only was he, like other OT prophets, a direct spokesman for God to call the nation to repentance, but he himself was also the subject of prophecy—the one who, according to Scripture, would announce the Day of Yahweh (v.10).

The form of the quotation shows influence from Exodus 23:20 (LXX) in the first clause (cf. Blomberg, "Matthew," in *CNTUOT*). Yet there is no doubt that the primary passage being cited is Malachi 3:1. The messenger in Malachi 3:1 (Elijah in Mal 4:5–6) prepares the way for the great and dreadful Day of Yahweh. The form of the text, adding "ahead of you" (probably by using Ex 23:20) in the first line, changing "before me" to "before you" in the second line, and adding "your," has the effect, on one interpretation, of making Yahweh address Messiah. On any reading of Malachi 3:1 (see France, *Jesus and the Old Testament*, 91–92 n. 31), Yahweh does not address Messiah; but inasmuch as the messenger prepares the way for Yahweh (Mal 4:5–6), with whom Jesus is constantly identified in the NT (see comments at 2:6; esp. 3:3), this periphrastic rendering makes Jesus' identity unambiguous (cf. France, *Jesus and the Old Testament*, 155). Even if Malachi 3:1 had been exactly quoted, the flow of the argument in Matthew demands that if John the Baptist is the prophesied Elijah who prepares the way for Yahweh (3:3; cf. Lk 1:76) or for the Day of Yahweh (Mal 4:5–6), and John the Baptist is Jesus' forerunner, then Jesus himself is the manifestation of Yahweh and brings in the eschatological Day of Yahweh (see Andrew S. Malone, "Is the Messiah Announced in Malachi 3:1?" *TynBul* 57 [2006]: 215–28).

Hill comments, "It is probable that the quotation has been inserted by the evangelist; it breaks the logical connection between verses 9 and 11, and anticipates the mysterious announcement in verse 14." It seems difficult to have it both ways. If the quotation anticipates v.14, then it must be left in place unless v.14 is also judged inauthentic. More important, v.10, far from breaking them up, ties v.9 and v.11 together. By citing Malachi, Jesus (v.10) has shown in what way John the Baptist is greater than a prophet: he is greater in that he alone of all the prophets was the forerunner who prepared the way for Yahweh-Jesus and personally pointed him out. While the OT prophets doubtless contributed to the corpus of revelation that pointed to Messiah, they did not serve as immediate forerunners. This is what makes John greater than a prophet (v.9)—indeed the greatest born of women (v.11; i.e., the greatest human being; cf. Job 14:1).

Thus far the argument flows coherently. But who is the "least in the kingdom of heaven," and how is he greater than John the Baptist? Many have found this comparison so difficult that some fanciful suggestions have been made. McNeile holds the kingdom to be entirely future: the least in the kingdom will *then* be greater than John *now* is. But will not John also be in the kingdom then? And how will this contribute to the argument? Others argue that *ho mikroteros* means not "the least" but "the younger," the "lesser" in a purely temporal sense. In this view it refers to Jesus: Jesus, though lesser through being younger, is greater than John the Baptist (so Chrysostom; Augustine; cf. BDF para. 61 [2]; O. Cullmann, "Ὁ ὀπίσω μου ἐρχόμενος," ConBNT 11 [1947]: 30; Zerwick, *Biblical Greek*, para. 149; Benedict T. Viviano, *Matthew and His World: The Gospel of the Open Jewish Christians: Studies in Biblical Theology* [NTOA 61. Göttingen: Vandenhoeck & Ruprecht, 2007], 81–94). This implies that John the Baptist is himself, according to Matthew, in the kingdom—a conclusion widely defended, largely on the grounds of comparing the ministries of John and Jesus (e.g., 3:2; 4:17; so, e.g., Walter Wink, *John the Baptist in the Gospel Tradition* [Cambridge: Cambridge Univ. Press, 1968], 33–35).

It must be admitted, however, that *ho mikroteros* is made to mean "the younger" chiefly because v.11 is so difficult. In view of the fact that a comparison establishing John as greater than the prophets immediately precedes this text, it is most natural to take *ho mikroteros* as meaning "the least" in the kingdom. This entails the view that John the Baptist was not himself in the kingdom. Parallels between John's and Jesus' preaching are readily explained (see comments at 4:17), and v.12 can best be taken that way as well (see comments below).

In what way, then, is the least in the kingdom greater than John the Baptist? The answer must not be in terms of mere privilege—namely, the least are greater because they live to see the kingdom actually inaugurated—but in terms of the greatness already established for John. He was the greatest of the prophets because he pointed most unambiguously to Jesus. Nevertheless, even the least in the kingdom is greater yet because, living after the crucial revelatory and eschatological events have occurred, he or she points to Jesus still more unambiguously than John the Baptist. "The issue here is not John's personal salvation, but his place in the scheme of salvation history. For all his crucial role as herald of the kingdom of heaven, John (together with all the prophets and godly people of the OT) belongs essentially to the old era, not the new" (France [NICNT]). This interpretation entirely suits the context and accomplishes three things.

1. It continues a defense of John by showing that his question (v.3), which springs neither from fickleness nor weakness (vv.7–8), does not make him forfeit his primacy among the prophets because of his being the forerunner of Jesus (vv.9–10), but that the question owes its origin to his still-veiled place in the redemptive history now unfolding.

2. By contrast it continues the theme of discipleship, whose essential function is to acknowledge Jesus before people (10:32–33), and it establishes that function as the disciples' essential greatness. Even the least in the kingdom points to Jesus Christ more clearly than all his predecessors, not excluding John. For they either live through the tumultuous events of the ministry, passion, and beyond, after which things are much clearer; or they enter the kingdom after these events, with the same clear understanding. Thus the ground is being laid for the Great Commission. Clear witness to Christ before men is not only a requirement of the kingdom (10:32–33) and a command of the resurrected Lord (28:18–20) but the true greatness of the disciple (v.11).

3. At the same time, by explaining John's greatness and his place in salvation history, this verse points back to the preeminence of Jesus himself.

12 This enigmatic saying has called forth a host of interpretations. These depend on several alternatives related to several exegetical turning points that can be combined variously. A complete list of the possibilities (for bibliography, see Chilton, *God in Strength*, 203ff.) must be passed over in favor of an interpretation that does justice both to the context and to the language. The turning points are three.

1. "From the days of John the Baptist until now." As already pointed out (vv.10–11), most commentators understand "until" in v.13 to be an exclusive usage, putting John within the kingdom (though most scholars hold that Lk 16:16 is an inclusive usage of "until"). Indeed, John P. Meier ("John the Baptist in Matthew's Gospel," *JBL* 99 [1980]: 383–405) makes it the crux of his interpretation of Matthew's treatment of the Baptist. The phrase "from the days of John the Baptist" is almost certainly a Semitic way of saying "from the time of the activity of John the Baptist" (cf. Jeremias, *New Testament Theology*, 46–47). John's ministry provides the terminus a quo, the phrase "until now" the terminus ad quem. But many argue that "until now" means "up until" Matthew's time of writing, not "up until" Jesus' time of speaking (e.g., Cope, *Matthew*, 75–76; Albright and Mann). This interpretation is rendered plausible (Albright and Mann) because the rest of the verse seems to picture violent men ransacking the kingdom (see comments below); and this certainly did not happen in the short time between the Baptist's death and this saying by Jesus during his earthly ministry.

A better synthesis emerges by taking the text strictly. The idiom "from ... " in Matthew *includes* the following term (cf. 1:17; 2:16; 23:35; 27:45). But the entire expression "from the days of John the Baptist" does not say that John inaugurates the kingdom but only that during his time of ministry it was inaugurated and (or) attacked. The expression does not even assume John's death; it assumes only that the crucial period of his ministry during which the kingdom was inaugurated lies in the past. Now this kingdom has begun, in however preliminary a way, with Jesus' preaching and powerful works during "the days of John the Baptist." Thus there is no reason why the Prophets and the Law should not prophesy "until John" in an inclusive sense (v.13)—an interpretation that not only agrees with Luke 16:16 but goes best with vv.9–11.

Whether the kingdom has been "forcefully advancing" (NIV) or attacked (see comments below), this has been going on from its inception under Jesus' ministry during the days of John the Baptist (there had to be temporal overlap if the forerunner was to prepare his way and point him out) "until now"—namely, until this point in Jesus' ministry. This does not mean that the activity (whether of forceful advance or of being attacked) stops at that point, any more than the same expression in John 2:10 (the only other place it occurs in the NT) means that everybody at the wedding instantly stopped drinking the best wine. The continuation is not the focus of interest.

2. "The kingdom of heaven has been forcefully advancing." The crux of the problem is the verb *biazetai* ("has been forcefully advancing," GK *1041*). The form is either middle or passive. If the former, the NIV rendering, or something like it, is right; if the latter, it means that the kingdom is being attacked (in a negative sense) or is being forcefully advanced (by God?) (cf. *TDNT*, 1:610–11). In Greek sources relevant to the NT, *biazetai* is considerably more common in the deponent middle than in the active or passive voices (in the NT the verb is found only here and in Lk 16:16), and this supports the NIV rendering of the clause (cf. BDAG, 175; *NIDNTT*, 3:711–12) as Ridderbos, NEB (text note), Hendriksen, Chilton, and others do. But many object to this rendering on one of two grounds: (1) it brings a notion of "force" to the kingdom contrary to the gospels' emphases, and (2) it deals poorly with the last clause of the text, since *biastēs* really must not be rendered "forceful man" (in a positive sense) but "violent man" (see comments below). The first objection is insubstantial. The kingdom has come with holy power and magnificent energy that has been pushing back the frontiers of darkness. This is especially manifest in Jesus' miracles and ties in with Jesus' response to the Baptist (Mt 11:5). Some kind of compulsion even of people is presupposed elsewhere (Lk 14:23). Moreover, the force implied by the middle deponent verb is not always violent or cruel (cf. BDAG). The second objection is important and brings us to the third part of the verse.

3. "And forceful men lay hold of it." Hendriksen, for instance, thinks the cognate noun *biastēs* ("forceful man") finds its meaning now established by the considerations discussed above for the meaning of the verb *biazetai* ("has been forcefully advancing"). The kingdom is making great strides; now is the time for courageous souls, forceful people, to take hold of it. This is no challenge for the timorous or fainthearted. This interpretation is possible but not convincing. The noun *biastēs* is rare in Greek literature (only here in the NT), but where it occurs it always has the negative connotations of violence and rapacity. Moreover, the verb *harpazō* ("lay hold of," GK *773*), a fairly common verb, almost always has the same evil connotations (a rare exception is Ac 8:39). For these reasons most commentators see a reference to violent men and then read the verb in the preceding clause as a passive: "the kingdom of heaven is suffering violence and violent men are seizing it"—so, more or less, KJV; NASB; Weymouth; NEB; Hill; Maier; E. Moore ("Βιάζω, ἁρπάζω and Cognates in Josephus," *NTS* 21 [1975]: 519–43); and many others. There are many conflicting views about who the violent men are—Zealots, Pharisees, evil spirits and their human hosts, Herod Antipas, Jewish antagonists in general. But the thrust is the same in any case.

Not satisfied with this, others have made suggestions, none convincing. The kingdom of heaven "has been taken by storm and eager men are forcing their way into it" (offered by J. B. Phillips [*New Testament in Modern English*] and C. B. Williams [*New Testament in the Language of the People*] and defended by Keener) is a rendering that combines the unlikelihood of a passive verb with the unlikelihood of a positive-connotative noun. James Swetnam (*Bib* 61 [1980]: 440–42) wants the verse to mean that from the time of John the kingdom has been suffering violence (passive verb) *of interpretation*; and those who are of like-minded violence—i.e., who understand the kingdom in the same way—are the ones who snatch it away. To the weaknesses of the last suggestion, this one adds an unparalleled meaning ("to suffer violence of interpretation") to the verb.

The best solution is to take the verb in its most likely voice, middle deponent, and the noun and verb of the last clause with their normal evil connotations: namely, from the time of John the Baptist (as explained above) until now, the kingdom of heaven has been forcefully advancing; and violent or rapacious men have been trying (conative present) to plunder it—so Pamment ("Kingdom of Heaven," 227–28), though she then makes the rendering nearly incoherent by saying the kingdom of heaven is exclusively future (see comments at 5:3). Furthermore, the verbs in the last two clauses are both in the present tense. If they are rendered as presents in English, the syntax is wrong: "From the time of John until now the kingdom is forcefully advancing, and violent men are pillaging it." But that acceptable Greek syntax calls in question Pamment's views on the futurity of the kingdom of heaven and sets up the picture of a tremendous, violent struggle being waged even as Jesus speaks. Certainly "Jesus considers his ministry to be a time when the Kingdom can be attacked as being present" (Hill; cf. Kümmel, *Promise and Fulfillment*, 121ff.).

If this is a form of antanaclasis (a figure of speech in which the same word is repeated in a different or even contradictory sense), based in this instance not on exactly the same word but on a cognate, the verse admirably suits the context. The argument up to v.11 has established John the Baptist's greatness, grounded in his ministry of preparing for and pointing out Christ; it has anticipated the witness of those in the kingdom who are even greater than John because the least of them testifies to Christ yet more clearly. Now, Jesus goes on to say, from the days of the Baptist—i.e., from the beginning of Jesus' ministry—the kingdom has been forcefully advancing (the point also made in Lk 16:16). But it has not swept all opposition away, as John expected (see comments at vv.2–4).

Simultaneous with the kingdom's advance have been the attacks of violent men on it. That is the very point John could not grasp. Now Jesus expressly affirms it. The statement is general because it does not refer to just one kind of opposition. It includes Herod's imprisonment of John (cf. Robinson, *Twelve New Testament Studies*, 44–45), the attacks by Jewish leaders now intensifying (9:34; 12:22–24), the materialism that craved a political Messiah and the prosperity he would bring but not his righteousness (11:20–24). Already Jesus has warned his disciples of persecution and suffering (10:16–42); the opposition was rising and would get worse. Meanwhile, not the aggressive zealots will find rest for their souls, but the weary, the burdened, the children to whom the Father has revealed the truth (11:25–30). The last-mentioned passage is the death knell of those who think the *biastai* are "forceful men" (in a positive sense); it is exactly what the chapter, taken as a whole, rules out. Instead, we are hearing the sound of divine grace, a note that becomes a symphony later in this gospel.

If this interpretation is sound, there seems little reason either for thinking that v.12 is out of place or for seeing in it the later creation of the church.

13 In view of the preceding, "until John" means up to and including John (cf. D. A. Carson, "Do the Prophets and the Law Quit Prophesying Before John? A Note on Matthew 11:13," in *The Gospels and the Scriptures of Israel* [ed. Craig A. Evans and W. Richard Stegner; JSNTSup 104; Sheffield: Sheffield Univ. Press, 1994], 179–94). The Baptist belongs to the last stage of the divine economy before the inauguration of the kingdom (as in Lk 16:16). Sigal (*Halakhah of Jesus*, 68–69) mishandles this verse because he treats it as if the Prophets and the Law must prophesy about John rather than until John. Some of what the OT says about John has been set out in v.10. Here the point is to set out the redemptive-historical turning point that has brought about the transformation of perspectives explained in vv.11–12. The two anomalies in the verse are (1) "the Prophets" precedes "the Law," an unusual order (cf. 5:17; 7:12), and (2) both "Prophets" and "Law" prophesy. Both anomalies serve the same purpose—a powerful way of saying that the entire OT has a prophetic function, a function it maintained up until, and including, John the Baptist.

In the twin settings of Matthew's "fulfillment" theme (see comments at 2:15; 5:17–20) and the role of John the Baptist (11:10), it is understood that now, after John the Baptist, that which Prophets and Law prophesied has come to pass—the kingdom has dawned and Messiah has come. This establishes the primary function of the OT in Matthew's gospel: it points to Jesus and the kingdom. This confirms our interpretation of 5:17–20. The *gar* ("for") thus ties 11:13 not to v.11 but to v.12 (confirming v.12 as an integral part of the argument). Verse 13 further explains that "from the days of John the Baptist"—i.e., from the beginning of Jesus' ministry—the kingdom has been forcefully advancing. The Prophets and the Law prophesied until then and, implicitly, prophesied of this new era. And from that time on, the fulfillment of the prophecy, the kingdom itself, has been forcefully advancing.

14–15 The argument returns to vv.9–10, stating explicitly what Jesus said there: John the Baptist was the prophesied "Elijah." This locates his place and function in the history of redemption and affirms again that what Jesus was doing was eschatological—he was bringing in the Day of Yahweh. The clause "if you are willing to accept it" does not cast doubt on the truth of the identification; but, like v.15, it acknowledges how difficult it was to grasp it, especially before the cross and the resurrection. For if the people had truly understood, they would necessarily have seen Jesus' place in salvation history as the fulfillment of OT hopes and prophecy. That is why the sonorous formula of v.15 is added (cf. 13:9, 43; 24:15; Rev 2:7, 11 et al.): the identification of John with prophesied Elijah has messianic implications that "those with ears" would hear. The formula is both a metaphorical description of and a challenge to spiritual sensitivity to the claims of the gospel.

NOTES

8 Here and in v.9, ἀλλά (*alla*, "but") is used after a rhetorical question, with the answer implied but suppressed. In other words, the Greek conjunction here adopts the force of Aramaic אֶלָּא (*ʾelāʾ*, "if not"). But this meaning of ἀλλά, *alla*, is also a feature of classical Greek; and the NIV, following McNeile, translates it "if not."

9 The meaning of τί (*ti*) affects punctuation: If "what," read τί ἐξήλθατε ἰδεῖν; προφήτην; (*ti exēlthate idein; prophētēn;*) as "What did you go out to see? A prophet?" If "why," read "Why did you go out to see a prophet?" The problem is compounded by an important variant that reverses the last two Greek words and makes impossible the former punctuation. But the textual evidence is strongest for the order given in the first reading above, and the parallel use of τί, *ti*, in vv.7–8 likewise favors "what." It is doubtful whether *Gospel of Thomas* 78, which prefers "why," is authentic.

12 Obviously related to the interpretation of this verse is the interpretation of the parallel in Luke 16:16. The clause "the good news of the kingdom of God is being preached" is an acceptable parallel to Matthew's "the kingdom of heaven has been forcefully advancing" and eliminates the perplexing verb βιάζεται (*biazetai*, "is forcefully advancing"). The problem lies in the last clause of Luke 16:16: καὶ πᾶς εἰς αὐτὴν βιάζεται (*kai pas eis autēn biazetai*), which might mean (1) "and everyone is forced into it" or, (2) more plausibly, "and everyone is forcing his way into it" (NIV). The latter might be taken in a positive sense, in which case it is not parallel to v.12 as we have interpreted it (see comments above); or in a negative sense dealing with opponents manifesting hostile intent, in which case the clause is parallel to v.12 as we have interpreted it, but the verb is being used in a different sense than in Matthew, where the negative part of the verse depends only on the cognate noun, not the verb. The question remains a difficult one (see discussion in Marshall, *Gospel of Luke*, 626–30).

14 It is difficult to know why, according to John 1:21, the Baptist should deny that he was Elijah. Modern scholarship for the most part assumes independent and mutually contradictory traditions about the Baptist that reached the separate evangelists, who passed them on without recognizing the problem. But other suggestions include (1) John denied he was Elijah because his questioners expected a literal fulfillment—if he had answered in the affirmative, they would therefore have heard an untruth—and (2) John the Baptist saw himself as the voice of one crying in the wilderness (cf. Jn 1:23) but did not himself recognize that he was also fulfilling the Malachi prophecy. The second alternative may have support from vv.7–15; for according to it, John's knowledge did not extend to the nuanced dimensions of Christian "already/not yet" eschatology, and he may well have been in the dark on other points.

(2) The unsatisfied generation (11:16–19)

16"To what can I compare this generation? They are like children sitting in the marketplaces and calling out to others:

17 "'We played the flute for you,
and you did not dance;
we sang a dirge,
and you did not mourn.'

18For John came neither eating nor drinking, and they say, 'He has a demon.' 19The Son of
Man came eating and drinking, and they say, 'Here is a glutton and a drunkard, a friend of
tax collectors and "sinners."' But wisdom is proved right by her actions."

COMMENTARY

16–17 See the close parallel in Luke 7:31–35. "Comparison" stands at the heart of Jesus' parables (see comments at 13:24). Here Jesus uses an analogy to show his view of "this generation" (v.16), a designation recurring in 12:41–42, 45; 23:36; 24:34 (cf. 12:39; 16:4; 17:17) and used of Jesus' generation in connection with their general rejection of himself as Messiah. This identification of "this generation" is confirmed here by the next pericope (vv.20–24). Rudolf Stier (*Words of the Lord Jesus*, 2:98) comments, "It cannot but be noted that the Lord, *nihil humani a se alienum putans* [judging nothing human to be without interest to himself], as he took notice of the rending of mended garments (Mt 9:16), and the domestic concerns of the children in their beds (Lk 11:7), so also observes the children's play in the marketplace, and finds in everything the material for the analogies of his wise teaching."

There are either two kinds of games (v.17), a wedding game and a funeral game, or, less likely, two cries within one game, but the children cannot be satisfied with either. Because men traditionally danced at weddings and women traditionally mourned at funerals, Jeremias (*Parables of Jesus*, 160–62) suggests the two groups of children are boys and girls mutually criticizing each other. Curiously, both Gundry and Davies and Allison follow this line, but see the boys and girls in opposite roles. In reality, the text makes nothing of gender distinctions in the children's play (rightly noted by France [NICNT]).

18–19 "For" shows that Jesus now gives the reason the behavior of "this generation" suggests the comparison he has drawn. John the Baptist lived ascetically, "neither eating nor drinking," i.e., neither indulging in dinner parties (cf. 3:4) nor drinking alcohol (cf. Lk 1:15). Although he drew crowds (vv.7–8) and many were willing to enjoy his light for a time (Jn 5:35), the people as a whole rejected him, even charging him with demon-possession. Jesus came eating and drinking (9:10–11; Lk 15:1–2; cf. Jn 2:1–11) and was charged with gluttony, drunkenness, and bad associations (v.19; cf. Pr 23:20). Like disgruntled children, "this generation" found it easier to whine their criticisms and voice their discontent than to "play the game." Jesus says in effect, "But all you do is to give orders and criticize. For you the Baptist is a madman because he fasts, while you want to make merry; me you reproach because I eat with publicans, while you insist on strict separation from sinners. You hate the preaching of repentance, and you hate the proclamation of the gospel. So you play your childish game with God's messengers while Rome burns!" (Jeremias, *Parables of Jesus*, 161–62).

But the criticism runs at a still deeper level. If they had understood John, they would have understood Jesus, and vice versa; the thought has links with vv.7–15 (Bonnard).

Here Jesus uses *Son of Man* not only as a self-reference but as a veiled messianic allusion (see comments at 8:20). For tax collectors and sinners, see comments at 5:46.

The closing proverb has provoked much debate because Luke has "all her children" and Matthew "her actions." This proved so difficult that copyists in many MSS assimilated Matthew to Luke, where the text is relatively firm (cf. Metzger, *Textual Criticism*, 30; O. Linton, "The Parable of the Children's Game," *NTS* 22 [1975–76]: 165–71). But the problem cannot be so easily evaded. Aramaic reconstructions are not convincing.

Luke's form is probably original. It is commonly interpreted to mean that the claims of wisdom are proved true by all her children—all who accept the message of wisdom's envoys, John and Jesus (cf. Lk 7:29–30; some do accept it: see Marshall, *Gospel of Luke*, 303–4). Why the change to "actions" in Matthew? Suggs (*Wisdom, Christology, and Law*, 36–58) argues that the proverb should not be read as the conclusion to the immediately preceding parable but to vv.2–18 and notes the use of *erga* ("actions," GK *2240*) in v.2 (NIV, "what Christ was doing"). On this basis he argues that the proverb in Matthew reflects Son of Man "wisdom" Christology. Wisdom is proved right by her actions, and those actions are the actions of Christ (vv.2–5). Jesus is therefore wisdom incarnate (similarly, but more cautiously, David R. Catchpole, "Tradition History," in *New Testament Interpretation* [ed. Marshall], 167–71; Dunn, *Christology*, 197–98; and many others).

Certainly wisdom, already personified in the OT (e.g., Job 28; Pr 1; 8) and developed in Jewish tradition into a quasipersonal hypostasis in heaven, an agent who (or which) expresses the mind of God (cf. *TDNT*, 7:469–526; Felix Christ, *Jesus Sophia* [Zurich: Zwingli, 1970], 13–60, 156–63), sometimes serves in the NT as a vehicle for Christology. Yet here wisdom is best understood in its more traditional association with God. God's wisdom is vindicated by her (wisdom's) actions. The Wisdom-Christology theory must be rejected here. The theme of Matthew 11 is not Christology but the place of John the Baptist (and therefore of Jesus) in salvation history. The addition of such a Christology in v.19b adds little to the argument, and Suggs's detailed reasons for defending this view entail reconstructions of church history fundamentally questionable on other grounds.

The proverb should be read in the light of the preceding parable: God's wisdom has been vindicated (*edikaiōthe*, GK *1467*; NIV, "is proved right"—but the aorist, contra Jeremias [*Parables of Jesus*, 162 n. 42] and Turner [*Syntax*, 73], should not be taken as gnomic in this highly specific context) by her actions—i.e., by the lifestyles of both John and Jesus, referred to in the previous verses. Wisdom in the OT is much concerned with right living. John and Jesus have both been criticized and rejected for the way they live. But wisdom, preeminently concerned about right living, has been vindicated by her actions: their respective lifestyles are both acknowledged as hers (for questions of authenticity, see *TDNT*, 8:431–32).

A similar approach best interprets Luke. The phrase "all her children" does not refer to all those who accept John and Jesus as wisdom's envoys: vv.29–30 do not picture the masses accepting them but, unlike the Pharisees and other leaders, merely hearing them gladly. The parable follows in which this generation is denounced for not truly understanding and participating. Wisdom's "children" are therefore John and Jesus, not the crowds. "All her children" does not militate against this, because the form is proverbial and meant to include all God's messengers, even those so radically different as John and Jesus. The two forms of the saying are therefore not very far apart. Luke focuses on the lifestyles of John and Jesus as wisdom's children, thus concentrating on their persons, Matthew on their actions.

Not only is this interpretation coherent and contextually suitable, but it wraps up the preceding section in which Jesus has been exonerating the Baptist by explaining his role in redemptive history and simultaneously castigating the people for their spiritual dullness. See D. A. Carson, "Matthew 11:19 / Luke 7:35: A Test Case for the Bearing of Q Christology on the Synoptic Problem," in *Jesus of Nazareth: Lord and Christ* (ed. Joel B. Green and Max Turner; Grand Rapids: Eerdmans, 1994), 128–46.

NOTES

16 KJV's "friends" is explained by minor textual support for ἑταίροις (*hetairois*, "friends") instead of ἑτέροις (*heterois*, "others").

19 Several have argued (including Linton ["Parable of the Children's Game," 177–78]) that the preposition ἀπό (*apo*; NIV, "by") could be rendered "over against," reflecting מִן קֳדָם (*min qᵉddām*). In that case, "children" is required: i.e., wisdom is proved right over against her children—the Pharisees and others who think they are right. But it is doubtful whether Greek readers would naturally think of ἀπό, *apo*, in this way, and such a meaning is nonsensical in Matthew.

2. The condemned and the accepted (11:20–30)

a. The condemned: woes on unrepentant cities (11:20–24)

OVERVIEW

See Luke 10:12–15, in the context of the commission to the seventy-two. The structure of the two passages is not close, the language moderately so. There is no particular reason to think that Matthew 11:20–24 is the original: "then" is a loose expression in this gospel (see comments at 3:13), and "began" (see comments at v.7) is not much tighter. Luke's context is not clearly original; the second person in 10:13–15 may argue against it (but see comments at v.24). But there is no way to rule out the possibility Jesus uttered these "woes" repeatedly as warnings.

The denunciation in the last pericope (vv.16–19) now becomes sharper. Structurally there are two series of warnings, each with the same sequence of warning (vv.21a, 23a), explanation (vv.21b, 23b), and comparison (vv.22, 24) (cf. Joseph A. Comber, "The Composition and Literary Characteristics of Matthew 11:20–24," *CBQ* 39 [1977]: 497–504).

20Then Jesus began to denounce the cities in which most of his miracles had been
performed, because they did not repent. 21"Woe to you, Korazin! Woe to you, Bethsaida!
If the miracles that were performed in you had been performed in Tyre and Sidon, they
would have repented long ago in sackcloth and ashes. 22But I tell you, it will be more
bearable for Tyre and Sidon on the day of judgment than for you. 23And you, Capernaum,
will you be lifted up to the skies? No, you will go down to the depths. If the miracles that
were performed in you had been performed in Sodom, it would have remained to this
day. 24But I tell you that it will be more bearable for Sodom on the day of judgment than
for you."

COMMENTARY

20 The verb *oneidizein* ("denounce," GK *3943*), used only here and in 5:11; 27:44 in Matthew, is a strong verb, conveying indignation along with either insults (as in 5:11) or justifiable reproach (as here; cf. BDAG, 710). The expression *hai pleistai dynameis autou* (lit., "his very many miracles," elative superlative; cf. Turner, *Grammatical Insights*, 34) is rightly rendered "most of his miracles." Jesus did not denounce these cities for vicious opposition but because, despite the fact that most of his miracles took place there—miracles that attested his messianic mission (vv.5–6)—they had not repented (see comments at 3:2; 4:17). The many miracles again remind us of the extent of Jesus' ministry (cf. 4:23; 8:16; 9:35; Jn 20:30; 21:25) and of the depth of responsibility imposed on those with more light. "Every hearer of the New Testament is either much happier (v.11), or much more wretched than them of old time" (Bengel, *Gnomon*, 169)—those who lived before Christ.

21–22 *Ouai* (GK *4026*) can mean doom or solemn warning ("woe") or pity ("alas"); both are mingled here. Warnings have been given before; now woes are pronounced. Korazin is mentioned in the NT only here and in Luke 10:13. Its ruins may probably be identified with Kirbet Keraze, about two miles northwest of Capernaum. The Bethsaida in question was probably the home of Andrew, Peter, and Philip (Jn 1:44; 12:21) on the west side of Galilee, not Bethsaida Julias on the northeast shores near the Jordan inlet. Tyre and Sidon were large Phoenician cities on the Mediterranean, not far away and often denounced by OT prophets for their Baal worship (Isa 23; Eze 26–28; Joel 3:4; Am 1:9–10; Zec 9:2–4). "Sackcloth" is a rough fabric made from the short hairs of camels and usually worn next to the skin to express grief or sorrow (2Sa 3:31; 1Ki 21:27; 2Ki 6:30; Joel 1:8; Jnh 3:5–8). Ashes were added in cases of deep emotion (cf. Job 42:6; Da 9:3), whether one put them on the head (2Sa 13:19; La 2:10), sat in them (Jnh 3:6), lay on them (Est 4:3), or even rolled in them (Jer 6:26; Mic 1:10). For "But I tell you" (v.22)—properly "Indeed I tell you" (here and in v.24)—see comments at 26:64.

Three large theological propositions are presupposed by Jesus' insistence that on the day of judgment (see comments at 10:15; cf. 12:36; Ac 17:31; 2Pe 2:9; 3:7; 1Jn 4:17; Jude 6), when he will judge (7:22; 25:34), things will go worse for the cities that have received so much light than for the pagan cities. The first is that the Judge has contingent knowledge: he knows what Tyre and Sidon would have done under such-and-such circumstances. The second is that God does not owe revelation to anyone, or else there is injustice in withholding it. The third is that punishment on the day of judgment takes into account opportunity. There are degrees of felicity in paradise and degrees of torment in hell (12:41; 23:13; cf. Lk 12:47–48), a point Paul well understood (Ro 1:20–2:16). The implications for Western, English-speaking Christendom today are sobering.

23–24 For Capernaum, see comments at 4:13. The city was not only Jesus' base (4:13), but he performed many specific miracles there (8:5–17; 9:2–8, 18–33; Mk 1:23–28; Jn 4:46–54). For the difficult textual variants, see Metzger (*Textual Commentary*, 30–31) and France (*Jesus and the Old Testament*, 243): the question, kept in the NIV (v.23), is probably right. Whether "go down" (conforming to Lk 10:15) or "will be brought down" (conforming to Isa 14:15) is correct, the thrust is clear; and the allusion to Isaiah 14:15 is unmistakable. The favored city of Capernaum, like self-exalting Babylon, will be brought down to Hades (see comments at 5:22). The OT passage is a taunt against the wicked and arrogant city, personified in its king; and Capernaum is lumped together with Babylon, which all Jews regarded as the epitome of evil (cf. Rev 17:5). The heaven-hades contrast can be metaphorical for exaltation-humiliation or the like (cf. Job 11:8; Ps 139:8; Am 9:2; Ro 10:6–7). But in view of the surrounding references to "day of judgment," Hades must be given more sinister overtones. Similarly, though Sodom (Ge 19) was proverbial for wickedness (cf. Eze 16:44–52), it will be easier on the day of judgment for "the land of Sodom" (so Gk., recalling that several cities were involved in the sin and the destruction) than for Capernaum (see comments at vv.21–22).

The "you" in "I tell you" (v.22) is plural, probably implying the crowd (v.7), since the singular "you" is used for the city (vv.23–24, Gk.). This means that using the second person to address the cities is no more than a rhetorical device of Jesus' preaching.

b. The accepted (11:25–30)

OVERVIEW

If vv.20–24 describe the condemned, vv.25–30 describe the accepted. Verses 25–30 can be broken into three parts: vv.25–26, 27, 28–30. The first two are paralleled by Luke 10:21–22. The unity of the three parts and the authenticity of each have been hotly debated. Contrary to earlier opinion (esp. E. Norden, *Agnostos Theos* [Stuttgart: Teubner, 1913]), the language is not that of Hellenistic mysticism (Norden proposed Sir 51 as the closest parallel) but is thoroughly Semitic (cf. Davies, *Christian Origins*, 119–44; Manson, *Sayings of Jesus*, 79; Jeremias, *New Testament Theology*, 24, 57–58), which means that the provenance is Palestinian. See Celia Deutsch, *Hidden Wisdom and the Easy Yoke: Wisdom, Torah, and Discipleship in Matthew* (JSNTSup 18; Sheffield, JSOT Press, 1987), 107–11, for detailed discussion of the Jewish conceptual background of vv.25–27. Further aspects of the authenticity question are discussed below (see A. M. Hunter, *Gospel and Apostle* [London: SCM Press, 1975], 60–67).

Jesus' prayer builds on his rejection (vv.16–24) while still recognizing his mission (cf. 10:5–42).

(1) Because of the revelation of the Father (11:25–26)

25At that time Jesus said, "I praise you, Father, Lord of heaven and earth, because you have hidden these things from the wise and learned, and revealed them to little children. 26Yes, Father, for this was your good pleasure."

COMMENTARY

25 The Greek *en ekeinō tō kairō* ("at that time") is a loose connective in Matthew (cf. 12:1; 14:1), loosely historical (it was about that time) and tightly thematic (this pericope must be read in terms of the preceding denunciation). Luke 10:21 has Jesus saying these words "at that hour" (*en autē tē hōra*; NIV, "at that time") when the seventy-two joyfully returned from their mission, an event Matthew does not record. Luke's connective relates to the success of the mission; Matthew's assumes that there has been some success (God has revealed these things to little children) but draws a sharper antithesis between the recipients of such revelation and the "wise and learned," who, like the inhabitants of the cities just denounced, understand nothing.

While *exomologoumai soi* ("I praise you") can be used in the sense of "I confess my sins" (cf. 3:6), the basic meaning is acknowledgment. Sins truly acknowledged are sins confessed. When this verb is used with respect to God, the person praying "acknowledges" who God is, the propriety of his ways, and the excellence of his character. At that point, acknowledgment is scarcely distinguishable from praise (as in Ro 14:11; 15:9; Php 2:11; cf. LXX of Ps 6:6; 7:18; 17:50 et al.).

Here Jesus addresses God as "Father" and "Lord of heaven and earth" (cf. Sir 51:10; Tob 7:16). These are particularly appropriate titles, because the former indicates Jesus' sense of sonship (see comments at 6:9) and prepares for v.27, while the latter recognizes God's sovereignty over the universe and prepares for vv.25–26. God is sovereign, free to conceal or reveal as he wills. God has revealed "these things"—the significance of Jesus' miracles (cf. vv.20–24), the messianic age unfolding largely unnoticed, the content of Jesus' teaching—to *nēpiois* ("little children," "childlike disciples," "simple ones," GK *3758*; see Jeremias, *New Testament Theology*, 111; comments at 18:1–5; cf. Jn 7:48–49; 1Co 1:26–29; 3:18); and he has hidden them from the "wise and learned."

Many restrict the "wise and learned" to the Pharisees and teachers of the law, but the context implies something broader. Jesus has just finished pronouncing woes on "this generation" (v.16) and denouncing entire cities (vv.20–24). These are "the wise and learned" (better, "the wise and understanding") from whom the real significance of Jesus' ministry is concealed. The point of interest is not their education, any more than the point of interest in the "little children" is their age or size. The contrast is between those who are self-sufficient and deem themselves wise and those who are dependent and love to be taught.

For revealing the riches of the good news of the kingdom to the one and hiding it from the other, Jesus uttered his praise to his Father. Zerwick (*Biblical Greek*, para. 452) argues that though the construction formally puts God's concealing and his revealing on the same level, in reality it masks a Semitic construction. See Romans 6:17, which reads literally, "But thanks be to God that you were servants of sin, but you obeyed from the heart the form of teaching with which you were entrusted." But this example does not greatly help here; for even when the construction is rendered concessively ("I praise you ... because, though you have hidden these things from the wise and learned, you have revealed them to little children"), God remains the one who reveals and conceals.

Yet we must not think that God's concealing and revealing are symmetrical activities arbitrarily exercised toward neutral human beings who are both innocent and helpless in the face of the divine decree. God is dealing with a race of sinners (cf. 1:21; 7:11) whom he owes nothing. Thus to conceal "these things" is not an act of injustice but of judgment—the very judgment John the Baptist was looking for and failed to find in Jesus (see comments at vv.2–6). The astonishing thing about God's activity is not that God acts in both mercy and judgment but who the recipients of that mercy and judgment are: those who pride themselves in understanding divine things are judged; those who understand nothing are taught. The predestination pattern is the counterpoint of grace.

26 Far from bemoaning or finding fault with his Father's revealing and concealing, Jesus delighted in it. The conjunction *hoti* is best understood as "because" or "for" (NIV): I thank you *because* this was your good pleasure; and that is what Jesus "acknowledges" or "praises." Whatever pleases his Father pleases him. "It is often in a person's prayers that his truest thoughts about himself come to the surface. For this reason, the thanksgiving of Jesus here recorded is one of the most precious pieces of spiritual autobiography found in the Synoptic Gospels" (Tasker, 121). Jesus' balance mirrored the balance of Scripture: he could simultaneously denounce the cities that did not repent and praise the God who does not reveal, for God's sovereignty in election is not mitigated by man's stubbornness and sin, while man's responsibility is in no way diminished by God's "good pleasure" that sovereignly reveals and conceals (cf. Carson, *Divine Sovereignty*, 205ff.).

NOTES

25 The Greek has ἀποκριθεὶς ὁ Ἰησοῦς εἶπεν (*apokritheis ho Iēsous eipen*, "Jesus answered and said"), not just ὁ Ἰησοῦς εἶπεν (*ho Iēsous eipen*, NIV, "Jesus said"); similarly 12:38; 17:4; 26:63 (text note.); 28:5, where there is no "question" to "answer." This simply reflects Hebrew idiom (Zerwick, *Biblical Greek*, para. 366).

(2) Because of the agency of the Son (11:27)

27 "All things have been committed to me by my Father. No one knows the Son except the Father, and no one knows the Father except the Son and those to whom the Son chooses to reveal him."

COMMENTARY

27 Despite contrary opinions, the arguments for the authenticity of this saying are very strong. Long rejected because it was thought to reflect Johannine theology, which was judged to be the product of late Hellenization, this verse has by and large gained the recognition of scholarship that the "knowledge" categories here are Jewish and the structure of the verse Semitic (cf. Jeremias, *Prayers of Jesus*, 45ff.). Dunn (*Christology*, 199–200) has shown that the closest parallels are in the election language of the OT, a strong argument for the unity of vv.25–27.

Hill denies the authenticity of the saying but candidly admits, "The greatest barrier to the acceptance of the genuineness of the verse is the supposition that Jesus could not have made such an absolute claim for himself." This turns in part on the observation that, apart from the fourth gospel, the absolute expression "the Son" is exceedingly rare. But significantly it does occur twice more in Matthew, at 24:36 (cf. Mk 13:32) and 28:19 (elsewhere, cf. 1Co 15:28; Heb 1:8). Jeremias (*Prayers of Jesus*, 50) argues that Jesus' habit of addressing God as "Father" could well have contributed to such a self-understanding on the part of Jesus; but even he thinks v.27 should be understood generically: "Just as only a father really knows his son, so only a son really knows his father." But even if he is right, in a context where (1) Jesus has just addressed God as "Father" (vv.25–26) and (2) makes himself a son in an exclusive sense (3) with the sole power to mediate knowledge of God, one must conclude that the "generic" statement Jeremias finds could be applied *only* to Jesus, and that in such a way as to make his sonship exclusive.

Past interpreters often said that "the Son" is never used in pre-Christian sources as a title for the Messiah. With the discovery of 4Q174 (*Florilegium*) 10–14, citing 2 Samuel 7:14 and applying to "the Branch" of David the words "I will be his Father and he shall be my Son," this judgment must be reconsidered. Though it may not be a direct messianic title, it was certainly used to refer to an apocalyptic figure who was the son of a king, presumably David, and thus picks up OT uses of "Son" (see Ps 2; comments at 2:15; 3:17; 16:13–16; cf. Fitzmyer, *Wandering Aramean*, 102–7; M. Hengel, *The Son of God: The Origin of Christology and the History of Jewish-Hellenistic Religion* [London: SCM Press, 1976]; Guthrie, *New Testament Theology*, 301ff.). As with "Son of Man" (see Reflections, p. 247), so with "Son of God": it appears that Jesus used a designation not firmly defined and open to several interpretations as part of his gradual self-disclosure, a revelation that could be fully grasped only after the cross and the resurrection. Thus for Matthew there is no doubt of what Jesus is saying, because Matthew's "Son" or "Son of God" categories must be seen against the backdrop, not only of the prologue, but also of 3:17.

The latter passage raises a still more basic point. Cannot Jesus himself be thought to originate some things? Was the church so rich in imagination and Jesus so imaginatively poor that all new developments in titles and theology must be ascribed only to the church? If 3:17 is historical, why should not Jesus think of himself as the Son in 11:27? Is it necessary to conclude, with Hill, that v.27 cannot be authentic because it sounds like the authority of the postresurrection Jesus in 28:18? And if the two do sound alike, why should we not therefore conclude that there is more continuity between the earthly ministry of Jesus and the resurrected Lord than most scholars are prepared to admit?

Verse 27 is a christological claim of prime importance, fitting easily into the context. After declaring that the Father gives true understanding of "these things" to "little children" (vv.25–26), Jesus now adds that he is the exclusive agent of that revelation. "All things" may have reference not to "all authority" (as in 28:18) but to "all divine knowledge," all knowledge of "these things" (in v.25). But because the Son has not only knowledge but the authority to choose those to whom he will reveal God, probably "all things" includes authority. The reciprocal knowledge of Son and Father where the Father is God presupposes a special sonship indeed. And this unique mutual knowledge guarantees that the revelation the Son gives is true.

Not least astonishing about this reciprocity is the clause "No one knows the Son except the Father." Even if it is rendered in Jeremias's way (above), in this exclusivistic context it makes a claim no mere mortal could honestly make. There is a self-enclosed world of Father and Son that is opened to others only by the revelation provided by the Son. "It is one thing to know by equality of nature, and another by the condescension of him who reveals" (Jerome, cited in Broadus, 252). This revelation is not only factual (the Son reveals "these things") but personal (the Son reveals "him"—the Father).

The Son reveals the Father to those whom he, from time to time, wills (present subjunctive; cf. Turner, *Syntax*, 107). Just as the Son praises the Father for revealing and concealing according to his good pleasure (v.26), so the Father has authorized the Son to reveal or not according to his will. The text places enormous emphasis on Jesus' person and authority. The thought is closely echoed both in John (3:35; 8:19; 10:15; 14:9; 16:15) and in the Synoptics (Mt 13:11; Mk 4:11—Jesus makes known the secrets of the kingdom; cf. Mt 10:37–39; 11:25; Lk 10:23–24; ch. 15). What is made clear in this passage is that sonship and messiahship are not quite the same. "Sonship precedes messiahship and is in fact the ground for the messianic mission" (Ladd, *Theology of the New Testament*, 165–67, esp. 167).

(3) Because of the Son's gentle invitation (11:28–30)

OVERVIEW

These verses are only in Matthew. Jesus is the one who alone reveals the Father (v.27). Jesus it is who invites, not "the wise and learned" (v.25), but "the weary and burdened" (v.28). The Son reveals the Father, not to gratify learned curiosity or to reinforce the self-sufficiency of the arrogant, but to bring "the little children" (v.25) to know the Father (v.27), to introduce the weary to eschatological rest (v.28)—or, as the angel once said to Joseph, so that Jesus Messiah might save his people from their sins (1:21).

Partly because these verses have some links with Sirach 51:23–27, where wisdom invites men to her yoke, several have argued that Matthew here identifies Jesus with hypostasized wisdom (e.g., Zumstein, *La condition du croyant*, 140ff.; Dunn, *Christology*, 200–201). But the contrasts between Sirach 51 and this passage are more impressive than the similarities. In the former, Sirach is inviting men to take on the yoke of studying Torah as the means of gaining acceptance and rest; in the latter, Jesus offers eschatological rest, not to the scholar who studies Torah, but to the weary. Jesus' teaching must be adopted, not Torah; and this stands, as the next pericopes show (12:1–8, 9–14), in welcome relief to a primarily legal understanding of the OT. Stanton (*Jesus of Nazareth*, 368–71) disputes that there is any link with Sirach. But whether or not he has gone too far in this conclusion, he is entirely right to point out that despite the common words "to me," "toil," "yoke," "find," "rest," and "soul" in the two passages, the configuration of the two sets is entirely different. In Sirach, the writer, the Wise Man, receives Wisdom's blessings and invites his readers to share in them. Here, however, Jesus is not the mediator of Wisdom's blessings "but issues 'Wisdom's' invitation in his own person. Wisdom's yoke is now his yoke, and it is he who offers rest to those who toil" (France [NICNT]).

28"Come to me, all you who are weary and burdened, and I will give you rest. 29Take my yoke upon you and learn from me, for I am gentle and humble in heart, and you will find rest for your souls. 30For my yoke is easy and my burden is light."

COMMENTARY

28 The "me" is grammatically unemphatic but in the wake of v.27 extremely important. Jesus invites the "weary" (the participle suggests those who have become weary through heavy struggling or toil) and the "burdened" (the passive side of weariness, overloaded like beasts of burden) to come to him;

and he (not the Father) will give them rest. There is an echo of Jeremiah 31:25, where Yahweh refreshes his people through the new covenant.

While there is no need to restrict the "burdens," it is impossible not to be reminded of the "heavy loads" the Pharisees put on men's shoulders (23:4; cf. 12:1–14; see M. Maher, "'Take my yoke upon you' [Matt. xi.29]," *NTS* 22 [1976]: 97–103). The "rest" (cf. use of cognate term in Heb 3–4) is eschatological (cf. Rev 6:11; 14:13) but also a present reality.

29–30 The "yoke" (*zygos*, GK *2433*), put on animals for pulling heavy loads, is a metaphor for the discipline of discipleship. If Jesus is not offering the yoke of the law (*Pirke Avot* 3:6, cf. Sir 51:26), neither is he offering freedom from all constraints. The "yoke" is Jesus' yoke, not the yoke of the law; discipleship must be *to him*. In view of v.27, "learn from me" cannot mean "imitate me" or "learn from my experience" (contra Stauffer, *TDNT*, 2:348–49) but "learn from the revelation that I alone impart" (cf. Josef Schmid, *Das Evangelium nach Matthäus* [Regensburg: Pustet, 1959]).

The marvelous feature of this invitation is that out of his overwhelming authority (v.27) Jesus encourages the burdened to come to him because he is "gentle and humble in heart." Matthew stresses Jesus' gentleness (18:1–10; 19:13–15). Apparently the theme is connected with the messianic servant language (Isa 42:2–3; 53:1–2; cf. Zec 9:9, cited in Mt 21:5) that recurs in 12:15–21. Authoritative revealer that he is, Jesus approaches us with a true servant's gentleness. For the present, his messianic reign must not be understood as exclusively royal.

On "rest" (*anapausis*, GK *398*), see v.28. Here the words "and you will find rest for your souls" are directly quoted from Jeremiah 6:16 (MT, not LXX).

The entire verse is steeped in OT language (cf. Gundry, *Use of the Old Testament*, 136); but if this is intended to be not just an allusion but a fulfillment passage, then Jesus is saying that "the ancient paths" and "the good way" (Jer 6:16) lie in taking on his yoke because he is the one to whom the OT Scriptures point. That yoke is "easy" ("good," "comfortable," GK *5982*), and his burden is light (v.30). The "rest" he promises is not only for the world to come but also for this one as well.

The implicit contrast between Jesus' yoke and that of others is not between antinomianism and legalism, for in a deep sense his demands (5:21–48) are far more radical than theirs; nor between salvation by law and salvation by grace (contra Barth, "Matthew's Understanding of the Law," 148 n. 2); nor between harsh attitudes among Jewish teachers of the law and Jesus' humane and humble approach (Klostermann). No, the contrast is between the burden of submission to the OT in terms of Pharisaic regulation and the relief of coming under Jesus' tutelage as under the authority of gentle Revealer to whom the OT, the ancient paths, truly pointed (cf. H. D. Betz, "The Logion of the Easy Yoke and of Rest [Matthew 11:28–30]," *JBL* 86 [1967]: 10–24).

3. Sabbath conflicts (12:1–14)

OVERVIEW

Opposition to Jesus had already surfaced (9:3, 11, 14, 34; 10:25; 11:19). Now it erupts in a concrete issue that generates enough hatred to lead Jesus' enemies to contemplate murder (v.14).

Matthew picks up the narrative from Mark 2:23 (cf. Mk 2:23–28; Lk 6:1–5) at the point where he had left the source as far back as Matthew 9:18. Only here does he speak of conflicts over the Sabbath (though cf. 13:54–58; 24:20).

The Jewish rules of conduct about Sabbath were extremely detailed; and it was wryly admitted that "the rules about the Sabbath ... are as mountains hanging by a hair, for [teaching of] Scripture [thereon] is scanty and the rules many" (*m. Ḥag.* 1:8). Yet for many Jews of Jesus' day, the Sabbath was a joyful festival, a sign of the covenant, a reminder of divine creation in six days, and, provided the rules were obeyed, a means of gaining merit for Israel (*Mek.* 20:16; 23:15; 26:13; *b. Šabb.* 10b). At many points there were diverse interpretations; and though the Pharisees were strict, the Qumran covenanters were stricter yet (CD 10:14–11:8). For detailed study, see Carson, "Jesus and the Sabbath," in *From Sabbath to Lord's Day*, 58–97.

a. Picking heads of grain (12:1–8)

[1]At that time Jesus went through the grainfields on the Sabbath. His disciples were
hungry and began to pick some heads of grain and eat them. [2]When the Pharisees saw
this, they said to him, "Look! Your disciples are doing what is unlawful on the Sabbath."
[3]He answered, "Haven't you read what David did when he and his companions were
hungry? [4]He entered the house of God, and he and his companions ate the consecrated
bread—which was not lawful for them to do, but only for the priests. [5]Or haven't you
read in the Law that on the Sabbath the priests in the temple desecrate the day and yet
are innocent? [6]I tell you that one greater than the temple is here. [7]If you had known what
these words mean, 'I desire mercy, not sacrifice,' you would not have condemned the
innocent. [8]For the Son of Man is Lord of the Sabbath."

COMMENTARY

1 "At that time" need not mean the same day as the events of ch. 11 but "at about that time" (see comments at 3:1; 11:25; cf. 13:1). Here it introduces an *example* of burdensome Pharisaic regulation (arising out of 11:28–30) along with the theme of rising opposition to Jesus that ties much of this section (11:2–13:53) together.

Various explanations have been advanced for what Jesus' disciples (presumably the Twelve) did. Some scholars have noted that only Matthew mentions their hunger and have suggested that they ate the grain out of necessity (Kilpatrick, *Origins*, 116; Willy Rordorf, *Sunday* [London: SCM Press, 1968]). But there is no necessity unless one has not eaten for days. The reference to hunger is simply part of the story. Why else would the disciples pick a little grain? Samuele Bacchiocchi's suggestion (*From Sabbath to Sunday* [Rome: Pontifical Gregorian Univ. Press, 1977], 50) that Jesus' rebuke (v.7) implies that the Pharisees should have taken Jesus and his disciples home for lunch after the synagogue service instead of criticizing them for picking heads of grain is fanciful.

Manson (*Sayings of Jesus*, 190) remarks that Jesus and his disciples were going from place to place on missionary work and so invests their act with kingdom significance. But why, then, were they not charged with exceeding a Sabbath day's journey (about eleven hundred meters; cf. *m. Soṭah* 5:3)? And what were the Pharisees doing there? The scene is reminiscent of a Sabbath afternoon stroll within the permitted distance. P. K. Jewett (*The Lord's Day* [Grand Rapids: Eerdmans, 1971], 37) suggests the disciples were making a path for Jesus, an idea based on Mark's "began to make their way." This will not do in Matthew and wrongly interprets Mark. A path cannot be made merely by picking heads of grain. At the time fields were not separated by fences but by landmark stones (cf. Dt 19:14). Paths went right across fields or closely skirted them, the grain being sown to the field's very edge and sometimes beyond (cf. 13:4); and the right to pluck grain casually (though not necessarily on the Sabbath) was established by Deuteronomy 23:25.

2 The Pharisees' charge that the disciples were breaking the law was based, not on their picking grain in someone else's field, but on the fact that picking grain—i.e., "reaping" (cf. *y. Šabb.* 7.2, 9.c)—was one of thirty-nine kinds of work forbidden on the Sabbath (*m. Šabb.* 7:2) under prevailing halakah. Though exceptions to these were granted in the case of temple service and where life was at stake, neither exception applied here. Sigal (*Halakhah of Jesus*, 160) argues that not all authorities prohibited what the disciples were doing; but *Šabbat* (Mishnah) 10:2, to which he refers, does not deal with casually picking grain in an open field and so is in any case irrelevant. At a much later period, the Gemara expressly permits picking grain by hand and eating it on the Sabbath but merely forbids the use of a tool (*b. Šabb.* 128a, b; cf. Bonnard). But this refinement is much later and may even owe something to Christian influence.

3–4 The use of counterquestion and appeal to Scripture was common, though not exclusively so, in rabbinic debates (cf. v.5; 19:4; 21:16, 42; 22:31). The account to which Jesus refers (1Sa 21:1–6) is from the "Former Prophets," as the Jews called these books. On the regulations regarding the consecrated bread (lit., "bread of the presentation"), see Exodus 25:30; Leviticus 24:5–9.

The "house of God" that David entered was the tabernacle (cf. Ex 23:19; Jdg 18:31; 1Sa 1:7, 24; 3:15; 2Sa 12:20; Ps 5:7), at that time at Nob, just south of Jerusalem. Both David and his companions ate what should have been eaten only by the priests and did so after lying to the priest about their mission. It is possible that this event took place on a Sabbath, since 1 Samuel 21:5–6 sounds as if the consecrated bread had just been changed. Many Jews understood the text that way (cf. Str-B, 1:618–19; *TDNT*, 7:22). But Jesus makes nothing of David's deceit nor depends on any supposition regarding the day on which it occurred. If it was on a Sabbath, others than the priests should not have eaten that bread; if it was not a Sabbath, the bread should not have been changed, let alone eaten by nonpriests.

The argument takes a common rabbinical form (cf. Sigal, *Halakhah of Jesus*, 162–63), namely, the juxtaposition of two apparently contradictory statements from Scripture in order to draw a halakic conclusion (a conclusion regarding regulations for conduct). On the one hand, David ate; on the other, it was unlawful for him to do so. Jesus' point is not simply that rules admit of exceptions but that the Scriptures themselves do not condemn David for his action; therefore the rigidity of the Pharisees' interpretation of the law is not in accord with Scripture itself (cf. Cranfield, *Mark*, 11–12; Lane, *Mark*, 117). The point is not "The Sabbath is delivered unto you, you are not delivered unto the Sabbath" (*Mek.* 26:13, cf. 2 Macc 5:19) but that the Pharisees' approach to the OT was wrong and could not explain the incident of David.

How, then, does this apply to Jesus and his disciples? They were not desperate and famished, unlike David and his men. It is not even clear how they were breaking any OT law, where commandments about the Sabbath were aimed primarily at regular work. The disciples were not farmers trying to do some illicit work but were itinerant preachers casually picking some heads of grain. Indeed, apart from halakic interpretations, it is not at all obvious that any commandment of Scripture was being broken. It seems, then, that Jesus used the David incident not merely to question the Pharisees' view of the Sabbath, for the David incident was not directly relevant. Rather he was questioning their approach to the law itself.

There is more. In the incident to which Jesus referred, regulations (even of the written law) were set aside for David "and his companions." Is there not, therefore, a case for setting aside regulations (which had no clear base in the written law) for Jesus and those with him (so Hooker, *Son of Man*, 97–98)? This analogy holds good only if Jesus is at least as special as David, and it is to this conclusion that the argument builds in the following verses.

5–6 Jesus' second appeal, preserved only in Matthew (doubtless because it was of interest to his Jewish-Christian readers), is from Torah in the narrow sense of Pentateuch (cf. Nu 28:9–10). Formally speaking, the Levitical priests "broke" the Sabbath every week (v.5), since the right worship of God in the temple required them to do some work (changing the consecrated bread [Lev 24:8] and offering the doubled burnt offering [Nu 28:9–10]). In reality, of course, the priests were guiltless. The law that established the Sabbath also established the right of the priests, formally speaking, to "break" it (for a similar argument, see Jn 7:21–23).

But how does this apply to Jesus and his disciples? The form of the argument is *qal waḥomer* (lit., "the light and the weighty," an a fortiori argument [see comments at 5:25–30]), a recognized procedure for establishing a halakic regulation (Daube, *New Testament and Rabbinic Judaism*, 67ff.). But this is valid only if the "one greater than the temple" (v.6) is truly greater. The "one greater" is neuter (the masculine variant is poorly attested), as in vv.41–42—i.e., "something greater" (NIV text note). The neuter, however, can refer to persons when some quality is being stressed rather than the individual per se (Turner, *Syntax*, 21).

So the question remains: Who or what is greater than the temple? B. Gerhardsson ("Sacrificial Service and Atonement in the Gospel of Matthew," in *Reconciliation and Hope* [ed. R. Banks; Exeter: Paternoster, 1974], 28), followed by David Hill ("On the Use and Meaning of Hosea vi.6 in Matthew's Gospel," *NTS* 24 [1978]: 115), argues that this refers to the service or worship of God in which Jesus was engaged. This is greater than the service of the temple performed by the priests. But Jesus and his disciples were not really "engaged" in such service while plucking heads of grain, the way the priests were engaged in worship on the Sabbath. Moreover, the comparison in the text is not with the service of the temple but with the temple itself.

Others have argued that what is greater than the temple is the love command (Sigal, *Halakhah of Jesus*, 163–66; cf. D. M. Cohn-Sherbok, "An Analysis of Jesus' Arguments Concerning the Plucking of Grain on the Sabbath," *JSNT* 2 [1979]: 31–41), finding support for this in the plea for mercy in v.7. But the supremacy of the love command has not yet been introduced (cf. 22:34–40). More important, the argument neglects the sequential-eschatological "is here." This refutes Sigal's insistence that Jesus is answering purely on the level of dispute over halakah. Instead, he is insisting that a new and greater development-thing-person has arrived at this point in history, something not there before. And the reference to "mercy" (v.7) is open to a better interpretation.

There are still other suggestions, but the most likely is that the "something greater" is either Jesus himself (Bornkamm, "End-Expectation and the Church," 35) or the kingdom (Lohmeyer). And in fact the two merge into one. If the kingdom, it is the kingdom Jesus is inaugurating; if Jesus, it is not only Jesus as a man but as Messiah, Son of David (vv.3–4), Son of Man (v.8), the one who ushers in the messianic age. Yet "Jesus" is perhaps marginally more plausible, not only because of the christological connections just alluded to, but also because of the parallel drawn by Jesus himself between his own body and the temple (26:61; cf. Jn 2:20–21).

Jesus' argument, then, provides an instance from the law itself in which the Sabbath restrictions were superseded by the priests because their cultic responsibilities took precedence: the temple, as it were, was greater than the Sabbath. But now, Jesus claims, "something" greater than the temple is here. And that, too, takes precedence over the Sabbath. This solution is entirely consistent with what we have perceived to be Jesus' attitude to the law in this gospel. The law points to him and finds its fulfillment in him (see comments at 5:17–48). Not only, then, have the Pharisees mishandled the law by their halakah (vv.3–4), but they have failed to perceive who Jesus is. The authority of the temple laws shielded the priests from guilt; the authority of Jesus shields his disciples from guilt. It is not a matter of comparing Jesus' action with the action of the priests; nor is it likely that Jesus is suggesting that all his disciples are priests (contra Lohmeyer). "Rather, it is a question of *contrasting* [new emphasis] [Jesus'] authority with the authority of the priests" (Carson, "Jesus and the Sabbath," 67).

7–8 Again (cf. v.3) Jesus rebuked the Pharisees for their failure to understand the Scriptures (cf. Jn 5:39), and this time he quoted Hosea 6:6, as he had once before (see comments at 9:13). The relevance of this quotation from the "Latter Prophets" depends on the Pharisees' attitude to the law being as worthy of condemnation as the attitude of those who relied superficially and hypocritically on mere ritual in Hosea's day. Jesus claims, in effect, that the Pharisees have not really grasped the significance of the law, and this is demonstrated by their halakah. The accusers stand accused; the disciples are explicitly declared "innocent." The Hosea quotation, with its emphasis on mercy, prompts Verseput (*Rejection of the Humble Messianic King*, 166–71) and others to argue that the most important issue in this Sabbath pericope is the mercy of God, rather than the authority of Jesus. But that is an unnecessary antithesis. The innocence of Jesus' disciples was not established on their being hungry but on the ground that something greater than the temple was present. In other words, the Son of Man is Lord of the Sabbath. Whether "for" (v.8) relates to v.6 or v.7 is unclear and of little consequence. If the former, it sums up Messiah's supremacy over the temple; if the latter, it does the same but also serves as explicit ground for the innocence of the disciples.

Some have argued that "Son of Man" here has corporate significance: the community of Jesus' disciples together is "Lord" of the Sabbath (e.g., T. W. Manson, "The Son of Man in Daniel, Enoch and the Gospels," *BJRL* 32 [1949–50]: 191). But this is based on a disputed understanding of "Son of Man" (see Reflections, p. 247) and on a misunderstood connection with Mark 2:27 (see Carson, "Jesus and the Sabbath," 62–65). In all three Synoptics, the Son of Man is David's son, Jesus the Messiah (Hill). But the title is ambiguous enough that few would grasp the point until after the resurrection, at which time few could miss it. The claim (v.8) is implicitly messianic, a claim that goes beyond the mere right to tamper with halakah. It places the Son of Man in a position to handle the Sabbath law any way he wills, or to supersede it in the same way that the temple requirements superseded the normal Sabbath restrictions (cf. Hooker, *Son of Man*, 100ff.).

NOTES

4 Moule (*Idiom Book*, 27) points out that ὅ οὐκ ἐξὸν ἦν αὐτῷ φαγεῖν (*ho ouk exon ēn autō phagein*, "which was not lawful for him to eat") is a mixed construction: the relative pronoun ὅ, *ho*, which refers to the eating of the bread in the preceding clause, seems to serve simultaneously as subject of οὐκ ἐξὸν ἦν, *ouk exon ēn*, and object of φαγεῖν, *phagein*. Moule suggests the clause is being treated as if it had begun with ἀλλά (*alla*, "but") or καίπερ (*kaiper*, "although").

The reading ἔφαγεν (*ephagen*, "he ate") has very strong attestation but is rejected by Metzger (*Textual Commentary*, 31) and UBS[4] in favor of ἔφαγον (*ephagon*, "they ate"), supported only by א B and one minuscule, on the grounds that it represents the nonparallel reading (cf. Mk 2:26: Lk 6:4). But the change may have gone the other way, in order to make it unambiguous that not only David but all his men ate—a fact clearly relevant to Jesus and his disciples. "He ate and his companions" is an acceptable but ambiguous way of saying in Greek "he and his companions ate."

b. Healing a man with a shriveled hand (12:9–14)

OVERVIEW

Luke (6:6–11) specifies that this event took place on another Sabbath (cf. Mk 3:1–6). Unlike the previous pericope, Jesus does not refer to Scripture. This time it is *his* activity that is in question, not that of his disciples; his argument, at first glance a stinging ad hominem, holds deeper implications.

The first-century Jews discussed at length what was permitted in caring for the sick on the Sabbath (e.g., *m. ʿEd.* 2:5; *m. Šabb.* 6:3; *Mek.* 22:2; 23:13). Jesus' attitude was more fundamental: it is lawful to do good on the Sabbath.

[9]Going on from that place, he went into their synagogue, [10]and a man with a shriveled hand was there. Looking for a reason to accuse Jesus, they asked him, "Is it lawful to heal on the Sabbath?"

[11]He said to them, "If any of you has a sheep and it falls into a pit on the Sabbath, will you not take hold of it and lift it out? [12]How much more valuable is a man than a sheep! Therefore it is lawful to do good on the Sabbath."

[13]Then he said to the man, "Stretch out your hand." So he stretched it out and it was completely restored, just as sound as the other. [14]But the Pharisees went out and plotted how they might kill Jesus.

COMMENTARY

9–10 "Going on from that place" is a Matthean connective to move the action from the field to the synagogue without reference to time. Regarding "their" synagogue, see comments at 10:17; 11:1. All three synoptists make plain the malice in the Pharisees' watching (Mark) and question (Matthew). In Mark and Luke, Jesus precipitates the action by calling forward the man with the shriveled hand; in Matthew this is omitted.

The form of the Pharisees' question in Matthew (v.10) is general. The customary Jewish ruling was that healing was permitted on the Sabbath when life was in danger (cf. *m.Yoma* 8:6; *Mek.* 22:2; 23:13), which of course did not apply here. Even so, what rabbinic discussion had in view was medical help by family members or professionals, not miraculous healings. But Jesus did not reply on that level.

11–13 For the third time in this gospel, Jesus' argument depends on a contrast between animals and men (cf. 6:26; 10:31) and presupposes the greater value of human beings based on their special creation: man alone was made in the image of God (Ge 1–2). This particular argument occurs only in Matthew; but a similar analogy is drawn in Luke 13:15; 14:5. In all three instances, Jesus assumed that the Pharisees would lift an animal out of a pit on the Sabbath—though the most that was allowed at Qumran was to do something that would enable the animal to help itself (CD 11:13–14). Sigal (*Halakhah of Jesus*, 169–70), in support of his too rigid theory that the Pharisees are to be identified as *perushim* (see Introduction, section 11.f), is reduced to thinking that *probaton hen* (v.11) should be taken literally to mean "one sheep," namely, the last one. But the expression probably means no more than "a sheep" (see comments at 8:19).

Jesus' argument is again *qal waḥomer* (see comments at vv.5–6): If a sheep, how much more a man (v.12)? Neither the sheep in the pit nor the man in Jesus' presence is in mortal danger. The question is simply one of doing good. This does not mean Jesus is saying that failure to do good is itself an evil thing (e.g., Klostermann; Cranfield, *Mark*, 120). Jesus is talking about what is "lawful," not what is required, and if it were absolutely true that failure to do good is *always* evil, there would be no possibility of any rest at all. Jesus' rhetorical question therefore has a narrower focus: Was the Sabbath a day for maleficent activity—such as their evil intentions in questioning him—or for beneficent action, such as the healing about to be done?

The healing (v.13), like that in 9:1–8, comes after the shocking word (in all three Synoptics) and therefore serves to confirm that word. The miracle itself says nothing of the man's faith, since the focus is not on him but on the Pharisees. Yet in light of the preceding interchange, it also confirms Jesus' claim to lordship over the Sabbath, as his healing in 9:1–8 confirmed his authority to forgive sins.

14 Much has been made of the fact that Matthew omits mention of the Herodians (Mk 3:6), as if that proves that the point of reference is now after AD 70, when the Herodians no longer existed and the sole opponents were the Pharisees (e.g., Hummel, *Auseinandersetzung*, 12ff.; Hill). But giving reasons for *omissions* in Matthew is extremely hazardous (see comments at 8:1–4). And in this instance it is noteworthy that Matthew mentions the Herodians in 22:16 and refers often to the Sadducees.

Sigal (*Halakhah of Jesus*, 175) wants *apolesōsin* ("destroy," GK *660*) to mean not "kill" but "put under the synagogue ban," because no Pharisee would consider executing another Jew merely over a halakic dispute. While he is correct in the latter supposition, the point is that these Sabbath confrontations are *not* mere disputes over halakah; they have to do with Jesus' fundamental messianic claims, a point vigorously denied by Sigal, who generally assigns a verse such as v.8 to later Christian theology and reduces the remainder to purely halakic categories. But it is very doubtful (contra Sigal) that Jesus tolerated the oral tradition implicit in much Jewish halakah (cf. Jeremias, *New Testament Theology*, 208–11). Moreover, the Sabbath-controversy pericopes cohere as they stand. This first mention of a plot to kill Jesus springs from disputes not about the legality of various Sabbath activities but about Jesus' authority. The Sabbath conflicts are not the cause of the plotting but its occasion. Therefore, Sabbath disputes were not mentioned at Jesus' trials; in themselves they were never as much an issue as Jesus' claim to be Sabbath's Lord.

4. Jesus as the prophesied Servant (12:15–21)

OVERVIEW

Verses 15–16 constitute a brief summary of Mark 3:7–12, omitting, among other things, a "Son of God" title. To this summary Matthew adds a fulfillment passage, citing Isaiah 42:1–4. Thus he interprets Jesus' healing ministry, not so much in terms of "Son of God" or even royal "Son of David" Christology, but in terms of Yahweh's Suffering Servant (see comments at 8:17).

This section simultaneously contrasts the hatred of the Pharisees (v.14) with Jesus' tranquility (v.19) and gentleness (v.20) and prepares the way for themes in the rest of the chapter (see comments below). Menken (*Matthew's Bible*, 51–65) rightly underscores the relation between this quotation and the verse before this pericope: that verse, v.14, is the first to provide a direct reference to Jesus' impending death, and so the effect of this quotation is to assert that Jesus' withdrawal from some conflict and his commitment to silence and gentleness indicate the true nature of his mission and purpose, which will be fully revealed only later, in his death and resurrection. See also Richard Beaton's chapter on the christological contribution of Isaiah 42:1–4 (*Isaiah's Christ in Matthew's Gospel* [SNTSMS 123; Cambridge: Cambridge Univ. Press, 2002], 174–91).

[15]Aware of this, Jesus withdrew from that place. Many followed him, and he healed all their sick, [16]warning them not to tell who he was. [17]This was to fulfill what was spoken through the prophet Isaiah:

18 "Here is my servant whom I have chosen,
the one I love, in whom I delight;
I will put my Spirit on him,
and he will proclaim justice to the nations.
19 He will not quarrel or cry out;
no one will hear his voice in the streets.

20 A bruised reed he will not break,
and a smoldering wick he will not snuff out,
till he leads justice to victory.
21 In his name the nations will put their hope."

COMMENTARY

15–17 Jesus often withdrew when opposition became intense (cf. 4:12; 14:13; 15:21; 16:5)—at least that was his custom until the appointed hour arrived (26:45; cf. Jn 7:8). This practice becomes for his disciples an example of moving from place to place (10:23). Thus his extensive ministry continued (cf. 4:23; 8:16; 9:35). Warnings to those healed to keep silent increased for the same reasons as before and with as little effect (cf. 8:4; 9:30). But Jesus' conduct under these pressures, Matthew perceives, was nothing less than the fulfillment of the Scriptures. Though the Pharisees might plot to kill him (v.14), he would not quarrel or cry out (v.19). Despite all Matthew has done to show Jesus to be the messianic Son of David and unique Son of God, he wants to separate himself from exclusively royal and militaristic interpretations of Messiah's role. He knows that the ministry of Jesus Messiah must also be understood as the fulfillment of the prophecies of the Suffering Servant.

18–21 This quotation (Isa 42:1–4), the longest in Matthew, is remarkable for its text form. The changes have been variously assigned to Matthew's "school" (Stendahl, *School of St. Matthew*, 107ff.), to a developing Christian apologetic (Lindars, *New Testament Apologetic*, 147–52), to the evangelist's redactional interests (Hill). Certainly there is a mixed text-character here (for details, see Gundry, *Use of the Old Testament*, 110–16; Blomberg, "Matthew," in *CNTUOT*), and the reason for each change is not easy to discern, though most of the quotation appears to be an independent rendering of the Hebrew rather than an adaptation of any manuscript in the LXX tradition.

The noun *pais* ("servant," v.18, GK *4090*) can also mean "son," though the Hebrew is unambiguously "servant." The servant in Isaiah 42 appears to be Israel. Matthew's application to Jesus is part of his common pattern of seeing Jesus as the ultimate Israel, the fulfillment of Israel (e.g., see comments at 4:1–11). Cope (*Matthew*, 44–45), in line with his generally plausible view that this quotation anticipates the major themes of the rest of Matthew 12, suggests that Matthew exploits the Son-Servant ambiguity to anticipate vv.46–50—his disciples are brothers and sisters, but he is the unique Son of the Father. This seems tenuous, for elsewhere in Matthew God is the Father of the disciples (e.g. 6:9, 26; 10:29) as well as of Jesus (though in a somewhat different sense). The link between this quotation and vv.46–50 is on a different level, a christological one—namely, Jesus cannot be understood in terms of the normal family relationships that bind humanity. He is God's chosen Servant, the one on whom God has poured out his Spirit with a specific mission in view. Therefore, his disciples, not his family, must be reckoned closest to him.

The words "whom I have chosen" (Heb., "whom I uphold") may have been borrowed by Matthew from the second line of Isaiah 42:1, or from Isaiah 43:10; 44:1 (thus making the quotation composite); "the one I love" carries overtones of 3:17; 17:5, because love and election are closely connected. God's "delight" in his servant and the mention of the Spirit God puts on him to a special degree (cf. Jn 3:34) remind us of both Jesus' baptism and his transfiguration (3:16–17; 17:5), where Jesus was called God's Son. Yet, far from subsuming Jesus' servant role under his sonship (Kingsbury), Matthew omits Mark's mention of "Son of God" (Mk 3:11) and here makes the servant motif preeminent (cf. Hill, "Son and Servant," 4–12).

This "servant" will proclaim "justice" to the nations. Neither the Hebrew *mišpāṭ* (GK 5477) nor Greek *krisis* (GK *3213*) easily suggests "the true faith" (JB). But the suggestion is not entirely without merit, since what is in view is "justice"—i.e., righteousness broadly conceived as the self-revelation of God's character for the good of the nations (cf. Isa 51:4), yet at the same time calling them to account. Concern for the Gentiles thus emerges again (cf. 1:1; 2:1–12; 3:9; 4:15–16; 8:5–13 et al.) in anticipation of the Great Commission (28:18–20).

But even within this chapter, the twin themes of Spirit and Gentiles are programmatic (Cope, *Matthew*, 32ff.; Hill, "Son and Servant," 10–11). God has poured out his Spirit on his Servant; so the exorcisms he performs by the Spirit constitute proof of the kingdom's inauguration (v.28). Therefore, blasphemy against that Spirit cannot be forgiven (see comments at v.32). Moreover, the pericope about the sign of Jonah (vv.38–41) returns to the theme of the place of the Gentiles in the merciful salvation of God and warns "this wicked generation" (v.45) once more.

The servant "will not quarrel or cry out" or raise his voice in the streets (v.19). The picture is not one of utter silence (else how could he "proclaim" justice [v.18]? cf. Jn 7:37) but of gentleness and humility (11:29), of quiet withdrawal (see comments at vv.15–17) and a presentation of his messiahship that is neither arrogant nor brash.

The first two lines of v.20 are very close to both LXX and MT. The double metaphor breathes compassion: the servant does not advance his ministry with such callousness to the weak that he breaks the bruised reed or snuffs out the smoldering wick (smoldering because it is either poorly trimmed or low on oil). This may include reference to Jesus' attitude to the sick (v.15). But the last clause of v.20 ("till he leads justice to victory"), apparently a paraphrase of Isaiah 42:3 ("in faithfulness he will bring forth justice") and Isaiah 42:4 ("till he establishes justice on earth") under influence of Habakkuk 1:4 (cf. Gundry, *Use of the Old Testament*, 114–15), suggests something more—namely, that he brings eschatological salvation to the "harassed and helpless" (9:36), the "weary and burdened" (11:28).

"Leads" is a trifle weak for *ekbalē* (GK *1675*): though the verb can have a wide semantic range, it requires something like "thrusts forth" in this context (used elsewhere in this chapter in vv.24, 26, 27 [2x], 28, 35 [2x]). What is pictured is a ministry so gentle and compassionate that the weak are not trampled on and crushed until justice, the full righteousness of God, triumphs. And for such a Messiah most Jews were little prepared (cf. *Pss. Sol.* 17:21). Small wonder that the Gentiles put their hope in his name (v.21, cf. Isa 11:10; Ro 15:12). The Hebrew reads (lit.) "the coastlands wait for his laws," but the word "coastlands" often signifies Gentiles (*ethnē*; NIV, "nations," GK *1620*). "Will put their hope" (*elpizō*, GK *1827*) is idiomatic for "look forward to" or "expect."

"Name" (*onoma*, GK *3950*) follows the LXX, even though the MT has "law" (*tôrâ*, "teaching," GK 9368). In view of the mixed text-character, which testifies to Matthew's ability and willingness to use the MT or to set it aside (unless, with Gundry [*Use of the Old Testament*, 115–16], we postulate that LXX here renders a lost Hebrew original), this must be thought strange if certain recent reconstructions of the importance of the law in Matthew are correct (see Introduction, section 11.c). However, if, as we have maintained, the law in this gospel serves primarily to point to Jesus, then it is not surprising that Matthew prefers the LXX term. For "in his name," see comments at 5:10–12.

5. Confrontation with the Pharisees (12:22–37)

a. The setting and accusation (12:22–24)

OVERVIEW

For a convenient summary of the parallels, see Albright and Mann. The analogous incident in 9:32–34 is not a doublet but a sample of the same outrageous charge that is raised in 12:24.

22Then they brought him a demon-possessed man who was blind and mute, and Jesus
healed him, so that he could both talk and see. 23All the people were astonished and said,
"Could this be the Son of David?"
24But when the Pharisees heard this, they said, "It is only by Beelzebub, the prince of
demons, that this fellow drives out demons."

COMMENTARY

22 The *tote* ("then") is very loose (see comments at 2:7; 11:20), and probably this event took place a good deal later (compare Mark and Luke). The NIV sounds as if the man suffered from three distinct ailments; the Greek, very condensed, puts blind and mute (*kōphos*, GK *3273*, as in 9:32) in opposition to "demon-possessed," suggesting the latter is the cause of the other two. The healing itself is told with admirable brevity, for it is not so much the miracle itself that captures the attention of the synoptists as the confrontation that follows.

23–24 The acute astonishment of the crowd (the verb *existanto* [GK *2014*], "were astonished," is used only here in Matthew, though it is common in Mark and Luke) prompted the question. Its form in Greek suggests the crowds were none too sure: "This couldn't be the Son of David, could it?" The question does not ask whether Jesus is a magician of the kind that popular superstition said David's son Solomon was (contra Loren L. Fisher, "Can This Be the Son of David?" in *Jesus and the Historian* [ed. F. T. Trotter; Philadelphia: Westminster, 1968], 82–97) but whether Jesus is the Messiah (see comments at 1:1; 9:27; 15:22). The Messiah was expected to perform miracles (cf. v.38), so the exorcism/healing stood in Jesus' favor. But perhaps his reticence, his nonregal sayings, and his servant ministry engendered doubt. Matthew's readers can see the connection between the Suffering Servant (vv.18–21) and the Son of David (vv.22–23), but those who witnessed Jesus' ministry could not view it in the light of the resurrection.

On "Beelzebub" (v.24), see comments at 10:25.

b. Jesus' reply (12:25–37)

OVERVIEW

While the structure of vv.25–37 is parallel to that of Mark 3:23–30, Matthew's length is surprising. Some but not all of Matthew's "response" section is closer to Luke than to Mark. Most likely, Matthew used both Mark and a "Q" source for this narrative. Part of Jesus' response in Matthew is scattered in Luke (cf. Lk 6:43–45; 11:17–23; 12:10), prompting some to think this passage is a composite of a number of independent sayings. While this is possible—the transitions are loose, and, unlike the five major discourses, the end of the response is not decisive—it is also possible that one of the two Lukan parallels (Lk 6:43–45) has been placed elsewhere for topical reasons and that the other (12:10) is simply a report of a similar saying. At any rate the argument in Matthew 12:25–37 is unified and coherent.

(1) The divided kingdom (12:25–28)

25 Jesus knew their thoughts and said to them, "Every kingdom divided against itself
will be ruined, and every city or household divided against itself will not stand. 26 If Satan
drives out Satan, he is divided against himself. How then can his kingdom stand? 27 And if
I drive out demons by Beelzebub, by whom do your people drive them out? So then, they
will be your judges. 28 But if I drive out demons by the Spirit of God, then the kingdom of
God has come upon you."

COMMENTARY

25–26 Jesus "knew their thoughts" (cf. 9:4). The narrative is condensed, and the "house" is not mentioned (cf. Mk 3:20, 23). The argument is clear: any kingdom, city, or household that develops internal strife will destroy itself. The same holds true for Satan's *basileia* ("kingdom," v.26, GK *993*), his exercise of authority among his minions (cf. H. Kruse, "Das Reich Satans," *Bib* 58 [1977]: 29–61). "For the prince of the demons to cast out his subjects would be virtually casting out himself, since they were doing his work" (Broadus, 269).

27 Whether the words *hoi huioi hymōn* (lit., "your sons") mean no more than "your people" (the Jews) or those instructed by the Pharisees (cf. 22:15–16, 23:9–15) is uncertain. Jesus' argument is ad hominem: he is saying "your sons" drive out demons on occasion (a not uncommon practice linked to some bizarre notions; cf. Josephus, *Ant.* 8.45–8 [2.5]; *J.W.* 7.185 [6.3]; Tob 8:2–3; Justin Martyr *Dial.* 85; cf. Ac 19:13), and I do this so powerfully that great damage is done to Satan's kingdom. So if I who do so much damage to his kingdom by my exorcisms perform them by Satan's power, by whom do your sons drive out demons?

28 Luke 11:20 has "the finger of God" instead of "the Spirit of God." Possibly the latter is original (cf. Dunn, *Jesus and the Spirit*, 44–46), but the matter is of little consequence since they both refer to the same thing (cf. Ex 8:19; Dt 9:10; Ps 8:3). Matthew's phrase makes a clearer connection with 12:18 (Isa 42:1) and a more specific contrast with Beelzebub (cf. Gundry). Only here and in 19:24; 21:31, 43 does Matthew have "kingdom of God" instead of "kingdom of heaven" (see comments at 3:2). This may reflect his source, common to Luke (though elsewhere, when following a source, Matthew changes to "kingdom of heaven" except at 19:24), or he may use "kingdom of God" stylistically to go with "Spirit of God." What is certain is that Jesus knows that his exorcisms, performed by the Spirit of God, prove that the kingdom age has already dawned.

Of course this also implies that Jesus is King Messiah without explicitly affirming it. Dunn (*Jesus and the Spirit*, 46–69) rightly emphasizes the realized eschatology but overstates his Spirit Christology when he adds, "The eschatological kingdom was present for Jesus only because the eschatological Spirit was present in and through him. In other words, it was not so much a case of 'Where *I* am there is the kingdom,' as, 'Where the *Spirit* is there is the kingdom'" (emphasis his).

Four considerations argue strongly against this view.

1. Dunn has introduced a disjunction alien to the text ("only because the eschatological Spirit was present," he says) and maintains the disjunction by interpreting Jesus' messianic claims in non-Spirit dress as anachronistic. Jesus knew *both* that he was unique, the promised Messiah, *and* that the eschatological Spirit was on him.

2. If Jesus' self-recognition turned exclusively on his ability to exorcise demons by the Spirit's power, then on what basis could he deny similar self-recognition to the "your people" (v.27) who also drove out demons? In other words, Spirit-prompted phenomena were not sufficient in themselves for Jesus' self-understanding, especially in the light of his own warnings in this respect (cf. 7:21–23).

3. Dunn has too quickly turned this pericope into a question of Jesus' self-understanding ("The eschatological kingdom was present for Jesus," he says), whereas on the face of it Jesus is arguing, not to convince himself, but manifestly to convince the Pharisees that the kingdom had come on them.

4. In his gospel's structure Matthew is less interested in Jesus' self-understanding than in his apologetics and fulfillment of OT prophecies (see the reference to Spirit in v.18).

NOTES

26 The first clause is an excellent instance of a "real" condition, εἰ (*ei*, "if") plus the indicative, in which the "reality" need not be admitted by the speaker but only assumed for the sake of argument (cf. *Grammar*, 1008; Zerwick, *Biblical Greek*, para. 306).

(2) The strong man's house (12:29)

[29]"Or again, how can anyone enter a strong man's house and carry off his possessions unless he first ties up the strong man? Then he can rob his house."

COMMENTARY

29 The opening *ē* (lit., "or"; cf. 7:9; 12:5; 20:15) here means "or look at it another way." Some Jewish expectation looked forward to the binding of Satan in the messianic age (*As. Mos.* 10:1; cf. Rev 20:2), and under this metaphor Jesus is the one who ties up the strong man (Satan) and carries off his "possessions" (*ta skeuē*; "vessels" preserves the metaphor of the house and has no relation to [demonic] possession except metaphorically). The argument has thus advanced: if Jesus' exorcisms cannot be attributed to Satan (vv.25–26), then they reflect authority greater than that of Satan. By this greater power Jesus is binding "the strong man" and plundering his "house." So the kingdom of heaven is forcefully advancing (see comments at 11:12).

(3) Blasphemy against the Spirit (12:30–32)

[30]"He who is not with me is against me, and he who does not gather with me scatters. [31]And so I tell you, every sin and blasphemy will be forgiven men, but the blasphemy against the Spirit will not be forgiven. [32]Anyone who speaks a word against the Son of Man will be forgiven, but anyone who speaks against the Holy Spirit will not be forgiven, either in this age or in the age to come."

COMMENTARY

30 Here several of Jesus' sayings are aphoristic. Their relation to the pericope is internal, not grammatical; and the relation to what precedes goes back to the tradition itself and cannot be ascribed to Matthew (cf. Lk 11:23).

The general thrust of v.30 is straightforward: in our relationship to Jesus there can be no neutrality. As to some issues and persons, neutrality is possible and may even be wise. But in the great struggle (vv.25–29), neutrality is impossible. The claims of the kingdom and the demands of Jesus are so exclusivistic that to be indifferent or apathetic to him is to be on the side of those who do not confess that he is the Messiah who brings in the kingdom of God (cf. 11:16–24).

Jesus' claim implies a high Christology, which is underlined by the harvest figure in v.30b (cf. 3:12; 6:26; Jn 4:36). Jesus is the one who will harvest in the last days, a function the OT regularly assigns to God. Hill (217) objects to the authenticity of the setting of this saying on the grounds that an affirmation about the impossibility of neutrality with respect to Jesus "is hardly likely to have been addressed to implacable opponents such as the Pharisees." But crowds were also present (v.23). And this form of statement could serve as both a rebuke to the Pharisees and a warning to the questioning crowd that failure to follow Jesus wholeheartedly is as dangerous as outright opposition.

The inverted saying—"whoever is not against us is for us" (Mk 9:40; Lk 9:50)—and this one "are not contradictory if the one was spoken to the indifferent about themselves and the other to the disciples about someone else" (McNeile, 177).

31–32 "And so"—*dia touto* (lit., "on account of this")—ties the statements about blasphemy against the Spirit (v.31) to the preceding verse. But the transition cannot easily be readily grasped until vv.31–32 are understood. Introduced by the solemn "I tell you" (see comments at 5:18), these statements constitute a pair, one from Mark (Mt 12:31 = Mk 3:28–29), one from Q (Mt 12:32 = Lk 12:10, in a different context; see comments above). "Blasphemy" (*blasphēmia*, GK *1060*) is extreme slander (see comments at 9:3), equivalent to "speaking against" (cf. 12:32). Blasphemy against God was viewed by Jews with utmost gravity (26:65); but here Jesus makes a sharp distinction between blasphemy against the Son of Man, which is forgivable, and blasphemy against the Spirit, which is not.

His statement is remarkable because one of the glories of the biblical faith is the great emphasis Scripture lays on the graciousness and wideness of God's forgiveness (e.g., Pss 65:3; 86:5; 130:3–4; Isa 1:18; Mic 7:19; 1Jn 1:7). A common interpretation of vv.31–32 is that they originated with a Christian prophet speaking for the exalted Jesus and are here read back into the life of the earthly Jesus. The blasphemy against the Son of Man is rejection of him by nonbelievers, and this is clearly forgivable when a person becomes a Christian. But blasphemy against the Holy Spirit is committed by a Christian (Christians after Pentecost would understand that only believers enjoy the Spirit) and is equivalent either to apostasy or to rejection of a Christian prophet's inspired message. For this there is no forgiveness (so Stendahl, "Matthew," in *Peake's Commentary*; and in a highly structured scheme, M. E. Boring, "The Unforgivable Sin Logion Mark III 28–29/Matt XII 31–32/Luke XII 10: Formal Analysis and History of the Tradition," *NovT* 18 [1976]: 258–79).

But there is strong and consistent evidence that the writers of the NT did not read words of Christian prophets back into the life of the historical Jesus (cf. J. D. G. Dunn, "Prophetic 'I'-Sayings and the Jesus Tradition: The Importance of Testing Prophetic Utterances within Early Christianity," *NTS* 24 [1978]: 175–98). It is highly unlikely that "Son of Man" would be used as an object of blasphemy without some qualifications about "Son of Man" (i.e., as "earthly Jesus only," etc.), which do not appear until Origen. Moreover, this does not explain what these sayings are doing in their gospel contexts (esp. Mark and Matthew).

The views of many older conservative scholars are also unhelpful. Broadus, for instance, ties blasphemy against the Holy Spirit to the "age of miracles" when the Spirit's power could be directly perceived—and rejected. But apart from the question of whether miracles take place now, Jesus elsewhere warned that miracles are not *necessarily* the criterion of true discipleship (7:21–23); i.e., they do not *necessarily* reveal the Spirit's presence and power.

Among the many other interpretations of this difficult incident, the best treats it in its setting during Jesus' life. The Pharisees have been attributing to Satan the work of the Spirit and have been doing so, as Jesus makes plain, in such a way as to reveal that they speak, not out of ignorance or unbelief, but out of a "conscious disputing of the indisputable" (the phrase is from G. C. Berkouwer, *Sin* [Grand Rapids: Eerdmans, 1971], 340; cf. 323–53, to which this exposition is indebted).

The distinction between blasphemy against the Son of Man and blasphemy against the Spirit is not that the Son of Man is less important than the Spirit, or that the first sin is prebaptismal and the second postbaptismal, still less that the first is against the Son of Man and the second rejects the authority of

Christian prophets. Instead, within the context of the larger argument, the first sin is rejection of the truth of the gospel (but there may be repentance and forgiveness for that), whereas the second sin is rejection of the same truth in full awareness that this is exactly what one is doing—thoughtfully, willfully, and self-consciously rejecting the work of the Spirit, even though there can be no other explanation of Jesus' exorcisms than that. It thus becomes a declaration that one is against God (see Verseput, *Rejection of the Humble Messianic King*, 236–38). For such a sin there is no forgiveness, "either in this age or the age to come" (cf. 13:22; 25:46)—a dramatic way of saying "never" (as in Mk 3:29).

If this interpretation is correct, the distinction between Son of Man and Spirit is relatively incidental. After all, blasphemy against the Spirit is also a rejection of Jesus' own claims: the christological implications of the sin are not diminished but increased in moving from "blasphemy against the Son of Man" to "blasphemy against the Spirit." This provides a clue for understanding how the unforgivable sin of which Jesus here speaks compares with the sins referred to in Hebrews 6:4–6; 10:26–31; and possibly 1 John 5:16. In each instance there is self-conscious perception of where the truth lies and the light shines—and a willful turning away from it. This is very different from Paul's persecution of the church (1Co 15:9), which was not unforgivable (1Ti 1:13).

C. K. Barrett (*The Holy Spirit and the Gospel Tradition* [London: SPCK, 1966], 106–7) discusses this matter wisely, except for his assumption that the sin is committed within the church and "because it denies the root and spring of the church's life, cannot rediscover the forgiveness by which the sinner first entered the community of the forgiven." But the biblical texts are more subtle than that. The author of Hebrews says, with a surprising combination of tenses, "We have come [perfect] to share in Christ if we hold firmly [aorist subjunctive] to the end the confidence we had at first" (Heb 3:14). In other words, our past participation in the blessings of the gospel is valid only if we continue in it. John presupposes the same thing—that those who leave the church show they never really belonged in it (1Jn 2:19; 2Jn 9). Even Hebrews 6:4–6; 10:26–31 show how much of the truth may be grasped, how much of the life of the age to come may be sampled, without coming to the place from which there is no turning back (cf. Philip E. Hughes, *A Commentary on the Epistle to the Hebrews* [Grand Rapids: Eerdmans, 1977]). This is apostasy, and it involves a break with what one has formally adhered to.

The universal witness of the NT is that apostasy if persisted in not only damns but shows that salvation was never real in the first place. The NT reveals how close one may come to the kingdom—tasting, touching, perceiving, understanding. And it also shows that to come this far and reject the truth is unforgivable. So it is here. Jesus charges that those who perceive that his ministry is empowered by the Spirit and then, for whatever reason—whether spite, jealousy, or arrogance—ascribe it to Satan, have put themselves beyond the pale. For them there is no forgiveness, and that is the verdict of the one who has authority to forgive sins (9:5–8).

The significance of the transitional words "and so" now becomes plain. Neutrality to Jesus is actually opposition to him (v.30); therefore Jesus gives this warning regarding those who blaspheme against the Spirit, since the self-professedly neutral person may not recognize the inherent danger of his or her position. See Graham A. Cole, *He Who Gives Life: The Doctrine of the Holy Spirit* (Wheaton, Ill.: Crossway, 2007); D. A. Carson, "Reflections on Assurance," in *Still Sovereign: Contemporary Perspectives on Election, Foreknowledge, and Grace* (ed. Thomas R. Schreiner and Bruce A. Ware; Grand Rapids: Baker, 2000), 247–76.

(4) Nature and fruit (12:33–37)

OVERVIEW

This section has no parallel in Mark, but it fits well into Matthew. A similar metaphor occurs in 7:16–19, but there the point is that Jesus' disciples must test character by conduct, whereas here it is that conduct, especially speech, reveals character. Therefore the only remedy is a radical change of heart. Parts of vv.33–34 are also reflected in Luke 6:43–45.

33"Make a tree good and its fruit will be good, or make a tree bad and its fruit will be
bad, for a tree is recognized by its fruit. 34You brood of vipers, how can you who are evil say
anything good? For out of the overflow of the heart the mouth speaks. 35The good man
brings good things out of the good stored up in him, and the evil man brings evil things
out of the evil stored up in him. 36But I tell you that men will have to give account on the
day of judgment for every careless word they have spoken. 37For by your words you will
be acquitted, and by your words you will be condemned."

COMMENTARY

33 It is possible to construe the expression "make a tree good ... bad" to mean "suppose a tree is good ... bad." But in that case, the word "and" fits badly, and the final "for" clause relates poorly to what precedes. Jesus is rather telling his hearers to make the tree good or bad, knowing that its fruit will be correspondingly good or bad, because a tree is recognized by its fruit (cf. Sir 27:6). To speculate on the means—pruning, grafting, watering, fertilizing—is to go beyond the metaphor.

34–35 Then Jesus drives the point home. "You brood of vipers" (see comments at 3:7; 23:33) was most likely addressed to the Pharisees in the crowd (cf. 12:23–24), though this is not certain (cf. 7:11). Verse 35 makes a tight connection with v.33: what a person truly is determines what he says and does. Out of the *perisseuma* ("overflow," GK *4354*—what remains, the excess) the "mouth speaks." *Perisseuma* is used here and in Luke 6:45 in reference to the heart, the center of human personality (see comments at 5:8). It is the mouth that reveals what is in the heart. How, then, can those who are evil say anything good? What is needed is a change of heart.

36–37 These two verses occur only in Matthew. That Jesus describes the evil of the "brood of vipers" in terms of their hearts or natures does not thereby excuse them. Far from it! A person will be held accountable on the day of judgment for "every careless word." The Greek *argos* ("careless," GK *734*) does not refer here to "unfounded" words (JB) but to words that might be thought "insignificant" (Stendahl, "Matthew," in *Peake's Commentary*) except for their revealing what is in the heart. Jesus is saying that every spoken word reflects the heart's overflow and is known to God. Therefore, words are of critical importance (cf. Eph 5:3–4, 12; Col 3:17; Jas 1:19; 3:1–12).

The change to the second person (v.37) implies that the saying may be proverbial. Here it heightens the warning that what one says about Jesus and his miracles reveals what one is and that he will be judged accordingly. Jesus' authority in saying this is staggering. It is not he who is being assessed when men ask, "Could this be the Son of David?" (v.23), or utter blasphemies (v.24); it is they who are being assessed, and by their words they will be judged.

NOTES

36 The syntax is difficult. If πᾶν ῥῆμα ἀργόν (*pan rhēma argon*, "every careless word") is construed as nominative, there is an awkward anacolouthon (... περὶ αὐτοῦ λόγον [*peri autou logon*, lit., "concerning his (or its) word"]; cf. 13:19); but this may be accusative by attraction to the relative ὅ (*ho*, "which").

c. Continued confrontation (12:38–42)

(1) Request for a sign (12:38)

38Then some of the Pharisees and teachers of the law said to him, "Teacher, we want to see a miraculous sign from you."

COMMENTARY

38 One might take *apekrithēsan* ("answered," GK *646*; NIV, "said") as meaning that the Pharisees and teachers of the law were continuing the controversy. This is possible, and the parallel in Luke 11:29–32 is sufficiently detached from its context to permit this interpretation. But *apekrithēsan* does not always have its full strength in Matthew (see comments at 11:25), so it seems best not to insist on the continuance of the controversy.

The Jewish leaders phrased their question respectfully ("Teacher"; see comments at 8:19) and asked for a "sign" (*sēmeion*, GK *4956*), not just for another miracle. Jesus had already done many miracles. OT and intertestamental Jewish literature shed light on the request (cf. *TDNT*, 7:208–21, 225–29; *TDOT*, 1:167–88; see 1Sa 2:30–33; 1Ki 20:1–14; Isa 7:10–25; *b. Sanh.* 98a; *b. B. Meṣ.* 59b; cf. O. Linton, "The Demand for a Sign from Heaven [Mk 8:11–12 and Parallels]," *ST* 19 [1965]: esp. 123ff.). A sign was usually some miraculous token to be fulfilled quickly, or at once, to confirm a prophecy. The Jews were not asking for just another miracle, since they had already persuaded themselves that at least some of those Jesus had performed were of demonic agency (v.24); they were asking for a "sign" performed on command to remove what seemed to them to be the ambiguity of Jesus' miracles. (In John, "sign" is not so much something people ask for as the evangelist's standard label for what the synoptists call "powers" or "wonders." The "signs" Jesus performs under John's pen bear implicit and explicit symbolic weight.)

(2) The sign of Jonah (12:39–42)

[39]He answered, "A wicked and adulterous generation asks for a miraculous sign! But none will be given it except the sign of the prophet Jonah. [40]For as Jonah was three days and three nights in the belly of a huge fish, so the Son of Man will be three days and three nights in the heart of the earth. [41]The men of Nineveh will stand up at the judgment with this generation and condemn it; for they repented at the preaching of Jonah, and now one greater than Jonah is here. [42]The Queen of the South will rise at the judgment with this generation and condemn it; for she came from the ends of the earth to listen to Solomon's wisdom, and now one greater than Solomon is here."

COMMENTARY

39–40 The Pharisees and teachers of the law did not, in Jesus' view, stand alone. They represented this "wicked and adulterous generation" (cf. 11:16–24). "Adultery" was frequently used by OT prophets to describe the spiritual prostitution and wanton apostasy of Israel (e.g., Isa 50:1; 57:3; Jer 3:8; 13:27; 31:32; Eze 16:15, 32, 35–42; Hos 2:1–7; 3:1). Here Jesus applies it to his contemporaries, as did his brother James later on (Jas 4:4). Israel had largely abandoned her idolatry and syncretism after the exile. But now Jesus insists that she is still adulterous in heart. In the past God had graciously granted "signs" to strengthen the faith of the timid (e.g., Abraham [Ge 15]; Gideon [Jdg 6:17–24]; Joshua [Jos 10]). Here, however, Jesus says that signs are denied "this wicked and adulterous generation," because they are never to be performed on demand or as a sop to unbelief (cf. 1Co 1:22).

In Mark 8:11–12, Jesus refuses to give any sign; but in Matthew and Luke (Q) the sign of Jonah is expected. This has led many to conclude that the reference to Jonah is an unauthentic, late addition (Stendahl, "Matthew," in *Peake's Commentary*; G. Schmitt ["Das Zeichen Jona," *ZNW* (1978): 123–29] suggests that the addition was made in the seventh decade AD through the influence of *Lives of the Prophets*). On the other hand, Taylor (*Mark*, 63) suggests Mark has abbreviated the original in the interests of his "messianic secret" theme so as to produce a flat refusal to provide a sign. But the difference between Mark and the other two synoptists may be more subtle. Rightly understood the sign, which is the exception in Matthew and Luke, is not a sign at all, as Jesus' opponents understood the word. It becomes a sign only for those with eyes to see. In that sense, there is no exception: Jesus offers no miraculous token on demand. That is Mark's point—a point not contradicted by the "exception" the other synoptists record.

But what is "the sign of Jonah"? This question is tied to the absence of v.40 from the parallel in Luke and its being regarded as a late addition. The argument, it is said, must therefore run from v.39 to v.41; and the sign of Jonah must be his preaching of repentance, a ministry in which Jesus has likewise been engaged. Verse 40 is, then, a late typological addition.

Nevertheless, a good case can be made for the authenticity of v.40 (cf. especially France, *Jesus and the Old Testament*, 80–82). Luke does not simply "drop out" Matthew 12:40. Rather, following the reference to the "sign of Jonah," Luke writes (11:30), "For as Jonah was a sign to the Ninevites, so also will the Son of Man be to this generation." He then includes the visit of the Queen of the South before returning to the men of Nineveh, who will rise up and condemn Jesus' contemporaries (cf. Mt 12:41). In other words, Luke, for whom Jonah's preaching is not a sign, does not support the alleged continuity between Matthew 12:39 and 12:41. If this is correct, then either v.40 is an enlargement of an original but cryptic Luke 11:30, or else Luke 11:30 is an effort to veil the specificity of an original Matthew 12:40. The latter view is more credible, for Luke has an obvious reason for making the saying more cryptic—namely, the reference to three days and three nights, so readily understood in Matthew's Jewish environment (see below), would be problematic to Luke's readers, who would see a conflict with the length of time Jesus was actually in the tomb. The same concern doubtless accounts for Justin Martyr's quoting (*Dial.* 107:1) Matthew 12:39 and saying that Jesus was speaking cryptically of the resurrection, though Justin does not actually quote v.40.

The rejection of v.40 is tied to the interpretation of the "sign of Jonah." If v.40 is removed, the "sign" is most likely the preaching. But this is intrinsically unlikely. In both Matthew and Luke, the sign is future to Jesus' utterance (Mt 12:39; Lk 11:30), which suits Jesus' death and resurrection but not his preaching. Verse 40, therefore, becomes an integral part of Matthew's pericope. And the contention of R. A. Edwards (*The Sign of Jonah* [London: SCM Press, 1971], 25ff.) that the sayings of this pericope are in the form of a new *Gattung*, a Christian invention after Jesus' time, has been disproved by lists of much older examples of the same form (cf. Daryl Schmidt, "The LXX Gattung 'Prophetic Correlative,'" *JBL* 96 [1977]: 517–22).

In "the sign of Jonah," then, "of Jonah" must be construed as an epexegetic genitive (Zerwick, *Biblical Greek*, para. 45; Turner, *Syntax*, 214). It is the sign that Jonah himself was, not the sign given him or presented by him. This interpretation commonly accepts the view that the Ninevites learned what had happened to Jonah and how he got to their city. Jonah himself thus served as a "sign" to the Ninevites, for he appeared to them as one who had been delivered from certain death (cf. *TDNT*, 3:409; Eugene H. Merrill, "The Sign of Jonah," *JETS* 23 [1980]: 23–30). As Jonah was three days and three nights in the belly of the fish, so the Son of Man—seen here in his suffering role (see comments at 8:20)—will be three days and three nights in the "heart [perhaps an echo of Jnh 2:3; cf. Ps 46:2] of the earth"—a reference to Jesus' burial, not his descent into Hades. That is to say, Jesus' preaching will be attested by a deliverance like Jonah's, only still greater; therefore, there will be greater condemnation for those who reject the significance of Jonah's deliverance.

Some scholars perceive the strength of the argument for the authenticity of this pericope but interpret v.40 as if it were referring to the "sign" of the coming Son of Man (24:30), or to Jesus' vague awareness that he must die sometime, or to the fact that Jesus by his suffering will carry the truth of God to the Gentiles as Jonah did. But this overlooks the connection between Jonah and Jesus established by the text. Grant the authenticity of v.40, and the only legitimate conclusion is that Jesus knew long in advance about his death, burial, and resurrection and saw his life moving toward that climax. The christological implications must not be avoided.

Jonah spent "three days and three nights" in the fish (Jnh 1:17). But if the normal sequence of Passion Week is correct (see comments at 26:17–30), Jesus was in the tomb only about thirty-six hours. Since they included parts of three days, by Jewish reckoning Jesus was buried "three days," or to put it another way, he rose "on the third day" (16:21). But this does not cover more than two nights. Some advocate a Wednesday crucifixion date (see comments at 26:17); but though that allows for "three days and three nights," it runs into difficulty with "on the third day." In rabbinical thought, a day and a night make an *onah*, and a part of an *onah* is as the whole (cf. Str-B, 1:649, for references; see also 1Sa 30:12–13; 2Ch 10:5, 12; Est 4:16; 5:1). Thus according to Jewish tradition, "three days and three nights" need mean no more than "three days" or the combination of any part of three separate days.

41 The first point of comparison between Jonah and Jesus is that they were both delivered from death—a deliverance that attested the trustworthiness of their preaching. The second point of comparison is the different responses of the hearers. The men of Nineveh repented. But even though "something [neuter, as in 12:6; NIV, 'one'] greater than Jonah is here"—the reference is to Jesus, not his deliverance, because the comparison is with Jonah, not his deliverance—the people of Jesus' day—"this generation" (cf. v.39)—did not repent. Therefore men of Nineveh (the nouns are anarthrous) "will stand up with" this generation at the final judgment; i.e., they will rise to bear witness against them (see comments at 11:20–24; on the Semitic legal idiom, see Mk 14:57; Black, *Aramaic Approach*, 134). Thus Jesus' "sign" does not meet the Jews' demand for a special token (see comments at v.38). Yet it is the only one he will provide. For his own followers, his authority will be grounded in his death and resurrection. And as for those who do not believe, they will only prove themselves more wicked than the Ninevites.

42 Jonah and Solomon are linked in other Jewish literature (cf. D. Correns, "Jona und Salomo," in *Wort in der Zeit* [ed. W. Haubeck and M. Bachmann; Leiden: Brill, 1980], 86–94). The nature of the link—Jonah and the queen with "this generation" rising at the judgment—strongly supports the view that for Jesus, Jonah was a historical person. The Queen of the South (the Arabian peninsula, which for the Jews was "at the ends of the earth"; cf. Jer 6:20; Joel 3:8 NASB) was the queen of Sheba (1Ki 10:1–13), who came to Jerusalem because of reports of Solomon's wisdom. But Jesus is "something greater" (see comments at v.41) than Solomon; Jesus is the Messiah, who will introduce the promised eschatological age. Therefore, the queen of Sheba will rise at the judgment to join the Ninevites in condemning the unbelieving generation of Jesus' time.

NOTES

41 The phrase εἰς τὸ κήρυγμα Ἰωνᾶ (*eis to kērygma Iōna*, "at the preaching of Jonah") cannot be final but establishes the ground for the Ninevites' repentance. On this rather rare use of εἰς, *eis*, see Turner, *Syntax*, 255; Zerwick, *Biblical Greek*, para. 106; BDF, para. 207; cf. Notes, 10:41.

d. The return of the evil spirit (12:43–45)

OVERVIEW

The parallel in Luke 11:24–26 is, as here, tied to the Beelzebub controversy, though the preceding verse is different (Lk 11:23 = Mt 12:30). Though many think Luke applies the parable to the individual and Matthew to the nation, this contrast is too facile. Luke omits (according to the best texts) the connective *de* ("and" or "but"). This suggests an independent saying that fits the movement of the chapter but is not meant to be tied too tightly to the verse preceding it. The warning in both Matthew and Luke is not (contra Marshall, *Gospel of Luke*, 479) aimed at "those who exorcise demons without giving a positive substitute to their patients." In both Matthew (12:27) and Luke (11:19) the comparison Jesus draws between himself and other exorcists is not meant to prove his superiority but to show that even Jewish exorcists achieve some success in their work by virtue not of Beelzebub but of God's power.

This story about the unclean spirit who after being driven out returns with seven wicked spirits goes beyond Jesus' comparison, for Luke (11:21–22) has shown Jesus' authority in binding Satan, and Matthew (12:39–42) has insisted that Jesus is greater than Jonah and Solomon. In other words, in both gospels this pericope is set in a milieu of veiled messianic claims. The point here and in Luke is that those who through the kingdom power of God experience exorcisms must beware of neutrality toward Jesus the Messiah, for neutrality opens the door to seven demons worse than the one driven out. Commitment to Jesus is essential. Thus the pericope supports Luke 11:23, which, like Matthew 12:30, rules out neutrality.

Against the broader background in Matthew of the Beelzebub controversy and the sign of Jonah, in sweeping out the house and ridding it of its demons, Jesus has been testifying to the presence of the kingdom (v.28). Yet many of that "wicked and adulterous generation" are so neutral toward him they require signs (v.38) and fail to see that one greater than Jonah and Solomon has come. Luke 11:23 does not mean that Matthew 12:43–45 and Luke 11:24–26 refer to individual demon-possession in contrast to the national rejection of Jesus Messiah portrayed in Matthew. On the contrary, both evangelists deal with the same issue, namely, the extreme danger of being neutral toward Jesus (see comments at v.45).

43"When an evil spirit comes out of a man, it goes through arid places seeking rest and does not find it. 44Then it says, 'I will return to the house I left.' When it arrives, it finds the house unoccupied, swept clean and put in order. 45Then it goes and takes with it seven other spirits more wicked than itself, and they go in and live there. And the final condition of that man is worse than the first. That is how it will be with this wicked generation."

COMMENTARY

43 When an evil spirit (see comments at 8:28; 10:1) leaves a man (lit., "the man," but the article presents a typical case), it goes "through arid places" in search of rest. This conforms to the view that demons have an affinity for such places (Tob 8:3; cf. Rev 18:2). Ultimately, however, they seek another body in order to do even more harm.

44 Verse 43 implies the possibility of repossession. While v.44 may be theoretically interpreted as a universal fact of experience, that would make Jesus' exorcisms an invitation to catastrophe. So it is better to take the language of the text as a Semitic paratactic conditional protasis to v.45 (i.e., "If the demon on his arrival finds the house unoccupied, etc."; cf. H. S. Nyberg, "Zum grammatischen Verständnis von Matth.12:44f.," ConBNT 13 [1949]: 1–11; Jeremias, *Parables of Jesus*, 197–98) or to take the details of the story as representing a dangerous contingency (Beyer, *Semitische Syntax*, 281–86).

45 Though the seven evil spirits may have been harder to drive out than just one (cf. Mk 5:9; 9:29), the text mentions only their greater wickedness. The man from whom the demon had been driven out is now in a far worse condition than before. Jesus' final statement in this pericope—"That is how it will be with this wicked generation" (omitted by Luke)—does not change the point of the story from one of demon-possession to the nation's failure to recognize Jesus, for both Matthew and Luke understand the story to demand recognition of Jesus Messiah. But what Matthew adds (1) closes off the main part of the pericope by referring again to "this wicked generation" (cf. v.39)—a common but overlooked Matthean device (see comments at 15:20)—and (2) makes the warning less cryptic than Luke (cf. v.40; Lk 11:30). Though Luke knows the danger into which the Jews' rejection of Jesus (Lk 21:20–24) will place them, this is not for him, as it is for Matthew, a major theme.

6. Doing the Father's will (12:46–50)

OVERVIEW

Here Matthew basically follows Mark 3:31–35 (cf. Lk 8:19–21; Jn 7:3–5), though he omits the background in Mark 3:20–21. As a result, these verses are not so much a confrontation between Jesus and his family as a statement about what it really means to be a disciple of Jesus and to be totally committed to him. The way for us to be as close to Jesus as his nearest and dearest is to do the will of his Father.

46While Jesus was still talking to the crowd, his mother and brothers stood outside,
wanting to speak to him. 47Someone told him, "Your mother and brothers are standing
outside, wanting to speak to you."
48He replied to him, "Who is my mother, and who are my brothers?" 49Pointing to his
disciples, he said, "Here are my mother and my brothers. 50For whoever does the will of my
Father in heaven is my brother and sister and mother."

COMMENTARY

46–47 The obvious implication is that Jesus is inside the house (cf. Mk 3:20, 31). Though v.47 is omitted in many MSS, probably by homoeoteleuton (words, clauses, or sentences with similar endings being dropped by oversight; both v.46 and v.47 end in *lalēsai* ["to speak"]), it was likely in the original text and clearly helps the sense of the pericope. While the verse might represent assimilation to Mark 3:32, this would not explain *tō legonti autō* ("to the one who had spoken to him," omitted from v.48 in the NIV), which presupposes v.47.

In Mark's account, a reason is given as to why Mary and Jesus' brothers were trying to see him: they were concerned because the press of the crowd was so great that Jesus was not finding time and space even to eat (3:20–21). In that context, Jesus' insistence that his disciples constitute his true family members might be taken to stem, in part, from Jesus' insistence that his family did not have the right to interfere with his God-given mission. Because Matthew's account, typically shorter than that of Mark, does not mention his family's concern, Jesus' comment about which people constitute his true family appears even sharper, though the main point is unchanged. Rather remarkably, David Sim (*Gospel of Matthew*, 191–92) thinks Matthew's account actually rehabilitates James and the natural family of Jesus by including his disciples "*within* his natural family" (emphasis added). It is hard to see why he draws this inference. The only argument he advances is that Mary is presented favorably in Matthew's birth narratives. Even this judgment is misplaced. Compared with Luke's account, Matthew's birth narratives are not much interested in Mary.

The most natural way to understand "brothers" is that the term refers to sons of Mary and Joseph and thus to brothers of Jesus on his mother's side. To support the dogma of Mary's perpetual virginity, a notion foreign to the NT and to the earliest church fathers, Roman Catholic scholars have suggested that "brothers" refers either to Joseph's sons by an earlier marriage or to sons of Mary's sister, who had the same name (cf. McHugh, *Mother of Jesus*, 200ff.). Certainly "brothers" can have a wider meaning than male relatives (Ac 22:1); yet it is very doubtful whether such a meaning is valid here, for it raises insuperable problems. For instance, if "brothers" refers to Joseph's sons by an earlier marriage, not Jesus but Joseph's firstborn would have been legal heir to David's throne. The second theory—that "brothers" refers to sons of a sister of Mary also named "Mary"—faces the unlikelihood of two sisters having the same name. All things considered, the attempts to extend the meaning of "brothers" in this pericope, despite McHugh's best efforts, are nothing less than far-fetched exegesis in support of a dogma that originated much later than the NT (see comments at 1:25; cf. Lk 2:7; see Broadus on 13:55–56).

48–50 Jesus' searching question (v.48) and its remarkable answer (vv.49–50) in no way diminish his mother and brothers but simply give the priority to his Father and doing his will. "For, had [Christ] not entered into earthly kinship solely for the sake of the higher spiritual relationship which He was about to found ...? Thus, it was not that Christ set lightly by His Mother, but that He confounded not the means with the end" (Edersheim, *Life and Times*, 1:577). Henceforth the disciples are the only "family" Jesus recognizes.

The metaphorical nature of v.49 is shown by the "ands" (v.50): "my brother and sister [Jesus had physical sisters; cf. 13:56] and mother" instead of " ... or ... or." We do not make ourselves Jesus' close relatives by doing the will of his heavenly Father. Rather, doing the Father's will *identifies us* as his mother and sisters and brothers (cf. 7:21). The doing of that will turns on obedience to Jesus and his teaching, according to Matthew, for it was Jesus who preeminently revealed the will of the Father (cf. 11:27). This means that Jesus' words in this pericope are full of christological implications, but they also establish the basic importance of the community now beginning to form around him, God's chosen Servant, who, despite rising opposition, will lead justice to victory (vv.18, 20).

B. Third Discourse: The Parables of the Kingdom (13:1–53)

1. The setting (13:1–3a)

[1]That same day Jesus went out of the house and sat by the lake. [2]Such large crowds gathered around him that he got into a boat and sat in it, while all the people stood on the shore. [3]Then he told them many things in parables, saying:

COMMENTARY

1 Matthew links the parabolic discourse in ch. 13 to the preceding controversies (either 12:38–50 or 12:22–37) and ends it with a formulaic conclusion (13:53), which implies that all these parables were given on this occasion. The statement "Jesus went out of the house" implies the same thing by setting a specific scene carried forward by 13:36.

Jesus "sat by the lake," taking the normal position of a teacher (see comments at 5:1–2). The explanation that Jesus' posture was a symbol drawn from apocalyptic literature representing God's sitting in judgment (cf. Rev 7:12; Kingsbury, *Parables of Jesus*, 23–24) is not only overly subtle and needlessly anachronistic but misunderstands the parables. Although in some parables Jesus portrayed himself as the Judge coming at the end of the age (esp. vv.40–43), such a judicial session is future. During his ministry Jesus' chosen role was that of a teacher who taught others about the kingdom so that they might teach others (see comments at vv.51–52).

2 This is the only one of the five major discourses in Matthew that is addressed not to the "disciples" (in the broad sense of 5:1–2) but to the crowds. Therefore, Matthew includes in it two major digressions (vv.10–23, 36–43), in which Jesus explained to his disciples the significance of parables and interpreted two of them. While these digressions doubtless took place after the public discourse, Matthew moves them back as parentheses so that the significance of the parables will not be lost to the reader. Some scholars contend that the crowds, unlike the Jewish leaders, are portrayed favorably, since they are the group Matthew wants immediately to reach. But that is far-fetched. In Matthew, Jesus has already criticized "this generation" (11:16–24) and can treat the Jewish leaders as typical of it (12:38–39). Here the crowds are not given "the secrets of the kingdom" (v.11).

Matthew changes Mark's "taught" (Mk 4:2) to "told" (v.3a)—a change that has encouraged many to suppose that he is turning the parables into "proclamation narratives" (e.g., W. Wilkens, "Die Redaktion des Gleichniskapitels Mark 4 durch Matth.," *TZ* 20 [1964]: 305–27). On the other hand, Kingsbury (*Parables of Jesus*, 28–31) holds that the change from "taught" to "told" owes everything to the structure of Matthew's gospel. After Matthew 12 Jesus never teaches or preaches to the Jews. So Matthew looks on this chapter as a sort of "apology." To base such large theological implications on the change of a single verb is not convincing, because Matthew often shows considerable independence in verbal expression. What he understands Jesus to be doing in the parables must be based on the exegesis of the whole chapter, and especially on that of vv.10–17, which purports to answer that very question. Kingsbury's view that Jesus does not teach or preach to the crowd after Matthew 12 is, in any case, manifestly wrong. Little of such teaching occurs before Matthew 12; most references to it are general (e.g., 4:23; 9:35). After Matthew 12 we find similar remarks (13:54; 15:10; 21:23; cf. 22:16; 26:55; and implicitly 14:13–36; 15:29–31). These and similar reconstructions attempt to see in the antithesis between the "crowds" and the "disciples" a covert disjunction between the church and the synagogue. J. Dupont ("Le point de vue," 221–59) analyzes these efforts in detail and shows that the language is simply not specific enough to draw such far-reaching conclusions. In particular, he shows that the disciples-crowds contrast relates to what is just or unjust and with either doing or not doing the will of the Father.

3a Jesus told the crowd "many things in parables." Before we examine them, however, three comments are necessary.

1. The history of the interpretation of parables is complex, and the number of new developments in parable scholarship has accelerated in recent years. This has been set forth concisely by J. G. Little ("Parable Research in the Twentieth Century," *ExpTim* 87 [1975–76]: 356–60; *ExpTim* 88 [1976–77]: 40–44, 71–75) and comprehensively by W. S. Kissinger (*The Parables of Jesus: A History of Interpretation and Bibliography* [Metuchen, N.J.: Scarecrow, 1979]), and more recently by Craig Blomberg (*Interpreting the Parables* [Downers Grove, Ill.: InterVarsity, 1990]) and Klyne Snodgrass (*Stories with Intent: A Comprehensive Guide to the Parables of Jesus* [Grand Rapids: Eerdmans, 2008]).

Commentators tended to interpret the parables more or less by appeal to allegory (with notable exceptions such as Augustine and, to a lesser extent, Calvin) until Adolph Julicher's huge study (*Die Gleichnisreden Jesu* [2 vols.; Tübingen: Mohr, 1910]), which contends that Jesus told not allegories but parables—simple stories with a single point. Traces of allegorical interpretation of parables in the Gospels must therefore be assigned to the postapostolic church. Studies by Dodd (*Parables of the Kingdom*) and Jeremias (*Parables of Jesus*) have proceeded along similar lines. Dodd has tried to show that some parables demonstrate the eschatological orientation of Jesus' preaching and the "presentness" of the kingdom, while Jeremias has established "laws" of parable transmission to determine how Jesus' simple stories were progressively changed in the process of oral and written retelling and application. Using these "laws," Jeremias has argued that we can strip off later accretions and discover what the historical Jesus really taught.

Two essays challenge Jeremias's view. Both Matthew Black ("The Parables as Allegory," *BJRL* 42 [1959–60]: 273–87) and Raymond E. Brown ("Parable and Allegory Reconsidered," *NovT* 5 [1962]: 36–45) convincingly demonstrate that the allegory-parable distinction is too facile, that Jesus himself occasionally derived more than one or two points from certain of his parables, and that all "allegorizing" of the parables cannot be automatically assigned to the postapostolic church. Two things follow: (1) what Jeremias calls allegorization does not by itself prove secondary accretion; (2) as McNeile, 186, observed long ago, a certain unavoidable ambiguity is built into the parables, for it is not always easy to distinguish illustrative details and details that are merely part of the story structure. While there is room for difference of opinion here, the slight loss in certainty of meaning is more than compensated for by the greater flexibility in understanding the parables.

Parable scholarship moved in a more productive direction with the publication of Hans Weder's *Die Gleichnisse Jesu als Metaphern* [Göttingen:

Vandenhoeck & Ruprecht, 1978], 69–75). Weder distinguishes parabolic (as opposed to allegorical) elements as those tied to the narrative flow and lacking independent existence both in the narrative and its interpretation. His work largely follows the studies of Eta Linnemann (*Parables of Jesus* [London: SPCK, 1966]), D. O. Via (*Parables*), and J. D. Crossan (*In Parables* [New York: Harper, 1973]), who say that what distinguishes parable from allegory is not that only the former has one central point but that the former alone ties all its elements to one another within the parable's framework. These interconnections are determined not so much by a one-to-one link with the historical or theological situation to which the parable refers as by the demands of the story—namely, the parable itself. Therefore, some parabolic elements may have a historical referent, others none. But where such "outside" connections are made, they are subsidiary to the connections "inside" the parable, the point of which is contained within the story's internal movement.

These are important insights. Reflection on such distinctions might make some commentators, who rightly see that some narrative parables cannot be reduced to one central meaning, refrain from labeling the additional points "allegorical," since that term in modern usage tends to call to mind not merely what is symbolic but what is laden with symbolism extraneous to the narrative. On the other hand, some of those who have developed important insights as to how the subsidiary points are tightly tied to the central narrative unfortunately tend to think deeply on the literary level but naively on the historical one. Many recent interpreters tend to be far less conservative than Jeremias in what they ascribe to the historical Jesus. And it is astonishing how often, once they have finished their interpretations, they exhort their readers to choose authentic existence, trust the benevolence of the universe, or the like. Whatever else Jesus was, he was no twentieth-century existentialist or a twenty-first-century student of narrative. Coupling these literary studies with insights from "the new hermeneutic," Mary Ann Tolbert (*Perspectives on the Parables: An Approach to Multiple Interpretations* [Philadelphia: Fortress, 1979]) tries to establish the legitimacy of interpreting the parables in different ways that depend largely on the stance of the interpreter, and she argues that the parables' "dynamic indeterminacy" (115) requires such an approach. Questions raised by such studies (and the German works on which many of them are based) cannot be handled here. For a responsible treatment of the issues involved, see A. C. Thiselton, *The Two Horizons* (Grand Rapids: Eerdmans, 1980). Those interested in charting how contemporary interpretation of parables has responded not only to hermeneutical trends but to powerful historical events might usefully read Tania Oldenhage, *Parables for Our Time: Rereading New Testament Scholarship after the Holocaust* (New York: Oxford Univ. Press, 2002). Over against such trends are those that try to tie the interpretation of any parable to the context of Jesus and/or of Matthew—to the cultural and social context of Jesus, for instance (e.g., Bailey, *Jesus Through Middle Eastern Eyes*), or to the particular audiences that Matthew specifies (e.g., Carter and Heil, *Matthew's Parables*).

Suffice it to say that historical doubts are not always tied as intimately to the genuine literary insights of these writers as they seem to think. Jesus, though he did indeed confront people and demand existential choices, did so within a message that was, and can still be, defined and defended propositionally. Moreover, the criteria for distinguishing between Jesus' parables and church accretions to them are becoming less and less justifiable. Although there are many *kinds* of parables (see below), Thiselton (*Two Horizons*, 12–15, 344–47) is right in pointing out how many of them are designed to capture the listener and make him a participant, overturning his worldview and leading him to call in question his most basic values. These convictions undergird the following exposition.

2. Some areas of disagreement might be eliminated if more attention were paid to the word "parable" itself (*parabolē*, GK *4130*). Behind it stands the Hebrew *māšāl* (GK 5442; twenty-eight of thirty-three instances in the OT are rendered *parabolē* in the LXX), a word referring to proverbs, maxims, similes, allegories, fables, comparisons, riddles, taunts, stories embodying some truth (Nu 23:7, 18; 1Sa 10:12; 24:13; Job 27:1; Pss 49:4; 78:2; Pr 1:6; Ecc 12:9; Isa 14:4; Eze 12:22; 17:2; 24:3; Mic 2:4; Hab 2:6). And *parabolē* in the NT comes close to duplicating this range (cf. *NIDNTT*, 2:743–60). Thus a parable can be a proverb (Lk 4:23; something John calls a *paroimia* [GK *4231*, "figure of speech," Jn 10:6; 16:25, 29; cf. Job 27:1 LXX]); a profound or obscure saying (Mt 13:35); a nonverbal symbol or image (Heb 9:9; 11:19); an illustrative comparison, whether without the form of a story (15:15; 24:32) or with (in the most familiar kind of "parable"—e.g., 13:3–9); an illustrative story not involving comparison of unlikes (e.g., the rich fool, Lk 12:16–21); and more. So it becomes obvious that much learned discussion actually focuses on only one or two kinds of NT "parables." Most, though not all, parables are extended metaphors or similes. Yet even so broad a definition as this eliminates some of the material listed above that NT writers label "parable." Most generalized conclusions about parables require painful exceptions, and, on the whole, it is best to deal inductively with parables while at the same time being aware of the questions posed by recent studies and the scholarly analyses of some parable material.

One of the most responsible of these is Boucher's work (*Mysterious Parable*), some of whose conclusions are adopted later (see comments at vv.10–17). But even Boucher narrows down parable to "a *narrative* having two levels of meaning" (p. 23) and confusingly defines allegory as merely "a device of meaning, and not in itself a literary form or genre" (p. 20), while insisting that allegory must extend a metaphor over a whole story, thus tying it inescapably to a form. By this definition some parables are allegories. Yet it is useful, for instance, to be able to distinguish allegories that are types from those that are not. Progress in understanding parables depends, it seems, on greater scholarly agreement over the semantics of the labels and on greater willingness to recognize the diversity of kinds of parables in the NT (cf. G. B. Caird, *The Language and Imagery of the Bible* [London: Duckworth, 1980], 161–67; Robert H. Stein, *The Method and Message of Jesus' Teachings* [Philadelphia: Westminster, 1978], 34–39.)

3. The structure of the third discourse (13:3–52) bears directly on its interpretation. Certain things are obvious. Two of the parables are also found in Mark and Luke—the sower and its interpretation (13:3–9, 18–23; Mk 4:3–9, 13–20; Lk 8:5–15) and the mustard seed (13:31–32; Mk 4:30–32; Lk 13:18–19). One is paralleled in Luke but not Mark (the yeast [13:33; Lk 13:20–21]), and the other four (or five; see below) are found only in Matthew. Mark 4:26–29 adds still another to this discourse, and both Mark 4:33 and Matthew 13:3 suggest there was a great deal more left unreported. For a useful survey of the themes developed by the parables in this chapter, see Carter and Heil, *Matthew's Parables*, 53–58.

These are the agreed-on facts, but the structure of the discourse as it stands is more disputed (cf. Dupont, "Le point de vue," 231–32; Kingsbury, *Parables of Jesus*, 12–15). The best analysis has been provided by David Wenham ("Structure of Matthew XIII," 516–22), who argues, with Lohmeyer and Kingsbury (*Parables of Jesus*), that v.52

is a parable (note the form "is like [plus dative]" and the opening words of v.53). The discourse may then be broken down into two parts of four parables each (vv.3–33, 44–52). The first four are addressed to the crowds, the last four to the disciples. Wenham's distinctive contribution lies in identifying the emergent chiastic structure. Of the first four parables, the first stands apart from the other three, separated by discussion about the purpose of parables (vv.10–17) and the interpretation of the parable (vv.18–23). It has a formally different introduction (the other three begin "Jesus told them another parable, 'The kingdom of heaven is like ...'"). The matching chiastic four in the second half begin with three parables with the same opening ("The kingdom of heaven is like ..."), separated from the fourth, which has a different beginning, by the explanation in vv.49–50 and the question and answer about the disciples' understanding of parables. The central section separating the two sets of parables (vv.34–43) divides the chiasm and further explains the function of parables while expounding one of them (see Outline, p. 80).

The implications are important.

1. Matthew reports two rationales for parables, one related to their function for outsiders and one related to their function for disciples.

2. The detailed structure reveals Matthew's skill as an author, and the alleged dislocations (esp. vv.12, 34–35), often taken to support Markan priority, turn out to be, not aporias (i.e., breaks that demand explanation), but integral parts of the outline (see below). This does not, of course, disprove Mark's priority here, but if Matthew is indeed prior or independent for all or part of this chapter (as Wenham argues in "Synoptic Problem Revisited"), it supports an important point, namely, that it is methodologically doubtful to think that the only access to information Matthew has when following Mark is Mark itself.

3. This structure also calls in question the traditional dispensational interpretation of the parables in this chapter. Typical is Walvoord's perspective (96–97, quoting Tasker, 134–35):

> "Jesus deliberately adopted the parabolic method of teaching at a particular stage in his ministry for the purpose of withholding further truth about himself and the kingdom of heaven from the crowds, who had proved themselves to be deaf to his claims and irresponsive to his demands.... From now onwards, when addressing the unbelieving multitude, he speaks only in parables, which he interprets to his disciples in private."

There is insight here. Walvoord rightly detects the note of judgment bound up with some parables. His position, however, is too cut-and-dried. First, remembering the broad definition of "parables" in the NT, it is doubtful we are to think that ch. 13 contains Jesus' first use of parables in Matthew (cf. 7:24–27; 9:15–17; 11:16–19). Second, if Walvoord were to respond that such passages are not labeled "parables," the historical problem recurs when any synoptic harmony is attempted (a procedure he would approve). Historically Jesus does not use parables for the first time at this stage in his ministry (cf. Lk 5:36; 6:39). What does seem likely is that rising opposition to Jesus encouraged his greater and greater use of parables (see comments at vv.10–17, 34–35). But there is little ground for the sudden switch in method Walvoord sees. Third, parables are not restricted to Jesus' ministry to outsiders. He also uses them positively for his disciples (see comments above). Fourth, there has been no extensive teaching to outsiders before this third discourse and none after it to test Walvoord's claim that Jesus' use of parables is a new departure here. We have only the fact that Jesus' preaching to outsiders is repeatedly mentioned but no extended samples of it (see comments at v.11).

2. *To the crowds (13:3b–33)*

a. The parable of the soils (13:3b–9)

3b"A farmer went out to sow his seed. 4As he was scattering the seed, some fell along the
path, and the birds came and ate it up. 5Some fell on rocky places, where it did not have
much soil. It sprang up quickly, because the soil was shallow. 6But when the sun came up,
the plants were scorched, and they withered because they had no root. 7Other seed fell
among thorns, which grew up and choked the plants. 8Still other seed fell on good soil,
where it produced a crop—a hundred, sixty or thirty times what was sown. 9He who has
ears, let him hear."

COMMENTARY

3b–7 The focus of the parable is not the sower (the article is used in v.3 to designate a class; cf. 12:43) but the soils. The farmer scatters the seed, which falls in various places. Paths run through and around the unfenced fields (see comments at 12:1). The earth paths are too hard to receive the seed, which is eaten by birds (v.4). "Rocky places" (v.5) are those in which the limestone bedrock lies close to the surface; there is little depth of soil. As the rainy season ends and the sun's heat increases, the shallow soil heats up quickly (v.6). The seeds sprout and promise to be the best of the crop (on the appropriateness of these details to the Palestinian setting, cf. P. B. Payne, "The Order of Sowing and Ploughing in the Parable of the Sower," *NTS* 25 [1978–79]: 123–29). But the unrelenting summer heat demands that plants send deep roots down for water, and the bedrock prevents this. Like grass on rooftops, the young plants wither before they can grow (Ps 129:6). Other seed falls into hedges of thorns that deprive the plants of sun and nourishment (v.7).

8–9 Some seed falls on good soil and produces crops of various yields, which, contrary to what many think, are not extremely high, symbolic of the fertility of the messianic age, but well within ordinary expectations (cf. Keener; Payne, "Authenticity of the Parable," 181–86). The same seed produces no crop, some crop, or much crop according to the soil's character. The final exhortation (v.9; see comments at 11:15) warns Jesus' hearers and Matthew's readers that the parable needs careful interpretation.

At this point, many commentators, believing vv.18–23 to be unauthentic, attempt to interpret vv.3b–9 without reference to vv.18–23. Their efforts fail to produce interpretations more believable than the one Matthew ascribes to Jesus. Typical is that of Hill, who says the parable means that just as every (Palestinian) sower does his work in spite of many frustrations, so the kingdom makes its way in spite of many difficulties. It will be established in time, with a sure and glorious harvest, but only after much loss. The parable has little to do with how to hear the word of God. But Hill's interpretation depends on treating the parable serially—i.e., the sower sows seed in all the bad places first! On the face of it, the differences lie in the soils, not in the order of sowing: i.e., the kingdom, while advancing now by the promulgation of the good news about the kingdom (4:23), is meeting many different responses.

b. Interlude (13:10–23)

(1) On understanding parables (13:10–17)

OVERVIEW

Matthew's treatment is not only longer than Mark's (Mk 4:10–12) and Luke's (Lk 8:9–10; 10:23–24), but it includes more OT Scripture and is structured with great care. The disciples' question (v.10) evokes Jesus' basic answer (vv.11–12), which is then applied in greater detail first to "them" (vv.13–15) and then to the disciples (vv.16–18). The latter two sections are a well-ordered chiasm whose inversion echoes OT form (e.g., Ps 89:28–37) and emphasizes the climax of judgment and mercy (so Kenneth E. Bailey, *Poet and Peasant* [Grand Rapids: Eerdmans, 1976], 61–62):

Therefore I speak to them in parables,

1 because seeing *they see not* and hearing *they hear not*, nor understand.
  2 And *it is fulfilled to them* the *prophecy* of Isaiah, which says,
    3 "Hearing you *shall hear* and shall *not understand*,
      4 and seeing you *shall see* and shall *not perceive*.
        5 For this people's *heart is* become dull
          6 and the *ears* are dull of hearing
            7 and their *eyes* they have closed,
            7' lest they should perceive with the *eyes*
          6' and hear with the *ear*
        5' and understand with the *heart* and should turn again and I should heal them."
      4' But blessed are *your eyes*, for they see,
    3' and your *ears*, for they *hear*.
  2' For truly I *say to you* that many *prophets* and righteous men
1' desired to see what you *see* and *did not see*, and to hear what you *hear* and *did not hear*.

10The disciples came to him and asked, "Why do you speak to the people in parables?"
11He replied, "The knowledge of the secrets of the kingdom of heaven has been given to you, but not to them. **12**Whoever has will be given more, and he will have an abundance. Whoever does not have, even what he has will be taken from him. **13**This is why I speak to them in parables:

"Though seeing, they do not see;
  though hearing, they do not hear or understand.

14In them is fulfilled the prophecy of Isaiah:

"'You will be ever hearing but never understanding;
you will be ever seeing but never perceiving.
15For this people's heart has become calloused;
they hardly hear with their ears,
and they have closed their eyes.
Otherwise they might see with their eyes,
hear with their ears,
understand with their hearts
and turn, and I would heal them.'

16But blessed are your eyes because they see, and your ears because they hear. 17For I tell you the truth, many prophets and righteous men longed to see what you see but did not see it, and to hear what you hear but did not hear it."

COMMENTARY

10 "The disciples" (Mk 4:10: "the Twelve and the others around him") approached Jesus, apparently in private. If this occurred at the end of the discourse, the plural "parables" would be well accounted for. Kingsbury (*Parables of Jesus*, 40–41) detects in the verb *proselthontes* ("came to him," GK *4665*) a "cultic connotation": the disciples approached Jesus "with the same reverence that would be due to a king or deity." He defends this doubtful view with a prejudicial selection of the evidence that could in some cases be taken that way, while ignoring contrary evidence regarding Matthew's use of the verb (cf. 4:3; 8:19; 9:14; 15:1, 30; 16:1; 17:24; 22:23).

Recent scholarship rightly sees in this chapter the distinction between the disciples and the crowds, presupposed by the above outline. But there has been a regrettable tendency to think Matthew has absolutized the distinction, idealized the disciples, and played down their lack of understanding (Barth, "Matthew's Understanding of the Law," 105ff.; Kingsbury, *Parables of Jesus*, 42ff.). This idealization, it is alleged, is very strong in vv.10–17 and emerges in v.10. The disciples ask why Jesus speaks to the crowds in parables, not what the parables mean—and this presupposes they already know. But Mark's question is ambiguous (4:10); Matthew typically has merely clarified the point. The critics' contention is based on an argument from silence. But if the disciples did understand the parable of the sower, why does Jesus proceed in a few verses to give them an explanation (vv.18–23)? And why do they ask for an explanation to a later parable (v.36)? The focus of Jesus' reply (vv.11–17) is not so much on the disciples' understanding as on the fact that the revelation is given to some and not to others and why. On this recurring question, see Trotter, "Understanding and Stumbling."

11–12 Jesus' answer cannot legitimately be softened. At least one of the functions of parables is to conceal the truth, or at least to *present it in a* *veiled way*. This point is strengthened if the *hoti* is not "recitative" (equivalent to the quotation marks in the NIV) but fully causal—"because." The disciples ask, "Why do you speak, etc.?" and Jesus replies, "Because the secrets of the kingdom have been given to the disciples but not to others." The strength of this translation turns not only on its suitability after "Why?" but also on the fact that *hoti* is nowhere else in the NT "recitative" after the particular formula used: *ho de apokritheis eipen* ("he replied," v.11; cf. Wenham, "Structure of Matthew XIII," 519 n. 5, and literature cited). The pronoun *autois* ("to them") does not refer first to the Jews in Matthew's day but to "the people" mentioned by the disciples in the previous verse.

Ta mysteria tēs basileias ("the secrets of the kingdom") is not explained; its meaning may be deduced by the context and by the use of *mysterion* ("secret") elsewhere. *Mysterion* (GK *3696*) has no obvious connections with pagan mystery religions but reflects a thoroughly Semitic background (cf. R. E. Brown, *The Semitic Background of the Term "Mystery" in the New Testament* [Philadelphia: Fortress, 1968]). It appears in the OT in Daniel (Aram. *rāz*; GK 10661), which refers to some eschatological secret, some portent of what God has decreed will take place in the future. The Greek term can also reflect the Hebrew *sôd* ("secret," "confidential speech," GK 6051), taken from the heavenly council (cf. Brown, *Semitic Background*, 2–6; *NIDNTT*, 3:502). The same range of meanings is found in the Dead Sea Scrolls. "Mysteries" are divine plans or decrees, often passed on in veiled language, known only to the elect, and usually relating to eschatological events.

For the "secrets of the kingdom" to be "given" the disciples suggests that to them certain eschatological realities are being revealed. What is revealed is not who Jesus is, the nature of God, or the power of love (all of which have been suggested); rather, the "mystery of the Kingdom is the coming of the Kingdom into history in advance of its apocalyptic manifestation" (Ladd, *Presence of the Future*, 219–42, esp. 222). That God would bring in his kingdom was no secret. All Jews looked forward to it. "The new truth, now given to men by revelation in the person and mission of Jesus, is that *the Kingdom which is to come finally in apocalyptic power, as foreseen by Daniel, has in fact entered into the world in advance in a hidden form to work secretly within and among men*" (ibid., 225, emphasis his).

It is unlikely that the plural "secrets," as opposed to Mark's "secret," refers to everything Jesus has taught (so Kingsbury, *Parables of Jesus*, 44–45). The strongest reason for the latter view is that some of the parables deal with ethical matters, not eschatology, reflecting, it is argued, the full gamut of Jesus' teaching (e.g., parables of the hidden treasure, of the pearl, of the unforgiving servant). But in reality, all such parables, as we shall see, necessarily presuppose some form of realized eschatology to make their ethical demands meaningful. The plural "secrets" is best accounted for as a typical Matthean preference for the plural (cf. Mt 4:3—Lk 4:3; Mt 8:26—Mk 4:39; Mt 26:15—Mk 14:11; and a regular changing of "crowd" to "crowds" at 12:46; 13:2; 14:22; 15:36; 21:46; 23:1; 27:20), or as a reflection of a non-Markan source (there are several Matthew–Luke "minor agreements" against Mark here; for details, see Wenham, "Synoptic Problem Revisited"), or perhaps as a reference to the multiple elements bound up with the basic eschatological truth that the age to come has already dawned.

The antithesis of v.12 is proverbial and repeated elsewhere (25:29; cf. Mk 4:25; Lk 8:18). It warns against taking spiritual blessings for granted and serves to increase gratitude and a sense of privilege among those who continue to enjoy them. What is lost in the second part of the antithesis is not the law but one's standing as the expected subject of the kingdom (cf. 8:11–12).

13 Jesus now explicitly applies his answer (vv.11–12) to those who are not disciples. Discussion of this verse turns on Matthew's change of *hina* plus subjunctive in Mark 4:12 ("in order that ...")—which implies that the parables' blinding outsiders is a function of divine election—to *hoti* ("because"), which means that Jesus speaks in parables because the people are spiritually insensitive. Though they "see," they do not *really* "see." There are four possible approaches to the above data.

1. Some argue that Matthew's change of *hina* to *hoti* is motivated by his editorial desire to blame the Jews or to establish a moral basis for their being rejected (e.g., Kingsbury, *Parables of Jesus*, 48–49; Dupont, "Le point de vue," 233–34). But this badly oversimplifies the matter because of the strong note on election in the best rendering of v.11 (see comments above).

2. Others suggest a sort of additive harmonization: "because" (*hoti*, Matthew) the willful rejecters refused to see and hear, Jesus spoke to them in parables "in order that" (*hina*, Mark-Luke) they might not (truly) see and hear (Hendriksen). This may be theologically sound, but it is doubtful whether simple addition best explains what Matthew has done.

3. Many attempt to soften the *hina* in Mark to lose its telic force ("in order that") and take on a consecutive force ("with the result that"; cf. NIV's ambiguous "so that"). Mark and Matthew would then be very close in thought in this verse. Certainly *hina* can have consecutive force in Hellenistic Greek, a distinct departure from the classical, but Mark has *hina ... mēpote* (lit., "in order that ... lest"; NIV, "so that ... otherwise"), and it is very difficult to give such an expression anything else than full telic force. Moule (*Idiom Book*, 143) recognizes the strength of this argument, but because he judges the notion of parables told to prevent any who are not predestined for salvation from hearing "too incongruous with any part of the NT period to be plausible," he is forced to appeal to Semitic idiom or even the much later linguistic development of causal *hina*. But attempts to ground Mark's *hina* in a Semitic mistranslation (cf. esp. T. W. Manson, *The Teachings of Jesus* [2nd ed.; Cambridge: Cambridge Univ. Press, 1935], 76ff.) have proved futile (cf. Gundry, *Use of the Old Testament*, 34–35 n. 1; Boucher, *Mysterious Parable*, 43–44). And appeals to rabbinic parables and their function have turned out to support the telic view, since rabbis did indeed use parables to mask truth: the rabbinic parable "is not a universalistic form" (D. Daube, "Public Pronouncement and Private Explanation in the Gospels," *ExpTim* 57 [1945–46]: 177).

4. Though the last two approaches are not convincing, the first can become plausible if presented with greater awareness of the relationship v.12 enjoys with v.11 and v.13. Verse 11 most likely embraces a strictly predestinarian viewpoint, more strongly than Mark 4:11 and doctrinally, though not verbally, like Mark 4:12. The reply to the disciples' question (v.10) is thus given in terms of election in v.11, which is further explained in v.12. Verse 13 recapitulates the reason for speaking in parables but now frames the reason, not in terms of election, but in terms of spiritual dullness. Matthew has already given Jesus' answer in terms of divine election (v.11); now he gives the human reason. While this brings him into formal conflict with Mark 4:12, he has already sounded the predestinarian note of Mark 4:12. Here Matthew includes much more material than Mark, and in the ordered structure (see parallelisms above) that results from the inclusion of such new material, verbal parallels are lost in favor of conceptual ones.

Three broader reflections help resolve the problem.

1. Biblical writers in both the OT and NT have, on the whole, fewer problems about the tension between God's sovereignty and human responsibility than do many moderns. This is not because they fail to distinguish purpose and consequence, as many affirm (e.g., Moule, *Idiom Book*, 142), but because they do not see divine sovereignty and human responsibility as mutually incompatible antitheses. In short, they are compatibilists and therefore juxtapose the two themes with little self-conscious awareness of any problem (cf. Ge 50:19–20; Jdg 14:4; Isa 10:5–7; Hag 1:12–14; Jn 11:49–52; cf. Carson, *Divine Sovereignty*).

2. Thus, even though he records Jesus' answer in terms of election, Mark does not thereby mean to absolve the outsiders of all responsibility. How could he, in the light of the interpretation of the parable of the sower he records (4:13–20), his record of John's demand for repentance (1:4), and much more? Matthew has taken up these themes in greater detail because he wishes simultaneously to affirm that what is taking place in the ministry of Jesus is, on the one hand, the decreed will of God and the result of biblical prophecy and, on the other hand, a terrible rebellion, gross spiritual dullness, and chronic unbelief. This places the responsibility for the divine rejection of those who fail to become disciples on their own shoulders while guaranteeing that none of what is taking place stands outside God's control and plan. The same sort of pairing has already been expressed in 11:25–30.

3. This sheds much light on the parables. It is naive to say Jesus spoke them so that everyone might more easily grasp the truth, and it is simplistic to say that the sole function of parables to outsiders was to condemn them. If Jesus simply wished to hide the truth from the outsiders, he need never have spoken to them. His concern for mission (9:35–38; 10:1–10; 28:16–20) excludes that idea. So he must preach without casting his pearls before pigs (7:6). He does so in parables: i.e., in such a way as to harden and reject those who are hard of heart and to enlighten—often with further explanation—his disciples. His disciples, it must be remembered, are not just the Twelve but those who are following him (see comments at 5:1–12) and who, it is hoped, go on to do the will of the Father (12:50) and do not end up blaspheming the Spirit (12:30–32) or being ensnared by evil more thoroughly than before (12:43–45). Thus the parables spoken to the crowds do not simply convey information or mask it but challenge the hearers. They do not convey esoteric content only the initiated can fathom but present the claims of the inaugurated kingdom and the prospects of its apocalyptic culmination in such a way that its implications are spelled out for those in the audience with eyes to see (overstated but rightly defended by Boucher, *Mysterious Parable*, 83–84).

The parable of the soils not only says that the kingdom advances slowly and with varied responses to the proclamation of that kingdom but also implicitly challenges hearers to ask themselves what kinds of soil they are. Those whose hearts are hardened and who lose what little they have do not participate in the messianic kingdom they have been looking for, and for them the parable is a sentence of doom. Those who have ears to hear, to whom more is given, perceive and experience the dawning of the messianic age; for them the parable conveys the mysteries of the kingdom. In the varied responses given to the challenge of the parables, God's act of judgment and his self-disclosure in Jesus are both seen to be taking place in exactly the same way that various "soils" respond to the "seed," which is the message about the kingdom (see comments at 15:10–13).

14–15 Stendahl (*School of St. Matthew*) and others advance several reasons for taking this quotation as a late gloss on the gospel, including an anomalous introductory formula, and insist that the quotation is tautologous after v.13. But parallels to this introductory formula are common in the LXX and other Greek-Jewish literature with which Matthew is familiar, and vv.14–15 are not strictly tautologous since they go on to stress the theme of fulfillment. Moreover, if Matthew follows Mark (4:12) in v.13, it is unlikely he abridged his source by omitting the entire last clause of Mark 4:12 ("otherwise they might turn and be forgiven"). The one area where Matthew almost invariably gives more material than the other synoptists is in OT quotations and allusions. "We must rather assume that verse 13 leads up to the formal quotation in verses 14, 15" (Gundry, *Use of the Old Testament*, 116–18). These two verses thus become the rough equivalent of Mark 4:12–13.

The text form is LXX (as also in Ac 28:26–27), which follows the MT of Isaiah 6:9–10 pretty closely, except that the LXX is a description of the people whereas the MT makes this a command to the prophet ("Be ever hearing, but never understanding.... Make the heart of this people calloused"). But this is not as significant a change as some have thought; for judging by the prophet's later messages, the words in Isaiah 6:9–10 are steeped in bitter irony. After all, Isaiah was not given this charge because the result was desirable but because it inevitably came on people who were calloused. So also in Jesus' day! The Messiah who comes to reveal the Father (11:25–27) succeeds only in dulling what little spiritual sense many of the people have, for they do not want to turn and be healed. Indeed, the context of Isaiah 6:9–10 reveals that their dullness will continue "until the cities lie ruined ... and the fields ruined and ravaged ... and the land is utterly forsaken. And though a tenth remains in the land, it will again be laid waste" (6:11–13). The reference is to the exile, but the events surrounding the exile are seen as a paradigm, the classic case of rejection of God and resulting judgment, repeated in Jesus' generation on a new level and so fulfilling the words of the prophecy. It is unclear whether any claim that Isaiah 6:9–10 has predictive force is implied (if so, see comments at 2:15). What is certain is the racial connection (cf. Ac 28:26–27; see also Jn 12:38–40). The failure of most Jews to discern spiritual realities was no new thing. Moreover, if the context of Isaiah 6:9–10 goes with the quotation, a strong hint of judgment accompanies the description.

The first two lines of the quotation are in the second person plural: the people are directly addressed. But v.15 gives us God's description of the people in the third person. This makes it at least possible to interpret the "otherwise" clauses (*mēpote*, "lest"), not as the people's purpose (they have closed their eyes lest they see and turn and be healed), but as God's judgment (they have closed their eyes as the result of divine judicial action, otherwise they might see and turn, etc.). The thought then becomes similar to 2 Thessalonians 2:11. Again, of course, neither Jesus nor Matthew would see anything incongruous in God's judicial hardening (see comments at v.13).

16–17 The disciples were blessed by God (see comments at 5:3; cf. Lk 10:23–24) and privileged above the crowd because they saw and heard (v.16) what "many prophets and righteous men" (v.17; see comments at 10:40–42) longed to see but did not. The reference is to OT prophets and others who were just before God—people who looked forward to the coming of the kingdom. Here one cannot help but include Simeon and Anna (Lk 2:25–38). Implicitly there is in Jesus' saying a rich christological and eschatological claim: no mere prophet could say as much as he did.

Those who think Matthew idealizes the disciples (see comments at v.10) observe that the parallel in Luke 10:23–24 contrasts Jesus' generation with earlier generations but argue that Matthew contrasts the disciples ("your" is emphatic) with the hard people of that same generation (cf. Barth, "Matthew's Understanding of the Law," 107). In fact Matthew does something of both. Verse 16, in connection with the preceding verses, contrasts the disciples with the calloused crowd, but v.17 contrasts them with prophets and righteous men of past generations. So the crowd in Jesus' day stands in the line of the willfully blind in the OT (vv.14–15), and Jesus' disciples stand in the line of the prophets (as in 5:11–12). The fulfillment motif is operating, showing that the division taking place in Jesus' time with the coming of the kingdom stands in succession to the divisions already spelled out in the Scriptures. The disciples are not idealized; they will later have to ask for an explanation (v.36). But by contrast with the crowds, they really did follow Jesus and gradually grasped the critical turning point in redemption history Jesus was even then introducing.

NOTES

14 The addition of a cognate participle or a cognate dative to a verb in order to strengthen the verb is a customary way for the LXX to render the Hebrew infinitive absolute (cf. BDF, para. 422; Zerwick, *Biblical Greek*, para. 369). Both are found here in this LXX quotation: ἀκοῇ ἀκούσετε (*akoē akousete*, lit., "in hearing you will hear"), βλέποντες βλέψετε (*blepontes blepsete*, lit., "seeing you will see"). In English these are confusing tautologies, and their meaning is rightly rendered by the NIV: "You will be ever hearing," or "you will be hearing acutely," etc.

(2) Interpretation of the parable of the soils (13:18–23)

OVERVIEW

Jeremias (*Parables of Jesus*, 62) thinks the interpretation provided in all three gospels (cf. Mk 4:14–20; Lk 8:11–15) is a later church creation, but we have already questioned the cogency of some of his criteria. Payne ("Authenticity of the Parable") has taken up the points in question and offered comprehensive rejoinders, some of which will be noted below. Here it is enough to say that (contra Jeremias, 79) not every point in the parable is interpreted allegorically. No explanation is given of the sower, the path, the rocky ground, or the diverse yield. What "allegorical" points are scored emerge naturally from the story (even the identification of the birds; see comments at v.19), once the main point of the extended metaphor is established—and this is why the very category "allegorical" is not the best one (see comments at v.3a). For a brief but fair defense of the authenticity of this interpretation of Jesus' parable, see France (NICNT) and the literature he cites.

The general point is that the "message about the kingdom" (v.19) receives a varied reception among various people, and that during this time of difficulty and frustration there is an implied delay while the seed produces in some soils its various yields. The interpretation therefore demands that each person look to himself as to how he "hears" the message. Broadus, 294, cites Chrysostom:

"Mark this, I pray thee, that the way of destruction is not one only, but there are differing ones, and wide apart from one another. Let us not soothe ourselves upon our not perishing in all these ways, but let it be our grief in whichever way we are perishing."

18"Listen then to what the parable of the sower means: 19When anyone hears the
message about the kingdom and does not understand it, the evil one comes and snatches
away what was sown in his heart. This is the seed sown along the path. 20The one who
received the seed that fell on rocky places is the man who hears the word and at once
receives it with joy. 21But since he has no root, he lasts only a short time. When trouble or
persecution comes because of the word, he quickly falls away. 22The one who received the
seed that fell among the thorns is the man who hears the word, but the worries of this life
and the deceitfulness of wealth choke it, making it unfruitful. 23But the one who received
the seed that fell on good soil is the man who hears the word and understands it. He
produces a crop, yielding a hundred, sixty or thirty times what was sown."

COMMENTARY

18 The *hymeis* ("you") is probably emphatic: in light of the great privilege extended to you, which prophets and righteous men wanted to enjoy and the calloused spurn, *you* listen.

19 Matthew omits "the farmer sows the word" (Mk 4:14) and plunges right into the significance of the various soils. This does not mean he is concerned with the ecclesiastical implications at the expense of the christological ones (so Kingsbury, *Parables of Jesus*, 72), since Mark himself does not identify the sower as Jesus. If he here depends on Mark, Matthew simplifies to get to the point. But David Wenham ("Interpretation of the Parable of the Sower") has provided a plausible source reconstruction that would invalidate redaction-critical conclusions in this pericope that depend on Markan priority. Possibly Matthew and Mark share a common source.

Neither "word" (Mark) nor "word of the kingdom" (Matthew; NIV, "message about the kingdom") indicates later ecclesiastical tradition (cf. Payne, "Authenticity of the Parable," 178–79; contra Jeremias, *Parables of Jesus*, 77–78; Hill). On the change from "word" to "word of the kingdom," compare Matthew's "gospel of the kingdom" (4:23; 9:35; 24:14). More difficult is the mixed metaphor: the seed appears to be "the message about the kingdom," but in the last sentence of the verse it is *ho para tēn hodon spareis* (lit., "he who was sown along the path"; the NIV has smoothed out the difficulty by treating the masculine participle as if it were neuter).

A similar problem occurs in Mark's parallel. Several ways for resolving the problem have been suggested. G. H. Box (*St. Matthew* [Edinburgh: T. C. & E. C. Jack, n.d.) and Alan Hugh McNeile are among those who take the text literally but think there is a purposeful link between the seed and human character, which grows from the seed. But surely the point of this part of the parable is that the seed is taken away before it has time to grow. Others have suggested some sort of ellipsis: "This is [the situation of] the seed sown along the path," understanding "This" to refer to the situation, not the seed or the person, which would also explain vv.20–23, though the masculine *houtos* ("this") instead of the neuter is somewhat surprising. Alexander and Hendriksen therefore opt for a fairly complex ellipsis: "He is the one that [in his reaction to the message resembles the reaction of the ground to the seed that] was sown along the path"—which is possible but rather finely drawn.

Wenham ("Interpretation of the Parable of the Sower") offers a complex but plausible source-critical solution; Payne ("Authenticity of the Parable," 172–77) proposes an underlying Aramaic too literally translated and observes that the Greek can be understood to mean, not "this is he who was sown along the path," but "this is the man who received the seed along the edge of the path" (JB; cf. NASB), understanding the passive participle *ho spareis* to mean, not "the one [seed] sown," but "the one [*soil*] sown." C. F. D. Moule ("Mark 4:1–20 Yet Once More," in *Neotestamentica et Semitica* [ed. Ellis and Wilcox], 112) has shown that the ambiguity is no indication that the interpretation is secondary; the same thing occurs in Colossians 1:6, 10, where the metaphor of growing and bearing fruit is applied first to the seed sown and then to the ground in which it is sown.

Two further features of this verse require explanation.

1. The words "in his heart" make the heart the place of decision, the center of personality (see comments at 5:8). Kingsbury (*Parables of Jesus*, 55) is wrong to conclude from this that the person in view actually becomes a Christian and church member and then rejects the message. He argues that the words "when anyone hears the message about the kingdom" are "tantamount to saying that he becomes a Christian." The conclusion is untenable if one considers the next words—"and does not understand it" (cf. the same verbs in vv.13–14). The hunt for anachronisms can distort scholarly judgment.

2. The evil one (cf. 6:13; 12:45; 13:38–39), called "Satan" in Mark 4:15 and "the devil" in Luke 8:12, has been symbolized by the birds, a point Via (*Parables*, 8) uses to argue that this interpretation goes beyond the range of the natural and understandable symbolism inherent in the parable and must therefore be judged guilty of falling into allegorizing. In fact, close study of birds as symbols in the OT and especially in the literature of later Judaism shows that birds regularly symbolize evil and even demons or Satan (cf. *b. Sanh.* 107a; see also Rev 18:2).

Jesus' interpretation is clear: Some people hear the message about the kingdom, but like hardened paths, they do not let the truth penetrate; before they really understand it the devil has snatched it away.

20–21 The language of these verses is often taken to reflect the apostolic age, not Jesus (cf. Jeremias, *Parables of Jesus*). But "root" (v.21) is appropriate to the extended agricultural metaphor, and "persecution" is amply treated by Jesus elsewhere in nonparabolic settings (e.g., 5:10–12, 43–44; 10:16–25; 24:9; see Payne, "Authenticity of the Parable," 177–80). Jesus' interpretation is coherent. The person who receives "the word" (same Gk. word as "message" in v.19) in a thoughtless way may show immediate signs of life and promise to be the best of the crop: he receives the truth "with joy" (v.20). But without real root, there is no fruit; and external pressures, trouble, and persecution (cf. 24:9, 21, 29), like sun beating on a rootless plant, soon reveal the shallowness of this soil. "At once" (*euthys*) he receives the word with joy and, as "quickly" (*euthys*), "falls away" (*skandalizetai*, GK *4997*; see comments at 5:29). Such temporary disciples are always numerous in times of revival and were so in Jesus' ministry (see comments at 12:32).

22 This person does not hear the word "with joy" (as in v.20) but simply never permits the message about the kingdom to control him. Life has too many other commitments that slowly choke the struggling plant, which never matures and bears fruit. The competing "thorns" are summed up under two headings—the "worries of this life" (lit., this "age" as opposed to the age to come; see comments at 6:25–34) and "the deceitfulness of wealth." The latter category, *hē apatē tou ploutou*, may possibly be rendered "the delight in wealth," since in late Greek *apatē* (GK *573*), which earlier meant "deceitfulness," came to mean "pleasure" or "delight," usually involving sin (e.g., 2Pe 2:13; cf. BDAG, 99). The idea is clear: worries about worldly things or devotion to wealth (cf. 1Ti 6:9) snuff out spiritual life. If "deceit" is understood, there is an added warning that these "thorns" are so subtle that one may not be aware of the choking that is going on. The warning is timeless. Moreover, it is as unconvincing to deduce from this verse that Matthew's church was wealthy (contra Kilpatrick, *Origins*, 124ff.; Kingsbury, *Parables of Jesus*, 61) as to deduce from 6:28–32 that his church was poverty-stricken. What must be avoided is unfruitfulness, for only fruitfulness, not its opposite, indicates spiritual life (cf. Jn 15:1–8). This person finds "all the seeming good effect is gone, leaving the soul a very thicket of thorns" (Broadus, 292).

23 By contrast with the negative results of the preceding verses, we now come to the person who hears the word and understands it (thus reverting to the categories of Isa 6:9–10 used in vv.13–15, 19). The use of *syniēmi* ("understand," GK *5317*) in vv.19, 23, a verb not found in the Markan parallels, has led some to say that "understanding" is a fundamental characteristic of discipleship in Matthew, and that his disciples have again become idealized (see comments at v.10): they are made to "understand" more than the disciples really did at this point in their pilgrimage (cf. Barth, "Matthew's Understanding of the Law," 107; Kingsbury, *Parables of Jesus*, 61–62). But this may be premature. Certainly *syniēmi* with its nine occurrences is an important part of Matthew's vocabulary. But Mark uses *syniēmi* five times, in a book about two-thirds the length of Matthew.

David Wenham ("Interpretation of the Parable of the Sower," 308–9 n. 5) has shown that granted Matthew's syntax in v.19, he could not very well have omitted *syniēmi* there. Its use in v.23 picks up the Isaiah quotation given more briefly in Mark. Moreover, v.23 does not apply the verb directly to the disciples but interprets the parable aphoristically; in so doing it is merely in line with Mark's "hear the word, *accept it*" (4:20, emphasis added). In this chapter the disciples are distinguished from the crowd, but their understanding is only relatively better (v.36), and they are not idealized. Misunderstanding of this point springs from too ready a willingness to read the later church into every phrase of the parable and from a failure to recognize the absolute categories that any competent preacher, including Jesus, uses (see comments at 6:5–8).

The interpretation, like the parable itself, ends positively. We must not fail to notice that the soil that produces only a small crop is nevertheless called "good" (cf. 25:22–23).

NOTES

23 The particle δή (*dē*, used for various kinds of emphasis) is normally employed in the NT in sentences of command or exhortation. This is the sole NT exception (though there are good classical parallels):

"he is just the man who, etc." (cf. BDF, para. 451 [4]). The anomaly has prompted a variant reading in the Western textual tradition.

c. The parable of the weeds (13:24–30)

OVERVIEW

This parable occurs only in Matthew. For the reasons why its interpretation (vv.36–43) is separated from it, see comments at v.3a regarding the structure of the chapter. A few (e.g., Manson, *Sayings of Jesus*, 143) have argued that this parable is not authentic but a creation of Matthew, constructed out of the parable of the seed growing quietly (Mk 4:26–29). But the similar language on which this theory is based owes more to the common agricultural setting than to borrowing. Though many affirm the authenticity of the parable but deny the authenticity of the interpretation (Dodd, *Parables of the Kingdom*, 183–84; Jeremias, *Parables of Jesus*, 81ff.; Kingsbury, *Parables of Jesus*, 65–66), the criteria for such distinctions are faulty (see comments at v.3a); specific arguments can be advanced to defend their joint integrity in this case (see comments at vv.36–43). David R. Catchpole ("John the Baptist, Jesus and the Parable of the Tares," *SJT* 31 [1978]: 557–70) unwittingly supports the view that the parable and its interpretation stand or fall together when, in the course of defending his reconstruction of a much shorter parable (vv.24b, 26b, 30b) that Matthew allegedly expanded, he expresses dissatisfaction with this parable because it includes elements that invite the "allegorizing" interpretations of vv.36–43.

The parable of the sower shows that though the kingdom will now make its way amid hard hearts, competing pressures, and even failure, it will produce an abundant crop. But one might ask whether Messiah's people should immediately separate the crop from the weeds; this next parable answers the question negatively: there will be a delay in separation until the harvest.

[24]Jesus told them another parable:"The kingdom of heaven is like a man who sowed
good seed in his field. [25]But while everyone was sleeping, his enemy came and sowed
weeds among the wheat, and went away. [26]When the wheat sprouted and formed heads,
then the weeds also appeared.

[27]"The owner's servants came to him and said,'Sir, didn't you sow good seed in your
field? Where then did the weeds come from?'

[28]"'An enemy did this,' he replied.

"The servants asked him,'Do you want us to go and pull them up?'

[29]"'No,' he answered,'because while you are pulling the weeds, you may root up the
wheat with them. [30]Let both grow together until the harvest. At that time I will tell the
harvesters: First collect the weeds and tie them in bundles to be burned; then gather the
wheat and bring it into my barn.'"

COMMENTARY

24 Jesus *parethēken* ("told") the people another parable (lit., "he set another before them"). This verb is used in the NT only here and in v.31 in the sense of teaching, though that meaning is attested elsewhere. "Them" must be the crowd, not the disciples (cf. vv.34, 36).

The kingdom of heaven is not "like a man" but "like the situation of a man who ..."; the "is like" formula reflects an Aramaic idiom meaning "It is the case with X as with Y" (cf. Jeremias, *Parables of Jesus*, 100–101; Zerwick, *Biblical Greek*, para. 65). But the peculiar tense used here (see Notes) also implies that the kingdom *has become* like the situation of a man who, etc. The thought is intriguing; for whereas Judaism was accustomed to delays in waiting for the coming of Messiah (cf. R. J. Bauckham, "The Delay of the Parousia," *TynBul* 31 [1980]: 3–36), what Jesus argues is both that the kingdom has come (see 4:17; 12:28) and that the Parousia is still delayed (i.e., the kingdom has become like a parable dealing with the *delay* of the kingdom's arrival).

25–26 "Sleeping" does not imply that the servants were neglectful but that the enemy was stealthy and malicious. What he sowed was *zizania* ("weeds"—almost certainly bearded darnel [*lolium temulentum*]), which is botanically close to wheat and difficult to distinguish from it when the plants are young. The roots of the two plants entangle themselves around each other; but when the heads of grain appear on the wheat, there is no doubt which plant is which (v.26). This weed the enemy sowed "among the wheat"; the Greek (*ana mesov*) suggests thorough distribution. The growing plants gradually become identifiable, and the servants tell their master about the weeds.

27 For *oikodespotēs* ("owner," GK *3867*), see comments at 10:25; 13:52. The servants are not identified; their function in the parable is to elicit information from the owner. In v.27, *kyrios* ("sir") has no special significance; but later Christian readers doubtless saw in it further evidence that the owner is the "Lord" Jesus. The interrogative pronoun *pothen* ("where") can refer to a person as well as to a location (cf. use in vv.54, 56; 21:25), as Jesus' answer (v.28) presupposes.

28–30 The owner blames an enemy (lit., "a man [who is] an enemy"; the construction occurs again in v.52). But the owner forbids his servants from attempting to separate weed from wheat until the harvest (v.29–30). Then, as the workers reap the field, only the wheat will be gathered; the weeds, apparently so plentiful they must first be gathered up and burned (v.30), contaminate the wheat no longer. "Harvest" is a common metaphor for the final judgment (see comments at 9:37–38). In this light, the "good seed" (v.24) cannot be the "word" or "message" of vv.19–23 but people who must face final judgment.

An astonishing number of scholars treat this parable as if there were behind it a Matthean church riddled with problem people, perhaps even apostates. So Jesus' answer in Matthew becomes, in effect, advice not to try to have a pure church, because the Lord will make the right distinctions at the end (cf. G. Barth, "Auseinandersetzungen um die Kirchenzucht im Umkreis des Matthäusevangelium," *ZNW* 69 [1978]: 158–77). But this is a major error in category. Nowhere in Matthew does "kingdom" (or "reign"—see comments at 3:2) become "church" (see comments at vv.37–39; 16:18). The parable does not address the church situation at all but explains how the kingdom can be present in the world while not yet wiping out all opposition. That must await the harvest. The parable deals with eschatological expectation, not ecclesiological deterioration.

NOTES

24 The normal way for synoptic parables of the sort "the kingdom is like" to express "is like" consists of ὁμοία ἐστίν (*homoia estin*, "is like") plus dative. In Matthew, however, this pattern sometimes changes to aorist passive ὁμοιώθη (*homoiōthē*, "has become like," here and in 18:23; 22:2) or to future passive ὁμοιωθήσεται (*homoiōthēsetai*, "will become like," 7:24, 26; 25:1). The future passive usages of the verb focus on the kingdom at its consummation, and the aorist passive on the kingdom as it has already been inaugurated (cf. Strecker, *Weg der Gerechtigkeit*, 214–15; Kingsbury, *Parables of Jesus*, 67; esp. Carson, "ὅμοιος Word-Group"). If so, Pamment's view ("Kingdom of Heaven"; see comments at 5:3; 11:12), that "kingdom of heaven" is always future, referring to the consummated kingdom, receives a fatal blow.

29 Only here in the NT does the adverb ἅμα (*hama*, "at the same time"; NIV, "when") function as an improper preposition "with," "along with" (plus dative, cf. Moule, *Idiom Book*, 81; BDF, para. 194 [3]).

d. The parable of the mustard seed (13:31–32)

[31]He told them another parable: "The kingdom of heaven is like a mustard seed, which a man took and planted in his field. [32]Though it is the smallest of all your seeds, yet when it grows, it is the largest of garden plants and becomes a tree, so that the birds of the air come and perch in its branches."

COMMENTARY

31–32 Close comparison with Mark 4:30–32 and Luke 13:18 suggests that Matthew may have slightly modified the Q form of this parable under Mark's influence. Yet it is easy to exaggerate the differences (see comments and chart at 19:1–2). Many have held that in Mark the contrast in size is of greatest importance, in Luke the process of growth, and that Matthew has conflated the two ideas. Such distinctions are too finely drawn. If size were for Mark the most important factor, one wonders why Mark's Jesus would choose a plant that reaches a height of only ten to twelve feet.

There is a better interpretation. In all three gospels the parable begins with a mustard seed (for the introductory formula and the verb *paretheken* ["he told"], see comments at v.24). This seed is designated "the smallest of all your seeds," but it becomes "the largest of garden plants" (*meizon tōn lachanōn*, v.32; see Notes). In rabbinical thought, the mustard seed was proverbial for smallness (cf. *m. Nid.* 5:2; Str-B, 1:669). It becomes a tree, large in comparison with the tiny seed, large enough for birds to perch in its branches (Matthew; Luke) or in its shade (Mark). The image recalls OT passages that picture a great kingdom as a large tree with birds flocking to its branches (Jdg 9:15; Eze 17:22–24; 31:3–14; Da 4:7–23).

But if the greatness of the kingdom is in view, why a mustard plant? The contrast in size between seed and plant does not itself establish the greatness of the kingdom. Contrary to Kingsbury (*Parables of Jesus*, 81) and Huffmann ("Atypical Features in the

Parables," 211), it is doubtful whether Jesus' point is that the kingdom grows supernaturally. Instead, the point is the organic unity of small beginning and mature end (cf. Dahl, *Jesus in the Memory*, 155–56). No pious Jew doubted that the kingdom would come and that it would be vast and glorious. What Jesus is teaching goes beyond that. He is saying there is a basic connection between the small beginnings taking place under his ministry and the kingdom in its future glory. Though the initial appearance of the kingdom may seem inconsequential, the tiny seed leads to the mature plant.

We can now see why Jesus chose the mustard seed. For him it was not essential to stress the greatness of the future kingdom; few would dispute that. It was more important that he find a metaphor emphasizing the kingdom's tiny beginning. Jacques Dupont ("Le couple parabolique du sénevé et du levain," in *Jesus Christus* [ed. Strecker], 331–45) has suggested another reason for this metaphor. He convincingly shows that the parables of the mustard seed and of the yeast, linked in Matthew and Luke but only the first occurring in Mark, actually belonged together from the beginning. He argues that Mark has structural reasons for dropping the parable of the yeast, and so his silence is scarcely determinative. But one of the links he finds between the two parables is the incongruity of both metaphors. He quotes authors who find the mustard plant an incongruous or even bizarre symbol for the kingdom, while everyone knows that yeast normally symbolizes evil (see comments at v.33). But that, Dupont says (pp. 344–45), is just the point. In both parables the strange choice of images evokes surprise, encourages the reader to penetrate the parable's meaning, and accords with other parables designed to jar the unthinking (e.g., the coming of the kingdom is like the coming of a thief in the night [24:43]).

NOTES

31 The construction ὅν λαβὼν ἄνθρωπος ἔσπειρεν (*hon labōn anthrōpos espeiren*, lit., "which having taken a man sowed") represents a Semitic auxiliary construction and occurs only here in the NT and at vv.33, 44; Luke 12:37; 13:19, 21.

32 The word μεῖζον (*meizon*, "the largest") is neuter and is therefore in agreement with τὸ σίναπι (*to sinapi*, "mustard," "mustard plant") rather than ὁ κόκκος (*ho kokkos*, "seed"). There is no smooth way of translating the anomaly.

e. The parable of the yeast (13:33)

33 He told them still another parable: "The kingdom of heaven is like yeast that a woman took and mixed into a large amount of flour until it worked all through the dough."

COMMENTARY

33 The general thrust of this parable is the same as that of the mustard seed. The kingdom produces ultimate consequences out of all proportion to its insignificant beginnings. Efforts by many dispensationalists (e.g., Walvoord) to interpret the yeast as a symbol for evil are not very convincing in this setting because they require the introduction of anachronistic ideas like "the professing church." Moreover, though yeast is normally associated with evil in the OT, this is *not always* so (cf. Lev 7:13; 23:15–18). Metaphors may have diverse uses; e.g., the lion at different times symbolizes both Satan and Jesus. In any case, the anomalous metaphor is here best explained along the lines suggested by Dupont ("Le couple"; see comments at vv.31–32).

If there is a distinction between this parable and the last one, it is that the mustard seed suggests extensive growth and the yeast intensive transformation. The yeast doesn't grow; it permeates, and its inevitable effect, despite the small quantity used, recalls Jesus' words in 5:13. In both parables it is clear that at present the kingdom of heaven operates, not apocalyptically, but quietly and from small beginnings.

There seems little merit in trying to identify the woman, any more than the man in v.31. Some have thought that *enekrypsen* (RSV, "hid"; NIV, "mixed," from *enkryptō*, GK *1606*) resonates with "hidden" (*kekrymmena*, from *kryptō*, GK *3221*) in vv.35, 44: "The Kingdom was inaugurated without display or pomp; its silent, secret character must have surprised those who were zealously impatient for its expected manifestation in power and glory" (Hill, 234). These comments, while relevant to the parable as a whole, read too much into the verb *enkryptō* itself. It simply means "put something into something," even in nonbiblical Greek (cf. BDAG, 274); the NIV's "mixed" is therefore not bad. Usage of *kryptō* in later verses of this chapter (vv.35, 44) is best interpreted in other ways.

NOTES

33 The phrase εἰς ἀλεύρου σάτα τρία (*eis alearou sata tria*, "into three satas of flour") is anomalous (an anarthrous noun that depends on a preposition is normally placed before a case governed by it) but not unprecedented (cf. BDF, para. 474 [4]).

Far more difficult is the expression σάτα τρία (*sata tria*, "three satas"). The NIV has "a large amount of flour," which is true enough, but it is not an unreasonable amount of flour, adopted for parabolic purpose, since the same amount was mixed by Sarah in Genesis 18:6. It probably represents the largest amount of flour a woman might make up into bread at one time. But how much is it? The NIV text note specifies "about 1/2 bushel or 22 liters." In fact, the standard reference works (including *ISBE*) adopt an unrecognized and conflicting pair of computations leading to mutually exclusive results. If one follows OT ratios and equivalences, τὸ σάτον (*to saton*) = Aram. סָאתָא (*sāʾtāʾ*) = Heb. סְאָה (*sᵊʾâ*) = 1/3 of an ephah or bath. Therefore, three satas, as here, equal 1 ephah, known to be 1/10 of a homer.

Now an ephah (or bath) is normally reckoned at about 22 liters. Measurements were imprecise in the ancient world, ranging substantially in place and time (cf. Jeremias, *Jerusalem*). That this estimate is approximately correct has been confirmed by an archaeological find that has measured what is almost certainly a "bath" jar and found it to have the capacity of about 21 liters (David Ussishkin, "Excavations at Tel Lachish—1973–1977," *TA* 5 [1978]: 87 n. 9; I am indebted to Hugh G. M. Williamson for this reference). This agrees with the NIV text note. But Josephus (*Ant.* 9.85 [4.5]) and other Jewish sources (cf. Str-B, 1:669–70) establish that one σάτον, *saton*, = 1½ *modii*, where 1 *modius* = 16 sextarii = approx. 8.75 liters (confirmed by Josephus, *Ant.* 8.57 [2.9], which says a bath contains 72 sextarii); and in that case σάτα τρία (three *sata*, as in v.33) = 1.5 x 3 x 8.75 = approx. 39.4 liters—a long way from the 22 suggested by the alternative computation.

Both approaches are unwittingly juxtaposed in the standard reference works *The Illustrated Bible Dictionary* (3:1637–39) and *The Interpreter's Dictionary of the Bible* (4:833–35), though the writer in the former mentions in passing that "the bath is variously calculated between 20.92 and 46.6 litres." The matter has not been finally resolved. D. J. Wiseman, in a private communication (December 2, 1980), suggests that the solution may be analogous to the "greater" and "lesser" (half) weights measures (cf. the approximately double "royal bath").

3. Pause (13:34–43)

OVERVIEW

Mark 4:33–34 concludes Mark's report of Jesus' parables on this occasion. But Matthew has already departed from Mark at 13:16–17 and 13:24–30 and by omitting Mark 4:21–29. Now he continues on his own. To believe he has simply modified Mark in this section is difficult because of the great differences between the two accounts. Speculating about Matthew's dependence on an earlier form of Mark (Schniewind) seems too uncontrolled. It is better to assume that Matthew had independent information (Lohmeyer).

a. Parables as fulfillment of prophecy (13:34–35)

34Jesus spoke all these things to the crowd in parables; he did not say anything to them
without using a parable. 35So was fulfilled what was spoken through the prophet:

"I will open my mouth in parables,
I will utter things hidden since the creation of the world."

COMMENTARY

34 The Greek's chiasm puts the emphasis on parables: Jesus did not speak to the crowds without using them. The first verb is aorist (*elalēsen*, "spoke"), referring to the situation at hand; the second is imperfect (*elalei*, "used to say"), implying that this was Jesus' constant custom. But *chōris parabolēs* ("without a parable") does not mean that he told nothing but parables to the crowd but that he said nothing to them without using parables. In short, parables were an essential part of his spoken ministry.

35 The quotation is from Psalm 78:2 (LXX 77), a psalm of Asaph. In addition to two difficult textual variants (see Notes), the text form is notoriously difficult to resolve. The first line follows the LXX exactly; hence it uses the plural *en parabolais* ("in parables") to translate the Hebrew *b^{e}māšāl* ("in a parable" or "in a wise saying"; for the meaning of these words, see comments at v.3a). But the singular is probably generic; so LXX has caught the main point. The second line means roughly the same thing as both the LXX and MT but is quite independent. The verb *ereuxomai* (lit., "I belch forth," "I utter") is an etymological rendering of the MT and may have been chosen above the LXX's *phthenxomai* ("I will utter") simply because it is stronger (Goulder, *Midrash and Lection*, 371); thus it may indicate the richness of the revelation: "I will pour forth things hidden" (as in Ps 19:2 [LXX 18:3]). Matthew's *kekrymmena* ("things hidden") is likewise closer to the Hebrew *ḥîdôt* ("enigmas," "dark sayings," GK 2648) than LXX's *problēmata* ("tasks," "problems").

But in what sense can Jesus' ministry in parables be said to be a fulfillment of Asaph's psalm? The problem does not arise just because the quotation is from a psalm. In 22:43–44, another psalm is quoted as prophecy. Matthew 11:11–13 has already established that the entire OT is in some sense prophetic (see comments at 2:15, 17–18; 5:17–20); 2 Chronicles 29:30 attests that Asaph is a "seer." The problem arises rather in the way Psalm 78:2 is applied to Jesus. Contemporary NT scholars almost universally agree that Matthew has taken Psalm 78:2 badly out of context. Psalm 78 repeats Israel's well-known history, none of which is "mysterious" or "hidden." But Matthew presents Jesus as uttering hidden things. He speaks to the people in parables, in a hidden way, whereas his disciples are enlightened and understand all things. Thus, though Mark 4:33 presents Jesus using the parables to communicate as much truth to the crowds as they could understand, Matthew sees parables as a means of hiding the truth from the outsiders (so, more or less, Lindars, *New Testament Apologetic*, 156–57; Kingsbury, *Parables of Jesus*, 88–90; Rothfuchs, *Erfüllungszitate*, 78–80; Hill).

Despite its popularity, this approach misunderstands both Psalm 78 and Matthew 13. It is true that Psalm 78 recounts the known history of Israel, but there is no escaping the fact that Psalm 78:2 nevertheless finds the psalmist declaring that he will open his mouth "in parables, wise sayings," and pour forth *ḥîdôt* ("enigmas," "dark sayings"). The point is that, though the history of the Jews, which Asaph relates, is well-known, the psalmist selects the historical events he treats and brings them together in such a way as to bring out things that have been riddles and enigmas "from of old." The pattern of history is not self-evident; but the psalmist will show what it is really all about. He enlarges on God's might at the time of the exodus and at other major turning points, a might exercised on behalf of his people. With these events the psalmist juxtaposes the people's persistent rebellion, the result being a vivid portrayal of God's justice and mercy and the people's obtuseness, need, and privilege.

The psalmist teaches all this by opening his mouth "in parables" (i.e., by comparing various things) and in so doing utters "things hidden from of old"—"things that we have heard and known, that our ancestors have told us" (NRSV, v.3), yet enigmatic and hidden. They are "deep and hidden teachings, which the events of the past embrace" (Louis Jacquet, *Les Psaumes* [Brussels: Duculot, 1975–81], 2:522). Thus the psalmist makes his deep points, as does Stephen in Acts 7, by comparing events in redemptive history.

We turn to Matthew 13:35 and discover a similar pattern. If Jesus pours forth things hidden from the beginning, does this mean that those things remain hidden, i.e., that Jesus pours forth teaching in so hidden a form that outsiders cannot understand them? That is what the popular interpretation of the passage requires, but its death knell is the final phrase: "from the beginning." Whatever that phrase means—the NIV has "since the creation of the world" (see Notes)—it modifies *kekrymmena* ("things hidden"), the unavoidable implication being that those hidden things are no longer hidden since Jesus has revealed them. Otherwise, Jesus is saying no more than this: "I will reveal things that have always been hidden so that they will remain hidden"—an unnatural way to take the sentence.

Apparently, then, as applied to Jesus the second line of the quotation pictures him as revealing things formerly hidden. This does not necessarily mean he is teaching entirely new things any more than the psalmist was teaching such things. In both cases, the patterns of redemptive history may be so stressed that when rightly interpreted they point toward new revelation—namely, they are fulfilled (see comments at 2:15; 5:17–20). This admirably suits v.52: the "teacher of the law who has been instructed about the kingdom of heaven is like the owner of a house who brings out of his storeroom new treasures as well as old." But Jesus teaches these hitherto hidden things "in parables," i.e., by comparing various things. The parables of this chapter are not exactly like the comparisons and wise sayings offered in Psalm 78. Yet the term "parable" can embrace both kinds of utterance. So we must be careful not to impose on the text too narrow an understanding of what a parable is.

It follows that vv.34–35 are much closer in thought to Mark 4:33–34 than is commonly believed. Jesus does teach the crowds, in parables, revealing new things. How much they understand is a different matter. Yet we have already seen that even 13:11–13 must not be taken to mean that in Matthew the parables for nondisciples are designed only to conceal. Actually they have a dual role, and here Matthew, rightly understanding the psalmist and reverting to the Hebrew from the LXX so as not to miss his desired nuance, insists that Jesus reveals new truth to the crowds.

But what are these "hidden things" Jesus is now uttering? In Psalm 78 they are "the righteous acts of God in redemption" (Lindars, *New Testament Apologetic*, 157). Likewise, that is what Jesus is now revealing—the righteous acts of God in redemption taking place in his teaching, miracles, death, and resurrection. Matthew insists that the OT Scriptures prophesied these things. They are not novel. If in one sense they have not been known before, it is because they have not all been brought together in the same pattern before. Jesus' kingdom parables to the crowds declare new things—secrets (v.11), hidden things (v.35). Yet they are secret and new chiefly because they depend on an approach to Scripture not unlike Asaph's—bringing together various pieces of previous revelation into new perspectives. Thus Messiah is Son of David but also Suffering Servant. Jesus is the royal King and Son of David foreseen in Scripture (21:4–11) but also the stricken Shepherd equally foreseen in Scripture (26:31). Who clearly foresaw that both streams would merge in one person?

Taken as a whole, Jesus' parables preserve the expectation of the apocalyptic coming of Messiah. They also introduce a new pattern of an inaugurated kingdom that anticipates the Parousia. Moreover, this pattern rests on Jesus' self-understanding as the Messiah who unites in himself streams of revelation from the old covenant that had not been so clearly united before.

The connection between Matthew 13:35 and Psalm 78:2 is thus very close. But what does Matthew mean when he says that Jesus' ministry of parables "fulfilled" the word spoken through the prophet? Elsewhere when psalms are treated as prophecies, there is normally a Davidic typology, but not so here. A number of things may have led

Matthew to this psalm. The phrase "in parables" may have drawn his attention to Psalm 78, but in itself that does not account for the notion of "fulfillment." But a second connection presents itself: it is possible that, as Psalm 78 recounts Israel's history, so Jesus is presented as the one who is the supreme embodiment of Israel and her history, the one who fulfills all the patterns of the OT regarding Israel. We have noticed this theme before in Matthew, though it is stronger in the fourth gospel.

But there may be a third and more subtle factor. Matthew understands that "prophecy" does not necessarily predict the future; it may reveal hidden things (cf. 26:68 with parallels in Mark and Luke). This sense of "prophecy" and its predictive sense "converge" in a passage such as 11:13, where, as we have seen, the entire OT Scripture (both Law and Prophets) "prophesy"; i.e., they comprehend certain patterns, types, predictions, declarations, which cumulatively look forward to him who "fulfills" them. Now in Psalm 78 Asaph claims to be explaining such earlier patterns in redemptive history, but in so doing, from a NT perspective he is also himself becoming a constituent element of the recorded redemptive history the NT explains. As such Psalm 78 becomes part of the "Law and Prophets" that prophesy. Blomberg ("Matthew," in *CNTUOT*) is not wrong to call this use of the OT the purest instance of typology. If part of this sacred record interprets and brings new truth out of an earlier part, it establishes a pattern that looks to one who will interpret and bring new truth out of the whole. Jesus, Matthew claims, fulfills that role and is exercising it in his own parabolic teaching.

NOTES

35 There are two important and extremely difficult variants in this verse.

1. Most MSS read διὰ τοῦ προφήτου (*dia tou prophētou*, "through the prophet"). A few witnesses in Jerome's day read διὰ Ἀσὰφ τοῦ προφήτου (*dia Asaph tou prophētou*, "through Asaph the prophet"); but none have come down to us, and "Asaph" is certainly an interpolation. But an impressive group of witnesses (א* H f^1 f^{13} 33 eth^{ms} et al.) read διά Ἠσαΐου τοῦ προφήτου (*dia Ēsaiou tou prophētou*, "through Isaiah the prophet"); precisely because the quotation does not come from Isaiah, the reading could lay claim to being the *lectio difficilior* that scribes would want to correct. On the other hand, transcriptional evidence favors the probability of adding a prophet's name where none is mentioned (e.g., 1:22; 2:5; 21:4; Ac 7:48). This factor is even more compelling in Matthew than elsewhere since the first evangelist tends not to name the prophet except when quoting Isaiah or Jeremiah, a habit that makes it less likely that he would falsely ascribe to Isaiah, a book with which he was intimately familiar, something extraneous to Isaiah. Scribal misascription is therefore more likely than misascription by Matthew.

2. A majority of the witnesses support the reading ἀπὸ καταβολῆς κόσμου (*apo katabolēs kosmou*, "from the foundation of the world"); a second reading, ἀπὸ καταβολῆς (*apo katabolēs*, "from the foundation"), is attested by a small but diversified number of Alexandrian, Western, and Eastern text types ($א^b$ B f^1 $it^{e,k}$ syr ^{c,s} eth et al.). Although the preponderance of external evidence supports inclusion of κόσμου, *kosmou*, the phrase "the foundation of the world" is so stereotyped in the NT (25:34; Lk 11:50; Jn 17:24; Eph 1:4, Heb 4:3; 9:26; 1Pe 1:20; Rev 13:8; 17:8) that there is far greater transcriptional probability that the word was added rather than omitted.

There is another reason for thinking the shorter text is original. While we have already seen that in the second line of the quotation Matthew stops following the LXX and apparently offers his own rendering of the MT, I did not discuss this closing phrase of the second line. The Hebrew here reads מִנִּי־קֶדֶם (*minnî-qedem*, "from of old"), which the LXX renders ἀπ' ἀρχῆς (*ap archēs*, "from the beginning"). Now the MT's "from of old" can mean "from the beginning" or "from eternity" (cf. parallelism in Pr 8:23; see also Dt 33:27; Ps 55:19). Yet the expression itself is indefinite and in the context of Psalm 78 may refer only to the beginning of the nation, since God's dealings with Israel constitute the focus of discussion. If so, then the LXX's "from the beginning" might sound too absolute, and this could account for Matthew's "from the foundation [i.e., of the nation]." Certainly καταβολή (*katabolē*, "foundation," GK *2856*) does not have to be taken to refer to the foundation of the world: cf. ἀποστάσεως καταβολή (*apostaseōs katabolē*, "the beginning of the insurrection") in Josephus, *J. W.* 2.260 (13.4) (other examples in BDAG, 515). The shorter expression in Matthew might then easily have been lengthened by later scribes. If this reasoning is right, then "since the creation of the world" (NIV) is wrong, and the probability that Matthew is treating his OT text thoughtfully and with profound theological understanding is all the more increased.

For fuller discussion of the technical questions of translation and related bibliography, see Gundry (*Use of the Old Testament*, 118–19); Rothfuchs (*Erfüllungszitate*, 79–80).

b. Interpretation of the parable of the weeds (13:36–43)

OVERVIEW

For a discussion of the authenticity of this interpretation, see comments at vv.3a, 24. The reasons for separating the parable from its interpretation relate to Matthew's plan for this chapter (see comments at vv.3a, 10–17) and on the need for a setting for this explanation to disciples only (cf. Bonnard).

Those who see more of Matthew's church than of Jesus in Matthew's gospel commonly identify the kingdom in vv.41, 43 with Matthew's church. There is, they argue, a double level of meaning. At one level the passage tells the church not to excommunicate its members because there will be a mixture of "wheat" and "weeds" in the church until the end of the age. For Hill this leads to an anomaly: 18:8–9, which he applies to church government, suggests excommunication. But it is doubtful whether Matthew ever confuses kingdom and church. These are two quite distinct categories (see comments at vv.37–39).

Hendriksen recognizes the distinction in principle but then ignores it, arguing (1) if tares are "sown *among* the wheat, not alongside of it or on some other field," then it is "natural to think of the intermingling of true and false members within the church"; (2) that the parables shed light on "mysteries" (v.11), and there is no "mystery" in both kinds of people living on the same earth, but it is "far more of a mystery ... that *within the church visible* God allows both the true and the merely nominal Christians to dwell side by side"; and (3) that the gathering "out of his kingdom" (v.41) assumes the weeds were inside, "in this case inside the church visible" (emphasis his).

In reply, (1) Jesus explicitly says the "field is the world" (v.38), not the church, so how could there be "some other field"? The intermingling is adequately explained if it takes place on the field of the world (see comments at v.38). (2) The "mysteries" of v.11 are bound up, not with the intermingling of good and evil per se, in church or world, but in a preliminary or inaugurated form of the kingdom that is not yet the apocalyptic and totally transforming kingdom belonging to the end of the age. (3) The gathering "out of his kingdom" (v.41) is perfectly clear on a synoptic understanding of "kingdom" (see comments at 3:2; 5:3; 13:41). But to say that "in this case" the expression refers to the church visible is to assume the very thing that must be proved (cf. Bonnard).

36Then he left the crowd and went into the house. His disciples came to him and said,
"Explain to us the parable of the weeds in the field."
37He answered, "The one who sowed the good seed is the Son of Man. 38The field is the
world, and the good seed stands for the sons of the kingdom. The weeds are the sons of
the evil one, 39and the enemy who sows them is the devil. The harvest is the end of the
age, and the harvesters are angels.
40"As the weeds are pulled up and burned in the fire, so it will be at the end of the
age. 41The Son of Man will send out his angels, and they will weed out of his kingdom
everything that causes sin and all who do evil. 42They will throw them into the fiery
furnace, where there will be weeping and gnashing of teeth. 43Then the righteous will
shine like the sun in the kingdom of their Father. He who has ears, let him hear."

COMMENTARY

36 The Greek *apheis tous ochlous* could mean either that Jesus sent the crowds away (KJV) or that he left them (NIV). The house referred to is the one Jesus left in order to preach to the crowds (v.1) and was located, presumably, in Capernaum. In Matthew's narrative, the house provides the setting both for Jesus' private explanations (vv.37–43, cf. vv.10–23) and for the parables aimed at his disciples (vv.44–52).

Whether the verb "explain" is *diasaphēson* (used elsewhere in the NT only in 18:31) or *phrason* (some MSS; used elsewhere in the NT only in 15:15) is uncertain but of little consequence. More important is the fact that the disciples need explanations (cf. 15:15–16). They are not distinguished from the crowds by their instant and intuitive understanding but by their persistence in seeking explanations. Jesus' disciples come to him and ask, and therefore a full explanation is given them (see comments at vv.10–13).

37–39 On "Son of Man," see Reflections, p. 247. The title recurs at 13:41: Jesus is the one who both sows the good seed and directs the harvest. One of the most significant details in Jesus' parables is the way key images that in the OT apply exclusively to God, or occasionally to God's Messiah, now stand for Jesus himself. These images include sower, director of the harvest, rock, shepherd, bridegroom, father, giver of forgiveness, vineyard owner, lord, and king (cf. Philip B. Payne, "Jesus' Implicit Claim to Deity in His Parables," *TJ* [1981]: 3–23).

"The field is the world" (v.38). This brief statement presupposes a mission beyond Israel (cf.

10:16–18; 28:18–20) and confirms that the narrower command of 10:5–6 is related exclusively to the mission of the Twelve during the period of Jesus' earthly ministry. Of greater importance in the history of the church has been the view that this actually means that the field is the church. The view was largely assumed by the early church fathers, and the tendency to interpret the parable that way was reinforced by the Constantinian settlement. Augustine made the interpretation official. Struggling against the Donatists, who were overzealous in their excommunication practices, he went so far as to say that a mixture of good and evil in the church is a necessary "sign" of the church (cf. his *Brev. coll.* and *Don.*). Most Reformers followed the same line. Calvin went so far as to say that the "world" here represents the church by synecdoche.

Ironically, some modern redaction criticism has returned to this interpretation because it sees more of Matthew's church than of Jesus in this gospel. Nevertheless, this interpretation is without exegetical foundation. The kingdom is a category flexible enough to be used simultaneously for the saving reign of God (so that "sons of the kingdom" can refer to those who are truly God's people, v.38) and for his reign more broadly considered (so that the kingdom in this sense might well embrace wheat and tares; see comments at 3:2; 5:3; 28:18). But it is not demonstrable that "church" ever has such semantic flexibility, or that "church" is ever confused with "kingdom" (cf. Ladd, *Theology of the New Testament*, 105ff.; Guthrie, *New Testament Theology*, 702–6).

In this parable and its interpretation, unlike the parable of the sower, the good seed stands for the sons of the kingdom—a healthy reminder that images can symbolize different things in different contexts (see comments at v.33). But "sons of the kingdom" has also changed its meaning from its use in 8:12. There it refers to those who by birth into the Jewish race have a covenant right to look forward to the messianic kingdom but who, by and large, are forfeiting that right. Here it refers to those who truly are the objects of messianic favor and participants in the messianic kingdom. For their sake, the "weeds" are now preserved, and at the "harvest" for their sake the "weeds" will be destroyed. These weeds are "the sons of the evil one." (On "sons of," see comments at 5:9; with the entire expression, cf. Jn 8:44; 1Jn 5:19.) The devil himself is the enemy (v.39); the harvest is the end of the age (see comments at 9:37; cf. Jer 51:33; Hos 6:11; Joel 3:13; *4 Ezra* 4:28–29; *2 Bar.* 70:2); and the harvesters are angels (24:30–31; 25:31; cf. 18:10; Lk 15:7; Heb 1:14; 1Pe 1:12; see also *1 En.* 63:1).

What must also be pointed out is how many features in the parable are not given nonsymbolic equivalents. These include the conversation between the man and his servants, the servants' sleep, and the fact that the wheat was sown before the tares. This selective use of elements in the story is not atypical of parables (see comments at v.3a), and the other elements should not be allegorized.

40–42 The identification of the actors is over, and the description of the action begins. As the weeds are "pulled up" (same verb as "collect" in v.30b, *syllegō*, GK *5198*) and burned, so it is at the end. The kingdom we have known as the kingdom of heaven or the kingdom of God is also seen as the kingdom of the Son of Man, Jesus' kingdom (cf. 20:21; 25:31; cf. Da 2:35; Rev 11:15). This is not the church (contra Bornkamm, "End-Expectation and the Church," 44; see comments above), for Jesus' reign after the resurrection extends to the farthest reaches of the universe (28:18). In that sense, "everything that causes sin and all who do evil" may be weeded out of his kingdom (v.41). For the meaning of *panta ta skandala* ("everything that causes sin"), see comments at 5:29; with "all who do evil" (lit., "those who do lawlessness"), compare 7:23.

The entire expression "everything that causes sin and all who do evil" appears to be a periphrastic rendering of the Hebrew of Zephaniah 1:3 (*hammakšēlôt ʾet-hāršāʿîm* [lit., "the stumbling blocks with the wicked"]), a phrase so difficult in its context that emendations have been suggested and the best MSS of the LXX omit it. The first of the two Hebrew words occurs elsewhere only at Isaiah 3:6, where it means "ruins." Hence the NIV translates the phrase in Zephaniah 1:3 as "The wicked will have only heaps of rubble." If this is correct, Matthew is either not referring to Zephaniah 1:3 or else is freely adapting it. But the Hebrew word may well mean "stumbling blocks," "offenses." For what it is worth, etymology supports it, and the Targum understands it that way. Thus in Zephaniah 1:3, the word may refer to idols, or, better yet, in a figurative manner to people seen as "things that cause offense." If so, Matthew's rendering is appropriate.

The "sons of the evil one" (v.38) may be metaphorically considered as "everything that causes sin" or, without any metaphor, "all who do evil." They, like the weeds, are thrown into the fiery furnace (v.42; see comments at 3:11; 5:22; cf. Jer 29:22; Da 3:6; Rev 20:15), where there will be weeping and gnashing of teeth (see comments at 8:12, cf. *4 Ezra* 7:36)—namely, eschatological doom. Nothing is made of the word "first" in v.30, and here the order is reversed. What is clear is that Jesus ascribes to himself the role of eschatological Judge that Yahweh assigns himself in the OT, including Zephaniah 1:3 (cf. France, *Jesus and the Old Testament*, 156–57).

43 In contrast to the evildoers, "the righteous will shine like the sun in the kingdom of their Father." The allusion is to Daniel 12:3 LXX, somewhat shortened by omitting *hoi synientes* (= Heb. *hammaśkilîm*, "those who are wise" or "those who understand"), further evidence that Matthew has not idealized the disciples as those who have understanding (see comments at vv.10–13, 19, 23, 36). Hill remarks that early in the tradition there may have been a wordplay on *maśkilîm* (Aram. *maśkiltîn*) ("wise" or "understanding") in v.43 and *makšēlôt* (Aram. *makśelān*) ("stumbling blocks" or "things that cause offense") in v.41. These righteous people (see comments at 5:20, 45; 9:13; 10:41; 13:17; 25:37, 46), once the light of the world (5:14–16), now radiate perfections and experience bliss in the consummation of their hopes.

The "kingdom of their Father" must not, as is commonly done, be set over against the kingdom of the Son of Man (v.41) on the supposed ground that the former alone is eternal, or that the Son of Man hands over the elect to him (1Co 15:24). The Son's postascension reign is a mediated reign. All God's kingly authority is given to Jesus (28:18) and mediated through him; for all that time the kingdom can be called the kingdom of God or the kingdom of the Son of Man or, more generally, the kingdom of heaven. But even when that mediation ceases, halted by the destruction of the last enemy (1Co 15:24–26), in Matthew's terminology it is still appropriate to call Jesus Messiah the King (20:31; 25:34; cf. 26:64), for the kingdom remains no less his.

NOTES

39 In the final two identifications of the list in vv.37–39, the subjective complement precedes the copula verb and becomes anarthrous, in conformity with the rules developed by E. C. Colwell and extended by Lane C. McGaughy (*Toward a Descriptive Analysis of EINAI* [Missoula, Mont.: SBL Press, 1972]). The absence of articles in συντέλεια αἰῶνός (*synteleia aiōnos*, "the end of the age") is therefore no evidence for a construction built on analogy to the Hebrew construct state (contra Hill), not least because the construction is very common in the NT (706 occurrences) and widely distributed.

4. To the disciples (13:44–52)

a. The parable of the hidden treasure (13:44)

OVERVIEW

For the way these parables relate to the structure of the chapter, see comments at vv.10–17.

The parables of the hidden treasure and the pearl are a pair; and pairing is not uncommon in Matthew (e.g., 5:14b–16; 6:26–30; 7:6; 9:16–17; 10:24–25; 12:25; 13:31–33; 24:43–51), an excellent way of reinforcing a point. Like the paired parables with which these two are chiastically coordinated (mustard seed and yeast, vv.31–33), these two make the same general point but have significant individual emphases.

Unlike the parables earlier in the chapter, these two do not deal so much with the hidden, inaugurated form of the kingdom and the concomitant delay of the Parousia as with the superlative worth of the kingdom of heaven. Yet even here, the previous eschatological structure underlies them, for in traditional Jewish apocalyptic, one could scarcely liken the kingdom to a man finding a treasure or buying a pearl. The kingdom was to come apocalyptically at the end of the age by an act of God alone. In contrast to this, some kind of realized or inaugurated eschatology is here presupposed.

44"The kingdom of heaven is like treasure hidden in a field. When a man found it, he hid it again, and then in his joy went and sold all he had and bought that field."

COMMENTARY

44 On the "is like" language, see comments at v.24. The kingdom is not simply like a treasure, but its situation is like the situation of a treasure hidden in a field. The Greek articles are generic (cf. Turner, *Syntax*, 179). Finding the treasure appears to be by chance. In a land as frequently ravaged as Palestine, many people doubtless buried their treasures; but as Huffman ("Atypical Features in the Parables," 213) points out, actually to find a treasure would happen once in a thousand lifetimes. Thus the extravagance of the parable dramatizes the supreme importance of the kingdom.

Derrett (*Law in the New Testament*, 1–16) has pointed out that under rabbinic law if a workman came on a treasure in a field and lifted it out, it would belong to his master, the field's owner; but here the man is careful not to lift the treasure out until he has bought the field. So the parable deals with neither the legality nor the morality of the situation (as with the parable of the thief in the night) but with the value of the treasure, which is worth every sacrifice. When the man buys the field at such sacrifice, he possesses far more than the price paid (cf. 10:39). The kingdom of heaven is worth infinitely more than the cost of discipleship, and those who know where the treasure lies joyfully abandon everything else to secure it.

Two alternative interpretations must be dismissed.

1. The first, represented by Walvoord, understands the treasure to represent Israel and Jesus as the man who sold everything to purchase her. He rejects the above view by making the parable mean that "a believer in Christ has nothing to offer and the treasure is not for sale" and proposes his own interpretation by noting that in Exodus 19:5 Israel is called God's treasure. But any view, including Walvoord's, can be made to look foolish by pressing a parable into a detailed allegory. For instance, one could rebut his view by showing that it entails Israel's being worth far more than the price paid, and that of course would constitute an implicit depreciation of Christ's sacrifice, which no thoughtful Christian would accept. One must come to grips with the nature of parables (see comments at v.3a). And "treasure" has a vast range of associations in the OT and NT; on what basis, then, does Walvoord select Exodus 19:5? Above all, his interpretation does not adequately handle the opening clause.

2. J. D. Crossan (*Finding Is the First Act* [Philadelphia: Fortress, 1979], esp. 93ff.) argues that "sold all he had" must be taken so absolutely that "all" includes the parable itself. One must give up the parable itself and, in abandoning all, abandon even abandonment. The parable is therefore a paradox, like the sign that reads "Do not read this sign." Crossan's interpretation is unacceptable for exegetical, literary, historical, and theological reasons: exegetical, in that this parable does not speak of "abandoning" or "giving up" things but of "selling," and one cannot imagine giving the parable away by selling it; literary, in that Crossan, like Walvoord, fastens on one word and rides it so hard that the nature of parables is overlooked; historical, in that ascription of such existentialist results to Jesus or to Matthew is so anachronistic as to make a historian wince; theological, in that his interpretation of "paradox" is defective and is used in undifferentiated ways. Crossan oscillates between paradox construed as a merely formal contradiction and paradox construed as antinomy or even incoherence.

b. The parable of the expensive pearl (13:45–46)

45"Again, the kingdom of heaven is like a merchant looking for fine pearls. 46When he found one of great value, he went away and sold everything he had and bought it."

COMMENTARY

45–46 The word *palin* ("again") ties this parable fairly closely to the preceding one (cf. 5:33). Walvoord recognizes that this parable is roughly equivalent to the last. But here, he says, the pearl represents not Israel but the church. The church, like the pearl, is formed organically, and "there is a sense in which the church was formed out of the wounds of Christ." This does not take us much beyond patristic allegorizing. The real connection with the last parable is the supreme worth of the kingdom. But here we deal with a merchant whose business it is to seek pearls and who chances on one of supreme value. Derrett (*Law in the New Testament*, 15) sees a rabbinic parallel: "One wins eternal life after a struggle of years, another finds it in one hour" (*b. ʿAbod. Zar.* 17a); contrast the conversions of Saul and the Ethiopian eunuch.

Unlike the man in the last parable, the merchant, though he sells everything he has to purchase the pearl, apparently pays a full price. Although he is an expert in pearls, this single find so far surpasses any other pearl the merchant has ever seen that he considers it a fair exchange for everything else he owns. Thus Jesus is not interested in religious efforts or in affirming that one can "buy" the kingdom; on the contrary, he is saying that the person whose whole life has been bound up with "pearls"—the entire religious heritage of the Jews?—will, on comprehending the true value of the kingdom as Jesus presents it, gladly exchange all else to follow him.

NOTES

45–46 The change from present tense (v.44) to aorist (vv.45–46) is not transparent but doubtless reflects the evangelist's decision to portray the action in v.44 as progression, and the action in vv.45–46 in a perfective fashion. The perfect tense πέπρακεν (*pepraken*, "sold," GK *4405*) is aspectually vague. There is no aorist active form for this verb.

c. The parable of the net (13:47–48)

47"Once again, the kingdom of heaven is like a net that was let down into the lake and caught all kinds of fish. 48When it was full, the fishermen pulled it up on the shore. Then they sat down and collected the good fish in baskets, but threw the bad away."

COMMENTARY

47–48 This parable, like the last two, is peculiar to Matthew. In the chiastic structure of the chapter, it is parallel to the parable of the weeds and has a somewhat similar meaning. But whereas the parable of the weeds focuses on the long period of the reign of God during which tares coexist with wheat and the enemy has large powers, the parable of the net simply describes the situation that exists when the last judgment takes place: the kingdom embraces "good" fish and "bad" fish, and only the final sweep of the net sorts them out. That is why the introductory formula uses the present tense (see comments at v.24; cf. Carson, "ὅμοιος Word-Group"). The chief concern of the parable is neither the consummated kingdom (which in Matthew would call forth a future tense—"the kingdom of heaven will become like") nor the inaugurated kingdom ("the kingdom of heaven has become like") but the situation that exists at the end. And, once again, kingdom and church must not be equated.

A *sagēnē* (lit., "dragnet," used only here in the NT) was drawn along between two boats or tied on shore at one end and put out by a boat at the other end, which was then drawn to land by ropes. "All kinds of fish" (v.47) might hint at the multiracial character of the subjects of the kingdom, but more probably this refers to "good" and "bad" fish (v.48). In the parable itself, "good fish" and "bad" have no moral overtones but refer simply to fish ceremonially suitable and large enough for eating and those for some reason unacceptable, respectively. The word *sapron* ("bad," GK *4911*) can mean "decayed," but here it simply means "worthless."

d. Interlude (13:49–51)

(1) Interpretation of the parable of the net (13:49–50)

[49]"This is how it will be at the end of the age. The angels will come and separate the wicked from the righteous [50]and throw them into the fiery furnace, where there will be weeping and gnashing of teeth."

COMMENTARY

49–50 Many separate the parable (vv.47–48), supposedly about the disciples on mission as "fishers of men," and the interpretation (vv.49–50), which transforms the parable into a "last judgment" scene. Hill insists this is "not a suitable ending, for the furnace is hardly the place for bad fish." But that is to confuse symbol with what is symbolized; the furnace is not for the fish but for the wicked. To be consistent, Hill (and many others, e.g., Jeremias, *Parables of Jesus*, 85; Strecker, *Weg der Gerechtigkeit*, 160–61) would also have to object that the tares, when burned (v.42), do not weep and gnash their teeth (Kingsbury, *Parables of Jesus*, 165–66 n. 143). The parable itself cannot easily be made to refer to the missionary activity of the church; for it describes a separation *when the net is full*, not a continuous separation. Nor may one attach some deep significance to the distinction between catching all the fish (v.47) and separating them (v.48)—as if the original parable referred to both the church's witness in catching men and the final separation (so Kingsbury, *Parables of Jesus*, 120)—any more than it is legitimate in interpreting the tares to divide the harvesting from the final separation of weeds and wheat. Both the parable and its interpretation point to the last judgment. On the angels and the image of the fiery furnace, see comments at vv.41–42.

But this does not mean that the parable and its interpretation are about the last judgment in the same way 25:1–13 (the ten virgins) and 25:31–46 (the sheep and the goats) are, the one warning of the need for readiness and the other establishing a basis for judgment. The focus here is on the state of the kingdom when the judgment occurs. Though it includes both the righteous and the wicked, a thorough sorting out will certainly take place.

(2) On understanding parables (13:51)

[51]"Have you understood all these things?" Jesus asked.
"Yes," they replied.

COMMENTARY

51 Both "Jesus says to them" and "Lord" (KJV) are late additions to the text; it is difficult to explain why they were dropped if part of the original text.

Jesus' question picks up the disciples' request for an explanation (v.36) but goes beyond it, since the question is introduced, not after v.43, but after three additional parables. The words "all these things" have been taken to refer to what Jesus means by his parables (Filson, Plummer, Schweizer) or to the unexplained parables (Robinson, *Twelve New Testament Studies*) or to the "secrets of the kingdom" in v.11 (Grundmann, Bonnard, Hill, Fenton). In fact, all these are so tightly linked that it is hard to imagine how one could understand one of these areas and not the other two.

This is the only place in this chapter where the disciples themselves are explicitly said to understand, and they say it by themselves. It is as wrong to say that Matthew has portrayed them as understanding everything as it is to say that they understood nothing. The truth lies between the extremes. The disciples certainly understood more than the crowds; on the other hand, they are shortly to be rebuked for their dullness (15:16). Like another positive response in this gospel (see comments at 20:22–23), this one cannot be simply dismissed as presumptuous enthusiasm (as if they think they know everything when in fact they know nothing), nor taken at face value (as if their understanding were in fact mature). In any event, the disciples' *claim* is not as important as the last parable to which it leads (for the structure of this section, see comments at v.3a, pp. 349–50).

e. The parable of the teacher of the law (13:52)

[52]He said to them, "Therefore every teacher of the law who has been instructed about the kingdom of heaven is like the owner of a house who brings out of his storeroom new treasures as well as old."

COMMENTARY

52 Interpretations of this difficult verse are legion. It has been variously held that it refers to scribes who become disciples of the kingdom (Jeremias, *Parables of Jesus*, 216) or join the Christian community (Hummel, *Auseinandersetzung*, 17ff.); that Matthew here refers to the way he himself functions within the community (C. F. D. Moule, "St. Matthew's Gospel," *SE* 2 [1964]: 98–99); that the verse demonstrates the existence of Christian "scribes" or "teachers of the law" in Matthew's church, men who exercise much the same role as scribes in Judaism (Kilpatrick, *Origins*, 111; Grundmann), or even that disciples within Christianity are more important than scribes within Judaism (Manson, *Sayings of Jesus*, 198–99); that each disciple who is able to qualify may present himself as a "teacher of the law" (Lagrange); that any scribe who understands what has been taught about the kingdom is like the lord of a house "who handles everything in a carefree manner, who does not save anything and even uses what is old" (van Tilborg, *Jewish Leaders*, 132; Walker, *Heilsgeschichte*, 27–29).

The verse's parabolic structure must be noted and a number of exegetical details explored before its meaning can be grasped or the significance of the introductory "therefore" rightly perceived. The "is like" formula (see comments at v.24) means "it is with a teacher of the law who has been instructed about the kingdom as it is with the owner of a house." The problem is to discern the point of the comparison. The *oikodespotēs* ("owner of a house," GK *3867*) is a frequent figure in Jesus' parables and can stand for God (21:33), Jesus (10:25), or disciples (24:43). Very often he is a figure who dispenses wealth in some way (20:1–16; 21:33–43). So here he brings out of his "storeroom" (same word as "treasure" in 2:11; 6:19–21; 12:35 [2x]; 13:44; 19:21) new things and old things. Why would an owner of a house do this? Presumably it is not simply to ogle his wealth but for some useful purpose. The point is that his treasure *includes* both the new and the old, and that he can use both.

The point of comparison becomes clearer when we remember that a *grammateus* ("scribe," GK *1208*) in Jesus' day might refer not only to rabbinic, Pharisaic scribes, who were theological interpreters of the Scriptures capable of rendering halakic decisions (rules for conduct), but to apocalyptic scribes. This is central to the thesis of David E. Orton (*The Understanding Scribe*). Matthew does not reject all "scribes" (NIV, "teachers of the law") but only those from the rabbinic/Pharisaic matrix. Orton's extended discussion (pp. 65–120) shows how "apocalyptic" scribes—scribes in the apocalyptic tradition—were devoted to understanding and interpreting hard sayings, dark sayings, apocalyptic sayings. Indeed, parables were part of their focus (cf. Sir 39:1–3). Since Jesus' disciples have now understood his parables, they can legitimately be called "scribes" themselves, as can all of his disciples with similar understanding. Jesus adds an explanatory expression: the scribe with whom he is concerned *mathēteutheis tē basileia tōn ouranōn* ("has been instructed about the kingdom of heaven"). Whether the verbal form is construed as deponent ("has become a disciple") or strictly passive ("has been made a disciple"), it is not at all clear that the dative expression means "about the kingdom of heaven"; in the one NT passage with similar construction (27:57), Joseph of Arimathea had become a disciple *of* Jesus, not *about* Jesus. By analogy, the scribes in this verse have become disciples *of the kingdom of heaven*.

If the preceding exegetical observations are correct, the points of comparison in the parable are two. The emphasis in the first part of the verse rests, not on the supposition that the scribe has been instructed *about* the kingdom and therefore understands, but that he has become a disciple *of* the kingdom and therefore his allegiance has been transformed. It is with such a person as with "the owner of a house"—a discipled scribe brings out of his storeroom new things and old.

The *thēsauros* ("storeroom," GK *2565*) so regularly stands for a man's "heart," its wealth and cherished values (see comments at 12:35), that we must understand the discipled scribe to be bringing things out of his heart—out of his understanding, personality, and very being. What he brings out are *kaina kai palaia*, not "new things as well as old" (NIV), which suggests the new things have been added to the old, but "new things and old things"—a subtle touch that reminds the alert reader that in Matthew the gospel of the kingdom, though new, takes precedence over the old revelation and is its fulfillment (cf. 5:17–20). The new is not added to the old; there is but one revelation, and its focus is the "new" that has fulfilled and thereby renewed the old, which has thereby become new (Bonnard). Thus the OT promises of Messiah and kingdom, as well as OT law and piety, have found their fulfillment in Jesus' person, teaching, and kingdom, and the scribe who has become a disciple of the kingdom now brings out of himself deep understanding of these things and their transformed perspective affecting all of life.

But the order is of great importance. The parable shows that a discipled scribe has this understanding, *not* that understanding generates discipleship. This conforms perfectly to the chapter's structure. The disciples are not defined as having understanding but are described as having been given revelation and understanding (vv.11–12). When the disciples ask for an explanation, they are given it (vv.36–43) and thus claim some measure of understanding (v.51). "Therefore" (v.52) a *discipled* scribe is like, etc. Discipleship to Jesus, recognition of the revelation he is and brings, and submission to the reign he inaugurates and promises are necessary prerequisites to understanding and bringing out from oneself the rich treasures of the kingdom (see comments at 25:31–46).

But there is a second point of comparison in the parable. The last one could have been made by stressing discipleship but omitting any reference to scribes. Scribes were "teachers of the Scriptures." If they are likened to the owner of a house who brings treasures out of his storeroom, the further implication is unavoidable: they are not bringing forth things new and old for purely private or personal reasons *but in their capacity as teachers*. Jesus' disciples claim they have understood what he has been teaching. "Therefore," he responds, discipled teachers of the Scriptures, if they have understood, must themselves bring out of their storeroom the treasures now theirs so as to teach others (cf. Trotter, "Understanding and Stumbling"). Implicitly this serves as "a warning against neglecting the old in the excitement of having discovered the new—as indeed the imagery of the parables of the treasure and the pearl might suggest" (France [NICNT]).

This interpretation admirably fits in with three other Matthean themes.

1. The disciples have a major responsibility in evangelizing and making disciples, both during Jesus' ministry (ch. 10) and after his departure (28:18–20).

2. In the latter instance, they are told to "disciple" the nations and teach them everything Jesus has commanded them: i.e., the focus of their mission is Jesus and the revelation—the new "fulfillment" revelation—he has brought.

3. This interpretation, which places some teaching responsibility on the disciples, also fits the purpose of the parables described in the comments at vv.12–17, 34–35. Indeed, part of the reason for private instruction may again be linked to the place of Jesus' earthly ministry in redemptive history, for what he tells his disciples in secret they are to proclaim from the rooftops (10:27). Jesus explains the parables to his disciples in private; they are to bring out of their treasure rooms "new things and old." Thus they are to understand the antecedent Scriptures correctly and show how they point to Jesus the Messiah and the dawning of the promised kingdom.

If this interpretation of v.52 is correct, then though "disciples" in this chapter most probably refers to the Twelve, they epitomize the church to come. In that event, "disciples" does not refer to a special group of "teachers of the law" within Matthew's community (see comments at 23:34) but to those who by Matthew's day were called Christians. Just as they have been aligned with prophets and righteous men from past ages (e.g., 5:11–12; 10:41), so are they aligned with "teachers of the law." In fact, only Jesus' "disciples" are able to bring forth new things and old; the Jewish teachers of the law could bring forth only the old.

5. Transitional conclusion: movement toward further opposition (13:53)

53When Jesus had finished these parables, he moved on from there.

COMMENTARY

53 On the Greek preliminary formula, see comments at 7:28–29.

The common view that v.53 properly introduces the following pericope fits neither that beginning nor the structure of Matthew. Gooding's claim ("Structure littéraire," 229) that v.24 is syntactically tied to v.53 is incorrect (cf. the same openings at 8:14; 9:23, where new pericopes are introduced). This verse, as Hill, 241, points out, "suggests that Jesus spoke all the preceding parables at once"—though he thinks this "is unlikely" (see comments at 5:1–12; 13:3a). What is clear is that Jesus' movement from Capernaum to "his hometown" (vv.53–54) turns out to be a further fulfillment of vv.14–15: these people will be ever hearing but never understanding.

NOTES

53 The verb μετῆρεν (*metēren*, "he moved on"), found in the NT only here and at 19:1 (again in a formulaic discourse ending), is normally transitive and probably owes its present intransitive force to Semitic influence (Moisés Silva, "New Lexical Semitisms?" *ZNW* 69 [1978]: 256).

V. THE GLORY AND THE SHADOW: PROGRESSIVE POLARIZATION (13:54–19:2)

OVERVIEW

The danger of outlines is oversimplification. Even genuine insight in outline form may eliminate or minimize various themes that occur in sections where the discovered "structure" does not allow for them. Matthew, as we have seen, can use structure effectively, and several complex structures have been found in, or imposed on, these chapters (cf. J. Murphy-O'Conner, "The Structure of Matthew XIV–XVII,"

RB 82 [1975]: 360–84; Gooding, "Structure littéraire," 248ff.). No detailed and comprehensive outline of these chapters is quite convincing; so it seems best to deal with them pericope by pericope.

The principal themes of these chapters are clear. There is a progressive polarization along several axes. As Jesus extends his ministry, the opposition sharpens (15:1–9; 16:1–14). When he reveals himself to his disciples, they clearly perceive some truth and entirely reject other truth (16:13–22; 17:1–13). As Jesus is increasingly opposed by Jewish leaders, so his own disciples become increasingly important (18:1–10). Over it all is the contrast between Christ's glory, goodness, and grace and the blind misunderstanding of the disciples (15:15–16, 33; 16:22; 17:4, 19; 18:21) and Jewish leaders (15:2, 8; 16:6, 12; 17:24) alike. And rising less ambiguously now is the shadow of the cross (16:21–22; 17:22–23).

A. Narrative (13:54–17:27)

OVERVIEW

In this section (13:54–17:27), Matthew follows Mark 6–9 fairly closely until Mark 9:33. Of course, Matthew leaves out all the material between Mark's parables and the rejection at Nazareth (namely, Mk 4:35–5:43) because he has presented it earlier (chs. 8–9).

1. Rejected at Nazareth (13:54–58)

OVERVIEW

Placing this pericope immediately after the discourse on parables extends the hostility and rejection of the scribes and Pharisees even to Jesus' hometown (cf. Mk 6:1–6). It is almost universally assumed that this is the same rejection recorded in Luke 4:16–30, which ties the event to OT prophecy. Though not unlikely, this is not certain. Unlike Luke, Mark and Matthew mention no hostility so great as to lead people to kill Jesus. If there were two incidents, the one recorded by the first two evangelists may reflect an abating of instinctive rage as the village's most famous son has grown in reputation in the area.

54Coming to his hometown, he began teaching the people in their synagogue, and they
were amazed. "Where did this man get this wisdom and these miraculous powers?"
they asked. 55"Isn't this the carpenter's son? Isn't his mother's name Mary, and aren't his
brothers James, Joseph, Simon and Judas? 56Aren't all his sisters with us? Where then did
this man get all these things?" 57And they took offense at him.

But Jesus said to them, "Only in his hometown and in his own house is a prophet without honor."

58And he did not do many miracles there because of their lack of faith.

COMMENTARY

54 On the formal connection between this verse and the preceding one, see comments at v.53.

Jesus' *patris* ("hometown," GK *4258*) is here understood to be Nazareth, explicitly named only by Luke (4:16; cf. Mt 2:23; 4:13). That Jesus taught extensively in the synagogues is certain (cf. 4:23; 12:9); but he did not limit himself to this environment. (On "their" synagogue, see comments at 4:23; 7:29; 9:35; 10:17; 11:1; 12:9–10.) The imperfect *edidasken* is probably inceptive (cf. the NIV's "began teaching").

The interrogative *pothen* ("where"; repeated in v.56) is not so much concerned with location as with source of authority (cf. v.27; see Bonnard). Do Jesus' wisdom and powers—his teaching and miracles, both evidences of his authority—reflect God's authority or something else (cf. 12:24)?

55–57a Obviously some of the questioners' motivation springs less from a serious desire to know whence Jesus derives his authority than from personal pique that a hometown boy has outstripped them. The questions (vv.55–56) do not call for answers but merely reveal that there has already been a denial of who Jesus is. Mark 6:3 has "the carpenter," not Matthew's "the carpenter's son" (v.55); but in a day when most lads followed their father's trade, both are correct. *Tektōn* can mean "carpenter"—one who works with wood—or perhaps even "builder," in a time and place when most homes were made of mud brick. Justin Martyr (*Dial.* 88.8, ca. AD 150) says Jesus was a maker of plows and yokes. The definite article ("*the* carpenter's son") suggests there was only one in town.

On the question of Jesus' brothers and sisters, see comments at 12:46–50. The four names listed (see Notes) are typically Jewish.

In one sense, of course, the questions of the people are understandable, if not justifiable. Here was a young artisan from a rough town, with no special breeding or education. Whence, then, his wisdom and miracles? (Incidentally, their questions render impossible the fanciful miracles ascribed to Jesus' childhood by the apocryphal gospels.) But by their questions the people merely condemn themselves: they cannot doubt the fact of his wisdom and miracles (v.56), yet they reject his claims (v.57). "They took offense at him" (*eskandalizonto en autō*), i.e., found in him obstacles to faith (see comments at 5:29; 11:6), even though the biggest obstacles were in their own hearts. It is sad that every time in the NT somebody is "scandalized" by someone, that someone is Jesus (see *TDNT*, 7:349; cf. 11:6; 26:31, 33; Mk 6:3; Lk 7:23).

57b–58 The proverb in v.57b recurs at Mark 6:4; Luke 4:24; John 4:44 (cf. Hennecke, *New Testament Apocrypha*, 1:109). Most often a person is better received at home than anywhere else, but if he enjoys an elevated position, the reverse is true.

Many say that v.58 softens Mark's "He could not do any miracles there, except lay his hands on a few sick people and heal them. And he was amazed at their lack of faith" (Mk 6:5–6). But two factors must be borne in mind: (1) Mark mentions some miracles, and Matthew, typically condensing, may be referring to these rather than commenting on Jesus' ability to do miracles; and (2) it is doubtful whether Mark's "could not" is ontological or absolute, for Mark records other miracles in which the beneficiaries exhibit no faith (feeding the five thousand, stilling the storm, healing the Gerasene demoniac). The "could not" is related to Jesus' mission: just as Jesus could not turn stones to bread without violating his mission (4:14), so he could not do miracles indiscriminately without turning his mission into a sideshow. The "lack of faith" (*apistia*, GK *602*, used only here in Matthew) of the people was doubtless a source of profound grief and frustration for Jesus (cf. *apistos*, "unbelieving," in 17:17) rather than something that stripped him of power.

NOTES

55 Many MSS read Ἰωσῆς (*Iōsēs*; KJV, "Joses") instead of Ἰωσήφ (*Iōsēph*; NIV, "Joseph"), doubtless following the Galilean pronunciation יוֹסֵי (*yôsê*) of the correct Hebrew יוֹסֵף (*yôsēp*).

56 The phrase πρὸς ἡμᾶς (*pros hēmas*, "with us") with the sense of position instead of motion (i.e., having the force of παρ' ἡμῖν [*par' hēmin*, "with us"]) represents a Hellenistic Greek far more fluid than its Attic forbear (cf. Moule, *Idiom Book*, 52).

2. Herod and Jesus (14:1–12)

a. Herod's understanding of Jesus (14:1–2)

[1]At that time Herod the tetrarch heard the reports about Jesus, [2]and he said to his attendants, "This is John the Baptist; he has risen from the dead! That is why miraculous powers are at work in him."

COMMENTARY

1–2 Of the two parallels (Mk 6:14–16; Lk 9:7–9), only Mark (6:17–29) goes on to give the story of John's death; and Matthew follows this account (14:3–12). On the chronological problem raised by a comparison of vv.1–2 and v.13, see comments at v.13.

The phrase "at that time" is very loose (see comments at 11:25; 12:1) and should not be tied to the previous pericope. Mark sets the scene after the mission of the Twelve, and certainly the multiplication of Jesus' influence through his disciples would upset Herod, one of whose motives in imprisoning the Baptist had been to thwart any threat to political stability (cf. Josephus, *Ant*. 18.116–19 [5.2]).

Herod Antipas, son of Herod the Great (see comments at 2:1), was tetrarch (v.1; see comments at 2:22), not king—though doubtless "king" was used popularly (Mk 6:14). His tetrarchy included Galilee (4:12) and Perea (19:1). Because John the Baptist's ministry had been exercised in Perea (Jn 1:28), he had come under Herod's power. Herod had been ruling more than thirty years, and at this time he lived primarily at Tiberias on the southwest shore of Galilee. Thus Jesus' ministry was taking place largely within Herod's jurisdiction.

How the reports of Jesus' ministry reached Herod is unknown; it may have been through Cuza (Lk 8:3). So extensive a ministry could not have been kept from Herod for long. His conclusion, that this was John the Baptist risen from the dead (v.2), is of great interest. It reflects an eclectic set of beliefs, one of them the Pharisaic understanding of resurrection. During his ministry John had performed no miracles (Jn 10:41); therefore Herod ascribes the miracles in Jesus' ministry not to John but to John "risen from the dead." Herod's guilty conscience apparently combined with a superstitious view of miracles to generate this theory.

b. Background: Herod's execution of John the Baptist (14:3–12)

[3]Now Herod had arrested John and bound him and put him in prison because of
Herodias, his brother Philip's wife, [4]for John had been saying to him:"It is not lawful for you
to have her." [5]Herod wanted to kill John, but he was afraid of the people, because they
considered him a prophet.
[6]On Herod's birthday the daughter of Herodias danced for them and pleased Herod so
much [7]that he promised with an oath to give her whatever she asked. [8]Prompted by her
mother, she said, "Give me here on a platter the head of John the Baptist." [9]The king was
distressed, but because of his oaths and his dinner guests, he ordered that her request be
granted [10]and had John beheaded in the prison. [11]His head was brought in on a platter
and given to the girl, who carried it to her mother. [12]John's disciples came and took his
body and buried it. Then they went and told Jesus.

COMMENTARY

3–5 Both Mark (6:16–29; cf. Lk 3:19–20) and Matthew insert this story as an excursus, a bit of explanatory background (see comments at v.13). As usual, Matthew is more condensed than Mark, yet does add one detail (see comments at v.12); but in this case it is doubtful whether Matthew is a condensation of Mark. More likely Matthew follows independent information (cf. Hoehner, *Herod Antipas*, 114–17). Many scholars have insisted the gospel reports of John's death and the report of Josephus (*Ant*. 18.116–19 [5.2]) cannot be reconciled, especially because Josephus assigns a political motive to the execution of the Baptist and the synoptists a moral and religious one. Hoehner (pp. 124–49) has exhaustively treated these problems and points out that the two motives are not as far apart as some have thought.

Herod's first wife was the daughter of Aretas (cf. 2Co 11:32), Arabian king of the Nabateans, whose land adjoined Perea on the south. To divorce her in favor of Herodias was politically explosive (see R. L. Webb, *John the Baptizer and Prophet: A Socio-Historical Study* [Sheffield: JSOT Press, 1991], 368). Indeed, some years later, border fighting broke out, and Antipas was defeated, but saved by Roman intervention. John's rebuke would be like a spark on tinder; and his powerful preaching about the nearness of the messianic kingdom fueled the expectations of the populace, not least for the reestablishment of the law by which John was rebuking Herod. Religious fanaticism with messianic overtones is more politically dangerous than mere political extremism. This Herod well knew. Josephus and the gospel writers blend together.

Herodias was married to Herod Philip (not Philip the tetrarch, Lk 3:1), son of Herod the Great and Mariamne II (for this identification, see Hoehner, *Herod Antipas*, 131–36), and therefore half brother to Herod Antipas. John probably did not denounce Antipas for divorcing his former wife, an action probably judged allowable (cf. *b. Ketub.* 57b; Jeremias, *Jerusalem*, 371 n. 60), but for incestuously marrying his half brother's wife (Lev 18:16; 20:21); and John probably kept on repeating his rebuke. John's courage in denouncing Herod distinguishes him from the Essenes (with whom many scholars associate him), for they tended to refuse to meddle in political life, no matter how evil it became (Bonnard). Herodias was not only Antipas's sister-in-law but also his niece, the daughter of his half brother Aristobulus; but for most Jews there was no bar to marrying a niece (see Hoehner, pp. 137–39 n. 4, for the literature). The larger offense may have sprung from the ritual impurity of marrying a brother's wife (while the brother was still alive; see Lev 20:21; cf. Webb, *John the Baptizer*, 366–67).

Some think Matthew's statement that "Herod wanted to kill John, but he was afraid of the people" (v.5) conflicts with Mark's picture of a Herod who wants to spare John but is pushed into killing him by Herodias (cf. Mk 6:19–21). The total situation is psychologically convincing. Like Ahab, Antipas was wicked but weak, and Herodias, like Jezebel, was wicked and ruthless. Herod's grief (not mere distress) in v.9 shows his ambivalence. Moreover, if he was "afraid of the people" because they held John to be a prophet (cf. 21:26, 46), then Matthew confirms Josephus's view that Herod's actions were largely motivated by politics.

6–8 "On Herod's birthday" (or, better, "At Herod's birthday feast" [see Notes]), Herodias's daughter by her former marriage, Salome, a girl between twelve and fourteen years of age (Hoehner, *Herod Antipas*, 151–56), danced before the king and his lords (v.6). The dance may have been very sensual, but the text does not say so. The outrageous morals of the Herodians suggest it, as does the low status of dancing girls. At any rate, Salome pleased Herod Antipas enough for him to put on the airs of a lavish and powerful emperor; petty ruler though he was, he imitated the grandiloquence of ancient Persian monarchs (Est 5:3, 6; 7:2)—the story also has certain parallels with a later oath made by the Roman emperor Gaius to Herod Agrippa (cf. Hoehner, pp. 165–67)—and with drunken dignity made a fool of himself. Salome, still young enough to ask her mother's advice, became the means for accomplishing Herodias's darkest desire—the death of the man whose offense had been telling the truth.

9–11 Though grieving because of his oath (the Greek is plural but refers to the single oath Herod had made: see comments at 2:20; Turner, *Insights*, 27; BDF, para. 142) and his loss of face before his guests if he were to renege on his vow (but see Notes, v.9), Herod gave the order. "Like most weak men, Herod feared to be thought weak" (Plumptre, 202). His oath should neither have been made nor kept. Decapitation (v.10), though sanctioned by Greeks and Romans, was contrary to Jewish law, which also forbade execution without trial.

The gospel writers have been charged with fabrication on the ground that the prompt execution of John would have quenched the merriment. But hardened men are unlikely to let a little gore spoil their merriment. While Alexander Jannaeus feasted with his concubines in a public place, he ordered eight hundred rebels to die by crucifixion, their wives and children being slaughtered before the eyes of the victims (Josephus, *Ant.* 13.380 [14.2]). When Cicero's head was brought to Fulvia, the wife of Antony, she spat on it and pierced its tongue with a pin in spite against the man who had opposed Antony. Jerome says Herodias did the same thing to the head of John. We do not know where Jerome got his information, and it may not be historical, but it would not have been out of character for a cruel and ruthless woman intent on aping the imperial court. So John died, the last of the OT prophets (11:9, 13) who through persecution became models for Jesus' disciples (5:11–12).

For the significance of *korasion* ("girl," v.11; GK *3166*), see Hoehner (*Herod Antipas*, 154–56).

12 Though both Mark and Matthew tell of the burial of John the Baptist's body by his disciples, only Matthew mentions their report to Jesus. This report does not become the reason for Jesus' withdrawal (see comments at v.13) but serves other purposes: (1) It draws John and Jesus together against the opposition; (2) it suggests, though it does not prove, a positive response to Jesus by John and his disciples following 11:2–6; and (3) it supports the view that Matthew often finishes his longer narrative pericopes by returning to the opening theme (see comments at 12:45; 15:20)—Herod hears reports of Jesus (v.1); Jesus hears reports of Herod (v.12). The frequency of this device gains importance in interpreting Matthew's later chapters.

NOTES

6 The Greek γενεσίοις δὲ γενομένοις (*genesiois de genomenois*, "at the birthday feast") is so difficult that it has generated a nest of variant readings. It appears to be a dative absolute, which, though apparently common in Plutarch, has no other certain example in the NT (cf. Moule, *Idiom Book*, 44–45).

9 There are two principal readings (1) λυπηθεὶς ὁ βασιλεὺς διά (*lypētheis ho basileus dia*), attested by B D Q f^1 f^{13} 700 $it^{a,b,d}$ et al.; (2) ἐλυπήθη ὁ βασιλεύς; διὰ δέ (*elypēthē ho basileus • dia de*), attested by ℵ C K (L omit *de*) L^c W X *Byz* et al. The first, adopted here, is supported by witnesses of Alexandrian, Western, and Caesarean text types but has an ambiguity: does the διά, *dia*, phrase qualify λυπηθεὶς, *lypētheis* ("grieving")—i.e., "the king, grieving because of his oath and his dinner guests, ordered, etc."—or ἐκέλευσεν (*ekeleusen*, "he ordered")—i.e., "the king was grieved; but because of his oath and his dinner guests, he ordered, etc."? The second reading, most likely secondary, removes the ambiguity (usually evidence of being secondary) and requires the second interpretation. The difference is one of emphasis only; but the harder reading may be taken to support the more nuanced interpretation of Herod's motives given above.

3. The feeding of the five thousand (14:13–21)

OVERVIEW

The feeding of the five thousand is found in all four gospels (cf. Mk 6:30–44; Lk 9:10–17; Jn 6:1–14; see comments at 15:32–39 = Mk 8:1–10). Comprehensive interpretations are too numerous to list. There is probably an implicit anticipation of the messianic banquet (see comments at 8:11), but the text focuses more on Jesus' compassion (v.14), on the responsibility of the disciples to minister to the crowds (v.16), and on this miracle of creation. Suggestions that what "really happened" was that the people started sharing their lunches have much more in common with late nineteenth-century liberalism than with the text. Those who see eucharistic significance in the event (Benoit, Gundry) make it meaningless at the time it occurred; the most that can be said is that after the institution of the Lord's Supper and after the passion and resurrection, some Christians may have seen parallels to the Eucharist (cf. Blomberg, *Contagious Holiness*, 103–4). John 6, often taken to support this, is not as convincing as is commonly thought (cf. Carson, "Historical Tradition," 125–26).

Possible OT allusions to Exodus 16 or 2 Kings 4:42–44 cannot be more than allusions, for the differences between this story and those are more significant than the similarities. Hence, as Davies notes (*Setting*, 48–49), that Matthew here develops a "new Moses" theme based on a manna typology (Ex 16) is unlikely since (1) none of the synoptists stresses the desert setting; (2) in the OT the manna was not to be kept, but here the fragments are to be kept; (3) Jesus ministers to a crowd from which he has tried to escape, and Exodus has no parallel to this. It is far more likely that this pericope shows that Jesus himself cannot be reduced to one of the ready-made categories of the day—prophet, rabbi, teacher of the law (cf. van der Loos, *Miracles of Jesus*, 634–37).

13When Jesus heard what had happened, he withdrew by boat privately to a solitary
place. Hearing of this, the crowds followed him on foot from the towns. 14When Jesus
landed and saw a large crowd, he had compassion on them and healed their sick.
15As evening approached, the disciples came to him and said, "This is a remote place,
and it's already getting late. Send the crowds away, so they can go to the villages and buy
themselves some food."
16Jesus replied, "They do not need to go away. You give them something to eat."
17"We have here only five loaves of bread and two fish," they answered.
18"Bring them here to me," he said. 19And he directed the people to sit down on the
grass. Taking the five loaves and the two fish and looking up to heaven, he gave thanks
and broke the loaves. Then he gave them to the disciples, and the disciples gave them to
the people. 20They all ate and were satisfied, and the disciples picked up twelve basketfuls
of broken pieces that were left over. 21The number of those who ate was about five
thousand men, besides women and children.

COMMENTARY

13–14 If "what had happened" refers to John's death, then the chronology is either contradictory (so Bultmann, *History of the Synoptic Tradition*, 351–52) or a return to a much earlier time, since the beginning of the chapter presupposes the Baptist's death (v.2). But vv.3–12 must be seen as an excursus: the section opens with *gar* ("for"), commonly used to introduce excursuses, and the *de* ("and") in v.13 is resumptive (cf. L. Cope, "The Death of John the Baptist in the Gospel of Matthew, or, The Case of the Confusing Conjunction," *CBQ* 38 [1976]: 515–19). Therefore, v.13 picks up from vv.1–2: when Jesus heard, namely, Herod's response to his preaching and miracles, he decided to withdraw. He had done so previously to escape the animus of the Pharisees (12:15); he now does so to avoid Antipas. But as elsewhere (e.g., Mk 7:24–25), it is not possible for Jesus to escape the crowds even when it is possible for him to leave a place. So he withdraws "privately" (*kat' idian*: the idea is that he does not tell the crowds, not that he leaves by boat all by himself; cf. Hagner).

Luke (9:10) specifies that the "solitary place" was in the region belonging to Bethsaida—i.e., Bethsaida Julias (see comments at 11:21) on the northeast shore of Galilee. The crowds ran "on foot" around the top of the lake, presumably crossing the upper Jordan at a ford two miles north of where the river enters Galilee. They "followed" Jesus, seeing where he was going and setting out after him; but arriving first, they were already there when he landed with his tired disciples (v.14). Lohmeyer finds profound symbolism—Jesus "withdraws" from the presence of God in prayer, like a high priest leaving the Holy of Holies, and presents himself to the people. But this is as uncontrolled a piece of allegorizing as any church father ever thought of. (On Jesus' never-failing compassion, see 9:36.)

15–17 "Evening" (*opsios*, GK *4070*) is a flexible word, referring to any period from midafternoon to just after sunset. The later period is in view in v.23; here the earlier one.

On the face of it, the conversation between Jesus and his disciples is straightforward, though very condensed compared with the other gospels. The "villages" to which the disciples wished to send the crowds were small, unwalled hamlets. Bread and fish were staples in Galilee, especially for the poor. John 6:9, 13 specifies *barley* loaves—the cheaper, coarser bread. The numbers "five" and "two" (v.17) are simply accurate details. Efforts to explain them (e.g., as referring to the Pentateuch and two tables of the Law) are as fanciful as Christian frescoes making them eucharistic symbols, which would turn fish into wine!

But in recent years the influence of Held ("Matthew as Interpreter of the Miracle Stories," 181–83) has convinced many that Matthew's changes of Mark (assuming absolute dependence in this pericope) demonstrate two other themes at work: (1) the disciples take part in the miracle, and so discipleship is prominent; (2) the omission of Mark 6:37b shows that though in Mark the disciples do not understand Jesus' words—"You [emphatic] give them something to eat" (v.16; i.e., they do not understand that they themselves should perform a miracle)—in Matthew they do understand but lack the requisite faith. This will not do.

1. Held is establishing a great deal on the basis of an omission in a book characterized by condensations and omissions, and he does not even raise the question whether Mark 6:37b was omitted for nontheological reasons.

2. Similarly, would a first-century reader of Matthew perusing this gospel without critically comparing it with Mark at every turn suspect that Matthew was any easier on the disciples than Mark was at this point?

3. Neither "understanding" nor "faith" is explicitly raised in this pericope.

4. Jesus' words "you give them something to eat" are not easy to understand, but whatever they mean, it is possible that the disciples do not understand them, even in Matthew. If (and this is doubtful, though Held seems to assume it) Jesus means that they should perform such a miracle, then their response (v.17) betrays their complete misunderstanding; for miracles of creation cannot be thought to require something first. If, on the other hand, Jesus is simply making them responsible to find out what is needed, buy food, or pray—if they remembered the miracle of the wine in Cana (Jn 2:1–11), they should have asked Jesus to meet the need, not send the people away—then their answer not only reveals limited vision but an approach to

the problem betraying a lack of both understanding and faith.

5. The disciples' role in the miracle is limited to the organization and distribution needed for a crowd of thousands. This can scarcely mean that the disciples contribute to the miracle. Indeed, the story could more easily be taken as contrasting Jesus with his disciples in this miracle than as elevating them to major roles.

18–21 Jesus alone multiplies the loaves and fishes. He gives the orders, gives thanks, and breaks the loaves (vv.18–19). The actions—looking up to heaven, thanking God, and breaking the loaves—are normal for any head of a Jewish household (cf. Moore, *Judaism*, 2:216–17; Str-B, 1:685–86; *m. Ber.* 6–8) and have no special eucharistic significance. A common form of prayer before eating was "Blessed art thou, O Lord our God, King of the universe, who bringest forth bread from the earth."

Matthew omits many details—the greenness of the grass, the groups of fifty and one hundred—but points out that all ate and were satisfied (v.20), perhaps an anticipation of the messianic banquet, and at least evidence that there was lots to eat! The twelve baskets (*kophinos*, GK *3186*, a stiff wicker basket) of leftovers and the size of the crowd (which might have been fifteen or twenty thousand total, if there were five thousand "men," v.21) also support the latter point. David Instone-Brewer (*Traditions of the Rabbis from the Era of the New Testament* [Grand Rapids: Eerdmans, 2004], 1:79–81) suggests that the reason for counting males only may be related to the rabbinic stipulations of different kinds of "grace" to be said for different numbers of males who were present (*m. Ber.* 7:3.) But the "twelve basketfuls" may be significant: that there were twelve tribes and twelve apostles—emphasized in 19:28—cannot be coincidence. Yet the precise significance is uncertain. The best suggestion may be that Messiah's supply is so lavish that even the scraps of his provision are enough to supply the needs of Israel, represented by the Twelve.

4. The walk on the water (14:22–33)

OVERVIEW

Many scholars since Bultmann (*History of the Synoptic Tradition*, 216) have surmised that two stories are woven together in Mark's account (6:45–52; cf. Jn 6:16–21)—an account of walking on the water and a later storm-calming miracle. But Scot McKnight ("The Role of the Disciples in Matthew and Mark: A Redactional Study" [Master's thesis, Trinity Evangelical Divinity School, 1980], 153–56) has shown the two to be integrally related. Some of the points arising from the differences between Mark and Matthew are briefly treated below.

On the theological thrust of the passage, see John P. Heil, *Jesus Walking on the Sea* (Rome: Biblical Institute Press, 1981), who notes the association in the OT between chaos and sea. The stilling of the sea is, therefore, not only christological in orientation but also eschatological: Jesus is even now stilling the deep.

[22]Immediately Jesus made the disciples get into the boat and go on ahead of him to the other side, while he dismissed the crowd. [23]After he had dismissed them, he went up

on a mountainside by himself to pray. When evening came, he was there alone, 24but the
boat was already a considerable distance from land, buffeted by the waves because the
wind was against it.

25During the fourth watch of the night Jesus went out to them, walking on the lake.
26When the disciples saw him walking on the lake, they were terrified. "It's a ghost," they
said, and cried out in fear.

27But Jesus immediately said to them: "Take courage! It is I. Don't be afraid."

28"Lord, if it's you," Peter replied, "tell me to come to you on the water."

29"Come," he said.

Then Peter got down out of the boat, walked on the water and came toward Jesus. 30But
when he saw the wind, he was afraid and, beginning to sink, cried out, "Lord, save me!"

31Immediately Jesus reached out his hand and caught him. "You of little faith," he said,
"why did you doubt?"

32And when they climbed into the boat, the wind died down. 33Then those who were in
the boat worshiped him, saying, "Truly you are the Son of God."

COMMENTARY

22 Why Jesus "made" (the verb is very strong and might be translated "compelled") the disciples go on ahead of him may be deduced from these bits of information: (1) he wanted to be alone to pray (v.23); (2) he wanted to escape the crowd with his disciples to get some rest (Mk 6:31–32); and (3) he may have dismissed the disciples forcefully to help tame a messianic uproar (Jn 6:15).

The omission of "Bethsaida" (Mk 6:45) in Matthew raises a difficult geographical problem. From the perspective of the site where the feeding took place, "to the other side" means the west shore, and that is where the boat ultimately landed, at Gennesaret (Mk 6:53 = Mt 14:34), a small triangular plain on the northwest shore of the lake (Kinnereth in the OT, 1Ki 15:20). John 6:17 specifies the town of Capernaum. But Mark (6:45) says Jesus sent his disciples "on ahead of him to the other side [in the best MSS] to Bethsaida, while he dismissed the crowd." This was most likely Bethsaida Julius, just up the coast to the north, on the same side of the lake. The apparent discrepancy has prompted some MSS of Mark to omit "to the other side." The explanation that the boat was blown off course and landed on the west side does not explain the reference to Bethsaida, if this is Bethsaida Julius.

The problem is knotty. The simplest solution is that defended by Westcott (*The Gospel according to St. John* [repr.; Grand Rapids: Eerdmans, 1981]) and Morris (*John*)—namely, Jesus sent the disciples off to cross the lake, with the command to wait for him on the eastern shore near Bethsaida Julius, but not beyond a certain time. The delay in waiting for Jesus would then account for the actual walking on the water not occurring until the fourth watch (v.25), i.e., after 3:00 a.m.

A bit of syntax may support this view. Matthew's *heōs hou* plus the aorist subjunctive verb should normally be rendered "until" (as in 13:33; 17:9; 18:34; though cf. 26:36)—i.e., the disciples were to "go on ahead" (*proagein*, GK *4575*) of him *until*, not *while*, he was free of the crowds, after which he hoped to join them, after some time alone in prayer; they would then cross "to the other side." Mark (6:45) specifies Bethsaida but has *heōs* plus the indicative [in the best MSS]: the disciples were to go "to Bethsaida while," not "until," he sent the crowds away.

23–24 If this interpretation is correct, then it is the length of Jesus' prayer time that delays his coming and sends the disciples across the lake on their own. On the phrase "into the hills," see comments at 5:1–2. The burden of Jesus' prayer is not revealed; but it is possible that the crowd's attempts to make him king (Jn 6:15) prompted him to seek his Father's face. If so, it is not a Matthean concern here (as is a similar crisis at 26:39).

The NIV's "a considerable distance" (v.24) masks a considerable textual difficulty. The most likely reading is "many *stadia* [one *stadion* was about two hundred yards] from land" (Metzger, *Textual Commentary*, 37). In any event, the boat was out toward the middle of the lake. If *enantios* is taken literally to mean "against" and not metaphorically to mean "hostile to," then the clause "the wind was against it," on the basis of the movements suggested above, refers to a strong wind from the west—a regular feature during the rainy season (Mark's "green grass" [6:39] confirms the season).

Many eager to find signs of the Matthean church take the boat as a symbol of that church—a community of disciples in stormy times (e.g., Bonnard, Schweizer). But if so, why did Peter want to step "out of the boat"?

25–27 The ancient Hebrew world divided the night from sunset to sunrise into three watches (Jdg 7:19; La 2:19), but the Romans used four (v.25); and their influence prevailed in the evangelists' chronologies. Jesus' approach to the boat, therefore, occurred between 3:00 a.m. and 6:00 a.m. Matthew omits the difficult words "He was about to pass by them" (Mk 6:48), on which see Lane (*Mark*, 235–36). The disciples were terrified (Mt 14:26), thinking they were seeing a *phantasma* ("apparition"; NIV, "ghost"; used in the NT only here and in Mk 6:49). There is no merit in the supposition that this is a transposed resurrection appearance. Jesus' "Take courage!" (v.27, as in 9:2, 22) and his "Don't be afraid" bracket the central reason for these calming exhortations: "It is I." Although the Greek *egō eimi* can have no more force than that, any Christian after the resurrection and ascension would also detect echoes of "I am," the decisive self-disclosure of God (Ex 3:14; Isa 43:10; 51:12). Once again, we find Jesus revealing himself in a veiled way that will prove especially rich to Christians after his resurrection (see comments at 8:20; cf. Carson, "Christological Ambiguities").

28 Verses 28–32 have no parallel in the other gospels; and two of the verbs ("to sink" and "to doubt") are used elsewhere in this gospel only in exclusively Matthean sections (18:6; 28:17). Perhaps Matthew was the first to commit this part of the story to writing, though the evidence from two verbs each used but once elsewhere is not commanding. This is the first of three scenes in which Peter receives special treatment, all in chs. 14–17 (cf. 16:13–23; 17:24–27). Benoit thinks that already in this story Peter gains primacy over the rest of the Twelve; but "if so, it is a primacy which reveals weakness in faith" (Hill). See comments at 14:31.

Peter's protasis ("if it's you") is a real condition, almost "since it's you." The request is bold, but the disciples had been trained for some time and given power to do exactly the sort of miracles Jesus was doing (10:1). What is more natural than for a fisherman who knew and respected the dangers of the Sea of Galilee to want to follow Jesus in this new demonstration of supernatural power?

29–31 How far Peter got is unclear (see Notes, v.29), but at Jesus' command he walked on the water (the plural "waters" in Greek may be in imitation of Hebrew, which uses "water" only in the plural; cf. Mk 9:22; Jn 3:23). But his outlook changed: when he saw the wind (synecdoche for the storm), he began to sink (v.30). It was not that he lost faith in himself (so Schniewind), but that his faith in Jesus, strong enough to get him out of the boat and walking on the water, was not strong enough to stand up to the storm. Therefore, Jesus calls him a man "of little faith" (v.31; see comments at 6:30; 8:26; esp. at 17:20); and his rhetorical question—"Why [see Notes] did you doubt?"—helps both Peter and the reader recognize that doubts and fears quickly disappear before a strict inquiry into their cause. Thus Peter in this pericope is both a good example and a bad example (cf. Brown et al., *Peter in the New Testament*, 83). His cry for help is natural, not a liturgical creation—Did not liturgy have to choose some formulas on which to build?—and Jesus' rescuing him is akin to God's salvation in the OT (Pss 18:16; 69:1–3; 144:7).

32–33 The climax of the story is not the stilling of the storm (v.32) but the confession and worship of the disciples: "Truly you are the Son of God" (v.33). This is the first time Jesus has been addressed by the disciples with this full title (cf. 16:16; 26:63; 27:40, 43, 54). But it already lurks behind 3:17 ("my Son"), and the devil has used it of Jesus (4:3, 6). It is most likely abbreviated to "the Son" in Jesus' self-references in 11:25–27. In the earlier passage (cf. 3:17), we have seen how the title would most likely have been understood by the disciples at the time and how it would have been fleshed out in light of the resurrection. On the absence of the Greek articles, see comments at 13:39.

The objection that v.33 so anticipates 16:16 as to make the latter anticlimactic is psychologically unconvincing. Similar reasoning would make the rebuke of Peter (16:21–23) following his grand confession (16:13–20) impossible or preclude defection from Jesus at his passion. The Synoptic Gospels show us that the disciples understand only by degrees. Therefore, their confessions of Christ must not be interpreted as if they had postresurrection understanding of him. One of the marks of the evangelists' fidelity to the historical development of the disciples' understanding of Christ lies precisely in this—that they show the disciples coming around to the same points again and again, each time at a deeper level of comprehension, but always with a mixture of misapprehension.

Exactly what the disciples meant by "Son of God" is uncertain. It is doubtful that at this point they understood the title in a genuine ontological sense (though they would later). It is even less likely that they thought of Jesus as a *theios anēr* ("divine man"), allegedly an understood category in Hellenistic Judaism for various miracle workers. Carl Holladay (Theios Anēr *in Hellenistic Judaism: A Critique of the Use of This Category in New Testament Christology* [Missoula, Mont.: Scholars Press, 1977]) has shown the category was not well defined, that it had no fixed content in our period, and that it was not that common (contra O. Cullmann, *The Christology of the New Testament* [2nd ed.; Philadelphia: Westminster, 1963], 277; E. Lövestam, "Wunder und Symbolhandlung: Eine Studie über Matthäus 14:29–31," *Kerygma and Dogma* 9 [1962]: esp. 135; and many others). Probably they used the title in a messianic way (see comments at 3:17; 11:25–30) but still with superficial comprehension.

Many feel that vv.32–33 decisively alter Mark 6:51–52 (cf. Held, "Matthew as Interpreter of the Miracle Stories," 204ff.). Mark, it is alleged, leaves a final impression of confusion. No mention is made of the disciples' worship; instead they are amazed and do not understand the previous miracle of the loaves, and their hearts are hardened. But Matthew portrays them worshiping and uttering an important christological confession, with no mention of amazement, hard hearts, or failure to understand.

These are indeed undeniable differences; but the two evangelists are not as far apart as one might think.

1. Mark says they are "amazed"; but the verb used is often associated, not with fear, but with joyful worship (Lev 9:24 LXX; similarly the cognate noun, Lk 5:26). When used in Mark, the word usually, but not always, denotes amazement in response to some divine self-disclosure, but without fear. Why should they be afraid? The storm had ceased!

2. The comment in Mark 6:52 that the disciples' hearts were hardened does not refer to their amazement but to an underlying attitude that could allow for amazement after having seen so much of Jesus' work. The same point could be deduced from Matthew, even though it is not spelled out there.

3. Matthew may have omitted the censure in Mark 6:52 because he thought it would be repetitive. He had already shown the fear and lack of faith of the disciples (vv.26–27). (On these points, see esp. Trotter, "Understanding and Stumbling.")

This is not to deny differences in emphasis between Matthew and Mark but to deny that the historical reality behind the two accounts is too small to sustain both emphases. Mark focuses on the disciples' "hardness" that continued despite another miracle like a previous one (cf. 8:23–27; Mk 4:35–41) by someone who could multiply loaves. Matthew hints at such unbelief through his narrative—he is capable of much more subtle characterization than Mark—and by the example of Peter (if he is a man of little faith, what about the rest of them?) but focuses explicitly on the disciples' confession of Jesus as God's Son. But even there, in view of later developments in Matthew, a reader might think that the disciples' confessions are much greater than their actual comprehension (see comments at 16:21–28).

NOTES

29 The principal textual options are (1) καὶ ἦλθεν (*kai ēlthen*, "and he came or went [to Jesus]") and (2) ἐλθεῖν (*elthein*, "to come,""to go"). The latter signifies intent, the former accomplishment. (The NIV does not translate the word.) The external evidence is neatly divided. Metzger's argument (*Textual Commentary*, 37) that "he went" was changed to "to go" because the former seemed to say too much may be right. But one might argue that "to go" seems to say too little, since the text claims that Peter actually walked on the water; yet, when Peter began to sink, Jesus needed only reach out his hand to seize him, which implies Peter had walked almost all the way.

31 Εἰς τί (*eis ti*, "Why"), probably equivalent to לָמָּה (*lᵉmâ*, "why"), is extraordinary. The customary form is διὰ τί (*dia ti*, "why"), as in 9:14. Turner (*Syntax*, 266–67) detects a subtle difference: the latter means "because of what" = "why," whereas the former means "in order to what" = "why"; and in this instance, the latter nuance in "why" makes good sense. Jesus does not ask "because of what" Peter doubted (any fool could see that!) but for what purpose, to what end: What was the point of his doubt, having come so far?

5. Transitional summary of constant and unavoidable ministry (14:34–36)

34When they had crossed over, they landed at Gennesaret. 35And when the men of that place recognized Jesus, they sent word to all the surrounding country. People brought all their sick to him [36]and begged him to let the sick just touch the edge of his cloak, and all who touched him were healed.

COMMENTARY

34–36 Gennesaret was the fertile plain on the northwest side of the lake (see comments at v.22), vividly described by Josephus (*J.W.* 3.516–21 [10.8]). The crowd's instant recognition of Jesus (v.35) showed the extent of his ministry; again, word-of-mouth reports led to crowds (cf. 3:5; 4:24). Like the woman with the hemorrhage (9:20–22), the people were satisfied if only they could touch the edge of his cloak (v.36)—and even that degree of faith brought thorough healing (the preposition compounded with the verb in *diesōthēsan* ["were healed," GK *1407*] is emphatic).

This little pericope stresses again the sweeping extent of Jesus' public ministry (cf. 4:23–25; 8:16; 9:35–36) and shows that Jesus' ministry extended to all the people, though his close disciples had special access to him and his more intimate instruction. Also, because the stricter groups, such as the Pharisees and the Essenes, counted it an abomination to rub shoulders in a crowd—one never knew what ceremonial uncleanness one might contract—Jesus' unconcern about such things neatly sets the stage for the confrontation over clean and unclean (15:1–20). As in 8:1–4; 9:20–22, he himself cannot become unclean; instead, he makes clean.

6. Jesus and the tradition of the elders (15:1–20)

OVERVIEW

Controversies become sharper and more theological as Matthew's narrative moves on. This controversy is of great importance in grasping Jesus' understanding of the law. Some have tended to draw radical conclusions as to Matthew's distinctive emphases by comparing this pericope with Mark 7:1–23 (e.g., Barth, "Matthew's Understanding of the Law," 86–89). The most prominent differences between Matthew and Mark are these: Matthew omits Mark 7:3–4, adds 15:12–14, omits Mark's interpretation (Mk 7:19) that Jesus made all foods clean, and adds 15:20b to keep the focus on food eaten with washed or unwashed hands. Thus, many argue that whereas in Mark Jesus annuls the law, in Matthew he does not do more than annul one small bit of halakah (rabbinic interpretation affecting conduct). These issues must be kept in mind in interpreting the text more closely. (See esp. Banks's balanced study, *Jesus and the Law*, 132–46.)

[1]Then some Pharisees and teachers of the law came to Jesus from Jerusalem and asked,
[2]"Why do your disciples break the tradition of the elders? They don't wash their hands
before they eat!"

[3]Jesus replied, "And why do you break the command of God for the sake of your tradition? [4]For God said, 'Honor your father and mother' and 'Anyone who curses his father
or mother must be put to death.' [5]But you say that if a man says to his father or mother,
'Whatever help you might otherwise have received from me is a gift devoted to God,' [6]he
is not to 'honor his father' with it. Thus you nullify the word of God for the sake of your
tradition. [7]You hypocrites! Isaiah was right when he prophesied about you:

8 "'These people honor me with their lips,
but their hearts are far from me.
9 They worship me in vain;
their teachings are but rules taught by men.'"

[10]Jesus called the crowd to him and said, "Listen and understand. [11]What goes into a
man's mouth does not make him 'unclean,' but what comes out of his mouth, that is what
makes him 'unclean.'"

[12]Then the disciples came to him and asked, "Do you know that the Pharisees were
offended when they heard this?"

[13]He replied, "Every plant that my heavenly Father has not planted will be pulled up by
the roots. [14]Leave them; they are blind guides. If a blind man leads a blind man, both will
fall into a pit."

[15]Peter said, "Explain the parable to us."

[16]"Are you still so dull?" Jesus asked them. [17]"Don't you see that whatever enters the
mouth goes into the stomach and then out of the body? [18]But the things that come out of
the mouth come from the heart, and these make a man 'unclean.' [19]For out of the heart come
evil thoughts, murder, adultery, sexual immorality, theft, false testimony, slander. [20]These are
what make a man 'unclean'; but eating with unwashed hands does not make him 'unclean.'"

COMMENTARY

1 "Then" (see comments at 2:7) certain Pharisees (see comments at 3:7; Introduction, section 11.f) and teachers of the law came to Jesus "from Jerusalem" (see comments at 2:3). These did not belong to the many such leaders scattered throughout the land but came from Jerusalem. They would probably, therefore, be held in special esteem (cf. Str-B, 1:691). But from Matthew's perspective, they were probably a quasiofficial deputation (cf. Jn 1:19) and a source of Jesus' most virulent opposition.

2 As in 9:14, the attack on Jesus comes through the behavior of his disciples, though elsewhere we learn that the disciples reflected his own practices (Lk 11:37–41). Matthew is much more condensed than Mark, for two reasons: (1) Unlike Mark, Matthew does not need to explain Jewish customs to his readers, and (2) Mark deals with an array of Pharisaic halakic regulations (Mk 7:1–3), whereas Matthew stresses the one issue of eating food with unwashed hands. It must be emphasized that this distinction says nothing about the sharpness of the Pharisees' attack on Jesus' response but only about the concentration of issues (see comments at v.20). (For other differences between Matthew and Mark, cf. Banks, *Jesus and the Law*, 132–34.)

The "tradition of the elders," the "tradition of men" (Mk 7:8; Col 2:8), "your tradition" (vv.3, 6; Mk 7:9, 13), and the "traditions of the fathers" (Gal 1:14) refer to the great corpus of oral teaching that commented on the law and interpreted it in detailed rules of conduct, often recording the diverse opinions of competing rabbis. This tradition in Jesus' time was largely oral and orally transmitted; but the Pharisees, though not the Sadducees, viewed it as having authority very nearly equal to the canon. Much of it was severely disputed in the first century (cf. J. Andrew Overman, *Matthew's Gospel and Formative Judaism: The Social World of the Matthean Community* [Minneapolis: Fortress, 1990], 62–68). It was later codified under Rabbi Judah the Prince (ca. AD 135–200) to form the Mishnah (cf. Str-B, 1:691–95; *TDNT*, 6:661–63; Moore, *Judaism*, 1:251–62). One entire tractate, *Yadayim*, deals with "hands" (i.e., *yādayim*), specifying such details as how much water must be used for effective ceremonial purification: e.g., "If a man poured water over the one hand with a single rinsing, his hand is clean; but if over both hands with a single rinsing, R. Meir declares them unclean unless he pours over them a quarter-log or more" (*m. Yad.* 2:1)—but it is not entirely clear how ritual washings demanded by some in the tradition of Pharisaism were observed by ordinary folk.

3–6 Jesus' words, in slightly different order in Mark, are less a response than a counterattack. He made a fundamental distinction between the authority of "the command of God" (as found in Scripture) and the halakic tradition, and he insisted that the Pharisees and teachers of the law were guilty of breaking the former for the sake of (lit., "on account of") the latter (v.3). The two texts cited are Exodus 20:12 and 21:17 (cf. Dt 27:16; Pr 1:8; 20:20; 30:17; 1Ti 5:3), and their point is clear enough. The English verb "curses" (v.4) is too narrow: *kakologeō* means "to insult," "to speak evil of," "to revile" (used in the NT only here and at Mk 7:10; 9:39; Ac 19:9). The one who speaks evil of his parents must surely be put to death (on the construction of the latter clause, cf. Zerwick, *Biblical Greek*, para. 60).

"But you" (v.5)—the "you" is emphatic—have evaded through your traditions God's command (v.6), broadly interpreted by Jesus to lay responsibility on children to take responsibility for their parents. Greed could keep a son from discharging this duty by prompting him to declare the goods or money that might have gone to support his parents *korban*, a gift devoted to God (cf. Lev 27:9, 16), set aside for the temple treasury (cf. *m. Ned.*, esp. 1, 9, 11; cf. Str-B, 1:711–17). Such a vow could be annulled in various ways. It would not mean that one could use the goods or money in question, but rather that he could withhold it from his parents (for legal questions, cf. Derrett, *Studies in the New Testament*, 1:112–17). Thus halakic tradition was nullifying the word of God (the textual variants "law of God" and "command of God" are not critical).

A further observation may be important, though it should not be overstressed. For Jesus and the kingdom, a man must be willing to put aside family loyalties and love Jesus supremely (10:37–39). Yet here Jesus accuses the Pharisees and teachers of the law of breaking God's command when they use similar arguments to support vows devoting certain gifts to God. Apparently neither Jesus nor Matthew sees any inconsistency here, because in their view Jewish halakah cannot take precedence over the law, whereas Jesus and the kingdom may do so because they "fulfill" it. Other factors are also relevant. The halakic regulations Jesus opposed permitted a son sometimes to act against his parents, whereas 10:37–39 presupposes family opposition against disciples. Not only is the rule different, but the victim is also different.

7–9 This is the first recorded instance of Jesus' calling the Pharisees and teachers of the law hypocrites (see comments at 6:2). Luke 11–12 probably refers to a later time. The charge was that, while they made a show of devotion to God, their religious traditions took precedence over God's will. In referring to Isaiah 29:13, Jesus did not say, "Isaiah was right when he said ... and now I make a secondary application," but, "Isaiah was right when he prophesied about you." Yet Isaiah 29:13 is addressed to men of Isaiah's day. What then did Jesus mean? There are three points of contact: in each case those warned (1) were Jews (2) from Jerusalem (3) with a religion characterized by externals that sometimes vitiated principle. Moreover, the Jews of Jesus' day thought of themselves as preserving ancient traditions; but Jesus said that what they were actually preserving was the spirit of those whom Isaiah criticized long before. The thought is close to, though different in categories from, 23:29–32.

The quotation essentially follows the shorter form of the LXX (for details, cf. Gundry, *Use of the Old Testament*, 14–16; Blomberg, "Matthew," in *CNTUOT*). The burden of the Scripture Jesus quotes is that the Pharisees and teachers of the law have displaced the true religion of the heart (v.8), of the entire personality and will, with a religion of form. Therefore, their worship is vain (v.9) and their teachings their own, with nothing of God's authority behind them.

The judgment is so sweeping that it calls into question not only the Jews' halakah but their entire worship and teaching.

10–11 Jesus' sharpest barb against the Pharisees and teachers of the law had been private. Now he teaches the crowd the same things. These two verses also answer the Pharisees' question (v.2) directly, not just by countercharge (vv.3–9).

What Jesus now says, the disciples call a "parable" (v.15; so also Mk 7:17; see comments at 13:3a). In presenting it to the crowd (v.10), Jesus exhorts them to understand; for the parable was not meant to be cryptic, though only few seemed to have grasped it at the time, and the disciples had trouble with it (vv.15–16). This confirms our earlier comments on Jesus' parables (13:10–17, 34–35). The verb *koinoō* ("make unclean," GK *3124*), here used (v.11) for the first of fourteen times in the NT, literally means "to render common"; but because to participate in what was common was for a practicing Jew to become ceremonially unclean, the customary NT meaning is very similar.

Perhaps Mark 7:15 is a shade more generalized than Matthew's form of the "parable" (v.11), but the differences are slight. "If Matthew really wished to exclude the kind of laxity represented by his Markan source, it is hard to see why he kept the potentially dangerous parable around which this whole controversy is constructed" (C. E. Carlston, "The Things That Defile (Mark 7:14) and the Law in Matthew and Mark," *NTS* 15 [1968–69]: 77). The language is so general it lets in everything Mark allows, even though the final application is to food eaten with unwashed hands (v.20). The form of the argument is from this principle to that application, the former being broader than the latter. Thus, though Matthew omits Mark's parenthetical interpretation (Mk 7:19b)—"(In saying this, Jesus declared all foods 'clean.')"—yet retention of the "parable" and its interpretation (vv.17–20) leads precisely to that conclusion.

12–14 These verses are peculiar to Matthew and reflect what took place after Jesus and his disciples had retired from the crowd and entered the house (cf. Mk 7:17). The disciples' question shows that the Pharisees understood enough of Jesus' parable to take offense (v.12). The disciples' request to have the parable explained (v.15) does not reveal them as being more obtuse than the Pharisees but shows that, in common with most Jews at the time, they held the Pharisees in high regard and therefore wanted to be certain of exactly what Jesus had said that offended them so badly. Therefore, vv.12–14 are not out of place. Jesus must disillusion his disciples as to the reliability of the Pharisees and teachers of the law as spiritual guides, as well as explain the parable. This is not to say that these verses turn the entire section (vv.1–20) into a personal attack on the Pharisees rather than on their use of the law (so Kilpatrick, *Origins*, 180); for the chief point for which they are blamed relates to their misunderstanding of the law.

Jesus uses two images. The first (v.13) predicts the rooting up of any plant the heavenly Father has not planted. Israel often saw herself as a plant God had planted (Ps 1:3; Isa 60:21; cf. 1QS 8:5; CD 1:7; *1 En.* 10:16; *Pss. Sol.* 14:2), and the prophets turned the image against them (Isa 5:1–7). Thus Jesus is not saying that every false doctrine will be rooted up (so Broadus) but that the Pharisees, the leaders of the Jewish people, are not truly part of God's planting. In other words, they do not truly belong to Israel. (On the use of "planting of Israel" and "uprooting of Israel" as metaphors, see Charette, *Theme of Recompense*, 44–48.) This shocking idea has already been hinted at in Matthew (3:9; 8:11–12) and will recur.

The second image (v.14) may depend on a title some Jewish leaders apparently took on themselves. They had the law, they reasoned, and therefore were fit to serve as "guides of the blind" (Ro 2:19; cf. Lk 6:39). This Jesus disputes. In his view they were "blind guides of the blind" (NIV text note, so the most likely variant, cf. Metzger, *Textual Commentary*, 39); and "both will fall into a pit" (cf. Lk 6:39). Though the Pharisees and teachers of the law had the scrolls and interpreted them in the synagogues, this does not mean they really understood them. On the contrary, they were blind and failed to comprehend the Scriptures they claimed to follow. Jesus' denunciation presupposes that anyone who truly understands "the word of God" (v.6) will discern who he is and follow him (cf. Jn 5:39–40). The Pharisees did not follow Jesus, so they did not understand and follow the Scriptures.

15–16 Peter speaks on behalf of the other disciples. Jesus' answer shows that the "parable" to which Peter refers is v.11. The disciples' failure to understand shocks Jesus. (1) *Kai* ("also")—are you, too, "still so dull?" Dullness might be understandable in others, but in you disciples? (2) *Akmēn* ("still," used only here in Matthew) may mean either "Are you *still* without understanding?" (Hill, McNeile) or "Are you still—*but not for long*—without understanding?" (Schlatter). The context strongly favors the former, and therefore the question, far from toning down the disciples' failure to grasp Jesus' teaching (so Schweizer), magnifies its enormity.

17–20 Verse 17 explains that "what goes into a man's mouth" (v.11) is merely food, which passes through the body and is excreted (lit., "is cast into a latrine"). On the sanitary conditions of the time, cf. Edward Neufeld, "Hygiene Conditions in Ancient Israel," *BA* 34 (1971): 42–66. Verses 18–20 explain that "what comes out of a man's mouth" (v.11), and what makes him unclean, comes from his heart (see comments at 12:34–35). Matthew's list of the heart's products (v.19) is shorter than Mark's. After the first, "evil thoughts," the list follows the same order as the sixth and seventh commandments, followed by *porneia* ("sexual immorality"; see comments at 19:3–12), the order of the eighth and ninth commandments, and finally "slander," which probably includes blasphemy (cf. 12:31). The list itself negates (as Banks [*Jesus and the Law*, 143–44] points out) Kilpatrick's suggestion (*Origins*, 38) that Matthew has transformed Mark's principle of morals into a precept of law.

It would be puerile to ask how every item on the list results directly in defiling speech. The point, as in 12:34–35, is that what a man truly is affects what he says and does. Jesus presupposes that the heart is essentially evil (cf. 7:11). But the burden of this pericope is to teach that what ultimately defiles a man is what he really is. Jesus is not spiritualizing the OT but insisting that true religion must deal with the nature of man and not with mere externals.

Because v.20b does not occur in Mark, many have thought it to be Matthew's way of limiting the application of the controversy to the single question of eating food with unwashed hands. Two things militate against this view: (1) Jesus deals with a broad principle touching *all* foods and applies it to this situation, but the application can be no more valid than the broader principle on which it is based; and (2) Matthew frequently ends his pericopes by referring back to the questions that precipitate them (see comments at 12:45; 14:12; 16:11–12; 17:13), so v.20b requires no more explanation than that.

The way one interprets this pericope relates to a larger understanding of how Matthew deals with Jesus' attitude to the law and the situation in his own church.

1. It goes beyond the evidence to argue, as does Ernst Käsemann (*Essays on New Testament Themes* [London: SCM Press, 1964], 101), that Jesus now abrogates the distinction between the sacred and the profane; or, as Lohmeyer does, that Jesus now distinguishes "word of God" from "word of man," even within Scripture itself; or, as McNeile does, that Jesus now undermines, as in Mark, *all* Mosaic distinctions between clean and unclean. He deals, principally, with the clean/unclean distinctions as to foods and applies this principle to foods eaten with unwashed hands.

2. On the other hand, it does not go as far as the exegetical evidence to pit Matthew against Mark so that the former, unlike the latter, is seen as absolutely restricting Jesus' words to the single problem of foods eaten with unwashed hands. Verses 3, 7–9, 11, 14, 17–19 cannot be taken so narrowly.

3. The approach that sees a Jewish-Christian church behind this pericope—whether still related to the synagogue or recently separated from it—is exegetically unsatisfying. Matthew is slightly more cautious than Mark and perhaps a shade less explicit, but that is not solid enough evidence to support G. Barth's reconstruction ("Matthew's Understanding of the Law") of the Matthean church. Though Ebionite groups doubtless flourished, Matthew did not belong to one or anything like one, for no Ebionite could write vv.11, 17–20.

4. Banks (*Jesus and the Law*, 140–41) contends that if Jesus explicitly repudiated the food laws contained in Leviticus 11 and Deuteronomy 14 (Da 1:8–16; cf. Jdt 10:5; Tob 1:10–11), then the hesitations of the primitive church on the issue (Ac 10:14–15; 15:28–29; Ro 14:14; Gal 2:11–14) are inexplicable. But Banks avoids falling into the trap of thinking that Jesus' original teaching on this matter was no more than Semitic hyperbole, with the meaning that "pollutions from within are more serious than pollutions from without" (p. 141; cf. Hos 6:6). Rather, he holds that Jesus' approach neither attacked nor affirmed the law but moved on a different level, expressing "an entirely new understanding of what does and does not constitute defilement" (p. 141). Abrogation was latent within the saying, but not more. This is a shade too timid.

The hesitations of the early church regarding the food laws are not inexplicable. A great deal of what Jesus taught became *progressively* clear to the church after the resurrection and did not immediately gain universal assent. The same is true of Jesus' words on Gentile conversion, on the Great Commission, on the delay of the Parousia. What can be said is that Jesus' teaching in this pericope (and in its Markan parallel) opens up an entirely fresh approach to the question of the law. It does not simply subordinate the ritual to the moral (these are not the categories appealed to); instead, it discounts the Pharisees' oral tradition while defending the law (vv.3–6) and yet insists that real "cleanness" is of the heart, thus discounting some of the law's formal requirements. What is indisputable is how seminal Jesus' treatment of this point proved to be in the early decades of the church after Pentecost (see, e.g., Ac 10–11; Gal 2:11–14; cf. J. D. G. Dunn, *Jesus, Paul and the Law* [London: SPCK, 1990]).

The only way to explain these phenomena is the one Matthew has already developed (see esp. 5:21–48): Jesus insists that the true direction in which the OT law points is precisely what he teaches, what he is, and what he inaugurates. He has fulfilled the law; therefore, whatever prescriptive force it continues to have is determined by its relationship to him, not vice versa. It is within this framework that Jesus' teaching in this pericope theologically anticipates Romans 14:14–18; 1 Corinthians 10:31; 1 Timothy 4:4; Titus 1:15, and that historically it took some time for the ramifications of Jesus' teaching to be thoroughly grasped, even by his own disciples. Once again it is a mark of Matthew's fidelity to the historical facts that he does not overstate Jesus' teaching, and a mark of his literary skill that he does not find it necessary to draw Mark's parenthetical conclusion (Mk 7:19b), even though he obviously shares it.

5. It follows that Jesus not only rejected the Pharisees and teachers of the law as authentic interpreters of Scripture (esp. vv.12–14) but assigned that role finally and absolutely to himself (cf. 5:21–48). Historically the conflict between Jesus and the traditional interpreters of Scripture would wax fierce and would ultimately take him to the cross; theologically, the fundamental distinctions between a Christian and a Jewish reading of Scripture must be traced to Jesus himself.

6. What concerned Jesus was not so much the form of religion as human nature. He wanted to see people transformed and their hearts renewed (cf. 6:1–33; 12:34–35; see comments at 25:31–46) because he came to save his people from their sins (1:21).

7. More healings (15:21–31)

a. The Canaanite woman (15:21–28)

OVERVIEW

It is by no means clear which way—if at all—the literary dependency of this pericope on Mark (cf. Mk 7:24–30) runs (cf. E. A. Russell, "The Canaanite Woman and the Gospels," in *Studia Biblica 1978* [ed. Livingstone], 2:263–82). Of greater interest is the placing of this pericope in both gospels. It not only records Jesus' withdrawal from the opposition of the Pharisees and teachers of the law (cf. 14:13) but contrasts their approach to the Messiah with that of this woman. They belong to the covenant people but take offense at the conduct of Jesus' disciples, challenge his authority, and are so defective in understanding the Scriptures that they show themselves not to be plants the heavenly Father has planted. But this woman is a pagan, a descendant of ancient enemies, and one who has no claim on the God of the covenant. Yet in the end, she approaches the Jewish Messiah and with great faith asks only for grace, and her request is granted (cf. 8:5–13).

This essentially christological approach to the pericope is more defensible than the one that sees in these verses guidance for Matthew's Jewish church in its relations to Gentiles—they could not claim immediate access to salvation, but exceptions would be made where there was deep faith (Hill). This begs too many issues. Would they, or would they not, then have to conform to all Jewish law? How do we know so much about Matthew's church (see Introduction, section 2)? What this explains to Matthew's readers (Matthew's "church," though this designation may give the wrong impression of a group hermetically sealed off from other churches) is not what attitude they ought to adopt toward Gentile evangelism, whether opposition or occasional acquiescence, but rather "how we got from there to here"—i.e., how the development of redemptive history changed the position of God's people from late OT concepts to the full Christian concept. This story is a step along the way, focused on the self-disclosure of the Messiah and his attitudes to his own mission, his pivotal role in salvation history. But if Matthew's Jewish-Christian readers want to learn more about what their attitude should be toward Gentile evangelism, they must also read the words of the resurrected and glorified Jesus after the climax of his self-disclosure (28:18–20).

The worst feature of many redaction-critical attempts to reconstruct Matthew's church and its problems is the implicit elimination of the salvation history insisted on by the Gospels themselves, a persistent refusal to believe that the evangelists are interested in writing about Jesus to explain him, and therefore "how we got from there to here," rather than to address their "churches" from the perspective of a theology infinitely flexible and shaped by contemporary problems alone. Once the perspective of redemptive history is granted, we may cheerfully acknowledge that the evangelists include material and write it down in such a way that it will prove of interest and/or use (not necessarily both) to their readers. But the loss of the historical perspective from which the evangelists claim to write leads to an unnecessary and basic distortion of their gospels.

21 Leaving that place, Jesus withdrew to the region of Tyre and Sidon. 22 A Canaanite
woman from that vicinity came to him, crying out, "Lord, Son of David, have mercy on me!
My daughter is suffering terribly from demon-possession."

23 Jesus did not answer a word. So his disciples came to him and urged him, "Send her
away, for she keeps crying out after us."

24 He answered, "I was sent only to the lost sheep of Israel."

25 The woman came and knelt before him. "Lord, help me!" she said.

26 He replied, "It is not right to take the children's bread and toss it to their dogs."

27 "Yes, Lord," she said, "but even the dogs eat the crumbs that fall from their masters'
table."

28 Then Jesus answered, "Woman, you have great faith! Your request is granted." And her
daughter was healed from that very hour.

COMMENTARY

21 Jesus "withdraws" (as in 2:12, 22; 4:12; 12:15; 14:13) to the region of Tyre and Sidon, cities on the Mediterranean coast lying about thirty and fifty miles respectively from Galilee. Kilpatrick (*Origins*, 130ff.) notes Matthew's interest in them (cf. 11:21–24) and suggests that Matthew and his church were there—a possibility, but without much supporting evidence. "The vicinity of Tyre" (Mk 7:24) leads us to ask whether Jesus actually entered the region of Tyre and Sidon or went only to the border—which would mean the woman came out to meet him. But Matthew 15:21 and Mark 7:31 make it clear that Jesus left Galilee and entered pagan territory. According to Mark 3:8 and Luke 6:17, some crowds had come from Tyre and Sidon to be helped by him, but there he would hardly be known.

22 The introductory *idou* (lit., "behold," untranslated in NIV) probably points to the extraordinary nature of the story. Mark (7:26) calls the woman "a Greek [i.e., a non-Jewess], born in Syrian Phoenicia." Matthew's use of the old term "Canaanite" shows that he cannot forget her ancestry: now a descendant of Israel's ancient enemies comes to the Jewish Messiah for blessing. *Exelthousa* (lit., "coming out") does not mean that she came out of that pagan region to meet Jesus but either that her ancestry was there or that she had left her home (Bonnard, Lohmeyer). Her calling Jesus "Son of David" shows some recognition of Jesus as the Messiah who would heal the people (see comments at 9:27; 12:23); "Lord" is ambiguous (see comments at 8:2). For other instances of demon-possession in this gospel, see comments at 4:24; 8:16, 28, 33; 9:32; 12:22.

23–24 That these verses are peculiar to Matthew is not surprising. Matthew's Jewish readers would be intensely interested in Jesus' doing a miracle to aid a Gentile, on Gentile territory. Mark's Gentile readers would, however, have needed much explanation had this saying been included in his gospel. Jesus had healed Gentiles before (4:24–25; 8:5–13), but always in Jewish territory.

Jesus' silence does not quiet the woman; so his disciples beg him to stop her persistent cries (v.23). If they mean "send her away without helping her," either they suppose she is annoying him or they themselves are being annoyed. But their words could also be taken to mean "send her away with her request granted" (so Meyer, Benoit). Indeed only this interpretation makes sense, because v.24 gives a reason for Jesus' not helping her rather than for not sending her away.

Bultmann (*History of the Synoptic Tradition*, 155), Arens (Ἦλθον-*sayings*, 315–19), and others judge Jesus' answer (v.24) to be inauthentic, largely on the grounds that "I was sent" sounds Johannine and thus for them is late and inauthentic. Regardless of this similarity, the particularism of the thought supports its authenticity, since the church, even before Paul, engaged in Gentile evangelism and could therefore hardly be thought to have created the saying (cf. Jeremias, *Jesus' Promise*, 26–28; Bonnard; Hill). The thought echoes 10:6, where the same language is used (lit., "the lost sheep of the house of Israel"). But even ch. 10 recognizes that one day the mission of the disciples will take them to Gentiles (10:18). But that time was not yet. Meanwhile, Jesus, doing the Father's will (cf. 11:27), recognized that his own mission was to Israel; and he delighted to do the will of him who sent him.

"The lost sheep of the house of Israel" either means "the lost sheep *among* the house of Israel"—i.e., some in the house of Israel are not lost—or "the lost sheep *who are* the house of Israel"—i.e., all Israel, regarded as lost sheep. The latter is correct, for in the identical expression at 10:6 the contrast is not between these lost sheep and others in Israel who are not lost but between these lost sheep and Gentiles or Samaritans. Flender (*Die Botschaft Jesu*, 23ff.) errs in the opposite direction, holding that Jesus sees himself gathering *all* Israel, not just a remnant. But Jesus is not so naive (cf. 7:13–14; 10:17–22, 34–37), for there is a categorical distinction between a target people and a converted people.

It appears, then, that Jesus wanted his disciples and the Canaanite woman to recognize "that his activities were circumscribed not only by the inevitable limitations of his manhood, but by the specific part that he had been called to play during his brief earthly life" (Tasker, 150). True, Jesus was "Son of David," as the woman said, but that did not give her the right to enjoy the benefits covenanted to the Jews. The kingdom must first be offered to them. The thought is like John 4:22: "Salvation is from the Jews." The Samaritan woman, like this Canaanite woman, had to recognize this—even if a time was coming when true worship would transcend such categories (Jn 4:23–26). Chae (*Jesus as the Eschatological Davidic Shepherd*, 216–17) rightly points out that the advance of thought in this pericope follows the flow of thought in Ezekiel 34–37 and beyond, on which the notion of "David" as eschatological Shepherd of his people depends: first he restores Israel, and then his reign extends to the nations.

25 The woman knelt (see comments at 2:2; 8:2) before Jesus (probably the imperfect is used to make the action more vivid) and cried, as only the mother of an afflicted child could, "Lord, help me!"

26 Still Jesus made certain that she grasped the historic distinction between Jew and Gentile. Jesus' short aphorism supposes that the "children" are the people of Israel and the "dogs" are Gentiles. The "crumbs" (v.27) do not designate the quantity of blessing bestowed; and still less does the table refer to the Eucharist (rightly Bonnard). The question is one of precedence: the children get fed *first*.

27 The woman's answer is masterly. "Yes, Lord," she agrees, "for even [not 'but even,' NIV; see Notes] the dogs eat the crumbs that fall from their masters' table." Those two words, "for even," reveal immense wisdom and faith. She does not phrase her answer as a counterstroke but as a profound acquiescence with the further implications of "dogs." She does not argue that her needs make her an exception, or that she has a right to Israel's covenanted mercies, or that the mysterious ways of divine election and justice are unfair. She abandons mention of Jesus as "Son of David" and simply asks for help, "and she is confident that even if she is not entitled to sit down as a guest at Messiah's table, Gentile 'dog' that she is, yet at least she may be allowed to receive a crumb of the uncovenanted mercies of God" (Tasker, 152; cf. Bailey, *Jesus through Middle Eastern Eyes*, 217–26). There may be no significance to the use of the diminutive "dogs" (*kynaria*, GK *3249*) in vv.26–27, because in Hellenistic Greek the diminutive force is often entirely lacking; but if there is such force here, it does not make the dogs more acceptable—i.e., "pet dogs" or "house dogs" as opposed to "wild dogs"—but more dependent: i.e., little, helpless dogs eat little scraps of food (*psichiōn*—equally diminutive in form). As does Paul in Romans 9–11, the woman preserves Israel's historical privilege over against all radical idealization or spiritualization of Christ's work, yet perceives that grace is freely given to the Gentiles.

28 The faith that simply seeks mercy is honored. Again Jesus speaks, this time with emotion (see Notes), and the woman's daughter is healed "from that very hour" (cf. 8:13; 9:22). The Clementine homilies (end of the second century) call the woman Justa and her daughter Berenice, but the names may have been invented.

NOTES

27 The words καὶ γάρ (*kai gar*; NIV, "but even") are used approximately thirty-nine times in the NT. In no other place does the NIV render them adversatively ("but even"), and there is no justification for doing so here. The natural translation is "for even." The Markan parallel (Mk 7:28) exhibits far more variants; but the correct reading almost certainly omits both γάρ (*gar*, "for") and ἀλλά (*alla*, "but") in favor of a simple "Lord, even the dogs," whose precise nuance is a shade more ambiguous.

28 The ejaculation ὦ (*ō*, "O [woman]," omitted in D) has emotional force (cf. BDF, para. 146 [1b], which contrasts this with use of the vocative "woman" without the word in Luke 22:57; John 2:4; 4:21; et al.), as seems usual in the Hellenistic Greek of the NT, with the exception of Acts, which prefers the classical usage (cf. Zerwick, *Biblical Greek*, para. 35).

b. The many (15:29–31)

OVERVIEW

Mark 7:31–37 tells of the healing of a deaf mute; Matthew provides a summary of more extensive healings (cf. T. J. Ryan, "Matthew 15:29–31: An Overlooked Summary," *Hor* 5 [1978]: 31–42; for other summaries, cf. 4:23–25; 9:35–38; 12:15–21; 14:14–36). Ryan points out the echoes of Isaiah 29:18–19; 35:5–6. Of greater consequence is the geographical location. Contrary to Bonnard, these healings and the subsequent feeding of the four thousand take place in Gentile territory—namely, in the Decapolis (see below). Jesus had already displayed the power of the kingdom here (8:28–34; Mk 5:20). His reluctance to respond to the request of the Canaanite woman (vv.21–28) must therefore turn not just on her being a Gentile or on this being Gentile territory (cf. 8:28–34), but more on her appealing to him as Son of David and on his being conscious of his primary aims during his earthly ministry. Because of her faith, making appeal to his mercy, the woman receives the "crumbs." Then lest anyone think the crumbs betray a restricted blessing for Gentiles, Matthew immediately tells us of the feeding of four thousand Gentiles. If Jesus' aphorism about the children and the dogs merely reveals *priority* in feeding, then it is hard to resist the conclusion that in the feeding of the four thousand Jesus is showing that blessing for the Gentiles is beginning to dawn.

[29]Jesus left there and went along the Sea of Galilee. Then he went up on a mountainside and sat down. [30]Great crowds came to him, bringing the lame, the blind, the crippled, the mute and many others, and laid them at his feet; and he healed them. [31]The people were amazed when they saw the mute speaking, the crippled made well, the lame walking and the blind seeing. And they praised the God of Israel.

COMMENTARY

29–31 "Jesus left there" refers to the region of Tyre and Sidon (v.21). But to which (not "along" which, as in the NIV; cf. Moule, *Idiom Book*, 50–51) side of the Sea of Galilee did he go? If to the west, he was in Jewish Galilee; if to the east, in predominantly Gentile Decapolis (see comments at 4:25). Mark 7:31 has Jesus traveling north from the vicinity of Tyre to Sidon, and then south and east to the Decapolis on the southeastern side of the lake, still outside Herod's jurisdiction (cf. 14:13). This places him not far from where he had healed the demoniacs and may account for the growing crowds.

But all this depends on reading Mark into Matthew. Could it be that Matthew simply does not care about where Jesus was at this point? No, the evidence suggests rather that he assumes it: (1) the clause "they praised the God of Israel" (v.31) uses language that only Gentiles would have used for praising God; (2) the remoteness of the place (v.33) suggests the eastern side of the lake; and (3) the number of "basketfuls of broken pieces" (v.37) left over avoids the symbolic "twelve" (cf. 14:20). More incidental bits of information point in the same direction (see below).

Jesus did many miracles over the course of several days (cf. vv.30–32). The order of the ailments varies in the MSS, possibly owing in part to homoeoteleuton (cf. Metzger, *Textual Commentary*, 40).

8. The feeding of the four thousand (15:32–39)

OVERVIEW

Many scholars hold that this miracle, reported here and in Mark 8:1–10, is a doublet of the feeding of the five thousand, though there is little agreement about why Matthew should include a doublet here. A few have thought the requirements of a liturgical calendar led him to do this—a theory lacking in substantial evidence. More common is the view that Mark put in the doublet to affirm that Gentiles as well as Jews will enjoy the messianic banquet. "The repetition of the story therefore serves theology, not history" (Hill).

This is not very satisfactory, for if even one of Mark's or Matthew's readers knew there was only one miraculous feeding, *and that of Jews*, the point about the Gentiles would be lost and the credibility of the two evangelists impugned. The events were within the lifetime of many of Matthew's readers. We are dealing with a few decades, not centuries. Thus the validity of the theological point depends here on the credibility of the historical record. Moreover, both Mark 8:17–19 and Matthew 16:9–11 report that Jesus referred to the two feedings as separate occasions. Even if one rejects the authenticity of what Jesus said, it argues that the evangelists themselves believed in two miraculous feedings.

Close comparison of the two miracles shows similarities only where there could scarcely be anything else: (1) they both take place in the country; (2) bread and fish appear in both, but this was the common food of the area; (3) Jesus gives thanks and breaks the bread, as one would expect him to (see comments at 14:19); (4) both portray the disciples distributing the food, a necessity because of the many thousands; and (5) both end in a boat trip, but so do many other stories located near Galilee, especially when Jesus desires to escape the crowds.

On the other hand, the differences between the two miracles are impressive (cf. Maier): (1) the different numbers, five thousand and four thousand; (2) the different locales, northeast shore and southeast shore of Galilee (clearest in Mark); (3) no mention of grass in the second story, implying a different season of the year; (4) a different supply of food at the beginning; (5) a different number of basketfuls of leftovers, and even different words for "basket"; and (6) the longer stay of the people in the second miracle (v.32).

It might be wise to remember that two feeding miracles by Moses (Ex 16; Nu 11) and Elisha are reported (2Ki 4:1–7, 42–44). The only impressive reason for taking this account as a doublet is the disciples' response in v.33, and this is best accounted for in other ways (see below).

32Jesus called his disciples to him and said, "I have compassion for these people; they
have already been with me three days and have nothing to eat. I do not want to send
them away hungry, or they may collapse on the way."
33His disciples answered, "Where could we get enough bread in this remote place to
feed such a crowd?"
34"How many loaves do you have?" Jesus asked.
"Seven," they replied, "and a few small fish."
35He told the crowd to sit down on the ground. 36Then he took the seven loaves and the
fish, and when he had given thanks, he broke them and gave them to the disciples, and
they in turn to the people. 37They all ate and were satisfied. Afterward the disciples picked
up seven basketfuls of broken pieces that were left over. 38The number of those who ate
was four thousand, besides women and children. 39After Jesus had sent the crowd away,
he got into the boat and went to the vicinity of Magadan.

COMMENTARY

32–33 On Jesus' compassion, see comments at 9:36. It appears that Jesus' preaching and miracles so captivated the people (cf. their exuberant praise, v.31) that they refused to leave him until he hesitated to dismiss them, fearing that many of them would collapse for hunger on their way home (v.32). Some had come a long distance (Mk 8:3). The response of the disciples is not surprising and not sufficient to prove this pericope a doublet of the feeding of the five thousand, for:

1. The disciples may have understood the feeding of the five thousand Jews as anticipating the messianic banquet. But, though they might have been prepared for Jesus to perform miracles of healing and exorcism on Gentiles as expressions of his mercy and compassion, they might still have been a long way from admitting that Gentiles could share in any anticipation of the messianic banquet.

2. According to John 6:26, after the feeding of the five thousand, Jesus rebuked the crowds for just

wanting food, and the disciples may therefore have thought better of bringing the subject up again.

3. More important, we must never lose sight of a human being's vast capacity for unbelief. After this healing, whether a doublet of the feeding of the five thousand or not, Jesus' disciples completely misinterpreted one of his enigmatic sayings because even then they did not understand that those with Jesus could never starve (16:5–12).

34–39 Here in v.36 the verb *eucharisteō* ("I give thanks," GK *2373*) is used, not *eulogeō* (lit., "I bless," GK *2328*), as in 14:19, though there is no substantial difference in meaning. The *spyridas* ("baskets," GK *5083*) were woven of rushes and used for fish or other food (cf. *kophinous* ["baskets"] in 14:20, GK *3186*). A. E. J. Rawlinson (*The Gospel According to St. Mark* [5th ed.; London: Methuen, 1942], 87) cites Juvenal to the effect that, at least in Rome, Jews commonly used *kophinous* to carry kosher food. If so, the use of *spyridas* in this setting may imply that the locale and its people were non-Jewish.

If the number of baskets of leftovers in 14:20 is symbolic, it is hard to see why the seven baskets here (v.37) are not symbolic (see comments at vv.29–31). The number seven may be significant because it is not twelve and therefore not allusive to the twelve apostles or twelve tribes. This seems more sensible than seeing an allusion to the seven deacons (Ac 6:1–6; so Lohmeyer)—an anachronistic view that ignores that (1) the seven in Acts 6 are not explicitly called deacons; (2) the church was then entirely Jewish; and (3) the twelve apostles exercised general oversight. It is barely possible that the seven baskets represent the fullness of the people of God now being touched by Jesus' power, as the twelve baskets bore an allusion to Israel; but what is surprising on this view is that the audience here was not apparently composed of both Jew and Gentile but only the latter.

As before, *hoi esthiontes* ("those who ate," v.38; on the tense, cf. Zerwick, *Biblical Greek*, para. 291) are all satisfied, and the men only are numbered. The whole crowd may have exceeded ten thousand.

The site of Magadan (v.39; see Notes) is unknown. Both Mark and Matthew now speak of a conflict with the Pharisees and Sadducees (16:1–4). If this occurred when Jesus and the disciples landed, it must have been on Jewish territory, probably on the western shores of Galilee.

NOTES

39 Mark 8:10 has τὰ μέρη Δαλμανουθά (*ta merē Dalmanoutha*, "the region of Dalmanoutha"); but we do not know where that is. The uncertainty of the site of Μαγαδάν (*Magadan*) has prompted several textual variants, including Μαγδαλάν (*Magdalan*) and Μαγδαλά (*Magdala*), which may have been influenced by a Semitic word for "tower" (Heb. מִגְדָּל [*migdāl*]; Aram. מִגְדְּלָא [*migdᵉlāʾ*]).

9. Another demand for a sign (16:1–4)

OVERVIEW

Doubtless there were many requests for signs (see comments at 12:38–40), as there continued to be after Jesus' resurrection and ascension (1Co 1:22–24). Moreover, itinerant preachers develop standard responses to standard questions. But this pericope (cf. Mk 8:11–13) has a crucial place in the narrative. Jesus has barely returned to Jewish territory when the opposition of Jewish leaders again surfaces, prompting him to leave the area once more, cross the lake, and head far north to Caesarea Philippi (v.13), where in God's providence and in the heart of Gentile territory, Peter makes the great confession that Jesus is the Messiah (v.16).

[1]The Pharisees and Sadducees came to Jesus and tested him by asking him to show them a sign from heaven.

[2]He replied, "When evening comes, you say, 'It will be fair weather, for the sky is red,'
[3]and in the morning, 'Today it will be stormy, for the sky is red and overcast.' You know how to interpret the appearance of the sky, but you cannot interpret the signs of the times.
[4]A wicked and adulterous generation looks for a miraculous sign, but none will be given it except the sign of Jonah." Jesus then left them and went away.

COMMENTARY

1 The single article in *hoi Pharisaioi kai Saddoukaioi* ("the Pharisees and Sadducees") implies that they acted together. Because the two groups were so frequently at odds theologically and politically, many think such united action improbable. Moreover, critical orthodoxy dates this gospel at about AD 85, a time when the Sadducees, closely connected with Jerusalem and the temple, destroyed in AD 70, no longer existed as a coherent force. Therefore, many feel that since only Pharisaism was dominant in Judaism at that time, this reference to the Sadducees implies no more than that Matthew vaguely remembered all official Judaism being opposed to Jesus.

A better approach is possible.

1. It is precarious to identify, without remainder, the Pharisees of Jesus' day and the rabbis of AD 85 (see Introduction, section 11.f), and the Sadducees did not continue as a group with genuine influence after AD 70. Matthew's use of these terms might therefore be taken as evidence for historical accuracy in the pre–AD 70 setting and not as an anachronism.

2. The introduction has already questioned critical orthodoxy regarding the date and setting of Matthew's gospel. A date in the ninth decade should not be lightly assumed. Overcoming that barrier, references to the Sadducees in the Synoptic Gospels can be taken to support the evangelists' accuracy. Would not failure to mention the Sadducees have raised questions about how close the evangelists were to what they were writing about? Why then should mention of them not argue for the evangelists' fidelity? If the Sadducees do not appear more often than they do, it is because they were a small group and closely tied to Jerusalem—a long way from Galilee, where Jesus exercised so much of his ministry. Indeed the controversy between Jesus and the Sadducees, recorded in 22:23–34; Mark 12:18–27; Luke 20:27–38, occurs in the south, where, too, there is much more frequent mention of "priests" and "chief priests," exactly what one would expect from an accurate historian.

3. The other references to the Sadducees in the Gospels are all in Matthew (3:7; 16:1, 6, 11, 12),

exactly as might be expected of a writer who often relies on the understanding of his Jewish readers.

4. Pharisees and Sadducees may here be lumped together because they represent the Sanhedrin, which included both groups (cf. Ac 23:6), or because a common opponent transforms enemies into friends (cf. Lk 23:12; cf. Ps 2:2). Also, Matthew elsewhere distinguishes between the two groups (22:33–34; see Introduction, section 11.f).

These men came to Jesus to "test" him (see comments at 4:1, 7; cf. 19:3; 22:18, 35), asking for "a sign from heaven" (see comments at 12:38).

2–3 Jesus' words here are omitted by a small but important group of witnesses. Jerome reports that most MSS known to him omit the words, and many scholars consider them an assimilation to Luke 12:54–56. But if that were so, one wonders why the wording is not closer. Lagrange, Metzger (*Textual Commentary*, 41), and others have postulated that the words are original but were dropped from some MSS by scribes living in climates such as Egypt, where a red sky in the morning (v.3) does not presage rain. The evidence is rather finely balanced, and it is probably best to include the words. If so, Jesus' point is clear enough: the Pharisees and Sadducees can read the "signs" that predict weather, but they remain oblivious to the "signs of the times" already happening. Here these "signs of the times" point neither to the future nor (contra Hoekema, *Bible and the Future*, 133) to what God has done in the past. Instead, they testify to Jesus and the kingdom now dawning (cf. 11:4–6; 12:28). The proof that they cannot discern the "signs" is that they ask for a sign (v.1)! For those with eyes to see, the "signs of the times," if not the kind of "sign" the Pharisees and Sadducees demanded, were already abundant.

4 But if a definitive sign is demanded, none but the sign of Jonah will be given (see comments at 12:39). Mark 8:12 is no exception. In one sense, both evangelists are right, for the Jews would not have recognized Jonah as the kind of sign they were after (so there was no exception, Mark), even though that was the only definitive sign Jesus would allow (so there was an exception, Matthew). For exposition, see comments at 12:38–42.

Mark also says that Jesus "sighed deeply." The controversies were wearying. Jesus leaves his opponents and withdraws by boat to the other side of the lake (v.5) and points north (v.13). But his withdrawal is emotional and judicial as well as geographical.

10. The yeast of the Pharisees and Sadducees (16:5–12)

OVERVIEW

This is Jesus' last and most important withdrawal from Galilee before his final trip south (19:1), and it continues to 17:20. Close comparison of these verses with Mark 8:13–21 shows significant differences. In particular, (1) Matthew omits Mark 8:17b–18; (2) Matthew 16:9–11a shortens and rearranges Mark 8:19–21; (3) Matthew adds vv.11b–12; and (4) Matthew refers to the yeast of the Pharisees and Sadducees, but Mark to the yeast of the Pharisees and of Herod.

What do we make of these differences? Some writers (e.g., Barth, "Matthew's Understanding of the Law," 114–16; Strecker [*Weg der Gerechtigkeit*, 193]; Zumstein [*La condition du croyant*, 203]) argue that Matthew minimizes the disciples' lack of understanding, so pronounced in Mark, and separates understanding from faith (see comments at 13:10–15). Though the differences must not be minimized, the question is: What prompts them?

The single-strand theological motivation advanced by many is reductionistic, when on the face of it numerous factors must be weighed.

1. Commentators on Mark complain that Mark 8:13–21 lacks cohesion or is verbose. In part, Matthew, as usual, is simply tightening things up and condensing his source.

2. Matthew 16:9 is still very negative. The disciples do not understand (a verb no weaker than the one used in Mark 8:17–18).

3. When they finally do understand (v.12), it is as a result of Jesus' explanation—as in the case of the parables (13:36–43; 15:15–16). The disciples are *beginning* to understand (Trotter, "Understanding and Stumbling"), exactly as we might expect from their position in salvation history.

4. Far from driving a wedge between faith and understanding, the charge in vv.8–9a links them. Yet faith in Christ is made the prerequisite to understanding Jesus' remark (see comments at 13:34–35). This makes explicit what is merely implicit in Mark.

5. Matthew's distinctive emphases, as compared with Mark, are two: first, he takes the story to the point where the disciples do achieve some understanding, whereas Mark leaves the outcome hanging. This rounded-off conclusion is typical of Matthew (see comments at 15:20). Second, in Matthew, Jesus specifies that the "yeast" metaphor refers to the "teaching" of the Pharisees and Sadducees, whereas in Mark it extends to Herod but is not explained. From the context of Mark we may deduce that yeast refers to "the disposition to believe only if signs which compel faith are produced" (Lane, *Mark*, 281), evidenced by the Pharisees in the preceding pericope and by Herod a short while before (Mt 14:1–2; Mk 6:14). Matthew may not be very different. Jesus is surely not telling his disciples to beware of *all* the teaching of the Pharisees and Sadducees. These two groups did not always agree, and Jesus can stand with the Sadducees against the Pharisees on the authority of halakah (rules of conduct derived from interpretations of Scripture, preserved in oral tradition) and with the Pharisees against the Sadducees on the resurrection (22:23–33). The "teaching of the Pharisees and Sadducees" to which Jesus refers (vv.5–12), therefore, is an attitude of unbelief toward divine revelation that could not perceive Jesus to be the Messiah (vv.1–4) but that tried to control and tame the Messiah they claimed to await. The disciples are to avoid that. This is why the next pericope (vv.13–20) is so important: Peter makes the confession that Jesus is the Messiah, not on the basis of manipulative signs, but by revelation from the Father.

5When they went across the lake, the disciples forgot to take bread. 6"Be careful," Jesus
said to them. "Be on your guard against the yeast of the Pharisees and Sadducees."
7They discussed this among themselves and said, "It is because we didn't bring any
bread."
8Aware of their discussion, Jesus asked, "You of little faith, why are you talking among
yourselves about having no bread? 9Do you still not understand? Don't you remember the
five loaves for the five thousand, and how many basketfuls you gathered? 10Or the seven
loaves for the four thousand, and how many basketfuls you gathered? 11How is it you

don't understand that I was not talking to you about bread? But be on your guard against the yeast of the Pharisees and Sadducees." [12]Then they understood that he was not telling them to guard against the yeast used in bread, but against the teaching of the Pharisees and Sadducees.

COMMENTARY

5–7 The setting may be the boat in which Jesus and his disciples cross the lake (v.5; see Notes). The conversation reveals the contrasting attitudes of Jesus and his disciples. He is still thinking about the malignity of the Pharisees and Sadducees (vv.1–4), and the disciples are thinking about food (15:29–38), which they forgot to bring. Mark 8:14 says they were down to one loaf. (For "Pharisees and Sadducees" governed by one article, see comments at v.1.)

"Yeast" (v.6) was a common symbol for evil (see comments at 13:33) and could therefore be applied to different kinds of wickedness (e.g., Lk 12:1; cf. Ex 34:25; Lev 2:11; 1Co 5:6–8), but always with the idea that a little of it could have a far-reaching and insidious effect. The disciples do not understand what Jesus is saying but find his words enigmatic and discuss them (v.7).

8–12 Because they were men of little faith (v.8; cf. 6:30; 8:26; 14:31), they came to an unimaginative conclusion (v.7; see Notes). Jesus could not have been talking about bread because he had already shown his power to provide all the bread they needed (vv.9–10; cf. 14:13–21; 15:32–39). He had performed two "food" miracles, and there had been basketfuls of leftovers each time.

Jesus' charge (v.11) against the disciples ran deep. Jesus had already denounced the Pharisees and Sadducees for their particular "teaching" that demanded manipulative signs instead of believing in the bountiful evidence already supplied. And now the disciples are perilously close to the same unbelief in Jesus' person and miracles. The miracles Jesus performs, unlike the signs the Pharisees demand, do not compel faith; but those with faith will perceive their significance. Moreover, it is just possible that Jesus was asking his disciples to recognize symbolic meaning in the numbers of leftover baskets, here reiterated (see comments at 14:20; 15:37). Jesus is the Messiah who spreads bounty and invites both the twelve tribes of Israel and the Gentiles to his messianic banquet. But whether or not this thought is valid, Jesus' criticism of his disciples was sharp.

Instead of explaining the meaning of his metaphor of the yeast, Jesus repeats it in both Matthew and Mark. This suggests that, great teacher that he is, he is trying to train his disciples to think deeply about the revelation he is giving and is not content to keep on spoon-feeding them. Only Matthew provides the interpretation (v.12); Mark leaves it to the reader to discern (but cf. Mt 15:19–20 and Mk 7:19).

NOTES

5 The NASB handles the tenses awkwardly: "The disciples came to the other side and had forgotten to take bread" (similarly ESV). The verb ἔρχομαι (*erchomai*, GK *2262*) can mean "I come" as well as "I go," and its aorist participle ἐλθόντες (*elthontes*) can indicate either action antecedent to ("having come," "having gone") or coordinate with ("coming," "going") the main verb. The NIV's "When they went ..., the disciples forgot" is coherent and renders the verbs accurately.

7 The ὅτι (*hoti*) could be (1) recitative: the disciples said, "We didn't bring any bread"; (2) causal: the disciples said, "[It is] because we didn't bring any bread"; or (3) an abbreviated form of τί ἐστιν ὅτι (*ti estin hoti*), introducing a question, "Why did we bring no bread?" In light of v.7a, where the disciples discuss Jesus' enigmatic saying among themselves, the second option is to be preferred.

11. Peter's confession of Jesus and its aftermath (16:13–23)

a. The confession (16:13–20)

OVERVIEW

Broadly speaking, Matthew and Mark treat Peter's confession similarly. All three Synoptics (cf. Mk 8:27–30; Lk 9:19–21) immediately follow it by Jesus' prediction of his sufferings, a theme Matthew develops (17:12, 22–23; 20:17–19). (For questions of structure, see comments at v.21; Introduction, section 14.)

The connections between this key passage and the rest of Matthew are intricate. Some have already been dealt with (see comments at vv.5–12). Peter recognizes Jesus as the Messiah by revelation, not by signs Peter dictates and thus uses to manipulate the Messiah. That Jesus is the Messiah leads inexorably to his self-disclosure as the suffering Messiah (vv.21–23), a theme anticipated earlier (see comments at 8:17; 10:24–25; 12:15–21). Moreover, the suffering of the Servant is not only redemptive (20:28) but exemplary (vv.24–26). Therefore, the fourth discourse (18:3–35) is grounded in Christology.

Peter's role in this passage has been analyzed hundreds of times and is further discussed below. At the risk of oversimplification, we may classify the positions defended in this century into two classes. The first thinks of Peter as a "typical" disciple who speaks for the other disciples, who in turn represent all believers. Thus, everything said about Peter becomes a lesson for all Christians (e.g., Strecker, *Weg der Gerechtigkeit*, 205). The second sees Peter as in some way unique. He becomes a kind of supreme rabbi on whom Jesus builds his church, a rabbi who guarantees and transmits the traditions of Jesus in Matthew's church (cf. esp. Hummel, *Auseinandersetzung*, 59ff.; C. Kahler, "Zur Form- und Traditionsgeschichte von Matth. xvi.17–19," *NTS* 23 [1977]: 36–58).

In a balanced essay, J. D. Kingsbury ("The Figure of Peter in Matthew's Gospel as a Theological Problem," *JBL* 98 [1979]: 67–83) has shown how both alternatives distort the text. The second will not stand. Matthew's gospel insists that only Jesus is to be called rabbi (23:8, 10) and that after his resurrection he himself will remain with his disciples to the end of the age (28:20; cf. 18:20). Moreover, if Peter is given power to bind and loose, so also is the church (18:18); and all of Jesus' followers are to be involved in discipling and teaching the nations (28:18–19). Yet the first view is also simplistic. Matthew 16:16–17 is intensely personal, not merely representative. Whatever the precise meaning of these verses, Matthew presents Peter as the "first" disciple to be called (4:18–20; 10:2–4) and now the first one truly to understand that Jesus is the promised Messiah, the Son of God. So these passages honor his "salvation-historical primacy" (Kingsbury's expression; cf. his "Figure of Peter"), and we must not do less.

For brief comments on problems connected with the authenticity of vv.17–19, see below.

[13]When Jesus came to the region of Caesarea Philippi, he asked his disciples, "Who do people say the Son of Man is?"

[14]They replied, "Some say John the Baptist; others say Elijah; and still others, Jeremiah or one of the prophets."

[15]"But what about you?" he asked. "Who do you say I am?"

[16]Simon Peter answered, "You are the Christ, the Son of the living God."

[17]Jesus replied, "Blessed are you, Simon son of Jonah, for this was not revealed to you
by man, but by my Father in heaven. [18]And I tell you that you are Peter, and on this rock
I will build my church, and the gates of Hades will not overcome it. [19]I will give you the
keys of the kingdom of heaven; whatever you bind on earth will be bound in heaven, and
whatever you loose on earth will be loosed in heaven." [20]Then he warned his disciples not
to tell anyone that he was the Christ.

COMMENTARY

13 Caesarea Philippi was built by Herod Philip the tetrarch (cf. 2:20, 22), who enlarged a small town on a terrace 1150 feet above sea level at the base of Mount Hermon, renaming it in honor of Caesar, "Philippi" being added to distinguish it from the coastal city of the same name. It lies twenty-five miles north of Galilee. Snow-capped Mount Hermon can be seen on a clear day from as far away as Nazareth, where Jesus grew up. The inhabitants were largely Gentile. Though Jesus exercised some broader ministry here (17:14; cf. Mk 8:34), primarily he gave himself to the Twelve. Matthew omits Mark's casual details (Mk 8:27).

In Mark and Luke, Jesus' question leaves out the "Son of Man": "Who do people say I am?" (For the title, see Reflections, p. 247.) This clear self-designation must have been somewhat ambiguous or else Jesus' question would have been fatuous. Which form of the question is original is not certain. But the fact that only Jesus uses the title in the Gospels, and that it can serve as a self-designation with some ambiguous messianic significance, favors the view that Matthew is original, while Mark and Luke preserve the self-designation ("I") but delete the title for fear that their non-Jewish readers, who have learned to see messianic significance in it but not Jesus' self-designation, might think the question odd.

14 Opinion on Jesus' identity was divided. Some thought he was John the Baptist risen from the dead—Herod Antipas's view (14:2). Those who thought he was Elijah saw him as forerunner to a Messiah still to come (see comments at 3:1–3; 11:9–10; 17:10–13; cf. Mal 4:5–6). Only Matthew mentions Jeremiah, the first of the so-called latter prophets in the Hebrew canon (see comments at 27:9–10). There may have been late Jewish traditions about Jeremiah's death that supported this identification (cf. 2 Macc 2:1–12; 15:14–15), and it is possible that some onlookers had been struck by the mixture of authority and suffering characteristic of Jesus' ministry and well exemplified by Jeremiah (cf. Bonnard). J. Carmignac ("Pourquoi Jérémie est-il mentionné en Matthieu 16:14?" in *Tradition und Glaube* [ed. G. Jeremias et al.; Göttingen: Vandenhoeck & Ruprecht, 1971], 283–98) suggests that Jesus, like Jeremiah, must have seemed to many like a prophet of doom because of his negative prognosis for Israel. The promise that both Isaiah and Jeremiah would be sent comes from a later source (*5 Ezra* 2:18) that is probably dependent on Matthew (cf. Stanton, *Gospel for a New People*, 269–70). On the entire question as to why Jeremiah should be listed as one of the options advanced by the disciples, see Knowles, *Jeremiah in Matthew's Gospel*, 82–95.

"One of the prophets" testifies to the diversity of eschatological expectations in Jesus' day, some of the people expecting a long series of prophetic forerunners. But no group was openly and thoughtfully confessing Jesus as Messiah. Probably aberrations such as 9:27; 15:22 were considered extravagant devices used by desperate people, not maliciously, but in deep hope that their own needs might be met. What we must recognize is that christological confession was not cut-and-dried, black or white. It was possible to address Jesus with some messianic title without complete conviction, or while still holding some major misconceptions about the nature of his messiahship, and therefore stopping short of unqualified allegiance or outright confession. If Peter had some misconception (vv. 22–23), how much more misconception would there be in disciples outside the Twelve? Thus, confessions like those in 9:27; 15:22 may not be so surprising.

15–16 The "you" is emphatic and plural (v.15). Therefore, at least in part, Peter serves as spokesman for the Twelve (as he often does: cf. 15:15–16; 19:25–28; 26:40; Mk 11:20–22; Lk 12:41; Jn 6:67–70; cf. Ac 2:37–38; 5:29). Peter's confession (v.16) is direct: "You are the Christ" (Mark 8:29); "The Christ of God" (Luke 9:20); "You are the Christ, the Son of the living God" (Matthew). (For discussion about Messiah = Christ, see comments at 1:1.)

Majority opinion assigns "the Son of the living God" to Matthean redaction, a sort of explanatory gloss. Yet this may be premature. Ben F. Meyer (*Aims of Jesus*, 185–97) has given good reason for accepting Matthew's form as authentic: (1) It better explains the genesis of the other forms, not only in Mark and Luke but also "the Holy One of God" in John 6:69, than does Mark's "You are the Christ"; (2) "Son of God" may well have had purely messianic significance in Peter's mind (see comments at 3:17; 11:27; 14:33), even though it came to indicate divinity (cf. Bonnard; see Reflections, pp. 251–52); and (3) other details in this pericope support Matthew's priority (see comments at vv.17–19). Guthrie (*New Testament Theology*, 305–6) reminds us that since the other synoptists record the application of "Son of God" to Jesus in other contexts, it is not intrinsically unlikely here.

17–19 Many scholars doubt the authenticity of these verses because they are missing in Mark and Luke. We may note that in addition to positions that simply deny that these words are authentic (e.g., Bultmann, *Theology of the New Testament*, 1:45), there are more sophisticated options. O. Cullmann (*Peter: Disciple-Apostle-Martyr* [London: SCM Press, 1953], 158–70) holds that the *saying* is authentic but not the *setting*, which originally lay during the passion period, in some such place as Luke 22:31–38. R. E. Brown et al. (*Peter in the New Testament*, 85ff.) argue that the origin of this saying lies in some tradition on the resurrection. Max Wilcox ("Peter and the Rock: A Fresh Look at Matthew xvi.17–19," *NTS* 22 [1976]: 73–88) believes that these verses spring from some ecclesiastical linking of Jesus as the Son with the "rejected stone" and related testimonia (Ps 118:22–23; Isa 8:14; 28:16), and that the possibility of linking "stone" with Peter's name prompted the transfer of this category from Jesus to Peter. Critical orthodoxy largely concurs that "church" is an anachronism; that the omission of the word "this" in the Greek text of Matthew 16:17 suggests that the words did not originally stand here (so Cullmann); and that words such as "blessed," "my Father," and "in heaven" are characteristically Matthean and are therefore probably inauthentic.

But Ben F. Meyer (*Aims of Jesus*, 185–97) has mounted a detailed defense of the authenticity of vv.17–19. Some of his points, plus one or two others, are included below.

1. "Blessed" is not exclusively Matthean, and "my Father in heaven" no more vitiates the authenticity of this saying than it does the authenticity of the opening line of the Lord's Prayer (6:9). This is so of any view of the relation between 6:9–13 and Luke 11:2–4, since a redactional formulation says nothing about authenticity unless we are thinking in terms only of *ipsissima verba*, not *ipsissima vox* (see Notes, 3:17).

2. The omission of "this" from the Greek in v.17 does not prove the saying was moved from some other place. Greek transitive verbs often omit the direct object where it is obvious. The verb in question, *apokalyptō* ("I reveal," GK *636*), is used transitively seven other times in the NT. Three of these require for clarity inclusion of the direct object. Of the remaining four (11:27; Lk 10:22; 1Co 2:10; Php 3:15), where the meaning is so clear that no direct object must be included, only one has it (Php 3:15). Matthew 16:17 fits the majority usage.

3. The use of "church" is not anachronistic; see comments at v.18.

4. Meyer (pp. 189–90) advances good reasons for doubting Mark's priority in this pericope but rightly points out that even if Matthew depends on Mark, this says nothing at all about the historical value of Matthew's redaction (pp. 71–72; see Introduction, sections 1–3).

5. The verb "reveal" has its closest links, not with any resurrection text, but with 11:25, where, as in v.17, "the Father's revealing is correlative to the insight of faith, and the correlation 'revelation/faith' is placed in the present of the ministry" (Meyer, p. 192). Similar things can be said for the next closest parallel, namely, 11:27.

Though the history of the interpretation of these verses is even more tortuous than the recent history of critical opinion about them, part of it has been well chronicled by Joseph A. Burgess (*A History of the Exegesis of Matthew 16:17–19 from 1781 to 1965* [Ann Arbor, Mich.: Edwards Brothers, 1976]).

17 For "Blessed," see comments at 5:3. Jesus is the "Son of the living God" (v.16); Peter is the "son of Jonah" (see Notes). Yet Jesus' Father has revealed to Peter the truth he has just confessed. Indeed, no one knows the Son except the Father (11:27; cf. Jn 6:44), who has now graciously revealed his identity to Peter. Such knowledge could not have originated in "flesh and blood"—a common Jewish expression referring to man as a mortal being (cf. 1Co 15:50; Gal 1:16; Eph 6:12; Heb 2:14; cf. Sir 14:18; 17:31.) We must neither minimize nor exaggerate this revelation of the Father to Peter. Similar confessions by others do not necessarily evoke similar theological conclusions (e.g., 21:9; 27:54); so Peter's confession assumes a God-given insight deeper than these. The formal parallel to Galatians 1:16 prompts Sim (*Gospel of Matthew*, 200–203) to find, once again, evidence of anti-Pauline polemic. One cannot help but reflect that B. P. Robinson ("Peter and His Successors: Tradition and Redaction in Matthew 16:17–19," *JSNT* 21 [1984]: 85–104) argues that Paul in Galatians 1:16 is dependent, rather, on precisely the kind of tradition here preserved in v.17 (noted also by France [NICNT]).

On the other hand, we need not suppose that the idea that Jesus was Messiah was here entering the apostles' minds for the first time. If so, Jesus' closest disciples were remarkably obtuse (see comments at 5:17–48; 7:21–23; 11:2–6). John's witness is surely sound. The disciples began following Jesus in the hope that he was the Messiah (Jn 1:41, 45, 49). But their understanding of the nature of Jesus' messiahship was hindered by their own expectations (see comments at vv.21–23), and they did not come into a full "Christian" understanding until after Easter. This verse marks a crucial stage along that growth in understanding and faith. Partial as it was, Peter's firm grasp of the fact that Jesus is the Messiah set him apart from the uncertainty and confusion of the crowd and could only be the result of the Father's disclosure. Indeed, the depth of Peter's conviction was the very thing that simultaneously made talk of Jesus' suffering and death difficult to integrate and prevented more serious defection when the one confessed as Messiah went to his death on a Roman cross.

18 *And I tell you* ...: Bernhard Weiss (*Das Matthäus-Evangelium* [Göttingen: Vandenhoeck & Ruprecht, 1898]) sees a contrast between Jesus and his Father, as if Jesus were saying, "Just as the *Father* revealed something to you and thereby honored you, so now I do the same." But the formula is common enough in places without such a contrast, and this may be an unwarranted refinement. The words simply point to what is coming.

that you are Peter ...: The underlying Aramaic *kêpāʾ* ("Cephas" in Jn 1:42; 1Co 15:5; Gal 1:18; et al.) was an accepted name in Jesus' day (see comments at 4:18). Though Ben F. Meyer (pp. 186–87) insists that Jesus gave the name "Cephas" to Simon at this point, Jesus merely made a pun on the name (4:18; 10:2; Mk 3:16; Jn 1:42). Yet Meyer is right to draw attention to the "rock" motifs on which the name Cephas is based (pp. 85–86, 194–95), motifs related to the netherworld and the temple (and so connoting images of "gates of Hades" and "church"; see below). The Greek *Kēphas* (Eng. "Cephas") transliterates the Aramaic, and *Petros* ("Peter") is the closest Greek translation. P. Lampe's argument ("Das Spiel mit dem Petrusnamen—Matt. xvi.18," *NTS* 25 [1979]: 227–45) that both *kêpāʾ* and *petros* originally referred to a small "stone," but not a "rock" (on which something could be built), until Christians extended the term to explain the riddle of Simon's name, is baseless. True, *petros* commonly means "stone" in pre-Christian literature, but the Aramaic *kêpāʾ*, which underlies the Greek, means "(massive) rock" (cf. H. Clavier, "Πέτρος καὶ πέτρα," *Neutestamentliche Studien* [ed. W. Eltester; Berlin: Topelmann, 1957], 101–3).

and on this rock ...: "Rock" now becomes *petra* (feminine), and on the basis of the distinction between *petros* (above) and *petra* (here), many have attempted to avoid identifying Peter as the rock on which Jesus builds his church. Peter is a mere "stone," it is alleged, but Jesus himself is the "rock," as Peter attests (1Pe 2:5–8) (so, among others, Lenski, Walvoord). Others adopt some other distinction; e.g., "upon this rock of revealed truth—the truth you have just confessed—I will build my church" (Allen). Yet if it were not for Protestant reactions against extremes of Roman Catholic interpretation, it is doubtful whether many would have taken "rock" to be anything or anyone other than Peter.

1. Although it is true that *petros* and *petra* can mean "stone" and "rock" respectively in earlier Greek, the distinction is largely confined to poetry. Moreover, the underlying Aramaic in this case is unquestionable, and most probably *kêpāʾ* was used in both clauses ("you are *kêpāʾ*, and on this *kêpāʾ*"), since the word was used both for a name and for a "rock." The Peshitta (written in Syriac, a language cognate with Aramaic) makes no distinction between the words in the two clauses. The Greek

makes the distinction between *petros* and *petra* simply because it is trying to preserve the pun, and in Greek the feminine *petra* could not very well serve as a masculine name. For a full discussion of the linguistic issues, see Chrys C. Caragounis, *Peter and the Rock* (BZNW 58; Berlin: de Gruyter, 1989), 9–16.

2. Paronomasia of various kinds is very common in the Bible and should not be belittled (cf. Barry J. Beitzel, "Exodus 3:14 and the Divine Name: A Case of Biblical Paronomasia," *TJ* 1 [1980]: 5–20; BDF, para. 488).

3. Had Matthew wanted to say no more than that Peter was a stone in contrast with Jesus the Rock, the more common word would have been *lithos* ("stone" of almost any size). Then there would have been no pun—and that is just the point!

4. The objection that Peter considers Jesus the rock is insubstantial because metaphors are commonly used variously, until they become stereotyped, and sometimes even then. Here Jesus builds his church; in 1 Corinthians 3:10, Paul is "an expert builder." In 1 Corinthians 3:11, Jesus is the church's foundation; in Ephesians 2:19–20, the apostles and prophets are the foundation (cf. Rev 21:14), and Jesus is the "cornerstone." Here Peter has the keys; in Revelation 1:18; 3:7, Jesus has the keys. In John 9:5, Jesus is "the light of the world"; in Matthew 5:14, his disciples are. None of these pairs threatens Jesus' uniqueness. They simply show how metaphors must be interpreted primarily with reference to their immediate contexts.

5. In this passage Jesus is the builder of the church, and it would be a strange mixture of metaphors that also sees him within the same clauses as its foundation.

None of this requires that conservative Roman Catholic views be endorsed (for examples of such views, cf. Lagrange, Sabourin). The text says nothing about Peter's successors, infallibility, or exclusive authority. These late interpretations entail insuperable exegetical and historical problems—e.g., after Peter's death, his "successor" would have authority over a surviving apostle, John. What the NT does show is that Peter is the first to make this formal confession and that his prominence continues in the earliest years of the church (Ac 1–12). But he, along with John, can be sent by other apostles (Ac 8:14), and he is held accountable for his actions by the Jerusalem church (Ac 11:1–18) and rebuked by Paul (Gal 2:11–14). He is, in short, *primus inter pares* ("first among equals"), and on the foundation of such men (Eph 2:20), Jesus built his church. That is precisely why Jesus, toward the close of his earthly ministry, spent so much time with them. The honor was not earned but stemmed from divine revelation (v.17) and Jesus' building work (v.18).

I will build my church ...: The term *ekklēsia* ("church," GK *1711*) occurs only here and at 18:17 in the Gospels. Etymologically, it springs from the verb *ekkaleō* ("call out from") and refers to those who are "called out"; but usage is far more important than etymology in determining meaning. In the NT, *ekklēsia* can refer to assemblies of people in a nonreligious setting (Ac 19:39), and once it refers to God's OT people, the "church" in the desert at the giving of the law (Ac 7:38; cf. Heb 2:12). But in Acts and in the Epistles it usually refers to Christian congregations or to all God's people redeemed by Christ. Therefore R. Bultmann ("Die Frage nach der Echtheit von Mt 16:17–19," *TBl* 20 [1941]: 265–79) argues that the use of *ekklēsia* in Matthew 16:18; 18:17 cannot be authentic. It refers to a practicing group of Christians, a separate community, or a Christian synagogue in contrast to the Jewish synagogues, and is presided over by Peter.

K. L. Schmidt (*TDNT*, 3:525) suggests that the Aramaic term behind *ekklēsia* in Matthew is a late term, *k*^{e}*nîštāʾ*, which could mean either "the people [of God]" or "a [separate] synagogue." In fact, the strongest linguistic evidence runs in another direction. Whenever *ekklēsia* in the LXX is translating Hebrew, the Hebrew word is *qāhāl* ("assembly," "meeting," "gathering," GK 7736), with reference to various kinds of "assemblies" (cf. *THAT*, 2:610–19), but increasingly used to refer to God's people, the assembly of Yahweh.

The Hebrew *qāhāl* has a broad semantic range and is not always rendered *ekklēsia*; sometimes in the LXX it is translated "synagogue" or "crowd." "Synagogue" customarily translates an entirely different Hebrew word (*ʿēdâ*, "corporate congregation," GK 6337), which the LXX never translates *ekklēsia* (on these words, see *NIDNTT*, 1:292–96). Thus *ekklēsia* ("church") is entirely appropriate in Matthew 16:18; 18:17, where there is no emphasis on institution, organization, form of worship, or separate synagogue. Even the idea of "building" a people springs from the OT (Ru 4:11; 2Sa 7:13–14; 1Ch 17:12–13; Pss 28:5; 118:22; Jer 1:10; 24:6; 31:4; 33:7; Am 9:11). "Jesus' announcement of his purpose to build his *ekklēsia* suggests ... that the fellowship established by Jesus stands in direct continuity with the Old Testament Israel" (Ladd, *Theology of the New Testament*, 110), construed as the faithful remnant with the eyes of faith to come to terms with the new revelation. Acknowledged as Messiah, Jesus responds that he will build his *ekklēsia*, his people, his church—which is classic messianism. "It is hard to know what kind of thinking, other than confessional presupposition, justifies the tendency of some commentators to dismiss this verse as not authentic. A Messiah without a messianic community would have been unthinkable to any Jew" (Albright and Mann, 195).

Implicitly, then, the verse also embraces a claim to messiahship. The "people of Yahweh" become the people of Messiah (cf. 13:41). If the Qumran community thinks of itself as the "people of the covenant," Jesus speaks of his followers as *his* people—his church—who come, in time, to see themselves as people of the new covenant established by Messiah's blood (26:28).

Jesus' "church" is not the same as his "kingdom" (contra Hill). The two words belong to different concepts, the one to "people" and the other to "rule" or "reign" (see comments at 13:28–30, 36–43). But neither must they be opposed to each other, as if both cannot occupy the same place in time (contra Walvoord). The messianic reign is calling out the messianic people. The kingdom has been inaugurated; the people are being gathered. So far as the kingdom has been inaugurated in advance of its consummation, so far also is Jesus' church an outpost in history of the final eschatological community. "The implication is inescapable that, in the establishment of the church, there was to be a manifestation of the kingdom or rule of God" (Stonehouse, *Witness of Matthew*, 235). When the kingdom is consummated, then Messiah's "assembly" shall also attain the richest blessings Messiah's reign can give. Nothing, therefore, can eliminate Messiah's church or prevent it from reaching that consummation.

and the gates of Hades will not overcome it. On Hades, see *NIDNTT*, 2:206–8; Str-B, 4:1016–29; comments at 5:22; 11:23. The "gates of Hades" have been taken to represent the strength of Satan and his cohorts (since "gates" can refer to "fortifications," Ge 22:17; Ps 127:5): the church, because Jesus is building it, cannot be defeated by the hosts of darkness. Other scholars focus not on "gates" but on "Hades" and, turning to Revelation 1:18, think this means that death will not prevent Messiah's people from rising at the last day. But "gates of Hades" or very similar expressions are found in canonical literature (Job 17:16; 38:17; Pss 9:13; 107:18; Isa 38:10), noncanonical Jewish literature (Wis 16:13; 3 Macc 5:51; *Pss. Sol.* 16:2), and pagan literature (Homer, *Il.* 9.312; *Od.* 11.277; Aeschylus, *Ag.* 1291; Euripides, *Hec.* 1), and seem to refer to death and dying. Hence the RSV: "The powers of death shall not prevail against it." Because the church is the assembly of people Jesus Messiah is building, it cannot die. This claim is ridiculous if Jesus is nothing but an overconfident popular preacher in an unimportant vassal state of first-century Rome. It is the basis of all hope for those who see Jesus as the Messiah who builds his people.

19 *I will give you the keys of the kingdom of heaven*: As in v.18, the promise goes beyond the days of Jesus' earthly ministry. What Jesus' disciples thought this meant at the time is uncertain. Perhaps they hoped that when Jesus established his earthly reign and defeated the Romans, they would hold major posts under his reign (cf. Bonnard). In the postresurrection period, the nature of this inaugurated kingdom became progressively clearer. Hannan (*Nature and Demands*, 143) is correct to observe that "the power Jesus grants with these keys must also be connected with the authority to interpret the Law correctly as Jesus himself has done."

Here, as in 7:21, the "kingdom" (see comments at 3:2; 5:3) is to be entered. The metaphor therefore changes. From being the rock-foundation of the church, Peter now becomes the one who wields the keys of the kingdom (as Alexander points out, the metaphor would be equally mixed if Jesus-rock-foundation "gives" the keys). The person with the keys has power to exclude or permit entrance (cf. Rev 9:1–6; 20:1–3). There may be an allusion here to the chief stewards of monarchs (Isa 22:15, 22). But we cannot go on without understanding the binding and loosing to which the keys are related.

whatever you bind … loosed in heaven …: Five separate and difficult questions must be considered to understand the force of this verse, and some answers must be tentative.

1. How are the future periphrastic perfects to be translated? The answers to the question are multifaceted, sometimes mutually contradictory, and in any case complex. During most of the twentieth century, the debate circled around whether or not the perfect tense is invariably used to signal action or state that has come about in the past with continuing effect. In 1938, J. R. Mantey ("The Mistranslation of the Perfect Tense in John 20:23, Matthew 16:19, and Matthew 18:18," *JBL* 58 [1939]: 243–49) argued that the perfects in all three instances must have their "normal" force (under the assumption, of course, that this temporal configuration is "normal"). The finite perfect in John 20:23 must be rendered "If you forgive anyone his sins, they have already been forgiven"; and when the perfect participle is given its "normal" force in the Matthean passages, the periphrastic future perfect in v.19 becomes "whatever you bind on earth *shall have been bound* in heaven, and whatever you loose on earth *shall have been loosed* in heaven" (similarly for 18:18). Mantey tied his understanding of the Greek perfect to the thesis that there is no evidence for "sacerdotalism or priestly absolution" in the NT.

In the same issue of *JBL*, H. J. Cadbury ("The Meaning of John 20:23, Matthew 16:19, and Matthew 18:18," 251–54) noted that the six perfects or future perfects in the three passages all occur in the apodosis of a general condition. The question, then, is "whether a perfect in the apodosis indicates an action or condition prior to the time of the apodosis" (p. 251); citing 1 John 2:5; James 2:10; Romans 13:8; 14:23, along with certain grammarians (e.g., BDF, para. 344; *Grammar*, 897–98, 908), he denied that this must be so. Although he thought the future an acceptable translation here, he suggested that in Matthew the perfects have the force "shall be once for all" (cf. Allen's "Whatsoever thou bindest *shall remain bound*, etc.," 177).

The matter was picked up by W. T. Dayton ("The Greek Perfect Tense in Relation to John 20:23, Matthew 16:19, and Matthew 18:18" [ThD diss., Northern Baptist Theological Seminary, 1945]) and once more by J. R. Mantey ("Evidence That the Perfect Tense in John 20:23 and Matthew 16:19 Is Mistranslated," *JETS* 16 [1973]: 129–38). Both works are marred by the tendency to cite quotations from grammarians in their favor without a fair handling of counterarguments. Of greater use are Dayton's short lists of periphrastic future perfects in Strabo, Lucian, and some papyri, for all these retain "normal" perfect force, even when used in the apodosis of a general condition. This is valuable comparative material, since periphrastic future perfects in the NT are rather rare, and there are no finite future perfects at all.

Before pursuing the grammatical question, it must be noted that, regardless of whether v.19 is translated as an English future perfect or as an English future, scholars have at times tried to bleed a bit too much theology out of their grammatical conclusions. For instance, if the tense is translated as a future ("shall be bound"), the passage could be taken to justify some form of extreme sacerdotalism without unambiguous defense elsewhere in the NT. But if it is translated as a future perfect ("shall have been bound"), it could be taken to support the notion that the disciple must therefore enjoy infallible communication from God in every question of "binding and loosing," a communication that is the role of the so-called charismatic gifts. Paul Elbert ("The Perfect Tense in Matthew 16:19 and Three Charismata," *JETS* 17 [1974]: 149–55) introduces them here with no sensitivity to broader questions of context, awareness of anachronism, or consciousness that the gifts do not provide infallible guidance (cf. 1Co 14:29). But in neither case do these conclusions *necessarily* follow. More moderate interpretations of both grammatical options are possible. The truth is that neither sacerdotalism nor a set of charismatic assumptions will stand or fall by these texts alone, though it may be helped or hindered by them.

Commentators and grammarians from the middle of the twentieth century on are divided on this question. Hendriksen, who finds Mantey's way of taking the perfects "artificial," opts for "shall be and shall definitely remain bound/loosed," a variation of Allen—and Hendriksen can scarcely be called a sacerdotalist. Many grammarians treat the perfect participle in this construction as little more than an adjective, with little "normal" perfect sense remaining (K. L. McKay, "On the Perfect and Other Aspects in New Testament Greek," *NovT* 23 [1981]: 289–329); Moule, *Idiom Book*, 18; cf. Lk 12:52, where it is very difficult to find any "normal" perfect force at all ["there will be ... divided": the parallel future passive in the next verse makes this clear]). But Turner (*Grammatical Insights*, 80–82; *Syntax*, 82) challenges these views. In disagreeing with Allen and Hendriksen, he points out that the future force is restricted to the auxiliary verb *estai* ("will be") and is not found in the participle, which must retain its "normal" perfect sense, thereby agreeing with Mantey. Turner further argues that this is even clearer in John 20:23, where the finite perfect, not the periphrastic future perfect, is used. Similarly Albright and Mann say, "The church on earth carries out heaven's decisions, not heaven ratifying the church's decisions," which is something of a caricature of the options.

What Turner (*Syntax*, 82–83) and Zerwick (*Biblical Greek*, para. 288–89) argue is that where finite perfects have some force other than the "normal" perfect in the NT, they tend to be in well-known stereotyped forms: *oida* ("I know," not "I have known"); *pepoitha* ("I am persuaded"); *hestēka* ("I stand"). Similar is the periphrastic future perfect in Hebrews 2:13. Although *esomai pepoithōs* means "I will put my trust" (NIV), not "I will have put my trust," this participle commonly takes on perfect form with present meaning. Likewise, when the perfect has an aorist force (Zerwick, *Biblical Greek*, para. 288–89; as at 13:46), there are normally good reasons for it, as when the verb is defective and has no aorist form (cf. BDF, para. 340ff.).

In some ways, this discussion of the semantics of the perfect participle was overlooking an obvious point. From the eighteenth century on, grammarians largely abandoned the attempt to discern in each Greek tense, in every mood, some reflection of time. Rather, outside the indicative, *Aktionsart* ("kind of action") was said to be reflected in the tenses; time was preserved only in the indicative mood. By the twentieth century, this was an almost universal perception of how the Greek verbal system "works." It is hard to think of a major figure who would dispute this analysis for the aorist and the present tenses. So why was time controlling so much of the discussion of the perfect *participle* in Matthew 16:19?

From the end of the twentieth century to the present, however, analysis of the Greek verbal system became more and more focused on verbal aspect theory. (For readers who are familiar with this theory, my summary of the dominant options in the next paragraph or two will make sense; readers who have not yet come to grips with the linguistic terminology in which verbal aspect is discussed might want to skip a paragraph or two, as this is not the place to outline theories that have become subtle and complex.) As far as the perfect tense is concerned, however, under verbal aspect theory three options now dominate: (1) Some hold that the Greek perfect, in all moods, is perfective in aspect, though they do not agree on other semantic components. Buist M. Fanning (*Verbal Aspect in New Testament Greek* [Oxford: Clarendon, 1990]) argues the perfect is perfective in aspect, past in time, and stative in *Aktionsart*. Mari Broman Olsen (*A Semantic and Pragmatic Model of Lexical and Grammatical Aspect* [New York: Garland, 1997]) thinks the perfect is perfective in aspect and present in tense, and without stativity. (2) Others, such as Kenneth L. McKay (*A New Syntax of the Verb in New Testament Greek: An Aspectual Approach* [SBG 5; New York: Lang, 1994]) and Stanley E. Porter (*Verbal Aspect in the Greek of the New Testament, with Reference to Tense and Mood* [SBG 1; New York: Lang, 1989]), hold that the perfect tense encodes stativity only; i.e., it is stative in aspect. McKay and Porter disagree primarily on whether this "stative" category applies to the subject of the verb or to the action/state of the verb. (3) Two scholars hold that the Greek perfect is imperfective in aspect; i.e., they hold that the perfect tense depicts action internally, as though unfolding (T. V. Evans, *Verbal Syntax in the Greek Pentateuch: Natural Greek Usage and Hebrew Interference* [Oxford: Oxford Univ. Press, 2001]; Constantine R. Campbell, *Verbal Aspect, the Indicative Mood, and Narrative: Soundings in the Greek of the New Testament* [SBG 13; New York: Lang, 2007]). With some hesitations and minor adjustments, I hold that the second (McKay and Porter) is the most defensible position. That means the perfect tense does not *by itself* establish time relations, but the state or condition established by the lexis of the verb in interaction with the context. Temporal relations are established not by the tense itself but by a wide array of deictic markers.

This leads us to the following conclusion: Where questions dealing strictly with Greek syntax are asked, it seems impossible to reach a firm decision that will satisfy a majority of readers. Perhaps we can make a little progress by asking paradigmatic questions: Why was the Greek perfect (Jn 20:23) or the Greek periphrastic perfect (Mt 16:19) used instead of something else? In John, both perfect verbs have acceptable present and future tenses used elsewhere; neither verb exhibits a preferential pattern for the perfect. The perfect participles in the periphrastic constructions of Matthew 16:19; 18:18 are based on the two verbs *lyō* ("I loose," GK *3395*) and *deō* ("I bind," GK *1313*). Evidence regarding the latter is ambiguous; it often occurs as a perfect participle in the NT, sometimes as an aorist participle, never as a present participle; so one might hold that its perfect participle form has purely adjectival or present force in some instances—a debatable point. But the former is unambiguous. *Lyō* has a full range of forms, and it is difficult to see why Matthew did not use either the future or the present participle in a periphrastic future if he was merely trying to denote expectation of what is to be. This result spills over onto *deō* ("I bind"), since the two verbs are so tightly linked in these verses. If we think exclusively in temporal categories, the relevant expressions must either be rendered "shall be bound/loosed" or "shall have been bound/loosed." But if the perfect encodes stative aspect, then the apodosis tells us the state of affairs ("bound/loosed") *without necessary reference to time, apart from what is discerned from the context.* We might paraphrase the apodosis, with magnificent temporal ambiguity, "stands bound/loosed" or the like. But what does this mean? To answer the question we must bring into the discussion a further range of exegetical details.

2. Does the "whatever" (*ho*) refer to things or people? Formally *ho* is neuter, and "things" might be expected. Moreover, the rabbis spoke of "binding" and "loosing" in terms of laying down halakah (rules of conduct): Shammai is strict and "binds" many things on the people, while Hillel allows greater laxity and "looses" them. It might be argued, then, that in Acts 15:10, Peter looses what certain Jewish believers want to bind. Yet despite this, it is better to take the binding and loosing in v.19 to refer to persons, not rules. The neuter *hosa* ("whatever") occurs in 18:18, where the context demands that persons are meant. Indeed, Greek often uses the neuter of people for classes or categories rather than for individuals. The context of v.19 supports this, for the "keys" in the preceding clause speak of permission for entering the kingdom or being excluded from it, not rules of conduct under heaven's reign. Acts 15:10 is scarcely an example of the opposite viewpoint, for there Peter does not proceed by legislative fiat. The church in Acts 15 seeks spiritually minded consensus, not imposed halakoth, and James is more prominent than Peter.

3. But exactly what is meant by this "binding and loosing" of persons, and is it absolute? And how is it related to the power of "the keys"? Substantial help comes from comparing Jesus' denunciation of the teachers of the law in Luke 11:52. There they are told that they "have taken away the key to knowledge" and have not only failed to enter [the kingdom] themselves but have "hindered those who were entering." Clearly, then, by their approach to the Scriptures, Jesus says they are making it impossible for those who fall under the malign influences of their teaching to accept the new revelation in Jesus and enter the kingdom. They take away "the key to knowledge."

In contrast, Peter, on confessing Jesus as Messiah, is told he has received this confession by the Father's revelation and will be given the keys of the kingdom—i.e., by proclaiming "the good news of the kingdom" (4:23), which by revelation he is increasingly understanding, he will open the kingdom to many and shut it against many. Fulfillments of this in Acts are not found in passages like 15:10 but in those like 2:14–39 and 3:11–26, so that by this means the Lord added to the church those who were being saved (Ac 2:47)—or, otherwise put, Jesus was building his church (Mt 16:18). But the same gospel proclamation alienates and excludes men, so we also find Peter shutting up the kingdom against certain people (Ac 4:11–12; 8:20–23). The periphrastic future perfects are then perfectly natural. Peter accomplishes this binding and loosing by proclaiming a gospel that has already been given and by making personal application on that basis (e.g., Simon Magus). Whatever he binds or looses will have been bound or loosed, as long as he adheres to that divinely disclosed gospel. He has no direct pipeline to heaven; still less do his decisions force heaven to comply. But he may be authoritative in binding and loosing because heaven has acted first (cf. Ac 18:9–10). Those he ushers in or excludes have already been bound or loosed by God according to the gospel already revealed and which Peter, by confessing Jesus as the Messiah, has most clearly grasped.

4. Does this promise apply to Peter only, to the apostolic band, or to the church at large? The interpretation given so far broadly fits a major theme of Matthew's gospel: the disciples were called to be fishers of men (4:19), to be salt (5:13) and light (5:14–16), to preach the good news of the kingdom (10:6–42), and, after the resurrection, to disciple the nations and teach them all that Jesus commanded (28:18–20). Within this framework, Matthew 16:18–19 fits very well. Unlike the messianic kingdom expected by so many Jews, which would come climactically without any agreement or action taken by human beings, Jesus announces something different. In full Christian perspective, the kingdom will be consummated in sudden, apocalyptic fashion at the Parousia, when God's actions are final and quite independent of human means. But now the keys of the kingdom are confided to Christians. They must proclaim the Good News, forbid entrance, and urge conversion. They constitute a small minority in a big world. Their mission will be to function as the eschatological *ekklēsia*, the people of God that Jesus is building within this world. Inevitably the assignment involves them in using the keys to bind and loose. These verses are therefore the result of the partially realized—and one day to be consummated—eschatology implicit in the NT.

Understanding the text in this way largely answers the question as to how far the promise applies, for the focus is no longer on the individual and what he or she does or does not represent but on that individual's place in salvation history. In one sense, Peter stands with the other disciples as fishers of men, as recipients of the Great Commission (notice in v.20 that Jesus warns *all* his disciples, not just Peter, to tell no one). In that sense, the disciples stand as paradigms for all believers during this period of redemptive history. But this does not exclude a special role for Peter or the apostles (see comments at v.18). Peter was the foundation, the first stone laid. He enjoys this "salvation-historical primacy," and on him others are laid. This results in certain special roles in the earliest years of the Christian church. But notions of hierarchy, sacerdotalism, or charismatic giftedness are simply irrelevant to the text.

Confirmation that this is the way v.19 is to be taken comes at 18:18. If the church, Messiah's eschatological people already gathered now, has to exercise the ministry of the keys, if it must bind and loose, then clearly one aspect will be the discipline of those who profess to constitute it. Thus the two passages are tightly joined: 18:18 is a special application of 16:19. Again, if we may judge from Paul's ministry, this discipline is a special function of apostles but also of elders and even of the whole church (1Co 5:1–13; 2Co 13:10; Tit 2:15; 3:10–11)—an inescapable part of following Jesus during this age of the inaugurated kingdom and of the proleptic gathering of Messiah's people. The church of Jesus the Christ is more than an audience. It is a group with confessional standards, one of which (namely, "Jesus is the Christ") here precipitates Jesus' remarks regarding the keys. The continuity of the church depends as much on discipline as on truth. Indeed, faithful promulgation of the latter both entails and presupposes the former.

It appears, then, that the text is not interested in whether Peter's (or the church's) decisions are infallible. Its concern is with the role Jesus' disciples must play within this new phase of redemptive history. To press the "whatever" absolutely not only misunderstands the context but fails to reckon with Jesus' tendency to use absolutist language, even when he cannot possibly mean to be taken that way (see comments at 5:33–37).

5. How is the contrast between "heaven" and "earth" to be understood? Our exegesis determines the answer. Some have understood the contrast temporally: What is bound or loosed now on earth will be bound or loosed then in heaven. But it is better to see God's realm breaking into the sinful, human realm. "Heaven" has revealed the gospel in the person of Jesus the Messiah, and heaven's rule has thereby broken in. (On the strange fact that the plural of "heaven" is used here in v.19, while the singular is used in 18:18, see Pennington, *Heaven and Earth*, 147–49.) Thus Jesus' disciples, in accordance with his gospel of the kingdom, take up the ministry of the keys and bind and loose on earth that which, with the coming of the kingdom, stands bound and loosed in heaven. The thought is akin to, though more comprehensive than, Acts 18:9–10.

20 Jesus' warning his disciples not to tell anyone that he was the Christ does not stem from personal reluctance to accept the title, nor from merely qualified acceptance subject to teaching that he was a suffering Messiah (vv.21–26), still less because all the commands to keep silent are church constructions designed to create a "messianic secret" to explain why Jesus failed openly to present himself to the people as Messiah. The categories are wrong. "Contrary to common misappropriation of the messianic secret, it was not Jesus' purpose to conceal his messianic identity. It was his purpose to set before Israel symbol-charged acts and words implying a persistent question: Who do you say that I am?" (Ben F. Meyer, *Aims of Jesus*, 305 n. 59; see also pp. 250, 309–10 nn. 119–20). Jesus steadily refused to make an explicit messianic claim, declining to bow to demands for a definitive sign (12:38–39; 16:4) and insisting that the "step into messianic faith would be taken only under the combined impact of his densely symbolic career and of a divine illumination disclosing its sense" (ibid., 250; cf. 11:4, 25–26; 16:17).

The disciples are now charged to exercise the same reticence. Having come to faith, they must not go beyond the Master himself in the means and limitations of his self-disclosure. The aim must not be to hide Jesus' identity from Israel or to keep it an esoteric secret but to guarantee (1) that the decisive factors in the conversion of men are not nationalistic fervor and impenitent messianic expectation but faith, obedience, and submission to Jesus; and (2) that the events leading to the cross are not to be short-circuited by premature disclosure. After the resurrection, there could be unqualified proclamation (cf. 10:27), but not yet. The disciples were beginning to comprehend the first of these two aims, but the second, as the next pericope shows, completely eluded them (see comments at 13:10–17, 34–35, 51–52).

NOTES

14 On the anomalous mixing of ἄλλοι (*alloi*, "others") and ἕτεροι (*heteroi*, "others"), see BDF, para. 306 (2).

17 Βαριωνᾶ (*Bariōna*) is a Greek transliteration of בַּר יוֹנָה (*bar yônâ*), where *bar* means "son of" (cf. English John*son*, Robin*son*, et al.). In John 1:42, Peter is called "son of John" (in Gr.; there is no transliteration from the Aram.). Probably Peter was called בַּר יוֹחָנָן (*bar yôḥānēn*, "son of Johanan"), and "Jonah" is a shortened form of "Johanan," whereas Ἰωάννης (*Iōannēs*, "John") is the closest Greek translation of the name.

18 Often cited as a parallel to Peter as a rock is Isaiah 51:1–2. But the analogy is not close. The point of the Isaiah passage is that Israel should remember her poor beginnings and be conscious of Yahweh's goodness toward her. Still less relevant, though formally closer, is the Jewish Midrash on Isaiah 51:1–2, where God, before creating the world, looks ahead until he finds Abraham and says, "Behold, I have found a rock on which I can build and found the world"; but there the point concerns Abraham's merits and worth, quite clearly not paralleled by Peter in Matthew 16. For rabbinic references and some of the impact of the exegesis on the Targums, see N. A. van Uchelen, "The Targumic Versions of Deuteronomy 33:15: Some Remarks on the Origin of a Traditional Exegesis," *JSS* 31 (1980): 199–209.

b. The first passion prediction (16:21–23)

21From that time on Jesus began to explain to his disciples that he must go to Jerusalem and suffer many things at the hands of the elders, chief priests and teachers of the law, and that he must be killed and on the third day be raised to life.

22Peter took him aside and began to rebuke him. "Never, Lord!" he said. "This shall never happen to you!"

23Jesus turned and said to Peter, "Get behind me, Satan! You are a stumbling block to me; you do not have in mind the things of God, but the things of men."

COMMENTARY

21 Kingsbury (*Structure*, 7ff.), following Lohmeyer, argues strongly that *apo tote* ("From that time"), both here and at 4:17, marks a major turning point in Matthew. Turning point there is, but it is not at all clear that the structure of the entire gospel is dominated by these twin foci. The same expression is found in 26:16, which marks a turning point in Judas Iscariot's pilgrimage but scarcely a major turning point in the book. On the contrary, the very nature of the expression links what follows with what precedes (see Introduction, section 14).

For the meaning of "began," see comments at 11:7, 20, and compare 16:22. At the very least the verb implies that Jesus gave this explanation again and again. This is not the first time he alludes to his death (cf. 9:15; 10:38; 12:40; cf. also Jn 2:19; 3:14), but it is the first time he discusses it openly with his disciples. The time for symbols and veiled language was largely over, now that they had recognized him as Messiah. That is probably the significance of the change from Mark's *didaskō* ("I teach") to Matthew's *deiknyō* ("I point out," "I show"—not, as in the NIV, "I explain"). Jesus had taught the passion earlier but in symbolic language. Now he shows these things to his disciples clearly. Matthew's verb (*deiknyō*) is equivalent to Mark's clause: "He spoke plainly about this" (Mk 8:32).

The prediction is remarkably detailed. Jesus must go to Jerusalem (cf. Lk 13:33), but the "must" of Jesus' suffering lies, not in unqualified determinism or in heroic determination (though some of both is present), but in willing submission to his Father's will. The nature of this "must" becomes clearest in the passion narrative: he *must* suffer and die in line with what Scripture stipulates (26:24, 31, 54, 56), prompting Davies and Allison to comment that "must" in Matthew "is the functional equivalent of γέγραπται ['it is written']" (2:656; cf. France [NICNT]). At Jerusalem, the killer of prophets (23:37), he will suffer many things (more details specified in 20:19) at the hands of the elders, chief priests, and teachers of the law—the three groups that largely constituted the Sanhedrin (see comments at 3:7; 26:59; one governing article, as in 16:1, 6; Pharisees would overlap with the first and third groups). There he would be killed and rise again the third day (see comments at 12:40).

The parallel in Mark 8:31 uses Son of Man language (see comments at 8:20; 16:13). The authenticity of this and other passion predictions has been widely discussed. Bultmann (*History of the Synoptic Tradition*, 151) flatly denies it. J. Jeremias and W. Zimmerli (*The Servant of the Lord* [London: SCM Press, 1965], 57ff.) approach the question by examining whether there are any Jewish antecedents to the notion of a suffering Messiah. Hill thinks Jesus foresaw confrontation in Jerusalem, typical of the prophets, and the possibility of suffering and death, but doubts that he could have spoken so explicitly. C. F. D. Moule ("From Defendant to Judge and Deliverer: An Inquiry into the Use and Limitations of the Theme of Vindication in the New Testament," *NTS* 3 [1952–53]: 40–53) argues that the "Son of Man" (Mk 8:31), related to the "saints of the Most High" in Daniel 7, is vindicated after trial and suffering; so if Jesus takes this title and role to himself, he might well perceive the need to suffer before being exalted (cf. 26:64).

Lindars (*New Testament Apologetic*, 60ff.) turns to Hosea 6:2 and suggests that historically Jesus spoke of resurrection, of being "raised to life," in a metaphor, as referring to the restoration of God's people. If so, what is surprising, especially in a book as studded with OT quotations as Matthew, is that Hosea is not mentioned, nor are his words clearly referred to, even allusively. On the face of it, our texts speak of Jesus' resurrection after being killed, not of Jesus' death followed by the restoration of God's people. Others have suggested that Jesus is thinking of Isaiah 53.

These approaches seek to make some part of Jesus' passion predictions historically credible through some historical antecedent on which Jesus allegedly based his predictions. While this is not wrong, it is too restrictive for dealing with one who claims exclusive and intimate knowledge of the Father (11:27). Is it reasonable to think that Jesus could have predicted the details of his passion only if he read about them somewhere? This is not to question the applicability of some of the OT allusions to him; it is rather to question the historical reductionism of some gospel research.

How much of Jesus' sayings about his death did the disciples understand before the events? The gospel evidence points in two complementary directions. On the one hand, the disciples understand perfectly well; otherwise, for instance, Peter could not possibly have rebuked Jesus (v.22). On the other hand, they cannot believe that Messiah will really be killed because their conceptions of the Messiah do not allow for a Suffering Servant. Therefore, Peter dares to rebuke Jesus, and the disciples begin to think that Jesus' predictions of his sufferings must be in some way nonliteral (Mk 9:10; Lk 9:45; see comments at 17:4).

22 Peter's rebuke reveals how little he understands the kind of messiahship Jesus has in mind. "Began" (cf. v.21) suggests that Peter gets only so far before Jesus cuts him off (v.23). Peter uses very strong language. "Never, Lord!" (see Notes) is a vehement Septuagintalism. "This shall never happen to you!" renders *ou mē* ("never") plus a future indicative, instead of the expected aorist subjunctive. The future indicative after *ou mē*, which makes a strong expression even stronger, is comparatively rare in the NT (only here and in 15:6; 26:35; Mk 13:31; 14:31; Lk 21:33; Jn 4:14; 6:35; 10:5; Heb 10:17; Rev 9:6; 18:14), and most of these occurrences have textual variants. Peter's strong will and warm heart linked to his ignorance produce a shocking bit of arrogance. He confesses that Jesus is the Messiah and then speaks in a way that implies he knows more of God's will than the Messiah himself.

23 That "Jesus turned" means "Jesus turned away from Peter" or "turned his back on Peter" is doubtful. The connection with what follows is too awkward. If Jesus told Peter to get out of his way, even metaphorically, it must have been that Jesus was confronting him face-to-face, not turning away from him. It is better to assume that Jesus turned toward Peter to speak to him, the detail implying an indelible historical reminiscence. The sharp rebuke is made up of three parts.

1. *Hypage opisō mou, Satana* (lit., "Go behind me, Satan") could, by itself, be a call to discipleship (cf. the same adverb in Mk 1:17, 20; 8:34) and therefore be a sharp reminder for Peter to remember that as a disciple he must follow, not lead. But this ill suits the vocative "Satan." The verb *hypagō* (GK *5632*) is therefore best taken in the way it is used in Matthew 4:10 ("Away from me, Satan"). It is not simply that Peter should get out of Jesus' sight but, as a stumbling block, out of Jesus' way.

2. A few moments earlier, Jesus had called Peter a rock. Now he calls him a different kind of "rock," a *skandalon* ("a stumbling block," GK *4998*; see comments at 5:29). This is one of several striking parallels between vv.13–20 and vv.21–23. As Satan offered Jesus kingship without suffering (4:8–9), so Peter does the same, adopting current expectations of victorious messianic conquest (*Pss. Sol.* 17; cf. Schürer, *History of the Jewish People*, 2:517–25, and bibliography, 488–92). Jesus recognizes the same diabolical source behind the same temptation. For him to acquiesce would be to rebel against the will of his Father. The notion of a suffering Messiah, misunderstood by Peter so that he became a stumbling block to Jesus, itself becomes, after the resurrection, a stumbling block to other Jews (1Co 1:23).

3. Peter was not thinking (the verb *phroneō* [NIV, "have in mind"], common in Paul, is used elsewhere in the NT only here, in Mk 8:33, and in Ac 28:22) God's thoughts (namely, that Jesus must go to Jerusalem and die, v.21), but men's thoughts (namely, that he must *not* go). In vv.13–17, Peter, unlike other men, did think God's thoughts because divine revelation was given him. Here, however, he has switched sides, aligning himself not only with men but with Satan.

Many scholars have thought the contrast between Peter in vv.13–20 and vv.21–23 so remarkable that they have worked out elaborate explanations. The most common view is that Peter is a stumbling block during Jesus' earthly ministry but becomes a foundation stone after the resurrection (Brown et al., *Peter in the New Testament*, 94). There is an element of truth in this because Jesus' promise to Peter (vv.17–19) does look to the future. But it looks to the future on the basis of the revelation Peter has *already* grasped (vv.16–17). This means that historically Peter did and did not understand. Along with the other disciples, he understood much more than the crowds; yet even so, he did not reach full understanding until after the resurrection. The juxtaposition of vv.13–20 and vv.21–23 clearly shows the (at best) qualified understanding of Jesus' disciples at this point in salvation history (cf. Trotter, "Understanding and Stumbling").

NOTES

21 The variants are very difficult. Most witnesses support ὁ Ἰησοῦς (*ho Iēsous*, "Jesus"); ℵ* B* sa[mss] bo offer Ἰησοῦς Χριστός (*Iēsous Christos*, "Jesus Christ"). The latter has early and important but very limited attestation. Its strength is that it admirably fits the context, after Jesus has just been confessed as being the Christ. By the same token, a copyist might well think the same. The title in the second reading is very rare, which makes it the *lectio difficilior* ("the harder reading"). Internal evidence is therefore ambivalent. On external grounds alone, the first reading is to be preferred. A few witnesses omit both, probably due to accidental deletion, something easily done in Uncial scripts, where the names were regularly abbreviated to $\overline{\text{IC}}$ and $\overline{\text{XC}}$ respectively.

22 Ἵλεώς σοι, κύριε (*Hileōs soi, kyrie*, "Never, Lord") has been understood two ways.

1. The word ἵλεως, *hileōs*, used in the NT only here and in Hebrews 8:12, is taken to mean "propitious," "merciful," "gracious"—and the entire expression is an abbreviation of something longer, either ἵλεως εἴη σοι ὁ θεός (*hileōs eiē soi ho theos*, "May God be merciful to you") or ἵλεως ἔσται σοι ὁ θεός (*hileōs estai soi ho theos*, "God will be merciful to you"). Coupled with what Peter says next, the rebuke is still there but in rather soft language: "This won't happen to you, Lord, for God will be merciful to you" or "may God be merciful to you" (cf. Moulton, *Grammar: Prolegomena*, 240; *TDNT*, 3:300–301).

2. It is far more likely that ἵλεως, *hileōs*, is merely a homonymic rendering of the Hebrew חָלִילָה (*ḥālîlâ*, "far be it from"). This is a common Septuagintalism and has the force in confrontational situations of a very strong "Never!" or "Be it far from you!" or "God forbid!" For references and discussion, see Turner, *Syntax*, 309; H. St. J. Thackeray, *A Grammar of the Old Testament in Greek According to the Septuagint* (Cambridge: Cambridge Univ. Press, 1909), 1:38; BDF, para. 128 (5).

12. The way of discipleship (16:24–28)

OVERVIEW

Matthew omits mention of the crowds (cf. Mk 8:34) and omits Mark 8:38 because he has provided a parallel thought elsewhere (10:33). In 16:27, Matthew adds some words from Psalm 62:12. This pericope does two things: (1) After the passion prediction in vv.21–23, it demands the disciples' willingness to deny themselves absolutely, a kind of death to self; (2) yet it assures us that the consummated kingdom will at last come. For the pericope's structure, see comments at v.28.

24Then Jesus said to his disciples, "If anyone would come after me, he must deny
himself and take up his cross and follow me. 25For whoever wants to save his life will lose
it, but whoever loses his life for me will find it. 26What good will it be for a man if he gains
the whole world, yet forfeits his soul? Or what can a man give in exchange for his soul?

[27]For the Son of Man is going to come in his Father's glory with his angels, and then he will reward each person according to what he has done. [28]I tell you the truth, some who are standing here will not taste death before they see the Son of Man coming in his kingdom."

COMMENTARY

24 Though addressed to Jesus' "disciples" (see comments at 5:1–2), the thought is expressed in widest terms—"if anyone." As in 10:33, Jesus speaks of "disowning" or "renouncing." The Jews renounced the Messiah (Ac 3:14); his followers renounce themselves (cf. Ro 14:7–9; 15:2–3). They "take up their cross" (cf. 10:38). Any Jew in Palestine would know that the man condemned to crucifixion was often forced to carry part of his cross (see comments at 27:32)—a burden and a sign of death. Though Jesus does not explicitly mention the mode of his death until a few days before it takes place (20:19), the impact of this saying must have multiplied after Golgotha. Death to self is not so much a prerequisite of discipleship to Jesus as a continuing characteristic of it (see comments at 4:19; cf. Jn 12:23–26). (On the differences between discipleship to Jesus and discipleship to first-century rabbis, see Bornkamm, *Jesus of Nazareth*, 144–45.)

25–26 The logic is relentless: *gar* ("for") begins vv.25, 26, 27. For the sense of v.25, see comments at 10:39. The orientation is eschatological. Saving one's *psychē* (NIV, "life," GK *6034*; see comments at 10:28) *now* will result in losing it *at the end*, and losing it now will result in finding it at the end. Verse 26 (cf. *2 Bar.* 51:15) furthers the argument by asking twin rhetorical questions, showing the folly of possessing all created abundance and wealth at the expense of one's *psychē*. The NIV here changes its rendering "life" (v.25) to "soul" (v.26). This is not necessarily wrong. The abrupt change from the physical to the spiritual is amply attested elsewhere (cf. 8:22; Jn 4:10; 6:27); but the change in English is perhaps too sharp (cf. Lk 9:25: "his very self"). The focus is still eschatological, and the loss is the eternal loss of one's soul = life = self (on the afterlife, see comments at 22:23–33). Terminology aside, the bargain is a bad one.

27 Not only Jesus' example (v.24; cf. 10:24–25) but the judgment he will exercise is an incentive to take up one's cross and follow him. The Son of Man (see comments at 8:20; 16:13) will come "in his Father's glory"—the same glory God his Father enjoys (cf. 26:64; Jn 17:1–5), another implicit claim to the status of deity—along with his angels, who both enhance his glory and serve as his agents for the eschatological ingathering (13:41; 24:31; 25:31–32; Lk 9:26). They are his angels. He stands so far above them that he owns them and uses them. At that time he will reward each person *kata tēn praxin autou* ("according to what he has done"). The language is that of Psalm 62:12, where Yahweh rewards his people, and the Yahweh-Jesus exchange is not uncommon. The use of *praxis* ("conduct," "deeds," GK *4552*) is Matthew's rendering of the Hebrew collective singular by a corresponding singular in Greek (Gundry, *Use of the Old Testament*, 138). For the concept of rewards, see comments at 5:12.

28 Many of the possible interpretations and difficult issues bound up with this verse have been treated at 10:23 and need not be repeated. Martin Kunzi (*Das Naherwartungslogion Markus 9.1 par:*

Geschichte seiner Auslegung [Tübingen: Mohr, 1977]) has an excellent history of interpretation.

The parallel in Mark 9:1 has a somewhat different "before" clause: "before they see the kingdom of God come with power." But this and Matthew's "before they see the Son of Man coming in his kingdom" may mean much the same thing, when it is remembered that "kingdom" is a dynamic concept (see comments at 3:2) and that "the coming of the Son of Man" also has a wide range of possible meanings (see comments at 10:23). The principal explanations of this verse may be briefly listed.

1. Dodd (*Parables of the Kingdom*, 53–54) interprets Mark's form of the saying as meaning "there are some who stand here who will never taste death until they have seen that the kingdom of God has come with power." In other words, the kingdom had come when Jesus was speaking (perfect participle *elēlythyian*), and the disciples "see"—i.e., perceive that this is so. But, as many have shown, this is an unnatural way of taking the verb "to see," and it introduces an insurmountable problem in Matthew, where the participle is *erchomenon* ("the kingdom of God coming").

2. Many have held that this verse refers to the transfiguration, the very next pericope in both Matthew and Mark. The problem is twofold. First, "some who are standing here will not taste death before they see" is an extraordinary way to refer to Peter, James, and John, who witness the transfiguration a mere six days later (17:1). Second, as magnificent as the transfiguration was, it is not entirely clear how the Son of Man comes in his kingdom (Matthew) or the kingdom comes in power (Mark) through this event.

3. Others take this to refer to the resurrection or to Pentecost. This view has been strenuously defended, but again it faces the difficulty that even these events are not far enough off to warrant the phrasing "some standing here who will not taste death."

4. Still others (Gaechter, Plummer) think the saying refers to the fall of Jerusalem (a view this commentary defends for 10:23). The chief problem is that the context does not encourage this interpretation here, as it does in 10:23. There is no mention of the cities of Israel, of persecution in synagogue settings, etc. Indeed, the preceding verse (v.27) appears to refer to the Parousia.

5. Others interpret this verse as referring to the Parousia but draw divergent conclusions. Some think the saying shows that Jesus expected history to end within a few years but was clearly wrong; others that "some who are standing here" refers not to those then standing there but to the final generation, prophetically foreseen. If Matthew believed that the former was what Jesus meant, we would expect a gospel full of the Thessalonian heresy, loaded with expectation of the second coming, because few of the first generation would still be alive. Instead, the disciples' mission is to continue to the end of the age (28:20). The second alternative means that the words were calculated to be misunderstood by "those who [were] standing here."

6. Bruce Chilton has offered a novel interpretation (*God in Strength*, 251–74; "An Evangelical and Critical Approach to the Sayings of Jesus," *Them* 3 [1977–78]: 78–85). He argues that "those not tasting death" is a technical reference to "immortals" such as Elijah and Enoch (cf. *Gen. Rab.* 9:6; *4 Ezra* 6:26), that what Jesus actually said was that the immortals, like Elijah and Moses in the transfiguration scene that immediately follows, do indeed witness the reality of the kingdom, understood as God's revelation on behalf of his people. If this is correct, then the problem of trying to find a suitable period to explain Jesus' prediction in v.28 and in Mark 9:1 is resolved: there is no prediction left. But Chilton's argument depends on adopting a doubtful reading in Mark 9:1 (cf. Kent Brower, "Mark 9:1: Seeing the Kingdom in Power," *JSNT* 6 [1980]: 30–31) and on reasoning that maintains that both Mark and Matthew so completely misinterpreted Jesus that they make him say

something quite different from what he really said. The word "here," despite Chilton's contention that it contrasts those not tasting death with Jesus' hearers, is most naturally understood to refer to them.

Moreover, most of Chilton's sources for nailing down "those not tasting death" ("taste death" itself simply means "die"; cf. Heb 2:9) as a special phrase for "immortals" are either certainly or probably late. Whereas some elements of Jewish tradition did treat Moses, along with Elijah, as a "deathless figure," the OT firmly insists that "Moses the servant of the LORD died" (Dt 34:5). Furthermore, what "those who are standing here" will see is, in Mark, the kingdom "coming with power" or "having come with power"—i.e., they see evidence of the kingdom's powerful operation. This is interpreted by Matthew to be the equivalent of "the Son of Man coming in [or perhaps 'with'; cf. BDF, para. 198 (2)] his reign"—i.e., they see evidence of the Son of Man's reigning authority. But Chilton's interpretation allows for none of this. In his view, the "deathless figures" merely perceive the reality of God's reign, and thus Chilton confuses the kingdom with evidence for the coming of the kingdom.

Jesus refers to those who "will not taste death," but Chilton treats them as if they are generically "those not tasting death." He does this by rightly pointing out that the words do not necessarily mean that those "standing" there will necessarily taste death after they have seen the kingdom coming in power. The words *ou mē ... heōs an* ("not ... until") reflect a Semitic construction, used in Genesis 28:15, in which God says to Jacob, "I will not leave you until I have done what I have promised you," which does not mean God will leave him afterwards. From this, Chilton deduces that "will not taste death until [NIV, 'before']" refers to "immortals," or "deathless figures," because the "until" does not necessarily mark the end of something. But this, though correct, misses two crucial points.

First, whether "those standing" must one day die or not, with this expression the part of the sentence before the "until" clause always expresses something new or the ending or changing of something. The main clause always demands sequence and change. For example, in the Genesis passage just quoted, "until" may not mean that God will then leave Jacob; but the main clause does mean that God will keep every word of his promises and remain with Jacob, at least "until" all the promises have been fulfilled. Likewise in Mark 9:1 and Matthew 16:28, the "until" clause (NIV, "before") does not necessarily mean those "standing" must die; but the verse as a whole does mean they will at some future time witness the powerful operation of the reign of God (Mark), the coming of the Son of Man with his reign (Matthew), and that *at least* until then they will not die. Thus, even Chilton's reconstruction does not eliminate the difficulty of determining what time period within salvation is in view. He has sidestepped the problem but not resolved it.

Second, the *ou mē ... heōs an* ("not ... until") construction can mean that at the "until" the action or state of the first clause will cease (as in 23:39). There are numerous NT occurrences of this construction (5:18, 26; 10:23; 16:28; 23:39; 24:34; Mk 9:1; 14:25; Lk 9:27; 12:59; 13:35; 21:32), and in addition there are important variations with the same meaning, none more so than Luke 2:26, where it had been revealed to Simeon that he would not see death "until" (*prin an* or *prin ē an* or *heōs an*) he saw the Lord's Christ, after which, apparently, he died. Many of these references give evidence of the termination of the action of the first clause when the time of the "until" clause has passed. Along with comments on the natural force of "here," these data suggest that the best way to take "some who are standing *here* will not taste death *until* they see the Son of Man coming with his reign" therefore depends solely on the meaning of "the Son of Man coming with his reign." If this is a reference to the Parousia, then the "some who are standing here" will not die even then; but in that case, Jesus' chronology would be very wrong. If it is a reference to the demonstrable evidences of powerful kingship, then "some who are standing here" will die at some point after seeing those evidences. Moreover, it must be said that Chilton's redaction-critical methods, though done with rigor, are so procrustean in distinguishing between the "traditional" and the "redactional" that they can produce only suspect results.

7. It seems best to take v.28 as having a more general reference—namely, not referring simply to the resurrection, to Pentecost, or the like, but to the manifestation of Christ's kingly reign exhibited after the resurrection in a host of ways, not the least of them being the rapid multiplication of disciples and the mission to the Gentiles. Some of those standing there would live to see Jesus' gospel proclaimed throughout the Roman Empire and a rich "harvest" (cf. 9:37–38) of converts reaped for Jesus Messiah. This best suits the flexibility of the "kingdom" concept in the Synoptic Gospels (see comments at 3:2; 10:23; 12:28) and the present context. Thus, v.28 does not refer to the same thing as 10:23. But the distinction is made, not on the basis that consistency is "the hobgoblin of little minds," but on the basis of context.

This pericope contains an important chiasm:

v.24: challenge to take up the cross and follow Christ in the immediate future
  v.25: incentive reward and punishment at the Parousia
    v.26: central weighing of values
  v.27: incentive reward and punishment at the Parousia
v.28: promise of witnessing the kingdom power of Jesus in the immediate future

The setting is quite different from that in 10:23. But if the evidence of the kingdom is seen in the church, this does not mean that the church and the kingdom are to be identified. Rather, at this point in salvation history, it is the power of the kingdom working through Jesus' disciples that calls the church into being (see comments at 13:36–43). Moreover, as Brower ("Mark 9:1," 32ff.) points out, the larger context also offers important insights. Though the transfiguration is not the fulfillment of v.28, it is related to it in an important way. Sections that stress suffering and the cross (vv.21–28; 17:9–13) envelop the transfiguration and bracket this clearest manifestation of divine glory by suffering. The way to glory is the way of the cross, and the reign of the Son of Man, which "some standing here" will see before they "taste death," will be inaugurated by the cross.

13. The Transfiguration (17:1–13)

a. Jesus transfigured (17:1–8)

OVERVIEW

This passage raises difficult literary, historical, and theological questions. The *literary* questions arise largely from the several important "minor agreements" of Matthew and Luke (9:28–36) against Mark (9:2–8), raising doubts about the adequacy of the two-source hypothesis (see Introduction, section 3). These have been scrutinized by F. Neirynck ("Minor Agreements of Matthew-Luke in the Transfiguration Story," in *Orientierung an Jesus* [ed. Hoffmann et al.], 253–66) and judged to be of greater relevance to the tendencies of Matthew and Luke than to source-critical relationships.

The *historical* questions arise because there have been numerous attempts to explain the origin of this story in some setting other than what the evangelists present. Schweitzer (*Quest of the Historical Jesus*, 380ff.) holds that when Jesus' dreams were shattered following the mission of the Twelve (he thought that mission would usher in the kingdom), he experienced an ecstatic, perhaps glossalalic, vision later reinterpreted by his disciples. This historical reconstruction depends on Schweitzer's broader theories, now long discredited (see comments at 10:23). More influential is Bultmann's view (*History of the Synoptic Tradition*, 259) that this story is a misplaced resurrection narrative. But this has been decisively rebutted by Robert H. Stein ("Is the Transfiguration [Mark 9:2–8] a Misplaced Resurrection Account?" *JBL* 95 [1976]: 79–96), who shows that in language and form the theory of Bultmann and many others will not work.

Bruce D. Chilton ("The Transfiguration: Dominical Assurance and Apostolic Vision," *NTS* 27 [1980]: 115–24) has followed up his interpretation of v.28 (see comments there) by positing that the genesis of the transfiguration narrative is his reconstruction of Jesus' saying behind v.28—namely, Jesus swears by "deathless witnesses" that the "kingdom," the revelation of "God in strength," continues in forceful operation. These "deathless witnesses" were understood by the disciples to be Moses and Elijah, a step not dominical but consistent with it. Then Peter, James, and John, who saw themselves as Aaron, Nadab, and Abihu with reference to the new Moses (i.e., Jesus), emphasized the continuity of Jesus' disclosure with the prophetic revelation of old in this "visio-literary fashion." Chilton's first and essential step we have seriously questioned, and the rest is little more than mere assertion without further supporting evidence. Even if his understanding of v.28 were correct, it would be difficult to see on what evidential grounds he holds that 17:1–8 is meant by the evangelist to be nonhistorical.

The *theological* questions arise because the story has so many nuances—allusions to Moses, his experience of glory and his role in redemptive history, Elijah and his role as eschatological forerunner, Jesus' baptism (the Voice from heaven saying much the same thing, cf. 3:17), the Parousia, perhaps the Shekinah glory, and others. The narrative is clearly a major turning point in Jesus' self-disclosure, and some attempt must be made to weave these themes together without merely allegorizing the passage. The best recent exposition is that of Liefeld ("Theological Motifs"). Also, G. H. Boobyer (*St. Mark and the Transfiguration Story* [Edinburgh: T&T Clark, 1942], 1–47) provides a useful survey of theological options.

1After six days Jesus took with him Peter, James and John the brother of James, and led
them up a high mountain by themselves. 2There he was transfigured before them. His face
shone like the sun, and his clothes became as white as the light. 3Just then there appeared
before them Moses and Elijah, talking with Jesus.
4Peter said to Jesus, "Lord, it is good for us to be here. If you wish, I will put up three
shelters—one for you, one for Moses and one for Elijah."

[5]While he was still speaking, a bright cloud enveloped them, and a voice from the cloud said, "This is my Son, whom I love; with him I am well pleased. Listen to him!"

[6]When the disciples heard this, they fell facedown to the ground, terrified. [7]But Jesus came and touched them. "Get up," he said. "Don't be afraid." [8]When they looked up, they saw no one except Jesus.

COMMENTARY

1 Precise time indicators like "after six days" are rare in the Synoptics apart from in the passion narrative. Luke's "about eight days after Jesus said this" (9:28) is based on a Greek way of speaking and means "about a week later." Numerous suggestions have been made as to why "six days" should be mentioned. Bonnard sees an allusion to the six days separating the Day of Atonement from the Feast of Tabernacles. In this view, the first explicit mention of Jesus' passion (16:21–23) occurs on the former day, and the transfiguration, with its "shelters" (v.4) or "tabernacles," on the latter. But it seems highly unlikely that Jesus and his disciples would travel from Caesarea Philippi to this mountain during the feast. Nor is there any direct evidence of its taking place that time of year. Others see a reference to Exodus 24:16 ("For six days the cloud covered the mountain, and on the seventh day the LORD called to Moses from within the cloud"). Such views are probably too subtle, especially for Luke! The "six days" may simply indicate the time it took to travel from one place (16:13) to another (17:1) and thus establish the fact, noted by all three synoptists, that the transfiguration took place within a few days of the prediction that Jesus must go to Jerusalem and be killed. The two passages must therefore be read together.

Mount Tabor, the traditional "high mountain," lies south of Galilee; but it is not at all "high" (about 1,900 feet), and going to it would have been a roundabout way of traveling from Caesarea Philippi to Capernaum (vv.22, 24; Mk 9:30, 33). Moreover, according to Josephus (*J.W.* 2.573 [20.6]; 4.54–55 [1.8]), it had a walled fortress at its summit. Mount Hermon, rising above Caesarea Philippi, is the most popular alternative (9,232 feet); but it is so high and cold at its summit—if indeed they went to the top—it seems a strange place to pass the night (Luke specifies they descended the next day). Immediately after their descent Jesus and the inner three faced crowds that included "teachers of the law" (Mk 9:14). This is almost inconceivable at Mount Hermon in Gentile territory. Liefeld ("Theological Motifs," 167 n. 27) has plausibly suggested Mount Miron (3,926 feet), the highest mountain within Israel and on the way from Caesarea Philippi to Capernaum. The "mountain" calls to mind Moses and Elijah, both of whom received revelation on a mountain (Ex 19; 24; 1Ki 19; for thorough comparison of this christophany with the theophanies experienced by Moses and Elijah respectively, see G. Juncker, "Jesus and the Angel of the Lord: An Old Testament Paradigm in New Testament Christology" [PhD diss., Trinity Evangelical Divinity School, 2001], 351–75), though here part of the purpose was to ensure privacy ("by themselves," v.1; "all alone," Mk 9:2).

Those Jesus "took with him" (the verb, contrary to some expositions, has no obvious connection with master-disciple relations; cf. its use in 2:13; 4:5,

12:45) were Peter, James, and John, the inner circle of the Twelve (see comments at 10:2, 20:20; 26:37; cf. Mk 5:37, and the continued friendship of Peter and John, Ac 8:14; Gal 2:9 [with a different James]).

2 Moses' face shone because it reflected something of God's glory (Ex 34:29–30). But as for Jesus, he himself was transfigured. The verb *metamorphoō* ("transfigure," "transform," "change in form," GK *3565*) suggests a change of inmost nature that may be outwardly visible (as here; cf. Ex 34:29; *2 Bar.* 51:3, 5) or quite invisible (Ro 12:2; 2Co 3:18). That Jesus was transfigured "before them" implies that it was largely for their sakes. Whatever confirmation the experience may have given Jesus, for the disciples it was revelatory. As they would come to realize, they were being privileged to glimpse something of his preincarnate glory (Jn 1:14; 17:5; Php 2:6–7) and anticipate his coming exaltation (2Pe 1:16–18; Rev 1:16). Their confession of Jesus as Messiah and his insistence that he would be a suffering Messiah (16:13–21; 17:9) were confirmed. Therefore, they had reason to hope that they would yet see the Son of Man coming in his kingdom (16:28). The contrast between what Jesus had just predicted would be his fate (16:21) and this glorious sight would one day prompt Jesus' disciples to marvel at the self-humiliation that brought him to the cross and to glimpse a little of the height to which he had been raised by his vindicating resurrection and ascension.

3 The word *idou* should not be pressed to mean "Just then" (NIV). It is used twice more in v.5, where it stresses the marvel of the experience (see comments at 1:20). Unlike Mark, Matthew puts Moses before Elijah, giving him slightly greater status, and only Matthew mentions the brightness of the cloud (v.5), reminiscent of the Shekinah glory (cf. Davies, *Setting*, 50–56). Both Moses and Elijah had eschatological roles: Moses was the model for the eschatological Prophet (Dt 18:18), and Elijah for the forerunner (Mal 4:5–6; Mt 3:1–3; 11:7–10; 17:9–13). Both had strange ends. Both were men of God in times of transition, the first to introduce the covenant and the second to work for renewed adherence to it. Both experienced a vision of God's glory, one at Sinai (Ex 31:18) and the other at Horeb (1Ki 19:8). Now, however, the glory is Jesus' glory, for it is he who is transfigured and who radiates the glory of deity. Both suffered rejection of various kinds (for Moses, cf. Stephen's summary, Ac 7:35, 37; for Elijah, cf. 1Ki 19:1–9; Mt 17:12). Together they may well summarize the Law and the Prophets. This is all the more plausible when we recall that these two figures very rarely appear together in Judaism or in the NT (possibly Rev 11:3; cf. Zec 4:14; *TDNT*, 4:863–64). All these associations gain importance as the narrative moves on and Jesus is perceived to be superior to Moses and Elijah and, indeed, to supersede them (vv.5, 8).

The verb *ōphthē* ("appeared," GK *3972*), sometimes used in connection with Jesus' resurrection, does not in itself suggest a resurrection setting, since Moses and Elijah are the ones who "appear," not Jesus.

4 Peter "answered" Jesus (NIV, "said"). The peculiar verb form (*apokritheis*, GK *646*) may mean that his suggestion was called forth by the circumstances, but more likely it has no force of "response" (see comments at 11:25). Just as Moses and Elijah, in their respective theophanies, spoke with *God*, so Peter and his companions speak with *Jesus*; in other words, this is not a "new Moses" Christology leading his people on a new exodus but an unveiling of who Jesus truly is, a theophany in the strongest sense (cf. Juncker, "Jesus and the Angel of the Lord," 364). Peter, speaking for the three ("it is good for us to be here"), sensing something of the greatness of what he, James, and John are seeing, suggests building three *skēnas* ("tabernacles," GK *5008*; NIV, "shelters"). While the word looks back to the tabernacle in the wilderness, forerunner of the temple, the idea of building "tabernacles" also reflects the Feast of Tabernacles, when Jews built shelters for themselves and lived in them for seven days (cf. Lev 23:42–43). The feast had eschatological overtones. So Peter may have been saying that in gratitude for witnessing Jesus' transfiguration and recognizing the imminent dawn of the messianic age, he would build three "tabernacles"—one for Jesus, one for Moses, and one for Elijah.

The rebuke that follows does not offer criticism of Peter's eschatology, nor even of its timing, but is administered solely because what Peter blurted out compromised Jesus' uniqueness. *Jesus* was transfigured; they must bear witness concerning him (v.5). Mark says Peter spoke out of fear, Luke that he made his suggestion as Moses and Elijah were about to leave. Mark and Luke point out the foolishness of Peter's remark. Matthew simplifies and so highlights the christological error of Peter.

Mark (9:5) has "Rabbi," Luke (9:33) "Master," and Matthew "Lord." Mark is probably original; Luke translates "Rabbi" by "Master" for his non-Jewish readers; and Matthew probably uses "Lord" in its general sense (see comments at 7:21), connoting no more respect than "rabbi." But why Matthew's different form of address? Perhaps it is to stress what Peter is doing. Earlier Peter had confessed Jesus as Christ and yet rebuked him because Peter did not understand the full meaning of "Christ." Here he again treats Jesus with respect ("Lord") but suggests something that compromises his identity. Matthew's readers know very well that "Christ" means more than messianic political conqueror and that "Lord" would in time include unqualified supremacy. But Peter does not yet know these things.

5 The "cloud" is associated, in both the OT and intertestamental Judaism, with eschatology (Ps 97:2; Isa 4:5; Eze 30:3, Da 7:13; Zep 1:15; cf. *2 Bar.* 53:1–12; *4 Ezra* 13:3; 2 Macc 2:8; *b. Sanh.* 98a) and with the exodus (Ex 13:21–22; 16:10; 19:16; 24:15–18; 40:34–38). Of the synoptists, only Matthew says that the cloud was "bright," a detail that recalls the Shekinah glory. The latter eschatological associations (Lk 21:27; 1Th 4:17) show Jesus in his role as the one who succeeds Moses, the eschatological prophet; the former associations (Ps 97:2 et al.) assure us that Jesus is the messianic King whose kingdom is dawning. But as Liefeld ("Theological Motifs," 170) points out, common to both sets of passages and to others as well is the more fundamental idea of the presence of God.

It is uncertain whether *epeskiasen* means "enveloped" (NIV) or "overshadowed" (cf. Ex 40:35). What the Voice from the cloud says is largely a repetition of 3:17, an apparent mingling of Psalm 2:7 and Isaiah 42:1, stressing that Jesus is both Son and Suffering Servant. This is the high point of the narrative (cf. S. Pedersen, "Die Proklamation Jesu als des eschatologischen Offenbarungsträgers," *NovT* 17 [1975]: 241–64). (Mark omits the allusion to Isa 42:1; but both Matthew and Luke, not to mention 2Pe 1:17, attest the connection in different ways; cf. Gundry, *Use of the Old Testament*, 36–37.) But if Matthew 3:17 identifies Jesus, this verse in its context goes further and places him above Moses and Elijah.

The additional words "Listen to him"—an allusion to Deuteronomy 18:15—confirm Jesus is the Prophet like Moses (Dt 18:15–18; cf. Ac 3:22–23; 7:37). This does not mean Jesus is another prophet of Moses' stature but the eschatological Prophet patterned on Moses as a type; for, as Liefeld has suggested ("Theological Motifs," 173), Moses' primary role here is typological, whereas Elijah's, not explained until vv.9–13, is eschatological. As Moses' antitype, Jesus so far outstrips him that when Moses is put next to him, men must "listen" to Jesus, as Moses himself said. The climax of biblical revelation is Jesus, the Son and Servant whom God loves and with whom God is well pleased. Even Moses and Elijah (the Law and the Prophets) assume supporting roles where he is concerned. This confirms our interpretation of 5:17–48; 11:11–15.

6–8 The effect of the transfiguration on the disciples reminds us of Daniel (Da 10:7–9; cf. Dt 5:25–26; Heb 12:19). The visible glory of deity brings terror, but Jesus calms his disciples' fears (cf. 14:26–27; Da 8:18; 10:18). Mark relates fear to Peter's foolish words; Matthew, to the disciples' response to the Voice from the cloud. Both are psychologically convincing; both make different points in the narrative. In Mark, fear helps explain Peter's folly. In Matthew, it magnifies the greatness of the transfiguration. Matthew alone tells us that at the divine splendor the disciples "fell facedown to the ground" (v.6), a prelude to their seeing no one "except Jesus" (v.8). These words are pregnant with meaning. Compared with God's revelation through him, all other revelations pale. Supporting, pointing, prophetic roles such revelation may enjoy, but that Jesus is God's Son (and here Matthew's readers must have remembered chs. 1–2) is primary. Therefore all must "listen to him!" (v.5).

The transfiguration was largely for the disciples (Jesus brought the inner three to it; he was transfigured before "them"; the Voice spoke to "them"; cf. Allison A. Trites, "The Transfiguration of Jesus: The Gospel in Microcosm," *EvQ* 51 [1979]: 77–78). This does not mean they understood it fully, but it was a crucial step in the symbol-charged self-disclosure of Jesus that would be much better understood (2Pe 1:16–19) following the resurrection. For the present, it indelibly confirmed the disciples' conviction that Jesus was the Messiah.

NOTES

4 BDF, para. 372 (2c), suggests that "If you wish," found only in Matthew, is Hellenistic for "please" (cf. French *s'il vous plaît*).

5 There have been many attempts to relate the words of the Voice from heaven to the story of the near sacrifice of Isaac in Genesis 22, as that story is developed in late Judaism into vicarious atonement motifs. But P. R. Davies and B. D. Chilton ("The Aqedah: A Revised Tradition History," *CBQ* 40 [1978]: 514–46) have clearly shown that such Jewish traditions did not develop until after AD 70.

b. The place of Elijah (17:9–13)

OVERVIEW

Luke has no parallel, but see Mark 9:9–13. Matthew omits Mark 9:10, and his handling of Mark 9:12–13 in vv.11–13 is so independent, though complementary, that some scholars (e.g., Schlatter, Lohmeyer) think Matthew here draws on an independent source.

9As they were coming down the mountain, Jesus instructed them, "Don't tell anyone what you have seen, until the Son of Man has been raised from the dead."

[10]The disciples asked him, "Why then do the teachers of the law say that Elijah must come first?"

[11]Jesus replied, "To be sure, Elijah comes and will restore all things. [12]But I tell you, Elijah has already come, and they did not recognize him, but have done to him everything they wished. In the same way the Son of Man is going to suffer at their hands." [13]Then the disciples understood that he was talking to them about John the Baptist.

COMMENTARY

9 In Matthew, this is Jesus' fifth and last command for the disciples to be silent (see comments at 8:4). This time, Jesus permits his disciples to tell everything after the Son of Man (see Reflections, p. 247) "has been raised from the dead." Jesus could scarcely have attached this permission to earlier warnings to keep silent (16:20), since he had not yet spoken clearly about his sufferings and death. Nevertheless, the same salvation-historical change—first silence, then proclamation—occurs as early as 10:27.

The command must have been in some ways disappointing and its lifting a delight. Why did Jesus impose it? Probably for two principal and complementary reasons:

1. The story would only stir up superficial political messianism, already a menace. If Jesus' closest disciples found it hard to understand a suffering and dying Messiah, how would the crowds fare until after the resurrection?

2. The strongest evidence for Jesus' messiahship would be his resurrection, by which he "was declared with power to be the Son of God" (Ro 1:4). Premature self-disclosure in a direct fashion, without the supreme "sign of Jonah," the resurrection (see comments at 12:40), would not only foster false expectations but also quickly disillusion those who held them. Thus, with his prospective converts in mind, Jesus knew it was better for their sakes to wait until after the resurrection before allowing Peter, James, and John to tell what they had seen.

This does not mean that Jesus' full glory could be known only through the resurrection. On the contrary, it means that though his true glory antedated the resurrection and was revealed to three intimates before the passion, it could be made known to others only after the resurrection.

10 Why did the disciples ask this question, connecting it (in Matthew) with *oun* (normally a logical connective, "therefore," "then")? There are two false solutions:

1. If Jesus was the Messiah, how were the disciples to answer the objection of the scribes that Elijah must *precede* Messiah's coming (Mal 4:5–6; cf. *m. ʿEd.* 8:7; *m. B. Meṣ.* 3:5; Str-B, 4:764–98; see comments at 11:7–15)? In this view, the *oun* follows the fact of Jesus' messiahship and the disciples' acceptance of Jesus' reiteration of his death and resurrection: *because* the disciples understand who Jesus is, they ask why then do the scribes insist Elijah precedes Messiah, since apparently Elijah has not yet appeared. This interpretation is intrinsically unlikely, as Mark's account shows. The disciples are there pictured "discussing what 'rising from the dead' meant" (Mk 9:10), thereby showing they did *not* truly understand what Jesus was talking about; and as a result of this discussion, they ask the question in Mark 9:11 and Matthew 17:10. Commentators on Mark assume

this is a second relevant question but do not show how it ties in with the disciples' discussion. Trench (*Studies in the Gospels*, 222) goes so far as to say that the disciples do not venture to raise the first subject and so move on to this one; Lagrange says Matthew omits Mark 9:10 because that text leads nowhere. Yet a tight connection can be established.

2. A few scholars have suggested that the disciples' question was prompted by an assumption that Elijah's appearance during the transfiguration was itself the fulfillment of Malachi 4:5, and then the question becomes, Why did Messiah (Jesus) appear before Elijah did, when the scribes say the order should be reversed (cf. Robertson, *Word Pictures*, 1:141)? But this interpretation suffers from the weakness of the former view (namely, that the disciples properly understand Jesus' teaching of v.9 and par.), while resting on the dubious assumption that the disciples would interpret this brief vision of Elijah as the fulfillment of a prophecy that promised that Elijah would "turn the hearts of the fathers to their children, and the hearts of the children to their fathers" (Mal 4:6).

The real connection is deeper. Elijah was expected to restore all things—to bring about a state of justice and true worship. If that were so, how could it be that Messiah would be killed in such a restored environment—killed, Jesus had told them only a week before, by elders, chief priests, and teachers of the law (16:21)? This interpretation makes sense both of Matthew's *oun* ("therefore") and of Mark 9:10. If Jesus as Messiah (whose messiahship the disciples do not now doubt) must *suffer*, then how could it be said that Elijah must first come *to restore all things*? Their confusion is not merely chronological, though that may be involved; it is their inability to find a framework in which they can believe that the Messiah could die.

11–12 Jesus' answer confirms this interpretation. He approves the teaching of the scribes but insists that another fact must be taken into account. The NIV's "To be sure, ... But" structure accurately reflects this duality (Gk. *men*,... *de*). On the one hand, Elijah comes "first" (*prōton*, in some MSS) and "will restore all things" (the combination of present and future tenses is less consistent than Mk 9:12 but reflects the OT prophecy: see Zerwick, *Biblical Greek*, para. 281). John's mission was a success (3:5–6; 14:5); on the other hand, though, "restore all things" must not be taken absolutely. The Baptist stood in succession of the OT prophets who were persecuted and even killed. The unrecognized fact is that although the scribes' *interpretation* is right—Elijah must precede the Messiah—their grasp of recent *history* is wrong, for Elijah has already come (v.12; cf. 11:14; Lk 1:17); but the people in general and the scribes and leaders in particular did not recognize him and did to him "everything they wished"—a vague expression hinting at John's rejection by most Jewish leaders (cf. 21:24–27) and his death, for which the Jewish leaders were not directly responsible. Gundry points out how this expression is sometimes linked with tyranny (Da 8:4; 11:6, 36; cf. Sir 8:15; 2 Macc 7:16).

Jesus' point is general: the Baptist (Elijah) did fulfill his mission, but he was killed doing it. In the same way, the Son of Man is going to suffer [cf. BDF, para. 315] "at their hands" (v.12b). If the Baptist's restoration of "all things" did not prevent his own death, why should Messiah be any better received?

13 Matthew's conclusion, not found in Mark, has provoked much speculation. G. Barth ("Matthew's Understanding of the Law," 106) takes it as further evidence for his idea that in Matthew "understanding" is essential to discipleship. Others think it to be a turning point in Matthew's narrative—the disciples now arrive at true understanding (e.g., Klostermann). Still others hold that this introduces a split between what the disciples understand and the teachers of the law don't (e.g., McNeile; Schweizer;

Meier, *Vision of Matthew*, 123). Though this has some validity, there are two other factors: (1) Matthew again rounds off a pericope by returning to the question first raised (see comments at 15:20); and (2) what the disciples understand is that John the Baptist is Elijah. It is not at all clear, however, that they have understood much more about the death and resurrection of the Son of Man, and it becomes very obvious during the passion narrative that they have not understood (cf. esp. 26:50–56). In short, this pericope marks another small step in the understanding of Jesus' disciples.

NOTES

9 Because Matthew has τὸ ὅραμα (*to horama*, GK *3969*; lit., "the vision"; NIV, "what you have seen") for Mark's ἃ εἶδον (*ha eidon*, "what they had seen"), many suggest that Matthew is seeking to explain the transfiguration in acceptable terms to his readers. But ὅραμα, *horama*, does not necessarily mean "vision" as a result of a dream or a trance; it can simply refer to what is seen (BDAG, 718). Therefore, too much should not be made of the difference between the two expressions.

14. The healing of an epileptic boy (17:14–20 [21])

OVERVIEW

All three synoptists (cf. Mk 9:14–29; Lk 9:37–43) put this miracle right after the descent from the Mount of Transfiguration. Matthew's account is much shorter than Mark's, which has led some to think Matthew used independent information here. It introduces Matthew 17:20 (the thrust of which occurs again at 21:21) and thus makes faith pivotal in the narrative. The contrast between the glory of the transfiguration and Jesus' disciples' tawdry unbelief (see v.17) is part of the mounting tension that magnifies Jesus' uniqueness as he moves closer to his passion and resurrection.

14When they came to the crowd, a man approached Jesus and knelt before him. 15"Lord,
have mercy on my son," he said. "He has seizures and is suffering greatly. He often falls into
the fire or into the water. 16I brought him to your disciples, but they could not heal him."
17"O unbelieving and perverse generation," Jesus replied, "how long shall I stay with
you? How long shall I put up with you? Bring the boy here to me." 18Jesus rebuked the
demon, and it came out of the boy, and he was healed from that moment.
19Then the disciples came to Jesus in private and asked, "Why couldn't we drive it out?"
20He replied, "Because you have so little faith. I tell you the truth, if you have faith as
small as a mustard seed, you can say to this mountain, 'Move from here to there' and it will
move. Nothing will be impossible for you."

COMMENTARY

14–16 Matthew's account, with its sudden introduction of the crowd (v.14), clearly presupposes some fuller narrative (cf. Mark). The word for "knelt" (*gonypeteō*, used in the NT only here and at 27:29; Mk 1:40; 10:17) has no overtones of worship but suggests humility and entreaty. For "Lord" (v.15; Mark has "Teacher"), see comments at 8:2; 17:4. *Selēniazetai* ("he has seizures") occurs only twice in the NT (see comments at 4:24), and is not connected with epilepsy (see France [TNTC]). Mark 9:18–20 describes the boy's symptoms more vividly. "Epilepsy" in this instance is associated with demon-possession (see comments at 8:28). The "disciples" who are unable to heal him are presumably the nine left behind when Jesus took Peter, James, and John with him when he was transfigured.

The disciples' failures are a recurring theme throughout this section (14:16–21, 26–31; 15:16, 23, 33; 16:5, 22; 17:4, 10–11). This failure in their healing ministry at first seems strange, since Jesus had clearly given them power to heal and exorcise demons (10:1, 8). Yet it is part of the pattern of the disciples' advance and failure. In other situations they had shown lack of faith (14:26–27, 31)—a reminder that their power to do kingdom miracles was not their own but, unlike magic, was entirely derivative and related to their own walk of faith.

17–18 Jesus' response is reminiscent of Deuteronomy 32:5, 20. *Apistos* (GK *603*) can mean either "untrustworthy" or "unbelieving." The latter is dominant here (cf. v.20); yet it does not mean "this generation" has no faith whatsoever but that unbelief is characteristic of "this generation." The perfect passive participle *diestrammenē* ("perverse") probably has adjectival force rather than denoting a state consequent on some previous action (see comments at 16:19). Juxtaposing "perverse" and "unbelieving" implies that the failure to believe stems from moral failure to recognize the truth, not from want of evidence, but from willful neglect or distortion of the evidence. *Diastrephō* ("pervert," GK *1406*) is used seven times in the NT (cf. Lk 9:41; 23:2; Ac 13:8, 10; 20:30; Php 2:15). In the last of these, Paul applies to the entire world the same words Jesus uses here.

But what does "generation" (*genea*, GK *1155*) cover? To be sure, it extends Jesus' excoriation beyond the disciples (cf. 11:16; 12:39–42; 16:4; 23:36; 24:34). But it goes past the evidence to hold with Walker (*Heilsgeschichte*, 35ff.) that the word here means "race," and therefore that the Jews are henceforth excluded from salvation, or to say with Frankemölle (*Jahwebund und Kirche Christi*, 21ff.) that Israel alone is being addressed. That the disciples' unbelief is central to Jesus' exasperation is made clear by Matthew's omitting Mark 9:23–24. If his description extends beyond them to the entire contemporary generation, it must principally extend also to all guilty of the same unbelief, regardless of their race.

The rhetorical questions—"How long shall I stay with you? How long shall I put up with you?"—express not only personal disappointment but also Jesus' consciousness of his heavenly origin and destiny. His disciples' perverse unbelief is actually painful to him. He must endure (NIV, "put up with") it, though this theme is stronger in Mark than in Matthew (cf. Mk 8:12 and Mt 16:4; Mk 3:5 and Mt 12:13). As for the miracle, Matthew describes it succinctly, leaving no doubt of Jesus' power to heal and exorcise demons (v.18). The boy is healed "from that moment" (lit., "from that hour"; cf. 9:22; 15:28).

19–20 [21] The disciples, presumably the nine who had tried and failed (v.16), ask Jesus, in private (cf. Mk 9:28), why "we" (emphatic) could not drive out the demon (v.19). The reason, Jesus says, is their *oligopistia* ("little faith," v.20; see Notes). Despite the etymology of the word, it probably does not refer so much to the littleness of their faith as to its poverty (so Bonnard). Little faith, like a little mustard seed, can be effectual; poor faith, like that of the disciples' here, is ineffectual. The noun occurs only here in Matthew, but the cognate adjective occurs at 6:30; 8:26; 14:31; 16:8, and always refers to disciples. Removal of mountains was proverbial for overcoming great difficulties (cf. Isa 40:4; 49:11; 54:10; Mt 21:21–22; Mk 11:23; Lk 17:6; 1Co 13:2). Nothing would be impossible for them—a promise that, like its analogue in Philippians 4:13, is limited by context, not by unbelief. Here it refers to the accomplishment of the works of the kingdom, for which they had been given authority.

Jesus' answer in Matthew is not the same as the one in Mark 9:29 ("This kind can come out only by prayer"), but if the comment on *oligopistia* ("poverty of faith") is correct, then at least the two answers are complementary, each shedding light on the other. At a superficial level, the disciples did have faith. They expected to be able to exorcise the demon. They had long been successful in this work, and now they are surprised by their failure. But their faith is poor and shoddy. They are treating the authority given them (10:1, 8) like a gift of magic, a bestowed power that works *ex opere operato*. In Mark, Jesus tells them that this case requires prayer—not a form or an approved rite, but an entire life bathed in prayer and its concomitant faith. In Matthew, Jesus tells his disciples that what they need is not giant faith (tiny faith will do) but true faith—faith that, out of a deep, personal trust, expects God to work.

NOTES

14 The genitive absolute here, in v.26, and in Acts 17:14 is defective—a participle without a substantive (cf. Zerwick, *Biblical Greek*, para. 50; Moule, *Idiom Book*, 203). This evokes the introduction of a pronoun in many later MSS, or a change in the participle to the nominative singular in a few of them.

17 In exclamations expressing very strong emotion, ὦ (*ō*, "O") is not restricted to the vocative but may color an entire sentence, which is often, as here, a question (cf. BDF, para. 146 [2]).

18 For the confusion between the prepositions ἀπό (*apo*, "from," "away from") and ἐκ (*ek*, "from," "out from") in Hellenistic Greek, see comments at 3:16.

20 Ὀλιγοπιστίαν (*oligopistian*, "little faith," or, better, "poor faith") is read by א B H f^1 f^{13} 33 700 892 et al., and ἀπιστίαν (*apistian*, "faithless," as in v.17) by the rest. But the first reading has strong witnesses; it is a NT hapax legomenon (single occurrence); its cognate is distinctively, if not exclusively, Matthean (6:30; 8:26; 14:31; 16:8); and the change to the second reading may well have been prompted by v.17, where the text is firm.

21 "But this kind does not go out except by prayer and fasting" is omitted by a powerful combination of witnesses. It is obviously an assimilation to the synoptic parallel in Mark 9:29. There is no obvious reason why, if original, it should have been omitted, and textual harmonization is quite demonstrably a secondary process.

15. The second major passion prediction (17:22–23)

OVERVIEW

This is the second major passion prediction (see comments at 16:21–23), though there are earlier allusions to Jesus' death (9:15; 10:38; 12:40) and one intervening specific reference (v.12b). Jesus not only foresees the inevitability of his death but, precisely because he knows this to be the Father's will (26:39), recognizes it as an essential part of the divine plan. But this death issues in the resurrection.

22When they came together in Galilee, he said to them, "The Son of Man is going to be betrayed into the hands of men. 23They will kill him, and on the third day he will be raised to life." And the disciples were filled with grief.

COMMENTARY

22 Thompson (*Matthew's Advice*, 13ff.) finds here the beginning of a new literary unit, ending at 18:35, based partly on the references to Galilee here and at 19:1. But the departure from Galilee (19:1) not only ends this brief stay but also this entire period of Jesus' northern ministry (4:23–25). From 19:1 on, Jesus moves toward Jerusalem and Judea. "When they came together" (the best reading) does not necessarily suggest new activities but the general time when Jesus and the inner circle of disciples joined the other nine in Galilee (see comments at vv.1, 14–20). No sooner are they all together after the transfiguration than Jesus again takes up the theme he introduced to them earlier (16:21–23). The verb *paradidosthai* ("to be betrayed," GK *4140*) is doubly ambiguous. First, it can have either a weak meaning ("to hand over") or a strong meaning ("to betray"), depending on context; second, the passive ("to be handed over") is perhaps a studied ambiguity, leaving it unclear whether God or Judas Iscariot is the one who hands Jesus over or betrays him respectively.

23 Mark and Luke say the disciples do not understand. Matthew, adept at fine characterization, establishes the same point by noting the disciples' grief. They are beginning to absorb the announcement of Jesus' death, but of his resurrection they have no comprehension.

16. The temple tax (17:24–27)

OVERVIEW

This incident is peculiar to Matthew (cf. Mk 9:33 for geographical detail). Its significance in Matthew depends heavily on its interpretation at several critical points.

[24]After Jesus and his disciples arrived in Capernaum, the collectors of the two-drachma tax came to Peter and asked, "Doesn't your teacher pay the temple tax?"

[25]"Yes, he does," he replied.

When Peter came into the house, Jesus was the first to speak. "What do you think, Simon?" he asked. "From whom do the kings of the earth collect duty and taxes—from their own sons or from others?"

[26]"From others," Peter answered.

"Then the sons are exempt," Jesus said to him. [27]"But so that we may not offend them, go to the lake and throw out your line. Take the first fish you catch; open its mouth and you will find a four-drachma coin. Take it and give it to them for my tax and yours."

COMMENTARY

24 Although the point is disputed (see comments at v.25), the *didrachma* (lit., "two drachmas") was probably not a civil tax in support of Rome (see comments at 22:15–22) but a Jewish "tax" levied on every male Jew between the ages of twenty and fifty in support of the temple and its services. The *didrachma*, worth one-half a *statēr* or shekel, was seldom minted at this time; and probably two people joined to pay a *tetradrachma* ("a four-drachma coin," 17:27) or shekel. Originally half a shekel was levied on each Jew at every census (Ex 30:11–16), the money going to support the tabernacle; after the exile one-third of a shekel was gathered annually. In Jesus' day the amount was two drachmas (half a shekel) annually. This is well attested in both Josephus (*Ant.* 3.193–96 [8.2]; 18.312 [9.1]) and Mishnah (*Šeqal.*). The imposition of this "tax" lacked the sanction of Roman law, but it was understood that the Jews would pay it.

25–26 Peter's defense of Jesus (v.25) is misguided. Once they are alone in the house (perhaps Peter's; cf. 4:13; 8:14), Jesus takes the initiative—whether he overheard Peter's response or knew it supernaturally is unclear—and asks Peter a provocative question. The vast literature on this pericope stems largely from Jesus' question being cast in *civil* terms: "kings of the earth," "duty," "taxes." The majority view today (e.g., Kilpatrick, *Origins*, 41–42; Walker, *Heilsgeschichte*, 101–3; Bonnard; Hill) holds that the original question was recast in the period after AD 70 (when Matthew is alleged to have been writing) to address questions faced by Christians about taxes paid to Rome. The effect of the pericope, then, is like that of 22:15–22, though Jesus' reported answer here is anachronistic. Jesus is made to say that the Son of God, and therefore Christians, *need* not pay taxes to Rome because of their allegiance to God but *should* do so in order not to cause offense. This will not do, for in Jesus' reply the "king" who collects the tax is Jesus' "Father." Therefore, this cannot refer to Rome.

Others (Thompson, *Matthew's Advice*, 50–68) suggest that this is the tax paid the post-Jamnia patriarchate and that the question Matthew is facing is whether Christians at his time of writing should bow to Jewish religious authority. This means not only that Jesus' question and Peter's answer are anachronistic but that the redaction here is inept. Would Jews at the end of the first century think of the Jamnia rabbis as kings or of Jesus Messiah as their son? The suggestion that the tax is the one imposed by Vespasian in support of the temple of *Jupiter Capitolinus* after the fall of Jerusalem (Josephus, *J.W.* 7.218 [6.6]—so H.W. Montefiore, "Jesus and the Temple Tax," *NTS* [1964–1965], 60–71 [cf. Hill], and others) is incredible. No Christian willingly advocated direct subsidy of pagan idolatry in order not to offend Rome, and on this reading Jesus' question becomes even more obscure.

Because of such difficulties, Richard J. Cassidy ("Matthew 17:24–27—A Word on Civil Taxes," *CBQ* 41 [1979]: 571–80) argues that the entire pericope deals, not with the temple tax, but with civil taxes. The terminology of v.25 supports him, but again it is less than clear how sonship to an imperial "king" fits Jesus.

It is better to allow the most likely interpretations of both v.24 and v.25 to stand—temple tax and civil tax respectively—but to recognize that, whereas v.24 establishes the topic of the entire pericope, v.25 is parabolic. This is suggested by the generalized "kings of the earth"—scarcely an adequate way to refer to Caesar. The point is that, just as royal sons are exempt from the taxes imposed by their fathers, so also Jesus is exempt from the "tax" imposed by his Father. In other words, Jesus acknowledges the temple tax to be an obligation to God; but since he is uniquely God's Son, therefore he is exempt (v.26). The focus of the pericope is thus supremely christological and, unlike 22:15–22, says nothing about responsibilities to Caesar.

27 Exempt though he is, Jesus will pay the tax so as not to offend (for the verb, see comments at 5:29). Thus he sets an example, later followed by Paul (1Co 8:13; 9:12, 22). The plural "we" and the four-drachma coin to pay for Jesus and Peter at first sight makes the above interpretation seem difficult. In what sense are we to suppose that Peter's reason for paying the tax is akin to Jesus'? Part of the explanation may lie in the freedom Jesus extends to his disciples: e.g., he alone is Lord of the Sabbath, and this has implications for his disciples (see comments at 12:1–8). More important, Jesus here implicitly frees his followers from the temple tax on the grounds that they, too, will belong to the category of "sons," though derivatively. Meanwhile, "disciples should avoid unnecessarily offending others (15:12–13 has shown that they cannot avoid all offense)" (Blomberg [NAC]).

Both the christological implication and the relevance to Peter and the disciples are made clear in the course of the narrative. Jesus has just been declared God's unique Son (v.5); yet his glory is veiled as he moves toward betrayal and death, thus establishing a pattern of humility for his followers (18:1–5). At the same time, Jesus' death and resurrection have again been introduced (vv.22–23), a foretaste of the lengthy passion and resurrection narratives about to begin and the means by which the Son of Man, in giving his life "as a ransom for many" (20:28), completes the redemptive act inaugurating the gathering of his "church" (16:18; 28:18–20). At that point, the redemptive-historical significance of the temple will end. Its claims for the two-drachma tax may continue until its destruction forty years later; the sons of God (cf. 5:9) are exempt. But that time is not yet. Like so many of Jesus' actions at this turning point, the full significance of what Jesus was saying could not be grasped, even by Peter, until after the resurrection.

The miracle itself has no close canonical parallel. This is the only place in the NT where a fish is caught with a hook (nets were normally used), though coins have occasionally been found in the mouths of fish caught in the Sea of Galilee. Some scholars point out that the event ("miracle"?) itself is not described, but only the command: "We do not know what resulted. Given Peter's track record of misunderstanding, it would be rash to hazard a guess" (Blomberg [NAC]; cf. France [TNTC]). But unless one speculates that Jesus is somehow speaking ironically or humorously (for which there is here very little evidence), the obvious implication is that Jesus *did* issue this command, regardless of how Peter did or did not carry it out. Extravagant symbolism for "fish" and "lake" (e.g., Neil J. McEleney, "Mt 17:24–27—Who Paid the Temple Tax?" *CBQ* 38 [1976]: 189–92) is fanciful. This spectacular way of paying the tax is something only Jesus could do; it therefore suggests that though Jesus as the unique Son is free from the law's demands, he not only submits to them but makes provision, as only he can, for the demands on his disciples (cf. Gal 4:4–5)—and this right after a passion prediction (17:22–23)! Perhaps, too, we are reminded of Jesus' humility. He who so controls nature and its powers that he stills storms and multiplies food now reminds Peter of that power by this miracle, while nevertheless remaining so humble that he would not needlessly cause offense (cf. 11:28–30; 12:20). The lesson in humility is for Peter and the other disciples. We have no evidence that the tax collectors witnessed it. (The nonhealing miracles in Matthew are almost always for the sake of the disciples; see Gerhardsson, *Mighty Acts*.) But humility is about to be explained to the disciples in some detail (18:1–35).

NOTES

26 As in v.14, the genitive absolute is defective and has led to many variants (cf. Metzger, *Textual Commentary*, 46).

27 Although some (e.g., Zerwick, *Biblical Greek*, para. 93) suggest ἀντί (*anti* "instead of," "in substitution for") here has the force of ὑπέρ (*hyper*, "on behalf of"), it is perhaps better to think of Exodus 30:11–16 as the background, remembering that this tax was perceived as a ransom payment instead of the person (cf. Turner, *Insights*, 173).

B. Fourth Discourse: Life under Kingdom Authority (18:1–19:2)

OVERVIEW

This fourth discourse, like the previous three, is bracketed by remarks suggesting that it was delivered on the one occasion specified (see comments at 5:1; 7:28–29). The chapter parallels Mark 9:33–50 to some extent but omits Mark 9:38–41 (cf. Mt 10:42). The differences between Mark and Matthew are so great that some scholars assume separate sources (e.g., Lohmeyer) or wisely advocate cautious agnosticism (e.g., Thompson, *Matthew's Advice*, 147–51).

Many writers compare Matthew 18 with 1QS, the Manual of Discipline at Qumran, and interpret it as regulation for the life of the Christian community. But two major reservations forbid too easy a comparison.

1. There is very little in Matthew 18 that has the flavor of regulation and much that deals with principles. The contrasts with 1QS are far more noticeable than the similarities. Even vv.15–17, the closest approximation to regulation, are far less concerned with mechanical details than with the importance and means of reconciliation. And the whole chapter shows up the carnality of the

opening question (v.1) and establishes a radical set of values for greatness in the kingdom.

2. The Qumran covenanters had little doubt about their identity or place in God's eschatological scheme. But here we are dealing with disciples at a critical turning point in salvation history, men of seriously defective understanding who remain such until after the cross.

1. Setting (18:1–2)

[1]At that time the disciples came to Jesus and asked, "Who is the greatest in the kingdom of heaven?"

[2]He called a little child and had him stand among them.

COMMENTARY

1–2 Mark (9:33–37) says that the disciples were disputing along the way, and when challenged, they fell silent. Luke (9:46–48) says Jesus discerned their thoughts. It is not difficult or unnatural to suppose that Jesus detected their rivalry (Luke), challenged them, and thereby silenced them (Mark), and that they then blurted out their question (Matthew). Alternatively, Matthew uses this brief question to summarize what was truly on their minds.

"At that time" (lit., "hour") may only mean "in that general phase of the ministry" (cf. 10:19; 26:45), but it alerts the reader to the transition from what precedes. "At that time," when Jesus has again spoken of his suffering and death, the disciples' grief (17:23) proves short-lived, and they busy themselves with arguing about who is greatest in the kingdom. Jesus has already said that there will be distinctions in the kingdom (5:19; cf. 1QS 3:19–25; 6:9–13), and recently three of them have been specially favored (17:1–3), while Peter has been repeatedly singled out (14:28–29; 15:15; 16:16–18, 22–23; 17:4, 24–27)—though sometimes for rebuke! Perhaps these things set off the dispute, which continues in the ambition of James, John, and their mother to the period right before the cross (20:20–23) and which embraces the jealousy of the other ten (20:24). Substantial misunderstanding of Jesus by his disciples is presupposed throughout Jesus' entire earthly ministry.

The "disciples" are probably the Twelve but may include others (cf. Thompson, *Matthew's Advice*, 83–84; see comments at 5:1–2). The child (v.2) may have been Peter's, if the house is his (17:25; Mk 9:33).

2. Humility and greatness (18:3–4)

[3]And he said:"I tell you the truth, unless you change and become like little children, you will never enter the kingdom of heaven. [4]Therefore, whoever humbles himself like this child is the greatest in the kingdom of heaven."

COMMENTARY

3–4 With the solemn introductory formula "I tell you the truth" (v.3; see comments at 5:18), Jesus warns his disciples that they must "change and become like little children," for unless they do, they will "never enter the kingdom of heaven." Clearly, the consummated kingdom is in view. The child is held up as an ideal, not of innocence, purity, or faith, but of humility and unconcern for social status. Jesus advocates humility of mind (v.4), not childishness of thought (cf. 10:16). With such humility comes childlike trust (cf. *TDNT*, 8:16–17). The disciples must change (lit., "turn," probably not to be taken as a Semitic auxiliary to "become," i.e., "become again a little child"; cf. J. Dupont, "Matthieu 18:3," in *Neotestamentica et Semitica* [ed. Ellis and Wilcox], 50–60) from their present conduct and attitudes and adopt this new norm or be excluded from the kingdom. Conversely, the person who truly humbles himself (see Notes, v.4) like this child is "the greatest in the kingdom of heaven." The expression completes a link with v.1, and the present tense may suggest that the disciple's greatness, doubtless made obvious in the consummated kingdom in the future, has already begun here as far as kingdom norms are concerned.

The thought is not far removed from 5:3 and vitiates any thought that the kingdom can be gained by personal merit or violent force (see comments at 11:12). It is to "little children" that the Lord of heaven and earth reveals his truth (11:25).

NOTES

4 The verb ταπεινώσει (*tapeinōsei*, lit., "will humble") is one of the few instances in which the distinction between a future indicative and an aorist subjunctive plus ἄν (*an*, untranslatable particle used to suggest some kind of contingency) is virtually obliterated (cf. BDF, para. 380 [2]).

3. The heinousness of causing believers to sin (18:5–9)

OVERVIEW

Although some read v.5 with vv.3–4, it is better to link it with vv.6–9, because (1) v.4 already rounds off vv.1–4 with a summary, and (2) vv.5–6 taken together constitute a neat promise-warning proverb (cf. Thompson, *Matthew's Advice*, 101–7). This pericope is held tightly together by its repeated use of *skandalon* ("stumbling block," GK *4998*) and the verb derived from it (see comments at 5:29); Paul calls such an obstacle a *proskomma* ("obstacle," "cause of stumbling," GK *4682*; cf. Ro 14:13; 1Co 8:9). Rabbinic literature contains denunciations of the evil of causing others to sin (cf. Bonnard), but never with reference to "little ones."

5"And whoever welcomes a little child like this in my name welcomes me. 6But if
anyone causes one of these little ones who believe in me to sin, it would be better for

him to have a large millstone hung around his neck and to be drowned in the depths of the sea.

7"Woe to the world because of the things that cause people to sin! Such things must come, but woe to the man through whom they come! 8If your hand or your foot causes you to sin, cut it off and throw it away. It is better for you to enter life maimed or crippled than to have two hands or two feet and be thrown into eternal fire. 9And if your eye causes you to sin, gouge it out and throw it away. It is better for you to enter life with one eye than to have two eyes and be thrown into the fire of hell."

COMMENTARY

5–6 This promise-warning couplet (like 12:32 in structure) advances the thought by turning attention from the self-humiliation of the true disciple (vv.3–4) to the way others receive such "little ones." The opening clauses of v.5 and v.6 are roughly parallel. The one who welcomes "a little child like this *in my name*" is not welcoming literal children but "children" defined in the previous verses—those who humble themselves to become like children, i.e., Jesus' true disciples. They are not welcomed because they are great, wise, or mighty but because they come in Jesus' name (v.5)—i.e., they belong to him. "In my name" (v.5), the parallel clause "who believe in me" (v.6), and the necessity of becoming childlike even to enter the kingdom (v.3) all confirm the view that those referred to in vv.5–6 are simply Jesus' disciples—Christians (to use a later term), not literal children or some smaller group of especially humble disciples (see Warfield, *Selected Shorter Writings*, 1:234–52; Trotter, "Understanding and Stumbling"). These "little ones" (cf. 25:40, 45) can stumble, even the greatest of them (14:28–31; 26:30–35); but whoever causes them to stumble (NIV, "to sin") stands in grave peril.

It is no objection to this identification of "little ones" with believers that Jesus is here addressing his disciples and not the world that is most in need of the warning, for (1) the "whoever" takes in everybody; (2) despite the fact that Jesus is speaking to disciples (v.1), he utters a woe on the world in v.7; (3) this suggests that the passage aims at encouraging the disciples who are going to have to face the world's opprobrium (as also 10:40–42); and (4) the warnings against the world, though not at this moment directed to the world, will in due course become part of the disciples' arsenal in their preaching.

The person who welcomes one of these "little ones," these disciples of Jesus, simply because they are his, welcomes Jesus himself (cf. 10:42). Presupposed is the world's animosity. Mere hospitality is not in view but hospitality given because of the "little ones'" link with Jesus. It is probably presupposed that hospitality motivated in this way would be shown only if the benefactor were already well disposed toward Jesus, or at least moving in that direction. The antithetic alternative, causing the "little ones" to stumble, does not mean that the "little ones" are led into apostasy. Rather, they are not welcomed but are rejected, ignored. This causes them to stumble in their discipleship. It may lead to serious sin; but, as in 10:40–42 and 25:31–46, the really grave aspect of the rejection is that it signifies rejection of Jesus.

Implicitly, the offense is gravely magnified when, with particular perversity, some wicked people self-consciously try to entice Christ's "little ones" into sin—but the evil is broader than that. Because it signals a rejection of Jesus as well as damaging his people, drowning at sea before the evil was committed is much preferable to eschatological judgment, the eternal fire of hell (vv.8–9) that awaits the perpetrators. Drowning was a not uncommon punishment in Greek and Roman society. Though rare in Jewish circles, it was done at least once in Galilee (Josephus, *Ant.* 14.450 [15.10]). Most millstones were hand tools for domestic use (see comments at 24:41); here it is the heavy stone pulled around by a donkey. The picture is more graphic than in Mark, the horror of the judgment sharpened.

7 The Greek text proclaims a "woe" (here, clearly, a proclamation of judgment, not of "sympathetic sorrow" [McNeile, 261], since Matthew heightens the judgment language; see comments at 23:13–32) on the "world," understood not merely as the neutral "setting for the struggle between belief and unbelief" (Thompson, *Matthew's Advice*, 109–10), but the source of all stumbling. Jesus pronounces this woe *apo tōn skandalōn*, which, contrary to the NIV, should not be rendered "because of the things that cause *people* to sin," as if the discussion had progressed from Jesus' "little ones" to "people" in general, but "because of stumbling blocks," i.e., of the things that cause the stumbling already referred to in v.6. Such things must come, but this does not mitigate the responsibility of those through whom they come (cf. Isa 10:5–12; Ac 4:27–28; see comments at 13:13). The necessity does not spring from divine compulsion but, like all things, falls within the sphere of his sovereignty so that he may use those very things to accomplish his plan and perfect his people (cf. 24:10–13; 1Co 11:19). Thus, on the one hand, the disciples are not to think such opposition strange, for Jesus himself has declared it must occur; on the other hand, they are assured that justice will be done in the end (cf. 26:24).

8–9 Jesus now abandons denunciation of the world's causing his disciples to stumble and tells his disciples they may prove to be not only victims but aggressors. The adversative *de* is given its full force: "*But*, beyond all this, if *your* hand" (v.8). This does not mean that the church, pictured as a body in anticipation of Paul's language (e.g., 1Co 12:12–27), is here exhorted to excommunicate offending members. The word "body" is not used, and the language is akin to that in 5:29–30. Certain attitudes nurtured by Jesus' disciples toward other believers could also be sinful; thus, instead of being enticed to sin by outsiders, they would cause their own stumbling. Perhaps the particular believer-to-believer attitude that most needs rooting out is pride, so vv.8–9 prepare for v.10.

The argument is clear. Jesus' followers must become like children in humility if they are to enter the kingdom (vv.3–4). Those who receive such "little ones" because they belong to him in effect receive Jesus; those who reject them, causing them to stumble, are threatened with condemnation (vv.5–6). Things causing Jesus' people to stumble are inevitable, yet damning (v.7). But the disciples themselves must beware. Failure to deal radically with similar sin in their own lives betrays their allegiance to the world and threatens them with the eternal fire of hell (see comments at 5:22). Jesus' disciples must deal as radically with pride as they were earlier commanded to deal with lust (5:29–30).

NOTES

7 The γάρ (*gar*, "for") retains its normal causal force but applies to the next clause, here introduced by πλήν (*plēn*, "but"). The content of the γάρ, *gar*, itself is parenthetical so far as the force of γάρ, *gar*, is concerned. The same construction is found elsewhere (cf. 22:14; 24:6; cf. Zerwick, *Biblical Greek*, paras. 474–75).

4. The parable of the lost sheep (18:10–14)

OVERVIEW

Verse 10 clearly follows vv.5–9; but because it also forms a neat inclusio with v.14, vv.10–14 must be read together in the light of the preceding pericope. This link raises important questions concerning the relation between this parable and the parable of the lost sheep in Luke 15:3–7, where it is addressed, not to disciples, but to Pharisees and teachers of the law, in defense of Jesus' attitude to sinners. Almost all scholars hold that one parable stands behind both gospels, and then they debate over which form and setting are most primitive (for discussion, see Jeremias, *Parables of Jesus*, 38ff.; Marshall, *Gospel of Luke*, 600–601; Hill), some arguing in favor of the form in *Gospel of Thomas* 107 (e.g., W. L. Petersen, "The Parable of the Lost Sheep in the *Gospel of Thomas* and the Synoptics," *NovT* 23 [1981]: 128–47; but cf. Blomberg, "Tendencies of the Tradition," 29–63, 96–100). All these views presuppose that at least one of the two settings defined by Matthew and Luke is a late creation by the church or by one of the evangelists to apply the parable to some new problem.

But if the original parable was "simple enough and rich enough to be applied to more than one situation" (Hill), why could not Jesus himself apply it to more than one situation? What methodological reasons are advanced for distinguishing between multiple usages by Jesus and multiple usages by the church? It is remarkable how different Matthew's and Luke's forms of the parable are when closely compared in the Greek text. Almost every relevant term is not the same as in the parallel, and the few that are the same are well within the bounds of repetition expected in an itinerant ministry (see comments at 5:1–2). The evidence suggests that these are two similar parables, both taught by Jesus, but with very different aims (see comments at 19:1–2 for the bearing of the problems of "Luke's central section" on this discussion). Matthew is not concerned with "faithful pastorship in the community" (Hill) but, following the preceding pericope, with the importance in Messiah's community of harming no member, of sharing the Father's concern that none of "these little ones" be lost. See discussion in France (NICNT) and in Thompson (*Matthew's Advice*, 168–74).

[10]"See that you do not look down on one of these little ones. For I tell you that their angels in heaven always see the face of my Father in heaven.

[12]"What do you think? If a man owns a hundred sheep, and one of them wanders away, will he not leave the ninety-nine on the hills and go to look for the one that wandered off? [13]And if he finds it, I tell you the truth, he is happier about that one sheep than about the ninety-nine that did not wander off. [14]In the same way your Father in heaven is not willing that any of these little ones should be lost."

COMMENTARY

10 [11] Verse 10 continues the note of humility struck at the discourse's beginning (vv.3–4) and the concern for "these little ones" (vv.5–9). There is no conflict between "you" and "these little ones." At this stage of their pilgrimage, even the disciples must change and become like little children (v.3). Jesus is discussing what will be normative when his passion and resurrection fully inaugurate the messianic community. Its members will be poor in spirit (5:3) and humble (18:3–4), and none will be admitted to it without these graces. If his disciples become like that, they will belong to the "little children"; if they look down on them, they will share in the woes (vv.8–9). The warning was not irrelevant. At least one disciple left Jesus.

Jesus says that the "little ones"—believers in him—must be treated with respect because "their angels in heaven" always see the face of the heavenly Father. Many believe this supports the idea of a guardian for each "little one." It is thought that these angels are "in heaven" means they are of highest rank and that their seeing the Father's face means they always have access to his presence. This is based largely on Jewish sources (cf. Str-B, 1:781ff.; 3:48ff., 437ff.; *TDNT*, 1:82, 86; see esp. Tob 12:14–15). Yet the idea will not bear close scrutiny.

It is true that angels are sent to minister to those who will inherit salvation (Heb 1:14). But nowhere in Scripture or Jewish tradition of the NT period is there any suggestion that there is one angel for one person. Daniel and Zechariah imply one angel for each nation. Appeal to Acts 12:15 does not help. Why should Peter's supposed guardian angel sound like Peter? And if ministering angels are sent to help believers, what are the angels in Matthew 18:10 doing around the divine throne instead of guarding those people to whom they are assigned? References in the Dead Sea Scrolls to angels who share in the community's worship (1QSa 2:9–10) or minister to the Lord (1QH 5:20–22) are even less relevant, for this context does not deal with corporate worship.

The most likely explanation is the one Warfield (*Selected Shorter Writings*, 1:253–66) defends. The "angels" of the "little ones" are their spirits after death, and they always see the heavenly Father's face. Do not despise these little ones, Jesus says, for their destiny is the unshielded glory of the Father's presence. The present tense (they "always see") raises no difficulty because Jesus is dealing with a class, not individuals. The same interpretation admirably suits Acts 12:15. What the assembled group thinks is standing outside is Peter's "spirit" (angel), which accounts for Rhoda's recognition of his voice.

But can the word "angel" be pressed into this interpretation? Certainly Jesus teaches that God's people in the resurrection "will be like the angels in heaven" as to marriage (22:30) and immortality (Lk 20:36). Similar language is also used in

2 Baruch 51:5, 12 (cf. also *1 En.* 51:4): the righteous will become angels in heaven, will be transformed into the splendor of angels, and will even surpass the excellency of angels. The evidence, though not overwhelming, is substantial enough to suppose that "their angels" simply refers to their continued existence in the heavenly Father's presence.

12–13 Here is another reason not to despise these "little ones": the shepherd—the Father (v.14)—is concerned for each sheep in his flock and seeks the one who strays (v.12). His concern for the one wandering sheep is so great that he rejoices more over its restoration than over the ninety-nine that do not stray (v.13). With a God like that, how dare anyone cause even one of these sheep to go astray?

14 Jesus drives the lesson home: the heavenly Father is unwilling for any of "these little ones" (see comments at vv.3–6) to be lost. If that is his will, it is shocking that anyone else would seek to lead one of "these little ones" astray. (Thompson, *Matthew's Advice*, 187–88, follows the line of thought admirably.) This love for the *individual* sheep is not at the expense of the entire flock but so that the flock as a whole may not lose a single one of its members. On God's preservation of his own, see comments at 12:32; 13:3–9, 19–23.

NOTES

11 This verse is omitted by the earliest witnesses of the Alexandrian, pre-Caesarean, Egyptian, and Antiochene text types. Inclusion in various forms appears to be an assimilation to Luke 19:10.

12 Some commentators argue that the verb πλανηθῇ (*planēthē*, "wanders away") signifies for Matthew apostasy from the Christian community (cf. 24:4–5, 11, 24). Two of these references (24:4–5) are taken from Mark 13:5–6, but Matthew ignores two other good references (Mk 12:24, 27). Πλανηθῇ, *planēthē*, has for Matthew no technical force, and in Matthew 22:29 cannot possibly refer to such apostasy. It is general and suits the pastoral setting of the parable. Doubtless Jesus' teaching looks forward to the established church, but there is no evidence here to support theories about Matthew's anachronisms.

5. Treatment of a sinning brother (18:15–20)

15"If your brother sins against you, go and show him his fault, just between the two of
you. If he listens to you, you have won your brother over. 16But if he will not listen, take one
or two others along, so that 'every matter may be established by the testimony of two or
three witnesses.' 17If he refuses to listen to them, tell it to the church; and if he refuses to
listen even to the church, treat him as you would a pagan or a tax collector.
18"I tell you the truth, whatever you bind on earth will be bound in heaven, and whatever you loose on earth will be loosed in heaven.
19"Again, I tell you that if two of you on earth agree about anything you ask for, it will be
done for you by my Father in heaven. 20For where two or three come together in my name,
there am I with them."

COMMENTARY

15 Jesus has just spoken to his disciples to warn them not to cause one of these "little ones" to stumble. Now the thought shifts. What the shift is depends on the variant reading chosen. If the words "against you" are included, Jesus is looking at offenses within the messianic community from the opposite perspective from the viewpoint of the brother against whom the sin is committed. If "against you" is omitted (see Notes), Jesus is telling the community as a whole how to handle the situation when a brother sins, and in the immediate context, the sin is that of despising another brother.

Either way, the proper thing is to confront the brother privately and "show him his fault." The verb *elenchō* (GK *1793*) probably suggests "convict" the brother, not by passing judgment, but by convicting him of his sin. The aim is not to score points over him but to win him over (same verb as in 1Co 9:19–22; 1Pe 3:1) because all discipline, even this private kind, must begin with redemptive purposes (Lk 17:3–4; 2Th 3:14–15; Jas 5:19–20; cf. Sir 19:13–17). Jesus assumes that the individual (second person singular) who personally confronts his brother will do so with true humility (vv.3–4; cf. Gal 6:1). If it is hard to accept a rebuke, even a private one, it is harder still to administer one in loving humility. Behind this verse stands Leviticus 19:17: "Do not hate your brother in your heart. Rebuke your neighbor frankly so you will not share in his guilt."

16 If private confrontation does not work, the next step (backed by Dt 19:15) is to take two or three witnesses (though the text form of the quotation is much disputed: cf. Gundry, *Use of the Old Testament*, 139; Blomberg, "Matthew" in *CNTUOT*). Doubtless this Deuteronomic law was designed for what we would call "secular" cases. But the distinction is artificial and should not be pressed, for the Israelite nation understood itself to be not a nation like others but a theocratic nation, God's chosen people. In conformity with his customary interpretation of the Scriptures, Jesus perceives the link joining his messianic community with ancient Israel.

It is not at first clear whether the function of the witnesses is to support the one who confronts his erring brother by bringing additional testimony about the sin committed (which would require at least three people to have observed the offense) or to provide witnesses to the confrontation if the case were to go before the whole church. The latter is a bit more likely, because Deuteronomy 19:15 deals with judicial condemnation (a step taken only by the entire assembly), not with attempts to convince a brother of his fault. By the united testimony of two or three witnesses, every matter "may be established" (*stathē*, lit., "may be made to stand"—though the rise of deponents in Hellenistic Greek, including the use of *stathē*, implies that "may stand" is a superior rendering; cf. Zerwick, *Biblical Greek*, para. 231; Turner, *Syntax*, 57).

17 The same three-step procedure is known elsewhere (1QS 5:25–6:1; cf. CD 9:2–3; Davies, *Setting*, 221ff.). Refusal to submit to the considered judgment of Messiah's people means that they are to treat the offender as "a pagan or a tax collector." It is poor exegesis to turn to 8:1–11; 9:9–13; 15:21–28 and say that such people should be treated compassionately. The argument and the NT parallels (Ro 16:17; 2Th 3:14) show that Jesus has excommunication in mind. That his words should be preserved in this form, with the mention of "pagan or a tax collector," suggests that the people for whom Matthew is writing are predominantly Jewish Christians. The NIV's "treat him as you would" catches the idea, but in the Greek expression "let him be to you as," the "you" is singular. This suggests that each member of the church is to abide by the corporate judgment and reminds the reader of the individual responsibility each believer has toward the others, already presupposed by the singular "your brother" in v.15.

18 For comments on the grammar and theology of this verse, see comments at 16:19. "The fact that God has given his people the role of declaring his will on earth does not mean that he is bound to add his divine sanction to anything they may think up" (France [NICNT]).

19–20 These two verses should not in this setting be taken as a promise regarding any prayer on which two or three believers agree (v.20). Scripture is rich in prayer promises (21:22; Jn 14:13–14; 15:7–8, 16), but if this passage deals with prayer at all, it is restricted by the context and by the phrase *peri pantos pragmatos* (NIV, "about anything"), which should here be rendered "about any judicial matter": the word *pragma* often has that sense (GK *4547*; cf. 1Co 6:1; BDAG, 859), a sense nicely fitting the argument in Matthew 18.

By contrast, J. Duncan M. Derrett ("'Where two or three are convened in my name ...': A Sad Misunderstanding," *ExpTim* 91 [1979–80]: 83–86) has argued that vv.19–20 do not deal with prayer at all. The two who agree are the offender and the one against whom the offense has been committed. They come to agreement on earth about any judicial matter they have been pursuing. The verb *aiteisthai* can refer to "pursuing a claim," as well as asking in prayer. The promise, then, is that if two individuals in the church come to agreement concerning any claim they are pursuing (presumably on the basis of the church's judgment, v.18), "it will be allowed, ratified (literally it shall succeed, come off) on the part of my heavenly Father" (Derrett, "Where two or three," 84). This is because God's will and purpose stand behind the binding and loosing of v.18 and also because ("for," v.20) the presence of Jesus is assured with the two or three who are (lit.) "brought together"—judges solemnly convened before the church and by the church to render a decision (see Notes, v.20). It is a truism of the biblical revelation that God's presence stands with the judges of his people (Ps 82:1).

Here as elsewhere, Jesus takes God's place. Jesus will be with the judges. As he has identified himself with God before (see comments at 2:6; 3:3; 11:4–6, 7–8), so he does again, and thus anticipates the broader promise of 28:20: he will be with his people "to the very end of the age" (cf. Kupp, *Matthew's Emmanuel*, 86–87, 185–88). Jesus thereby implicitly points forward to a time when, as "God with us" (1:23), he will be spiritually present with the "two or three" and with all his followers; and he presupposes that this time will be of considerable duration (see comments at 24:1–3).

NOTES

15 Εἰς σέ (*eis se*, "against you") is omitted by ℵ B f[1] cop[sa, bo mss] Origen Basil[3/6] Cyril. If the omission was original, the words were added very early, perhaps to make the general case (suggested by the omission) apply more tightly to the sins of the immediate context. But one might equally argue that omission was an early change designed to generalize the passage. Moreover, because η (*ē*), ῃ (*ē*), and ει (*ei*) were all pronounced the same way in NT times, it is easy to see how ἁμαρτήσῃ [εἰς σέ] (*hamartēsē* [*eis se*], "sins against you") could foster errors in writing down dictation. UBS[4] and NA[27] include the words with square brackets, indicating considerable doubt.

The aorist indicative ἐκέρδησας (*ekerdēsas*, "you have won over") after a future condition is to some extent futuristic itself (cf. BDF, para. 333 [2]).

19 The word οὗ (*hou*, "which") is one of only three instances in Matthew in which the relative is attracted to the case of its antecedent (cf. 24:50; 25:24; cf. Zerwick, *Biblical Greek*, para. 16).

20 Derrett ("Where two or three") suggests that the "two or three" [judges] reflect known Jewish legal practice. Each of the disputing parties would nominate his own "judge," a layman known to be impartial, and these two would try to settle the problem. If this effort failed, they would approach a third, unconnected with the disputants, who worked with the others either along the lines of arbitration or adjudication. The parallel is very neat and nicely accounts for Jesus' "two or three." My chief hesitation comes from the fact that Jesus has just told the complainant to "tell it to the church" (v.17), not to judges appointed by the disputants. Here the Dead Sea Scrolls (referred to above) may offer a closer parallel. Moreover, Derrett assumes that the "two" in v.19 and the "two or three" in v.20 are not the same individuals but disputants and judges respectively. But these points are not decisive. We have as parallels not only 1 Corinthians 5, where the entire church meets on an issue, but also 1 Corinthians 6:4, where the church becomes involved through appointed judges. Matthew 18:19–20 remains difficult; at this point we must be content with a balance of probabilities.

6. Forgiveness (18:21–35)

a. Repeated forgiveness (18:21–22)

21Then Peter came to Jesus and asked, "Lord, how many times shall I forgive my brother when he sins against me? Up to seven times?"
22Jesus answered, "I tell you, not seven times, but seventy-seven times."

COMMENTARY

21–22 "Then" is probably to be taken strictly (see comments at 3:13). The issue is not the adjudication of the church, still less the absolute granting of forgiveness by the church (only God and Jesus can forgive sins in so absolute a fashion), but personal forgiveness (cf. 6:14–15). In rabbinic discussion, the consensus was that a brother might be forgiven a repeated sin three times; on the fourth, there is no forgiveness. Peter, thinking himself bighearted, volunteers "seven times" in answer to his own question—a larger figure often used, among other things, as a "round number" (cf. Lev 26:21; Dt 28:25; Ps 79:12; Pr 24:16; Lk 17:4).

Jesus' response (v.22) alludes to Genesis 4:24 (see Notes): Lamech's revenge is transformed into a principle of forgiveness. In this context, Jesus is not saying that seventy-seven times is the upper limit, nor that the forgiveness is so unqualified it vitiates the discipline and procedural steps just taught (vv.15–20). Rather he teaches that forgiveness of fellow members in his community of "little ones" (brothers) cannot possibly be limited by frequency or quantity; for, as the ensuing parable shows (vv.23–35), all of them have been forgiven far more than they will ever forgive (cf. Chris Brauns, *Unpacking Forgiveness: Biblical Answers for Complex Questions and Deep Wounds* [Wheaton: Crossway, 2008]; D. A. Carson, *Love in Hard Places* [Wheaton: Crossway, 2002]).

NOTES

21 The Greek is literally "How many times will my brother sin against me and I will forgive him?"—an excellent example of parataxis under Semitic influence, especially in interrogative sentences (cf. BDF, para. 471 [2]; Zerwick, *Biblical Greek*, para. 453, who compares Isa 50:2).

22 The Greek could just barely be taken to mean 70 x 7 (490) instead of 70 + 7 (77), but it follows the LXX of Genesis 4:24 exactly, which is a rendering of the Hebrew 77. For discussion and bibliography, see Gundry, *Use of the Old Testament*, 140.

b. The parable of the unmerciful servant (18:23–35)

23"Therefore, the kingdom of heaven is like a king who wanted to settle accounts with
his servants. 24As he began the settlement, a man who owed him ten thousand talents
was brought to him. 25Since he was not able to pay, the master ordered that he and his
wife and his children and all that he had be sold to repay the debt.
26"The servant fell on his knees before him. 'Be patient with me,' he begged, 'and I will
pay back everything.' 27The servant's master took pity on him, canceled the debt and let
him go.
28"But when that servant went out, he found one of his fellow servants who owed him
a hundred denarii. He grabbed him and began to choke him. 'Pay back what you owe me!'
he demanded.
29"His fellow servant fell to his knees and begged him, 'Be patient with me, and I will pay
you back.'
30"But he refused. Instead, he went off and had the man thrown into prison until he
could pay the debt. 31When the other servants saw what had happened, they were greatly
distressed and went and told their master everything that had happened.
32"Then the master called the servant in. 'You wicked servant,' he said, 'I canceled all that
debt of yours because you begged me to. 33Shouldn't you have had mercy on your fellow
servant just as I had on you?' 34In anger his master turned him over to the jailers to be
tortured, until he should pay back all he owed.
35"This is how my heavenly Father will treat each of you unless you forgive your brother
from your heart."

COMMENTARY

23 "Therefore," since Jesus requires his followers to forgive, the kingdom of heaven has become like (not "is like"; see comments at 13:24) a king who ...: the reference is to the kingdom already being inaugurated. The reign of God establishes certain kinds of personal relationships, portrayed by this parable, whose point is spelled out in v.35. It quite misses the point to identify kingdom and church and argue that just as the king, though merciful, must be severe in judging the unforgiving, so the church must follow a similar pattern (so Hill). "Kingdom" and "church" are distinct categories (see comments at 13:37–39), and the immediate context has returned to the question of *repeated, personal* forgiveness (vv.21–22) and the reasons for it. Those in the kingdom serve a great king who has invariably forgiven far more than they can ever forgive one another. Therefore, failure to forgive excludes one from the kingdom, whose pattern is to forgive.

The "servants" (*douloi*, lit., "slaves," GK *1528*) may include high-ranking civil servants in a huge colonial empire, for the amount of indebtedness is astronomical (v.24). Yet Jesus may simply be using hyperbole to make clear how much the heirs of the kingdom have really been forgiven.

24–27 We glimpse some idea of the size of the indebtedness when we recall that David donated three thousand talents of gold and seven thousand talents of silver for the construction of the temple, and the princes provided five thousand talents of gold and ten thousand talents of silver (1Ch 29:4, 7). Some recent estimates suggest a dollar value of twelve million, but with inflation and fluctuating precious metal prices, this could be over a billion dollars in today's currency. (For "talent," see comments at 25:15.)

Such indebtedness could not possibly be covered by selling the family into slavery (v.25). Top price for a slave fetched about one talent, and one-tenth that amount or less was more common. The practice of being sold for debt was sanctioned by the OT (Lev 25:39; 2Ki 4:1), but such slaves had to be freed in the Year of Jubilee (every fiftieth year). (For Jewish and Gentile slavery in Jesus' day, cf. Str-B, 4:697–716; Jeremias, *Jerusalem*, 312ff., 345ff.)

In this parable, selling the slave and his family does not mean the debt is canceled but rather highlights the servant's desperate plight. With neither resources nor hope, he begs for time and promises to pay everything back (v.26)—an impossibility. So the master takes pity on him and cancels the indebtedness (v.27). The word *daneion* ("loan," a hapax legomenon) suggests that the king mercifully decides to look on the loss as a bad loan rather than embezzlement, but by v.32 he abandons that terminology and calls it a "debt."

28–31 The servant's attitude is appalling. The amount owed him is not insignificant. Though worth but a few dollars in terms of metal currency, a hundred denarii (v.28) represented a hundred days' wages for a foot soldier or common laborer. Yet the amount is utterly trivial compared with what has already been forgiven him. The similarity of his fellow servant's plea (v.29) to his own (v.26) does not move this unforgiving man. He has him thrown into a debtor's prison (v.30). Even an inexpensive slave sold for five hundred denarii, and it was illegal to sell a man for a sum greater than his debt. But the other servants (v.31), deeply distressed by the inequity, tell the master everything (*diesaphēsan* is a strong verb meaning "explained in detail," not merely "told" [NIV]; it occurs in the NT only here and at 13:36).

32–34 When the servant owes ten thousand talents, the king forgives him, but when the servant shows himself unforgiving toward a fellow servant, the king calls him wicked (v.32) and, forgoing selling him, turns him over to the "torturers" (*basanistais*, not merely "jailers," NIV); the word reminds us of earlier warnings in this chapter (vv.6, 8–9). The servant is to be tortured till he pays back all he owes (v.34), which he can never do.

35 Jesus sees no incongruity in the actions of a heavenly Father who forgives so bountifully and punishes so ruthlessly, and neither should we. Indeed, it is precisely because he is a God of such compassion and mercy that he cannot possibly accept as his those devoid of compassion and mercy. This is not to say that the king's compassion can be earned. Far from it, the servant is granted freedom only by virtue of the king's forgiveness. As in 6:12, 14–15, those who are forgiven must forgive, lest they show themselves incapable of receiving forgiveness.

NOTES

28 Ἀπόδος εἴ τι ὀφείλεις (*apodos ei ti opheileis*, lit., "pay back, if you owe anything") is not an expression of pitiless logic (Meyer, *Aims of Jesus*) but the Hellenistic equivalent of ἀπόδος ὅ τι ἂν ὀφείλῃς (*apodos ho ti an opheilēs*; NIV, "pay back what you owe"; cf. BDF, para. 376).

30 In negations, the aorist is normally used, "because usually the action as a whole is negated" (BDF, para. 327). When the imperfect is used in negations, the author is choosing to present the action in process, as durative or iterative. In this light, οὐκ ἤθελεν (*ouk ēthelen*, "he refused") may be the evangelist's way of suggesting that the man repeatedly refused, that he maintained a sustained unwillingness (as in 22:3).

32 BDF (para. 328) points out that—especially in verbs to command, order, request, or send—if an action is complete in itself but the accomplishment of a second action toward which the first points is represented as unaccomplished or still outside the scope of the assertion, then the first verb commonly takes the imperfect, not the aorist. Hence the use of aorist παρεκάλεσάς με (*parekalesas me*, "you begged me to"), pointing toward the forgiveness (ἀφῆκά σοι [*aphēka soi*, "I canceled ... yours"]), in the context means that "the simple request sufficed" (similarly at 26:53).

7. Transitional conclusion: introduction to the Judean ministry (19:1–2)

1When Jesus had finished saying these things, he left Galilee and went into the region of Judea to the other side of the Jordan. 2Large crowds followed him, and he healed them there.

COMMENTARY

1–2 For the formula used in this transition and the manner in which it points ahead, see comments at 7:28–29. Jesus "left" (*metairō*; for the verb, see comments at 13:53) Galilee and began to make his way toward Jerusalem, traveling by way of Perea, on the east side of the Jordan, thus avoiding Samaria—at least that is the customary explanation (19:1). But it is possible that *peran tou Iordanou* (lit., "across the Jordan") modifies "Judea" on the west bank. This implies that the writer describes the movements from a stance on the east bank (so Slingerland, "Transjordanian Origin"; see comments at

4:15). The parallel in Mark 10:1 is difficult because of the textual uncertainty concerning *kai* ("and [across the Jordan]"). If the *kai* is original, Mark is thinking of *two* areas—Judea *and* Perea ("across the Jordan"). But Matthew's expression "the other side of Jordan" could be taken as an awkward adverbial modifier of "went": Jesus "went across the Jordan [by that route] into the region of Judea."

The large crowds (v.2) and the many healings show that Jesus did in Judea what he had already done in Galilee. But the many summaries of Jesus' ministry in this gospel (cf. 4:23; 9:35; 14:13–14; 15:30–31), along with showing how busy Jesus was, have another function. Because this gospel contains so many discourses, "the picture of Jesus might easily become that of a *prophet*, attended by certain signs and wonders but with one single main task: to speak." These summaries help maintain balance and declare the full-orbed ministry of the Messiah (Gerhardsson, *Mighty Acts*, 36, emphasis his).

Behind these two verses lurks a very complex problem in synoptic harmony. Although Matthew and Mark are roughly parallel from Matthew 14 to the end, here Luke goes his own way. He pictures Jesus going through Samaria (Lk 9:51–56) and then begins a lengthy series of accounts, some having no synoptic parallel and others appearing to be parallel to earlier material in Mark and Matthew, material Matthew has omitted (e.g., cf. Lk 11:14–36 with Mt 12:22–45; Mk 3:20–30; and Lk 12:22–31 with Mt 6:25–34). Not until Luke 18:15 does Luke rejoin Matthew (19:13) and Mark (10:13), thereafter running roughly parallel with them. The long section, Luke 9:51–18:14 (though the precise ending is disputed), formerly called Luke's "travel narrative" but now commonly referred to as his "central section," is a problem for commentators on Luke, not Matthew; but it cannot be ignored by any synoptic commentator, because the way we perceive Luke's "central section" bears directly on the question of how many of the pericopes in Luke 9:51–18:14 are taken as real parallels to similar ones in the other Synoptics.

Because in Luke's "central section" Jesus is regularly portrayed as heading for Jerusalem (9:51–53; 13:22; 17:11), some have argued that there is a direct route to Jerusalem, with various side trips, but the chronology and topography become so tortuous as to render this unbelievable. Others see the three chief references to Jerusalem as parallels to (1) Jesus' journey to Jerusalem at the Feast of Tabernacles (Jn 7:2–10), (2) Jesus' journey south at the time of the raising of Lazarus (Jn 11:17–18), and (3) the journey terminating in the final Passover and the cross. Therefore, the entire "travel narrative" stands under the shadow of the cross. This is possible, but it raises more questions of gospel chronology and harmony than can be discussed here; in particular, it means that none of the apparent parallels to similar synoptic material can possibly spring from the same historical event. That, too, is just possible and is defended by many older commentators (e.g., Broadus). But it is unlikely that an evangelist like Luke—whose "orderly account" (1:3) clearly organizes much material in topical, not chronological or geographical, order—abandons this in 9:51–18:14.

Therefore, even if (as I am willing to assume) Luke's central section is framed by certain historical journeys to Jerusalem, used theologically to point to the final journey, it is only to be expected that topical material is also incorporated, because many of Luke's transitions between pericopes (when he uses them at all) are chronologically imprecise. What this means for a commentator on Matthew is that each apparent parallel between a pericope in Matthew and one in Luke's "central section" must be assessed on its own merits. In some cases, they probably refer to the same event, in others not; and in some instances, the evidence may be such that a convincing decision is impossible.

Craig Blomberg ("Tradition-History in the Parables Peculiar to Luke's Central Section" [PhD diss., University of Aberdeen, 1982]) has made some careful comparisons. In Blomberg's chart, column *a* lists the total number of words in Luke's account that appear in identical form in the synoptic parallel, *b* lists the number of words common to both texts but in different lexical or grammatical forms, and *c* the number of words in Luke that are clear synonyms for corresponding words in the other text. Column *d* provides the percentage of words in Luke falling into category *a*, and column *e* the percentage falling into *a*, *b*, or *c*.

Lukan parable	Synoptic parallel	Number of words in Luke	*a*	*b*	*c*	*d*	*e*
12:39–40	Mt 24:43–44	34	29	2	3	85.3	100.0
13:20–21	Mt 13:33	21	15	4	1	71.4	95.2
12:42–46	Mt 24:45–51	102	83	5	4	81.4	90.2
8:5–8	Mk 4:3–9	76	44	11	7	57.9	81.5
7:31–35	Mt 11:16–19	76	45	14	2	59.2	80.3
11:11–13	Mt 7:9–11	48	34	2	2	70.8	79.2
13:18–19	Mt 13:31–32	38	19	5	4	50.0	73.7
20:9a–16a	Mk 12:1–9	120	64	11	6	53.3	67.5
14:5	Mt 12:11	17	2	6	1	11.7	52.9
6:47–49	Mt 7:24–27	83	21	16	3	25.3	48.2
19:12–27	Mt 25:14–30	253	54	23	28	21.3	41.5
15:4–7	Mt 18:12–14	81	15	12	2	18.5	35.8
14:16–24	Mt 22:2–10	159	10	14	4	6.3	17.6
12:35–38	Mk 13:33–37	67	2	4	3	3.0	13.4

The chart reveals three groups of parables: (1) those with considerable verbal similarity, 53.3%–85.3% in column *d*, and 67.5%–100% in column *e*; (2) those with very little verbal similarity, 3.0%–6.3% in column *d*, and 13.4%–17.6% in column *e*; and, bunched between these two extremes, (3) those with a significant but not high verbal similarity, 18.5%–25.3% in column *d*, and 35.8%–52.9% in column *e*. As far as these statistics are concerned, one might be tempted to think that parables in group 1 probably have a common source, parables in group 2 are distinct, and parables in group 3 have to be handled one by one. This is largely the way they have worked out in this commentary.

Yet, other mitigating factors must be kept in mind. For instance, if a parable is brief and aphoristic, then high verbal similarity is less likely to indicate a common source. The parable may have been repeated many times. Again, contrary to Jeremias (*Parables of Jesus*, 33ff.), P. B. Payne ("Metaphor as a Model for Interpretation of the Parable of the Sower" [PhD diss., Cambridge University, 1975], 308–11) has shown in detail that in almost all instances, the audience claimed by the evangelist for any parable found in two or more Synoptic Gospels does not contradict the audience claimed by another synoptic evangelist for what appears to be the same parable. If the gospel writers are careful to preserve the correct audience in all but two cases, one suspects that if there is independent reason in those two cases to think the parallels may not be parallels but *independent* parables, that is reasonable evidence to believe the alleged parables were separate stories with similar plot lines and vocabularies from the beginning. One such case is the parable of the lost sheep (see comments at 18:10–14), which falls at the bottom of the intermediate group on the accompanying chart (cf. Blomberg, "Tradition-History," ch. 2).

While the work of Blomberg and Payne is largely restricted to the parables in Luke's central section (or, in Payne's case, to synoptic parables), their methods and general observations are applicable to other materials in that section that are paralleled in Matthew (see comments at 18:10–14; 22:2–10; 24:43–44; 25:14–30).

VI. OPPOSITION AND ESCHATOLOGY: THE TRIUMPH OF GRACE (19:3–26:5)

OVERVIEW

On the dangers and difficulties of constructing detailed outlines, see comments at 13:54–58. Yet, certain themes in these chapters (19:3–26:5) are crystallized. The opposition to Jesus becomes more heated and focused; the stances of Jesus and the Jewish leaders become more irreconcilable. Jesus not only reveals more of himself and his mission to his disciples but centers more attention on the end, the ultimate eschatological hope, the consummation of the kingdom. Within these two poles, opposition and eschatology, the grace of God toward those under the kingdom becomes an increasingly dominant theme. Without ever using the word "grace," Matthew returns to this theme repeatedly (e.g., 19:21–22; 20:1–16). But grace does not mean there is no judgment (23:1–39). Rather, it means that despite the gross rejection of Jesus; the chronic unbelief of opponents, crowds, and disciples alike; and the judgment that threatens both within history and at the end, grace triumphs and calls out a messianic people who bow to Jesus' lordship and eagerly await his return.

By and large, 19:3–26:5 follows the structure of Mark; but there are substantial additions (20:1–16; 21:28–32; 22:1–14), expansions (esp. 23:1–39; cf. Mk 12:38–44), alterations (esp. Mt 21:10–17), and additional parables in the Olivet Discourse (ch. 25).

A. Narrative (19:3–23:39)

1. Marriage and divorce (19:3–12)

OVERVIEW

For three reasons the first pericope in this section of Matthew has called forth an enormous quantity of comment and exposition: (1) It deals with a perennially burning pastoral issue in society and in the church; (2) it includes some notoriously difficult words and phrases (see esp. v.9); and (3) its relation to the parallel in Mark 10:2–12 is hotly disputed. Only some of these issues can be directly addressed here. (For the cultural background to marriage in the Bible, see Keener; Edwin M. Yamauchi, "Cultural Aspects of Marriage in the Ancient World," *BS* 135 [1978]: 241–52; Michael L. Satlow, *Jewish Marriage in Antiquity* [Princeton: Princeton Univ. Press, 2001].)

3Some Pharisees came to him to test him. They asked, "Is it lawful for a man to divorce his wife for any and every reason?"
4"Haven't you read," he replied, "that at the beginning the Creator 'made them male and female,' 5and said, 'For this reason a man will leave his father and mother and be united to his wife, and the two will become one flesh'? 6So they are no longer two, but one. Therefore what God has joined together, let man not separate."
7"Why then," they asked, "did Moses command that a man give his wife a certificate of divorce and send her away?"
8Jesus replied, "Moses permitted you to divorce your wives because your hearts were hard. But it was not this way from the beginning. 9I tell you that anyone who divorces his wife, except for marital unfaithfulness, and marries another woman commits adultery."
10The disciples said to him, "If this is the situation between a husband and wife, it is better not to marry."
11Jesus replied, "Not everyone can accept this word, but only those to whom it has been given. 12For some are eunuchs because they were born that way; others were made that way by men; and others have renounced marriage because of the kingdom of heaven. The one who can accept this should accept it."

COMMENTARY

3 Pharisees (see comments at 3:7) are often found in Matthew's gospel testing or opposing Jesus in some way (12:2, 14, 24, 38; 15:1; 16:1; 19:3; 22:15, 34–35). Their "test," here, was probably delivered in the hope that Jesus would say something to damage his reputation with the people or even seem to contradict Moses. Perhaps, too, they hoped that Jesus would say something that would entangle him in the Herod-Herodias affair so that he might meet the Baptist's fate. Machaerus was not far away (see comments at 14:3–12).

The question whether it is right for a man to divorce his wife "for any and every reason" (the NIV has rightly rendered a difficult phrase; cf. Turner, *Insights*, 61) hides an enormous diversity of Jewish opinion. Among the Qumran covenanters, divorce was judged illicit under all circumstances (CD 4:21; esp. 11QT^a 57:17–19; see J. R. Mueller, "The Temple Scroll and the Gospel Divorce Texts," *RevQ* 38 [1980]: 247ff.).

In mainstream Palestinian Judaism, opinion was divided roughly into two opposing camps. Both the school of Hillel and the school of Shammai permitted divorce (of the woman by the man; the reverse was not considered) on the grounds of *ʿerwat dābār* ("something indecent," Dt 24:1), but they disagreed on what "indecent" might include. Shammai and his followers interpreted the expression to refer to gross indecency, though not necessarily adultery; Hillel extended the meaning beyond sin to all kinds of real or imagined offenses, including an improperly cooked meal. The Hillelite R. Akiba permitted divorce in the case of a roving eye for prettier women (*m. Giṭ.* 9:10).

On any understanding of what Jesus says in the following verses, he agrees with neither Shammai nor Hillel. Even though the school of Shammai was stricter than Hillel, it permitted remarriage when the divorce was not in accordance with its own halakah (rules of conduct) (*m.* ʿ*Ed.* 4:7–10), and if Jesus restricts grounds for divorce to sexual indecency (see comments at v.9), then he differs fundamentally from Shammai. Jesus cuts his own swath in these verses, as Sigal (*Halakhah of Jesus*, 104ff.) rightly points out, and he does so in an age when in many Pharisaic circles "the frequency of divorce was ... an open scandal" (Hill). Josephus, for instance, himself a divorcé, was a Pharisee; and in his view divorce was permitted "for any causes whatsoever" (Josephus, *Ant.* 4.253 [8.23]).

Thus the setting of the divorce question in this pericope is different from 5:31–32. There divorce is set in a discourse that gives the norms of the kingdom and the sanctity of marriage; here it is set in a theological disputation that raises the question of what divorces are allowed. For a helpful chart comparing the two passages, see David Turner's commentary.

4–6 Jesus aligns himself with the prophet Malachi, who quotes Yahweh as saying, "I hate divorce" (2:16), and also refers to creation (2:14–15). Jesus cites first Genesis 1:27 and then Genesis 2:24. The Creator made the race "male and female" (v.4). The implication is that the two sexes should be united in marriage. But lest the implication be missed, the Creator then said that "for this reason" (v.5)—because God made them so—a man will leave father and mother, be united to his wife, and become one flesh (cf. Sir 25:26; Eph 5:28–31).

The words "for this reason" in Genesis 2:24 refer to Adam's perception that the woman was "bone of my bones and flesh of my flesh" because she had been made from him and for him—i.e., the man and the woman were in the deepest sense "related." The same thing is implied by Genesis 1:27—i.e., the "one flesh" in every marriage between a man and a woman is a reenactment of and testimony to the very structure of humanity as God created it.

"So" (*hōste* here is "simply an inferential particle" [Moule, *Idiom Book*, 144]), Jesus concludes, the husband and wife are no longer two but one, and that by God's doing (v.6). If God has joined them together, according to the structure of his own creation, divorce is not only "unnatural" but rebellion against God. God and man are so far apart on this issue that what God unites, man divides.

Jesus' response cuts through a great deal of casuistry and sets forth a dominant perspective that must not be lost in the exegetical tangles of v.9. Two profound insights must be grasped.

1. Although Jewish leaders tended to analyze adultery in terms not of infidelity to one's spouse but of taking someone else's wife (cf. *m. Ketub.* and *m. Qidd.*), Jesus dealt with the sanctity of marriage by focusing on the God-ordained unity of the couple.

2. Jesus essentially appealed to the principle, "The more original, the weightier," an accepted form of argument in Jewish exegesis (cf. Paul in Gal 3:15–18), and it is impossible to go further back than creation for the responsibilities of mankind. If marriage is grounded in *creation*, in the way God has made us, then it cannot be reduced to a merely covenantal relationship that breaks down when the covenantal promises are broken (contra David Atkinson, *To Have and to Hold: The Marriage Covenant and the Discipline of Divorce* [London: Collins, 1979], 114ff.). But the argument in this instance

leaves unanswered the question of how the Mosaic law is to be taken, and therefore the stage is set for the Pharisees' next question.

7–8 The Pharisees refer to Deuteronomy 24:1–4, which they interpret to mean something like this: "If a man takes a wife ... and she does not find favor in his eyes ... he shall write a bill of divorce ... and shall send her away from his house" (so also Vul.). But the Hebrew more naturally means something like this: "If a man takes a wife ... and she does not find favor in his eyes ... and he writes a bill of divorce ... and he sends her away from his house ... and her second husband does the same thing, then her first husband must not marry her again" (presumably because that would be a kind of incest; cf. Zerwick, *Biblical Greek*, para. 458; G. J. Wenham, "The Restoration of Marriage Reconsidered," *JJS* 30 [1979]: 36–40). In other words, Moses did not command divorce but permitted it for *ʿerwat dābār* ("something indecent"); and the text is less concerned with explaining the nature of that indecency (the precise expression is found in only one other place in the OT: Dt 23:14, with reference to human excrement) than with prohibiting remarriage of the twice-divorced woman to her first husband. Divorce and remarriage are therefore presupposed by Moses; i.e., he "permitted" them (v.8).

The general thrust of Mark 10:2–9 is the same as in Matthew 19:3–8. But there (1) the Pharisees ask their test question without "for any and every reason"; (2) Jesus mentions Moses' command; (3) the Pharisees reply in terms of what Moses permitted; and (4) only then does Jesus offer his basic perspective in terms of the creation ordinance. The net effect of the two passages this far is the same. But it is not easy to reconstruct the historical details. Matthew seems more concerned about the thrust of the exchange than about who said what first.

Both Matthew and Mark show that Jesus taught that Moses' concession reflected not the true creation ordinance but the hardness of men's hearts. Divorce is not part of the Creator's perfect design. If Moses permitted it, he did so because sin can be so vile that divorce is to be preferred to continued "indecency." This is not to say that the person who, according to what Moses said, divorced his spouse was actually committing sin in so doing; but the fact that divorce could even be considered testified that there had already been sin in the marriage. Therefore, any view of divorce and remarriage (taught in either Testament) that sees the problem only in terms of what may or may not be done has already overlooked a basic fact: divorce is never to be thought of as a God-ordained, morally neutral option but as evidence of sin, of hardness of heart. The fundamental attitude of the Pharisees to the question was wrong.

It should be noted also that Jesus, when speaking of the sin of the people, invariably refers to their sin or your sin, never our sin (cf. 6:14–15).

But what was the "indecency" in Moses' day that allowed for divorce? "Something indecent" could not be equated with adultery, for the normal punishment for that was death, not divorce (Dt 22:22)—though it is not at all clear that the death penalty was in fact regularly imposed for adultery (cf. Henry McKeating, "Sanctions against Adultery in Ancient Israelite Society," *JSOT* 11 [1979]: 57–72). Nor could the indecency be suspicion of adultery, for which the prescribed procedure was the bitter-water rite (Nu 5:11–31). Yet the indecency must have been shocking. Ancient Israel took marriage seriously. The best assumption is that the indecency was any lewd, immoral behavior, sometimes including, but not restricted to, adultery—e.g., homosexuality or sexual misconduct that fell short of intercourse.

9 Four problems contribute to the difficulty of understanding this verse. The first is textual. The "except" clause appears in several forms, doubtless owing to assimilation to 5:32, but there can be no doubt that an "except" clause is original. Though some MSS add a few more words (e.g., "and the divorcée who marries another commits adultery"), the diversity of the MS additions and the likelihood of assimilation to 5:32, not to mention the weight of external evidence, support the shorter text (cf. Metzger, *Textual Commentary*, 47–48).

The second problem concerns the meaning of *porneia* (NIV, "marital unfaithfulness," GK *4518*; KJV, "fornication"). H. Baltensweiler (*Die Ehe im Neuen Testament* [Zurich: Zwingli, 1967], 93) thinks that it refers to marriage within prohibited degrees (Lev 18), i.e., to incest. Many others, especially Roman Catholic scholars, have defended that view in some detail (cf. J. A. Fitzmyer, "The Matthean Divorce Texts and Some New Palestinian Evidence," *TS* 37 [1976]: 208–11). Appeal is often made to 1 Corinthians 5:1, where "a man has his father's wife" (his stepmother). But it should be noted that even here Paul gives no indication he is dealing with an incestuous marriage but only an incestuous affair. It is very doubtful whether Paul or any other Jew would have regarded an incestuous relationship as marriage: Paul would not have told the couple to get a divorce but to stop what they were doing. And in the next chapter, Paul uses the same word (*porneia*) to describe prostitution (1Co 6:13, 16).

Others have argued that *porneia* refers to premarital unchastity (A. Isaksson, *Marriage and Ministry in the New Testament* [Lund: Gleerup, 1965], 135ff.; Mark Geldard, "Jesus' Teaching on Divorce," *Churchman* 92 [1978]: 134–43); if a man discovers his bride is not a virgin, he may divorce her. This has the advantage (it is argued) of being no *real* exception to Jesus' prohibition of divorce, making it easier to reconcile Matthew and Mark, who omits the "except" clause. Moreover, it provides a neat background for the disciples' shock (v.10), for if *porneia* refers to every sexual sin, Jesus is saying no more than what many rabbis taught. The latter objection is best treated at v.10. The former is a possible way of reconciling Matthew and Mark, but there are many other possibilities; and there is no reason to adopt this one if *porneia* is being squeezed into too narrow a semantic range.

Still others hold that *porneia* here means "adultery," no more and no less (e.g., T. V. Fleming, "Christ and Divorce," *TS* 24 [1963]: 109). Certainly the word can include that meaning (Jer 3:8–9 LXX; cf. Sir 23:23). Yet, in Greek the normal word for adultery is *moicheia* (GK *3657*). Matthew has already used *moicheia* and *porneia* in the same context (15:19), suggesting some distinction between the words, even if there is considerable overlap. A. Mahoney ("A New Look at the Divorce Clauses in Mt 5:32 and 19:9," *CBQ* 30 [1968]: 29–38) suggests *porneia* refers to spiritual harlotry, a metaphor often adopted by the OT prophets. Jesus then prohibits divorce except where one spouse is not a Christian. But it is almost impossible to conceive how such a response, couched in such language, could have any relevance (let alone intelligibility) to the disputants here. Moreover, Paul knows no dominical word on the subject of mixed marriages (1Co 7:12), and the answer he provides (1Co 7:12–16) seems somewhat stricter.

The reason these and many other creative suggestions have been advanced lies in the difficulty of the verse as a whole, both in its immediate context and as a parallel to Mark-Luke. But it must be admitted that the word *porneia* itself is very broad. In unambiguous contexts, it can on occasion refer to a specific kind of sexual sin. Yet even then, this is possible only because the specific sexual sin belongs to the larger category of sexual immorality. *Porneia* covers the entire range of such sins (cf. *TDNT*, 6:579–95; BDAG, 854; Joseph Jensen, "Does *Porneia* Mean Fornication? A Critique of Bruce Malina," *NovT* 20 [1978]: 161–84) and should not be restricted unless the context requires it.

The third problem is why Matthew alone of the Synoptic Gospels includes the "except" clause, and the fourth is just what that clause means. These may be handled together. Proposed solutions are legion, but there are eight important ones.

1. Some hold that the except clause here and in 5:32 is really no exception at all. The preposition *epi* plus the dative can have the sense of addition: "in addition to" or even "apart from" (cf. Lk 3:20; Col 3:14; Zerwick, *Biblical Greek*, para. 128). In this verse, the words should be rendered "not apart from sexual promiscuity," and similar reasoning applies to the slightly different construction in 5:31: "whoever repudiates his wife, in addition to the *porneia* [for which he repudiates her], causes her to be defiled by adultery." There is then no exception to Jesus' prohibition of divorce as reported in Mark-Luke. But all this requires almost impossible Greek. When *epi* has this "additive" force, it is nowhere preceded by *mē* ("not"), which most naturally introduces an exception. Dupont (*Mariage et divorce*, 102–6) has clearly shown that a real exception is meant.

2. A number of commentators hold that Matthew has simply taken over Mark's pericope but liberalized it. The absolute prohibition was no longer possible in the Matthean church, and so the except clause was introduced (so David R. Catchpole, "The Synoptic Divorce Material as a Traditio-Historical Problem," *BJRL* 57 [1974–75]: 92–127; R. H. Stein, "Is It Harmful for a Man to Divorce His Wife?" *JETS* 22 [1979]: 115–21; idem, *Mark* [BECNT 2; Grand Rapids: Baker, 2008]). The particular reason for adding the exception is variously put: (1) Jesus' absolute prohibition was meant to be only a guideline, which the evangelists felt free to adapt—after all, "Jesus was not a legalist" (Stein); (2) Matthew felt it necessary to align Jesus with the school of Shammai in the context of rabbinic debates in his day (Bornkamm, "End-Expectation and the Church," 25–26); and (3) *porneia* refers to incestuous marriages, not uncommon among Gentiles, so Matthew added the except clause because an increasing number of Gentile converts were entering his predominantly Jewish church, and Jesus' prohibition of divorce must not be thought to apply to their illicit marriages (Mahoney, "New Look"; cf. Benoit, Bonnard).

But all these views have serious problems.

a. There is serious debate about whether Matthew has actually *added* something to the tradition or whether he is independent of Mark at this point.

b. To stigmatize an absolute prohibition by suggesting it would make Jesus a "legalist" is to beg a number of questions. Could not any absolute prohibition be subjected to the same cavalier labeling? The word "legalist" is a loaded word that can refer either to someone who sets up absolutes or to someone who thinks he is accepted by God on the basis of his obedience. In the first sense, Jesus is a "legalist" (e.g., 22:37–38); in the second sense, he is not. But only the first sense is relevant to this verse.

c. It is not clear why Matthew would feel it necessary to align his gospel with a particular rabbinic school that, as he knew, already existed in Jesus' day. There is no new situation, in this respect, in AD 85.

d. The new situation suggested by Mahoney ("New Look") is not very plausible because it requires an unnatural reading of *porneia*. It assumes that Matthew would see an incestuous "marriage" as a genuine marriage subject to divorce (instead of a sinful affair that must be terminated), and it introduces an unsupported major anachronism.

e. Moreover, simple alignment with the school of Shammai is implausible in a book demanding a righteousness surpassing that of the Pharisees (5:20) and in a context where Jesus' teaching on divorce evokes a cynical response from the disciples (v.10).

3. Others argue that *porneia* simply means "adultery" in this context and that Jesus is interpreting the *ʿerwat dābār* ("something indecent") of Deuteronomy 24:1 in this way. This does not necessarily

mean that Matthew softens Mark. As Hill points out, in Jewish circles of the first century, Jewish law *required* a man to divorce an adulterous wife (*m. Soṭah* 5:1), and this may well be assumed by the other gospels "as an understood and accepted part of any teaching on the subject of divorce" but spelled out only in Matthew. This interpretation probably narrows down the meaning of *porneia* too far; but apart from that, the objections against it can be satisfactorily answered (see comments below at point 8).

4. Bruce Vawter, in two articles ("The Divorce Clauses in Mt 5:32 and 19:9," *CBQ* 16 [1954]: 155–67; and "Divorce and the New Testament," *CBQ* 39 [1977]: 528–48), argues strongly that the except clauses have been misunderstood. They are preteritions, i.e., exceptions to the proposition itself, not simply to the verb. The except clause in v.9 therefore "means that *porneia* [which he takes to be equivalent to the 'something indecent' of Dt 24:1] is not involved"—i.e., "I say to you, whoever dismisses his wife—the permission in Deuteronomy 24:1 notwithstanding—and marries another, commits adultery." Similarly, in Matthew 5:32, he understands the crucial phrase to mean "quite apart from the matter of *porneia*." Vawter is followed by Banks (*Jesus and the Law*, 156–57). The effect of this interpretation is similar to point 1: Matthew allows no more of an exception than Mark, and Jesus specifically abrogates the Mosaic permission. It makes good sense of the disciples' next remarks (v.10)—though Jesus' rejoinder (vv.11–12) seems a bit of a letdown in a book in which the redactional pattern is *not* to have Jesus agree with his misunderstanding disciples but to reemphasize the point just made (cf. Q. Quesnell, "'Made Themselves Eunuchs for the Kingdom of Heaven' (Mt 19:12)," *CBQ* 30 [1968]: 340ff.). Moreover, it is not at all obvious that the except clauses are preteritions; certainly the earliest Greek commentators did not take them that way, as Quesnell (p. 348) points out.

5. What Quesnell himself argues is that Jesus by using the verb *apolyō* (v.9) permits, in the case of the wife's marital infidelity, separation but not divorce (similarly G. J. Wenham, "May Divorced Christians Remarry?" *Churchman* 95 [1981]: 150–61; Dupont, *Mariage et divorce*, 93–157), and therefore no remarriage under any circumstances (cf. esp. William A. Heth and Gordon J. Wenham, *Jesus and Divorce: The Problem with the Evangelical Consensus* [Nashville: Abingdon, 1984]; Andrew Cornes, *Divorce and Remarriage: Biblical Principles and Pastoral Practice* [Grand Rapids: Eerdmans, 1993]; it should be noted that Heth subsequently changed his mind [see his "Jesus on Divorce: How My Mind Has Changed," *SBJT* 6:1 (2002): 4–29]). Such separation without possibility of remarriage was unheard of in Jewish circles and, of course, would have been much stricter than the school of Shammai; and this prompts the disciples' reaction (v.10). But two considerations stand against this view. First, *apolyō* has already been used in v.3 with the undoubted meaning "to divorce." It is unwarranted to understand the same verb a few verses later in some other way, unless there is some compelling contextual reason for the change. Again, though it is formally true that the except clause is syntactically linked to the divorce clause, not the remarriage clause, this is scarcely decisive. Locating the except clause anywhere else would breed even more ambiguity. For instance, if it is placed before the verb *moichatai* ("commits adultery," GK *3656*), the verse might be paraphrased as follows: "Whoever divorces his wife and marries another, if it is not for fornication that he divorces one and marries another, commits adultery." But this wording suggests that fornication is being advanced as the actual *reason* for marrying another, and not only for the divorce—an interpretation that borders on the ridiculous. Moreover, if the remarriage clause is excluded, the thought becomes nonsensical: "Anyone who divorces his wife, except for *porneia*, commits adultery"—surely

untrue unless he remarries. The except clause must therefore be understood to govern the entire protasis. For detailed treatment of the syntax of conditionals with multiple protases, see Charles Edward Powell, "The Semantic Relationship Between the Protasis and the Apodosis of New Testament Conditional Constructions" (PhD diss., Dallas Theological Seminary, 2000), esp. 361–62. We may paraphrase as follows: "Anyone who divorces his wife and marries another woman commits adultery—though this principle does not hold in the case of *porneia*."

6. John J. Kilgallen ("To What Are the Matthean Exception-Texts [5:32 and 19:9] an Exception?" *Bib* 61 [1980]: 102–5) suggests that the except clauses need only mean that in some cases divorce is not adulterous rather than that in some cases divorce is not morally wrong. He renders 5:32: "Everyone who divorces his wife (except in the case of *porneia*) makes her adulterous." But in the case of *porneia*, he does not *make* her adulterous; she is *already* adulterous (similarly Westerholm, *Jesus and Scribal Authority*, 118–19, and the literature he cites). This is not convincing, for the Greek does not read "makes her adulterous" or "makes her an adulteress," but "makes her commit adultery" (the passive infinitive does not mean "to become an adulter[ess]" but "to commit adultery"; cf. BDAG, 657). If the woman has already committed *porneia*, doubtless divorce (and the remarriage that would ensue) could scarcely be said to make her an adulteress, but such divorce and remarriage would make her commit adultery. And this approach does not work in v.9, where the result is not that the man makes his wife commit adultery but that he commits adultery.

7. More recently, David Instone-Brewer has written two books and several articles offering a new synthesis. The most important of these publications is his *Divorce and Remarriage in the Bible: The Social and Literary Context* (Grand Rapids: Eerdmans, 2002). There is an outstanding amount of careful comparative material in his work, but on the crucial point where he makes his most significant synthetic and pastoral contribution, Instone-Brewer's argument appears to be seriously flawed. In brief, he argues that Jesus' arguments must be read not only against the background of Deuteronomy 24:1–4 (which is why they were treated above) but also against the background of Exodus 21:10–11: "If [a man] marries another woman, he must not deprive the first one of her food, clothing and marital rights. If he does not provide her with these three things, she is to go free, without any payment of money." Whatever the restrictions here in v.9, Instone-Brewer argues that 1 Corinthians 7:15 (where Paul asserts that if the unbelieving spouse leaves, the believing spouse "is not bound in such circumstances") surely includes the kind of abandonment mentioned in Exodus 21:10–11. In other words, spousal neglect in the domains of food, clothing/shelter, and sexual rights is ground for divorce and remarriage.

Although Instone-Brewer mounts as good a case as can be made for this view, it is open to severe criticisms. Strictly speaking, Exodus 21:10–11 is directed at the man who is adding another wife and who might be tempted to abandon the first one, not talking about marriage responsibilities in general. Jesus (and Paul too, for that matter) cuts so independent a swath in the domain of marriage and divorce, grounding his arguments on creation, that even an OT text that is *specifically* introduced, such as Deuteronomy 24:1–4, gets somewhat modified in its emphasis. So what right do we have to assume that Jesus and Paul are simply taking over Exodus 21:10–11 as an assumption? Does Instone-Brewer think that the law demanding that priests never marry a widow or a prostitute but only a virgin (Lev 21:13–15) should be imposed on all Christians today, since, according to Peter, we are all priests? Or should the test for an unfaithful wife be operative today (Nu 5:11–31; Dt 22:13–21)? These are not trick questions, nor are they trivial questions. What is missing from Instone-Brewer's work is a believable theory of how these laws *ought* to be integrated with the demands of the new covenant. At the end of the day, his stance depends on an argument from silence: neither Jesus nor Paul has distanced himself from Exodus 21:10–11, so these must remain legitimate grounds for divorce and remarriage. I doubt that Instone-Brewer can apply that hermeneutical approach to the OT very consistently. Meanwhile, what Jesus and Paul *do* say *explicitly*—as here in v.9—seems to exclude the broad category of "spousal neglect" that he wishes to include.

8. It seems best, then, to permit both *porneia* and the except clause to retain their normal force. Jesus is then saying that divorce and remarriage always involve evil; but as Moses permitted it because of the hardness of human hearts, so also does he—but now on the sole grounds of *porneia* (sexual sin of any sort). The principal exegetical difficulties surrounding this view may be treated as follows:

a. Formally Jesus is abrogating something of the Mosaic prescription; for whatever the *ʿerwat dābār* ("something indecent") refers to (Dt 24:1), it cannot easily be thought to refer to adultery, for which the prescribed punishment was death. That this was rarely carried out (McKeating, "Sanctions against Adultery"; cf. Joseph in 1:19–20) is beside the point. As a legal system, irrespective of whether it was enforced, the Deuteronomic permission for divorce and remarriage could scarcely have adultery primarily in view. But *porneia* includes adultery, even if not restricted to it. Jesus' judgments on the matter are therefore both lighter (no capital punishment for adultery) and heavier (the sole exception being sexual sin) than the Mosaic code.

b. This exception does not contradict Jesus' strong words in vv.4–8, despite frequent insistence on the contrary. In vv.4–8, Jesus lays out the true direction in which Scripture points (cf. Jesus' treatment of oaths, 5:33–37, where there is also formal abrogation of a Mosaic command). Even here, Jesus acknowledges that the Mosaic concession springs not from divine desire but human hard-heartedness. Would Jesus say human hearts were any less hard in his own day? Might there not, therefore, be some exception to the principle he lays out, precisely because *porneia* was not on the Creator's mind in Genesis 1–2? More important, sexual sin has a peculiar relation to Jesus' treatment of Genesis 1:27; 2:24 (in Mt 19:4–6), because the indissolubility of marriage he defends by appealing to those verses from the creation accounts is predicated on sexual union ("one flesh"). Sexual promiscuity is, therefore, a de facto exception. It may not necessitate divorce; but permission for divorce and remarriage under such circumstances, far from being inconsistent with Jesus' thought, is in perfect harmony with it.

c. Although it is commonly held that the except clauses are secondary and bring Matthew into a clash with Mark, the issue is not so simple. Not a few scholars hold that, at least on this point, Matthew 19:9 is authentic and that Mark omits the obvious exception (e.g., Schlatter; Isaksson, *Marriage and Ministry*, 75–92; D. L. Dungan, *The Sayings of Jesus in the Churches of Paul* [Philadelphia: Fortress, 1971], 122–25).

Catchpole ("Synoptic Divorce Material"), on the other hand, argues for Markan priority on the ground that the aporias he finds in Matthew 19:3–12 can all be explained by recognizing that they have been introduced precisely where Matthew has changed Mark. His argument has some weight only if the aporias are real; but the four he mentions are either imagined or explainable in other ways. For instance, Catchpole holds that v.9 does not cohere with vv.4–8, and this problem can be remedied only by the removal of the except clause in v.9 which is precisely the new bit Matthew has added. But we have shown above at point 8b that v.9 *does* cohere with vv.4–8. This does not prove that Matthew did not depend on Mark, but it forbids claiming he *did*. And even if Mark's priority prevails in this pericope, Matthew's redactional additions cannot be assumed to be nonhistorical unless we have evidence that Matthew had access to no other information (see Introduction, sections 1–3). We conclude, therefore, that there is no decisive evidence for literary dependence either way, and that there is no overwhelming reason why the except clauses, both here and in 5:32, should not be authentic.

Certainly, on the interpretation adopted here, Matthew and Mark-Luke have this in common: they abrogate any permission for divorce in Deuteronomy 24:1 if that permission extends, or is thought to extend, beyond sexual sin. If Mark has priority, the except clause in Matthew seems best explained along the line suggested by Hill above at point 3; if the reverse, or if the two gospels preserve independent accounts of the same incident, Mark may think the exception so obvious (because it concerns sexual infidelity, the heart of the union according to Genesis) as not to be worth mentioning. Moreover, the exception is particularly appropriate to Jesus' day and to Matthew's Jewish readers, for though Jesus had formally dismissed the Mosaic divorce provisions and substituted marital unfaithfulness as the sole basis of a rupture of the "one flesh," this exception collided with the Mosaic sentence of stoning in such cases—a fact of which Jewish audiences were doubtless aware. With the death penalty for marital *porneia* effectively abolished, "the termination of the relationship might appropriately be effected by divorce" (James B. Hurley, *Man and Woman in Biblical Perspective* [Leicester: InterVarsity, 1981], 104; cf. John Murray, *Divorce* [Philadelphia: Presbyterian & Reformed, 1953], 51ff.).

d. The final problem is whether this interpretation adequately accounts for the disciples' reaction (v.10). Before turning to this, we may observe that Mark 10:12 makes the same responsibilities and privileges concerning divorce and remarriage extend to the woman as well as the man—probably a pointed rebuke of Herodias (cf. Lane, *Mark*, 358). Mark omits the except clause and retains the remark about women, Matthew the reverse. (Further discussion of the related question of the so-called Pauline privilege [1Co 7:15]—i.e., beyond what was said above at point 7—must be left to commentaries on 1 Corinthians.)

10–12 Dupont (*Mariage et divorce*, 161–222) argues that these verses deal, not with celibacy, but with continence after divorce. Believing that no remarriage is legitimate, Dupont argues that the divorced believer must remain continent "for the sake of the kingdom"—i.e., in order to enter it—because remarriage would be adulterous. Somewhat similar is Francis J. Moloney's position ("Matthew 19:3–12 and Celibacy: A Redactional and Form-Critical Study," *JSNT* 2 (1979): 42–60, esp. 47ff.). But in addition to the difficulties entailed by holding that no remarriage is permitted (see comments at v.9), "eunuch" is a strange figure for continence after marriage, especially since if the divorced spouse died, the survivor could remarry (Dupont's view).

There is a better way to look at these verses. First, the disciples' reaction (v.10) must not be exaggerated. Unlike v.25, there is no mention of astonishment. Jesus, though not forbidding *all* divorce and remarriage, has come close to the school of Shammai on the grounds for exceptions, while taking a far more conservative stance than Shammai on who may remarry. In the light of the position, tacitly adopted by most Jews, that marriage was a duty, the disciples rather cynically conclude that such strictures surely make marriage unattractive. This virtually makes the appeal of marriage contingent on liberal divorce and remarriage rights—a stance that fails miserably to understand what Jesus has said about the creation ordinance.

Verse 11 can then be understood in one of two ways. *Ton logon touton* (lit., "this word"—regardless of whether *touton* is original, since *ton* can be a mild demonstrative) refers either to Jesus' teaching in vv.4–9 or to the disciples' misguided remark in v.10. The NIV's "this teaching" (v.11) favors the former, but this is unlikely, for it makes Jesus contradict himself. After a strong prohibition, it is highly unlikely that Jesus' moral teaching dwindles into a pathetic "But of course, not everyone can accept this."

It helps little to say (with Bonnard) that those to whom the teaching is given are Christians who must follow Jesus' moral standards but that others cannot accept what he says, for Jesus' appeal has been to the creation ordinance, not to kingdom morality. It is better to take "this word" to refer to the disciples' conclusion in v.10: "it is better not to marry." Jesus responds that not everyone can live by such a verdict, such abstinence from marriage. But some do, namely, those to whom it is given—those born eunuchs, those made eunuchs by men (possibly in groups like the Essenes, but more likely a reflection of the rabbinic distinction between two types of eunuch: the impotent and the castrated—the latter very often for some high court position where there were royal women (cf. Ac 8:26–39; Str-B, 1:805–7)—and those who have made themselves eunuchs because of the kingdom of God. The latter is not a commendation of self-castration but of renunciation of marriage in light of the disciples' remark, "it is better not to marry."

Jesus, like Paul after him (1Co 7:7–9), is prepared to commend celibacy "because of the kingdom" (not "for the sake of attaining it," but "because of its claims and interests"; cf. J. Blinzler, "Εἰσὶν εὐνοῦχοι: Zur Auslegung von Mt 19:12," *ZNW* 28 [1957]: 254–70). Thus, far from backing down at the disciples' surliness, Jesus freely concedes that for those to whom it is given "it *is* better not to marry"; and "The one who can accept this should accept it." But it is important to recognize that neither Jesus nor the apostles see celibacy as an intrinsically holier state than marriage (cf. 1Ti 4:1–3; Heb 13:4), nor as a condition for the top levels of ministry (Mt 8:14; 1Co 9:5), but as a special calling granted for greater usefulness in the kingdom. Those who impose this discipline on themselves must remember Paul's conclusion: it is better to marry than to burn with passion (1Co 7:9).

Two final observations: (1) The authenticity of v.12 has been admirably defended by T. Matura ("Le celibat dans le Nouveau Testament," *NRTh* 107 [1975]: 481–500); and (2) Jesus' remarks betray a certain self-conscious independence of the OT law, which excluded eunuchs from the assembly of Yahweh (Dt 23:1; cf. Lev 22:24; Str-B, 1:806–7; see Schweizer). One cannot forget the conversion of the Ethiopian eunuch (Ac 8:26–40), who, though he would have been excluded from the assembly of Yahweh, was joyfully welcomed to the assembly of Messiah.

NOTES

5 On the use of εἰς σάρκα μίαν (*eis sarka mian*, "one flesh") instead of a predicative nominative, see Moule, *Idiom Book*, 183, 208; Zerwick, *Biblical Greek*, para. 32.

10 Οὕτως (*houtōs*, lit., "thus") here takes on a relatively rare adjectival function (NIV, "this"; cf. BDF, para. 434 [1]).

Contrary to B. F. Meyer (*Aims of Jesus*), αἰτία (*aitia*) here means not "cause" but "case" or "situation" (NIV; cf. BDF, para. 5 [3b]).

2. Blessing little children (19:13–15)

[13]Then little children were brought to Jesus for him to place his hands on them and pray for them. But the disciples rebuked those who brought them.

[14]Jesus said, "Let the little children come to me, and do not hinder them, for the kingdom of heaven belongs to such as these." [15]When he had placed his hands on them, he went on from there.

COMMENTARY

13 "Then" is ambiguous (see comments at 2:7). Children in Jesus' day were often brought to rabbis and elders to be blessed, customarily by placing hands on them (cf. Ge 48:14; Nu 27:18; Ac 6:6; 13:3; see also Mt 9:18, 20; Mk 10:16). The disciples "rebuked them" (lit.): both the context and the synoptic parallels show that "them" refers, not to the children, but to "those who brought them" (NIV).

Why did the disciples stoop to this rebuke? Perhaps they were annoyed that Jesus was being delayed on his journey to Jerusalem; perhaps they felt they were being interrupted in their important discussion. Although children in the Judaism of the time were deeply cherished, they were thought in some ways to be negligible members of society. Their place was to learn, to be respectful, to listen. But two deeper insights suggest themselves: (1) the preceding pericope (vv.3–12) implicitly stresses the sanctity of the family, and vv.13–15 continue by saying something important about children; and (2) in 18:1–9, children serve as models for humility, patterns for Jesus' "little ones"; yet Jesus' disciples, his "little ones," show little humility here.

14 Jesus does not want the little children prevented from coming to him, not because the kingdom of heaven belongs to them, but because the kingdom of heaven belongs to those like them (so also Mark and Luke, stressing childlike faith). Jesus receives them because they are an excellent object lesson in the kind of humility and faith he finds acceptable.

NOTES

14 O. Cullmann (*Baptism in the New Testament*, 71–80) finds in μὴ κωλύετε (*mē kōluete*, "do not hinder") an echo of a primitive baptismal formula, because this verb refers to baptism elsewhere (3:14; Ac 8:36; 10:47; 11:17). He does not argue that here Jesus teaches infant baptism but that the church transmitted the story in such a way that Christians would remember an event in Jesus' ministry "by which they might be led to a solution of the question of infant baptism" (p. 78). Apart from the propriety of finding a solution to a later problem in a story all agree does not address it, the suggestion that μὴ κωλύετε, *mē kōluete*, was a technical term that connoted baptism is very doubtful. The verb occurs twenty-three times in the NT, and only five of these relate to baptism. The four (outside this passage) allegedly referring to baptism fail to establish a clear baptismal formula: in 3:14 John tries "to deter" Jesus; in Acts 8:36 the Ethiopian eunuch asks what "prevents" him from being baptized; and the remaining two occurrences (Ac 10:47; 11:17) justify the baptism of the Gentile Cornelius on the grounds that the Spirit had fallen on him.

3. Wealth and the kingdom (19:16–30)

a. The rich young man (19:16–22)

OVERVIEW

Some of the differences between Matthew and Mark-Luke (cf. Mk 10:17–31; Lk 18:18–30) are so sharp (see vv.16–17) that they have frequently served as tests for redaction criticism. Many, of course, are of little significance. Matthew introduces the central figure as "a man" and later says he was "young" (v.20). Mark (10:17) says nothing about his age but provides more details of the initial meeting: it was "as Jesus started on his way" that a man "ran up" to him and "fell on his knees before him." These and many similar differences have been treated elsewhere (cf. Carson, "Redaction Criticism," 119ff.). The nub of the problem turns on vv.16–17 and parallels.

16Now a man came up to Jesus and asked, "Teacher, what good thing must I do to get
eternal life?"
17"Why do you ask me about what is good?" Jesus replied. "There is only One who is
good. If you want to enter life, obey the commandments."
18"Which ones?" the man inquired.
Jesus replied, "'Do not murder, do not commit adultery, do not steal, do not give false
testimony, 19honor your father and mother,' and 'love your neighbor as yourself.'"
20"All these I have kept," the young man said. "What do I still lack?"
21Jesus answered, "If you want to be perfect, go, sell your possessions and give to the
poor, and you will have treasure in heaven. Then come, follow me."
22When the young man heard this, he went away sad, because he had great wealth.

COMMENTARY

16–17 A certain man—identified by all three evangelists as rich, by Matthew (v.20) as young, and by Luke (18:18) as a ruler—asks Jesus what he must do to inherit "eternal life" (v.16). The latter expression refers to a life "approved by God and to which access to the kingdom (present and eschatological) is promised (cf. the rabbinic 'life of the age to come')" (Hill; cf. 7:14; 25:46; see Hill, *Greek Words*, 163–201).

The problem arises when Matthew is compared with Mark and Luke. In the latter, the questioner asks, "Good teacher, what must I do to inherit eternal life?" (Lk 18:18). Jesus replies, "Why do you call me good? No one is good—except God alone" (v.19). In Matthew, however, the questioner asks, "Teacher, what good thing must I do to inherit eternal life?" (v.16). "Good" no longer modifies "teacher," and therefore Jesus' response is correspondingly adapted: "Why do you ask me about what is good? There is only One who is good" (v.17). A majority of modern scholars hold that Matthew has transformed the exchange because, at his later time of writing, the church can no longer live with the suggestion that Jesus himself is not sinless.

It is logically possible to achieve harmonization by mere addition ("*Good* teacher, what *good* thing?" followed by Jesus giving both answers); indeed, later copyists of NT manuscripts sometimes opted for such an approach (hence KJV). But the procedure is notoriously implausible. The evangelists, as we have often witnessed, are far more concerned with Jesus' *ipsissima vox* than his *ipsissima verba* (see Notes, 3:17); and we do the Scriptures disservice when we fail to consider the implications. Nevertheless, the christological explanation ventured by many is equally implausible. A better understanding of the text is gained from the following observations.

1. Stonehouse (*Origins*, 93–112) has convincingly demonstrated that christological concerns do not stand at the heart of *any* of the three synoptic accounts. The argument of G. M. Styler ("Stages in Christology in the Synoptic Gospels," *NTS* 10 [1963–64]: 404–6) that Matthew reflects a growing interest in ontology is especially weak. Styler argues that, unlike Mark, Matthew believes Jesus is divine. But Hill rightly points out that Matthew still preserves the words "There is only One who is good," a clear reference to God; and the alteration says nothing about Jesus' status in relation to God. Moreover, Styler has adopted a historical reconstruction of the development of doctrine that not all find convincing (cf. D. A. Carson, "Unity and Diversity: On the Possibility of Systematic Theology," in *Scripture and Truth* [ed. Carson and Woodbridge], 65ff.), especially here where Luke, probably writing after Matthew or at least very close to him, senses no embarrassment in Mark's words but records them verbatim—and this despite the fact that Luke elsewhere feels free to drop bits that could be taken as detrimental to Jesus. We must, therefore, look for nonchristological explanations for Matthew's alteration.

2. The thrust of the passage in both Mark and Matthew must be grasped. Irrespective of what "good" refers to, the man approaches Jesus with a question showing how far he is from the humble faith that, as Jesus has just finished saying, characterizes all who belong to the kingdom (vv.13–15). He wants to earn eternal life, and in the light of v.20, he apparently thinks there are good things he can do, beyond the demands of the law, by which he can assure his salvation. Many Jews believed that a specific act of goodness could win eternal life (Str-B, 1:808ff.); this young man, assuming this opinion is correct, seeks Jesus' view as to what that act might be. Whatever differences exist between Matthew and Luke, Jesus' response is not designed either to confess personal sin (Mark) or to call in question his own competence to discuss what is good (Matthew), for such topics are not in view (see B. B. Warfield, "Jesus' Alleged Confession of Sin," *PTR* 12 [1914]: 127–228). Instead Jesus calls into question his interlocutor's inadequate understanding of goodness. In the absolute sense of goodness required to gain eternal life, only God is good (cf. 1Ch 16:34; 2Ch 5:13; Ps 106:1; 118:1, 29). Jesus will not allow anything other than God's will to determine what is good. By approaching Jesus in this way (esp. vv.16, 20), the young man reveals simultaneously that he wants something beyond God's will (v.20) and that he misconstrues the absoluteness of God's goodness.

3. In this light, Matthew's phrasing of the initial exchange between Jesus and the young man focuses on the issue central for both Matthew and Mark

more clearly than Mark does. To that extent it also ties this pericope more closely to the preceding one than Mark does. This young man stands in stunning contrast to those to whom, according to Jesus, the kingdom belongs. This may help explain Matthew's wording.

4. Within this framework, Mark 10:18 no more calls into question Jesus' sinlessness than Matthew 19:17 calls into question Jesus' competence to judge what is good. Apart from the assumption of Mark's priority without either evangelist having access to other traditions, it is difficult to see why, if we charge Matthew with eliminating the possibility that readers might think Jesus could sin, we should not charge Mark with eliminating the possibility that some readers might think Jesus could not pronounce on what was good. Both charges would miss the central point of both Matthew and Mark.

5. "If you want to enter life, obey the commandments" (v.17) does not mean that Matthew, unlike Mark, thinks eternal life is *earned* by keeping the commandments. After all, Mark himself is about to report Jesus' exhortation to keep specific commandments. The entire debate has been bedevilled by a false split between grace and obedience to the will of God. No less staunch a supporter of grace than Paul can insist that without certain purity a man cannot inherit the kingdom (1Co 6:9–10). Jesus tells this young man, in similar vein, what good things he must do if he is to gain eternal life, precisely because he perceives his questioner has little understanding of such things. But that is still far from telling him that by doing these things he will *earn* eternal life.

6. But why, then, has either Matthew or Mark edited the exchange? Or, if the two reports are independent, or if Matthew depends on Mark but has eyewitness knowledge of the events, how is it possible that both accounts can be accepted as trustworthy representations of the same incident? Lohmeyer suggests that the variations stem from different translations of an Aramaic report of the incident. Better yet is a reconstruction of the incident that, though not simple additive harmonization, provides a historical basis broad enough to support reports of both Matthew and Mark-Luke and fits well within the normal latitude the evangelists show in their reportage. This reconstruction is worked out in more detail elsewhere (Carson, "Redaction Criticism"). Briefly, it suggests the young ruler's question was, "Good teacher, what must I do to inherit eternal life?" and that Jesus' reply was, "Why do you ask *me* questions regarding the good? There is only One who is good, namely, God."

18–20 Jesus lists the sixth, seventh, eighth, ninth, and fifth commandments of Exodus 20 in that order. He omits "do not defraud" (Mk 10:19, apparently an application of the eighth and ninth) and adds "love your neighbor as yourself" (Lev 19:18; cf. Mt 22:34–40). On the text form, compare Gundry (*Use of the Old Testament*, 17–19) and K. J. Thomas ("Liturgical Citations in the Synoptics," *NTS* 22 [1975–76]: 205–14). The man's impulsive reply is reflected by Paul (Php 3:6; cf. Str-B, 1:814) on a certain understanding of the law, but the man's further words, "What do I still lack?" show his uncertainty and lack of assurance of ever being good enough for salvation, as well as his notion that certain "good works" are over and above the law (cf. Str-B, 4:536ff., 559ff.). He enjoyed wealth (v.22) while suffering barrenness of soul.

21–22 Many have taken these verses to indicate a two-tier ethic. Some disciples find eternal life, and others go further and become perfect by adopting a more compassionate stance (e.g., Harrington; *NIDNTT*, 2:63). But G. Barth ("Matthew's Understanding of the Law," 95ff.) convincingly disproves this exegesis. In particular the young man's question in v.20, "What do I still lack?" clearly refers to gaining eternal life (v.17), and Jesus' answer in v.21 must be understood as answering the question.

A two-tier Christianity is implicitly contradicted by 23:8–12, and the same word ("perfect") is applied to all of Jesus' disciples in 5:48. Matthew shows no strong tendency toward asceticism. Therefore, the basic thrust of v.21 is not "Sell your possessions and give to the poor" but "Come, follow me."

What the word "perfection" suggests here is what it commonly means in the OT—undivided loyalty and full-hearted obedience. This young man could not face that. He was willing to discipline himself to observe all the outward stipulations and even perform supererogatory works, but because of his wealth, he had a divided heart. His money was competing with God, and what Jesus everywhere demands as a condition for eternal life is absolute, radical discipleship. This entails the surrender of *self.* "Keeping the individual commandments is no substitute for the readiness for self-surrender to the absolute claim of God imposed through the call of the gospel. Jesus' summons in this context means that true obedience to the Law is rendered ultimately in discipleship" (Lane, *Mark*, 367). Warren Carter (*Households and Discipleship: A Study in Matthew 19–20* [JSNTSup 103; Sheffield: JSOT Press, 1994]) has an excellent discussion on how wealth was viewed in the ancient world (pp. 127–43) but badly misses the point when he assumes that this young man's wealth was gained by oppression (p. 388). There is not a hint of that in the text.

Formally, of course, Jesus' demand in v.21 goes beyond anything in OT law (cf. Banks, *Jesus and the Law*, 163). Equally remarkable is the fact that the focus on *God's will* (vv.17–19) should culminate in following *Jesus*. The explanation of this is that Jesus is prophesied by the OT. The will of God as revealed in Scripture looks forward to the coming of Messiah (see comments at 2:15; 5:17–20; 11:11–13). Absolute allegiance to him, with the humility of a child, is essential to salvation. The condition Jesus now imposes not only reveals the man's attachment to money but shows that all his formal compliance with the law is worthless because none of it entails absolute self-surrender. What the man needs is the triumph of grace, for as the next verses show, entering the kingdom of heaven is impossible for him (v.26). God, with whom all things are possible, must work. The parable in 20:1–16 directly speaks to this issue. But the young man is deaf to it. He leaves because if a choice must be made between money and Jesus, money wins (cf. 6:24).

NOTES

20 Here and elsewhere (Allen, xxiii), Matthew uses the aorist active verb—this time ἐφύλαξα (*ephylaxa*, "I have kept")—rather than the middle Mark uses—but the distinction is hardly worth mentioning (cf. Moule, *Idiom Book*, 24).

b. Grace and reward in the kingdom (19:23–30)

[23]Then Jesus said to his disciples, "I tell you the truth, it is hard for a rich man to enter
the kingdom of heaven. [24]Again I tell you, it is easier for a camel to go through the eye of a
needle than for a rich man to enter the kingdom of God."

[25]When the disciples heard this, they were greatly astonished and asked, "Who then can be saved?"

[26]Jesus looked at them and said, "With man this is impossible, but with God all things are possible."

[27]Peter answered him, "We have left everything to follow you! What then will there be for us?"

[28] Jesus said to them, "I tell you the truth, at the renewal of all things, when the Son of Man sits on his glorious throne, you who have followed me will also sit on twelve thrones,
judging the twelve tribes of Israel. [29]And everyone who has left houses or brothers or
sisters or father or mother or children or fields for my sake will receive a hundred times as
much and will inherit eternal life. [30]But many who are first will be last, and many who are
last will be first."

COMMENTARY

23–24 Jesus is not saying that all poor people and none of the wealthy enter the kingdom of heaven (see comments at 3:2). That would exclude Abraham, Isaac, and Jacob, to say nothing of David, Solomon, and Joseph of Arimathea; it would also sanction the lazy and wicked poor, sometimes excoriated in the book of Proverbs. (For a balanced treatment of these themes, see Craig L. Blomberg, *Neither Poverty Nor Riches: A Biblical Theology of Possessions* [NSBT 7; Downers Grove, Ill.: InterVarsity, 1999].) The point of Jesus' teaching lies elsewhere. Most Jews expected the rich to inherit eternal life, not because their wealth could buy their way in, but because their wealth testified to the blessing of the Lord on their lives. Jesus' view is a different and more sober one. (On "I tell you the truth," see comments at 5:18.) The proverbial saying of v.24 refers to the absolutely impossible. The camel was the biggest animal in Palestine (a similar proverb in Babylonian Talmud [*b. Ber.* 55b] prefers "elephant" to "camel" because elephants were not uncommon in Babylon). Attempts to weaken this hyperbole by taking "needle," not as a sewing needle, but as a small gate through which an unladen camel could just squeeze—and only on his knees—are misguided. This conjecture may come from some of Jerome's allegorizing (cf. Broadus).

25–26 "Saved" is equivalent to entering the kingdom of God (v.24) or obtaining eternal life (v.16). The disciples, reflecting the common Jewish view of the rich, are astonished and ask that if rich men, blessed of God, cannot be saved, then who *can* be? Jesus agrees: "With man this [the salvation of anyone] is impossible, but with God all things are possible" (v.26; cf. Ge 18:14; Job 42:2; Lk 1:37).

27–28 Peter, impressed by "impossible" and speaking for his fellow disciples, thinks Jesus' words are unfair to the Twelve. Peter emphatically replies, "We have left everything to follow you" (cf. 4:20). Even here, he and the others are thinking in terms of deserving or earning God's favor. Yet Jesus does not castigate his disciples for being mercenary. They have made sacrifices and deserve an answer. But what he says—that the blessing to come, whether belonging exclusively to the Twelve at the renewal (v.28) or to all believers now (vv.29–30), far surpasses any sacrifice they might make—implies that it is a gentle rebuke.

Verse 28 has no parallel in Mark and only a loose one in Luke 22:28–30. The solemn "I tell you the truth" points to something important. Jesus looks forward to the session of the Son of Man (see comments at 8:20). He will sit on his "glorious throne" (lit., "throne of glory"; see Zerwick, *Biblical Greek*, para. 41; Turner, *Syntax*, 214; cf. 7:22; 16:27; 25:31–34) at the *palingenesia* ("renewal" of all things), a word used only twice in the NT, the other occurrence dealing with "rebirth ... by the Holy Spirit" (Tit 3:5). Here it has to do with the consummation of the kingdom (RSV, "in the new world"). (For its use elsewhere, see *TDNT*, 1:686–89; *NIDNTT*, 1:184–85; cf. 13:32; Ac 3:21; Ro 8:18–23, 2Pe 3:13; Rev 21:1, 5; 1QS 4:25.)

Contrary to Schweizer, there is no allusion to the endless Stoic cycles of conflagration and "renewal"; the idea moves strictly within Jewish teleological and apocalyptic expectation. But the remarkable feature of this verse is that the Twelve will "sit on twelve thrones," sharing judgment with the Son of Man. The idea that believers will at the consummation have a part in judging is not uncommon in the NT (Lk 22:30; 1Co 6:2). What is less clear is whether (1) the twelve apostles exercise judgment over the twelve tribes of Israel physically and racially conceived, or whether (2) the twelve apostles will exercise some kind of judgment over the entire church, symbolized by "Israel" (cf. Rev 21:12–14), or whether (3) the Twelve represent the entire assembly of Messiah, who will exercise a juridical role over racial Israel. The third supposition has no scriptural parallel; the second is possible but an unnatural way of taking "Israel" in a book that, though applying OT promises to Gentiles and Jews alike—namely, the "church" of Messiah—distinguishes between the two. The most plausible interpretation is the first one. At the consummation, the Twelve will judge the nation of Israel, presumably for its general rejection of Jesus Messiah. (On the symbolism, see Joseph M. Baumgarten, "The Duodecimal Courts of Qumran, Revelation, and the Sanhedrin," *JBL* 95 [1976]: 59–78, esp. 70–72; France, *Jesus and the Old Testament*, 65–66.)

29–30 Jesus now extends his encouragement to all his self-sacrificing disciples (cf. Mk 10:30). The promise is not literal (one cannot have one hundred mothers). God is no man's debtor. If one of Jesus' disciples has, for Jesus' sake, left, say, a father, he will find within the messianic community a hundred who will be as a father to him—in addition to inheriting eternal life (v.29).

The proverbial saying (v.30) is one Jesus repeats on various occasions. Here he immediately illustrates it by a parable (20:1–16), climaxed by the proverb in reverse form (20:16) as a closing bracket. It indicates something of the reversals under the king's reign. Attempts to restrict the application of this parable to one setting are not successful.

1. Some say the rich become poor at the consummation and the poor rich (cf. vv.16–29), as in Luke 16:19–31 (the story of Lazarus and the beggar). But such reversals are not absolute. Zacchaeus (Lk 19:1–10) was a rich man to whose house salvation came; Abraham, to whose "bosom" the beggar went, had great wealth.

2. Many of the Fathers hold that the first/last idea refers to Jews and Gentiles respectively. Doubtless it may, but this theme is not dominant in these chapters.

3. Some think the proverb assumes that the disciples had been arguing about priority on the basis of who was first called, to which Jesus responds that "the last will be first ..." But this better suits the situation in Matthew 18 than in ch. 19.

4. It seems preferable, therefore, to take the proverb as a way of setting forth God's grace over against *all* notions that the rich, powerful, great, and prominent will continue so in the kingdom. Those who approach God in childlike trust (vv.13–15) will be received and advanced in the kingdom beyond those who, from the world's perspective, enjoy prominence now.

4. The parable of the workers (20:1–16)

OVERVIEW

On parables generally, see comments at 13:3a. From this one, found only in Matthew, we learn how "the last" person can become "first" (19:30)—by free grace (see esp. v.15). Bailey (*Jesus through Middle Eastern Eyes*, 355) rightly points out that the common title given this parable, namely, "The Parable of the Workers," misdirects the reader's focus. The parable is primarily not about the workers at all but about "the amazing grace and compassion of the employer" (ibid.; cf. Jeremias, *Parables of Jesus*, 37). The point is not that those who work just an hour do as much as those who work all day (unlike a Jewish parable ca. AD 325 that tells of a man who, on those grounds, is paid a month's wages for a few hours' discussion), nor that the willingness of the latecomers matches that of the all-day workers (contra *TDNT*, 4:717 and n. 91), nor that Gentiles are the latecomers in contrast to the Jews (the context knows no such distinctions), nor that all men are equal before God or that all kingdom work is equal. Still less acceptable is Derrett's lengthy explanation (*Studies in the New Testament*, 1:48–75). He rightly holds that the entire parable portrays working conditions in the first century, but the eleventh-hour men, entitled to a certain minimum wage, actually get more. But Derrett's view depends on late sources for minimum wage laws, and he assumes that the grapes were urgently in need of harvesting and that it must have been Friday afternoon—none of which the text implies.

Huffmann ("Atypical Features in the Parables," 209–10) is right. The parable begins with a topical scene and introduces atypical elements to surprise the reader and make a powerful point. "Jesus deliberately and cleverly led the listeners along by degrees until they understood that if God's generosity was to be represented by a man, such a man would be different from any man ever encountered" (p. 209).

[1]"For the kingdom of heaven is like a landowner who went out early in the morning to hire men to work in his vineyard. [2]He agreed to pay them a denarius for the day and sent them into his vineyard.

[3]"About the third hour he went out and saw others standing in the marketplace doing nothing. [4]He told them, 'You also go and work in my vineyard, and I will pay you whatever is right.' [5]So they went.

"He went out again about the sixth hour and the ninth hour and did the same thing.
6About the eleventh hour he went out and found still others standing around. He asked
them, 'Why have you been standing here all day long doing nothing?'
7"'Because no one has hired us,' they answered.
"He said to them, 'You also go and work in my vineyard.'
8"When evening came, the owner of the vineyard said to his foreman, 'Call the workers and pay them their wages, beginning with the last ones hired and going on to the
first.'
9"The workers who were hired about the eleventh hour came and each received a
denarius. 10So when those came who were hired first, they expected to receive more. But
each one of them also received a denarius. 11When they received it, they began to grumble against the landowner. 12'These men who were hired last worked only one hour,' they
said, 'and you have made them equal to us who have borne the burden of the work and
the heat of the day.'
13"But he answered one of them, 'Friend, I am not being unfair to you. Didn't you agree
to work for a denarius? 14Take your pay and go. I want to give the man who was hired last
the same as I gave you. 15Don't I have the right to do what I want with my own money? Or
are you envious because I am generous?'
16"So the last will be first, and the first will be last."

COMMENTARY

1–2 On the formula "the kingdom of heaven is like," see comments at 13:24. The normal working day was ten hours or so, not counting breaks. The landowner in the parable finds his first set of men at about 6:00 a.m. (*hama prōi* means "at dawn"; NIV, "early in the morning"; on the construction, see Moule, *Idiom Book*, 82) and agrees to pay each worker a denarius (v.2)—the normal wage for a foot soldier or day laborer (Tob 5:14 [LXX 5:15]; cf. Tacitus, *Ann.*, 1.17; Pliny, *Nat.* 33.3).

3–7 There were twelve "hours" from dawn to sundown. The third hour (v.3) would be about 9:00 a.m., the sixth about noon, and the eleventh about 5:00 p.m. The marketplace would be the central square, where all kinds of business were done and casual labor hired. Why the landowner kept returning to hire more men—lack of foresight, not finding enough workers earlier in the day at the marketplace, the poor work of the first laborers—is not spelled out and, therefore, cannot be the key to the parable. The third-hour men are promised "whatever is right" (v.4); trusting the landowner's integrity, they work on that basis (v.5). The last group (v.6) were standing around ("idle" [KJV] is a late addition) because no one had hired them (v.7).

8–12 Some take "when evening came" as an allusion to the judgment, but this is doubtful. It is essential to the story in a time when laborers were customarily paid at the end of each day (cf.

Lev 19:13). The foreman is told to pay each man (lit.) "the wage"—the standard day-laborer's wage. Who gets paid first is crucial: it is only because the last hired receive a day's wage (v.9) that those first hired expect to get more than they bargained for (v.10). They "grumble against" (v.11) the owner because he has been generous to others and merely just to them. They have borne "the heat" of the day (*kausōn*, v.12; either direct sunlight or hot wind [BDAG, 536]), which could drive workers from the field; though fairly paid, they feel unfairly treated because others who worked much less received what they did. Nothing in the parable implies that Jews have borne the burden of the law and now Gentile outcasts are made equal to them.

13–15 "Friend" suggests that this rebuke is only a mild one. "I am not being unfair to you"—I am not cheating you, defrauding you (cf. M. Black, "Some Greek Words with Hebrew Meanings in the Epistles and Apocalypse," in *Biblical Studies* (ed. J. R. McKay and J. F. Miller; London: Collins, 1976], 142ff.). The owner has paid the agreed-on wage (v.14). If he wants to pay others more, that is his business. Provided he has been just in all his dealings, does he not have the right to do what he wants with his money (v.15)? The NIV translates "is your eye evil" (lit. Gk.) by "are you envious," because the "evil eye" was an idiom used to refer to jealousy (cf. Dt 15:9; 1Sa 18:9; see comments at 6:22–23).

These rhetorical questions (vv.13b–15) show that God's great gifts, simply because they *are* God's, are distributed, not because they are earned, but because he is gracious. Jesus is not laying down principles for resolving union-management disputes. On the contrary, "the principle in the world is that he who works the longest receives the most pay. That is just. But in the kingdom of God the principles of merit and ability may be set aside so that grace can prevail" (Kistemaker, *Parables of Jesus*, 77–78). See also Notes, 5:12; cf. G. de Ru, "The Conception of Reward in the Teaching of Jesus," *NovT* 8 [1966]: 202–22.

16 God's grace makes some who are last first. The point of the parable is not that all in the kingdom will receive the same reward but that kingdom rewards depend on God's sovereign grace (cf. v.23). For the inclusio around the parable, see comments at 19:30.

NOTES

5 The expression οἱ δὲ ἀπῆλθον (*hoi de apēlthon*) at the beginning of this verse can plausibly be rendered "But they went away" (as Charette, *Theme of Recompense*, 115 n. 2, observes). The meaning of the parable would not thereby change; rather, its lesson would not apply to this particular group that "went away" instead of working. More likely, then, the expression should be rendered "So they went" (NIV) or "And off they went" (France [NICNT]), so as not to have an anomalous group stuck in the middle of the parable.

10 The article in τὸ ἀνὰ δηνάριον (*to ana dēnarion*) is anaphoric, i.e., "a denarius to each man as to the others who preceded"; cf. BDF, para. 266 (2).

15 "Or" is omitted by some MSS, with the evidence rather evenly divided (cf. Metzger, *Textual Commentary*, 50–51).

16 Many MSS add to the end of the verse "for many are invited, but few are chosen." The shorter reading is Alexandrian and Western. The longer reading, if original, might have been dropped by homoeoteleuton; but it is equally possible the extra words are an assimilation to 22:14 (so Metzger, *Textual Commentary*, 5).

5. Third major passion prediction (20:17–19)

OVERVIEW

See comments at 16:21–23; 17:9, 22–23; for the synoptic parallels, see Mark 10:32–34; Luke 18:31–34. Here there is the first mention of the mode of Jesus' death and of the Gentiles' part in it (only the Romans could crucify people). These three verses may look back to the preceding parable by implying the grounds of God's grace—namely, what his Son did on the cross. Also, just as 19:13–15 sets the stage for 19:16–30, so 20:17–19 sets it for vv.20–28. While Jesus faces crucifixion, his disciples, still blind to the nature of his messiahship, squabble over their places in the kingdom.

[17]Now as Jesus was going up to Jerusalem, he took the twelve disciples aside and said
to them, [18]"We are going up to Jerusalem, and the Son of Man will be betrayed to the chief
priests and the teachers of the law. They will condemn him to death [19]and will turn him
over to the Gentiles to be mocked and flogged and crucified. On the third day he will be
raised to life!"

COMMENTARY

17 "Going up" does not necessarily mean that Jesus has left Perea, crossed the Jordan, passed through Jericho, and begun the ascent to Jerusalem; it had become customary to speak of "going up" to Jerusalem regardless of where one was in Palestine, as in England one "goes up" to London from every place except Oxford or Cambridge. We should, therefore, not be surprised to find Jesus still in Jericho (v.29). Before setting out for Jerusalem, doubtless to attend the festival, Jesus took the Twelve aside from the throngs of pilgrims choking the roads to Jerusalem at such times (see comments at 21:9). Only the Twelve were even remotely ready to hear this passion prediction.

18–19 Jerusalem was the focal point of Jewish worship. We are going there, Jesus says, because there the Son of Man will be betrayed and crucified. He will be "condemned"—his death will result from legal proceedings. Mention of the resurrection is brief (v.19) and apparently not understood (cf. Lk 18:34)—though in Matthew, the disciples' misunderstanding is not spelled out as in Luke but exemplified by the succeeding story (vv.20–28), which Luke omits.

6. Suffering and service (20:20–28)

OVERVIEW

Luke parallels Matthew both before and after this pericope but omits it (cf. Mk 10:35–45). He has a somewhat similar account (Lk 22:24–30), but it is probably a different occasion. Carter (*Matthew and the Margins*, 399) demonstrates how vv.17–19 mesh nicely with these verses. Jesus' death and resurrection hold the sections together, and the question of who is ruling, and what it means to rule, continues.

Again the question of rank returns (cf. 18:1–5). Despite Jesus' repeated predictions of his passion, two disciples and their mother are still thinking about privilege, status, and power.

S. Légasse ("Approche de l'Épisode préévangélique des Fils de Zébédée [Mark x.35–40 par.]," *NTS* 20 [1974]: 161–77) represents those who discount the historicity of this narrative largely on the hypothesis that "cup" and "baptism" are theological symbols around which a fictional episode was woven to convey certain theological truths. Bultmann (*History of the Synoptic Tradition*, 24) goes further and says that even the "prospect" of James's and John's death could not have been implied until after their martyrdom. The grounds for such theorizing are slender indeed. Why cannot theologically loaded terms be used in a historical narrative? Bultmann's critique reflects presuppositional antisupernaturalism in its most naive form. Jesus predicts his death (vv.17–19), and when two of his disciples ask for preferential treatment, it is entirely natural that he should ask them if they are prepared to face similar suffering and death (cf. 5:10–12; 10:37–39). Moreover, it is highly unlikely the church would invent a story so damaging to two of its leading apostles.

20Then the mother of Zebedee's sons came to Jesus with her sons and, kneeling down,
asked a favor of him.
21"What is it you want?" he asked.
She said, "Grant that one of these two sons of mine may sit at your right and the other
at your left in your kingdom."
22"You don't know what you are asking," Jesus said to them. "Can you drink the cup I am
going to drink?"
"We can," they answered.
23Jesus said to them, "You will indeed drink from my cup, but to sit at my right or left is
not for me to grant. These places belong to those for whom they have been prepared by
my Father."
24When the ten heard about this, they were indignant with the two brothers. 25Jesus
called them together and said, "You know that the rulers of the Gentiles lord it over them,
and their high officials exercise authority over them. 26Not so with you. Instead, whoever
wants to become great among you must be your servant, 27and whoever wants to be first

must be your slave — [28]just as the Son of Man did not come to be served, but to serve, and to give his life as a ransom for many."

COMMENTARY

20 In Mark, John and James approach Jesus themselves; here, it is through *their mother*. Many find this historically improbable because in v.22 Jesus responds to her sons only. But the following points make the obvious synthesis plausible:

1. According to v.20, the mother *and her sons* approach Jesus, the implication being that all three are asking this favor, with the mother as the speaker.

2. This is confirmed by the other apostles' indignation (v.24), showing that James and John as well as their mother were involved.

3. That the mother should be the one to approach Jesus becomes the more plausible if she is Jesus' aunt on his mother's side — not certain, but not unlikely (see comments at 10:2; 27:56).

4. By adding the mother, Matthew cannot be shielding James and John. They still get the same response as in Mark. Matthew has no obvious theological motive for introducing their mother; he is simply recording a historical detail.

5. That the request should come from James and John, whether through their mother or not, accords with what we know of their aggressiveness (cf. Mk 9:38; Lk 9:54).

The "kneeling down" is not "worship" of deity but may imply homage to the one increasingly recognized as King Messiah (see comments at 2:2).

21 The "right hand" and "left hand" suggest proximity to the King's person and so a share in his prestige and power. Such positions increase as the King is esteemed and has absolute power (cf. Pss 16:11; 45:9; 110:1; Mt 26:64; Ac 7:55–56; cf. Josephus, *Ant.* 6.235 [11.9]). Mark has "in your glory," Matthew "in your kingdom." Mark's phrase clearly points to the Parousia, "when Jesus is enthroned as eschatological judge" (Lane, *Mark*, 379). Hill proposes that the "kingdom" in Matthew is the kingdom of Christ (13:41–43; 25:31–46), identified as the church; and the change from "glory" to "kingdom" therefore means that the original story is now being applied to competition for leadership in the church. But we have already seen that "kingdom" is never identified with "church" in Matthew (see comments at 13:37–39), and Christ's kingdom is equivalent to the kingdom of heaven (13:41; 20:21; 25:31). Because the "kingdom" comes in stages, there is no substantial difference between Matthew and Mark. The kingdom here is the reign of Messiah at the consummation. The link with 19:28 — a verse that speaks (cf. Gk.) of both "throne" and "glory" — is unmistakable. What the sons of Zebedee want and their mother asks for is that they might share in the authority and preeminence of Jesus Messiah when his kingdom is fully consummated — something they think to be near at hand without the cross or any inter-advent period.

22 The additional words "and to be baptized with the baptism that I am baptized with" (KJV) — and similarly in v.23 — are almost certainly an assimilation to Mark 10:38–39. Jesus' answer is not severe but mingles firmness with probing. It is often ignorance that seeks leadership, power, and glory; the brothers do not know what they are asking. To ask to reign with Jesus is to ask to suffer with him, and not only do they not know what they are asking for (cf. 10:37–39; Ro 8:17; 2Ti 2:12; Rev 3:21);

they have as yet no clear perceptions of *Jesus'* sufferings. To ask for worldly wealth and much honor is often to ask for anxiety, temptation, disappointment, and envy; in the spiritual arena, to ask for great usefulness and reward is often to ask for great suffering (cf. 2Co 11:23–33; Col 1:24; Rev 1:9). "We know not what we ask, when we ask for the glory of wearing the crown, and ask not for grace to bear the cross in our way to it" (Matthew Henry).

The "cup" (cf. 26:39) characteristically refers, in OT imagery, to judgment or retribution (cf. Ps 75:8; Isa 51:17–18; Jer 25:15–28). If the disciples grasped anything of Jesus' passion predictions, they probably thought the language was partly hyperbolic (Jesus did use hyperbole elsewhere [e.g., 19:24]) and referred to the eschatological conflict during which Messiah's side would suffer losses; but these could scarcely be too severe for one who could still storms and raise the dead. Thus, by their bold response, James and John betray their misunderstandings of the timing of the dawn of the kingdom in all its glory (cf. Lk 19:11), and equally of the uniqueness and redemptive significance of Jesus' sufferings (cf. v.28) now imminent.

23 Jesus answers them first on their own terms before speaking of his own death as a ransom (v.28). In a sense, they can and will drink from his cup of suffering. James would become the first apostolic martyr (Ac 12:2), and John (if it is the same one) would suffer exile (Rev 1:9). But it is not Jesus' role to determine who sits on his right hand and his left. Here, as elsewhere (see comments at 11:27; 24:36; 28:18; cf. Jn 14:28), Jesus makes it clear that his authority is a derived authority. These positions have already been assigned by the Father. Jesus cannot assign them at a mother's request.

24–27 The indignation of the ten doubtless sprang less from humility than jealousy plus the fear that they might lose out. If these verses scarcely support egalitarianism—choice positions, after all, will be allotted—they demonstrate that interest in egalitarianism may mask a jealousy whose deepest wellsprings are not concern for justice but "enlightened self-interest." The disciples revert to the squabbling of an earlier period (Mk 9:33–37; cf. Mt 18:1). Jesus calls them together and draws a contrast between greatness among *ta ethnē* ("pagans" or "Gentiles," v.25) and greatness among heirs of the kingdom. The "pagans" or "Gentiles" who would spring to mind were Romans; power and authority characterized their empire. The NIV's "lord it over" gives a false impression. Jesus is not criticizing abuse of power in political structures—the verb never has that meaning (cf. K. W. Clark, "The Meaning of [κατα] κυριεύειν," in *Studies in New Testament Language* [ed. Elliott], 100–105) and should be translated "exercise lordship over," parallel to "exercise authority over" in the next line—but insists that the very structures themselves cannot be transferred to relationships among his followers.

Greatness among Jesus' disciples is based on service. Anyone who wants to be great must become the *diakonos* ("servant," v.26, GK *1356*) of all. Here *diakonos* does not mean "deacon" or "minister" (KJV) in the modern church use. One of the ironies of language is that a word like "minister," which in its roots refers to a helper, one who "ministers," has become a badge of honor and power in religion and politics. But lest the full force of his teaching be lost, Jesus repeats it in v.27 with the stronger word *doulos* ("slave," GK *1528*; cf. 1Co 9:19; 2Co 4:5). In the pagan world, humility was regarded not so much as a virtue but as a vice. Imagine a slave being given leadership! Jesus' ethics of the leadership and power in his community of disciples are revolutionary.

28 At this point, Jesus presents himself—the Son of Man (see comments at 8:20)—as the supreme example of service to others. The verse is clearly important to our understanding of Jesus' view of his death. Three related questions call for discussion.

1. *Authenticity*. Many reject the authenticity of v.28, or at least of v.28b (and, correspondingly, Mark 10:45; most recently, see McKnight, *Jesus and His Death*, 356–57), on the grounds that it ill suits the context, since Jesus' atoning death cannot be imitated by his disciples, that nowhere else is he reported as speaking of his death in this way, and that the language reflects the influence of the Hellenistic church. On the contrary, the language has been shown to be Palestinian (Jeremias, *Eucharistic Words*, 179–82), and Jesus speaks of his death in not dissimilar terms when instituting the Lord's Supper (26:26–29) and also in Luke 22:37, assuming that it relates to a different occasion. It is quite common in the NT, both in words ascribed to Jesus and elsewhere, to begin with the disciples' need to die to self and end up with Jesus' unique, atoning death as an ethical example—or, conversely, to begin with Jesus' unique death and find it applied as an example to the disciples (16:21–28; Jn 12:23–25; Php 2:5–11; 1Pe 2:18–25). There are no substantial reasons for denying the authenticity of this saying (cf. S. H. T. Page, "The Authenticity of the Ransom Logion [Mark 10:45b]," in *Gospel Perspectives* [ed. France and Wenham], 1:137–61), and its nuances seem much more in keeping with the way Jesus progressively revealed himself (cf. Carson, "Christological Ambiguities") than with a clear-cut, postresurrection apostolic confession.

2. *Meaning*. It is natural to take "did not come" as presupposing at least a hint of Jesus' preexistence, though the language does not absolutely require it. He came not to be served, like a king dependent on countless courtiers and attendants, but to serve others. Stonehouse (*Witness of Matthew*, 251ff.; *Origins*, 187) rightly points out that the verse assumes that the Son of Man had every right to expect to be served, but he served instead. Implicit is a self-conscious awareness that the Son of Man who, because of his heavenly origin, possessed divine authority was the one who humbled himself, even to the point of undergoing an atoning death. The tripartite breakdown of the Son of Man references (see Reflections, p. 247) is to this extent artificial. The display of divine glory shines most brightly when it is set aside for the sake of redeeming man by a shameful death. This stands at the very heart of Jesus' self-disclosure and of the primitive gospel (1Co 1:23: "We preach Christ [Messiah] crucified").

The Son of Man came to give his life as a ransom for many. Deissmann (*Light from the Ancient East*, 331–32) points out that *lytron* ("ransom," GK *3389*) was most commonly used as the purchase price for freeing slaves; there is good evidence that the notion of "purchase price" is always implied in the NT use of *lytron* (cf. Morris, *Apostolic Preaching*, 11ff.). Others, however, by examining the word in the LXX, conclude that, especially when the subject is God, the word means "deliverance" and the cognate verb "to deliver," without reference to a "price paid" (cf. Hill, *Greek Words*, 58–80; McKnight, *Jesus and His Death*, 357). The matter may be difficult to decide in a passage like Titus 2:14. Is wickedness a chain from which Jesus by his death *delivers* us, or a slave owner from whom Jesus by his death *ransoms* us? The parallel in 1 Peter 1:18 suggests the latter, even though (as Turner, *Christian Words*, 105–7, insists) there is never any mention in the NT of the one to whom the price is paid, and in 20:28, this meaning is virtually assured by the use of *anti* ("for"). The normal force of this preposition denotes substitution, equivalence, exchange (cf. *NIDNTT*, 3:1179–80). "The life of Jesus, surrendered in a sacrificial death, brought about the release of forfeited lives. He acted on behalf of the many by taking their place" (ibid., 1180).

"The many" underlines the immeasurable effects of Jesus' solitary death: the one dies, the many find their lives "ransomed, healed, restored, forgiven," a great host no man can number (cf. J. Jeremias,

"Das Lösegeld für Viele," *Judaica* 3 [1948]: 263). But it should be remembered that "the many" can refer, in the Dead Sea Scrolls and the rabbinic literature, to the elect community (cf. Ralph Marcus, "'Mebaqqer' and Rabbim in the Manual of Discipline vi:11–13," *JBL* 75 [1956]: 298–302). This suggests Jesus' substitutionary death is payment for and results in the eschatological people of God. This well suits "the many" of Isaiah 52:13–53:12.

3. *Dependence on Isaiah 53.* C. K. Barrett ("The Background of Mark 10.45," in *New Testament Essays* [ed. A. J. B. Higgins; Manchester: Manchester Univ. Press, 1959], 1–18; idem, "Mark 10.45: A Ransom for Many," in *New Testament Essays* [London: SPCK, 1972], 20–26), Hooker (*Son of Man*, 140–47), and others have argued that there is no allusion to Isaiah in Mark 10:45 and Matthew 20:28. They argue this on two grounds: linguistic and conceptual. Linguistically, they point out that the Greek verb *diakoneō* ("I serve," v.28) and its cognates are never used in the LXX to render *ʿebed* ("servant" of Isaiah's "Servant Songs," GK 6269) and its cognates. But the evidence is slight, and the conceptual parallels close—Isaiah's Servant benefits people by his suffering, and so does Jesus. Hooker is certainly incorrect in restricting *diakoneō* to *domestic* service (cf. France, "Servant of the Lord," 34). Both France and Moo (*Old Testament in the Gospel Passion Narratives*, 122–27) have also shown that "to give his life" springs from Isaiah 53:10, 12, and that *lytron* ("ransom") is not as impossible a rendering of *ʾāšām* ("a guilt offering") as some allege. The Hebrew word *ʾāšām* includes the notion of substitution, at least of an equivalent. The guilty sinner offers an *ʾāšām* to remove his own guilt; in Leviticus 5, *ʾāšām* refers to compensatory payment. Thus, though *ʾāšām* has more sacrificial overtones than *lytron*, both include the idea of payment or compensation. Most scholars have also recognized in "the many" a clear reference to Isaiah (cf. esp. Dalman, *Jesus-Jeshua*, 171–72). The implication of the cumulative evidence is that Jesus explicitly referred to himself as Isaiah's Suffering Servant (see comments at 26:17–30) and interpreted his own death in that light—an interpretation in which Matthew has followed his Lord (see comments at 8:17; 12:15–21).

Both Mark (10:45) and Matthew (here) tie their understanding of this verse not only to the immediate pericope but to their entire gospel narrative (see Bolt, *Cross from a Distance*, ch. 2).

NOTES

21 Compare this use of εἰπὲ ἵνα (*eipe hina*, "Grant that") with the use in 4:3. "Command that" is the idea common to both. The mother believes Jesus need only say the word for it to be done.

28 For an interesting and extended gloss on this verse, see Metzger, *Textual Commentary*, 53.

7. Healing two blind men (20:29–34)

OVERVIEW

Mark (10:46–52) and Luke (18:35–43) mention only one blind man, and Mark names him (Bartimaeus, 10:46); but Matthew habitually gives fuller details on numbers of persons (cf. 8:28). This story is not a doublet of 9:27–31, which stresses faith and ends with a command to be silent. It lacks those twin foci but has other purposes. It pictures Jesus still serving and again links his healing ministry with his death (v.28; see comments at 8:17). Moreover, it reminds us that the one going up to Jerusalem to give his life as a ransom for many is the Messiah, the Son of David, whose great power, used mercifully (v.30) and compassionately (v.34), is not used to save himself.

29As Jesus and his disciples were leaving Jericho, a large crowd followed him. 30Two
blind men were sitting by the roadside, and when they heard that Jesus was going by,
they shouted, "Lord, Son of David, have mercy on us!"
31The crowd rebuked them and told them to be quiet, but they shouted all the louder,
"Lord, Son of David, have mercy on us!"
32Jesus stopped and called them. "What do you want me to do for you?" he asked.
33"Lord," they answered, "we want our sight."
34Jesus had compassion on them and touched their eyes. Immediately they received
their sight and followed him.

COMMENTARY

29 Matthew and Mark say that Jesus was "leaving," Luke that he was "entering," Jericho. While there are several possible reasons for this, none is certain. Many "explanations" are inadequate: that Jesus healed one blind man on entering the town and two on leaving; that the healings occurred while Jesus was going "in and out"; that Jesus went through Jericho (Lk 19:1) without finding lodging and on his way out healed the blind men, met Zacchaeus, and returned to his place—so that Jesus' "leaving" was really his "entering." Calvin's "conjecture," followed by many, is that Jesus on his way into the city did not respond to the petitions of the blind men (perhaps in order to increase their faith; cf. 15:21–28) but healed them on his way out. Marshall (*Gospel of Luke*, 692–93) offers a literary explanation—namely, Luke made the change to accommodate the ensuing Zacchaeus story that takes place in Jericho and that Luke wants to place as a climax. One might have thought that Luke's simpler course would have been to drop any mention of Jericho in this healing, since he gains nothing by it and his alteration brings him into conflict with Mark.

Many avoid geographical contradiction by noting that in this period there were *two* Jerichos—an older town on the hill, largely in ruins, and the new Herodian town about one mile away (cf. Josephus, *J.W.* 4.459 [8.3]). In this view, Matthew and Mark, under Jewish influence, mention the old town Jesus was leaving; Luke the Hellenist refers to the new one, which Jesus is entering. This may well be the explanation. But there is no certain evidence that the old town was still inhabited at this time, and we do not know the local names of the two sites.

Jericho was not only the home of Jesus' ancestor Rahab (1:5) but was also a day's journey from

Jerusalem. The "large crowd" implies more than messianic excitement; it also reflects the multitudes of pilgrims from Galilee and elsewhere heading to Jerusalem for the feast.

30 The rather common suggestion that Matthew increases the number of blind men to two because two was the minimum number of witnesses for attesting Jesus' messiahship is misguided. To *experience* the healings would not prove Jesus was the Messiah. He might simply be a prophet. On the other hand, if the miracle confirmed or promoted belief in Jesus' messiahship, it might do so as easily for *those who witnessed the miracle* as for those who experienced it. The "large crowd" would have provided witnesses aplenty. The "two," therefore, has no theological motivation but shows personal knowledge of the events. There may have been many blind people in the Jericho area; for the region produced large quantities of balsam, believed to be very beneficial for many eye defects (cf. Strabo, *Geogr.* 16.2.41). These two were sitting by the roadside, doubtless begging (Mark-Luke); hearing that Jesus was passing, they cried out, "Lord, Son of David, have mercy on us!" (in the most likely text; cf. Metzger, *Textual Commentary*, 53–54). On the title "Son of David" in relation to healing, see comments at 9:27.

31–34 Matthew's account is simple but stresses that Jesus mercifully healed the men despite the opposition of the crowds (v.31) that, like the disciples (cf. 19:13–15), wanted to bask in his glory but not practice his compassion. After this healing, unlike 9:30, there is no command to be silent. That point in Jesus' ministry has been reached when more public self-disclosure could not change the course of events. The two healed men joined the crowds following Jesus (20:34), pressing on to the Passover they expected and the cross they did not.

8. Opening events of Passion Week (21:1–23:39)

a. The triumphal entry (21:1–11)

OVERVIEW

Alistair Wilson (*When Will These Things Happen?* 85–99) suggests that the first three pericopes of this chapter—the triumphal entry, the cleansing of the temple, and the cursing of the fig tree—depict incidents that are "prophetic acts" mirroring those of Hosea, Jeremiah, and Ezekiel. T. W. Manson ("The Cleansing of the Temple," *BJRL* 33 [1951]: 271–82) suggests the feast in question is Tabernacles (autumn), not Dedication (winter) or Passover (spring). Because Jesus died at Passover, Manson spreads Matthew 21–28 (and parallels) over six months instead of six days. His view rests largely on the observation that figs do not usually appear on the trees around Jerusalem until June and September, which seems to rule out Passover (usually April) as the right period for 21:18–21. But figs are regularly found in Jericho much earlier—and sometimes also in Jerusalem—and Manson's view introduces some difficult problems in the passion chronology.

For the moment we shall assume that this trip to Jerusalem occurred a few days before the Passover on which Jesus was crucified. Matthew does not mention the stay at Bethany (Jn 12:1–11), where Jesus arrived "six days before Passover," probably Friday evening (at the beginning of the Sabbath) before Passion Week, and stayed there for Sabbath, entering Jerusalem on Sunday. Apparently Jesus went back and forth to Bethany throughout the week (21:17). (For a detailed chronology of Passion Week, see Hoehner, *Chronological Aspects*; on the question of authenticity, see Dhyanchand Carr, "Jesus, the King of Zion: A Traditio-Historical Enquiry into the So-called 'Triumphal' Entry of Jesus" [PhD diss., University of London, 1980], 128–218, 350–92.)

1 As they approached Jerusalem and came to Bethphage on the Mount of Olives, Jesus
sent two disciples, 2 saying to them, "Go to the village ahead of you, and at once you will
find a donkey tied there, with her colt by her. Untie them and bring them to me. 3 If anyone
says anything to you, tell him that the Lord needs them, and he will send them right away."
4 This took place to fulfill what was spoken through the prophet:

5 "Say to the Daughter of Zion,
'See, your king comes to you,
gentle and riding on a donkey,
on a colt, the foal of a donkey.'"

6 The disciples went and did as Jesus had instructed them. 7 They brought the donkey
and the colt, placed their cloaks on them, and Jesus sat on them. 8 A very large crowd
spread their cloaks on the road, while others cut branches from the trees and spread them
on the road. 9 The crowds that went ahead of him and those that followed shouted,

"Hosanna to the Son of David!"
"Blessed is he who comes in the name of the Lord!"
"Hosanna in the highest!"

10 When Jesus entered Jerusalem, the whole city was stirred and asked, "Who is this?"
11 The crowds answered, "This is Jesus, the prophet from Nazareth in Galilee."

COMMENTARY

1–2 The Roman military road from Jericho to Jerusalem was about seventeen miles long and climbed three thousand feet. It passed through Bethany and nearby Bethphage ("house of figs"), which lay on the southeast slope of the Mount of Olives, then crossed over the mount and the Kidron Valley and entered Jerusalem (v.1). The mount itself stands about three hundred feet higher than the temple hill and about one hundred feet higher than the hill of Zion, affording a spectacular, panoramic view of the city.

Jesus sent two disciples (unnamed, but cf. Lk 22:8) ahead to Bethphage (for the grammar, cf. *Grammar*, 643–44) to fetch the animals (v.2). The distinguishing feature of the synoptic accounts, as opposed to John 12, is that Jesus arranged for the ride. The applause and the crowds were not manipulated; they would have occurred in any case. But the ride on a colt, because it was planned, could only be an acted parable, a deliberate act of symbolic self-disclosure for those with eyes to see or, after the resurrection, with memories by which to remember and integrate the events of the preceding weeks and years. Secrecy was being lifted.

3 "Lord" (also Mark-Luke) might mean "owner"; but then the disciples' response would be untrue, unless Jesus owned the animals, which is extremely unlikely. The title might refer to Yahweh—the animals are needed in Yahweh's service. But the most natural way to take "Lord" is Jesus' way of referring to himself. This step is in keeping with the authority he has already claimed for himself and fits this late period of his ministry, when he revealed himself with increasing clarity. J. Gresham Machen (*The Origin of Paul's Religion* [New York: Macmillan, 1928, 1947], 296–97) notes that even the church's ascription of "Lord" to Jesus in a full christological sense finds its roots in Jesus' self-references.

4–5 It is possible that Matthew presents these verses as having been spoken by Jesus. The perfect *gegonen* should then be translated, "This has taken place" (v.4), spoken somewhat proleptically because the order had been given (see comments at 1:22). The alternative is to take the verses as Matthew's comment. This requires taking the perfect as either having aoristic force or meaning, "This stands as something that happened." John's statement that the disciples did not understand all this at the time (12:16) does not necessarily support the alternative, since Jesus said many things they did not understand at the time (cf. Jn 2:20–22).

A few MSS add "Zechariah" or "Isaiah" to "prophet," doubtless because the quotation comes from both. The introductory words of the quotation are from Isaiah 62:11, and the rest from Zechariah 9:9. The omitted words "righteous and having salvation" (Zec 9:9) may be understood as implicitly included, or omitted because the chief stress is on Jesus' humility (Stendahl, *School of St. Matthew*, 118–20).

The text form of the quotation (v.5) is disputed, but at least the latter parts depend directly on the MT (cf. Gundry, *Use of the Old Testament*, 120–21; Blomberg, "Matthew," in *CNTUOT*). The last word, *hypozygion*, means a "beast of burden," which in Palestine was usually a donkey. Such an animal was sometimes ridden by rulers in times of peace (Jdg 5:10; 1Ki 1:33; cf. Rev 19:11). Jews certainly understood Zechariah 9:9 to refer to the Messiah, often in terms of the Son of David (Str-B, 1:842–44; cf. Ham, *Coming King*, 47). Therefore, for those with eyes to see, Jesus was not only proclaiming his messiahship and his fulfillment of Scripture but showing the kind of peace-loving approach he was now making to the city.

Many scholars find difficulty with the fact that Matthew alone of the four evangelists mentions *two* animals—a donkey and her colt (vv.2, 7)—and only he cites the Hebrew text so fully that the unwary might think there *were* two animals. The Hebrew, of course, refers to only one beast. The last line is in parallelism with the next-to-the-last line and merely identifies the "donkey" (line 3) as a colt (a young male donkey). But it is quite unreasonable to suggest that Matthew, who demonstrably had a good command of Hebrew (cf. Gundry, *Use of the Old Testament*, 198), added the extra animal to fit a text he radically misunderstood (contra McNeile, Schniewind). Nor is it more reasonable to assume that Matthew knows there actually were two animals and quotes Zechariah because the prophet's words might barely refer to two, for his Jewish readers would not likely be convinced. Still less likely is the appeal to unassimilated sources (cf. R. Bartnicki, "Das Zitat von Zach IX, 9–10 und die Tiere im Bericht von Matthäus über dem Einzug Jesu in Jerusalem (Mt XXI, 1–11)," *NovT* 18 [1976]: 161–66).

The most reasonable suggestion is that Mark's "which no one has ever ridden" prompted Matthew to mention both animals (cf. Stendahl, *School of St. Matthew*, 118–20; Longenecker, *Biblical Exegesis*, 148–49). Gundry (*Use of the Old Testament*, 198–99) holds that Matthew witnessed the scene. Matthew's reference to both animals is his way of highlighting what the other synoptists affirm—the animal Jesus rode on *was* "a colt." If we assume that Matthew understood Hebrew, the full quotation affirms that Jesus rode on the "colt," not its mother. Mark and Luke say the animal was so young that it had never been ridden. In the midst, then, of this excited crowd, an unbroken animal remains calm under the hands of the Messiah who controls nature (8:23–27; 14:22–32). Thus the event points to the peace of the consummated kingdom (cf. Isa 11:1–10). Though Matthew may have something of the same thing in mind, in addition he stresses that Jesus fulfills Scripture even in this detail—that the animal he rode was a colt. Without warrant is the appeal to Midrash, at least in its technical, fourth-century sense (see Introduction, section 12.b). Although Jewish midrashic writers occasionally give a separate meaning to each part of Hebrew parallelism (cf. examples in Carr, "Jesus, the King of Zion"), the continuity of the Midrash lies in the passage being expounded, not in the narrative explanations. But here the continuity lies in the narrative. Still less credible is the allegorizing of many of the Fathers, and even of J. P. Lange: the donkey symbolizes Jews accustomed to the yoke of the law, and the colt hitherto untamed Gentiles ("The old theocracy runs idly and instinctively by the side of the young church, which has become the true bearer of the divinity of Christ" [*CHS*, 372]).

6–8 The two disciples returned from their errand and put their cloaks (their outer garments; see comments at 5:40) on the beasts—both animals were in the procession (v.7). Jesus sat "on them." Not a few critics take the antecedent of "them" to be the animals and ridicule the statement. But as Plummer remarks, "The Evangelist credits his readers with common sense." The antecedent of "them" may be the cloaks, or the plural may be a "plural of category" (cf. "He sprang from the horses"; cf. Turner, *Insights*, 41; see comments at 2:20). Less convincing is appeal to very weak textual traditions: he sat on *it* or they sat him on *it* (thereon, KJV; cf. Broadus; BDF, para. 141).

A "very large crowd" (v.8, the Gk. superlative is merely elative; cf. Moule, *Idiom Book*, 98) spread their cloaks on the road, acknowledging Jesus' kingship (cf. 2Ki 9:13). Still others "cut branches" and "spread them" (the Gk. imperfects make the action vivid) on the road. It has been argued that cutting down tree branches well suits the activities of the Feast of Tabernacles, when the people built "booths" to live in for the week (cf. Lev 23:41–42). But those "branches" were substantial boughs, big enough to support a lean-to; these "branches," thrown before the animals, were not more than twigs. The somewhat parallel entrance of Simon Maccabaeus into Jerusalem (1 Macc 13:51; 2 Macc 10:7) does not depend on the season of the year but on the man.

9 Crowds ahead and behind may be incidental confirmation of two other details. First, John 12:12 speaks of crowds coming out of Jerusalem to meet Jesus. Apparently the Galilean pilgrims accompanying Jesus and the Jerusalem crowd coming out to greet him formed a procession of praise. Second, the fact that the Jerusalem crowds knew he was approaching supports the stopover in Bethany, which allows time for the news to spread. Messianic fervor was high, and perhaps this contributed to Jesus' desire to present himself as the Prince of Peace.

The words of praise come primarily from Psalm 118:25–26. "Hosanna" transliterates the Hebrew expression that originally was a cry for help: "Save!" (cf. 2Sa 14:4; 2Ki 6:26). In time, it became an invocation of blessing and even an acclamation, the latter being the meaning here (cf. Gundry, *Use of the Old Testament*, 41–43). "Son of David" is messianic and stresses the kingly role Messiah was to play (cf. Mark, Luke, and John for explicit references to "kingdom" or "king"). "He who comes in the name of the Lord" is cited by Jesus himself a little later (23:39; cf. 3:11; 11:3), but some scholars object that if this phrase had been a messianic acclamation by the people, the authorities would have stepped in. The words, they say, must be a formula of greeting to pilgrims on the way to the temple.

Such an assessment betrays too stark an "either-or" mentality to weigh the evidence plausibly. "Son of David" in the previous line is unavoidably messianic, and the authorities *do* raise objections (v.16). But crowd sentiments are fickle. On the one hand, acclamation can rapidly dissipate, so instant action by the authorities was scarcely necessary; on the other hand, it is foolish to antagonize the crowd at the height of excitement (cf. 26:4–5, 16). "Hosanna in the highest" is probably equivalent to "Glory to God in the highest" (Lk 2:14). The people praise God in the highest heavens for sending the Messiah and, if "Hosanna" retains some of its original force, also cry to him for deliverance.

Two final reflections on this verse are necessary. First, Psalm 118 was not only used at the Feast of Tabernacles (*m. Sukkah* 4:5) but also at the other two major feasts, Dedication and Passover—at the latter as part of "the great Hallel" (Pss 113–18). The use of Psalm 118 is, therefore, no support for Manson's suggestion (see Overview, 21:1–11). Second, Walvoord's interpretation stumbles badly: "They recognized that he was in the kingly line, although they do not seem to have entered into the concept that he was coming into Jerusalem as its King." On the contrary, it is hard to think of the crowd's making fine distinctions between "kingly line" and "king." Moreover, one growing thrust of this gospel is, as we have seen, that even where Jesus was perceived, however dimly, as King Messiah, he was not perceived as Suffering Servant. In the expectations of the day, it was fairly easy for the crowd, after hearing Jesus' preaching and seeing his miracles, to ascribe messiahship to him as much in their hope as in conviction. But it was far harder for them to grasp the inevitability of his suffering and death and the expansion of the "people of God" beyond the Jewish race.

10–11 Only Luke (19:41–44) pictures Jesus weeping over the city as he approaches it. Mark 11:11 establishes chronology; Matthew's information stands alone. Jesus probably entered Jerusalem through what some now call Saint Stephen's gate, near the north entrance to the outer court of the temple. As the city was stirred earlier (2:3), so here (21:10): news of Jesus' presence is inevitably disturbing. "Who is this?" does not mean that Jesus was virtually unknown in Jerusalem, and so needed to be identified (Bonnard), but "Who really is this about whom there is so much excitement?" The answer of the crowds accurately reflects the historical setting. Many of his contemporaries saw him as a prophet (cf. 16:14; 21:46) "from Nazareth in Galilee"—his hometown and primary field of ministry respectively. The phrase probably also connotes surprise that a prophet should come from so unlikely a place (see comments at 2:23). In the light of the messianic acclamation (v.9), some may well have seen Jesus as the eschatological Prophet (Dt 18:15–18; cf. Jn 7:40, 52; Ac 3:22; 7:37), though there is no more than a hint of that here. Yet there is also no evidence that Matthew deprecates the people's understanding as faulty, preferring "Son of God" (contra Kingsbury, 22, 88–89).

NOTES

3 Zerwick (*Biblical Greek*, para. 280) rightly points out that the verb ἐρεῖτε (*ereite*, lit., "you will say"; NIV, "tell") is one of the rare instances when a future indicative in the NT has, pragmatically, imperatival force (apart from passages where the NT cites the LXX).

11 Note this use of ἀπό (*apo*, "from, "away from") to denote place of origin instead of ἐκ (*ek*, "from," "out from"; cf. BDF, para. 209 [3]).

b. Jesus at the temple (21:12–17)

OVERVIEW

Matthew is considerably more condensed than Mark (Mk 11:11–19; cf. Lk 19:45–48; Jn 2:13–22). Matthew omits, among other things, Mark's more precise chronology, all mention of the habit of carrying merchandise through the temple courts, and reference to the Gentiles in the quotation from Isaiah 56:7. It is doubtful whether Matthew's silence in any of these things reflects major theological motivation (but see comments at 21:13). Matthew focuses on the cleansing of the temple as the work of the Son of David (vv.9, 15) and as of as much messianic significance as any of Jesus' miracles.

The great majority of contemporary scholars believe there was only one cleansing of the temple and debate about whether the synoptists or John put it at the right time in Jesus' ministry. Although some argue that the event occurred early in Jesus' ministry (John), more side with the Synoptics in placing it late. Certainly we have ample evidence that the evangelists arranged some materials topically; yet there are, in this instance, numerous reasons for the possibility, indeed the likelihood, of two separate cleansings—something most commentators never seriously consider. France's (NICNT) "The suggestion ... that it happened twice is about as probable as that the Normandy landings took place both at the beginning and the end of the Second World War" sacrifices a meaningful analogy for a sly chuckle. No one suggests the Normandy landings took place *only* at the beginning of that war, though quite a few think the temple cleansing took place *only* at the beginning of Jesus' ministry. No one thinks the Normandy landings occurred twice; historically, many Christian thinkers have held there were two cleansings, and a ridiculous (if funny) analogy does not interact seriously with their arguments.

1. Leon Morris (*John*, 288ff.) has shown the striking differences between the details John provides and those the Synoptics provide. If there was but one cleansing, some of these differences became surprising; if there were two cleansings, they became quite reasonable.

2. Those who hold that John's placing of the cleansing is topical usually assume that he does so to lead up to the saying, "Destroy this temple, and I will raise it again in three days" (Jn 2:19), part of his "replacement" theme—namely, that Jesus himself replaces much of the Jewish cultic milieu. But this view fails to provide any reason for shifting the temple's cleansing so as to make it an *early* theme in Jesus' ministry. Moreover, in this particular case, the temple replacement theme is reflected in the

trial of Jesus in two of the Synoptics (Mt 26:61; Mk 14:58). Indeed, the fact that the witnesses regarding Jesus' "destroy this temple" utterance, which is tied to the cleansing in John 2 but *not* to the cleansing in Holy Week, could not get their stories straight (Mk 14:59) makes sense if they were trying to recall something two or three years earlier rather than two or three days earlier.

3. If the Synoptics fail to mention the earlier cleansing, this may go back to their omission of Jesus' entire early Judean ministry.

4. Some hold that if Jesus had inaugurated his ministry by cleansing the temple, the authorities would not have let him do it a second time. But two or three years have elapsed. The money changers and merchants, protected by the temple police, doubtless returned the day after the first cleansing. But it is doubtful that tight security would have been kept up for months and years. This second cleansing took a few dramatic minutes and could not have been prevented, and its prophetic symbolism quickly spread throughout Jerusalem.

5. It is difficult to tell from the Gospels how much the cleansing(s) of the temple contributed to official action against Jesus, and to overstate the evidence is easy. But a second cleansing as Passover drew near was far more likely to have led to the authorities' violent reaction than the first one.

[12]Jesus entered the temple area and drove out all who were buying and selling there.
He overturned the tables of the money changers and the benches of those selling doves.
[13]"It is written," he said to them, "'My house will be called a house of prayer,' but you are
making it a 'den of robbers.'"
[14]The blind and the lame came to him at the temple, and he healed them. [15]But when
the chief priests and the teachers of the law saw the wonderful things he did and the children shouting in the temple area, "Hosanna to the Son of David," they were indignant.
[16]"Do you hear what these children are saying?" they asked him.
"Yes," replied Jesus, "have you never read,

"'From the lips of children and infants
you have ordained praise'?"

[17]And he left them and went out of the city to Bethany, where he spent the night.

COMMENTARY

12 Jesus entered the *hieron* ("temple area," GK *2639*). Temple service required provision to be made for getting what was needed for the sacrifices—animals, wood, oil, etc.—especially for pilgrims from afar. The money changers converted the standard Greek and Roman currency into temple currency, in which the half-shekel temple tax had to be paid (cf. 17:24–27). (For some of the customs and regulations, cf. *m. Šeqal.*; Edersheim, *Life and Times*, 1:367–74.) But letting these things go on at the temple site transformed a place of solemn worship into a market where the hum of trade mingled with the bleating and cooing of animals and birds. Moreover, especially on the great feasts, opportunities for extortion abounded. Jesus drove the lot out.

13 Jesus here refers to Scripture, much as he did when confronted by the devil (4:1–10). His first words are from Isaiah 56:7. Isaiah looked forward to a time when the temple would be called a house of prayer. But now, at the dawn of the messianic age, Jesus finds a "den of robbers." The words come from Jeremiah 7:11, which warns against the futility of superstitious reverence for the temple, compounded with wickedness that dishonors it. This suggests that the Greek *lēstai* ("robbers," GK *3334*) should be given its normal meaning of "nationalist rebel" (see comments at 27:16). The temple was meant to be a house of prayer, but they had made it "a nationalist stronghold" (cf. C. K. Barrett, "The House of Prayer and the Den of Thieves," in *Jesus und Paulus* [ed. Ellis and Grässer], 16).

The point is even clearer in Mark, who retains "house of prayer for all nations" (Isa 56:7 uses the longer form once, and the shorter one once). The temple was not fulfilling its God-ordained role as witness to the nations but had become, like the first temple, the premier symbol of a superstitious belief that God would protect and rally his people, irrespective of their conformity to his will. The temple would therefore be destroyed (vv.18–22; 24:2). Matthew does not omit "for all nations" because he writes after the temple has been destroyed and, therefore, recognizes the promise in Isaiah is no longer capable of fulfillment. Even Mark knows that the temple cannot stand and that this temple could never become a rallying place "for all nations." The omission may simply be for conciseness, but it shifts the contrast from "temple mission–nationalist stronghold" (Mark) to "house of prayer–nationalist stronghold" (Matthew)—a shift that focuses attention more on spiritual neglect and mistaken political priorities than on neglect of what the temple was really for. These are the things Jesus denounces.

The Lord whom the people see now comes to his temple (Mal 3:1). Purification of Jerusalem and the temple was part of Jewish expectation (cf. *Pss. Sol.* 17:30). So for those with eyes to see, Jesus' action was one of self-disclosure and an implicit claim to eschatological authority over the Holy Place. That the purification would entail destruction and building a new temple (Jn 2:19–22) none but Jesus could yet foresee.

14 Verses 14–15 are found only in Matthew. Not only is v.14 the last mention of Jesus' healing ministry, but it takes place *en tō hierō* ("at the temple [site]") and probably within the temple precincts in the Court of the Gentiles. It was not uncommon for the chronically ill to beg at the approaches to the temple (Ac 3:2), but where the lame, blind, deaf, or otherwise disabled could go in the temple area was restricted. The Court of the Gentiles was open to them all, and there were even crippled priests. But restrictions were imposed when the disability required certain kinds of cushions, pads, or supports that might introduce "uncleanness" (cf. Jeremias, *Jerusalem*, 117–18).

Most Jewish authorities forbade any person who was lame, blind, deaf, or mute from offering a sacrifice, from "appearing before Yahweh in his temple." The Qumran covenanters wanted to go further and exclude all cripples from the congregation, the messianic battle, and the messianic banquet (1QSa 2:5–22; 1QM 7:4–5). But Jesus heals them, thus showing that "one greater than the temple is here" (12:6). He himself cannot be contaminated, and he heals and makes clean those who come into contact with him. These two actions—cleansing the temple and the healing miracles—jointly declare his superiority over the temple (Heil, "Significant Aspects of the Healing Miracles," 283–84) and raise the question of the source of his authority (v.23).

15–16 The "chief priests and the teachers of the law" (see comments at 2:4; 26:59) express indignation, not so much at what he has done, as at the acclamation he is receiving for it. The children cry out, "Hosanna to the Son of David" (see comments at v.9), and if Jesus is prepared to accept such praise, then "the wonderful things" he is doing must have messianic significance. When challenged, Jesus supports the children by quoting Psalm 8:2, introducing it with his "have you never read" (v.16), which exposes the theological ignorance of the Scripture experts (cf. 12:3; 19:4; 21:42; 22:31). God *has* ordained praise for himself from "children and infants" (lit., "infants and sucklings"—nursing sometimes continued among the Jews to the age of three: cf. 2 Macc 7:27). Jesus' answer is a masterstroke and simultaneously accomplishes three things.

1. It provides some kind of biblical basis for letting the children go on with their exuberant praise and thus stifles, for the moment, the objections of the temple leaders.

2. At the same time, thoughtful persons, reflecting on the incident later (especially after the resurrection), perceive that Jesus was saying much more. The children's "Hosannas" are not being directed to God but to the Son of David, the Messiah. Jesus is therefore not only acknowledging his messiahship but justifying the praise of the children by applying to himself a passage of Scripture applicable only to God (see Notes).

3. The quotation confirms that the humble perceive spiritual truths more readily than the sophisticated (cf. 19:13–15). The children have picked up the cry of the earlier procession and, lacking inhibitions and skepticism, enthusiastically repeat the chant, arriving at the truth more quickly than those who think themselves wise and knowledgeable.

17 During the festivals Jerusalem was crowded. So Jesus spent his last nights at Bethany, on a spur of the eastern slopes of the Mount of Olives (cf. Mk 11:19; Lk 21:37). The home where he stayed was probably that of Mary, Martha, and Lazarus.

NOTES

16 Part of the interpretation given above depends on the view that Psalm 8 is not messianic. This is almost certainly the case. Even application of Psalm 8:5–7 to Jesus in 1 Corinthians 15:27; Hebrews 2:6–8 is due, not to the psalm's messianic character, but to Jesus' role in introducing humanity to the heights God designed for it, as most expositors now acknowledge. The treatment of Psalm 8 as messianic by ancient Jewish authorities in the Targum on Psalm 8 (cf. F. J. Maloney, "The Targum on Psalm 8 and the New Testament," *Salesianum* 37 [1975]: 326–36) almost certainly postdates the NT.

c. The fig tree (21:18–22)

OVERVIEW

This story is found only here and in Mark, where it is split into two parts (11:12–14, 20–26), with the temple's cleansing in between. Chronologically, Mark is more detailed. If the triumphal entry was on Sunday, then, according to Mark, the cursing of the fig tree was on Monday, and the disciples' surprise at the tree's quick withering, along with Jesus' words about faith, were on Tuesday. Matthew has simply put the two parts together in a typical topical arrangement. He leaves indistinct (v.20) the time when the disciples saw the withered fig tree, though he implies it was the same day. Compare the condensation in 9:18–25.

While William R. Telford (*The Barren Temple and the Withered Tree* [Sheffield: JSOT Press, 1980]) admirably surveys earlier studies, his own is less helpful. The idea that "this mountain" (v.21) refers to the temple, thus making the cursing of the fig tree a sign of the temple's doom, is unlikely. More probably it refers to the Mount of Olives as a sample of any mountain. Telford's exhaustive examination of the uses of "fig tree" as a metaphor does no more than show that "fig tree" could be applied metaphorically to many different things, but only the context of each occurrence of the metaphor is determinative. Still less convincing is the view that this story is a mere dramatization of the parable in Luke 13:6–9 (so van der Loos, *Miracles of Jesus*, 692–96); apart from the question of whether such "historicization" of parabolic material ever occurs, the latter treats *delay* in judgment, whereas the present passage is concerned with *imminent* judgment.

It is commonly held that vv.20–22 and the corresponding Markan material is a separate tradition unrelated to the original. Preferable is the view that the awkward transition reflects the historical chronology, which Mark preserved. Cursing the fig tree is, then, an acted parable related to cleansing the temple and conveying a message about Israel. But when the next day the disciples see how quickly the fig tree has withered, their initial—and shallow—response is to wonder how it was done—and this leads to Jesus' remarks on faith. So this single historical event teaches two theological lessons.

18 Early in the morning, as he was on his way back to the city, he was hungry. 19 Seeing a
fig tree by the road, he went up to it but found nothing on it except leaves. Then he said
to it, "May you never bear fruit again!" Immediately the tree withered.
20 When the disciples saw this, they were amazed. "How did the fig tree wither so
quickly?" they asked.
21 Jesus replied, "I tell you the truth, if you have faith and do not doubt, not only can you
do what was done to the fig tree, but also you can say to this mountain, 'Go, throw yourself
into the sea,' and it will be done. 22 If you believe, you will receive whatever you ask for in
prayer."

COMMENTARY

18–19 Somewhere on the road between Bethany and Jerusalem, Jesus approached a fig tree in the hope of assuaging his hunger. Mark tells us that though it was not the season for figs, the tree was in leaf. Fig leaves appear about the same time as the fruit or a little after. The green figs are edible, though sufficiently disagreeable as not usually to be eaten till June. Thus the leaves normally point to every prospect of fruit, even if not fully ripe. Sometimes, however, the green figs fall off and leave nothing but leaves. All this Matthew's succinct remark—"He ... found nothing on it except leaves" (v.19)—implies; his Jewish readers would infer the rest. This understanding of the text confirms the chronology established at vv.1–11. If these events took place at Dedication, when figs were plentiful, not only would Mark's explicit statement be incorrect (11:13), but in both Matthew and Mark, Jesus' cursing of the tree would be harder to understand, for if he was hungry, he could simply go to the next tree.

Many commentators think otherwise and suppose that by omitting Mark's statement, "it was not the season for figs," Matthew has eliminated a moral difficulty. Why should Jesus curse a tree for not bearing fruit when it was not the season for fruit? But this theory misses the point. That it was not the season for figs explains why Jesus went to this particular tree, which stood out because it was in leaf. Its leaves advertised that it was bearing, but the advertisement was false. Jesus, unable to satisfy his hunger, saw an opportunity to teach a memorable object lesson and cursed the tree, not because it was not bearing fruit, whether in season or out, but because it made a show of life that promised fruit, yet was bearing none.

Most scholars interpret the cursing of the fig tree as a symbolic cursing of the people of Israel for failing to produce faith and righteousness, as evidenced primarily in their attitude to Jesus. The fig tree, then, becomes akin to the imagery of the vine in Isaiah 5:1–7 or the figs in Jeremiah 8:13; 24:1–8: sterility, the absence of fruit, or bad fruit—all lead to judgment. Walvoord objects, insisting there is no place in the Bible where a fig tree serves as a type of Israel (Jeremiah 24:1–8 is dismissed because the good and bad figs refer to captives versus those who remain in the land). The gospel pericope is a lesson on faith and the miraculous, no more. But if the common interpretation will not stand, Walvoord's reductionism cannot withstand close scrutiny either.

1. Mark's arrangement of the material, with the temple's cleansing sandwiched between the two parts, must be taken into account. Even Matthew, who condenses Mark's arrangement and eliminates the division of the pericope into two, places this immediately after the cleansing of the temple and right before the questioning of Jesus' authority. We have learned to respect Matthew's arrangement of pericopes enough to see them as linked; therefore, to read vv.18–22 as nothing more than a lesson on faith forfeits the obvious links.

2. Jeremiah 24:1–8 may provide a closer parallel than Walvoord thinks, for even in the Gospels Jesus is not saying that all Jews fall under whatever curse this may be; after all, his disciples at this point in history were all Jews. In the Synoptics, as in Jeremiah, there is a division between Jew and Jew.

3. Yet even if Jeremiah 24:1–8 is not very close a parallel, one cannot make too much of the fig tree's not being a type of Israel, for one could similarly argue that there is no other example in the Bible of Jesus' performing a miracle *simply* to teach faith, without there being some organic connection with the narrative.

This does not mean the common interpretation—that the fig tree represents Israel, cursed for not bearing fruit—is correct. In light of the discussion on the relation between leaves and fruit, Jesus is cursing those who make a show of bearing much fruit but are spiritually barren. This has four advantages.

1. It deftly handles both Mark and Matthew on the fig tree and its leaves.

2. It directs the attack against the hypocrites among the Jewish people, a constant target in all four gospels but especially in Matthew (e.g., 6:2, 5, 16; 7:5; 15:7; 22:18; and we now approach 23:1–39!).

3. It is compatible with the cleansing of the temple, which criticizes, not the Jewish children and their praise, or the Jewish blind and lame who came to be healed (vv.14–15), but those who used the temple to make a large profit and those who stifled the children's praises of Messiah. These, like

this leafy fig tree, Jesus finds full of advertised piety without any fruit—and them he curses.

4. Unlike other passages (3:9; 8:11–12), there is no mention of something being taken from the Jews and given to Gentiles. The cursing of the fig tree is an acted parable cursing hypocrites, not Jews or Judaism.

The cursing of the fig tree is not so far out of character for Jesus as some would have us believe. The same Jesus exorcised demons so that two thousand pigs were drowned (8:28–34), drove the animals and money changers out of the temple precincts with a whip, and says not a little about the torments of hell. Perhaps the fact that the two punitive miracles—the swine and the fig tree—are not directed against people should teach us something of Jesus' compassion. He who is to save his people from their sin and its consequences resorts to prophetic actions not directed against his people, in order to warn them of the binding power of the devil (the destruction of the swine) and of God's enmity against all hypocritical piety (the cursing of the fig tree).

20–22 Though it is uncertain whether v.20 is a question or an exclamation (cf. Moule, *Idiom Book*, 207), the effect is the same. The substance of Jesus' response has already been given in 17:20, which implies that the figure of a mountain cast into the sea was common in Jesus' teaching. Here, however, attention shifts "from the smallest effective amount of faith to the opposition of faith to doubt" (Hill). The miracle Jesus selects to teach the power of faith—throwing a mountain into the sea (v.21)—is no more than a hyperbolic example of a miracle. But because the Dead Sea can be seen from the Mount of Olives, some have suggested an allusion to Zechariah 14:4 (Lane, *Mark*, 410)—namely, what the disciples must pray for is the coming eschatological reign. This seems unlikely, for Zechariah speaks of the splitting of the Mount of Olives rather than its removal into the sea.

Jesus used the fig tree to teach the power of *believing* prayer, an extrapolation on the theme of faith, the lesson just taught by the immediate withering of the fig tree. But belief in the NT is never reduced to forcing oneself to "believe" what he does not really believe. Instead it is related to genuine trust in God and obedience to and discernment of his will (see comments at 19:20; cf. D. A. Carson, *The Farewell Discourse and Final Prayer of Jesus* [Grand Rapids: Baker, 1980], 43, 108–11). Though exercised by the believer, such faith reposes on the will of the God who acts.

NOTES

19 Μίαν (*mian*, lit., "one") here has the force of enclitic τὶς (*tis*, "a certain," "a"); see comments at 8:19; 9:18; cf. 19:16; 21:24; BDF, para. 247 (2).

d. Controversies in the temple court (21:23–22:46)

OVERVIEW

This long section (21:23–22:46) is characterized by a number of controversies with various Jewish leaders, along with several parables that must be interpreted in the light of such controversies. In Mark's chronology, these controversies apparently took place on Tuesday, the third day of Passion

Week. It was customary to stop well-known teachers and ask them questions (cf. 22:16, 23, 35), and the crowds delighted in these exchanges. Eventually Jesus turned primarily to the crowds and addressed them without excluding the Pharisees and teachers of the law (ch. 23); then, as evening fell, he retired to the Mount of Olives and gave his last "discourse" to his disciples (chs. 24–25).

(1) The question of authority (21:23–27)

OVERVIEW

In the first exchange between Jesus and various Jewish leaders (vv.23–27), Matthew follows Mark (11:27–33) fairly closely (cf. Lk 20:1–8).

[23]Jesus entered the temple courts, and, while he was teaching, the chief priests and the
elders of the people came to him. "By what authority are you doing these things?" they
asked. "And who gave you this authority?"
[24]Jesus replied, "I will also ask you one question. If you answer me, I will tell you by what
authority I am doing these things. [25]John's baptism—where did it come from? Was it from
heaven, or from men?"
They discussed it among themselves and said, "If we say, 'From heaven,' he will ask,
'Then why didn't you believe him?' [26]But if we say, 'From men'—we are afraid of the
people, for they all hold that John was a prophet."
[27]So they answered Jesus, "We don't know."
Then he said, "Neither will I tell you by what authority I am doing these things."

COMMENTARY

23 Jesus' teaching takes place in the "temple courts," probably in one of the porticos surrounding the Court of the Gentiles. The chief priests were high temple functionaries, elevated members of the priestly aristocracy who were part of the Sanhedrin (see comments at 2:4); the elders were in this case probably nonpriestly members of the Sanhedrin, heads of the most influential lay families (cf. Jeremias, *Jerusalem*, 222ff.). In other words, representative members of the Sanhedrin, described in terms of their clerical status rather than their theological positions (e.g., Sadducees and Pharisees), approached Jesus and challenged his authority to do "these things"—namely, the cleansing of the temple, the miraculous healings, and perhaps also his teaching (v.23). Their first question was not narrowly theological but concerned Jesus' authority; yet their concern in asking who gave him this authority (cf. Ac 4:7) sprang less from a desire to identify him than from a desire to stifle and perhaps ensnare him.

24–26 Jesus' reply is masterful. He responds to their question with a question of his own, a common enough procedure in rabbinic debate (cf. Daube, *New Testament and Rabbinic Judaism*, 151–55). "John's baptism" (v.25) is a way of referring to the Baptist's entire ministry (cf. v.25b and the reference to *believing* John, not simply being *baptized* by him). Jesus asks whether that ministry was from heaven or from men. He does not raise this question as a simple rebuke—as if to say that if the authorities cannot make up their minds about John, neither will they be able to do so about him. His question is far more profound. If the religious authorities rightly answer it, they will already have the correct answer to their own question. If they respond, "From heaven," then they are morally bound to believe John—and John pointed to Jesus (see comments at 11:7–10; cf. Jn 1:19, 26–27; 3:25–30). They would, therefore, have their answer about Jesus and his authority. If they respond, "From men" (v.26), they offer the wrong answer—but they will not dare utter it for fear of the people. The religious authorities share Herod's timidity (14:5).

Far from avoiding the religious leaders' question, Jesus answers it so that the honest seeker of truth, unswayed by public opinion, will not fail to see who he is, while those interested only in snaring him with a captious question are blocked by a hurdle their own shallow pragmatism forbids them to cross. At the same time, Jesus' question rather strongly hints to the rulers that their false step goes back to broader issues than Jesus' identity. If they cannot discern Jesus' authority, it is because their previous unbelief has blinded their minds to God's revelation.

27 "We don't know," they said—which is not so much a lie as a misrepresentation of the categories that bound them in public indecision. Their equivocation gave Jesus a reason for refusing to answer their question. Rejection of revelation already given is indeed a slender basis on which to ask for more. In one sense, the Sanhedrin enjoyed not only the right but the duty to check the credentials of those who claimed to be spokesmen for God. But because they misunderstood the revelation already given in the Scriptures and rejected the witness of the Baptist, the leaders proved unequal to their responsibility. They raised the question of Jesus' authority; he raised the question of their competence to judge such an issue.

(2) The parable of the two sons (21:28–32)

OVERVIEW

This is the first of three parables by which Jesus rebukes not only the Jewish leaders but all members of the Jewish nation who do not receive God's Messiah (vv.28–32, 33–46; 22:1–14; cf. Wesley G. Olmstead, *Matthew's Trilogy of Parables: The Nation, the Nations and the Reader in Matthew 21.28–22.14* [SNTSMS 127; Cambridge: Cambridge Univ. Press, 2003]). The first and third of these are peculiar to Matthew. There is no convincing evidence that this first parable is only a variation of Luke 15:11–32. Helmut Merkel ("Das Gleichnis von den 'ungleichen Söhnen,'" *NTS* 20 [1974]: 254–61) argues that the entire parable is inauthentic, but his approach—isolating, sometimes on doubtful grounds, Matthew's redaction and wondering if enough of the parable is left for us to posit an authentic core—is so one-sided that few follow it. It is much more common to deny the authenticity of v.32 (e.g., Strecker, *Weg der Gerechtigkeit*; 153; Ogawa, "Paraboles de l'Israël véritable?" 121ff.), or of the last clause of v.32 (van Tilborg, *Jewish Leaders*, 52–54). Jeremias (*Parables of Jesus*, 80–81) argues for the authenticity of the whole.

That the verb *metamelomai* ("change one's mind," GK *3564*) occurs in the Synoptics only in Matthew (vv.29, 32; 27:3) is scarcely evidence against authenticity (so Strecker) because (1) the figures are so low (three occurrences) as to be statistically useless—one might as cogently argue that the verse is Pauline since Paul uses the verb once; (2) its use in this parable (v.29) might as easily suggest the entire parable is traditional; and (3) even if the language is Matthean—and the evidence is not conclusive either way—such considerations are not themselves conclusive concerning content (see Introduction, section 2). The entire parable makes excellent sense in context; indeed, van Tilborg (*Jewish Leaders*, 47–52) has convincingly argued that all three parables belong together as a block, even if Matthew has tightened the connections. This supports the view that 21:23–22:46 constitutes a block of confrontations and warnings that took place on the one occasion (see comments at v.23).

28"What do you think? There was a man who had two sons. He went to the first and said, 'Son, go and work today in the vineyard.'

29"'I will not,' he answered, but later he changed his mind and went.

30"Then the father went to the other son and said the same thing. He answered, 'I will, sir,' but he did not go.

31"Which of the two did what his father wanted?"

"The first," they answered.

Jesus said to them, "I tell you the truth, the tax collectors and the prostitutes are entering the kingdom of God ahead of you. **32**For John came to you to show you the way of righteousness, and you did not believe him, but the tax collectors and the prostitutes did. And even after you saw this, you did not repent and believe him."

COMMENTARY

28 The particular wording "What do you think?" is distinctively Matthean (17:25–18:12; 22:17). The parable is introduced without any preamble other than the question. The normal way to take *prōtō* ("first") and *heterō* ("other," v.30; some MSS, *deuterō*, "second") in this context is "older" and "younger" son respectively (Derrett, *Studies in the New Testament*, 1:78).

29–31 The last point has a useful bearing on the complex textual problem in these verses. The evidence is neatly set out by Metzger (*Textual Commentary*, 55–56), along with some useful bibliography (cf. Derrett, *Studies in the New Testament*, 1:76ff.). When the textual evidence is sifted, three choices remain.

1. The older son says no but repents and goes; the second son says yes but does nothing. Who performs the father's will? The first.

2. The older son says yes but does nothing; the second son says no but repents and goes. Who

performs the father's will? The younger, or the latter, or the second.

3. The older son says no but repents and goes; the second son says yes but does nothing. Who performs the father's will? The latter.

Clearly 3 is the hardest reading; and from the time of Jerome, some have defended it for precisely that reason (e.g., J. Wellhausen, *Das Evangelium Matthaei* [Berlin: Reimer, 1904]). But not only is this reading weakly attested (Jerome knew of some Greek MSS supporting it, but only versional evidence remains today); it is either nonsensical, or else we must say the Jews are represented as perversely giving a farcical answer to avoid the application to themselves. This is not very convincing. If we do not adopt the position of Westcott and Hort, who suggest that a primitive textual error lies behind all extant copies, we must choose between 1 and 2. Many choose 1—as the NIV—largely on the grounds that it has somewhat better external attestation than 2 and that the change from 1 to 2 can easily be envisaged. For one thing, if the first son actually went, the second might not be necessary. Also, it was natural to identify the older son with the disobedient one and the younger son with the obedient one, once the interpretation of the Fathers was widely adopted—namely, that the disobedient son stands for the Jew (who chronologically came first), and the obedient son stands for Gentile sinners. The first of these two arguments is irrelevant. There is nothing whatsoever to suggest that only one son was needed in the vineyard. The second argument is, by itself, more convincing, but it needs to face another possibility.

Derrett has shown that in the world of Jesus' day, option 2 is psychologically far more natural. The older son is somewhat pampered and favored because he is the heir, whereas the younger son is sullen and resentful but has to go out of his way to prove himself to his father. The change from 2 to 1 may have occurred if copyists supposed that in this context the father stands for John the Baptist (so, e.g., Jeremias, *Parables of Jesus*), whom tax collectors and prostitutes, open sinners, first denied and then believed. The evidence does not admit of certain resolution, but perhaps the balance of probabilities slightly favors the NASB (option 2 rather than the NIV).

Either way the story is fairly straightforward. *Metamelomai* ("changed his mind," v.29) may or may not be followed by change of purpose in the NT, unlike *metanoeō* ("repent," GK *3566*). For the first time, Jesus openly makes a personal application of one of his parables to the Jewish leaders. "I tell you the truth" (v.31; see comments at 5:18), he solemnly begins, "the tax collectors and the prostitutes enter the kingdom of God—and you do not"—for so the verb *proagō* (GK *4575*) must be translated here, rather than "are entering ... ahead of you" (NIV; cf. Jeremias, *Parables of Jesus*, 101 n. 54; *TDNT*, 8:105 n. 158; BDF, para. 245a [3]).

The shock value of Jesus' statement can be appreciated only when the low esteem in which tax collectors were held (see comments at 5:46), not to mention prostitutes, is taken into account. In our day of soft pornography in the media, we are not shocked by "prostitutes." But Jesus is saying that the scum of society, though it says no to God, repents, performs the Father's will, and enters the kingdom, whereas the religious authorities loudly say yes to God but never do what he says, and therefore they fail to enter. Their righteousness is not enough (cf. 5:20). Thus the parable makes no distinction between Jew and Gentile but between religious leader and public sinner.

32 This verse links the parable to the preceding pericope, where the importance of believing John has already been established (vv.23–27). John pointed the way to the kingdom (11:12), which sinners are now entering (v.31). The NIV interprets v.32 in much the same way; strictly speaking, though, the Greek text says, "John came to you in the way of righteousness," not "John came to show you the way of righteousness." This probably means that John came preaching God's will about what was right (cf. "the way of God," 22:16; see Przybylski, *Righteousness in Matthew*, 94–96). But in Matthew's thought, John's preaching includes the demand for ethical reformation in light of the imminent coming of the kingdom (cf. 3:2–3). In this way John pointed to Jesus and the kingdom's superior righteousness (5:20). But the religious leaders did not believe John's witness, even after seeing society's vilest sinners repenting and believing him and his message.

NOTES

32 Hill (*Greek Words*, 124–25), Przybylski (*Righteousness in Matthew*, 94–96), and others rightly insist that δικαιοσύνη (*dikaiosynē*, "righteousness," GK *1466*) in Matthew means "righteousness that is practiced," "performing the will of God." But this does not necessarily mean that practicing righteousness in itself gains entrance into the kingdom, for if Matthew says that John taught men to repent, he equally makes clear that John's ministry pointed to Jesus and the kingdom. If John is believed, men are led to Jesus. "Righteousness" or, better, "doing what is right, in accordance with the Father's will," includes not merely ethics narrowly conceived but believing Jesus and welcoming him as Messiah. The Father's will focuses on Jesus (11:25–27), who comes not only to set an example but to give his life as a ransom for many (20:28) and to inaugurate the new covenant in his blood (26:27–28). Word studies on "righteousness" by Hill and Przybylski, sound as they are, must not blind us to the larger themes in Matthew with which "righteousness" is inextricably connected.

(3) The parable of the tenants (21:33–46)

OVERVIEW

This parable has long been a battleground for complex debate. It is marginally easy to account for synoptic differences (cf. Mk 12:1–12; Lk 20:9–19) by postulating both a Markan and a Q recension, but this is by no means certain (see chart and discussion at 19:1–2).

On the face of it, the parable continues to make a statement against the Jewish religious authorities and others in the nation of Israel who reject Jesus. The metaphorical equivalences are obvious: the landowner is God, the vineyard Israel, the tenants the leaders of the nation, the servants the prophets, and the son is Jesus Messiah. Such obvious metaphors have troubled many scholars, who detect late "allegorizing," which, they judge, could not have been part of the original parable but belongs only to the church's interpretation of it.

The reconstructed parable is, therefore, given other interpretations (cf. Jeremias, *Parables of Jesus*, 76; Dodd, *Parables of the Kingdom*, 124–32) so far removed from the texts as we have them that others have despaired of reconstructing the original. W. G. Kümmel ("Das Gleichnis von den bösen Weingärtnern [Mark 12.1–9]," *Aux Sources de la Tradition Chrétienne* [ed. O. Cullmann and P. Menoud; Neuchatel: Delachaux et Niestlé, 1950], 120–38) argues that the creative milieu from which this parable springs is neither Galilee nor the ministry of Jesus, but the first-century church influenced by its own interpretation of Isaiah 5. The following observations, however, point in a different direction.

1. We have already noted (see comments at 13:3a) that to draw a rigid line between a one-point "parable" and a parable with several intertwined points, or between or "parable" and "interpretation," has no methodologically secure base.

2. Certainly Jesus himself faced opposition from the religious leaders of his people and day. There is no historical reason to think he could not himself have referred to Isaiah 5 in this connection, and there is substantial formal literary reason for thinking that the parable, as the Synoptics preserve it, fits in with some of Jesus' established patterns of teaching (cf. Ellis, "New Directions," 299–315, esp. 312–14).

3. Recognizing these things, some scholars have argued that the "son" motif in the parable itself depends on the logic of the story and therefore must not be judged inauthentic (Hill; cf. J. Blank, "Die Sendung des Sohnes," in *Neues Testament und Kirche* [ed. Gnilka], 11–41). This is surely right. But to assign the identification of this "son" as Jesus only to the church seems a rather artificial expedient. Even the most skeptical approach to the Gospels acknowledges that Jesus enjoyed a sense of special sonship to the Father. It is almost inconceivable, therefore, that Jesus could use this "son" language in defending his mission and not be thinking of himself. It is far more natural to read the "son" language of the parable as yet another veiled messianic self-reference, especially in light of the use of "Son of God" as a messianic title in 4Q174 (see comments at 2:15; 3:17; 11:27).

4. As far as source criticism is concerned, it will no longer do to postulate that *Gospel of Thomas* 65–66 preserves the original form of the parable. K. R. Snodgrass ("The Parable of the Wicked Husbandmen: Is the *Gospel of Thomas* Version the Original?" *NTS* 21 [1975]: 142–44), along with reviewing the evidence that argues that the omissions in Thomas owe something to gnostic influence, shows the dependence of this version on the Syriac Gospels.

33"Listen to another parable: There was a landowner who planted a vineyard. He put a
wall around it, dug a winepress in it and built a watchtower. Then he rented the vineyard
to some farmers and went away on a journey. 34When the harvest time approached, he
sent his servants to the tenants to collect his fruit.

35"The tenants seized his servants; they beat one, killed another, and stoned a third.
36Then he sent other servants to them, more than the first time, and the tenants treated
them the same way. 37Last of all, he sent his son to them. 'They will respect my son,' he said.

38"But when the tenants saw the son, they said to each other, 'This is the heir. Come, let's
kill him and take his inheritance.' 39So they took him and threw him out of the vineyard
and killed him.

40"Therefore, when the owner of the vineyard comes, what will he do to those tenants?"

41"He will bring those wretches to a wretched end," they replied, "and he will rent the
vineyard to other tenants, who will give him his share of the crop at harvest time."

42Jesus said to them, "Have you never read in the Scriptures:

"'The stone the builders rejected
has become the capstone;

the Lord has done this,
and it is marvelous in our eyes'?

43"Therefore I tell you that the kingdom of God will be taken away from you and given to a people who will produce its fruit. 44He who falls on this stone will be broken to pieces, but he on whom it falls will be crushed."

45When the chief priests and the Pharisees heard Jesus' parables, they knew he was talking about them. 46They looked for a way to arrest him, but they were afraid of the crowd because the people held that he was a prophet.

COMMENTARY

33–34 This parable is apparently addressed not only to Jewish rulers (v.23) but to the crowds in the temple courts, not excluding the rulers (cf. Lk 20:9). "Another" (v.33) links this parable with the last one (cf. plural "parables" in v.45). Verses 33–34 clearly allude to Isaiah 5:1–7 and Psalm 80:6–16. Jesus' parable is an old theme with new variations. The pains the landowner takes show his care for the vineyard. He builds a wall to keep out animals and a watchtower to guard against thieves and fire, and he digs a winepress to squeeze the grapes right there. All this shows his confidence that his vineyard will bear fruit. The tenant farmers take care of the vineyard during the owner's absence and pay rent in kind.

The "servants" are the owner's agents sent "to collect his fruit." Mark stipulates merely "some of the fruit of the vineyard"; some overly zealous critics think *tous karpous autou* (NIV, "his fruit"; but possibly "its fruit" [i.e., the vineyard's] as in v.43, where the "its" refers to the kingdom) in Matthew represents the *whole* crop. That any first-century reader would take words referring to rent this way is very doubtful (v.33). Mark mentions one servant at a time but says that many others were sent (cf. v.36); again, it is very doubtful that any profound theological issue hangs on the differences.

35–37 The verb *derō* ("beat," GK *1296*) can also mean "flay" or "flog" and stands for general bodily ill-treatment (cf. Jer 20:1–2; 37:15; for Micaiah, see 1Ki 22:24). Killing the prophets is attested in the OT (1Ki 18:4, 13; Jer 26:20–23), as is stoning (2Ch 24:21–22; cf. Mt 23:37; Heb 11:37). The landowner sends more servants (some commentators detect an allusion to the Jewish distinction between "former" and "latter" prophets), who are treated in the same brutal way (v.36). "Last of all" (v.37) he sends his son—there is a note of pathos here—hoping the tenants will respect him. This is not as implausible as it might seem to a Western reader (cf. Derrett, *Studies in the New Testament*, 2:97–98); here it shows the landowner's forbearance with his wicked tenant farmers (cf. Ro 2:4) and motivates the ultimate implacability of his wrath.

38–41 The action of the tenants is consistently callous. Precisely how it applies to Jesus is not entirely clear. Many object that the Jewish leaders did not recognize Jesus and did not desire to kill Messiah and usurp his place. But these objections miss the mark and encounter the danger of making the details of the parable run on all fours. Matthew does not take as tolerant a view as some modern scholars do of the way the Jewish leaders discharged their responsibility. Elsewhere he shows (23:37) their fundamental unwillingness to come to terms with Jesus' identity and claims because they did not want to bow to his authority. True, their attitude was not, according to the synoptic record, "This is the Messiah; come, let us kill him"; yet, in the light of the Scriptures, their rejection of him was no less culpable than if it had been that. Therefore, though all the parable's details may not be pressed, rejection of the son (v.39) by the leaders *is* the final straw that brings divine wrath on them.

For six months Jesus has been telling his disciples that the rulers at Jerusalem will kill him (16:21; 17:23; 20:18). Now he tells the rulers themselves, albeit in a parable form, which, at some level, the leaders understand (vv.45–46). Undoubtedly, some who heard Peter a few weeks later (Ac 2:23–37; 3:14–15) were the more convicted when they remembered these words of Jesus.

Many take the order of events—"threw him out of the vineyard and killed him" (Matthew and Luke in the best texts), the reverse of Mark (12:8)—as the result of an attempt to align the parable a little more closely with Jesus' passion: he was taken outside the city wall and then crucified (a point made by all four gospels). This is possible. But if Matthew and Luke here depend on Q, it is at least equally possible that they preserve the original order, and Mark has a climactic arrangement: the tenants kill the son and throw him out of the vineyard. Nothing in the parable suggests that the vineyard stands for Jerusalem.

In Matthew alone, Jesus elicits the self-condemning response (vv.40–41) of the hearers of the parable, thus concluding his teaching in this parable instead of simply presenting it. Of course, the conclusion remains his, regardless of how he gets it across. The NIV nicely preserves the verbal assonance in the Greek ("wretches ... wretched end").

42 In the NT, only Jesus asks, "Have you never read?" (12:3; 19:4; 21:16; Mk 12:10); in each case, he is saying, in effect, that the Scriptures point to him (Jn 5:39–40). The quotation is from Psalm 118:22–23 (LXX, which faithfully renders the MT; see Notes). Luke adds a free translation of Isaiah 8:14 (cf. Isa 28:16), which appears in v.44. "Stone" symbolism was important in the early church (Ac 4:11, Ro 9:33; 1Pe 2:6) to help Christians understand why Jesus was rejected by so many of his own people; doubtless its effectiveness was enhanced by Jesus' use of it.

Jesus now turns to the image of a building. The "capstone" (lit., "head of the corner") is most probably the top stone of roof parapets, exterior staircases, and city walls (cf. Derrett, *Studies in the New Testament*, 1:61). Psalm 118 may have been written about David, the type of his greater Son. All the "builders"—Goliath, David's own family, even Samuel—overlooked or rejected David, but God chose him. So in Jesus' day the builders (leaders of the people) rejected David's antitype, Jesus. But God makes him the Capstone. Alternatively, and more probably, the psalm concerns Israel. The nation was despised and threatened on all sides, but God made it the capstone. Jesus, who recapitulates Israel (see comments at 2:15) and is the true center of Israel, receives similar treatment from his opponents, but God vindicates him (cf. 23:39).

The building metaphor makes no explicit allusion to the church; the point is christological, not ecclesiastical. The reversal of what man holds dear, the elevation of what he rejects, can only be the Lord's doing—"and it is marvelous in our eyes."

43 This verse, found only in Matthew (cf. van Tilborg, *Jewish Leaders*, 54–58), further explains the parable. Up to this time, the Jewish religious leaders were the principal means by which God exercised his reign over his people. But the leaders failed so badly in handling God's "vineyard" and rejecting God's Son that God gave the responsibility to another people who would produce the kingdom's fruit (cf. 7:16–20). For a somewhat similar explanation, see Stonehouse (*Witness of Matthew*,

230). Strictly speaking, then, v.43 does not speak of transferring the locus of the people of God from Jews to Gentiles, though it may hint at this insofar as that locus now extends far beyond the authority of the Jewish rulers (cf. Ac 13:46; 18:5–6; 1Pe 2:9); instead, it speaks of the ending of the role the Jewish religious leaders played in mediating God's authority (see comments at 23:2–3; so also Ogawa, "Paraboles de l'Israël véritable?" 127–39, though he unsuccessfully questions the authenticity of v.43).

44–46 Jesus' words are confirmed by what "the chief priests [mostly Sadducees] and the Pharisees" (v.45)—the two principal voices of authority in the Judaism of Jesus' day—understood this parable to mean: "they knew he was talking about them." Verse 44 is inserted in many MSS. It is certainly dominical but may be an assimilation to Luke 20:18. A "capstone," if too low, could be tripped over by an unwary person, sending him over the parapet; if too light or insecurely fastened, leaning against it could dislodge it and send it crashing onto the head of some passerby (v.44). There is probably an allusion to both Isaiah 8:14–15 and Daniel 2:35. This despised stone (v.42) is not only chosen by God and promoted to the premier place; it is also dangerous.

The pericope ends with magnificent yet tragic irony (v.46). The religious leaders and others who do not accept God's Messiah are told they will reject Jesus and be crushed. But instead of taking the warning, they hunt for ways to arrest him, hindered only by fear of the people who accept Jesus as a prophet (see comments at v.11), and so trigger the very situation they have been warned about—a dramatic example of God's poetic justice. God in the Scriptures foretells this very event. These men, prompted by hatred, rush to bring it to pass.

NOTES

42 The words αὕτη (*hautē*, "this") and θαυμαστή (*thaumastē*, "marvelous") are feminine and could be construed with κεφαλή (*kephalē*, "head," as in "head of the corner" = "capstone"); more likely, this LXX feminine is a slavish rendering of the Hebrew, which has no neuter and often uses feminine for general ideas; i.e., זאת (*zōʾt*, "this") = αὕτη, *hautē*, and so forth (cf. BDF, para. 138 [2]). The case of λίθον (*lithon*, "stone") has been determined by inverse relative attraction (cf. BDF, para. 295; Zerwick, *Biblical Greek*, para. 19).

On εἰς (*eis*, "for") plus an accusative as a substitute for the predicate nominative, see Zerwick, *Biblical Greek*, para. 32.

46 On εἰς (*eis*, "for") as substitute for the predicate accusative—an unmistakable trace of Semitic influence—see BDF, para. 157 (5); Turner, *Syntax*, 266; Zerwick, *Biblical Greek*, para. 70.

(4) The parable of the wedding banquet (22:1–14)

OVERVIEW

The similarities between this parable and the one in Luke 14:16–24 lead most commentators to take them as separate developments of the same tradition, found also in the *Gospel of Thomas* (64). This almost inevitably leads to the view that Matthew is later on the grounds that it is more "allegorizing" (but see comments at 13:3a) and that 22:6–7, 11–13 are secondary (e.g., Ogawa, "Paraboles de l'Israël véritable?" 140), vv.11–13 perhaps representing another parable. Some go so far as to argue that the Thomas version is the most primitive of the three (but see Blomberg, "Tendencies of the Tradition," esp. 81ff.). Even when there is perfunctory recognition that Jesus may have repeated the same parable on many different occasions and applied it in quite different ways, the text is subjected to ingenious theories that "explain" all the differences with no attempt to explain the methodological grounds on which one may distinguish two historical accounts of the same or similar parables from one account considerably modified in the tradition and placed in an entirely different setting. (To cite one of many examples, see Robert W. Funk, *Language, Hermeneutic, and the Word of God* [New York: Harper, 1966], 163–87; for discussion on the general problem, see Introduction, section 6, and comments at 5:1–12.)

Until we have unambiguous criteria, it seems wise to accept Matthew's setting and report and Luke's setting and report (for detailed discussion, see Stonehouse, *Origins*, 35–42). This is especially so here because of the very small degree of verbal similarity between Matthew and Luke (see chart and discussion at 19:1–2).

In this instance, the differences between Matthew and Luke are striking:

- in Luke, the story concerns "a certain man"; in Matthew, "a king"
- in Luke, a great supper; in Matthew, a wedding banquet for the king's son
- in Luke, one invitation; in Matthew, two
- in Luke, the invited guests make excuses; in Matthew, they refuse and turn violent
- in Luke, the invited guests are passed by; in Matthew, they are destroyed.

Each parable makes admirable sense in its own setting. Whereas the skeptic may judge such suitability to be due to editorial tampering, one may equally conclude from the evidence itself that the suitability of the two parables in their respective settings stems from two historical situations.

Regardless of textual provenance, Blickenstaff (*While the Bridegroom*, 46–76) finds the violent ending so repulsive that she offers a "resistant reading" in which the king is not God but a vicious tyrant, the bridegroom is not Jesus but a rude and judgmental human character, and the wedding feast cannot possibly represent any reign of God that any thoughtful follower of Jesus might want to enter. Similarly, John S. Kloppenborg (*The Tenants in the Vineyard: Ideology, Economics, and Agrarian Conflict in Jewish Palestine* [WUNT 195; Tübingen: Mohr, 2006]) compares and contrasts this parable with its ostensible parallel in the *Gospel of Thomas* and thinks the latter is closer to the original and is more "realistic." While eschewing the "ideological bias" of those who disagree with them, both writers seem remarkably insensitive to the degree to which they are shaped by their own ideologies.

The alleged evidence for later "allegorizing" in Matthew, in addition to being of doubtful worth as an index of later editorial activity (since more and more scholars recognize that parables and allegorizing are not mutually exclusive), must be set against the view that Luke's very simplicity may argue for the lateness of his account. Both criteria—allegorizing and simplicity—are practically useless for determining historical settings. And if Matthew's parable is much harsher than Luke's, may this not owe something to the historical situation—open confrontation with the Jewish leaders during Passion Week, which sets it considerably later than in Luke?

If the parable of the tenants exposes Israel's leaders' neglect of their covenanted duty, this one condemns the contempt with which Israel as a whole treats God's grace. The parable of the wedding banquet is, therefore, not redundant.

[1]Jesus spoke to them again in parables, saying: [2]"The kingdom of heaven is like a king who prepared a wedding banquet for his son. [3]He sent his servants to those who had been invited to the banquet to tell them to come, but they refused to come.

[4]"Then he sent some more servants and said, 'Tell those who have been invited that I have prepared my dinner: My oxen and fattened cattle have been butchered, and everything is ready. Come to the wedding banquet.'

[5]"But they paid no attention and went off — one to his field, another to his business. [6]The rest seized his servants, mistreated them and killed them. [7]The king was enraged. He sent his army and destroyed those murderers and burned their city.

[8]"Then he said to his servants, 'The wedding banquet is ready, but those I invited did not deserve to come. [9]Go to the street corners and invite to the banquet anyone you find.' [10]So the servants went out into the streets and gathered all the people they could find, both good and bad, and the wedding hall was filled with guests.

[11]"But when the king came in to see the guests, he noticed a man there who was not wearing wedding clothes. [12]'Friend,' he asked, 'how did you get in here without wedding clothes?' The man was speechless.

[13]"Then the king told the attendants, 'Tie him hand and foot, and throw him outside, into the darkness, where there will be weeping and gnashing of teeth.'

[14]"For many are invited, but few are chosen."

COMMENTARY

1 *Apokritheis* (NASB, "answered"; untranslated in NIV) may reflect Jesus' response to the Jewish leaders' desires (21:45–46), but it is probably merely formulaic (see comments at 11:25).

2–3 For "kingdom of heaven," see comments at 3:2. This kingdom has become like the following story (cf. Carson, "ὅμοιος Word-Group"). The kingdom has already dawned; invitations to the banquet have gone out and are being refused. The son's wedding banquet doubtless hints at the messianic banquet, but this must not be pressed too hard, for when that banquet comes, there is no possibility of acceptance or refusal.

The king's son is clearly the Messiah, not uncommonly represented as a bridegroom (9:15; 25:1; Jn 3:29; Eph 5:25–32; Rev 21:2–9). Prospective guests to a major feast were invited in advance and then notified when the feast was ready, but these guests persistently refuse (imperfect tense).

4–5 The king not only graciously repeats his invitation but describes the feast's greatness in order to provide an incentive to attend it. *Ariston* ("dinner," GK *756*) properly means "breakfast." It refers to the first of two meals, usually taken about mid-morning (unlike Lk 14:16, where the word *deipnon* [GK *1270*] refers to the evening meal). But large wedding feasts went on for days in the ancient world. This *ariston* is, therefore, just the beginning of prolonged festivity. By v.13 the celebration is continuing at night. Those invited stay away for mundane and selfish reasons (v.5). They slight the king, whose invitation is both an honor and a command, and the marriage of whose son is a time for special joy.

6–7 The scene turns violent. Some of those invited treat the king's messengers outrageously (*hybrizō* is stronger than "mistreat," GK *5614*). Enraged, the king sends his army (see Notes), destroys the murderers, and burns their city (v.7). Many object that vv.6–7 introduce an unexpectedly violent tone, but it is unexpected *only* if Luke 14:16–24 is presumed to be the more primitive form of the story. Matthew's readers, who have just finished 21:38–41, would not find vv.6–7 out of place. Nor is there a veiled allusion to AD 70 (contra Hummel, *Auseinandersetzung*, 85–86, and many others): Reicke ("Synoptic Prophecies," 123) has shown how implausible this is because the language belongs to the general OT categories of judgment (see Introduction, section 6).

8–10 The situation having gone beyond that at normal wedding banquets, these shocking developments make their points that much more effectively. The king sends his servants to *tas diexodous tōn hodōn* ("the street corners," v.9)—probably the forks of the roads, where they would find many people. They extend the king's invitation to all and succeed in drawing in all kinds of people, "both good and bad" (v.10). That Jesus is reported as saying this in Matthew clearly shows that the superior righteousness (5:20) believers must attain to enter the kingdom is not merely rigorous obedience to law. After all, this gospel promises a Messiah who saves his people from their sins (1:21; 20:28). Those who are now being invited to come to the banquet are not Gentiles but the despised within Israel. "When the elite do not come, they are replaced by those of the lower social orders, not of a different ethnicity" (Carter, *Matthew and the Margins*, 436).

11–13 Whether one is good or bad, there is an appropriate attire for this wedding feast. Evidence that the host in first-century Palestinian weddings furnished appropriate attire is inadequate and probably irrelevant to what Matthew is saying. The guest's speechlessness proves he knows he is guilty, even though the king gently calls him "friend" (v.12; cf. 20:13). In view of "good or bad" (v.10), it is difficult to believe that the wedding clothes symbolize righteousness, unless we construe it as a righteousness essential not to enter but to remain there. It is better to leave the symbolism a little vague and say no more than that the man, though invited, did not prepare acceptably for the feast. Thus, though the invitation is very broad, it does not follow that all who respond positively actually remain for the banquet. Some are tied (presumably so they can't get back in) and thrown outside into the darkness, where final judgment awaits (v.13).

14 The *gar* ("for") introduces a general, pithy conclusion explaining the parable (see comments at 18:7; Zerwick, *Biblical Greek*, paras. 474–75). Many are invited, but some refuse to come, and others who do come refuse to submit to the norms of the kingdom and are therefore rejected. Those who remain are called "chosen" (*eklektoi*, GK *1723*), a word implicitly denying that the reversals in the parable in any way catch God unawares or remove sovereign grace from his control. At the same time, it is clear from all three parables (21:28–22:14) that not the beginning but the end is crucial.

NOTES

2 The plural γάμους (*gamous*, lit., "wedding feasts," GK *1141*), as in vv.3–4 (though singular in vv.8, 11–12), may suggest a feast with successive stages (cf. English "nuptials"; see *TDNT*, 1:648–57).

7 The words τὰ στρατεύματα αὐτοῦ (*ta strateumata autou*, lit., "his armies") might lead the English reader to think of vast numbers of soldiers but is probably no more specific than the English idiom "sending in the army" or "police."

(5) Paying taxes to Caesar (22:15–22)

OVERVIEW

Matthew now rejoins Mark (12:13–17) and Luke (20:20–26) in a series of confrontations, the third of which Luke omits. In each one, Jesus is confronted in an attempt to show he is no better than any other rabbi, or even to ensnare him in serious difficulties. Not only does Jesus respond with superlative wisdom, but he ends the exchanges by challenging his opponents with a question of his own they cannot answer (vv.41–46)—another bit of veiled self-disclosure. All this probably takes place in the temple courts on Tuesday of Passion Week.

15Then the Pharisees went out and laid plans to trap him in his words. 16They sent their
disciples to him along with the Herodians. "Teacher," they said, "we know you are a man of integrity and that you teach the way of God in accordance with the truth. You aren't swayed by men, because you pay no attention to who they are. 17Tell us then, what is your
opinion? Is it right to pay taxes to Caesar or not?"

18But Jesus, knowing their evil intent, said, "You hypocrites, why are you trying to trap
me? 19Show me the coin used for paying the tax." They brought him a denarius, 20and he
asked them, "Whose portrait is this? And whose inscription?"

21"Caesar's," they replied.

Then he said to them, "Give to Caesar what is Caesar's, and to God what is God's."

22When they heard this, they were amazed. So they left him and went away.

COMMENTARY

15–16a "Then" (*tote*) may have purely temporal force (Mark and Luke have "and"), but there is probably a logical connection as well: "then"—after Jesus' further self-disclosure and ample warning to the Jewish leaders—the Pharisees went out from the temple courts where Jesus was preaching (21:23) and "laid plans to trap him in his words." Mark (12:13) says that "they" (presumably "the chief priests, the teachers of the law and the elders," 11:27) sent "some of the Pharisees and Herodians" to ensnare Jesus. Matthew says the Pharisees laid the plan and sent their disciples along with Herodians (v.16). Many think this difference reflects Matthew's "anti-Pharisaic bias." But several cautions must be sounded.

1. If Mark's "they" includes "the chief priests, the teachers of the law and the elders," we must remember that most of the latter two groups were Pharisees. Both gospels, therefore, recognize the Pharisees' part in this confrontation.

2. Matthew's motive for making the Pharisees instigators does not have to be "anti-Pharisaic bias," any more than mention of the Sadducees in v.23 and synoptic parallels reflects "anti-Sadducean bias." It may owe something to literary balance—an explicit party in v.23, an explicit party in v.15. Or it may even reflect historical awareness since the Sadducees, most of whom got along with the Roman overlord better than the Pharisees, would be less likely to think up this first confrontation.

3. Both Matthew and Mark specify that Pharisees and Herodians approached Jesus, and the reason is obvious. Unlike most of the Jews, the Herodians openly supported the reigning family of Herod and its pro-Roman sympathies. Clearly, both Pharisees and Herodians are more than mere envoys; they are active participants, seeking to put Jesus between a rock and a hard place.

A common enemy makes strange bedfellows, and common animus against Jesus erupts in plans to trip him up by fair means or foul. The verb *pagideuō* ("ensnare," "entrap," used only here [v.15] in the NT) reveals the motive. This is no dispassionate inquiry into a proper attitude to the Roman overlord. Paying the poll tax was the most obvious sign of submission to Rome. In AD 6, Judas of Galilee led a revolt against the first procurator because he took a census for tax purposes (Josephus, *Ant.* 18.3 [1.1]). Zealots claimed the poll tax was a God-dishonoring badge of slavery to the pagans. The trap, then, put Jesus in the position where he would either alienate a major part of the population or else lay himself open to a charge of treason.

16–17 The title "Teacher" and the long preamble (v.16) reflect flattery and pressure for Jesus to speak. If he does not reply after such an introduction, then he is not a man of integrity and is swayed by men. The question "Is it right?" is theological, as all legal questions inevitably were to a first-century Jew. The question raised here, and others like it, exercised the rabbis (e.g., *b. Pesaḥ.* 112b, *b. B. Qam.* 113a).

By NT times "Caesar," the family name of Julius Caesar, had become a title (cf. Lk 2:1, of Augustus; 3:1, of Tiberius; Ac 17:7, of Claudius; 25:8–12; Php 4:22, of Nero). The reference here is to Tiberius. The wording of the question, with its deft "or not," demands a yes or a no.

18–20 Jesus will not be forced into a reductionistic reply. He recognizes the duplicity of his opponents. "Trap" (v.18) is not *pagideuō* (as in v.15) but *peirazō* ("test" or "tempt," as in 4:1; 16:1). Jesus chooses to answer them on his own terms and asks for the coin (*nomisma*, a NT hapax legomenon) used for paying this tax (22:19). That he has to ask may reflect his own poverty or the fact that he and his disciples had a common purse. It was customary, though not absolutely essential, to pay the tax in Roman currency; and that such coins bore an image of the emperor's head along with an offensive inscription ("Tiberius Caesar, son of the divine Augustus" on one side and "*pontifex maximus*"—which Jesus would understand as "high priest"—on the other) would offend most Palestinian Jews. They hand Jesus a denarius (v.19), and, as in 21:23–27, he asks his questioners a question—this time one they have to answer (v.20).

21–22 Superficially, Jesus' answer accords with Jewish teaching that men ought to pay taxes to their foreign overlords, since the great, even the pagan great, owe their position to God (cf. Pr 8:15; Da 2:21, 37–38). But Jesus' answer (v.21) is more profound than that and can be fully understood only in the light of religion-state relations in first-century Rome. The Jews, with their theocratic heritage, were ill equipped to formulate a theological rationale for paying tribute to foreign and pagan overlords, unless, like the Jews of the exile, they interpreted their situation as one of divine judgment. But it was not only Jewish monotheism that linked religion and state. Paganism customarily insisted even more strongly on the unity of what we distinguish as civil and religious obligations. Indeed, some decades later, Christians faced the wrath of Rome because they refused to participate in emperor worship—a refusal the state judged to be treason.

Seen in this light, Jesus' response is not some witty way of getting out of a predicament; rather, it shows his full awareness of a major development in redemption history. Jesus does *not* side with the Zealots or with any who expect his messiahship to bring instant political independence from Rome. The messianic community he determines to build (16:18) must render to whichever Caesar is in power whatever belongs to that Caesar, while never turning from its obligations to God. The lesson was learned by both Paul and Peter (Ro 13:1–7; 1Pe 2:13–17). Of course, Jesus' reply is not a legal statute resolving every issue. Where Caesar claims what is God's, the claims of God have priority (Ac 4:19; 5:29; much of Revelation). Nevertheless, Jesus' pithy words not only answer his enemies but also lay down the basis for the proper relationship of his people to government. The profundity of his reply is amazing (v.22), but some of his enemies, no doubt disappointed at their failure to ensnare him, later on lie to pretend that their snare had worked (Lk 23:2).

On the theological bearing of this pericope on Romans 13, see D. A. Carson, *Christ and Culture Revisited* (Grand Rapids: Eerdmans, 2008), passim.

NOTES

16 The clause οὐ γὰρ βλέπεις εἰς πρόσωπον ἀνθρώπων (*ou gar blepeis eis prosōpon anthrōpōn*, lit., "you do not look to the face of men") is idiomatically translated by the NIV, "you pay no attention to who [men] are." The expression probably has the same force as לֹא תַכִּיר פָּנִים (*lōʾ takîr pānîm*, "you shall not respect persons [NIV, 'show partiality']," Dt 16:19; cf. Lev 19:15): cf. Sigal, *Halakhah of Jesus*, 74–75; contra Derrett, *Law in the New Testament*, 313ff.

21 Some have interpreted ἀπόδοτε (*apodote*, "give," GK *625*) to mean "pay back": Give back to God what he has given you, and to Caesar what he has given you. Although the verb can have that force, it need only mean "give" or "pay." The latter is more suitable in this context because in no real sense does Caesar "give back" his subjects' tax money. They pay what is his due, what properly belongs to him, not what he has given them.

(6) Marriage at the Resurrection (22:23–33)

OVERVIEW

The questioners' intent is as malicious as in the last pericope. They hope to embroil Jesus in a theological debate where he must choose sides; instead, the exchange again demonstrates his wisdom and authority (cf. Mk 12:18–27; Lk 20:27–40).

23 That same day the Sadducees, who say there is no resurrection, came to him with a
question. 24 "Teacher," they said, "Moses told us that if a man dies without having children,
his brother must marry the widow and have children for him. 25 Now there were seven
brothers among us. The first one married and died, and since he had no children, he left
his wife to his brother. 26 The same thing happened to the second and third brother, right
on down to the seventh. 27 Finally, the woman died. 28 Now then, at the resurrection, whose
wife will she be of the seven, since all of them were married to her?"
29 Jesus replied, "You are in error because you do not know the Scriptures or the power
of God. 30 At the resurrection people will neither marry nor be given in marriage; they will
be like the angels in heaven. 31 But about the resurrection of the dead — have you not read
what God said to you, 32 'I am the God of Abraham, the God of Isaac, and the God of Jacob'?
He is not the God of the dead but of the living."
33 When the crowds heard this, they were astonished at his teaching.

COMMENTARY

23 "That same day" (lit., "in that hour") places this confrontation in the same situation as the former one. Pharisees believed in a resurrection from the dead, basing their belief in part on Isaiah 26:19 and Daniel 12:2. But Sadducees did not believe in a resurrection. Both body and soul, they held, perish at death (cf. Ac 23:8; see Josephus, *Ant.* 18.12–17 [1.3–4]; *J. W.* 2.162–66 [8.14]). In Jesus' time, Judaism as a whole held surprisingly diverse views of death and what lies beyond it (cf. G. W. E. Nickelsburg, *Resurrection, Immortality, and Eternal Life in Intertestamental Judaism* [Cambridge: Harvard Univ. Press, 1972]; Keener). In support of his view that Matthew was written so late that it retains only vague and inaccurate impressions of Sadducees (who largely died out after AD 70), Hummel (*Auseinandersetzung*, 18–20) argues that this verse says that only *some of* the Sadducees say there is no resurrection; the Greek text knows no such restriction, whatever variant is chosen (see Notes).

24–28 Like the Pharisees and Herodians, the Sadducees approach Jesus with insincere respect ("Teacher"; cf. v.16). They begin by citing the Mosaic levirate law (Dt 25:5–6). The text form in Matthew either is a little closer to the Hebrew than in Mark and Luke, or else assimilates more closely to Genesis 38:8 (LXX). According to biblical law, if a man dies without children (the plural is generalizing: Zerwick, *Biblical Greek*, para. 7; see comments at 2:20), his younger brother is to marry the widow and "have children for him," i.e., sire children who would legally be heirs of the deceased brother. Levirate marriage antedates Moses in the canon (Genesis 38:8); i.e., Moses regulated the practice but did not initiate it. The OT gives us no case of it, though levirate law stands behind Ruth 1:11–13; 4:1–22. Probably in Jesus' day, the law was little observed, the younger brother's right to decline taking precedence over his obligation.

Though the case brought by the Sadducees (vv.25–27) *could* have happened, it is probably hypothetical, fabricated to confound Pharisees and others who believed in resurrection. Their question presupposes that resurrection life is an exact counterpart to earthly life. If so, the resurrected woman (v.28) must be guilty of incestuous marriages (see comments at 19:9) or arbitrarily designated the wife of one of the brothers. And if so, which one? Or—and this is the answer the Sadducees pressed for—the whole notion of resurrection is absurd.

29–30 In Jesus' mind, the Sadducees were denying Scripture because they approached its clear teaching on the subject (Isa 26:19; Da 12:2; cf. Job 19:25–27), assuming that if God raises the dead, he must bring them back to an existence just like this one. Jesus' response was acute. The Sadducees, Jesus insists, betray their ignorance of the Scriptures, which *do* teach resurrection, and of the power of God, who is capable of raising the dead to an existence quite unlike this present one. "For" (*gar*, untranslated in NIV)—introducing an explanation as to how the power of God will manifest itself—"in" (*en*, not "at" [NIV], viewing the resurrection, not as a single event, but as a state inaugurated by the event) "the resurrection" there will be a change in sexual relationships (v.30). In this way we shall be "like the angels in heaven," and marriage as we know it will be no more. In fact, Jesus' use of angels contains a double thrust since the Sadducees denied their existence (cf. Ac 23:8).

Some have concluded from Jesus' answer that in heaven there will be no memory of earlier existence and its relationships, but this is a gratuitous assumption. The greatness of the changes at the resurrection (cf. 1Co 15:44; Php 3:21; 1Jn 3:1–2) will doubtless make the wife of even seven brothers (vv.24–27) capable of loving all and the object of the love of all—as a good mother today loves all her children and is loved by them.

31–32 Jesus now turns from the power of God to the word of Scripture (cf. v.29). He may have drawn the passage to which he appeals (Ex 3:6) from the Pentateuch because the Sadducees prized the Pentateuch more highly than the rest of Scripture. "Have you not read?" (v.31) is a rebuke (see comments at 21:42).

If God is the God of Abraham, Isaac, and Jacob even when addressing Moses, hundreds of years after the first three patriarchs died, then they must be alive to him (v.32), "for to him all are alive" (Lk 20:38). God is the eternal God of the covenant, a fact especially stressed wherever reference is made to the patriarchs (e.g., Ge 24:12, 27, 48; 26:24; 28:13; 32:9; 46:1, 3–4; 48:15–16; 49:25). He always loves and blesses his people; therefore it is inconceivable that his blessings cease when his people die (cf. Pss 16:10–11; 17:15; 49:14–15; 73:23–26). Yet, at first glance, the text Jesus cites is sufficient, along the lines of this argument, to prove immortality but not resurrection. Two observations largely alleviate the problem.

1. The Sadducees denied the existence of spirits as thoroughly as they denied the existence of angels (Ac 23:8). Their concern was, therefore, not to choose between immortality and resurrection but between death as finality and life beyond death, whatever its mode.

2. The mode that was the principal (though certainly not exclusive) option in Palestinian piety was a rather shadowy existence in Sheol followed by final resurrection.

Our problem is that we force on the text a Neoplatonic dualism and demand a choice between immortality and resurrection (cf. Warfield, *Selected Shorter Writings*, 1:339–47). The point is simply "that God will raise the dead because he cannot fail to keep his promises to them that he will be their God" (Marshall, *Gospel of Luke*, 743), read against the background of biblical anthropology and eschatology (cf. also F. Dreyfus, "L'argument scripturaire de Jésus in faveur de la résurrection des morts [Mark 12:26–27]," *RB* 66 [1959]: 213–24—though he handles Lk 20:37–38 rather disappointingly).

33 Matthew does not tell us that the Sadducees are convinced but that the crowds are astonished at Jesus' teaching. The cause of the astonishment is probably Jesus' authority and incisive insight into biblical truth (cf. 7:28–29; 13:54; 22:22). Luke (20:39) remarks that some teachers of the law, almost certainly of Pharisaic persuasion, responded, "Well said, teacher!"

NOTES

23 The two principal readings are "Sadducees saying" and "Sadducees, those who say" (for textual details, see Metzger, *Textual Commentary*, 58). The former is likely original, both on external evidence and because it almost suggests the Sadducees began the conversation with a denial, an unprecedented approach (though it is possible their "saying" is understood to be an aside, under their breath as it were). The second reading is then a partial assimilation to Mark 12:18; Luke 20:27. But even if the second reading is original, it is quite unnecessary to suppose "those who say" refers to some part of the Sadducees. The words most plausibly belong in apposition: "Sadducees, i.e., those who say." Matthew treats the verb ἔρχονται (*erchontai*, come) in Mark 12:18 as a historical present, and if "saying" is a dependent participle, it takes on the same temporal force as Matthew's προσῆλθον (*prosēlthon*, "came").

31 This is the only place in the NT that speaks of resurrection τῶν νεκρῶν (*tōn nekrōn*, "of the dead"), though Romans 1:4 uses the anarthrous expression. More common is the insertion of the preposition ἐκ (*ek*, "from"). Despite various theories to explain these differences, the diverse forms are probably synonymous.

(7) The greatest commandments (22:34–40)

OVERVIEW

The account as we have it is not in Luke (cf. Mk 12:28–34), though Luke 10:25–28 has something similar introducing the parable of the Good Samaritan. Because there are several verbal agreements between Matthew and Luke against Mark, it is usually held that the "double commandment" came down separately in Mark and Q (cf. R. H. Fuller, "The Double Commandment of Love," in *Essays on the Love Commandment* [ed. Schottroff et al.], 41–56). This is quite possible. The Lukan pericope (10:25–37) is so loosely connected to its setting that it could have come from almost any period in Jesus' ministry.

On the other hand, the rabbis of Jesus' day were much exercised to find summary statements of OT laws and establish their relative importance. In all probability, the question arose enough times in Jesus' ministry that he developed a fairly standard response to the question. In Luke, Jesus elicits the correct answer from the expert in the law rather than providing it himself, but we have already seen this kind of diversity when the synoptists recount the same event (e.g., Mk 12:9 and Mt 21:40–41; cf. Mk 12:35–36 and Mt 22:42–44); thus the distinction may not be significant. More telling is the fact that the pericope in Luke focuses primarily not on the question of the greatest commandment but on the question of how to inherit eternal life. While this is scarcely conclusive, it may suggest quite separate occasions (cf. Ellis, "New Directions," 310–12).

[34]Hearing that Jesus had silenced the Sadducees, the Pharisees got together. [35]One of them, an expert in the law, tested him with this question: [36]"Teacher, which is the greatest commandment in the Law?"

[37]Jesus replied: "'Love the Lord your God with all your heart and with all your soul and with all your mind.' [38]This is the first and greatest commandment. [39]And the second is like it: 'Love your neighbor as yourself.' [40]All the Law and the Prophets hang on these two commandments."

COMMENTARY

34 Mark says that teachers of the law—most of whom were Pharisees—posed the question (12:28) and gives a rather positive picture of the man. But Matthew maintains the polemical tone and portrays this confrontation as owing something to the machinations of the Pharisees, who saw how Jesus had silenced the Sadducees. Historically, the Pharisees' leaders sent one of their "disciples" (cf. v.16)—himself a Pharisee—who turned out to be more sympathetic than his seniors. Mark focuses on the confrontation; Matthew looks at its core from the perspective of the Pharisees who plotted it. (For similar dissension among high Jewish authorities when assessing Jesus, see Jn 7:45–52; Ac 5:33–39.)

35–36 The *nomikos* ("expert in the law," GK *3788*, assuming this is the correct reading and not an interpolation from Luke) is here a Pharisee, a "scribe" or "teacher of the law" considered particularly learned (v.35). The "law," of course, is Scripture, perhaps especially the Pentateuch. But because Scripture was applied to every area of life—including all civil matters—by means of certain interpretive rules and a vast complex of tradition, such an expert was, by modern standards, both a learned theologian and a legal expert. He "tested" Jesus, asking which is the greatest commandment (v.36; the positive is used for the superlative, a not uncommon way to speak of a group or class; cf. Moulton, *Grammar: Accidence*, 442; BDF, para. 245 [2]; Zerwick, *Biblical Greek*, para. 146).

The Jews quite commonly drew distinctions among the laws of Scripture—great and small, light and heavy. Jesus does something similar in 23:23. *Testament of Issachar* 6 gives certain Scriptures as the epitome of the law; and Akiba's "negative golden rule" (see comments at 7:12) is proclaimed as "the whole law. The rest is commentary" (cf. *b. Šabb.* 31a). Yet the Jewish evidence is not univocal. *Mekilta* Exodus 6 and *Sifre* Deuteronomy 12:8; 19:11 speak of the equal importance of all commandments (cf. Str-B, 1:902ff.). We must allow not only for diversity of opinion among Jewish authorities but also for various opinions with different aims. Moreover, equality of various laws can refer to equality of reward for keeping them; Akiba's dictum was a response to a Gentile challenge to explain the whole law during the time he could stand on one leg.

Verse 36 shows that the question of the expert was probably a hotly debated one (cf. Urbach, *Sages*, 1:345–65). The scene is like an ordination council, where the candidate is doing so well that some of the most learned ministers ask him questions they themselves have been unable to answer—in the hope of tripping him up or of finding answers.

37–39 Jesus first quotes Deuteronomy 6:5 (part of the Shema [Dt 6:4–9; 11:13–21; Nu 15:38–41]) and then Leviticus 19:18. The first is from the MT, the second from the LXX (cf. Gundry, *Use of the Old Testament*, 22–25; Blomberg, "Matthew," in *CNTUOT*). From the viewpoint of biblical anthropology, "heart," "soul," and "mind" (v.37) are not mutually exclusive but overlapping categories, together demanding our love for God to come from our whole person, our every faculty and capacity. "First and greatest" (v.38) refers to one, not two, qualities. The "and" is explicative; i.e., this command is primary because it is the greatest. The second (v.39) also concerns love, this time toward one's "neighbor," which in Leviticus 19:18 applies to a fellow Israelite or resident alien, but which Luke 10:29–37 expands to anyone who needs our help.

Bringing these two texts together does not originate with Jesus, as Luke's parallel suggests (confirmed also by *T. Iss.* 5:2; 7:6; *T. Dan* 5:3, if these texts are pre-Christian).

40 This verse is distinctive though enigmatic. "All the Law and the Prophets hang on [lit., 'are suspended from'] these two commandments." The following observations bring out the principal points of this summary.

1. The two commandments, Jesus says, stand together. The first without the second is intrinsically impossible (cf. 1Jn 4:20), and the second cannot stand without the first—even theoretically—because disciplined altruism is not love. Love in the truest sense demands abandonment of self to God, and God alone is the adequate incentive for such abandonment. Moreover, in Leviticus 19, from which the second commandment is quoted, the grounding of the stipulations is frequently given: "I am the LORD"—i.e., the grounding is in the first commandment.

2. But in what sense do the Law and the Prophets "hang" on these two commandments? It is unlikely that the verb implies "derivation"—that the Law and the Prophets can be deduced from these two commandments (so K. Berger, *Die Gesetzesauslegung Jesu* [Neukirchen-Vluyn: Neukirchener Verlag, 1972], 227–32). Jesus has expanded the initial category ("the greatest commandment in the Law," v.36) to include all Scripture ("all the Law and the Prophets"). So even if "all the Law" could be derived from these two commandments, how could the same be said of "all the Prophets"?

3. It is equally unlikely that Jesus is appealing to these two commandments to abolish the necessity of formal adherence to all other law, thus entirely abandoning the rabbinical approach to the law and perhaps even making the love commandments a kind of hermeneutical canon for interpreting all OT law. This view, in one form or another, is very popular (cf. Barth, "Matthew's Understanding of the Law," 76–78; Bornkamm, *Geschichte*, 37–45; Hummel, *Auseinandersetzung*, 51ff.; see esp. B. Gerhardsson, "The Hermeneutic Program in Matthew 22:37–40," in *Jesus, Greeks, and Christians* [ed. R. Hamerton-Kelly and R. Scroggs; Leiden: Brill, 1976], 129–50). This radical interpretation of Jesus' answer is said to be necessary to make sense of the fact that this confrontation is a test (Barth, "Matthew's Understanding of the Law," 78). But the test can be understood in other ways (see comments at v.36). The fact that Jesus' opponents are testing him does not require his answer to be radical, any more than in vv.23–33. There is no positive evidence in the text to support this view, if a better one can be found; and Moo ("Jesus and the Authority of the Mosaic Law") has rightly pointed out that in no case in the Gospels does love serve as grounds for abrogating any commandment (the Sabbath controversies are no exception, since there concern for fellow human beings is recognized as one important factor within the Sabbath law itself; see comments at 12:1–13). Indeed, Barth ("Matthew's Understanding of the Law," 78) is reduced to pitting the love commands against the "jot and tittle" of 5:18, though both are taught by Jesus.

4. W. C. Kaiser ("Weightier and Lighter Matters") rightly points out that this passage is in keeping with the prophetic tradition of the OT, which equally demands a heart relationship with God (Dt 10:12; 1Sa 15:22; Isa 1:11–17; 43:22–24; Hos 6:6; Am 5:21–24; Mic 6:6–8; cf. Pr 15:8; 21:27; 28:9). Sterile religion, no matter how disciplined, was never regarded as adequate. Unfortunately, Kaiser then arbitrarily links this pericope too closely with a passage such as Matthew 23:23–24 and argues that Jesus is saying that "the meticulous scribes and punctilious Pharisees ... *must penetrate to the more significant and abiding aspects of the law*" (p. 185, emphasis mine). But that is just what Jesus does not say at this point. The relative "greatness" of this command or some other one has no connection whatsoever in synoptic pericopes to continuity or discontinuity between the Testaments.

5. Nevertheless, Kaiser's initial linking of vv.34–40 with the OT tradition demanding heart religion is valid. This matter is well treated by Moo ("Jesus and the Authority of the Mosaic Law"). There is no question here of the priority of love over law—i.e., one system over another—but of the priority of love within the law. These two commandments are the greatest because all Scripture "hangs" on them; i.e., nothing in Scripture can cohere or be truly obeyed unless these two are observed. Love is "the primary hermeneutical principle for interpreting and applying the law" (Mohrlang, *Matthew and Paul*, 95). The entire biblical revelation demands heart religion marked by total allegiance to God, loving him and loving one's neighbor. Without these two commandments, the Bible is sterile. This pericope prepares the way for the denunciations of 23:1–36 and conforms fully to Jesus' teaching elsewhere. "Love is the greatest commandment, but it is not the *only* one; and the validity and applicability of other commandments cannot be decided by appeal to its paramount demand" (Moo, p. 12). The question of the continuity or discontinuity of OT law within the teaching of Jesus is determined not with reference to the love commands but by a salvation-historical perspective focusing on prophecy and fulfillment (see comments at 5:17–48).

NOTES

40 It is doubtful whether Paul (Ro 13:8–10) goes beyond the interpretation given above (cf. C. E. B. Cranfield, *The Epistle to the Romans* [Edinburgh: T&T Clark, 1975, 1979], 2:673–79). This does not mean that Cranfield's entire view on the law in Paul is to be endorsed but that he rightly perceives the relation between love and law. For discussion of the place of law in the history of redemption, see *From Sabbath to Lord's Day* [ed. Carson]; Stephen Westerholm, *Perspectives Old and New on Paul* (Grand Rapids: Eerdmans, 2004).

(8) The son of David (22:41–46)

OVERVIEW

After silencing the Jewish leaders, Jesus in turn asks them a question. His purpose is not to win a debate but to elicit from them what the Scriptures themselves teach about the Messiah, thus helping people to recognize who he really is. The passage speaks to crucial christological and hermeneutical issues (see comments at vv.43–44). Although many commentators hold that this pericope represents a debate between the synagogue and the church, or within the church, in Matthew's day, Bock (*Blasphemy and Exaltation*, 220–22) rightly points out how unlikely it is that the church, which happily and frequently confessed Jesus to be the Son of David, would invent a story that appears to question the legitimacy of that confession.

The synoptic parallels (Mk 12:35–37; Lk 20:41–44) do not show that Jesus' questions were addressed to the Pharisees, or that they replied (see comments vv.34–40). The historical setting is the temple courts, where crowds and leaders mingled together and alternately listened to the teacher from Nazareth and fired questions at him (21:23–23:36). Matthew's details probably stem from his memory of the events. That he mentions the Pharisees may reveal his desire to show his readers where the Pharisees were wrong. But one cannot be dogmatic about this, since Matthew omits Mark's gentle snub: "The large crowd listened to him with delight" (12:37), which shows that Mark, too, knows that Jesus aimed his exegesis of Psalm 110 against the biblical experts of his day.

41While the Pharisees were gathered together, Jesus asked them, **42**"What do you think about the Christ? Whose son is he?"

"The son of David," they replied.

43He said to them, "How is it then that David, speaking by the Spirit, calls him 'Lord'? For he says,

44 "'The Lord said to my Lord:
"Sit at my right hand
until I put your enemies
under your feet."'

45If then David calls him 'Lord,' how can he be his son?" **46**No one could say a word in reply, and from that day on no one dared to ask him any more questions.

COMMENTARY

41–42 Jesus' question (v.41) focuses on the real issue—Christology, not resurrection or taxes—that turned the authorities into his enemies. The Messiah's identity according to the Scriptures must be determined. One way to do that is to ask whose son he is (v.42). The Pharisees gave the accepted reply: "The son of David"—based on passages such as 2 Samuel 7:13–14; Isaiah 11:1, 10; Jeremiah 23:5 (see comments at 1:1; 9:27–28; cf. Moore, *Judaism*, 2:328–29; Guthrie, *New Testament Theology*, 253–56; Fitzmyer, *Essays on the Semitic Background*, 113–26; Longenecker, *Christology of Early Jewish Christianity*, 109–10).

43–45 This view, though not wrong, is too simple because, as Jesus points out, David called the Messiah his Lord (v.43). How, then, could Messiah be David's son? The force of Jesus' argument depends on his use of Psalm 110, the most frequently quoted OT passage in the NT. The Davidic authorship of the psalm, affirmed by the psalm's superscription, is not only assumed by Jesus but is essential to his argument. If the psalm was written by anyone else, then *David* did not call Messiah his Lord. The phrase "speaking by the Spirit" not only assumes that all Scripture is Spirit-inspired (cf. Ac 4:25; Heb 3:7; 9:8; 10:15; 2Pe 1:21) but here reinforces the truth of what David said so it may be integrated into the beliefs of the hearers (cf. "and the Scripture cannot be broken," Jn 10:35). The text of Psalm 110:1, quoted by all three Synoptics, is essentially Septuagintal (cf. Gundry, *Use of the Old Testament*, 25; on the variants, see Fee, "Modern Text Criticism," 163–64). The "right hand" (v.44) is the position of highest honor and authority (cf. 19:28; Ps 45:9).

Many but not all Jews in Jesus' day regarded Psalm 110 as messianic (cf. Str-B, 4:452–65; Edersheim, *Life and Times*, appendix 9; David M. Hay, *Glory at the Right Hand: Psalm 110 in Early Christianity* [Nashville: Abingdon, 1973], 11–33). Most modern scholars say that Psalm 110 was not Davidic but was written *about* David or some other king, making "my Lord" a monarchical reference by an unknown psalmist. Because Psalm 110 is so frequently quoted in the NT, some scholars try to establish the "entry" of the psalm into Christian tradition, associating it with, say, "the pre-Pauline formula in Romans 1:3f." (D. C. Duling, "The Promises to David and Their Entrance into Christianity," *NTS* 20 [1974]: 55–77) or Pentecost (M. Gourgues, "Lecture christologique du Psaume cx et Fête de la Pentecōte," *RB* 83 [1976]: 1–24). A pattern is then plotted for the score of NT uses of Psalm 110, on which Matthew 22:41–46 (plus par.) appears too late to be authentic words of Jesus.

Nevertheless there are many arguments for an interpretation more in conformity with the texts as we have them.

1. That Psalm 110 is about the king makes sense only if the superscription is ignored. If David is indeed the author, as both the psalm's superscription and Jesus insist, then either the psalm deals with some figure other than David or else David, caught up in high prophetic vision, is writing about himself in the third person.

2. The latter is by no means implausible. But we have already seen that much prophecy and fulfillment is in OT paradigms pointing forward, sometimes with the understanding of the OT writers, sometimes not (see comments at 2:15; 5:17; 8:16–17). David is regularly portrayed, even in the OT, as the model for the coming Anointed One, and David himself understood at least something of the messianic promise (2Sa 7:13–14).

3. Psalm 110 uses language so reckless and extravagant ("forever," v.4; the mysterious Melchizedek reference, v.4; the scope of the king's victory, v.6) that one must either say the psalm is using hyperbole or that it points beyond David. That is exactly the sort of argument Peter uses in Acts 2:25–31 concerning another Davidic psalm (Ps 16).

4. Psalm 110 contains no allusion to the much later Maccabeans, who were priest-kings, for they were priests who became "kings," whereas the figure in Psalm 110 is a king who becomes a priest.

5. As the text stands, this pericope has important christological implications. The widely held, if not dominant, view was that the coming Messiah would be the son of David (cf. *Pss. Sol.* 17). Jesus not only declares that view inadequate, but he insists that the OT itself tells us it is inadequate. If Messiah is not David's son, *whose son is he*? The solution is given by the prologue to Matthew (chs. 1–2) and by the voice of God himself (3:17; 17:5): Jesus is the Son of God. Even the title "Son of Man" (see comments at 8:20) offers a transcendent conception of messiahship.

6. However, in spite of Bultmann (*History of the Synoptic Tradition*, 136–37) and many others,

this does not mean that Jesus or Matthew is *denying* that the Messiah is David's son, replacing this notion with a more transcendent perspective. This gospel repeatedly recognizes that Jesus the Messiah is Son of David, not only by title (1:1; 9:27; 15:22; 20:30–31; 21:9, 15; cf. 12:23) and by the genealogy (1:2–16), but also by its portrayal of Jesus as King of the Jews (2:2; 21:5; 27:11, 29, 37, 42: cf. Hay, *Glory at the Right Hand*, 116–17). What Jesus does is synthesize the concept of a human Messiah in David's line with the concept of a divine Messiah who transcends human limitations (e.g., Ps 45:6–7; Isa 9:6; Jer 23:5–6; 33:15–16; Zec 12:10 [MT]; 13:7 [NASB]), even as Matthew elsewhere synthesizes kingship and the Suffering Servant. The OT itself looked forward to one who would be both the offshoot and the root of David (Isa 11:1, 10, cf. Rev 22:16).

7. Even the fact that Jesus' use of Psalm 110:1 was susceptible to an interpretation denying that the Messiah must be of Davidic descent argues strongly for the authenticity of this exegesis of the psalm, for it is unlikely that Christians would have placed this psalm on Jesus' lips when his Davidic sonship is taught throughout the NT (in addition to Matthew, cf. Mk 10:47–48; 11:10; Lk 1:32; 18:38–39; Ro 1:3; 2Ti 2:8; Rev 3:7; 5:5; 22:16). Jesus' question (v.45) is not a denial of Messiah's Davidic sonship but a demand for recognizing how Scripture itself teaches that Messiah is more than David's son.

8. Against those who hold that this transcendent sonship could have arisen as an issue only after the passion (e.g., Lindars, *New Testament Apologetic*, 46–47), we must ask why Jesus himself could not have expressed the paradox of Messiah's dual paternity since he certainly knew God as uniquely his "Father" (see esp. 11:27) and applies the transcendent title "Son of Man" to himself as well.

9. If this approach is substantially correct, then the entrance of Psalm 110 into Christian theology is traceable to Jesus himself. Moreover, it can be credibly argued that *his* approach to the OT is adopted by the NT writers, even when they do not focus on the same OT texts to which he gave his primary attention.

10. Finally, the text has some eschatological implications, even though they are not of primary interest. Messiah is pictured at God's right hand of authority during a period of hostility from God's enemies, a hostility to be crushed at the end (cf. 28:18–20).

46 In Mark, the opponents' silence (12:34) concludes the pericope of the greatest commandment. Matthew uses this comment to finish the entire section of confrontations (21:23–22:46). Many who were silenced were not saved; so Jesus' enemies went underground for a short time before the crucifixion. Yet even their silence was a tribute. The teacher who never attended the right schools (Jn 7:15–18) confounds the greatest theologians in the land. And if his question (v.45) was unanswerable at this time, a young Pharisee, who may have been in Jerusalem at the time, was to answer it in due course (Ro 1:1–4; 9:5).

NOTES

44 The variants "under your feet" and "your footstool" (cf. NA[27]) were easily exchangeable in Greek because of (1) similarity in the Greek terms ὑποκάτω (*hypokatō*, "under") and ὑποπόδιον (*hypopodion*, "footstool"); (2) the demonstrable influence of Psalm 8:6; and (3) the obvious relation between the two expressions (a footstool by definition is under one's feet). On the significance of the idea, see Joshua 10:24; Psalm 47:3.

e. Seven woes on the teachers of the law and the Pharisees (23:1–36)

OVERVIEW

Structurally, it is difficult to decide just where Matthew 23 belongs. Because it is essentially discourse, some have held that it either belongs to Matthew 24–25 or else is a separate discourse and must be treated as such. But the different audiences (23:1; 24:3) separate ch. 23 from chs. 24–25, as do their distinct, though related, themes. Nor is Matthew 23 a discourse on a par with the five major discourses of Matthew; it lacks the characteristic discourse ending (see comments at 7:28–29). Moreover, from a thematic viewpoint, Matthew 23 is best perceived as the climax of the preceding confrontations (cf. Keener; Garland, *Intention of Matthew 23*, 41–46).

Solutions to many of the important questions raised by Matthew 23 gradually emerge from exegesis of the whole, but several preliminary considerations will point the way ahead.

1. The literary origins of this chapter are disputed. Some see vv.1–12 as free expansion—by Matthew of Mark 12:38–39, and vv.13–36 of Mark 12:40. Others hold that Mark has reduced material in Matthew because he is not interested in this debate, and still others that the two gospels spring at this juncture from separate traditions. There is no way of proving the rightness of one of these options. Yet it must be said that Matthew's material is remarkably coherent and, when viewed dispassionately (see below), believably dominical. Even the changes of addressees (vv.1, 13, 37) admirably suit the larger context (21:23–22:46), with crowds and authorities milling around and coming and going, and the preacher addressing first this part of his audience, then that. The chapter *may* be a montage of sayings—there is ample evidence that Luke often compiled sayings in that way, without pretense of doing otherwise; on the other hand, there is no good reason for thinking vv.2–36 cannot be a report of what Jesus said on this occasion.

2. Attempts to define the situation in Matthew's church on the basis of this chapter are precarious. These turn on attitude toward the law (cf. vv.2–3, 23) or toward the Jewish religious leaders and lead to extended debate as to whether Matthew's church has broken from the synagogue and is therefore appealing to it, denouncing it from without, or is still trying to win it over from within. Objections to the contrary, there is no real anachronism to warrant such discussion, which is scarcely more than fanciful, though learned, speculation. Obviously, Matthew claims to be telling us what Jesus says, not what the church says. Even if we assume that Matthew's choice of what he includes largely reflects the situation at the time he wrote, it is naive to think twenty-first-century scholars can reconstruct the situation in detail (see Introduction, section 2). A certain amount of personal interest or a need to show his readers "how we got from there to here" may have led Matthew to many of his choices. The space he allots to it implies that he is interested in the continuity between the OT people of God and the church, the people of the Messiah, and how it happened that so many Jews, including the religious authorities, rejected Jesus. But Paul had similar aims in writing Romans, and no one thinks the church at Rome is theologically akin to Matthew's church in this respect.

3. The literary context of the chapter is extremely important. Not only does Matthew 23 climax a series of controversies with the Jewish religious authorities (21:23–22:46), but it immediately

follows the christologically crucial confrontation of 22:41–46. The question "What do you think about Christ?" raised by Jesus (22:42), "was not simply a theological curiosity which could be thrashed out in the seminar room," as Garland (*Intention of Matthew 23*, 24) puts it; it stands at the heart of the gospel. The failure of the Pharisees to recognize Jesus as the Messiah prophesied in Scripture is itself already an indictment, the more so since they "sit in Moses' seat" (see comments at v.2); the woes that follow are, therefore, judicial and go some way toward explaining the prophesied destruction of Jerusalem in the Olivet Discourse (24:4–25:46).

4. Thus Jesus' strong language in this chapter ("fools," "hypocrites," "blind guides," "son of hell") is not the language of personal irritation at religious competition, nor the language of a suffering church tired of the restrictions and unbelief of the synagogue in the ninth decade AD, but the language of divine warning (cf. vv.37–39) and condemnation. Those who see Matthew 23 as inconsistent with the Sermon on the Mount (esp. 5:43–48; e.g., Mohrlang, *Matthew and Paul*, 99–100) neglect two things: (1) they overlook the limitations inherent to the sermon itself—the love Jesus demands of his followers is more radical and more discriminating than modern liberal sentimentality usually allows—and (2) the Sermon on the Mount, not less than Matthew 23, also presents Jesus as eschatological Judge who pronounces solemn malediction on those he does not recognize and who fail to do his word (7:21–23). To read Matthew 23 as little more than Matthew's pique about AD 85 is not only without adequate historical and literary justification but fails dismally to understand the historical Jesus, who not only taught his followers to love their enemies and gave his own life in supreme self-sacrifice but proclaimed that he came not to bring peace but a sword (10:34) and presented himself as eschatological Judge (e.g., 7:21–23; 25:31–46).

(1) Warning the crowds and the disciples (23:1–12)

1 Then Jesus said to the crowds and to his disciples: 2 "The teachers of the law and the
Pharisees sit in Moses' seat. 3 So you must obey them and do everything they tell you. But
do not do what they do, for they do not practice what they preach. 4 They tie up heavy
loads and put them on men's shoulders, but they themselves are not willing to lift a finger
to move them.

5 "Everything they do is done for men to see: They make their phylacteries wide and the
tassels on their garments long; 6 they love the place of honor at banquets and the most
important seats in the synagogues; 7 they love to be greeted in the marketplaces and to
have men call them 'Rabbi.'

8 "But you are not to be called 'Rabbi,' for you have only one Master and you are all
brothers. 9 And do not call anyone on earth 'father,' for you have one Father, and he is in
heaven. 10 Nor are you to be called 'teacher,' for you have one Teacher, the Christ. 11 The
greatest among you will be your servant. 12 For whoever exalts himself will be humbled,
and whoever humbles himself will be exalted."

COMMENTARY

1 Perhaps a year earlier, Jesus had begun to denounce the Pharisees (15:7). Subsequently, he warned his disciples of the teaching of the Pharisees and Sadducees (16:5–12). Now his warnings and denunciations are public. Current scholarship tends to see "crowds" and "his disciples" either as unhistorical, perhaps an invented transition (Walker, *Heilsgeschichte*, 68–70), or else as an ambiguous pastiche of historical reminiscence and contemporizing, the "crowds" referring to Jews in Matthew's day and "disciples" to Christians in his day. All this is groundless. In the setting—the temple courts a few days before Passover (21:23)—crowds along with "disciples" and some religious authorities are to be expected. Matthew mentions both groups because he sees that the essential thrust of Jesus' warnings is to compel men to follow him—the Messiah as defined in 22:41–46—or the religious leaders. And those who do the latter will share their leaders' condemnation. The scene is therefore set for Jesus' lament over Jerusalem (vv.37–39) and the judgment that follows (chs. 24–25; cf. Garland, *Intention of Matthew 23*, 34–41).

2 Only here in Matthew do the Greek words behind "teachers of the law" and "Pharisees" take separate articles, implying two separate groups (cf. *Grammar*, 758–59). Therein lies a problem, for whereas "scribes" (NIV, "teachers of the law") had teaching authority, the Pharisees as such did not. Many were laymen without authority or responsibility to teach. Grundmann suggests that *kai* ("and") is epexegetical ("scribes, that is, the Pharisees"); Gaechter, that the phrase is a hendiadys ("scribes of the Pharisees"). But both views are unnatural and do not account for the use of "Pharisees" in ch. 23.

On the other hand, some hold that "Pharisees" represents Matthew's opponents in AD 85 and is therefore anachronistically inserted into the gospel (Kilpatrick, *Origins*, 113; Bonnard; and many others). Garland (*Intention of Matthew 23*, 44 n. 32, and 218–21), however, has pointed out that Luke attacks the Pharisees as vigorously as Matthew; yet no one holds that Pharisaic Judaism was a major concern for Luke's church. Walker (*Heilsgeschichte*, 20), van Tilborg (*Jewish Leaders*, 106), and Garland (pp. 43–46) conclude that all categories of Jewish leaders (Pharisee, scribe, Sadducee, chief priest, etc.) in Matthew lose all historical distinction and become synonymous, ciphers for Jewish leadership in general that failed to recognize Jesus as Messiah. But some passages preserve fine historical distinctions (e.g., 21:23), and it is intrinsically unlikely that a writer as sensitive to Jewish background as Matthew would use words so clumsily. The problem is one of demanding too narrow a definition of certain categories and, when they don't fit, charging the writer with anachronism.

A better approach is possible (see Carson, "Jewish Leaders"). The "teachers of the law," most of them Pharisees in Matthew's time, were primarily responsible for teaching. "Pharisee" defines a loose theological position, not a profession like "teacher." The two terms are distinct, even if there is much overlap on the personal level. An analogy might be the Puritan John Owen's denouncing "the prelates and Roman Catholics" and then continuing his discourse with epithets like "you prelates, you Catholics," "you prelates, Catholics." "Prelates" defines roles but does not mean that the only prelates are Catholics (some were Anglicans); the other—"Catholics"—defines theological position but does not require all Catholics to be prelates. This is how Jesus was attacking a theological position and those who promulgated it. Garland (*Intention of Matthew 23*, 117–23) argues that even if the ostensible targets of the "woes" are Jewish leaders, his immediate pastoral concern is to warn Christian leaders against similar hypocrisy.

These leaders "sit in Moses' seat." E. L. Sukenik (*Ancient Synagogues in Palestine and Greece* [London: Oxford Univ. Press, 1934], 57–61) has shown that synagogues had a stone seat at the front where the authoritative teacher, usually a *grammateus* ("teacher of the law," GK *1208*), sat. Moreover, "to sit on X's seat" often means "to succeed X" (Ex 11:5; 12:29; 1Ki 1:35, 46; 2:12; 16:11; 2Ki 15:12; Ps 132:12; cf. Josephus, *Ant.* 7.353 [14.5]; 18.2 [1.1]). This would imply that the "teachers of the law" are Moses' legal successors, possessing all his authority—a view the scribes themselves held (*m. Sanh.* 11:3; cf. Sir 45:15–17; *m. ʾAbot* 1:1; *m. Yebam.* 2:4; 9:3). Nevertheless, there is no convincing evidence that this seat was actually described in the first century as the "chair of Moses" (cf. Davies and Allison; Kenneth G. C. Newport, *The Sources and* Sitz im Leben *of Matthew 23* [JSNTSup 117; Sheffield: Sheffield Academic, 1995], 119–24).

3 The astounding authority conceded "the teachers of the law and the Pharisees" in v.2 becomes explicit in v.3. Even if the emphasis in v.3 falls at the end, where Jesus denounces the Jewish leaders' hypocrisy, the beginning of the verse gives them full authority in all they teach, even if they do not live up to it. *Panta hosa* ("everything") is a strong expression and cannot be limited to "that teaching of the law that is in Jesus' view a faithful interpretation of it"; it covers *everything* the leaders teach, including the oral tradition (Garland, *Intention of Matthew 23*, 48–49; contra Allen; Plummer; Stonehouse, *Witness of Matthew*, 196–97; and others). Nor does the text say their authority rests in their roles but not in their doctrine; on the contrary, v.3 affirms their doctrine but condemns their practice. Meier (*Law and History*, 106, 119, 156) argues that this pertains only to Jesus' earlier ministry but not to the church from the resurrection on. But this settles nothing, because Jesus has during his ministry repeatedly criticized the scribes and Pharisees for their teaching, not least their oral tradition (5:21–48; 15:3–14; 16:12), and will do so again (23:16–36), and he has just finished exposing their ignorance of the Scriptures (22:41–46).

Many scholars hold that vv.2–3 reflect an earlier tradition—a time when Matthew's church was still part of and under the authority of the Jewish leaders—and that somehow that early tradition was awkwardly preserved in a book that, on the whole, reflects later theological developments. But it is doubtful whether there ever was such a time (cf. Ac 3–4); in any case, the theory makes Matthew an extraordinarily incompetent editor.

The way around this thorny point, according to Schweizer, is to recognize that Matthew preserves vv.2–3 because the rupture between synagogue and church has not yet taken place—and so Matthew incorporates vv.2–3 to mollify and if possible win Jewish opponents, while at the same time giving a qualified interpretation of the statement in line with 5:17–20. The remarkable thing, however, is that vv.2–3 are not in themselves qualified but are about as strong as can be imagined. If Matthew was interested in preventing a threatening rupture in the alleged union between synagogue and church, why does he not elsewhere mitigate his strong denunciation of the Jewish leaders' teaching and include the praise of the scribe (Mk 12:34)? First-century readers were no less alert than we. Could they not see that the gospel repeatedly criticizes the Pharisees' doctrine, making the assurance of vv.2–3 empty and mocking?

Before proposing a solution, we must consider the force of v.4.

4 The Qumran covenanters called the Pharisees "the expounders of smooth things," because their casuistry made life easier than the covenanters themselves approved. To reconcile this Dead Sea Scrolls evidence with v.4, some have held that though the Pharisees made things easier for themselves, proving the covenanters right, they made it harder for everyone else; thus v.4 is correct (cf. Hill). The distinction is doubtful. Most Pharisees, including rabbis, worked in some full-time trade. They were not secluded scholars but active members of society. It is hard, therefore, to see how their rulings could benefit only themselves. We must not forget that the Dead Sea Scrolls came out of a monastic community that would negatively judge all rules less rigorous than their own. The real question about v.4 is whether (1) it contrasts in some way with vv.2–3 or (2) it merely illustrates v.3b. The latter will not stand close scrutiny (cf. Garland, *Intention of Matthew 23*, 50ff.).

Verse 4 speaks of the leaders' putting "heavy loads on men's shoulders"—laying down irksome rules—and then refusing "to lift a finger" to help. This does not mean they were unwilling to obey burdensome rules themselves (contra Bornkamm, "End-Expectation and the Church," 24; Schweizer) but that they refused to help those who collapsed under their rules (Manson, *Sayings of Jesus*, 101; McNeile; Filson; Garland, *Intention of Matthew 23*, 51). This is the natural interpretation of *kinēsai* ("to move," GK *3075*; cf. BDAG, 545) and fits the allusion to 11:28–30. Thus the Pharisees are unlike Jesus, whose burden is light and who promises rest. But this means that v.4 does more than illustrate v.3b; it shows how the Pharisees are by their teaching doing more harm than good.

Thus vv.2–3 stand alone in their emphasis; their contexts flatly contradict them. It will not do to treat vv.2–3 as a concession to the leaders that Matthew then modifies, a "rhetorical preparation" drawn from conservative tradition that the evangelist proceeds to modify (Banks, *Jesus and the Law*, 176; Garland, *Intention of Matthew 23*, 54–55), for the tension is too sharp. The only way to make sense of the text is to follow Jeremias (*New Testament Theology*, 210) and France (NICNT), who see in vv.2–3 an instance of biting irony bordering on sarcasm. This position is self-consistent and does not weaken the strong statements in vv.2–3. Moreover, it is strengthened by the verb *ekathisan* ("sit," GK *2767*) in v.2. The aorist is not normally translated as a present. In response, many point out that the same aorist verb is used in Mark 16:19; Hebrews 1:3; 8:1; 10:12; Revelation 3:21—all of which refer to Jesus as still sitting. But that misses the point. The emphasis in each of these instances is not that Jesus is still sitting, though that is doubtless presupposed, but on the fact that as a result of his triumph he *sat down*. The aorist does not *require* that the action be at one point in time; it is the context that in each of these instances presupposes it. Moreover, the gnomic aorist in the indicative mood (which is how the NIV's "sit" takes the Greek in v.2) is so rare in the NT that it should not be our first option. But if vv.2–3a are ironic, then the aorist can have its natural force: the teachers of the law and the Pharisees *sat down* in Moses' seat (NASB, "have seated themselves," which may be overtranslated but has the right idea). The Jewish religious leaders have "presumed" to sit in Moses' seat (so Adalbert Merx, *Das Evangelium Matthaeus* [Berlin: Reimer, 1902]; Moulton, *Grammar: Prolegomena*, 458; Zahn). It is, of course, of no help to say that such a translation must be followed in v.3a by "therefore, pay no attention to what they say" (contra Plummer; Banks, *Jesus and the Law*, 175; Garland, *Intention of Matthew 23*, 48), for v.3a continues the irony. This generates a neat chiasm:

A: v.2—the leaders have taken on Moses' teaching authority—irony
    B: v.3a—do what they say—irony
    B': v.3b—do not do what they do—nonironical advice
A': v.4—their teaching merely binds men—nonironical advice

Thus the first two elements are ironic, and the last two reveal in reverse order the painful futility of following the teachers of the law. Jesus warns the crowds and his disciples in the sharpest way possible. The reluctance of many scholars to admit that vv.2–3 are biting irony overlooks the tone of much of this chapter (e.g., vv.23–28) and superb parallels elsewhere in the NT (e.g., 1Co 4:8a, 10).

5–7 These verses illustrate some of the leaders' practices not to be copied (v.3b; cf. Mk 12:38–39; Lk 20:46). Jesus accuses them of being time servers and applause seekers (cf. 6:1–18). "Phylacteries" (v.5) were small leather or parchment boxes containing a piece of vellum inscribed with four texts from the law (Ex 13:1–10, 11–16; Dt 6:4–9; 11:13–21). They were worn on the arm or tied to the forehead (Ex 13:9, 16; Dt 6:8; 11:18, though originally these passages were probably metaphorical). The peculiar term used here only in the NT has pagan associations ("amulet") and may insinuate that the *tôṭāpōt* ("frontlets," as they were called, though they are now referred to by Jews as *tᵉpillîn* [lit., "prayers"]) had become like pagan charms (cf. *ZPEB*, 4:786–87; Str-B, 4:250–76; Urbach, *Sages*, 1:130, 366–67).

To show their piety to the world, these leaders made large, showy phylacteries. The same ostentation affected the length of tassels, worn by all Jews (including Jesus, 9:20; 14:36) on the corners of the outer garment, in obedience to Numbers 15:37–41 and Deuteronomy 22:12. (The view that *kraspeda* ["tassels," GK *3192*] means "borders" [KJV] of garments is unlikely in this context; cf. BDAG, 564; on the details of Jewish ritualism, see Schürer, *History of the Jewish People*, 2:479ff.)

Seeking a reputation for piety goes with seeking places of honor at great dinners or the most important seats—as close as possible to the law scrolls—in the synagogues (v.6). "Rabbi" (v.7), the transliteration of the Hebrew word meaning "my master" or "my teacher," was used in Hillel's time, a generation before Jesus, but it probably did not signify official ordination until after the fall of Jerusalem. The title, originally merely a mark of respect, was applied to Jesus (26:25, 49; Jn 1:38; 3:26). But like other common terms, it became inflated. By Talmudic times a rabbi's status was immense. His disciple had to obey him without question, never walk beside or in front of him, never greet him first, and so forth (cf. Moses Abelbach, "The Relations between Master and Disciple in the Talmudic Age," in *Essays Presented to Chief Rabbi Brodie* [ed. H. J. Zimmels; London: Soncino, 1966–1967], 1:1–24; Albright and Mann). The situation had not developed so far in Jesus' day, but if the process had begun, one can well imagine Jesus' exposing it (esp. in light of 18:1–5; 20:25–28; see Introduction, section 11.f).

8–10 The "you" (v.8) is emphatic, but this does not mean that vv.8–10 are out of place in an address before a mixed audience. It is not implausible that out of the crowd Jesus is here speaking primarily to his disciples, just as he later addresses the Pharisees directly (vv.13–36). A good preacher knows that forthright words about what is required of believers can be at the same time a powerful incentive to decision on the part of the sympathetic but uncommitted. These verses could, therefore, serve as warning not to follow the "teachers of the law and the Pharisees" while laying down normative patterns for relationships among Jesus' disciples.

Unlike the religious authorities, Jesus says, his disciples are not to be called "Rabbi" (v.8), for they have but one *didaskalos* (GK *1437*; better rendered "Teacher" than "Master"). The "one Teacher" is not God but Jesus himself (cf. v.10), but either way, in view of 22:41–46; 23:4, 13–36, this verse not only proscribes self-exaltation in teaching divine things but rejects the authority of the religious teachers of Jesus' day. Such authority has been taken from them (see comments at 21:43). Among those who follow Jesus, a brotherly relationship (see comments at 5:22–24, 47; 18:15, 21, 35; 25:40; 28:10) is required.

Verse 9 moves from "Rabbi" or "Teacher" to "father." To the best of our knowledge, rabbis were not directly addressed as "fathers." Some have, therefore, argued that the text is referring to the patriarchs and is saying, "Do not rely on your racial tie to Abraham, Isaac, and Jacob" (cf. 3:9; so J.T. Townsend, "Matthew xxiii.9," *JTS* 12 [1961]: 56–59; Schweizer; and others). Nothing in the context supports this, still less the suggestion that Greek Stoicism stands in the background (van Tilborg, *Jewish Leaders*, 138). But K. Kohler ("Abba, Father: Title of Spiritual Leader and Saint," *JQR* 13 [1900–1901]: 567–80) showed long ago that "the fathers" became a very common way of referring to earlier teachers of the law, especially the great masters (cf. Urbach, *Sages*, 1:186; 2:906 n. 38; hence the Mishnaic tractate *ʾAbot*, "The Fathers"). The practice may have stretched back to the days of the prophets (cf. 2Ki 2:12).

"On earth" does not mean the "fathers" were alive in Jesus' time but simply contrasts them with the Father in heaven. Their domain is not exalted enough to warrant the latter title. This explains the change from the passive ("do not be called," vv.8, 10) to the active ("do not call [i.e., someone else," v.9): "do not be called" would be inappropriate since the title was not bestowed until after the teachers of law died and were memorialized. There may be an allusion to Malachi 2:7–10. Like the priests of Malachi's day whose teaching caused many to stumble, so the revered Jewish fathers have so misinterpreted Scripture that they must not be called "fathers." There is but one Father, God.

But where, then, is the voice of authoritative teaching? Jesus returns to that theme in v.10, completing an A-B-A chiasm. Thus v.10 largely repeats v.8, using a different word for "Teacher" (see Notes); but it is not repetitious, still less anticlimactic, because it ends by identifying the sole Teacher as the Christ, the Messiah (Kingsbury, *Structure*, 93). This not only picks up the theme of 1:1 and 16:16 but echoes the confrontation in 22:41–46 regarding Messiah. Jesus' enemies, the certified teachers of Israel, could not answer basic biblical questions about the Messiah. Now he, Jesus the Messiah, declares in the wake of that travesty that he himself is the only one qualified to sit in Moses' seat—to succeed him as authoritative Teacher of God's will and mind.

Two further observations need to be made. First, it is untrue to Jesus' teaching to deduce from this passage that no Jewish leader was sympathetic to his cause or that there is no place for distinctions in roles or respect for leaders in his church, any more than his prohibition of oaths (5:33–37) means it is unchristian to swear an oath in court. Certainly Jesus was not justifying that particularly perverse pride that cloaks itself in discourtesy. Yet once this has been noted, we must say that the risen Christ is as displeased with those in his church who demand unquestioning submission to themselves and their opinions and confuse a reputation for showy piety with godly surrender to his teaching as he ever was with any Pharisee.

Second, the continuing modern discussion as to what these verses show about the structure of Matthew's church finds no valid source here. For instance, Hummel (*Auseinandersetzung*, 27–28) holds that vv.8–10 show that there must have been a sort of Christian rabbinate in Matthew's day that Matthew was combating or attempting to guide. That may be so, but the text does not say so. In any case, other reasons for Matthew's including this material spring readily to mind. If Matthew *is* concerned to show Christian-Jewish readers of his own day "how we got from there to here," and if this material is basically authentic, no further reason is needed. The truth is that we know about Matthew's situation only from what he chose to write about Jesus, not a late first-century church.

11–12 The substance of v.11 is in 20:26: Matthew repeatedly emphasizes humility. For instances of exalting oneself, see comments at 20:20–28;

of humbling oneself, see comments at 18:4 (cf. Pr 15:33; 22:4; Jas 4:6; 1Pe 5:5–6). "Will be your servant," "will be humbled," and "will be exalted" are pure futures without imperatival force (contra Zerwick, *Biblical Greek*, para. 280). The latter two could not be otherwise; so v.11 should be read the same way. The principle enunciated in these verses reflects not natural law but kingdom law: the eschatological reward will humble the self-exalted and exalt the self-humbled, after the pattern in Ezekiel 21:26. What is commended is humility, not humbug; service, not servility. The supreme example—the Messiah himself—makes this clear (20:26–28), for his astonishing humility and service to others was untainted by servility and was perfectly compatible with exercising the highest authority. Having done the greatest service, he has been most highly exalted.

NOTES

4 For the variant "and hard to carry" (as in Lk 11:46), see Metzger, *Textual Commentary*, 59–60.

8 For literature on the question of whether this use of "Rabbi" is anachronistic, see Garland, *Intention of Matthew 23*, 58; Sigal, *Halakhah of Jesus*.

9 The Greek word order suggests the rendering "for, for you there is only one Father—the heavenly Father" (Moule, *Idiom Book*, 166).

10 Καθηγητής (*kathēgētēs*, "teacher") is used only here in the NT. Many suggestions have been made as to why it should replace "rabbi" and διδάσκαλος (*didaskalos*, "teacher") in v.8. Some have assumed it to be Matthew's translation for Gentile readers (Grundmann; Strecker, *Weg der Gerechtigkeit*, 217) or an addition to dissociate Jesus from Hellenistic teachers as much as from "teachers of the law" (Frankemölle, *Jahwebund und Kirche Christi*, 99–100). C. Spicq ("Une Allusion au Docteur de Justice dans Matthieu, XXIII, 10?" *RB* 66 [1959]: 393–96) suggests the word is the Greek equivalent of the Hebrew מוֹרֶה (*môreh*, "teacher), used in the Dead Sea Scrolls for the "Teacher of Righteousness" at Qumran. Jesus is then seen as denouncing the sectarian religious authorities as well as the scribes. But the linguistic evidence is unconvincing, and it seems wiser to take καθηγητής, *kathēgētēs*, as a synonym for διδάσκαλος, *didaskalos*, possibly prompted by homophony with ἐκάθισαν (*ekathisan*, "they sat down") and καθέδρα (*kathedra*, "seat") in v.2. "This would be further evidence that the authority of the scribes and Pharisees is null and void for Matthew" (Garland, *Intention of Matthew 23*, 60 n. 100).

(2) The seven woes (23:13–32)

OVERVIEW

Compare the six woes of Luke 11:37–54. The overlaps are considerable, but the differences in order and wording are no less remarkable. The three chief options are (1) Luke preserves the correct setting, and Matthew adds the woes to the end of 23:1–12; (2) Matthew preserves the correct setting, and Luke inserts some of the woes into his narrative; and (3) Jesus pronounced such woes on the Pharisees fairly frequently, perhaps following the pattern of the six woes of Isaiah 5:8–23 or the five woes of Habakkuk 2:6–20. (For discussion, see Marshall, *Gospel of Luke*, 491–93.)

The seven woes Matthew records fit into a neat chiastic pattern:

A: First woe (v.13)—failing to recognize Jesus as the Messiah
  B: Second woe (v.15)—superficially zealous, yet doing more harm than good
    C: Third woe (vv.16–22)—misguided use of the Scripture
      D: Fourth woe (vv.23–24)—fundamental failure to discern the thrust of Scripture
    C': Fifth woe (vv.25–26)—misguided use of the Scripture
  B': Sixth woe (vv.27–28)—superficially zealous, yet doing more harm than good
A': Seventh woe (vv.29–32)—heirs of those who failed to recognize the prophets

What stands out is the centrality of rightly understanding the Scriptures—a theme that is reflected in all the preceding controversies and is no less related to Jesus' rejection of the claims of the teachers of the law.

(a) First woe (23:13 [14])

13"Woe to you, teachers of the law and Pharisees, you hypocrites! You shut the kingdom of heaven in men's faces. You yourselves do not enter, nor will you let those enter who are trying to."

COMMENTARY

13 [14] Verse 14 must be taken as an interpolation, derived from Mark 12:40; Luke 20:47. This is made clear, not only by its absence from the best and earliest Matthew MSS, but from the fact that the MSS that do include it divide on where to place it—before or after v.13. (For the meaning of v.14, see Derrett, *Studies in the New Testament*, 8–27.)

Verse 13 contains the first of seven "woes." A "woe" can be a compassionate "alas!" (24:19), a strong condemnation (11:21), or a combination of the two (18:17; 26:24). In Matthew 23, condemnation predominates, but it is neither vindictive nor spiteful so much as judicial. Jesus the Messiah pronounces judgment.

"Teachers of the law" and "Pharisees" are anarthrous from here on throughout the chapter (see comments at 2:4; 3:7; 23:2; Introduction, section 11.f). (For "hypocrites," see comments at 6:2; for "kingdom of heaven," see comments at 3:2.) The syntax of v.13 (see Notes) assumes that the messianic reign has begun. The teachers of the law and the Pharisees are "hypocrites" since they claim to teach God's way but refuse to enter the messianic kingdom and hinder those who try to do so. This does not refer to their casuistry that obscured fundamental questions of conduct and made it difficult for people to obey God's law fully, though this is the dominant interpretation (e.g., Hill). Conduct is not mentioned here, only entrance into the kingdom. Though proper conduct is essential, it admits no one into the kingdom.

The last controversy (22:41–46) reveals the real failure: the teachers of the law and the Pharisees do not enter the kingdom because they refuse to recognize who Jesus is. When the crowds begin to marvel at Jesus and suggest he may be the Messiah, the authorities do all they can to dissuade them (cf. 9:33–34;11:19; 12:23–24; 21:15). The sheep of Israel are "lost" (10:6; 15:24) because the shepherds have led them astray. The "woe" pronounced on the authorities is, therefore, of a piece with 18:6–7.

NOTES

13 The present substantival participle τοὺς εἰσερχομένους (*tous eiserchomenous*, "those entering") need not in itself have present force but can refer to sustained effort in the past (as in 2:20; for discussion, see BDF, para. 339 [3]; *Grammar*, 858–64, 891–92; Zerwick, *Biblical Greek*, para. 274). However, in the context of the present finite verb οὐδὲ ... ἀφίετε (*oude ... aphiete*, "nor ... do you permit"), there can be no doubt that the action envisaged by both participle and finite verb is portrayed as simultaneous with the speaker's words.

(b) Second woe (23:15)

15"Woe to you, teachers of the law and Pharisees, you hypocrites! You travel over land and sea to win a single convert, and when he becomes one, you make him twice as much a son of hell as you are."

COMMENTARY

15 External sources for assessing the Pharisees' zeal to win converts are not easy to interpret. Scholars are sharply divided as to how much proselytism took place, and how successful it was. A sizable body of primarily older scholarship argues that the first century AD until the fall of Jerusalem marks a remarkable period of Jewish missionary zeal (see esp. B. J. Bamberger, *Proselytism in the Talmudic Period* [Cincinnati, Ohio: Hebrew Union, 1939]; W. G. Braude, *Jewish Proselytizing in the First Five Centuries of the Common Era* [Providence, R.I.: Brown Univ. Press, 1940]; F. M. Derwacter, *Preparing the Way for Paul: The Proselyte Movement in Later Judaism* [New York: Macmillan, 1930]; Jeremias, *Jesus' Promise*, 11ff.; cf. Ro 2:24). Clearly both Philo and Josephus (esp. the latter's *Against Apion*) constitute attempts to commend Judaism to outsiders. Not the least important fact, as W. Paul Bowers observed ("Studies in Paul's Understanding of His Mission" [PhD diss., Cambridge University, 1976]), is that there is no evidence that Jews in any way opposed Paul's or anyone else's Christian Gentile mission; rather, what they disputed was the basis of admission to the people of God.

On the other hand, Scot McKnight (*A Light among the Gentiles: Jewish Mission in the Second Temple Period* [Minneapolis: Fortress, 1991], esp. 106–8) argues that much of the Pharisees' activity, especially in Palestine, was aimed at converting to their views those who had already become loose adherents of Judaism (cf. Josephus, *Ant.* 20.34–48 [2.3–4]). Whether the scribes and Pharisees were winning raw pagans or sympathizers of Judaism, they were winning them to their own position. Such converts, therefore, would not be converts to Judaism but to Pharisaism. Pharisees and teachers of the law would travel extensively to make one "proselyte"—a word used in the NT only here and in Acts 2:11; 6:5; 13:43, and one that at this time probably refers to those who have been circumcised and have pledged to submit to the full rigors of Jewish law, including the oral tradition for which the Pharisees were so zealous.

Jesus did not criticize the *fact* of the Pharisees' extensive missionary effort but its *results*: the "converts" became twice as much a "son of hell" (see comments at 5:22) as the scribes and Pharisees who won them—i.e., someone who belongs to hell and is destined for hell. This means that the Pharisees' interpretations and the rules deduced from Scripture became so fully those of their converts that they "out-Phariseed" the Pharisees. Psychologically, this is entirely possible, as every teacher of converts knows. As for the converts of whom Jesus was speaking, the Pharisees' teaching locked them into a theological frame that left no room for Jesus Messiah and therefore no possibility of entering the messianic kingdom.

(c) Third woe (23:16–22)

16"Woe to you, blind guides! You say, 'If anyone swears by the temple, it means nothing; but if anyone swears by the gold of the temple, he is bound by his oath.' 17You blind fools! Which is greater: the gold, or the temple that makes the gold sacred? 18You also say, 'If anyone swears by the altar, it means nothing; but if anyone swears by the gift on it, he is bound by his oath.' 19You blind men! Which is greater: the gift, or the altar that makes the gift sacred? 20Therefore, he who swears by the altar swears by it and by everything on it. 21And he who swears by the temple swears by it and by the one who dwells in it. 22And he who swears by heaven swears by God's throne and by the one who sits on it."

COMMENTARY

16–22 See comments at 5:33–37 for the background and thrust of these verses. The striking designation "blind guides" (v.16) was introduced at 15:14. The "temple" here is *naos* (see comments at 4:5).

Because of the references to the temple—its gold, altar, and offerings—a surprising number of scholars focus on Matthew's attitude toward the cultic aspects of the temple (Hummel, *Auseinandersetzung*, 78–82; van Tilborg, *Jewish Leaders*, 105). This quite misses the point (Gaston, *No Stone*, 94). The pericope simply uses the language of the cultus in discussing the kinds of distinctions in oaths often favored in Jewish circles. Saul Lieberman (*Greek in Jewish Palestine* [New York: Jewish Theological Seminary, 1942], 115–43), after studying the difficult and conflicting Jewish evidence, argues that the rabbis fought the abuses of oaths and vows among the unlearned masses. This is doubtless so. But the way they fought them was by differentiating between what was binding and what was not. In that sense, wittingly or unwittingly, they encouraged evasive oaths and therefore lying. Jesus cut through these complexities by insisting that men must tell the truth.

Some writers have supposed that 5:33–37—which, formally at least, abolishes oaths—contradicts 23:20–22, which maintains that all oaths are binding but does not abolish them. In fact, however, vv.20–22 provide the rationale for 5:33–37. All oaths are in some way related to God. All are, therefore, binding, and thus evasive oaths are disallowed. On the other hand, the heart of the issue is telling the truth. It is probably a new kind of casuistry that, failing to see this, insists that Jesus in 5:33–37 abolishes all oaths of every kind.

In the context of Matthew 23, Jesus charges the teachers of the law and the Pharisees with mishandling the Scriptures they claimed to defend and promulgate.

REFLECTIONS

References to the temple and the cultus, which no longer existed after AD 70, do not prove that this gospel was composed before that date, since Matthew, writing later, may be incorporating older material and describing what Jesus said at the time of his ministry. But the pericope is consistent with an early date. More important, if we think instead that Matthew writes about AD 85 but carefully preserves the right tense and distinctions appropriate to Jesus' ministry, why should we not expect him to be equally careful elsewhere?

(d) Fourth woe (23:23–24)

23"Woe to you, teachers of the law and Pharisees, you hypocrites! You give a tenth of your spices—mint, dill and cummin. But you have neglected the more important matters of the law—justice, mercy and faithfulness. You should have practiced the latter, without neglecting the former. 24You blind guides! You strain out a gnat but swallow a camel."

COMMENTARY

23–24 The OT law on tithing (Dt 14:22–29) specifies grain, wine, and oil, though Leviticus 27:30 is more comprehensive. Certainly in the first century, there was debate about how far the law of tithing should extend. The consensus was to include greens and garden herbs (v.23; Str-B, 1:932). Jesus does not condemn scrupulous observance in these things ("without neglecting the former") but insists that to fuss over them while neglecting the "more important matters of the law" (cf. 22:34–40)—justice, mercy, and *pistis* (GK *4411*; here rightly translated "faithfulness")—is to strain out a gnat but swallow a camel (v.24), both unclean creatures.

Several points deserve notice.

1. The "weightier" matters are not the "more difficult" or "harder" but the "more central," "most decisive" (Ridderbos, *Coming of the Kingdom*, 302) or (as in NIV) "more important" versus "peripheral"

or trifling ones (cf. *TDNT*, 1:554, 558; Kaiser, "Weightier and Lighter Matters," 184).

2. Yet it goes much too far to interpret vv.23–24 as expanding the love command into the central feature of the law (see comments at 22:34–40 and literature cited there; also Garland, *Intention of Matthew 23*, 139).

3. In essence, what Jesus accuses the teachers of the law and the Pharisees of is a massive distortion of God's will as revealed in Scripture. At a fundamental level, they fail to focus on the thrust of Scripture, a point made with equal force in the two references to Hosea 6:6 in this gospel (see comments at 9:9–13; 12:1–14).

4. The chiastic structure of the "woes" centers on this fourth one, where the basic failure of the Pharisaic teachers is laid bare. Moving out from this center, it becomes clear that where Scripture is interpreted by the Pharisees, there is danger of misappropriation of truth (woes 3 and 5) and of corrupting other people (woes 2 and 6), coupled with blindness to true revelation when it comes supremely in the person of Jesus the Messiah (woes 1 and 7).

5. All this presupposes that Jesus holds readers of the OT responsible for discerning its purpose and recognizing its most important emphases (see comments at 22:40). Only those who do this please God and recognize the Messiah (cf. Lk 24:44–46; Jn 5:39–40).

6. The current debate over the words "without neglecting the former"—namely, whether they show Jesus or Matthew as a very conservative interpreter of the law, or whether they can possibly come from the historical Jesus (cf. Garland, *Intention of Matthew 23*, 140 n. 66; Westerholm, *Jesus and Scribal Authority*, 58–59)—badly misses the point. For neither Jesus nor Matthew do these verses focus on the problem of continuity/discontinuity between the OT and the reign of Jesus Messiah but on the relative importance of material within the OT. Jesus describes what the Pharisees should have done; he is not here questioning how the "former" will relate to the reign he now inaugurates (12:28) or the church he will build (16:19), any more than in vv.16–22 he discusses what role the temple altar plays under the new covenant.

NOTES

24 Black (*Aramaic Approach*, 175–76) points out that in Aramaic this saying would be something of a pun, since "gnat" and "camel" sound much alike: קַלְמָא (*qalmāʾ*) and גַּלְמָא (*galmāʾ*) respectively.

(e) Fifth woe (23:25–26)

25"Woe to you, teachers of the law and Pharisees, you hypocrites! You clean the outside of the cup and dish, but inside they are full of greed and self-indulgence. 26Blind Pharisee! First clean the inside of the cup and dish, and then the outside also will be clean."

COMMENTARY

25–26 The most common interpretation of these verses is that Jesus begins with the metaphor of the cup and dish (v.25a), reveals his nonmetaphorical concerns in the last words of v.25, then returns to his metaphor in v.26 now that its real purpose has been exposed. The Pharisees have been occupied with external religion instead of that of the inner person. Within themselves they remain "full of greed and self-indulgence [*akrasia*, found in the NT only here and in 1Co 7:5]." In the metaphor, cleaning the inside is basic and guarantees cleanliness of the outside.

Jacob Neusner ("First Cleanse the Inside," *NTS* 22 [1976]: 486–95) holds, largely on form-critical grounds, that pre–AD 70 Judaism was divided on the issue of clean vessels. The Hillelites thought that cleaning the inside of a vessel declared it "clean." The Shammaites, predominant before AD 70, held it was necessary to cleanse both inside and outside; the one did not affect the status of the other (cf. *m. Kelim* 2:1; 25:1, 7–9; *y. Ber.* 8:2). Consequently, Jesus could not be refuting the Hillelites (who did not become predominant until after AD 70), telling them *first* to cleanse the inside, since they would have cleaned *only* the inside. Rather, the admonition was for the Shammaites.

From this debate about cleansing, it is argued, the saying was variously interpreted and applied (cf. Lk 11:41) in metaphorical ways. Garland (*Intention of Matthew 23*, 148–50) thinks the first part of v.25 is literal but was taken over by Matthew to make his point. In his view, the *ek* clause should not be rendered "full of greed and self-indulgence" but "full *because* of greed and self-indulgence" (Turner, *Syntax*, 260; Schweizer, McNeile, and others think this is possible). In other words, Matthew turns the original saying into one that says the inside is most important but then draws "attention to the fact that the vessels were filled with food and drink which was [*sic*] obtained unjustly and consumed intemperately—a circumstance which cultic washing could not cleanse—and ultimately made the entire issue moot" (Garland, *Intention of Matthew 23*, 149).

This interpretation will not do. The Pharisees were not as a class intemperate in food and drink but abstemious (cf. Lk 18:11–12). Moreover, if they were full *because* of greed and self-indulgence, the preceding "but" is nonsensical: the first clause should read "you empty the cup and dish," not "you clean the outside." Rather, the kind of historical background envisaged by Neusner is being used by Jesus to point away from the ceremonial question altogether. The Pharisees (here Shammaites) debate about what must be cleansed for a cup to be clean, without seeing that they themselves need to become inwardly clean. This approach is very close to the traditional interpretation of these verses (above; cf. Westerholm, *Jesus and Scribal Authority*, 85–90). Yet it also hints that Jesus holds that OT ceremonial distinctions have moral implications the avoiding of which betrays deep misunderstanding.

"Blind Pharisee!" (v.26, the singular has generic force), says the one who came to save his people from their sin (1:21), "first clean the inside ..., and then the outside also will be clean." "Inside" does not here encourage privatized pietism but total moral renewal in terms of "justice, mercy and faithfulness." The "outside," the bits of religious observance easily seen by men, will then take care of itself.

(f) Sixth woe (23:27–28)

[27]"Woe to you, teachers of the law and Pharisees, you hypocrites! You are like whitewashed tombs, which look beautiful on the outside but on the inside are full of dead men's bones and everything unclean. [28]In the same way, on the outside you appear to people as righteous but on the inside you are full of hypocrisy and wickedness."

COMMENTARY

27–28 During the month of Adar, just before Passover, it was customary to whitewash with lime graves or grave sites that might not be instantly identified as such (v.27), in order to warn pilgrims to steer clear of the area and avoid ritual uncleanness from contact with corpses (cf. *m. Šeqal.* 1:1; *m. Kelim* 1:4; *m. Moʿed Qaṭ.* 1:2; *m. Maʿaś. Š.* 5:1). Such uncleanness would prevent participation in the Passover (*m. Kelim* 1:4; for similar concerns, see Jn 11:55; 18:28). But in that case, whitewashed tombs would not have been objects of beauty ("which look beautiful on the outside") but of disgust. They were places to be shunned (cf. Lk 11:44, which mentions neither whitewash nor beauty).

Various solutions have been put forward (for a list, see S.T. Lachs, "On Matthew 23:27–28," *HTR* 68 [1975]: 385–88). Perhaps the best proposal is Garland's (*Intention of Matthew 23*, 150–57), who suggests that the graves were beautiful because of their structure (cf. v.29), not their whitewash. Monuments were normally considered pure unless marked with whitewash; so if the memorial was built right over a grave, it would probably be whitewashed. Thus Jesus' mention of whitewashing has nothing to do with the beauty of sepulchers but is a further thrust at the Pharisees based on their distinctive preoccupation with avoiding defilement from corpses (cf. *b. B. Qam.* 57a; *b. B. Meṣ.* 85b). Jesus is saying that the scribes and Pharisees are sources of uncleanness just as much as the whitewashed graves are. There may also be an allusion to the white linen clothes that some men, impressed with their own eminence, used to wear (cf. *b. Qidd.* 72a; *b. Šabb.* 25b; *b. Ned.* 20b; Josephus, *J.W.* 2.123 [8.3]).

In the context of Matthew 23, the point Jesus was making is not that the scribes and Pharisees were deliberate and self-conscious but that in their scrupulous regulations they appeared magnificently virtuous but were actually contaminating the people. This woe parallels the second (v.15). The supreme irony is that their preoccupation with their law (*nomos*, GK *3795*) left them steeped in *anomia*—a general term for "wickedness" (v.28, GK *490*; cf. 13:41; see *TDNT*, 4:1085–86), but which may here suggest that their fundamental approach to the law was in fact, from the perspective of Jesus' hermeneutic, plain "lawlessness."

(g) Seventh woe (23:29–32)

[29]"Woe to you, teachers of the law and Pharisees, you hypocrites! You build tombs for the prophets and decorate the graves of the righteous. [30]And you say, 'If we had lived

in the days of our forefathers, we would not have taken part with them in shedding the blood of the prophets.' [31]So you testify against yourselves that you are the descendants of those who murdered the prophets. [32]Fill up, then, the measure of the sin of your forefathers!"

COMMENTARY

29–30 Derrett (*Studies in the New Testament*, 2:68ff.) denies that Pharisees in Jesus' day would have been involved in building memorial tombs, but his evidence is late and may well represent reaction against earlier excesses (cf. Garland, *Intention of Matthew 23*, 164). Herod led the way in tomb building (cf. Josephus, *Ant.* 16.179–82 [7.1]; 18.108 [4.6]; 20.95 [4.3])—to atone for his attempts to plunder them! Jewish building was more likely to be commemorative; by erecting monuments, the religious leaders thought themselves morally and spiritually above their forebears who had persecuted the prophets whose monuments they were building (v.29). They believed that they would not have joined their forebears in murdering the prophets (v.30)—just as many Christians today naively think they would have responded better to Jesus than the disciples or the crowds that cried, "Crucify him!"

31 But the distinction the Jews draw in v.30 Jesus now denies. Their own saying (not the tomb building) testifies against them. They speak of their forefathers and so acknowledge themselves to be the sons (NIV, "descendants") of those who shed the blood of the prophets. But Jesus sees further irony here, based on the ambiguity of "fathers" and "sons" (see comments at 5:9). The Jews think in terms of their physical descent. Jesus responds by saying in effect that they are sons all right—more than they realize. They show their paternity by resembling their fathers. While piously claiming to be different, they are already plotting ways to put an end to Jesus (21:38–39, 46).

32 The conclusion is defiant and ironical. The idea behind "the measure of the sin" is that God can tolerate only so much sin; then, when the measure is "full," he must respond in wrath (cf. Ge 15:16; 1Th 2:14–16). The idea is common in the intertestamental literature (e.g., *Jub.* 14:16; *1 En.* 50:2; 2 Esd 4:36–37; 4Q185 2:9–10), but never before was the concept applied to Israel.

(3) Conclusion (23:33–36)

[33]"You snakes! You brood of vipers! How will you escape being condemned to hell?
[34]Therefore I am sending you prophets and wise men and teachers. Some of them you will
kill and crucify; others you will flog in your synagogues and pursue from town to town. [35]And
so upon you will come all the righteous blood that has been shed on earth, from the blood
of righteous Abel to the blood of Zechariah son of Berekiah, whom you murdered between
the temple and the altar. [36]I tell you the truth, all this will come upon this generation."

COMMENTARY

33 See comments at 3:7 and 12:34 for the epithets. The transition from the preceding verse is clear: If the teachers of the law and Pharisees are filling up the measure of the sin of their forefathers, how can they possibly escape the condemnation of hell (see comments at 5:22; 23:15)?

34 If this verse shares a common source (Q?) with Luke 11:49 (see comments at 23:1–12), the differences between Matthew and Luke are noteworthy, though perhaps not quite so problematic as many think. The most noteworthy feature is the change from "the wisdom of God" (NIV, "God in his wisdom") as the sender of the emissaries to an emphatic "I." Not only is there little doubt that Christians identified Jesus with God's wisdom, but he who assigned to himself messianic titles and even OT texts referring exclusively to Yahweh would not have hesitated to make the same identification. Matthew's interpretation is, therefore, not necessarily wrong, even if a single saying stands behind both Luke and Matthew; it certainly has the result of emphasizing Jesus' authority (cf. Orton, *Understanding Scribe*, 154–55).

Hare (*Theme of Jewish Persecution*, 87–88) thinks the introductory *dia touto* ("Because of this," Lk 11:49; "Therefore," v.34) is drastically altered. In Luke, it refers to Luke 11:47–48—a tacit admission of blood-guiltiness for the prophets' death and for which reason "the wisdom of God" sends more prophets so that "this generation" (Lk 11:50) will be accountable. In Matthew, however, vv.32–33 separate the tacit admission from *dia touto* ("Therefore," v.34) so that the connective no longer explains God's wisdom in the past but an act Jesus performed in the present. But Hare's contrast is exaggerated. It is formally correct that *dia touto* in Luke 11:49 explains a statement made in the past by the wisdom of God. But this explains only that a statement was made, not the statement's content—which refers to an act done in the present, namely, Jesus' sending emissaries. Thus the two renderings of *dia touto* are very close and share the same function: they point out that because of the Jewish leaders' wicked reception of God's messengers, more messengers will "therefore" be sent; and they will be treated the same way. This will fill up the full measure of iniquity, and judgment will fall.

Luke (11:49) has "prophets and apostles," Matthew "prophets and wise men and teachers." The "wise man" and the "teacher" were "materially identical" (Garland, *Intention of Matthew 23*, 175; cf. *TDNT*, 8:505–7) at this time. Both Matthew and Luke here look forward to the sending out of Christian missionaries—disciples of Jesus (cf. 5:10–12; 9:37–38; 28:18–20). The terms used do not reflect post–AD 70 terminology (cf. van Tilborg, *Jewish Leaders*, 140–41).

Matthew adds "crucify." There is no evidence Jews used crucifixion as a mode of capital punishment after 63 BC. "Crucify" may mean "cause to be crucified" (as in Ac 2:36; 4:10), surely a better possibility than Hare's suggestion (*Theme of Jewish Persecution*, 89–92) that the words "and crucify" are a gloss on what Matthew wrote. Garland (*Intention of Matthew 23*, 177) holds that "and crucify" refers to Jesus' death. But this, too, requires a causative sense and seems strange when it is Jesus who is sending the emissaries to their deaths and Jesus who is (in this view) among those sent and killed. Perhaps v.34 echoes 10:24–25: the servant is not above his master. If Jesus is to be crucified, his servants may expect the same.

35 The very messengers who were beaten and killed for calling the people to repentance in the mystery of providence fill up the measure of the people's sin (v.32)—namely, shedding righteous blood of God's emissaries from Abel to Zechariah (see Notes). Verse 35 anticipates 27:24–25: Pilate tries to evade responsibility for crucifying Jesus, and the Jews clamor for that same dreadful responsibility because of their skepticism about who Jesus is. On the question of alleged anti-Semitism, see comments at 26:57–68.

36 All along in this chapter, the teachers of the law and the Pharisees have been Jesus' primary target. Now the reference is to "this generation," because the leaders represent the people (see comments at 21:43); and the people, despite Jesus' warnings, do not abandon their leaders for Jesus Messiah. This sets the stage for the concluding lament over Jerusalem (vv.37–39).

NOTES

34 On flogging, see comments at 10:17; on persecution from city to city, see 10:23; Acts 9:2; 13:50–51; 14:4–7; 17:10–15. On indifference toward and harsh treatment of OT prophets, see 1 Kings 18:4, 13; 19:10, 14; 2 Kings 17:13–17; 1 Chronicles 16:22; 2 Chronicles 24:19; 36:14–16; Psalm 105:15; Jeremiah 7:25–26; 25:4; 26:5, 20–23; 29:19; 35:15; 44:4; Lamentations 2:20; 4:16.

35 Abel is the first victim of murder in the Scriptures (Ge 4:8). The identity of this "Zechariah son of Berekiah" is problematic. Principal possibilities include:

1. It could refer to Zechariah the father of John the Baptist, but there is no evidence he was martyred.

2. It could be Zechariah son of Baris or Baruch or Bariscaeus (MSS vary), who was murdered by two Zealots in the temple (Josephus, *J.W.* 4.334–44 [5.4]). But there is no evidence he was a prophet or a martyr, and though he was killed ἐν μέσῳ (*en mesō*, "in the midst") of the temple precincts, it is unlikely he was killed between the actual sanctuary and the altar unless he was a priest, and there is no evidence for this.

3. It could be a reference to the OT prophet Zechariah son of Berekiah (Zec 1:1). But there is no account of his being killed.

4. It may be a Zechariah of whom we have no knowledge (Albright and Mann). This is possible but without proof.

5. Another possibility is Zechariah the son of Jehoiada (2Ch 24:20–22). His murder took place in the courtyard of the temple and is related toward the end of what was probably the last book in the Hebrew canon. The sweep runs (to use Christian terms) "from Genesis to Revelation." The problem is the patronymic. There is a possible solution. Just as Zechariah the prophet is alternately given his father's patronymic (Zec 1:1) or his grandfather's (Ezr 6:14), so it is possible Jehoiada was the grandfather (not father) of the Zechariah of 2 Chronicles 24—a suggestion that Jehoiada's living to be 130 years old (2Ch 24:15) makes more plausible, since Zechariah's ministry immediately followed Jehoiada's death. An otherwise unknown Berekiah would, therefore, have had time to sire Zechariah, live to a good age, and die before the death of his own father gave him opportunity to serve as chief priest. That would allow time for a father named Berekiah. But we do not know. Substantive text-critical uncertainties in the relevant traditions (esp. LXX) complicate the problem. For literature and discussion, see Gundry, *Use of the Old Testament*, 86–88; Garland, *Intention of Matthew 23*, 182–83.

f. Lament over Jerusalem (23:37–39)

OVERVIEW

Almost exact verbal equivalence between these verses and Luke 13:34–35 makes it nearly certain that both Matthew and Luke are following the same written source (Q?) and, therefore, that at least one of the two evangelists displaced this prayer from its setting in the life of Jesus. Certainly the lament is more integral to the setting in Matthew than in Luke (cf. Suggs, *Wisdom, Christology, and Law*, 64–66; Garland, *Intention of Matthew 23*, 187–97). Jesus undoubtedly lamented over the city on other occasions (Lk 19:41–44), and the broad compassion of his words is characteristic (Mt 9:35–38).

The effect of the lament is twofold. First, it tinges all the preceding woes with compassion (note the doubling of "Jerusalem" [cf. 2Sa 18:33; 1Ki 13:2; Jer 22:29; Lk 10:41; 22:31]). There is also a change of number from Jerusalem to people of Jerusalem: literally, "the (one) [singular] killing the prophets and stoning the (ones) sent to her [singular; NIV, 'you who kill the prophets and stone those sent to you'] ... your [singular] children ... your [plural] house ... you [plural] will not see." The effect is to move from the abstraction of the city to the concrete reality of people. Jesus' woes in Matthew 23, therefore, go far beyond personal frustrations; they are divine judgments that, though wrathful, never call in question the reality of divine love (see comments at 5:44–45).

Second, the christological implications are unavoidable, for Jesus, whether identifying himself with God or with wisdom, claims to be the one who has longed to gather and protect this rebellious nation. Phrased in such terms, Jesus' longing can belong only to Israel's Savior, not to one of her prophets. The authenticity of the lament is frequently denied on the ground that the historical Jesus could not possibly have said it (e.g., Suggs, *Wisdom, Christology, and Law*, 66). But it is a strange criticism that a priori obliterates any possibility of listening to the text in such a way as to hear a historical Jesus who was not only conscious of his transcendent origins but who in many ways laid claims to his origins as part of his compassionate and redemptive self-disclosure.

37"O Jerusalem, Jerusalem, you who kill the prophets and stone those sent to you, how often I have longed to gather your children together, as a hen gathers her chicks under her wings, but you were not willing. 38Look, your house is left to you desolate. 39For I tell you, you will not see me again until you say, 'Blessed is he who comes in the name of the Lord.'"

COMMENTARY

37 Verses 37–39 preserve Jesus' last recorded public words to Israel. Jerusalem, the city of David, the city where God revealed himself in his temple, had become known as the city that killed the prophets and stoned those sent to her. Stoning to death, prescribed in the law of Moses for idolatry

(Dt 17:5, 7), sorcery (Lev 20:27), and several other crimes, is also laid down in the Mishnah (*m. Sanh.* 7:4) for false prophets. It could also be the outcome of mob violence (21:35; Ac 7:57–58) or conspiracy, which apparently is how Zechariah died (2Ch 24:21). "How often" may look back over Israel's history — namely, Jesus' identifying himself with God's transcendent, historical perspective (Jn 8:58); more probably, "how often" refers to the duration of Jesus' ministry. During it, he "often" longed to gather and shelter Jerusalem (by metonymy including all Jews) as a hen her chicks (cf. Dt 32:11; Pss 17:8; 36:7; 91:4), for despite the woes, Jesus, like the "Sovereign LORD" in Ezekiel 18:32, took "no pleasure in the death of anyone."

38 This verse may allude to both Jeremiah 12:7 and 22:5 (see Notes). "Your house" in this context could refer to Jerusalem, since the lament is first addressed to her (Klostermann, McNeile), to Israel (Schniewind, Green; cf. Gal 4:25–26 for a similar use of "Jerusalem"), or to the temple in whose precincts Jesus was preaching (21:23; 24:1) and whose destruction was about to be predicted (24:2; cf. Manson [*Sayings of Jesus*, 127]; Davies [*Setting*, 298]). There seems to be no need to choose only one of these options; all three are closely allied and rise and fall together. If "desolate" (*erēmos*, GK *2245*) is not part of the text (see Notes), the verse means "your house is abandoned to the consequences of your misdeeds" (Plummer). More probably, *erēmos* is original and makes the implied destruction explicit. Your "house" is left to you (i.e., abandoned), whether by God (as in Jer 12:7) or Jesus (cf. 24:1), who is "Immanuel," "God with us" (1:23; cf. Garland, *Intention of Matthew 23*, 202–3, who traces God's abandonment of the temple, not least in Eze 8–11). The verb "left" (*aphietai*, GK *918*) can mean "abandoned to enemies," not just "abandoned." But since the ideas are related, a choice is unnecessary.

39 E. Haenchen ("Matthäus 23," *ZTK* 48 [1951]: 56) holds that in vv.33–36, "Wisdom" (cf. Lk 11:49) looks *forward* prophetically to sending the prophets, but in vv.37–39, it looks *back* on the sending of prophets. The latter passage must, therefore, be anachronistic. But the temporal relation between the two passages is not so sharp. If vv.33–36 look forward to the sending of the prophets, they also speak of judgment on "this generation." If vv.37–39 look backward on prophets already killed, the reference is to the way Jerusalem has acted in the *past* (v.37), a past that is even now bringing judgment (v.38), and that looks *forward* to future consummation (v.39).

The quotation is from Psalm 118:26 (also in 21:9; see 21:42 for another quotation from this psalm). The words may have been used by the priests in greeting the worshipers at the temple. Jesus, too, the true locus of Israel, must come, victorious and exalted, and receive greetings and homage from the religious authorities (cf. France, *Jesus and the Old Testament*, 58–59). Because of its location in Luke, "until" could refer to Palm Sunday, when people cried such words (Lk 19:38; cf. Mt 21:9); but as Marshall (*Gospel of Luke*, 576–77) points out, if Palm Sunday is in view in Luke, the cries of the people are but an ironic fulfillment that still looks forward to the consummation.

What Matthew refers to is perfectly clear. The Greek literally translated reads, "You will not see me from now [*ap' arti*] until you say"; and *ap' arti* is tied to the consummation (cf. 26:29, 64). Thus v.39 looks, not to Jesus' resurrection appearances, but to his second coming. When he returns, all will acknowledge him. The context strongly implies that the Parousia spells judgment (cf. 24:30–31; Php 2:9–11; Rev 1:7), but the quotation of Psalm 118 keeps open the way Jesus will be received as consuming Judge or welcomed King (cf. Benoit; Goulder, *Midrash and Lection*, 429–30; contra Garland, *Intention of Matthew*

23, 207–9 and the literature there cited). But whatever the outcome, the immediate prospect is disaster: "for I tell you, you will not see me, etc."; i.e., the proof that judgment is imminent is that Jesus turns away and will not be seen again until the End.

So Jesus leaves the temple and goes away (24:1); and his words, which have dealt with judgment on Israel and with the consummation, evoke his disciples' two-pronged question (24:3) and lead to the Olivet Discourse (chs. 24–25).

NOTES

38 If ἔρημος (*erēmos*, "desolate," GK *2245*) is omitted, as in B L[1 184] it[ff2] et al., the allusion is to Jeremiah 12:7 alone; if included, there may also be an allusion to Jeremiah 22:5 (cf. Gundry, *Use of the Old Testament*, 88). Westcott and Hort, relying too heavily on B, omit it, but the external evidence is strong for inclusion in Matthew, even if omission in Luke—where the evidence is much weaker and principally Western—is more likely (cf. Garland, *Intention of Matthew 23*, 200–201 n. 120). The presence of the word makes the judgment theme slightly more emphatic.

B. Fifth Discourse: The Olivet Discourse (24:1–26:5)

OVERVIEW

Few chapters of the Bible have elicited more disagreement among interpreters than Matthew 24 and its parallels in Mark 13 and Luke 21. The history of the interpretation of this chapter is immensely complex. G. R. Beasley-Murray's *Jesus and the Future* (London: Macmillan, 1954) is an admirable guide for works up to 1954; David Wenham's "Recent Study of Mark 13" (*TSF Bulletin* 71 [Spring, 1975]: 615; 72 [Summer 1975]: 19) succinctly summarizes and critiques several works up to 1975, including A. L. Moore, *The Parousia in the New Testament* (Leiden: Brill, 1966); Lars Hartman, *Prophecy Interpreted: The Function of Some Jewish Apocalyptic Texts and of the Eschatological Discourse, Mark 13 Par.* (Lund: Gleerup, 1966); R. Pesch, *Naherwartungen: Tradition und Redaktion in Markus 13* (Düsseldorf: Patmos, 1968); Gaston, *No Stone*; and France (*Jesus and the Old Testament*); G. R. Beasley-Murray (*Jesus and the Last Days* [Peabody, Mass.: Hendrickson, 1993]). In addition, there are now major commentaries on each of the Synoptic Gospels, not least Matthew (see Davies and Allison, Nolland, France [NICNT], Keener, and esp. Luz, whose survey of the history of interpretation is most helpful), not to mention a plethora of articles and essays. Some of the difficulties and exegetical turning points, and a little of the literature, must be cursorily introduced:

1. The literary nature of chs. 24–25 and of the parallels in Mark and Luke has occupied much scholarly attention. For a century or two before and after Jesus, writings now described as "apocalyptic literature" flourished in Jewish and Christian circles. At best, the label is not precise, and the genre's various forms tend to fray around the edges. G. E. Ladd ("Why Not Prophetic-Apocalyptic?" *JBL* 76 [1957]: 192–200) has wisely suggested that the NT apocalypses, especially this chapter and most

of Revelation, read like a merging of apocalyptic and prophetic literature. The symbolism is not as sharp as in works indisputably apocalyptic, and the "above-below" dualism typical of apocalyptic is here rather muted. Other features of this discourse are often noted, especially the frequent imperatives, whether in the second person ("Watch out that no one deceives you," v.4; "See to it that you are not alarmed," v.6) or the third person ("Let no one in the field go back," v.18).

2. As for the sources, first there is the question of whether the synoptists have simply put together a pastiche of Jesus' sayings (some of which may represent an "Olivet Discourse"), mingled with other traditions, or have selected and shaped material deriving from a single historical utterance. They undoubtedly give the latter impression. Matthew, with his framing formulas (see comments at 5:12; 7:28–29), is especially clear about this. Though this view is a minority one, nevertheless it can be strenuously argued that each evangelist felt his report of the discourse to be coherent. And if this is so, it seems too much to postulate, on the basis of disputable conceptual and grammatical discrepancies, unambiguous sources stemming from various traditions.

Second, the relation among the three synoptic accounts is still disputed. Some have argued that Luke 21 is sufficiently distinctive to spring from a separate tradition. Touching on both of these questions, David Wenham argues for a source-critical solution, not only tying together all the Synoptic Gospel records of this discourse, but also uniting them into a single comprehensive record. While Wenham's reconstruction is far from certain, the fact that he is able to develop his view so rigorously shows the dangers of the facile historical and literary disjunctions of which many critics are so fond.

Third, the Olivet Discourse is studded with OT quotations and allusions that add to the complexity.

Fourth, the discourse itself is undoubtedly a source for the Thessalonian epistles (cf. G. Henry Waterman, "The Sources of Paul's Teaching on the 2nd Coming of Christ in 1 and 2 Thessalonians," *JETS* 18 [1975]: 105–13; David Wenham, "Paul and the Synoptic Apocalypse," in *Gospel Perspectives* [ed. France and Wenham], 2:345–75) and Revelation (cf. G. K. Beale, "The Use of Daniel in Jewish Apocalyptic Literature and in the Revelation of St. John" [PhD diss., Cambridge University, 1980], 260–64; more recently, idem, *The Book of Revelation* [NIGTC; Grand Rapids: Eerdmans, 1999]; idem, *1–2 Thessalonians* [IVPNTC; Downers Grove, Ill.: InterVarsity, 2003]). If so, then we may say that Jesus himself sets the pattern for the church's eschatology.

3. This last statement presupposes the authenticity of the discourse material in the Gospels. This is frequently denied, however, on the ground that the "prophecy" of the fall of Jerusalem must in reality be *ex eventu*, based on the event itself. This will not do because, apart from antisupernatural presuppositions, Reicke ("Synoptic Prophecies") has shown the language in the Olivet Discourse prophesying the fall of Jerusalem to be largely in OT categories. Not only is it general; it does not describe any detail peculiar to the known history of the Jewish War (AD 66–73). Reicke goes so far as to conclude that the Olivet Discourse as found in any of the Synoptics *could not* have been composed after AD 70, and therefore the Synoptics themselves have earlier dates (see Introduction, section 6).

4. Numerous details in the text are much disputed and hard to understand: the meaning of "the abomination that causes desolation" (24:15), the significance of "let the reader understand" (v.15), whether the "coming of the Son of Man" (vv.27, 30) refers to his return at the consummation or to something else (the resurrection, Pentecost, the fall of Jerusalem, and the growth of the church have

all been suggested), the extent of "this generation" (v.34). The ideal solution is the one that treats all of these in the most natural way possible.

5. A disputed term, not in the text but in the forefront of interpretive theory, is "imminent," which has two related but distinct problems. One concerns the expectations of the historical Jesus and is linked to the way the various parts of the discourse relate to one another and to v.34: "I tell you the truth, this generation will certainly not pass away until all these things have happened." How "imminent" did Jesus think the coming of the Son of Man was (see below, under point 6)?

The other problem concerns the meaning of the word "imminent" as used in theological—especially evangelical—discussion. A dictionary defines it as "impending"; as applied to Christ's return, an "imminent return of Christ" would then mean Christ's return was near, impending. Hardly anyone uses "imminent" that way but understands it in a specialized, theological sense to mean "at any time": "the imminent return of Christ" then means Christ may return at any time. But the evangelical writers who use the word divide on whether "imminent" in the sense of "at any time" should be pressed to mean "at any second" or something looser, such as "at any period" or "in any generation."

Resolution turns on two issues. First, how are the various "signs" presaging Christ's return to be related to an "imminent" return? The dispensational response is to postulate two returns (or, as they hold, one return in two stages): one before any of the "signs" appear, a "rapture" that removes the church alone and that could take place at any second; the other after the signs appear, a return that consummates history as we know it. Most will agree that no passage in the Bible unambiguously teaches a two-stage return. The theory is in the best sense a theological harmonization—certainly not a wrong approach in itself—of disparate texts.

Other theories clamor for attention, including that of J. Barton Payne (*The Imminent Appearing of Christ* [Grand Rapids: Eerdmans, 1962]), who proposes that with the events of AD 70 now behind us, all the remaining "signs" are so general that they may be "fulfilled" in any generation. Distinctions regarding "imminency" therefore become moot. Other theories are not lacking. Unfortunately, the meaning of "imminent" is so comprehensive a question that each theory is in fact an entire eschatological scheme, complete with detailed exegesis and sweeping synthesis. While the approach of this commentary is inductive and limited primarily to the text of Matthew, some implications for the debate will be spelled out in due course.

Second, on what is the "any second" view of imminency based and how well does it withstand close scrutiny? The truth is that the biblical evidence nowhere unambiguously endorses the "any second" view and frequently militates against it (as has often been demonstrated; cf. R. H. Gundry, *The Church and the Tribulation* [Grand Rapids: Zondervan, 1973], esp. 29ff.; Craig Blomberg and Sung Wook Chung, eds., *A Case for Historic Premillennialism: An Alternative to "Left Behind" Eschatology* [Grand Rapids: Baker, 2009]; Benjamin L. Merkle, "Could Jesus Return at Any Moment? Rethinking the Imminence of the Second Coming," *TJ* 26 [2005]: 279–92). Not only do all the relevant NT verbs for "looking forward to" or "expecting" or "waiting for" have a semantic range including necessary delay, but many NT passages also implicitly rule out an "any second" imminency (24:45–51 [see below]; 25:5, 19; Lk 19:11–27: Jn 21:18–19 [cf. 2Pe 1:14]; Ac 9:15; 22:21; 23:11; 27:24). Yet the terms "imminent" and "imminency" retain theological usefulness if they focus attention on the eager expectancy of the Lord's return characteristic of many NT passages, a return that could take place soon, i.e., within a fairly brief period of time, without specifying that the period must be one second or less! This is not as rigid as the "any second" view, and it more fairly represents the exegetical evidence.

6. But the most difficult interpretive questions concern the structure of the discourse—how the parts relate to each other, to the initial questions of the disciples, and to the whole. On the face of it, the disciples' questions and the tenor of the discourse argue that Jesus is dealing with at least two issues—the fall of Jerusalem and the return of the Son of Man. But these two issues appear to be so tightly intertwined that it is impossible to separate them, and therefore Jesus or Matthew wrongly (as it turned out) tied them together.

Many modern scholars adopt this view. It is given a new twist by Desmond Ford (*The Abomination of Desolation in Biblical Eschatology* [Washington, D.C.: University Press of America, 1979], 76). He argues that Jesus meant to say that the Parousia would immediately succeed the fall of Jerusalem, all within the generation of his hearers, but that this was in reality a contingent promise, like Jonah's "Forty more days and Nineveh will be overturned" (Jnh 3:4). Hence "it is possible that he [Jesus] believed that if the early church proved faithful to its missionary commission, and if the chastened Jewish nation repented, the end would transpire in the same Age."

But the parallel with Jonah is not very close, if only because the Parousia is invariably treated in the NT as qualitatively unlike all other divine visitations. It alone marks the end of history, the final outpouring of judgment and blessing, and thus is not an event that can be postponed. More important, v.22 seems to say that God will hasten the consummation, not postpone it, for the days of tribulation are shortened. And nowhere in the NT is there any clear suggestion that the delay of the Parousia was the result of the church's sin (2Pe 3:12 is not a genuine exception). Yet Ford's view highlights the problem of the relation between the fall of Jerusalem and the Parousia.

At the risk of oversimplification, we may lump together some other major interpretations of the Olivet Discourse according to their treatment of this problem.

a. In 1864, T. Colani published his "little apocalypse" theory, postulating that the historical Jesus exhibited no interest in any future kingdom. As far as Jesus was concerned, the kingdom was exclusively present. The genesis of Mark 13 and parallels, therefore, must be accounted for as a tract by first-century Jewish Christians facing persecution just before AD 70. The answer of the historical Jesus to the disciples' questions was simply Mark 13:32 (Mt 24:36). Few follow Colani now, though some have tried to find in the Olivet Discourse not one "little apocalypse" but a number of different sources. Taken together, such theories follow a unifying method: the material in the discourse is assumed to be so disparate that it can be accounted for only by appealing to distinct sources not very well integrated by the evangelist-redactor. But too many details in the various theories seem unconvincing and fail to deal adequately with how each synoptist thought of the material he was editing. If he detected some unity, it must be found; and if found, then what methodological principle distinguishes between the unity imposed by a synoptist-redactor and a unity latent in a discourse delivered by Jesus? Indeed, one could make an a priori case for the apparent textual discrepancies based, not on the synoptist's failure to integrate separate sources, but on its condensed and selective reporting of much longer unified material in terms understandable to the first readers but more susceptible to misunderstanding today.

b. Perhaps the most common approach to the interpretation of the Olivet Discourse today is that which holds that Jesus responds *both* to the question regarding the destruction of Jerusalem *and* to the expectation of the *parousia* of the Son of Man, but that these two themes are so intertwined it is almost impossible to untangle them—or, alternatively, if a commentator thinks they *can* be untangled from verse to verse, there is little convincing rationale for the tangled skein. This mixed reading, combining interest in both the fall of Jerusalem and Jesus' second coming, goes back at least as far as Augustine. Those of evangelical heritage—exemplified, for instance, by Broadus and Lane (*Mark*)—want to hold the pieces together somehow but frankly acknowledge the difficulty. Broadus holds that vv.15–21, 34 foretell the destruction of Jerusalem, and at least vv.29–31 foretell the Lord's return; but "every attempt to assign a definite point of division between the two topics has proved a failure." If Christ's return is placed between v.28 and v.29, then v.34 is difficult; if after v.34, v.36, or v.42, how are we to interpret vv.30–31, 36? The solution is that the two are purposely intertwined, perhaps under some kind of "prophetic foreshortening." The near event, the destruction of Jerusalem, serves as a symbol for the far event. (In addition to the commentaries, see Hoekema, *Bible and the Future*; Ridderbos, *Coming of the Kingdom*, 477–510.) This approach is possible but has two weaknesses. It has to skate gingerly around the time references in the discourse (e.g., "immediately after the distress of those days," v.29; "this generation," v.34), and it leads some of its adherents to the view that on the *timing* of the Parousia Jesus was in error (e.g., Beasley-Murray, *Baptism*). Verse 36 is scarcely sufficient to support all this, since it is one thing to admit ignorance and another to be quite mistaken. Those who simply find the text so alien to the worldviews of their own time wrestle valiantly with the history of interpretation, the nature of apocalyptic metaphor, the structure of the passage, and the like but are inclined to conclude, "In part the text's language and images cannot be understood, and they appear to be fantasy. History and 'trans-history,' reality and images, human behavior and events from the beyond, world and God appear to be interrelated in a way that defies efforts to unravel them" (Luz, 183).

c. A number of scholars have denied that any part of the Olivet Discourse deals with the fall of Jerusalem; all of it concerns the Parousia. One form or another of this theory is held by Lagrange, Schlatter, Schniewind, and Zahn. Lagrange thinks the "abomination of desolation" deals with Jerusalem but not the "great distress" (v.21). In large measure, this approach is a resuscitation of the dominant approach in the patristic period before Augustine. Almost all who hold this view today are forced to say that Luke 21:20–24, which is unavoidably historical, stems from another discourse or has been consciously modified by Luke. The latter suggestion seems a desperate expedient in support of a weak theory. It is very difficult to imagine that a Christian reader of any of the Synoptics at any period during the first one hundred years of the existence of these documents would fail to see a reference to the destruction of Jerusalem. Methodologically, this approach belongs with those who flatten the discourse in other ways—e.g., by claiming that it represents a continuous account of Christian history.

d. An older view (e.g., Alexander), now again popular (Tasker; J. M. Kik, *Matthew Twenty-Four* [Swengel: Bible Truth Depot, 1948]), resuscitating the work of the Antiochene John Chrysostom, given fresh exegetical support thirty-five years ago by France (*Jesus and the Old Testament*, 231–39) and newly made popular by a number of scholars, e.g., Wright (*Jesus and the Victory of God*); Wilson (*When Will These Things Happen?*); Garland (*Reading Matthew*); Jeffrey A. Gibbs (*Jerusalem and Parousia: Jesus' Eschatological Discourse in Matthew's Gospel* [St. Louis, Mo.: Concordia, 2000]), and Bolt (*Cross from *a Distance*, ch. 3), holds that the fall of Jerusalem is in view in the discourse until the end of v.35. Only with the opening of v.36 does the second advent come into view. This interpretation, often called the preterist view, has the advantage of being neat. There is a clear division between the two parts of the discourse, and it eliminates flipping back and forth or appealing to "prophetic foreshortening" or the like. Its proponents point out that this interpretation answers both questions posed by the disciples. The first, concerning the destruction of Jerusalem and its temple, elicits the anticipation of an answer in v.15 ("When you see ...") but finds an explicit answer only in vv.29–31. The verses before v.29 tell of great anguish *preceding* the events of AD 70. But unless vv.29–35 deal with the fall of Jerusalem itself, it is held, the disciples' first question is never satisfactorily answered.

If someone objects that vv.29–35 more naturally read as a prophecy foretelling the second advent than the destruction of Jerusalem, this, we are told, would not be so obvious to the first readers. The celestial disturbances (v.29) are figurative, symbolic of political and national disasters (as in Isa 13:10; 34:4). The coming of the Son of Man in glory and power (v.30) is not Jesus' return to earth but, as in Daniel 7, a heavenly coming for vindication, a reference either to Jesus' vindication after the resurrection or to the fall of Jerusalem itself (26:64 is then commonly interpreted the same way). The sending of the "angels" is the commissioning of "messengers" or "missionaries" to gather the elect in the church (v.31), for despite the Lord's judgment on the Jews, the gathering in of the elect continues through the preaching of the gospel. (For the sake of completeness, it should perhaps be added that this is an array of "mixed" views that usually add little in terms of believability. For instance, Davies and Allison, like those listed under this heading, see a major structural break after 24:35 but in general are closer to point b above than to point d. Brant Pitre [*Jesus, the Tribulation and the End of the Exile* (WUNT 203; Tübingen: Mohr, 2005)]) largely follows N. T. Wright, not only in Wright's understanding of this Olivet Discourse but also in Wright's overemphasis on the "end of the exile" theme, but argues that the exile in question does not begin with the Babylonian captivity but with the Assyrian captivity of the northern kingdom.)

Casey (*Son of Man*, 172ff.) has raised some criticisms, a few of them cogent, as has Edward Adams (referenced below). Detailed rebuttal is impossible, but the following difficulties in this interpretation must be faced.

(1) Even if v.15 speaks only of the beginning of the Jerusalem distress (and this is debated), if France's view is right, it is hard to explain how vv.21–22 could describe the mere preliminaries to Jerusalem's fall. Verse 22 speaks of those days being cut short. Surely this does not mean the preliminaries to the fall of Jerusalem were cut short for the elect's sake, for that would entail the conclusion that the fall itself was a display of mercy on the elect.

(2) Although vv.14–22 do not explicitly mention the fall of Jerusalem, the same can be said with even greater vigor of vv.29–35. Similarly, if vv.29–35 do not mention the coming of the Son of Man *to the earth*, the same can be said of 1 Thessalonians 4:16, where in my opinion that is implied. In any case, there may be other reasons for Jesus not mentioning the fall of Jerusalem explicitly in vv.15–22. The cryptic "let the reader understand" (v.15) may be thought hint enough of the true import of Jesus' reference to Daniel's "abomination that causes desolation"; it may even be that the synoptists thought the Jerusalem reference obvious. Apparently Luke thought so (cf. Lk 21:20–24; see comments at v.15 below).

(3) France, Wright, and others argue that since Daniel 7:27 interprets Daniel 7:13 as referring to

"the saints, the people of the Most High," the reference to the coming of the Son of Man in Mark 13:26 (Mt 24:30) must have a corporate dimension. The coming of the Son of Man in these passages must refer to Jesus *and his people* as the replacement of Jews in the light of the destruction of the temple in AD 70. It follows that the sending out of the "angels" in the next verse (Mk 13:27; Mt 24:31) refers to the sending of missionaries to gather in the multinational, multiethnic people of God. But the "coming" (*parousia*) of Christ or of the Son of Man, along with related expressions, is so regularly associated with the coming of Jesus at the end of the age in connection with the resurrection from the dead (e.g., compare closely Mt 13:40–41; 16:27; 25:31; 1Co 11:26; 15:23, 52; 16:22; cf. 1Th 2:19; 3:13; 4:14–17; 5:23; 2Th 1:7; 2:1, 8; Jas 5:7–8; 2Pe 1:16; 3:4, 10–12; 1Jn 2:28; Rev 1:7) that it would take overwhelmingly convincing reasons to overturn this set of associations. Here are references to the Son of Man's coming, angels gathering the elect, trumpet call, clouds, glory, tribes of the earth mourning, celestial disturbances—all unambiguously related to the second advent. See also Frank Thielman, *Theology of the New Testament* (Grand Rapids: Zondervan, 2005), 719. Of course, there can be no objection to coming-of-the-Son-of-Man language occasionally referring to something other than the Parousia (see comments at 10:23; 16:28), yet when these occur, the interpretive problems are invariably notoriously complex. See comments at these last-referenced texts below.

(4) This approach to vv.29–35 is psychologically unconvincing for two reasons. First, it demands a close connection between the fall of Jerusalem and the Gentile mission (v.31), when in fact the Gentile mission had been prospering, first informally and then formally, for several decades. The fall of the temple doubtless helped support Christian theology about Jesus as the true sacrifice, priest, and temple, but it did not clearly motivate Gentile mission per se. Why, then, should the link be tendered here, almost as the climax of the pericope? Second, even on the basis of the interpretation under review, Christians saw the destruction of Jerusalem as a terrible thing and the onslaught by the pagan Romans as an abomination. If they also saw it as Jesus' vindication and as judgment on the Jewish nation, that is comprehensible enough; but could they see it as fulfillment of Daniel 7? Daniel 7 portrays something glorious and wonderful, the end of the pagan emperor's reign, yet AD 70 marks success by the pagan emperor. Even if one supposes that the Synoptics are operating under a reverse typology—the OT pagans being now equated with the Jews—is it psychologically convincing to hold that antipathy between Jews and Christians was running so high that the latter could be told the sack of Jerusalem was their "redemption" (Lk 21:28)?

(5) In both an essay and a book, Edward Adams ("The Coming of the Son of Man in Mark's Gospel," *TynBul* 56 [2005]: 39–61; *The Stars Will Fall from Heaven: Cosmic Catastrophe in the New Testament and Its World* [LNTS 347; London: T&T Clark, 2007]) has taken on this view directly, especially with respect to its treatment of the parallel passage in Mark 13 (he says much less regarding Mt 24). The nub of Adams's argument (in "Coming") is that Mark's use of Daniel 7:9–14 is *not* about enthronement/vindication only. Mark links Daniel 7:13 with other OT texts (not least Zec 14:3) and other images that anticipate God's coming to the earth. These links establish that what Jesus (in Mark) has in mind is his coming as exalted Lord from heaven to earth at the end of history. In other words, although images of trumpets and signs in the sky *can* be used for something other than the end, in *many* OT texts an array of such images are conjoined to signal cosmic catastrophe and the onset of the end with the final visitation

of God in consummating judgment and blessing. These images are similarly conjoined in Mark and Matthew. The preterist view is salvageable only by taking the images one by one and showing that each one *can* be used of something other than such a cosmic catastrophe. Putting them together is what the OT texts repeatedly do, in contexts of cosmic catastrophe, and observing that the Olivet Discourse forges similar links makes that preterist reading singularly unlikely, despite its recent rise in popularity. In his recent commentary (NICNT), France has responded to Adams's essay, arguing that his own interpretation makes better sense of the coming-of-the-Son-of-Man language in Mark 8:38 (in the light of Mk 9:1; the corresponding passages in Matthew are 16:28; 17:1). But this assumes that the three crucial coming-of-the-Son-of-Man passages in Matthew (10:23; 16:28; 24:30) all refer to the same thing, and I have given extensive reasons in each passage to call that assumption into question (see comments at 10:23; 16:28). Moreover, Matthew 24:30 itself contains an allusion to Zechariah 12:10–12, and other similar NT use of this passage, as Adams has pointed out, supports the view that the verse refers to the Parousia. (France did not have opportunity to respond to the much more detailed argument of Adams in the latter's *Stars Will Fall*.) Turner rightly points out that the preterist interpretation of 24:31 is particularly strained. The trumpet sounds and the "angels" (missionaries?) gather the elect from the four winds; this does not sound like missionary activity, especially in the light of the apocalyptic threats of final judgments that prevail in all of the immediately ensuing parabolic material, which seems to be telling readers how to wait for the end (esp. 24:39, 44, 50–51; 25:13, 30, 46).

(6) There are already hints early in the discourse (esp. in Matthew) that the reader is to bear in mind that there are at least two topics under discussion, not one: the fall of Jerusalem and the second advent (cf. vv.3, 5, 14, 23–27). Thus, since the reader is already primed to expect mention of the second advent, it would be difficult for him to take vv.29–31 in any other way.

e. A strong minority of evangelicals adopts one form or another of the dispensationalist interpretation of the discourse (A. C. Gaebelein; Walvoord; cf. John F. Walvoord, "Christ's Olivet Discourse on the End of the Age," *BS* 128 [1971]: 109–16; *BS* 129 [1972]: 20–32, 99–105, 206–10, 307–15). Perhaps the most common view along these lines takes vv.36–40 to refer to a secret "rapture of the church," which could take place at any second, and vv.4–28 (or vv.15–28) to refer to the great tribulation, lasting seven years and culminating in the second advent (vv.29–35). Walvoord adds refinements. He holds that v.2 refers to the destruction at AD 70. The disciples' question of v.3 is in *three* parts, the first of which, dealing with the fall of Jerusalem, Jesus does not answer.

At this point, there is a curious intersection of views with writers like Hare (*Theme of Jewish Persecution*, 177–79), who argues that Matthew, writing after the events of AD 70, eliminates all reference to the destruction of Jerusalem and "eschatologizes" even vv.15–28 and so does not answer the disciples' first question. Under Hare's view of Matthew's editorial activity, the strange thing is that Matthew retains that first question. The entire discourse, in Walvoord's view, deals with the general characteristics of the age (vv.4–14), the great tribulation (vv.15–25), and the second advent (vv.26–31), because the "rapture" is not revealed until Paul. Thus "taken" in vv.40–41 means "taken in judgment." "This generation" (v.34) Walvoord takes to mean either "this race" or something like "the generation that is alive when the great tribulation starts."

This interpretation is difficult to discuss adequately without delving into dispensationalism, including its "parenthesis" view of the church, something beyond the range of this commentary. If dispensationalism were unambiguously defined elsewhere in Scripture, then the least to be said for its interpretation of Matthew 24 is that it is self-consistent and makes sense of the time indicators (e.g., "Immediately after the distress of those days," v.29, etc.). Even then, however, this interpretation faces several difficulties, one or two of them well-nigh insuperable.

(1) It is forced to adopt a possible but extraordinarily unlikely meaning for "this generation" (v.34; see below).

(2) It rests heavily on Matthew's report of the Olivet Discourse and makes less sense of the parallels in Mark and Luke. One of many examples of its problems is Matthew's recording the disciples' question differently from Mark and Luke; Walvoord's interpretation of the discourse depends almost entirely on Matthew. Even if through harmonizing Walvoord can show that v.3 best preserves the tripartite nature of the disciples' historical question, one must still ask why Mark and Luke have it as they do. If the discourse as they present it can be adequately explained only by reference to the disciples' question as Matthew preserves it, then Mark and Luke cannot be intelligently read without referring to Matthew.

(3) Much dispensationalism, especially the older kind, holds that the "rapture" is not mentioned in this chapter and justifies this view on the ground that Jesus is not talking to the church but to Jews. Dispensationalists use this disjunction to justify a number of theological points, but they are insensitive to historical realities. Even after Pentecost the earliest church was entirely Jewish. Here, before the passion, Jesus is not addressing the church in its post-Pentecost sense; but he is addressing, not his Jewish opponents, but his Jewish disciples who will constitute the church. Rigid application of this doubtful disjunction between Jews and church likewise banishes the church from the Sermon on the Mount, but it fails to observe that 18:15–20, dealing with the church, is also addressed, before the passion, to Jewish disciples.

(4) Granted the dispensational interpretation, Jesus' answer must have not only been opaque to his auditors but almost deceptive. Their first question concerns Jerusalem's judgment. But since a substantial part of Jesus' answer is couched in terms dealing with Jerusalem's destruction, how could the disciples think Jesus was *not* answering their question but describing a *second* destruction of the city, unless Jesus explicitly disavowed their understanding? But he does nothing of the kind. So perhaps it is not surprising that the dispensational identification of vv.15–28 *exclusively* with the great tribulation after the rapture of the church, whether revealed or unrevealed, finds no exponent until the nineteenth century. The dispensational approach to the Olivet Discourse must be judged historically implausible in reference to both the history of Jesus and the history of interpretation.

f. The view of Matthew 24 this commentary advocates finds clear breaks in the Olivet Discourse, thus differing from the second option, but deals with the location and significance of these breaks in a slightly novel way. David Wenham and I, to our mutual surprise, came to independent but similar conclusions about the Olivet Discourse. Sustained discussion benefited us both and enabled both of us to develop the original ideas, with the result that I cannot say exactly what each of us contributed to the thinking of the other. The first edition of this commentary appeared before the publication of Wenham's work; almost immediately afterward, his *The Rediscovery of Jesus' Eschatological Discourse* appeared. It confirmed that in structure and flow of thought he and I are much on the same page, though his work is far more detailed than my own and far more confident about source alignments than I am able to be. But here I gratefully acknowledge indebtedness to him.

In my understanding of the Olivet Discourse, the *disciples* think of Jerusalem's destruction and the eschatological end as a single complex web of events. This accounts for the form of their questions. Jesus warns that there will be delay *before* the End—a delay characterized by persecution and tribulation for his followers (vv.4–28), but with one particularly violent display of judgment in the fall of Jerusalem (vv.15–21; Mk 13:14–20; Lk 21:20–24). Immediately after the days of that sustained persecution characterizing the interadvent period comes the second advent (vv.29–31; cf. Guthrie, *New Testament Theology*, 795–96). The warning in vv.32–35 describes the whole tribulation period, from the ascension to the second advent. The tribulation period will certainly come, and the generation to which Jesus is speaking will experience all its features that point to the Lord's return. But the exact time of that return no one but the Father knows (vv.36–44). This structure works out in all three Synoptics (though with significant differences in emphasis), and the main themes developed have important ties with other NT books. The disciples' questions are answered, and the reader is exhorted to look forward to the Lord's return and meanwhile to live responsibly, faithfully, compassionately, and courageously while the Master is away (24:45–25:46). Gundry objects to this analysis largely on the ground that the text seems to be flipping back and forth between the two events. But Gundry really does not interact with the *textual* evidence for such flips and the reasons advanced for them.

1. Setting (24:1–3)

OVERVIEW

Unlike Mark (12:41–44) and Luke (21:1–4), Matthew omits the story of the widow's offering, thus linking the Olivet Discourse more closely to the "woes" in Matthew 23. This does not mean that Matthew 24–25 continues a single discourse—the setting, audience, and principal themes all change. But Matthew does tie the prediction of desolation (23:37–39) to the destruction of the temple (24:2; for discussion, see Hummel, *Auseinandersetzung*, 85–86; J. Lambrecht, "The Parousia Discourse," in *L'Évangile selon Matthieu* [ed. Didier], 314–18; France [NICNT], who ties 24:1–2 more tightly to ch. 23, and 24:3 to chs. 24–25).

[1]Jesus left the temple and was walking away when his disciples came up to him to call
his attention to its buildings. [2]"Do you see all these things?" he asked. "I tell you the truth,
not one stone here will be left on another; every one will be thrown down."
[3]As Jesus was sitting on the Mount of Olives, the disciples came to him privately. "Tell
us," they said, "when will this happen, and what will be the sign of your coming and of the
end of the age?"

COMMENTARY

1 Jesus' departure from the *hieron* ("temple complex," GK *2639*) may be symbolic (see comments at 23:39). It also gives the disciples a chance to call Jesus' attention to its various structures. In Mark and Luke, the disciples call Jesus' attention to the beauty of the temple buildings and the great stones on which it rests (cf. Josephus, *Ant.* 15.391–402 [11.3]; *J.W.* 5.184–226 [5.16]; Tacitus, *Hist.* 5.8.12). Whether or not the disciples thought they were speaking piously, they show they have underestimated or even misunderstood the force of Jesus' denunciations in Matthew 23 and Luke 11. They still focus on the temple, on which Jesus has pronounced doom, since the true center of the relation between God and man has shifted to himself. In Matthew 23 Jesus has already insisted that what Israel does with him, not the temple, determines the fate of the temple and of Israel nationally.

2 Because *tauta panta* ("all these things") is neuter and "buildings" (v.1) feminine, some have suggested that Jesus' question refers, not to the buildings, but to the discourse in Matthew 23, especially v.36, and should be rendered "You do understand [metaphorically 'see'] these things, don't you?" the positive answer being suggested by the presence of the particle *ou* ("not," untranslated in NIV). This may be oversubtle. The Greek demonstrative pronoun may have an irregular antecedent for various reasons (*Grammar*, 704). Moreover, the particle *ou*, anticipating a positive response, detracts from this novel interpretation, for if Jesus thinks his disciples have understood, why then does he go on immediately to answer their question unequivocally? But if the sentence is taken in the usual way (NIV), then the expectation of a positive response is most natural—of course the disciples see the buildings! (Moule is nevertheless right in saying that English idiom prefers an open question here; cf. *Idiom Book*, 159.)

Jesus' forecast of the destruction of the temple complex is unambiguous, cast in OT language (cf. Jer 26:6, 18; Mic 3:12) and repeated variously elsewhere (23:38; 26:61; Lk 23:28–31).

3 The Mount of Olives (see comments at 21:1, 17) is an appropriate site for a discourse dealing with the Parousia (cf. Zec 14:4). Mark specifies that Peter, James, John, and Andrew (the first four in Mt 10:2) asked the question privately. Whether this means that they were the only disciples present or that they were the ones who raised the question is uncertain, since "privately" in both Matthew and Mark sets the disciples apart from the crowds, not some disciples from others. The form of the question varies from gospel to gospel, with Matthew showing the greatest independence. Yet if we make the reasonable assumption that in the disciples' minds their question as to the temple's destruction and the signs that will presage it are linked to the end of the age and Jesus' return (cf. 16:27–28; 23:39; Lk 19:11–27), there is little problem. Matthew makes explicit what was implicit and what Jesus recognized as implicit in their question.

"The end of the age" is used six times in the NT (13:39, 40, 49; 24:3; 28:20; Heb 9:26), five of which are in Matthew and look to final judgment and the consummation of all things. (Heb 9:26 sees the cross as introducing the coming age and thereby marking out "the end of the ages" [NIV].) *Parousia* ("coming," GK *4242*) is found twenty-four times in the NT, four of which are in Matthew 24 (vv.3, 27, 37, 39). The term can refer to "presence," "arrival," or "coming"—the first stage of "presence"—and need not have eschatological overtones (2Co 7:6; 10:10). Yet *parousia* is closely tied with Jesus' glorious "appearing" or "coming" at the end of human history. (For views of its relation to NT eschatology, see Turner, *Christian Words*, 40–48; *NIDNTT*, 2:898–935.)

2. The birth pains (24:4–28)

a. General description of the birth pains (24:4–14)

OVERVIEW

Alexander goes too far in saying that Jesus' purpose in these verses "is not to tell what are but what are not the premonitions of the great catastrophe to which he refers." Instead, all things (vv.5–7) are signs that Jesus is coming back, and they all will be manifest before the generation Jesus is addressing has died. But though these things show that the end is near, none of them stipulates how near, and the tenor of the warning is that the delay will be substantial and that during this period Jesus' disciples must not be deceived by false messiahs.

4Jesus answered: "Watch out that no one deceives you. 5For many will come in my
name, claiming, 'I am the Christ,' and will deceive many. 6You will hear of wars and rumors
of wars, but see to it that you are not alarmed. Such things must happen, but the end is
still to come. 7Nation will rise against nation, and kingdom against kingdom. There will be
famines and earthquakes in various places. 8All these are the beginning of birth pains.
9"Then you will be handed over to be persecuted and put to death, and you will be
hated by all nations because of me. 10At that time many will turn away from the faith and
will betray and hate each other, 11and many false prophets will appear and deceive many
people. 12Because of the increase of wickedness, the love of most will grow cold, 13but
he who stands firm to the end will be saved. 14And this gospel of the kingdom will be
preached in the whole world as a testimony to all nations, and then the end will come."

COMMENTARY

4–5 One of the greatest temptations in times of difficulty is to follow blindly any self-proclaimed savior who promises help. It is the temptation to repose confidence (v.4) in false christs. Those who "come in my name" (v.5) may refer to those who come as Jesus' representatives, but because of the words that follow, we must assume that their claim goes further. They claim to be Messiah, Christ himself. They come "in his name," as if they were he. Would-be deliverers have appeared in every age, not least the first century (Ac 5:36; Josephus, *Ant.* 20.97–99 [5.1], 160–72 [8.56], 188 [8.10]; *J.W.* 2.259 [8.5], 433–56 [17.910]; 6.285–87 [5.2]). That this governs vv.4–28 is made clear by the second half of the literary inclusio (vv.26–28) that brackets the section. (On Mark's parallel "I am he," see Lane, *Mark*, 457 n. 43.)

6–8 "Birth pains" (v.8) in this context (elsewhere in the NT in Ac 2:24 ["agony"]; 1Th 5:3) stems from such OT passages as Isaiah 13:8; 26:17; Jeremiah 4:31; 6:24; Micah 4:9–10. By this time it was almost a special term for "the birth pangs of the Messiah," the period of distress preceding the messianic age (see Str-B, 1:905; 4:977–78; *TDNT*, 9:667–74; cf. *2 Bar.* 27:1–30:1; *b. Šabb.* 118a; *b. Sanh.* 98b). But the "wars and rumors of war,... famines and earthquakes" (vv.6–7, of which there were not a few in the first century; cf. Alford, *New Testament for English Readers*, 1:163) do not so point to the end as to validate the false christs' claims. Jesus' followers are not to be alarmed by these events. "Such things must happen"; yet the end is still to come (v.6). These are only "the beginning of [the] birth pains" that stretch over the period between the advents. Why "must [they] happen"? The reason may be hidden in God's providence, which can provide a haven for faith (cf. 26:54). But it may also be that during this time of inaugurated reign before the messianic age attains its splendor, conflict is inevitable, precisely because the kingdom is only inaugurated. The conflict extends not only to families (10:34–37) but to nations and even nature (cf. Ro 8:20–21; Col 1:16, 20).

The effect of these verses, then, is not to curb enthusiasm for the Lord's return but to warn against false claimants and an expectation of a premature return based on misconstrued signs.

9–13 *Tote* ("then," v.9) is an elusive word (see comments at 2:7). In Matthew 24 alone it occurs in vv.9, 10, 14, 16, 21, 23, 30, 40. Translated "then" in v.9, it occurs as "At that time" in v.10. Certainly there is no suggestion of sequence between v.8 and v.9; it is during the "birth pains" that Jesus' disciples will be persecuted and killed. "You" quite clearly extends beyond the immediate disciples and includes all the followers Jesus will have. Persecution would break out early (cf. Ac 4:1–30; 7:59–8:3; 12:1–5; Rev 2:10–14) and keep on during the "birth pains," against a background of hatred by the whole world (cf. Ac 28:22).

Thlipsis ("persecution," "tribulation," "distress," GK *2568*) occurs four times in Matthew, three in this chapter (13:21; 24:9, 21, 29), and relates significantly to the chapter's structure (see comments at vv.21, 29). Jesus establishes *thlipsis* as characteristic of this age (cf. 10:16–39)—a time when many will "turn away" (*skandalisthēsontai*, GK *4997*) from the faith (for the verb, see comments at 5:29; 13:21, 57) and hate each other (24:10).

In this chapter, there are several allusions to Daniel (cf. Da 11:35; linguistically some LXX MSS of Da 11:41; see D. Wenham, "A Note on Matthew 24:10–12," *TynBul* 31 [1980]: 155–62; esp. Trotter, "Understanding and Stumbling") and a certain parallelism between v.10 and vv.11–12. Those who turn away from the faith are deceived by false prophets, and those who hate each other do so because wickedness abounds and the love of most grows cold (cf. Trotter). Professing believers are either included in this description or are the focus of interest; but only those who endure—in love (v.12) and despite persecution (vv.9–11; cf. Rev 2:10)—will be saved (v.13). They must "stand firm" (endure) to the end. Individual responsibility persists to the end of life, but corporate responsibility to the final consummation. Part of the effect of this "tribulation," therefore, is to purify the body of professed disciples. Those who endure are saved, as in Daniel 11:32, 34–35, and elsewhere in Matthew (see comments at 12:32; 13:21, 41; cf. 2Ti 2:3, 10–13; 3:11; Heb 10:32; 11:27; 12:2–3; Jas 1:12; 5:11).

The reasons for falling away may differ. In 13:21, the cause is *thlipsis* ("persecution" or "tribulation"), and in 24:10–12, it is false prophets (see comments at 7:15–23). But even here, the false prophecy finds some of its appeal in the matrix of trouble and persecution (vv.4–9) from which it emerges. Matthew cares little whether faith is lost owing to fear of physical violence or to deception effected by false prophets. The result is the same and is to be expected throughout this age (cf. 7:15–23; 24:24; Ac 20:29–30; 2Pe 2:1; 1Jn 4:1).

14 But none of this means that the gospel of the kingdom (see comments at 4:23) is not preached or that its saving message does not spread throughout the world. Despite persecution—and often because of it (Ac 8:1, 4)—the Good News is "preached" (*kērychthēsetai*, GK *3062*; see comments at 4:17) "as a testimony to all nations." The expression is itself neutral (see comments at 8:4), and the gospel will bring either salvation or a curse, depending on how it is received. Thus the theme of Gentile mission is again made explicit (see comments at 1:1; 2:1–12; 3:9; 4:15–16; 8:11–12; 21:43; 28:18–20).

NOTES

10 The reciprocal pronoun ἀλλήλους (*allēlous*, "one another"), used twice in this verse, can scarcely be strictly reciprocal in either case.

b. The sharp pain: the fall of Jerusalem (24:15–21)

OVERVIEW

Although many commentators hold that Matthew (but probably not Mk and certainly not Lk) here portrays not just the fall of Jerusalem but also the great tribulation before Antichrist comes (e.g., Hill), the details in vv.16–21 are too limited geographically and culturally to justify that view. For other interpretations, see comments at the beginning of this chapter. For justification of a pericope termination at v.21 instead of the more common v.22, see below (on vv.21–22).

15"So when you see standing in the holy place 'the abomination that causes desolation,' spoken of through the prophet Daniel—let the reader understand—**16**then let those who are in Judea flee to the mountains. **17**Let no one on the roof of his house go down to take anything out of the house. **18**Let no one in the field go back to get his cloak. **19**How dreadful it will be in those days for pregnant women and nursing mothers! **20**Pray that your flight will not take place in winter or on the Sabbath. **21**For then there will be great distress, unequaled from the beginning of the world until now—and never to be equaled again."

COMMENTARY

15 *Oun* ("so") can serve as either an inferential or merely a transitional conjunction (cf. BDAG, 736–37; BDF, para. 451.1, plus appendix; *Grammar*, 119–92; Turner, *Syntax*, 337–38), which can sometimes be left untranslated; it does not introduce something *temporally* new. If it retains any inferential force in this passage, it is very light—"accordingly, when you see ... then flee." Having characterized the entire age during which the gospel of the kingdom is preached as a time of *thlipsis* ("distress"), Jesus goes on to talk about one part of it when there will be particularly "great distress."

To bdelygma tēs erēmōseōs means "the abomination characterized by desolation," leaving it unclear whether the abomination "causes" desolation (NIV; cf. McNeile, "the abominable thing that layeth waste"; NRSV, "the desolating sacrilege") or is simply a token of it. The former is more likely. The expression occurs three times in Daniel (9:27; 11:31; 12:11; cf. 8:13, "rebellion that causes desolation"). Daniel 11:31 clearly refers to the desecration under Antiochus Epiphanes (168 BC; cf. 1 Macc 1:54–61), who erected an altar to Zeus over the altar of burned offering, sacrificed a swine on it, and made the practice of Judaism a capital offense. The other references in Daniel are more disputed. Matthew and Mark agree with the LXX of Daniel 12:11 only; "[despite] the primary importance of Daniel 9:27 for the meaning of the expression, 12:11 is contextually the more suitable reference so far as the gospels are concerned, because allusions to Daniel 11:40–12:13 surround this reference to the abomination of desolation" (Gundry, *Use of the Old Testament*, 48).

Jesus, then, is identifying Daniel 9:27 and 12:11 with certain events about to take place; the parenthetical "let the reader understand" is designed to draw the attention of the *reader of Daniel* to the passages' true meaning. This parenthetical aside is not a Matthean addition (unless one holds to Matthew's priority), for it is already in Mark. Matthew clearly understood it, not as an aside by Mark to draw the attention of his readers to the importance of this gospel text, but as an aside by Jesus to draw the attention of his hearers who read Daniel to the importance of Daniel's words; hence Jesus' mention of "the prophet Daniel." Whether the identification Jesus makes is a prediction fulfillment or a typological fulfillment depends largely on how one understands the various "abomination of desolation" passages in Daniel.

But to what event does Jesus make this text from Daniel refer? Some have suggested Caligula's plan to set up a pagan altar and standards in the temple precincts (AD 40), a plan never carried out; but the description in the following verses cannot apply to that. The obvious occasion, in general terms, is AD 70, though certain difficulties must be faced. Although *topos* ("place," GK *5536*) can refer to the city of Jerusalem (cf. BDAG, 1011), the normal meaning of *topos hagios* ("holy place") is the temple complex (cf. BDAG; see Isa 60:13; 2 Macc 1:29; 2:18; Ac 6:13; 21:28). But by the time the Romans had actually desecrated the temple in AD 70, it was too late for anyone in the city to flee.

Mark's language is less explicit—"standing where it does not belong" (Mk 13:14) instead of "standing in the holy place." Luke resolves the matter: "When you see Jerusalem being surrounded by armies, you will know that its desolation is near" (Lk 21:20)—but now there is no explicit mention of "the abomination of desolation." Possibly Jesus said something ambiguous, such as Mark reports. Luke, writing for a Gentile audience less concerned with Daniel, emphasizes the aspect of warning. Matthew, believing the allusions to Daniel important for his Jewish audience because Jesus drew attention to them, makes explicit reference to "the abomination of desolation" and to "the holy place," since the setting up of the abomination in the holy place is the inevitable result of the pagan attack.

By the time the Roman military standards (an eagle in silver or bronze over the imperial bust, to which soldiers paid homage not far removed from worship) surrounded Jerusalem, the city was defiled. Some have held that though Luke refers to the approaching armies, Matthew and Mark refer to the Zealot excesses that polluted the temple before AD 70 (including murder and the installation of a false high priest; cf. Josephus, *J.W.* 4.147–57 [3.6–8], 162–92 [3.10], 334–44 [5.4]), when there was still time to flee (e.g., Lane, *Mark*, 469; Gaston, *No Stone*, 458ff.). In any case, there is reasonably good tradition that Christians abandoned the city, perhaps in AD 68, about halfway through the siege.

16–19 The instructions Jesus gives his disciples about what to do in view of v.15 are so specific that they must be related to the Jewish War. The devastation would stretch far beyond the city; people throughout Judea should flee to the mountains, where the Maccabeans had hidden in caves. Most roofs were flat (cf. Dt 22:8; Mk 2:4; Ac 10:9)—pleasant places in the cool of the day. Verse 17 implies such haste that fugitives will not take time to run downstairs for anything to take with them but will run from roof to roof to evacuate the city as quickly as possible (cf. Josephus, *Ant.* 13.140 [5.3]). People in the fields will not have time to go home for their cloaks (see comments at 5:40). It will be especially dreadful (lit., "woe," here like a compassionate "alas!") for pregnant women and nursing mothers.

20 Flight is obviously harder in winter. As for fleeing on the Sabbath, travel would become more difficult because few would help, and many would try to prevent traveling farther than a Sabbath day's journey. Jesus clearly expects these events to take place while the strict Sabbath law is in effect.

21 "For" introduces the reason for flight in vv.17–20: *thlipsis* ("distress," "tribulation") and unprecedented suffering (cf. Da 12:1; 1 Macc 9:27; Rev 7:14; see Gundry, *Use of Old Testament*, 49–50). The savagery, slaughter, disease, and famine (mothers eating their own children) were monstrous (cf. Josephus, *J.W.* 5.424–38 [10.2–3]), "unequaled from the beginning of the world until now," and, according to Jesus, "never to be equaled again." There have been greater numbers of deaths—six million in the Nazi death camps, mostly Jews, and an estimated twenty million under Stalin—but never so high a percentage of a great city's population so thoroughly and painfully exterminated and enslaved as during the fall of Jerusalem.

From this "great distress" Jesus' followers were to flee. Eusebius (*Hist. eccl.* 3.5.2–3) says that during the siege under Titus (who did not replace his father Vespasian as commanding officer until AD 69, after the death of Galba), many were permitted to leave (cf. Josephus, *J.W.* 5.420–23 [10.1]). Others hold that the Christians left in 66 or 68.

That Jesus in v.21 promises that such "great distress" is never to be equaled implies that it cannot refer to the tribulation at the end of the age; for if what happens next is the millennium or the new heaven and the new earth, it seems inane to say that such "great distress" will not take place again. At the same time, by these remarks Jesus finishes his description of Jerusalem in Matthew and Mark (Luke goes to 21:24). (For the way Luke's version of the discourse fits this framework, see Wenham, *Rediscovery of Jesus' Eschatological Discourse*.)

NOTES

18 Only here and in Luke 7:38 is ὀπίσω (*opisō*, "back") used as an adverb (cf. Moule, *Idiom Book*, 86).

c. Warnings against false messiahs during the birth pains (24:22–28)

22"If those days had not been cut short, no one would survive, but for the sake of the
elect those days will be shortened. 23At that time if anyone says to you, 'Look, here is the

Christ!' or, 'There he is!' do not believe it. [24]For false Christs and false prophets will appear and perform great signs and miracles to deceive even the elect—if that were possible. [25]See, I have told you ahead of time.

[26]"So if anyone tells you, 'There he is, out in the desert,' do not go out; or, 'Here he is, in the inner rooms,' do not believe it. [27]For as lightning that comes from the east is visible even in the west, so will be the coming of the Son of Man. [28]Wherever there is a carcass, there the vultures will gather."

COMMENTARY

22 Many problems in interpreting the Olivet Discourse relate to the assumption that "those days" refers to the period described in vv.15–21 and also to v.29. But there are excellent reasons for concluding that vv.22–28 refer to the general period of distress introduced by vv.4–14 and that, therefore, "those days" refers to the entire period of which vv.15–21 are only one part—the "great distress" (v.21).

1. The term "elect" (in Matthew only at 22:14; 24:22, 24, 31; plus the variant at 20:16) most naturally refers to all true believers, chosen by God; thus it is reasonable to assume that it does so here.

2. Similarly, *pasa sarx* (lit., "all flesh"; NIV, "no one"; see Notes) normally refers to all mankind and is more sweeping than "no one in Jerusalem."

3. The themes of the ensuing verses have already been taken up as characteristics of the entire age (vv.4–14), especially the warning against false christs (cf. vv.4–5).

4. It has already been shown that v.21 makes a suitable ending to vv.15–21.

5. Wenham (*Rediscovery of Jesus' Eschatological Discourse*) posits a neat presynoptic tradition that embraces the content of all three gospels and suggests reasons for individual selection of materials. That tradition (slightly modified from Wenham) runs approximately as follows:

Matthew 24:15–20 = Mark 13:14–18 = Luke 21:20–24
Matthew 24:21 = Mark 13:19
Matthew 24:22–28 = Mark 13:20–23
Matthew 24:29–42 = Mark 13:24–37 = Luke 21:25–36

Right or wrong as to source-critical details, this reconstruction at least makes sense of the relationship among the Synoptics at this point and supports a logical break between v.21 and v.22 of Matthew 24.

6. Further literary and structural arguments suggest that vv.4–28 must be taken as one time period, with vv.15–21 a critical part of it (see comments at v.29).

While none of these arguments are decisive, all are reasonable and help us understand the whole discourse. If they are correct, then v.22 tells us that this age of evangelism and distress—wars, famines, persecution, hatred, false prophets—will become so bad that, if not checked, no one will survive. The last hundred years have seen two world wars and the threat of extinction by nuclear holocaust, and witnessed more Christian martyrs than in all the previous nineteen centuries put together. Jesus' prediction does not seem far-fetched. But the age will not run its course; it will be cut short. (For a somewhat similar idea, see the Jewish apocalypse *2 Bar.* 20:12; 83:1.) This promise enables believers to look for God's sovereign, climactic intervention without predicting dates.

23–25 Empty-headed credulity is as great an enemy of true faith as chronic skepticism. Christian faith involves the sober responsibility of neither believing lies nor trusting imposters. As false christs and false prophets proliferate (v.24), so will their heralds (v.23). Jesus' disciples are not to be deceived, even by spectacular signs and miracles (see comments at 7:21–23; 16:1; for the terms, see 12:38; 18:12–13; cf. 24:4–5, 11). The imposter is perennial (Dt 13:14; Rev 13:13).

Ei dynaton ("if that were possible") no more calls into question the security of the elect (contra I. H. Marshall, *Kept by the Power of God* [rev. ed.; Minneapolis: Bethany, 1975], 72–73) than it calls into question the inevitability of Jesus' cup (26:39). If "deceive" is telic (i.e., "in order to deceive"; see Notes), the "if possible" refers to the intent of the deceivers: they intend to deceive, if possible, even the elect—without any comment on how ultimately successful such attacks will be. "If that were possible" clearly suggests that "deceive" is not ecbatic (i.e., "with the result that"). That Jesus tells these things in advance (v.25) not only warns and strengthens his followers (cf. Jn 16:4) but also authenticates him (cf. Dt 13:14; Jn 14:29).

26–27 It is pointless to look for Messiah's return in the desert (cf. 4:1) or in inner rooms (cf. 6:6)—whether in some desert monastic community or in some hidden, unrecognized enclave for insiders (cf. Stendahl, "Matthew," in *Peake's Commentary*). Far from it! The coming of the Son of Man (see comments at 8:20; here his coming is clearly identified as "your [Jesus'] coming," v.3, and Messiah's coming, vv.23–24) will be public, unquestionable, and not confined to some little group of initiates. As the lightning (cf. Ps 97:4; Zec 9:14) comes out of the east but is everywhere visible, as far away as the west (Broadus), so also the coming of the Son of Man will be visible to all people everywhere (*TDNT*, 8:433–34).

28 Here Jesus quotes a proverb (cf. Job 39:30; Lk 17:37). "Eagle" (KJV) is wrong: "vulture" (NIV) is correct. *Aetos* can mean eagle, kite, or vulture, but eagles are not normally carrion eaters. The proverb itself is a difficult one.

1. Calvin, following some of the Fathers, sees it as portraying God's children, gathering to feed on Christ. But identifying carrion with Christ is strange indeed!

2. Others see an allusion to Roman military eagles, with the Roman forces swarming over corrupt Jerusalem. But eagles are not vultures; and the preceding verse relates to the Parousia, not the fall of Jerusalem.

3. Hill and others think that the vultures' gathering indicates that the Parousia is near. But there must be carrion before the vultures gather, so the symbolism breaks down, because the "signs" attest the reality only after the fact.

4. Manson (*Sayings of Jesus*, 147) emphasizes the swiftness of the coming of the Son of Man—the carrion is no sooner there than the vultures swoop down (Eze 17:3, 7; Rev 4:7; 8:13). But in passages where the *aetos* ("eagle" or "vulture") symbolizes speed, it is understood to mean an "eagle." Why then assign it to a setting where it must be taken as a vulture?

5. The proverb may be a colorful way of saying that things come to pass at just the right time (Broadus); thus the proverb applies here and in Luke 17:37 to the Parousia of the Son of Man. Concluding this broader section (vv.4–28) is this thought: Do not be too eager for Christ's coming, or you will be deceived by false claimants (vv.23–26). When he comes, his coming will be unmistakable (v.27), in God's own time (v.28)—a time when the world will be ripe for judgment (Zahn; see comments at v.6).

6. This enigmatic proverb may simply mean that it will be as impossible for humanity not to see the coming of the Son of Man (cf. v.27) as it is for vultures to miss seeing carrion (Klostermann). This makes sense of the immediate context. Jesus' disciples are not to be seduced by some claim to a secret and largely unseen putative coming (like that which the Jehovah's Witnesses claim to have taken place in 1914). Animals regularly go off somewhere and die, and their time and place of death are unnoted. But where there is a carcass over which vultures are hovering, everyone can see that a death has taken place. Similarly with respect to the coming of Christ. It will be as visible and as undeniable as lightning flashing across the heavens (v.27); it will be as public as hovering vultures make any death public. As a colleague put it in a private communication, "The return of the Son of Man will not have taken place *at* all if it is not visible *to* all."

NOTES

22 On the aorist verbs in this verse, see Zerwick, *Biblical Greek*, para. 317. The οὐ ... πᾶς (*ou ... pas*, lit., "not ... all") construction is often said to represent the Hebrew לֹא כֹּל (*lōʾ ... kōl*), equivalent to Greek οὐδείς (*oudeis*, "no one"; e.g., Zerwick, *Biblical Greek*, para. 446; but the Semitizing stretches even farther to οὐκ ... πᾶσα σάρξ (*ouk ... pasa sarx*, lit., "not ... all flesh," i.e., no person).

24 The construction ὥστε πλανῆσαι (*hōste planēsai*, "to deceive") would most naturally be expected to be consecutive, and so it may be (Moule, *Idiom Book*, 143); but the same construction can have final force (Zerwick, *Biblical Greek*, para. 352), as does the parallel expression in Mark 13:22.

3. The coming of the Son of Man (24:29–31)

OVERVIEW

Matthew essentially follows Mark (13:24–27; cf. Lk 21:25–28) but adds the allusion to Zechariah about mourning (v.30) and the trumpet call (v.31).

29"Immediately after the distress of those days

"'the sun will be darkened,
and the moon will not give its light;
the stars will fall from the sky,
and the heavenly bodies will be shaken.'

30"At that time the sign of the Son of Man will appear in the sky, and all the nations of
the earth will mourn. They will see the Son of Man coming on the clouds of the sky, with
power and great glory. 31And he will send his angels with a loud trumpet call, and they will
gather his elect from the four winds, from one end of the heavens to the other."

COMMENTARY

29 For general arguments that vv.29–31 refer to the Parousia, not the coming of the Son of Man in the events of AD 70, see comments at vv.1–3. Mark brackets the last section (Mk 13:5–23 parallels Mt 24:4–28) with *blepete* ("watch out," GK *1063*) in Mark 13:5, 23. Matthew has nothing similar, but the effect is the same because v.29 begins the new stage with "Immediately after the distress [*thlipsis*] of those days," a clear reference back to the *thlipsis* of vv.9, 22, not to the "great distress" of vv.15–21. Thus the celestial signs and the coming of the Son of Man do not immediately follow "the abomination that causes desolation" but "the distress of those days"—i.e., of the entire interadvent period of *thlipsis*.

The cosmic portents (cf. esp. Isa 13:9–10; 34:4; but also Eze 32:7; Joel 2:31; 3:15; Am 8:9; Rev 6:12) are probably meant to be taken literally, because of the climactic nature of the Son of Man's final self-disclosure. Yet this is not certain, since in some political contexts, similar expressions are used metaphorically (see comments at vv.1–13).

30 "The sign of the Son of Man" has been interpreted in three principal ways.

1. Some of the Fathers after the Constantinian settlement thought it referred to Constantine's vision of a cross in the sky, with the words "In this sign, conquer"—an interpretation both anachronistic and fanciful.

2. More commonly, "the sign" is assumed to be Jesus' coming, with "of the Son of Man ... in the sky" being taken as standing in epexegetical relation to "the sign." The Jews had repeatedly asked for a sign (12:38; 16:1; cf. Jn 2:18), and the disciples had just asked for the sign of his coming (v.3). The supreme "sign" is his parousia at the end of the age. This interpretation is possible, though perhaps a bit forced. When the Jews asked for a sign, Jesus referred them to "the sign of Jonah" (12:39–41), not to his parousia. His disciples' more specific question (v.3) was partially answered by vv.4–28, with a fuller answer in vv.32–35.

3. T. F. Glasson ("The Ensign of the Son of Man [Matt. xxiv, 30]," *JTS* [1964]: 299–300) offers the best explanation. He points out that careful comparison of vv.30–31 with the synoptic parallels shows Matthew has added mention of both "sign" and "trumpet." But *sēmeion* ("sign," GK *4956*) commonly meant "ensign" or "standard" both in pagan Greek literature and in the LXX; and "standard" and "trumpet" are both regularly associated with the eschatological gathering of the people of God (cf. v.31; Isa 11:12; 18:3; 27:13; 49:22; Jer 4:21; 6:1; 51:27; 1QM 3:14:2). Therefore, *sēmeion* has two different meanings in this chapter (vv.3, 30)—a phenomenon common enough in the NT. Theologically, this means that the kingdom is being consummated. The standard, the banner of the Son of Man, unfurls in the heavens, as he himself returns in splendor and power. This view is rightly taken up by many today (e.g., Davies and Allison, Turner).

The event will prompt "all the nations of the earth" to mourn, an allusion to Zechariah 12:10–12, probably directly from the MT (see Gundry, *Use of the Old Testament*, 53; Blomberg, "Matthew" in *CNTUOT*; cf. Jn 19:37; Rev 1:7). In Zechariah, the reference is to the tribes of Israel in the land, and the mourning is that of repentance. Those who follow Kik (*Matthew Twenty-Four*) and France (*Jesus and the Old Testament*) want to keep the first link with the OT (the tribes of Israel) but not the second (the mourning; see comments at vv.1–3). Most scholars see the mourning (v.30) as that of despair, not repentance (Rev 1:7, 6:15–17), and I have already argued for the translation "all the nations of the earth" (NIV) over "all the tribes of the land." So it seems that neither link with the OT is simple, and we must probe for a deeper link.

What we discover is an implicit a fortiori argument. In Zechariah 12, Yahweh enables the house of David and Judah to crush its enemies; as a result, the Jews weep, apparently in contrition for their past sins in light of Yahweh's merciful deliverance and salvation (cf. Zec 13:1–2). But it is the Gentile enemies who are crushed. If, then, the Jews face judgment and mourning (vv.15–21), even though not only Jerusalem but also *all nations* (v.9) have hated Jesus' disciples, *how much more* will all the nations of the earth, to whom the gospel has been preached (v.14), also mourn at the Parousia, when the lost opportunities and the persecution of Jesus through persecuting his disciples are seen as they truly are?

The next allusion in v.30 is to Daniel 7:13–14. Some have objected that, since in Daniel's vision "one like a son of man" approaches the throne of "the Ancient of Days" and does not descend to earth, v.30 and parallels cannot be speaking about the Parousia, which requires the descent to earth. The objection misses the point. In Daniel, "one like a son of man" approaches God to receive all authority, glory, and sovereign power—"an everlasting dominion that will not pass away." In the framework of NT eschatology, we may imagine Jesus the Son of Man receiving the kingdom through his resurrection and ascension, his divine vindication, so that now all authority is his (28:18). Yet it is equally possible to think of him receiving the kingdom at the consummation, when his reign or kingdom becomes direct and immediate, uncontested and universal. Unless one thinks of the location of the Ancient of Days in some physical and spatial sense, it is hard to imagine why Christ's approaching God the Father to receive the kingdom might not be combined with his returning to earth to set up the consummated kingdom. This interpretation goes well with the vivid context.

The Son of Man, whose standard has been unfurled, comes "on [*epi*] the clouds of heaven" (cf. 26:64; Rev 14:14–16). It is doubtful whether sharp distinctions are to be drawn between this expression and "in [*en*] a cloud" (Lk 21:27; cf. Mk 13:26) or "with [*meta*] the clouds of heaven" (Mk 14:62 [NIV, "on"]; Rev 1:7). The clouds symbolize God's presence (see comments at 17:5): Immanuel ("God with us") comes "with power and great glory." The latter phrase not only ensures that the coming is universally witnessed and unmistakably plain (cf. vv.26–28, 30) but may allude to Isaiah 11:10: the nations will rally to "the Root of Jesse," and his place of rest will be (lit.) "the Glory" (cf. M. G. Kline, "Primal Parousia," *WTJ* 40 [1977–78]: 274).

31 The sound of a loud trumpet (cf. Isa 27:13; 1Co 15:52; 1Th 4:16) is an eschatological figure (see comments at v.30). Only with considerable difficulty can v.31 be interpreted as referring to Christian missions; its natural linguistic relations are in 13:41. For "his elect," see comments at 22:14; 24:22. The "four winds" represent the four points of the compass (Eze 37:9; Da 8:8; 11:4)—the elect are gathered from all over (cf. 8:11), "from one end of the heavens to the other" (from every place under the sky), since that is how far the gospel of the kingdom will have been preached (v.14). Although all nations of the earth will mourn, nevertheless the elect are drawn from them.

4. The significance of the birth pains (24:32–35)

32"Now learn this lesson from the fig tree: As soon as its twigs get tender and its leaves
come out, you know that summer is near. 33Even so, when you see all these things, you

know that it is near, right at the door. [34]I tell you the truth, this generation will certainly not pass away until all these things have happened. [35]Heaven and earth will pass away, but my words will never pass away."

COMMENTARY

32–33 This "lesson" (*parabolē*, GK *4130*, lit., "parable"; see comments at 13:3a; 15:15) of the fig tree (cf. 21:18–22) is based on the common observation that the twigs get tender before summer and arouse expectations of summer (v.32). Although the Greek is ambiguous, the NIV's "you know" (v.33) is preferable to the KJV's imperative ("know"). The "parable" points to the relation between "all these things" and "it is near" (v.33). It is uncertain whether the antecedent of "it" is the Parousia or Jesus, the Son of Man. Jesus sometimes spoke of himself in the third person (v.31) and may be doing so here. But whatever "it" refers to, it is certainly the nearness of the second advent that is in view.

"All these things" is more problematic. If the words include the celestial signs and *the Parousia itself* (vv.29–31), then vv.32–33 are illogical, because any distinction between "all these things" and "it is near" would be destroyed. Thus many have suggested that vv.32–33 constitute a displaced parable—once again making the synoptists out to be less intelligent than their critics two millennia later. The more natural way to take "all these things" is to see them as referring to the distress of vv.4–28, the tribulation that comes on believers throughout the period between Jesus' ascension and the Parousia.

Having warned his disciples of the course of this age (vv.4–28) and told them of its climax in the Parousia (vv.29–31), Jesus in these verses answers the part of his disciples' questions (v.3) dealing with timing. He makes two points. First, "all these things" (vv.4–28) must happen, and then the Parousia is "near, right at the door"—"imminent." In other words, the Parousia is the next major step in God's redemptive purposes. Second, this does not mean that the period of distress pinpoints the Parousia, for "no one knows about that day or hour" (vv.36–42).

34 "I tell you the truth" emphasizes the importance of what it introduces. "This generation" (see comments at 11:16; 12:41–42; 23:36; cf. 10:23; 16:28) can only with the greatest difficulty be made to mean anything other than the generation living when Jesus spoke. Even if "generation" by itself can have a slightly larger semantic range, to make "*this* generation" refer to all believers in every age, or the generation of believers alive when eschatological events start to happen, is highly artificial. Yet it does not follow that Jesus mistakenly thought the Parousia would occur within his hearers' lifetime. If our interpretation of this chapter is right, all that v.34 demands is that the distress of vv.4–28, including Jerusalem's fall, happens within the lifetime of the generation then living. This does *not* mean that the distress must end within that time but only that "all these things" must happen within it. Therefore, v.34 sets a terminus a quo for the Parousia; it cannot happen until the events in vv.4–28 take place, all within a generation of AD 30. But there is no terminus ad quem to this distress other than the Parousia itself, and "only the Father" knows when it will happen (v.36).

35 The authority and eternal validity of Jesus' words are nothing less than the authority and eternal validity of God's words (Ps 119:89–90; Isa 40:6–8).

5. The day and hour unknown: the need to be prepared (24:36–41)

a. The principle (24:36)

36"No one knows about that day or hour, not even the angels in heaven, nor the Son, but only the Father."

COMMENTARY

36 Many commentators read v.36 with the preceding paragraph; but it goes much better with the following verses, which constitute an exhortation to vigilance precisely because, the day and the hour being unknown to humanity, life goes on as it always has. The *gar* ("for") at the beginning of v.37 must not be overlooked, as in the NIV.

The gist of v.36 is clear enough. Jesus' disciples are morally bound to repress all desires to know what no one knows but the Father—not even angels (cf. 18:10; *4 Ezra* 4:52) or the Son (see Notes). If the Son himself does not know the time of the Parousia, "how cheerfully should we his followers rest in ignorance that cannot be removed, trusting in all things to our heavenly Father's wisdom and goodness, striving to obey his clearly revealed will, and leaning on his goodness for support" (Broadus). Moreover, it is ridiculous quibbling divorced from the context to say that though the day and hour remain unknown, we ascertain the year or month.

Jesus' self-confessed ignorance on this point has generated not a little debate. In fact, it is part of the NT pattern of his humiliation and incarnation (e.g., 20:23; Lk 2:52; Ac 1:7; Php 2:7). John's gospel, the one of the four gospels most clearly insisting on Jesus' deity, also insists with equal vigor on Jesus' dependence on and obedience to his Father—a dependence reaching even to his knowledge of the divine. How NT insistence on Jesus' deity is to be combined with NT insistence on his ignorance and dependence is a matter of profound importance to the church; attempts to jettison one truth for the sake of preserving the other must be avoided. (For an attempt to work some of these things out, see Carson, *Divine Sovereignty*, 146–60.)

NOTES

36 The words "nor the Son," while textually secure in Mark 13:32, are disputed here. The omission is supported by most late MSS and by ℵ[a]. Such omission may have been prompted by the doctrinal difficulty presented by the words, but it is mildly surprising that Mark 13:32 has not suffered similar distortion. One might in fact argue that the omission in Matthew is original and that the words were added by assimilation to Mark. The most convincing argument in favor of retaining the words in Matthew is grammatical (cf. Metzger, *Textual Commentary*, 62). The curious suggestion of Jeremias (*Prayers of Jesus*, 37), that "nor the Son" is a late addition in both Matthew and Mark that makes explicit the implications of "but only the Father," is not only without textual warrant but also an intrinsically unlikely christological development.

b. Analogy of the days of Noah (24:37–39)

[37]"As it was in the days of Noah, so it will be at the coming of the Son of Man. [38]For in the days before the flood, people were eating and drinking, marrying and giving in marriage, up to the day Noah entered the ark; [39]and they knew nothing about what would happen until the flood came and took them all away. That is how it will be at the coming of the Son of Man."

COMMENTARY

37–39 (See also Mk 13:33 and Lk 17:28–32, though the latter is in a different context and has quite different structure and wording.) The *gar* ("for") in the best MSS further elucidates v.36: that the coming of the Son of Man takes place at an unknown time can be true only if, in fact, life seems to be going on pretty much as usual—just as in the days before the flood (v.37). People follow their ordinary pursuits (v.38). Despite the distress, persecutions, and upheavals (vv.4–28), life goes on: people eat, drink, and marry. There is no overt typological usage of the flood as judgment here, nor any mention of the sin of that generation. Yet Jesus' warning may well have given rise to 1 Peter 3:20–21. Jesus expects ceaseless vigilance of his followers, for the final climax of human history will suddenly come on ordinary life. In the human condition, massive distress and normal life patterns coexist. For the believer the former points to the end; the latter warn of its unexpectedness.

c. Two in the field; two with a mill (24:40–41)

[40]"Two men will be in the field; one will be taken and the other left. [41]Two women will be grinding with a hand mill; one will be taken and the other left."

COMMENTARY

40–41 These two vignettes do not "stress the sharp cleavage caused by the coming of the Son of Man, *rather than* the unexpectedness of the event" (Hill, emphasis mine), but the unexpectedness of the event by means of the sudden cleavage. Two men are working in a field; one is taken, the other left (v.40). Two women work their hand mill (v.41)—one normally operated by two women squatting opposite each other with the mill between them, each woman in turn pulling the stone around 180 degrees. The two are apt to be sisters, mother and daughter, or two household slaves. Yet no matter how close their relationship, one is taken, the other left (cf. 10:35–36). It is neither clear nor particularly important whether "taken" means "taken in judgment" (cf. v.39, though the verb "took ... away" differs from "taken" in vv.40–41) or "taken to be gathered with the elect" (v.31).

6. Parabolic teaching: variations on watchfulness (24:42–25:46)

a. The homeowner and the thief (24:42–44)

OVERVIEW

The exact relation between vv.42–51 and Mark 13:33–37 is obscure and has not been satisfactorily explained. On the nature of parables, see comments at Matthew 13:3a; on comparison with Luke 12:39–40, see discussion and chart at Matthew 19:1–2. Each of the five parables in 24:42–25:46 deals with some aspect of watchfulness. But watchfulness is not always passive: duties and responsibilities must be discharged (24:45–51), and foresight and wisdom are important (25:1–13). Responsible living under Jesus' directives is rewarded in the end (24:14–46).

42"Therefore keep watch, because you do not know on what day your Lord will come.
43But understand this: If the owner of the house had known at what time of night the thief was coming, he would have kept watch and would not have let his house be broken into.
44So you also must be ready, because the Son of Man will come at an hour when you do not expect him."

COMMENTARY

42–44 The first parable teaches both the unexpectedness of the return of "your Lord" (*kyrios hymōn*, v.42)—an expression that not only is identical to "the master" in the next parable (v.45) but lays the foundation for the church's cry "Come, O Lord!" (1Co 16:22)—and the willingness of the church to call Jesus *ho kyrios* ("the Lord"), a title hitherto reserved in its religious use by the Jews for God himself (1Co 12:3; Php 4:5; 2Th 2:2; Jas 5:7; see comments at 8:2; 17:4, 14–16; 21:3; 22:41–46). It might be better to take *ginōskete* not as an imperative (NIV, "understand," v.43, GK *1182*) but as an indicative ("you know"): the disciples know the owner of a house would watch if he knew when the thief was coming (on the tenses of the verb, see Zerwick, *Biblical Greek*, para. 317), so the thief could not break in (on the verb, see comments at 6:19). Since no one knows at what time or during what "watch" the thief might strike, constant vigilance is required. "So you also must be ready" (v.44), because in this one respect—the unexpectedness of his coming—the Son of Man (see comments at vv.37, 39; 8:20) resembles a thief.

b. The two servants (24:45–51)

OVERVIEW

The good servant is prepared for his Lord at any time, is faithful throughout his delay, and in the end is highly rewarded. The wicked servant is faithless in his responsibilities, abusive to fellow servants, and lax in waiting for his master's return, and he ultimately earns the punishment that is his due (see chart and comments at 19:1–2; cf. 21:34–36; Mk 13:34–37; Lk 12:35–38, 42–46).

45"Who then is the faithful and wise servant, whom the master has put in charge of the
servants in his household to give them their food at the proper time? 46It will be good for
that servant whose master finds him doing so when he returns. 47I tell you the truth, he
will put him in charge of all his possessions. 48But suppose that servant is wicked and says
to himself, 'My master is staying away a long time,' 49and he then begins to beat his fellow
servants and to eat and drink with drunkards. 50The master of that servant will come on
a day when he does not expect him and at an hour he is not aware of. 51He will cut him
to pieces and assign him a place with the hypocrites, where there will be weeping and
gnashing of teeth."

COMMENTARY

45–47 The *doulos* ("servant," GK *1528*) in this parable is the head over all the domestics. This, however, does not so much limit the application of the parable to leaders as establish that their responsibilities entail good personal relationships (v.49), requiring exemplary conduct and precluding harshness and lording it over others. The good servant is faithful and "wise" (i.e., prudent, judicious—cf. 7:24; 10:16), doing what is assigned him. When his master returns (v.46), he is *makarios* ("blessed," GK *3421*; NIV, "will be good"; see comments at 5:3) and promoted (v.47; cf. 25:21). In Mark 13:37, Jesus applies the necessity of watching to "everyone."

48–51 If the servant is wicked (v.48) and lacking faithfulness and wisdom (v.45), he may convince himself that the master "is staying away a long time"—perhaps a subtle hint that the Parousia could be considerably delayed (cf. 25:19). The wicked servant uses the delay to abuse his fellow servants and carouse (v.49). (For "begins to beat," see 11:7, 20.) But the wicked servant, surprised and unprepared for his master's return (v.50), is put with the "hypocrites" (v.51). His lot is with the punishment given those most constantly held up as vile in this gospel (6:2, 5, 16; 15:7; 23:13–29). The master "will cut him to pieces" (cf. 1Sa 15:33; Heb 11:37; Sus 55; on the punishments accorded Jewish slaves, see Str-B, 4:698–744). *Dichotomeō* literally is "I cut in two" (found in the NT only here and Lk 12:46). Alleged parallels in 1QS 1:10–11; 2:16–17; 6:24–25; 7:1, 2, 16; 8:21–23 are unconvincing. The Hebrew "cut off from the midst of the sons of light" refers to excommunication. Here, however, the wicked servant is not cut off from anything; he is cut in pieces—a most severe and awful punishment—and joins the hypocrites in weeping and grinding of teeth (cf. 8:12).

NOTES

50 This is one of only three places in Matthew where the relative pronoun is attracted to the case of its antecedent (see comments at 18:19; cf. 25:24).

c. The ten virgins (25:1–13)

OVERVIEW

This parable has been widely discussed. Hill, largely following Jeremias (*Parables of Jesus*, 51–53), notes the "allegorical" elements (bridegroom's coming = coming of the Son of Man; ten virgins = expectant Christian community; tarrying = delay of the Parousia; rejection of the foolish virgins = final judgment) and claims there is evidence for thinking these to be later additions by the church. This view is strengthened, it is claimed, by the fact that the equation Messiah = bridegroom is virtually unknown in late Judaism (cf. Jeremias, p. 52) and first appears in 2 Corinthians 11:2. The story Jesus actually told, stripped of its "allegorical accretions," involved wedding preparations and warned his hearers of the impending eschatological crisis. But this will not do. We have already seen that source criticism of gospel parables based on theoretical distinctions between "parable" and "allegory" is ill founded (see comments at 13:3a). The idea of Messiah as bridegroom springs from such OT passages as Isaiah 54:4–6; 62:4–5; Ezekiel 16:7–34; Hosea 2:19. There Yahweh is portrayed as the "husband" of his people. We have noted how readily Jesus in his parables places himself in Yahweh's place (see comments at 13:37–39). Moreover, both John the Baptist (Jn 3:27–30) and Jesus himself (9:15; Mk 2:19–20) have already made the equation Jesus = Messiah = bridegroom, unless we deny the historicity of these passages. But the parable makes sense in its own setting and as it stands.

While dispensationalists divide on whether this parable relates to the "rapture" of the church (A. C. Gaebelein) or the second advent, following the tribulation (Walvoord), both views introduce eschatological structures that do not emerge naturally from the text (see comments at v.13).

W. Schenk ("Auferweckung der Toten oder Gericht nach den Werken: Tradition und Redaktion in Matthäus xxv 13," *NovT* 20 [1978]: 278–99) reconstructs a very simple "original" parable in which all the virgins have enough oil but only five of them sleep. When the bridegroom comes, they all enter and enjoy the feast. The point is that when the bridegroom comes, some are asleep and some are awake, but all enjoy the festivities (as in 1Th 4:15–17). But Matthew has allegorized this parable and required a store of good works (oil) as qualification for entry. It is hard to decide which of Schenk's options is more wrong—his reconstruction of the alleged original or his interpretation of the parable as it stands in Matthew.

Blickenstaff (*While the Bridegroom*, 78–109) continues her "resistant reading" of select parables found in Matthew and insists the bridegroom is simply rude and cannot possibly represent Jesus or God; this is merely more prejudice and violence against women. Scarcely less idiosyncratic is J. M. Ford ("The Parable of the Foolish Scholars," *NovT* 9 [1967]: 107–23), who, arguing largely from late rabbinic sources, claims the virgins represent Jewish scholars, the lamps Torah, and the oil good deeds. The foolish virgins are Jewish scholars who study Torah but who fail to practice good deeds. They are, therefore, excluded from the Chamber of Instruction.

Such ingenuity ignores both the narrative and the context, as J. M. Sherriff ("Matthew 25:1–13: A Summary of Matthean Eschatology?" in *Studia Biblica 1978* [ed. Livingstone], 2:301–5) has pointed out. The plot turns on the bridegroom's delay. The foolish virgins do not *forget* to bring oil; rather, the delay of the bridegroom shows they did not bring enough. The oil cannot easily apply to "good works" or "Holy Spirit." It is merely an element in the narrative showing that the foolish virgins were unprepared for the delay and so shut out in the end. In a real sense, it is the bridegroom's delay that distinguishes the wise from the foolish virgins. Any interpretation that ignores this central element in the story is bound to go astray (cf. G. Bornkamm, *Geschichte*, 49–50). The context similarly shows that the overriding theme is preparedness for the coming of the Son of Man. Even when this involves certain forms of behavior (24:45–51; 25:14–30), that behavior is called forth by the unexpectedness of the master's return.

From this perspective, vv.1–13 fit well into this sequence of parables and agree with what we know Jesus taught. There is no good reason for doubting their authenticity or retreating to one of several reconstructed cores. The first parable (24:42–44) warns of the unexpectedness of Messiah's coming. The second (24:45–51) shows that more than passive watchfulness is required: there must be behavior acceptable to the master, the discharge of allotted responsibilities. This third parable (25:1–13) stresses the need for preparedness in the face of an unexpectedly long delay.

[1]"At that time the kingdom of heaven will be like ten virgins who took their lamps and
went out to meet the bridegroom. [2]Five of them were foolish and five were wise. [3]The
foolish ones took their lamps but did not take any oil with them. [4]The wise, however, took
oil in jars along with their lamps. [5]The bridegroom was a long time in coming, and they all
became drowsy and fell asleep.

[6]"At midnight the cry rang out: 'Here's the bridegroom! Come out to meet him!'

[7]"Then all the virgins woke up and trimmed their lamps. [8]The foolish ones said to the
wise, 'Give us some of your oil; our lamps are going out.'

[9]"'No,' they replied, 'there may not be enough for both us and you. Instead, go to those
who sell oil and buy some for yourselves.'

[10]"But while they were on their way to buy the oil, the bridegroom arrived. The virgins
who were ready went in with him to the wedding banquet. And the door was shut.

[11]"Later the others also came. 'Sir! Sir!' they said. 'Open the door for us!'

[12]"But he replied, 'I tell you the truth, I don't know you.'

[13]"Therefore keep watch, because you do not know the day or the hour."

COMMENTARY

1 *Tote* ("At that time") is sufficiently vague in Matthew's usage (see comments at 2:7; 24:9) that not much can be built on it. The most natural way to take it here is as a reference to the coming of the Son of Man (cf. 24:29–31, 36–44). "At that time" the kingdom of heaven will become like the story of the ten virgins (so the Gk.; cf. Carson, "ὅμοιος Word-Group")—i.e., the parable deals with the onset of the consummated kingdom.

The setting is fairly clear, given what we know of the marriage customs of the day (cf. Broadus; Jeremias, *Parables of Jesus*, 173–74; *TDNT*, 4:1100; esp. H. Granquist, *Marriage Conditions in a Palestinian Village* [2 vols.; Helsingfors: Central-tryckeriet, 1931, 1935]; Bailey, *Jesus through Middle Eastern Eyes*, esp. 271–73). Normally the bridegroom with some close friends left his home to go to the bride's home, where there were various ceremonies, followed by a procession through the streets—after nightfall—to his home. The ten virgins may be bridesmaids who have been assisting the bride; they expect to meet the groom as he comes from the bride's house (cf. Kistemaker, *Parables of Jesus*, 130), though this is uncertain. Everyone in the procession was expected to carry his or her own torch. Those without a torch would be assumed to be party crashers or even brigands. The festivities, which might last several days, would formally get under way at the groom's house.

That the bride is not mentioned in the best MSS (see Notes) has been variously interpreted. Some have thought this is the trip to the bride's house or that this is one of those rare occasions when all the festivities took place at her home, because the groom lived at a considerable distance. But then the bride's father, not the groom, would have refused entrance to the foolish virgins. To demand the presence of the bride is to demand that the parable walk on all fours; mention of her is not essential to the story.

For the meaning of *parthenos* ("virgin," GK *4221*), see comments at 1:23. The point is not these girls' virginity, which is assumed, but simply that they are ten (a favorite round number; e.g., Ru 4:2; Lk 19:13; Josephus, *J.W.* 6.423–24 [9.3]) maidens invited to the wedding. The "lamps" (not the same word as in 5:15) are here either small oil-fed lamps or, more plausibly, torches whose rags would need periodic dowsing with oil to keep them burning. In either case, the prudent would bring along a flask with an additional oil supply.

2–5 The "wise" are called such because they are prepared (v.4) for the bridegroom's delayed coming. Both wise and foolish wait and doze (v.5); no praise or blame attaches to either group for this. There is no point in seeing hidden meanings in the oil or sleep. The sole distinction between the two groups is this: the wise bring not only oil in their lamps but an extra supply in separate jars, while the foolish bring no oil (either no extra oil or no oil at all [cf. Robertson, *Word Pictures*, 1:196; Hendriksen; Lenski]; if the latter, then the lamps going out [v.8] is the sputtering of wicks or rags that burn brightly but don't last). The wise are prepared for delay; the foolish expect to meet the groom but are either utterly unprepared or unprepared if he is delayed. And the bridegroom is a long time coming (24:48; 25:19).

6–9 At midnight, symbol of eschatological climax, "the cry rang out"—an admirable paraphrase of *kraugē gegonen* (lit., "a cry has arisen"; the perfect is unusual and probably dramatic; cf. Moule,

Idiom Book, 14, 202; BDF, para. 343 [3]). All the virgins wake up and trim their lamps (v.7), but the lamps of the foolish virgins quickly go out (present tense, "are going out," contra the KJV's "are gone out"). Apart from the identification of "oil" with "grace," Matthew Henry's observation is pertinent: "They will see their need of grace hereafter, when it should save them, who will not see their need of grace now, when it should sanctify and rule them" (p. 291). The wise virgins cannot help them. Whether the text reads "there may not be enough" or "there will certainly not be enough" (see Notes), the effect is the same: the foresight and preparedness of the wise virgins cannot benefit the foolish virgins when the eschatological crisis dawns (vv.8–9). Preparedness can be neither transferred nor shared.

10–12 The bridegroom comes, the wise virgins enter, and the door is shut (cf. 7:22–23; Lk 13:25). The intense cries of the ill-prepared and foolish latecomers—"Sir! Sir!" (on the doubling, cf. BDF, para. 493 [1]; 7:21–23; 23:37)—are of no avail (v.11). Because this parable concerns the consummation, the refusal to recognize or admit the foolish virgins (v.12) must not be construed as calloused rejection of their lifelong desire to enter the kingdom. Far from it; it is the rejection of those who, despite appearances, never made preparation for the coming of the kingdom.

13 The theme is reiterated once more (cf. 24:36, 42, 44, 50). Jeremias (*Parables of Jesus*, 52) and others suggest this verse is a late addition to the parable, since it is at variance with the fact that both the wise and the foolish virgins fell asleep. But this misses the purpose of v.13. "Keep watch" does not mean "keep awake," as if an ability to fight off sleep were relevant to the story. Rather, in light of the entire parable, the dominant exhortation of this discourse is repeated: Be prepared! Keep watching!

NOTES

1 The words "and the bride," attested by D X* Θ f^1 et al., may have been added out of a sense of propriety, a desire for a well-rounded story in which the bride should be present. Alternatively, one might argue that the words were original but omitted out of the widely held view that Christ would come and fetch his bride, the church. These and other internal considerations (how much did copyists know about marriage customs in Jesus' day?) are indecisive. On external evidence alone, omission is more likely original.

9 The two readings are (1) μήποτε οὐκ ἀρκέσῃ (*mēpote ouk arkesē*, "no, there may not be enough"), supported by ℵ A L Z (Θ) f^{13} et al.; and (2) μήποτε οὐ μὴ ἀρκέσῃ (*mēpote ou mē arkesē*, perhaps "no, there will certainly not be enough"), attested by B C D K W Δ et al. The second option might be taken to introduce into the parable the notion of the absolute untransferability of the oil. But three things must be borne in mind: (1) though the grammatical points are much discussed, there is some ground for thinking that by NT times the second construction (οὐ μὴ, *ou mē*, plus the subjunctive) could itself be softened to the first meaning (cf. Zerwick, *Biblical Greek*, para. 444); (2) on internal grounds, the first reading is considerably more likely, since copyists might well wish to change an οὐκ, *ouk*, to an οὐ μὴ, *ou mē*, before the subjunctive; and (3) the effect on the story is the same—whether the wise virgins are certain they will not have enough oil to share or doubt that they will, the outcome is the same; and the reasons differ but little.

d. The talents (25:14–30)

OVERVIEW

This parable goes beyond the first three (24:42–25:13) in that it expects the watchfulness of the servants to manifest itself during the master's absence, not only in preparedness and performance of duty, even if there is a long delay, but in an improvement of the allotted "talents" until the day of reckoning.

The parable is frequently compared with Luke 19:11–27, the parable of the ten minas. The majority opinion today is that there is only one original and that most likely Luke has borrowed from Matthew's version or from a precursor of it (cf. Marshall, *Gospel of Luke*, 700–703; esp. Davies and Allison; see chart and comments at 19:1–2). Borrowing the other way is scarcely conceivable. Would Matthew, for instance, be likely to eliminate the "king" theme found in Luke? The language of the two pericopes is rather different, and most of the differing details cannot be reconciled on normal grounds. The few parallels are well within the bounds of the speech variation of any itinerant preacher. Moreover, the emphasis in each of the two parables is somewhat different, and Luke's is tightly tied to the Zacchaeus episode. The somewhat similar parable in the later noncanonical Gospel of the Nazarenes (Hennecke, *New Testament Apocrypha*, 1:149) is undoubtedly secondary and dependent on Matthew. On the whole, it seems best to side with certain older commentators (Plummer, Zahn) who discern two separate parables.

[14]"Again, it will be like a man going on a journey, who called his servants and entrusted
his property to them. [15]To one he gave five talents of money, to another two talents, and to
another one talent, each according to his ability. Then he went on his journey. [16]The man
who had received the five talents went at once and put his money to work and gained
five more. [17]So also, the one with the two talents gained two more. [18]But the man who had
received the one talent went off, dug a hole in the ground and hid his master's money.

[19]"After a long time the master of those servants returned and settled accounts with
them. [20]The man who had received the five talents brought the other five. 'Master,' he said,
'you entrusted me with five talents. See, I have gained five more.'

[21]"His master replied, 'Well done, good and faithful servant! You have been faithful
with a few things; I will put you in charge of many things. Come and share your master's
happiness!'

[22]"The man with the two talents also came. 'Master,' he said, 'you entrusted me with two
talents; see, I have gained two more.'

[23]"His master replied, 'Well done, good and faithful servant! You have been faithful with a
few things; I will put you in charge of many things. Come and share your master's happiness!'

[24]"Then the man who had received the one talent came. 'Master,' he said, 'I knew that
you are a hard man, harvesting where you have not sown and gathering where you have

not scattered seed. [25]So I was afraid and went out and hid your talent in the ground. See, here is what belongs to you.'

[26]"His master replied, 'You wicked, lazy servant! So you knew that I harvest where I have not sown and gather where I have not scattered seed? [27]Well then, you should have put my money on deposit with the bankers, so that when I returned I would have received it back with interest.

[28]"'Take the talent from him and give it to the one who has the ten talents. [29]For everyone who has will be given more, and he will have an abundance. Whoever does not have, even what he has will be taken from him. [30]And throw that worthless servant outside, into the darkness, where there will be weeping and gnashing of teeth.'"

COMMENTARY

14 The introduction to this parable in the Greek is somewhat abrupt (lit., "for as," without mention of the kingdom, "it" [NIV]; or a verb [NIV, "will be"]; the closest parallel is Mk 13:34). Probably this parable is so tightly associated with the last one as to share its introduction (see comments at v.1).

Slaves in the ancient world could enjoy considerable responsibility and authority. The man going on a journey entrusts his cash assets to three of his slaves who are understood to be almost partners in his affairs and who may share some of his profits (cf. Derrett, *Law in the New Testament*, 18). The departure and the property are integral parts of the story and should not be allegorized (to refer to the ascension and the gifts of the Spirit), though doubtless some early readers after Pentecost read these into the text.

15 Modern English uses the word "talent" for skills and mental powers God has entrusted to people, but in NT times the *talanton* ("talent," GK *5419*) was a unit of exchange. Estimates of its value vary enormously for four reasons.

1. A talent could be of gold, silver, or copper, each with its own value. *Argyrion* in v.18, a word that can mean either "money" or "silver," may hint at the second option.

2. The talent was first a measure according to weight—between fifty-eight and eighty pounds (twenty-six to thirty-six kilograms)—and then a unit of coinage, one common value assigned it being six thousand denarii.

3. Although it is possible to calculate by weight or metallic value, another problem remains. For instance, eighty pounds of silver at fifteen dollars an ounce would mean that a talent was worth about nineteen thousand dollars. But modern inflation changes silver values so quickly that prices are soon obsolete. Yet such equivalences are passed on from generation to generation of reference texts (e.g., BAG [1957] and BAGD [1979] have the same figures; mercifully, BDAG [2000] updates).

4. It may be more sensible to compare the talent with modern currency in terms of earning power. If a talent was worth six thousand denarii, then it would take a day laborer twenty years to earn so much—perhaps three hundred thousand dollars. If the weight was of gold (cf. the TNIV's "bag of gold"), then the value was much greater yet. On any reckoning, the NIV's footnote ("more than a thousand dollars") is much too low.

So the sums are vast—much larger than in Luke 19:11–27, where a "mina" (one hundred drachmas) is very close to one hundred denarii, or one-third of a year's wages (perhaps five thousand dollars). Moreover, in Matthew's parable, the talents are distributed according to the master's evaluation of his slaves' capacities, whereas in Luke, each slave is given the same amount. In Matthew, therefore, the parable lays intrinsic emphasis on the principle "to whom much is given, from him also shall much be required."

Attempts to identify the talents with spiritual gifts, the law, natural endowments, the gospel, or whatever else lead to a narrowing of the parable with which Jesus would have been uncomfortable. Perhaps he chose the talent or mina symbolism because of its capacity for varied application.

16–18 "At once" relates to the slave's promptness to put the money to work (NIV), not with the owner's departure (KJV; cf. Metzger, *Textual Commentary*, 63). The point is that the good slaves felt the responsibility of their assignment and went to work without delay. The NIV's "put his money to work" does not mean the slave invested the money in some lending agency. Rather, he set up some business and worked with the capital to make it grow. But one slave, unwilling to work or take risks, merely dug a hole and buried the money (v.18). This was safer than the deposit systems of the time. (In Luke's parable, the money of the last slave is hidden in a piece of cloth.)

19–23 The accounting begins "after a long time" (v.19), the implication being that the consummation of the kingdom will be long delayed (24:48; 25:5). "Settled accounts" (*synairei logon*) is a standard commercial term (cf. Deissmann, *Light from the Ancient East*, 118–19). The first slave, who doubled his five talents (v.20), is praised, especially for his faithfulness, and given two things (vv.21, 23): increased responsibility and a share in his master's *chara* ("joy," as in Jn 15:11). But we should not conclude that the sole reward of fulfilled responsibility is increased responsibility. The eschatological setting, coupled with the promise of joy that bursts the natural limits of the story, guarantees that the consummated kingdom provides glorious new responsibilities and holy delight (cf. Ro 8:17).

The parallelism of vv.22–23 with vv.20–21 is not exact but close (cf. 7:26–27 with 7:24–25) and reflects a Semitic cast. The second slave has been faithful with what has been given him (v.22) and hears the same words as his more able fellow slave (v.23). Probably the "many things" assigned the two men are not exactly the same. The point is not egalitarianism, whether here (cf. 13:23) or in the consummated kingdom, but increased responsibility and a share in the master's joy to the limits of each faithful slave's capacity.

24–25 The third slave accuses his master of being a "hard" (*sklēros*, GK *5017*) man. The word, both in Greek and English, can mean various things (elsewhere in the NT it is found only in Jn 6:60; Ac 26:14; Jas 3:4; Jude 15). The slave is saying that the master is grasping, exploiting the labor of others ("harvesting where you have not sown"), and putting the slave in an invidious position. Should he take the risk of trying to increase the one talent entrusted to him, he would see little of the profit. If he failed and lost everything, he would incur the master's wrath. Perhaps, too, he is piqued at having been given much less than the other two (cf. Derrett, *Law in the New Testament*, 26); so, in a rather spiteful act, he returns to his master what belongs to him, no more and no less (v.25).

What this slave overlooks is his responsibility *as a slave* to his master and his obligation to discharge his assigned duties. We must not read the parable with modern Western eyes as an exercise in negotiations between capitalist owners and trade union workers, the latter having the right to go on strike and withdraw their labor. This slave's failure betrays not only his lack of love for his master, which he masks by blaming his master and excusing himself, but his own responsibilities *as a slave* (the modern rendering "servant" does not capture the original). Only the wicked slave blames his master. "There, the foolish virgins failed from thinking their part too easy—here, the wicked servant [fails] from thinking his too hard" (Alford, *New Testament for English Readers*, 1:173–74). Grace never condones irresponsibility; even those given less are obligated to use and develop what they have.

Is it necessary to point out that this parable no more condones slavery than comparing Jesus' coming to that of a thief (24:42–44) condones theft?

26–27 The master condemns the slave on the basis of the slave's own words, which prove his guilt (v.26). If the master was so hard and grasping, should not the slave have put the money where it would have been relatively safe, earned interest, and required no work (v.27)?

The OT forbade Israelites from charging interest to one another (Ex 22:25; Lev 25:35–37; Dt 23:19; cf. Ps 15:5; usury is from the Lat. *usura*, "use," and came to refer to the interest charged for the use of money), but interest on money loaned to Gentiles was permitted (Dt 23:20). Doubtless the law was frequently broken (e.g., Ne 5:10–12). By NT times, Jewish scholars already distinguished between "lending at interest" and "usury" (in the modern sense). According to Roman law the maximum rate of interest was 12 percent (cf. W. W. Buckland, *A Textbook of Roman Law* [3rd ed.; Cambridge: Cambridge Univ. Press, 1963], 465). It is wrong to assume that Jesus is here either supporting or setting aside the OT law. The question does not arise, for Jesus' parables are so flexible that he sometimes uses examples of evil to make a point about good (e.g., Lk 16:19; 18:18).

28–30 The talent entrusted to this wicked slave is taken from him; the relationship between master and slave is severed (cf. Derrett, *Law in the New Testament*, 28). It is given to the man who now has ten talents, following the kingdom rule (v.29) Jesus had already taught in 13:12. Moreover, there is OT warrant for this pattern. On this basis, the kingdom of Israel was stripped from Saul and given to David (cf. 21:43). The wicked slave is "worthless" (*achreios*, used only here [v.30] and in Lk 17:10), for to fail to do good and use what God has entrusted to us to use is grievous sin, which issues not only in the loss of neglected resources but in rejection by the master, banishment from his presence, and tears and gnashing of teeth.

The parable insists that the watchfulness that must mark all Jesus' disciples does not lead to passivity but to doing one's duty, to growing, to husbanding and developing the resources God entrusts to us, until "after a long time" (v.19) the master returns and settles accounts. Christ's followers, his slaves, are responsible for improving their Master's assets. For those of good heart, this will be more than a responsibility; it will be a challenge, a joy, a privilege. The parable applies widely and cannot be restricted to Christian leaders or Jews who fail to recognize their Messiah.

e. The sheep and the goats (25:31–46)

OVERVIEW

Strictly speaking, this passage is not a narrative parable. Its only parabolic elements are the shepherd, the sheep, the goats, and the actual separation. Moreover, because the pericope is unique to Matthew, criticism based on close parallels is impossible. It clearly functions in this discourse somewhat as 10:40–42 (with which it has some connections) does in the second discourse. Almost everyone praises the simplicity and power of the passage. Alford remarks, "It will heighten our estimation of the wonderful sublimity of this description, when we recollect that it was spoken by the Lord *only three days before his sufferings*" (*New Testament for English Readers*, 1:176, emphasis his). But there is disagreement over the meaning and literary history of these eloquent words.

For a detailed history of the interpretation of this parable, see Sherman W. Gray, *The Least of My Brothers: Matthew 25:31–46: A History of Interpretation* (SBLDS 114; Atlanta: Scholars Press, 1989).

1. A majority of scholars understand "the least of these brothers of mine" (vv.40, 45) to refer to all who are hungry, distressed, needy. The basis of acceptance into the kingdom is thus established by deeds of mercy and compassion. This interpretation is often allied with a misunderstanding of 22:34–40 (see comments there). The overall interpretation can take on varying forms as it relies on source-critical conclusions or particular views of the "Son of Man" (U. Wilckens, "Gottes geringste Brüder—zu Mt 25:31–46," in *Jesus und Paulus* [ed. Ellis and Grässer], 363–83; David R. Catchpole, "The Poor on Earth and the Son of Man in Heaven: A Reappraisal of Matthew xxv.31–46," *BJRL* 61 [1978–79]: 355–97).

Most authors stress the Jewish parallels relating to compassion and almsgiving. Bornkamm ("End-Expectation and the Church," 23–24) holds that the parable (as we shall call it) eliminates distinction not only between Jews and Gentiles but also between Jesus' disciples and unbelievers. All will ultimately be judged by their response to human need, and on this basis, some from each group will be numbered among the sheep (cf. P. Christian, *Jesus und seine geringsten Brüder* [Leipzig: St. Benno, 1975], who holds this is a sermon for the Christian church concerning the eschatological significance of human solidarity). J. Friedrich's *Gott im Brüder?* (Stuttgart: Calwer, 1977) includes much useful information about how this pericope has been interpreted; but its basic point—that Matthew narrowed down to Christians Jesus' teaching that the eschatological judgment would decide the fate of all men according to their response to all human need—is unconvincing because it rests on a redaction-critical methodology of dubious worth. Robert Smith (*Matthew* [ACNT; Minneapolis: Augsburg, 1989], 299) writes, "In his vision Jesus speaks about being identified with the world's outcasts, and in his passion he actively and actually identifies with them. The Son of God ... stands deliberately and voluntarily in the shoes of the powerless, the weak, the defenseless, the hated, the tortured." Powerfully stated, possibly at some level true—but is it the point of this parable?

The weakness of this general position is the identification of the least of Jesus' brothers with the poor and needy without distinction. There is no parallel for this, but there are one or two excellent alternative interpretations with strong NT parallels.

2. If the first interpretation extends "one of the least of these brothers of mine" too far, the second does not go far enough. Several scholars (e.g., J. R. Michaels, "Apostolic Hardships and Righteous Gentiles," *JBL* 84 [1965]: 27–37; J. Mánek, "Mit wem identifiziert sich Jesus (Matt 25:31–46)?" in *Christ and Spirit in the New Testament* [ed. B. Lindars and S. S. Smalley; Cambridge: Cambridge Univ. Press, 1973], 15–25) argue that Jesus' "least brothers" are apostles and other Christian missionaries, the treatment of whom determines the fate of all men. Those who receive them receive Christ; those who reject them reject Christ (cf. 10:40–42). This interpretation is much closer to the text than the first one. The only hesitation

concerns the restriction to apostles and missionaries in any technical sense. Appeal to Matthew 10 cuts two ways: though that mission was first restricted to the Twelve, it is clear that Jesus was looking beyond the Twelve to all true disciples, who without exception must confess him before men (10:32–33). Proclaiming the gospel of the kingdom to all nations (24:14) takes place in obedience to a universal mandate (28:18–20), and the suffering that Jesus envisages for his disciples (24:9–13) is not restricted to missionaries, even if sometimes theirs is a special share of it. Without detracting from the Twelve, Matthew's report of Jesus' words makes it clear that all true disciples are his emissaries.

3. Another restrictive interpretation is that of George Gay ("The Judgment of the Gentiles in Matthew's Theology," in *Scripture, Tradition, and Interpretation* [ed. W. W. Gasque and W. S. LaSor; Grand Rapids: Eerdmans, 1978], 199–215). Relying on Matthew 18, Gay holds that three mutually exclusive groups are involved: those outside the Christian community who think they are part of it, those inside the community but not the "little ones," and the "little ones" within the community. The basis for judgment is the attitude of professing believers to the "little ones," Jesus' favorites. The judgment is therefore not the judgment of the nations ("It would be unfair and illogical to judge the unrepentant who have never made any commitment to Jesus and know nothing of the demands of the kingdom on the same basis" [p. 210]).

But Matthew 18 does not support Gay's tripartite distinction, and 12:46–50 makes it clear that Jesus' brothers are his disciples. Moreover, the language of vv.31–32, 46, including a reference to "all the nations" gathered before the Son of Man "on his throne in heavenly glory," cannot easily be made to apply to anything as restricted as Gay suggests.

4. Dispensational writers see a reference to the second coming, after the church has been removed at the rapture. Jesus' "brothers" are Jews who have been converted during the tribulation, and the "nations" are converted Gentiles (the "sheep") because they side with the converted Jews during this period. But unconverted Gentiles (the "goats") continue to oppose Jesus' brothers (Jews converted during the tribulation). The sheep enter the millennial kingdom with Jesus' "brothers." "All the nations" (v.32), therefore, excludes Jews—though it is doubtful whether the same interpretation would be pressed in 28:18–20. Some older writers argue that the judgment determines what nations as opposed to individuals are admitted to the millennial kingdom, but see comments at 28:18–20. One or two nondispensationalist writers (e.g., Allen) think the "brothers" are Christian Jews.

This interpretation fails unless the dispensational interpretation of Matthew 24–25 is sustained, something we have rejected on other grounds (see comments at 24:13). Moreover, there is no such pinpointing in the passage itself. Jesus never speaks of Jews as his brothers, though he does speak of his disciples in that way (12:46–50).

5. By far the best interpretation is that Jesus' "brothers" are his disciples (12:48–49; 28:10; cf. 23:8). The fate of the nations will be determined by how they respond to Jesus' followers, who, "missionaries" or not, are charged with spreading the gospel and do so in the face of hunger, thirst, illness, and imprisonment. Good deeds done to Jesus' followers, even the least of them, are not only works of compassion and morality but reflect where people stand in relation to the kingdom and to Jesus himself. Jesus identifies himself with the fate of his followers and makes compassion for them equivalent to compassion for himself (cf. Kistemaker, *Parables of Jesus*, 146ff.; Manson, *Sayings of Jesus*, 251; G. E.

Ladd, "The Parable of the Sheep and the Goats in Recent Interpretation," in *New Dimensions* [ed. Longenecker and Tenney], 191–99; Witherington; Turner; Blomberg [NAC]; see Mt 10:40–42; Mk 13:13; Jn 15:5, 18, 20; 17:10, 23, 26; Ac 9:4; 22:7; 26:14; 1Co 12:27; Heb 2:17).

To the objection that this interpretation does not preserve an adequate distinction between the "sheep" and "the least of these brothers of mine," the answer is that (1) a similar ambiguity occurs in Matthew 18; (2) this interpretation emphasizes the kind of loving relationships that must exist within the Christian community, a constant theme in the NT; and (3) it prepares the way for the surprise shown by both sheep and goats (vv.37–39, 44) and for some important theological implications (see below). Moreover, it is entirely in line with the way the resurrected Jesus ties himself to his persecuted church when he confronts the church's archpersecutor on the Damascus Road (Ac 9:4).

31"When the Son of Man comes in his glory, and all the angels with him, he will sit on
his throne in heavenly glory. 32All the nations will be gathered before him, and he will
separate the people one from another as a shepherd separates the sheep from the goats.
33He will put the sheep on his right and the goats on his left.
34"Then the King will say to those on his right, 'Come, you who are blessed by my Father;
take your inheritance, the kingdom prepared for you since the creation of the world. 35For
I was hungry and you gave me something to eat, I was thirsty and you gave me something
to drink, I was a stranger and you invited me in, 36I needed clothes and you clothed me, I
was sick and you looked after me, I was in prison and you came to visit me.'
37"Then the righteous will answer him, 'Lord, when did we see you hungry and feed you,
or thirsty and give you something to drink? 38When did we see you a stranger and invite
you in, or needing clothes and clothe you? 39When did we see you sick or in prison and go
to visit you?'
40"The King will reply, 'I tell you the truth, whatever you did for one of the least of these
brothers of mine, you did for me.'
41"Then he will say to those on his left, 'Depart from me, you who are cursed, into the
eternal fire prepared for the devil and his angels. 42For I was hungry and you gave me
nothing to eat, I was thirsty and you gave me nothing to drink, 43I was a stranger and you
did not invite me in, I needed clothes and you did not clothe me, I was sick and in prison
and you did not look after me.'
44"They also will answer, 'Lord, when did we see you hungry or thirsty or a stranger or
needing clothes or sick or in prison, and did not help you?'
45"He will reply, 'I tell you the truth, whatever you did not do for one of the least of these,
you did not do for me.'
46"Then they will go away to eternal punishment, but the righteous to eternal life."

COMMENTARY

31 Nowhere in this discourse does Jesus explicitly identify the "Son of Man" (see comments at 8:20) with himself (24:27, 30, 37, 39, 44). But since this epithet is used in answer to the question "What will be the sign of your coming?" (24:3), the inference is inescapable. There are clear allusions to Zechariah 14:5 (cf. Da 7; Joel 3:1–12); but the role of eschatological Judge is, like many other things (see comments at 13:37–39), transferred without hesitation from Yahweh to Jesus. The Son of Man will come "in [his] heavenly glory" (cf. 16:27; 24:30; 1Th 4:16; 2Th 1:8); "nothing earthly could furnish the images for an adequate description" (Broadus). He sits on his throne, not only as Judge, but as King (see v.34); all divine authority is mediated through him (28:18; cf. 1Co 15:25; Heb 12:2). (On the role of the angels, see 13:41–42; 24:31; 2Th 1:7–8; Rev 14:17–20.)

32–33 Presupposed is the fulfillment of 24:14. "All the nations" (*panta ta ethnē*) means "all peoples" and clearly implies that "all the nations" includes more than Gentiles only (see comments at 28:18–20). As the gospel of the kingdom is preached to Gentiles as well as Jews (see comments at 1:1; 2:1–12; 3:15–16; 8:11), so also must all stand before the King.

In the countryside, sheep and goats mingled during the day. At night they were often separated. Sheep tolerate the cool air, but goats have to be herded together for warmth. In sparse grazing areas the animals might be separated during the day as well. But now these well-known, simple, pastoral details are freighted with symbolism. The right hand is the place of power and honor.

34–40 The change from "Son of Man" (see Reflections, p. 247) to "King" (vv.31, 34) is not at all unnatural; the Son of Man in Daniel 7:13–14 approaches the Ancient of Days to receive "a kingdom," and here that kingdom is consummated (see comments at 24:30). The kingship motif has long since been hinted at or, on occasion, made fairly explicit to certain persons (see comments at 3:2; 4:17; 5:35; 16:28; 19:28; 27:42). Yet Jesus still associates his work with his Father, something he loves to do (10:32–33; 11:25–27; 15:13; 16:17, 27; 18:10, 19; 20:23; 26:29, 53; and many references in John). He addresses the sheep, "Come, you who are blessed by my Father" (v.34). "Blessed" is not *makarioi* (as in 5:3) but *eulogēmenoi* (as in 21:9; 23:39). They are "blessed" inasmuch as they now take their inheritance (Ro 8:17; Rev 21:7), which presupposes a relationship with the Father. That inheritance is the kingdom (see comments at 3:2) prepared for them "before the creation of the world" (Jn 17:24; Eph 1:4; 1Pe 1:20). This glorious inheritance, the consummated kingdom, was the Father's plan for them from the beginning.

The reason they are welcomed and invited to take their inheritance is that they have served the King's brothers (cf. Isa 58:7). The thought is antithetical to Paul only if we think this is all Matthew says and that all Paul says touches immediately on grace. Both assumptions are false: 2 Corinthians 5:10 is related to the thought of this parable, and Matthew has other things to say about the salvation of men and women (1:21; 11:25–30; 20:28). The reason for admission to the kingdom in this parable is more evidential than causative. This is suggested by the surprise of the righteous (vv.37–39; see comments below). When he is questioned, the King replies that doing the deeds mentioned to the least of his brothers is equivalent to doing it to him (v.40), and by implication to refuse help to the King's brothers is sacrilege (Calvin).

There is no awkwardness in the scene that requires a disjunction between the sheep (the righteous) and "the least of these brothers of mine," for in pronouncing sentence on each one, the King could point out surrounding brothers who had been compassionately treated.

41–45 The condemnation is even more awful than in 7:23. The "goats" are cursed; they are banished from the King's presence and sent to the eternal fire. Hell is here described in categories familiar to Jews (see comments at 3:12; 5:22; 18:8; cf. Jude 7; Rev 20:10–15). The kingdom was prepared for the righteous (v.34). Hell was prepared for the devil (see comments at 4:1) and his angels (demons; see comments at 8:31; cf. Jude 6; Rev 12:7) but now also serves as the doom of those guilty of the sins of omission of which Jesus here speaks—they have refused to show compassion to King Messiah through helping the least of his brothers. There is no significance in the fact that the "goats" address Jesus as "Lord" (v.44), for at this point there is no exception to confessing Jesus as Lord (cf. Php 2:11).

More important is the surprise of the sheep (vv.37–39) and the goats (v.44), a major part of the parable, though rarely discussed. Three things can be said with confidence.

1. Contrary to what some have suggested (e.g., Gay, "Judgment of the Gentiles"), neither the sheep nor the goats are surprised at the place the King assigns them but at the reason he gives for this—namely, that they are admitted or excluded on the basis of how they treated Jesus. Thus there is no need to say the goats expected to be welcomed or the sheep expected to be rejected.

2. Zumstein (*La condition du croyant*, 348) is right to point out that the surprise of the righteous makes it impossible to think that works of righteousness win salvation. How the sheep and the goats treated Jesus' brothers was not for the purpose of being accepted or rejected by the King; they did not act the way they did because they themselves recognized that what they were doing, or not doing, was done, or not done, with respect to Jesus himself. The sheep did not show love to gain an eschatological reward, nor did the goats fail to show it to flout eschatological retribution.

3. The parable, therefore, presents a test eliminating the possibility of hypocrisy. If the goats had thought that their treatment of Jesus' "brothers" would gain them eschatological felicity, they would doubtless have treated them compassionately. But Jesus is interested in a righteousness of the whole person, a righteousness from the heart (see comments at 5:20; 13:52). As people respond to his disciples, or "brothers," and align themselves with their distress and afflictions, they align themselves with the Messiah, who identifies himself with them (v.45). True disciples will love one another and serve the least brother with compassion; in so doing they unconsciously serve Christ. Those who have little sympathy for the gospel of the kingdom will remain indifferent and, in so doing, reject King Messiah. So Paul learned at his conversion! Determined to persecute Christians, he heard the Voice from the heavenly glory declaring, "I am Jesus, whom you are persecuting" (Ac 9:5).

We must not think that the Bible is unconcerned for the poor and the oppressed (Dt 15:11; Mt 22:37–40; 26:11; Gal 2:10; 6:10; cf. Tim Keller, "The Gospel and the Poor," *Them* 33:3 [2008]: 8–22). But that is not the center of interest here.

46 The same word, "eternal" (*aiōnion*, GK *173*), modifies "punishment" as modifies "life." *Aiōnion* can refer to life or punishment in the age to come, or it can be limited to the duration of the thing to which it refers (as in 21:19). But in apocalyptic and eschatological contexts, the word connotes not only "pertaining to the [messianic] age" but, because that age is always lived in God's presence, also "everlasting" (cf. BDAG, 33; *NIDNTT*, 3:826–33). (On penal notions in NT theology, see J. I. Packer,

"What Did the Cross Achieve? The Logic of Penal Substitution," *TynBul* 25 [1974]: 3–45.)

The final separation of "sheep" and "goats" is a recurring theme in the NT, including Matthew (e.g., 7:21–23; 13:40–43). Some have argued that this doctrine has turned many people into infidels; but so have other Christian doctrines. The question is not how men respond to a doctrine but what Jesus and the NT writers actually teach about it. Human response is a secondary consideration and may reveal as much about us as about the doctrine being rejected. Nevertheless, two things should be kept in mind: (1) As there are degrees of felicity and responsibility in the consummated kingdom (e.g., 25:14–30; cf. 1Co 3:10–15), so also are there degrees of punishment (e.g., 11:22; Lk 12:47–48); and (2) there is no shred of evidence in the NT that hell ever brings about genuine repentance. Sin continues as part of the punishment and the ground for it.

7. Transitional conclusion: fourth major passion prediction and the plot against Jesus (26:1–5)

1When Jesus had finished saying all these things, he said to his disciples, 2"As you know, the Passover is two days away—and the Son of Man will be handed over to be crucified."
3Then the chief priests and the elders of the people assembled in the palace of the high priest, whose name was Caiaphas, 4and they plotted to arrest Jesus in some sly way and kill him. 5"But not during the Feast," they said, "or there may be a riot among the people."

COMMENTARY

1–2 For the other major passion predictions, see comments at 16:21; 17:22–23; 20:18–19. One last time, Matthew uses the formula by which he brings all his discourses to a close (v.1; see comments at 7:28–29). In the narrative line of Matthew, this pericope is a masterpiece of irony. The judge of the universe, King Messiah, the glorious Son of Man, is about to be judged. After Jesus' warnings against hypocrisy (23:12–31) and his demand for righteousness that involves the whole person (25:31–46), the plot moves on by stealth and by a morally bankrupt expediency (26:4–5). The passion begins.

The Passover began Thursday afternoon with the slaughter of the lamb. "Two days" (v.2) must be somewhat under forty-eight hours, or the "two days" would be "three days" (see comments at 12:40). According to the tentative chronology (see comments at 21:23–22:46; 23:1–36; 24:13), Jesus speaks these words on the Mount of Olives late Tuesday evening, which, by Jewish reckoning, would be the beginning of Wednesday.

The "Son of Man" (see comments at 8:20) is here both glorious and suffering; as often, the themes merge. The Passover is two days away, and it is during that festival, Jesus now reveals for the first time, that the Son of Man will be handed over (for reasons to take the Greek present as a future, see Moule, *Idiom Book*, 7) to be crucified. Thus Jesus provides a framework for his disciples to interpret his death correctly after it happens—a framework alluded to a little more clearly in the institution of the Lord's Supper (vv.17–29).

3–5 *Tote* ("then," v.3) is such a loose connective (see comments at 2:7) that it does not mean that the Jewish leaders began to plot only after Jesus had delivered his final passion prediction (vv.1–2). Certainly the opposition had been rising for some time (cf. 12:14; 21:45–46). On the other hand, by placing vv.3–5 immediately after vv.1–2, Matthew gives the narrative the flavor of God's sovereign control. The leaders may plot, but if Jesus dies, he dies as a voluntary Passover sacrifice (vv.53–54; Jn 10:18).

Matthew mentions the chief priests and elders, probably meaning the clerical and lay members of the Sanhedrin (see comments at 21:23). The word *aulē* can mean "courtyard," "farm" or "farmyard," "temple court," or the "prince's court," hence, "palace" (NIV). Caiaphas is called the high priest in Matthew and John (Jn 11:49); Luke (Lk 3:2; Ac 4:6) specifies Annas. There is no real conflict. Annas was deposed by the secular authorities in AD 15 and replaced by Caiaphas, who lived and ruled until his death in AD 36. But since according to the OT the high priest was not to be replaced until after his death, the transfer of power was illegal. Doubtless some continued to call either man "high priest." Certainly Annas, Caiaphas's father-in-law (Jn 18:13), continued to exercise great authority behind the scenes. This joint high priesthood is presupposed by Luke 3:2 and probably by John 18, where the most natural reading of the passage names Caiaphas as high priest in v.13 but Annas as high priest in v.19 (cf. v.24).

The combination of *synagō* ("assembled," GK *5251*) and *symbouleuomai* (from *bouleuomai*, "plotted," GK *5205*) in vv.3–4 strongly suggests an allusion to Psalm 31:13. Psalm 31 is the lament of a righteous sufferer and the source of Jesus' word from the cross in Luke 23:46 (cf. Moo, *Old Testament in the Gospel Passion Narratives*, 234–35). Earlier that day, the leaders had wanted to arrest Jesus but dared not do so for fear of the people (21:46; apparently earlier attempts had also failed, Jn 7:32, 45–52). Now they decide to do away with Jesus (v.4), recognizing that they must do this by *dolos* ("stealth," "cunning," "guile," GK *1515*) so as not to excite the crowds and start a riot (v.5).

The leaders were right in fearing the people. Jerusalem's population swelled perhaps fivefold during the feast; with religious fervor and national messianism at a high pitch, a spark might set off an explosion. They decided to suspend action, but Judas's offer to hand Jesus over at a time and place when the crowds were not present was too good an opportunity to pass up (vv.14–16). Thus in God's providence, the connection between Passover and Jesus' death that he had just predicted (vv.1–2) came about.

VII. THE PASSION AND RESURRECTION OF JESUS (26:6–28:20)

OVERVIEW

Because of the structure the five discourses impose on Matthew, some scholars (Bacon, *Studies in Matthew*; Stendahl, *School of St. Matthew*, 20ff.) have thought that the passion and resurrection narratives (26:6–28:20) stand outside the main framework, perhaps as a kind of epilogue to balance the "prologue" (chs. 1–2). But I have argued (see Introduction, section 14; comments at 28:18–20) that the familiar pattern of narrative elements followed by discourse teaching continues here in a *sixth* section. In this case, however, the "teaching" part of the narrative-and-teaching structure is continued by the church after

Jesus' ascension (28:18–20). From another viewpoint, the passion and resurrection must, as in all the gospels, be seen as the climax toward which a great deal of the earlier narrative has been moving.

As often noted, Matthew from now on follows Mark quite closely, though he omits Mark 14:51–52; 15:21b, adds certain bits (e.g., 27:3–10, 51–53), provides a completely independent ending, and offers a number of minor changes (e.g., some third-person reports in Mark are now given in direct speech). Many attempts have been made to identify what is exclusively Matthean in the passion narrative; but not a few such attempts suffer from reductionism. For instance, Dahl (*Jesus in the Memory*, 37–51) holds that Matthew's account is designed to highlight differences between church and synagogue. The former has accepted Jesus as Messiah; the latter has rejected and condemned him (cf. Trilling, *Das wahre Israel*, 66–74). Others think Jesus' passion in Matthew has an ethical cast, designed to help young disciples learn obedience (e.g., Strecker, *Weg der Gerechtigkeit*, 183–84). Many others see various christological elements in Matthew's account. Barth ("Matthew's Understanding of the Law") claims that by his suffering and death, Jesus fulfills God's redemptive plan and establishes the kingdom; Kingsbury stresses the confession of Jesus as "Son of God." (For an excellent survey, see D. Senior, "The Passion Narrative in the Gospel of Matthew," in *L'Évangile selon Matthieu* [ed. Didier], 343–57.)

Virtually every theme thought to be particularly strong in Matthew can be shown to be present in one or more of the other gospels. For instance, that the events are all under God's control or that Jesus dies voluntarily is even more strongly attested in John than in Matthew. This is not to deny that Matthew has his own contribution to make. Instead it is to say that what Matthew offers is a great deal of commonly held theology, presented with a rich allusiveness and a complex intertwining of themes, subtly blended to lay stress on one part or another of the narrative and capped with a few additions unknown in any other source. Thus it is best to examine Matthew's material inductively and trace its unfolding.

A. The Passion (26:6–27:66)

1. Anointed at Bethany (26:6–13)

OVERVIEW

The first pericope (vv.6–13) is problematic because of its disputed relation to other gospel accounts (Mk 14:3–9; Jn 12:2–8; cf. Lk 7:36–50). Some ancient commentators (e.g., Origen) thought there were three anointings: (1) Luke 7:36–50, in Galilee; (2) John 12:2–8, a few days earlier than the third; and (3) Mark 14:3–9 and Matthew 26:6–13. Most modern scholars believe that there was only one anointing and that variations in details arose during oral transmission and because of the hortatory use by each evangelist (cf. R. Holst, "The One Anointing of Jesus: Another Application of the Form-Critical Method," *JBL* 95 [1976]: 435–46), but there is no consensus among these scholars as to the original setting or purpose of the story.

On the whole, a third alternative seems preferable: there were two anointings, one in Galilee (recorded by Luke) and the other in Bethany (recorded by Matthew, Mark, and John; so Broadus; McNeile; A. Legault, "An Application of the Form

Critique Method to the Anointings in Galilee and Bethany," *CBQ* 16 [1954]: 131–45; France [NICNT]; Turner). The only real similarities between the two incidents are the anointing by a woman and the name Simon. But "Simon," like "Judas," was a very common name, and the two incidents differ in many details. In Luke, the woman is a "sinner"; in the other account, there is no mention of this, and John says she is Mary of Bethany. In Luke, the host is a Pharisee, in a Galilean home; here the host is "Simon the leper," at a home in Bethany. In Luke, the host is critical of the woman's actions; here the disciples criticize her.

Small differences among Matthew, Mark, and John are fairly easily reconciled. John may place the incident where he does because he has just spoken of Bethany and will mention that town no more; but his links with the historical setting seem fairly strong, and the most natural interpretation of his account is that the anointing took place before the triumphal entry (Jn 12:2, 12). Mark and Matthew, on the other hand, provide no chronological connection, only a thematic one. Out of Jesus' rebuke to the disciples, Judas Iscariot sets his course of betrayal (cf. Jn 12:46). To object to this two-incident theory on the grounds that the methodology and many of the presuppositions "are out of date due to the scholarly advances in the disciplines of form and redaction criticism ... [so that there is] no trajectory or *tendency* to explain the complexities of the final editions of the stories" (Holst, "The One Anointing," 435, emphasis his) is to make these tools intrinsically incapable of recognizing two superficially similar incidents.

6While Jesus was in Bethany in the home of a man known as Simon the Leper, 7a
woman came to him with an alabaster jar of very expensive perfume, which she poured
on his head as he was reclining at the table.
8When the disciples saw this, they were indignant. "Why this waste?" they asked. 9"This
perfume could have been sold at a high price and the money given to the poor."
10Aware of this, Jesus said to them, "Why are you bothering this woman? She has done
a beautiful thing to me. 11The poor you will always have with you, but you will not always
have me. 12When she poured this perfume on my body, she did it to prepare me for burial.
13I tell you the truth, wherever this gospel is preached throughout the world, what she has
done will also be told, in memory of her."

COMMENTARY

6–7 For Bethany, see comments at 21:17. Contrary to common opinion, John does not say this took place at the home of Lazarus, Mary, and Martha; he may mean only that the well-known family was present. That Martha served is quite in keeping with village life at the time. Mark and Matthew set the scene in the home of "Simon the Leper," who was presumably cured—or else all there were violating Mosaic law. The action of the woman was not unprecedented: a distinguished rabbi might have been so honored. The evangelists stress the cost of the "perfume" (v.7, most likely a fairly viscous fluid, possibly from the nard plant native to India), which was extracted from the thin-necked alabaster flask by snapping off the neck. According to John 12:3, the nard was worth about three hundred denarii—approximately a year's salary for a working man.

8–9 Matthew mentions "the disciples" (v.8), Mark "some of those present," and John "Judas Iscariot." If the three accounts represent the same incident, it could be that, just as Peter voiced the sentiments of the group (v.35) and was answered directly by Jesus, so with Judas. Matthew shows the disciples' failure to understand what is taking place, not only in the anointing, but also in who Jesus truly is and in the rush of events toward the cross (see comments at 16:21–28; 17:22–23; 20:18–19). Doubtless there were thousands of really poor people within a few miles of this anointing. Whatever Judas's motives (Jn 12:6), some people at least were motivated by righteous indignation (v.9); thus in Jesus' view they revealed their distorted values and blindness as to the unique redemptive event about to take place.

10–11 The Greek *gnous de* ("Aware of this") is also behind 16:8 ("Aware of their discussion"). It is possible that Jesus' knowledge is here supernatural, but perhaps the complaints were whispered and came to Jesus' attention because they troubled the woman. Jesus begins his rebuke by accusing the disciples of "bothering" her (v.10; the Greek idiom, found in the NT only here and in Lk 11:7; Gal 6:17, is a strong one). What they call waste, Jesus calls "a beautiful thing."

Hill's claim that Jesus' further statement (v.11) "distinguishes between a good work (i.e., almsgiving) and one done with reference to himself while he is present (with his disciples, and also as the 'living Christ' in the Matthean church)" entirely misses the point. Jesus distinguishes between giving to the poor and the extravagance lavished on himself *on the grounds that he will not always be there to receive it.* Far from referring to Jesus' spiritual presence in the church, Matthew distinguishes between Jesus' earthly presence and his postascension spiritual presence (28:20). His followers will always find poor people to help (cf. Dt 15:11); they will not always have the incarnate Jesus with them. Implicitly, the distinction Jesus makes is a high christological claim, for it shows not only that he foresees his impending departure but also that he himself, who is truly "gentle and humble in heart" (11:29), *deserves* this lavish outpouring of love and expense.

Lane (*Mark*, 493–94) follows F. W. Danker, ("The Literary Unity of Mark 14:1–25," *JBL* 85 [1966]: 467–72) in suggesting that Psalm 41 may also be alluded to here—a psalm that speaks of the poor yet righteous sufferer who is betrayed by his closest friend, yet vindicated by God in the end. Jesus is the poor, righteous Sufferer par excellence, and the opportunity to help him in any way will soon be gone forever.

12 The anointing does not designate Jesus as Messiah but "prepares" him for his burial after dying the death of a criminal, for only in that circumstance would the customary anointing of the body be omitted (cf. D. Daube, "The Anointing at Bethany and Jesus' Burial," *AThR* 32 [1950]: 187–88). Jesus' defense of the woman does not necessarily mean that the woman understood what she was doing, though it allows this. Jesus may well be using the anointing to intimate again his impending crucifixion (cf. v.2).

13 Interpretations of this verse, with its solemn promise, differ. Jeremias (*Prayers of Jesus*, 112–24; *Jesus' Promise*, 22) takes the saying as authentic but says that *hopou* here means not "wherever" (NIV) but "when"—i.e., when the triumphal news of this gospel is proclaimed by God's angel (cf. Rev 14:6–11) at the Parousia, before all the world, then her act will be remembered. Jeremias thus avoids any prediction by Jesus of a worldwide mission. But this uses "gospel" strangely and is too tightly linked with assumptions about what Jesus could or could not have said. Jesus did foresee Gentiles entering the kingdom (8:11) in response to his disciples' preaching, and that the word of God would be preached in the world (13:37; 24:14). Thus the groundwork has already been laid for this saying and also for the Great Commission (28:18–20).

The most natural interpretation of v.13 is that the woman and her deed would be remembered "wherever" the "gospel of the kingdom" would be preached (cf. Moore, *Judaism*, 203–4). Broadus remarks, "This very remarkable promise ... was already in process of fulfillment when John wrote his gospel, probably sixty years afterwards; for he distinguishes this Bethany from the one beyond Jordan (Jn 1:28) by calling it (Jn 11:1) the village of Mary (placed first) and Martha; and then makes all definite and clear by adding, 'It was that Mary who anointed the Lord with ointment', etc. He has not yet in his gospel told the story of the anointing, but he assumes that it is familiar to all Christian readers."

2. Judas's betrayal agreement (26:14–16)

OVERVIEW

All the gospels speak of Judas's important role in Jesus' death (cf. Mk 14:10–11; Lk 22:3–4); but none explains what motives prompted his treachery. Like most human motives, his were mixed and doubtless included avarice and jealousy combined with profound disappointment that Jesus was not acting like the Messiah he had expected.

14Then one of the Twelve—the one called Judas Iscariot—went to the chief priests 15and asked, "What are you willing to give me if I hand him over to you?" So they counted out for him thirty silver coins. 16From then on Judas watched for an opportunity to hand him over.

COMMENTARY

14–16 While *tote* ("then") is generally difficult to translate (see comments at 2:7), here (v.14) there is probably a logical connection with the preceding pericope. In Judas's view, Jesus was acting less and less regal and more and more like a defeatist on his way to death. If Matthew's anointing (vv.6–13) is the same as the one in John 12:1–8, Judas may also have been smarting from Jesus' rebuke. Moreover, *if* his name ties him in with the Zealot movement (see comments at 10:4), then his disappointment is the more understandable, though not more excusable. He approaches the "chief priests" (see comments at 21:23). (One may ask in passing why Matthew makes no mention of the Pharisees if his antipathy toward them is as strong as some say.)

The chief priests "counted out for him thirty silver coins" (v.15); Matthew's language (lit., "they weighed out to him"), unlike Mark's, is the distinctive language of the LXX and calls to mind Zechariah 11:12, to which Matthew will return in 27:3–10 (Moo, *Old Testament in the Gospel Passion Narratives*, passim). In Zechariah 11, thirty pieces of silver is a paltry amount ("the handsome price at which they priced me" [Zec 11:13] is ironic)—

the value of a slave accidentally gored to death by an ox (Ex 21:32). That Jesus is lightly esteemed is reflected not only in his betrayal but in the low sum agreed on by Judas and the chief priests.

REFLECTIONS: CHRONOLOGICAL CONSIDERATIONS

The traditional date of Jesus' death is AD 30. But Hoehner (*Chronological Aspects*, 65–93) has made a plausible case for AD 33, though the exact year has little effect on the exegesis. More important is the problem of the relationship between the Synoptic Gospels and John. The Synoptics seem to indicate that Jesus and his disciples ate the Passover meal the evening before the crucifixion (see esp. Mk 14:12–16; 15:1–25, and par.), whereas John seems to suggest that the Passover lamb was slaughtered at the moment Jesus was being put to death, which would, of course, mean that he and his disciples did not eat the Passover at the Last Supper (see esp. Jn 18:28; 19:14).

The question is of more than chronological interest, for quite apart from harmonization of disparate historical records, the meaning of the Lord's Supper is affected by its connection with Passover. The literature about this question is immense. The aim here is to list some of the principal options and defend briefly the interpretation adopted here. Essential bibliography includes Hoehner, *Chronological Aspects*, 81–90; Jeremias, *Eucharistic Words*, 41ff.; Str-B, 2:847–52; A. Jaubert, *The Date of the Last Supper* (Staten Island, N.J.: Alba, 1965); E. Ruckstuhl, *Chronology of the Last Days of Jesus* (New York: Desclee, 1965); G. Ogg, "The Chronology of the Last Supper," in *Historicity and Chronology in the New Testament* (ed. D. E. Nineham; London: SPCK, 1965), 75–96; J. B. Segal, *The Hebrews Passover from the Earliest Times to AD 70* (London: Oxford Univ. Press, 1963); S. Dockx, *Chronologies néotestamentaires et Vie de l'Église primitive* (Paris: Duculot, 1976), passim; Marshall, *Last Supper*, esp. 57ff., and Table 4 (184–85); Moo, *Old Testament in the Gospel Passion Narratives*, 318–23; and the major commentaries on the gospels.

1. Many scholars maintain that the discrepancies are not historically reconcilable—that either the Synoptics are right or John is. There are many indications that the synoptists understand the Last Supper to be a Passover meal (see Jeremias, *Eucharistic Words*, 41–62; Marshall, *Last Supper*, 59–62). Therefore, attempts to turn the meal into something else—a *qidduš* (prayer meal), though this was unknown until several centuries later, or a *haburah* (fellowship meal) eaten just before Passover—are not convincing. That the meal was not Passover supper but that such elements are read back into it is a counsel of despair, especially in light of the Passover associations as early as 1 Corinthians 11.

Any theory of this kind depends on its explanation of why the discrepancy was introduced. If the Synoptics are historically correct (Jeremias), perhaps John changed the date to correspond with his Jesus/Passover lamb typology; if John is historically correct (Ogg), perhaps the synoptists changed the date to make the Last Supper fit the Passover symbolism. Either way, it is necessary to trace a theological development; but to date no such work has proved convincing. To argue that John has identified Jesus with the Passover lamb by so flimsy a device as changing two or three chronological references is not very credible in a book abounding with explanatory statements (1:42; 2:21–22; 12:38; 13:18 et al.). In fact, only the Synoptics mention the day the lambs were sacrificed (Mk 14:12; Lk 22:7). Finding theological motivation for a putative change in the Synoptics is even more problematic because of the highly disputed question of which evangelist preserves the oldest form of the institution of the Lord's Supper (cf. Marshall, *Last Supper*, 30ff.).

2. The second group of options brings together various theories of calendrical disputes in the first century. Jaubert argues that Jesus, as reported by the synoptists, was using a solar calendar known to us from *Jubilees* and apparently adopted at Qumran. Passover always occurred on *Tuesday* evening (14–15 Nisan), so Jesus and his men ate their Passover that night. But the "official" Pharisaic lunar calendar, followed by the fourth gospel, places the cross and the sacrifice on the *lunar* 14–15 Nisan (Thursday-Friday, from nightfall to nightfall). In a somewhat different scheme, some have argued that the Pharisees and Sadducees adopted different calendars (Str-B), or that Jesus followed a Galilean (i.e., Pharisees') calendar (Synoptics) and John reports on the basis of the Judean (Sadducees') equivalent (so Hoehner).

At least all these theories based on diverse calendars join in affirming that Jesus and his disciples ate a Passover meal, whatever the date. But beyond that, all these calendrical solutions have severe drawbacks. Part of Jaubert's view, for instance, turns on a third-century document (the *Didascalia Apostolorum*) concerned with justifying current fasting practices by appeal to Passion Week, rather than giving any useful historical information about that week. There is no evidence that Jesus followed a sectarian calendar, and quite certainly sacrifices were not offered in the temple on any day other than the "official" (lunar calendar) day. Moreover, all four evangelists seem to agree that Jesus was arrested the evening before his crucifixion and that, despite objections, there was enough time between his arrest Thursday night and his crucifixion Friday to allow for the various events discussed below. Some of the other theories are highly suspect because of poor attestation in primary sources and are little more than last resorts.

3. The third approach is to attempt historical harmonization between John and the Synoptics as they stand. Of these attempts, one, pursued at various times in church history, is reasonably successful.

Matthew 26:17 speaks of "the first day of the Feast of Unleavened Bread." According to Leviticus 23:6 and Numbers 28:17, Jews were forbidden to use yeast in their bread for seven days from 15 Nisan. However, Exodus 12:18 says that yeast should be removed from the house on 14 Nisan; there is some evidence that Jews customarily removed it at noon on 14 Nisan so as to have everything ready in good time. Thus Josephus can in one place speak of the beginning of the feast as occurring on 15 Nisan (*Ant.* 3.248–50 [10.5]) and in another as occurring on 14 Nisan (*J.W.* 5.99 [3.1]; cf. *Ant.* 2.315–16 [15.1]). Matthew seems to presuppose Thursday, 14 Nisan. According to Exodus 12:6 and Numbers 9:3, the Jews were directed to kill the paschal lamb "at twilight" (NIV), i.e., "between the two evenings," which in Jesus' day meant middle to late afternoon until sundown (Dt 16:6). Hence Josephus (*J.W.* 6.423 [9.3]) says the lambs were killed from the ninth to the eleventh hour (3:00 p.m. to 5:00 p.m.) and that on one occasion the number killed was 256,500—almost certainly an inflated figure.

It seems, then, that Jesus' disciples entered the city shortly after noon on Thursday, 14 Nisan, procured the room, took a lamb to the temple court and killed it, roasted it with bitter herbs (Ex 12:8–9), and made other arrangements for the meal, including the purchase of wine and unleavened bread. Matthew 26:19 explicitly says they "prepared the Passover." After nightfall on Thursday evening, when it was 15 Nisan, Jesus joined his disciples, and they ate the Passover. On these points the Synoptics agree; and this places Jesus' death on Friday, 15 Nisan, probably about 3:00 p.m.

The following passages in John are the most difficult to harmonize with this scheme (cf. D. A.

Carson, *The Gospel according to John* [PNTC; Grand Rapids: Eerdmans, 1991].)

John 13:1. "It was just before the Passover Feast" need not set the stage for the meal, which was about to be eaten, but for the footwashing. The footwashing took place before the "Passover Feast." John 13:2 in the best texts does not contradict this. We should not read "supper being ended" (KJV) but the "meal was being served" (NIV).

John 13:27. "What you are about to do, do quickly." John adds (v.29) that some of those present thought Jesus was telling Judas to buy what was necessary for the feast, or else give something to the poor. How could they think this if they were just then *finishing* the feast? But one may also ask why, if the feast was still twenty-four hours away, anyone would think that there would be any rush to buy things. It is more reasonable to think that the disciples thought Judas needed to make some purchases for the *continuing* "Feast of Unleavened Bread"—e.g., some more unleavened bread. Since the next day, still Friday, 15 Nisan, was a high feast day and the day after a Sabbath, it was best to do things immediately. By Jewish reckoning, the high feast day (15 Nisan) had begun that Thursday evening, but purchases were more than likely still possible, though inconvenient. After all, one could buy necessities even on a Sabbath if it fell before a Passover, provided it was done by leaving something in trust rather than paying cash (*m. Sanh.* 23:1). Moreover, it was customary to give alms to the poor on Passover night. The temple gates were left open from midnight on, and beggars congregated there (cf. Jeremias, *Eucharistic Words*, 54; Ruckstuhl, *Chronology of the Last Days*, 132). It is difficult to imagine why the disciples would think on any other night that Judas was being sent out for this purpose; the next day would have done as well.

John 18:28. Jesus stands before Pilate. "By now it was early morning, and to avoid ceremonial uncleanness the Jews did not enter the palace; they wanted to be able to eat the Passover." The precise nature of this "ceremonial uncleanness" is highly disputed. Certainly Jews had to purify themselves for Passover (cf. 2Ch 30:18; Ezr 6:19–21; cf. Jn 11:55; 12:1), and Pilate respected the Jews' scruples (Jn 18:28–29). Contamination might come from the road dust brought in by foreign visitors (cf. *m. Ber.* 9:5), or from contact with Gentiles who had eaten or touched something unclean (e.g., a corpse or a menstruating woman). While there are numerous other possibilities, uncleanness from any of these sources could have been eliminated at the end of one day by a purifying wash at sundown (cf. Lev 15:5–11, 16–18; 22:5–7; see *y. Pesaḥ.* 36b, 92b), and then the Passover could be eaten. Thus, close attention to John's text and the historical background makes it unlikely that John 18:28 can be used to defend the view that Jesus ate a meal the evening before Passover night. Instead, 18:28 is more plausibly interpreted in one of two other ways.

1. It is possible that the priests had intended to eat the Passover that night, but, pressed by their temple duties and the thousands of sacrifices they had to perform, interrupted by Judas's unexpected offer of instant betrayal, and delayed by the headlong pace of the ensuing judicial examinations, they had not yet eaten their own Passover. This view is unlikely if Exodus 12:8–10, forbidding delay of the Passover dinner beyond midnight (*m. Pesaḥ.* 10:9; *m. Zebaḥ.* 5:8), was strictly interpreted. But these traditions may be late, and *Mekilta* Exodus says that some rabbis interpreted Exodus 12:8–10 as being satisfied if the Passover were eaten by dawn. Even so, these Jewish leaders were being caught out by at least two or three hours.

2. More plausibly, "to eat the Passover" in John 18:28 may refer not to the Passover meal itself but to the continuing feast, and in particular to the *ḥagigah*,

the feast offering offered on the morning of the first full paschal day (cf. Nu 28:18–19). This could explain the Jews' concern: ritual purification could be regained by nightfall but not by the morning *ḥagigah*. Of course, the *ḥagigah* could be eaten later in the week, but it is unlikely that the leaders, conscious of their public status, would be eager to delay it unless absolutely unavoidable. Deuteronomy 16:3 speaks of eating the Passover food of unleavened bread for seven days. It may be, then, that the leaders wanted to avoid ritual uncleanness in order to continue full participation in the entire feast. Moreover, this becomes the more plausible if our treatment of John 19:31 is correct. Morris's objection (*John*, 778–79) that one may concede that "the Passover" can refer to Passover plus the Feast of Unleavened Bread but certainly not to the Feast of Unleavened Bread without the Passover meal may be setting up a straw man, for the interpretation being defended here does not claim that "the Passover" here refers to the Feast of Unleavened Bread *apart from* the Passover meal itself but to *the entire Passover festival*. Ritual uncleanness at this point in the festival would force temporary withdrawal from the festivities, from "eating the Passover."

John 19:14. Referring to the day of Jesus' crucifixion, the verse reads, "It was *paraskeuē tou pascha*" (lit., "the Preparation of the Passover"). There is strong evidence to suggest that *paraskeuē* ("Preparation [Day]," GK *4187*) had already become a technical name for Friday, since Friday was normally the day on which one prepared for the Sabbath (Saturday); and we have no evidence that the term was used in the evangelist's time to refer to the eve of any festal day other than the Sabbath (cf. C. C. Torrey, "The Date of the Crucifixion according to the Fourth Gospel," *JBL* 50 [1931]: 241). In this context, then, *tou pascha* means "of Passover Week" or "of the Passover festival." Several diverse strands of evidence support this meaning of *pascha*. Josephus (*Ant.* 14.21 [2.1]; cf. 17.213 [9.3]; *J.W.* 2.10 [1.3]) uses "Passover" to refer to the entire Feast of Unleavened Bread, unless he is directly dependent on an OT passage, when he tends to keep the two distinct (*Ant.* 3.248–51 [10.5]; cf. BDAG, 784). The same extended usage is found not only in *m. Pesaḥ.* 9:5 but in the NT (cf. Lk 22:1: "the Feast of Unleavened Bread, called the Passover," and probably also such passages as Jn 2:23, 6:4; 13:1; 19:31, 42). Thus John 19:14 most probably means "Friday in Passover Week" (hence the NIV, "the day of Preparation of Passover Week"); this understanding of *pascha* reinforces the comments made above in the John 18:28 paragraph.

John 19:31. "And the next day was to be a special Sabbath." The most plausible view is that this does not refer to the day of the Passover meal but to Saturday, which would be considered a "high" or "special" Sabbath, not only because it fell during the Passover Feast, but because on the second paschal day, in this case a Sabbath (Saturday), the very important sheaf offering fell (cf. Str-B, 2:582; Philo, *Spec.* 2).

John 19:36. This verse refers to Exodus 12:46 to explain that Jesus, the Passover Lamb, did not have any of his bones broken. Some have thought this suggests that Jesus must have died while the lambs were being slaughtered. But this does not follow. John makes no such temporal connection, and the theological connection could spring either from the tradition regarding the witness of John the Baptist (Jn 1:29, 36) or from Jesus' words at the institution of the Lord's Supper, reported by the synoptists and Paul.

~

It seems, then, that the fourth gospel can be fairly harmonized with the Synoptics as far as the chronology of the Last Supper and Jesus' death are concerned.

One final question remains: How could conscientious Jews be party to a trial and execution on a feast day, which, in terms of prohibitions and legal procedure, was to be regarded as a Sabbath (cf. Ex 12:16; Lev 23:7; Nu 28:18; *m. Beṣah* 5:2)? But Mishnah (*Sanh.* 11:4) insists that the execution of a rebellious teacher *should* take place on one of the three principal feasts so that all the people would hear and fear (cf. Dt 17:13; Str-B, 2:826). Jeremias (*Eucharistic Words*, 79) examines other events reported in the Gospels (e.g., Jesus' burial) and alleged to be inconsistent with the sabbatical nature of Passover feast day and concludes that "the passion narratives portray no incident which could not have taken place on Nisan 15." There are numerous irregularities connected with the Sanhedrin trial; these, however, bear only marginally on the chronological problems and are treated in situ (see comments at 26:57–68).

Therefore, we seem to be on safe ground in arguing that the Last Supper was a Passover meal and that some of its associations must be seen in that light.

For an alternative view, see France [NICNT].

3. The Lord's Supper (26:17–30)

a. Preparations for the Passover (26:17–19)

17On the first day of the Feast of Unleavened Bread, the disciples came to Jesus and
asked, "Where do you want us to make preparations for you to eat the Passover?"
18He replied, "Go into the city to a certain man and tell him, 'The Teacher says: My
appointed time is near. I am going to celebrate the Passover with my disciples at your
house.'" 19So the disciples did as Jesus had directed them and prepared the Passover.

COMMENTARY

17 Problems of chronology and some of the steps needed to prepare for the Passover are discussed in the Reflections section above. A few more details shed light on the situation. Toward midafternoon of Thursday, 14 Nisan, the lambs (one per "household"—a convenient group of perhaps ten or twelve people) would be brought to the temple court, where the priests sacrificed them. The priests took the blood and passed it in basins along a line until it was poured out at the foot of the altar. They also burned the lambs' fat on the altar of burnt offerings. The singing of the *Hallel* (Pss 113–18) accompanied these steps.

After sunset (i.e., now 15 Nisan), the "household" would gather in a home to eat the Passover lamb, which by this time would have been roasted with bitter herbs. The head of the household began the meal with the thanksgiving for that feast day (the Passover *qidduš*) and for the wine, praying over the first of four cups. A preliminary course of greens and bitter herbs was, apparently, followed by the Passover *haggadah*—in which a boy would ask the meaning of all this and the head of the household would explain the symbols in terms of the exodus (cf. *m. Pesaḥ.* 10:4–5)—and the singing of the first part of the *Hallel* (Ps 113 or Pss 113–14). Though the precise order is disputed, apparently a second cup of wine introduced the main course, which was followed by a third cup, known as the "cup of blessing," accompanied by another prayer of thanksgiving. The participants then sang the rest of the *Hallel* (Pss 114–18 or 115–18) and probably drank a fourth cup of wine. Thus the preparations about which the disciples were asking were extensive.

18–19 Matthew's account is much simpler than Mark's. *Pros ton deina* ("to a certain man") refers to somebody one cannot or does not wish to name (v.18). A case can be made that the home belonged to the father of John Mark (Zahn), but this is far from certain. It is not clear whether Jesus had made previous arrangements or called on supernatural knowledge (cf. 21:13). Either way, Jesus was carefully taking charge of this final Passover meal. Jesus' words "My appointed time is near" were probably purposely ambiguous. To the disciples and the owner of the house, they might have implied Jesus' timing for the Passover meal and prior arrangements for it. In the light of Easter, the words must refer to the impending crucifixion, the fulfillment of Jesus mission.

The disciples do as Jesus has "directed" (v.19) or "instructed" them (*syntassō* is used in the NT only here and in 21:6; 27:10). *Syntassō* does not relate to discipleship, as many maintain, and still less to Jesus' authority in any abstract sense. Instead, it prepares the way for the Last Supper and Jesus' death and demonstrates that he is quietly and consciously taking the steps to complete his mission of tragedy and glory.

b. Prediction of the betrayal (26:20–25)

OVERVIEW

Matthew agrees with Mark in placing this scene before the words of institution, whereas Luke's briefer account gives the impression that Judas did not leave until after those words. We cannot be certain which gospel has preserved the chronological sequence; perhaps the Lukan account betrays greater marks of condensation and topical arrangement. Matthew omits the allusion to Psalm 41:9 preserved in Mark 14:18 but adds the brief exchange between Jesus and Judas in v.25 (cf. Mk 14:18–21; Lk 22:21–23; Jn 13:21–30).

20When evening came, Jesus was reclining at the table with the Twelve. 21And while
they were eating, he said, "I tell you the truth, one of you will betray me."
22They were very sad and began to say to him one after the other, "Surely not I, Lord?"
23Jesus replied, "The one who has dipped his hand into the bowl with me will betray
me. 24The Son of Man will go just as it is written about him. But woe to that man who
betrays the Son of Man! It would be better for him if he had not been born."
25Then Judas, the one who would betray him, said, "Surely not I, Rabbi?"
Jesus answered, "Yes, it is you."

COMMENTARY

20–22 The Passover meal could not be eaten until after sundown; and for those living within Palestine, it had to be eaten inside Jerusalem or not at all. That is why we find Jesus reclining at a table in a room in the city "when evening came." Once the meal begins—we do not know at what stage—Jesus solemnly says, "I tell you the truth, one of you will betray me" (v.21). The disciples respond uniformly. One after another, as the enormity of the charge sinks in, each man asks, "Surely not I, Lord?" (v.22).

23 The NIV's "The one who has dipped his hand into the bowl" attempts to render an aorist participle (*ho embapsas*); contrast the present tense "one who dips" in Mark 14:20 (*ho embaptomenos*). Nevertheless the NIV is misleading. It gives the impression that a particular "one" is in view, when in fact most, if not all, of those present would have dipped into the same bowl as Jesus, given the eating styles of the day. Jesus' point is that the betrayer is a friend, someone close, someone sharing the common dish, thus heightening the enormity of the betrayal. The identification in John 13:22–30 probably took place just after this. If the main course, the roast lamb, was being eaten, the "bowl" would contain herbs and a fruit puree, which would be scooped out with bread.

24 For "woe," see comments at 23:13; for "Son of Man," see Reflections, p. 247. Here the Son of Man is simultaneously the glorious messianic figure who receives a kingdom and the Suffering Servant; indeed, the former highlights the evil of the person who hands him over to the latter role. No OT quotation explains "as it is written of him"; but one may think of OT passages such as Isaiah 53:7–9; Daniel 9:26, or else suppose that an entire prophetic typology (see comments at 2:15; 5:17–20) is in view, such as the Passover lamb, or some combination of the two.

The divine necessity for the sacrifice of the Son of Man, grounded in the Word of God, does not excuse or mitigate the crime of betrayal (cf. Ac 1:16–18; 4:27–28). Nor is this an instance of divine "overruling" after the fact. Instead, divine sovereignty and human responsibility are both involved in Judas's treason, the one effecting salvation and bringing redemption history to its fulfillment, the other answering the promptings of an evil heart. The one results in salvation from sin for Messiah's people (1:21), the other in personal and eternal ruin (cf. Carson, *Divine Sovereignty*, 130–32).

25 This exchange, preserved only in Matthew, magnifies Judas's effrontery and brackets the words of institution (vv.26–30) with the deceit of the betrayer (v.25) and the empty boast of the one who would disown Jesus with oaths (vv.31–35). Doubtless Judas felt he had to speak up; silence at this stage might have given him away to the others. Both here and in v.49, Judas uses "Rabbi" (see comments at 8:19; 23:7), which, in the pre-Easter setting, was probably more unambiguously honorific than the versatile *kyrios* ("Lord," v.22). As in v.22, the form of the question (using *mēti*) anticipates a negative answer, but the expected answer bears no necessary relation to the real answer (BDF, para. 427 [2]). Jesus' response is identical in Greek to that in v.64. It is affirmative but depends somewhat on spoken intonation for its full force. It could be taken to mean "You have said it, not I"; yet, in fact, it is enough of an affirmative to give Judas a jolt without removing all ambiguity from the ears of the other disciples. See comments at v.64.

c. The words of institution (26:26–30)

OVERVIEW

John records nothing of the words of institution. Matthew and Mark are fairly close in their formulations, as are Luke and Paul, but Luke and Paul are sufficiently distinct to make it better to speak of three accounts instead of two (cf. Mk 14:23–26; Lk 22:19–20; 1Co 11:23–25). The numerous text-critical variations confirm the tendency toward assimilation, especially in material at the heart of Christian liturgy. The literature attempting to trace Jesus' exact words and to determine which of the synoptic forms is most primitive is immense (cf. Jeremias, *Eucharistic Words*, 96–105; Marshall, *Last Supper*, 30–56). Marshall's caution is sensible: "It must be emphasized that there is no good reason for supposing that any one of the three versions must necessarily be closer to the original form of the account than any of the others" (p. 38).

We may go farther and ask why we must limit ourselves to just one "original account." There were eleven or twelve witnesses. We have repeatedly referred to the evangelists' interest in reporting Jesus' *ipsissima vox*, not his *ipsissima verba* (see Notes, 3:17). The various criteria for getting behind this (number of Semitisms, redaction-critical distinctions) are inadequate. A good translation may reduce Semitisms but preserve authentic content; redaction criticism may determine that some statement is traditional but cannot prove authenticity or, conversely, that some formulation is redactional without disproving authenticity. We must be satisfied with the sources we have. (On the question of discerning by critical means Jesus' understanding of his own death, see H. Schürmann, "Wie hat Jesus seinen Tod bestanden und verstanden? Eine methodenkritische Besinnung," in *Orientierung an Jesus* [ed. Hoffmann et al.], 325–63; Guthrie, *New Testament Theology*, 436–48.)

Close comparison of Mark and Matthew reveals few distinctive elements in Matthew. The first evangelist, unlike Mark, has "eat" in v.26 and replaces "they all drank from it" (Mk 14:23) with "Drink from it, all of you" (v.27). Matthew is usually judged more "liturgical" (Lohmeyer; Stendahl, *School of St. Matthew*; Hill). This, though possible, is no more than a guess; we know almost nothing about first-century liturgy, and the variations are no more revealing in this regard than variations between Mark and Matthew in "nonliturgical sections."

Appeal to liturgical influence is commonplace in current NT scholarship, and therefore the frequent assumption of such influence lends credibility to the claim; this, however, is in urgent need of reexamination. There may have been considerable diversity in the formulations used in church worship even *within each congregation*, as today in many nonliturgical denominations. Once again, we must confess that our sources are inadequate for a confident conclusion. What is certain is that Jesus bids us commemorate, not his birth, nor his life, nor his miracles, but his death (vv.26–29; cf. 20:28).

26 While they were eating, Jesus took bread, gave thanks and broke it, and gave it to his disciples, saying, "Take and eat; this is my body."

[27]Then he took the cup, gave thanks and offered it to them, saying, "Drink from it, all of you. [28]This is my blood of the covenant, which is poured out for many for the forgiveness of sins. [29]I tell you, I will not drink of this fruit of the vine from now on until that day when I drink it anew with you in my Father's kingdom."

[30]When they had sung a hymn, they went out to the Mount of Olives.

COMMENTARY

26 This is the second thing Matthew records that takes place "while they were eating" (cf. v.21). Jesus takes *artos*, which can refer to "bread" generally (4:4; 6:11; 15:2, 26) but more commonly refers to a loaf or cake (4:3; 12:4; 14:17, 19; 15:33–34; 16:5–12). This loaf was unleavened (cf. Ex 12:15; 13:3, 7; Dt 16:3). He then gives thanks, probably with some such traditional formula as "Blessed art thou, O Lord our God, King of the universe, who bringest forth bread from the earth." He breaks it, distributes it (if the imperfect indicative variant is original, it may imply that he personally gave the bread to each of them), and says, "Take and eat; this is my body."

Few clauses of four words have evoked more debate than the last one. But three things must be said.

1. The words "this is my body" had no place in the Passover ritual; as an innovation, they must have had stunning effect, an effect that would grow with the increased understanding gained after Easter.

2. Both the breaking and the distributing are probably significant. The bread (body) is broken, and all must partake of it. The sacrificial overtones are clearer in vv.27–28, but the unambiguous sacrificial language connected with Jesus' blood requires that v.26 be interpreted in a similar way.

3. Much of the debate on the force of "is" (In what sense is the bread Jesus' body?) is anachronistic. The verb itself has a wide semantic range and proves very little. "Take this, it means my body" (Moffatt) has its attractions, though it is scarcely less ambiguous. But what must be remembered is that this is a Passover meal. The new rite Jesus institutes has links with redemption history. As the bread has just been broken, so will Jesus' body be broken; and just as the people of Israel associated their deliverance from Egypt with eating the paschal meal prescribed as a divine ordinance, so also Messiah's people are to associate Jesus' redemptive death with eating this bread by Jesus' authority. On the development of the theology of the Lord's Supper across the centuries, see Howard Clarke's admirable summary (*Gospel of Matthew and Its Readers*, 207–19); at greater length, see Gordon T. Smith, ed., *The Lord's Supper: Five Views* (Downers Grove, Ill.: InterVarsity, 2008).

27 Assuming this is a Passover meal, this "cup" (with or without the article, by assimilation to Mk 14:23 or Lk 22:17 respectively) is probably the third, the "cup of blessing." Jesus again gives thanks, probably with some such prayer as "Blessed art thou, O Lord our God, King of the universe, Creator of the fruit of the vine." The wine was not grape juice, though it was customary to cut the wine with a double or triple quantity of water. Unlike Mark, Matthew records not the performance but the command: "Drink from it, all of you." As in Luke and Paul, this has the effect of describing exclusively what Jesus did, not what the disciples did. It should be noted that the participle *eucharistēsas* ("gave thanks"), cognate with *eucharistia* ("thanksgiving"), has given us the word "Eucharist." Some Protestants have avoided the term because of its associations with the traditional Roman Catholic Mass, but the term itself is surely not objectionable.

28 This verse is rich in allusions; so attempts to narrow down its OT background to but one passage are reductionistic. "Blood" and "covenant" are found together in only two OT passages (Ex 24:8; Zec 9:11). Lindars (*New Testament Apologetic*, 132–33) represents those who think the allusion must be to the latter, because allusion to the former would presuppose a typological exegesis not used so early in the tradition. But this fails to reckon with the extensive use of typology at Qumran, and the textual affinities are clearly in favor of Exodus 24:8 (see Gundry, *Use of the Old Testament*, 57–58; Moo, *Old Testament in the Gospel Passion Narratives*, 301–11.). The conclusion seems to be that, once again, we can penetrate near the heart of Jesus' own understanding of his relation to the OT (see comments at 5:17–20; 9:16–17; 11:9–13; 12:28; 13:52). And it is his understanding that sets a paradigm, not only for Matthew (see comments at 1:23; 2:15, 23; 8:16–17; 12:15–21; 13:35) but for other NT writers also (e.g., Heb 9:20). Equally without support are those theories that hold the covenant language to be original but not the blood sacrifice language, making the primary allusion to Jeremiah 31:31–34; or that the sacrifice language is original but not the concept of covenant, making the primary allusion to the OT sacrificial system or to Isaiah 52:13–53:12. The primary reference is to Exodus 24:8, though other allusions are certainly present.

This means that Jesus understands the violent and sacrificial death he is about to undergo (i.e., his "blood"; cf. Morris, *Apostolic Preaching*, 112–28; A. M. Stibbs, *The Meaning of the Word 'Blood' in Scripture* [London: Tyndale, 1954]) as the ratification of the covenant he is inaugurating with his people, even as Moses in Exodus 24:8 ratified the covenant of Sinai by the shedding of blood. "Covenant" is thus a crucial category (cf. *NIDNTT*, 1:365–72; Ridderbos, *Coming of the Kingdom*, 200–201; Morris, *Apostolic Preaching*, 65–111; John J. Hughes, "Hebrews ix 15ff. and Galatians iii 15ff.; a Study in Covenant Practice and Procedure," *NovT* 21 [1979]: 27–96; cf. Heb 8:1–13; 9:11–10:18, 29; 13:20). The event through which Messiah saves his people from their sins (1:21) is his sacrificial death, and the resulting relation between God and the messianic community is definable in terms of covenant, an agreement with stipulations—promises of blessing and sustenance and threats of cursing, all brought here into legal force by the shedding of blood.

Luke and Paul use the adjective "new" before covenant and thus allude to Jeremiah 31:31–34. Mark almost certainly omits the adjective; the textual evidence for the word in Matthew is finely divided. But the passage from Jeremiah was almost certainly in Jesus' mind, as Matthew reports him, because "for the forgiveness of sins" reflects Jeremiah 31:34. Matthew has already shown his grasp of the significance of Jesus' allusion to covenant terminology in general and to the "new covenant" in particular; in 2:18 (see comments there) he cites Jeremiah 31 so as to show that he interprets the coming of Jesus as the real end of the exile and the inauguration of the new covenant.

The words *to peri pollōn ekchynnomenon* ("which is poured out for many") could not fail to be understood as a reference to the Passover sacrifice in which so much blood had just been "poured out" (see comments at v.17). They also connote other sacrificial implications (e.g., Lev 1–7, 16), especially significant since at least *Jesus'* crucifixion did entail much bloodshed. The Mishnah (*Pesaḥ*. 10:6), which in this instance may well preserve traditions alive in

Jesus' day, uses Exodus 24:8 to interpret the Passover wine as a metaphor for blood that seals a covenant between God and his people. Jeremias (*Eucharistic Words*, 222ff.) theorizes that the reason no mention is made of the Passover lamb in our accounts is that Jesus had already identified himself as the Lamb. This is possible because the failure to mention the lamb in any of the Synoptics is startling. But like most arguments from silence, it falls short of proof. Yet the allusions to the Passover—not least being the timing of the Last Supper—are cumulatively compelling.

It appears, then, that Jesus understands the covenant he is introducing to be the fulfillment of Jeremiah's prophecies and the antitype of the Sinai covenant. His sacrifice is thus foretold both in redemption history and in the prophetic word. The exodus becomes a "type" of a new and greater deliverance; and as the people of God in the OT prospectively celebrated in the first Passover their escape from Egypt, anticipating their arrival in the Promised Land, so the people of God here prospectively celebrate their deliverance from sin and bondage, anticipating the coming kingdom (see comments at v.29).

Some take the preposition *peri* ("for [many]") to mean "on account of many" or "because of many" (BDF, para. 229 [1]). But it is more likely equivalent in meaning to the *hyper* (NIV, "for [many]") of the parallel in Mark (Moule, *Idiom Book*, 63; Zerwick, *Biblical Greek*, para. 96) and possibly has the force of *anti* in 20:28 (cf. Morris, *Apostolic Preaching*, 63, 172, 204, 206). As Karl Barth noted, the three prepositions point to Christ's "activity as our Representative and Substitute.... They cannot be understood if—quite apart from the particular view of the atonement made in him which dominates these passages—we do not see that in general these prepositions speak of a place which ought to be ours, that we ought to have taken this place, that we have been taken from it, that it is occupied by another, that this other acts in this place as only he can, in our cause and interest" (quoted in Morris, *Apostolic Preaching*, 63). For "many," see comments at 20:28.

"For the forgiveness of sins" (cf. Heb 9:22) occurs in the words of institution only in Matthew and alludes to Jeremiah 31:31–34. Because the identical phrase is found in Mark 1:4 to describe the purpose of John's baptism but is omitted from the parallel in Matthew (3:1–2, 11), many suggest that Matthew purposely suppressed the phrase there because he wanted to attach it here and connect it exclusively to the work of Jesus Messiah. This is possible. NT writers understand that repentance and forgiveness of sin are tied together as tightly in the OT as in the period following Jesus' death, even though Jesus' death provides the real basis for forgiveness, a basis long promised by revelatory word, cultic act, and redemptive event. In one sense, Mark might be willing to speak of John's baptism as a "baptism of repentance for the forgiveness of sins," while in another, Matthew might be more interested in the ultimate ground of that "forgiveness of sin" and so reserve the phrase for Jesus. But several cautions should be kept in mind.

1. Matthew so regularly condenses Mark that it is usually risky to base too much on an omission.

2. Even in Matthew, John's baptism requires repentance (3:11) that demands confession of sin (3:6). It is hard to believe that Matthew thought that those who thus repented and confessed their sins were not forgiven!

3. Matthew may have slightly abbreviated the report of the Baptist's preaching (3:2) to maintain formal similarity to Jesus' early preaching (4:17).

4. In any case, a more important connection with v.28 is to be found in 1:21. It is by Jesus' death, by the pouring out of his blood, that he will save his people from their sins.

One more OT allusion is worth emphasizing. As in 20:28, it is very probable that Jesus is also portraying himself as Isaiah's Suffering Servant (cf. Moo, *Old Testament in the Gospel Passion Narratives*, 127–32; France, "Servant of the Lord," 37–39). This is based on three things: (1) "my blood of the covenant" calls to mind that the servant is twice presented as "a covenant for the people" (Isa 42:6; 49:8)—i.e., he will reestablish the covenant; (2) *ekchynnomenon* ("poured out," GK *1772*) may well reflect Isaiah 53:12; and (3) "for many" again recalls the work of the Servant in Isaiah 52:13–53:12 (see comments at 20:28).

29 The "fruit of the vine" is a common Jewish way of referring in prayers to wine (cf. *m. Ber.* 6:1). Contrary to Jeremias (*Eucharistic Words*, 207–18), Jesus' promise does not mean that he is abstaining from the cup of wine in this first "Lord's Supper" (cf. Hill). Rather, just as the first Passover looks forward not only to deliverance but to settlement in the land, so also the Lord's Supper looks forward to deliverance and life in the consummated kingdom. The disciples will keep this celebration until Jesus comes (cf. 1Co 11:26); but Jesus will not participate in it with them until the consummation, when he will sit down with them at the messianic banquet (Isa 25:6; *1 En.* 72:14; see comments at 8:11; cf. Lk 22:29–30) in his Father's kingdom, which is equally Jesus' kingdom (cf. Lk 22:16, 18, 29–30; see comments at 16:28; 25:31, 34). This point is greatly strengthened if we assume that Jesus speaks after drinking the *fourth cup* (see comments at v.17).

The four cups were meant to correspond to the fourfold promise of Exodus 6:6–7. The third cup, the "cup of blessing" used by Jesus in the words of institution, is thus associated with redemption (Ex 6:6); but the fourth cup corresponds to the promise "I will take you as my own people, and I will be your God" (Ex 6:7; cf. Daube, *New Testament and Rabbinic Judaism*, 330–31; Lane, *Mark*, 508–9). Thus Jesus is simultaneously pledging that he will drink the "bitter cup" immediately ahead of him and vowing not to drink the cup of consummation, the cup that promises the divine presence, until the kingdom in all its fullness has been ushered in. Then he will drink the cup with his people. This is a veiled farewell and implies a sustained absence (see comments at 24:14; 25:5, 19). The Lord's Supper, therefore, points both to the past and to the future, both to Jesus' sacrifice at Calvary and to the messianic banquet.

30 The "hymn" normally sung was the last part of the *Hallel* (Pss 114–18 or 115–18). It was sung antiphonally. Jesus as the leader would sing the lines, and his followers would respond with "Hallelujah!" Parts of it must have been deeply moving to the disciples when after the resurrection they remembered that Jesus sang words pledging that he would keep his vows (Ps 116:12–13), ultimately triumph despite rejection (Ps 118), and call all nations to praise Yahweh and his covenant love (Ps 117). It may be that Jewish exegesis had already interpreted Psalm 118:25–26 as a reference to Messiah's parousia (Jeremias, *Eucharistic Words*, 255–62).

NOTES

29 BDF, para. 12 (3), points out that ἀπάρτι (*aparti*) is ambiguous. It should most likely be taken as ἀπ' ἄρτι (*ap' arti*; NIV, "from now on"), but it could be construed as Ionic and Attic ἀπαρτί (*aparti*, "exactly," "certainly"), as, possibly, in Revelation 14:13. But the customary rendering fits the context well and should be given the benefit of the doubt.

4. *Prediction of abandonment and denial (26:31–35)*

OVERVIEW

Mark (14:27–31) and Matthew place this pericope after Jesus and his disciples have left the Upper Room. Luke (22:31–38) implies that its contents occur before the departure for the Mount of Olives; John (13:36–38) clearly places it during the supper and before the farewell discourse. The abruptness with which Mark begins this pericope suggests that he displaced it, perhaps to keep intact the theological coherence of the preceding pericope. Matthew does the same thing and for the same reason: this use of *tote* ("then") is inconsequential (see comments at 2:7). It seems likely, therefore, that John gives us the historical sequence at this point, while Matthew and Mark place this pericope where it will emphasize the gravity of the disciples' defection and Peter's denial. Matthew adds some touches, such as the personal pronouns in v.31 (emphasis mine): "*You* will all fall away *on account of me*"—*you*, of all people, on account of *me*, your Messiah, by your own confession. Moreover, in laying out in advance much of the tragedy of the coming hours, the pericope shows that Jesus is not a blind victim of fate but a voluntary sacrifice, and simultaneously he is preparing his disciples for their dark night of doubt.

31Then Jesus told them, "This very night you will all fall away on account of me, for it is
written:

"'I will strike the shepherd,
and the sheep of the flock will be scattered.'

32But after I have risen, I will go ahead of you into Galilee."
33Peter replied, "Even if all fall away on account of you, I never will."
34"I tell you the truth," Jesus answered, "this very night, before the rooster crows, you
will disown me three times."
35But Peter declared, "Even if I have to die with you, I will never disown you." And all the
other disciples said the same.

COMMENTARY

31 "This very night" makes clear how very soon the disciples' defection and Peter's denial will happen. The intimacy of the Last Supper is shortly to be replaced by disloyalty and cowardice. The disciples will all "fall away" on account of Jesus. They will find him an obstacle to devotion and will forsake him (for the verb, see comments at 5:29). As the quotation from Zechariah makes clear, their falling away is related to the "striking" of the Shepherd. Jesus has repeatedly predicted his death and resurrection, but his disciples are still unable to grasp how such things could happen to the Messiah to whom they have been looking (16:21–23; 17:22–23; see comments at v.33).

Yet Jesus' words "for it is written" show that the disciples' defection, though tragic and irresponsible, does not fall outside God's sovereign plan. The textual questions relating to Zechariah 13:7 are complex (cf. Gundry, *Use of the Old Testament*, 25–28; Moo, *Old Testament in the Gospel Passion Narratives*, 182ff.; Blomberg, "Matthew," in *CNTUOT*; see Jn 16:32): apparently the quotation rests on a pre-Christian recension of the LXX or on the MT (Ham, *Coming King*, 213), or on some combination of both. There is no reason to think that Zechariah's words have been altered to fit the events of Jesus' passion and thereby accord with Christian tradition to make the "prophecy" after the event seem to be scriptural (Jeremias, *New Testament Theology*, 297–98). The change to the future *pataxō* ("I will strike") from the imperative *pataxate* ("strike") is the only word that provides nominal support for this theory. However, the grammatical change was probably necessitated by the omission of a definite subject when the Zechariah passage was condensed (France, *Jesus and the Old Testament*, 107–8), rather than by the pressure of an *ex eventu* "prophecy" or by a stress on the divine initiative for theological reasons—something already accomplished by "it is written." Even if it is the "sword" that does the striking in the MT, it does so at Yahweh's command.

Matthew alone (cf. Mark) includes "of the flock" in the second line of the quotation (following LXX), but to what does "the flock" refer? In light of the context of Zechariah 13:1–6, many have suggested that a wicked prophet is in view there. But this is incompatible with "the man who is close to me [i.e., to Yahweh]" (Zec 13:7b). Instead, Yahweh pictures a day when, owing to the prevailing apostasy, the Shepherd who is close to him (as opposed to the false shepherd in Zec 11) is cut down and the sheep scattered. In 13:8–9 most of the sheep perish; but one-third are left, after being refined, to become "my people"—those who will say, "Yahweh is our God." If Jesus' quotation of Zechariah in the Gospels presupposes the full context of Zechariah 13:7, then the rejected Shepherd theme of Zechariah 9–11 is assumed, and the disciples themselves join Israel, the sheep of God, in being scattered as the result of the "striking" of the Shepherd. Their falling away "this very night" continues to the cross and beyond and is emblematic of the coming dispersion of the whole nation. But a purified remnant, a "third," will survive the refining and make up the people of God, "my people." Thus, at the very instant Jesus' disciples show by their scattering that they temporarily side with the unbelieving and apostate nation, God is taking action to make them his true people.

32 Lohmeyer originated the notion that this verse refers to Jesus' future parousia, not his resurrection appearances. The Parousia is to take place, Lohmeyer thinks, in Galilee. But R. H. Stein ("A Short Note on Mark xiv.28 and xvi.7," *NTS* 20 [1974]: 445–52) has conclusively shown that v.32 must refer to a resurrection appearance. Others see in the verb *proagō* (which may mean either "will go ahead" [NIV] or "will lead" [as does a shepherd]) a continuation of the shepherd imagery. But the most natural way to take the verse, and one that vitiates the frequent insistence that it ill suits its context, is that of Stonehouse (*Witness of Matthew*, 170–73). The prediction that the shepherd will be stricken and the sheep scattered might suggest, apart from any further word, that the disciples would return disconsolate to their homes in Galilee, leaving Jesus behind in a grave in Judea. But this new word (v.32) promises that after Jesus has risen, he will arrive in Galilee before they get there; he will "go ahead of [them]."

33 Some have objected that Jesus' prediction of the scattering of *all* the disciples (v.31) conflicts with Peter's following Jesus into the high priest's courtyard (e.g., G. Klein, "Die Verleugnung des Petrus:

Eine traditionsgeschichtliche Untersuchung," *ZTK* 58 [1961]: 297; M. Wilcox, "The Denial-Sequence in Mark xiv.26–31, 66–72," *NTS* 17 [1970–71]: 426–36). But this overlooks the fact that all the disciples actually fled (v.56) and that Peter followed only "at a distance" (v.58) and then denied Jesus. At the end of the day, all the sheep were scattered; all had fallen away.

Peter does not respond directly to Jesus' quotation, nor to his promise to meet him in Galilee. But this does not mean that vv.31b–32 are misplaced redactional additions, for Peter's reply is psychologically convincing. On the one hand, he has learned more about Jesus than he knew at Caesarea Philippi (16:21–28); as a result he is able to accept the idea of suffering for both Jesus and himself. On the other hand, his notion of suffering is bound up with the heroism of men like the Maccabean martyrs, not with voluntary sacrifice—hence v.51 (cf. Jn 18:10). He is prepared for suffering but is not yet ready for what he thinks of as defeat. More important, he reacts on a primal level to Jesus' prediction in v.31a: "It would be natural for him to be too taken up with the implied slur on his loyalty to pay much attention to anything else" (Cranfield, *Mark*, 429).

34 Jesus' "I tell you the truth" (see comments at 5:18) introduces another warning about how near Peter's own defection is: "this very night," indeed, "before the rooster crows." If the idea of *two* cock crowings, preserved only in certain MSS of Mark 14:30, 68, 72, is original (and it may not be; cf. John W. Wenham, "How Many Cock-Crowings? The Problem of Harmonistic Text-Variants," *NTS* 25 [1978–79]: 523–25), then the "difference is the same as that between saying 'before the bell rings' and 'before the second bell rings' (for church or dinner)" (Alexander). Apparently it was usual for roosters in Palestine to crow about 12:30, 1:30, and 2:30 a.m. (Hans Kosmala, "The Time of the Cock-Crow," *ASTI* 2 [1963]: 118–20; *ASTI* 6 [1967–68]: 132–34); so the Romans gave the term "cock-crow" to the watch from 12:00 to 3:00 a.m. Despite Peter's claims of undeviating loyalty (v.33), Jesus says that Peter is within hours of disowning (same verb as in 16:24) him three times.

35 The language of Peter's protest (the rare subjunctive of *dei*) shows that he does not really think that Jesus' death is likely; he still has his visions of heroism. Nor is he alone in his brash protestations of loyalty—only quicker and more vehement than his peers.

5. Gethsemane (26:36–46)

OVERVIEW

Scholars usually see in this pericope an exhortation to foster vigilance and prayerfulness in the face of temptation (cf. Mk 14:32–42; Lk 22:40–46; Jn 12:28–33; 13:21; 16:32). Though this is doubtless present, far more central is the light the pericope sheds on Jesus' perception of what he is about to do. If the exegesis of v.39 is correct, we must ask why this Jesus who has for so long calmly faced the prospect of death (16:21; 17:22–23; 20:17–19; 26:1–2) should now seem to be less courageous than the Maccabean martyrs or the many thousands of his disciples who have faced martyrdom with great courage. The anguish in Gethsemane is not lightly to be passed over; three times Jesus prayed in deep emotional distress. The answer is found even in this first gospel.

The pericope must be interpreted in light of 1:21 and 20:28, on the one hand, and, on the other, in light of the reader's recognition that Jesus is the Messiah, the Son of God, "God with us," whose sacrificial death inaugurates the new covenant (vv.26–30) and redeems his people from their sins. Small wonder that NT writers make much of Jesus' unique and redemptive death (Ro 3:21–26; 4:25; 5:6, 9; 1Co 1:23; 2Co 5:21; Heb 2:18; 4:15; 5:7–9; 1Pe 2:24).

Jesus did not suffer martyrdom. Can anyone imagine the words of v.53 on the lips of a Maccabean martyr? Many of Jesus' followers throughout the centuries willingly suffer martyrdom because of the strength Jesus' death and resurrection give them. But Jesus went to his death knowing that it was his Father's will that he face death completely alone (27:46) as the sacrificial, wrath-averting Passover Lamb. As his death was unique, so also was his anguish; and our best response to it is hushed worship (see K. Schilder, *Christ in His Suffering* [trans. H. Zylstra; Grand Rapids: Eerdmans, 1938], 289–309); J. I. Packer and Mark Dever, *In My Place Condemned He Stood: Celebrating the Glory of the Atonement* [Wheaton, Ill.: Crossway, 2008], not least the extensive bibliography by Ligon Duncan).

36Then Jesus went with his disciples to a place called Gethsemane, and he said to them,
"Sit here while I go over there and pray." 37He took Peter and the two sons of Zebedee
along with him, and he began to be sorrowful and troubled. 38Then he said to them, "My
soul is overwhelmed with sorrow to the point of death. Stay here and keep watch with me."
39Going a little farther, he fell with his face to the ground and prayed, "My Father, if it is
possible, may this cup be taken from me. Yet not as I will, but as you will."
40Then he returned to his disciples and found them sleeping. "Could you men not keep
watch with me for one hour?" he asked Peter. 41"Watch and pray so that you will not fall
into temptation. The spirit is willing, but the body is weak."
42He went away a second time and prayed, "My Father, if it is not possible for this cup to
be taken away unless I drink it, may your will be done."
43When he came back, he again found them sleeping, because their eyes were heavy. 44So
he left them and went away once more and prayed the third time, saying the same thing.
45Then he returned to the disciples and said to them, "Are you still sleeping and
resting? Look, the hour is near, and the Son of Man is betrayed into the hands of sinners.
46Rise, let us go! Here comes my betrayer!"

COMMENTARY

36–38 "Gethsemane" means "oil press," from which the *chōrion* ("place"; usually a field or an enclosed piece of ground [cf. Jn 18:4, "went out"] to which the press was attached) derived its name. Jesus and his disciples often frequented this spot (Jn 18:1–2) on the western slopes of Mount Olivet, separated from Jerusalem by the Kidron. Eight disciples remain at some distance, perhaps outside the enclosure, and the inner three join him (v.37). Jesus, with stern self-control, has so far masked his anguish;

now he begins "to be sorrowful [*lypeisthai*, which connotes deep grief] and troubled" (*adēmonein*, found in the NT only here, in the par. in Mk 14:33, and in Php 2:26, and connoting deep distress).

Jesus' next words—"My soul is overwhelmed with sorrow" (v.38)—are almost a quotation from the refrain of Psalms 42–43 (LXX). The phrase *heōs thanatou* ("to the point of death") is so common in the LXX (e.g., Isa 38:1) that it should not be thought an allusion to Jonah 4:9 (contra Gundry, *Use of the Old Testament*, 59) but "merely a reflection of the OT-tinged language which Jesus used" (Moo, *Old Testament in the Gospel Passion Narratives*, 241). It suggests a sorrow so deep it almost kills (Taylor, *Mark*, 553; Hill; and many others), not that Jesus is so sorrowful he would rather be dead (contra Bultmann, *TDNT*, 4:323 n. 2). Having revealed his deepest emotions and thus given his disciples the most compelling of reasons to do what he asks, he tells them to stay and "keep watch with me" while he goes a little farther on to pray alone. His words could be taken as no more than a request to protect him from intrusion in his deep anguish (cf. many older commentaries). But his words "with me" (only in Matthew) imply that he wanted them to keep awake and go on praying.

39 Jesus prays, prostrate in his intense anguish. He addresses God as "my Father" (see comments at 6:9); Mark preserves the Aramaic *Abba*. The "cup" (*potērion*, GK *4539*) refers not only to suffering and death but, as often in the OT (Pss 11:6 [NIV, "lot"]; 75:7–8; Isa 51:19, 22; Jer 25:15–16, 27–29; 49:12; 51:57; La 4:21; Eze 23:31–34; Hab 2:16; Zec 12:2; cf. Job 21:20; Ps 60:3; Isa 63:6; Ob 16), also to God's wrath (cf. C. E. B. Cranfield, "The Cup Metaphor in Mark xiv.36 and Parallels," *ExpTim* 59 [1947–48]: 137–38; *TDNT*, 6:153; Blaising, "Gethsemane," 339–40; Brown, *Death of the Messiah*, 168–70). The frequent OT allusions in the passion narrative demand an OT meaning for *potērion* instead of "cup of death" in other Jewish literature. Thus the meaning here is fuller than in 20:22–23 and anticipates 27:46.

In one sense, all things are possible with God (cf. Mk 14:36; see comments at 19:26); in another, some things are impossible. The two passages (Mk 14:36 and Mt 26:39) complement each other: All things are possible with God, and so, if it is morally consistent with the Father's redeeming purpose that this "cup" (Matthew) or "hour" (Mark) be taken from Jesus, that is what he deeply desires. But more deeply still, Jesus desires to do his Father's will. Though the precise wording of the synoptic accounts varies somewhat, if the prayer was of some duration ("one hour," v.40), and if Jesus after his resurrection told his disciples its contents, or if the disciples were within earshot, some variation in the tradition is not surprising. Jesus' deep commitment to his Father's will cannot be doubted. But in this crisis, the worst since 4:1–11, Jesus is tempted to seek an alternative to sin-bearing suffering as the route by which to fulfill his Father's redemptive purposes. As with his self-confessed ignorance in 24:36, Jesus may simply not have known whether any other way was possible. He prays in agony; and though he is supernaturally strengthened (Lk 22:43), he learns only that the cross is unavoidable if he is to obey his Father's will.

Blaising ("Gethsemane," 337) proposed an alternative exegesis. He observes that, whatever the wording in the Synoptics, the conditional clause is grammatically "first class," a so-called real condition, which he interprets as follows: "This class of condition assumes the condition to be a reality, and the conclusion follows logically and naturally from that assumption" (cf. *Grammar*, 1007). From this, Blaising concludes that what Jesus is asking for is possible with the Father and that Jesus knows it; so he cannot be asking that the cup (i.e., his passion) not come to him, an impossibility, for Jesus has repeatedly spoken of it, but that the cup not *remain* with him. In other words, Jesus is tempted to fear that the "cup" of God's wrath will not pass away from him after he has drunk it but that it will consume him forever, and there would be no resurrection. He prays with faith, because he knows it is the Father's will: "Father, as you have promised in your Word, take the cup from me after I drink it; yet this is not my will alone; it is your will that this be done" (Blaising, p. 343).

This interpretation has certain attractions, yet along with several questionable details, it has two insuperable difficulties.

1. Despite Blaising's appeal to A. T. Robertson (i.e., *Grammar*, 1007), even under this slightly dated classification of conditionals, a first-class condition in Greek does not necessarily assume the reality of the protasis but only that the protasis is as real as the apodosis. The speaker assumes the reality of the protasis for the sake of argument but does not thereby indicate that the condition described in the protasis is, in fact, real. Were Blaising to apply his understanding of first-class conditional clauses to Matthew 12:26–27 and Mark 3:24–26, the result would be theologically incoherent, as Robertson himself recognizes (*Grammar*, 1008; cf. Zerwick, *Biblical Greek*, paras. 303ff.).

2. Blaising introduces a novel interpretation, but only the traditional view continues the line of temptation Jesus has earlier found most difficult to confront—namely, the temptation to avoid the cross (see comments at 4:1–11; 16:21–23).

40–41 Jesus returns to his disciples—i.e., the inner three—and finds them sleeping (Lk 22:45 adds "exhausted from sorrow"). Jesus' question is addressed to Peter but is in the plural and therefore includes them all (see comments at 16:16; 26:33–35). Though "one hour" need not be exact, it certainly indicates that Jesus has been praying for some time. "Watch and pray" could be a hendiadys (see Notes); alternatively, it may suggest two components: spiritual alertness and intercession.

It is doubtful that "so that you will not fall into temptation" (v.41) means only "so that you will stay awake and not fall into the temptation to sleep." Indeed, Jesus' prediction of their spiritual defection that "very night" (v.31) should have served as an urgent call to prayer. So now he tells them that only urgent prayer will save them from falling into the coming "temptation" (see comments at 4:1; 6:13). Even in his own extremity, when he needs and seeks his Father's face, Jesus thinks of the impending but much lesser trial his followers will face. He speaks compassionately: "The spirit is willing, but the body [*sarx*, 'flesh,' GK *4922*] is weak." This is not a reference to the Holy Spirit but makes a "distinction between man's physical weakness and the noble desires of his will" (Hill; idem, *Greek Words*, 242). But though compassionate, these words, which doubtless hark back to v.35, are not an excuse but a warning and incentive (Broadus). Spiritual eagerness is often accompanied by carnal weakness—a danger amply experienced by successive generations of Christians.

42–44 Some interpreters have seen a certain progression in Jesus' three prayers, but Matthew says that Jesus said "the same thing" (v.44). The variations between v.39 and v.42 must therefore be incidental. "May your will be done" mirrors one of the petitions of the prayer Jesus taught his disciples (6:10). As Jesus learned obedience (Heb 5:7–9), so he became the supreme model for his own teaching. In the first garden, "Not your will but mine" changed paradise to desert and brought man from Eden to Gethsemane. Now "Not my will but yours" brings anguish to the man who prays it but transforms the desert into the kingdom and brings man from Gethsemane to the gates of glory.

45–46 The word *loipon* as an adverb does not naturally mean "still" (NIV) or "meanwhile" but points to the future ("henceforth") or is inferential ("it follows that"). Therefore, Jesus' words should not be taken as a question (NIV) but as a gently ironic command (see KJV, "Sleep on now, and take your rest"; cf. the irony in 23:23; see Moule, *Idiom Book*, 161). The hour of the passion is near: it is too late to pray and gain strength for the temptations ahead. His disciples may as well sleep. The Son of Man (see comments at 8:20) is betrayed into the hands of sinners; he who is the resplendent, messianic King takes the path of suffering. Doubtless Jesus could see and hear the party approaching as it crossed the Kidron with torches and climbed up the path to Gethsemane. The sleepers for whom he would die have lost their opportunity to gain strength through prayer. By contrast, Jesus has prayed in agony but now rises with poise and advances to meet his betrayer.

NOTES

39 The distinctions Thrall (*Greek Particles*, 67–70) draws between Mark's (14:36) ἀλλά (*alla*, "but") and Matthew's πλήν (*plēn*, "but") are dubious because the former adversative particle has so broad a semantic range.

41 If the ἵνα (*hina*, "that") clause is dependent only on the verb "pray," then it is probably not final (as in 5:29) and gives the content of the prayer. If it depends on "watch and pray" together, it may have telic force.

43 The periphrastic pluperfect ἦσαν ... βεβαρημένοι (*ēsan ... bebarēmenoi*, lit., "were having been weighed down"; NIV, "were heavy") provides a good instance in which the perfect passive participle probably has no more than adjectival force (cf. Moule, *Idiom Book*, 19)—or, better put, it should be read in line with aspect theory as expressing stativity, not in some complex and unbelievable temporal grid.

6. The arrest (26:47–56)

47While he was still speaking, Judas, one of the Twelve, arrived. With him was a large
crowd armed with swords and clubs, sent from the chief priests and the elders of the
people. 48Now the betrayer had arranged a signal with them: "The one I kiss is the man;
arrest him." 49Going at once to Jesus, Judas said, "Greetings, Rabbi!" and kissed him.
50Jesus replied, "Friend, do what you came for."
Then the men stepped forward, seized Jesus and arrested him. 51With that, one of Jesus'
companions reached for his sword, drew it out and struck the servant of the high priest,
cutting off his ear.
52"Put your sword back in its place," Jesus said to him, "for all who draw the sword will
die by the sword. 53Do you think I cannot call on my Father, and he will at once put at my
disposal more than twelve legions of angels? 54But how then would the Scriptures be
fulfilled that say it must happen in this way?"

[55]At that time Jesus said to the crowd, "Am I leading a rebellion, that you have come out with swords and clubs to capture me? Every day I sat in the temple courts teaching, and you did not arrest me. [56]But this has all taken place that the writings of the prophets might be fulfilled." Then all the disciples deserted him and fled.

COMMENTARY

47 Judas Iscariot (see comments at 10:4; 26:14–16, 25; 27:3–10) arrived with armed men. What he received payment for was probably information as to where Jesus could be arrested in a quiet setting with little danger of mob violence. He may have first led the "large crowd" to the upper room and, finding it empty, surmised where Jesus and his disciples had gone (cf. Jn 18:1–3). The "large crowd" accompanying Judas had been sent "from the chief priests and the elders of the people"—the clergy and lay members of the Sanhedrin (see comments at 21:23). Luke 22:52 says some chief priests and elders accompanied the crowd. The military terms in John 18:3, 12 suggest that some Roman soldiers were among the number, along with temple police and some others. Although many scholars have argued that no Romans were involved at this time, it is not unlikely that some were present. Especially during the feasts the Romans took extra pains to ensure public order, so a request for a small detachment from the cohort would not likely be turned down. Thus Pilate might have had some inkling of the plot from the beginning, and if he shared it with his wife, it might help explain her dream (27:19).

48–50 The need for pointing out the right man was especially acute, not only because it was dark, but because, in a time long before photography, the faces of even great celebrities would not be nearly as widely known as today. To identify Jesus, Judas chose the kiss (thereby turning it into a symbol of betrayal). "Greetings, Rabbi!" (v.49; see comments at 8:19; 23:8), a tragic mockery, was for the crowd's ears, not Jesus'.

"Friend" (v.50) is an openhearted but not intimate greeting. Brown (*Death of the Messiah*, 256–57) stresses the ironic function in all its uses in Matthew (cf. 20:13; 22:12). The next words, *eph ho parei* ("what you came for"), are notoriously ambiguous. If the relative pronoun *ho* functions as a direct interrogative pronoun, the expression means "Why [lit., 'for what'] have you come?" (NIV text note; cf. Zerwick, *Biblical Greek*, para. 223; Turner, *Insights*, 69–71; idem, *Syntax*, 49–50; BDF, paras. 495–96), and some verb like "do" must he supplied (NIV text; cf. BDF, para. 300 [2]). If the clause is an imperatival statement, its force is like John 13:27 and reflects Jesus' newly regained poise and his sovereignty in these events. If it is a question, it elicits no information but administers a rebuke steeped in the irony of professed ignorance that knows very well why Judas has come.

51–54 "With that" is the NIV's acceptable effort to render *idou* in this context (cf. "Look," v.45; "Here," v.46; untranslated, v.47; see comments at 1:20). Many are skeptical of the authenticity of this passage, finding it out of keeping with the restrained spirit of the pericope as a whole and wondering why the offending disciple was not arrested. Moreover, it is the latest gospel that names Jesus' sword-wielding disciple (Peter) and his target (Malchus [Jn 18:10]). This might suggest that the story was growing and gaining accretions. Noteworthy are the following points.

1. The restraint belongs to Jesus, not the pericope. Moreover, we have already seen that earlier protestations of loyalty (vv.33–35) were probably grounded in some form of nationalistic messianism; so Peter's response is scarcely unexpected.

2. Peter's response is psychologically convincing. After repeated warnings of defection, Peter may have felt that the crucial test of loyalty had arrived. He is magnificent and pathetic — magnificent because he rushes in to defend Jesus with characteristic courage and impetuousness, pathetic because his courage evaporates when Jesus undoes Peter's damage, forbids violence, and faces the passion without resisting.

3. However one interprets the difficult verses in Luke 22:36–38, they show that the disciples had two swords with them; if Peter actually wielded the sword, other disciples had the same idea (Lk 22:49). On the likelihood of a disciple carrying a sword, see Brown, *Death of the Messiah*, 268–71.

4. There were probably many reasons why Peter was not arrested. Jesus not only quickly cooled the situation but healed the wound (omitted by Matthew). It was one thing to escort a nonresisting prisoner quietly back to the city; it was another to escort twelve men, eleven of them frightened and ready to fight. In any case, before decisive action could be taken, the disciples fled in the darkness (v.56).

5. Over the centuries, pious Christian imaginations have provided names for those not named in the NT (cf. B. M. Metzger, "Names for the Nameless in the New Testament," in *New Testament Studies* [ed. Metzger], 23–43). Within the NT the evidence is mixed. Whatever order the Synoptics were written in, we must note that Matthew may preserve a name omitted by Mark (Mt 26:57; Mk 14:53) or drop a name preserved by Mark (Mt 9:18; Mk 5:22). Matthew and Luke both drop Mark's Bartimaeus (Mk 10:46) and Alexander and Rufus (Mk 15:21). Add to this the fact that many scholars now insist that John does not represent late tradition, and there remains little reason for skepticism concerning this sorry scene.

Some take Jesus' response — "for all who draw the sword will die by the sword" (v.52) — as a call to pacifism, whereas others observe that Jesus told Peter to put his sword "back in its place," not to throw it away. Both views ask the text to answer questions of no immediate relevance. The least we can say is that violence *in defense of Christ* is completely unjustified; certainly v.52 separates Jesus from the Zealots. "Whether these words ... can be taken as the basis for a thoroughgoing pacifism will depend on a wider assessment of the relevant biblical material. But as a proverbial observation (cf. Rev 13:10) on the tendency of violence to recoil on those who perpetrate it Jesus' aphorism reflects common experience, even though not every historical example conforms to this pattern" (France [NICNT]). Moreover, a simple request to his Father would bring twelve legions of angels (a full Roman legion was six thousand; cf. *ZPEB*, 3:907–8) to his assistance — perhaps one legion for Jesus and one for each of the Eleven (v.53). This is more than the eyes of faith seeing help, as in 2 Kings 6:17; it is the knowledge that help is available while refusing to use it (cf. Jn 10:18). In addition, Jesus' stance regarding his own death is grounded on the fact the "Scriptures" (plural, v.54) must be fulfilled (see comments at vv.24, 31; cf. Lk 24:25–26). This divine "must" (*dei*) is not for Jesus sheer inevitability, since he still believes it possible to gain instant aid from his Father. Instead, it is the commingling of divine sovereignty and Jesus' unflagging determination to obey his Father's will.

Many commentators note that in 1QM 7:6 the angels are represented as joining forces with the righteous at the End. Jesus himself elsewhere pictures angelic participation at the consummation (e.g., 13:41; 24:30–31). But at this point in redemptive history, the angels are not called on. Jesus faces this battle alone, and the consummation of all things is not yet.

55–56 Every day for the preceding week, and presumably on earlier visits to the Holy City, Jesus had been teaching in the temple courts; yet the authorities had not arrested him. Why then do they seize him now as if he were a rebel (*lēstēs*, GK *3334*; see comments at 27:16)? The implication is that there is no need to arrest him secretly and violently, except for reasons in their own minds that reveal more about them than about him. "At that time" (lit., "In that hour") seems a rather heavy-handed transition, but perhaps what follows it was a well-known saying of Jesus among Christians to whom Matthew was writing, and he is pointing out that this was the time when he spoke it.

After questioning the display of force by those who arrested him, Jesus said, "This has all taken place [see comments at 1:22; 21:4] that the writings [or 'Scriptures'] of the prophets might be fulfilled." Mark (14:49) simply has "But the Scriptures must be fulfilled." Matthew gives us more, doubtless because he is more interested in the prophetic nature of the Scriptures (see Introduction, section 11.b). "The writings of the prophets," therefore, probably does not exclude the Law and the Writings, for elsewhere Moses and David are also considered "prophets." The reference is to the Scriptures (as in v.54), their human authors being considered primarily as prophets, not lawgivers, wise men, or psalmists.

All the disciples then fulfill one specific prophecy (see comments at v.31) and flee. Mark 14:51–52 adds the account of the young man who flees naked. Probably at this time Jesus is bound (Jn 18:12).

7. Jesus before the Sanhedrin (26:57–68)

OVERVIEW

Few topics have caused more tension between Jews and Christians than the trial of Jesus. Those who have committed abominable atrocities against the Jews have often based their actions on the ground that Jews are the murderers of their Messiah, or God-killers, and have all too frequently turned to Matthew 27:25 for backing. As a reaction to this reprehensible attitude, more recent study (both Jewish and Christian) has argued that the Jews were very little involved and that most of the blame should be placed on the Romans. An excellent survey of Jewish and Christian exegesis of the trial narratives, from 1770 to the late 1960s, is given by Catchpole (*Trial of Jesus*); further representative treatments, in addition to commentaries and articles, are included in our bibliography under Blinzler (*Trial of Jesus*), Sherwin-White (*Roman Society*, ch. 2), and Benoit (*Jesus and the Gospel*, 123–66). See also S. G. F. Brandon, *The Trial of Jesus of Nazareth* (London: Batsford, 1968); E. Bammel, ed., *The Trial of Jesus* (London: SCM Press, 1970); Haim Cohn, *The Trial and Death of Jesus* (New York: Ktav, 1977); Paul Winter, *On the Trial of Jesus* (2nd ed.; Berlin: de Gruyter, 1974).

Though there is no consensus, the dominant view in current scholarship runs something like this: The four gospel accounts of the trial before the Sanhedrin cannot readily be reconciled. But the fourth gospel, though making clear that both Jewish and Roman authorities were involved from the beginning (Jn 18:3, 12), stresses that the Sanhedrin did not have the power to inflict the death penalty (Jn 18:31) and places much more emphasis on the Roman trial. By contrast, the Synoptics lay more blame on the Jews, and Matthew goes so far as to tell us that Pilate washed his hands of the whole affair, while the Jews called down curses on themselves (27:24–25). On the face of it, John's account is the more historically reliable, whereas the Synoptics are more seriously tainted by later church-synagogue tensions. In short, anti-Semitism has colored their narratives.

This is confirmed, it is alleged, when all the illegalities of the Jewish proceedings are noted. The Mishnah (*Sanh.*) makes it clear that legal procedure in capital cases forbade night trials, required at least two consecutive days, and provided for private interrogation of witnesses. The breaches in law are so numerous as to be unbelievable, and one Jewish writer (Cohn, *Trial and Death of Jesus*) has gone so far in reconstructing the evidence that he concludes the Sanhedrin actually tried to save Jesus from the Roman courts. Any trace of evidence that counters this thesis he ascribes to the polemic of later deteriorating church-synagogue relationships, compounded with the natural desire in Christian writers to avoid blaming the powerful Roman authorities.

Yet some things must not be overlooked.

1. The problem of illegalities in Jesus' trial is more complex than is customarily recognized. We have already shown (see Reflections, p. 597) that executions under certain circumstances could take place on a major feast day. Other irregularities include (1) the proceedings that apparently took place in Caiaphas's home, not the temple precincts; (2) Jesus' not being offered a defense attorney; (3) his being charged with blasphemy without actually blaspheming in the legally defined sense, which required that the accused actually pronounce the name of God; (4) the verdict's being rushed through at night without the minimum two days required in capital cases, which had the effect of banning the new opening of capital trials from the day before Sabbaths or festival days (*m. Sanh.* 4:1). But quite apart from the difficult problem of dating Mishnaic traditions—for the sake of argument we may agree that they all date back to the beginning of the first century or earlier—five factors challenge the idea that legal considerations invalidate the authenticity of the Gospels on these points.

a. Some Mishnaic stipulations, not least in the tractate *Sanhedrin*, are almost certainly theoretical formulations only, which never had the force of obeyed law. Is there any independent historical evidence, for instance, that "burnings" of the sort described in *Sanhedrin* 7:2 ever took place?

b. Dalman (*Jesus-Jeshua*, 98–100) provides references to other occasions of flagrant breach of judicial regulations on the ground that "the hour demands it."

c. Similarly, there is evidence that expediency partially motivated the religious authorities (cf. Jn 11:49–50). This could account for numerous irregularities. If the leaders feared mob violence, haste was required. Moreover, it was legitimate to execute certain criminals on feast days but not on the Sabbath. If Jesus was arrested Thursday night (Friday by Jewish reckoning), things had to move swiftly if he was to be buried by dusk on Friday, the onset of Sabbath. An all-night session of the Jewish authorities was demanded by the fact that Roman officials like Pilate worked very early in the morning and then refused to take on new cases for the rest of the day. If Jesus could not be presented to Pilate by early Friday morning, the case would drag on until after Sabbath—along with mounting risks of mob violence.

d. The sources are sufficiently difficult that we do not know the precise relationship between the Pharisees of Jesus' day and the rabbis who compiled Mishnah. Even if Sigal (*Halakhah of Jesus*; see Introduction, section 11.f) has exaggerated the distinctions, we may not always be wise in reading rabbinic regulations back into Jesus' day. For instance, the narrow and technical definitions of blasphemy in Mishnah may not have been popular with all Pharisees. After all, large parts of the population held to extraordinarily broad notions of blasphemy: Josephus (*Ant.* 20.108 [5.2]) records that an angry crowd accused a Roman soldier of blasphemy because he had exposed his genitals to them. And we have *no* evidence for the way the Sadducees understood blasphemy.

e. We may go farther. A strong, if not entirely convincing, case can be made for distinguishing between "Sanhedrin" and "Beth Din." The NT speaks of the former; the relevant Mishnaic tractate, though traditionally called *Sanhedrin*, in fact speaks almost thirty times of the latter and only three times of the former. From this, some have deduced that what the Gospels describe is *not* the "Sanhedrin" in the religious, scholarly sense but the "Sanhedrin" that was essentially political and, to some extent, corrupt (cf. E. Rivkin, "Beth Din, Boule, Sanhedrin: A Tragedy of Errors," *HUCA* 46 [1975]: 181–99). Even if this distinction does not prove valid, it must be admitted that "a way of removing an undesirable enemy is usually found when the will is there" (S. Rosenblatt, "The Crucifixion of Jesus from the Standpoint of Pharisaic Law," *JBL* 75 [1956]: 319 [though Rosenblatt does not accept the accounts as we have them in the Gospels]). Catchpole (*Trial of Jesus*, 268–69) has convincingly shown that "the debate about illegalities should be regarded as a dead end, and at most able to make only a minor contribution."

2. More distinction is found between John and the Synoptics and between Matthew and Mark-Luke than is actually there. Although John places more emphasis on the Roman trial, only in John 19:12, and never in the Synoptics, do we find *the Jews* manipulating Pilate in order to secure a guilty verdict and a capital sentence. It is surely false to attribute the lesser prominence of Pilate in the Synoptics to Christian concern to get on with Rome; for long before the evangelists wrote, Pilate was deposed and banished by Rome. Moreover, it is not at all clear that Matthew sees 27:24 as an effective absolution for Pilate. Matthew frequently records denunciations of hypocrisy and expects persecution from Gentile "governors and kings" (10:18–19). Equally, it is not at all clear that 27:25 should be interpreted to mean that all Jews remain under a continuing curse. The first disciples were Jews to a man; and the fact that Matthew clearly insists the authorities were afraid of mob action (26:3–5) shows he understands that many Jews were enthusiastically, if superficially, *for* Jesus, even if few of them were committed disciples.

3. But if such sharp distinctions between John's treatment of the trial and that of the Synoptics are scarcely supported by the text, even less defensible are sharp disjunctions. The attempt to blame the Romans and exonerate the Jews finds little support in the fourth gospel; but even if it were an unquestionable theme there, responsible historiography attempts a synthesis of the sources, not a priori historical disjunctions—one of the classic "historians' fallacies" (cf. Fischer, *Historians' Fallacies*). And a believable synthesis is indeed possible (see below).

4. John 18:31, frequently cited to absolve the Sanhedrin, is not only historically credible (cf. Sherwin-White, *Roman Society*, 35–43; Catchpole, *Trial of Jesus*, 247–48) but also provides an important clue to the roles played by Jews and Romans. All the gospels attest, repeatedly and in highly diverse ways, that many Jewish leaders wanted Jesus' removal because of his claims of messianic author-

ity, coupled with his popularity among the populace at large and the unexpected kind of "messiah" he was proving to be—and especially his failure to show more respect to the religious authorities. When he finally came into their hands, political circumstances forced them to seek the death sentence from Pilate. For this purpose, it was necessary for the Jewish leaders to tinge the charges against Jesus with political color. Thus he was made to seem less a Messiah than a competitor of Caesar. Only by a very selective handling of the evidence (e.g., Brandon, *Trial of Jesus*) can one conclude that the political charge came first, making Jesus some kind of Zealot rebel.

5. The Holocaust and other atrocities have blinded the eyes of both Jewish and Christian historians. Not a few modern Jews insist that the Holocaust is the result of centuries of bigoted Christian tradition and that Christian solidarity entails corporate Christian guilt. Yet they would be loath to assume that Jewish solidarity entails for the Jewish race a corporate Jewish guilt because of the contribution of a few Jews to the death of Jesus. Meanwhile Christian historians, alive to the legacy of Western Christendom's persecution of the Jews, are embarrassed into making irresponsible judgments against the historical evidences as a sort of atonement for past injustices. It is easier to blame the Romans, who are not present to defend themselves, than to face the survivors of the Holocaust with unpleasant historical realities. The wisest scholars of both sides have seen this. The Jewish scholar Samuel Sandmel (*We Jews and Jesus* [New York: Oxford Univ. Press, 1965], 141) writes, "Perhaps we might be willing to say to ourselves that it is not at all impossible that some Jews, even leading Jews, recommended the death of Jesus to Pilate. We are averse to saying this to ourselves, for so total has been the charge against us that we have been constrained to make a total denial."

It is helpful to remember that, whatever Christendom has done, the NT writers, most if not all of whom were Jews, can scarcely or reasonably be labeled "anti-Semitic." Matthew and the other evangelists certainly blame some Jews for Jesus' death. They also blame some Romans. But the reasons for the blame are historical, theological, spiritual—not ethnic. The Twelve are Jews; and after the crucifixion, a Jew from Arimathea (27:57–60) shows great concern for Jesus' burial. The NT writers assess people by their response to Jesus, whom they have come to know as King Messiah and Son of God, not by their race.

6. From the viewpoint of NT theology, Christians must repeatedly remind themselves of two things. First, from a theological perspective, every Christian is as guilty of putting Jesus on the cross as Caiaphas. Thoughtful believers will surely admit that their own guilt is the more basic of the two, for if we believe Matthew's witness, and Jesus could have escaped the clutches of Caiaphas (v.53), then what drove Jesus to the cross was his commitment to the Father's redemptive purposes. While this does not excuse Caiaphas and his peers, it keeps Christians from supercilious judgment of the Jews. Second, even if first-century Christians, whether Jews or Gentiles, rightly saw God's judgment in the destruction of Jerusalem and Judea (AD 66–73), that could not give them the right to put themselves in God's place and execute his judgment for him. Judgment belongs only to God. Any other view, including that which has often dominated Christendom, fails to recognize essential NT distinctions between the kingdom and the church (see comments at 13:37–39).

At this point we should consider one of several ways in which the complementary accounts of Jesus' passion in our gospels can be reasonably harmonized so as to show how the proceedings against Jesus could have been completed within the few hours the chronology permits. There were two trials—one Jewish and the other Roman. The Jewish trial began with an informal examination by Annas (Jn 18:12–14, 19–23), perhaps while members of the Sanhedrin were being hurriedly gathered. A decision by a session of the Sanhedrin (vv.57–68; Mk 14:53–65) was followed by a formal decision at dawn and a dispatch to Pilate (27:1–2; Lk 22:66–71). The Roman trial began with a first examination before Pilate (vv.11–14; Jn 18:28–38a) and was quickly followed by Herod's interrogation (Lk 23:6–12) and the final appearance before Pilate (27:15–31; Jn 18:38b–19:16). This reconstruction is merely tentative, but it usefully coordinates the biblical data.

57Those who had arrested Jesus took him to Caiaphas, the high priest, where the
teachers of the law and the elders had assembled. 58But Peter followed him at a distance,
right up to the courtyard of the high priest. He entered and sat down with the guards to
see the outcome.
59The chief priests and the whole Sanhedrin were looking for false evidence against
Jesus so that they could put him to death. 60But they did not find any, though many false
witnesses came forward.
Finally two came forward 61and declared, "This fellow said, 'I am able to destroy the
temple of God and rebuild it in three days.'"
62Then the high priest stood up and said to Jesus, "Are you not going to answer? What
is this testimony that these men are bringing against you?" 63But Jesus remained silent.
The high priest said to him, "I charge you under oath by the living God: Tell us if you are
the Christ, the Son of God."
64"Yes, it is as you say," Jesus replied. "But I say to all of you: In the future you will see
the Son of Man sitting at the right hand of the Mighty One and coming on the clouds of
heaven."
65Then the high priest tore his clothes and said, "He has spoken blasphemy! Why do
we need any more witnesses? Look, now you have heard the blasphemy. 66What do you
think?"
"He is worthy of death," they answered.
67Then they spit in his face and struck him with their fists. Others slapped him 68and
said, "Prophesy to us, Christ. Who hit you?"

COMMENTARY

57 For the relationship between Annas and Caiaphas, see comments at v.3. If both men concurred in finding Jesus guilty and recommending the death penalty, the action would more likely win the acceptance of both the populace and the Romans than if only one agreed. Well-to-do homes were often built in a square shape with an open, central courtyard. If Annas lived in rooms on one wing of the court, then it is possible that he interviewed Jesus (Jn 18:19–24) in one wing while the Sanhedrin was assembling in another (the NIV's "had assembled" is too strong; the Greek verb requires no more than "assembled"). Not much time would be required.

Matthew mentions the teachers of the law and the elders; Mark 14:53 adds the chief priests, to whom Matthew refers in v.59. There is probably little significance to such variations, but they warn us against reading too much into particular details. No Pharisees are mentioned, though doubtless many teachers and lay elders belonged to that party. Their absence from Matthew's passion account is important for two reasons. First, it calls into question theories that pit the Matthean church against "Pharisees" of AD 85; for if Matthew sees the Pharisees as prime enemies of Jesus, why are they not mentioned in this final confrontation? Second, it accurately reflects the little we know about Jerusalem politics at the time. The Pharisees doubtless exercised throughout the land strong theological and social influence and through the synagogues in the towns and villages a great deal of moral persuasion and some political power. But for the Sanhedrin, where the final act of confrontation with Jewish leaders was played out, the shape of power was different. The high priest, almost certainly a Sadducee, presided; the priests, primarily if not exclusively Sadducees, enjoyed large and perhaps dominant influence, and the Pharisees exercised power only through the decision of the entire assembly.

58 Peter followed Jesus "at a distance," midway between courage (v.51) and cowardice (v.70) (Bengel, *Gnomon*). John 18:15–16 provides additional information on how Peter secured entrance to the high priest's courtyard. Peter joined the "servants" (the term is general but probably includes both household servants and temple police—hence the NIV's "guards") around the courtyard fire, waiting to see the outcome.

59–63a If there was but one central Sanhedrin (see above), it was composed of three groups: leading priests (see comments at 21:23), teachers of the law, and elders. It had seventy members plus the high priest, but a mere twenty-three made a quorum. The "whole Sanhedrin" need not mean that everyone was present (cf. Lk 23:50–51) but only that the Sanhedrin as a body was involved. We do not know what proportion of the seventy came from constituent groups or whether the proportion had to be preserved in the quorum.

Many equate this meeting of the Sanhedrin with the one at daybreak described by Luke (22:66–71). But Matthew seems to make a distinction between the two (cf. 27:12). Perhaps the later meeting was in the temple precincts (the usual place) and was more fully attended; if so, Luke may well be conflating the proceedings.

Matthew says the Sanhedrin was looking "for false evidence" (*pseudomartyria*, v.59, GK *6019*) and obtained it from "false witnesses" (*pseudomartyres*, v.60). It is unlikely this means that the Sanhedrin sought liars only; if so, why not simply fabricate the evidence? Rather, the Sanhedrin, already convinced of Jesus' guilt, went through the motions of securing evidence against him. When people hate, they readily accept false witness; and the Sanhedrin eventually heard and believed just about what it wanted. Matthew knew that Jesus was not guilty and could not be, so he describes the evidence as "false."

The two men who came forward (v.60) may or may not have been suborned (cf. Ac 6:11). At least two witnesses were required in a capital case. In Greek, *houtos* does not necessarily carry a sneering tone (NIV, "This fellow," v.61; similarly v.71) but may serve as an emphatic pronoun or equivalent to the British "this chap." Their witness had some element of truth but was evilly motivated and disregarded what Jesus meant in John 2:19–21 (the reference is not to Mt 24:2, where only disciples were present; see comments at 21:12–17). John did not interpret Jesus' saying allegorically (Hill) but typologically. Though some will insist that even typological exegesis must be traced to the later church, we have already noted enough typological exegesis in Jesus' own teaching (see comments at 26:28) to acknowledge that Jesus himself led the way in this regard. Interpreted with crass literalism, Jesus' words might be taken as a threat to desecrate the temple, one of the pillars of Judaism. Desecration of sacred places was almost universally regarded as a capital offense in the ancient world—and in this, Jews were no different from the pagans (e.g., Jer 26:1–19; *t. Sanh.* 13:5; *b. Roš Haš.* 17a).

But what do Jesus' words in John 2:19–21 mean? If Jesus sees himself as the antitype of the Passover lamb, the true Suffering Servant, the revelation of the Father, and the fulfillment of OT Scriptures (e.g., vv.27–30; cf. 5:17–20; 11:25–30), it is not at all unlikely he would also see himself as the true temple, the ultimate point of meeting between God and man. In that case, John's words accurately reflect Jesus' thought.

We have penetrated very close to the heart of the dispute between early Christianity and Judaism as attested elsewhere in the NT—a dispute that may be summarized by a series of questions: What is the nature of the continuity between the old covenant and the new? Must Gentiles become Jews before they can become Christians? In what sense and to what degree does the Mosaic law have binding force on Jesus' followers? The place of the temple is one element in that debate, raised in earliest Christianity (Ac 6:13–14) but traceable back to Jesus himself and a contributing factor to his own condemnation (cf. G. K. Beale, *The Temple and the Church's Mission* (NSBT 17; Downers Grove, Ill.: InterVarsity, 2004).

The NIV and NASB are probably correct in translating v.62 as two questions from the high priest (cf. BDF, paras. 298 [4]; 299 [1]). He probably hoped Jesus would incriminate himself. But, true to Isaiah 53:7, Jesus kept silent (v.63a; cf. Moo, *Old Testament in the Gospel Passion Narratives*, 148–51).

63b The high priest, frustrated by Jesus' silence, tried a bold stroke that cut to the central issue: Was Jesus the Messiah or was he not? The question has been raised before in one form or another (see comments at 12:39–42; 16:1–4; 21:1–11, 14–16, 23) and may have been prompted in the high priest's mind by Jesus' mention of the temple, since some branches of Judaism anticipated a renewal of the temple's glory when Messiah came (cf. Lane, *Mark*, 535). But whether or not this explains his motive, the high priest boldly charges Jesus to answer "under oath by the living God" (cf. McNeile; Benoit, *Jesus and the Gospel*, for justification of this rendering).

The form of the question in Mark 14:61 is slightly different: "Are you the Christ [see comments at 1:1; 2:4], the Son of the Blessed One?" Instead of the latter, Matthew uses his preferred title, "the Son of God." The two titles are formally equivalent, and both may have been used at various points in the trial (cf. Jn 19:7). "Son of God" in Judaism can be equivalent to Messiah (see comments at 2:15; 3:17; 11:27; 16:13–20).

The outcome is now inevitable. If Jesus refuses to answer, he breaks a legally imposed oath. If he denies he is the Messiah, the crisis is over—but so is his influence. If he affirms it, then, given the commitments of the court, Jesus must be false. After all, how could the true Messiah allow himself to be imprisoned and put in jeopardy? The gospels' evidence suggests that the Sanhedrin was prepared to see Jesus' unequivocal claim to messiahship as meriting the death penalty, and their unbelief precluded them from allowing any other possibility.

64 Perhaps this is what is meant by Jesus' "good confession" (1Ti 6:13). There are four points of interest.

1. Unlike the unambiguous "I am" in Mark 14:62, Matthew uses an expression, found also in 26:25, that many have taken to be purposely ambiguous (e.g., Turner, *Insights*, 72–75). But David Catchpole ("The Answer of Jesus to Caiaphas (Matt. xxvi.64)," *NTS* 17 [1970–71]: 213–26) has convincingly shown that the expression is "affirmative in content, and reluctant or circumlocutory in formulation." Certainly Caiaphas understood it as positive (v.65). The next clause, beginning with *plēn legō hymin* ("But I say to all of you"), found also in 11:22, 24, means something like "Indeed I tell you": there is likely no adversative force (Thrall, *Greek Particles*, 72–78). Instead it expresses an expansion or a qualification (Catchpole, "Answer of Jesus," 223) of the preceding statement. Jesus speaks in this way, not because Caiaphas has spoken the truth of him without any revelation (Kingsbury, *Structure*, 74), but because Caiaphas's understanding of "Messiah" and "Son of God" is fundamentally inadequate. Jesus is indeed the Messiah and so must answer affirmatively. But he is not quite the Messiah Caiaphas has in mind, so he must answer cautiously and with some explanation.

2. That explanation comes in allusions to two passages: Psalm 110:1 (see comments at 22:41–46) and Daniel 7:13 (see comments at 8:20; 24:13, 30–31). Jesus is not to be considered primarily a political Messiah but as the one who, in receiving a kingdom, is exalted high above David and at the Mighty One's right hand, the hand of honor and power (cf. 16:27; 23:39; 24:30–31; 26:29). This is Jesus' climactic self-disclosure to the authorities, and it combines revelation with threat.

3. Jesus uses "Son of Man" (see comments at 8:20) instead of "Christ" or "Son of God" (cf. v.63). Efforts to interpret Son of Man in terms of Son of God (Kingsbury, *Structure*, 113ff.) badly miss the point (cf. Hill, "Son and Servant"). The titles are parallel, and each is messianic. Certainly Caiaphas understands "Son of Man" that way. The most ambiguous title now reveals the most about Jesus: it is his self-designation, associated with the glory of the Parousia but uttered at the culmination of Jesus' ministry and in the face of suffering and death.

4. The Greek phrase *ap' arti* (lit., "from now"; NIV, "in the future"; see comments at v.29) is difficult (see Casey, *Son of Man*, 189). Some have found it so difficult that they say v.64 must refer, not to the Parousia, but to the resurrection (e.g., Lars Hartman, "Scriptural Exegesis in the Gospel of St. Matthew and the Problem of Communication," in *L'Évangile selon Matthieu* [ed. Didier], 145). But if "from now" or "from now on" ill suits the delay till the Parousia, it is equally unsuited to the delay until the resurrection and the ascension (see comments at 28:18–20). Moreover, the records show that the high priest and other august leaders were not witnesses of the resurrection; for according to the NT, no human being saw the actual event happen.

The best explanation of v.64 is that Jesus is telling the members of the Sanhedrin ("you" is plural) that from then on they would not see him as he now stands before them but only in his capacity as undisputed King Messiah and sovereign Judge. "From now on" (i.e., "in the future" [NIV]) that is the way they will see him. Jesus' reference is "to the state of authority which Jesus will enjoy continuously at the right hand of God" (France [NICNT]). Matthew does not include the word "only" or the like (e.g., "From now on you will only see the Son of Man sitting on the right hand ...") because it would imply a possibility they might not see him at all, which is not true. The phrase "from now on" makes this a forceful warning that at least some Sanhedrin members doubtless remembered after the resurrection.

65–66 Rending garments (v.65) was prescribed for blasphemy (*m. Sanh.* 7:5) but can also express indignation or grief (cf. 2Ki 18:37; Jdt 14:19; 1 Macc 11:71; Ac 14:14). It appears that the definition of "blasphemy" varied over the years (see Overview, 26:57–68; cf. Jn 5:18; 10:33; see the careful evaluation provided by Bock, *Blasphemy and Exaltation*). Whether the Sanhedrin thought Jesus was blaspheming because he claimed to be Messiah, because he put himself on the Mighty One's right hand, or because God had not especially attested who Jesus was (a requirement in certain rabbinic traditions) is uncertain. The decision of the assembled members of the Sanhedrin appears to have been by acclamation. "Worthy" (*enochos*, v.66, GK *1944*) is the same word used in 5:21. Jesus is "liable" to the death penalty, mandated for blasphemy (Lev 24:16).

67–68 Although Luke portrays the examination and condemnation only at the trial that takes place after dawn (parallel to Mt 27:1–2), even he has this outrage first (Lk 22:63–65), which, in agreement with Matthew and Mark, suggests that some decisions had already been made. Though "they" (v.67) might well mean the members of the Sanhedrin, it might also refer to those under their control, their immediate servants (cf. Lk 22:63–65). In any case, the messianic claims of the accused do not impress the Sanhedrin; and the indignities to which he is now subjected are probably meant to deride his false pretensions. The true Messiah would vanquish all foes and, according to some Jewish traditions, would be able to judge by smell without the need of sight (see Lane, *Mark*, 539–40 and references there; cf. *Pss. Sol.* 17:37ff.). But here is Jesus, spit on, punched, slapped (cf. Isa 50:6; the verb for "slapped" is also used in 5:39 and may mean "clubbed"), blindfolded (Mk 14:65; Matthew does not mention this detail), and taunted without displaying any power.

"Prophesy" (v.68) does not here imply foretelling the future but revealing hidden knowledge (cf. 11:13): Messiah should be able to tell who hit him, even when blindfolded. The easiest way to explain Matthew's not mentioning blindfolding while including "Who hit you?" (not in Mark) is that Matthew and Mark have each kept one part of what Luke has kept intact (see Notes, v.68). In any case, Jesus remains silent, confirming their suspicions while fulfilling Isaiah 53:7.

NOTES

61 The peculiar expression διὰ τριῶν ἡμερῶν (*dia triōn hēmerōn*, "in three days") uses the preposition in its primary sense of "between," which then extends to the notion of interval (contra B. F. Meyer, *Aims of Jesus*; cf. Zerwick, *Biblical Greek*, para. 115; Moule, *Idiom Book*, 56).

63 Some MSS preserve only καί (*kai*, "and"), others καὶ ἀποκριθείς (*kai apokritheis*, "and he answered"), and a few ἀποκριθεὶς οὖν (*apokritheis oun*, "therefore he answered"). Although some have argued that the shortest reading came about because copyists felt "answered" was inappropriate immediately after a statement about Jesus' silence, Metzger (*Textual Commentary*, 65) says the majority of the UBS Committee preferred the shortest reading on the external evidence. But it is difficult to imagine why "answered" would have been introduced into the shortest reading, and easy to understand how the second reading could have generated the other two. If original, "answered" must be understood as in 11:25.

68 Although this is a remarkably clear "minor agreement" of Matthew and Luke (22:64) against Mark (14:65), it is scarcely adequate to overturn Mark's priority (see Introduction, section 3); but at very least it suggests that more independent accounts of the synoptic passion narratives were circulating (cf. Lk 1:1–4) than is commonly recognized. Some detect Luke's dependence on Matthew here. The literary relationships are too complex to sort out with certainty; but in view of the apparent independence of Luke's trial narrative as a whole, it seems wise to think that on this one point—the *combination* of the blindfolding and the question "Who hit you?"—Luke has preserved the *historical* connection, of which Matthew and Mark have each given one part.

8. Peter's denial of Jesus (26:69–75)

OVERVIEW

The four gospel accounts, though brief (cf. Mk 14:66–72; Lk 22:54–62; Jn 18:15–18, 25–27; see comments at v.34 on two cock crowings [Mark]), contain substantial differences, and a variety of solutions have been proposed. Matthew and Mark are in close agreement and list three denials: (1) before a servant girl, in the courtyard; (2) before another girl, but out by the gateway; (3) before bystanders, apparently in the court. Luke also lists three: (1) before a servant girl, apparently near the fire; (2) before another person, place not specified; (3) before yet another person, still in the courtyard (22:60–61). The three denials recorded by John are (1) before a servant girl, at the door; then, after a break in the narrative, (2) before some people—the verb is plural but may be a generalizing one—(3) before one of the high priest's servants, a relative of Malchus.

Several things may be said.

1. Some attempts to harmonize the texts have resulted in Jesus' predicting three denials at each of *two* different times, making six denials (cf. H. Lindsell, *The Battle for the Bible* [Grand Rapids: Zondervan, 1976], 174–76). This is not only intrinsically unlikely but introduces major source-critical problems never addressed and handled.

2. It may help us to look at the location of the relevant pericopes in the four gospels. If our treatment of the trial sequence is correct (see Overview, 26:57–68), Matthew and Mark do not record the examination before Annas but simply say that Peter followed Jesus into the courtyard. Then they place Peter's three denials after the preliminary trial before the Sanhedrin. Luke records neither the examination before Annas nor the preliminary trial before the Sanhedrin and therefore places Peter's three denials before recording the Sanhedrin trial at dawn. John has nothing about the Jewish trial (though it may be hinted at in 19:24) except Jesus' examination before Annas. If Peter's first denial took place about the time of that examination, it is understandable that John separates it from the other two, which he describes after Jesus has been led before Caiaphas.

3. The order of the first two denials may be reversed between John and the Synoptics (cf. the order of the temptations; see comments at 4:1–11), but which gospel has the historical order cannot easily be determined. John has "the girl at the gate" asking the first question and implies, but does not state, that this occurs on Peter's way in. Matthew and Mark have Jesus move back out to the gate as the setting for their second denial. Several possibilities come to mind, but no adequate way of testing them.

4. Remaining differences are minor and are capable of many solutions. Problems arise from

the brevity of the accounts. In a setting around a fire, two or three may speak up at once (see comments at vv.69–70); or, more probably, the plural in the second denial (in John's order) is generalizing (as in Mt 2:20). The differences in the reports of the denial cannot adequately be accounted for on redactional grounds.

69Now Peter was sitting out in the courtyard, and a servant girl came to him. "You also
were with Jesus of Galilee," she said.
70But he denied it before them all. "I don't know what you're talking about," he said.
71Then he went out to the gateway, where another girl saw him and said to the people
there, "This fellow was with Jesus of Nazareth."
72He denied it again, with an oath: "I don't know the man!"
73After a little while, those standing there went up to Peter and said, "Surely you are one
of them, for your accent gives you away."
74Then he began to call down curses on himself and he swore to them, "I don't know
the man!"
Immediately a rooster crowed. 75Then Peter remembered the word Jesus had spoken:
"Before the rooster crows, you will disown me three times." And he went outside and wept
bitterly.

COMMENTARY

69–70 The article "a" in "a servant girl" masks an idiomatic use of "one" (*mia*, v.69; see comments at 8:19; 21:19; cf. Moule, *Idiom Book*, 125). Her remark to Peter reflects both an accusation and her curiosity. "Jesus of Galilee" (Mk 14:67: "that Nazarene, Jesus") is the kind of derogatory remark one might expect from a Jerusalemite convinced of her geographical and cultural superiority. Peter denies her words "before them all" (v.70), implying that several people were listening and that some may have joined in the questioning. The form of Peter's denial is akin to a formal, legal oath (cf. *m. Šebu.* 8:3).

71–72 Peter "went out" to the gateway, apparently retiring from the brighter light of the fire into the darkness of the forecourt. Again he denies the accusation, this time with an oath. "Oath" here (v.72) does not refer to "swearing" as we know it in profanity; rather, Peter invokes a solemn curse on himself if he is lying and professes his "truthfulness" by appealing to something sacred (see comments at 5:33–34; 23:16–22).

73–75 A little more time elapses. Luke says "about an hour later" (22:59). In any age, accent in speaking varies with geography (e.g., Jdg 12:5–6), and Peter's speech shows him to be a Galilean (cf. Hoehner, *Herod Antipas*, 61–64). That one of those present at Peter's denial said that his accent proved him to be a disciple of Jesus shows how much Jesus' ministry had been in Galilee and how relatively few of his disciples were from Judea. Having lied twice, Peter finds himself forced to lie again, this time with more oaths (v.74). Immediately the rooster crows, a bitter reminder (v.75) of Jesus' words (v.34). He who thought he could stand has fallen terribly (cf. 1Co 10:12). Luke tells us that Jesus looked at Peter—perhaps through a window or as he was being led across the courtyard. If we cannot credit the legend that after this Peter never heard a cock crow without weeping, we may justifiably assume that Peter's bitter tears led to his being "poorer in spirit" (5:3) the remainder of his days than he had ever been before.

From this point on, Matthew does not mention Peter again.

Dorothy Jean Weaver (*Matthew's Missionary Discourse: A Literary Critical Analysis* [JSNTSup 38; Sheffield: Sheffield Academic Press, 1990], 149) offers a more optimistic reading of this paragraph. At least Peter followed Jesus to the high priest's house, she observes, and then he remembered Jesus' prediction—and together these facts demonstrate that "Peter is still active as a disciple." But oh, the betrayal and the tears!

9. Formal decision of the Sanhedrin (27:1–2)

OVERVIEW

Whether this formal decision was reached as a final stage of the first meeting or at a separate meeting held either in Caiaphas's house or the temple precincts, we cannot say with certainty (see comments at vv.57–68). But Luke 22:66 implies a meeting in the council chamber (Catchpole, *Trial of Jesus*, 191–92).

[1]Early in the morning, all the chief priests and the elders of the people came to the decision to put Jesus to death. [2]They bound him, led him away and handed him over to Pilate, the governor.

COMMENTARY

1 *Symboulion elabon* ("came to the decision") is a Latinism for *consilium capere* (cf. *Grammar*, 109; BDF, para. 5 [3b]) and does not mean "hold a council" (Hill). On the other hand, Catchpole (*Trial of Jesus*, 191) seems to go too far in denying that it refers to the same event as Luke 22:66–71. The term can refer to a plot (as in 12:14; 22:15) and also to an agreed-on decision (28:12) as here. *Hōste* plus the infinitive here clearly refers to intention (cf. Zerwick, *Biblical Greek*, para. 352; Moule, *Idiom Book*, 140). Probably, too, the religious authorities decided just how to present their case to Pilate. If their own concern was Jesus' "blasphemy" (26:65), they were nevertheless more likely to get Pilate to sentence him to death by stressing the royal side of messiahship rather than blasphemy, as to Pilate that would suggest treason (cf. Ac 17:5–9 for a similar reference to treason).

2 Jesus is led to Pontius Pilate, the "governor" (for the variant, see Metzger, *Textual Commentary*,

65). "Governor" is here a general title (cf. 10:18; 1Pe 2:14); Pilate was in fact appointed prefect or procurator by Tiberius Caesar in AD 26 (cf. *IDB*, 3:1229–31; *ZPEB*, 4:790–93). Prefects governed small, troubled areas. In judicial matters they possessed powers like those of the far more powerful proconsuls and imperial legates; in short, they held the power of life and death, apart from appeal to Caesar. Following the banishment of Archelaus in AD 6, Judea and Samaria were made into one Roman province governed by a prefect or procurator who normally lived at Caesarea but often came to Jerusalem during the feasts to be close to any potential trouble spots.

Extrabiblical sources portray Pilate as a cruel, imperious, and insensitive ruler who hated his Jewish subjects and took few pains to understand them (e.g., Josephus, *Ant.* 18.35 [2.2], 55–62 [3.12], 177–78 [6.5]; *J.W.* 2.169–77 [9.2–4]; Philo, *Legat.* 38; cf. Hoehner, *Herod Antipas*, 172–83; one hesitates to mention a novel in a commentary, but the novel by Paul L. Maier is extraordinarily faithful to first-century documents: *"Pontius Pilate": A Documentary Novel* [1968; repr., Grand Rapids: Kregel, 1990]). He stole korban (see comments at 15:5) money to build an aqueduct, and when the population of Jerusalem rioted in protest, he sent in soldiers, who killed many. He defiled Jerusalem more than once (cf. Lk 13:1). These known facts about Pilate are often thought to render the gospel accounts incredible, for here Pilate is portrayed as weak, ineffectual, and cowardly, judicially fair enough to want to release Jesus but too cowardly to stand up to the Sanhedrin's browbeating tactics. This transformation of Pilate's character, it is claimed, results from the evangelists' desire to exculpate the Romans and condemn the Jews.

Hoehner (*Chronological Aspects*, 105–14) responds to these problems with his crucifixion date of AD 33, after Pilate had set up the embossed shields in Jerusalem that Tiberius Caesar directly ordered removed, and *after* the execution of Pilate's patron, the anti-Semite Sejanus (d. 19 Oct. AD 31), whose death endangered Pilate. At this time, the Sanhedrin would have found it easier to make direct and telling application to the emperor. In Hoehner's view, Pilate appears weak in the gospels because he has just been severely rebuked by Caesar and fears that the Jews' threat (Jn 19:12) could lead to another rebuke. By AD 33, Pilate's administration had become so bad that in AD 36 he was recalled and finally banished.

Even without this chronology, far too wide a historical gap between the Pilate of the gospels and the Pilate of extrabiblical sources is being assumed.

1. Modern psychology helps us understand that the weak, insecure, selfish man elevated to a position of authority may become despotic and insensitive. Thus the evidence about Pilate may be complementary rather than disjunctive.

2. Pilate hated the Jews and especially the Jewish leaders. In the crisis forced on him by the Sanhedrin, though he may have seemed to be *for* Jesus, in reality he was probably *against* the Sanhedrin. His final decision betrayed no trace of sympathy for the Sanhedrin; rather, the Jews' threat (Jn 19:12) could well have intimidated so corrupt a man at any point in his career.

3. Jesus was not the criminal or guerrilla fighter with whom Pilate was familiar. Jesus' silence and poise, the wisdom of his brief answers, and the dreams of Pilate's wife (v.19) may have prompted less drastic action than Pilate usually took.

4. Arguably, v.24 does not exculpate Pilate or reserve exclusive blame for the Jews (see comments at vv.24–25). Instead, as in vv.3–5, Matthew uses irony to say that no one connected with this crisis could escape personal responsibility.

5. Both the Sanhedrin trial and the trial before Pilate were necessary for capital punishment. With-

out the Sanhedrin, Pilate would never have taken action against Jesus unless he had become convinced Jesus was a dangerous Zealot leader; without Pilate, the Sanhedrin might whip up mob violence against Jesus but not a legally binding death sentence (cf. Jn 18:31).

10. The death of Judas (27:3–10)

OVERVIEW

This account is peculiar to Matthew, though Acts 1:16–19 also records Judas's death. The differences between the two are considerable; many scholars hold that Acts 1:16–19 or something like it circulated as a bit of independent tradition Matthew adapted to develop his "fulfillment" theme further. But Benoit (*Jesus and the Gospel*, 189–207) finds greater historical accuracy in Matthew than in Acts. Many believe the only historically fixed points are Judas's sudden death and the purchase of a piece of land called "the Field of Blood" (cf. Stendahl, *School of St. Matthew*, 120–27; Lindars, *New Testament Apologetic*, 116–22). But if Matthew developed a fulfillment theme by adding to or changing an earlier tradition, numerous difficulties, including even misnaming the prophet (v.9), show that he botched the job.

Hill's suggestion that Matthew placed the story of Judas's suicide here to show that Judas's remorse depends on the Sanhedrin's decision, not Pilate's, is only a possibility. No matter where Matthew located the pericope, it would interrupt the narrative at this point; and other reasons may have led him to place it here. Senior (*Passion Narrative*, 346–52) suggests several reasons, including the observation that this placement has the effect of setting the treachery of Judas alongside Peter's betrayal. This has the effect of comparing Judas with Peter and therefore of inviting the reader to ponder why one life turned out one way and the other another way (France [NICNT]). Perhaps Matthew's prime interest in this pericope is to continue the fulfillment theme—that not only Jesus' death but the major events surrounding it were prophesied in Scripture. Verse 4 again stresses Jesus' innocence and sees the fulfillment of another of Jesus' predictions (26:24), which sets up an apologetic tool (cf. "to this day," v.8). In any case, neither Peter's tears nor Judas's remorse can remove their guilt.

3When Judas, who had betrayed him, saw that Jesus was condemned, he was seized
with remorse and returned the thirty silver coins to the chief priests and the elders.
4"I have sinned," he said, "for I have betrayed innocent blood."
"What is that to us?" they replied. "That's your responsibility."
5So Judas threw the money into the temple and left. Then he went away and hanged
himself.
6The chief priests picked up the coins and said, "It is against the law to put this into the
treasury, since it is blood money." 7So they decided to use the money to buy the potter's
field as a burial place for foreigners. 8That is why it has been called the Field of Blood to

this day. [9]Then what was spoken by Jeremiah the prophet was fulfilled: "They took the thirty silver coins, the price set on him by the people of Israel, [10]and they used them to buy the potter's field, as the Lord commanded me."

COMMENTARY

3 On "the chief priests and elders," here governed by a single article suggesting a single entity (the Sanhedrin), see comments at 21:23. Verse 3 looks back to 10:4; 26:14–16, 20–25. Judas's "remorse" is not necessarily repentance, though the two Greek verbs *metamelomai* (here and in 21:29) and *metanoeō* can overlap.

4 Judas recognizes not only that he is guilty of betrayal but that Jesus, whom he has betrayed, is "innocent" (cf. Metzger, *Textual Commentary*, 66). Strangely, Davies and Allison think Judas's regret signals genuine repentance; but see Keener for a response. The Jewish leaders' callous response "What is that to us?" is both a Semitic and a classical idiom (cf. BDF, paras. 127 [3], 299 [3]). But their own words condemn them, for it *should* have been something to them. Judas has betrayed innocent blood; they have condemned innocent blood. "That's your responsibility" (lit., "you will see [to it]," as in v.24), they say—a remark correct in content but wrong in implying that they are absolved.

5–8 Exactly where Judas threw the money is uncertain (see Notes). He then went out and hanged himself. *Apēnxato* ("hanged himself") occurs in 2 Samuel 17:23 LXX. On this basis, some have made lengthy comparisons between Judas and Ahithophel—the one a treacherous friend of David, the other a treacherous friend of David's greater Son (e.g., B. F. Meyer, *Aims of Jesus*; McNeile); but that Matthew intended such a comparison is doubtful (cf. Moo, *Old Testament in the Gospel Passion Narratives*, 189–91).

The chief priests, in accord with Deuteronomy 23:18, refuse to allow the blood money to supplement the funds of the *korbanas* ("treasury," v.6; used only here in the NT—the place where a consecrated article is deposited and cognate with *korban*; see comments at 15:5; Josephus, *J.W.* 2.175 [9.4]). Many scholars suggest that elements of the OT quotation (vv.9–10) have generated these "historical" details. They hold that the Hebrew *yôṣēr* ("potter," GK 3450) in Zechariah 11:12–13 was either confused with *ʾôṣār* ("treasury," GK 238) or that the latter was found in Matthew's copy of Zechariah (as in Peshitta). Alternatively, *yôṣēr* can mean "smith," i.e., a worker in metals, and is so rendered by the LXX. Does Zechariah, therefore, throw his money "to the potter" (NIV), to the treasury, or to the temple foundry, which made temple vessels and coins? The problem with this alternative to the MT is that if Matthew (or the tradition he used) understood the OT to refer to the treasury, then where did he find his reference to "potter" (vv.7, 10)? The OT text is indeed difficult, though a better analysis is possible (see below). What is clear is that Matthew is again pointing out the propensity of the Jewish leaders for ceremonial probity even in the face of gross injustice (cf. 12:9–14; 15:19; 23:23; 28:12–13; cf. Jn 18:28).

With this probity in view, the chief priests decide (same construction as in v.1) to buy the potter's field to meet a public need (v.7)—an accepted use of ill-gotten gains (cf. Str-B, 1:37; Jeremias, *Jerusalem*, 140). The potter's field, used for the burial of foreigners, probably did not belong to "the potter" (surely there was more than one potter in Jerusalem) but was a well-known place, perhaps the place where potters had long obtained their clay. If depleted, it might have been offered for sale. There are no reliable early traditions of its location, though Matthew's "to this day" shows it was well-known when he wrote. The best assumption is that it lay in the valley of Hinnom near the juncture with the Kidron.

There are three significant differences between these verses and Acts 1:18–19.

1. Matthew says that the chief priests bought the field; Acts, that Judas did. But if the priests bought it with Judas's money, it may well have been regarded as his. More important, the language in Acts is finespun: "With the reward of unrighteousness, he acquired [*ktaomai*, not necessarily 'bought'] a field" (literal translation). "The money bought him a burial-place; that was to him the sole financial outcome of the iniquitous transaction" (Broadus, 558).

2. Matthew says Judas hanged himself; Acts, that "he fell headlong, his body burst open and all his intestines spilled out." This does not imply a disease, or that Judas tripped, as some have held. If Judas hanged himself, no Jew would want to defile himself during the Feast of Unleavened Bread by burying the corpse, and a hot sun might have brought on rapid decomposition until the body fell to the ground and burst open. Alternatively, one long tradition in the church claims Judas hanged himself from a tree branch that leaned over a ravine (of which there are many in the area); when the branch broke, whether before or after he died, Judas fell to a messy end. We are not so much beset by contradictory accounts as by paucity of information, making it difficult to decide which of several alternatives we should choose in working out the complementarity of the two accounts.

3. Matthew seems to ascribe the name "Field of Blood" to its being purchased with blood money; Acts, to the fact that Judas's blood was shed there. But again the paucity of information faces us with several possibilities. All of the circumstances must have become public knowledge; and one reason, far from ruling out the other, actually complements it—provided that Judas died in the field purchased by the priests. Perhaps the priests bought the field (not necessarily the same day—Sunday would have been adequate), and Judas, informed as to what had been done with the blood money and driven to despair by futile remorse, decided to commit suicide in a field for the burial of aliens to Israel's covenants.

Moreover, we must at least raise the question whether Acts 1:18–19 associates "Field of Blood" with Judas's blood. "Everyone in Jerusalem heard about this" (Ac 1:19)—but does "this" refer to Judas's body splitting open, without mention of blood, or to securing the field with blood money, also without explicit mention of blood? This is not an attempt at forced harmonization. But if it is bad historiography to squeeze two diverse accounts of one incident into a contrived union, it is equally bad historiography to mistake an instance of too little information for contradiction.

9–10 Four aspects of this complex quotation need discussion.

1. *The ascription to Jeremiah.* On the face of it, the quotation is in part a rough rendering of Zechariah 11:12–13 (though France [NICNT] is not wrong to call it "a mosaic of scriptural motifs"), with "I took" changed to "they took," and the price interpreted as referring to the sum paid for Jesus. The only obvious allusions to Jeremiah are 18:2–6; 32:6–7—Jeremiah did visit a potter, and he did buy a field. But though some of the language of those passages may have influenced Matthew 27:9–10, it is difficult to imagine why Matthew mentioned Jeremiah instead of Zechariah, even though Jeremiah is important in this gospel (cf. 2:17; 16:14). Highly improbable "solutions" abound. Some have

followed the minor textual variant "Zechariah" instead of "Jeremiah"; others have argued for an original text with no mention of the prophet's name, attributing "Jeremiah" to a copyist's error; many have assumed that Matthew made a minor error; others have appealed to a hypothetical writing of Jeremiah now lost; others have held that Jeremiah wrote Zechariah 9–11—though it is surely "a critical anachronism" (Morison) to see Matthew as anticipating modern source theories; and still others assume that Matthew is referring to the entire collection of prophetic books grouped under the name of the first book (though it is not at all certain that Jeremiah was first in Matthew's day). France [NICNT] and Knowles (*Jeremiah in Matthew's Gospel*) think Jeremiah is mentioned because this is a pastiche of OT allusions of which only the Jeremiah text actually mentions buying a field.

The most believable solution comes from Hengstenberg (*Christology of the Old Testament*, 2:1095ff.) and is developed by Gundry (*Use of the Old Testament*, 122–27), Senior (*Passion Narrative*, 359ff.), and especially by Moo (*Old Testament in the Gospel Passion Narratives*, 168–69). They note that no extant version of Zechariah 11 refers to a field. Matthew's attributing the quotation to Jeremiah suggests we ought to look to that book. Jeremiah 19:1–13 (not Jer 18 or 32) is the obvious candidate. There Jeremiah is told to purchase a potter's jar and take some elders and priests to the Valley of Ben Hinnom, where he is to warn of the destruction of Jerusalem for her sin, illustrated by smashing the jar. A further linguistic link is "blood of the innocent" (Jer 19:4). Thematic links include renaming a locality associated with potters (19:1) with a name ("Valley of Slaughter") denoting violence (19:6). The place will henceforth be used as a burial ground (19:11), as a token of God's judgment. In the last clause in Matthew's quotation, "as the Lord commanded me" (27:10), Lindars (*New Testament Apologetic*, 121) sees an allusion to Exodus 9:12; Moo (*Old Testament in the Gospel Passion Narratives*, 196–97) has shown this is at best tenuous.

We have not yet tried to explain what Matthew understands by these OT texts or what he means by "fulfillment." But it is fair to say that the quotation appears to refer to Jeremiah 19:1–13, along with phraseology drawn mostly from Zechariah 11:12–13 (MT in both cases), with the concluding clause a traditional "obedience formula" (cf. R. Pesch, "Eine alttestamentliche Ausführungsformel im Matthäus-Evangelium," *BZ* 10 [1966]: 220–45) used to paraphrase the opening words of Zechariah 11:13: "And the LORD said to me." Such fusing of sources under one "quotation" is not unknown elsewhere in Scripture (e.g., Mk 1:2–3; in Matthew, see 2:6; 11:10; 21:5; cf. 2Ch 36:21, verbally drawn from Lev 26:34–35, yet ascribed to Jeremiah [25:12; 29:10; cf. Gundry, *Use of the Old Testament*, 125]; see comments at 3:17). Jeremiah alone is mentioned, perhaps because he is the more important of the two prophets, and perhaps also because, though Jeremiah 19 is the less obvious reference, it is the more important as to prophecy and fulfillment.

2. *Prophecy and history*. Many scholars hold that Matthew presents as history a number of "fulfillments" that did not happen. Rather he deduces that they must have happened because his chosen OT texts predict, as he understands them, that such events would take place. To this there are two objections. First, the more complex and composite a quotation (as here), the less likely is it that the "fulfillment" was invented. It is far easier to believe that certain historical events led Matthew to look for Scriptures relating to them. We may then ask how he has treated these Scriptures, but that is a separate problem. Second, when we examine Matthew's quotation clause by clause, we can see impressive reasons for holding that the narrative does not grow out of the prophecy. To give

but one instance, the "thirty silver coins" (v.3) are mentioned in Zechariah 11:13; but Mark speaks of betrayal money without mentioning Zechariah. Even if Mark does not specify the amount, the *fact* that Judas had been paid became well-known, independent of any Christian interpretation of Zechariah 11:12–13, and it is not unreasonable to suppose that the *amount* of money also became common knowledge.

3. *Meaning*. How did Matthew understand the OT texts he was quoting? The question is not easy, because the two dominant OT passages themselves can be variously explained. It appears that in Zechariah 11, the "buyers" (v.5) and the three shepherds (vv.5, 8, 17) represent Israel's leaders, who are slaughtering the sheep. God commands Zechariah to shepherd the "flock marked for slaughter" (v.7), and he tries to clean up the leadership by sacking the false shepherds. But he discovers that not only is the leadership corrupt, but the flock detests him (v.8). Thus Zechariah comes to understand the Lord's decision to have no more pity on the people of the land (v.6).

Zechariah decides to resign (11:9–10), exposing the flock to ravages. Because he has broken the contract, Zechariah cannot claim his pay (presumably from the "buyers"); but they pay him off with thirty pieces of silver (v.12). But now Yahweh tells Zechariah to throw this "handsome price at which they priced me" (probably ironical; see Notes) to the potter in the "house of the LORD," i.e., the temple (v.13). Temple ritual required a constant supply of new vessels (cf. Lev 6:28); so a guild of potters worked somewhere in the temple precincts. Certainly Jeremiah could point to a potter as he preached and could purchase pottery somewhere near the temple (Jer 18:6; 19:1).

The purpose of Zechariah's action is uncertain. Because a *yôṣēr* (lit., "shaper") was both a potter and a metal worker, it may be that the money in Zechariah 11:12–13 was thrown to the *yôṣēr* so that it would be melted down and turned into a figurine, a little "god." The people did not want the Lord's shepherd, and so they will be saddled with a silver figurine (cf. Eze 16:17; Hos 2:8)—betrayal money, in effect, since it pays off the good shepherd, who would have kept the people true to the Lord's covenant and who has been rejected by the people. The result can only be catastrophic judgment (Zec 11:14–17).

The parallel between Zechariah 11 and Matthew 26–27 is not exact. In Zechariah, the money is paid to the good shepherd; in Matthew, it is paid to Judas and returned to the Jewish leaders. In Zechariah, the money goes directly to the "potter" in the temple; in Matthew, after being thrown into the temple, it purchases "the potter's field"—though at this point the influence of Jeremiah 19 has been introduced (see below). Nevertheless, the central parallel is stunning: in both instances, Yahweh's shepherd is rejected by the people of Israel and valued at the price of a slave. And in both instances, the money is flung into the temple and ends up purchasing something that pollutes.

The reference to Jeremiah 19 (see point 1 above) provides equally telling parallels. The rulers have forsaken Yahweh and made Jerusalem a place of foreign gods (v.4); so the day is coming when this valley, where the prophecy is given and the potter's jar smashed, will be called the Valley of Slaughter, symbolic of the ruin of Judah and Jerusalem (vv.6–7). Similarly in Matthew, the rejection of Jesus (Yahweh; see comments at 2:6, 3:3; 13:37–39) leads to a polluted field, a symbol of death and the destruction of the nation about to be buried as "foreigners."

4. *Fulfillment*. In the light of these relationships between the events surrounding Jesus' death and the two key OT passages that make up Matthew's quotation, what does the evangelist mean by saying that the prophecy "was fulfilled"? As in 2:17, the form

of this introductory formula shrinks from making Judas's horrible crime the immediate result of the Lord's word, while nevertheless insisting that all has taken place in fulfillment of Scripture (cf. 1:22 with 2:17). Beyond that there is a tendency to apply standard Jewish categories to this use of the OT by Matthew. For instance, J. W. Doeve (*Jewish Hermeneutics in the Synoptic Gospels and Acts* [Assen: Van Gorcum, 1954], 185–86) characterizes 27:3–10 as "haggadah," a creative story the starting point of which was the link between "innocent blood" in v.4 and in Jeremiah 26:15, which led on by associations of word and theme to Jeremiah 19 and 32 and Zechariah 11:13. But "innocent blood" is not an uncommon expression and is, therefore, an inadequate link between Matthew and Jeremiah. Lindars (*New Testament Apologetic*, 116–22) detects an elaborate midrashic development along somewhat different lines, and Stendahl (*School of St. Matthew*, 120–26, 196–98) finds a parallel in midrash pesher at Qumran. Though these are invaluable studies, several cautions are needed.

France (*Jesus and the Old Testament*, 206–7) draws attention to two differences between Matthew's use of the OT in this passage and the pesharim at Qumran, which claimed that various OT texts were in reality referring to certain recent historical events. First, Matthew changes the wording far more than was done at Qumran; second, he respects the central intentions of the OT authors far more than at Qumran. These two points are linked. Matthew does not need to devise far-fetched explanations for each word and phrase, because in each case he has truly represented the central theme. The verbal differences he introduces in citing the OT are not an embarrassment to him, because he is not claiming that the OT text is a prophecy to be fulfilled by a simple one-on-one pattern. Pesher claims that what the OT text refers to is the specified historical event; there are close parallels to this claim elsewhere in the NT (e.g., Ac 2:16). But what we find in Matthew, including 27:9–10, is not *identification* of the text *with* an event but *fulfillment* of the text *in* an event, based on a broad typology governing how both Jesus and Matthew read the OT (see comments at 2:15; 8:17; 13:35; 26:28, 54).

Because of this typological model, Matthew introduces the commonly noticed changes: the one on whom a price is set is no longer the prophet ("me," Zec 11:13) but Jesus ("him," v.9). Even Matthew's use of the concluding obedience formula—"as the Lord commanded me"—is best accounted for as a hint of the prophecy-fulfillment pattern. Here "me" can refer only to the prophet, yet Matthew keeps it, even though he changes other parts of the quotation to "him" because he believes that in obeying the Lord, the prophet—whether Jeremiah or Zechariah—was setting forth typological paradigms that truly did point to Jesus and the greatest rejection of all.

"Midrash" and "haggadah" are deceptive categories. We have maintained that Matthew did not make up the events he relates to illustrate Scripture but that they stand as independent historical realities he now relates to Scripture. Normally, late midrash (the only kind that is well defined; see Introduction, section 12.b) begins with the text as the point of departure, but in Matthew, the narrative is the point of departure. The element of "fulfillment" is not present in midrash in the way it is everywhere presupposed in the NT.

This is not a surreptitious plea to divorce Matthew from his Jewish roots. Doubtless it is correct to say that Matthew uses "midrashic techniques," at least on the level of what Moo (*Old Testament in the Gospel Passion Narratives*) calls "appropriation techniques"—i.e., devices by which an OT text is applied to or appropriated by events contemporary with the evangelist. But such procedures are so universally used that the expression "midrashic techniques" conceals more than it reveals; it is a little like saying "interpretive techniques." What must not be overlooked is that, unlike any other broad hermeneutical category used by the Jews, NT approaches to the OT are steeped in a salvation-historical perspective that finds in the sacred text entire patterns of prophetic anticipation (see comments at 2:15; 5:17–20; 8:17; 11:11–13; 13:34–35). In this sense, Matthew sees in Jeremiah 19 and Zechariah 11 not merely a number of verbal and thematic parallels to Jesus' betrayal but a pattern of apostasy and rejection that must find its ultimate fulfillment in the rejection of Jesus, who was cheaply valued and rejected by the Jews and whose betrayal money was put to a purpose that pointed to the destruction of the nation (see comments at 15:7–9; 21:42).

NOTES

5 The question of where Judas threw the money is beset by two problems.

1. O. Michel (*TDNT*, 4:882–85) and G. Schrenk (*TDNT*, 3:235) argue that there is no necessary difference between ναός (*naos*, "temple [sanctuary]," GK *3724*) and ἱερόν (*hieron*, "temple [and its precincts]," GK *2639*). If so, then the use of the former in this verse means no more than that Judas threw the money somewhere in the temple area. But a fairly strong case can be made for maintaining a distinction between the words in Matthew's usage. Ναός, *Naos*, is used only of the temple proper, the sanctuary, in 23:16–17, 21; 27:51, and, metaphorically, in 26:61; 27:40, whereas ἱερόν, *hieron*, is used of the temple and its precincts in 4:5; 21:12, 14–15, 23; 24:1; 26:55 (cf. Garland, *Intention of Matthew 23*, 199 n. 117). It is possible that ἱερόν, *hieron*, is a trifle forced in 12:5; but since it is the encompassing term and not all the priests' functions took place in the temple proper, the use still admits the traditional distinction between the terms. That leaves only 27:5; but in the narrow sense of ναός, *naos*, Judas would normally not have been allowed to enter. That may be just the point. Feeling damned already, he has nothing more to lose; in desperation he runs into the temple proper and flings down his money before he can be stopped. Thus he deeply incriminates the priests, a further example of 23:35.

2. It is very difficult to decide between the variant εἰς τὸν ναόν (*eis ton naon*, "into the temple") and ἐν τῷ ναῷ (*en tō naō*, "in the temple") (cf. Metzger, *Textual Commentary*, 66).

8 The time of the aorist passive ἐκλήθη (*eklēthē*, here "it has been called") is established by the deixis of the ἕως (*heōs*, "until") clause that follows (cf. E. de W. Burton, *Syntax of the Moods and Tenses in New Testament Greek* [Edinburgh: T&T Clark, 1894], para. 18; Moule, *Idiom Book*, 14; somewhat similar, 28:15).

9 Although thirty shekels is the price of a slave (Ex 21:32), some argue (e.g., Joyce Baldwin, *Haggai, Zechariah, Malachi* [TOTC; London: Tyndale, 1972], 183–86) that the amount is not paltry. The Code of Hammurabi distinguishes an ordinary citizen from a slave by saying that when either is gored to death by an ox, the payment in the former case is one-half mina and in the latter one-third mina, when a mina was probably worth about fifty shekels. Doubtless the biblical law puts more value on a human life, slave or not, but the fact remains that thirty shekels is a slave's price. If Baldwin is correct, then "the handsome price" of Zechariah 11:13 is not ironic but must be an indication of how willing the buyers were to get rid of this shepherd. This seems unlikely since Zechariah is going to leave anyway. If, however, "the handsome price" is meant sardonically, this makes good sense, for even if the amount represents a substantial sum, it is still the price of a slave and representative of how God's prophet is valued by an apostate people.

The same kind of irony probably stands behind the paronomasia of v.9: τὴν τιμὴν τοῦ τετιμημένου ὃν ἐτιμήσαντο (*tēn timēn tou tetimēmenou hon etimēsanto*, lit., the price of the one whose price had been priced ["by the sons of Israel]").

10 The third person plural ἔδωκαν (*edōkan*, "they gave"; NIV, "they used") is to be preferred above the first person singular ἔδωκα (*edōka*, "I gave") because the OT text and the "me" of the next clause would be strong inducement to change to the first person (cf. Senior, *Passion Narrative*, 356).

11. Jesus before Pilate (27:11–26)

OVERVIEW

John gives the most details of the trial before Pilate; Luke adds the account of the intervening trial before Herod; Matthew follows Mark rather closely, but vv.19, 24–25 have no parallel (cf. Mk 15:2–15; Lk 23:2–25; Jn 18:28–19:16).

The setting is uncertain. It might be the Tower of Antonia, on the northwest corner of the temple area; more probably, it is Herod's old palace on the west side of the city near the Jaffa gate (cf. Josephus, *Ant.* 20.110 [5.3]; *J.W.* 2.328 [15.5]; Philo, *Legat.* 38). The word "Praetorium" (v.27) can refer to a princely palace as readily as to a judicial or military seat. Probably Herod Antipas, tetrarch of Galilee, would also stay in his father's palace whenever he came to Jerusalem, which could explain the ease with which Jesus' brief interview with Herod (Lk 23:8–12) was arranged.

11 Meanwhile Jesus stood before the governor, and the governor asked him, "Are you
the king of the Jews?"
"Yes, it is as you say," Jesus replied.
12 When he was accused by the chief priests and the elders, he gave no answer. 13 Then
Pilate asked him, "Don't you hear the testimony they are bringing against you?" 14 But Jesus
made no reply, not even to a single charge—to the great amazement of the governor.
15 Now it was the governor's custom at the Feast to release a prisoner chosen by the
crowd. 16 At that time they had a notorious prisoner, called Barabbas. 17 So when the crowd
had gathered, Pilate asked them, "Which one do you want me to release to you: Barabbas, or Jesus who is called Christ?" 18 For he knew it was out of envy that they had handed
Jesus over to him.
19 While Pilate was sitting on the judge's seat, his wife sent him this message: "Don't have
anything to do with that innocent man, for I have suffered a great deal today in a dream
because of him."
20 But the chief priests and the elders persuaded the crowd to ask for Barabbas and to
have Jesus executed.

[21]"Which of the two do you want me to release to you?" asked the governor.
"Barabbas," they answered.
[22]"What shall I do, then, with Jesus who is called Christ?" Pilate asked.
They all answered, "Crucify him!"
[23]"Why? What crime has he committed?" asked Pilate.
But they shouted all the louder, "Crucify him!"
[24]When Pilate saw that he was getting nowhere, but that instead an uproar was starting, he took water and washed his hands in front of the crowd. "I am innocent of this man's blood," he said. "It is your responsibility!"
[25]All the people answered, "Let his blood be on us and on our children!"
[26]Then he released Barabbas to them. But he had Jesus flogged, and handed him over to be crucified.

COMMENTARY

11 For more about Pilate, see comments at vv.1–2. Matthew's report, in which Pilate asks, "Are you the king of the Jews?" presupposes the background of Luke 23:2 and John 18:28–33. The Sanhedrin's concern with Jesus' "blasphemy" becomes his claim to kingship, a charge of treason with overtones of Zealot sedition, capped with a claim that Jesus refuses to pay taxes (see comments at 22:15–22). In Roman trials, the magistrate normally heard the charges first, questioned the defendant and listened to his defense, sometimes permitted several such exchanges, and then retired with his advisers to decide on a verdict, which was then promptly carried out. The first step, the charge by the Jewish leaders, led to this particular formulation of Pilate's question to Jesus. Jesus answers, as in 26:25, 64, in an affirmative but qualified way. He is indeed the king of the Jews, but not exactly in the sense Pilate might think. The nature of Jesus' kingship is defined in the more detailed exchange John reports (18:34–37).

Verse 11 is important theologically as well as historically. It stands behind the inscription on the cross (v.37) and prepares the way for Christianity, which rests on the conviction that Jesus of Nazareth, who rose from the dead, is indeed the promised Messiah, the King of the Jews—basic themes in Matthew even in the prologue. In other words, the vindicated Lord is the crucified Messiah (cf. N. A. Dahl, *The Crucified Messiah* [Minneapolis: Augsburg, 1974], 10–36).

12–14 Persistent charges by "the chief priests and the elders" evoke only silence from Jesus. If Jesus had said nothing at all, Pilate would be bound to condemn him (Sherwin-White, *Roman Society*, 25–26), since in the Roman system the defense depended heavily on the defendant's response. But Jesus *has* spoken (v.11). Now, surrounded by unbelief and conscious that the hour has come, he makes no reply (v.14). Thus he continues to fulfill Isaiah 53:7 (see comments at 26:63). Pilate's "great amazement" (v.14) appears to be mingled with respect for Jesus and antipathy for the Jewish leaders, and so he takes tentative steps to release the prisoner. Meanwhile Jesus' silence testifies mutely to his willingness (cf. 26:53) to suffer as "a ransom for many" (20:28).

15 In Roman law, an imperial magistrate could acquit a prisoner not yet condemned or pardon one already condemned; but the gospel accounts make this a regular custom, apparently associated with Judea alone (on the grammar, see Moule, *Idiom Book*, 59). Blinzler (*Trial of Jesus*, 218–21), followed by Lane (*Mark*, 552–53), has shown that *m. Pesaḥim* 8:6 ("they may slaughter [namely, a Passover lamb] for one ... whom they have promised to bring out of prison") presupposes some kind of regular paschal amnesty; the tractate in question is universally recognized as recording very old traditions.

16 "Barabbas" seems a strange name. "Bar Abba" means "son of Abba," i.e., "son of the father." But there is evidence that the name or nickname was not unknown in rabbinic families (cf. Str-B, 1:1031). Perhaps Barabbas was the son of a famous rabbi (on such a use of "father," see comments at 23:9). Some MSS preserve his name as "Jesus Barabbas" (see Notes), but with what authority we cannot now be certain. Matthew says he was an *episēmos* (NIV, "notorious") prisoner. The NIV's translation implies Barabbas was universally reprobated, but the Greek is neutral ("notable," "conspicuous"); in the only other NT occurrence of the word, the NIV renders it "outstanding" (Ro 16:7). The point is not academic, for Barabbas was no ordinary villain but a *lēstēs* (Jn 18:14; cf. Mk 15:7; Lk 23:19). Although *lēstēs* (GK *3334*) can refer to a robber (as perhaps in Jn 10:1), it more probably refers to insurrectionists (cf. 26:55; Jn 18:40); Josephus constantly uses it of the Zealots. Neither theft nor violent robbery was a capital offense, but insurrection was. Revolts and bloodshed fostered by guerrilla action were common (cf. Josephus, *Ant.* 18.3–10 [1.1], 60–62 [3.2]; Lk 13:1), and Barabbas had been caught. In the eyes of many of the people he would not be a "notorious" villain but a hero.

It may be that the two who were crucified with Jesus were co-rebels with Barabbas, for 27:38 calls them *lēstai* ("rebels," "guerrillas," or "insurrectionists" is better than the NIV's "robbers"), and their crucifixion indicates they were judged guilty of more than robbery. The fact that three crosses were prepared strongly suggests that Pilate had already ordered that preparations be made for the execution of the three rebels. If so, Jesus the Messiah actually took the place of the rebel [Jesus] Barabbas because the people preferred the political rebel and nationalist hero to the Son of God.

17–18 The "crowd" was not a crowd of Jesus' accusers but of those trying to influence the selection of the prisoner who would receive the paschal amnesty (cf. Mk 15:8). It is possible, though far from certain, that the crowd, knowing little as yet of the arrest and trial of Jesus Christ, was voicing its support for "Jesus" (i.e., Jesus Barabbas—if the variant is supported), and Pilate mistook their pleas as support for Jesus Christ (cf. Lane, *Mark*, 554 n. 29).

What is certain is that Pilate sized up the real motivation of the Jewish leaders (v.18). They had no special loyalty to Rome; so if they were accusing Jesus of being a traitor to Rome, he must have been disturbing them for other reasons, and they were simply using Pilate to eliminate Jesus' challenge to them. Pilate, with his network of spies and informers, would be aware of how much popularity Jesus Christ enjoyed among the people at large. He could hardly have been unaware of the upsurge of acclaim the previous Sunday (21:1–16). He thought to administer a reversal to Sanhedrin policy by using the paschal amnesty to encourage the crowd to free Jesus; therefore he offered them a choice: Barabbas or Jesus "who is called Christ." The last clause may be contemptuous.

19 In AD 21, it had been proposed in the Roman Senate that no provincial magistrate could be accompanied by his wife (cf. Tacitus, *Ann.* 3.33–35). The proposal was defeated, so Pilate's wife was on hand to speak of her dream. If Roman troops were involved in Jesus' arrest (see comments at 26:47–56), Pilate and perhaps his wife would have been informed. Her dream calls to mind the five dreams of Matthew 1–2; but it is quite unlike them and may not have been supernatural. God gave the earlier dreams for guidance to be obeyed, but this dream combines suffering with intimations of gloom. In any event, the interruption of Pilate's wife while he was sitting "on the judge's seat" (cf. Josephus, *J.W.* 11.301 [14.8]) further stresses Jesus' innocence (the NIV rightly renders *dikaios* by "innocent," GK *1465*) and gives the chief priests and elders a few moments to influence the crowd. On the idiom "Don't have anything to do with," see Turner, *Insights*, 43–47.

20–23 Matthew and Mark both insist that the leaders ("chief priests," Mark; "chief priests and elders," Matthew) helped persuade the crowd (v.20). But it is wrong to infer that either Matthew or Mark is whitewashing the crowd (contra Hill et al.), for then "all the people" (v.25) would make no sense. Historically, the description of the crowd's response is comprehensible enough. They have come to demand Barabbas's release (see comments at v.17). When they are confronted with the choice of Barabbas or Jesus (v.21), both of whom were widely popular, their momentary faltering is resolved by their leaders. If the crowd must choose between Pilate's choice and the Sanhedrin's choice, especially if the Sanhedrin members are circulating stories of Jesus' "blasphemy," then there can be little doubt on which side of the issue they will come down. In Judea it was common to confront the Roman authorities with as noisy and large a delegation as possible (cf. Josephus, *Ant.* 18.269–72 [8.3]). And now mob mentality begins to take over.

Tactically Pilate has blundered. Trying to save face, he asks more questions. The first (v.22) offers the hope of milder sentence (high treason could be punished by crucifixion, facing wild animals in the arena, or banishment); the second (v.23) attests Jesus' innocence (on the NIV's sensitive rendering of *gar* [lit., "for"], see BDF, para. 423 [1]). But mob psychology prevails (cf. Ac 19:34). The demand for crucifixion also assured that the executed person would be declared accursed (see Overview, 27:32–44).

The people indicate their preference for a murderous, nationalistic guerrilla leader over their Messiah, who exhorted the people to love their enemies and said he would die as a ransom for many. As Luke points out, it would not be long before Peter would remind the people of Israel at large (not just the leaders), "You handed [Jesus] over to be killed, and you disowned him before Pilate, though he had decided to let him go. You disowned the Holy and Righteous One and asked that a murderer be released to you" (Ac 3:13–14).

24 It is customary to interpret this verse as Matthew's fictitious attempt to show Pilate's positive response to his wife's advice (v.19) and place guilt on the Jews (cf. v.25). But this is not the most natural interpretation.

1. To the best of our knowledge, this hand washing was not a Roman custom. After living several years among the Jews he detested, Pilate picked up one of their own customs (Dt 21:6; cf. Ps 26:6) and contemptuously used it against them. On the other hand, Gundry goes too far in suggesting that Matthew has "Christianized" Pilate. It is one thing to say Pilate thought Jesus was innocent; it is another to say Matthew pictures Pilate as a Christian (see Helen K. Bond, *Pontius Pilate in History and Interpretation* [SNTSMS 100; Cambridge: Cambridge Univ. Press, 1998], 124–37).

2. There is little reason to think the hand washing incompatible with the proceedings, because, whatever his motives, Pilate tried repeatedly to release Jesus. He sent him to Herod (Luke), suggested that

the paschal amnesty be applied to him, proposed a compromise with a scourging (Luke), tried to turn the case back to Jewish authorities (John), remonstrated before pronouncing sentence (John), and here washes his hands. Matthew gives us only two of these steps, and so it is difficult to see why he should be charged with exculpating the Romans simply because one of his two is the only one not mentioned by the other evangelists.

3. If Matthew were interested in exculpating Pilate, would he have included the soldiers' savage mockery of Jesus (vv.27–31)?

4. Pilate's claim to be "innocent of this man's blood" is no stronger than Luke 23:14. Why, then, should this verse in Matthew be thought to color the first gospel's passion narrative uniquely?

5. We cannot be certain that Pilate actually thought his action would excuse him. It may have reflected his contempt for the Jews or have been a taunt. And even if he thought he had exculpated himself, he should have known better. Plumptre quotes Ovid's lines (*Fasti* 2:45): "Too easy souls, who dream the crystal flood / Can wash away the fearful guilt of blood."

6. But regardless of what Pilate thought, Matthew does not think the hand washing exonerated Pilate. We have already seen how Matthew shows that all connected with Jesus' death are guilty (see comments at vv.2, 4–5). Now Matthew insists that Pilate's action was not prompted by desire for justice but by political and moral cowardice and fear of a mob. The Romans expected their magistrates to maintain peace. An uproar, especially one tinged with complaint to Caesar (John), would be enough to intimidate a corrupt governor whose past has caught up with him (see comments at 26:57–68). So when Pilate says, "It is your responsibility" (27:24), Matthew intends his readers to remember the same words spoken by the chief priests and elders to Judas (v.4).

7. Too much of the debate about v.24 implies that the text merely reflects church-synagogue relations at the end of the first century, with little connection with the trial of Jesus. This has led to so many historical disjunctions as to be no longer credible. Is it not remarkable that the fourth gospel, which in recent literature is also regularly interpreted as a clash between church and synagogue, should contain much more about the Roman trial than the Synoptics?

25 To Pilate's words, "all the people" answer, "Let his blood be on us and on our children!" The idiom is familiar (2Sa 1:16; 3:28; Ac 18:6; 20:26). In the narrative, this is a swift retort to Pilate's taunt and mob pressure for him to pronounce the verdict. But it clearly is more than that. How much more? Many say that by "all the people" Matthew is saying that *the Jews as a whole* reject Jesus (Frankemölle, *Jahwebund und Kirche Christi*, 204–11) and, therefore, have incurred collective guilt. Thus v.25 becomes a prophecy of the destruction of Jerusalem and the nation; and a new people of God, the church, take over. There is some truth in this view, but it needs qualification.

1. Matthew probably means "all the people" to refer to the entire crowd that cries, "Let his blood be on us," rather than limiting these words to the chief priests and elders (see comments at v.20).

2. Even if there is symbolism (as there appears to be) whereby the crowd's response reflects the response of the nation as a whole (cf. 23:37–39), Matthew certainly knows that *all* the first disciples were Jews. Thus the gospel's denunciations of the Jews are not more severe than those of many OT prophets, and in both instances it is understood that a faithful remnant remains. So what Matthew actually says cannot be judged as anti-Semitic. It is only when Matthew's account is read as a description, not of Jesus' trial, but of later church-synagogue relations, that it begins to bear anti-Semitic nuances

fostered, not by the trial itself, but by the expansion of the remnant to include Gentile believers. Thus the anachronism of the church-synagogue conflict, consciously adopted by more liberal critics and unconsciously presupposed by more conservative ones, injects into the passion narratives more "anti-Semitic" bias than was actually present in the events they describe. If v.25 joins Matthew 25 in anticipating the judgment of AD 70, it does so in a way akin to Jeremiah's prophecies of the exile and not with the often cynical detachment of Gentile believers from the Fathers on.

26 Among the Jews, scourging was limited to forty lashes (Dt 25:3; cf. 2Co 11:24), but the Romans were restricted by nothing but their strength and whim. The whip was the dreaded *flagellum*, made by plaiting pieces of bone or lead into leather thongs. The victim was stripped and tied to a post. Severe flogging not only reduced the flesh to bloody pulp but could open up the body until the bones were visible and the entrails exposed (cf. *TDNT*, 4:510–12; Josephus, *J.W.* 2.612 [21.5]; 6.304 [5.3]). Flogging as an independent punishment not infrequently ended in death. It was also used to weaken the prisoner before crucifixion. Jesus' flogging took place before the verdict (cf. Lk 23:16, 22; Jn 19:1–5; cf. Blinzler, *Trial of Jesus*, 222ff.) and so was not repeated after the verdict. Repetition would doubtless have killed him. Pilate, after further entreaty (Jn 19:1–16), "handed him over to be crucified"; the words recall the Suffering Servant (Isa 53:6, 12 LXX).

NOTES

16–17 Only witnesses of the Caesarean text (e.g., Θ f^1 700* syr^s) preserve the name "Jesus" before "Barabbas"; but Origen knows the reading, as do several marginal glosses (in one uncial, S, and in about twenty minuscules), and it is probably presupposed in the ancestors of B 1010. The external evidence is not strong enough to be at all certain; on the whole, it is more likely that scribes deleted the name out of reverence for Jesus than added it in order to set a startling if grotesque choice before the Jews. The problem is compounded in v.17, where, in an uncial script, the abbreviated form of the accusative of "Jesus" could be easily lost by haplography (YMIN$\overline{\text{IN}}$). See Metzger, *Textual Commentary*, 67–68. UBS[4] and NA[27] include "Jesus" in brackets.

12. The soldiers' treatment of Jesus (27:27–31)

OVERVIEW

Many think it unlikely that troops (auxiliary soldiers recruited from the non-Jewish population of Palestine and under Pilate's direct control) would mock a prisoner just scourged; but close parallels are not hard to find (Philo, *Flacc.* 6.36–39; Cassius Dio, *Hist.* 15.20–21; cf. Luther R. Delbrueck, "Antiquarisches zu den Verspottungen Jesu," *ZNW* 41 [1942]: 124–45). This pericope is meant to fulfill 17:22–23; 20:17–19 (cf. Mk 15:16–20; Jn 19:2–3).

27Then the governor's soldiers took Jesus into the Praetorium and gathered the whole company of soldiers around him. 28They stripped him and put a scarlet robe on him, 29and then twisted together a crown of thorns and set it on his head. They put a staff in his right hand and knelt in front of him and mocked him. "Hail, king of the Jews!" they said. 30They spit on him, and took the staff and struck him on the head again and again. 31After they had mocked him, they took off the robe and put his own clothes on him. Then they led him away to crucify him.

COMMENTARY

27 That the governor's troops are the ones involved in these shameful actions belies any suggestion that Matthew exculpates Pilate (see comments at v.24). The "Praetorium" is probably the old palace of Herod (see Overview, 27:11–26; cf. Benoit, *Jesus and the Gospel*, 167–88); the soldiers take Jesus into the palace courtyard. The "whole company" would number six hundred if the cohort were at full strength and all were on duty, but more likely the expression refers simply to all the soldiers present.

28–31 Here we have humanity at its worst—a scene of vicious mockery. The Jews have mocked Jesus as Messiah (26:67–68); here the Roman soldiers ridicule him as king. Matthew's readers recognize that the soldiers speak more truly than they know, for Jesus is both King and Suffering Servant. The "robe" (*chlamys*, in the NT only here and in v.31) is probably the short red cloak worn by Roman military and civilian officials (v.28). Mark and John describe it as "purple," Matthew as "scarlet." Commentators have speculated that this redactional change serves to symbolize blood and its concomitant suffering. Such efforts are strained. The ancients did not discriminate among colors as closely as we do, and BDAG (855) adduces a reference in which a Roman soldier's cloak is said to be "purple." The "purple" (Mark; John) calls to mind the robes worn by vassal kings (cf. 1 Macc 10:20, 62; 11:58; 14:43–44), and the "scarlet" (Matthew) shows what the garment probably was—a trooper's cloak.

For a crown (v.29) the soldiers plaited a wreath of thorns from palm spines or acanthus (Brown, *Death of the Messiah*, 866–67, lists other possible plants) and crushed it down on Jesus' head in imitation of the circlet on the coins of Tiberius Caesar (cf. *TDNT*, 7:619–24, 632–33). Whether this "crown" was left on Jesus' head after this mockery, the text does not say. Later Christian art depicts the crown still there as Jesus hung from the cross, though Brown (*Death of the Messiah*, 244–45) notes that the earliest Christian depiction of the resurrection pictures Jesus without the crown of thorns. The staff they put in his hand stood for a royal scepter, and the mocking "Hail, King of the Jews!" corresponded to the Roman acclamation "Ave, Caesar!" and capped the flamboyant kneeling. Not content with the ridicule and the torture of the thorns, they spat on him (v.30) and used the staff, the symbol of his kingly authority, to hit him on the head "again and again" (not required by the imperfect tense of the verb but perhaps hinted at).

"After they had mocked him" (v.31; the time is established by the flow of the narrative, not by the [aorist] tense; see comments at v.8; cf. Moule, *Idiom*

Book, 16), they dressed him again in his own clothes and led him off to be crucified. Normally a prisoner went naked to his place of execution and was scourged along the route. That this custom was not followed with Jesus may be because he had already been flogged and more flogging might have killed him. Or it may reflect an attempt not to offend too many Jewish sensibilities during a feast time. Jesus was led away by the execution squad of four soldiers, dragging the crosspiece to which his hands would be nailed (Jn 19:17, 23).

One cannot help but observe that the mocking soldiers meant their cry, "Hail, king of the Jews!" to be mockingly ironic; the words meant the opposite of what they formally say. But Matthew sees a deeper irony: Jesus *is* the king of the Jews, a theme the evangelist has emphasized since first introducing it in 1:1.

13. The crucifixion and mocking (27:32–44)

OVERVIEW

Two thousand years of pious Christian tradition have largely domesticated the cross, making it hard for us to realize how it was viewed in Jesus' time. Two excellent studies discuss the relevant evidence (M. Hengel, *Crucifixion* [London: SCM Press, 1977]; J. A. Fitzmyer, "Crucifixion in Ancient Palestine, Qumran Literature and the New Testament," *CBQ* 40 [1978]: 493–513). Crucifixion was unspeakably painful and degrading. Whether tied or nailed to the cross, the victim endured countless paroxysms as he pulled with his arms and pushed with his legs to keep his chest cavity open for breathing and then collapsed in exhaustion until the demand for oxygen demanded renewed paroxysms. The scourging, the loss of blood, the shock from the pain all produced agony that could go on for days, ending at last by suffocation, cardiac arrest, or loss of blood. When there was reason to hasten death, the execution squad would smash the victim's legs. Death followed almost immediately, either from shock or from collapse that cut off breathing.

Beyond the pain was the shame. The later rabbis excluded crucifixion as a form of capital punishment for just this reason, though there is some evidence that the Pharisees, their probable predecessors, did not oppose it in principle (cf. David T. Halperin, "Crucifixion, the Nahum Pesher, and the Rabbinic Penalty of Strangulation," *JJS* 32 [1981]: 32–46). In ancient sources, crucifixion was universally viewed with horror. In Roman law, it was reserved only for the worst criminals and lowest classes. No Roman citizen could be crucified without a direct edict from Caesar.

Among Jews, the horror of the cross was greater still because of Deuteronomy 21:23: "Anyone who is hung on a tree is under God's curse." In Israelite law, this meant the corpse of a judicially executed criminal was hung up for public exposure that branded him as cursed by God. The words were also applied in Jesus' day to anyone crucified; therefore, the Jews' demand that Jesus be crucified rather than banished was aimed at arousing maximum public revulsion toward him. But in Christian perspective the curse on Jesus at the cross fulfills all OT sacrifices; it is a curse that removes the curse from believers—the fusion of divine, royal prerogative and Suffering Servant, the heart of the gospel, the inauguration of a new humanity, the supreme model for Christian ethics, the ratification of the new covenant, and the power of God

(1Co 1:23–24; Gal 3:13; Ro 5:12–21; Col 2:14; Heb 1–13; 1Pe 2:18–25; cf. Mt 3:17; 8:17; 16:21, 24–25; 20:25–28; 21:38–42; 26:26–29).

All four gospels record the crucifixion. No gospel says much about the crucifixion itself; the details were all too well-known, and theological interest does not lie so much in crucifixion per se as in the attendant circumstances and their significance. Each evangelist gives his narrative an independent cast by what he includes or omits, though these differences are often exaggerated. Matthew largely follows Mark; but whereas Mark alludes to the OT, Matthew tends to be somewhat more explicit (v.34, Ps 69:21; v.35, Ps 22:18; v.39, Ps 22:7; v.43, Ps 22:8). The dominant note of the pericope is the continuing mockery (Bonnard); but the mockery by an awful irony reveals more than the mocker thinks, for Jesus is indeed King of the Jews (v.37), the new meeting place with God (v.40), the Savior of men (v.42), the King of Israel (v.42), and the Son of God (v.43).

The date is 15 Nisan AD 30 or 33, and the time fairly early in the morning, as the interchanges with Pilate and Herod and the scourging and the mocking need not have consumed more than two to three hours.

32 As they were going out, they met a man from Cyrene, named Simon, and they forced
him to carry the cross. 33 They came to a place called Golgotha (which means The Place of
the Skull). 34 There they offered Jesus wine to drink, mixed with gall; but after tasting it, he
refused to drink it. 35 When they had crucified him, they divided up his clothes by casting
lots. 36 And sitting down, they kept watch over him there. 37 Above his head they placed the
written charge against him: THIS IS JESUS, THE KING OF THE JEWS. 38 Two robbers were crucified
with him, one on his right and one on his left. 39 Those who passed by hurled insults at him,
shaking their heads 40 and saying, "You who are going to destroy the temple and build it in
three days, save yourself! Come down from the cross, if you are the Son of God!"
41 In the same way the chief priests, the teachers of the law and the elders mocked him.
42 "He saved others," they said, "but he can't save himself! He's the King of Israel! Let him
come down now from the cross, and we will believe in him. 43 He trusts in God. Let God
rescue him now if he wants him, for he said, 'I am the Son of God.'" 44 In the same way the
robbers who were crucified with him also heaped insults on him.

COMMENTARY

32 "As they were going out" presupposes "of the city," not "from the Praetorium," as Mark says that Simon was coming in "from the country." Executions normally took place outside the city walls (Lev 24:14; Nu 15:35–36; 1Ki 21:13; Ac 7:58), symbolizing still further rejection (cf. Heb 13:13). This suggests that Jesus, weak as he was, managed to carry the crossbeam as far as the city gates (cf. Jn 19:17). There the soldiers forced Simon to assume the load. His name suggests, but does not prove, that he was a Jew. He came from Cyrene, an old Greek settlement on the coast of North Africa (Ac 2:10; 6:9; 11:20; 13:1). Mark says that he was the father of Alexander and Rufus, who may be referred to in Acts 19:33

and Romans 16:13 and were obviously well-known to Mark's readers; but because the names were common, these passages may refer to other persons.

In 1941, N. Avigad ("A Depository of Inscribed Ossuaries in the Kidron Valley," *IEJ* 12 [1962]: 1–12) published an account of the discovery of a burial cave belonging to Cyrenian Jews, located on the southwest slope of the Kidron and dating from pre–AD 70. An ossuary from this find is twice inscribed in Greek: "Alexander son of Simon." But we cannot be certain the same family is in view.

The efforts of Christian piety to make Simon's act a deed of sympathetic magnanimity are invalid. Simon had no choice, and the text says nothing about his sympathy for Jesus.

33 The site of Golgotha (transliteration of Aram. *gûlgaltāʾ* ["skull"]) is uncertain. Gordon's Calvary is not an option (cf. Parrot, *Golgotha*, 59–65). The most likely place is one near the Church of the Holy Sepulchre, in an area outside the northern wall, on a hill near the city wall (Jn 19:20), and not far from the road (Mt 27:39). Our English "Calvary" comes from the Latin *calva* ("a skull").

34 Mark says they offered Jesus wine mingled with myrrh, and he refused it; Matthew, that they offered him wine mingled with gall, and he tasted it and then refused it. A common explanation is that Mark describes a custom in which women of Jerusalem, responding to Proverbs 31:6–7 (the alleged custom is Jewish, not Roman), prepared a drink of wine and [frank]incense—Mark's mention of myrrh instead of frankincense is variously explained (e.g., Lane, *Mark*, 124)—as a narcotic to ease the pain of the sufferers (*b. Sanh.* 43a). This Jesus refused so as to drink the full draught of suffering with all his senses intact. Matthew then changed "myrrh" (Mark) to "gall" in order to link the event to Psalm 69:21.

Though this interpretation remains popular, another one is more convincing (cf. Moo, *Old Testament in the Gospel Passion Narratives*, 249–52). Neither Mark nor Matthew mentions women, and both imply that the soldiers administered the drink. Moreover, that Matthew says Jesus tasted it before refusing it argues against the view that it was a customary narcotic to dull pain, for if customary, he would know what it contained. Why should he have tasted it if he would in the end refuse it? It is much better to assume that the gesture in both Matthew and Mark was not one of compassion but of torment.

Myrrh may have been used with wine to strengthen the drink (*TDNT*, 7:458), but it has no effect on pain (cf. John Wilkinson, "The Seven Words from the Cross," *SJT* 17 [1964]: 77 n.1). But myrrh tastes bitter; so a large dose of it mingled with wine would make the latter undrinkable. Whether customary or not, the drink was offered to Jesus; but it was so bitter he refused it, and, according to this view, the soldiers were amused. Mark keeps the word "myrrh" to describe the content, and Matthew uses "gall" to describe the taste and to provide a link with Psalm 69:21. In both Hebrew and Greek, the words for "gall" in Psalm 69:21 (*rōʾš* and *cholē* respectively) refer to various bitter or poisonous substances. Like David, Jesus looked for sympathy but found none (Ps 69:20).

35 The victim was either tied or nailed to the crossbeam (in Jesus' case, the latter), which was then hoisted to its place on the upright. The feet were sometimes tied or, as in this instance, nailed to the upright. Crosses were made in various shapes—an X, a T, or the traditional cross (✝). The last is in view here (v.37). How high the victim was from the ground varied from a few inches to several feet—in Jesus' case, the latter (v.48; Jn 19:29). The Romans crucified their victims naked. Whether they permitted a loincloth to avoid transgressing Jewish stipulations (*m. Sanh.* 6:3) is unknown. The victim's clothes customarily became the perquisite of the executioners; here they divided them—probably an inner and outer garment, a belt, and a pair of sandals—among themselves by casting lots, oblivious to the OT lament in Psalm 22:18 that John 19:23–24 says was now fulfilled. (The variant reading in Matthew, preserved in the NIV text note, is an assimilation to John.) Mark says this took place at the third hour, about 9:00 a.m.

36 This verse is peculiar to Matthew. The soldiers kept watch to prevent rescue (men were known to have lived after being taken down from a cross). Perhaps Matthew gives us this detail to eliminate any suggestion that Jesus was removed from the cross without dying.

37 The statement of the crime was often written on a white tablet in red or black letters and displayed on the cross. The charge against Jesus, written in Hebrew, Greek, and Latin (Jn 19:20), is highly ironic. Pilate, though desiring to offend the Jews (Jn 19:19–22), wrote more of the truth than he knew. Pilate rubs the noses of the Jews in their vassal status. To a Jew, "king of the Jews" meant "Messiah"; so the charge on which Jesus was executed was, according to Pilate, that he was a messianic pretender. Matthew's Christian reader will remember the intertwining strands of royal Son and Suffering Servant and see their climax here.

38 On the two *lēstai* ("rebel guerrillas"; NIV, "robbers"), see comments at v.16. The King of the Jews is crucified along with rebels. Matthew may be thinking of Isaiah 53:12, but this is uncertain (cf. Moo, *Old Testament in the Gospel Passion Narratives*, 154–55).

39–40 Crucifixion was always carried out publicly as a warning to others. With the day of the paschal meal behind them (see Reflections, p. 593) and the restrictions of Sabbath not to begin until sundown, there was time and opportunity for people to walk by on the nearby road and "hurl insults" (*blasphēmeō*, 27:39, as in 9:3; 12:31; 26:65) at Jesus. The verb in this context must be taken in the more "secular" sense of "slander" or "hurl insults" (NIV), but by using it Matthew may intend his readers to think back to the more "theological" sense of 12:31; 26:65 (cf. Bock, *Blasphemy and Exaltation*, passim; France [NICNT]). Shaking their heads, and so calling to mind the derision in Psalms 22:7; 109:25; Lamentations 2:15 (see Knowles, *Jeremiah in Matthew's Gospel*, 203–4), the passersby threw up the charge in Matthew 26:60–61. The Greek should probably be rendered "You who were trying to destroy the temple and rebuild it in three days" (v.40; cf. Jn 2:20; see BDF, para. 339 [3]; Turner, *Syntax*, 80–81). The derision was palpable and identifies the mockers as those who had witnessed the proceedings of the Sanhedrin or had some report of them (cf. 26:61). The reason such a charge was brought against Jesus at his trial was that the Romans, in an effort to keep religious peace in their religiously diverse empire, made it an offense—a capital offense—to desecrate any temple. If Jesus' strange words could be taken in that sense, his opponents had him on a capital charge. The parallel in Mark (14:58–59) shows the witnesses could not agree on this point. This inability to agree stands in happy harmony with the fact that Jesus' actual words along these lines are reported only in John's gospel *toward the beginning of his public ministry* in conjunction with an early cleansing of the temple (2:20).

The second taunt, "If you are the Son of God," not only harks back to the trial (26:63), but for Matthew's readers recalls a dramatic parallel (4:3, 6). Through the passersby, Satan was still trying to get Jesus to evade the Father's will and avoid further suffering (Lohmeyer; cf. 16:21–23). Once more there is double irony. The mockers identify Jesus as the one who destroys and rebuilds the temple in three days, meaning, of course, exactly the opposite—that is the nature of irony. But Matthew perceives a deeper irony. By his death and resurrection, Jesus *does* become the temple, the great meeting place between God and sinners, signaled, in Matthew's gospel, by the destruction of the curtain of the *old* temple (v.51; cf. G. K. Beale, *The Temple and the Church's Mission: A Biblical Theology of the Dwelling Place of God* (NSBT; Downers Grove, Ill.: InterVarsity, 2004).

41–43 The "chief priests, the teachers of the law and the elders" represent all the principal groups of the Sanhedrin (see comments at 21:23; 26:59). They do not address Jesus directly but speak of him in the third person, in a stage whisper meant for his ears. "He saved others" (v.42) is probably an oblique reference to Jesus' supernatural healing ministry. "But he can't save himself" is cutting because it questions that same supernatural power. But there is level upon level of meaning. For the Christian reader, "save" has full eschatological overtones. Matthew has introduced the verb in 1:21, thereby establishing that Jesus' mission was to *save* his people from their sins. And though Jesus *could* have saved himself (26:53), he could not have saved himself if he was to save others. Here, too, there is double irony. The mockers verbally stipulate that he saves others—but in a context where they are really saying that he cannot be much of a savior if he cannot save himself. But Matthew himself perceives a deeper irony. It is precisely by *not* saving himself that he saves others. The mockers' "*can't* save himself" is doubtless physical—he is nailed to a cross. Matthew understands that, morally speaking, he *can't* save himself precisely because he came to do his Father's will, not because the nails hold him in place—and the Father's will is that by Jesus' not saving himself he will save others.

The taunt "He's the king of Israel" substitutes the covenant term "Israel" for "the Jews" in Pilate's words (v.11) and is in fact the normal Palestinian form of Jesus' claim (cf. *TDNT*, 3:359–62, 375–76). The words "Let him come down from the cross, and we will believe in him" have several levels of meaning. They constitute a malicious barb directed at Jesus' helplessness, while having the effrontery to suggest that the leaders' failure to believe was his fault. The taunt piously promises faith if Jesus will but step down from the cross; but the reader knows that, in the mystery of providence, if Jesus did step down, there would be no "blood of the covenant ... for the forgiveness of sins" (26:26–29), no ransom (20:28), no salvation from sin (1:21), no theological basis for healing (8:16–17), no gospel of the kingdom to be proclaimed to nations everywhere (28:19–20), no fulfillment of Scripture (5:17–18).

In an unconscious allusion to Psalm 22:8 (as Caiaphas uttered an unconscious prophecy in Jn 11:49–52), the religious leaders launch their third taunt: "He trusts in God" (v.43). This prepares the way for the cry of desolation (see comments at v.46). The leaders recognize that Jesus' claim to be the "Son of God" was at least a claim to messiahship and perhaps more. Assuming that God must crown every effort of Messiah with success, they conclude that Jesus' hopeless condition is proof enough of the vanity of his pretensions. Again, their malice masks the ironic redemptive purposes of God. On the one hand, as Christian readers know, God will indeed vindicate his Son at the resurrection; Matthew ends his gospel, not at Matthew 27:56, but at 28:20 (cf. Ac 2:23–24; Ro 1:3–4). On the other hand, the leaders are right. Jesus is now facing his most severe test, the loss of his Father's presence, leading to the heartrending cry of the following verses (esp. v.46).

44 The *lēstai* ("robbers"; see comments at v.16) crucified with him join in the abuse (cf. Lk 23:39–43; Zerwick, *Biblical Greek*, para. 7).

14. The death of Jesus (27:45–50)

[45]From the sixth hour until the ninth hour darkness came over all the land. [46]About the ninth hour Jesus cried out in a loud voice, *"Eloi, Eloi, lama sabachthani?"*—which means, "My God, my God, why have you forsaken me?"

[47]When some of those standing there heard this, they said, "He's calling Elijah."

[48]Immediately one of them ran and got a sponge. He filled it with wine vinegar, put it on a stick, and offered it to Jesus to drink. [49]The rest said, "Now leave him alone. Let's see if Elijah comes to save him."

[50]And when Jesus had cried out again in a loud voice, he gave up his spirit.

COMMENTARY

45 The darkness that "came over all the land" from noon until 3:00 p.m. (that is what "sixth hour" and "ninth hour" refer to) was a sign of judgment and/or tragedy. The Greek *gē* here means "land" rather than "earth," since the darkness was meant to be a sign relating both to Jesus' death and to the Jewish people; beyond the borders of Israel, the darkness would lose this significance. Str-B (1:1040–42) gives numerous rabbinic parallels, and Johann Jakob Wettstein an array of Greek and Latin authors. But the most telling background is Amos 8:9–10, and to a lesser extent Exodus 10:21–22. Both passages portray darkness as a sign of judgment, but Amos mentions noon and the turning of religious feasts into mourning, and says, "I will make that time like mourning for an only son" (Am 8:10; see comments at 2:15). The judgment is, therefore, a judgment on the land and its people (cf. Best, *Temptation and the Passion*, 98–99). But it is also a judgment on Jesus, for out of this darkness comes his cry of desolation (v.46). The cosmic blackness hints at the deep judgment that was taking place (20:28; 26:26–29; Gal 3:13).

It is futile to argue whether the darkness was caused by an eclipse of three hours (!) or by atmospheric conditions caused by a sirocco or something else, not because it did not happen, but because we do not know how it happened, any more than we know how Jesus walked on the water or multiplied the loaves. The evangelists are interested chiefly in the theological implications that rise out of the historical phenomena.

46 The "cry of desolation" raises two important questions.

1. In what language did Jesus utter it? Almost all recognize that the words echo Psalm 22:1 (for a list of exceptions, see Moo, *Old Testament in the Gospel Passion Narratives*, 264–65). But among the variant readings of a confused textual history (see Notes), Matthew keeps "*Eli, Eli*" (NIV, "*Eloi, Eloi*"), representing a Hebrew original, and Mark "*Eloi, Eloi*," representing an Aramaic original. The remaining words, "*lama sabachthani*," are Aramaic. Many suggest that Jesus quoted Psalm 22:1 in Hebrew, reverting to the ancient language of Scripture in his hour of utmost agony. Only this, it is argued, accounts for the confusion with "Elijah" in v.47 and provides a plausible explanation for the rendering "my power" (*hē dynamis mou*, presupposing Semitic *ḥêlî*) in the apocryphal *Gospel*

of Peter. In this view Mark, or an early copyist of Mark, has turned Jesus' words into Aramaic, recognizing that Jesus more commonly spoke Aramaic than Hebrew.

However, though Jesus was probably at least trilingual (Hebrew, Aramaic, Greek—with perhaps some Latin), the overwhelming textual evidence for the rest of the cry supports an Aramaic original. Even Matthew's Hebraic-sounding *Eli* may in fact support an Aramaic original, because the Targum (written in Aramaic) to Psalm 22:1 has *ʾēlî*. Apparently some Aramaic speakers preserved the Hebrew name for God in the same way some English speakers sometimes refer to him as Yahweh. The evidence of the *Gospel of Peter* is not decisive because "my power" may not rest on a Semitic original but may be an independent periphrasis for God, akin to Matthew 26:64. Moreover, on the lips of a dying man crying out in agony, *Eloi* could as easily be mistaken for Elijah as *Eli* (cf. Broadus; Lagrange; Gundry, *Use of the Old Testament*, 63–66; Moo, *Old Testament in the Gospel Passion Narratives*, 264–75). Jesus' cry was most probably in Aramaic; and at least some of the variants stem from the difficulty of transliterating a Semitic language into Greek, and others from the influence of the OT.

2. What does this psalm quotation signify? A large number of commentators have interpreted the cry against the background of the *whole* of Psalm 22, which begins with this sense of desolation but ends with the triumphant vindication of the righteous sufferer. The chief difficulty is that though OT texts are frequently cited with their full contexts in mind, they are never cited in such a way that the OT context effectively annuls what the text itself affirms (Bonnard). If the context of Psalm 22 is carried along with the actual reference to Psalm 22:1, the reader of the gospel is to understand that the vindication comes with the resurrection in Matthew 28, not that Jesus' cry reflects full confidence instead of black despair.

Equally futile is the suggestion of Schweizer and others that these words constitute a more or less standard cry of a pious man dying with the words of a psalm on his lips. But why *this* psalm when others would be more suitable? Evidence for such a use of Psalm 22 is sparse and late. It is better to take the words at face value: Jesus is conscious of being abandoned by his Father. For one who knew the intimacy of Matthew 11:27, such abandonment must have been agony; and for the same reason, it is inadequate to hypothesize that Jesus felt abandoned but was not truly abandoned (contra Bonnard; Green; McNeile; Senior, *Passion Narrative*, 298), because "it seems difficult to understand how Jesus, who had lived in the closest possible fellowship with the Father, could have been unaware whether he had, in fact, been abandoned" (Moo, *Old Testament in the Gospel Passion Narratives*, 274).

If we ask in what ontological sense the Father and the Son are here divided, the answer must be that we do not know because we are not told. If we ask for what purpose they are divided, the ultimate answer must be tied in with Gethsemane, the Last Supper, passion passages such as 1:21; 20:28 (see also 26:26–29, 39–44), and the theological interpretation articulated by Paul (e.g., Ro 3:21–26). In this cry of dereliction, the horror of the world's sin and the cost of our salvation are revealed, a fact that should be clear from surrounding details: (1) The verb "to save," used in the preceding verses, has forced us to remember that Jesus came to save his people from their sins (1:21). (2) The darkness covering the land must signal something like the loss of the light of the Father's presence. (3) The result of Jesus' death is the tearing of the temple curtain (v.51), signaling full and free access into the presence of the holy God, which is possible only because sin has been paid for and the judgment of God averted. (4) This verse, cited from Psalm 22, must be read in the light of 27:43, also drawn from Psalm 22 (as we have seen). The mockers cry, "He trusts in God"—meaning, of course, with their sarcastic attempts at irony, precisely the opposite. Jesus' ostentatious trusting of his Father must be dismissed as a failure or a joke, for look where it has gotten him! But once again, Matthew perceives a deeper irony: Jesus *does* trust in God, in precisely the same way, though doubtless at a deeper level, than David trusted in God, yet cried out in abandonment. Trusting God and being abandoned are not mutually exclusive—not in David's experience, and not in Jesus' experience. Jerome H. Neyrey (*Honor and Shame in the Gospel of Matthew* [Louisville, Ky.: Westminster, 1998], 152–61) shows that this cry is, in this sense, a true prayer, a mark of piety, cried precisely because Jesus *is* in the same profound way abandoned, which was God's purpose all along, as Jesus' prayers in Gethsemane attest. God's answer to this cry of desolation, then, is in the utter vindication of vv.51–54.

In the words of Elizabeth Barrett Browning:

> Yea, once, Immanuel's orphaned cry his universe
> hath shaken—
> It went up single, echoless, "My God, I am
> forsaken!"
> It went up from the Holy's lips amid his lost
> creation,
> That, of the lost, no son should use those words
> of desolation!

Browning wrote these lines, of course, as part of her homage to William Cowper. For all his brilliance, Cowper suffered several rounds of suicidal depression. Browning powerfully asserts that Jesus cried, "My God, I am forsaken!" so that for all eternity William Cowper would not have to. Jesus cried, "My God, I am forsaken!" so that for all eternity Don Carson would not have to—"That, of the lost, no son should use those words of desolation!"

47 According to 2 Kings 2:1–12, Elijah did not die but was taken alive to heaven in a whirlwind. Some Jewish tradition, perhaps as old as the first century, held that he would come and rescue the righteous in their distress (cf. *TDNT*, 2:930–31; Str-B, 4:769–71).

48–49 See comments at v.34. The allusion is again to Psalm 69:21. What is not clear is whether the offer of a drink is meant as a gesture of mercy or as mockery. The gospel parallels are somewhat ambiguous. The best explanation is that of mockery. *Oxos* (lit., "vinegar," GK *3954*) probably refers to "wine vinegar" (NIV), sour wine diluted with vinegar drunk by foot soldiers; but this does not make the offer a compassionate act, since its purpose may have been to prolong life and agony, while with false piety the onlookers say they will wait for Elijah to rescue him (v.49). But if the Father has abandoned Jesus, will Elijah save him? The offer of a drink not only fulfills Scripture but makes the cry of desolation (v.46) all the bleaker.

It is not clear whether Luke 23:36, where mockery is clearly intended, properly parallels Matthew 27:34 or 27:48–49. John's gospel (19:28–29) is interested only in the Scripture's fulfillment, not whether mockery is intended.

50 This loud cry reminds us once more of Jesus' hideous agony. Matthew's "he gave up his spirit" ("spirit" here is equivalent to "life") suggests Jesus' sovereignty over the exact time of his own death. It was at this moment, when he was experiencing the abyss of his alienation from the Father and was being cruelly mocked by those he came to serve, that he chose to yield his life as a "ransom for many" (see comments at 20:28).

NOTES

46 Instead of ηλι or ηλει (*ēli* or *ēlei*,) from the Hebrew אֵלִי (*ʾēlî*, "my God"), some MSS agree with Mark 15:34: ελωι (*elōi*), from the Aramaic אֱלָהִי (*ʾᵉlāhî*, "my God"), the long *ō* in Greek representing the Semitic *ā* by influence of Hebrew *ʾᵉlōhay*. It is perhaps more probable that some MSS of Matthew have been assimilated to Mark than to the MT. For other variants, see Metzger, *Textual Commentary*, 70, 119.

49 The future participle σώσων (*sōsōn*, "to save") here functions as a supplement to the main verb. The construction is rare in the NT (cf. BDF, paras. 351 [1], 418 [4]; Zerwick, *Biblical Greek*, para. 282).

15. Immediate impact of the death (27:51–56)

51 At that moment the curtain of the temple was torn in two from top to bottom. The
earth shook and the rocks split. 52 The tombs broke open and the bodies of many holy
people who had died were raised to life. 53 They came out of the tombs, and after Jesus'
resurrection they went into the holy city and appeared to many people.
54 When the centurion and those with him who were guarding Jesus saw the earthquake and all that had happened, they were terrified, and exclaimed, "Surely he was the
Son of God!"
55 Many women were there, watching from a distance. They had followed Jesus from
Galilee to care for his needs. 56 Among them were Mary Magdalene, Mary the mother of
James and Joses, and the mother of Zebedee's sons.

COMMENTARY

51a There were two temple curtains, one dividing the Most Holy Place from the Holy Place and the other separating the Holy Place from the court. Tearing the latter would be more public, but tearing the inner curtain could hardly be hushed up. Jewish parallels are interesting (*b. Yoma* 39b reports the doors of the temple opened of their own accord during the forty years before the destruction of the temple) but difficult to interpret. The inner curtain is presupposed in Hebrews 4:16; 6:19–20; 9:11–28; 10:19–22. Destruction of the outer curtain would primarily symbolize the forthcoming destruction of the temple, while destruction of the inner curtain would primarily symbolize open access to God (Best, *Temptation and the Passion*, 99); but destruction of either curtain could point in both directions.

There is more. If the death of Jesus opened up a fresh access to God that made the OT sacrificial system and the Levitical high priesthood obsolete, then an entire change in the Mosaic covenant must follow. It is impossible to grapple with Matthew's fulfillment themes (see comments at 5:17–20; 11:11–13) and see how even the law points prophetically to Messiah and hear Jesus' promise of a new covenant grounded in his death (26:26–29) without seeing that the tearing of the veil signifies the obsolescence of the temple ritual and the law governing it. Jesus himself is the New Temple, the meeting place of God and man (see comments at 26:61); the old is obsolete. The rent veil does indeed serve as a sign of the temple's impending destruction—a destruction conceived not as a brute fact but as a theological necessity. For extensive discussion, see Daniel M. Gurtner, *The Torn Veil: Matthew's Exposition of the Death of Jesus* (SNTSMS 139; Cambridge: Cambridge Univ. Press, 2007).

51b–53 On problems concerning the historicity of this narrative, see D. Wenham, "Resurrection Narratives" (esp. 42–46). Only Matthew reports it, but it is of a piece with the tearing of the temple curtain. Both are part of the initial impact of Jesus' death, along with the centurion's exclamation (v.54). Moreover, the earthquake apparently links them. It is possible that Matthew sees the earthquake (v.51b), itself a symbol of judgment and theophanic glory (cf. 1Ki 19:11; Isa 29:6; Jer 10:10; Eze 26:18; see esp. the background materials gathered by R. J. Bauckham, "The Eschatological Earthquake in the Apocalypse of John," *NovT* 19 [1977]: 224–33), as the means of tearing the curtain as well as opening the tombs. The temple area lies on a geological fault; and the Muslim shrines on the site today have been damaged by tremors from time to time (cf. D. Baly, *The Geography of the Bible* [New York: Harper, 1974], 25).

But the resurrection of the *hagioi* ("saints," i.e., "holy people," v.52) remains extraordinarily difficult for two reasons. First, its extreme brevity and lack of parallels raise many unanswered questions: What kind of bodies do these "holy people" have? Do they die again? How many people saw them? How public were these appearances? Second, a quick reading of the text gives the impression that though the holy people were raised when Jesus died, they did not leave the tombs and appear to the citizens of the "holy city" until after Jesus' resurrection (v.53). What were they doing in between?

The passage has elicited various explanations. Some think it a displaced resurrection account, originally connected with the earthquake of 28:2. Others have thought it a primitive Christian hymn. D. Senior ("The Death of Jesus and the Resurrection of the Holy Ones [Matthew 27:51–53]," *CBQ* 38 [1976]: 312–29), in addition to criticizing some other views, represents the view that these verses are a midrash, a symbolic representation of certain theological ideas about the triumph of Jesus and the dawning of the new age. But apart from questions of literary genre (see Introduction, section 12.b), one wonders why the evangelist, if he had nothing historical to go on, did not invent a midrash with fewer problems.

J. W. Wenham ("When Were the Saints Raised?" *JTS* 32 [1981]: 150–52) offers an alternative view. He has convincingly argued that a full stop should be placed, not after "split" (v.51), but after "broke open" (v.52). The tearing of the curtain and the opening of the tombs together symbolize the first of twin foci in Jesus' death and resurrection. On the one hand, Jesus' sacrificial death blots out sin, defeats the powers of evil and death, and opens up access to God. On the other, Jesus' victorious resurrection and vindication promise the final resurrection of those who die in him.

The resurrection of "the holy people" begins a new sentence and is tied up only with Jesus' resurrection. So Matthew does not intend his readers to think that these "holy people" were resurrected when Jesus died and then waited in their tombs until Easter Sunday before showing themselves. The idea is a trifle absurd anyway; there is no reason to think they were any more impeded by material substance than was the resurrected Lord, the covering rock of whose grave was removed to let the witnesses in, not to let him out. The "holy people" were raised, came out of the tombs, and were seen by many after Jesus rose from the dead. There is no need to connect the earthquake and the breaking open of the tombs with the rising of "the holy people"; the two foci must be differentiated.

On several details we are told little. For instance, it is unclear whether the resurrection of the "holy people" was to natural bodies (cf. Lazarus, Jn 11) or to supernatural bodies. The latter is perhaps more likely; in that case they did not return to the tombs, and their rising testifies that the last day had dawned. Where they ultimately went Matthew does not say. Were they "translated"? Nor does he tell us who they were; but the language implies, though it does not prove, that they were certain well-known OT and intertestamental Jewish "saints," spiritual heroes and martyrs in Israel's history (cf. the terminology in Isa 4:3; Da 7:18; Tob 8:15; *1 En.* 38:45; *T. Levi* 18:10–11). If so, then Matthew is telling us, among other things, that the resurrection of people who lived before Jesus Messiah is as dependent on Jesus' triumph as the resurrection of those who come after him. The idea is not fanciful, given Matthew's grasp of prophecy and fulfillment (see comments at 5:17; Introduction, section 11.a).

One must still reflect on why the evangelist placed the account here instead of in ch. 28. He probably had at least three reasons.

1. The pericope would disrupt the narrative in Matthew 28.

2. The account is held together by two foci—Jesus' death and resurrection. Therefore, Matthew's putting it with the resurrection pericopes would have possibly been even more awkward than putting it with the passion pericopes. Linking the cross and the empty tomb in a unified theological application is not without its difficulties, regardless of whether the pericope in question is placed with the story of the cross or with the account of the resurrection.

3. More positively, the placement of this pericope with other verses dealing with the immediate impact of Jesus' death may be peculiarly appropriate since they, too, point to the future. No Christian reader who saw in the torn curtain a reference to judgment on the temple would fail to see the new means opening up for the meeting of God and man, a means dependent on Jesus' resurrection and continued ministry. Similarly, the confession that Jesus was the Son of God (v.54) would appear to thoughtful readers as a deeper truth than the centurion and his men could have known, for Matthew 28 lies just ahead. Furthermore, if the text had ended at "broke open" (v.52) and resumed with v.54, the reader would have been given a wholly wrong impression. Jesus' work on the cross is tied to his impending resurrection; together they open up the new age and promise eschatological life.

54 Despite the fact that "Son of God" is one of several major christological titles in Matthew, it also appears in Mark as the climax of the passion (Mk 15:38–39). What is not certain is exactly what the soldiers meant by "Son of God" (cf. Blair, *Jesus in the Gospel of Matthew*, 60–68). They may have used the term in a Hellenistic sense, "a son of God" referring to a divine being in a pagan sense. But the governor's soldiers were probably non-Jewish natives of the land (see comments at v.27). If so, or even if they were Romans who had been assigned to Palestine for some time, they may well have understood "Son of God" in a messianic sense (see comments at 26:63). Certainly the anarthrous noun "Son" can mean "*the* Son" instead of "a Son" in this construction (cf. Moule, *Idiom Book*, 116). What the soldiers meant by the expression and what Matthew meant need not be exactly the same thing.

The darkness, the earthquake, and the cry of desolation convinced the soldiers that this was no ordinary execution. The portents terrified them and probably led them to believe that these things testified to heaven's wrath at the perpetration of such a crime, in which the soldiers had participated. But this confession tells us something more: Jesus as the promised Messiah and unique Son of God is seen most clearly in his passion and death; but again the Jewish religious establishment, mistaking the nature of his messiahship, mocked him with the very title (vv.41–44) by which the pagans now confessed him (see comments at 8:5–13; 15:21–28).

55–56 Along with the soldiers, certain women, generally not highly regarded in Jewish society, watched to the bitter end. They kept their distance, whether through timidity or modesty. Though last at the cross, they were first at the tomb (28:1). Not only do they provide continuity to the narrative, but they prove that God has chosen the lowly and despised things of the world to shame the wise and strong (cf. 1Co 1:27–31). These women were Galileans who often traveled with the disciples to care for Jesus' needs out of their own resources (cf. Lk 8:2–3).

Comparison of the lists of names in Matthew, Mark (15:40), and John (19:25) produces these results:

Matthew	**Mark**	**John**
Mary Magdalene	Mary Magdalene	Jesus' mother
Mary the mother of James and Joses	Mary the mother of James the younger and Joses	Jesus' mother's sister
Mother of Zebedee's sons	Salome	Mary the wife of Clopas
		Mary Magdalene

If we make two assumptions—(1) that John's second entry is distinguished from his third (i.e., they are not in apposition) and (2) that John's list of four includes the list of three in Matthew and Mark—then certain things become probable. First, the mother of Zebedee's sons was called Salome, unless a different woman is here introduced. Second, if Mary the mother of James and Joseph (or Joses) is Jesus' mother (cf. 13:55), then Jesus' mother and Mary Magdalene appear on all three lists. That would make Salome Jesus' mother's sister—his aunt on his mother's side. Others suppose that Mary the wife of Clopas is the mother of James and Joses, who are not Jesus' half brothers. Yet the result still equates Salome and Jesus' aunt on his mother's side. Although none of this is certain, it would help explain 20:20.

16. The burial of Jesus (27:57–61)

OVERVIEW

Because of Deuteronomy 21:22–23, Jesus' body, according to Jewish custom, could not remain on the cross overnight. The Roman custom was to let bodies of crucified criminals hang in full view until they rotted away. If they were buried at all, it was only by express permission of the imperial magistrate. Such permission was usually granted to friends and relatives of the deceased who made application, but never in the case of high treason.

[57]As evening approached, there came a rich man from Arimathea, named Joseph, who
had himself become a disciple of Jesus. [58]Going to Pilate, he asked for Jesus' body, and
Pilate ordered that it be given to him. [59]Joseph took the body, wrapped it in a clean linen
cloth, [60]and placed it in his own new tomb that he had cut out of the rock. He rolled a big
stone in front of the entrance to the tomb and went away. [61]Mary Magdalene and the
other Mary were sitting there opposite the tomb.

COMMENTARY

57 The approaching evening—about 6:00 p.m. at that time of year—would mark the end of Friday and the beginning of Sabbath. Mark and Luke portray Joseph of Arimathea (the place is uncertain, but the best guess is Ramathaim, northwest of Lydda) as a prominent member of the Sanhedrin; Luke says Joseph had not consented to the Sanhedrin's action. Only Matthew mentions he was rich. This may direct attention to Isaiah 53:9–12: though Jesus was numbered with the transgressors, yet in his death he was with the rich. To own a new tomb and use the quantity of spices reported by John, Joseph must have been well-to-do. Matthew tells us Joseph had become a disciple (on the verbal forms, see BDF, para. 148 [3]; Zerwick, *Biblical Greek*, para. 66; see comments at 13:52; 28:19); he learned from Jesus and to some extent was committed to following him, even if his discipleship was secret (Jn 19:38).

58–60 Matthew's account is more condensed than Mark's, who mentions Pilate's checking that Jesus was actually dead and describes Joseph's purchases. Joseph's initiative is remarkably courageous; and Pilate granted his request only because he was convinced that Jesus was not really guilty of high treason (v.58). Joseph could not have acted alone: removal of the body, washing, the weight of spices, and other preparations would be too much for one man with limited time. John mentions the assistance of Nicodemus; probably their servants also helped. Matthew does not mention the seventy-five pounds of spices (Jn 19:39) wrapped up with Jesus in the linen cloth.

The Church of the Holy Sepulchre is most probably the correct site of the tomb (cf. Parrot, *Golgotha*). Some centuries earlier, the place had been a stone quarry, and the resulting rugged face became a place where tombs were cut from the rock. Joseph had prepared this tomb for his own use (v.60), but now he laid Jesus' body in it. Tombs were of various kinds. Many were sealed with some sort of boulder wedged into place to discourage wild animals and grave robbers. But an expensive tomb consisted of an antechamber hewn out of the rock face, with a low passage (cf. "bent over," Jn 20:5, 11) leading into the burial chamber, which was sealed with a cut disk-shaped stone that rolled in a slot cut into the rock. The slot was on an incline, making the grave easy to seal but difficult to open. Several men might be needed to roll the stone back up the incline. This sort of tomb is presupposed in the gospel records (cf. Parrot, *Golgotha*, 43ff.).

61 No mourning was permitted for those executed under Roman law. The women followed with broken but silent grief and watched the burial. In addition to Joseph of Arimathea and Nicodemus, the women saw Jesus buried. This must be factual, since the Jews placed little value on the testimony borne by women (*m. Roš Haš.* 1:8). The witness of the women also prepares the way for 28:1. That Jesus was actually buried became an integral part of gospel proclamation (cf. 1Co 15:4).

17. The guard at the tomb (27:62–66)

OVERVIEW

This pericope is peculiar to Matthew. It is often viewed as a piece of "creative writing" designed to provide "witnesses" to the resurrection (Schniewind) or to provide "evidence" that Jesus' body had not been stolen. But there are several things in favor of the pericope's historicity.

1. It must be taken with 28:11–15. Thus, the account of the guards at the tomb does less to assure us that the body was not stolen than to provide background for the report that it was.

2. This may be the reason why the other evangelists omit it. In the circles they were writing for, the report circulated by the Jews may not have been current, so no explanation was necessary. In Matthew's Jewish environment, he could not avoid dealing with the subject. But to think that this story was made up out of whole cloth *by Christians* makes little sense: "It is hardly likely that Christians would have invented such a convenient weapon for their critics if the story were not already in circulation" (France [NICNT]; cf. Wright, *Resurrection of the Son of God*, 636–40).

3. Matthew has regularly given information in the passion narrative that the other evangelists omit (e.g., vv.19, 34–35, 62–63); and it is methodologically wrong to doubt the historicity of all details that lack multiple attestation—not least because such "multiple attestation" may sometimes go back to one literary source.

4. If Matthew were trying to prove Jesus' body was not stolen, why does he not have the guards posted immediately instead of waiting until the next day (v.62)?

5. On the other hand, the chief priests and the Pharisees would not necessarily be defiling themselves by approaching Pilate on the Sabbath, provided they did not travel more than a Sabbath day's journey to get there and did not enter his residence (cf. Jn 18:28). Their action is not implausible if they still saw some potential threat in the remains of the Jesus movement. A few more details are mentioned below. (See also D. Wenham, "Resurrection Narratives," esp. 47–51.)

[62]The next day, the one after Preparation Day, the chief priests and the Pharisees went to Pilate. [63]"Sir," they said, "we remember that while he was still alive that deceiver said, 'After three days I will rise again.' [64]So give the order for the tomb to be made secure until the third day. Otherwise, his disciples may come and steal the body and tell the people that he has been raised from the dead. This last deception will be worse than the first."

[65]"Take a guard," Pilate answered. "Go, make the tomb as secure as you know how." [66]So they went and made the tomb secure by putting a seal on the stone and posting the guard.

COMMENTARY

62 This strange way of referring to the Sabbath (for "Preparation Day," see Reflections, p. 596) cannot reasonably be taken to spring from Matthew's desire to use the word he omitted at v.57 (Mk 15:42; so Bonnard, Hill): Matthew is nowhere committed to using all of Mark's words. Rather, this may be a way to avoid using the word "Sabbath," which can be ambiguous during a feast, since it could refer to the last day of the week or to a feast Sabbath.

63–64 "Sir" (*kyrie*) is merely a polite form of address. For the phrase "after three days," see comments at 12:40. The objection that this scene is implausible because it shows the Jewish leaders believing something the disciples themselves cannot yet believe is insubstantial. They may have heard something of the content of 16:21; 17:9; 20:19 from Judas. Whatever the source of their information, they certainly do not *believe* Jesus' prediction. They are merely afraid of fraud—a fear fostered perhaps by the report that Jesus' body, against all judicial custom (see Overview, 27:57–61), had been taken down from the cross and returned to Jesus' disciples by Joseph and Nicodemus. This could also account for the delay in the request to post a guard (vv.62, 64). The disciples disbelieved Jesus' words about rising again, not because they could not understand the plain words, but because they had no frame of reference capable of integrating a dying and rising Messiah into their own messianic expectations. Shattered by the demoralizing turn of events, they cowered in fear (Jn 20:19), unable and even unwilling to trust their judgment and understanding on anything except the terrible fact that their Messiah had been crucified.

The Jews could take no military action without Roman sanction; so they asked Pilate that a guard be posted against the possibility of the body being stolen (v.64). Jesus' "first deception" was his claim to messiahship; his "last deception" was his claim that he would rise from the dead. Now they hold Jesus to be "that deceiver." Later Jewish polemic against Jesus often accuses him of being an "imposter" and someone guilty of "fraud" (cf. Stanton, *Gospel for a New People*, 171–80; Wright, *Jesus and the Victory of God*, 439–42). From their viewpoint, the Jewish leaders are protecting themselves and the people from deception; from Matthew's perspective, they are deceiving themselves.

65–66 The Greek *echete koustōdia* could be imperative (NIV, "Take a guard"), but it is more likely indicative (NRSV, "You have a guard of soldiers"; cf. KJV). Pilate refuses to use his troops but tells the Jewish authorities that they have the temple police at their disposal; and he grants the leaders permission to use them. This explains why, after the resurrection, the guards reported to the chief priests, not to Pilate (28:11). Pilate's answer in v.65 must therefore be construed as cynical. He is saying, "You were afraid of this man when he was alive; now he is dead, and you are still afraid! By all means, secure the tomb as tightly as possible, if you think that will help. But use your own police." So guards are posted, and the stone sealed with cord and an official wax seal (v.66). But "death could not keep his prey." With the dawn, all the efforts to eliminate Jesus Messiah from the stage of redemptive history are held up for heavenly derision (Ps 2:4) in the irresistible triumph of the resurrection.

B. The Resurrection (28:1–15)

OVERVIEW

Because the resurrection is central to Christian theology, few subjects have received more attention. Paul goes so far as to say that if Christ was not raised from the dead, Christian faith is vain, and we are still dead in our sins (1Co 15:12–17). Useful examples of redaction-critical approaches to the resurrection narratives are provided by N. Perrin, *The Resurrection Narratives* (London: SCM Press, 1977), and especially John E. Alsup, *The Post-Resurrection Appearance Stories of the Gospel-Tradition* (Stuttgart: Calwer, 1975). Older works, such as B. F. Westcott's *The Gospel of the Resurrection: Thoughts on Its Relation to Reason and History* (New York: Macmillan, 1906), are too readily passed over in the contemporary debate. Some works raise questions that turn on relatively new literary and philosophical angles. A useful place to begin is with G. E. Ladd, *I Believe in the Resurrection of Jesus* (Grand Rapids: Eerdmans, 1975); Daniel P. Fuller, *Easter Faith and History* (Grand Rapids: Eerdmans, 1965); W. L. Craig, "The Bodily Resurrection of Jesus," in *Gospel Perspectives* (ed. France and Wenham), 1:47–74; idem, "The Empty Tomb of Jesus," in *Gospel Perspectives*, 2:173–200; idem, *Assessing the New Testament Evidence for the Historicity of the Resurrection of Jesus* (Lewiston: Mellen, 1989). But by far the most important work to appear in perhaps a century on this subject is that of Wright (*Resurrection of the Son of God*).

The textual problems at the end of Mark compound the difficulties in sorting out literary relationships. Most now hold that Mark intended to end his gospel with 16:8, though some still cling to the authenticity of the "long ending" (Mk 16:9–20); others suggest some such ending as Matthew 28:9–10. What is certain is that, for those who wish to attempt it, the various resurrection appearances can be harmonized in at least three different ways (cf. Broadus; Ladd, *I Believe in the Resurrection*, 91–93). But it is more important to come to grips with the distinctive emphasis of each NT writer.

The considerable number of "minor agreements" between Matthew and Luke over against Mark strongly suggests that Matthew and Luke either shared as one source a written account of some resurrection appearances or borrowed from each other. The theological implications of the resurrection are not treated at length by the evangelists, but the theme constantly recurs in Paul (e.g., Ro 4:24–25; 6:4; 8:34; 10:9; 1Co 15; 2Co 5:1–10, 15; Php 3:10–11; Col 2:12–13; 3:1–4; 1Th 4:14). Thought-provoking works in this area include W. Künneth, *The Theology of the Resurrection* (trans. J. W. Leitch; London: SCM Press, 1965); T. F. Torrance, *Space, Time and Resurrection* (Edinburgh: Handsel, 1976); Richard B. Gaffin, *The Centrality of the Resurrection* (Grand Rapids: Baker, 1978).

1. The empty tomb (28:1–7)

1 After the Sabbath, at dawn on the first day of the week, Mary Magdalene and the other Mary went to look at the tomb.

[2]There was a violent earthquake, for an angel of the Lord came down from heaven and, going to the tomb, rolled back the stone and sat on it. [3]His appearance was like lightning, and his clothes were white as snow. [4]The guards were so afraid of him that they shook and became like dead men.

[5]The angel said to the women, "Do not be afraid, for I know that you are looking for Jesus, who was crucified. [6]He is not here; he has risen, just as he said. Come and see the place where he lay. [7]Then go quickly and tell his disciples: 'He has risen from the dead and is going ahead of you into Galilee. There you will see him.' Now I have told you."

COMMENTARY

1 The Greek *opse de sabbatōn* can be understood as meaning "late on the Sabbath"; then the next phrase would mean "as it began to dawn toward the first day of the week." Taken together, these two temporal phrases must mean one of two things: (1) unlike Mark 16:1, not to mention the consistent witness of the NT, the events described take place on *Saturday* evening, the end of the Sabbath; or (2) this is evidence for a scheme of counting days from sunrise to sunrise, and the events take place early Sunday morning.

Instead, it is far better to take *opse* as an irregular preposition, meaning "after" (so NIV; cf. BDF, para. 164 [4]; *Grammar*, 645–46; Moule, *Idiom Book*, 86). "After the Sabbath" is then a general time indicator; i.e., the women would not walk far during the Sabbath, so they waited until after the Sabbath. But by then, Saturday night was drawing on. So early on the first day of the week (i.e., at dawn; cf. BDAG, 386), Mary Magdalene and "the other Mary"—the other one mentioned in 27:56 (still others are mentioned in Mk 16:1; Lk 24:10)—"went to look at the tomb." Mark says they "bought spices so that they might go to anoint Jesus' body." It has been argued that Matthew must make the change to "late on the Sabbath" because he alone introduces the account of the posting of the guard (26:62–66), which would make admittance by the women impossible. The women would not have come once the guards were posted; so they must be presented as slipping in earlier. But if the women stayed home on the Sabbath and the guard was not posted until the Sabbath, would the women be likely to learn of it until they arrived on Sunday morning?

Matthew's brief "to look at the tomb" preserves the theme of witness (27:56, 61); but in addition, it may reflect an ancient Jewish tradition that says Jews visited the tombs of the deceased until the third day to ensure that the party was truly dead (cf. Thomas R. W. Longstaff, "The Women at the Tomb: Matthew 28:1 Re-examined," *NTS* 27 [1981]: 277–82).

2–4 The clause introduced by "for" (v.2) suggests that the violent earthquake (see 27:51) either came with the "angel of the Lord" (on angels, see comments at 1:20; 18:10) or was the means the angel used to open the tomb. In Matthew and Luke, the angel is more clearly portrayed as an angel than in Mark ("a young man dressed in a white robe," 16:5). But the distinction should not be pressed, as angelic beings often appear in human form in the

OT; and Mark's young man is clearly an angel (cf. Lane, *Mark*, 586–87; see Josephus, *Ant.* 5.277 [8.2]). The guards witnessed the earthquake, saw the angel, and "became like dead men" (v.4—i.e., "fainted in terror" or the like). There is no implication that the earthquake had anything to do with releasing Jesus. The stone was rolled back, the seal broken, and the soldiers made helpless, not to let the risen Messiah escape, but to let the first witnesses in.

Too much speculative theologizing has accompanied some modern treatments of these verses. In particular there is nothing to suggest that the soldiers were in any sense pagan witnesses of the resurrection. They neither heard the angel's words nor saw the risen Jesus; and they would shortly lie about what really had happened (vv.11–15). Furthermore, it is doubtful whether Matthew intended to contrast the soldiers' terror, based on their failure to understand, with the joy of the women, who received the word of revelation. There is no evidence that the women witnessed the earthquake and the first descent of the angel; moreover, their joy was mingled with fear (v.8), for the angel's "Do not be afraid" (v.5) is meaningless unless they were afraid. What is stunningly clear is the restrained sobriety of these accounts as compared with the later apocryphal gospels (e.g., *Gospel of Peter*, 9:35–11:44).

5–7 The angel speaks (lit., "answered"; see comments at 11:25) words that allay the women's fears (cf. Mk 16:5–7; Lk 24:4–8). The empty tomb by itself is capable of several explanations (cf. Jn 20:10–15). This explanatory word of revelation narrows the potential interpretations down to one: Jesus has risen from the dead (v.6), a truth to be confirmed by personal appearances. In Matthew and Luke, but not in Mark, the fact of Jesus' resurrection, announced by the angel, is also tied into Jesus' promises "as he said" (cf. 16:21; 17:23; 20:18–19). This is one of several significant "minor agreements" of Matthew and Luke against Mark in the resurrection narratives. The women are invited to see the place where Jesus lay and commanded to go "quickly" (v.7, a happy touch) to give his disciples the joyous message. Unlike Mark, Matthew does not explicitly mention Peter.

Jesus had promised to go ahead of his disciples into Galilee (see comments at 26:32); the angel now reminds them of this (v.7). The present tense *proagei* ("is going ahead," GK *4575*) cannot mean that Jesus is already on his way, because (1) v.10 places him still in Jerusalem, and (2) a verb like "go ahead," if pressed to mean Jesus was actually traveling, "would also seem to presuppose that the disciples also were on the way to Galilee" (Stonehouse, *Witness of Matthew*, 173). The verb is not a progressive present but a vivid future. As he promised, Jesus will arrive in Galilee before they do and meet them there, contrary to their expectation (see comments at 26:32; 28:10).

2. First encounter with the risen Christ (28:8–10)

8So the women hurried away from the tomb, afraid yet filled with joy, and ran to tell
his disciples. 9Suddenly Jesus met them. "Greetings," he said. They came to him, clasped
his feet and worshiped him. 10Then Jesus said to them, "Do not be afraid. Go and tell my
brothers to go to Galilee; there they will see me."

COMMENTARY

8–9 With mingled fear and joy, the women run to tell their news to the disciples (v.8), when "suddenly" (the probable force of *idou*, "behold," in this context) Jesus meets them (v.9). "Greetings" (*chairete*, GK *5897*) is a normal Greek salutation (cf. 26:49). The women clasp his feet (possibly a generalizing plural; see Turner, *Insights*, 76; cf. Jn 20:11–14) and worship him. *Prosekynēsan* ("worshiped," GK *4686*) can mean simply "knelt before" (see comments at 8:2). The same verb occurs in the only other resurrection appearance in Matthew (v.17) and encourages the view that the "kneeling" has instinctively become worship.

10 Like the angel (v.5), Jesus stills the women's fears and gives them a similar commission. Some have held that "my brothers" raises the status of Jesus' eleven surviving disciples. This ignores the use of the term in Matthew; for apart from the places where "brothers" denotes a natural relationship, the term is employed of spiritual relationship—even before the passion—explicitly referring to the fellowship of those who acknowledge Jesus as Messiah (18:15; 23:8; cf. 5:22–24; 7:3–5; 18:21, 35). In the two other places where Jesus uses the full expression "my brothers" (12:49–50; 25:40), it refers to all Jesus' disciples and cannot possibly be limited to the apostles (cf. Stonehouse, *Witness of Matthew*, 176–77).

Therefore, the natural way to interpret "my brothers" here is not as a reference to the Eleven but to all those attached to his cause who were then in Jerusalem, most of whom had followed him from Galilee to Jerusalem as his "disciples" (see comments at 5:12; 26:32; 28:7). There were many others in addition to the Twelve who had followed Jesus (e.g., 20:17; 21:8–9, 15; 27:55; cf. 20:29; 21:46; 23:1). Apart from the Galileans, Joseph of Arimathea was certainly not Jesus' sole disciple from the Jerusalem region (19:13–15; 27:57–61).

If this interpretation of Jesus' words is reasonable, several interesting conclusions or possibilities are evident.

1. The view that interprets the "some" of v.17 as a reference to others than the apostles is supported, and the resurrection appearance of vv.16–20 may well be equivalent to the appearance before five hundred reported by Paul (1Co 15:6).

2. Obviously Matthew does not tell all he knows or recount every resurrection appearance of which he has information. Therefore, it is tendentious to argue that vv.10, 16–20 meant that Matthew thinks Jesus appeared to his disciples only in Galilee and denies any Jerusalem appearances.

3. The interpretation of v.10 offered here looks back to 26:32; 28:7: Jesus now confirms his earlier promise that, far from being left behind as a rotting corpse when his disciples return to Galilee, he will precede them there and meet them there. But now, after the resurrection, he makes the promise a command and includes all his "brothers." Taken this way, v.10 is far from eliminating other appearances to the believers (cf. Lk 24:13–49; Jn 20:3–9, 11–29) before they return to Galilee. It is simply that Matthew, for his immediate purposes, is not interested in them.

4. But why not? Or why does Matthew record only the resurrection appearance to the women and the appearance in Galilee to his followers? Some have suggested that Galilee is introduced because it is the place of revelation and ministry, whereas Jerusalem is the place of rejection and judgment (see E. Lohmeyer, *Galiläa und Jerusalem* [Göttingen: Vandenhoeck & Ruprecht, 1936], 36ff.; R. H. Lightfoot, *Locality and Doctrine* [London: Hodder and Stoughton, 1938], 66ff., 128ff.). But one must wonder whether enough weight has been assigned to various facts, namely, that Jesus' ministry was not only to Galilee but to

the whole of Israel (10:6, 23; 15:24); opposition was directed against Jesus in Galilee as well as in Jerusalem, where the plots to kill him were hatched; at Jerusalem Jesus revealed himself as King in fulfillment of Zechariah's prophecy (21:1–7); and Jerusalem, called the "holy city" (4:5; 27:53), peculiarly drew out Jesus' compassion (23:37–39), whereas cities in Galilee were excoriated (11:20–24).

Why, then, Matthew's record of a resurrection appearance in Galilee? The answer surely lies in the combination of two themes that have permeated the entire gospel. First, the Messiah emerges from a despised area (see comments at 2:23) and first sheds his light on a despised people (see comments at 4:15–16); for the kingdom of heaven belongs to the poor in spirit (5:3). For this reason, too, the risen Jesus first appears to women, whose value as witnesses among Jews is worthless (see comments at 27:55–56, 61; 28:1, 5–7). Second, "Galilee of the Gentiles" (4:15) is compatible with the growing theme of Gentile mission in this gospel (see comments at 1:1; 2:1–12; 4:15–16; 8:5–13; 10:18; 12:21; 13:37; 15:21–28; 24:14 et al.) and prepares for the Great Commission (28:18–20).

3. First fraudulent denials of Jesus' resurrection (28:11–15)

OVERVIEW

There is no sure way of dating the writing of *this* pericope by the closing words, "to this very day" (v.15). To conclude from this pericope that Matthew had in mind a period ten or fifteen years after the fall of Jerusalem (so Bonnard) stretches the evidence too far. Matthew simply intends this paragraph to be an explanation of the stolen-corpse theory and an apologetic against it. He may also be drawing out a startling contrast: the chief priests use bribe money to commission the soldiers to spread lies, while the resurrected Jesus uses the promise of his presence to commission his followers to spread the gospel (vv.16–20).

11While the women were on their way, some of the guards went into the city and
reported to the chief priests everything that had happened. 12When the chief priests
had met with the elders and devised a plan, they gave the soldiers a large sum of money,
13telling them, "You are to say, 'His disciples came during the night and stole him away
while we were asleep.' 14If this report gets to the governor, we will satisfy him and keep
you out of trouble." 15So the soldiers took the money and did as they were instructed. And
this story has been widely circulated among the Jews to this very day.

COMMENTARY

11 Some of the guards (presumably the rest waited to be officially relieved) reported, not to Pilate, but to the chief priests; probably they were temple police (see comments at 27:65–66). When

Matthew says the guards reported "everything that had happened," he is not suggesting that they actually witnessed the resurrection, but the earthquake, angel, and empty tomb (Bonnard).

12–14 It is very difficult to believe that Roman soldiers of Pilate would admit falling asleep (v.13)—that would be tantamount to suicide. But the temple police could more easily be bribed—even though it took "a large sum of money" (v.12)—and could more easily be protected from Pilate's anger. The plan devised (see comments at 12:14; 27:1) by the chief priests and elders (see comments at 21:23) proves to Matthew that their pious promises to believe if Jesus would only come down from the cross (27:42) were empty. Once again, the instinctive concern of the Jewish leaders relates to expedience and the people's reaction, not to the truth. The story they concoct shows how desperate they are for an explanation, for if the guards were asleep, they could not know of the alleged theft; and if one of them awoke, why was not an alarm sounded, and why were the disciples not arrested? Molesting graves was a serious offense in the ancient world, subject at times to the death penalty. The famous "Nazareth Inscription," recording an ordinance of Caesar to that effect, confirms this, though the relation of this inscription to Jesus' death and burial is uncertain (cf. B. M. Metzger, "The Nazareth Inscription Once Again," in *Jesus und Paulus* [ed. Ellis and Grässer], 221–38).

It is equally improbable that the timid and fearful disciples could have mustered up the courage to open Jesus' tomb and run the risk of a capital indictment, or that the Jewish authorities would have failed to prosecute the disciples if they had possessed a scrap of evidence pointing to the disciples' guilt. Nor was the "large sum of money" an adequate measure of how far the Jewish leaders would go, for to "satisfy" the governor may well have involved further bribery (cf. parallels in Wettstein's Greek New Testament).

15 And this, Matthew explains, was the origin of the "widely circulated" Jewish explanation for the empty tomb, still common in the days of Justin Martyr (*Dial.* 108).

C. The Risen Messiah and His Disciples (28:16–20)

OVERVIEW

Partly because there is no close gospel parallel to these verses, and partly because as the conclusion to Matthew's gospel they have great significance, an enormous amount of study has centered on these verses. Much of it has gone into trying to distinguish between tradition and redaction or into establishing the *Gattung* or literary genre (e.g., B. J. Malina, "The Literary Structure and Form of Matthew 28:16–20," *NTS* 17 [1970–71]: 87–103; J. Lange, *Das Erscheinen des Auferstandenen im Evangelism nach Matthäus* [Würzburg: Echter, 1973]; Hubbard, *Matthean Redaction*). The most believable opinion is that of Hubbard, who avoids the classifications of his predecessors (enthronement hymn, official decree, covenant renewal manifesto) and opts for a commissioning narrative patterned after similar OT commissionings (e.g., Ge 12:1–4; Ex 3:1–10; Jos 1:1–11; Isa 6; 49:1–6). After examining twenty-seven such narratives and finding a basic form consisting of seven elements, Hubbard finds five of them in 28:16–20: introduction (v.16), confrontation (vv.17–18a), reaction (v.17b), the commission (vv.19–20a), reassurance (v.20b). Missing are the protest before the reassurance and a conclusion stating the work is being carried out.

But several questions persist. Hubbard himself concedes that the form is not monolithic even in the OT; and absence of two of the seven common elements is disconcerting, the more so since Matthew's final clause is a perfectly suitable conclusion to his gospel. More important, all the OT commissions Hubbard refers to are to individuals, whereas this one is to the disciples as a group. Some of the OT commissions are in reality the establishment of covenants; and if Frankemölle (*Jahwebund und Kirche Christi*, 42ff.) has somewhat exaggerated this theme in Matthew, it cannot be entirely ignored in a book that promises a new covenant (26:26–29) and seeks to demonstrate the continuity with and fulfillment of the OT covenant people in the messianic community being gathered around Jesus.

It seems best to conclude with John P. Meier ("Two Disputed Questions in Matthew 28:16–20," *JBL* 96 [1977]: 407–24; cf. O'Brien, "Great Commission," 254–67) that this pericope does not easily fit any known literary form and must not be squeezed into a poorly fitting mold. Yet Meier's principal reason for this conclusion could be strengthened. He argues that these verses constitute a tradition so heavily redacted by the evangelist that conformity to a *Gattung* (or form) shaped primarily by oral transmission is, in principle, unlikely. That may be so, but this conclusion by no means makes impregnable judgments about the way the material came into Matthew's hands (see Introduction, section 2). Above all, the temptation to ascribe authenticity to "tradition" but not to "redaction" must be resisted (cf. Carson, "Redaction Criticism"; Beasley-Murray, *Baptism*, 77ff.).

Some have distinguished between "Christ-epiphanies" (appearances of the resurrected Christ on earth, as in v.9) and "Christophanies" (appearances of the resurrected Christ from heaven, as at Paul's conversion, Ac 9; cf. Dunn, *Jesus and the Spirit*, 116, 123). Those who make this helpful distinction are uncertain how to classify the resurrection appearance of 28:16–20. The dilemma is a false one. There has been no mention of the ascension; moreover, Paul seems to put his own experience of the risen Christ into a class of one (1Co 15:8), the sole "Christophany," which must also be distinguished from John's visionary experiences (e.g., Rev 1:12–16).

It is often pointed out that vv.16–20 recapitulate many of Matthew's themes. The point can be overstressed (e.g., Peter F. Ellis, *Matthew: His Mind and His Message* [Collegeville, Minn.: Liturgical, 1974]; Kupp, *Matthew's Emmanuel*, identifies connections between, on the one hand, Mt 1–2 and, on the other, 27:51–28:20) but remains an important insight that ties up several loose ends. The most obvious connection between the end of this gospel and its beginning is the way v.20, "And surely I am with you always, to the very end of the age," is thematically tied to "Immanuel" (1:23).

1. Jesus in Galilee (28:16–17)

16Then the eleven disciples went to Galilee, to the mountain where Jesus had told them
to go. 17When they saw him, they worshiped him; but some doubted.

COMMENTARY

16 "Then" translates the mildly adversative *de* ("but"), not *tote* (see comments at 2:7). The fraudulent explanation of the empty tomb was purchased with a bribe and was widely circulated (vv.11–15), *but* the Eleven (designated as such in the NT only here and four times in Luke and Acts) do what Jesus says and go to Galilee. They go "to the mountain where Jesus had told them to go"; the subordinate clause makes the expression *eis to oros* ("to the mountain") specific, though by itself it customarily means "into the hills." We do not know what mountain is meant, but the verse presupposes the arrangements implicit in 26:32; 28:7, 10. Associating the Great Commission (vv.18–20) with Galilee not only has nuances with Jesus' humble background and the theme of Gentile mission (see comments at v.10) but "ensures that the risen Christ and his teaching are not thought of as a substitute for, but as continuous with, Jesus' ministry and teaching in Galilee" (Hill).

17 Doubt about Jesus' resurrection is expressed elsewhere (Lk 24:10–11; Jn 20:24–29), but only by those who have heard reports of Jesus' resurrection without actually seeing him. This verse is therefore unique. Two difficulties must be considered.

1. Does "some" refer to "some of the Eleven" or to "some others" in addition to the Eleven? The question is partly decided by one's interpretation of v.10, though more can be said. If *proskyneō* (GK *4686*) here means not merely "kneel" or "make obeisance to" but "worship" (see comments at v.9), then the "eleven disciples" and the "some" probably constitute two groups; for doubt about who Jesus is or about the reality of his resurrection does not seem appropriate for true worship. Especially if Matthew was an eyewitness, it is easy to believe that he describes a scene vivid in his own memory without taking all the precautions that would remove questions from the minds of readers who were not there. As a result, both here and in v.10, Matthew in an incidental fashion alludes to the larger crowd without providing useful specifics. Moreover, *hoi de*, here as in 26:67, means "but some," in contrast with those already mentioned, rather than "but they" (cf. Gundry). While this solution is not certain, the problem is not helped by suggesting that "some" refers to those in Matthew's community who have doubts (Hill).

2. But why was there doubt at all? The verb used (*edistasan*, "[some] doubted") occurs in the NT only here and in 14:31 and does not denote intellectual disbelief but hesitation (cf. JB, "though some hesitated"; see I. P. Ellis, "'But some doubted,'" *NTS* 14 [1967–68]: 574–80). That is one of the reasons why the suggestion of J.-P. Sternberger ("Le doute selon Mt 28:17," *ETR* 81 [2006]: 429–34) is not credible. He argues on the basis of symmetry in 28:16–20 that this verb must mean the opposite of "worshiped," or something similar, and paraphrases, "Some were convinced, while others refused to believe." But "refused to believe" is simply not what the Greek verb means. Even so, why did they hesitate, and why does Matthew include this information here? Even if others than the Eleven are the ones who hesitate, this does not solve the problem; it merely shifts it from the Eleven to other followers of Jesus.

Several solutions have been proposed, few of them convincing. There is no evidence of scribal emendation. It is barely possible that some doubted not the fact of the resurrection but just who this person was (Hendriksen, Grosheide, Filson, Walvoord et al.). The pattern would then be somewhat akin to Luke 24:16; John 21:4–14, where the resurrected Jesus is not instantly recognized. But it must be admitted that this introduces a very subtle distinction into Matthew 28. Moreover, the parallels in Luke and John are not all that close, since Luke says the two on the Emmaus road "were kept from recognizing him," and John's narrative has other uncertainties—distance from shore and the aside in John 21:12b. Neither Luke nor John uses the verb found here in Matthew. The most that can be said for this interpretation is that other passages show that Jesus in his postresurrection appearances was not always instantly recognized. Far less likely is the view of L. G. Parkhurst ("Matthew 28:16–20 Reconsidered," *ExpTim* 90 [1978–79]: 179–80), who says that some doubted, not who Jesus was, nor the facticity of the resurrection, but the propriety of worshiping the resurrected Jesus; and this hesitation Jesus dispels by the words of 28:18: "All authority ... has been given to me." Somewhat similar is the position of Gundry, who argues that vv.17–20 are Matthew's way of saying that only Jesus' word quiets doubt, and even the resurrection appearances will not do this. According to Gundry, we "could hardly ask for better evidence of the authority of Jesus' teaching in Matthew's theology." But thematically v.18 is tightly related to v.19, not v.17. It is not at all clear that v.18 alleviates the doubt of v.17 (cf. Dunn, *Jesus and the Spirit*, 124; and to the contrary, Barth, "Matthew's Understaning of the Law," 132). At very least, we must admit that the text does not say that all doubts were removed, as is the case in Luke 24 and John 21. More important, Matthew's use of *proskyneō* ("worship") has been sufficiently ambiguous (see comments at 8:2; 28:9) that he would have needed to use a stronger verb such as *latreuō* ("worship," "serve [God]") if he were trying to make the various points Parkhurst and Gundry suggest.

Perhaps it is best to conclude that, especially if the "some" refers not to the Eleven but to other followers, the move from unbelief and fear to faith and joy was for them a "hesitant" one. The Eleven, who according to the other gospels had already seen the risen Jesus at least twice (Peter at least three times, Thomas at least once), respond instantly with worship on the occasion of this new epiphany, but some (others) hesitated—without further specification as to their subsequent belief or doubt. If this is what Matthew means, he may be using this historical reminiscence to stress the fact that Jesus' resurrection was not an anticipated episode that required only enthusiasm and gullibility to win adherents among Jesus' followers. Far from it, they still were hesitant; and their failure to understand his repeated predictions of his resurrection, compounded with their despair after his crucifixion, worked to maintain their hesitancy for some time before they came to full faith. Jesus' resurrection did not instantly transform men of little faith and faltering understanding into spiritual giants. One suspects that the "hesitation" (not doubt) sprang from the fact that the "risen Jesus both was and was not 'the same' as he had been before.... There was a mystery about him which even those who knew him best were now unable to penetrate" (Wright, *Resurrection of the Son of God*, 643–44; cf. France [NICNT]).

Another thing (not dealt with by Matthew) was necessary, namely, the endowment of the Spirit at Pentecost. Matthew's concise account presupposes this—for it is impossible that any evangelist could have been ignorant of that transforming event—but omits it in favor of pressing on to the Great Commission, which ties together some of his own thematic interests.

2. The Great Commission (28:18–20)

18Then Jesus came to them and said, "All authority in heaven and on earth has been
given to me. 19Therefore go and make disciples of all nations, baptizing them in the

name of the Father and of the Son and of the Holy Spirit, [20]and teaching them to obey everything I have commanded you. And surely I am with you always, to the very end of the age."

COMMENTARY

18 "All" dominates vv.18–20 and ties these verses together: *all* authority, *all* nations, *all* things (NIV, "everything"), *all* the days (NIV, "always"). The authority of Jesus Messiah has already been heavily stressed in this gospel (e.g., 7:29; 10:1, 7–8; 11:27; 22:43–44; 24:35; cf. Jn 17:2). Therefore, it is incautious, if not altogether wrong, to claim that the resurrection conferred on Jesus an authority incomparably greater than what he enjoyed before his crucifixion. The truth is more subtle. It is not that anything he teaches or does during the days of his flesh is *less* authoritative than what he now says and does. Even during his ministry, his words, like God's, cannot pass away (24:35); and he, like God, forgives sin (9:6). It is not Jesus' authority per se that becomes more absolute. Rather, the spheres in which he now exercises absolute authority are enlarged to include all heaven and earth, i.e., the universe. This authority has been "given" him by the Father; and so, of course, the Father is exempt from the Son's authority (cf. 1Co 15:27–28). The Son becomes the one through whom *all* God's authority is mediated. He is, as it were, the mediatorial King. This well-defined exercise of authority is given Jesus as the climactic vindication of his humiliation (cf. Php 2:5–11), and it marks a turning point in redemptive history, for Messiah's "kingdom" (i.e., his "king-dominion," the exercise of his divine and saving authority; see comments at 3:2; 13:37–39) has dawned in new power. Certainly such claims challenge the sweep of the authority and mission of the Roman Empire (so Carter, *Matthew and the Margins*, 549–50), but the vision is primarily theological and cosmic, not merely political. This is still clearer if we accept the view that there is a conscious allusion here to Daniel 7:13–14 (cf. France, *Jesus and the Old Testament*, 142–43): the Son of Man, once humiliated and suffering, is given universal authority (same word in the LXX).

Contrary to France, it does not follow from this that Matthew 26:64 and Mark 14:62 refer to this exaltation and not the Parousia. In the first place, the chief priests in no way witnessed this coming of the Son of Man; in the second place, we have repeatedly observed how the coming of the Son of Man to kingly authority cannot be reduced to a single moment in redemptive history.

19 "Therefore" is probably the correct reading; but even if the word is absent, the logical connection is presupposed by the flow of the commission. Two features tie the command to Jesus' universal authority.

1. Because he *now* has this authority, *therefore* his disciples are to go and make disciples—i.e., the dawning of the new age of messianic authority changes the circumstances and impels his disciples forward to a universal ministry he himself never engaged in during the days of his flesh, "except in reluctant anticipation" (Stendahl, "Matthew," in *Peake's Commentary*). His promotion to universal authority serves as an eschatological marker inaugurating the beginning of his universal mission.

2. Because of that authority, his followers may go in the confidence that their Lord is in sovereign

control of "everything in heaven and on earth" (cf. Ro 8:28).

In the Greek, "go"—like "baptizing" and "teaching"—is a participle. Only the verb "make disciples" (see below) is imperative. Some have deduced from this that Jesus' commission is simply to make disciples "as we go" (i.e., wherever we are) and constitutes no basis for going somewhere special in order to serve as missionaries (e.g., Gaechter; R. D. Culver, "What Is the Church's Commission?" *BS* 125 [1968]: 243–53). There is something to this view, but it needs three careful qualifications.

1. When a participle functions as a circumstantial participle dependent on an imperative, it frequently gains some imperatival force (cf. 2:8, 13; 9:13; 11:4; 17:27; cf. C. Rogers, "The Great Commission," *BS* 130 [1973]: 258–67). Only the context can decide the question.

2. While it remains true to say that the main imperatival force rests with "make disciples," not with "go," in a context that demands that this ministry extend to "all nations," it is difficult to believe that "go" has no imperatival force.

3. From the perspective of mission strategy, it is important to remember that the Great Commission is preserved in several complementary forms that, taken together, can only be circumvented by considerable exegetical ingenuity (e.g., Lk 24:45–49; Jn 20:21; Ac 1:8; cf. Mt 4:19; 10:16–20; 13:38; 24:14).

The main emphasis, then, is on the command to "make disciples," which in Greek is one word, *mathēteusate*, normally an intransitive verb, here used transitively (a not uncommon Hellenization; cf. BDF, para. 148 [3]; Zerwick, *Biblical Greek*, para. 66; see comments at 13:52; 27:57). "To disciple a person to Christ is to bring him into the relation of pupil to teacher, 'taking his yoke' of authoritative instruction (11:29), accepting what he says as true because he says it, and submitting to his requirements as right because he makes them" (Broadus). Disciples are those who hear, understand, and obey Jesus' teaching (12:46–50). The injunction is given at least to the Eleven, but to the Eleven in their own role as disciples (28:16). Therefore, they are paradigms for *all* disciples. Plausibly, the command is given to a larger gathering of disciples (see comments at vv.10, 16–17). Either way, it is binding on all Jesus' disciples to make others what they themselves are—disciples of Jesus Christ.

The words *panta ta ethnē* ("all nations") have been understood primarily in two ways.

1. They refer to all Gentiles—i.e., all nations except Israel. Israel has forfeited her place, and now the preaching of the gospel must be kept from her (so Hare, *Theme of Jewish Persecution*, 147–48; Walker, *Heilsgeschichte*, 111–13; D. R. A. Hare and D. J. Harrington, "'Make Disciples of All the Gentiles' (Mt 28:19)," *CBQ* 37 [1975]: 359–69).

2. They refer to all people, including Israel (so Trilling, *Das wahre Israel*, 26–28; Hill; Hubbard, *Matthean Redaction*, 84–87; John P. Meier, "Nations or Gentiles in Matthew 28:19?" *CBQ* 39 [1977]: 94–102; O'Brien, "Great Commission," 262–63).

Certainly *ta ethnē* in its eight occurrences in Matthew (4:15; 6:32; 10:5, 18; 12:18, 21; 20:19, 25) normally denotes Gentiles, often pagans; but 21:43, where *ethnos* is used anarthrously, is an instance where "people" does not exclude Jews. Moreover, contrary to Hare and Harrington, a good case can be made for saying that the full expression, *panta ta ethnē*, used four times in Matthew (24:9, 14; 25:32; here), uses *ethnē* in its basic sense of "tribes," "nations," or "peoples" and means "all peoples [without distinction]" or "all nations [without distinction]," thereby including Jews. Could Matthew really be excluding Israel as one source of the hate his followers will have to endure (24:9)? Would he say that any Jewish Christians in any church known to him should not be baptized and taught?

More telling yet, Matthew's gospel is now, in its final verses, returning to the theme introduced in the very first verse (see comments at 1:1)—that the blessings promised to Abraham and through him to all peoples on earth (Ge 12:3) are now to be fulfilled in Jesus the Messiah. And when that covenant promise is reiterated in Genesis 18:18; 22:18, the LXX uses the same words found here: *panta ta ethnē*. The expression is comprehensive. In line with all the anticipatory hints of Gentile witness in Matthew's gospel (1:1; 2:1–12; 4:15–16; 8:5–13; 10:18; 13:38; 24:14 et al.), it would be as wrong to conclude that only Gentiles are in view as it would be to set up another restriction and see this commission as a command to evangelize only Jewish tribes.

Adherents of the church growth movement have in the past attempted to justify their entire "people movement" principle on the basis of this phrase, used here and elsewhere, arguing that *ethnos* properly means "tribe" or "people" (most comprehensively, perhaps, by H. C. Goerner, *All Nations in God's Purpose* [Nashville: Broadman, 1979]). The latter point is readily conceded, but the conclusion is linguistically illegitimate. Plural collectives may have all-embracing force, whether in Greek or English. Doubtless God may convert people by using a "people movement," but to deduce such a principle from this text requires a "city movement" principle based on Acts 8:40, where the same construction occurs with the noun "cities." In neither case may missiologists legitimately establish the normativeness of their theories.

The aim of Jesus' disciples, therefore, is to make disciples of all people everywhere, without distinction. Hill insists that such a command cannot possibly be authentic: "Had Christ given the command to 'make disciples of all nations,' the opposition in Paul's time to the admission of Gentiles to the church would be inexplicable. It must be assumed that the church, having learned and experienced the universality of the Christian message, assigned that knowledge to a direct command of the living Lord." But we have already seen how slow the disciples were to grasp what Jesus taught. More important, Acts and the Epistles betray no trace of opposition whatsoever to the *fact* of a Gentile mission. The debate between Paul and his Judaizing opponents was over *the conditions of entrance* into the Christian community (see comments at 23:15). The many hints throughout Jesus' ministry that show he anticipated a Gentile ministry after some delay (see comments at 10:16–20, 13:37–39; 24:14) would make it incongruous for him to have not given some commission about this.

The syntax of the Greek participles for "baptizing" and "teaching" forbids the conclusion that baptizing and teaching are to be construed solely as the means of making disciples (cf. Allen, Lagrange, Schlatter), but their precise relationship to the main verb is not easy to delineate. Neither participle is bound to the other or to the main verb with the conjunction *kai* or a particle, and therefore "they must be viewed as dependent on one another or depending in differing ways on the chief verb" (Beasley-Murray, *Baptism*, 89; cf. BDF, para. 421). Most likely some imperative force is present, since the disciples are certainly to baptize and teach; but computer studies of the Greek NT have shown that although a participle dependent on an imperative normally gains imperatival force when it precedes the imperative, its chief force is not normally imperatival when it follows the imperative. Luke 6:35 has a close syntactic parallel: "And lend [*danizete*] to them without expecting to get anything back [*apelpizontes*]." Not expecting anything in return is certainly not the *means* of the lending, but it is modal in that it characterizes the lending; and at the same time at least some imperatival force tinges the participle, even if the participle is primarily modal.

Similarly, baptizing and teaching are not the *means* of making disciples, but they characterize it. Envisaged is that proclamation of the gospel that will result in repentance and faith, for *mathēteuō* ("I disciple") entails both preaching and response. The response of discipleship is baptism and instruction. Therefore, baptism and teaching are not coordinate—either grammatically or conceptually—with the action of making disciples. The masculine pronouns *autous* ("them," vv.19–20) hint at the same thing, since *ethnē* ("nations") is neuter: the "them" who are baptized and taught are those who have been made disciples. But this is uncertain, because the case of "them" may be *ad sensum* (i.e., merely according to the general sense). In any case, it would certainly misconstrue the text to absolutize the division between discipleship and baptism-instruction. The NT can scarcely conceive of a disciple who is not baptized or is not instructed. Indeed, the force of this command is to make Jesus' disciples responsible for making disciples of others, a task characterized by baptism and instruction.

Those who become disciples are to be baptized *eis* (NIV text note, "into") the name of the Trinity. Matthew, unlike some NT writers, apparently avoids the confusion of *eis* (strictly "into") and *en* (strictly "in"; cf. Zerwick, *Biblical Greek*, para. 106) common in Hellenistic Greek; if so, the preposition "into" strongly suggests a coming-into-relationship-with or a coming-under-the-lordship-of (cf. Allen; Albright and Mann). For more on baptism, see comments at 3:6, 11, 13–17. It is a sign both of entrance into Messiah's covenant community and of pledged submission to his lordship (cf. Beasley-Murray, *Baptism*, 90–92).

The triple formula containing Father (or God), Son (or Christ), and Spirit occurs frequently in the NT (cf. 1Co 12:4–6; 2Co 13:14; Eph 4:4–6; 2Th 2:13–14; 1Pe 1:2; Rev 1:4–6). Individually these texts do not prove there is any Trinitarian consciousness in the NT, since other threefold phrases occur (e.g., "God and Christ Jesus and the elect angels," 1Ti 5:21). But contributing evidence makes it difficult to deny the presence of Trinitarian thought in the NT documents: (1) the frequency of the God-Christ-Spirit formulas; (2) their context and use: it is impossible, for instance, to imagine baptism into the name of God, Christ, and the elect angels; (3) the recognition by NT writers that the attributes of Yahweh may be comprehensively applied to Jesus and, so far as we have evidence, to the Spirit (cf. C. F. D. Moule, *The Holy Spirit* [London: Mowbrays, 1978], 24–26).

Many deny the authenticity of this Trinitarian formula, however, not on the basis of doubtful reconstructions of the development of doctrine, but on the basis of the fact that the only evidence we have of actual Christian baptisms indicates a consistent monadic formula baptism in Jesus' name (Ac 2:38; 8:16; 10:48; 19:5; similarly, passages such as Ro 6:3). If Jesus gave the Trinitarian formula, why was it shortened? Is it not easier to believe that the Trinitarian formula was a relatively late development? But certain reflections give us pause.

1. It is possible, though historically improbable, that the full Trinitarian formula was used for pagan converts, and "in the name of Jesus" for Jews and proselytes. But this is doubtful, not least because Paul, Apostle to the Gentiles, never uses a Trinitarian formula for baptism.

2. Trinitarian ideas are found in the resurrection accounts of both Luke and John, even if these evangelists do not report the Trinitarian baptismal formula. The faith to be proclaimed was in some sense Trinitarian from the beginning. "This conclusion should not come as a great surprise: the Trinitarian tendencies of the early church are most easily explained if they go back to Jesus Himself; but the importance of the point for our study is that it

means that Matthew's reference to the Trinity in ch. 28 is not a white elephant thoroughly out of context" (D. Wenham, "Resurrection Narratives," 53).

3. The term "formula" is tripping us up. There is no evidence we have Jesus' *ipsissima verba* here and still less that the church regarded Jesus' command as a baptismal formula, a liturgical form the ignoring of which was a breach of canon law. The problem has too often been cast in anachronistic terms. E. Riggenbach (*Der Trinitarische Taufbefehl Matt. 28:19* [Gütersloh: Bertelsmann, 1901]) points out that as late as the *Didache*, baptism in the name of Jesus and baptism in the name of the Trinity coexist side by side. The church was not bound by precise "formulas" and felt no embarrassment at a multiplicity of them, precisely because Jesus' instruction, which may not have been in these precise words, was not regarded as a binding formula.

20 Those who are discipled must be not only baptized but also taught. The content of this instruction (see comments at 3:1 for *kērygma* ["preaching," GK *3060*] and *didachē* ["teaching," GK *1439*]) is everything Jesus commanded the first disciples. Five things stand out.

1. The focus is on Jesus' commands, not OT law. Jesus' words, like the words of Scripture, are more enduring than heaven and earth (24:35); and the peculiar expression "everything I have commanded you" is, as Trilling (*Das wahre Israel*, 37) has pointed out, reminiscent of the authority of Yahweh (Ex 29:35; Dt 1:3, 41; 7:11; 12:11, 14). This confirms our exegesis of 5:17–20. The revelation of Jesus Messiah at this late stage in salvation history brings the fulfillment of everything to which the OT Scriptures pointed and constitutes their valid continuity; but this means that the focus is necessarily on Jesus.

2. Remarkably, Jesus does not foresee a time when any part of his teaching will be rightly judged needless, outmoded, superseded, or untrue. *Everything* he has commanded must be passed on "to the very end of the age."

3. What the disciples teach is not mere dogma steeped in abstract theorizing but content to be *obeyed*.

4. It then follows that by carefully passing on everything Jesus taught, the first disciples—themselves eyewitnesses—call into being new generations of "ear-witnesses" (O'Brien, "Great Commission," 264–65). These in turn pass on the truth they received. So a means is provided for successive generations to remain in contact with Jesus' teachings (cf. 2Ti 2:2).

5. Christianity must spread by an internal necessity or it has already decayed, for one of Jesus' commands is to teach all he commands. Failure to disciple, baptize, and teach the peoples of the world is already itself one of the failures of our own discipleship.

But the gospel ends, not with command, but with the promise of Jesus' comforting presence, which, if not made explicitly conditional on the disciples' obedience to the Great Commission, is at least closely tied to it. "Surely" captures the force of *idou* here (see comments at 1:20). He who is introduced to us in the prologue as Immanuel, "God with us" (1:23; cf. 18:20), is still God with us, "to the very end of the age." The English adverb "always" renders an expression found in the NT only here—namely, *pasas tēs hēmeras*, strictly "the whole of every day" (Moule, *Idiom Book*, 34). Not just the horizon is in view, but each day as we live it. This continues to the end of the age (for this expression, see comments at 13:39–40, 49; 24:3; cf. Heb 9:26)—the end of history as we know it, when the kingdom will be consummated. Perhaps there is a small hint of judgment. The church dare not drift, because it, too, rushes to the consummation. The period between the commission and the consummation is of indefinite length; but whatever its duration, it is the time of the church's mission and of preliminary enjoyment of her Lord's presence.

Matthew's gospel ends with the expectation of continued mission and teaching. The five preceding sections always conclude with a block of *Jesus'* teaching (3:1–26:5); but the passion and resurrection of Jesus end with a commission *to his disciples* to carry on that same ministry (see Introduction, section 14) in the light of the cross, the empty tomb, and the triumphant vindication and exaltation of the risen Lord. In this sense, the gospel of Matthew is not a closed book until the consummation. The final chapter is being written in the mission and teaching of Jesus' disciples.

MARK

WALTER W. WESSEL AND MARK L. STRAUSS

Introduction

The gospel of Mark is a succinct, vivid, and action-packed account of the ministry, suffering, death, and resurrection of Jesus Christ. Jesus appears suddenly on the scene as the mighty and authoritative Messiah and Son of God, teaching with great authority, driving out demons, healing the sick, and even raising the dead. He calms the sea with a word and feeds the multitudes with a few loaves and fish. This person is truly God's Messiah, the promised Savior! The narrative takes a startling turn, however, as Jesus predicts that he will be rejected by Israel's leaders and will suffer and die a terrible death in Jerusalem. Yet this future is no tragedy or accident of fate. All along it was part of God's purpose and will for Jesus to suffer and die as a ransom payment for sins, bringing salvation to his people and to the whole world. The gospel of Mark is a call for believers to take up their cross and follow Jesus on the path through trials and suffering to salvation.

Mark presents the narrative in an appealing way; he tells the good news about Jesus Christ so simply that a child can understand it. Nevertheless, his gospel also contains "some things that are hard to understand," as Peter said of Paul's letters (2Pe 3:16). Like a pool of pure water, Mark is far deeper than it looks.

1. THE PLACE OF MARK'S GOSPEL IN BIBLICAL STUDIES

a. The Historical Neglect of Mark's Gospel

Today the gospel of Mark occupies a prominent place in biblical studies. It was not always so. Even though early tradition associated this gospel with the apostle Peter, it soon was relegated to a position inferior to that of the other gospels. In MSS that include the Gospels, Mark never occupies the first position (except in Codex Bobiensis), and sometimes it occupies the last (e.g., in codices Bezae and Washington). There are few quotations from Mark in the writings of either the apostolic fathers or the second-century apologists. Augustine thought it was an abridgment of Matthew's gospel, despite the fact that in almost every case where there are parallels, Mark's treatment is more detailed. The first commentary on Mark we have any record of is the one by Victor of Antioch in the fifth century AD. He sought in vain to find other commentaries on Mark and finally had to resort to gleaning incidental remarks on its text that he found in commentaries on the other gospels. From the time of Victor till the rise of modern biblical criticism, little attention was paid to Mark's gospel. It is not difficult to explain this neglect. Mark was not written by an apostle (as Matthew and John were), its language was rough and ungrammatical; and it was generally believed to be an abridgment of Matthew. So for centuries Mark remained in the shadows.

b. Emerging from the Shadows: Markan Priority and Growing Interest in the Gospel

In the nineteenth century a dramatic change came. When as a result of modern biblical studies scholars concluded that Mark was the first gospel to be written and that both Matthew and Luke used Mark in some form as a major source for writing their gospels, interest in Mark's gospel skyrocketed. The theory of "Markan priority" became one of the "sure results" of nineteenth-century biblical scholarship. This theory is usually credited to H. J. Holtzmann.[1] Much work on the synoptic problem pointing in the direction of the priority of Mark had been done in Germany before Holtzmann's time, especially by J. B. Koppe, K. Lachmann, G. E. Lessing, H. S. Reimarus, and B. Weisse; but it was Holtzmann who put it all together and popularized the theory.

The immediate response to Holtzmann's work brought Mark's gospel to a place of prominence, especially in the Life-of-Jesus movement of the nineteenth century. Mark was seen as the original gospel, containing the uninterpreted historical facts about Jesus of Nazareth. Whereas Matthew and Luke represented expansions and interpretations of the story of Jesus, Mark was considered to be pure gospel. And since this gospel, with its emphasis on the humanity of Jesus, lent itself in such a remarkable way to the preconceived christological notions of the nineteenth-century liberal theologians, they warmly embraced it. R. P. Martin observes that "with the Life-of-Jesus movement Mark's gospel came into its own, after centuries of neglect. Studies in literary criticism, gospel order, and theological implicates all contrived to push this gospel into a prominent place."[2]

The critical study of Mark's gospel was in full swing. Martin Kähler raised serious doubts about the Life-of-Jesus movement's understanding of Mark's gospel by pointing out the kerygmatic nature of the Markan material (i.e., it contains essentially preaching rather than historical materials).[3] Even more devastating was William Wrede's *The Messianic Secret*.[4] Mark, Wrede argued, is far from being a simple, historical account of the life of Jesus. The truth is, the author had a theological ax to grind. Before the resurrection, belief in Jesus as the Messiah never occurred to anyone. When, however, that belief did arise, there was an attempt to read it back into the accounts of Jesus. The messianic secret in Mark is such an attempt. Wrede's theory was so radical that it did not receive widespread acceptance (see comments at 9:9). Nonetheless,

1. H. J. Holtzmann, *Die synoptischen Evangelien* (Leipzig: Wilhelm Engelmanns, 1863).
2. R. P. Martin, *Mark: Evangelist and Theologian* (Grand Rapids: Zondervan, 1972), 37.
3. Martin Kähler, *The So-called Historical Jesus and the Historic, Biblical Christ* (Philadelphia: Fortress, 1964; German ed., 1896).
4. William Wrede, *The Messianic Secret* (Greenwood, S.C.: Attic, 1971; German ed., 1901).

it succeeded in undermining further the assumption that Mark was a straightforward historical account of the life of Jesus.

c. Form Criticism: Mark as a Repository of Oral Traditions

The next stage in the church's historical study of Mark's gospel came as form criticism—a school of gospel criticism that dominated Markan studies from about 1919 to 1954. Its chief architects were the German scholars R. Bultmann, M. Dibelius, and K. L. Schmidt. The main assumption of form criticism is that the units of gospel tradition circulated orally before they were written down and that in the oral period these units were shaped, even created, by the *Sitz im Leben* (life setting) of the early Christian community. This tradition, already formed and shaped, was collected and pieced together into our canonical gospels. Thus the gospel writers were essentially scissors-and-paste men—collectors, compilers, vehicles of tradition. The gospels themselves are more the products of the community than of the individual authors to whom they are ascribed. Furthermore, they record the history of the church more than the history of Jesus.

This approach to the Gospels doubted the possibility of an account of Jesus in any truly historical sense. Schmidt insisted that there were only separate units of tradition artificially put together, usually on a topical rather than a chronological basis; and since these units reflect more the life of the church than that of Jesus, they have little historical value.

Form criticism also undercut the tradition that Mark is based on the eyewitness reminiscences of Peter. It held that this gospel is not to be regarded as a factual apostolic account of Jesus' life but is rather a community product, evoked and shaped by the vicissitudes of early Christianity.

d. Redaction Criticism: Mark as a Purposeful Theological Work

With the emergence of redaction criticism in the 1950s and 1960s, a more positive and constructive approach to the Gospels began. This new direction for Markan studies was initiated by Willi Marxsen. Form criticism, as we have seen, had not assigned any significant role to the gospel writers. They were mere collectors of tradition. Redaction criticism turned attention to the editorial role of the gospel writers (a redactor being an editor). The chief concern was how these authors handled the tradition, both oral and written, that came into their hands. While form criticism dealt with the individual units of tradition, redaction criticism focused on each gospel as a whole and on the distinctive manner in which each evangelist wrote. It is particularly interested in the evangelists as theologians, i.e., as arrangers and shapers of the tradition in order to fulfill a particular theological purpose or set of purposes. Thus this approach recognizes a third life setting in the production of the Gospels. Not only are there (1) the life setting of Jesus and (2) that of the early church, but there is also (3) that of the evangelist himself. Redaction criticism deals especially with investigating this third *Sitz im Leben*.

In Marxsen's hands, redaction criticism does less than justice to the historicity of Mark by treating much of the gospel as the creative work of the evangelist. This approach, however, results more from Marxsen's faulty presuppositions about the nature of the tradition than from his interpretive method. In the hands of more conservative scholars, redaction criticism respects the historical reliability of the Gospels while offering valuable insights into the author's theological purpose and plan.

e. Narrative Criticism: Mark as Story

The last thirty years have seen the emergence of a variety of new literary methods for the study of the Gospels.[5] The most influential of these methods is narrative criticism, which seeks to study the Gospels as literary wholes rather than as editorial compilations. Groundbreaking narrative critical work on Mark's gospel was done by David Rhoads and Donald Michie.[6]

Both redaction and narrative criticism study the Gospels in their final forms, but the focus of the former is on the history of the text, the manner in which the evangelists edited their sources. Redaction critics have tended to focus on alterations and additions while mostly ignoring those traditions the evangelists brought over unchanged from their sources. Narrative criticism seeks to correct this oversight by examining each gospel as a literary unity without concern for putative sources. Narrative critics point out that the Gospels are first and foremost *stories* or *narratives* and should be studied as such. Drawing on categories from modern literary studies, narrative critics point to elements common to all stories, such as narrator, plot, character, and setting.

While redaction critics speak of historical authors' functioning as redactors, narrative critics focus on the narrator—the voice that is heard telling the story. All stories have narrators, though they can function in various ways. Narrators may speak in the first person, as a character in the story, or stand external to the story in the third person. All the gospel narrators speak in the third person (though Luke's second volume, Acts, has several first-person sections). Narrators may express limited knowledge of events and characters or may "omnisciently" describe the internal motivations of characters. The gospel narrators generally take the omniscient approach, as shown by their describing the thoughts of Jesus and his opponents at various points. The narrators expect the reader to adopt their point of view and to trust their words as reliable.

Though both form and redaction critics speak of pericopes—discrete units of oral and written tradition—narrative critics describe events, scenes, and acts that carry the drama forward. *Plot* refers to the progress of the story as it moves through causative actions from conflict to crisis to climax and finally to resolution. In addition to plot, all narratives have characters and settings. *Characters* may function in positive (protagonist) or negative (antagonist) roles, or somewhere in between. They can be complex and unpredictable ("round characters") or simple and stereotyped ("flat characters"). Jesus, of course, is the chief protagonist of all four canonical gospels. Satan, demons, and religious leaders are the primary antagonists. The disciples are on Jesus' side, but they waver—especially in Mark's gospel—and appear in constant danger of failure. The crowds move in various directions but are generally fickle and unreliable. *Setting* refers to all the elements associated with the narrative world of the text, including local, temporal, and social settings. The Gospels, for example, are set in the first-century world of Judaism, during the Roman Empire's rule of Palestine. More localized settings such as the wilderness, the Sea of Galilee, and the city of Jerusalem are also significant.

These and other literary categories are utilized by narrative critics to describe the narrative world of the text and the manner in which the story functions to produce its desired effect.[7]

---

5. In addition to narrative criticism, other recent methods that have been utilized to study Mark include rhetorical criticism, canonical criticism, structuralism, reader-response criticism, and feminist and liberationist approaches.
6. David Rhoads and Donald Michie, *Mark as Story: An Introduction to the Narrative of a Gospel* (Philadelphia: Fortress, 1982).
7. A good introduction to the methods and categories of narrative criticism can be found in Mark Allen Powell's *What Is Narrative Criticism?* (Minneapolis: Fortress, 1990).

The greatest strength of narrative criticism is that it recognizes the literary character of the Gospels. The evangelists chose narrative as the genre through which to communicate the Jesus event, and narrative criticism takes this genre seriously. Much insight can be gained from studying the progress of their plots, the characterization of the players, and the significance of various settings. A potential weakness of narrative criticism is rejection of the historical nature of the gospel. Some narrative critics treat the Gospels more as novels than as historical narrative. Yet the gospel writers clearly had historical as well as literary and theological concerns in mind as they produced their works.

The present commentary is eclectic in its methodology and draws insights from both redaction and narrative criticism. We will assume an historical author who drew from both written and oral sources to produce the gospel. At the same time, we will treat the gospel as a literary unity and follow the narrative as it progresses from conflict to resolution. Since most NT scholars hold to Markan priority, the redaction of Matthew and Luke may be discerned through studying their alterations of Mark. Redaction criticism is more difficult for Mark, since its sources are no longer directly available to us. Though evidence of Mark's sources may sometimes be detected through language and stylistic variation, conclusions in that regard are subjective and remain speculative; therefore, narrative criticism—studying the gospel narrative as a whole—is a particularly valuable tool for studying Mark's dramatic and fast-paced story.

2. GENRE

Mark's story, like those of Matthew, Luke, and John, came to be known in the early church as "gospel" (*euangelion*, GK *2295*; see Justin Martyr, *1 Apol.* 66:3). But what is a gospel? A vigorous debate has taken place in recent years concerning the genre of the Gospels and their relationship to other ancient literature. Some scholars have claimed that the Gospels are unique in the ancient world, that they represent a *sui generis* created by the early Christians. This view was particularly popular among form critics, who considered the Gospels to be nonliterary collections of oral traditions, or "folk literature." The Gospels were treated as products of the Christian community rather than of individual authors.

The last thirty years have seen much greater emphasis on the Gospels as literary works. Today scholars recognize that the gospel writers were not merely collectors of traditions but were true literary artists who intentionally crafted their narratives. This recognition has generated renewed interest in the relationship of the Gospels to other ancient literary forms. A growing consensus recognizes that the Gospels have much in common with certain Greco-Roman works, especially the broad category of writings known as "biographies" or "lives" (*bioi*) of famous people.[8] But the reader should note that the Gospels are not biographies in a modern sense; they do not provide a full historical account of the background, birth, life, and death of a historical figure. Mark, for example, tells us nothing about the birth or family background of Jesus. Ancient Greco-Roman *bioi* were written to preserve the memory and celebrate the virtues, teachings, and exploits of great philosophers, statesmen, and rulers. Examples of this general category are Plutarch's *Parallel Lives*, Suetonius's *Lives of the Caesars*, and the Jewish philosopher Philo's *Life of Moses*. Since the Gospels arose in

8. See Richard A. Burridge, *What Are the Gospels? A Comparison with Graeco-Roman Biography* (2d ed.; Grand Rapids: Eerdmans, 2004).

the Greco-Roman world of the first century, it is profitable to compare them to writings of that era and to identify the literary features and narrative techniques they have in common.

The Gospels are also unique in many ways. They were not written simply to preserve the memory or pass on the teachings of a great leader or teacher. The writers believed that with the coming of Jesus, God's plan of salvation was being fulfilled. They wrote, therefore, to proclaim the good news of salvation and to call people to faith in Jesus Christ, the risen Lord and Savior. Mark writes as a preacher and emphasizes Jesus' saving ministry. (About one-third of his gospel is devoted to Jesus' passion.) He calls his work a "gospel" because it contains the good news proclaimed.

This understanding of Mark's gospel as "proclamation" should not be used to deprecate the historical nature of the material it contains. The preaching enshrined by the gospel arose out of the historical events of the career of Jesus. Without that history, the good news that constitutes the gospel does not exist. Eduard Schweizer, after stressing the kerygmatic ("proclamatory") nature of Mark's gospel, remarks, "And yet it is really a history book, since Mark knows that these essentials [of the preached good news] will not be found anywhere except in the record of the events of these years [of the ministry of Jesus]."[9]

We may summarize by identifying Mark's gospel as *historical narrative motivated by theological concerns*. The gospel is similar in many respects to ancient *bioi*, yet also unique. Mark writes "story," but it is a narrative firmly anchored in the historical events of the man Jesus of Nazareth. His motivation is not merely historical but also theological; he arranges and interprets the tradition to address the needs and concerns of his hearers. His ultimate goal is to proclaim the good news of salvation accomplished by God through the life, death, and resurrection of God's Son, Jesus Christ, and to call people to faith in him.

3. AUTHORSHIP

a. Early Tradition and Internal Considerations

Although the gospel of Mark—like the other three gospels—is anonymous, there is a strong and early tradition that Mark was its author and that he was closely associated with the apostle Peter, from whom he obtained his information about Jesus. The earliest reference is found in the writings of the church historian Eusebius, who quoted from a lost work (*Exegesis of the Lord's Oracles*) written by Papias, bishop of Hierapolis, about AD 140. Papias, in turn, quotes "the Elder," probably the elder John, referred to elsewhere by Eusebius. The quotation in Eusebius is as follows:

> The Elder said this also: Mark, who became Peter's interpreter, wrote accurately, though not in order, all that he remembered of the things said or done by the Lord. For he had neither heard the Lord nor been one of his followers, but afterwards, as I said, he had followed Peter, who used to compose his discourses with a view to the needs of his hearers, but not as though he were drawing up a connected account of the Lord's sayings. So Mark made no mistake in thus recording some things just as he remembered them. For he was careful of this one thing, to omit none of the things he had heard and to make no untrue statements therein.[10]

9. Eduard Schweizer, *The Good News According to Mark* (London: SPCK, 1971), 24.
10. Eusebius, *Hist. eccl.* 3.39.15.

This tradition suggests several important points about Mark's gospel: (1) behind Mark is the eyewitness account and apostolic authority of Peter; (2) Mark did not write his account about Jesus in chronological sequence; (3) nevertheless Mark was careful to record accurately what Peter said.

The Papias tradition, with its insistence on the apostolic, eyewitness source of Mark's gospel, runs counter to the form-critical understanding of the tradition. Yet to accept Mark's dependence on Peter does not rule out Mark's role as the redactor and narrator of the received tradition. There may even be a hint of this possibility in Papias's reference to Mark's consequential arrangement of the tradition. If the tradition he received from Peter was in the form of disconnected homilies, Mark had much work to do in transforming Peter's preaching into a gospel narrative. This task would allow him the freedom to impress on the received tradition his own theological concerns with a view to the special needs of the community he addressed. There seem no compelling reasons for rejecting the Papias tradition—even if Papias's immediate concern was to establish the apostolic authority of Mark in the face of Marcion's championing of the gospel of Luke.[11]

Another early tradition, the Anti-Marcionite Prologue to Mark (AD 160–80; preface attached to the gospel of Mark in a number of Old Latin MSS), mentions Mark as a gospel writer and connects him with Peter. The passage, which is fragmentary, reads, " ... Mark declared, who is called 'stump-fingered' because he had short fingers in comparison with the size of the rest of his body. He was Peter's interpreter. After the death of Peter himself he wrote down this same gospel in the regions of Italy." The two items of additional information found here are (1) Mark wrote his gospel after the death of Peter, and (2) he wrote it in Italy.

Irenaeus (ca. AD 180) adds his testimony in agreement with the Anti-Marcionite Prologue: "And after their [Peter's and Paul's] death, Mark, the disciple and interpreter of Peter, himself also handed down to us in writing the things preached by Peter."[12]

The first line of the Muratorian Canon (ca. AD 200) that has been preserved reads, "at which he was present so he wrote them down." The immediate context of the line makes it clear that "he" refers to Mark and "which" refers to the preaching of Peter.

The importance of the tradition cited above is increased by its geographical spread. At least three different church centers are represented: Hierapolis (Papias), Rome (Anti-Marcionite Prologue and the Muratorian Fragment), and Lyons (Irenaeus).[13] The tradition is repeated later by Tertullian of North Africa and Clement of Alexandria.

In addition to the early tradition, several other considerations point to Markan authorship and his association with Peter.

- It seems unlikely that the church would have deliberately assigned the authorship of a gospel to a person of secondary importance such as Mark, who was neither one of the Twelve nor otherwise prominent in the early church, unless there were strong historical reasons for doing so.

11. See Martin, *Mark: Evangelist and Theologian*, 80–83.

12. Irenaeus, *Haer.* 3.1.2.

13. See William L. Lane, *The Gospel According to Mark* (NICNT; Grand Rapids: Eerdmans, 1974), 10.

- The earliest titles we have on gospel MSS identify them simply as "According to Matthew," "According to Mark," etc. While some critics claim these titles were added in the middle of the second century in order to provide authority to anonymous documents, Martin Hengel has argued that these titles were attached to the Gospels very early, as soon as they began to be distributed to various church communities. Such titular attachment would be necessary, he says, in order to distinguish one gospel from another. Hengel also points to the remarkable unanimity of titles, which can only be accounted for by such early attestation. If the titles were added later, each church would have given them different titles.[14]
- The early church tradition that Mark became the apostle Peter's companion also holds up under scrutiny. This connection to the most prominent of Jesus' disciples would explain why the gospel found immediate acceptance within the church. Assuming Markan priority, it would also explain why Matthew and Luke would readily accept its authority and use it as a source for their own works. The association of Mark with Peter finds incidental support in 1 Peter 5:13, where Peter sends greetings from "my son Mark."

B. John Mark in the Biblical Tradition

So who was this Mark who was associated with Peter in the early tradition and identified as the author of the gospel? Although Mark was a common name in both Greek and Latin, the most likely candidate is the John Mark of the NT. He is first mentioned in connection with his mother, who lived in the house in Jerusalem that Peter went to after his release from prison (Ac 12:12). Mark accompanied Paul and Barnabas, the latter of whom was Mark's cousin, when they returned to Antioch from Jerusalem after the famine-relief visit (Ac 12:25). Mark next appears as a "helper" (*hypēretēs*) to Paul and Barnabas on their first missionary journey (Ac 13:5). Mark's precise function is not clear; but whatever its nature, it brought him into close relationship with Paul and Barnabas.

Unfortunately, Mark did not last long as a missionary helper. At Perga in Pamphylia, he deserted to return to Jerusalem (Ac 13:13). Paul must have felt strongly about Mark's behavior on this occasion, because when Barnabas proposed taking Mark on the second journey, Paul flatly refused—a decision that caused Barnabas to separate from Paul (Ac 15:36–39). Barnabas took Mark and sailed for Cyprus. No further mention is made of either of them in the book of Acts.

In the epistles Mark is seen with Paul at Rome at the time of the writing of Colossians. It is clear this Mark is the same man, since Paul calls him "the cousin of Barnabas." Paul sends Mark's greetings and adds, "You have received instructions about him; if he comes to you, welcome him" (Col 4:10; cf. Phm 24, written at the same time). Apparently, Mark was at this point just beginning to win his way back into Paul's confidence. By the end of Paul's life, Mark was back in full favor. From Rome Paul wrote to Timothy, "Get Mark and bring him with you, because he is helpful to me in my ministry" (2Ti 4:11). Peter also witnesses to Mark's presence in Rome about this time (1Pe 5:13).

In summary, we may say that though strictly speaking Mark's gospel is anonymous, the early tradition of the church identifies the author as Mark, who was closely associated with the apostle Peter and from

14. See Martin Hengel, *Studies in the Gospel of Mark* (Philadelphia: Fortress, 1985), 74–81.

whom he received the tradition of the things said and done by the Lord. This tradition probably did not come to Mark as a finished, sequential account of the life of Jesus but in the form of the preaching of Peter—preaching that had been directed to the needs of the early Christian community. It is this material, arranged and shaped by Mark, that forms the nucleus of this gospel.

It is important to keep in mind, however, that the author does not explicitly identify himself. This was not *his* gospel, it was the gospel of Jesus Christ, the common inheritance of the church. The intentional anonymity and relative uncertainty of authorship should also serve as a caution while reading the gospel. The reader should allow the narrative to speak for itself rather than imposing on it presumed traits about John Mark's personality gleaned from elsewhere in the NT. To suggest, for example, that John Mark's failure on Paul's first missionary journey is expressed in the failure of the disciples in the gospel risks imposing something foreign and perhaps unintended on the narrative. The same may be said about the likely historical setting and original audience of the gospel. Though we will suggest below that Mark's gospel was probably written to the persecuted church in Rome, this suggestion remains a hypothesis and should not govern the exegesis of the text.

4. ORIGIN AND DESTINATION

a. A Single Destination?

Modern research on the Gospels has tended to assume that each of the four was written to a particular Christian community to address certain needs and concerns associated with that community. A further assumption is that the author was a member of that community, so that the provenance (place of writing) and the destination are the same. Within this framework, scholars seek to "read between the lines" of individual gospel stories to reconstruct the communal situation in which that gospel arose. In its extreme form, this perspective claims that the Gospels tell us more about the concerns of Christian communities than about the historical Jesus.

This single-destination assumption for the Gospels has been recently challenged by Richard Bauckham and others.[15] Bauckham argues that the Gospels were not written to individual Christian churches but instead were intended for the broader Christian community. Evidence for this view are the communication and travel among Christian groups represented in Paul's letters and other early Christian writings. First-century churches were not isolated communities but parts of a close network of churches scattered throughout the Roman Empire. In such an environment, the evangelists are unlikely to have written and addressed their works to a single church. A more general audience is also suggested by the literary interdependence of the Gospels. The likelihood that both Matthew and Luke used Mark as one of their sources suggests that Mark's gospel was widely circulated among first-century churches. Bauckham asserts that scholars have wrongly compared the Gospels to the letters of Paul, which *are* addressed to specific communities to address needs and concerns within them. Yet Paul's letters were substitutes for his presence. No such analogy holds for the Gospels, since the authors are assumed to be members of the community

15. See, e.g., Richard Bauckham, ed., *The Gospels for All Christians: Rethinking the Gospel Audiences* (Grand Rapids: Eerdmans, 1998).

to which they are writing. They would more naturally have addressed the concerns of that community through oral instruction rather than through written literature. "Indeed, why should [the gospel writer] go to the considerable trouble of writing a gospel for a community to which he was regularly preaching?"[16]

Bauckham's conclusions have much to commend them and provide an important corrective to the notion of isolated Christian communities, each with its own idiosyncratic beliefs. Yet he probably goes too far in denying a specific occasion and destination for the Gospels. Joel Marcus points out that the anonymity of the Gospels may itself point to a local address, since no byline would have been necessary.[17] Furthermore, the fact that all three Synoptic Gospels survived, despite their similarities and differences, suggests that they were written in and for distinct Christian communities. Matthew and Luke likely viewed their works as authoritative replacements for Mark. Yet Mark survived, thus suggesting local support for each of the Synoptics and some distance between their target audiences. Nor is it as odd as Bauckham asserts that the writers would produce written works for their own communities. The goal of such literature might be to record authoritative teaching for the next generation, especially as eyewitnesses pass from the scene. Marcus points to several examples of early Jewish and Christian literature—including the sectarian writings of the Dead Sea Scrolls—that appear to have been written specifically for the community in which they arose.

There is also evidence in the Gospels themselves for a specific destination. Mark's reference in 15:21 that Simon of Cyrene was "the father of Alexander and Rufus" is most easily explained if Mark's audience personally knew Simon's sons. Since Alexander and Rufus are not mentioned elsewhere in Christian literature, it seems unlikely that an author would have intended this reference to be for all churches everywhere. In fact, both Matthew and Luke independently omit the reference, presumably because it would have meant little to their readers.

While this debate between a general and a specific audience remains unresolved, the truth probably lies between two extremes. The gospel writers were certainly members of Christian communities and would most naturally have written with the needs and concerns of their own church (or churches) in mind. At the same time, it is unlikely that these communities were isolated from the larger network of first-century churches or that they practiced their own distinct and unique versions of Christianity. Even if the gospel writers wrote first and foremost with regard to the needs of their own communities, they would have kept a broader Christian audience in mind in the expectation that their work would be copied and distributed among other churches.

b. A Roman Origin and Destination

The most widely suggested place of origin and intended destination of Mark's gospel is Rome and the persecuted church there. Early church tradition locates the writing of the gospel either "in the regions of Italy" (Anti-Marcionite Prologue) or in Rome (Irenaeus, Clement of Alexandria). These church fathers also closely associate Mark's writing of the gospel with the apostle Peter. The above evidence is consistent with (1) the historical likelihood that Peter was in Rome toward the end of his life and probably was martyred there and (2) the biblical evidence that Mark was in Rome about the same time and was closely

16. Richard Bauckham, "For Whom Were the Gospels Written?" in *The Gospels for All Christians*, 29.

17. Joel Marcus, *Mark 1–8: A New Translation with Introduction and Commentary* (AB 27; New York: Doubleday, 2000), 26–27.

associated with Peter (cf. 2Ti 4:11 and 1Pe 5:13, where the word "Babylon" is probably a cryptogram for "Rome"). Further, quotations from Mark's gospel first appear in 1 Clement 15:2 and Hermas (*Sim.* 5:2), both of which writings are associated with Rome.

The only contrary witness in the early tradition is given by Chrysostom, who locates Mark's writing in Egypt (*Hom. Matt.*); but he has probably misunderstood the statement of Eusebius: "They say that Mark set out for Egypt and was first to preach there the gospel which he composed."[18]

Internal evidence also points to a Roman, or at least a Gentile, origin and destination for the gospel. Mark explains Jewish customs that would be unfamiliar to Gentile readers (7:2–4; 15:42). He translates Aramaic words into Greek (3:17; 5:41; 7:11, 34; 15:22). He uses Latinisms and Latin loanwords. While this feature by itself could not confirm a Roman audience (since Latinisms were used through the Roman Empire), the large number of them—especially in comparison with Matthew and Luke—would suggest a readership in or around Rome. Hengel notes especially the explanation of the Greek coin *lepton* as a *quadrans*, a Roman coin (12:42), and the courtyard (*aulē*) as the Praetorium (15:16). Such explanations would have been unnecessary to an audience in the East.[19] Mark also reveals a special interest in persecution and martyrdom (8:34–38; 13:9–13), subjects particularly relevant to Roman Christians. And finally, the immediate acceptance and widespread influence of his gospel (Matthew and Luke having built their gospels on Mark) suggests a powerful church behind it. No church better fits that description than Rome.

c. Other Suggestions for Origin and Destination

While a Roman origin for Mark's gospel remains a hypothesis, other suggested locations—such as Syria (D. Lührmann, D. Bartlett, J. Marcus) or Galilee (W. Marxsen, E. Lohmeyer, W. H. Kelber)—garner even less support. The Galilean proposal is adduced primarily from the fact that Mark places so much emphasis on Galilee throughout the gospel. This feature alone, however, is hardly sufficient to seal the case. Jesus' early Galilean ministry and his choice of Galilean disciples are surely based on firm historical traditions. There is no evidence that Mark emphasized Jesus' Galilean ministry to reflect his own community's life situation. A more robust defense has been put forth for Syria. Joel Marcus doubts the Roman hypothesis since the persecution described in the gospel—especially in Mark 13—does not really fit the persecution in Rome under the emperor Nero.[20] (On Nero's actions, see pp. 686–87.) In the Olivet Discourse, Jesus speaks of standing before governors and kings, being handed over to local councils, and being flogged in the synagogues (13:9). These afflictions sound much more like the sporadic persecutions experienced by Christian missionaries throughout the empire than the concentrated actions of a single emperor toward Christians in Rome. If the context were Rome, Marcus argues, we would expect more specific allusions to a Nero-like pagan king something like the descriptions of the "beasts" in Daniel 7 and Revelation 13. The "abomination of desolation" in the temple (Mk 13:14) cannot refer to Nero since he never visited or planned to visit Palestine. Marcus also rejects the linguistic data adduced for a Roman audience. In 12:42

18. Eusebius, *Hist. eccl.* 2.16.1.

19. Hengel, *Studies in the Gospel of Mark*, 29.

20. Marcus, *Mark 1–8*, 30–33.

and 15:16, Mark is not substituting Western terms for Eastern equivalents "but explaining imprecise Greek words by means of precise Latin ones."[21]

While noting important shortcomings with a Roman provenance, Marcus lacks much positive support for Syria. He bases his conclusion primarily on the assumption that Mark 13 and the gospel in general mirror the events of the Jewish revolt of AD 66–73. Galilee is an unlikely location, he claims, since the gospel assumes a primarily Gentile audience and since Galilee would have been in a state of war—hardly a community with the time, resources, or inclination to produce a gospel. Syria, on the other hand, was a predominantly Gentile region close enough to experience the effects of the war. This fact alone, however, does not produce a convincing case for a Syrian origin. While Mark may indeed see storm clouds on the horizon for Jerusalem (13:14: "let the reader understand"), there is little necessity to conclude that he is viewing these events from Syria. The gospel tradition that Jesus did in fact predict the destruction of Jerusalem is very strong, thus making it likely that Mark 13 is recording authentic dominical tradition rather than composing after-the-fact "prophecy." Even without assuming the reality of divine prophecy, Jesus could have predicted the events of AD 70. Other prophets and doomsayers of Jesus' day predicted the city's destruction.[22] Mark's descriptions of the siege are quite general, and they do not seem to have been written after the fact from an eyewitness perspective. Furthermore, as Marcus himself notes, the persecutions described in Mark 13:9–12 look more like sporadic local persecutions than a single cataclysmic event such as the siege and destruction of the holy city.

Other evidence Marcus adduces for a Syrian origin is even weaker. He claims Jesus' castigation of the religious authorities for allowing the temple to become "a den of thieves" (Mk 11:17; cf. Jer 7:11) may point to the seizure of the temple by a group of revolutionary zealots during the war. This action may also constitute the "abomination of desolation" of Mark 13:14. Further, according to Marcus, the fact that the revolution was apparently led by messianic pretenders may explain Mark's ambivalence toward the Davidic lineage of the Messiah. These proposals seem strained at best. Better interpretations of these texts may be found in Mark's larger theological and narrative purposes. Jesus' condemnation of the temple sellers, like his cursing of the fig tree, is almost certainly a broader indictment of Israel's spiritual state rather than an allusion to a specific event during the Jewish War. While Mark's description of Jesus' messianic identity certainly exhibits ambivalence toward the popular image of a conquering Davidic king, this is part of his larger redefinition of the meaning of Jesus' messiahship. Messianic pretenders of various sorts appeared in Israel throughout the first century, not only during the war.

While Marcus's conclusions should caution against too much optimism concerning a Roman provenance, his sparse arguments are hardly enough to overturn the cumulative weight of church tradition and internal considerations in favor of Rome. Yet while we acknowledge a Roman origin for Mark as most likely, this perspective will not control our exegesis of the gospel's individual passages. As noted above, introductory issues such as authorship, date, provenance, and destination are matters of conjecture with reference to the Gospels and should take second place to an analysis of the narrative and theological themes of the Gospels themselves.

21. Ibid., 32.

22. See Josephus, *J.W.* 6.5.3.

5. DATE

As with the place of origin, it is not possible to date the writing of Mark's gospel with certainty. Some evidence suggests a date in the 50s or early 60s of the first century: (1) Clement of Alexandria claimed Mark wrote while Peter was ministering in Rome.[23] Eusebius adds that Peter came to Rome when Claudius was emperor, in other words, sometime between AD 41–54.[24] (2) Since Peter is in Jerusalem in Acts 15, around AD 49, then he must have come to Rome after that date, perhaps in the early 50s. That Peter seems to have been in Corinth—or was at least known to the Corinthians—before Paul wrote 1 Corinthians, around AD 55 (see 1Co 1:12; 3:22; 9:5), may also suggest Peter's westward travels in the 50s (cf. the Asia Minor destination of 1 Peter). (3) Church tradition tells us Peter was martyred during the persecutions of the emperor Nero, around AD 64–67. This would allow for a date anytime from the mid 50s to the early 60s. A date in the 50s would fit a solution of the Synoptic Problem that sees Mark as the first gospel written. If Luke used Mark as a source, and if he completed Acts while Paul was still in prison in Rome (ca. AD 62; see Ac 28:30–31), then Mark must have been written prior to this imprisonment, i.e., in the 50s or very early 60s.

Most scholars, however, prefer a date in the late 60s or post-AD 70. Both Irenaeus and the Anti-Marcionite Prologue claim that Mark's gospel was written *after* the death of Peter. Irenaeus says that Paul also was dead at the time of its writing.[25] These claims would mean a terminus a quo (earliest possible date) for Mark of AD 64, the year of the martyrdom of Peter, or if Irenaeus is correct, AD 67, the most likely year of Paul's death.

Concerning internal evidence, the general tone of persecution throughout the gospel could go with either the earlier or later dates, since such trials characterized the church from its earliest days. But the cryptic narrative aside in Mark 13:14, "let the reader understand," in the context of Jerusalem's destruction (13:2) seems to suggest that Mark has the Jewish War of AD 66–74 in view. Scholars are divided, however, as to whether Mark writes in the time leading up to the war, during its early stages, or after Jerusalem's destruction in AD 70. A date before AD 70 seems most likely, since Mark descriptions are very general and—as noted above—do not seem to have been composed after the fact. Also, the likely use of Mark by Matthew and Luke would argue against a date much later than AD 70. Although we cannot be certain, the best estimate seems to be in the last half of the decade AD 60–70. This date embraces the period immediately following the great fire of AD 64, when intense persecution began to be directed against Christians in Rome. Many believe that Mark wrote to meet this crisis in the Roman church.

6. OCCASION AND PURPOSE

Concerning the occasion and purpose of Mark's gospel, scholars have tended toward three general directions, seeing the gospel's purpose as primarily catechetical, pastoral, or theological.

Catechetical: The need to preserve apostolic tradition for posterity. As the original apostles were beginning to pass from the scene, Mark saw the need to record for posterity the apostolic witness concerning

---

23. Clement of Alexandria, *Hypotyposeis* 6; cited by Eusebius, *Hist. eccl.* 2.15; 6.14.5–7.

24. Eusebius, *Hist. eccl.* 2.14.6.

25. Irenaeus, *Haer.* 3.1.1.

Jesus. As we have seen, the church fathers repeatedly stress Mark's intention to record Peter's teaching. One argument sometimes used against this purpose is the church's preference for oral teaching over written material, so there would be little perceived need for a written record of the acts and teachings of Jesus. This argument, however, overgeneralizes the situation. While it is certainly true that oral tradition was highly valued in Jewish and Christian contexts and that a church father such as Papias stated his preference for the oral word over the written,[26] there is much evidence for the great respect given to the written word as a means of passing down authoritative tradition: the great reverence for Torah in Judaism, the large body of Second Temple Jewish literature, and the widespread reproduction and dissemination of the early Christian letters and gospels. In this milieu it is not difficult to envisage Mark's desire to provide a written record of the "gospel" of Jesus being proclaimed by the church.

Pastoral: A call to the church to persevere through persecution. A second suggested purpose for the gospel centers on Mark's call for cross-bearing discipleship in the face of persecution. As we have seen, Mark's gospel has been traditionally associated with Rome and the persecuted church there. More particularly, the occasion has been identified as the persecutions instigated by the emperor Nero in the mid 60s of the first century. In AD 64, a devastating fire broke out in Rome. More than half the city was destroyed; and strong rumors persisted, despite all attempts to quash them, that Nero had himself deliberately set it as an attempt at "urban renewal." Tacitus, the Roman historian, describes the situation that followed:

> But neither human help, nor imperial munificence, nor all the modes of placating heaven, could stifle scandal or dispel the belief that the fire had taken place by order. Therefore, to scotch the rumor, Nero substituted as culprits, and punished with the utmost refinements of cruelty, a class of men, loathed for their vices, whom the crowd styled Christians. Christus, the founder of the name, had undergone the death penalty in the reign of Tiberius, by sentence of the procurator Pontius Pilatus, and the pernicious superstition was checked for a moment, only to break out once more, not merely in Judaea, the home of the disease, but in the capital itself, where all things horrible or shameful in the world collect and find a vogue. First, then, the confessed members of the sect were arrested; next, on their disclosures, vast numbers were convicted, not so much on the count of arson as for hatred of the human race. And derision accompanied their end: they were covered with wild beasts' skins and torn to death by dogs; or they were fastened on crosses, and when daylight failed were burned to serve as lamps by night. Nero had offered his gardens for the spectacle, and gave an exhibition in his circus, mixing with the crowd in the habit of a charioteer, or mounted on his car. Hence, in spite of a guilt that had earned the most exemplary punishment, there rose a sentiment of pity, due to the impression that they were being sacrificed not for the welfare of the state but to the ferocity of a single man.[27]

If the gospel of Mark was written sometime during the period AD 65–67, this passage from Tacitus sheds much light on its life setting. The Roman church was experiencing the fires of persecution. Even martyrdom was not unknown among its members. Mark's purpose in writing was intensely practical. F. C. Grant has observed, "He was writing a book for the guidance and support of his fellow Christians in a situation of intense crisis. The martyrdoms had fallen off, but there was no assurance—with Nero on

---

26. See Eusebius, *Hist. eccl.* 3.39.4.
27. Tacitus, *Ann.* 15.44.

the throne—when they might begin again; the last days could not be far off (ch. 13), and every Christian's lamp must be trimmed, every Christian's loins girded for the struggle."[28]

While the Neronian persecutions represent a likely occasion, it is not the only possible one. The gospel may reflect an earlier period, such as the riots between Jews and Jewish Christians in Rome in AD 49–50. These disputes prompted the emperor Claudius to expel the Jewish population from Rome (see Ac 18:2).[29] Mark's reference in 13:9 suggests that—at least in part—he is addressing the sporadic outbursts of violence against Christians coming both from the synagogue and from governmental officials. Mark's theme of patient endurance of suffering could then fit either the earlier or later dates suggested above for the gospel.

The way Mark prepares his Christian readers for suffering is by placing before them the passion experience of Jesus. Jesus' way was a *via dolorosa* ("way of suffering"). The way of discipleship for Christians is the same way—the way of the cross. About one-third of Mark's gospel is devoted to the death of Jesus. The theme of suffering appears not only in the account of the passion of Jesus; many explicit and veiled references occur elsewhere in the life of Jesus in Mark: in the temptation experience (1:12–13), in the misunderstanding on the part of his family (3:21, 31–35) and people generally (3:22, 30), in his statements about the cost of discipleship (8:34–38), and in his references to persecutions (10:30, 33–34, 45; 13:8, 11–13).

In addition, as R. P. Martin (following W. Popkes), has pointed out, it may be that *meta to paradothēnai ton Iōannēn* in 1:14 should be translated "after John was delivered over to death" rather than "after John was delivered over to prison." If this suggestion is correct, then Mark's interest in John is more theological than historical. He wants to show that "the fate of John and the fate of Jesus run parallel; and both end by their being delivered up by God to death."[30] On this understanding, the implication for the church is clear: faithfulness and obedience as a follower of Jesus Christ will inevitably lead to suffering and perhaps even death.

Theological: The need to correct false or inadequate teachings within the church. Many scholars have suggested a theological occasion and purpose for the gospel. W. Marxsen, in his groundbreaking redaction-critical work on the gospel, claimed that Mark wrote for an *eschatological* purpose—calling the Jerusalem church to flee to Galilee to await the imminent return of Christ. Such a highly specific purpose seems unlikely, since it zeroes in on a verse or two without taking adequate account of Mark's other themes and theology. W. H. Kelber also focuses on eschatology and Galilee, but he proposes a different Markan purpose.[31] With the failure of the kingdom to come in the context of the destruction of Jerusalem and the temple, Mark writes to redefine the kingdom in terms of both time and place. It will take place later than expected and in Galilee rather than Jerusalem.

Many scholars have suggested a *christological* purpose for Mark's gospel, namely, that Mark wrote to emphasize a particular side of Jesus' identity or to correct false or inadequate teachings about Jesus in the church. William Wrede's *The Messianic Secret* was the first major attempt in this direction. As noted above (p. 674), Wrede claimed that Mark invented the messianic secret—whereby Jesus silences those proclaiming his messianic identity—in order to explain Jesus' otherwise unmessianic life. Wrede's thesis has not been

28. F. C. Grant, *The Gospel According to St. Mark* (IB 7; New York: Abingdon, 1951), 633–34.

29. See Suetonius, *Claud.* 25.4.

30. Martin, *Mark: Evangelist and Theologian*, 67.

31. See W. H. Kelber, *The Kingdom in Mark: A New Place and a New Time* (Philadelphia: Fortress, 1974).

widely accepted, especially since the "secret" is constantly broken throughout Mark's gospel (see comments at 9:9). Other christological themes have been proposed. T. J. Weeden suggested that Mark wrote to combat a "divine-man" Christology that identified Jesus as a kind of first-century magician and miracle worker.[32] In response, Mark stresses the sacrificial death of the suffering Son of Man. Others, such as E. Schweizer and R. P. Martin, have suggested that Mark's very human portrait of Jesus was intended to correct the heresy of Docetism, which denied Jesus' true humanity.[33] Martin claims that the occasion for the writing of Mark's gospel should be traced to the "situation which arose after Paul's death or at least, in areas where the influence of Paul's kerygmatic theology had sufficiently been diluted as to suggest a loss of grip on the historical events underlying his kerygma."[34] Mark seeks to correct a Christology that is exalting the divine-man status of Jesus at the expense of his true humanity. Thus in Mark we find the emphasis on Jesus' true humanity, underscored by his sufferings.

Robert Gundry sees in Mark's gospel an *apologetic and evangelistic* purpose. He calls the work an apology for the cross. Mark's primary purpose is not "to keep Christians from apostatizing out of shame for the cross ... but to convert non-Christians despite the shame of the cross."[35]

Not all of these purposes are mutually exclusive, of course, and it is likely that Mark wrote for a variety of reasons. The recurrent church traditions related to Peter and Mark's identification of his work as a written version of the apostolic "gospel" suggest that, at least in part, he is writing to establish an authoritative written record of the Jesus tradition. Second, Mark's strong emphasis on Jesus' powerful messianic identity, together with his equally strong clarification that the Messiah must suffer and die, suggest a theological and christological purpose. Mark seeks to show that Jesus is indeed the Messiah—God's anointed one—not just despite his suffering but also *because* he obeyed the Father's will by taking the path through suffering to glory. Finally, Jesus' repeated calls to his disciples for cross-bearing discipleship also suggest a pastoral and paraenetic purpose. Mark is no ivory-tower theologian. As R. P. Martin has noted, "The nature of the Christian life, as he understands it, carries the same pattern as his Christology. The disciple is bidden to take up his cross and then follow the Lord who entered his glory by way of suffering and outward defeat."[36]

7. LITERARY FEATURES

a. Language and Style

The vocabulary of Mark's gospel is rather limited. He uses 1,270 different words, of which 80 are peculiar to him among the NT writers. Luke's gospel, by contrast, contains 250 words not found elsewhere in the NT.

Mark is fond of transliterating Latin words (at least ten of them) into Greek, and occasionally his Greek shows an underlying Latin construction or expression (cf. *symboulion edidoun* [3:6], *rhapismasin ... elabon* [14:65], and *tini to hikanon poiēsai* [15:15]).

32. See T. J. Weeden, *Mark: Traditions in Conflict* (Philadelphia: Fortress, 1971).

33. See Schweizer, *Good News According to Mark*, 380–86; Martin, *Mark: Evangelist and Theologian*, 153–56.

34. Martin, *Mark: Evangelist and Theologian*, 161.

35. Robert H. Gundry, *Mark: A Commentary on His Apology for the Cross* (Grand Rapids: Eerdmans, 1993), 1026.

36. Martin, *Mark: Evangelist and Theologian*, 161.

A more important influence on Mark's language is Aramaic. He occasionally preserves the original Aramaic words that Jesus used—such as *talitha koum* (5:41), *korban* (7:11), *ephphatha* (7:34), and *Abba* (14:36)—and utilizes Aramaic stylistic features. Some of the more obvious evidences of such features are Mark's use of parataxis (parallel clauses connected by "and") in preference to subordinating clauses; the use of *polla* ("many") as an adverb; the introduction of direct speech with the participle *legōn* ("saying"); the use of the *ērxato* ("began") as a redundant verb; and the use of the genitival pronoun. This strong Aramaic influence accounts in large measure for the rough, ungrammatical Greek often found in Mark's gospel. A. E. J. Rawlinson likens Mark's Greek to that spoken by the lower classes at Rome, especially those who might have come from Palestine or Syria and who spoke Aramaic as their mother tongue.[37]

Although Mark's facility with the Greek language does not match that of Luke or other NT writers, he manages to achieve a remarkably forceful, fresh, and vigorous style. He uses the historical present (present tense verbs used to describe a past event) over 150 times (Matthew 93 times; Luke 11 times). While characteristic of a rougher, less-refined Greek (probably spoken by the author as a second language), the historical present also gives the narrative a vivid and realistic feel, like an on-the-spot report by a newscaster. Translated literally, the account of Jesus' calming of the sea reads, "Leaving the crowd, they are taking him along with them in the boat ... there is arising a fierce gale of wind ... and they are waking him and saying to him ..." (Mk 4:36–38). Mark is also fond of the Greek word *euthys*, an adverb often translated "immediately" (42 times; Matthew 5 times; Luke only once). While the word does not always mean "just then," its effect is forcefully to propel the narrative forward. Intimate details such as one would expect from an eyewitness abound: e.g., the reaction of the crowds (1:27; 2:12); the emotional responses of Jesus (1:41, 43; 3:5; 7:34); and the reactions of the disciples (9:5–6, 10; 10:24, 32).

Another important feature of Mark's style is his vigorous interaction with his readers,[38] accomplished by his (1) directly addressing them (cf. 2:10, where the words "But that you may know that the Son of Man has authority on earth to forgive sins" may be a parenthetical statement by Mark addressed to his Roman readers [see comments at 2:10], and 7:19: "In saying this, Jesus declared all foods clean"); (2) addressing his readers through the words of Jesus (cf. 13:37: "What I say to you, I say to everyone: 'Watch!'"); (3) rhetorical questions addressed to them (cf. the question that ends the account of the stilling of the waves, asked by the disciples but addressed to Mark's readers: "Who is this? Even the wind and the waves obey him" [4:41]). Mark wants his readers to be participants, not mere observers. He wants them to respond to what he tells them about Jesus by saying of him, "He is the Christ, the Son of God."

b. Intercalation or "Sandwiching"

One of Mark's most distinctive literary devices is intercalation—the "sandwiching" of one event between the beginning and end of another. For example, Mark sandwiches Jesus' clearing of the temple in the middle of the account of the cursing and withering of a fig tree (11:12–25). Mark also intercalates the Beelzebul controversy between two episodes relating to Jesus and his family (3:20–35), and the raising of

37. A. E. J. Rawlinson, *The Gospel According to St. Mark* (London: Methuen, 1949), xxxi.

38. See Lane, *The Gospel According to Mark*, 26.

Jairus's daughter frames the healing of the woman with a blood disease (5:21–43). Mark's purpose in using this device is to allow the two events to interpret one another. For example, the withering of the fig tree, like the temple clearing, symbolizes God's judgment against Israel for her unbelief. The rejection of Jesus by his own family symbolically mirrors the rejection by Israel's leaders; and Jairus's need for faith in Jesus is modeled in the faith of the sick woman. Many of Mark's most distinctive themes are illuminated through this rhetorical device.

c. Sets of Threes

Mark often organizes his material topically and is especially fond of patterns of three. Three boat scenes reveal the disciples' lack of faith and comprehension (4:35–41; 6:45–52; 8:14–21). Three times Jesus predicts his death and then teaches his disciples about servant leadership (8:31–38; 9:31–37; 10:32–45). In the Olivet Discourse, Jesus three times calls his disciples to alertness (13:33, 35, 37) and then three times finds them sleeping in Gethsemane (14:37, 40–41). Peter disowns Jesus three times (14:68, 70–71), and the crucifixion is divided into three three-hour intervals (15:25, 33–34). Like a good preacher, the narrator uses repetition to drive his point home.

d. Irony

Mark's central christological theological theme—the Messiah who suffers—is an ironic paradox, and irony plays a major role throughout Mark's narrative.[39] Much of this irony is situational. The opponents of Jesus accuse him of being in league with Satan when, in fact, *they* are opposing God's purpose and kingdom (3:22). They seek to trap him with flattery by calling him a man of truth who teaches the true way of God (12:13–14). Ironically, though the religious leaders do not believe this commendation, the reader knows that it is true. These same leaders mock Jesus on the cross by saying he should come down and save himself if he is truly "the Christ, the King of Israel" (14:31–32). The reader knows that Jesus could indeed come down, but they also know that it is precisely *because* he is the Christ, the King of Israel, that he is suffering as a ransom for sins. It is by refusing to save himself that Jesus will bring salvation to others.

8. BIBLIOGRAPHY

The following is a selective list of commentaries and monographs on Mark, confined for the most part to those referred to in the commentary (they will be referred to simply by the author's name [and initials only when necessary to distinguish two authors of the same surname]). In instances where the same author has written a commentary as well as (a) book(s) and/or (an) article(s), the commentary will be referred to by the author's name, and the book(s)/article(s) by the author's name and short title.

References to resources that do not appear in the bibliography will carry full bibliographic details at the first mention and thereafter a short title.

39. See J. Camery-Hoggat, *Irony in Mark's Gospel: Text and Subtext* (SNTSMS 72; Cambridge: Cambridge Univ. Press, 1992).

A. Commentaries

Anderson, Hugh. *The Gospel of Mark*. New Century Bible Commentary. Grand Rapids: Eerdmans, 1981.
Bratcher, R. G., and E. A. Nida. *Translator's Handbook on Mark*. Leiden: Brill, 1961.
Brooks, James A. *Mark*. New American Commentary. Nashville: Broadman, 1991.
Calvin, John. *Commentary on a Harmony of the Evangelists*. 3 vols. Grand Rapids: Baker, 1979.
Cranfield, C. E. B. *The Gospel According to Saint Mark*. Rev. ed. Cambridge: Cambridge Univ. Press, 1977.
Donahue, John R., and Daniel J. Harrington. *The Gospel of Mark*. Sacra pagina 2. Collegeville, Minn.: Liturgical Press, 2002.
Edwards, James R. *The Gospel According to Mark*. Pillar New Testament Commentary. Grand Rapids: Eerdmans, 2002.
Evans, Craig A. *Mark 8:27–16:20*. Word Biblical Commentary 34B. Nashville: Nelson, 2001.
France, R. T. *The Gospel of Mark*. New International Greek Testament Commentary. Grand Rapids: Eerdmans, 2002.
Garland, David E. *Mark*. NIV Application Commentary. Grand Rapids: Zondervan, 1996.
Gould, E. P. *The Gospel According to Saint Mark*. International Critical Commentary. Edinburgh: T&T Clark, 1932.
Grant, F. C. *The Gospel According to St. Mark*. Interpreter's Bible. New York: Abingdon, 1951.
Guelich, Robert A. *Mark 1–8:26*. Word Biblical Commentary 34a. Waco, Tex.: Word, 1986.
Gundry, Robert H. *Mark: A Commentary on His Apology for the Cross*. Grand Rapids: Eerdmans, 1993.
Hiebert, D. E. *The Gospel According to Mark*. Chicago: Moody, 1974.
Hooker, Morna D. *The Gospel According to St. Mark*. Peabody, Mass.: Hendrickson, 1992.
Hunter, A. M. *The Gospel According to Saint Mark*. Torch Bible Commentary. London: SCM, 1967.
Hurtado, Larry. *Mark*. New International Bible Commentary. Peabody, Mass.: Hendrickson, 1989.
Lane, William L. *The Gospel According to Mark*. New International Commentary on the New Testament. Grand Rapids: Eerdmans, 1974.
Lohmeyer, E. *Das Evangelism des Markus*. Kritisch Exegetischer Kommentar über das Neue Testament. Göttingen: Vandenhoeck & Ruprecht, 1967.
Malina, Bruce J., and Richard L. Rohrbaugh. *Social-Science Commentary on the Synoptic Gospels*. Minneapolis: Fortress, 1992.
Marcus, Joel. *Mark 1–8: A New Translation with Introduction and Commentary*. Anchor Bible 27. New York: Doubleday, 2000.
Mitton, C. L. *The Gospel According to Mark*. London: Epworth, 1957.
Moloney, Francis J. *The Gospel of Mark: A Commentary*. Peabody, Mass.: Hendrickson, 2002.
Moule, C. F. D. *The Gospel According to Mark*. Cambridge Bible Commentary. Cambridge: Cambridge Univ. Press, 1965.
Nineham, D. E. *Saint Mark*. Pelican Gospel Commentary. Baltimore: Penguin, 1963.
Plummer, A. *The Gospel According to St. Mark*. Cambridge Greek Testament Commentary. Cambridge: Cambridge Univ. Press, 1914.
Rawlinson, A. E. J. *The Gospel According to St. Mark*. Westminster Commentaries. London: Methuen, 1949.
Schweizer, Eduard. *The Good News According to Mark*. London: SPCK, 1971.
Swete, H. B. *The Gospel According to St. Mark*. Macmillan New Testament Commentaries. London: Macmillan, 1927.
Taylor, Vincent. *The Gospel According to St. Mark*. London: Macmillan, 1952.
Witherington III, Ben. *The Gospel of Mark: A Socio-Rhetorical Commentary*. Grand Rapids: Eerdmans, 2001.

B. Monographs

Beasley-Murray, G. R. *A Commentary on Mark Thirteen*. London: Macmillan, 1957.
Bock, Darrell. *Blasphemy and Exaltation in Judaism: The Charge against Jesus in Mark 14:53–65*. Grand Rapids: Baker, 2000.
Brown, Raymond. *The Death of the Messiah: From Gethsemane to the Grave. A Commentary on the Passion Narratives in the Four Gospels*. New York: Doubleday, 1994.
Bultmann, R. *History of the Synoptic Tradition*. Rev. ed. Oxford: Blackwell, 1972.
Dalman, Gustav. *Sacred Sites and Ways*. London: SPCK, 1935.
Dodd, C. H. *The Parables of the Kingdom*. Rev. ed. London: Charles Scribner's Sons, 1961.

Dwyer, T. *The Motif of Wonder in the Gospel of Mark.* Journal for the Study of the New Testament Supplement Series 128. Sheffield: Sheffield Academic Press, 1996.

Hengel, Martin. *The Charismatic Leader and His Followers.* New York: Crossroad, 1981.

———. *Crucifixion in the Ancient World and the Folly of the Cross.* Philadelphia: Fortress, 1977.

———. *The Son of God: The Origin of Christology and the History of Jewish-Hellenistic Religion.* Philadelphia: Fortress, 1976.

———. *Studies in the Gospel of Mark.* Philadelphia: Fortress, 1985.

Hull, J. M. *Hellenistic Magic and the Synoptic Tradition.* Studies in Biblical Theology 28. London: SCM, 1974.

Jeremias, Joachim. *Jerusalem in the Time of Jesus.* Minneapolis: Fortress, 1979.

———. *The Parables of the Kingdom.* Rev. ed. New York: Charles Scribner's Sons, 1963.

———. *The Prayers of Jesus.* Philadelphia: Fortress, 1978.

Ladd, G. E. *A Theology of the New Testament.* Rev. ed. Grand Rapids: Eerdmans, 1993.

Manson, T. W. *The Teaching of Jesus: Studies of Its Form and Content.* 2d ed. Cambridge: Cambridge Univ. Press, 1935.

Marcus, Joel. *The Way of the Lord: Christological Exegesis of the Old Testament in the Gospel of Mark.* Louisville, Ky.: Westminster/John Knox, 1992.

Marshall, I. H. *The Origins of New Testament Christology.* Downers Grove, Ill.: InterVarsity, 1976.

Martin, R. P. *Mark: Evangelist and Theologian.* Grand Rapids: Zondervan, 1972.

Marxsen, W. *Mark the Evangelist.* Nashville: Abingdon, 1969.

McKnight, Scot. *Jesus and His Death: Historiography, the Historical Jesus, and Atonement Theory.* Waco, Tex.: Baylor Univ. Press, 2005.

Metzger, Bruce M. *A Textual Commentary on the Greek New Testament.* Rev. ed. Stuttgart: German Bible Society, 1994.

Myers, C. *Binding the Strong Man: A Political Reading of Mark's Story of Jesus.* Maryknoll, N.Y.: Orbis, 1988.

Sanders, E. P. *Judaism: Practice and Belief 63 BCE–66 CE.* Philadelphia: Trinity International, 1992.

Strauss, Mark L. *The Davidic Messiah in Luke-Acts: The Promise and Its Fulfillment in Lukan Christology.* Journal for the Study of the New Testament Supplement Series 110. Sheffield: Sheffield Academic Press, 1995.

Theissen, G. *The Miracle Stories of the Early Christian Tradition.* Studies of the New Testament and Its World. Edinburgh: T&T Clark, 1983.

Van der Loos, Hendrik. *The Miracles of Jesus.* Leiden: Brill, 1965.

Wrede, William. *The Messianic Secret.* Greenwood, S.C.: Attic, 1971. Original German ed. *Das Messiasgeheimnis in den Evangelien.* Cambridge: James Clarke, 1901.

Wright, N. T. *Jesus and the Victory of God.* Minneapolis: Fortress, 1996.

———. *The Resurrection of the Son of God.* Christian Origins and the Question of God. Minneapolis: Fortress, 2003.

9. OUTLINE

- I. Prologue (1:1–13)
  - A. The Heading (1:1–3)
  - B. John Prepares the Way (1:4–8)
  - C. The Baptism of Jesus (1:9–11)
  - D. The Temptation of Jesus (1:12–13)
- II. The Early Galilean Ministry (1:14–3:6)
  - A. The Gospel Proclaimed (1:14–15)
  - B. Authority in Calling the First Disciples (1:16–20)
  - C. Authority in Exorcisms and Healings (1:21–45)
    - 1. Driving Out an Evil Spirit (1:21–28)
    - 2. Healing Simon Peter's Mother-in-law (1:29–31)
    - 3. Healing Many People (1:32–34)
    - 4. Leaving Capernaum (1:35–39)
    - 5. Healing a Leper (1:40–45)
  - D. Conflict with the Religious Leaders (2:1–3:6)
    - 1. Healing a Paralytic (2:1–12)
    - 2. Eating with Sinners (2:13–17)
    - 3. A Question about Fasting (2:18–22)
    - 4. The Lord of the Sabbath (2:23–3:6)
      - a. Picking grain on the Sabbath (2:23–28)
      - b. Healing on the Sabbath (3:1–6)
- III. The Later Galilean Ministry (3:7–6:6a)
  - A. Withdrawal to the Lake (3:7–12)
  - B. Selection of the Twelve (3:13–19)
  - C. Jesus, His Family, and the Beelzebul Controversy (3:20–35)
    - 1. Charged with Insanity (3:20–21)
    - 2. Charged with Demon-Possession (3:22–30)
    - 3. Jesus' True Family (3:31–35)
  - D. Parables about the Kingdom of God (4:1–34)
    - 1. Parable of the Sower (4:1–9)
    - 2. Secret of the Kingdom of God (4:10–12)
    - 3. Interpretation of the Parable of the Sower (4:13–20)
    - 4. Parables of the Lamp and the Measure (4:21–25)
    - 5. Parable of the Secretly Growing Seed (4:26–29)
    - 6. Parable of the Mustard Seed (4:30–32)
    - 7. Summary Statement on Parables (4:33–34)
  - E. Triumph over Hostile Powers (4:35–5:43)
    - 1. Calming the Storm (4:35–41)

2. Healing the Demon-Possessed Man (5:1–20)
3. Healing a Sick Woman and Raising Jairus's Daughter (5:21–43)

F. Rejection at Nazareth (6:1–6a)

IV. Withdrawal from Galilee (6:6b–8:30)
A. Sending Out the Twelve (6:6b–13)
B. Death of John the Baptist (6:14–29)
C. Feeding of the Five Thousand (6:30–44)
D. Walking on the Water (6:45–52)
E. Healings near Gennesaret (6:53–56)
F. Commands of God and Human Traditions (7:1–13)
G. True Defilement (7:14–23)
H. The Faith of the Syrophoenician Woman (7:24–30)
I. Healing a Deaf and Mute Man (7:31–37)
J. Feeding the Four Thousand (8:1–10)
K. Requesting a Sign from Heaven (8:11–13)
L. The Yeast of the Pharisees and Herod (8:14–21)
M. Healing a Blind Man at Bethsaida (8:22–26)
N. Recognizing Jesus as Messiah (8:27–30)

V. The Journey to Jerusalem (8:31–10:52)
A. First Prediction of the Passion (8:31–33)
B. Requirements of Discipleship (8:34–9:1)
C. The Transfiguration (9:2–8)
D. The Coming of Elijah (9:9–13)
E. Healing a Boy with an Evil Spirit (9:14–29)
F. Second Prediction of the Passion (9:30–32)
G. A Question about Greatness (9:33–37)
H. Driving Out Demons in Jesus' Name (9:38–41)
I. Demanding Requirements of Discipleship (9:42–50)
J. Teaching on Divorce (10:1–12)
K. Blessing the Children (10:13–16)
L. Riches and the Kingdom of God (10:17–31)
M. Third Prediction of the Passion (10:32–34)
N. The Request of James and John (10:35–45)
O. Restoring Blind Bartimaeus's Sight (10:46–52)

VI. The Jerusalem Ministry (11:1–13:37)
A. The Triumphal Entry (11:1–11)
B. The Unfruitful Fig Tree (11:12–14)
C. The Cleansing of the Temple (11:15–19)
D. The Withered Fig Tree and Sayings on Faith and Prayer (11:20–25[26])
E. The Question about Jesus' Authority (11:27–33)

F. The Parable of the Tenants (12:1–12)
G. The Question about Paying Taxes to Caesar (12:13–17)
H. The Question of Marriage at the Resurrection (12:18–27)
I. The Question concerning the Great Commandment (12:28–34)
J. The Question about David's Son (12:35–37)
K. The Warning about the Teachers of the Law (12:38–40)
L. The Widow's Offering (12:41–44)
M. The Olivet Discourse (13:1–37)
1. Prophecy of the Destruction of the Temple (13:1–2)
2. The Disciples' Twofold Question (13:3–4)
3. Warnings against Deceivers and False Signs of the End (13:5–8)
4. Warnings of Persecution and Strife and a Call to Steadfastness (13:9–13)
5. The Abomination that Causes Desolation, and the Necessity of Flight (13:14–23)
6. The Coming of the Son of Man (13:24–27)
7. The Lesson of the Fig Tree (13:28–31)
8. The Necessity of Watchfulness (13:32–37)
VII. The Passion and Resurrection Narrative (14:1–16:8[9–20])
A. The Plot to Arrest Jesus (14:1–2)
B. The Anointing at Bethany (14:3–9)
C. The Betrayal by Judas (14:10–11)
D. The Last Supper (14:12–26)
1. Preparation of the Meal (14:12–16)
2. Announcement of the Betrayal (14:17–21)
3. Institution of the Lord's Supper (14:22–26)
E. The Prediction of Peter's Denial (14:27–31)
F. The Agony of Gethsemane (14:32–42)
G. The Betrayal and Arrest (14:43–52)
H. Jesus before the Sanhedrin (14:53–65)
I. Peter's Denial of Jesus (14:66–72)
J. The Trial before Pilate (15:1–15)
K. The Mocking of Jesus (15:16–20)
L. The Crucifixion (15:21–32)
M. The Death of Jesus (15:33–41)
N. The Burial of Jesus (15:42–47)
O. The Resurrection Announced (16:1–8)
Appendix: The Longer Ending (16:9–20)

Text and Exposition

I. PROLOGUE (1:1–13)

OVERVIEW

The first few paragraphs of Mark's gospel serve as an introduction or prologue to the work as a whole. Yet there is considerable debate concerning its parameters. A few commentators (e.g., E. Haenchen, W. Schmithals) see the prologue as continuing only through v.8, since vv.1–8 summarize the ministry of John the Baptist and Jesus first appears on the scene in 1:9. Others (e.g., C. E. B. Cranfield; W. L. Lane; R. H. Gundry; R. T. France) take the prologue through v.13, since these verses serve as a preview and introduction to Jesus' ministry, which begins in v.14. Still others (e.g., J. Marcus; R. A. Guelich) consider the introduction to extend to v.15 because of the inclusio between the *euangelion* (GK *2295*, "good news") of 1:1 and the two occurrences of *euangelion* in vv.14–15. Either of the latter two suggestions makes good sense, since vv.14–15 form a bridge and transition from the introduction of the gospel to the Galilean ministry of 1:16–3:6. The prologue introduces the good news about Jesus (1:1), which is proclaimed for the first time in vv.14–15. We will treat vv.14–15 as the introduction to the next section.

Verses 1–13 can be divided into four parts, the heading introducing the beginning of the gospel as the fulfillment of Scripture (vv.1–3), the ministry of John (vv.4–8), the baptism of Jesus (vv.9–11), and Jesus' temptation (vv.12–13).

A. The Heading (1:1–3)

1 The beginning of the gospel about Jesus Christ, the Son of God.
2 It is written in Isaiah the prophet:

"I will send my messenger ahead of you,
who will prepare your way"—
3 "a voice of one calling in the desert,
'Prepare the way for the Lord,
make straight paths for him.'"

COMMENTARY

1 The first verse functions as a kind of title. It is not clear, however, whether it is intended to refer to the entire gospel, the prologue (vv.1–13 or vv.1–15), the ministry of John the Baptist (vv.1–8), or only the scriptural quotations in vv.2–3. All four make good sense contextually. Since v.2 begins with "just as" (*kathōs*), which normally links with the preceding sentence, the beginning must point at least in part to the scriptural quotations of vv.2–3. Mark seeks to show that the beginning of the gospel was in fulfillment of Scripture. These scriptural quotations in turn point to the ministry of John, the description of which follows (vv.4–8), and throughout the NT the beginning of the gospel is consistently linked to John's ministry (Mt 11:12; Lk 16:16; Jn 1:6; Ac 1:22; 10:37; 13:24). At the same time, the whole book may be seen as "the beginning of the gospel" since it describes the origin of the message of salvation Mark and his community are presently proclaiming. It is also possible that in using the word *archē* (GK 794, "beginning") Mark intentionally echoes the opening verse of the LXX (*en archē*, "in the beginning"; Ge 1:1; cf. Jn 1:1), from a desire that his readers realize his book recounts a new beginning, in which God reveals the good news of Jesus Christ. Taken in this way, the first verse would be not only a title for the entire book but also a claim to its divine origin.

The word "gospel" comes from the old English "godspel" ("good news") and—as noted above—translates the Greek *euangelion*. The Greek word originally meant the reward for bringing good news but later came to mean the good news itself. It was used in the ancient world for announcements such as victory in battle or the enthronement of a ruler. An inscription celebrating the birthday of the Roman emperor Augustus speaks of "good news [*euangelia*] to the world" (*TDNT* 2:722, 724–25). In the OT, the announcement of God's end-time deliverance of his people is sometimes referred to as "good news." Isaiah 52:7 reads, "How beautiful on the mountains are the feet of those who bring good news ... who proclaim salvation, who say to Zion, 'Your God reigns!'" (cf. Ps 96:2; Isa 40:9; 61:1). Jesus probably drew from this OT imagery when he began proclaiming "the good news" that the kingdom of God was at hand. God's great day of salvation had arrived. The early church imitated this use when they identified as "gospel" the message of God's salvation available through the death and resurrection of Jesus Christ. Paul writes in 1 Thessalonians, one of the earliest NT books (ca. AD 50–51), that "our gospel [*euangelion*] came to you not simply with words, but also with power, with the Holy Spirit and with deep conviction" (1:5). Here, as elsewhere, the *euangelion* is the proclamation of the good news about Jesus Christ.

Mark does not identify his book as "*a* gospel" (a particular literary genre); rather, his book recounts *the beginning of the gospel*, how the proclamation of salvation available through Jesus Christ came to be. The book is a written version of the oral proclamation calling people to faith in Jesus. Although Mark does not call his work a gospel, it appears to have been Mark's use of the term that prompted the church to refer to such written accounts as "gospels." "Mark's book has come to be called *a* gospel because it contains *the* gospel—the announcement of the Christian good news" (Moule, 8).

In the rendering "about Jesus Christ," the translators of the NIV have interpreted the Greek genitival construction as an objective genitive: Jesus is the object and content of the gospel. The other main interpretive option is a subjective genitive, "by Jesus Christ," which certainly fits the near context, in which Jesus preaches the good news (vv.14–15). Some interpreters believe the genitive is intentionally ambiguous, with Jesus portrayed as both subject and object—the proclaimer and the proclaimed. This intention is possible, and the parallel "gospel of God" in v.14 suggests similar ambiguity. Jesus' proclamation there is both from God and about God. Against such a dual reference is the linguistic reality that an author *usually* has one sense in mind when writing (unless there is an intentional pun). If a decision must be made, the evidence tips in favor of the objective genitive, since Mark has in view the whole Jesus event—his life, death, and resurrection.

"Jesus" is the Greek form of *Joshua*, which means "Yahweh is salvation" or "salvation of Yahweh." It is the name revealed by the angel to Joseph before Jesus was born, and it was given as descriptive of his mission—"and you are to give him the name Jesus, because he will save his people from their sins" (Mt 1:21). "Christ" (*christos*) is the Greek word for "anointed," behind which is the Hebrew *māšîaḥ*, from which the English word "messiah" ("anointed one") derives. By the time Mark writes, Christians were regularly using the term as a second name for Jesus ("Jesus Christ"), yet in Mark, where it occurs only seven times, the term always carries a titular sense, "the Messiah" (1:1; 8:29; 9:41; 12:35; 13:21; 14:61; 15:32). The TNIV appropriately revises the NIV's "Jesus Christ" to "Jesus the Messiah" (see comments at 8:29 for a fuller discussion of the title).

Some MSS omit the last phrase of v.1, "the Son of God." A decision regarding its originality is very difficult from a textual standpoint. On the one hand, there are good reasons for including the phrase as original. (1) The evidence from the MSS is strong (see Notes at the end of this section). (2) The word's omission may be accounted for by *homoeoteleuton* (a technical term meaning "same ending"), whereby a scribe accidentally omitted the two words *huiou theou*, "Son of God," because the two previous words (*Iēsou Christou*) have the same endings. (3) Son of God is an important theme in Mark's gospel (cf. 1:11; 3:11; 5:7; 9:7; 12:6; 13:32; 14:36, 61; 15:39). The ministry of Jesus begins with the Father's announcement of Jesus' divine sonship at his baptism (1:11) and climaxes with the declaration of the centurion at the foot of the cross, "Surely this man was the Son of God" (15:39).

On the other hand, there is weighty evidence that the phrase is not original to the verse: (1) Some early texts lack it, and several early church writers omit it. (2) It is difficult to imagine how a scribe could have carelessly omitted the words at the very beginning of the book (long before copying fatigue set in). (3) A theologically astute scribe would have been aware of the importance of the title in Mark's gospel and may have introduced it for this very reason.

The scales would seem to tip slightly toward the phrase's original inclusion. Most English versions include it with a note alerting the reader to the alternative. Whether or not the phrase was original does not change the fact that "Son of God" is a critically important title in Mark' s gospel. Taylor, 120, remarks, "Beyond question this title represents the most fundamental element in Mark's Christology."

2–3 Mark cites the OT to show that any true understanding of the ministry of Jesus—the beginning of the gospel—must be firmly grounded there. The verb translated "is written" (v.2) is in the perfect tense. It denotes completed action in the past with continuing results. "It was written and still is" is the sense. The frequency with which this tense of the verb is used by the NT writers to introduce OT quotations underscores their strong belief in the unchanging authority of the Scriptures.

In the KJV (cf. NKJV), "in the prophets" is read for "in Isaiah the prophet." The MS attestation for this reading is very weak. It doubtless arose because the quotations that follow are not only from Isaiah but also include one from Malachi. The first part of the quotation in v.2 agrees verbatim with the LXX of Exodus 23:20a. The second part is from the Hebrew of Malachi 3:1 but differs from both the Hebrew and LXX in reading "your way" instead of "the way before me." By this change in persons, allowance was made for a messianic interpretation of this passage. These two texts were similarly combined by the rabbis (cf. *Exod. Rab.* 23:20), who apparently identified Elijah (Mal 3:1; 4:5–6) with the messenger of Exodus 23:20.

The quotation in v.3 is taken from the LXX's text of Isaiah 40:3, the only difference being the substitution by Mark (or perhaps he found the text already altered) of "of him" for "of our God." This applies the statement to Jesus, since the antecedent is "Lord," a title the early church used for Jesus.

Mark brings together these OT texts in a striking way. He probably found the Exodus text already combined with Malachi 3:1. The two passages occur together in the "Q" text Matthew 11:10// Luke 7:27, and, as noted above, were probably already linked in Jewish rabbinic tradition. The Exodus text originally referred to God's promise of a messenger "to guard you on the way and to bring you to the place I have prepared" (Ex 23:20), i.e., through the wilderness to the Promised Land. Malachi took up this Exodus text and gave to it an eschatological application with reference to a messenger (identified in Mal 4:5–6 as "Elijah") who would go before the Lord to prepare God's people for the great and dreadful "day of the LORD." Mark goes further by linking a third text to this matrix—Isaiah 40:3. In its original context, this Isaiah text predicted a *new exodus*, the Lord's glorious return to his people in their Babylonian exile to lead them in triumph back to the Promised Land. Isaiah depicts a voice calling for the preparation of the way "in the desert" for the coming of Yahweh to his people. Whereas the Hebrew text of Isaiah linked the desert to the preparation of a way, Mark follows the LXX in connecting the desert to the messenger. John the Baptist is the messenger in the desert who will prepare the way for a new and greater exodus deliverance, the revelation of God's salvation in Christ.

So why does Mark identify the prophecy as coming from "Isaiah" if it is a mixed citation? Some suggest Mark was simply mistaken; others, that he is citing from a book of "testimonies," a collection of OT texts that Christians used in their apologetic confrontations with Jews and God-fearers, and that three citations were collected under an "Isaiah" heading. A better solution is that Mark is thinking of the broader context of Isaiah and seeks to present the coming of Jesus as the fulfillment of Isaiah's portrait of God's end-time salvation. Rikki Watts (*Isaiah's New Exodus in Mark* [Grand Rapids: Baker, 2000]) sees Mark's reference to Isaiah as part of an Isaianic "new exodus" motif that runs as a thread throughout Mark's narrative. As the only editorial OT citation in Mark's gospel, this opening text is programmatic for his gospel; it invokes the prophecies of the Isaianic new exodus as the conceptual framework for his whole work. According to Watts, "for Mark the long-awaited coming of Yahweh as King and Warrior has begun, and with it, the inauguration of Israel's eschatological comfort: her deliverance from the hands of the nations, the journey of her exiles to their home and their eventual arrival at Jerusalem, the place of Yahweh's presence" (p. 90).

Watts traces this threefold Isaianic scheme through Mark's gospel. Isaiah's themes of Yahweh-Warrior's defeating Israel's enemy and their idols, and his healing of the people through the ministry of the Servant, correspond to Jesus' exorcisms of demons and healings in the Galilean ministry (Mark 1–7). In Isaiah Yahweh's healing of "blind" Israel and his leading them along the new exodus "way" indicate Israel's need to accept his wisdom as part of her deliverance. Similarly in Mark the restoration of sight in the new exodus "way" entails the "blind" disciples' acceptance of the suffering Messiah (Mk 8–10). Finally, Watts seeks to show that just as the return from the Babylonian exile failed to live up to expectations, so Jesus' arrival in Jerusalem fails to achieve the anticipated glorious enthronement expected in Jerusalem. Instead of being welcomed, Jesus is rejected by the religious leaders and executed (Mk 11–16). The negative response to Jesus, along with their rejection of John, means that, in accordance with Malachi 4, Yahweh's coming to his temple in Jesus is for judgment and a curse.

Another scholar who stresses the pervasive influence of Isaiah in Mark is Joel Marcus (see his *The Way of the Lord*). According to Marcus, Isaiah's "Way of the Lord" is the critical metaphor for Mark's account, with Jesus portrayed as marching through the wilderness as divine warrior, defeating his demonic enemies and establishing God's reign. As noted in the Introduction (pp. 683–84), Marcus locates the provenance of Mark's gospel in Syria during the period of the Roman siege and destruction of Jerusalem. Contrary to claims by the Jewish revolutionaries that God would bring in his kingdom through the destruction of the Romans, Mark presents Jesus as the true divine warrior who defeats Satanic enemies through his sacrificial death on the cross.

Whether the new exodus motif is the controlling one for Mark or merely one among many OT and Isaianic motifs Mark utilizes, it is clear that the citation here places not only the ministry of John but also the whole Jesus event under the banner of the prophetic fulfillment of Scripture.

NOTES

1 See Cranfield, 34–35, for ten possible referents for "the beginning."

The difficulty in reaching a conclusion on the reading υἱοῦ θεοῦ (*huiou theou*, "Son of God") is that the internal and external evidence seem to move in different directions. The transcriptional internal evidence (the tendency of copyists) would favor omission, since it is difficult to see how or why a scribe would omit the phrase. The intrinsic internal evidence (the tendency of authors) favors inclusion because of the title's importance throughout Mark. The external textual evidence favors inclusion, since the title is found in the great majority of MSS. It is, however, missing from the important uncial Sinaiticus (א), though a corrector has added it in the margin. The patristic evidence is difficult to evaluate, since the church fathers sometimes paraphrased or abbreviated their scriptural quotations. Origen omits the phrase, while Irenaeus includes it in two quotations, then omits it in a third. J. Slomp ("Are the Words 'Son of God' in Mark 1:1 Original?" *BT* 28 [1977]: 143–50) has a complete discussion of the evidence.

3 The urgency of the action is stressed by the use of the aorist imperative ἑτοιμάσατε (*hetoimasate*, "Prepare now!"). In the OT passage cited (Isa 40:3), κύριος (*kyrios*, "Lord") refers, of course, to Yahweh. Here it refers to the Lord Jesus.

B. John Prepares the Way (1:4–8)

OVERVIEW

Unlike Matthew and Luke, Mark has no nativity narrative. It is possible that the traditions concerning the birth and infancy of Jesus were unknown to him. More likely they were not useful for Mark's purpose. His concerns are kerygmatic and theological; i.e., he wants to highlight the saving facts and their theological meaning for the church. Thus he immediately begins with the ministry of John the Baptist as the forerunner of the Messiah and the fulfillment of Scripture. This is precisely where Peter begins in his proclamation of the gospel in Acts 10:37: "You know what has happened throughout Judea, beginning in Galilee after the baptism that John preached."

4 And so John came, baptizing in the desert region and preaching a baptism of repentance
for the forgiveness of sins. 5 The whole Judean countryside and all the people of Jerusalem
went out to him. Confessing their sins, they were baptized by him in the Jordan River.
6 John wore clothing made of camel's hair, with a leather belt around his waist, and he
ate locusts and wild honey. 7 And this was his message: "After me will come one more
powerful than I, the thongs of whose sandals I am not worthy to stoop down and untie.
8 I baptize you with water, but he will baptize you with the Holy Spirit."

COMMENTARY

4 John appears suddenly, as "baptizing in the desert region." The word *erēmos* (GK *2245*, "desert," "wilderness") does not necessarily refer to dry, arid land, but means essentially uninhabited territory in contrast to the cultivated and inhabited areas. The specific reference here, however, is to the arid regions west of the Dead Sea. (Matthew 3:1 locates John's ministry in the Judean desert.) This general area was the abode of the Qumran sect. It is possible that John came in contact with these people. He certainly must have known of them. What influences they exerted on him are not known. Perhaps his ascetic life and stern discipline were derived from them. However, neither his baptismal practices nor his great emphasis on ethical conduct and eschatological judgment seems to have come from them.

The wilderness is a significant location in Israel's history. It was a place of deliverance and of revelation, as God brought Israel out of Egypt and made his covenant with them at Mt Sinai. It was also a place of testing and failure, as Israel repeatedly disobeyed God and so wandered there for forty years. The tradition of deliverance, together with predictions of an eschatological "new exodus" from Isaiah and the prophets (see comments at v.3), resulted in the expectation among some Jews that God's final salvation would emerge from the desert. Josephus (*J.W.* 2.13.4–5 §§259–63; 6.6.3 §351) refers to various messianic pretenders and revolutionaries who gathered followers in the wilderness (cf. Ac 21:38; Mt 24:26). Such eschatological speculation was likely a factor in the choice by the Qumran community of a wilderness location near the Dead Sea (cf. Cranfield, 42).

The background to John's baptism has been a matter of much debate. Some scholars have seen parallels to the ceremonial washings practiced by the Essenes and other Jewish groups. As an act of ceremonial cleansing, individuals would dip themselves into a *miqveh*, or immersion pool. At Qumran, such washings, like John's, represented a turning from sin to participate in the eschatological community of God (1QS 5:13–14). Yet John's baptism is different in that it appears to be a onetime event rather than a repeated ritual. Others have pointed to the Jewish practice of proselyte (new convert) baptism. This parallel would be particularly striking since it would mean John is telling his fellow Jews that they must repent and be saved just like Gentiles. He is calling the apostate nation to become the people of God once again. While this interpretation would fit well the message of John (cf. Mt 3:6; Lk 3:8), it is uncertain whether Jews practiced proselyte baptism in the first century.

Whether related to proselyte baptism or something else, John's baptism was an appeal to the nation to repent. He was calling together the remnant of Israel to become the restored people of God. John comes preaching "a baptism of repentance for the forgiveness of sins." "Of repentance" is probably a genitive of quality. It was a repentance-baptism John was preaching; i.e., the baptism indicated that repentance had already occurred or accompanied it. *Metanoia* (GK *3567*, "repentance") can mean to change one's mind, attitude, and/or actions. Behind John's use is probably the Hebrew *šûb* ("to turn back," "return"), which in the OT often carries the sense of returning to God, reorienting one's life to a relationship with him. The end result (*eis*, "for") is the forgiveness of sins. God's direct response to true repentance is forgiveness.

5 John's preaching caused great excitement. Mark writes, "The whole Judean countryside and all the people of Jerusalem went out to him." The verb "went out" (*exeporeueto*) is in the imperfect tense and suggests that they "kept going out" to him. Although there is an element of hyperbole in Mark's report, it nevertheless implies that John's preaching aroused much interest and created a great stir. Jerusalem is at least twenty miles from the Jordan River and about four thousand feet above it. It was hard going down the rugged Judean hills to the Jordan and even harder coming back.

The message and popularity of John the Baptist is attested by Josephus, the only primary source reference to John outside the NT. Josephus describes a particular battle in which Herod Antipas suffered defeat, and then says rumors spread that Herod's loss was a result of God's judgment for his execution of John the Baptist. In this context Josephus (*Ant.* 18.5.2 §§116–17) briefly describes John's ministry:

> John ... the Baptist ... was a good man, and commanded the Jews to exercise virtue, both as to righteousness towards one another, and piety towards God, and so to come to baptism; for that the washing [with water] would be acceptable to him, if they made use of it, not in order to the putting away [or the remission] of some sins [only], but for the purification of the body; supposing still that the soul was thoroughly purified beforehand by righteousness.

Josephus's account agrees in general with the Gospels, although he does not expressly refer to John's eschatological message or to his role as forerunner of the Messiah. This omission is not surprising, since Josephus held pro-Roman and anti-Zealot views, as evidenced by his blaming the destruction of Jerusalem on insurrectionists and brigands who made messianic claims and stoked false eschatological hopes among the people. Josephus probably omits John's eschatological message of coming judgment either because he was unaware of it or, more likely, because he found such teaching repugnant in view of the events surrounding Jerusalem's destruction.

Based in part on Josephus's account, some scholars have claimed that John's message, while eschatological in focus, had nothing to do with Jesus; rather, he was expecting God alone to come and bring in the day of the Lord. It was later Christians, it is said, who transformed John into the forerunner of Jesus the Messiah. Yet the evidence suggests otherwise. John's statement about being unworthy to untie the sandals of the Coming One (attested independently in the fourth gospel and the Synoptics [Jn 1:27; Mt 3:11; Mk 1:7; Lk 3:16]) suggests John was expecting a human successor. Similarly, John's later doubts about Jesus are inexplicable unless he already had some messianic expectations concerning him (Lk 7:18–35; Mt 11:2–19). It is unlikely that the church would create an episode in which John (the herald and forerunner of the Messiah!) raised doubts about Jesus' messianic status.

6 The appearance of the Baptist, clad in "clothing made of camel's hair, with a leather belt around his waist," recalls the description of Elijah's clothing (2Ki 1:8) and is intended to present John as a prophetic figure. He is more than an ascetic or holy man living in the wilderness; he is a prophet called by God to a message of impending judgment to God's people. His food consisted of locusts and wild honey. In Leviticus 11:21–22, locusts are listed among clean foods. The Dead Sea Scrolls even provide instructions on how to eat them (CD 12.13–15). The wild honey is almost certainly bees' honey and not, as has sometimes been suggested, carob pods or sap from various trees in the area. Like his clothing, John's food reflects his simple desert lifestyle. He is "living off the land" without comforts or luxuries, a man dedicated wholly to God's purpose.

7 Mark's account of John's message is very brief. Mark includes nothing of John's pointed ethical admonitions to the Pharisees and Sadducees (Mt 3:7–10), to the crowds (Lk 3:10–11), or to the tax collectors and soldiers (Lk 3:12–14). Instead he focuses on the coming of the Stronger One (v.7), who will baptize with the Holy Spirit (v.8). So great is this Stronger One that John does not consider himself worthy even to untie his sandals. Removing someone's sandals was a lowly task appropriate only for a slave. The statement is particularly striking in the light of a later rabbinic tradition that removing a master's sandals was too low a task to require even of one's Hebrew slave (*Mek. Exod.* 21:2). Another tradition states that while the disciple of a rabbi should perform all the duties of a slave for his master, the removing of his shoes is excepted (*b. Ketub.* *96a*). John identifies himself as lower than a disciple and even a slave of the Messiah.

8 John next contrasts his baptism with that of the Coming One (v.8). John's baptism is water baptism; that of the Coming One is Holy Spirit baptism. Again, the emphasis is on the superiority (this time in terms of ministry) of the Coming One to John. Water baptism is an external rite that cleanses the physical body. Spirit baptism involves true spiritual cleansing. Moule's comment, 10, is to the point: "The Baptist evidently meant that the great Coming One would not merely cleanse with water but would bring to bear, like a deluge, the purging, purifying, judging presence of God himself." While Mark's readers would likely think of the dramatic episode of Pentecost as the primary fulfillment of this prophecy (Ac 2), its significance goes beyond that event. The OT prophets spoke of the coming age of salvation as the age of the Spirit, the time when God would pour out his Spirit on his people (Isa 32:15; Eze 36:26–27; 39:29; Joel 2:28–29). Spirit baptism, therefore, likely encompasses more than Pentecost by referring to the whole Jesus event, including the Spirit-empowered ministry of Jesus in healing, exorcising, raising the dead, and forgiving sins, and the Spirit's inauguration of the age of salvation in and through the church.

While Mark clearly considers the Stronger One to be Jesus, there is also a measure of intentional ambiguity in the passage. In their OT contexts, Malachi 3:1 and Isaiah 40:3 do not speak of the Messiah but of the coming of Yahweh for judgment and salvation. Furthermore, according to the OT it is Yahweh himself who will pour out his Spirit in the last days (Eze 36:26–27; 39:29; Joel 2:28). This ambiguity of referents appears to be Mark's way of affirming that, in some sense, "the coming of Jesus *is* the eschatological coming of God" (France, 70)—a very high Christology indeed.

NOTES

4 Grant, 649, thinks that βάπτισμα μετανοίας (*baptisma metanoias*) is "a Semitism, meaning 'a baptism which symbolized or expressed repentance.'"

6 The Hebrew phrase in 2 Kings 1:8, sometimes translated "he was a hairy man" (NASB), probably instead means "wearing a cloak of animal hair" (France, 69; so NIV, TEV, NAB, RSV, etc.).

C. The Baptism of Jesus (1:9–11)

OVERVIEW

Jesus likely began his public ministry sometime around AD 27, when he was about thirty years old (Lk 3:23). His childhood and youth were spent in Nazareth in Galilee (Mt 2:23; Lk 3:39), though Mark shows little interest in such details. He begins instead with two events that preceded Jesus' public ministry: his baptism by John and his temptation by the devil. In Mark the baptismal narrative confirms Jesus' identity as the Son of God and expresses the Father's approval of his person and mission.

9 At that time Jesus came from Nazareth in Galilee and was baptized by John in the
Jordan. 10 As Jesus was coming up out of the water, he saw heaven being torn open and
the Spirit descending on him like a dove. 11 And a voice came from heaven: "You are my
Son, whom I love; with you I am well pleased."

COMMENTARY

9 "At that time" is a free translation of *kai egeneto en ekeinais tais hēmerais* ("and it came to pass in those days") and represents one of the frequent "seams" or connecting links in Mark's gospel. These seams are Mark's way of putting together the stories about Jesus and often are helpful in probing into his theological concerns. From a narrative perspective, the phrase announces that a new scene in the drama has begun. It also carries an OT and Semitic sound recalling the biblical narratives of the past and suggesting the link between Mark's story and its biblical roots.

Jesus comes to John from the tiny backwater village of Nazareth in Galilee. Nazareth is never mentioned in the OT, in the Jewish Talmud, or by Josephus, and most Judeans in the south probably would never have heard of it (France, 75; cf. Nathanael's disparaging remarks in Jn 1:46). It seems hardly an appropriate place of origin for the messianic "Stronger One" whom John has been heralding. Yet here is part of the mystery that pervades Mark's narrative. Jesus apparently comes out of nowhere, both in terms of details about his birth and background and in the insignificance of his origins.

10 The NIV does not translate the adverb *euthys* ("immediately," "then," "subsequently") in this verse, since the temporal rendering of the participle "as Jesus was coming up ..." already provides the sense of immediacy expressed through the adverb. As noted in the Introduction (p. 689), the frequent use of this adverb is characteristic of Mark and gives his gospel a certain breathlessness that drives the narrative forward.

Mark seems to suggest that only Jesus saw "heaven being torn open and the Spirit descending on him like a dove," though he may have been so focusing on Jesus' experience that he says nothing of John's. Mark's use of the verb *schizō* (GK *5387*, "tear," "rend") to describe what happened to the heavens shows his graphic style of writing. The tearing open of the heavens is meant to signify a cosmic event. The language echoes Isaiah 64:1: "Oh, that you would rend the heavens and come down, that the mountains would tremble before you" (cf. *T. Levi* 18:512: "The heavens shall be opened ... the Father's voice ... sin shall come to an end ... and Beliar shall be bound by him"). Matthew and Luke use the ordinary word *anoigō* ("open"). Mark's point may be that what is torn open cannot be closed (Garland, 48). There may also be an intentional inclusio with 15:38, where the curtain of the temple is "torn in two" at the crucifixion. Just as the Father's announcement of Jesus' divine sonship will be echoed in the cry of the centurion at the cross (1:11; 15:39), so the tearing of the heavens at the baptism previews the tearing of the curtain veil (1:9; 15:38). Both renderings suggest access to God's presence made available through the coming of Jesus.

The descent of the Spirit "like a dove" may mean the Spirit looked like a dove or more likely that the descent was similar to a bird's flight. Whether there is symbolism here and what it means have been widely discussed. Some see an allusion to Genesis 1:2, where the Spirit "hovers" over the waters at creation. Jesus could be identified by Mark with the new creation. Others suggest an allusion to Genesis 8:8–12, where Noah's dove represents God's gracious deliverance after judgment.

Whatever else the descent of the Spirit on Jesus meant, it clearly indicates his empowerment for ministry as the Messiah. Isaiah 11 predicts the coming Messiah will be one on whom the Spirit of God will rest: "the Spirit of wisdom and of understanding, the Spirit of counsel and of power, the Spirit of knowledge and of the fear of the LORD." In Luke's gospel this connection is made even clearer, with the Spirit's descent identified as Jesus' "anointing" as Messiah (i.e., "Anointed One"): "The Spirit of the Lord is on me, because he has anointed me" (Lk 4:18; cf. 3:21–22; 4:1, 14).

11 The voice from heaven signifies the Father's affirmation of Jesus' person and mission. God's words allude to two, and perhaps three, OT passages. "You are my son" comes from Psalm 2:7, where Yahweh ("the LORD") announces the king's divine sonship and legitimate rule from Mount Zion (cf. 2Sa 7:14). "With you I am well pleased" echoes Isaiah 42:1, where the faithful and suffering servant of Yahweh is identified as God's chosen one. Finally, "whom I love" may represent an Isaac/Jesus typology from Genesis 22:2, where Isaac is Abraham's only son "whom you love." Abraham's willingness to offer his beloved son would be analogous to God's offering of his Son. If all three allusions are present, this single announcement makes the extraordinary claim that Jesus is the promised Messiah who will offer himself as a sacrifice for his people.

The main emphasis, however, is on the unique sonship of Jesus as God confesses Jesus to be his Son. From the perspective of the reader, the identity of Jesus is no secret. As Ernest Best, (*The Temptation and the Passion* [SNTSMS 2; Cambridge: Cambridge Univ. Press, 1965], 168) writes, "The gospel is not a mystery story in which the identity of the main character has to be guessed; from the outset it is made clear who this is—the Son of God." Yet from the perspective of the characters in the story, Jesus' identity and mission will be revealed only gradually. As noted above, Mark seems to underscore that the baptismal voice was a personal experience between Jesus and the Father ("*he saw* heaven being torn open ... '*you* are my Son'"; contrast Mt 3:17: "*This* is my Son"). In the episodes that follow, the spirit world is aware of Jesus' identity, as demons repeatedly recognize Jesus as the "Holy One of God," "the Son of God," and the "Son of the Most High God" (1:24, 34; 3:11; 5:7). Human recognition does not come until Peter's confession ("you are the Christ," 8:29), yet Peter still fails to comprehend the suffering role of the Christ. In the end, only the centurion at the cross gets it right by seeing that it is through suffering and death that Jesus is revealed to be the Son of God (15:39).

The baptism underscores the Father's approval of his Son. He knows the mission that has been given to the Son. At the very beginning of Jesus' fulfillment of that mission, God states his confidence in him. Lane, 58, points out that "the first clause of the declaration (with the verb in the present tense of the indicative mood) expresses an eternal and essential relationship. The second clause (the verb is in the aorist indicative) implies a past choice for the performance of a particular function in history."

The baptism of Jesus by John was a problem for some people in the early church. Why did Jesus submit himself to a baptism of repentance for the forgiveness of sins? In Matthew's account John is reluctant to baptize Jesus: "I need to be baptized by you, and do you come to me?" (Mt 3:14). Jesus replies, "It is proper for us to do this to fulfill all righteousness" (v.15). "All righteousness" is probably a reference to God's plan and purpose for Jesus. Part of that plan was the complete identification of Jesus at the outset of his ministry with human beings and their sin (cf. 2Co 5:21). He is also identifying with the ministry of John and with those who are responding to John's call for repentance.

NOTES

11 "Whom I love" is a translation of ὁ ἀγαπητός (*ho agapētos*). Since seven out of fifteen times in the LXX ἀγαπητός, *agapētos*, translates the Hebrew יָחִיד, *yāḥîd* ("only"), some commentators translate it "only" here (cf. I. H. Marshall, "Son of God or Servant of Yahweh? A Reconsideration of Mark 1:11," *NTS* 15 [1965]: 326–36). The verb εὐδόκησα (*eudokēsa*, "I am well pleased") may be taken as a timeless aorist or perhaps as representing the Hebrew stative perfect. The meaning then would be that God is always pleased with the Son.

D. The Temptation of Jesus (1:12–13)

OVERVIEW

Mark's account of the temptation is very brief. He devotes only two verses to it, whereas Matthew has eleven and Luke thirteen. No specific temptations are described, and no outcome is recorded. By omitting this information Mark probably wants to emphasize that Jesus' entire ministry was one continuous conflict with Satan and not limited to a few temptations in the desert during a period of forty days. The narrative that follows will vividly describe this continuing engagement with Satan and his demonic agents. By opening his gospel with Jesus' temptation by Satan and repeated encounters with demons (1:24, 27, 34), Mark sets the whole gospel in the context of a spiritual struggle between God and Satan, with cosmic and eschatological implications.

12At once the Spirit sent him out into the desert, 13and he was in the desert forty days, being tempted by Satan. He was with the wild animals, and angels attended him.

COMMENTARY

12 Mark emphasizes the close connection between the baptism and the temptation by the use of his characteristic word *euthys* ("at once"). The submission of Jesus by his identification with humanity's failure and sin at the baptism is continued by his subjection to the onslaughts of Satan. The same Holy Spirit who came on Jesus at the baptism drives him into the desert.

Mark uses stronger language than either Matthew or Mark when he says that the Spirit "drove," "impelled," or "cast out" Jesus into the wilderness (*ekballō*, GK *1675*, a term often used of exorcism). The verb likely does not indicate that the Spirit acted against Jesus' will, but rather reiterates the overwhelming presence of the Spirit in Jesus' life and the urgency of the task ahead.

13 The forty days have symbolic significance and recall the experiences of Moses (Ex 24:18) and Elijah (1Ki 19:8, 15) in the desert. They are also analogous to Israel's forty years in the wilderness, a time of testing and preparation. Although Israel repeatedly failed through disobedience and unfaithfulness, Jesus' success—though not explicitly stated—is implied in the episodes that follow, where Jesus acts in the power of the Spirit to teach, heal, and defeat Satan's demonic agents.

Among the Synoptics, only Mark makes the puzzling statement that Jesus was "with the wild beasts." Some have suggested this note is meant to imply a return to Paradise, since Adam was with the animals in the garden of Eden. More likely the reference to wild animals portrays the wilderness as a place of barrenness and danger, thus heightening the fierceness of Jesus' temptation experience. This perspective also fits better with Mark's statement that the angels were ministering to Jesus. Such service was necessary because of the desolation and peril of the place.

NOTES

12 Since Mark most often uses ἐκβάλλω (*ekballō*, GK *1675*] of the expulsion of demons (eleven times) and in this passage combines it with the vigorous word εὐθύς (*euthys*, "at once"), it ought to be translated by something stronger than the NIV's "sent out." "Force is certainly involved. There is no need, however, to infer resistance or unwillingness on the part of Jesus" (cf. Bratcher and Nida, 32).

II. THE EARLY GALILEAN MINISTRY (1:14–3:6)

OVERVIEW

The purpose of this section is to describe the opening stage of the Galilean ministry. The introductory statement (1:14–15) forms a transition from the ministry of John to that of Jesus. This transition is followed by the account of the calling of the first disciples (vv.16–20), Jesus' ministry in and around Capernaum (vv.21–34), and a series of conflict stories (2:1–3:6) that reach their climax in a plot to put Jesus to death (3:6). The central theme is the *authority of Jesus* and the opposition it provokes. Jesus demonstrates his authority as Messiah and Son of God by proclaiming the message of the kingdom, calling disciples, teaching with authority, healing the sick, casting out demons, and forgiving sins. Opposition comes first from demons and then from the religious leaders—thereby emphasizing just where the battle lines are drawn in the spiritual struggle ahead.

A. The Gospel Proclaimed (1:14–15)

14After John was put in prison, Jesus went into Galilee, proclaiming the good news of
God. 15"The time has come," he said. "The kingdom of God is near. Repent and believe the
good news!"

COMMENTARY

14 The opening of Jesus' public ministry is related to that of John the Baptist. Not until "after John was put in prison" (v.14) did Jesus begin his ministry. Mark will later describe the imprisonment and subsequent execution of John in a narrative flashback (6:14–29). His interest here is to show that John, the forerunner, completed his God-appointed task before Jesus began his ministry. There is both continuity and discontinuity between Jesus and John. While John is the forerunner, Jesus is the Messiah. Their messages are also similar, yet distinct. John proclaims the need to repent in the light of the soon arrival of eschatological judgment. Jesus also calls for repentance, but he announces the *arrival* of God's presence and kingdom through his own words and actions. What for John is still future comes to fulfillment in Jesus. This continuity/discontinuity between Jesus and John is reflected elsewhere in the Gospels. In Luke Jesus announces, "The Law and the Prophets were proclaimed until John. Since that time, the good news of the kingdom of God is being preached" (Lk 16:16). John has one foot in both ages—the age of promise and the age of fulfillment. He is the last and greatest of the OT prophets (Mt 11:9–11; Lk 7:26–28) and the herald of the messianic age of salvation.

Although Mark gives neither the exact place nor the precise time of the beginning of Jesus' ministry (he shows little interest in such details), he says that the content of Jesus' preaching is "the good news of God." God is both its source (subjective genitive) and object (objective genitive); it is from God and about God. The gospel is good news, the very best news ever to come to the hearing of humanity, because it contains the message of forgiveness, restoration, and new life in Christ Jesus (cf. 2Co 5:17).

15 Jesus witnesses to God's action for human salvation by saying, "The time has come." Time here is not simply a chronological reference—it refers to the eschatological time of salvation (cf. Gal 4:4). Redemptive history has been building to this climactic moment. "[Jesus] marks the fulfillment of the special salvation-time which is distinguished from all other time" (Schweizer, 45).

The concept of the kingdom of God is basic to the teaching of Jesus. Although the term "kingdom of God" does not occur in either the OT or the Apocrypha, the idea is abundantly present in both. The OT is full of such statements as "the LORD will reign for ever and ever" (Ex 15:18); "the LORD is enthroned as King forever" (Ps 29:10); and "I am the LORD, your Holy One, Israel's Creator, your King" (Isa 43:15).

An examination of such passages reveals that the Lord's kingship is both a present reality (God is exercising his authority now) and a future hope (God will reign in the eschaton—the end—when he finally puts down all opposition to his reign). His kingship can refer to a dynamic *reign*, God's spiritual authority in the lives of his people, or a static *realm*, a messianic kingdom centered in Jerusalem. In short, the kingdom could be conceived as present and future, a reign and a realm. The apocalyptic Judaism of Jesus' day acknowledged the present reality of God's sovereign authority but placed greatest emphasis on the future and eschatological dimensions of the kingdom. The persecuted people of God longed for the day when God would intervene in human history to actualize his reign and establish his kingdom on earth.

The same tension between the kingdom of God as both present and future exists in the teaching of Jesus in Mark. Jesus speaks of "receiving" the kingdom of God like a little child (10:15) and the difficulty of entering for those who are rich (10:23–25; cf. 9:47). The parable of the growing seed describes the kingdom as the slow growth from seed to plant until the day of harvest (4:26–29). Similarly, the parable of the mustard seed represents the kingdom as a tiny seed that grows into a great tree (4:30–32). In both parables the kingdom is something that begins with Jesus' ministry and is consummated at his return. After driving out the demons from a possessed man and being accused of being in league with Beelzebul, Jesus replied, "But if I drive out demons by the Spirit of God, then the kingdom of God has come upon you" (Mt 12:28; cf. Lk 11:20). In Jesus' actions, God's rule has invaded this world. It is present with people.

But in other sayings the kingdom is spoken of as still future. Jesus speaks of those who in the future will see the kingdom of God come with power (Mk 9:1) and refers to a future time when he will drink wine again in the kingdom of God (14:25). Joseph of Arimathea is longing for the kingdom of God (15:43), and at the triumphal entry the people express their hope in "the coming kingdom of our father David!" (11:10). While this latter passage could reflect a *misapprehension* on the part of the people, the future establishment of the kingdom is implied in Jesus' teaching concerning the coming of the Son of Man "with great power and glory ... to gather the elect" (13:26–32; cf. 8:38; 13:33–34; 14:62). This teaching of the future establishment of God's reign is in line with the expectations of apocalyptic Judaism.

Jesus' central message here, "the kingdom of God is near," itself suggests this ambiguity between present and future aspects of the kingdom. The Greek verb *ēngiken* (perfect tense of *engizō*, GK *1581*) could be translated as either "has arrived" or "has come near." It could denote presence either now or in the future and may be intentionally ambiguous.

The solution to the dilemma of both a present and a future kingdom is not to be found in rejecting one or the other (as, e.g., in realized eschatology's rejection of a future kingdom and consistent eschatology's rejection of a present kingdom). The ambiguity is best explained by seeing the kingdom as intimately related to *the person of Jesus*. The kingdom has come near because the king is present. It has drawn near *spatially* (in Jesus' person) and *temporally* (since it ushers in the events of the end). God's reign is evident in Jesus' healings, exorcisms, and nature miracles. His disciples experience the power of the kingdom—driving out demons and healing the sick—through *his* authority (5:7, 13). If the kingdom is directly related to the person of Jesus, then it is ultimately achieved through his death on the cross, the ransom for sins. The kingdom is realized not through conquest but through sacrifice. It will be consummated when he returns in power and glory.

The appropriate response is repentance and faith. There is an urgency about the nearness of God's kingdom. Since it ushers in the end, it speaks of judgment. Jesus proclaims God's kingdom so that people will repent and believe the gospel.

NOTES

14 The words translated "was put in prison" represent the Greek word παραδοθῆναι (*paradothēnai*, GK *4140*, "to be delivered over"). The NIV assumes the delivering over was to prison. It is possible, however, especially if Mark is more interested in theology than historical sequence, that the delivering over is to death (see comments at 6:14–29). By this means, Mark wants to heighten the similarity between John's and Jesus' ministries. They both end in death. Thus the shadow of the cross falls over the ministry of Jesus at its very outset.

On "the good news of God," see comments at 1:1. Dan Wallace (*Greek Grammar Beyond the Basics* [Grand Rapids: Zondervan], 119) calls the combination of subjective and objective genitives a "plenary genitive."

15 The verb πιστεύω (*pisteuō*, "believe") is followed by the preposition ἐν (*en*, "in")—the only occurrence of this combination in the NT. It probably means simply "believe the gospel" (the "in" being an example of "translation Greek"; i.e., the Greek carries over the Hebrew idiom).

B. Authority in Calling the First Disciples (1:16–20)

OVERVIEW

Jesus has begun to preach his message. Now he must gather around him disciples whom he can teach so that they may become sharers in that message. God's reign does not operate in a void. It assumes a people—a people subject to that rule. It involves the formation of a community. Verses 16–20 contain two "call narratives," analogous in many respects to Elijah's call of Elisha in 1 Kings 19:21.

After the dramatic announcement of the kingdom of God (the climax and turning point of redemptive history!), the recipients of Jesus' call are surprisingly unexceptional—a few common fishermen going about their daily lives. Already in Mark's gospel the fulfillment of the promise is taking a surprising turn. R. T. France, 94, writes, "The kingdom of God comes not with fanfare but through the gradual gathering of a group of socially insignificant people in an unnoticed corner of provincial Galilee."

Three of these four men—Simon, James, and John—will form in Mark's gospel the core of Jesus' disciples, sometimes referred to as the "inner circle" (5:37; 9:2; 14:33; with Andrew in 13:3). Simon will not be identified as "Peter"—the name Jesus gave him—until 3:16, where Mark lists the twelve disciples.

16As Jesus walked beside the Sea of Galilee, he saw Simon and his brother Andrew
casting a net into the lake, for they were fishermen. 17"Come, follow me," Jesus said, "and
I will make you fishers of men." 18At once they left their nets and followed him.
19When he had gone a little farther, he saw James son of Zebedee and his brother John
in a boat, preparing their nets. 20Without delay he called them, and they left their father
Zebedee in the boat with the hired men and followed him.

COMMENTARY

16 Jesus found Simon and his brother Andrew along the shore of the Sea of Galilee. This beautiful body of water—682 feet below sea level, fourteen miles long, and six miles wide—is an inland lake. (Luke calls it the "Lake [*limnē*] of Gennesaret" [5:1]; another designation was "Sea of Tiberias.") Much of Jesus' ministry took place near this lake. In NT times there were numerous towns along its shores, especially the northern and western ones. Since its waters abounded with fish, the local fishing industry flourished. Simon and Andrew were "casting a net" (*amphiballontas*) into the sea—probably from shore, but possibly from a boat—when Jesus called them. They were probably using a round throw net, a common way of fishing around Galilee. The net would be about fifteen feet across and weighted around the edges. When thrown, it would sink to the bottom, trapping the fish. It could then be gathered in and the fish removed.

17–18 Mark says nothing of a previous encounter of these two disciples with Jesus (cf. Jn 1:35–42). Even if he was aware of such a tradition, it is doubtful whether he would have used it. Mark wants to show the urgency of the situation, as consistent with the eschatological significance of Jesus' mission.

In its Markan context, "Come, follow me" is a call to discipleship, a relationship of loyalty to a master teacher. Jesus' call is different from the common pattern of Jewish rabbis, whose students would seek out and attach themselves to a particular teacher to learn the Law and pass on the traditions of the fathers. In contrast, Jesus—the teacher—seeks out and authoritatively calls particular disciples to himself. He expects their immediate response and full devotion to his person and to the message of the kingdom of God (cf. Hengel, *Charismatic Leader and His Followers*, 51).

The wordplay in English between being "fisher*men*" and "fishers of *men*" is not present in the Greek, since the Greek word "fishers" (*halieis*) does not have "men" as a component part. The striking contrast to which Jesus calls these men is between catching *fish* and catching *people* (*anthrōpoi*). The image of fishing for people appears in the OT, always in the context of judgment (e.g., Jer 16:16; Eze 29:4–5; 38:4; Am 4:2; Hab 1:14–17). This connotation may be present here in the light of the eschatological implications of Jesus' kingdom proclamation. If so, however, Jesus reverses the image, and the fish are caught for salvation rather than judgment. Jesus calls Simon and Andrew to the urgent task of rescuing people from the impending judgment that the coming of the kingdom entails. The urgency demands an immediate response. "At once" (*euthys*) the two fishermen left their nets and followed him (v.18). Though Mark's favorite term *euthys* does not always carry the sense of immediacy (cf. 1:21), here that is precisely the point. Jesus' authoritative call provokes *immediate* obedience.

19–20 The same call is now extended to James and John, sons of Zebedee. The phrase sometimes translated "mending their nets" (KJV, NKJV, NASB) does not necessarily mean "repair" but carries the sense of "putting in order." This would entail washing, folding, and mending the nets in preparation for the night's fishing (cf. Cranfield, 71). The NIV and TNIV accurately render it as "preparing their nets."

Like Peter and Andrew, James and John respond without any hesitation to Jesus' call (*euthys*, v.20). In their case something of the price of discipleship is indicated by the breaking of family ties—the leaving of their father's business. The mention of the hired men may imply that Zebedee was a man of wealth. It may also be included to indicate that by leaving their father to follow Jesus, James and John were not leaving him entirely alone to run his fishing business. The OT and Judaism strongly affirm the need for children to respect and honor their parents (cf. 7:10–12; 10:19). Yet Jesus also calls for a radical reorientation of family ties (3:34–35; 10:28–29). The main emphasis in this call, as in that of Simon and Andrew, is the authority of Jesus and the immediate response it provokes.

NOTES

18 The verb ἀκολουθέω (*akoloutheō*, GK *199*, "follow") is frequently used in the Gospels "to describe attachment to the person of Jesus, personal surrender to his summons, and acceptance of his leadership" (Taylor, 169). For an excellent statement of the concept of discipleship in Mark's gospel, see Schweizer, 49.

C. Authority in Exorcisms and Healings (1:21–45)

1. Driving Out an Evil Spirit (1:21–28)

OVERVIEW

In vv.21–34 Mark records what seems to have occurred on one memorable Sabbath day. The first incident occurred in the synagogue in Capernaum. "Synagogue" can refer either to the local congregation or to the building in which the congregation met. The synagogue apparently originated in the Babylonian exile as the result of Jews' meeting together for prayer and the study of the Torah. In NT times synagogues were found all over the Hellenistic world wherever there were sufficient numbers of Jews to maintain one. The synagogue became Judaism's most enduring institution.

21They went to Capernaum, and when the Sabbath came, Jesus went into the
synagogue and began to teach. 22The people were amazed at his teaching, because he
taught them as one who had authority, not as the teachers of the law. 23Just then a man in
their synagogue who was possessed by an evil spirit cried out, 24"What do you want with
us, Jesus of Nazareth? Have you come to destroy us? I know who you are — the Holy One
of God!"
25"Be quiet!" said Jesus sternly. "Come out of him!" 26The evil spirit shook the man
violently and came out of him with a shriek.
27The people were all so amazed that they asked each other, "What is this? A new
teaching — and with authority! He even gives orders to evil spirits and they obey him."
28News about him spread quickly over the whole region of Galilee.

COMMENTARY

21 Capernaum was the home of Simon Peter and became a kind of base of operations for Jesus' Galilean ministry. Tell Hum, located on the northwestern corner of the Sea of Galilee, almost certainly marks the site of Capernaum. The remains of a fourth-century synagogue are present today and may well sit atop the synagogue of Jesus' day. On the Sabbath Jesus enters the synagogue with his disciples (who then disappear from the narrative until v.29) and "began to teach" (*edidasken*, inceptive or ingressive imperfect). Jesus, like Paul (cf. Ac 13:15), uses the "freedom of the synagogue"— a Jewish custom that permitted recognized visiting teachers to preach in the synagogue by invitation of its leaders. The sermon or homily would normally be exposition on the daily readings from the Law and the Prophets (cf. Lk 4:15–30, where Jesus exposits Isa 61:1–2).

22 Characteristically, Mark does not provide the content of Jesus' preaching (it would certainly have concerned the good news of the kingdom; see 1:15). Mark often identifies Jesus as a teacher yet provides fewer examples of the content of this teaching than the other synoptic writers. Mark's interest is rather on the authority with which Jesus speaks and the amazed reaction of the people. The verb rendered "were amazed" is *exeplēssonto* (cf. 6:2; 7:37; 10:26; 11:18), a compound from *plēssō* (GK *4448*, "strike, smite"). It has a very strong meaning. People were astonished at Jesus' teaching "because he taught them as one who had authority, and not as the teachers of the law."

The NIV and TNIV regularly translate *grammateis* as "teachers of the law." Most readers of the Bible know them as "scribes." Sometimes called "lawyers" (*nomikoi*; see Lk 7:30; 10:25; 11:45) or "law teachers" (*nomodidaskaloi*; see Lk 5:17), they were experts in the interpretation and application of the law of Moses. Many were Pharisees (Mk 2:16; Ac 23:9), though there were also Sadducees and priests among them (cf. Mt 2:45; 21:15). The scribes traced their origin back to the priest Ezra, who established postexilic Judaism based on the law (Ezr 7:6–26; Ne 8:1–9). Jesus often came into conflict with them, especially over the issue of the authority of his words and actions. The scribes generally taught by citing the "traditions of the fathers," the authoritative traditions of those who had come before them ("Rabbi so-and-so says such-and-such"). Jesus spoke instead with authority directly from God.

23 Suddenly the synagogue service was disrupted by the cry of a man "possessed by an evil spirit." The word translated "evil" in the NIV (*akathartos*, GK *176*) normally carries the sense of "unclean" or "defiled." An "unclean spirit" is a Jewish way of referring to a demon, a spirit-being in opposition to God. Mark uses "unclean spirit" (eleven times) and "demon" (fourteen times) synonymously. For the second time in Mark, Jesus comes in conflict with the power of Satan (cf. 1:13), thus emphasizing again the spiritual nature of this struggle.

Although the belief that sickness or deviant behavior can be attributed to demon-possession has often been relegated in modern times to superstition or obscurantism, recent developments in the study of the occult and demonism have tended to leave the question more open. Reports of demon-possession now come not only from distant and remote mission fields but also from the most sophisticated of our urban centers. A postmodern worldview and the recognition that science cannot explain every experience of phenomena in the world have also produced greater openness to the reality of the spirit world. In this context the NT accounts of demonism do not seem so bizarre after all.

24 Although v.23 states that the man cried out, it was really the controlling demon who shouted. Notice that Jesus speaks directly to the demon in v.25. The phrase rendered in the NIV "What do you want with us?" (lit., "What to us and to you?") is a Hebrew idiom that can carry the sense "What do you have against us?" (cf. Jdg 11:12; 1Ki 17:18) or "What relationship do we have with you?" (cf. 2Ki 3:13; Hos 14:8; see Marcus, 187). Both carry the implication "Leave us alone!" (cf. France, 103). The "us" shows that the demon speaks for his fellow demons too, thus reiterating the spiritual nature and eschatological significance of Jesus' coming. Not just one demon but the whole demonic realm quakes in fear at the recognition that Jesus has come to conquer their realm and to rescue those enslaved by Satan. The inbreaking power of the kingdom of God will overwhelm the ramparts of Satan. The question "Have you come to destroy us?" could just as well be a statement of fact (since punctuation marks were added later to the MSS): "You have come to destroy us!" Whether a question or a statement, the demons recognize the eschatological significance of Jesus' arrival and the judgment against them that it entails. In the same eschatological vein, John writes that "the Son of God appeared ... to destroy the devil's work" (1Jn 3:8).

The utterance of the name of Jesus and his title "the Holy One of God" may have been an attempt by the demon to get control over Jesus. In the ancient world, knowledge of the name of a spirit-being was widely considered a way of gaining power over it. In the pseudepigraphic Jewish-Christian work *Testament of Solomon*, Solomon uses a magic seal ring given to him by Michael the archangel to learn the names of various demons and then coerce their help in building the temple (*T. Sol.* 1:7). Though this work postdates the NT, its traditions probably come from much earlier (cf. Josephus, *Ant.* 8.2.5 §§42–49, where Solomon's gifts of exorcism are described).

The title "Holy One of God" is not used of the Messiah in the OT, though it is appropriate for the one set apart to accomplish God's salvific purposes. It is used of Aaron in Psalm 106:16 and Elisha in 2 Kings 4:9. The title may be used here in contrast to the "unclean" spirit, since in Hebrew thought *hagios* (GK *41*, "holy") is roughly synonymous with *katharos* (GK *2754*, "clean"). While the demon is "unclean" or defiled, Jesus is "holy," in unity with the purpose of God.

25–26 Unlike other exorcists of his day, Jesus needed no secret formulas, incantations, or magical objects to exorcise the demon. He accomplished the task through his own authority. After ordering it to "Be quiet!" (v.25), Jesus simply spoke a word of power, and the evil spirit convulsed the man "and came out of him with a shriek" (v.26).

Why did Jesus command silence, since the demon was correctly identifying Jesus as the Holy One of God, whose mission was to destroy Satan's agents? The command should be seen first of all as evidence of Jesus' authority and complete mastery over the forces of Satan. It may also be Jesus' attempt to avoid "bad press," since the demons would inevitably distort his message. Jesus seeks to define his messiahship and mission on his own terms rather than through demonic recognition or the popular expectations of the people. The command to silence is unlikely to be part of a "messianic secret" invented by Mark (see Introduction, p. 674, and comments at 9:9). Jesus' fame will spread soon enough in Mark's narrative (see 1:28).

27–28 Mark again reports the reaction of the people. Their amazement, which also reveals some alarm, prompted them to ask one another, "What is this?" The answer stresses both the newness of Jesus' teaching and its authority. They had had no previous experience with this kind of teaching. Jesus' authority was inherent within himself and therefore did not have to appeal to spells or incantations to exorcise the demon. One command accomplished it. The inevitable result was that Jesus' fame was spread "over the whole region of Galilee" (v.28). The amazement of the crowds coupled with the popularity that results is an important theme throughout Mark's gospel (see Dwyer, *Motif of Wonder*).

NOTES

24 See Hull, *Hellenistic Magic*, 67–69, for the use of a name to gain mastery over a demonic presence.

25 Guelich, 58, suggests that commands for silence were standard procedure for an exorcism.

2. *Healing Simon Peter's Mother-in-law (1:29–31)*

OVERVIEW

Mark indicates that this healing occurred immediately after the synagogue service and so was part of the long day of ministry in Capernaum described in vv.21–34. It is still the Sabbath, so the passage confirms that Jesus has no qualms about healing on that day (cf. 3:1–6). The eyewitness details suggest the account may have come from Peter's own recollection.

29 As soon as they left the synagogue, they went with James and John to the home of Simon and Andrew. 30 Simon's mother-in-law was in bed with a fever, and they told Jesus about her. 31 So he went to her, took her hand and helped her up. The fever left her and she began to wait on them.

COMMENTARY

29–31 Jesus leaves the synagogue and enters the house of Simon and Andrew, which appears to have been close by. The fact that Peter was married is also attested by Paul (1Co 9:5). Peter's mother-in-law is described as sick with a "fever" (vv.30–31), a general description that may refer to a symptom or to the disease itself. In the light of Jesus' growing reputation as a miracle worker, the statement "they told Jesus about her" is probably not just a point of information but actually an indirect request for healing. The healing is described simply: "He went to her, took her hand and helped her up" (v.31). Whereas Jesus performed the previous exorcism with a command (v.25), here he heals with a touch—a common pattern in Mark (1:41; 5:41; 6:5; 7:32–33; 8:23–25; cf. 3:10; 5:27; 6:56). Touching is a sign of compassion and identification with the sufferer.

The narrator notes that as the fever left her, she got out of bed and began to serve the needs of her guests (probably by preparing food for them). The statement about her service likely has two purposes: to show that the cure was instantaneous and complete and to demonstrate her restoration to spiritual service. The purpose of healing is to empower for service. There is no negative or demeaning sense in her actions. Even the Son of Man came to serve, not to be served (10:45). The statement also recalls the ministry of the angels to Jesus in the desert (1:13).

NOTES

29 Archaeologists have discovered an ancient house in Capernaum that may have been the home of Peter and Andrew. It is located just south of the synagogue, and inscriptions in the ruins suggest it was venerated by early Christians. An octagonal church was built over the site in the fifth century.

31 The term translated "left" (ἀφίημι, *aphiēmi*, GK *918*) is a strong one for this context ("forsook") and indicates once again Jesus' authority.

3. Healing Many People (1:32–34)

[32]That evening after sunset the people brought to Jesus all the sick and demon-possessed. [33]The whole town gathered at the door, [34]and Jesus healed many who had various diseases. He also drove out many demons, but he would not let the demons speak because they knew who he was.

COMMENTARY

32–34 "That evening after sunset" would be, according to Jewish reckoning, the following day, since the Sabbath ends at sundown. The Sabbath having ended, people could now bring, without breaking the Jewish law, their sick and demon-possessed to Jesus.

Mark has provided individual examples of an exorcism (v.26) and a healing (v.31); now he gives a summary of Jesus' healing and exorcism ministry in Galilee. The previous events were not isolated cases: "Jesus healed many" and "drove out many demons" (v.34). The reference to "many" is not exclusive. Mark is not saying that some were *not* healed (though that case is possible; see 6:5–6), but that Jesus healed *many*, not just one or a few. The reference to "the whole town" gathered at the door (v.33) is no doubt hyperbole meant to show the extraordinary popularity Jesus' miracles are generating.

Mark distinguishes between diseases of various kinds and demonic possession. While the gospel writers sometimes attribute illnesses to demonic influence, there is no indication here or elsewhere in the Gospels that all illness is demonic, as some in the ancient world believed.

Again, Jesus muzzles the demons, "because they knew who he was" (v.34). Luke is more specific: "because they knew he was the Christ" (Lk 4:41). This reluctance by Jesus to have the demons name him is probably both a demonstration of his authority over them and a reflection of his desire to reveal through his own words and deeds what kind of Messiah he was (one quite different from the popular conception). Jesus may also be seeking to avoid the accusation—which will shortly come (3:22)—that such demonic recognition means he is in league with Satan.

4. Leaving Capernaum (1:35–39)

[35]Very early in the morning, while it was still dark, Jesus got up, left the house and went off to a solitary place, where he prayed. [36]Simon and his companions went to look for him, [37]and when they found him, they exclaimed: "Everyone is looking for you!"

[38]Jesus replied, "Let us go somewhere else — to the nearby villages — so I can preach there also. That is why I have come." [39]So he traveled throughout Galilee, preaching in their synagogues and driving out demons.

COMMENTARY

35 Although Mark makes no explicit connection between v.35 and the preceding paragraph, he seems to be giving a sequence of events. Jesus, after a busy and no doubt exhausting evening of healings and exorcisms, got up very early the next morning and sought a quiet place to pray. The description of this as a "desert" (*erēmos*) place does not mean the wilderness, since there is no such place around Capernaum, but rather a place of solitude where Jesus can rejuvenate in the presence of his Father. There could, however, be a distant echo to Jesus' wilderness temptation, since that, too, was a time of solitude and preparation (the same word *erēmos* is used). Garland, 74, notes that here Jesus will again face temptation, as the disciples seek to lure him back "to the scene of so many personal triumphs and to where he has such a tremendous following."

In the other two places in Mark's gospel where Jesus prays, he is faced with a crisis (6:46; 14:32–41). Here, too, there is a crisis: the temptation to stay in a place of security and success rather than to fulfill the mission God has given to him. They are only interested in what he can do to heal their physical afflictions. So Jesus seeks the strength that only communion and fellowship with the Father can provide.

36–37 The disciples (here called "Simon and his companions"— not *mathētai*, perhaps because they are not acting like disciples) do not understand Jesus or his need for communion with the Father. So they go to look for him. Mark uses the strong verb *katadiōkō* ("track down," "hunt," usually in a hostile sense). The people are eager to find Jesus in order to see more miracles, and the disciples enthusiastically join in the search. Apparently, they think Jesus will be pleased to know that everyone is looking for him (v.37). They do not understand that this popular acclaim is not what Jesus desires.

38–39 Jesus' reply shows that his healings and exorcisms could be hindrances to understanding who he really was. The people of Capernaum were interested in him as a popular miracle worker only. So Jesus suggests that he and the disciples move on to other villages so that he might "preach there also" (v.38). His coming into the world was to proclaim God's good news and all that was involved in discipleship and suffering.

This purpose is not to diminish the importance of the healings and exorcisms. Both carried eschatological significance and were closely linked to Jesus' preaching of the kingdom of God. The exorcisms are evidence that the reign of God is overwhelming and is defeating the powers of sin and Satan. The healings confirm that the eschatological restoration of creation predicted by Isaiah and the prophets is taking place through Jesus' words and deeds (cf. Mt 11:5; Lk 7:22). While healings and exorcisms thus had a critically important place in Jesus' Galilean ministry (v.39), they were meant to confirm and support, rather than to usurp, the primary purpose for which he had come: to proclaim the good news of the kingdom of God. These verses are evidence that Mark wrote — at least in part — to counter those who placed too much emphasis on Jesus as a miracle worker and not enough on his salvation-bringing task of suffering as an atoning sacrifice for sins (Mk 10:45).

NOTES

35 The redundant and somewhat awkward Greek expression πρωῒ ἔννυχα λίαν (*prōi ennucha lian*) means something like "early in the morning, while it was still exceedingly dark." It emphasizes Jesus' need to carve out time alone with God in the midst of a hectic ministry.

5. Healing a Leper (1:40–45)

OVERVIEW

The pericope of the healing of a leper (1:40–45) serves as a connecting link between the sections before and after (1:21–39; 2:1–3:6). Like the episodes of healing and exorcism in 1:21–39, the miracle demonstrates Jesus' kingdom authority and his power to allay human suffering. It also results in increased popularity and the crush of the crowds (v.45). The episode links to the section that follows (2:1–3:6) because it concerns ritual purity, uncleanness, and the OT law, the issues that will provoke conflicts between Jesus and the scribes and Pharisees. Curiously, Jesus—who will be criticized in the following episodes for laxity toward the law—instructs the man to follow the procedure for ritual cleanness set out in the law of Moses (1:45).

40A man with leprosy came to him and begged him on his knees, "If you are willing, you
can make me clean."
41Filled with compassion, Jesus reached out his hand and touched the man. "I am
willing," he said. "Be clean!" 42Immediately the leprosy left him and he was cured.
43Jesus sent him away at once with a strong warning: 44"See that you don't tell this to
anyone. But go, show yourself to the priest and offer the sacrifices that Moses commanded
for your cleansing, as a testimony to them." 45Instead he went out and began to talk freely,
spreading the news. As a result, Jesus could no longer enter a town openly but stayed
outside in lonely places. Yet the people still came to him from everywhere.

COMMENTARY

40 The word "leprosy" (*lepra*) was used in biblical times to designate a wide variety of skin diseases. It was not limited to modern-day leprosy, or Hansen's disease. The descriptions given in Leviticus 13–14 suggest a variety of skin disorders, including psoriasis, lupus, ringworm, and others.

Because of the uncertainties of diagnosis and the difficulties in distinguishing highly contagious diseases from relatively harmless ones, the OT set out strict guidelines for the examination and isolation of these skin disorders (Lev 13–14). If found to be "leprous" after examination by the priest, the diseased individual would be isolated from the rest of the congregation and was required to wear torn clothes, cover the lower part of the face, and cry out "Unclean! Unclean!" whenever approached. As long as the disease remained, the person had to live alone outside the camp of the Israelites (Lev 13:45–46). Whatever variety of skin disorder this man had, it had been identified as "leprous" and so resulted in uncleanness and separation. His suffering was therefore social and religious as well as physical.

Instead of keeping his distance from Jesus, as the law demanded, the leprous man came directly to him and fell down on his knees to make his plea. He had no doubt that Jesus could heal him. He only wondered whether Jesus was willing. It is sometimes easier to believe in God's power than in his mercy.

41–42 On the assumption that the correct reading of v.41 is "being angered" ("Jesus was indignant," TNIV) and not "filled with compassion" (NIV; see Notes), the question arises, Why? Many answers have been suggested (see Cranfield, 92). Jesus cannot be angry with the leper, for the Lord immediately shows compassion on the man by touching him. Perhaps Jesus is deeply grieved at the ravaging effect of disease on the human condition, the result of a fallen creation (cf. Jn 11:35). Or perhaps Jesus recognizes this particular disease as demonic, so that his anger was focused neither on the man nor on the disease but on Satan, whose work he came to destroy. Understood in this way, the incident becomes another example of the fierce conflict between Jesus and Satan that plays such an important part in this gospel. Like Jesus' exorcisms and other healings, this one has eschatological significance, evidence of the power of the kingdom of God at work in Jesus (cf. Mt 11:5; Lk 7:22; Marcus, 210).

Jesus also expressed compassion. He reached out and touched the unclean leper—an act that, according to the Mosaic law, incurred defilement. Calvin, 1:374, says: "By his word alone he might have healed the *leper*; but he applied, at the same time, the touch of his hand, to express the feeling of compassion. Nor ought this to excite our wonder, since he chose to take upon him our flesh, that he might cleanse us from our sins."

Jesus' touching of the leper not only resulted in the man's being cured (v.42) but also revealed Jesus' attitude toward the ceremonial law. He boldly placed love and compassion over ritual and regulation. Instead of being defiled by the leprosy, Jesus brings purification to the man. In the new age of salvation, the movement of uncleanness will be reversed. The command to Israel to come out and be separate will become the command to go into the world as salt and light, to become agents of transformation. Believers are not defiled by the world but bring healing and sanctification to it (cf. 1Co 7:14).

43–44 As Jesus silences the demons who recognize him, so now he commands the healed man to keep quiet. Both verbs in v.43, like the statement of anger in v.41, appear to be unusually harsh. "Sent him away" is from *ekballō* (see Notes, 1:12), which often is used of driving out demons; and *embrimaomai* (GK *1839*, "with a strong warning") is a word that originally meant "to snort like a horse." While the command is clearly forceful, the words do not necessarily convey anger (cf. Gundry, 96–97). Jesus is not rebuking the man in anger but is warning him forcefully: "Now listen, and listen good. Get to the priest immediately, and don't tell anyone about this!"

The reason for the command is likely similar to the muting of demons. Jesus wants to define his messiahship on his own terms rather than through the expectations of others. Jesus also recognizes that widespread acclaim for his miracles will create a level of popularity that will hinder the essential purpose of his ministry, namely, to proclaim the kingdom of God. In fact, however, Jesus' widespread popularity is exactly what develops (see v.45).

Jesus also instructs the leper to show himself to the priest and to offer sacrifices that were required by the Mosaic law. These procedures are given in detail in the laws of leprosy in Leviticus 14:2–31. Mark's purpose may be to show that Jesus did not oppose the law per se, but only the hypocritical and casuistic way in which it was applied by the Pharisees. More likely, Jesus has societal and personal concerns in mind. The man needed to perform these rituals to be accepted back into the Jewish community.

The last phrase—"as a testimony to them"—could be understood in at least four different ways: (1) evidence for the priests and the people of Jesus' faithfulness to the law; (2) evidence *for their benefit* of Jesus' messianic authority in the healing (for the phrase used positively, see 13:9); (3) evidence *against* them to be used at the final judgment, assuming they will reject Jesus despite the healing (for the phrase used in this negative sense, see 6:11 and possibly also 13:9); or simply (4) evidence that the man was truly clean, and so restored to society. The first probably places too much emphasis on legalistic questions, which are not Jesus' primary concern. The second and third are even less likely, since they would contradict Jesus' command to silence. The fourth is the most natural reading, namely, that the appearance and sacrifices before the priest are testimonies of the man's ritual cleanness and so his restoration to the community.

45 Despite Jesus' command, the leper could not contain himself and proclaimed far and wide what Jesus had done for him. The results were both positive and negative. On the one hand, more and more people heard about Jesus. On the other, the growing masses curtailed his public ministry. He avoided going into the towns and chose rather to stay in more isolated places. But even in his isolation people managed to find him and "came to him from everywhere."

NOTES

41 The translators of the NIV may have been correct in following the reading σπλαγχνισθείς (*splanchnistheis*, GK *5072*, "filled with compassion"), since the MS evidence strongly favors it. However, it is difficult to explain how the alternate reading ὀργισθείς (*orgistheis*, "being angry") came into existence. It is much easier to explain the scribal origin of σπλαγχνισθείς, *splanchnistheis*, as the result of embarrassment over the ascription of anger to Jesus. Metzger, 65, counters that copyists did not remove references to Jesus' anger elsewhere (3:5; 10:14), but in those cases the anger is understandable from the context. Here it is much more difficult. It is especially significant that Matthew and Mark do not have σπλαγχνισθείς, *splanchnistheis*, in their parallels (though they use the term elsewhere). Why would they eliminate a reference to Jesus' compassion? Their omission of Mark's ὀργισθείς, *orgistheis*, is easily explainable. Opting for the rendering ὀργισθείς, *orgistheis*, here is also consistent with the use of ἐμβριμάομαι (*embrimaomai*, "speak harshly to") in v.43, which has an element of indignation or anger in it. The TNIV accurately renders, "Jesus was indignant."

A demonic explanation for the leprosy is possible, since scale disease is ascribed to an evil spirit in *b. Ketubim 61b* and perhaps already in the Qumran scrolls (4Q272; see Marcus, 209, citing J. Baumgarten, "The 4Q Zadokite Fragments on Skin Disease," *Journal of Jewish Studies* 41 [1990]:153–65).

43 The use of the same verb ἐμβριμάομαι (*embrimaomai*, GK *1839*) in 14:5 is sometimes said to indicate that anger is intended, but even in that context the verb could mean that they spoke forcefully and with strong emotion rather than with actual anger. In human emotions, the line between forcefulness and indignation can be very thin.

D. Conflict with the Religious Leaders (2:1–3:6)

OVERVIEW

The five episodes recounted in 2:1–3:6 represent a distinct section in Mark's gospel, a section that focuses on Jesus' controversies with the religious leaders. It concludes with the plot of the Pharisees and Herodians to kill Jesus (3:6) and is framed at the beginning and end by statements of Jesus' growing popularity and the crush of the crowds (1:45; 3:7). The previous account of the healing of the leper hinted at controversy as Jesus touched a man with leprosy in apparent violation of the laws of purity. Now Jesus comes into open conflict with the teachers of the law.

1. Healing a Paralytic (2:1–12)

OVERVIEW

The account of the healing of the paralytic is an appropriate transition from the healing stories of ch. 1, for it involves elements of both healing and controversy. The story also continues the theme of Jesus' authority so prominent throughout his Galilean ministry. In the first miracle of the gospel, the exorcism in the Capernaum synagogue, Jesus' authority in teaching was contrasted with that of the scribes (1:22). Now—again in Capernaum—the scribes challenge his authority to forgive sins.

It has been suggested (e.g., Bultmann, Schweizer, Taylor) that vv.1–12 are the conflation of two stories. The first (vv.1–5a, 10b–12) is a miracle story, and the other (vv.5b–10a) is a separate story about the forgiveness of sins. This kind of conclusion was typical of form-critical analysis, which assumed oral stories always moved from the simple to the complex. Such a conclusion, however, represents an overly simplistic analysis of oral tradition by assuming too much standardization for oral forms and hard-and-fast "rules" of transmission. In fact, oral traditions sometimes move from complex to simple, and oral "forms" are not as fixed as is sometimes assumed. Dissecting the present passage fails to recognize the internal consistency of the narrative and the close relationship between the healing of the body and the forgiveness of sins. Whatever its possible origins, it clearly represents a unity in Mark's gospel.

1 A few days later, when Jesus again entered Capernaum, the people heard that he had
come home. 2 So many gathered that there was no room left, not even outside the door,
and he preached the word to them. 3 Some men came, bringing to him a paralytic, carried
by four of them. 4 Since they could not get him to Jesus because of the crowd, they made
an opening in the roof above Jesus and, after digging through it, lowered the mat the
paralyzed man was lying on. 5 When Jesus saw their faith, he said to the paralytic, "Son,
your sins are forgiven."

6 Now some teachers of the law were sitting there, thinking to themselves, 7 "Why does
this fellow talk like that? He's blaspheming! Who can forgive sins but God alone?"

8 Immediately Jesus knew in his spirit that this was what they were thinking in their
hearts, and he said to them, "Why are you thinking these things? 9 Which is easier: to say to
the paralytic, 'Your sins are forgiven,' or to say, 'Get up, take your mat and walk'? 10 But that
you may know that the Son of Man has authority on earth to forgive sins ..." He said to the
paralytic, 11 "I tell you, get up, take your mat and go home." 12 He got up, took his mat and
walked out in full view of them all. This amazed everyone and they praised God, saying,
"We have never seen anything like this!"

COMMENTARY

1 Jesus had been away from Capernaum for several days while traveling throughout Galilee. He now returns to the town that has served as his base of operations in the northern part of the country. While Jesus' popularity prevented him from "openly" entering a town (1:45), he is able to slip back into Capernaum on this occasion. The Greek phrase *en oikō* could mean "in a house" but often carries the idiomatic sense "home." It may refer here to the home of Peter and Andrew, which appears to have been Jesus' temporary residence while in Capernaum (1:29). Little can be kept secret in a village community, and the report soon goes out that Jesus is back in town.

2 The house quickly filled with people, and the overflow was so great that the space outside the door was blocked. They no doubt flocked to him because they wanted to see him perform more miracles. But Jesus was not working miracles inside the house. He was doing what he came to do: preaching the gospel to the people (1:38).

3–4 In order to understand the action these verses describe, it is necessary to visualize the layout of a typical peasant's house in first-century Palestine. It was usually a small, one-room structure with a flat roof. Middle Eastern roofs were often used for storage, drying fruit, and for sleeping on warm summer nights. Access was by means of an outside stairway or ladder built against an outside wall of the house (cf. modern escape ladders on the outsides of multistoried apartment complexes). The roof itself was usually made of wooden beams with thatched and compacted earth in order to shed the rain.

The four men brought a paralyzed man to the house where Jesus was preaching (v.3); but when they saw the size of the crowd, they realized it was impossible to enter by the door. So they carried him up the outside stairway to the roof (v.4). There they dug up the compacted thatch and earth (no doubt dirt showered down on those inside the house below) and lowered the man through the now-exposed beams to the floor below.

5 Jesus recognized the ingenuity and persistence of the men as evidence of faith. "Their faith" is primarily the faith of the friends, though it could also include that of the paralyzed man. Jesus often heals in response to faith in Mark (5:34, 36; 9:23–24; 10:52; cf. Mt 15:28), and that is what the crowd—and the implied reader—is expecting. Jesus' words are meant to be surprising and even shocking: "Son, your sins are forgiven."

It is possible that the man's disease resulted from his sinful behavior, but Jesus does not say so. Scripture affirms that disease *may* result from individual sins (Dt 28:27; Ps 107:17–18; Jn 5:14; Ac 5:1–11; 1Co 11:30; 1Jn 5:16), but it certainly has other causes too (Job 1:8; Lk 13:1–5; Jn 9:2–3). Yet all disease and suffering is ultimately related to the fallen state of humanity, so that the dawn of eschatological salvation brings both forgiveness and healing (Isa 29:18, 23; 32:3; 33:34; Jer 31:34; 33:8; 36:3). Jesus' proclamation of the kingdom of God means that the time of healing and forgiveness has arrived.

6 Mark has already mentioned the teachers of the law in 1:22, where their teaching is contrasted with Jesus' authoritative teaching. Here they become directly involved with Jesus. Luke 5:17 says that they had come from "every village of Galilee and from Judea and Jerusalem." Presumably, at this early stage in Jesus' ministry they were present more from curiosity than animosity. That will soon change.

7 Jesus' statement in v.5 that "your sins are forgiven" could be taken as a divine passive meaning "God has forgiven you," with Jesus functioning as God's spokesperson. The OT priests pronounced God's forgiveness of repentant sinners who brought sacrificial offerings to the temple, and a prophet such as Nathan could pronounce David forgiven on the basis of his repentance (2Sa 12:13). But Jesus' functioning as God's spokesperson is clearly not how Mark intended his readers to hear Jesus' words, since the teachers of the law immediately accuse Jesus of blasphemy, and since in v.9 Jesus explicitly declares his own authority to forgive sins.

The Mishnah defines blasphemy narrowly as the act of pronouncing the divine name (*m. Sanh.* 7:5); but Bock (*Blasphemy and Exaltation*, ch. 2) and others have shown that the term could be used for a much wider range of offenses against God. To lay claim to God's sole prerogative to forgive sins would certainly have qualified. If the scribes are correct about who Jesus is, their reasoning is flawless. In Jewish teaching even the Messiah could not forgive sins. The manner in which the accusation is expressed, "Who can forgive sins except One—God" (with Greek *heis*, "one," instead of *monos*, "only," "alone"), may indicate an allusion to the Shema, the classic Jewish statement of monotheism from Deuteronomy 6:4: "Hear, O Israel: The LORD our God, the LORD is one." Jesus is accused of usurping God's unique position.

8–9 The teachers of the law had not openly expressed their misgivings about Jesus' actions. They were "thinking in their hearts" that he had blasphemed. There is irony here. Just as they are inwardly castigating Jesus for claiming a prerogative of God, Jesus is reading their minds—demonstrating the divine attribute of omniscience!

Jesus challenges them with the question, "Which is easier: to say to the paralytic, 'Your sins are forgiven,' or to say, 'Get up, take your mat and walk'?" (v.9). Of course, as Jesus meant the words, neither of the two was easier. Effecting both was equally impossible for human beings and equally possible for God. To the teachers of the law, it was easier to make the statement about forgiveness, for who could verify its fulfillment? But to say, "Get up ... and walk"—the authority to issue that command could indeed be verified by an actual, observable healing. Jesus' question takes the form of a rabbinic-style "lesser-to-greater" (*qal waḥomer*) argument. If someone can do the "harder" (in this case, physically heal someone), it will prove the "easier" (here the forgiving of sins) has also been accomplished.

10–11 Some commentators have taken the first part of v.10—"But that you may know that the Son of Man has authority on earth to forgive sins"—to be a narrative aside addressed to Mark's readers rather than a statement to the scribes. This view is meant to solve the problem of the awkwardness of the parenthetic remark, "he said to the paralytic," in the second half of the verse, and also to reserve Jesus' public use of the title "Son of Man" until after the crucial incident of 8:29. The title "Son of Man" occurs only two times before 8:31 (here and in 2:28) but twelve times from then onward as Jesus' title for self-disclosure to his disciples (cf. G. H. Boobyer, "Mark 2:10a and the Interpretation of the Healing of the Paralytic," *HTR* 47 [1954]: 115–20; Lane, 96–98; Cranfield, 100).

While this interpretation is possible, nothing in the context suggests a change of addressees. The "you" of v.10 is most naturally taken as the scribes addressed in vv.8–9. A narrative aside would lose much of the dramatic effect of the episode, where Jesus claims the very authority the scribes deny him in v.7. Jesus' pronouncement *is* the critical point of the episode. Most telling against this view is the fact that the gospel writers never use the title "Son of Man" in their editorial comments (with a possible exception being Mk 2:28, which is also disputed).

"Son of Man" is Jesus' most common self-designation in the Gospels. In the OT the Hebrew designation *ben ʾādām* ("son of man") means "a human being" (see Ps 8:4), and Jesus' use of the title certainly points to his humanity. Yet there is further significance to the title. The OT book of Daniel speaks of "one like a son of man," an exalted messianic figure who comes with the clouds of heaven and receives authority, glory, and sovereign power from God, setting up an eternal kingdom that will never be destroyed (Da 7:13–14; cf. *1 En.* 34–53). On several occasions in Mark, Jesus identifies himself with this messianic figure (8:38; 13:26–27; 14:62). Historically, Jesus probably preferred the title because it expressed his identity without the political and military connotations that titles such as "Christ" and "son of David" carried in first-century Judaism. He could use it to define his messiahship on his own terms. In Mark's narrative Jesus uses the title to demonstrate his messianic authority (2:10, 28), affirm his mission of service and suffering (8:31; 9:9, 12; 10:33–34), and predict his return in glory to save and to judge (8:38; 13:26–27; 14:62).

What does it mean that the Son of Man has authority to forgive sins "on earth"? There are three main possibilities for the meaning of the phrase: (1) a sphere of influence, in contrast to the Father's authority in heaven; (2) "here and now" (i.e., during Jesus' earthly ministry, perhaps in contrast to the Son of Man's future authority in heaven); (3) as qualifying "sins," and so meaning "earthly sins" (i.e., those committed by human beings). The first is most likely, not in the sense of limiting Jesus' authority, but rather to show that divine authority to forgive sins is not the exclusive right of the Father in heaven—it is now rightfully exercised by the Son of Man on earth (cf. France, 129).

The words "he said to the paralytic" constitute a parenthesis to explain that the following words are addressed not to the teachers of the law but to the paralytic. Presumably, Jesus indicated his change by some sort of gesture.

12 The healing verified the claim to grant forgiveness. As surely as actual healing followed Jesus' statement "Get up" (v.11), so actual forgiveness resulted from his saying "your sins are forgiven." Hunter, 38, writes, "He did the miracle which they could see that they might know that he had done the other one that they could not see."

The man responded immediately (*euthys*; not translated in NIV). "In full view of them all" (i.e., the entire crowd and especially the teachers of the law, who had challenged Jesus' authority to forgive sins), the ex-paralytic walked out. Again, the response of the crowd (presumably the "all" includes the teachers of the law) was one of amazement, and Mark records the added response of their giving praise to God for what had happened. Never before had they witnessed anything like this event.

The significance of this story is not to be understood primarily in terms of the compassion that moves Jesus to heal the man's paralyzed body. The emphasis is on the forgiveness of sins, the root cause of all sickness and disease. In this act of forgiveness Jesus was declaring the presence of God's kingdom.

NOTES

2 "He preached the word to them" translates ἐλάλει αὐτοῖς τὸν λόγον (*elalei autois ton logon*). The word λόγον, *logon* (GK *3364*), is here used of the "message of salvation," the "good news" (BDAG, 599).

4 Theissen (*Miracle Stories*, 52–53) notes that it is a common theme in healing accounts that an obstacle blocks the suppliant from approaching Jesus (5:27–28, 35; 10:46–48; cf. Lk 19:3). Overcoming the obstacle is a sign of faith and is rewarded with healing.

5 See Marcus, 221, for more on the scriptural connection between sin and disease.

7 Some have claimed that a fragmentary text from Qumran, *The Prayer of Nabonidus* (4Q242), presents a Jewish exorcist as claiming to forgive the sins of Nabonidus. But the text is fragmentary and its meaning is disputed. See Marcus, 217, for details. Even if the text makes this claim, it would represent one very small exception to the rule.

2. Eating with Sinners (2:13–17)

OVERVIEW

This episode is the second in the series of five conflicts with the religious leaders. Each controversy is highlighted by an authoritative pronouncement by Jesus. The call of Levi introduces another key Markan motif: the humble recipients of God's salvific blessings. Forgiveness of sins and healing come not to the self-righteous religious leaders but to sinners and outcasts who respond with faith and repentance to Jesus' kingdom proclamation. Jesus has just announced his authority to forgive sins (2:10); he now calls a notorious sinner in need of forgiveness.

Two short incidents make up this scene. The first is a *call narrative* in which Jesus beckons the tax collector Levi to come and follow him in discipleship. The second is a *pronouncement story* that climaxes in an authoritative statement by Jesus. The narrative is intended to set up this climactic pronouncement.

13 Once again Jesus went out beside the lake. A large crowd came to him, and he
began to teach them. 14 As he walked along, he saw Levi son of Alphaeus sitting at the tax
collector's booth. "Follow me," Jesus told him, and Levi got up and followed him.
15 While Jesus was having dinner at Levi's house, many tax collectors and "sinners" were
eating with him and his disciples, for there were many who followed him. 16 When the
teachers of the law who were Pharisees saw him eating with the "sinners" and tax collectors, they asked his disciples: "Why does he eat with tax collectors and 'sinners'?"
17 On hearing this, Jesus said to them, "It is not the healthy who need a doctor, but the
sick. I have not come to call the righteous, but sinners."

COMMENTARY

13 The scene begins with the call of Levi. The only connecting word Mark uses is *palin* ("once again"), which makes it clear that what follows is a separate unit of tradition. The setting is the shore of Lake Galilee. Jesus' popularity with the crowds was still very evident—"a large crowd came to him, and he began to teach them."

14 There may be a change of scene here, with Jesus finishing his teaching and then walking beside the sea. Or Jesus may have done his teaching on this occasion as rabbis often did theirs—"as he walked along." In either case, Jesus comes upon Levi the son of Alphaeus at his tax collector's booth. The parallel text in the first gospel identifies this tax collector as "Matthew" (Mt 9:9) and lists him as one of the twelve disciples (Mt 10:3). Although Mark and Luke also list Matthew as one of the twelve (Mk 3:18; Lk 6:15), neither one explicitly identifies Levi the tax collector with Matthew the disciple. Many commentators believe that the author of the first gospel has merged two stories involving different individuals in order to make this episode a call to discipleship. But the easier and more likely explanation is that "Matthew" and "Levi" are two names for the same person. "Levi" may have been his given name and "Matthew" ("gift of God") his apostolic name (cf. "Simon Peter"). Or perhaps both names were given at birth. Another one of the twelve is named "James son of Alphaeus," perhaps Levi's brother.

Jesus found Levi at the "tax collector's booth"—probably the tollbooth on the road that ran from Damascus through Capernaum to the Mediterranean coast. Levi was likely employed by Herod Antipas, the tetrarch of Galilee, as a tax collector for goods in transit. A traveler from either Herod Philip's territory or the Decapolis would naturally pass through Capernaum on entering Galilee. The Jews despised their fellow tax collectors because of their duplicity with the oppressive rulers (both the Romans and their client kings, such as Herod Antipas) and their reputation for dishonesty and corruption. Extortion was common, for tax collectors made their living from the money they could collect over and above taxes owed. The Mishnah prohibits even receiving alms from a tax collector at his office, since the money is presumed to have been gained illegally (*m. B. Qam.* 10:1). If a tax collector entered a house, all that was in it became unclean (*m. Ṭehar.* 7:6). The rabbis went so far as to permit lying to tax collectors to protect one's property (*m. Ned.* 3:4). It is possible that Levi was a Levite (a descendant of

Jacob's son Levi, whose tribe was charged with serving in the temple; Nu 1:50; 3:12, etc.), since most people named "Levi" in the first century were in fact Levites (see Marcus, 225). If the Levi in Mark was indeed a Levite, he would have been particularly despised by his countrymen for choosing such a contemptible vocation over a religious one.

The parallel call of the four fishermen in 1:16, 18 confirms that Levi's call is one to discipleship. There was much at stake for Levi in accepting Jesus' challenge. Fishermen could easily go back to fishing after taking a "leave of absence" (as some of the disciples did after Jesus' crucifixion), but for Levi there would be little possibility of his returning to his occupation. No doubt his post would have been filled very soon after he left it, for jobs as tax collectors were highly sought after as sure ways to "get rich quick."

15 The Greek *katakeisthai auton* ("while he was reclining") carries the connotation of a formal banquet or dinner party, at which guests would recline on cushions around a low table (cf. Joachim Jeremias, *Eucharistic Words of Jesus* [Minneapolis: Fortress, 1977], 48–49). The dinner was probably Levi's farewell party before he left to become one of Jesus' disciples, or perhaps he simply wanted to gather his friends together so that they, too, could have an opportunity to meet Jesus. While the Greek text refers ambiguously to "his house" and could refer to either Jesus or Levi, the context suggests that Levi's house is intended. The parallel in Luke explicitly says that Levi made a great feast at his house (Lk 5:29).

The phrase "eating with Jesus [NIV, 'him']" (*synanekeinto tō Iēsou*) suggests that the tax collectors and sinners were having dinner *with Jesus*. Although at Levi's home, Jesus assumes the role of the host. Lane, 106, comments, "When this is understood, the interest of the entire pericope centers on the significance of Messiah eating with sinners. The specific reference in v.17 to Jesus' call of sinners to the Kingdom suggests that the basis of table-fellowship was *messianic forgiveness*, and the meal itself was an anticipation of the messianic banquet" (emphasis his).

"For there were many who followed him" shows that Jesus' following included more than the twelve disciples. It also stresses Jesus' growing popularity among those treated with contempt by the religious establishment. Jesus' reputation for associating with notorious sinners and offering God's forgiveness to them clearly piqued the interest of these people. Here was a rabbi who actually welcomed contact with them.

16 Table fellowship carried great significance in the ancient world; to dine with someone meant acceptance of that person. That Jesus would include in his most intimate circle a man associated with such a disreputable profession and would sit at table with tax collectors and sinners was too much for the teachers of the law.

The Pharisees appear here for the first time in Mark's gospel. The Greek phrase *hoi grammateis tōn Pharisaiōn* ("the scribes of the Pharisees") means those teachers of the law who were also Pharisees. Not all Pharisees were scribes, but many were. Little is known of either the origin or the predecessors of the Pharisees. The probability is that they were the successors of the *Hasidim*, the pious Jews who joined forces with Mattathias and his sons during the Maccabean period. They later split off in opposition to the Hellenizing tendency of the later Hasmoneans (the ruling dynasty that arose from the Maccabees). They first appear under the name "Pharisees" during the reign of the Hasmonean John Hyrcanus (135–104 BC). The most distinctive characteristic of the Pharisees was their strict adherence to Torah—not only the written law but also the oral law, a body of traditions that expanded and elaborated the OT law (the "traditions of the elders," 7:3). According to some rabbinic traditions, both the written and oral law had been given to Moses on Mount Sinai (*m. ᵓAbot* 1:1–2). Josephus (*J.W.* 1.5.2 §110) wrote, "The Pharisees [are] a body of Jews with the reputation of excelling the rest of their nation in the observances of religion, and as exact exponents of the laws."

Although many Pharisees were doubtless pious and godly men, others were characterized by jealousy, hypocrisy, and religious formalism. Jesus did not criticize them for their goals of purity and obedience, but for their hypocrisy. He accused them of saying one thing but doing another, of raising their interpretations (mere "human traditions") to the level of God's commandments (7:8), and of becoming obsessed with externals while neglecting the more important matters of the heart—justice, mercy, and faithfulness. For their part, the separatist Pharisees attacked Jesus' association with tax collectors and sinners and the way he placed himself above Sabbath regulations (2:23–28). Despite these differences Jesus was much closer theologically to the Pharisees than to the Sadducees, for with the Pharisees he shared belief in the authority of Scripture, the resurrection, and the coming of the Messiah. Jesus' frequent conflicts with the Pharisees arose because he challenged them on their own turf and because they viewed him as a threat to their leadership and influence over the people.

The consorting of Jesus with people who openly refused to keep the requirements of the law prompted the question, "Why does he eat with tax collectors and 'sinners'?" "Sinners" in this passage could be a technical term for those who failed to maintain the high standards of ritual purity kept by the Pharisees. A scrupulous Pharisee would not eat at the home of a common Israelite (those known as *ᶜam ha-ᵓaretz*, "people of the land"), since the Pharisees could not be sure that the commoner's food was ceremonially clean or that it had been properly tithed (*m. Demai* 2:2). Yet if "sinners" here designated commoners, Jesus and his disciples would also be so classified. More likely, "sinners" in this context means the truly wicked, those viewed by the general populace as evildoers. Jesus offers God's forgiveness to those who have transgressed his law.

17 No statement of Jesus in this gospel is more profound than this one. Jesus begins with a proverb and then clarifies it with reference to his ministry. "Only the sick need a doctor" was a common proverb in both Jewish and non-Jewish circles. A doctor ministers not to healthy persons but to the sick. The application is that Jesus came not to call the "righteous" (i.e., the self-righteous) but "sinners" (i.e., not merely people who refuse to carry out the details of the law but those who are alienated from the life of God). Jesus' call is to salvation; and in order to share in it, a person must first recognize his need of it. A self-righteous person is incapable of recognizing that need, but a sinner can. Hunter, 40–41, writes, "It would be true to say that this word of Jesus strikes the keynote of the gospel. The new thing in Christianity is not the doctrine that God saves sinners. No Jew would have denied that. It is the assertion 'that God loves and saves them *as sinners*.' ... This is the authentic and glorious doctrine of true Christianity in any age" (emphasis his).

NOTES

13–17 For more, see J. Dewey, *Markan Public Debate: Literary Technique, Concentric Structure, and Theology in Mark 2:1–3:6* (SBLDS 48; Chico, Calif.; Scholars Press, 1980); A. Hultgren, *Jesus and His Adversaries* (Minneapolis: Augsburg, 1979).

13 The verb ἐδίδασκεν (*edidasken*) is probably an inceptive or ingressive imperfect emphasizing the beginning of the action: "he began to teach."

14 The confusion of Levi's identity is also evident in a textual variant, with some Western and Caesarean MSS reading "James son of Alphaeus" in this verse. This is no doubt a scribal harmonization under the influence of Mark 3:18, where James is identified as one of the Twelve. A copyist assumed that since James and Levi had the same father, they were the same person (see Hooker, 94; Witherington, 119).

15 For the view that it was Jesus' house, not Matthew's, see E. S. Malbon, "TĒ OIKIA AUTOU: Mark 2.15 in Context," *NTS* 31 (1985): 282–92.

17 *Mekilta* to Exodus 15:26 has the following proverb: "If they are not sick, why do they need a physician?" According to Plutarch (*Apophthegmata laconica*, 230–31), Pausanias said of philosophers that "doctors ... are not to be found among the well but customarily spend their time among the sick." See Gundry, 129, for other references.

3. A Question about Fasting (2:18–22)

OVERVIEW

In this third of five controversies involving the religious leaders, Jesus is questioned as to why his disciples do not fast as a sign of their piety. Jesus uses the question to make a profound parabolic statement about the eschatological significance of his mission.

[18]Now John's disciples and the Pharisees were fasting. Some people came and asked Jesus, "How is it that John's disciples and the disciples of the Pharisees are fasting, but yours are not?"

[19]Jesus answered, "How can the guests of the bridegroom fast while he is with them? They cannot, so long as they have him with them. [20]But the time will come when the bridegroom will be taken from them, and on that day they will fast.

[21]"No one sews a patch of unshrunk cloth on an old garment. If he does, the new piece will pull away from the old, making the tear worse. [22]And no one pours new wine into old wineskins. If he does, the wine will burst the skins, and both the wine and the wineskins will be ruined. No, he pours new wine into new wineskins."

COMMENTARY

18 The law required fasting only on the Day of Atonement (Lev 16:29, 31; 23:27–32; Nu 29:7), but after the exile the Jews observed four other annual fasts (Zec 7:5; 8:19). A fifth fast was added in association with the festival of Purim (Est 9:31). In NT times the stricter Pharisees fasted twice a week (Monday and Thursday; cf. Lk 18:12; *Did.* 8:1; *b. Taʿan. 12a*). The phrase "the disciples of the Pharisees" is unique in the NT (but cf. Lk 5:33). It presents some difficulty, for the Pharisees were a religious sect, not teachers, and so did not have disciples. However, some Pharisees were also scribes (NIV, "teachers of the law") and as such did have disciples. "Disciples of the Pharisees" may also be used in a nontechnical sense to refer to people who were influenced by the teachings and practice of the Pharisees.

Mark does not say why these two groups were fasting. A variety of reasons could prompt the practice: sorrow, repentance, humility, self-denial, or preparation for service. The Pharisees' "disciples" were probably observing one of the biweekly fasts. John's disciples may have been fasting because he was in prison, or perhaps in anticipation of the messianic age (see Lane, 113). The latter explanation would fit the three parables that follow, which contrast the old age of promise with the new age of fulfillment. Whatever the specific reason for fasting, it was meant to be a sign of true piety. Mark does not specify who asks the question, but it may have been the scribes of the Pharisees referred to in the previous passage. The question is an implicit claim to higher spirituality. Though the question is about Jesus' disciples, it clearly challenges his own example. If he is so spiritual, why does he not encourage his disciples to live up to the high religious standards set by others?

19–20 Jesus answers in a parable. A Jewish wedding feast was a particularly joyous occasion. The guests joined in celebrations that sometimes lasted a week. To fast during that time of great joy and festivity would be unthinkable. Jesus indicates that he is the bridegroom and his disciples the guests. His presence should be a time of joyful celebration, not of mourning and sorrow. The wedding imagery also likely carries eschatological significance. Although the Messiah is never explicitly described as a bridegroom in the OT (but cf. Isa 62:5), the age of salvation is often portrayed with feasting and wedding imagery—the "messianic banquet" (Isa 25:6–8; 65:13–14; cf. Lk 13:29; Mt 8:11; *TDNT* 4:1103). The age of promise is giving way to the age of fulfillment, and with it a time of joyful celebration. Jesus' words here have parallels to the parable of the children in the marketplace in the "Q" passage (Mt 11:16–19; Lk 7:31–35). Jesus there compares John's ministry to a funeral dirge (indicating sorrow and repentance) and his own ministry to a celebratory dance. John called for fasting and repentance in solemn anticipation of the coming age of salvation. Jesus called for joyful celebration, for the time of salvation had arrived.

Yet Jesus does not reject the spiritual value of fasting. While he remains with them they will rejoice, not fast; but he will not always be with them. When he is taken away (v.20), fasting will be appropriate. The mention of the removal of the bridegroom has sometimes been explained as a later addition, with the church reading the death of Jesus back into his life. Yet there is little warrant for this conclusion. First, the reference to death is veiled. Jesus only speaks of the bridegroom as being "taken from them," not specifically of death (though see Notes, v.20). More important, there is no reason—even from a merely human perspective—why Jesus could not have foreseen and predicted his death. He faced serious opposition from the religious authorities, who considered him as being in league with Beelzebul (3:22–27), a blasphemer (2:7), a false prophet (14:65), and a Sabbath breaker (2:23–28; 3:1–6). He must have foreseen that this conflict could result in death. Jesus also often spoke of the persecution and murder of the OT prophets and identified himself with them (6:4; 12:1–11; cf. Mt 5:12; 13:57; 23:29–39; Lk 6:23, 26; 11:47–50; 13:33–35).

21–22 The short parables here at first seem an odd change of subject from the marriage analogy. Yet they follow the same theme of inappropriate actions in the light of the dawning age of salvation. Patching an old garment with a new cloth and putting new wine into old wineskins are just as inappropriate as fasting at a wedding feast. The new age of salvation means a new way of life and a new orientation toward God.

The two parables make the same point. A patch of unshrunk cloth sewn on a garment will shrink when washed and thus tear the garment. The new is incompatible with the old. So also is new wine in old wineskins. In ancient times wine was kept in animal skins. New skins were soft and pliable and would stretch when wine that had not yet completed fermentation was put in them. Old wineskins that were already stretched would become brittle and unable to stretch further. The gas from the new wine fermenting in them would burst them, thus destroying both the wine and the wineskin.

Jesus' point is that the coming of the kingdom represents a new work that God is doing. Jesus is not merely promoting a reform movement within Judaism (i.e., "patching" the old); rather, his coming is the turning point of human history—it marks the transition from the age of promise to the age of fulfillment. Everything has changed.

NOTES

19 The Greek idiom οἱ υἱοὶ τοῦ νυμφῶνος (*hoi huioi tou nymphōnos*, "children of the bridechamber") could mean either the wedding guests or the attendants of the groom.

20 The verb ἀπαρθῇ, *aparthē* ("will be taken away") is from ἀπαίρω (*apairō*, GK *554*, "take away," "remove") and occurs in the NT only here and in the parallels in Matthew and Luke. According to Bratcher and Nida, 92, "the verb as such does not state whether the removal is natural or sudden and violent. The context of the whole saying, however, implies a violent removal that will provoke sorrow (cf. the use of the verb in the LXX Isa 53:8 [where, however, the simple form αἴρω, *airō*, is used])."

22 The phrase "new wine in new wineskins" is a verbless clause in Greek and may have been a slogan in the wine industry.

See John 2:1–12 for another episode in which new "choice wine" likely represents the messianic banquet and the dawning age of salvation.

4. The Lord of the Sabbath (2:23–3:6)

OVERVIEW

The fourth and fifth controversy stories in this series both concern Jesus' apparent violation of the Sabbath. The first confirms that the Sabbath was made for the benefit of human beings and that Jesus himself is Lord of the Sabbath. The second shows that the meeting of human needs takes precedent over legalistic Sabbath restrictions. Both, like so many episodes in these early chapters of Mark, confirm Jesus' extraordinary authority as Messiah.

a. Picking grain on the Sabbath (2:23–28)

OVERVIEW

The specific time or place of this incident is not given, though the mention of kernels of grain might suggest the season is early summer. The theme of the incident, not its chronological position in the life of Jesus, is what determined its inclusion at this point in Mark's gospel. The conflict centers on the keeping of the Sabbath—an issue far more important in Judaism than the question of fasting.

[23]One Sabbath Jesus was going through the grainfields, and as his disciples walked
along, they began to pick some heads of grain. [24]The Pharisees said to him, "Look, why are
they doing what is unlawful on the Sabbath?"
[25]He answered, "Have you never read what David did when he and his companions
were hungry and in need? [26]In the days of Abiathar the high priest, he entered the house
of God and ate the consecrated bread, which is lawful only for priests to eat. And he also
gave some to his companions."
[27]Then he said to them, "The Sabbath was made for man, not man for the Sabbath. [28]So
the Son of Man is Lord even of the Sabbath."

COMMENTARY

23–24 The main point of contention was not the act of harvesting the heads of grain. Such activity was explicitly allowed in the law: "If you enter your neighbor's grainfield, you may pick kernels with your hands, but you must not put a sickle to his standing grain" (Dt 23:25). What the Pharisees objected to was harvesting grain on the Sabbath. In the Mishnah, reaping is one of the thirty-nine acts forbidden to do on the Sabbath (*m. Šabb.* 7:2).

25–26 Jesus meets the accusation of the Pharisees with a counterquestion. The incident he refers to is recorded in 1 Samuel 21:1–6. David and his companions were hungry and ate the consecrated bread—the twelve loaves baked of fine flour arranged in two rows or piles on the table in the Holy Place. Fresh loaves were brought into the sanctuary each Sabbath to replace the old ones, which were then eaten by the priests (cf. Ex 25:30; 35:13; 39:36; Lev 24:5–9; see Josephus, *Ant.* 3.10.7 §§255–56). Although the action of David was contrary to the law, he was not condemned in Scripture for it. Jesus does not claim that the Sabbath law has not been technically broken but that such violations under certain conditions are warranted. Human need is a higher law than religious ritual.

Yet there is more to this episode than the meeting of human needs. It is also about authority to overrule the Sabbath. David was the Lord's anointed (1Sa 16), the future king of Israel, through whose ancestors the Messiah—the "son of David"—would come (2Sa 7:14–17). By pointing to David's example, Jesus is making an implicit claim to possess authority equivalent to David's. Later in Mark, Jesus will present a conundrum to the Pharisees by pointing out that David's "son"—the Messiah—is also David's "Lord" (12:35–40; cf. Ps 110:1–2). There is an implicit lesser-to-greater argument here: If David did not sin by eating the consecrated bread, how much less did David's greater son and Lord sin by doing so.

There is a historical difficulty related to the reference to Abiathar in v.26, since it was actually Ahimelech, Abiathar's father, who gave the consecrated bread to David (1Sa 21:1, 6). The difficulty is revealed by the fact that neither Matthew nor Luke records the phrase in the parallel passages, and it is not found in several MSS. There are several possibilities. Mark could simply have confused the names. The OT itself seems at times to confuse Ahimelech and Abiathar (cf. 1Sa 22:20 with 2Sa 8:17; 1Ch 18:16; 24:6). In defense of Mark's historicity, however, the text does not actually say that David came to Abiathar, but that these events occurred *epi Abiathar archiereōs*, "in the [time] of Abiathar, the high priest" (NIV, "in the days of ... "). Abiathar is closely linked with David during David's reign, so his mention could constitute a general reference to that period. A similar reference appears in Luke 3:2, where both Annas and Caiaphas are identified as high priests during Jesus' ministry. Though Caiaphas was the official high priest, his father-in-law Annas—earlier deposed by the Romans—wielded enormous influence over the priesthood. (Five of his sons and one son-in-law served as high priests after him.) Another possibility is to translate the preposition *epi* as "in the account of," as is done in Mark 12:26 (*epi tou batou*, "in the account of the bush"). First Samuel 21–22 could be called "the account of Abiathar," since it was he who escaped to David when the priests were massacred at Nob (22:20). Either of these solutions is possible, though neither is entirely satisfactory. We must admit we simply do not know what meaning Mark intended.

27–28 Jesus concludes with a double pronouncement. The first affirms that the Sabbath was not created for its own sake; it was a gift of God to human beings. Its purpose was not to put people in a kind of straitjacket. It was for their good—to provide rest from labor and opportunity for worship (see Ex 23:12; Dt 5:14).

The second pronouncement, "So the Son of Man is Lord even of the Sabbath" (v.28), is sometimes treated as an aside by the narrator rather than a statement by Jesus himself. In this case Mark would be telling his readers that Jesus' authoritative pronouncement in v.27 confirms that he is indeed Lord of the Sabbath. One reason for this interpretation is that apart from here and in 2:10, Jesus does not speak of himself as the "Son of Man" in Mark's gospel until after Peter confesses that he is the Messiah (8:29). From that point on Jesus uses the term repeatedly of himself (8:31, 38; 9:9, 12, 31; 10:33; 13:26; 14:21, 41, 62; see comments at 2:10). While this interpretation is possible, against it is the fact that in every other case in the Gospels, "Son of Man" appears as a self-designation by Jesus rather than in an editorial comment of the evangelist. It seems best to view its use here as Jesus' own pronouncement about his authority.

Another question concerns the original meaning of the pronouncement. "Son of man" in Hebrew (*ben ʾādām*) means "human being," and this sense would fit the context. Jesus has just said that the Sabbath was created for human beings (v.27). He now concludes that consequently (*hōste*, "so") human beings have authority over the Sabbath. The Sabbath was created to be the servant—not the lord—of human beings. While this meaning makes good sense in its first-century context, it cannot be Mark's primary intent. The readers of the gospel would know that Jesus had assumed "Son of Man" as a messianic title. In the Markan context there is no doubt that Jesus is referring to *himself* as Lord over the Sabbath. Throughout this section of his gospel, Mark has been demonstrating Jesus' extraordinary authority in calling disciples, teaching, healing diseases, driving out demons, and forgiving sins. Now he indicates Jesus' authority even over the Sabbath command.

The second saying may therefore be something of a pun. Following as it does on the first pronouncement (v.27), it could mean that human beings have authority to exercise the spirit of the Sabbath over legalistic obligations to it, since the Sabbath was instituted for their benefit. But as the Davidic Messiah and quintessential human being ("*the* Son of Man"), who will bring salvation to all humanity, Jesus is the true and ultimate Lord of the Sabbath. The eschatological implications should not be missed. With his kingdom proclamation Jesus is establishing something new ("new wine," v.22): bringing in a new age—the age of salvation—and giving new significance to the Sabbath rest (cf. Heb 12:9–11).

NOTES

27 Jesus' pronouncement was not as radical for his day as some would think. Rabbi Simeon ben Menasya (ca. AD 180) said, "The Sabbath has been committed to you and not you to the Sabbath" (Mekilta, *Shabbata 1* to Ex 31:14; cf. *b.Yoma 85b*).

b. Healing on the Sabbath (3:1–6)

OVERVIEW

This last in a series of five conflict stories (2:1–3:6) comes hot on the heels of the previous Sabbath controversy. This episode serves as an initial climax to escalating hostility against Jesus and concludes with his enemies' plotting to destroy him (3:6).

[1]Another time he went into the synagogue, and a man with a shriveled hand was there.
[2]Some of them were looking for a reason to accuse Jesus, so they watched him closely to
see if he would heal him on the Sabbath. [3]Jesus said to the man with the shriveled hand,
"Stand up in front of everyone."

[4]Then Jesus asked them, "Which is lawful on the Sabbath: to do good or to do evil, to
save life or to kill?" But they remained silent.

[5]He looked around at them in anger and, deeply distressed at their stubborn hearts,
said to the man, "Stretch out your hand." He stretched it out, and his hand was completely
restored. [6]Then the Pharisees went out and began to plot with the Herodians how they
might kill Jesus.

COMMENTARY

1 Again Mark gives no details of time or geographical location, except that the episode occurred in a synagogue on the Sabbath. The synagogue in Capernaum may be intended, for it was Jesus' base of operations in Galilee (see 1:21). A man with a "shriveled hand"—apparently some sort of paralysis—is present in the synagogue.

2 Mark does not specifically identify the opposition here. Though he uses the indefinite "some," the opposition's identity is nonetheless clear. (Cf. v.6, where the Pharisees are mentioned, and Luke 6:7, which says that they were the "Pharisees and the teachers of law.") Since Jesus had already raised suspicions in their mind because of his unorthodox actions, they were present in the synagogue not to worship God but to spy on Jesus ("they watched him closely"). They "were looking for a reason to accuse Jesus." Their motives were wrong from the start. The statement "to see if he would heal him on the Sabbath" makes it clear that the Pharisees were convinced of Jesus' power to perform miracles. The issue was not "could he?" but "would he?"

The rabbis of Jesus' day debated whether providing medical help on the Sabbath violated the Sabbath command. It was generally agreed that doing so was allowed in extreme emergencies or when a life was in danger. The Mishnah says that "whenever there is doubt whether life is in danger this overrides the Sabbath" (*m. Yoma* 8:6; cf. CD 11:9–10; *m. Šabb.* 14:3–4). A midwife could also work on the Sabbath since birth could not be delayed. Since here the man's physical life is not in immediate danger, the scribes and Pharisees would have viewed his healing on the Sabbath as a violation of the law (cf. Lk 13:14). Evidently no objection had been raised when Jesus earlier drove out a demon on the Sabbath (1:21–28), but that infringement may have been overlooked because the demon took the initiative and disrupted the service. Jesus was correcting a chaotic situation rather than initiating an "unnecessary" healing.

3–4 Jesus was fully aware of the designs of the opposition. Once again he is exercising divine prerogative by reading minds (cf. 2:8). Yet instead of acting carefully in the situation, he commanded the man to stand up and take "center stage" so that everyone in the synagogue could see what he was going to do (v.3). By doing so, he is directly and publicly challenging his opponents. Only here in the Gospel of Mark does Jesus himself initiate a healing without being approached, thus further emphasizing the intentionality of his actions. There is no motif of secrecy here!

The religious leaders had not posed a question to Jesus, but he knew what was racing through their minds. So he asked them, "Which is lawful on the Sabbath: to do good or to do evil, to save life or to kill?" (v.4). The statement is couched in the typical language of rabbinic legal debate, "Is it lawful ...?" The two statements are parallel, with the second specifying the first. The answers to both are obvious: It is clearly better to do good than to do evil and to save a life than to kill. The rabbis themselves allowed the saving of a life on the Sabbath. The problem is not the meaning of the statement but its relevance to the present situation. In this case the man's life does not seem to be in danger, and so it would seem to be neither evil nor murder to leave the healing of his hand for another day. But Jesus is not simply making a legal ruling. He is using hyperbole to make a more profound point. The callous attitude of the Pharisees toward human suffering was itself evil, and so tantamount to murder. Calvin, 2:54, noted that "there is little difference between manslaughter and the conduct of him who does not concern himself about relieving a person in distress." The Pharisees are more concerned with the minutiae of the law than its benefit for people. They have missed the heart of God, who gave the law for humanity's good.

Even worse, the entire reason for their presence is to accuse Jesus of violating the Sabbath. As elsewhere in Mark's gospel, there is heavy irony here. While Jesus is doing good by alleviating human suffering, the Pharisees are present for an evil purpose and will soon be plotting murder (v.6)—all on the Sabbath!

Furthermore, the whole passage must be placed in the eschatological context of Jesus' ministry. While healing a paralyzed hand may not appear to be a life-saving action, *all* of Jesus' miracles reveal the inbreaking power of the kingdom of God and the restoration of creation. Jesus, in defeating disease and Satan, is redeeming the world. His work of "saving lives" by offering God's healing and forgiveness is appropriate at any time and in any place. The sacred days and places of Judaism, such as the Sabbath and the temple, will be given new spiritual significance in the dawning age of salvation.

The Pharisees respond with silence—perhaps because they have no answer to give. No one could question Jesus' point that it is always better to do good than evil and to save life rather than to murder. But from a narrative perspective, their silence also indicates rhetorical defeat. As he will do again in 11:33, Jesus has silenced and thus defeated his opponents.

5 Anger is rarely directly attributed to Jesus. The only other place in the Gospels where he is said to be angry is in the disputed reading in Mark 1:41. While there the anger was difficult to understand, here it is clearly justified. It is "righteous indignation"—what a good person feels in the presence of stark evil. Such anger was particularly appropriate to this situation. But even such justifiable anger was couched in compassion. The tenses of the verbs are important here. The looking "around at them in anger" was momentary (aorist tense), but the being "deeply distressed" was continuous (present tense).

Jesus' distress was caused by their "stubborn hearts," i.e., their consistent failure to recognize who he really was. Nineham, 110, writes, "Their opposition rested on a fundamental misunderstanding—an inability, or refusal, to see that Jesus was God's eschatological agent and that his sovereign freedom with regard to law and custom sprang from that fact." The "heart" in Hebrew thought was the seat of the mind and will as well as the emotions, and "hardness of heart" is a common OT expression for Israel's refusal to respond to the message of God's prophets (Jer 3:17; 7:24; 13:10, etc.; cf. Ro 11:25; 2Co 3:14). Later in the gospel, the disciples will experience a similar lack of spiritual discernment (6:52; 8:17).

When Jesus ordered the man to stretch out his hand, he obeyed; and it was instantly and completely restored. It is significant that Jesus heals with a simple word. France, 151, comments, "If this was 'work,' it was of a very nonphysical variety." Yet in their hostility and jealousy the Pharisees are blind to this point, as well as to the fact that it must be *God* working through Jesus who has healed the man.

6 H. Van der Loos (*Miracles of Jesus*, 438) writes, "The consequence of the healing was neither surprise nor acclamation, but increased enmity." The Pharisees, joined now by the Herodians, began to plot Jesus' death. The term "Herodian" occurs only here and in 12:13 (par. Mt 22:16) and is not further explained. It probably refers to influential Jews who were friends and backers of the Herodian dynasty. In Galilee they would have supported Herod Antipas, son of Herod the Great and tetrarch of Galilee and Perea. This friendship also meant that these Pharisees backed the rule of Rome, from which the Herods received their authority. The alliance of the Herods with the Pharisees is unusual, since the Pharisees would have viewed any king not descended from the line of David—including the Herods—to be illegitimate (cf. *Pss. Sol.* 17–18). The odd coalition arose from a common enemy, for both groups viewed Jesus as a threat to their influence and authority in Galilee. Their scheming introduces an ominous tone to the narrative and recalls for Mark's readers Jesus' previous reference to the time "when the bridegroom will be taken from them" (2:20).

III. THE LATER GALILEAN MINISTRY (3:7–6:6a)

OVERVIEW

Mark's summarizing statement (3:7–12) indicates that here begins a new section of his gospel, one sometimes called the later Galilean ministry. The section is framed on one side by the appointment of the Twelve (3:13–19) and on the other by Jesus' sending them out to preach and heal (6:6b–13). It is characterized by increasing polarization of people who are either for or against Jesus. The twelve men whom he chooses as his special disciples stand over against his own family (3:20–21, 31–35) and over against the religious leaders, who claim he drives out demons by Satan's power (3:22). The religious leaders thereby blaspheme the Holy Spirit—the Power at work in Jesus' miracles—and Jesus responds by teaching in parables to conceal the truth from them (4:1–34). The rejection of Jesus by his own people continues in 6:1–6a as Jesus faces hostility and rejection from the townspeople of Nazareth. The pervading theme is that a person is either on the side of God and Jesus or on the side of Satan. The people of God are not defined by physical descent or national identity but by their identification with Jesus the Messiah and their willingness to do the will of God (3:35).

The manifestation of Jesus' power against hostile forces also intensifies in this section as Jesus calms the angry sea (3:35–41), defeats a "legion" of demons (5:1–20), heals the sick, and even raises the dead (5:21–43). The clash of forces for and against God's reign increases and the battle lines are more clearly drawn.

A. Withdrawal to the Lake (3:7–12)

[7]Jesus withdrew with his disciples to the lake, and a large crowd from Galilee followed.
[8]When they heard all he was doing, many people came to him from Judea, Jerusalem,
Idumea, and the regions across the Jordan and around Tyre and Sidon. [9]Because of the
crowd he told his disciples to have a small boat ready for him, to keep the people from
crowding him. [10]For he had healed many, so that those with diseases were pushing
forward to touch him. [11]Whenever the evil spirits saw him, they fell down before him and
cried out, "You are the Son of God." [12]But he gave them strict orders not to tell who he was.

COMMENTARY

7 Why did Jesus withdraw? Matthew states that it was because Jesus "knew" (another indication of divine omniscience) of the plot of the religious authorities to kill him (12:14–15), and Mark's narrative implies the same thing. Since the time had not yet come for a serious confrontation, he withdrew to the Lake of Gennesaret. This withdrawal, however, did not separate him from the crowds, and a "great multitude" followed him.

8 The crowds came to Jesus not only from Galilee but also from Jerusalem and Judea (south), Idumea (southeast of Judea), across the Jordan (east), and Tyre and Sidon (northwest). Scholars have debated the significance of this geographical list. Some claim it represents the extent of Jesus' ministry as described in Mark (so Lane, Schweizer). While possible, this view confronts the problem that in Mark's gospel Jesus does not visit Idumea. Another possibility is that the list represents the boundaries of Israel of old (so Garland); but the list's omission of "Samaria" would then be surprising. A third suggestion is that the list represents "Jewish Palestine," in other words, those areas with a large Jewish population (so Klostermann). But then the list's inclusion of "Tyre and Sidon" is unusual. It is perhaps best not to push too hard for a theological motive. Mark may simply provide a representative sample to show that people are coming from far and wide—even from predominantly Gentile regions. In the light of 7:24–30, the reference to Tyre and Sidon may hint at the Gentile mission.

Some of these geographical terms merit comment. After the destruction of Jerusalem in 587 BC, Idumea was invaded and conquered by the Edomites, who came from the east and settled there. Judas Maccabeus carried out several successful campaigns against the Idumeans, and during the reign of John Hyrcanus they were forced to adopt Judaism. Herod the Great was an Idumean, and several of his sons played important roles in the political history of Palestine. "Tyre and Sidon" is widely used to mean "the northwestern area of Palestine." The "regions across the Jordan" probably included Perea and Decapolis, both of which were under the political control of Herod Antipas, as was Galilee.

Mark notes that the crowds came because they heard "all that he was doing." While Jesus himself places primacy on the proclamation of the kingdom (1:38), the crowds come primarily for the healings and miracles.

9–10 Only Mark includes the detail about the boat. The introduction of the disciples and a boat sets the stage for later events in Mark's gospel, in which a boat will form the setting for several key miracle stories (4:35–41; 5:1–20; 6:31–32, 45–52). It is unclear whether the purpose of the boat here was to provide escape in case the crowd became unruly, or as a podium to avoid the press of the crowd. The similar scene in 4:1–2 suggests the latter is more likely. The picture is of great numbers of people pressing forward ("falling upon [*epipiptō*] him") just to touch Jesus in the hope that by doing so they might be healed (v.10). Jesus often heals by touch in the Gospels (1:41; 7:33; 8:22), and Mark here presents the popular notion in the ancient world that people could be healed by simply touching the garment of a gifted healer (cf. 5:25–34; 6:56; 2Ki 13:21; Ac 5:15–16; 19:11–12). Jesus' statement in 5:34 ("your faith has healed you") suggests that—for Mark at least—this healing power is not a magical force emanating from the healer, but rather God's reward for faith in Jesus' authority to heal.

11–12 Here again Jesus comes into conflict with the demonic. The evil spirits recognized who Jesus was—even if the crowds did not. While the crowds "fell upon" Jesus (*epipiptō*), the demons "fall before" (*prospiptō*) him in submission to his authority. Their crying out "You are the Son of God" is best understood as a "futile attempt to render him harmless. These cries of recognition were designed to control him and to strip him of his power, in accordance with the conception that knowledge of the precise name or quality of a person confers mastery over him" (Lane, 130). "Son of God" in this context is a true designation of who Jesus is, expressed by his bitter foes, the demons. Jesus silenced the outcries of the demons (v.12) because the time for the clear revelation of who he was had not yet come, and the demons were hardly appropriate heralds of him.

NOTES

7–8 Mark uses the Greek word πλῆθος (*plēthos*) to designate the crowds only in these two verses. The presence of this and other hapax legomena (words used only once) in this summarizing statement suggests that here Mark is using a source rather than freely composing.

7 The Greek verb translated "withdrew" is ἀναχωρέω (*anachōreō*), used only here in Mark. It is not clear whether it contains the idea of forced withdrawal. MM, 40, gives examples from the papyri of its meaning "take refuge."

REFLECTIONS

In short, the summary of vv.7–12 reviews and intensifies prior themes of Mark's gospel. The crowds who have followed him now threaten to overwhelm him with their numbers and intensity. The demons who previously recognized his identity as "the Holy One of God" (1:24) here proclaim him to be "the Son of God," the christological title that most epitomizes Jesus' identity in Mark's gospel (1:11; 9:7; 15:39).

B. Selection of the Twelve (3:13–19)

OVERVIEW

Mark has narrated the call of four fishermen brothers (1:16–20) and Levi the tax collector (2:13–17), and he has referred repeatedly to Jesus' "disciples," a group of followers distinct from the crowds (2:15–16, 18, 23; 3:7, 9). Now he appoints a special group of twelve from among this larger group. From this point on in Mark's gospel, the term "disciples" is used almost exclusively of the Twelve (see R. P. Meye, *Jesus and the Twelve* [Grand Rapids: Eerdmans, 1968]).

13 Jesus went up on a mountainside and called to him those he wanted, and they came
to him. 14 He appointed twelve—designating them apostles—that they might be with
him and that he might send them out to preach 15 and to have authority to drive out

demons. [16]These are the twelve he appointed: Simon (to whom he gave the name Peter);
[17]James son of Zebedee and his brother John (to them he gave the name Boanerges,
which means Sons of Thunder); [18]Andrew, Philip, Bartholomew, Matthew, Thomas, James
son of Alphaeus, Thaddaeus, Simon the Zealot [19]and Judas Iscariot, who betrayed him.

COMMENTARY

13 Luke (6:12) says that Jesus spent a night in prayer before choosing the Twelve. The phrase *eis to oros* ("into the mountain") is a Greek idiom that can mean "into the hills," here indicating the Galilean hill country near the lake. No precise location is indicated, but for Mark the reference likely has theological significance. The mountain was a place of revelation in Israel's history (Ex 3), and mountains function in a similar way in the Gospels (esp. Mt 5:1; 14:23; 15:29; 17:1; 28:16). On the mountainside Jesus called "those he wanted, and they came to him." As in the previous call narratives, Jesus' authority is on center stage. Contrary to the model of first-century discipleship, according to which students would seek out a teacher, Jesus takes the initiative, and they respond immediately to his call (cf. 1:18, 20; 2:14).

14–15 It may be that the twelve men Jesus appointed were the same men he called in v.13, but more likely he is selecting from a larger group he summoned to the mountain. The words "designating them apostles" is textually doubtful and may be a harmonization to Luke 6:13. While Luke often refers to the Twelve as "the apostles" (6:13; 9:10; 17:5; 22:14; 24:10), Mark does so only in 6:30, where the term does not seem to function as a title but as a description of "those who were sent."

The appointment of the Twelve has profound theological significance. A first-century Jew would have immediately recognized some connection to the twelve tribes of Israel. Jesus intentionally chooses twelve disciples, thus indicating that he viewed this movement as in some sense the eschatological renewal and restoration of Israel (cf. Mt 9:28; Lk 22:30). The fact that Jesus does not identify himself as one of the Twelve is also significant. He stands over and above the restored Israel as her Messiah and Lord.

The purpose for which the Twelve were appointed was twofold: (1) "that they might be with him"; and (2) "that he might send them out to preach and to have authority to drive out demons." Discipleship is first and foremost about attachment to the Master, being with Jesus and learning from him (cf. Lk 10:38–42). The Twelve were to live with Jesus, travel with him, converse with him, and follow his model. Mark's gospel indicates that much of Jesus' time was occupied with their training. Yet the training was not an end in itself, for second, they were to be sent out (in Mark's gospel not until 6:7). Their ministry was to consist of preaching the good news and driving out demons (v.15). It is significant that this is the same ministry Jesus has been performing. The Twelve are to serve as his representatives and expand the scope of his ministry. The primary theme of Mark's gospel up to this point has been Jesus' *authority* as inaugurator of the kingdom of God. Now Jesus delegates this kingdom-authority to his disciples. As we have seen, the proclamation of the good news and driving out demons are closely related. The salvation Jesus brings is of cosmic significance: it involves the defeat of Satan and the spiritual forces of evil. The omission of healing here—another important part of Jesus' ministry (the parallel in Matthew 10:1 adds it)—is probably not significant and results from the summarizing nature of Mark's statement.

16–19 There are three other lists of the apostles in the NT (Mt 10:2–4; Lk 6:14–16; Ac 1:13). Simon Peter always heads these lists as the most prominent disciple, and he appears throughout the Gospels and Acts as representative of the others. Mark notes that Jesus gave Simon the nickname "Peter," meaning "rock" (Gr., *petros*; Aram., *kēphas*; cf. Jn 1:42), though no explanation for it is given here. The gospel's narrative depicts Peter as impetuous and wavering—anything but a rock! Yet Jesus saw in him great potential. Peter will be the first disciple to acknowledge Jesus is the Messiah (Mk 8:29). In Matthew, Jesus entrusts to Peter the "keys" of the kingdom and, according to one common interpretation, predicts that he will serve as a foundation stone for the apostolic church (Mt 16:13–20; cf. Ac 2:14–41).

In Mark's list (cf. Ac 1:13), Peter is followed by James and John, the sons of Zebedee, though Matthew (10:2) and Luke (6:14) place Peter's brother Andrew second. The elevation of James and John before Andrew likely results from their functioning with Peter as a kind of "inner circle" of disciples (cf. 5:37; 9:2; 14:33). James and John were nicknamed by Jesus *Boanerges*, an Aramaic term that Mark interprets as "Sons of Thunder" (v.17) and that probably described their disposition, i.e., as having something of the thunderstorm in it (cf. 9:38; 10:35–37; cf. Lk 9:54). Andrew was called with Peter to be a disciple (1:16–18) and plays a more prominent role in John's gospel (1:40–44; 6:8–9; 12:20–22). In Mark he appears only incidentally at 1:16, 29 and 13:3.

Philip appears only here in Mark, though (like Andrew) he is more prominent in John's gospel (1:43–48; 6:5–7; 12:21–22; 14:8–9). Philip is a Greek name, and John 1:44 tells us that Philip was from Bethsaida, the hometown of Peter and Andrew. Bartholomew (v.18) is not a personal name but a patronymic (identified by the name of his father) meaning "son of Tolmai." It has often been speculated he is the Nathanael of John 1:45 (cf. Jn 21:2, where Nathanael appears with others who are apostles). Matthew is doubtless to be identified with Levi (2:14; cf. Mt 9:9), but Mark makes no point to that effect. Thaddaeus is probably the Judas son of James of Luke's lists (Lk 6:16; Ac 1:13). Some MSS in Matthew refer to him as Lebbaeus, perhaps in an attempt to identify him with Levi the tax collector. Simon is called the *kananaion*, a Greek term sometimes mistranslated as "Canaanite," a place name (from Canaan or Cana). In fact, *kananaion* is a transliteration of an Aramaic term meaning "the Zealot." Luke accurately calls him "Simon the Zealot [*zēlotēs*]," which may describe his religious zeal (cf. Gal 1:14; Ac 22:3) or could refer to his association with the party of Zealots, who were bent on the violent overthrow of the Roman authorities (see Martin Hengel, *The Zealots* [Edinburgh: T&T Clark, 1989], 69–70). The problem with the latter view is that it is uncertain whether the term "Zealots" was used of insurrectionists prior to the Jewish revolt of AD 66–74.

Judas's surname is given as Iscariot (v.19), and he is identified as the man who betrayed Jesus. "Iscariot" probably means "man from Karioth." The location of Karioth (Kerioth) is uncertain but may be identified either with Kerioth Hezron (Jos 15:25), twelve miles south of Hebron, or Kerioth in Moab (Jer 48:24). If either identification is accurate, Judas may have been the only non-Galilean among the Twelve. Other, less likely, possibilities are that "Iscariot" comes from the Latin *sicarius*, referring to an insurrectionist or freedom fighter, or that it derives from an Aramaic term meaning "the lie" and refers to his status as a false disciple. In this latter case it would be an epithet given by the church after the fact.

NOTES

14 The phrase οὓς καὶ ἀποστόλους ὠνόμασεν (*hous kai apostolous ōnomasen*) has important external evidence in B ℵ Θ f^{13} Syr[h,mg] and Cop, but is questionable based on the internal evidence. Intrinsically, it is uncharacteristic of Mark's style; transcriptionally, a scribe is more likely to have added it than to have omitted it. The UBS's apparatus assigns it a "C" rating, which indicates considerable doubt as to its authenticity.

On the eschatological restoration of Israel, see Isaiah 49:6; Ezekiel 45:8; Sirach 36:10; 48:10; *Psalms of Solomon* 17:26–32; *Sibylline Oracles* 2:17076; *Testament of Joseph* 19:1–7; cf. Witherington, 151.

17 The etymology of Βοανηργές, *Boanērges*, is uncertain. For details, see Guelich, 162.

REFLECTIONS

It was a strange group Jesus chose to be his disciples. Four of them were fishermen, one a despised tax collector, another possibly a member of a radical and violent political party. Of six of them we know practically nothing. All of them were laymen. There was not a preacher or an expert in the Scriptures in the lot. Yet it was with these people that Jesus established his church and disseminated his good news to the ends of the earth.

C. Jesus, His Family, and the Beelzebul Controversy (3:20–35)

OVERVIEW

Here we encounter the first example of Mark's intercalation or "sandwiching"—one of his favorite literary devices—whereby one story is interrupted by another, with the two mutually interpreting each other (cf. 5:21–43; 6:7–30; 11:12–25; 14:1–11; see Introduction, pp. 689–90). In this case the story of the relationship between Jesus and his family (3:20–21, 31–35) is interrupted by the Beelzebul controversy (vv.22–30). Both stories concern those related to Jesus by blood or kinship—his family and relatives in the first place and his fellow Jews in the second. Both groups reject his ministry: his family thinks he has gone insane (v.21), while the Jewish religious leaders claim he is possessed by Satan and allied with him (v.22). Jesus responds by refuting the leaders' claim and then by defining true spiritual relationships as based not on physical descent or ethnic identity but on obedience to God's will (v.35).

1. *Charged with Insanity (3:20–21)*

[20]Then Jesus entered a house, and again a crowd gathered, so that he and his disciples were not even able to eat. [21]When his family heard about this, they went to take charge of him, for they said, "He is out of his mind."

COMMENTARY

20–21 Again Jesus was being pressed by the crowds. The house (probably of Peter and Andrew; cf. 1:29; 2:1–4) was so packed with people demanding his attention that both he and his disciples were prevented from eating. This reference to Jesus' family is the first one in Mark's gospel (see Notes). When they hear that he was so engrossed in his work that he failed even to care for his physical needs, they decide to go to Jesus and "take charge of him" (v.21), a phrase that probably means they wanted to take him back to Nazareth and thus remove him from the strain of having so many people constantly pressing on him to meet their physical and spiritual needs. The verb translated "take charge" is *krateō* (GK *3195*); it is used of arresting someone in 6:17; 12:12; 14:1, 44, 46, 49, 51. Jesus' family wanted to take charge of him because they feared that overwork had affected him mentally—he was "out of his mind." These words are shocking, but as Mitton, 26, writes, "If they reveal his family's failure to understand him, they are also a measure of their concern for him." In a culture in which honor and shame were critically important, there may also have been an attempt to prevent shame on the family caused by Jesus' unorthodox behavior.

NOTES

21 The Greek phrase οἱ παρ' αὐτοῦ (*hoi par' autou*) is an idiom that can indicate family, relatives, or friends. The continuation of the story in v.31 suggests that here immediate family is meant, though extended family may also be included. The theological significance is that these were Jesus' own people.

2. *Charged with Demon-Possession (3:22–30)*

OVERVIEW

Mark uses the change in scene to heighten the suspense and to allow for the passage of time. Jesus' family was located in Nazareth. Jesus himself was probably in Capernaum at this time; so his family had to travel to Capernaum to get him and take him home. Mark fills in this gap of time with an account of the Beelzebul controversy. The change of scene and intercalation also has theological significance, as both episodes concern the rejection of Jesus by his own people (cf. Jn 1:11) and the spiritual relationships that define the true people of God (vv.31–35).

[22]And the teachers of the law who came down from Jerusalem said, "He is possessed by Beelzebub! By the prince of demons he is driving out demons."
[23]So Jesus called them and spoke to them in parables:"How can Satan drive out Satan?
[24]If a kingdom is divided against itself, that kingdom cannot stand. [25]If a house is divided against itself, that house cannot stand. [26]And if Satan opposes himself and is divided, he cannot stand; his end has come. [27]In fact, no one can enter a strong man's house and carry off his possessions unless he first ties up the strong man. Then he can rob his house. [28]I tell you the truth, all the sins and blasphemies of men will be forgiven them. [29]But whoever blasphemes against the Holy Spirit will never be forgiven; he is guilty of an eternal sin."
[30]He said this because they were saying, "He has an evil spirit."

COMMENTARY

22 Mark notes that the teachers of the law had come down from Jerusalem. One always comes "down" from Jerusalem, not only because it is higher than Galilee in elevation, but also because it is the holy city of God. The reference to the scribes of Jerusalem suggests an official delegation sent by the city's religious leadership. Jesus has come in conflict with scribes in Galilee already, but now word of his actions has reached Jerusalem and caused concern in high places, both literally and figuratively! The narrative conflict escalates.

Two closely related accusations are made against Jesus. The first is, "He is possessed by Beelzebul." Exorcists were sometimes thought to be possessed by a powerful spirit, and the scribes here accuse Jesus of being under satanic control. The origin of the name "Beelzebul" is uncertain. It was probably originally a title of the Canaanite god Baal, meaning "Baal of the Exalted Dwelling." In time it came to be used of Satan, the "Prince of Demons" (v.22; cf. *T. Sol.* 3:2–5; 4:2; 6:1–3). Jesus' response in v.23 ("How can Satan drive out Satan?") confirms that he understood the name as a reference to Satan. A similar accusation is made in John 10:20 ("He is demon-possessed and raving mad"). That demon-possession and insanity were often closely related in the ancient world (though not all insanity was considered demonic) further links this episode with the previous one about Jesus' family.

The second accusation is related to the first. The scribes say that Jesus is not only possessed by Satan but is actually in collusion with him; he drives out demons by Satan's power. In Matthew and Luke this accusation is prompted by the account of the healing of the blind-and-dumb demoniac (cf. Mt 12:22; Lk 11:14); Mark relates it more generally to Jesus' previous exorcisms. Later Jewish polemic made similar claims, namely, that Jesus practiced sorcery and led Israel astray (*b. Sanh.* 43a; cf. Justin Martyr, *Dial.*, 69; Origen, *Cels.* 1.6).

23–27 Jesus replies to the charge "in parables" (v.23), which in this context means by making a comparison or by speaking proverbially. The term usually occurs in the context of controversy in

Mark's gospel. Jesus uses parables both to reveal and conceal the truth (see on 4:2, 11–12). His argument here is twofold. First, if he is casting out demons by Satan's power, then Satan is actually working against himself. But that would be absurd. Just as a (figurative) house (i.e., a household; v.25) or a kingdom (v.24) cannot stand if it is divided against itself or opposes itself, so Satan will bring about his own destruction by working against himself (v.26). The obvious and logical conclusion is that Jesus cannot be in collusion with Satan, since Satan would never be so foolish as to attack himself.

Jesus' second point confirms that Satan's realm, though not at war with itself, is indeed under attack. The image changes to one of household robbery. In order to enter the house of a strong man and plunder it, one must first tie up the strong man (v.27). The strong man is Satan. Through his exorcisms Jesus is entering Satan's realm, binding him, and "plundering" his goods. Satan's "possessions" (*ta skeuē autou*) is probably a reference to people in bondage to Satan. The language here recalls John the Baptist's reference to Jesus as the "more powerful one" in 1:7–8. It also echoes Isaiah 49:24–25, where the Lord is portrayed as a mighty warrior who will rescue his people—captives and plunder—from the enemies who have captured them.

When the binding of Satan took place is not indicated. It may refer to Jesus' temptation in the wilderness (1:12–13), though Mark (unlike Matthew and Luke) gives no details concerning the outcome of this encounter. It could also refer to each individual exorcism as an act of binding and release of captives. More likely it refers generally to the victory of the kingdom of God through Jesus' exorcisms and healings. Jesus' coming represents the decisive victory over Satan and ensures his ultimate doom. While binding language is sometimes used of individual exorcisms in Judaism (cf. Tob 8:3), more often it refers to the antediluvian imprisonment of fallen angels or, as here, to the eschatological defeat of the forces of evil (cf. Isa 24:21–22; Rev 20:1–3; *T. Levi* 18:12; *1 En.* 54:3–5; 69:28; see France, 173). Through Jesus' actions the kingdom of God is overwhelming and defeating the kingdom of Satan. This general eschatological sense also means that the language of binding must not be pressed too far—it does not mean complete restraint but rather decisive victory. Though his fate is sealed, Satan remains active in the world until his final destruction in the end.

28–30 The pronouncement Jesus makes is meant to be solemn and authoritative: "I tell you the truth"—Jesus' first of thirteen uses of the phrase *amēn legō hymin* in Mark's gospel. The phrase appears over fifty times in the Synoptics, always on the lips of Jesus, and in all strata of the gospel tradition. In John's gospel (twenty-five times), the word *amēn* is doubled for emphasis: "Truly, truly I say to you." The term is a transliteration of the Hebrew word meaning "confirmed" or "verified," and in the OT it is always used at the end of a saying to confirm its validity (Dt 27:15; Ps 41:13; etc.). Jesus used it in a unique and unprecedented manner at the *beginning* of his sayings to demonstrate the authority with which he spoke. Rather than appealing to the mediated authority of predecessors, as the rabbis did, Jesus appeals to his own unique authority and self-authenticating testimony. The closest OT parallel is the solemn declaration of the prophets, "Thus says the LORD." Jesus appears to be claiming that his words represent the very words of God.

The content of this authoritative statement is that forgiveness is available for all sins and blasphemies except one. That exception is blasphemy against the Holy Spirit (v.29). What is this unpardonable sin? The narrator provides an explanation in v.30: "He said this because they were saying, 'He has an evil spirit.'" Jesus had done what any unprejudiced person would have acknowledged as a good thing. He had freed an unfortunate man from the power and bondage of evil (cf. Mt 12:22; Lk 11:14). This he did through the power of the Holy Spirit, but the teachers of the law ascribed it to the power of Satan. In the full light of day, when the testimony of God's Spirit was right before them, they turned to darkness.

The words of v.29—"will never be forgiven; he is guilty of an eternal sin"—have caused great anxiety and pain in the history of the church. Many have wondered whether they have committed the "unpardonable sin." Surely what Jesus is speaking of here is not an isolated act but a settled condition of the soul—the ultimate and deliberate rejection of the work of the Spirit in an individual's life. And if the person involved cannot be forgiven, it is not so much that God refuses to forgive as that the sinner refuses God's forgiveness.

NOTES

22 The Israelites evidently mocked the name Beelzebul by changing it to *Beelzebub*, "Lord of the Flies" (see Jdg 10:6; 2Ki 1:2–3, 6). The Vulgate and Syriac versions use Beelzebub (cf. KJV, NIV), no doubt under the influence of 2 Kings 1:2. But there is no evidence for this reading in the Greek MSS. For the disputed background to Beelzebul, see L. Gaston, "Beelzebul," *TZ* 18 (1962): 247–55.

27 The adversative conjunction ἀλλά (*alla*, "but," "on the contrary") at the beginning of this verse indicates that while Satan's kingdom is not in civil war, it is in fact under attack—by the kingdom of God.

28 On Jesus' use of ἀμήν, *amēn*, see Joachim Jeremias's classic study, *The Prayers of Jesus*, 108–15. See also J. D. G. Dunn, *Jesus and the Spirit* (Philadelphia: Westminster, 1975), 79.

3. Jesus' True Family (3:31–35)

31Then Jesus' mother and brothers arrived. Standing outside, they sent someone in to
call him. 32A crowd was sitting around him, and they told him, "Your mother and brothers
are outside looking for you."
33"Who are my mother and my brothers?" he asked.
34Then he looked at those seated in a circle around him and said, "Here are my mother
and my brothers! 35Whoever does God's will is my brother and sister and mother."

COMMENTARY

31 Mark now turns back to the family of Jesus. By inserting (intercalating) the account of the Beelzebul controversy into the family episode he has both heightened the suspense and allowed for traveling time from Nazareth to Capernaum. The rejection of Jesus by the religious leaders parallels the rejection by his family and reminds the reader that it is Jesus' own people who are rejecting him. These developments allow Jesus to define true spiritual relationships in the kingdom of God.

The family arrived at Jesus' location but did not enter, presumably because of the size of the crowd.

Instead they stood outside (*exō*) and sent someone in to call him. Only Jesus' mother (the only reference to her in Mark's gospel) and his siblings are mentioned specifically. Joseph is not mentioned; presumably, he was not living at this time. The Greek word *adelphoi* can mean either "brothers" or "siblings" (i.e., "brothers and sisters"), and the latter may be intended here. Jesus' sisters will be explicitly mentioned in 6:3. Possible evidence for the presence of Jesus' sisters is the analogy in v.35, where Jesus' spiritual family includes "my brother and sister and mother."

Mark shows no interest or concern in the later church debate over whether these siblings were (1) born to Mary after Jesus was born, (2) Joseph's children by a previous marriage, or (3) only cousins of Jesus (as the Roman Catholic Church has historically asserted; see comments at 6:3). For Mark the point of the story is the climactic pronouncement in vv.34b–35 that true spiritual relationships are defined not by blood or birth but by common allegiance to the will and purpose of God.

32–35 When Jesus was told that his family was looking for him, he responded by asking the rhetorical question, "Who are my mother and my brothers [and sisters]?" (v.33). Then with a sweep of his eyes over those seated in a circle around him, he identified his true family: "Here are my mother and my brothers [and sisters]" (v.34). This statement would certainly have included the Twelve but also the "crowd" (*ochlos*, GK *4063*, v.32) gathered around him—the wider group of his followers. Jesus' point is that in the age of salvation there are spiritual ties that are closer than blood or family ties. Jesus' true family consists of all those who obey the will of God (v.35)—in Mark's narrative world, those who are responding positively to Jesus' proclamation of the kingdom of God.

Jesus' words are particularly shocking in the "dyadic" (group-oriented) culture of the Middle East, where respect and loyalty for family and clan were (and are) among the highest values. While Jesus does not reject or repudiate his own family, he places spiritual relationships on a higher plane. It can easily be imagined what this statement meant to the original readers of Mark's gospel. F. C. Grant, 694, writes, "In place of broken family relations, ostracism and persecution, was the close and intimate relation to the Son of God." The striking spatial contrast between Jesus' physical family, who are "outside" (*exō*; vv.31–32), and his spiritual family, who are "sitting around him" inside, will be taken up in the next chapter (see comments at 4:11). A reversal is taking place in Mark's gospel: those who have traditionally been insiders to God's blessings—the religious leaders and the physical heirs of Abraham's promise—will become the outsiders. And those who were formerly outsiders (sinners, tax collectors, Gentiles) will become the insiders and recipients of God's salvation.

In view of the Jewish attitude of respect and honor toward one's parents—an attitude adopted by the church—the historicity of these two family scenes (vv.20–21; vv.31–35) can scarcely be denied, for the church would never have invented a story that put the family of Jesus in such bad light.

NOTES

31 On Jesus' siblings, see R. J. Bauckham, *Jude and the Relatives of Jesus in the Early Church* (Edinburgh: T&T Clark, 1990).

32 Some MSS include καὶ αἱ ἀδελφαι σου, *kai hai adelphai sou* ("and your sisters") in v.32.

D. Parables about the Kingdom of God (4:1–34)

OVERVIEW

This section is one of the few in Mark's gospel devoted to teaching. Although Mark frequently depicts Jesus as teaching (1:21; 2:13; 6:2, 6), only here and in 13:2–37—and perhaps in 7:1–13—does he give any sustained account of the content of his teaching.

Mark 4 contains four of Jesus' parables: the parable of the sower and its interpretation (vv.1–20), the parable of the lamp (vv.21–25), the parable of the secretly growing seed (vv.26–29), and the parable of the mustard seed (vv.30–32). Parables are the most striking feature in the teaching of Jesus. Although he did not invent this form of teaching (since parables are found both in the OT and in the writings of the rabbis), he used it in a way and to a degree unmatched before his time or since.

The Sunday school definition of a parable—"an earthly story with a heavenly meaning"—carries some truth but is inadequate to explain the context and complexity of Jesus' parables. Many of his parables are indeed stories from ordinary life used to drive home a spiritual or moral truth. But they are not always stories. Sometimes they are brief similes, comparisons, analogies, or even proverbial savings. The Greek word *parabolē* may carry any of these senses. The corresponding word most often used in the OT is *māšāl*, which can denote anything from a simple metaphor to an elaborate story. Nor is the description of parables as carrying "heavenly meaning" adequate. Jesus' parables do not teach general religious truth but are always dynamically related to his proclamation of the kingdom of God (see Dodd, *Parables of the Kingdom*; Jeremias, *Parables of the Kingdom*).

For centuries parables were interpreted allegorically; i.e., each element of the story was assigned a specific meaning. Thus Augustine found in the parable of the Good Samaritan references to Adam, Jerusalem, the Devil and his angels, the Law and the Prophets, and Christ and the church. This allegorical approach was challenged in the late nineteenth century by Adolf Jülicher (2 vols.; *Die Gleichnisreden Jesu* [Tübingen: Mohr, 1899]), who claimed Jesus' parables were not allegories but similitudes—extended similes intended to convey only one point. Allegorical elements were rejected by Jülicher as inauthentic additions made by the later church to relate the parables to Jesus' ministry. While Jülicher provided an important corrective to the church's tendency toward fanciful allegorization, he surely went too far in rejecting all allegorical elements in Jesus' parables. Most commentators today recognize that Jesus' parables sometimes carry allegorical elements and various dimensions of meaning. The important thing is to relate these allegorical elements first and foremost to Jesus' proclamation of the kingdom and subsidiary meanings to the central message of the parable. For example, the central message of the parable of the prodigal son is God's gracious forgiveness offered to sinners through the ministry of Jesus (Luke 15:11–32). But this main emphasis does not mean that the older brother in the parable cannot allegorically represent the religious leaders who stand in opposition to Jesus. The brother's refusal to come to the prodigal's reunion party is an important subtheme representing the religious leaders' refusal to welcome sinners as Jesus does.

Of the four parables in ch. 4, the first (parable of the sower) is the most important for Mark and becomes a defining passage not only for Jesus' teaching in parables but also for his teaching as a whole. Between the parable (vv.1–9) and its interpretation (vv.13–20), Jesus privately explains to his disciples the reason he speaks in parables and the hiddenness of his teaching to those whose hearts are hardened (vv.10–12). This section relates in turn to the three previous episodes, in which Jesus' family rejects him and the religious leaders accuse him of driving out demons by Satan's power (3:20–34). Jesus in response warns of the unforgivable "blasphemy of the Holy Spirit"—intentionally turning to darkness while in the light of the truth—and redefines the nature of true spiritual relationships. The religious leaders, who were once "insiders" to God's promises, now become "outsiders" whose hearts are hardened to the spiritual insights about the kingdom of God that the parables reveal.

The key theme throughout Mark 4 is the need to hear and respond to the truth. Jesus begins the parable with the command to "Listen!" (v.3; cf. v.24) and ends with the exhortation, "He who has ears to hear, let him hear" (v.9), a refrain repeated in v.23. The parable itself is interpreted with reference to the need not only to "hear" God's word, but also to respond to it (vv.15–16, 18, 20). The problem with the "outsiders"—the religious leaders—is that they are seeing but not perceiving, hearing but not comprehending (v.12, citing Isa 6:9–10). They have heard Jesus' testimony and seen his miracles but have refused to respond. The disciples, by contrast, are now insiders to the truth—they hear the parable and perceive its significance. Verse 34 notes that while speaking to others only in enigmatic parables, Jesus was explaining them privately to his disciples.

For good surveys of the purpose of the parables in the ministry of Jesus see R. H. Stein, *An Introduction to the Parables of Jesus* (Philadelphia: Westminster, 1981), and C. L. Blomberg, *Interpreting the Parables* (Downers Grove, Ill.: InterVarsity, 1990).

1. Parable of the Sower (4:1–9)

1 Again Jesus began to teach by the lake. The crowd that gathered around him was
so large that he got into a boat and sat in it out on the lake, while all the people were
along the shore at the water's edge. 2 He taught them many things by parables, and in his
teaching said: 3 "Listen! A farmer went out to sow his seed. 4 As he was scattering the seed,
some fell along the path, and the birds came and ate it up. 5 Some fell on rocky places,
where it did not have much soil. It sprang up quickly, because the soil was shallow. 6 But
when the sun came up, the plants were scorched, and they withered because they had no
root. 7 Other seed fell among thorns, which grew up and choked the plants, so that they
did not bear grain. 8 Still other seed fell on good soil. It came up, grew and produced a crop,
multiplying thirty, sixty, or even a hundred times."
9 Then Jesus said, "He who has ears to hear, let him hear."

COMMENTARY

1–2 Mark introduces the situation in which Jesus spoke this parable using the indefinite "again" (v.1) but gives us no specific information as to when it was told. The location was by Lake Galilee. The presence of the large crowd shows Jesus' popularity as a teacher. The crowd was so large that he found it convenient to use a small boat pushed out from the shore as his podium, teaching while sitting in the boat. Whether this is the same boat "made ready" for him in 3:9 is uncertain; if it is the same boat, the teaching reported in ch. 4 may have been given on that occasion and is only summarized in 3:9–11.

3–9 The parable of the "sower" (*ho speirōn*; NIV, "farmer,") begins and ends with a call for careful attention (vv.3, 9), thus suggesting that its meaning may not be self-evident. Alert minds are needed to comprehend its truth. As noted above, the theme of "hearing" runs throughout the chapter (vv.12, 15–16, 18, 20, 23–24).

The parable is structured around two sets of three. (Mark is fond of patterns of three—see Introduction, p. 690). Three typical seeds fail to produce a harvest because they fall, respectively, beside the path, on rocky ground, or among thorns. Other seeds fall on good ground and produce, respectively, thirty-, sixty-, and one hundredfold. The three failed seeds contrast with the three productive ones.

Like all of Jesus' parables, this one must be understood first and foremost in the context of Jesus' ministry and his proclamation of the kingdom of God. Jesus is the sower who is spreading the good news among the towns and villages of Israel. Yet the primary focus in the parable is not on Jesus but on the response of his hearers. While traditionally called the "parable of the sower," the story mentions the farmer only at the beginning. The main point is what happens to the seed as it falls on fertile or infertile ground, hence the various responses to Jesus' preaching.

Why does the sower apparently scatter the seed so carelessly rather than in neatly plowed furrows? Since Joachim Jeremias's seminal study (*The Parables of the Kingdom*, 11–12, 149–51), it has been widely claimed that in first-century Palestine sowing preceded plowing. The Jewish book of *Jubilees* (second century BC) speaks of crows as stealing the grain "before they plowed in the seed" (*Jub.* 11:11; cf. *b. Šabb.* 73*b*; *t. Šabb.* 7:2). In this case the farmer would be doing exactly what is expected—sowing seed randomly in broadcast fashion and expecting to return to plow it into the soil later. Any delay in plowing would result in the failures Jesus describes. While this scenario is possible, K. D. White ("The Parable of the Sower," *JTS* 15 [1964]: 300–307) has challenged Jeremias's claims. He argues that the normal Mediterranean practice was one of multiple plowings, both before and after sowing. In this case, Jesus might be implying that the good news is being sown far and wide in the hopes of drawing a harvest from every possible corner.

Presumably, the seed sown "along [or 'beside'] the path" does not take root because it is never plowed into the soil and so is left exposed to the birds. Luke 5:8 adds that it was "trampled on." The "rocky places" (*petrōdēs*) of the second seed must mean a thin layer of topsoil on bedrock, since it is the lack of soil and "no root" that allows the sun to wither it. There is a logical progression in the development of the three types of seed as each fails at a different stage: the first never germinates; the second sprouts but dies; the third becomes a plant but is choked by weeds. All fail to produce fruit.

In contrast to the three failed types of seed are the three successful ones, which yield thirty-, sixty-, and one hundredfold. Scholars debate the nature of this yield. Some argue that a typical harvest would be a fivefold or at most tenfold increase, so the reference to thirty, sixty, and one hundred is remarkable and even miraculous (cf. Witherington, 165; Marcus, 293). More likely, these numbers do not refer to the total harvest but to the number of grains per plant. Ancient sources speak of individual plants' producing thirty-five kernels on average and of good plants yielding sixty or even a hundred grains. In this case Jesus would be describing an abundant harvest but not an unrealistic one (cf. Guelich, 195).

Fruitfulness and barrenness are common images in the OT and Judaism for spiritual receptivity or dullness and often appear in eschatological contexts. Barrenness appears, significantly, in Isaiah's parable of the vineyard (Isa 5:1–7), which will be taken up and modified by Jesus in the parable of the tenant farmers (Mk 12:1–12). As noted above, this Markan parable shows considerable parallels with the present one and serves as an important climax in Mark's narrative. It is also significant that Jesus is about to quote Isaiah 6:9–10 in v.12, a passage contextually related to Isaiah's parable of the vineyard. It is Israel's unfruitfulness that will bring spiritual blindness and ultimately judgment.

Some commentators claim that Jesus' original parable placed all of the emphasis on the eschatological harvest the kingdom would bring and that the interpretation which follows concerning individual responses to "the word" (vv.14–20) is a later interpretation imposed by the church. This scenario is unlikely, however, since the various responses of the seed are an integral part of the parable. It makes several points at once: Jesus is the sower of the kingdom message; the failures and successes of the seed depend on the receptivity of the hearers; and the ultimate success of the kingdom issues in a bountiful harvest.

Jesus concludes with the exhortation, "He who has ears to hear, let him hear" (v.9), thus framing the parable in another call for spiritual discernment (vv.3, 9). Such discernment is necessary in the light of the surprising and unexpected manner in which the kingdom is appearing.

NOTES

3 On the debate concerning the nature of sowing in first-century Palestine, see P. B. Payne, "The Order of Sowing and Ploughing in the Parable of the Sower," *NTS* 25 (1978/1979): 123–29.

4–8 The pattern of two sets of three is more clear in the Greek than the English, since the words translated "some ... some ... other ..." in vv.4, 5, and 7 are singular in Greek (ὃ μὲν ... ἄλλο ... ἄλλο, *ho men ... allo ... allo*), while the word translated "other" (ἄλλα, *alla*) in v.8 is plural.

REFLECTIONS

Various commentators have noted the relationship between Jesus' first and last parables in Mark's gospel, those of the sower (4:1–9) and the tenant farmers (12:1–12). Both stories function as paradigms for Jesus' ministry; both describe the response to his message and ministry; both use agricultural imagery containing allegorical elements. The parable of the sower comes immediately after the rejection by the religious leaders and introduces the theme that they are now blind to his teaching. The parable of the tenant farmers also relates to the leaders' rejection but has the opposite result. While previously blinded to the meaning of the parables, now they get it! Ironically, they recognize that Jesus is speaking the parable against them and so seek to arrest him (12:12). The parable of the tenants not only allegorizes Jesus' ministry and his rejection; it actually provokes that rejection and so carries forward God's purpose and plan for the suffering Messiah.

2. Secret of the Kingdom of God (4:10–12)

[10]When he was alone, the Twelve and the others around him asked him about the parables. [11]He told them, "The secret of the kingdom of God has been given to you. But to those on the outside everything is said in parables [12]so that,

"'they may be ever seeing but never perceiving,
and ever hearing but never understanding;
otherwise they might turn and be forgiven!'"

COMMENTARY

10 The question about the parables, in view of the answer given by Jesus, must have been directed toward their purpose in his teaching. The plural "parables" is used because more is in view in Jesus' answer than the parable of the sower. Jesus had spoken other parables, and the disciples were inquiring into the purpose of parables generally. Mention is made of "others around him," i.e., followers of Jesus whom Mark distinguishes from the Twelve. This indicates that Jesus' teaching is not narrowly limited to the Twelve. He is no Gnostic revealer whose esoteric teaching is only for the fortunate few. He came to reveal the truth to all who were open to receiving it.

11–12 These verses are among the most difficult in the entire gospel. It is important to look carefully at the terminology. The word translated "secret" (v.11) is *mystērion* (GK *3696*). In the Gospels it occurs only here and in the synoptic parallels (Mt 13:11; Lk 8:10), Paul uses it frequently in his epistles (twenty-one times); and it is found in the book of Revelation four times (1:20; 10:7; 17:5, 7). In the NT it does not mean something mysterious or enigmatic. Nor is it something only for the initiated few. The emphasis is on God's disclosure to human beings of what was previously unknown. It is proclaimed to all, but only those who have faith really understand. Here in Mark the secret is the disclosure that the kingdom of God has drawn near in the person of Jesus Christ, or perhaps as Ladd (*Theology of the New Testament*, 92) suggests, it "is that the Kingdom that is to come finally in apocalyptic power, as foreseen in Daniel, has in fact entered into the world in advance in a hidden form to work secretly within and among human beings."

The secret has been given to the disciples because they have responded in faith, "but to those on the outside everything is said in parables." "Those on the outside" alludes to ch. 3 and the rejection of Jesus by the teachers of the law and by his own family (see the play on "insiders" vs. "outsiders" in 3:31–32). "Everything" does not mean the teaching only but also the entire significance of Jesus' person and mission. For those with hard hearts, all things come "in parables." Here the word *parabolē* takes on the meaning of "riddle," a meaning well within the range of the word.

12 The introductory conjunction (*hina*, "so that") is not part of the OT quotation but is Mark's own insertion. The quotation is from Isaiah 6:9–10, which in the Hebrew text is a command. Mark's attachment of "so that" to this command is not surprising, since in Semitic thought a command may be used to express a result.

Mark follows the text of the LXX; however, he omits the strong statements of the first part of v.10—"Make the heart of this people calloused, make their ears dull, and close their eyes"—and he changes the LXX's "and I heal them" (*kai iasomai autous*) to "and be forgiven" (*kai aphethē autois*). Mark's following the Targum in doing so suggests that the original quotation goes back to an Aramaic source (and so likely to Jesus himself).

Taken at face value, the statement seems to be saying that the purpose of parables is that unbelievers ("those on the outside," v.11) may not receive the truth and be converted. That this statement was thought to be difficult theologically may be seen in Matthew's changing *hina* ("in order that") to *hoti* ("with the result that"; the NIV translates *hina* with the ambiguous "so that") and in Luke's dropping the *mēpote* ("otherwise") clause.

Several recent attempts have been made to weaken the sense of purpose implied by *hina*:

(1) It is held that *hina* is used in the text to mean the same thing as *hoti*. Thus Jesus is not speaking of the purpose of parables but their result.

(2) Mark has mistranslated the original Aramaic word *de*. It means "who," not "in order that." Thus the text should read, "The secret of the kingdom of God has been given to you. But to those on the outside *who* are ever seeing but never perceiving ... everything is said in parables" (Manson, *Teaching of Jesus*, 76–80; emphasis added).

(3) The Greek *mēpote* (NIV, "otherwise") goes back to the Aramaic *dîlmaʾ*, which can mean "unless" instead of "lest." If the latter meaning applies here, Jesus is saying that they will be blinded "unless they turn and are forgiven" (Jeremias, *Parables of the Kingdom*, 17).

(4) *Hina* is an introductory formula to the free translation of Isaiah 6:9–10. On this understanding, *hina* would be almost equivalent to *hina plērōthē*, "in order that it might be fulfilled" (Jeremias, 17; Lane, 159).

(5) The *hina* is epexegetical and qualifies or interprets v.11b (a function of *hina* found in 9:12). In this case, the quotation from Isaiah is simply an explanation of what it means to receive everything in parables and could be translated "that is ...." Guelich, 211–12, adopts this view and then interprets *mēpote* as an indirect question meaning not "lest" but "if they had," so leaving open the possibility of forgiveness (cf. Manson, *Teaching of Jesus*, 78).

(6) The quotation is meant to be ironic, and the last line could be translated "because the last thing they want is to turn and have their sins forgiven!" (B. Hollenbach, "Lest They Should Turn and Be Forgiven: Irony," *BT* 34 [1983]: 312–21).

All these solutions have difficulties. While *hina* sometimes means "so that" (see BDAG, 477), Mark never uses it elsewhere in this sense. Views 2 and 3 are purely hypothetical, with little supporting evidence. In any case, while they propose what *Jesus*—speaking Aramaic—may have originally intended, they do not help resolve the difficulty in Mark, where the combination of *hina* and *mēpote* strongly suggests purpose. Solution 4 has merit but founders on the fact that Mark elsewhere does not use *hina* to mean "in order that it might be fulfilled." View 5 provides a tidy solution but depends on unusual meanings for both *hina* and *mēpote*. View 6 probably contains elements of truth, especially since irony runs throughout the Markan narrative (see Introduction, p. 690). Yet irony is notoriously difficult to identify on the printed page. As France, 201, notes, "Irony must therefore always be a slippery tool for the exegete, and can too easily be invoked as a counsel of despair." While the last line may contain a hint of irony (by suggesting that such blindness may not be totally irreversible), it does not negate the strong sense of purpose that runs throughout the verse.

The most natural interpretation remains that of purpose. Two contexts help to illuminate the significance of the quotation. The first is the context of Isaiah, in which the statement has a judicial function. Isaiah is commanded to keep preaching to Israel despite the fact that it will do no good. God has already pronounced Israel's judgment. Because of her sin, God is sending the Assyrians as his agents of judgment. The prophet's message will fall on deaf ears not only because of Israel's hard-heartedness but now also because God has determined what he is going to do. Israel's intransigence is not only the *reason* God will judge, but it is now also the *means* by which his purpose will be achieved. It is the same in the context of Mark. As we have seen, in ch. 3 Israel's leaders reject the clear evidence of God's work in Jesus' ministry and thereby blaspheme the Holy Spirit (3:28–29). The religious "insiders" now become outsiders whose fate is sealed. Yet this by no means thwarts God's purpose, which will be accomplished not just despite their unbelief but actually *through* it. Israel's rejection of Jesus is the means by which salvation will be achieved (8:31; 9:31; 10:33–34). Jesus therefore teaches in parables both to *reveal* the truth to those who are receptive and to *conceal* it from those whose hearts are hardened. It is not foreign to the teaching of Scripture that God in his wisdom hardens some in order to carry out his sovereign purposes (cf. Ex 8:15, 32; 9:12; 10:1; Ro 11:25–32).

3. Interpretation of the Parable of the Sower (4:13–20)

OVERVIEW

Many modern scholars reject the authenticity of this passage because it allegorizes the parable. It is thought to be the work of the early church rather than the authentic teaching of Jesus. Here we have a good example of allowing unproved presuppositions to dominate exegesis: Jesus never used allegory; here we have allegory—so it must not be from Jesus. The logic is sound, but the presupposition is faulty. Moule's word, 36, is to the point: "There is no evidence that Jesus never used allegory; and this is such a good and natural allegory, in which each point is itself a quite straightforward miniature parable, that Jesus may well have used it." There is nothing in the interpretation of the parable that is contrary to the teachings of Jesus. Thus there is no reason to reject it as not having come from him.

[13]Then Jesus said to them, "Don't you understand this parable? How then will you understand any parable? [14]The farmer sows the word. [15]Some people are like seed along

the path, where the word is sown. As soon as they hear it, Satan comes and takes away the
word that was sown in them. 16Others, like seed sown on rocky places, hear the word and
at once receive it with joy. 17But since they have no root, they last only a short time. When
trouble or persecution comes because of the word, they quickly fall away. 18Still others, like
seed sown among thorns, hear the word; 19but the worries of this life, the deceitfulness of
wealth and the desires for other things come in and choke the word, making it unfruitful.
20Others, like seed sown on good soil, hear the word, accept it, and produce a crop—
thirty, sixty or even a hundred times what was sown."

COMMENTARY

13 Jesus' statement contains a slight rebuke. The implication is that the meaning of the parable of the sower should be clear to those with receptive hearts. There is also the suggestion that this parable has a special function, since it concerns receptivity to Jesus' message. It is a parable about the parables (see France, 204). If the disciples do not get this one, how will they understand the meaning and significance of Jesus' ministry as a whole? The spiritual dullness of the disciples expressed here will grow increasingly severe throughout the gospel (4:40; 7:18; 6:52; 8:17–18, 32; 9:19, 32) until they are even in danger of becoming outsiders themselves (8:17–18).

14–15 This parable must be understood first and foremost in the context of Jesus' ministry. The "farmer," though not specifically identified here, is Jesus himself; and the "word" is the message of the kingdom (cf. Mt 13:19), i.e., the coming of the reign of God in Jesus' person and work. The parable's emphasis on the negative rather than positive responses is understandable in the context of chs. 2–3, where Jesus has faced increasing opposition and rejection. We must also keep in mind that Mark is writing to a Christian community, which would no doubt apply the parable to its own life setting and proclamation of the gospel. As always when reading the Gospels, a person must keep in mind both the setting of Jesus and that of the early church.

In the interpretation of the parable, Jesus describes in more detail the kind of reception the message of the kingdom receives. The imagery is somewhat fluid, since in v.15 the recipients appear to be the soil in which the seed is sown (the birds snatch the word that was sown "in them"), while in subsequent verses the recipients appear to be the seed itself, which either bears fruit or does not (vv.16–18, 20). The tension arises from the nature of the agricultural analogy, in which the seed represents both the message sown and the crop produced (cf. NLT and NASB, which retain the emphasis on soils throughout).

The first seed never takes root at all, because it is sown on (or beside [*para*]) the hard-beaten path (v.15). Some reject the message of the kingdom immediately. In Mark's narrative one thinks of the scribes and Pharisees, who appear from the start as Jesus' opponents. The identification of Satan as the thieving birds confirms that for Mark this struggle is a spiritual one of cosmic proportions: the kingdom of Satan is at war with the kingdom of God (cf. *Jub.* 11:11). Those who reject Jesus are under the deceptive influence of the Evil One.

16–17 Another hindrance to proper reception of the word is to be found in persecution and trials. The seed on rocky ground represents those who receive the word joyfully but whose faith is short-lived (*proskairos*) because they have no root "in themselves" (Gk.; untranslated in NIV). No real transformation of their life has taken place. In Mark's narrative we can think of the fickle crowds, who follow Jesus for the miracles and the free meals but who want no part in self-sacrificial discipleship. If Mark is writing to the persecuted church in Rome, this word would have been particularly relevant by sounding a warning to any who, because of persecution and trials, may have been thinking of defecting from the faith. The word translated "fall away" (v.17) is *skandalizō*, (GK *4997*), which often means "cause to sin" (see 9:42–47). Here it carries the sense of desertion or falling away. It will be used by Jesus in this sense in 14:27, 29 to predict the disciples' own defection at Jesus' arrest.

18–19 The third group of hearers are "like seed sown among thorns" (v.18). At first they seem to make good progress, but the word is choked out (1) by "the worries of this life" (v.19)—a reference to whatever distracts people from the really important things—what Taylor, 260, calls "anxiety arising out of the times"; (2) by "the deceitfulness of wealth"—deceitful because it gives to its possessor a false sense of security (a problem particularly evident in society today); and (3) by "the desires for other things"—an all-inclusive statement targeting everything that would choke out the sown word and prevent it from being productive. In Mark's narrative one thinks especially of the rich young man, who was too attached to his worldly wealth to lay it all aside and follow Jesus (10:17–22).

20 Some seed does fall on good soil and is productive. The kind of people spoken of here are open and receptive to the word of the kingdom. They are not hard, shallow, or preoccupied. So the message gets through to them and issues in a productive life. In them truth becomes virtue. The nature of the fruit produced is not specified in the parable or its interpretation, but in the context of Jesus' ministry it must refer to adopting the kingdom principles Jesus has been proclaiming.

NOTES

19 The Greek word αἰών (*aiōn*) in αἱ μέριμναι τοῦ αἰῶνος (*hai merimnai tou aiōnos*, "the worries of this life") means "this age" and is often contrasted in the NT with the age to come. The NIV translates ἀπάτη (*apatē*, GK *573*) as "deceitfulness." In Hellenistic Greek it may carry the meaning "pleasure" or "delight" and may do so here (cf. BDAG, 99).

4. Parables of the Lamp and the Measure (4:21–25)

OVERVIEW

The sayings in vv.21–25 appear to be a composite gathered together here by Mark. In Luke they occur in the same basic order following the parable of the sower (Lk 8:16–18), but in Matthew they appear separately in a variety of different contexts (Mt 5:15; 7:2; 10:26; 13:12; 25:29). Parallel sayings also appear elsewhere in Luke (Lk 11:33; 12:2; 19:26). Verses 21, 22, and 25 also have parallels in the Gnostic *Gospel of Thomas* (see *Gos. Thom.* 5–6, 33, 41, 108b).

In Mark the collection is carefully structured as two trilogies, both introduced by *kai elegen autois* ("and he was saying to them"; vv.21a, 24a). In each trilogy a concrete or pictorial expression (about a lamp and a measure, respectively) is followed by two parallel proverbial sayings (one in synonymous parallelism, one in antithetical parallelism) explaining the significance of the concrete saying. Between the two trilogies are two exhortations to listen (vv.23, 24a).

"And he was saying to them ..."

"Do you bring in a lamp ..." (v.21)	concrete statement
"For whatever is hidden ..." (v.22a)	proverbial explanations in
"And whatever is concealed ..." (v.22b)	synonymous parallelism
"If anyone has ears to hear ..." (v.23)	exhortation to listen

"And he was saying to them ..."

"Consider carefully ..." (v.24a)	exhortation to listen
"With the measure you use ..." (v.24b)	concrete statement
"Whoever has ..." (v.25a)	proverbial explanations in
"Whoever does not have ..." (v.25b)	antithetical parallelism

In addition to this literary balance, there is a conceptual balance in the two groups of sayings. The first trilogy (vv.21–22) relates to the eventual *revelation* of all things that are concealed; the second (vv.24b–25) relates to the continued *hiddenness* of the truth for those whose hearts are hard.

21He said to them, "Do you bring in a lamp to put it under a bowl or a bed? Instead,
don't you put it on its stand? 22For whatever is hidden is meant to be disclosed, and
whatever is concealed is meant to be brought out into the open. 23If anyone has ears
to hear, let him hear."
24"Consider carefully what you hear," he continued. "With the measure you use, it will be
measured to you—and even more. 25Whoever has will be given more; whoever does not
have, even what he has will be taken from him."

COMMENTARY

21–23 Mark's statement *erchetai ho lychnos* (lit, "does the lamp come ...") is unusual, for *erchetai* normally has a personal subject. This construction, together with Mark's use of the definite article (*ho*), has suggested to some that the lamp here refers to Jesus himself (cf. Lane, 165–66; Cranfield, 164;

Hooker, 133). The other possible interpretation is that the lamp refers to the message of the kingdom of God, the coming of which Jesus has been proclaiming (cf. France, 208). Both interpretations fit the context, since Jesus and the kingdom have appeared now in a veiled or hidden manner but will be fully revealed in the future. The two ideas are in fact very close since, as Lane, 166, points out, "the secret of the Kingdom of God ... is present in the person of Jesus." Furthermore, the return of the Son of Man in glory is associated with the consummation of the kingdom (13:26–27).

The purpose of the lamp (*lychnos*) is to be put on a lampstand and not under a bowl (*modios*) or a bed. A *lychnos* is a clay lamp filled with oil. A *modios* is a grain measure holding about two gallons. The bed (*klinē*) could be a bed or a dining couch. In Matthew the saying appears in the Sermon on the Mount and refers to the good deeds Jesus' disciples should shine on the world. Here, as the following proverbs explain, the point is that the present hiddenness of Jesus and the kingdom will not always be. Hidden things are meant to be brought into the open (v.22). It is not made explicit who the revealer is (God, Jesus, the disciples?) or when the revelation will take place. The revealer and revelation could be the glorious return of Christ and the consummation of the kingdom, or the disciples and their proclamation of the gospel following Jesus' death and resurrection. The latter fits well with Jesus' command to his disciples in 9:9 that his glory, revealed at the transfiguration, should not be proclaimed "until the Son of Man had risen from the dead." In either case, the statement balances the secrecy motif that runs throughout Mark's gospel. Though at present Jesus guards his identity and privately explains the secret of the kingdom of God to his disciples, this hiddenness is temporary and is simply the means by which God is accomplishing his salvific purpose. The time will come when all such mysteries will be revealed and the glory of Christ and the kingdom will be evident to all.

As with the parables, such teaching requires spiritual discernment, so the exhortation of 4:9 is repeated: "If anyone has ears to hear, let him hear" (v.23).

24 The second trilogy of "parables" begins with another exhortation to spiritual perception: "Consider carefully what you hear." The concrete proverb Jesus quotes ("with the measure you use ...") comes from the grain industry and relates to reciprocity. It occurs in other contexts in Matthew (7:2) and Luke (6:38) with different applications. In Matthew it refers to the danger of judging others, since the person who judges will be judged by the same standard. Luke's point is similar, but more generally refers to receiving back what one gives, whether in judgment, forgiveness, or an attitude of sharing. In rabbinic literature the proverb often relates to divine judgment mediated justly (*m. Soṭah* 1:7; *b. Sanh. 100a*; cf. France, 211). Here in Mark the meaning is illuminated by the broader context and the proverbs that follow: the more one listens to the word of Jesus with spiritual perception and appropriates it, the more the truth about Jesus will be revealed.

25 The two explanatory (antithetical) proverbs that follow also occur in other contexts (Mt 13:12; 25:29; Lk 19:26). In Matthew 25:29 and Luke 19:26 (the parables of the talents and minas, respectively), the meaning relates to good stewardship of the resources God has provided. Matthew 13:12 occurs in Jesus' explanation of the reason he teaches in parables and relates to spiritual discernment that comes to those receptive to Jesus' kingdom teaching. Here the context and meaning are similar. Those who are open and receptive to the message of the kingdom now will receive greater and greater spiritual insight from further teaching.

Those who are closed-minded and unresponsive will become more and more blind to spiritual realities. Even the little spiritual perception they have will be taken away.

5. Parable of the Secretly Growing Seed (4:26–29)

26He also said, "This is what the kingdom of God is like. A man scatters seed on the
ground. 27Night and day, whether he sleeps or gets up, the seed sprouts and grows,
though he does not know how. 28All by itself the soil produces grain — first the stalk, then
the head, then the full kernel in the head. 29As soon as the grain is ripe, he puts the sickle
to it, because the harvest has come."

COMMENTARY

26–28 Only Mark records this parable. Its emphasis is different from that of the parable of the sower. There the importance of proper soil for the growth of the seed and the success of the harvest are stressed. Here the mysterious power of the seed itself to produce a crop is emphasized.

The parable relates to the kingdom of God and, more particularly, how that kingdom grows. All the farmer does is plant the seed on suitable ground. He does not make the seed grow. He does not even understand how it grows (v.27). But it does grow, and "all by itself the soil produces grain" (v.28). The point of the parable is as follows: "As seedtime is followed in due time by harvest, so will the present hiddenness and ambiguousness of the kingdom of God be succeeded by its glorious manifestation" (Cranfield, 168).

A similar emphasis is suggested by Jeremias (*Parables of the Kingdom*, 152–53):

> The fruit is the *result* of the seed; the end is implicit in the beginning. The infinitely great is already active in the infinitely small. In the present, and indeed in secret, the event is already in motion.... Those to whom it has been given to understand the mystery of the Kingdom (Mark 4–11) see already in its hidden and insignificant beginnings the coming kingdom of God.

The point of the parable is *not* that disciples of Jesus should cease all activity and let spiritual growth just happen. Unlike the parable of the sower, this one does not address the response or receptivity of the hearers. The point rather is that the sovereign God is in charge of human history, and he will bring it to its destined conclusion. Neither the surprising and unexpected nature of the kingdom Jesus is proclaiming nor the powerful influence of those who oppose him will negate the power or presence of the kingdom. Jesus' followers can be assured that it will come, and it will come in power.

29 The last two clauses may provide additional insight into the purpose of the parable. "He puts the sickle to it, because the harvest has come" echoes Joel 3:13 [4:13], so suggesting that the harvest spoken of is the eschatological judgment. In the face of opposition, persecution, and trials, God's people can be assured that the harvest day is coming when God will deliver the righteous, judge the wicked, and right every wrong.

6. Parable of the Mustard Seed (4:30–32)

[30]Again he said, "What shall we say the kingdom of God is like, or what parable shall we use to describe it? [31]It is like a mustard seed, which is the smallest seed you plant in the ground. [32]Yet when planted, it grows and becomes the largest of all garden plants, with such big branches that the birds of the air can perch in its shade."

COMMENTARY

30–32 This parable is the third and last of those about the seed sown. The mustard seed is "the smallest seed you plant in the ground" (v.31). The mustard seed was proverbial for its small size (Mt 17:20; *m. Naz.* 1:5; *m. Nid.* 5:2), but it is not in fact the smallest known seed (e.g., the seed of the black orchid is smaller). Jesus obviously was not giving a lesson in botany. The mustard seed was, however, the smallest seed his audience was familiar with. When grown, it becomes a huge treelike shrub—sometimes ten or more feet high—larger than other garden plants (v.32). Matthew and Luke hyperbolically refer to it as a "tree" (*dendron*; Mt 13:32; Lk 13:19).

The main point of the parable is that the kingdom of God (v.30) develops like the mustard seed. After insignificant and weak beginnings it will someday become great and powerful. It is uncertain whether the detail about the birds' taking shelter in the tree's shade has any significance. Some interpreters see in it a mention of the inclusion of the Gentiles in the kingdom (cf. Marcus, 331). Support for this view may come from several OT passages that Mark's parable seems to echo. Ezekiel's two parables of cedar trees (Eze 17:23; 31:6) and Nebuchadnezzar's dream in Daniel 4:10–12, 14, 21 draw on common ancient Near Eastern imagery to describe the growth of great empires as large trees under which birds and beasts come for rest and protection. Ezekiel 31:6 explicitly identifies these seekers of refuge as "all great nations" living in the shade of the Assyrian empire.

There may be a further implication in the parable's imagery. Various scholars have noted how unusual is the choice of a mustard plant for such a parable (cf. Witherington, 172; J. D. Crossan, *The Historical Jesus* [San Francisco: HarperSanFrancisco, 1991], 277–79). For a symbol of the greatness of the kingdom, one would expect a stately tree, such as a cedar of Lebanon (cf. the Ezekiel and Daniel texts above), not a big bush! The mustard plant, in fact, was often seen in a negative light. Pliny the Elder (*Nat.* 19.170–71) wrote that the plant "grows entirely wild, though it is improved by being transplanted: but on the other hand when it has once been sown it is scarcely possible to get the place free of it, as the seed when it falls germinates at once." Perhaps in addition to describing the remarkable growth of the kingdom, the parable also suggests that the spreading kingdom "was a threat to the existing garden or field of early Judaism. If Jesus' proclamation took root, it stood in danger of subverting existing kingdom visions and power structures in Israel" (Witherington, 172).

7. *Summary Statement on Parables (4:33–34)*

33With many similar parables Jesus spoke the word to them, as much as they could understand. 34He did not say anything to them without using a parable. But when he was alone with his own disciples, he explained everything.

COMMENTARY

33–34 Mark ends this section of parables with a statement about Jesus' use of them. "With many similar parables" reiterates that Mark has provided merely a sampling of Jesus' broader teaching ministry. Parables (here the word has its broad meaning to include similitudes, riddles, etc.) constituted Jesus' primary method of speaking the word (i.e., the word of the kingdom—God's reign revealed in Jesus himself) to "them"—the crowd (v.33). The phrase "as much as they could understand" (*kathōs ēdynanto akouein*) does not mean "just enough for their level of understanding." The point here is not that Jesus gave just the right dose of truth so they could easily grasp it; rather, in line with the purpose of parables (see comments at vv.11–12), it means that the people's comprehension depended on whether or not they were able to hear (*ēdynanto akouein*). For those with hearts open to the kingdom message, the parables illuminated the truth. For those with closed minds and hearts, the parables blinded the eyes.

Verse 34 confirms that this sense is the one intended. "He did not speak anything to them without using a parable" means, on the one hand, that Jesus taught almost exclusively using stories and analogies. On the other hand, it means that everything he taught functioned parabolically, i.e., to *reveal* or to *conceal*, depending on the hearer's attitude of heart. Alone with the disciples (here probably meaning both the Twelve and other followers—those "insiders" who had opened their hearts to Jesus and the kingdom), "he explained everything." It should be added that while the parables are functioning as a word of judgment against those who are rejecting the kingdom, this word is not yet final, not yet a *fait accompli*. There is no impermeable boundary in the narrative between the "insiders" and "outsiders" (even the disciples will waver), and Jesus continues to proclaim the message to all who will listen. Yet unless they respond with a receptive heart, the word will continue to fall on deaf ears.

E. Triumph over Hostile Powers (4:35–5:43)

OVERVIEW

Jesus' teaching in parables is followed in Mark by a series of miracle stories that demonstrate Jesus' authority over various kinds of hostile powers: a storm at sea (4:35–41), a legion of demons (5:1–20), an incurable disease (5:25–34), and death itself (5:21–24, 35–43). The significant diversity represents all aspects of fallen creation (natural disasters, demonic influence, disease, and death).

From the perspective of Mark's narrative it reveals the inbreaking power of the kingdom of God, which will ultimately bring restoration to all things.

A common thread that runs through these episodes is the seemingly hopeless condition of the individuals involved (Garland, 190). The disciples fear for their lives in the storm-tossed sea (4:38); the Gerasene demoniac is so wild with demons that chains cannot even hold him (5:2–5); the sick woman has spent everything she had on doctors without hope for a cure (5:25–26); and Jairus sees his daughter succumb to the seemingly irreversible fate of death (5:35). The point is that no obstacle is too great for Jesus' power.

1. Calming the Storm (4:35–41)

OVERVIEW

Mark's narrative purpose in this episode is twofold: to demonstrate the awesome authority of the Son of God over the forces of nature, and to reveal the inadequate faith of the disciples. Though they are the "insiders" to whom the secret of the kingdom of God is being revealed (4:11–12), they have not yet arrived. Whether the seed of the word will fully take root in them and produce a harvest remains an open question (v.20).

There are a number of interesting parallels to the story of Jonah in this episode: a great life-threatening storm (Jnh 1:4); the main character's sleeping despite the storm's violence (1:5) and being awakened by a frightened crew looking for help (1:6); the immediate cessation of the storm by divine intervention (1:15); and the awe and fear thus inspired (1:16).

35That day when evening came, he said to his disciples, "Let us go over to the other
side." 36Leaving the crowd behind, they took him along, just as he was, in the boat. There
were also other boats with him. 37A furious squall came up, and the waves broke over the
boat, so that it was nearly swamped. 38Jesus was in the stern, sleeping on a cushion. The
disciples woke him and said to him, "Teacher, don't you care if we drown?"
39He got up, rebuked the wind and said to the waves, "Quiet! Be still!" Then the wind
died down and it was completely calm.
40He said to his disciples, "Why are you so afraid? Do you still have no faith?"
41They were terrified and asked each other, "Who is this? Even the wind and the waves
obey him!"

COMMENTARY

35–36 Note the details in the story: the mention of the time of day, the statement about the "other boats," the position of Jesus in the boat, the mention of the cushion, the sharp rebuke made by the disciples, and their terror and bewilderment. Taken together these details suggest the report of an eyewitness.

The story is literarily connected to Jesus' teaching in parables by its occurring on "that day" (v.35). Jesus has been teaching the people from a boat pushed out from the shore a short distance (see v.1). Evening has come; so Jesus decides to go over to the other side of the lake (v.35). Mark mentions no reason for this decision. Perhaps Jesus simply wanted to escape from the crowds for a little while and renew his strength. The disciples respond to Jesus' request by taking Jesus "just as he was, in the boat" (v.36). This comment probably means "without going to shore." That is, Jesus wanted to go directly to the other side of the lake in the same boat he had been teaching the people from and without the delay his going ashore might have caused.

The mention of "other boats with him" (v.36) suggests the trip involved more than the Twelve. We are not told what happened to the other boats. Perhaps they were driven back to the western shore of the lake.

37 The geographic location of the Sea of Galilee makes it particularly susceptible to sudden, violent storms. It is situated in a basin surrounded by mountains. Though at night and in the early morning the sea is usually calm, when storms come at those times they are all the more treacherous. The storm is described as a "furious squall" (*lailaps megalē anemou*, lit., "great windstorm") that was driving the waves into the boat so that it was being swamped. G. A. Smith's description (*The Historical Geography of the Holy Land* [New York: Armstrong & Son, 1909], 441–42) of the Sea of Galilee's susceptibility to storms is illuminating: "The atmosphere, for the most part, hangs still and heavy but the cold currents, as they pass from the west, are sucked down in vortices of air, or by the narrow gorges that break upon the lake. Then arise those sudden storms for which the region is notorious."

38 Jesus, tired from a long day's teaching, was in the stern of the boat, asleep on a cushion. "The cushion" (*to proskephalaion* [with the definite article) was apparently kept on board for those not involved in sailing or fishing, and Jesus used it as a pillow for his head (cf. Lane, 176). Only here in the Gospels is Jesus said to have slept; but he did, of course, get tired and need sleep like any other human being. The fact that Jesus could sleep through such a violent storm heightens the drama and produces a stark contrast between the disciples' fear and Jesus' peaceful trust in God (cf. Lev 26:6; Job 11:19; Pss 3:5; 4:8; Pr 3:24).

There is a tone of both panic and rebuke in the disciples' cry, "Teacher, don't you care if we drown?" Both Matthew and Luke soften the pointedness of this question, Matthew with the prayer, "Lord, save us! We're going to drown!" and Luke with, "Master, Master, we're going to drown!" Their response in Mark is in line with two Markan themes: the veiled nature of Jesus' messiahship and the dullness of the disciples' faith.

39 Jesus rebuked the wind and spoke to the waves. The verbs *epitimaō* (GK *2203*, "rebuke") and *phimoō* (GK *5821*, "muzzle," "be quiet") are found in the description of the exorcism of Mark 1:25, and various commentators have suggested that the storm is being viewed here as a satanic force in opposition to Jesus (cf. Marcus, 339; Guelich, 267; Moloney, 99). While this suggestion is possible, without other contextual indicators it is unlikely. The primary point, rather, is that Jesus has *divine* authority over the forces of nature. In the OT God himself is described as anthropomorphically "rebuking" the sea, thus demonstrating his sovereign control over all nature (2Sa 22:16; Pss 18:15; 104:7; 106:9; Isa 50:2; Na 1:4). While Mark probably does not view the sea as demonic, like other ancient people he likely views it as a place of chaos, danger, and death. Jesus' words, therefore, bring order from chaos, and peace and safety from the danger of death.

The result was that "the wind died down and it was completely calm." The Greek contrasts the "great storm" of v.37 (*lailaps megalē*) with the "great calm" of v.39 (*galēnē megalē*). The miracle indicates a theophany. In the psalms Yahweh is celebrated as Lord of the storm and sea. Psalm 89:9 says, "You rule over the surging sea; when its waves mount up, you still them." In Psalm 107:23–32, Yahweh "spoke and stirred up a tempest that lifted high the waves" (v.25). Yet when his people cry out to him, "He stilled the storm to a whisper; the waves of the sea were hushed" (v.29; cf. Pss 65:7; 104:6–7).

40 Jesus also rebuked his disciples for their lack of faith. The preferred reading (*oupō*, "not yet"; NIV, "still") indicates that Jesus had expected them by this time to have demonstrated more mature faith. "Faith" here means faith in God's saving power as it is present and active in the person of Jesus. This rebuke of the disciples is the first of several scoldings by Jesus for their lack of understanding and faith (cf. 7:18; 8:17–18, 21, 32–33; 9:19).

41 "Were terrified" describes the feeling of awe that came over the disciples as a result of Jesus' mighty act. While previously they were afraid of the storm, now they fear the awesome authority of Jesus himself. This occasion revealed something about him that they had not experienced before. So they wondered, "Who is this? Even the wind and the waves obey him!" For the reader of Mark, the answer is "the Christ, the Son of God!" (1:1). Yet the awestruck disciples do not yet know what to make of this Jesus, who apparently wields the very authority of God.

REFLECTIONS

The calming of the storm on Lake Galilee is a good example of a nature miracle, a feat of power that demonstrates authority over the natural world (cf. 6:30–44, 45–52; 8:1–10; 11:12–13, 20–23). Miracles of this kind seem to present the greatest problem for modern critics. The NT, however, makes clear that Jesus Christ is not only Lord over his church but also Lord of all creation. "For by him all things were created: things in heaven and on earth, visible and invisible, whether thrones or powers or rulers or authorities; all things were created by him and for him" (Col 1:16). The Creator-Lord also controls what he has created. "He is before all things, and in him all things hold together" (Col 1:17). It is inadequate to explain this miracle by coincidence or to relegate it to myth or imagination. One's conclusion about the historicity of this and similar stories in the Gospels will inevitably depend on one's Christology. If Jesus was the strong Son of God, as he claimed to be, a miracle of this kind is not inconsistent with that claim.

It is not difficult to imagine what effect this story had on the members of the persecuted (Roman?) church for whom Mark wrote his gospel. It assured them that the strong Son of God would go with them into the storm of opposition and trial.

2. Healing the Demon-Possessed Man (5:1–20)

OVERVIEW

Jesus had demonstrated his power over the forces of nature by stilling the winds and the waves. Now he demonstrates his power over the forces of evil by driving out demons from a possessed man. The two stories go together; they both reveal Jesus' divine authority.

[1]They went across the lake to the region of the Gerasenes. [2]When Jesus got out of the
boat, a man with an evil spirit came from the tombs to meet him. [3]This man lived in the
tombs, and no one could bind him any more, not even with a chain. [4]For he had often
been chained hand and foot, but he tore the chains apart and broke the irons on his feet.
No one was strong enough to subdue him. [5]Night and day among the tombs and in the
hills he would cry out and cut himself with stones.

[6]When he saw Jesus from a distance, he ran and fell on his knees in front of him. [7]He
shouted at the top of his voice, "What do you want with me, Jesus, Son of the Most High
God? Swear to God that you won't torture me!" [8]For Jesus had said to him, "Come out of
this man, you evil spirit!"

[9]Then Jesus asked him, "What is your name?"

"My name is Legion," he replied, "for we are many." [10]And he begged Jesus again and
again not to send them out of the area.

[11]A large herd of pigs was feeding on the nearby hillside. [12]The demons begged Jesus,
"Send us among the pigs; allow us to go into them." [13]He gave them permission, and the
evil spirits came out and went into the pigs. The herd, about two thousand in number,
rushed down the steep bank into the lake and were drowned.

[14]Those tending the pigs ran off and reported this in the town and countryside, and
the people went out to see what had happened. [15]When they came to Jesus, they saw
the man who had been possessed by the legion of demons, sitting there, dressed and in
his right mind; and they were afraid. [16]Those who had seen it told the people what had
happened to the demon-possessed man—and told about the pigs as well. [17]Then the
people began to plead with Jesus to leave their region.

[18]As Jesus was getting into the boat, the man who had been demon-possessed begged
to go with him. [19]Jesus did not let him, but said, "Go home to your family and tell them
how much the Lord has done for you, and how he has had mercy on you." [20]So the man
went away and began to tell in the Decapolis how much Jesus had done for him. And all
the people were amazed.

COMMENTARY

1 "Across the lake" means on the eastern side. That the population of this region was largely Gentile is shown by the name Decapolis (see comments at v.20) and the presence of a large herd of pigs—animals considered unclean by Jews and therefore unfit to eat (Lev 11:7–8). The theme of spiritual impurity or uncleanness runs through the narrative. The man is possessed by "unclean" (*akathartos*, GK *176*) spirits; he is living among tombs (unclean by virtue of the corpses); the demons are sent into unclean animals, which are destroyed. Through Jesus, the kingdom of God is invading and purifying the defiled realm of Satan.

The name of the place where the miracle was performed is disputed. The correct reading in Mark is the "region of the Gerasenes" (so NIV).

The textual variants (see Notes) arose because Gerasa, located about thirty miles southeast of the lake, seemed too far removed. However, Mark says the "region" of the Gerasenes, which apparently included the entire district extending down from the city to the lake. Another possibility is that Gerasa is to be identified with the ruins of Kersa (Koursi), a village on the eastern shore. Not far from this site is a cliff within forty meters of the shore and some old tombs.

2 From this verse it would appear that Jesus, on stepping out of the boat, was immediately confronted by the possessed man. Verse 6 clarifies the situation. The man actually saw Jesus from a distance and came running to him. Since it was already evening (cf. 4:35) when they started across the lake, by the time they reached the other side it was probably dark.

3–5 The possessed man lived in the tombs. Often in Palestine people were buried in natural caves or in tombs cut out of the limestone rock. These enclosures provided good shelter for anyone desiring to live in them. It was a natural place for a possessed man to dwell, for popular belief held that tombs were the favorite haunts of demons. This wretched man had probably been driven from ordinary society into the tombs.

Typical of his vivid style of storytelling is Mark's detailed description of the man's condition (vv.3b–5; cf. Lk 8:29). Efforts had been made to control the demoniac, but without success. Although bound "hand and foot," he had broken the chains; and no one was strong enough to subdue him. He would wander about at night while crying out and cutting himself. Solitary and self-destructive behavior was often associated with demon-possession. The Jerusalem Talmud describes people who go out alone at night as sleeping in graveyards, ripping their clothes, and losing what is given to them (*y. Ter.* 1:1 [*40b*]).

6 The NIV correctly translates *prosekynēsen autō* as "fell on his knees in front of him" rather than as "worshiped" (KJV). The act was one of submission rather than worship. The possessed man shows respect because he recognizes that he is confronted with one greatly superior to him.

7–8 The demon addresses Jesus by shouting "at the top of his voice." The NIV's "What do you want with me?" captures the sense of the Greek idiom, "What to me and to you?" (see comments at 1:23–24). This exasperated outburst is the equivalent of "Why are you bothering me! Leave me alone!" The demoniac recognizes that he is in the presence of the One who threatens his very existence.

In addressing Jesus the man uses Jesus' personal name. As at 1:24, this recognition reveals the profound spiritual and eschatological significance of Jesus' ministry. While human beings—even his own disciples (4:41)—puzzle at his identity, the demons know exactly who he is: the mighty "Son of the Most High God," who has come to destroy them! As noted earlier (see comments at 1:24), in the ancient world identifying a spirit being by name was considered a way of gaining control over it, so the demons may be trying to exert spiritual influence over Jesus. That the demons are seeking to gain some control is evident from the oath in the next phrase. The NIV's imperative "Swear to God ..." misses the Greek idiom, where it is the demon who swears by God's name (*orkizō se ton theon*; cf. TNIV, "In God's name don't torture me!"). The tormentor now changes his role; he pleads exemption from torment. This may be a reference to eschatological punishment (cf. 1:24: "Have you come to destroy us?"). The kingdom of God means the ultimate defeat of Satan and his minions. Matthew adds "before the appointed time" (8:29), which captures the sense that Jesus has authority in the present to pronounce eschatological judgment against the demons.

Verse 8 is a narrative aside, an explanation by Mark to make clear why the man was acting so excitedly. Jesus had ordered the demon to come out of the man. With v.8 understood in this way, there is no need to follow the suggestion of some commentators that v.8 originally preceded v.7.

9 To Jesus' demand for his name, the demoniac replies, "Legion." A Roman legion consisted of over six thousand men, but the explanation "for we are many" indicates that the reference is meant to be general rather than specific. The man has been overwhelmed not just by one demon but actually by a great host of demons. Whatever the number, it will be enough to panic two thousand pigs (v.13). Whether any other significance attaches to the name "Legion" is uncertain. The demons' giving it may be their futile attempt to avoid providing a true name and so succumbing to Jesus' power. Or it may intend to sound threatening by pointing to a large demonic presence (cf. Lane, 185). The latter possibility is less likely considering the possessed man's consistent attitude of submission toward Jesus (vv.6–7, 10).

Some commentators, noting the military language here and elsewhere in the episode, have suggested that Mark is here weaving a political allegory concerning Jesus' mission to liberate Palestine from Roman military occupation (so Myers, *Binding the Strong Man*, 190–94; Theissen, *Miracle Stories*, 255–56). This explanation seems unlikely, however, especially since the episode takes place in Gentile rather than Jewish territory.

10 Both the singular and the plural occur here—"He begged ... not to send them"—probably in an attempt by Mark to indicate that the multitude of demons are speaking through the lips of the demoniac. What they request is that they not be sent out of the "area" or "region" (*chōra*). The exact meaning of their plea is uncertain. It could simply mean they do not want to wander aimlessly on the earth (cf. Mt 12:43–45; Lk 11:24–26). Or it may reflect the popular conception that demons are assigned to particular localities (cf. Hooker, 145). In Luke (8:31) the request is that they not be sent into the Abyss, the place of confinement before judgment (Rev 20:1–3). The requests in Mark and Luke may carry the same meaning; for to be sent out of their appointed region would mean confinement in the Abyss to await judgment (2Pe 2:4; Jude 6). Another possibility is that the demons hope that even apart from their human host they will be able to maintain some of the authority they have gained in this region. This last suggestion fits well their request to enter the pigs.

11–13 The presence of a large herd of swine in the Decapolis is not surprising. This region, on the eastern shore of the Sea of Galilee, was largely Gentile. At first it seems odd that Jesus, who throughout the episode shows full command of the situation, would allow the demons to bargain for their fate. Yet the results reveal that he is still fully in control, as the demons get more than they bargained for. Spooked (literally) by the demons, the whole herd of two thousand rushes down a cliff and perishes in the sea. As Garland, 205, notes, "From a Jewish perspective, the scene is a joke: unclean spirits and unclean animals are both wiped out in one fell swoop, and a human being is cleansed."

Ancient and modern interpreters have struggled with the ethical question of why Jesus would allow such an apparently senseless loss of animal life, not to mention the economic loss to the pigs' owners. The most common answer is that Jesus needed to give tangible evidence to the man and to the people that the demons had actually been exorcised. The loss of life served the greater good of revealing Jesus' authority and provoking faith in him (cf. T. C. Oden and C. A. Hall, eds., *Mark* [ACCS 2; Downers Grove, Ill.: InterVarsity, 1998], 66–67). Neither Mark nor the other gospel writers seem concerned with this question. All apparently assume that these material losses pale in comparison to the eternal significance of one man's deliverance from bondage to Satan.

14–15 The result of the stampede and destruction of the pigs was the flight of the herdsman to "the town" (probably the chief town of the district) and "countryside" to tell what had happened (v.14). This brought the people to the scene of the miracle. When they arrived, they could scarcely believe their eyes! The man who had been known as "crazy," who had been so violent that he could not even be controlled by chains, they now saw sitting quietly (v.15). Before he had roamed naked through the tombs (cf. Lk 8:27); now he was "dressed." Previously he was possessed by powerful evil forces; now he was in his "right mind." Calvin, 2:436, makes a pointed application: "Though we are not tortured by the devil, yet he holds us as his slaves, till the Son of God delivers us from his tyranny. Naked, torn, and disfigured, we wander about, till he restores us to soundness of mind."

Instead of rejoicing because of the marvelous deliverance of the man from his pathetic state, the people "were afraid." Their fear was no doubt caused by the presence of one with the power to perform such a miracle.

16–17 When the eyewitnesses to the event reported what had happened (v.16), both to the man and to the pigs, the people decided it was time for Jesus to leave their region (v.17). In fact, they pleaded with him to leave. Why? They were afraid (v.15). They recognized that a mighty force was at work in Jesus and that they could neither understand nor control it. If it destroyed an entire herd of pigs, might not this power strike again with even more serious consequences? Fear, ignorance, and selfishness because of the material loss through the destruction of the pigs dominated their considerations rather than compassion for the former demoniac. So they asked Jesus to leave, and he did. Garland, 206, points to the irony in the response:

> The demons had begged Jesus to let them stay in the region (5:10); the townspeople now beg Jesus to leave the region. They are more comfortable with the malevolent forces that take captive human beings and destroy animals than they are with the one who can expel them. They can cope with the odd demon-possessed wild man who terrorizes the neighborhood with random acts of violence. But they want to keep someone with Jesus' power at lake's length.

18–19 Jesus had come to the eastern side of the lake by boat (v.2). Now he was about to return the same way. Not surprisingly, the formerly possessed man wanted to go with him. He was eager for Jesus' company, for no one had ever showed him such love and compassion. The man's request stands in striking contrast to the reaction of the townspeople. While they plead for Jesus to leave them (v.17), the man begs for the opportunity to stay with him. The kingdom either attracts or repels, depending on whether one has eyes to see and ears to hear (4:12).

Yet Jesus does not allow the man to come with him. Instead he gives him the much more difficult task of returning home to his family to bear testimony to what was done for him. The command to "go home to your family [or 'your people']" is particularly significant in the light of the solitary and self-destructive life the man had been leading. Jesus' healing brought restoration of normal human relationships.

The further command, "Tell them how much the Lord has done for you" (v.19), is in marked contrast to Jesus' instructions to the cleansed leper in 1:44—"See that you don't tell this to anyone." A probable reason for the change is that in the case of the demoniac Jesus was in Gentile territory, where there would be little danger that popular messianic ideas about him might be circulated. It was in Jewish territory that this possibility was always present. Or perhaps in this man's case, Jesus realized that the true nature of his person and mission was perceived; so the man could be trusted to convey to others the truth about Jesus.

20 The man obeyed without argument and "began to tell in the Decapolis how much Jesus had done for him." The Decapolis was a league of ten originally free Greek cities located on the east of Lake Galilee and the Jordan River (except for Scythopolis). They had been organized on the Greek model during the Seleucid period, brought under Hasmonean control by John Hyrcanus, and liberated by the Roman general Pompey. These cities heard the testimony of the former demoniac and responded with amazement. Anderson, 150, suggests that Mark may regard this incident "as the inauguration of the mission to the Gentiles." Whether or not this view is correct, Jesus' ministry in the Gentile region "across the sea" (v.1) certainly foreshadows the proclamation of the gospel to all nations.

Mark exhibits a very high Christology when Jesus' command to "tell them how much the Lord has done for you" (v.19) results in the man's telling "how much Jesus had done for him" (v.20). The work of Jesus is the work of God (cf. France, 233; Marcus, 354).

NOTES

1 There are three different readings of the place name: Γερασηνῶν (*Gerasēnōn*, "Gerasenes"), original in Mark; Γαδαρηνῶν (*Gadarēnōn*, "Gadarenes"), found in Matthew; and Γεργεσηνῶν (*Gergesēnōn*, "Gergesenes"), a reading attributable to Origen. Taylor, 278, writes, "The textual variations are due to the fact that Gerasa (30 miles to the southeast) and Gadara (6 miles to the southeast) are too far from the lake, and to the necessity of finding a site where the mountains run down steeply into the lake."

3 Contact with the dead rendered a Jew ceremonially unclean (Nu 19:11, 14, 16; Eze 39:11–15). In Isaiah 65:3–4 unbelieving Israel is described as a people "who sit among the graves and spend their nights keeping secret vigil; who eat the flesh of pigs."

20 Throughout Mark's gospel amazement and awe are common responses to Jesus' words and deeds (1:22, 27; 2:12; 5:20; 6:2; 7:37; 11:18).

3. Healing a Sick Woman and Raising Jairus's Daughter (5:21–43)

OVERVIEW

Mark's collection of four episodes demonstrating Jesus' triumph over hostile powers (4:35–5:43) climaxes with a story of the healing of a woman with a bleeding disorder and the raising of Jairus's daughter. These two accounts may have been brought together with the healing of the demoniac because all of them have to do with ritual uncleanness. According to Jewish law contact with Gentiles, demoniacs, graves, blood, or death made one ceremonially unclean. In none of these episodes does Jesus shirk back from unclean things. He is not defiled by them but rather brings healing and restoration to all he touches. The kingdom of God is salt and light, transforming and renewing a fallen world.

The raising of Jairus's daughter and the healing of the woman exhibit Mark's common literary technique of intercalation, whereby one story is sandwiched between the beginning and end of another (cf. 3:20–35; 5:21–43; 6:7–30; 11:12–25; 14:1–11, 53–72; see Introduction, pp. 689–90). The account of the woman's healing (vv.25–34) interrupts Jesus' journey to Jairus's home (vv.21–24; vv.35–43). As with other intercalations in Mark, the two episodes share a common theme and mutually interpret one another. The theme here is faith. In both cases faith is exhibited as each character approaches Jesus despite social and cultural obstacles. Jairus, a man with high social standing, humbles himself by falling at Jesus' feet and begging Jesus to heal his daughter (v.22). The woman, whose blood disorder places her on the fringe of Jewish social and religious life, is boldly willing to approach Jesus and even touch him. In both cases Jesus affirms such faith and boldness. He tells the woman that her faith has made her well (v.34), and he encourages Jairus to have faith despite his daughter's death (v.36).

21When Jesus had again crossed over by boat to the other side of the lake, a large
crowd gathered around him while he was by the lake. 22Then one of the synagogue rulers,
named Jairus, came there. Seeing Jesus, he fell at his feet 23and pleaded earnestly with
him, "My little daughter is dying. Please come and put your hands on her so that she will
be healed and live." 24 So Jesus went with him.
A large crowd followed and pressed around him. 25And a woman was there who had
been subject to bleeding for twelve years. 26She had suffered a great deal under the care
of many doctors and had spent all she had, yet instead of getting better she grew worse.
27When she heard about Jesus, she came up behind him in the crowd and touched his
cloak, 28because she thought, "If I just touch his clothes, I will be healed." 29Immediately
her bleeding stopped and she felt in her body that she was freed from her suffering.
30At once Jesus realized that power had gone out from him. He turned around in the
crowd and asked, "Who touched my clothes?"
31"You see the people crowding against you," his disciples answered, "and yet you can
ask, 'Who touched me?'"
32But Jesus kept looking around to see who had done it. 33Then the woman, knowing
what had happened to her, came and fell at his feet and, trembling with fear, told him the
whole truth. 34He said to her, "Daughter, your faith has healed you. Go in peace and be
freed from your suffering."
35While Jesus was still speaking, some men came from the house of Jairus, the synagogue ruler. "Your daughter is dead," they said. "Why bother the teacher any more?"
36Ignoring what they said, Jesus told the synagogue ruler, "Don't be afraid; just believe."
37 He did not let anyone follow him except Peter, James and John the brother of James.
38When they came to the home of the synagogue ruler, Jesus saw a commotion, with
people crying and wailing loudly. 39He went in and said to them, "Why all this commotion
and wailing? The child is not dead but asleep." 40But they laughed at him.

After he put them all out, he took the child's father and mother and the disciples who were with him, and went in where the child was. [41]He took her by the hand and said to her, *"Talitha koum!"* (which means, "Little girl, I say to you, get up!"). [42]Immediately the girl stood up and walked around (she was twelve years old). At this they were completely astonished. [43]He gave strict orders not to let anyone know about this, and told them to give her something to eat.

COMMENTARY

21 Again the scene shifts. Jesus has returned to the western side of the lake. (He had been asked to leave the eastern side.) Here great crowds greet him. The specific place where the incident occurred is not given, but most commentators conjecture that it was near Capernaum, Jesus' base of operations during his Galilean ministry (see 1:21).

22 Jesus was probably busy teaching when he was interrupted by the plea of "one of the synagogue rulers." Synagogue rulers (*archisynagōgoi*) were laymen whose responsibilities were administrative, not priestly, and included such things as looking after the building and supervising the worship. Sometimes in the NT the reference is singular, referring to the individual with oversight over a particular synagogue (cf. Lk 8:49; 13:14; Ac 18:8, 17). At other times it is plural and seems to refer to a council of elders (cf. Ac 13:15). At Antioch, Paul and Barnabas were invited by the synagogue rulers to participate in the service (Ac 13:15). The title may have sometimes been honorary and was given to prominent members of the congregation (Lane, 190 n. 38). The plural sense seems to be Mark's meaning here, since he describes Jairus as "one of the synagogue rulers."

23–24 Jairus's need was so urgent that he jettisoned all dignity and pride, fell at Jesus' feet, and begged for help (v.23). Jairus had apparently heard about Jesus and believed that he could heal his child. Mark records no oral reply by Jesus to Jairus's requests. Here Jesus does not speak; he acts. He set out with Jairus to go to the child, and a large crowd—probably of curiosity seekers—followed along (v.24).

Typical of his abbreviated style, Matthew telescopes Mark's account so that Jairus presents his daughter as having already died (Mt 9:18). Only Luke records that this girl was Jairus's only daughter (Lk 8:42).

25–26 The story of the healing of the woman with a hemorrhage is sandwiched between the report of the illness of Jairus's daughter and the action of Jesus in raising her to life. The precise nature of the woman's ailment is not stated. Probably some sort of menstrual disorder caused the bleeding that had persisted for twelve years. Such a condition not only damaged her health but also rendered her ceremonially unclean, thus limiting her participation in Israel's religious life (cf. Lev 15:19–33; Eze 36:17). In contrast to Jairus, she is something of an outcast. Mark includes vivid details: she had suffered much under the care of many doctors, had spent all she had, and instead of getting better her condition had gotten worse (v.26). Luke (a physician!) understandably tones down this verse by removing the negative reference to doctors and saying only that "no one could heal her" (Lk 8:43).

27–29 The reports the woman had heard about Jesus' healings and her belief that he could help her prompted her coming to him. But her faith seemed to be mixed with a measure of superstition. She apparently shared the then common belief that the power of a person was transmitted to his clothing (v.27; cf. 3:10; 6:56; and the similar belief related to Paul's clothing in Ac 19:12 and to Peter's shadow in Ac 5:15). So she went into the crowd and, because of her ceremonial uncleanness, approached Jesus surreptitiously from the rear. She thought, "If I just touch his clothes, I will be healed" (v.28). When she did so, her bleeding stopped immediately, and she felt a soundness in her body that assured her she had been healed (v.29). Though she was motivated in part by superstition, Mark makes clear in v.34 that it was her faith, not magic, that produced the healing.

30–32 Not only had something happened to the woman when she touched Jesus' clothes, but Jesus knew that something had happened to him too. Healing energy had gone out of him for someone's benefit. Insisting on knowing who it was, he asked, "Who touched my clothes?" To his disciples this question seemed stupid in view of the crush of the crowd all about him (v.31). (Both Matthew and Luke soften the harshness of the disciples' response to Jesus.) The lack of understanding on the part of Jesus' disciples and their strong reply may have been caused by their concern to get Jesus to Jairus's house, where a real emergency existed. The question raised by Jesus would only cause delay. From a narrative perspective, Jesus' question and the disciples' response emphasize his supernatural perception (cf. 2:8; 3:4; 5:30; 12:15). Only the Son of God could detect a desperate touch in a jostling crowd; so he "kept looking around" to find who it was (v.32). His purpose was not to rebuke her but to make personal contact with her, to let her know he cared about her needs. She also needed to know that it was her faith, not her superstitious belief, that had caused God to heal her. The apparent tension between Jesus' supernatural insight concerning the touch and his uncertainty about who did it is not meant to highlight Jesus' limited knowledge, but rather to heighten the drama. Jesus intentionally causes the woman to announce the healing publicly and so reaffirm her faith.

33 The woman responded to Jesus' searching eyes. She knew what had happened to her; and, though "trembling with fear," she came forward, prostrated herself before Jesus, and "told him the whole truth." To do so must have taken great courage, especially since she was regarded as ceremonially unclean.

34 Jesus addressed the woman as "daughter"—the only occurrence in the Gospels of Jesus' addressing a woman by that word. It was intended to ease her fear and provide assurance that her action was not wrong. Jesus may also be identifying her as a member of his true family in accordance with his comments in 3:31–35 about those who are his true mother and brothers and sisters. He made clear to her that it was her faith (in Jesus, or God) that had healed her (cf. 2:5; 5:36; 9:23–24; 10:52). The Greek word translated "healed" is *sōzō* (GK *5392*, "saved"). Here both physical healing and spiritual salvation are in mind. In Mark's gospel the two go together closely (cf. 2:1–12).

The phrase "Go in peace" is a traditional Jewish formula of leave taking ("shalom"; cf. Jdg 18:6; 1Sa 1:17). The word "peace" here "means not just freedom from inward anxiety, but the *wholeness* or *completeness* of life that comes from being brought into a right relationship with God" (Anderson, 154, emphasis his; cf. *TDNT* 2:911).

By Jesus' last statement to the woman—"be freed from your suffering"—he actively participated in her healing and confirmed God's will to make her well. This may also be Jesus' encouragement to go out and live her life in accord with the freedom and peace she has now been given.

35 While Jesus was still speaking to the woman, "some men" brought Jairus the news of the death of his daughter. Since death is final, they advised him not to bother Jesus any longer. Jairus had already demonstrated faith by coming to Jesus. But now his faith is about to be tested even further. Does Jesus have power even over death?

36 Jesus overheard what the messengers said but ignored it. In an effort to encourage Jairus, he said, "Don't be afraid; just believe." Jesus' word of assurance must have been just what Jairus needed. He in no way tried to dissuade Jesus from resuming his journey to the child's bedside.

37 At this point Jesus decided to separate himself from the crowd following him. A momentous miracle is about to take place, and he would have only a chosen few witness it. The particularly close relationship between Jesus and Peter, James, and John (9:2; 14:33; cf. 13:3) no doubt prompted his selecting them to see this miracle.

38 When Jesus arrived at Jairus's house, a great commotion was taking place. Swete, 107, puts it succinctly: "The Lord has dismissed one crowd only to find the house occupied by another." As was the custom, professional mourners had been secured; and they were already at work. One Bible scholar writes, "The lamentations consisted of choral song or antiphony, accompanied by hand-clapping" (Van der Loos, *Miracles of Jesus*, 568). Since Jairus occupied a prominent position in the Jewish community, the number of professional mourners was large. So along with members of his family, they were making a great uproar.

39 On entering the house, Jesus asked why they were making such a commotion since the child was not dead but only asleep. On the surface this statement is enigmatic. It could mean that she had slipped into a comatose state, from which he would awaken her. Yet a careful reading of the text confirms that this statement was Jesus' way of indicating that he proposed to bring her back from the dead. Since her death was not final, he spoke of it as sleep (cf. Jn 11:11–14). Luke's account explicitly indicates that Jesus raised the girl from the dead: "Her spirit returned, and at once she stood up" (Lk 8:55; cf. Mt 9:18).

40 The mourners, however, misunderstood Jesus' reference to sleeping to mean that she was not really dead. So they laughed at him. Tears were quickly changed to laughter—a clear indication of the superficiality of the grief of the professional mourners. Jesus did not want any noisy crowd present when he performed this stupendous miracle; so he put the mourners out. Their lack of sensitivity disqualified them from being present at such a beautiful event. Only Jesus' three most intimate disciples and the mother and father were allowed to enter the room where the dead child lay.

41 Jesus stood by the side of the child and took her hand (again healing is associated with Jesus' touch; cf. 1:41) and spoke the Aramaic words "*Talitha koum*," which Mark conveniently translates for his Gentile readers: "Little girl, I say to you, get up!" Mark is the only evangelist who preserves the original Aramaic here. Aramaic was the language of Palestine in the first century AD and was probably the language Jesus and his disciples normally spoke. However, since they came from Galilee, which was surrounded by the Gentile Decapolis and by Syrian Phoenicia, it seems highly likely that they also knew and on occasion spoke Greek. The suggestion that the original Aramaic words were preserved because Mark wanted to provide Christian healers with certain verbal prescriptions in the original language is far-fetched and must be rejected. Mark usually uses foreign words in contexts that do not have to do with miracle stories (cf. 3:17; 7:11; 11:9; 14:36; 15:22, 34). The only exceptions are this passage and 7:34 (the healing of the deaf and mute man). The more likely reason for the preservation of the exact words is an eyewitness recollection (probably Peter's) and the profound impact the event had on those who witnessed it. Jesus' words would have been still ringing in their ears as they, in astonishment, watched the girl get up from her bed. As again and again the early church recounted the extraordinary event, the dramatic climax would be Jesus' authoritative command, "*Talitha koum!*"

42 The young girl responded immediately to Jesus' words. Not only did she stand up; she also began to walk around. Swete, 109, writes, "Strength returned as well as life." The narrator's comment that she was twelve years old is probably an historical reminiscence, another eyewitness detail. It could also be meant to explain that she was old enough to get up by herself (Taylor, 297). The reaction of the five witnesses to the miracle (Peter, James, John, and the parents) was one of complete amazement (v.20).

43 Jesus gave two orders to the witnesses. First, they were not to reveal the facts about the miracle. It has been suggested that since keeping them quiet was impossible—too many people had known of the death of the girl, and it was not likely that her parents could hide her—we have here an example of the artificiality of the Markan messianic-secret motif. Cranfield, 191, correctly replies that Jesus did not think that the miracle could be kept "absolutely private, but simply that he wanted it kept as private as possible—no one was to know about it who need not. There was at least a chance of avoiding unnecessary publicity." As elsewhere in the gospel, Jesus does not want superficial excitement over the miracles to overshadow the fundamental message of the kingdom. There is also likely a continuation of the theme of "insiders" versus "outsiders" that has been running through the gospel. Jesus' messianic dignity is revealed to some (the five witnesses to the miracle) who can be entrusted with it, but veiled to those (such as the noisy mourners) who cannot.

Jesus' second order was that they should give the girl something to eat—evidence of his concern for ordinary human needs. It may also be meant to provide proof that the girl was really alive (cf. Lk 24:39–43; see Garland, 223).

In the preceding episodes Jesus has demonstrated his authority over the forces of nature, demonic hordes, and sickness. Now he defeats the greatest of all threats—death itself. E. Earle Ellis (*The Gospel of Luke* [NCB; Greenwood, S.C.: Attic 1966], 134) sums up the theological meaning of this miracle: "Like its younger brother, sickness, death is an enemy. But it must yield to the powers of the messianic kingdom present in Jesus. In the presence of Christ, death becomes a 'sleeping.' ... 'Finis' is transformed into prelude. Until the *parousia* its sting remains, but its ultimate threat is broken. If we 'believe,' we need not live in dread: 'fear not!'"

NOTES

21–43 The fact that the episode follows Mark's pattern of intercalations is not to deny the historicity of the chronology, and it is likely the two stories formed a unity in the tradition Mark received. The narrative bears the marks of an eyewitness account and follows a logical sequence. Some have claimed that the two stories were originally brought together because both concerned women and because of the "twelve years" associated both with the illness and the little girl's age. More likely the numbers are merely coincidental.

25 Ritual uncleanness of this kind was a significant issue among the rabbis of Judaism and a whole tractate in the Mishnah is devoted to it (*Niddah*). Women could not enter the temple during their menstrual period (Josephus, *J.W.* 5.5.6 §227).

39 The word καθεύδω (*katheudō*, GK *2761*) has three meanings in the NT: "sleep" in the literal sense (cf. Mt 8:24; 13:25; 25:5; 26:40, 43, 45; Mk 4:27, 38; 13:36; 14:37, 40–41; Lk 22:46; 1Th 5:7); "sleep" in the figurative sense (1Th 5:6); and "sleep" in the sense of death (1Th 5:10; cf. Da 12:2). It is in the last sense that it is used here. Jesus says that she is not (permanently) dead, but she is asleep (dead, but only briefly, because she is soon to be raised to life).

F. Rejection at Nazareth (6:1–6a)

OVERVIEW

This episode returns to the theme of Jesus' rejection by his own people, which began with the controversy stories of 2:1–3:6, climaxed with the Beelzebul incident and the visit by his family (3:20–34), and found explanation in Jesus' teaching in parables (4:11–12). Now Jesus visits his hometown and is rejected by his relatives and those with whom he grew up.

In Luke's gospel the visit to Nazareth is recounted in an expanded version and is moved forward to serve as the inauguration of Jesus' ministry (Lk 4:16–30). For Luke it serves as a programmatic foreshadowing of Jesus' whole ministry and the rejection he will receive from his own people. In Mark, the episode is a confirmation of the earlier theme that Israel is divided between those who are responding to the kingdom and those who are rejecting it. In this way it sets the stage for the subsequent mission of the Twelve, when the disciples will travel through Israel replicating Jesus' teaching and healing ministry (6:6b–13).

[1]Jesus left there and went to his hometown, accompanied by his disciples. [2]When
the Sabbath came, he began to teach in the synagogue, and many who heard him were
amazed.
"Where did this man get these things?" they asked. "What's this wisdom that has been
given him, that he even does miracles! [3] Isn't this the carpenter? Isn't this Mary's son and
the brother of James, Joseph, [14] Judas and Simon? Aren't his sisters here with us?" And
they took offense at him.
[4]Jesus said to them, "Only in his hometown, among his relatives and in his own house is
a prophet without honor." [5]He could not do any miracles there, except lay his hands on a
few sick people and heal them. [6a]And he was amazed at their lack of faith.

COMMENTARY

1 If Capernaum was the scene of the healing of Jairus's daughter, the movement of Jesus described here was to the southwest through the hill country of Galilee. Nazareth is not specifically mentioned here or in Matthew, but it is obviously meant (cf. Mk 1:9, 24; Jn 1:45–46). The Greek word *patris* usually means "home country" but may also be used of one's hometown. Even though Jesus was born in Bethlehem, since his family lived in Nazareth and he had been brought up there, it was natural to regard it as his hometown.

The incident Mark records here should not be thought of as a personal visit by Jesus to his family. Rather, he comes as a rabbi accompanied by his disciples, "a detail dropped in Matthew, but important for Mark, because in this part of the gospel he is concerned with their training" (Cranfield, 193). The presence of the disciples is also important because they are the "insiders," Jesus' new family (3:34–35), who in contrast to his own people are receiving the secrets of the kingdom of God (3:20–35; 4:11–12).

2 On the Sabbath, Jesus went into the synagogue and began to teach. (On the custom that allowed visiting teachers to give the scriptural exposition in the synagogue, see comments at 1:21.) This occasion may have been the first time Jesus' fellow townspeople had heard him teach, and many of them were amazed (cf. 1:22, 27; 11:18). But with some of them there was an undercurrent of doubt, as their questions imply: "Where did this man get these things?" and "What's this wisdom that has been given to him, that he even does miracles!" What was the source of his teaching and his miracles? Although we do not know of any miracles Jesus had performed in Nazareth, his reputation as a miracle worker had spread abroad.

3 The hostility of Jesus' townspeople toward him comes out more clearly in the rhetorical questions in this verse. "Isn't this the carpenter?" The Greek term translated "carpenter" (*tekton*) is a general one, referring to someone who built with materials such as stone, wood, or metal. Joseph and his sons may have been primarily stonemasons who built homes and public buildings. Or they may have made farm tools, household items, or furniture. In either case the townspeople are saying, "Isn't he just a common, ordinary fellow who makes his living with his hands like the rest of us? How is it that he's parading as a rabbi and miracle worker?" The second question, "Isn't this Mary's son?" seems also to be derogatory, for it was not customary among Jews to describe a man as the son of his mother even when the father was not alive (cf. Taylor, 299–300). Behind this question may be the rumor, circulated during Jesus' lifetime, that Jesus was illegitimate (cf. Jn 4:41; 9:29; see Origen, *Cels.* 1.28–32; *b. Sanh. 67a*; Marcus, 375).

It is unlikely that the brothers and sisters of Jesus mentioned here were actually cousins (Jerome's view). Greek has a distinct word for cousin (*anepsios*; cf. Col 4:10). Nor were they likely Joseph's children by a previous marriage (Epiphanius's view). No mention of these children is made in the birth narratives of either Matthew or Luke. Both Jerome and Epiphanius were influenced by the Roman Catholic dogma of the perpetual virginity of Mary (Jerome's theory also made possible the virginity of Joseph!). Neither view finds much support in Scripture. The children mentioned were probably born to Mary and Joseph according to natural biological processes subsequent to the virgin birth of Jesus (Helvidius's view). James was probably the oldest and was certainly the best known of Jesus' brothers. He was closely identified with the church of Jerusalem (cf. Ac 12:17; 15:13; 21:18; 1Co 15:7; Gal 1:19; 2:9, 12) and was probably the author of the epistle of James (Jas 1:1). Both Josephus (*Ant.* 20.9.1 §200) and Eusebius (*Hist. eccl.*

2.33) preserve accounts of his violent death. Jude was probably the author of the epistle of Jude (Jude 1). We know nothing of Joseph or Simon.

The verb translated "they took offense" is *skandalizō* (GK *4997*). "The idea conveyed by the Greek verb is that of being offended and repelled to the point of abandoning (whether temporarily or permanently the word does not specify) belief in the word (cf. Lk 8:13) or one's relation with Jesus (14:27, 29)" (Bratcher and Nida, 139–40).

4 Jesus responded to the doubts raised about the legitimacy of his teaching and his miracles with a proverb that has parallels in both Jewish and Greek literature (see examples in W. D. Davies and D. C. Allison Jr., *The Gospel According to St. Matthew* [ICC; Edinburgh: T&T Clark, 1991], 2:459–60). The sense is captured in the English proverb "familiarity breeds contempt." The people of Nazareth were incapable of appreciating who Jesus was because, like Jesus' own family, they identified him with themselves so closely.

Here is the only place in Mark's gospel where Jesus identifies himself as a prophet (though it is a favorite theme in Luke: 4:24; 7:16, 39; 11:47–51; 13:33–34; 24:19; Ac 3:22; 7:37). Elsewhere in Mark, Jesus is identified as a prophet only in popular speculation (6:15; 8:28). Here (as commonly throughout Luke), the proverb suggests that Jesus will experience the common fate of prophets: suffering and even death. Mark will shortly narrate the martyrdom of another prophet, John the Baptist (vv.17–29).

5 Verse 5 opens with "one of the boldest statements in the Gospels, since it mentions something that Jesus could not do" (Taylor, 301). It is unlikely that Mark means Jesus did not have the power to do more miracles. The inability was related to the moral situation. One of the great emphases of Mark's gospel is that Jesus performs his miracles in response to faith (2:5; 4:40; 5:34, 36; 9:23–24; 10:52; 11:22–24), a point just made in the previous miracles (5:21–43). With this self-imposed limitation, and in the climate of unbelief, it is completely appropriate for Mark to write that "he could not do any miracles there ...."

Of course there is also a "delightful irony" (as France puts it), in the added clause "except lay his hands on a few sick people and heal them." For most people "a few healings" could hardly be called "doing no miracles" (France, 244). The point is that, even under the restraints of unbelief, the kingdom of God keeps squeezing through. The tiny mustard seed grows on through the night. The tragedy for the townspeople of Nazareth was that Jesus could have done *so much more* if they had only believed.

6a Jesus expressed amazement at their lack of faith. Apparently, he did not expect such a response from his neighbors. It is significant that, in this gospel where people are constantly astonished and amazed at Jesus' words and deeds (cf. v.2), only here is amazement ascribed to Jesus himself. The one who elsewhere knows the thoughts of others and seems fully in control of every situation is taken aback, stunned, at the response he has received! From a literary perspective Jesus' reaction reveals the severity and significance of their unbelief. Those who should be the most receptive to the gracious work of God through Jesus' ministry in fact turn out to be the most resistant to it. Those who should be insiders turn out to be outsiders, blind and deaf to the message of the kingdom.

NOTES

3 Matthew calls Jesus "the carpenter's son" (13:55), but only Mark says he was a "carpenter" (τέκτων, *tektōn*). The variant reading "son of a carpenter" is an obvious assimilation to Matthew. Origen (*Cels.* 6.36) says that none of the Gospels current in his day call Jesus a "carpenter." Origen's statement was apparently due to either (1) a lapse of memory or (2) his acceptance of a Markan text assimilated to Matthew (probably because he preferred not to think of the Son of God as involved in so menial an occupation).

For the view that Jesus' siblings were children born to Joseph by a previous marriage, see R. J. Bauckham, *Jude and the Relatives of Jesus in the Early Church* (Edinburgh: T&T Clark, 1990); "The Brothers and Sisters of Jesus: An Epiphanian Response to John P. Meier," *CBQ* 56 (1994): 698–700.

4 In addition to the synoptic parallels (Mt 13:57; Lk 4:4), the proverb appears in John 4:44, *Gospel of Thomas* 31, and P.Oxy. 1:5 [I, 31–36].

On the suffering role of the OT prophets see 1 Kings 13:4; 18:13; 19:2; 22:26–27; 2 Kings 1:9; 6:31; 2 Chronicles 24:21; Jeremiah 18:18, 23; 26:11, 20–23; 36–38.

IV. WITHDRAWAL FROM GALILEE (6:6b–8:30)

OVERVIEW

This fourth section of Mark's gospel finds Jesus withdrawing from the territory of Galilee for the purpose of expanding his ministry and (especially) further instructing his disciples. Though one incident of public teaching occurs in the section 7:1–23, the primary focus of Jesus' teaching is now on the Twelve. The section begins with the mission of the Twelve, followed by an account of the various views that people held concerning Jesus' identity (6:14–16), including the view of Herod Antipas and the parenthetic story of the death of John the Baptist (6:17–29). Next are several complexes of incidents including two stories of Jesus' feeding the multitudes—the five thousand (6:30–44) and then the four thousand (8:1–10). Jesus moves from Galilee into the territory of Tyre and Sidon and then back through Galilee to the Decapolis. The section concludes with Peter's confession that Jesus is the Messiah (8:27–30). This last episode represents a critical climax and turning point in the narrative. From Peter's confession onward Jesus begins to teach his disciples about the suffering role of the Messiah (8:31–33; 9:12, 30–32; 10:32–34) and will start his symbolic journey to Jerusalem, where he will suffer and die as a ransom for many (10:45).

A. Sending Out the Twelve (6:6b–13)

OVERVIEW

At the beginning of the previous section (3:7–6:6a), Jesus appointed the Twelve "that they might be with him and that he might send them out to preach and to have authority to drive out demons" (3:14–15). They have fulfilled the first half of this commission already by personally watching him and learning from him. Now they will move on to the second part: preaching, healing, and casting out demons (6:7, 12–13). Mark is not departing from his emphasis on Jesus, however, since the disciples function as an extension of his ministry throughout Israel. They are his representatives. Though the message Jesus told them to preach is not explicitly stated, in v.12 we learn that "they went out and preached that people should repent." This statement (and the whole of Mark's narrative) confirms that as Jesus' representatives their message was the same as his: "The kingdom of God is near. Repent and believe the good news!" (Mk 1:15).

Some interpreters treat this episode as the conclusion of the previous section (3:7–6:6a) rather than as the introduction to the next one (6:6b–8:30; see Lane, 205–10). It follows naturally that Jesus, after being rejected in his hometown (6:1–6a), would expand his ministry beyond Galilee through his disciples. As noted in the previous paragraph, this passage also forms a fitting sequel to the appointment of the Twelve (3:13–19), since the preaching and healing ministry appointed to them is here initiated. While the passage is certainly transitional, it seems best to treat it with the following section since it both represents the expansion beyond Galilee, which characterizes this section, and, from a literary perspective, forms part of an intercalation that continues through 6:31. The episode concerning the death of John the Baptist (6:17–29) is "sandwiched" between accounts of the beginning and end of the mission of the Twelve (6:6b–13, 30–31).

As noted in the Introduction (pp. 689–90) and just witnessed in 5:21–43, intercalation is one of Mark's favorite literary techniques, with the two episodes mutually interpreting one another. The relationship between the mission of the Twelve and the account of John's death is not as clear as others but may focus on the cost of discipleship. The disciples set out on a mission for which they will have to sacrifice a great deal, perhaps even their own lives. John the Baptist is the model of the disciple who gives up everything for the kingdom.

[6b]Then Jesus went around teaching from village to village. [7]Calling the Twelve to him,
he sent them out two by two and gave them authority over evil spirits.
[8]These were his instructions: "Take nothing for the journey except a staff—no bread, no
bag, no money in your belts. [9]Wear sandals but not an extra tunic. [10]Whenever you enter
a house, stay there until you leave that town. [11]And if any place will not welcome you or
listen to you, shake the dust off your feet when you leave, as a testimony against them."
[12]They went out and preached that people should repent. [13]They drove out many
demons and anointed many sick people with oil and healed them.

COMMENTARY

6b There is some question as to whether the second half of v.6 should go with vv.1–6a or vv.7–13. If with the former, it means that as a result of his rejection at Nazareth, Jesus decided to inaugurate a village ministry. If with the latter, it was as a result of the village ministry that he decided to send out the Twelve, presumably to increase his own ministry through them. Most translations take verse 6b with vv.7–13 (so NIV, NLT, NCV, CEV, NEB, CSB). A few connect it with 1–6 (so NKJV) or treat it as a separate paragraph (so RSV, ESV).

7 Jesus had carefully prepared his disciples for this mission. He had called them with the promise, "I will make you fishers of men" (1:17). He had appointed them to be with him and to preach and drive out demons (3:14–15). They had witnessed his mighty acts and listened to his wise words. He had withdrawn on several occasions to give them special attention (3:7; 4:10). Now it was time for them to be sent out.

The verb translated "sent" is *apostellō* (GK *690*), which carries with it the idea of official representation. Lane, 260, writes, "Jesus authorized the disciples to be his delegates with respect to both word and power. Their message and deeds were to be an extension of his own." The Twelve were sent two by two, apparently a Jewish custom (cf. 11:1; 14:13; Ac 13:2, 4; 16:40). The purpose of their going in pairs was likely so that the truthfulness of their testimony about Jesus might be established "on the testimony of two or three witnesses" (Dt 17:6; cf. 19:15; Nu 35:30; *b. Sanh. 26a, 43a*).

Exercising "authority over evil spirits" was part of the commission of the Twelve (cf. 3:15). Mark especially highlights Jesus' power to exorcise demons—evidence of the spiritual and cosmic significance of his mission. Here that power is given to the Twelve as his representatives.

8–9 Inherent in the commission of the Twelve was absolute trust in God to supply all their needs. Here the physical needs are emphasized. They were to take only what they had on their backs, with the allowance of a staff as the sole exception. No bread (i.e., food of any kind), no bag, and no money could be taken. The bag (*pēra*) may be a leather knapsack or traveler's bag; or perhaps the passage has in mind the more specialized meaning of "beggar's bag" (BDAG, 811). In this case, Jesus may be saying they should not be like itinerant Greek philosophers such as the Cynics, who claimed freedom from possessions but then begged for their food (cf. Hengel, *Charismatic Leader and His Followers*, 28; Guelich, 322). The word for money is *chalkos*, a small copper coin, which could be translated "small change" (BDAG, 1076).

The amount of clothing, too, was to be minimal. Sandals were allowed and only one tunic (v.9). An extra tunic would come in handy at night, for it could be used as a covering from the chilly night air. Jesus probably issued this prohibition because he wanted the disciples to trust God for the provision of hospitality for each night.

How universal are these guidelines? Since they were given to the disciples for this particular mission, it would be inappropriate to assume that they are blanket guidelines for all missionary activity. (Notice, e.g., how Jesus' instructions in Luke 22:35–38 modify earlier guidelines.) Cranfield, 200, correctly comments: "The particular instructions apply literally only to this brief mission during Jesus' lifetime; but in principle, with the necessary modifications according to climate and other circumstances, they still hold for the continuing ministry of the church. The service of the Word of God is still a matter of extreme urgency, calling for absolute self-dedication." The impression one receives from Jesus' instructions is that the mission on which he is about to send the Twelve is both extremely urgent and demands total dependence on God.

10 Jesus gave the instruction here to protect the good reputation of the disciples. Whenever they accepted hospitality in a home, they were to lodge there until they left that town, even if more comfortable or attractive lodgings were offered to them. The human tendency would be gradually to move up the social ladder as friendships were developed with more influential people. Such actions would show unchristian favoritism (Jas 2:1–13), create spiritual disunity, and run contrary to the missionary's absolute dependence on God.

11 Jesus knew that the mission of the Twelve would not always be accepted. Had not he also been rejected by many? So he instructed them on how to act in such circumstances. The shaking of the dust from their feet may be understood in the light of the Jewish custom of removing carefully the dust from both clothes and feet before reentering Jewish territory (*m. Ohalot* 2:3; *m. Ṭehar.* 4:5l; *b. Šabb. 15b*). For the Jews, heathen dust was defiling. The significance of the act here is to declare the place to be heathen and to make it clear that those who rejected the message must now answer for themselves, as apparently meant by the phrase "as a testimony against them." The disciples' message, like that of Jesus, brings judgment as well as salvation.

12–13 Mark now describes the actual mission of the Twelve. It was clearly patterned after Jesus' own ministry. Three activities are described: (1) preaching repentance (v.12); (2) driving out demons (v.13); and (3) healing the sick (v.13)—all of them associated with Jesus' ministry. By these activities they were demonstrating that the kingdom of God had come with power, and so were extending the ministry of Jesus.

NOTES

8 The parallel accounts in the other Synoptics present an apparent contradiction, since Luke's does not allow for a staff (9:3) and Matthew's does not allow for either sandals or a staff (10:10). Many harmonizing solutions have been suggested, from that of an early scribal error to the proposal that two different staffs were intended: walking sticks were allowed, but not a shepherd's staff (cf. E. Power, "The Staff of the Apostles: A Problem in Gospel Harmony," *Bib* 4 [1923]: 241–66). While these or other solutions are certainly possible, it is perhaps better simply to acknowledge that the answer is uncertain.

B. Death of John the Baptist (6:14–29)

OVERVIEW

The account of the death of John the Baptist is intercalated or "sandwiched" between the beginning and end of the mission of the Twelve (vv.6b–13; v.30). This episode is more than a digression to explain what happened to John after he was imprisoned (cf. 1:14); it highlights the cost of discipleship and foreshadows the ultimate model for discipleship, namely, Jesus himself. Lane, 215, points out that in the scheme of Mark's gospel there are two "passion narratives": the passion of John and the passion of Jesus. The passion of the forerunner is a precursor to the passion of the Messiah. It is significant that Mark devotes fourteen verses to the death of John but only three to his ministry. Various commentators have noted numerous parallels between the deaths of Jesus and John. In both there is an arrest (6:27; cf. 14:46; 15:1), a death plot (6:19; cf. 14:1), fear (6:20; cf. 11:18, 32; 12:12; 14:2), an innocent man executed under pressure (6:26; cf. 15:10, 14–15), and burial by followers (6:29; cf.

15:45–46; see Guelich, 328). In both cases, the civil ruler (Herod/Pilate) hesitates to execute the person but then does so under pressure and through the scheming of others (Herodias/the chief priests; cf. Hurtado, 82–83; Witherington, 213, 216).

The account also parallels classic OT encounters between prophet and king, where the humble and ragged prophet of the Lord boldly confronts the powerful, yet morally challenged monarch. Especially relevant are the confrontations between Elijah and Ahab (1Ki 17–22), whose pagan queen Jezebel harbored the same animosity toward Elijah that Herodias bore toward John (1Ki 19:1–2). The parallel is especially telling in the light of John's identification in Mark's gospel as an Elijah-like figure (1:2, 6; 9:11–13). Calvin, 2:222, comments: "We behold in John an illustrious example of that moral courage, which all pious teachers ought to possess, not to hesitate to incur the wrath of the great and powerful, as often as it may be found necessary: for he, with whom there is acceptance of persons, does not honestly serve God."

14 King Herod heard about this, for Jesus' name had become well known. Some were
saying, "John the Baptist has been raised from the dead, and that is why miraculous
powers are at work in him."
15 Others said, "He is Elijah."
And still others claimed, "He is a prophet, like one of the prophets of long ago."
16 But when Herod heard this, he said, "John, the man I beheaded, has been raised from
the dead!"
17 For Herod himself had given orders to have John arrested, and he had him bound and
put in prison. He did this because of Herodias, his brother Philip's wife, whom he had married. 18 For John had been saying to Herod, "It is not lawful for you to have your brother's
wife." 19 So Herodias nursed a grudge against John and wanted to kill him. But she was not
able to, 20 because Herod feared John and protected him, knowing him to be a righteous
and holy man. When Herod heard John, he was greatly puzzled; yet he liked to listen to
him.
21 Finally the opportune time came. On his birthday Herod gave a banquet for his high
officials and military commanders and the leading men of Galilee. 22 When the daughter of
Herodias came in and danced, she pleased Herod and his dinner guests.
The king said to the girl, "Ask me for anything you want, and I'll give it to you." 23 And he
promised her with an oath, "Whatever you ask I will give you, up to half my kingdom."
24 She went out and said to her mother, "What shall I ask for?"
"The head of John the Baptist," she answered.
25 At once the girl hurried in to the king with the request: "I want you to give me right
now the head of John the Baptist on a platter."
26 The king was greatly distressed, but because of his oaths and his dinner guests, he
did not want to refuse her. 27 So he immediately sent an executioner with orders to bring

John's head. The man went, beheaded John in the prison, [28]and brought back his head on a platter. He presented it to the girl, and she gave it to her mother. [29]On hearing of this, John's disciples came and took his body and laid it in a tomb.

COMMENTARY

14 The flashback account of John's death is introduced in the context of popular speculation concerning Jesus and Herod's superstitious concerns that John has risen from the dead. The "King Herod" mentioned here is Antipas, son of Herod the Great and Malthace. When his father died, he became tetrarch ("ruler of the fourth part") of Galilee and Perea. He was not officially granted the title of "king." It was, in fact, his ambition to secure that title for himself that led to his downfall in AD 39 under Caligula (cf. Josephus, *Ant.* 18.7.1–2 §§240–56; *J.W.* 2.9.6 §§181–83). Mark may be using the title of "king" here ironically, or perhaps he is reflecting local custom (cf. Taylor, 308).

If the paragraph that begins with v.14 goes with the one that precedes it, then the "this" refers to the mission of the Twelve. Herod heard about it. Quite possibly the disciples of Jesus traveled as far as Tiberias on the western shore of Lake Galilee, where Herod had built his capital and named it after the ruling Caesar, Tiberias. On the other hand, the "this" of v.14 may be a reference to the mighty works of Jesus. This latter view seems likely, for the entire discussion focuses on the question of Jesus' identity.

Since the NIV (probably correctly) accepts the reading *elegon* ("some were saying") instead of *elegen* ("he [Herod] was saying"), what follows are popular views of who Jesus was. The speculation that Jesus was John the Baptist raised from the dead must have arisen among those who had not heard of Jesus until after John's death. Or perhaps (though less likely) the sense is that the spirit of John had now been transferred to Jesus in the same way that the spirit of Elijah was passed on to Elisha (2Ki 2:15; France, 253). John the Baptist did not perform miracles while he was alive, but apparently his resurrection status was thought to give him that power.

15 Another popular view identified Jesus with Elijah. There was much speculation in Judaism concerning the eschatological return of Elijah—speculation arising especially from Malachi 3:1; 4:5 and Elijah's ascent to heaven without dying (2Ki 2:1–12; cf. Sir 48:10; *4 Ezra* 6:26; Justin Martyr, *Dial.* 8, 49; *TDNT* 2:928–34). John the Baptist had also spoken of Jesus as "the Coming One," a title popular speculation may have identified with Elijah (cf. Mal 3:1; 4:6).

A third view was that "he is a prophet, like one of the prophets of long ago." This meaning could refer to the return of an actual OT prophet such as Elijah, or someone of the same authority and succession as the OT prophets. The latter is more likely, since the word "prophet" does not have the article and since the comparative adverb *hōs* clarifies that Jesus is "like" one of the OT prophets.

16 Herod's view—that Jesus was John the Baptist raised from the dead—arose not so much from what he had heard about Jesus as from the proddings of a guilty conscience, since Herod had been directly responsible for John's death. As with the popular speculation mentioned in v.14, Herod's view of Jesus suggests that he had not heard about Jesus prior to the death of John. Herod had gotten rid of one meddlesome prophet only to have another show up—perhaps they were one and the same!

The mention of the death of John causes Mark to interrupt the account of the mission of the Twelve in order to tell the story of John's murder.

17–18 Several historical questions have been raised about Mark's account of John's death, most of them arising from differences with Josephus, who also records the death of John (*Ant.* 18.5.2 §§116–19). We will discuss these differences below and in the notes.

John the Baptist had been arrested by Herod Antipas (v.17), who put him in prison for denouncing Herod's adulterous union with Herodias, the wife of his brother Philip (v.18). The Mosaic law prohibited a man from marrying his brother's wife (cf. Lev 18:16; 20:21), except in the case of Levirate marriage after the brother's death (Dt 25:5–10). Further, Herodias was the daughter of Aristobulus, one of the sons of Herod the Great; so she was a niece of Herod Antipas (and, for that matter, of Philip as well). In Jewish eyes, Herod's divorce and his marriage to Herodias while Philip still lived would have been viewed both as adulterous and incestuous.

Josephus (*Ant.* 18.5.2 §119) says that John was put in prison at Machaerus, the fortress situated in Perea, on the eastern side of the Dead Sea. Mark does not identify the place of John's imprisonment, but the reference to the Galilean dinner guests (v.21) has suggested to some that he is thinking of somewhere in Galilee. Either location is possible. Herod may have moved John to Galilee prior to his execution, or Herod may have brought his guests to Machaerus (which Josephus [*J.W.* 7.6.2 §§172–77] describes as both a formidable fortress and magnificent palace).

Josephus (*Ant.* 18.5.2 §118) emphasizes the general political motives behind Herod's actions and claims that Herod feared John's influence and power among the people. Mark emphasizes the particular issue in John's preaching that prompted Herod's concerns and the specific circumstances of the execution. The two accounts are complementary rather than contradictory. In order to marry Herodias, Herod had to rid himself of the daughter of King Aretas IV, whose kingdom lay just to the east of Perea. The situation between Herod and Aretas was already sensitive, and the divorce eventually led to war (cf. Josephus, *Ant.* 18.5.1 §§109–15). John's preaching against Herod's divorce and remarriage, therefore, had the potential to cause real political trouble at home.

19–20 Herodias had not taken John's condemnation of her marriage lightly. In fact, she was infuriated by him and wanted to kill him. Herodias knew that "the only place where her marriage certificate could safely be written was on the back of the death warrant of John" (T.W. Manson, *The Servant Messiah* [London: Cambridge Univ. Press, 1953], 40). She was thwarted in her design because Herod protected John (v.20). Motivated by fear and recognition of John's righteous and holy character, Herod refused to allow him to be put to death. Swete, 123, writes, "Herod was awed by the purity of John's character, feared him as the bad fear the good." Yet "he liked to listen to him," though he did not understand and was "greatly puzzled" by what he said. France, 257, notes that these verses set up the contrast "strongly reminiscent of the story of Ahab and Jezebel (whose 'target' was, of course, John's model Elijah), which the rest of the story will work out between a resolutely hostile Herodias and a wavering Antipas, who will eventually be tricked into pronouncing sentence against his better judgment."

21–23 Herodias finally got the opportunity she was waiting for. Herod celebrated his birthday with a banquet to which he invited the military and political leaders of his tetrarchy. At this festive occasion Herodias's daughter danced before the guests (v.22). Mark does not name the daughter, though some MSS read "his daughter Herodias," so suggesting mother and daughter had the same name (see Notes). Josephus (*Ant.* 18.5.4 §136) identifies the daughter of Herodias as Salome. The dance was probably an erotic one. Objections to the historicity of the account have been raised on the basis of the unlikelihood of such a performance by a princess, but the low morals in Herod's court would not be inconsistent with it. Herod and his dinner guests were pleased with her performance—so much so that Herod offered her up to half his kingdom (v.23). The words "up to half my kingdom" may have been a kind of proverbial way of expressing openhanded generosity and were not to be taken literally (cf. 1Ki 13:8; Est 5:3, 6; 7:2). For Mark's readers the offer would be ironic since Herod was not truly a king and since he served only at the whim of Rome. The kingdom was not his to give away. It is also ironic that Herod will eventually be exiled through a failed attempt to gain this kingship.

24–25 The girl left the banquet hall to seek the advice of her mother. Herodias may have intentionally sent the girl into the banquet hall to dance as part of her scheme to get rid of John. Or perhaps she simply took advantage of the opportunity when it presented itself. The latter is slightly more likely, since the girl does not reply to Herod immediately but rather goes to ask her mother. There seems to be no premeditated plan. At the same time, Mark does not mention any surprise on the daughter's part when her mother made the request, thus suggesting the mother's disdain for John had been passed on to her daughter. When the girl returns to request John's head, she actually adds two things: she wants John's head "right now" and she wants it "on a platter" (v.25).

26–28 Herod was in a quandary. Up to this point he had been able to protect John; but now, "because of his oaths and his dinner guests," he could hardly refuse the girl. The weak and vacillating ruler caves in under social pressure (cf. the role of Pilate in 15:9–15). Reluctantly (v.26 says he "was greatly distressed"), he ordered an executioner to be sent to the prison to decapitate John (v.27). John's head was brought to Herod (v.28), who presented it to Salome; and she gave it to her mother.

29 Mark ends the shocking story with the coming of John's disciples to take the body and give it a proper burial. Herod no doubt thought he was now finished with the righteous prophet he both feared and respected. But he wasn't. The ministry of Jesus stirred up Herod's memories of John and his fears returned once more. Josephus (*Ant.* 18.5.2 §119) says that when Herod's army was defeated by the Nabataeans in AD 30, the Jews thought it was a "punishment upon Herod and a mark of God's displeasure against him."

NOTES

17 For a fuller discussion of the differences between Mark and Josephus, see H. Hoehner, *Herod Antipas* (SNTSMS 17; Cambridge: Cambridge Univ. Press, 1972), 110–71; Cranfield, 208–9; Lane, 215–16; Taylor, 310–11.

There is some confusion concerning the first husband of Herodias, since Josephus refers to him as Herod (*Ant.* 18.5.4 §136), while Mark calls him Philip. Some claim Mark has confused this man with

Herod Philip, son of Herod the Great and Cleopatra and tetrarch of Iturea and Traconitis (Lk 3:1). The problem is easily resolved when we realize that "Herod" is a family name given to all of Herod the Great's sons and that Philip was almost certainly the first name of the man Josephus simply calls "Herod," the son of Mariamne II.

20 Some MSS read πολλὰ ἐποίει (*polla epoiei*, "he did many things"), but the reading adopted by the NIV, πολλὰ ἠπόρει (*polla ēporei*, "he was greatly puzzled"), has the stronger MS support. It also seems consistent with what we know of Herod's character.

22 The earliest MSS read θυγατρὸς αὐτοῦ Ἡρῳδιάδος (*thugatros autou Hērōdiados*, "his daughter Herodias"). The NLT translates, "Then his daughter, also named Herodias, came in ...." Most versions follow the reading θυγατρὸς αὐτῆς τῆς Ἡρῳδιάδος (*thugatros autēs tēs Hērōdiados*), which probably means "the daughter of Herodias herself" (with αὐτῆς, *autēs*, used intensively; cf. NASB, "And when daughter of Herodias herself came in"). Since Josephus identifies the girl as Salome, the best solution seems to be to regard αὐτοῦ, *autou*, as an early scribal error and αὐτῆς, *autēs*, as the original reading.

26 The depth of the distress experienced by Herod at Salome's request for the head of John the Baptist is expressed graphically by the Greek word περίλυπος (*perilypos*, GK *4337*, "greatly distressed"). This word is the same one used to describe Jesus' agony in Gethsemane (Mk 14:34).

C. Feeding of the Five Thousand (6:30–44)

OVERVIEW

The importance of the feeding of the five thousand for the early church is evident from the fact that it is the only miracle that appears in all four gospels. In Mark's narrative the episode plays an important role. It begins with an elaborate introduction (6:35–38), is looked back to on two different occasions (6:52; 8:17–21), and has a sequel in the feeding of the four thousand (8:1–10). Its position immediately following the account of Herod's feast is also striking: "In contrast to the drunken debauchery of the Herodian feast, Mark exhibits the glory of God unveiled through the abundant provision of bread in the wilderness where Jesus is Israel's faithful shepherd" (Lane, 227). The prideful sham-king Herod makes a mockery of justice by executing the noble prophet of God over a foolish oath. In contrast, the true shepherd-king Jesus shows real compassion for the flock of Israel by gently teaching them and providing for their needs.

The account echoes important passages in the OT: (1) Elisha's feeding of one hundred men with twenty barley loaves and some grain (2Ki 4:42–44); (2) the miraculous feeding of the people of Israel with manna in the desert (Ex 16; Nu 11; cf. Jn 6:14–40); and (3) the "messianic banquet," God's eschatological promise to feed and shepherd his people (Isa 25:6–8; 65:13–14). The latter two are particularly significant, since Mark repeatedly refers to the place where the feeding occurs as a "desert" or "wilderness" (*erēmos*, GK *2245*) place (vv.31–32, 35). The implication is that Jesus is a new Moses shepherding God's people in the wilderness and leading them on a new exodus deliverance (cf. Lane, 225–33; Ulrich Mauser, *Christ in the Wilderness* [London: SCM, 1963]).

30 The apostles gathered around Jesus and reported to him all they had done and
taught. 31 Then, because so many people were coming and going that they did not even
have a chance to eat, he said to them, "Come with me by yourselves to a quiet place and
get some rest."

32 So they went away by themselves in a boat to a solitary place. 33 But many who saw
them leaving recognized them and ran on foot from all the towns and got there ahead
of them. 34 When Jesus landed and saw a large crowd, he had compassion on them,
because they were like sheep without a shepherd. So he began teaching them many
things.

35 By this time it was late in the day, so his disciples came to him. "This is a remote
place," they said, "and it's already very late. 36 Send the people away so they can go to
the surrounding countryside and villages and buy themselves something to eat."

37 But he answered, "You give them something to eat."

They said to him, "That would take eight months of a man's wages! Are we to go and
spend that much on bread and give it to them to eat?"

38 "How many loaves do you have?" he asked. "Go and see."

When they found out, they said, "Five—and two fish."

39 Then Jesus directed them to have all the people sit down in groups on the green
grass. 40 So they sat down in groups of hundreds and fifties. 41 Taking the five loaves and
the two fish and looking up to heaven, he gave thanks and broke the loaves. Then he
gave them to his disciples to set before the people. He also divided the two fish among
them all. 42 They all ate and were satisfied, 43 and the disciples picked up twelve basketfuls
of broken pieces of bread and fish. 44 The number of the men who had eaten was five
thousand.

COMMENTARY

30 Mark now concludes the account of the mission of the Twelve after having interrupted it with the flashback to the death of John the Baptist. The disciples returned to Jesus from their mission of preaching, driving out demons, and healing and reported to him "all they had done and taught." Only here does Mark use the word "apostles" (*apostoloi*) for the disciples. (Its occurrence in 3:14 is textually doubtful.) Mark is probably not using it as a formal title for the Twelve ("the Apostles"), but rather in the functional sense, "those who were sent," recalling Jesus' commission in 6:7 (where the verb *apostellō* is used).

31–32 The disciples had just returned from what was apparently an intensive mission. Their activities had created much interest. So many people were coming and going that the disciples had no time even to eat (v.31; cf. 3:20). Since the disciples were doubtless tired from their missionary activities and from the demands of the crowds, Jesus decided to seek rest for them. Where specifically they went we are not told. Mark merely says it was a "quiet" and "solitary [*erēmos*, 'desert'] place" (v.32). Luke identifies the location as near Bethsaida (9:10), a town on the northeastern side of the lake. But Mark seems to have the northwestern shore in mind, for after the miracle, the traditional site of which is Tabgha—near Capernaum, on the northwestern shore—the disciples will cross the lake toward Bethsaida (6:45; cf. France, 264).

Further, the best way for Jesus and his disciples to have gotten away from the crowds was by boat. If the "solitary place" were on the northeastern side of the lake, the crowd that followed by land would have had to cross the Jordan where it flows into Lake Galilee. According to Dalman (*Sacred Sites and Ways*, 161), doing so *could* have been possible: "On October 10, 1921, I saw that it was almost possible to cross over the Jordan dry-shod, just where it enters into the lake. An absolutely dry bar lay before the mouth." However, in the spring of the year, when this event apparently took place (cf. v.39, "green grass"), the Jordan would have had more water in it.

33–34 Perhaps the little boat faced a strong headwind that slowed it down. At any rate the crowd was able to walk around the lake and arrive at the landing place ahead of the boat.

Jesus had every right to be annoyed with the crowd. They had prevented him and his disciples from getting a much-needed rest. But instead of being irritated, he responded compassionately and lovingly (v.34). He saw the multitude as "sheep without a shepherd."

The phrase is a common one in the OT, indicating a lack of leadership and care (Nu 27:17; 1Ki 22:17; Isa 13:14; Eze 34:5; Zec 13:7). The context of Numbers 27:17 is the wilderness wanderings and the appointment of Joshua to succeed Moses. In Ezekiel 34:23, 25, God promises to raise up a new David to shepherd his wayward flock (cf. Zec 13:7, which is also messianic). Mark seems to be working with these themes. Jesus, like Moses, leads his people into the wilderness, and, like David, he provides rest for them (cf. Lane, 226; Mauser, *Christ in the Wilderness*, 135). It is significant that in Isaiah 11:1–11 and elsewhere in the OT the "new exodus" theme is identified with the coming Messiah from David's line (Strauss, *Davidic Messiah*, 292–97).

35–36 Jesus' disciples became concerned for the crowd. It was late in the day, and since they were in a desolate place, there was little possibility of obtaining food. Their suggestion was that the crowd be dismissed so they could get food for themselves in the neighboring towns and villages (v.36). This seemed to be a simple way for them to satisfy their hunger.

37 Jesus did not concur with the suggestion of his disciples that the food needed to feed the crowd was to be supplied from the resources of the neighboring towns and villages. The disciples themselves were to supply it! Jesus uses the emphatic personal pronoun to make the message plain: "*You* give them something to eat."

The reply of the disciples indicates how startled they were at Jesus' command. They could only think of the impossible amount of money it would take to feed a crowd such as this one. Two hundred denarii represented the pay a common laborer earned in a period of about eight months (cf. Mt 20:2–15, where the usual pay for a day's wage is one denarius). Not even that amount of money would buy enough bread for everyone to eat (cf. Jn 6:7: "for each one to have a bite").

38 Jesus was not thinking of bread bought in the neighboring villages for two hundred denarii or whatever it might cost to supply the people. Before proceeding with his approach to the problem, he asked his disciples what was the present status of the food supply. When they inquired, they found it to be meager: five loaves and two fish—a mere pittance in view of the number of people to be fed. The loaves, John tells us (6:9), were barley loaves. Unlike our modern loaves of bread, these loaves were flat and round (about eight inches in diameter) and could scarcely feed more than one person.

39–40 At Jesus' direction (v.39), the disciples arranged the crowd into groups of hundreds and fifties (v.40). The phrases used to describe this arrangement are interesting. In v.39 Jesus says they should sit *symposia symposia*. A *symposion* was a group of people gathered for a banquet or drinking party, so the idiom means something like "divided into dinner parties." Verse 40 says they sat down *prasia prasia*. A *prasia* (etymologically, a "bed of leeks") was a garden plot, so the sense is "organized into rows or plots" (BDAG, 860, 959). Together they convey the orderly arrangement of the crowd to facilitate the distribution of the food. The verbs used in vv.39 and 40 for the people to sit down (*anaklinō*, *anapiptō*) reinforce the festive imagery, since they were commonly used in the Greco-Roman world of reclining around a banquet table.

Various commentators have suggested that the arrangement is intended to recall the Mosaic camp in the wilderness, where officials are appointed over "thousands, hundreds, fifties and tens" (Ex 18:21, 25; cf. Nu 31:14; Dt 1:15). The sectarians at Qumran applied this imagery to themselves as the assembly of the eschatological Israel in the wilderness (1QS 2:21–23; 1QSa 1:14–15; 1:28–2:1; 1QM 4:1–17; CD 13:1). If Mark has this imagery in mind, he may again be intentionally presenting Jesus as "the eschatological Savior, the second Moses, who transforms the leaderless flock into the people of God" (Lane, 230).

Mark notes that the grass was green (v.39), perhaps to invoke the image of the Lord as the Shepherd who brings the sheep to feed in green pastures (Ps 32:1–2). Historically, the green grass suggests that the incident took place in the late winter or early spring, when the grass in Galilee turns green after the rains.

41 Jesus did what any pious Jew would have done before eating—he prayed. The Mishnah provides an example of an ancient prayer of thanksgiving before a meal: "Blessed art thou, Lord our God, King of the world, who bringest forth bread from the earth" (*m. Ber.* 6:1). Jesus may have prayed something similar on this occasion. Lifting one's eyes toward heaven is a common posture for prayer (Job 22:26–27 LXX; Pss 121:1; 123:1).

This passage has clear verbal parallels with the institution of the Lord's Supper (Mk 14:22), which itself has strong links to the OT imagery of the messianic banquet (cf. 14:25). In John's gospel the connection to both the OT wilderness feedings and the Eucharist is even more explicit, as Jesus identifies himself as the "bread of life" and the "bread from heaven" in the discourse that follows the feeding (Jn 6:32–33, 35, 41).

As to how the miracle was performed, Mark does not give us so much as a hint. He simply says that Jesus broke the loaves, divided the fish, and gave them to the disciples to distribute among the people.

42–44 Not only were all the people fed and their hunger satisfied (v.42), but there was more left over at the end than there had been at the beginning—twelve basketfuls (v.43). The reference to leftover provisions is another parallel to the Elisha story in 2 Kings 4:42, where the Lord promises, "They will eat and have some left over." The number twelve may symbolically point to the twelve tribes of Israel, though it may simply point to the leftovers collected by the twelve disciples.

Mark says that the number of the men who had eaten was about five thousand (v.44)—a number that could easily have been calculated because of the division of the crowd into groups of hundreds and fifties. The number seems to refer to family units, since the word translated "men" is not *anthrōpoi*, the common word for "human beings," but rather *andres*, which normally means adult males. Matthew makes this meaning clear by adding "besides women and children" (14:21). The number is very large when one realizes that the neighboring towns of Capernaum and Bethsaida had only two to three thousand people.

Since Mark usually notes the reaction of people to the miracles of Jesus, it is perhaps significant that here he does not note the reaction of the crowd (contrast John 6:14–15). This omission seems to indicate that the miracle was meant especially for the disciples and is part of Jesus' self-revelation to them (see v.52; 8:17–21).

NOTES

32 The easiest solution to the apparent discrepancy between the location of the miracle in Mark and Luke is that Mark's reference to a departure toward Bethsaida after the miracle (6:45) is an early scribal error, and that the miracle actually occurred near Bethsaida on the northeastern side of the lake. This would also fit Mark's statement that the disciples' boat trip after the miracle ended up in Gennesaret (v.53; on the northwestern shore). Unfortunately, there is no MS evidence for such an error. Another harmonizing solution proposes that Luke is referring to a different town called Bethsaida, one on the northwestern corner of the lake, close to Chorazin and Capernaum (see Mt 11:21, 23). In this case, Luke, like Mark, would be describing a westward journey from one Bethsaida to another Bethsaida, and then back after the miracle. But there is no historical evidence for such a town (except perhaps John's opaque reference to Bethsaida as a town "of Galilee"; Jn 12:21; cf. France, 264). Furthermore, although this solution would bring the accounts of Mark and Luke into harmony, it would conflict with John's reference to a westward departure (toward Capernaum) after the miracle (6:17) and Mark's statement that the trip ended in Gennesaret (6:53).

38 The phrase "you give them something to eat" may echo 2 Kings 4:42, where Elisha says, "Give it [the barley bread] to the people to eat."

43 The word for basket (κόφινος, *kophinos*) refers to a kind of basket especially associated with the Jews, since the satirist Juvenal (*Sat.* 3.14; 6.542) twice mocks Jewish travelers for always taking along such baskets. Lane, 231 n. 109, refers to them as "small wicker baskets that every Jew carried with him as a part of his daily attire" that "were used to hold such items as a light lunch and general odds and ends." BDAG, 563, describes the type as "a large, heavy basket, probably of var. sizes, for carrying things."

44 The gathering of such a large body of men (without women and children?), and the apparently military language of organization ("fifties and hundreds"), has caused some commentators to speculate that, historically, this event might have been an attempt by zealous Galileans to launch an insurrection with Jesus as their leader. John's account in particular gives this impression since after the feeding Jesus withdraws quickly to the mountain, "knowing that they intended to come and make him king by force" (Jn 6:15). Whatever the historical situation, Mark does not develop this aspect but focuses instead on Jesus' compassion for the people.

REFLECTIONS

Since the emergence of critical biblical scholarship, attempts have been made to explain away this miracle rationally. Most common is the suggestion that this miracle was not one of multiplication but of sharing. The willingness of one person to share his own meager provisions resulted in a contagious and spontaneous response from the crowd, and soon hidden stores of food were available for all. Such explanations are pure speculation arising solely from antisupernatural presuppositions. There is no doubt but that Mark and the other gospel writers understood the actions of Jesus to have been miraculous, and there is no hint in the narrative that the event was ever understood differently.

D. Walking on the Water (6:45–52)

OVERVIEW

Two main themes appear in this episode: the extraordinary power of Jesus and the spiritual incomprehension of the disciples. The account is the second of Jesus' miracles on Lake Galilee recorded by Mark. In the first miracle Jesus calmed a storm at sea (4:35–41); now he walks on water, thus demonstrating similar mastery over the forces of nature. Both episodes have a strong theophanic character as Jesus reveals power and authority normally associated with God. In both situations, the disciples appear in danger or difficulty prior to the miracle, and in both they respond with amazement and fear. Both records also give a negative comment about their faith—the first coming from Jesus (4:40), the second from the narrator (6:52). The latter is more severe; it refers to their "hardness of hearts" and initiates a series of episodes in which the spiritual dullness and failings of the disciples will be highlighted (8:17–21, 32; 9:19, 34; 10:13, 37–38).

Both Matthew (14:22–33) and John (6:16–21) record this miracle and, like Mark, connect it with the feeding of the five thousand. Only Matthew includes the additional details about Peter's getting out of the boat and coming to Jesus (14:28–31). The agreement between the Synoptics and John confirm that the accounts of the feeding miracle and walking on water appeared together in the tradition Mark received. Luke, who has followed Mark quite closely up to this point, here departs from his order and omits the material from Mark 6:45–8:26 (sometimes called Luke's "Great Omission").

To try to rationalize this incident—as some have done in the past—by suggesting that what the disciples really saw was Jesus wading through the shallows at the edge of the shore is ridiculous. The text makes it clear that the boat was in the middle of the lake and that Jesus came to it there. The episode defies rationalistic explanations. One must either dismiss the whole event as a fanciful legend or accept it as an eyewitness account of a truly miraculous event.

45Immediately Jesus made his disciples get into the boat and go on ahead of him
to Bethsaida, while he dismissed the crowd. 46After leaving them, he went up on a
mountainside to pray.

[47]When evening came, the boat was in the middle of the lake, and he was alone on land.
[48]He saw the disciples straining at the oars, because the wind was against them. About
the fourth watch of the night he went out to them, walking on the lake. He was about to
pass by them, [49]but when they saw him walking on the lake, they thought he was a ghost.
They cried out, [50]because they all saw him and were terrified.
Immediately he spoke to them and said, "Take courage! It is I. Don't be afraid." [51]Then he
climbed into the boat with them, and the wind died down. They were completely amazed,
[52]for they had not understood about the loaves; their hearts were hardened.

COMMENTARY

45 While Mark records no reaction of the crowd to the multiplication of the loaves and fish, John speaks of an attempt to make Jesus king (Jn 6:15). Historically, Jesus may have feared a messianic uprising as a result of the miracle and for that reason "immediately" made his disciples get into the boat and go on ahead of him to Bethsaida. Yet no messianic aspirations are explicitly mentioned by Mark, who has presented the miracle as a compassionate banquet provided by Jesus and an act of self-revelation directed toward the disciples.

As noted in the previous section (v.32), Bethsaida's location on the northeastern side of Lake Galilee suggests that the disciples are sailing eastward across the northern part of the lake (but see Notes, v.32). The city was officially called "Bethsaida Julias," named after Julias, the daughter of the Roman emperor Augustus, by Herod Philip when he elevated the village to the status of a city (cf. Josephus, *Ant.* 18.2.1 §28).

After sending his disciples away in the boat, Jesus stayed to dismiss the crowd. Part of his purpose may have been to calm their messianic aspirations.

46 Mark's mention of Jesus' praying may be further evidence of the critical nature of the situation. On only three occasions in this gospel does Jesus withdraw to pray, and each time some sort of crisis is involved: (1) after the excitement and activity of a busy Sabbath in Capernaum (1:35), (2) after the multiplication of the loaves and fish (6:46), and (3) in Gethsemane after the Lord's Supper (14:32–36). Each incident involves the temptation not to carry out God's mission—a mission that would ultimately bring suffering, rejection, and death. These crises seem to represent an ascending scale and reach their climax in the agony of Gethsemane.

47–48 The time of this incident is "evening" (v.47). Since it was "already very late" in the afternoon (v.35) before the feeding of the five thousand, "evening" here must mean late at night. How Jesus "saw" the disciples straining at the oars (v.48) is not clear, whether through supernatural insight in the darkness (so Garland, 261), by the glow of moonlight (so Cranfield, 225), or in the light of early dawn (so France, 271). What is clear is that Jesus came in response to the struggle they were having. Apparently, the wind was blowing from the north or northeast and had blown the disciples off their course. They were "straining at the oars"—an indication of a stiff headwind. Jesus came to them "walking on the lake" at about the fourth watch (sometime between 3:00 and 6:00 a.m.). According to Roman reckoning (which Mark follows), the night was divided into four watches: 6:00 to 9:00 p.m., 9:00 p.m. to midnight, midnight to 3:00 a.m., and 3:00 to 6:00 a.m.

Like the calming of the storm and the multiplication of the loaves, walking on water has strong theophanic significance. In the OT God himself "treads on the waves" (Job 9:8) and makes a way through the sea (Ps 77:19; Isa 43:16).

The Greek phrase *kai ēthelen parelthein autous* could be translated "he wanted to pass them by," for the verb *thelō* (GK *2527*) normally carries the sense of desire or intention. This reading gives the impression that Jesus' intended to walk right past the disciples. Various suggested alternative interpretations follow.

(1) The NIV, taking the Greek verb *thelō* in the sense of *mellō* ("about to"; cf. Cranfield, 226), renders the phrase "he was about to pass by them."

(2) The text may represent not the intention of Jesus but the impression of an eyewitness as to what was happening: "it seemed to the disciples as though he intended to pass them by" (cf. France, 272).

(3) The verb "pass by" may carry the sense of "spare from catastrophe" (cf. Am 7:9), so that the idiom means something like "he wanted to save them" (H. Fleddermann, "'And He Wanted to Pass by Them' [Mark 6:48c]," *CBQ* 45 [1983]: 389–95).

(4) The verse may mean that Jesus intended to pass by them to show himself and so reveal his power and protection. The point is that Jesus' ability to walk on water should dispel all possible fears the disciples might otherwise have (cf. Hurtado, 90–91).

(5) There may be an intentional echo of OT passages in which God reveals himself by "passing by" or "passing before" his people (cf. Lane, 236; Garland, 263–64; Marcus, 426). In Exodus 33:18–23 Moses asks to see God's glory, and the Lord replies that no one can see his face and live; however, God will "pass by" the cleft of the rock and Moses will see his back: "I will cause all my goodness to pass in front of you, and I will proclaim my name, the LORD, in your presence" (Ex 33:19 [TNIV]). Similarly, in 1 Kings 19:11–12—when Elijah despairs that he is the only faithful person left in Israel—the Lord says "Go out and stand on the mountain before the LORD, for the LORD is about to pass by." God then reveals himself, not in a mighty wind, an earthquake or a fire, but in a quiet whisper. We have here, then, the language of theophany. Jesus intends to "pass by" in order to reveal his divine glory to the disciples.

Although a decision regarding the meaning of the phrase is difficult, the last option seems the most likely, especially in the light of the strong theophanic significance of walking on water and the exodus imagery here and in the immediately preceding feeding miracle.

49–50 Although the disciples did not recognize Jesus at first—they thought they had seen some sort of ghost (*phantasma*, v.49)—Jesus calmed their fears with words of assurance: "Take courage! It is I. Don't be afraid" (v.50). It has been suggested—in line with the theophanic nature of the whole episode—that the statement "It is I" identifies Jesus with God's self-revelation as the "I AM WHO I AM" (Ex 3:14; cf. Jn 8:58). A direct allusion to Exodus 3:14 seems unlikely, however, since in the context the words are intended to assure the disciples that he is not a ghost, not dramatically to reveal his divine nature. Such an explicit self-identification would be highly unusual in Mark's narrative, where Jesus repeatedly reveals divine attributes through his actions but never explicitly declares his own deity. It is probably better to regard the expression here simply as Jesus' way of identifying himself ("It is I—Jesus").

51 Here another miracle is presupposed. When Jesus climbed into the boat, "the wind died down." Though less explicitly than in 4:35–41, Jesus again reveals sovereign lordship over the wind and waves. The response of the disciples to both miracles is that they "were completely amazed." As so often in Mark, the power of God at work through Jesus results in shock and amazement (1:22, 27; 2:12; 5:15, 20, 42; 6:2; 7:37; 11:18). Yet here the implications are negative. By this time the disciples should not be shocked at Jesus' actions but should be comprehending the power of the kingdom of God at work in him.

52 Mark relates his explanation of the disciples' panic at seeing Jesus walking on the water and their amazement at the calming of the wind to their failure to understand the multiplication of the loaves. Had they understood about the loaves, i.e., that the sovereign Lord of the universe was in action there, they would have been prepared to understand his walking on water and calming waves. Their problem was a christological one. Not unlike Jesus' opponents—the "outsiders" of 4:10–11 (Isa 6:9–10)—"their hearts were hardened" (v.52). From this point on, Mark will paint the disciples in increasingly dark tones. In 8:14–21 Jesus will directly confront their inability to understand the feeding miracle, again with language reminiscent of Isaiah 6:9–10. Like the persecuted church of Mark's day, the disciples will need to decide whose side they are really on—and what price they are willing to pay for their allegiance to the kingdom of God.

NOTES

45 Fred Strickert ("The Coins of Philip," in *Bethsaida: A City by the North Shore of the Sea of Galilee*, ed. Rami Arav and Richard A. Freund [Kirksville, Mo.: Truman State Univ. Press, 2004], 1:165–89) claims that Bethsaida was not named for Augustus's biological daughter Julia but for Augustus's wife Livia, who was adopted as the emperor's daughter into the Julian family and given the name "Julia" after her husband's death.

48 Witherington, 221 n. 67, notes that in Sirach 24:5–6 personified Wisdom traverses the sea. This motif is significant since in a number of gospel passages Jesus appears to be presented as the incarnation of divine Wisdom (see Witherington, *Jesus the Sage: The Pilgrimage of Wisdom* [Minneapolis: Fortress, 2000]).

E. Healings near Gennesaret (6:53–56)

[53]When they had crossed over, they landed at Gennesaret and anchored there. [54]As soon as they got out of the boat, people recognized Jesus. [55]They ran throughout that whole region and carried the sick on mats to wherever they heard he was. [56]And wherever he went—into villages, towns or countryside—they placed the sick in the marketplaces. They begged him to let them touch even the edge of his cloak, and all who touched him were healed.

COMMENTARY

53 Jesus stayed with the disciples in the boat and crossed over with them to Gennesaret. The name refers to the plain north of Magdala on the western side of the lake, or perhaps to a city on the plain (see Dalman, *Sacred Sites*, 128). Depending on the location of the feeding miracle and the direction in which they were rowing (see Notes, v.32), this either means that they completed their journey westward from Bethsaida (Lk 9:10) or that, although headed for Bethsaida (Mk 6:45), they turned around because of the contrary winds and returned to the western side of the lake. In any case, Jesus and the disciples return to the place of their greatest popularity and most significant ministry.

54–56 This passage serves as a summary of Jesus' work in Galilee before he withdraws to other regions. It resembles the summaries in 1:32–34 and 3:7–12, except that no mention is made either of teaching or exorcising demons; rather, Mark's emphasis here is on Jesus' reputation as a healer—the primary reason for his widespread fame (vv.54–55).

Mark notes the desire of the people to touch Jesus' garments and be healed (v.56; cf. 5:27–29). The NIV's reference to the "edge" (*kraspedon*) of Jesus' cloak may refer to the tassels that pious Jews wore on the fringe of their outer garments (as commanded by God in Nu 5:37–39 and Dt 22:12). The word carries this sense in Matthew 23:5. We must assume on the basis of Mark 5:34 that, whether or not some of the people held superstitious beliefs, it was not the mere touch of Jesus' garments that produced the healings but rather their faith, to which Jesus responded.

Some commentators have suggested that the summary is meant to be negative and that the people are only interested in Jesus' miracles, not in the transformation that comes through the kingdom. While the subsequent narrative may hint at the validity of this suggestion, the primary point is Jesus' immense popularity and the enthusiastic response of the crowds to his presence. It should be noted that in contrast to the tepid response of unbelieving Nazareth (6:4–5), Mark indicates that "all" who touched him here were healed (v.56).

NOTES

53 The great fertility of the soil in the plain of Gennesaret enabled it to support a relatively large population. Josephus (*J.W.* 3.10.8 §518) says of it, "One may call this place the ambition of nature, where it forces those plants that are naturally enemies to one another to agree together."

F. Commands of God and Human Traditions (7:1–13)

OVERVIEW

This episode is linked with 7:14–23 by the common theme of purity, or what it means to be holy or undefiled before God. It is similar to the conflict stories found in 2:1–3:6 but is placed here (along with vv.14–23) to function as an introduction to the extension of the ministry of Jesus to the Gentiles in vv.24–30 (the Syrophoenician woman), in vv.31–37 (the deaf and mute man in the Decapolis) and, less obviously, in 8:1–10 (the feeding of the four thousand). There is a cohesive flow to the narrative as Jesus first challenges traditional Jewish notions of purity and defilement and then ventures into "defiled" Gentile territory with the gospel message.

The present episode is divided into two parts: (1) the accusation by the Pharisees in vv.1–5 (including Mark's parenthetic remark in vv.3–4), and (2) Jesus' response in vv.6–13. When the Pharisees accuse Jesus' disciples of not living by the high standards of ritual purity they themselves maintain, Jesus goes on the offensive by countering that it is they who are living impure lives. They honor God with their words yet deny him with their hearts by exalting their human traditions over God's commandments. Jesus then provides a specific example of their doing so: they devote gifts exclusively to God as an excuse for withholding them from their needy parents.

[1]The Pharisees and some of the teachers of the law who had come from Jerusalem
gathered around Jesus and [2]saw some of his disciples eating food with hands that were
"unclean," that is, unwashed. [3](The Pharisees and all the Jews do not eat unless they give
their hands a ceremonial washing, holding to the tradition of the elders. [4]When they come
from the marketplace they do not eat unless they wash. And they observe many other
traditions, such as the washing of cups, pitchers and kettles.)

[5]So the Pharisees and teachers of the law asked Jesus, "Why don't your disciples
live according to the tradition of the elders instead of eating their food with 'unclean'
hands?"

[6]He replied, "Isaiah was right when he prophesied about you hypocrites; as it is written:

"'These people honor me with their lips,
but their hearts are far from me.
[7] They worship me in vain;
their teachings are but rules taught by men.'

[8]You have let go of the commands of God and are holding on to the traditions of men."

[9]And he said to them: "You have a fine way of setting aside the commands of God
in order to observe your own traditions! [10]For Moses said, 'Honor your father and your
mother,' and, 'Anyone who curses his father or mother must be put to death.' [11]But you
say that if a man says to his father or mother: 'Whatever help you might otherwise have
received from me is Corban' (that is, a gift devoted to God), [12]then you no longer let him

do anything for his father or mother. [13]Thus you nullify the word of God by your tradition that you have handed down. And you do many things like that."

COMMENTARY

1 Another delegation of fact-finding religious leaders (Pharisees and teachers of the law) comes down from Jerusalem to investigate the Galilean activities of Jesus. The first such visit provoked the Beelzebul controversy (3:22–30), which, as we have seen, was a key crisis point in Mark's narrative used to distinguish the "insiders" who were responding to the kingdom message from the "outsiders" who were rejecting it (see comments at 3:20–34; 4:10–12). The reference to Jerusalem again reminds the reader where the center of hostility toward Jesus lies and foreshadows his Jerusalem passion.

2 What the Pharisees and scribes discovered was that Jesus' disciples did not wash their hands before eating. Their complaint was not, of course, that the disciples were being unhygienic. The question was one of ceremonial purity. The term translated "unclean" in the NIV (*koinos*, GK *3123*, "common") is used here in the sense of "defiled" (TNIV), in contrast to what is "holy" or set apart to God. Mark explains for his Gentile readers that *koinos* means "unwashed" (i.e., in the prescribed manner).

As in the question about fasting in 2:18, the issue here does not concern an OT command but a Pharisaic tradition. The OT did not command hand washing before meals but did require ritualistic washings for the priests before offering sacrifices (Ex 30:19–21; 40:12, 30–32). The Pharisees took these priestly commands and applied them to themselves, not only with reference to sacrifices but also to all food. Perhaps their intention in doing so was in recognition that Israel was intended to be a "kingdom of priests" (Ex 19:6). It is uncertain whether the Pharisees expected all Israelites to live by these standards or whether they are here applying them to the disciples because of Jesus' reputation as a religious leader.

3–4 Verses 3–4 are parenthetical (so NIV and TNIV). Mark felt it necessary to explain to his Gentile readers the Jewish custom of ceremonial hand washing. Mark's application of the custom not only to the Pharisees but also "all the Jews" (v.3) may be a generalization for his Gentile audience to identifying this custom as specifically Jewish. Gundry, 358–60, however, sees evidence for the widespread practice of hand washing among the Jews of Jesus' day.

The "tradition of the elders" (vv.3, 5) consisted in a great mass of oral tradition that had arisen about the OT law. About AD 200 it was written down in the Mishnah, but in Jesus' day it was still in oral form. The purpose of this oral tradition was to provide guidelines for all areas of life. If the OT law was silent or too general about a particular subject, the tradition would seek to provide specific applications for diverse situations. The goal was to "build a fence" around the law to protect against its violation. An entire division of the Mishnah is devoted to the question of ceremonial purity (*Ṭeharot*, "cleannesses"). The rabbis came to view these oral traditions as fully authoritative and even claimed they had been given to Moses by God on

Mount Sinai and passed down from one generation to the next (*m.* ʾ*Abot* 1:1–2).

In v.4, Mark gives an example of the custom. The Greek phrase *ap' agoras* ("from the marketplace") is cryptic and may mean "things bought from the marketplace" or "when they come from the marketplace." If the former meaning is adopted, the verse would be translated, "They do not eat things bought from the marketplace unless they wash them." But the NIV and most versions are probably correct, for the verb *baptisōntai* is in the middle voice and so could mean "wash themselves." After being in the marketplace and coming into contact with Gentiles or even nonobservant Jews, the Pharisees would wash themselves to ensure their ritual cleanness. By way of further explanation, Mark adds that the Pharisees "observe many other traditions, such as the washing of cups, pitchers and [copper] kettles."

5–8 To the question as to why Jesus' disciples acted as they did, Jesus answered by quoting a passage from Isaiah, preceded by his own comment: "Isaiah was right when he prophesied about you hypocrites" (v.6). The word "hypocrite" (*hypokritēs*, GK *5695*) originally meant "play actor" and refers here to people whose worship is merely outward and not from the heart. Though the term is common in Matthew (thirteen occurrences), Mark uses it only here. In saying that Isaiah had prophesied about them, Jesus did not mean that Isaiah had in mind the Pharisees and the teachers of the law when he originally wrote these words but that his denunciation of the religious leaders of his day fit those of Jesus' day. The quotation (Isa 29:13) is from the LXX, which differs slightly from the MT in the last sentence. The MT says "their fear [or reverence] of me consists of commandments taught by men." The LXX says "vainly they worship me, teaching human commandments and teachings." Both make essentially the same point—that their traditions and regulations pay mere lip service but show no true heart for God. Their outward appearance of piety is a lie, because it is not accompanied by a "total life commitment to the one who is the true object of religious devotion" (Anderson, 185).

In v.8, Jesus contrasts the "commands of God" with the "traditions of men." It is clear that this great body of Jewish tradition had failed to get to the heart of God's commands. It was supposed to fence in the law so that the people would not infringe on it. In practice, however, the Pharisees were abandoning God's law while holding fast to human traditions.

9 In v.9, Jesus repeats and expands the claim of v.8 by emphasizing that the Pharisaic traditions were even being used to overrule or invalidate God's commands. The statement is sarcastic and ironic: "You are very good at setting aside God's command to hold fast to your tradition!" The Pharisees, Jesus says, had turned doing so into an art form.

10–12 Jesus cites here a specific example. The first quotation is from the LXX of Exodus 20:12 (cf. Dt 5:16) and is a statement of the fifth commandment. The second quotation is from the LXX of Exodus 21:16[17]. In the latter the seriousness of the failure to keep the fifth commandment is underscored—death is the penalty for anyone who curses his father or mother (v.10). But by means of the tradition, the responsibility of children to their parents could be easily circumvented (v.11). A son need only declare that what he had intended to give to his father and mother be considered "Corban," i.e., a gift devoted to God; then it could no longer be designated for his parents. By devoting the gift to God, a son did not necessarily promise it to the temple, nor did he prevent its use for himself. What he did do was legally to exclude his parents from benefiting from it (v.12). So the very purpose for which the fifth commandment was given was set aside by the tradition. This loopholing is what is meant by "nullifying" (*akyrountes*, GK *218*) the word of God (v.13).

13 The phrase "and you do many things like that" parallels Mark's "and they observe many other traditions" (v.4) and carries the same derogatory tone. It emphasizes that this example is merely one of the many ways in which the true spirit of God's law is being ignored or arbitrarily dismissed by the Pharisees.

NOTES

2 The word κοινός (*koinos*, "unclean") occurs again in v.5—and the verbal form κοινόω (*koinoō*, GK *3124*) in vv.15, 18, 20, 23. It appears to be the theme word for the entire section (vv.1–23). In classical Greek, κοινός, *koinos*, means "common," in contrast to ἴδιος (*idios*, "private"). It sometimes has the classical meaning in the LXX, but in 1 Maccabees 1:47, 62 it has the sense of "ritually unclean," which is its meaning here in Mark (cf. Ac 10:14, 28; 11:8; Rev 21:27).

There is a lively debate concerning whether or not the Pharisees considered themselves bound by the priestly obligations set out in the law. For different views, see J. Neusner, *From Politics to Piety: The Emergence of Pharisaic Judaism* (Englewood Cliffs, N.J.: Prentice Hall, 1973) and E. P. Sanders, *Judaism*.

3 The NIV translates the Greek phrase ἐὰν μὴ πυγμῇ νίψωνται τὰς χεῖρας (*ean mē pygmē nipsōntai tas cheiras*) as "unless they give their hands a ceremonial washing." The word πυγμῇ, *pygmē*, is literally "with a [the] fist," but the sense is uncertain. It could mean (1) with the clenched fist of one hand rubbing the palm of the other, (2) up to the wrist or elbow, (3) with a handful of water (cupped hand), or something else. The difficulty prompted some copyists to omit it (Δ syr[s] cop[sa] Diatessaron[p]) and others to substitute another word that to them made better sense, such as πυκνά (*pykna*, "often" or "thoroughly"; ℵ W it[b,1] vg al) or *momento* ("in a moment," it[a]) or *primo* ("first," it[d]; cf. Metzger, 80).

4 Some MSS add "and reclining couches [or 'beds']" to the list of things washed. Metzger, 80–81, points out that this phrase may have been added under the influence of the legislation in Leviticus 15 (which discusses uncleanness of a bed caused by semen or menstrual blood) or else omitted accidentally through homoeoteleuton (having the same genitive plural ending as the previous words), or deliberately because the idea of washing beds seemed incongruous.

6 Regarding ὑποκρίτης (*hypokritēs*, GK *5695*, "hypocrite"), "The thought here is probably not so much that the people concerned were consciously acting a part as that there was a radical inconsistency in their lives.... If they were themselves deceived as well as deceiving others, their situation was more, not less serious" (Cranfield, 235).

In the rabbinic literature the Hebrew term *qorbān* (GK 7933) is often used in a formula to set aside something to God, thus rendering it unavailable for human use (*m. Ned.*; cf. Josephus, *Ant.* 4.4.4 §§72–73). The term appears to have been used primarily to protect one's property against use by another. J. A. Fitzmyer ("The Aramaic *Qorbān* Inscription from Jebel Hallet Et-turi and Mk 7:11/Mt 15:5," *JBL* 78 [1959]: 60–65) cites an ossuary inscription of the early first century AD that reads, "All that a man may find to his profit in this ossuary is *qorbān* to God from him who is within it." Since the OT forbade the breaking of oaths (Nu 30:2; Dt 23:21–23), the rabbis debated whether a *qorbān* oath could be broken if it conflicted with other commandments or produced hardship for others. In the case of the fifth commandment, the Mishnah seems to favor the release of the vow for the sake of the parents (*m. Ned.* 8:1–9:1). Jesus clearly knew of cases in which rabbis took a harder line and gave precedence to the oath.

G. True Defilement (7:14–23)

OVERVIEW

That these verses are closely related to vv.1–13 and represent a continuation of that episode is evident from Jesus' statement in v.15, which answers the question about ceremonial purity raised by the Pharisees and teachers in v.5. Jesus teaches that defilement does not come from external objects or food but from a person's attitude of heart.

This passage also has important parallels to Jesus' teaching in Mark 4. Jesus here "calls the crowd to him" (v.14), just as in ch. 4 "a large crowd" gathered to him (4:1–2). Just as Jesus taught in parables in ch. 4, so here Jesus' statement about the cause of uncleanness (v.15) is identified as a "parable" (v.17). Jesus also prefaces his statement with a prophetic call to hear ("Listen to me, everyone, and understand this," v.14), echoing the twin calls to hear that frame the parables in ch. 4 ("If anyone has ears to hear, let him hear," 4:9, 23). As in 4:10, Jesus here interprets the "parable" privately to his disciples (v.17). Yet strikingly, the spiritual dullness that in 4:11–12 characterizes the "outsiders," who were blind and deaf to the parables, is here attributed to the disciples (v.18). As noted above, this theme of the disciples' spiritual insensitivity builds throughout this section of the gospel (6:7–8:26) and will climax in 8:14–21, where the disciples are in grave danger of going the way of the scribes and Pharisees (see Overview, 8:14–21; comments at 8:15).

As France, 277, points out, there is something of an internal tension between this passage and the previous one. There Jesus challenged the human traditions that were being used to manipulate and distort the OT law of God. Here he apparently challenges the OT law itself by openly declaring that food mandated as unclean in the OT (Lev 11; 17) does not in fact defile a person. How can this tension be resolved?

The answer, as always, must be found in the context of Jesus' proclamation of the kingdom of God and the new age of salvation that is arriving through his words and deeds. Jesus is making two distinct but equally important points: (1) The religious leaders are characterized by hypocrisy and hard-heartedness. While holding fast to their human traditions, they are ignoring the true spirit of God's commands. They need to repent and turn to God. (2) But there is more going on here than a call to reform Israel's religious leadership. Jesus is not just patching up old wineskins; he is inaugurating the new age, with new wine and new wineskins (see 2:21–22). This dawning is God's eschatological salvation. The OT covenant given to Israel is being fulfilled through Jesus' words and deeds and will be superseded by a new covenant established through his death on the cross (14:24). In this new age, salvation is not the exclusive privilege of Israel but will go forth to all nations and peoples. The dietary laws given to Israel under the old covenant will no longer be mandated for the new-covenant people of God.

Furthermore, as the following episodes will make clear, Mark is doing more in this passage than defending the Christian claim that the OT dietary laws are not binding on believers. He is announcing that Gentiles are no longer to be considered "unclean." God's salvation is for all people everywhere.

[14]Again Jesus called the crowd to him and said, "Listen to me, everyone, and understand this. [15]Nothing outside a man can make him 'unclean' by going into him. Rather, it is what comes out of a man that makes him 'unclean.'"

[17]After he had left the crowd and entered the house, his disciples asked him about this parable. [18]"Are you so dull?" he asked. "Don't you see that nothing that enters a man from the outside can make him 'unclean'? [19]For it doesn't go into his heart but into his stomach, and then out of his body." (In saying this, Jesus declared all foods "clean.")

[20]He went on: "What comes out of a man is what makes him 'unclean.' [21]For from within, out of men's hearts, come evil thoughts, sexual immorality, theft, murder, adultery, [22]greed, malice, deceit, lewdness, envy, slander, arrogance and folly. [23]All these evils come from inside and make a man 'unclean.'"

COMMENTARY

14–15 (16) Jesus has been speaking directly to the Pharisees and the teachers of the law. Now he calls the crowd around him because he wants to make public the crux of his teaching about what is clean.

Jesus states clearly what does and does not make a person unclean (v.15). What is external cannot defile a person. Food, for example, cannot do so—not even if it is eaten with unwashed hands or labeled unclean by kosher food laws. This statement would have startled Jesus' hearers, since the Jews viewed the OT dietary laws as sacrosanct. Though startling, however, the statement is not out of line with Jesus' actions elsewhere. He freely eats with tax collectors and sinners in contexts where the food was unlikely to be kosher (cf. 2:16), and he has no qualms about touching a leper (1:41), the corpse of Jairus's daughter (5:41), or a hemorrhaging woman (5:27–29)—all actions that in Judaism would have rendered him ceremonially unclean (cf. Guelich, 376). Jesus is adamant that such external things do not make a person unclean, but rather those things that come from within, out of the heart and the will—ungodly thoughts, words, desires, and motives.

Verse 16 does not appear in the NIV because, though it is present in the majority of the MSS, it does not occur in the important Alexandrian witnesses. Metzger, 81, writes, "It appears to be a scribal gloss (derived perhaps from 4:9 or 4:23), introduced as an appropriate sequel to ver. 14."

17–18 After leaving the crowd Jesus enters a house, where the disciples ask him about the meaning of this "parable." The term here means an aphorism or proverb. (For this broad sense of parable, see Overview, 4:1–34.) Some interpreters have suggested that the house is Peter's at Capernaum. While it is a possibility—since the noun is without the definite article—no specific house is likely intended.

There is irony in the fact that, although the disciples have spent considerable time with Jesus and belong to the inner circle of his concern, they are slow to grasp the meaning of his teaching. Jesus expressed surprise at this slowness. The Greek conjunction *kai* could be translated as comparing the disciples to the crowds: "Are you *also* so dull?" This meaning would be similar to the sense in ch. 4, where Jesus first rebukes the disciples, "Don't you understand this parable?" but then gives its explanation. Or *kai* could be translated "Are you *indeed* so dull," with the implication, "After all the time I've spent with you, do you still not comprehend spiritual truth?"

19 After rebuking the disciples, Jesus continues with his explanation. The reason why nothing entering a person from the outside defiles him is because it enters into the stomach, not the heart, and then is eliminated from the body. And it is in the heart that the true issues of life lie. In Semitic expression the heart is the center of human personality and determines a person's actions and inaction (cf. Isa 29:13: "These people come near to me with their mouth and honor me with their lips, but their hearts are far from me").

In v.19b, Mark explains for his readers with a parenthetic statement the significance of Jesus' teaching about ceremonial purity. As R. P. Martin (*Mark*, 220) points out, this statement has its eye on a situation such as those in the Pauline mission churches in which questions of clean and unclean foods (cf. Ac 10:9–16; 11:5–10; see Ro 14:13ff.) and idol meats became live issues (cf. 1Co 8:10). According to Martin, this section in Mark 7 may be the most obvious declaration of Mark's purpose as a Christian living in the Greco-Roman world who wishes to publicize the charter of Gentile freedom by recording Jesus' detachment from Jewish ceremonialism and to spell out the application to his readers.

If Peter stands behind Mark's gospel, these words are particularly apropos in the light of Acts 10:15, where God directly reveals to Peter that he should call nothing impure that God has pronounced clean. It is also significant that just as the unclean animals in Peter's vision symbolize the Gentiles, so Mark is developing this theme in relation to the subsequent stories of Jesus' encounters with Gentiles.

20–23 The introduction to v.20 (*elegen de hoti*) could be understood as either direct discourse ("and he was saying ...") or indirect discourse ("and he was saying *that* ..."). Some commentators opt for the latter and suggest that what follows is Mark's further interpretation (cf. v.19b) or explanation of Jesus' teaching in vv.15–19a. The catechistical structure of vv.19b–23 may perhaps lend support to this possibility, but it is far from certain or necessary. Even if it is Mark's interpretation, it is not inconsistent with Jesus' teaching in vv.15–19a.

The main force of the passage is the same as in v.15b, which, in fact, is repeated in v.20. The source of uncleanness in anyone is the heart (v.21), for it is there that the true issues of life lie. The list of vices that follows is unique among the sayings of Jesus (Taylor, 345) but has many parallels elsewhere in the NT (Ro 1:29–31; 1Co 5:10–11; 2Co 2:20–21; Gal 5:19–21; Col 3:5–8; 1Ti 1:9–12; 2Ti 3:2–5; cf. 1Pe 4:3, 15). There are also many parallels in Judaism (1QS 4.9–11) and in Greco-Roman philosophical traditions (see Marcus, 459). The list is difficult to classify; it seems to move from overt sins to sinful attitudes or dispositions. "Evil thoughts" stand first, which suggests that what follows arises from them. *Porneia* (GK *4518*, "sexual immorality") is a broader term than *moicheia* (GK *3657*, "adultery"), for *porneia* describes illegitimate sexual relations generally, while adultery is limited to (always illicit) sex outside one's marriage. *Aselgeia* (GK *816*, "lewdness") suggests open and shameless immorality. *Pleonexiai* (GK *4432*, "greed," v.22) may have sexual overtones, since it is frequently associated (as here) with words indicating sexual sins (e.g., Eph

4:19; 5:3; Col 3:5; 2Pe 2:3). *Ophthalmos ponēros* (GK *4505*, "envy") is literally "evil eye," a Semitic term for "stinginess" (cf. Dt 15:9; Sir 14:10; 31:13) or, perhaps better, "envious jealousy." *Blasphēmia* (GK *1060*, "slander") includes speaking evil of either God or human beings. *Aphrosynē* (GK *932*) means "foolish" in the sense found in OT Wisdom literature, where the fool is not someone who is intellectually deficient but rather one with low moral and ethical standards who ignores God's authority.

NOTES

15 This saying appears both in Matthew's parallel and also in the *Gospel of Thomas* (14).

Rawlinson, 96, tones down this statement of Jesus by arguing that since the Hebrew and Aramaic know no comparative degree, what Jesus is saying is that "pollutions from within are more serious than pollutions from without." But this interpretation fails to see the revolutionary nature of Jesus' teaching concerning the law.

17 Here, as in 9:28, 33 and 10:10, the place where Jesus reveals the true meaning of his teaching is in a "house."

19 The Greek here is a very earthy expression that points out that food enters the stomach and then goes "into the latrine" (εἰς τὸν ἀφεδρῶνα, *eis ton aphedrōna*).

H. The Faith of the Syrophoenician Woman (7:24–30)

OVERVIEW

Why does Mark place this incident here? As noted above, it follows naturally the preceding incidents in which Jesus breaks with the Jewish oral law and particularly the law of ceremonial cleanness. Jews normally had no relationship with Gentiles because associations with them made Jews ritually unclean. Jesus now shows by example that those oral laws are invalid and deliberately associates himself with a Gentile woman.

A related purpose is to emphasize the mission to the Gentiles. The gospel of the kingdom is not limited to Israel, even though historically it came to her first (cf. v.27). Mark regards this story of the Syrophoenician woman as a natural consequence of Jesus' attitude toward the ceremonial law (vv.1–23); and by including it here, Mark wants to assure his Gentile readers that the "good news" is for them, as it was for the Syrophoenician woman.

The relationship established here between unclean foods (vv.1–23) and God's acceptance of a Gentile (vv.24–30) parallels Acts 10–11, where Peter's vision of unclean animals prepares him for the conversion of the Gentile centurion Cornelius.

[24]Jesus left that place and went to the vicinity of Tyre. He entered a house and did not
want anyone to know it; yet he could not keep his presence secret. [25]In fact, as soon as she

heard about him, a woman whose little daughter was possessed by an evil spirit came and fell at his feet. 26The woman was a Greek, born in Syrian Phoenicia. She begged Jesus to drive the demon out of her daughter.

27"First let the children eat all they want," he told her, "for it is not right to take the children's bread and toss it to their dogs."

28"Yes, Lord," she replied, "but even the dogs under the table eat the children's crumbs."

29Then he told her, "For such a reply, you may go; the demon has left your daughter."

30She went home and found her child lying on the bed, and the demon gone.

COMMENTARY

24 "Left that place" translates *ekeithen* ("from there") and may refer to the house (v.17) or to Gennesaret (6:53). As in the account of the Gerasene demoniac (5:1–20), Jesus leaves Jewish territory and enters a Gentile region. Phoenicia (now Lebanon), in which the city of Tyre was located, bordered Galilee to the northwest. Why Jesus went there or how far he penetrated into this territory we are not told. Mark usually leaves such details up to the imagination of the reader. Apparently, Jesus did not go there for public ministry. He went into a house "and did not want anyone to know it." This comment suggests that he went there to get out of the public eye, perhaps to rest and to prepare himself spiritually for what he knew lay ahead of him. But his hope for a time of quiet retirement was thwarted. His fame had apparently spread beyond the borders of Galilee into the territory of Phoenicia, and "he could not keep his presence secret." The insistent pursuit by the needy crowds despite Jesus' attempt at retreat has become a common theme in Mark (1:32–38, 45; 2:1–2; 3:7–13; 6:31–34). Mark uses this theme to display Jesus' extraordinary popularity and also to highlight the priorities of his ministry—proclaiming the kingdom and training his disciples.

25–26 One of the persons who sought out Jesus was a Gentile woman. No doubt she had heard about his healing powers and came to him because her daughter was possessed by a demon (v.25). Mark says that the woman was "a Greek, born in Syrian Phoenicia" (v.26). By nationality the woman was a Syrophoenician, thus not an ethnic Greek. "Greek" may instead be equivalent here to "Gentile" (as distinct from Jew). Paul often uses the term in this sense (Ro 1:16; 2:9–10; 3:9; 10:12; 1Co 12:13; Gal 3:28). Or the term may mean Greek as opposed to Aramaic speaking. In those days Phoenicia belonged administratively to Syria. So Mark probably used Syrophoenician to distinguish this woman from the Libyo-Phoenicians of North Africa.

Mark's description of the daughter's possession by an "unclean spirit" (*pneuma akatharton*; cf. 1:23, 26; 3:30; 5:2, 8; 7:25; 9:25) reiterates the theme of impurity found in the previous episode. From external appearances, the woman has everything going against her. She is a Gentile, a woman, and her daughter is possessed by a defiling spirit—all of which factors would render her off-limits for close contact with a Jewish rabbi such as Jesus. Again, Mark shows Jesus as breaking down the traditional Jewish boundaries of impurity and exclusivity.

27–28 Jesus' conversation with this woman was likely in Greek, not Aramaic. There is no reason why Jesus, raised in Galilee, would not have known Greek.

In the villages and towns of Palestine, he would ordinarily have used Aramaic. But in the coastal cities of the Gentiles, he would have spoken Greek.

At first sight Jesus' reply appears offensive and ethnocentric. He draws a sharp contrast between the "children" of the household—representing Israel—and the "dogs"—representing the Gentiles. The identification of Israel as God's children was a common metaphor in the OT and Judaism (Ex 4:22–23; Dt 14:1; Isa 1:2; 44:2; Jer 3:19; Hos 11:1; *m. ʾAbot* 3:15; Ro 9:4). Jews did not view dogs as loving pets but as detestable scavengers (1Ki 14:11; 21:19–24; Isa 56:10–11; Ps 22:16; *m. Kil.* 8:6), and the term came to be used in a derogatory sense for Gentiles (*1 En.* 89:42–49; cf. Php 3:2; Rev 22:15).

Two factors may help to mute the severity of Jesus' statement. First, he does not deny that the dogs (= Gentiles) will get some food but only that the children (= Israel) must be fed *first*. The parallel in Matthew is much stronger. It drops the reference to "first" and emphasizes that Jesus was sent *only* to the lost sheep of Israel (Mt 15:24, 26). Second, the term for dog here is not the usual Greek *kyōn* but the diminutive *kynarion*. Some commentators claim Jesus is referring to "puppies" or household pets rather than to scavengers (Lane, 262; cf. D. Rhoads, *Reading Mark* [Minneapolis: Fortress, 2004], 78). There may be some truth to this idea, since in the woman's reply these dogs are pictured under the table rather than in the street (v.28). But in Koine Greek the force of the diminutive had considerably weakened, and Mark commonly uses such forms with little diminutive sense. While Jesus probably has in mind small domesticated dogs rather than wild scavenger dogs, the statement can hardly be viewed as a compliment. These animals are not cuddly puppies being pampered like family members; rather, they are scrap eaters hanging around the garbage. The most that can be said is that Jesus softens what could have been an even more derogatory insult.

It is better to resolve the tension in the passage by recognizing that Jesus is being intentionally provocative in order to elicit the correct response from the woman. He is testing her to see whether she will claim what is rightfully hers, namely, the opportunity to receive God's blessings in the new age of salvation. As France, 296, points out, misunderstandings of the passage arise from not reading it through to the end, where the encounter builds to a wholly positive conclusion (vv.29–30). Jesus "appears like the wise teacher who allows, and indeed incites, his pupil to mount a victorious argument against the foil of his own reluctance."

The term "first" (*prōton*) in the phrase "*First* let the children eat" carries eschatological and salvation-historical significance similar to Paul's conclusion in Romans 1:16: "first to the Jews, then to the Gentiles" (cf. Marcus, 463). The Jews have both temporal and theological priority in God's plan of salvation, since "theirs is the adoption; theirs the divine glory, the covenants, the receiving of the law, the temple worship and the promises" (Ro 9:4). Yet the day was coming when Gentiles, too, would participate fully in the blessings of salvation. R. P. Martin (*Mark*, 222) correctly identifies *prōton* as indicating "the passing of the exclusive privilege of Israel. The period immediately following the birth of the Jerusalem church saw the time of Israel's opportunity when the children 'first' would be fed." Later, provision would be made for Gentiles. So far as this woman was concerned, the "later" time had already come, because Jesus responded compassionately to her needs.

28 The woman's reply is remarkable. It is humble and respectful, yet assertive and insightful. She addresses Jesus as "Lord" (*kyrie*, GK *3261*)—the only time Jesus is so addressed in Mark. Though in the context the term is simply one of respect for Jesus' position ("sir"), for Mark's readers it would echo their worship of Jesus as sovereign Lord. The woman acknowledges that Jesus has spoken the truth concerning the priority of salvation for the Jews ("Yes, Lord"), and even humbly accepts the designation "dogs." Yet she refuses to accept that her position means total exclusion from God's banquet table. Even the dogs get fed in time. Without denying Jesus' assertion, she contends that God's salvation-historical purpose must also include the Gentiles.

29 Jesus was pleased with the woman's reply. It revealed her humility, persistent faith, and spiritual insight. He responds that "for such a reply" her daughter had been healed and the demon had departed. This phrase could mean "with this answer you have changed my mind," but more likely it means "with this answer you have passed the test." The point of the story is not that Jesus is suddenly persuaded that Gentiles should receive God's salvation blessings; rather (as in the previous episode), he is indirectly teaching something about the nature of the kingdom of God. When Jesus expresses the common view of his countrymen ("we Jews are the recipients of God's blessings; you Gentiles are mere dogs"), he is verbally challenged and outmaneuvered by a Gentile woman! Marcus, 470, notes that this occasion is the only one in the Gospels on which Jesus loses an argument to someone. The point, of course, is that Jesus wins by losing. By accepting the woman's superior argument, he allows this "outsider" to express a fundamental truth of the gospel: In the kingdom age, salvation will be for all who respond in faith, regardless of ethnic identity.

30 The woman returned home and discovered the truth of what Jesus had said. Here is the only instance of healing at a distance found in Mark's gospel. She found her daughter lying on the bed (perhaps as the result of the final convulsion of the demon as it came out of her; cf. 9:26), and the demon gone.

NOTES

26 On Jesus' ability to speak Greek, see S. E. Porter, "Jesus and the Use of Greek in Palestine," in *Studying the Historical Jesus*, ed. B. Chilton and C. A. Evans (NTTS 19; Leiden: Brill, 1994), 123–54.

27 The term "daughter" appears in both diminutive (θυγάτριον, *thygatrion*, v.25) and nondiminutive (θυγατρός, *thygatros*, v.26) forms in the passage, and two different terms for children, one diminutive (παιδίον, *paidion*, vv.28, 30) and one nondiminutive (τέκνα, *tekna*, v.27) are also used (cf. the diminutive ψιχία, *psichia*, v.28), thus raising doubt as to whether κυναρίον (*kynarion*) carries any special diminutive force.

I. Healing a Deaf and Mute Man (7:31–37)

OVERVIEW

None of the other evangelists record this story. Mark includes it here because it gives an account of another healing in Gentile territory, thus connecting it with the episodes that precede and follow. As in the accounts of the Gerasene demoniac (5:1–20) and the Syrophoenician woman (7:24–30), Jesus enters a Gentile region, where he performs a healing in confirmation that God's eschatological salvation is for Gentiles as well as Jews. There are also significant parallels to the healing of the blind man at Bethsaida, the account of which follows in 8:22–26. In both episodes Jesus is approached by the man's friends, takes him off alone to be healed, touches the organ to be healed (ears and tongue in one case; eyes in the other), heals using spittle, and seeks to keep the miracle quiet afterward. Though Mark does not explicitly say so, both miracles seem intended to confirm that Jesus is accomplishing the eschatological signs of messianic salvation predicted by Isaiah the prophet: "Then will the eyes of the blind be opened and the ears of the deaf unstopped" (Isa 35:5; see comments at v.32 below).

31 Then Jesus left the vicinity of Tyre and went through Sidon, down to the Sea of Galilee
and into the region of the Decapolis. 32 There some people brought to him a man who was
deaf and could hardly talk, and they begged him to place his hand on the man.
33 After he took him aside, away from the crowd, Jesus put his fingers into the man's
ears. Then he spit and touched the man's tongue. 34 He looked up to heaven and with a
deep sigh said to him, *"Ephphatha!"* (which means, "Be opened!"). 35 At this, the man's ears
were opened, his tongue was loosened and he began to speak plainly.
36 Jesus commanded them not to tell anyone. But the more he did so, the more they
kept talking about it. 37 People were overwhelmed with amazement. "He has done
everything well," they said. "He even makes the deaf hear and the mute speak."

COMMENTARY

31 The geographic references introducing the passage are difficult, and some commentators have accused Mark of a deficient knowledge of Palestinian geography. Jesus journeys northward from Tyre through Sidon, then apparently in a southeasterly direction through the territory of Herod Philip, to the eastern side of the Sea of Galilee and into the territory of the Decapolis. The textual tradition indicates that the copyists had problems with this circuitous journey (see Notes). From a historical perspective, the journey is certainly not geographically impossible, especially since Mark is not giving a day-by-day itinerary but simply a general summary of places Jesus visited. From a narrative and theological perspective, Mark presents Jesus as expanding his ministry to the Gentile regions surrounding Galilee. The Decapolis (the territory of the ten Greek cities; see comments at 5:20) was largely Gentile, but there were also a significant number of Jews living there.

32 Mark says that the man brought to Jesus was "deaf and could hardly talk" (NLT, "a deaf man with a speech impediment"). The term translated "deaf" (*kōphos*) can mean deaf, mute, or both (cf. BDAG, 580). Mark clarifies with the adjective *mogilalos* (GK *3652*), a rare word that means either "unable to speak" or "could speak only with difficulty." The latter is probably meant, since after the cure he is able to speak "plainly" (*orthōs*). The description appears to be the common situation in which deafness results in poor or unintelligible speech.

The word *mogilalos* appears only here in the NT and only once in the Greek OT (LXX), in a context of great importance to the meaning of this story. Mark almost certainly has in mind Isaiah 35:6, a poetic description of the messianic age: "Then will the lame leap like a deer, and the tongue of the dumb [*mogilalos*] shout for joy." Later rabbis understood this text as fulfilled in the age of the Messiah (*Gen. Rab.* 95; *Midrash Tehillim* 146.8). By using this rare word, Mark echoes this OT passage and places the miracle in an eschatological context. Jesus' healings are the Isaianic signs of messianic salvation, evidence of the coming of the kingdom of God.

The people brought the deaf and mute man to Jesus and begged him to lay his hands on the man. Although the text does not explicitly say so, they obviously wanted Jesus to heal him. "They begged" (*parakaleō*, GK *4151*) shows their concern for him, and Jesus responds. The mute man could make no intelligible request for himself.

33 Jesus "took him aside, away from the crowd." The primary purpose for this seems to have been to keep the miracle a secret, since Jesus commands silence in v.36. It may also have been to deal more personally with the man. Mark often emphasizes Jesus' personal contact with the people he heals.

Mark describes Jesus' healing technique in greater detail than usual. While Jesus often heals in Mark with touch (1:31, 41; 5:23; 6:5; 8:25), only here and in 8:23, 25 does he touch the organs affected. Hull (*Hellenistic Magic*, 83) suggests that Jesus puts his fingers into the man's ears to create a passage out for an evil spirit causing the deafness, but the account contains no reference to demon-possession. More likely, Jesus is symbolically unblocking the ears. Mark does not say where Jesus spat, but it was probably into his hand before touching the man's tongue with a moistened finger. The use of saliva for healing is unusual in the Gospels (only here, in 8:23, and in Jn 9:6) but was common and highly regarded in the ancient world among both Jews and Gentiles (see Gundry, 389; Hull, 76–78). Especially prized was the spittle of powerful and famous people. The Roman historian Tacitus (*Hist.* 4:81) tells the story of a blind man who was healed by the saliva of the emperor Vespasian (cf. Suetonius, *Vesp.* 7). Evidently saliva was viewed as containing the life force of the person and so conveying their power to others.

Modern Christians often struggle with Jesus' technique here. If magical, it seems out of touch with Jesus' other miracles, where he heals not with rituals and incantations but in the power of the Spirit and from his own authority as Messiah and agent of the kingdom of God. If medicinal, it seems equally inappropriate as primitive and unscientific. Yet we must not force twenty-first-century expectations onto a first-century event. Whether Jesus viewed his technique as merely symbolic or truly efficacious cannot be determined from the text. What is clear is that Jesus' actions were intended to provoke faith in a tangible and meaningful way. Calvin, 2:271–72, comments:

> The laying on of hands would of itself have been sufficiently efficacious, and even, without moving a finger, he might have accomplished it by a single act of his will, but it is evident that he made abundant use of outward signs, when they were found to be advantageous. Thus, by touching the tongue with spittle, he intended to point out that the faculty of speech was communicated by himself alone; and by putting his fingers into the ears, he showed that it belonged to his office to pierce the ears of the deaf.

34 Jesus' looking up to heaven is best understood as an attitude of prayer (cf. Jn 11:41; 17:1), and perhaps it was also a way of showing the man that God was the source of his power. The "deep sigh" could be (1) part of the healing technique (so Marcus, 474; Gundry, 383–84); (2) an indication of Jesus' deep emotional involvement (so France,

234); (3) Jesus' heartache over the ravages of disease (so Witherington, 234); or (4) a sign of heartfelt prayer. This last suggestion is the most likely, since the phrase is closely linked with looking up into heaven. Van der Loos (*Miracles of Jesus*, 327) writes that it was "the 'sighing' of the prayer, the sighing that accompanied the concealed communion of Jesus with the Father. If this looking up and sighing had been permanent technical aspects of the modus operandi of Jesus, we should definitely find references to them in early Christianity, but what we find there is that it is repeatedly stated that healing was simply performed only 'in the name of Jesus'!"

The healing itself comes not through any technique but through the authoritative command of Jesus: "*Ephphatha!*" According to his custom, Mark explains the meaning of this Aramaic word to his readers: "Be opened!" Jesus' use of Aramaic is not surprising here, since the Gentiles of Decapolis spoke a dialect of Aramaic (as well as Greek). It is also possible that the man was a Jew. But why does Mark record the Aramaic word in this particular case? There is no indication from the text that the utterance is a magical formula of any kind; rather, as in 5:41, the profound nature of the healing no doubt left an impression on those present, and the actual word that Jesus uttered was remembered and passed down as the climax to the story.

35 The effect of the command was instantaneous. The man's ears were opened, his tongue loosed, and he spoke "plainly" (*orthōs*). As noted above, his doing so implies he had not been completely mute but instead had a speech impediment that resulted from the deafness (v.32).

36 Jesus again ordered the crowd not to divulge the miracle, but this command produced no effect at all. The more he insisted on their not talking about it, the more they blazed the miracle abroad. Both themes have become commonplace in Mark: Jesus' command for silence (1:34, 44; 3:12; 5:37, 43) and the failure of people to obey it (1:45; 2:1–2; 3:7–12; 6:33). What is unusual here is that earlier in this same region of the Decapolis Jesus had encouraged the Gerasene demoniac to proclaim to others what had happened to him (5:19–20). Why the change? Mark does not say, although 7:24 may give us a clue, since there we learn that Jesus' fame had spread even to the Gentile regions around Tyre. The same was likely true of the Decapolis. While in an earlier period Jesus could safely tell the healed man to proclaim far and wide what happened to him, safety in doing so was no longer possible—even in a Gentile region. As elsewhere in the gospel, Jesus' reasons for enjoining silence are probably twofold. First, Jesus wants to define his messiahship on his own terms rather than through the expectations of others. Second, Jesus recognizes that exuberant messianic expectations among the crowds could touch off a messianic insurrection and so hinder the essential purpose of his ministry: to proclaim the kingdom of God and accomplish his God-appointed mission.

37 Another result of the healing was that the people were "overwhelmed" (*hyperperissōs*, a true hapax legomenon [a word occurring only once in Greek literature] that means "beyond measure," "in the extreme"). The statement "he has done everything well" reminds us of Genesis 1:31: "God saw all that he made, and it was very good." The reminder is not unsuitable, for in a profound sense Jesus' work is indeed "a new creation." The last sentence, "He even makes the deaf hear and the mute speak," again recalls the messianic significance of this miracle with words that reflect Isaiah 35:5–6 (already anticipated by the use of *mogilalos* in v.32):

> Then will the eyes of the blind be opened
> and the ears of the deaf unstopped.
> Then will the lame leap like a deer,
> and the mute tongue shout for joy.

There can be no doubt that for Mark the significance of this miracle was the proclamation of the gospel in the territory of the Gentiles, a sign of the messianic activity of Jesus.

NOTES

31 The best representatives of the Alexandrian and the Western texts, in addition to important Caesarean witnesses, support the reading ἦλθεν διὰ Σιδῶνος (*ēlthen dia Sidōnos*, "he went through Sidon"). This reading indicates that Jesus took a circuitous route by traveling from Tyre north through Sidon, then southeast across the Leontes, south past Caesarea Philippi to the east of the Jordan River, into the territory of the Decapolis to the east of Lake Galilee. The alternative reading καὶ Σιδῶνος ἦλθεν (*kai Sidōnos ēlthen*, "and he went to Sidon") arose because copyists either had difficulty with Mark's geography and deliberately changed the text, or they, being influenced by the well-known expression "Tyre and Sidon," introduced it accidentally (cf. Metzger, 82).

J. Feeding the Four Thousand (8:1–10)

OVERVIEW

The theme of Jesus' ministry in Gentile territory continues with the account of the feeding of four thousand people. Though there is no explicit identification of the crowd here as Gentile, the location of the miracle in Decapolis, the episodes concerning Gentiles that precede it, or the parallel with the feeding of five thousand (Jews) in ch. 6, all these features suggest a Gentile milieu for this miracle. Further, Jesus has already confirmed to the Syrophoenician woman that the Gentile "dogs" would receive their share of the "bread" after the Jewish "children" have received theirs (6:27–29). Some commentators suggest that the numbers involved also point in this direction. The numbers five and twelve associated with the first feeding could be seen as "Jewish numbers," representing the five books of Moses and the twelve tribes of Israel. The number seven (loaves/baskets) in the second feeding could perhaps relate to the seventy Gentile nations in Genesis 10 or to the seven commandments in the Noahic covenant (Ge 9:4–6; cf. Witherington, 236). Though this last analogy is tenuous at best, the cumulative evidence comprises a credible case that Mark is intentionally developing the theme of the expansion of the gospel to the Gentiles.

Lane, 269, points to another literary pattern that seems to be at work in Mark's narrative, namely, a structural parallel between the sections 6:31–7:37 and 8:1–30:

6:31–44	Feeding the Multitude	8:1–9
6:45–56	Crossing the Sea and Landing	8:10
7:1–23	Conflict with the Pharisees	8:11–13
7:24–30	Conversation about Bread	8:13–21
7:31–36	Healing	8:22–26
7:37	Confession of Faith	8:27–30

The motif behind this structure seems to be spiritual understanding—or lack of it. Jesus sounds a call to spiritual understanding in 7:14–18, but after each feeding miracle the disciples fail to understand (6:52; 8:14–21). The miracles of healing—the opening of the ears of the deaf man (7:31–36) and the eyes of the blind man (8:22–26)—are symbolic of and prepare the way for the opening of the spiritual understanding of the disciples.

The striking similarity between this feeding miracle and the one in 6:34–44 raises the question of whether, historically, one or two feedings took place. The majority of scholars believe that only one happened, and they take 8:1–9 as a "doublet" of 6:34–44. Doublets are two versions of the same event that, in the history of transmission, came to be treated as two separate events. Matthew in particular has a number of stories commonly treated as doublets (Mt 9:27–31 = 20:29–34; 9:32–34 = 12:22–24; 12:38–39 = 16:1–4). In Mark, by contrast, this episode is the only one that may fit this category. The strongest argument for a doublet here is the disciples' apparent failure to remember the first feeding (see comments at v.4 below).

If the passage is indeed a doublet, there are two options as to its origin: either (1) a single story developed into two in the pre-Markan tradition, or (2) Mark himself duplicated the story in order to provide a Gentile feeding to balance his earlier Jewish one. Neither of these possibilities seems likely. Against the first is the fact that the differences in the two stories run counter to the normal pattern of oral transmission. As stories are passed down by word of mouth, central features tend to stay the same, while details of the story line vary. In the feeding miracles we see exactly the opposite. The central features that are emphasized—the number fed, the meager portions utilized, and the baskets left over—are all different, while the general story line remains the same (cf. France, 306).

The second option remains: Mark has intentionally rewritten the feeding of the five thousand and changed the numbers. But his having done so also seems unlikely. The episode contains a number of non-Markan words and grammatical forms, so suggesting he has taken it from the tradition rather than written it himself (cf. Guelich, 402). As noted above, nowhere else do we find evidence of doublets in Mark. While Mark's redactional hand is certainly evident in the way he edits traditional material to suit his narrative purpose, there is no evidence for his wholesale creation of events. Furthermore, Mark intentionally highlights the fact of two separate events, first by narrating both feedings and then by having Jesus explicitly refer to two distinct miracles (8:18–21).

The accounts certainly are similar. Yet their differences suggest that on two different occasions Jesus fed a multitude. For a more detailed discussion and defense of two separate feedings, see Gundry, 398–401.

1During those days another large crowd gathered. Since they had nothing to eat,
Jesus called his disciples to him and said, 2"I have compassion for these people; they have
already been with me three days and have nothing to eat. 3If I send them home hungry,
they will collapse on the way, because some of them have come a long distance."
4His disciples answered, "But where in this remote place can anyone get enough bread
to feed them?"
5"How many loaves do you have?" Jesus asked. "Seven," they replied.

[6]He told the crowd to sit down on the ground. When he had taken the seven loaves and given thanks, he broke them and gave them to his disciples to set before the people, and they did so. [7]They had a few small fish as well; he gave thanks for them also and told the disciples to distribute them. [8]The people ate and were satisfied. Afterward the disciples picked up seven basketfuls of broken pieces that were left over. [9]About four thousand men were present. And having sent them away, [10]he got into the boat with his disciples and went to the region of Dalmanutha.

COMMENTARY

1 "During those days" probably connects this incident with the preceding one (7:31–37). The point seems to be that Jesus remained in the Decapolis, on the eastern side of Lake Galilee, and hence in Gentile territory. The presence of a large crowd is implied. They had been with Jesus for three days, while probably receiving instruction from him. Taylor, 358, points out that "the reference to 'three days' is peculiar to the narrative, distinguishing it from 6:35–44, in which the crossing, the meal, and the recrossing all take place on the same day."

2–3 Jesus, not the disciples (as in 6:35–36), recognized the physical needs of the crowds. He was moved with compassion for them because they had had nothing to eat for three days. Another difference in this account is that Jesus immediately dismisses the idea that the crowd should be sent away for food ("If I send them home hungry, they will collapse on the way" [v.3]), whereas in 6:36 the disciples definitely ask him to send them away.

The comment that some of the people had come from "afar" (*makrothen*; NIV, "a long distance") may be another indication of a Gentile theme, since this term is used in the LXX of Gentile lands (Jos 9:6; Isa 60:4; Jer 46:27). Similar terminology appears in the NT (cf. *makran* in Ac 2:39; 22:21; Eph 2:11–12; see F. Danker, "Mark 8:7," *JBL* 83 [1963]: 215; Guelich, 404; Hurtado, 109–10).

4 The disciples' reply seems to indicate that they had completely forgotten the feeding of the five thousand, which is perhaps the strongest argument against the view that there were two separate feedings. But the argument is not as strong as it appears. Several things may be said in rebuttal to it (cf. Cranfield, 205): (1) A considerable period of time may have elapsed between the two events. (2) Even mature believers (which the disciples were not!), having experienced God's power and provision, have subsequently acted in unbelief. (3) The reluctance of Jesus to perform miracles must have so impressed itself on the disciples that they did not expect to meet every crisis in that fashion. (4) Some allowance must be made for the assimilation of the language of the two accounts because of their repeated use in teaching and worship. (5) The disciples' answer here is put in terms of the difficulty of finding enough food for such a huge crowd rather than sending them away to get their own, as in 6:36.

5–7 Only seven loaves were available to feed the crowd. Again the details differ from the account in ch. 6. There is no ordering of the people into groups of hundreds and fifties. They are simply asked to sit on the ground where they are (v.6). The narrative appears to downplay the fish (not mentioned until v.7), perhaps to highlight the eucharistic-sounding language of v.6 (cf. Lk 22:19; 1Co 11:24). They are merely "a few small fish" and are served as a second course in v.7. Jesus gives thanks separately for the bread and the fish, and after each prayer the disciples distribute the food to the people. The NIV does not distinguish between *eucharisteō* ("give thanks," v.6) and *eulogeō* ("bless," v.7); it translates both as "give thanks." The difficulty copyists had with the idea of Jesus' "blessing" the fish is reflected by the variant *eucharistēsas* ("having given thanks") in v.7 and by the omission of *auta* ("them," referring to the fish) in the same verse. Normally in Jewish tradition the blessing accompanied the breaking of the bread, not the main course, and it was God, not the food, who was blessed (Guelich, 406–7). Mark, treating *eucharisteō* and *eulogeō* as essentially synonymous, probably alternated between them for purely stylistic reasons and assumed his predominantly Gentile readers would not be concerned with a departure from traditional Jewish blessing formulas.

8 As always, Jesus' provision was sufficient—"the people ate and were satisfied." But it was also more than sufficient. Seven basketfuls of leftovers (of which there were twelve in ch. 6) were collected by the disciples. The number seven could indicate "completeness" or may simply reflect the original seven loaves. The use of *spyris* for "basket" here instead of *kophinos* (6:43) may also suggest two different occasions. A *spyris* is a large basket—Paul was lowered from the wall of Damascus in one (Ac 9:25)—whereas a *kophinos* is a wicker basket in which Jews ordinarily carried their food or possessions when journeying. This again may be part of a Jew/Gentile distinction in the two feedings miracles, since a *spyris* is a more general term, while the *kophinos* was associated especially with the Jews (see comments at 6:43).

9–10 Again the details are different. The crowd numbered "about four thousand." In the previous feeding, Mark specifically refers to five thousand "men" (*andres*). Here no gender is specified (the parallel in Mt 15:38 refers to " ... men, besides women and children"). Jesus got into the boat with his disciples (v.10). In the previous feeding he had the disciples get into the boat and go to Bethsaida, while he stayed back to dismiss the crowd.

The identity of Dalmanutha is unknown, and this reference to it is unique in ancient literature. Matthew (15:39) says Jesus went to the "vicinity of Magadan," which is also unknown, but the name may be a variant form of "Magdala," a town on the northwestern shore of Lake Galilee. (Some MSS of Matthew read Magdala.) Dalmanutha and Magadan may have been names for the same place, or two places located near each other, both on the western shore of the lake.

K. Requesting a Sign from Heaven (8:11–13)

OVERVIEW

This paragraph at first sight seems puzzling and abrupt. "Jesus crosses the sea, exchanges three sentences with the Pharisees, then immediately crosses back" (Marcus, 502). Yet Mark has an important reason for placing it here. Structurally, the passage forms a parallel in this section (8:1–30) with 7:1–23 in the previous section (6:31–7:37; see Overview, 8:1–10). Both incidents relate to conflict with the Pharisees. Mark's purpose seems to be twofold. First, the passage represents a reiteration and climax of Jesus' conflicts with the Pharisees in the first half of his gospel (2:16, 18, 24; 3:6; 7:1, 5).

Throughout these chapters the Pharisees have repeatedly appeared as Jesus' intractable opponents by challenging his authority and questioning his adherence to the law. In presenting Jesus as refusing to give them a sign (v.12) and then decisively "leaving" them (v.13), Mark brings to narrative climax Jesus' Galilean engagement with the Pharisees. Until his entrance in Jerusalem and the controversies that follow, he will concentrate almost exclusively on his disciples (except in 10:2). In this regard the passage reminds the reader of 3:22–30, where Jesus accuses the Pharisees of blaspheming the Holy Spirit and then treats them as "outsiders" through his teaching in parables (4:11). With a new pronouncement of judgment ("no sign will be given," v.12), Jesus decisively turns away from the Pharisees.

Mark's second purpose is to draw a comparison and contrast with the disciples. This passage sets the stage for the next, where Jesus will warn the disciples of the spiritual blindness and deafness that come with the "yeast of the Pharisees" (vv.14–21). In the episodes that follow, the disciples will demonstrate pride and spiritual dullness and teeter on the brink of failure. The reappearance of the Pharisees here reminds the reader that there are two paths the disciples may take: the obedient and suffering way of the kingdom pursued by Jesus, or the way of rejection and spiritual blindness taken by the Pharisees.

**11The Pharisees came and began to question Jesus. To test him, they asked him for
a sign from heaven. 12He sighed deeply and said, "Why does this generation ask for a
miraculous sign? I tell you the truth, no sign will be given to it." 13Then he left them, got
back into the boat and crossed to the other side.**

COMMENTARY

11 When Jesus lands in Dalmanutha (v.10) the Pharisees come out "to question" him (v.11). The verb *syzēteō* (GK *5184*) can mean "ask," in a neutral sense (1:27; 9:10), but is more often used in Mark in the negative sense of disputing (cf. 11:18; 12:12; 14:1)—clearly the sense here. The request for a sign was not sincere but was posed to "test" him (*peirazō*, GK *4279*). The same word will be used in 10:2 and 12:15 of attempts to discredit Jesus with difficult questions.

The test here was for Jesus to produce a "sign [*sēmeion*, GK *4956*] from heaven." This sign is unlikely to be simply a miracle (as commonly in John's gospel), since signs in Mark generally differ from "wonders" or "miracles" (*dynameis*; cf. Guelich, 413). Furthermore, considering Jesus' reputation as a miracle worker—repeatedly stressed throughout Mark—the Pharisees are unlikely to have denied that he had performed miracles. In 3:22 they acknowledge his exorcisms but attribute them to Satan. More likely the Pharisees are asking for "outward compelling proof of divine authority" (Cranfield, 257), confirmation that his authority and actions were *from God*—the more common OT and Jewish understanding of "sign" (Dt 13:1–2; 1Sa 2:30–33; 10:1–8; Isa 7:10–14; *b. Sanh. 98a*). The qualification "from heaven" could mean some kind of apocalyptic display in the sky, such as that of Mark 13:24–25 (cf. *4 Ezra* 5:4; 7:39), but more likely is a periphrasis for "from God." The demand, therefore, is that Jesus would provide confirmatory proof that his authority is from God.

12 Jesus responded to their request by "sighing deeply." The word *anastenazō*, found only here in the NT, likely describes Jesus' grief and disappointment when faced with the unbelief of those who, because of their spiritual privileges, ought to have been more responsive to him (cf. Taylor, 362; Lane, 277). There is a note of impatience in Jesus' question, "Why does this generation ask for a miraculous sign?" The designation "this generation" (*hē genea hautē*) likely carries a pejorative sense (cf. 8:38; 9:19), recalling the sinful generation of the flood and the wilderness (Ge 7:1; Ps 95:10–11; Dt 1:35; 32:5, 20; cf. E. Lövestam, *Jesus and "This Generation"* [ConBNT 25; Stockholm: Almqvist & Wiksell, 1995], 24–26; Marcus, 501; Moloney, 158). The wilderness recollection is more important here, especially in the light of the Mosaic and wilderness associations of the feeding miracles. Marcus, 504, writes, "Like the evil generation, which perished in the wilderness and never attained the promised land, the Pharisees and their followers will not receive what they request."

The second sentence of this verse is a particularly strong statement by Jesus. It is introduced by the solemn asseveration "I tell you the truth" (*amēn legō hymin*), which has occurred only once earlier in Mark (3:28). The pronouncement itself—translated by the NIV as "no sign will be given to it"—reads literally, "if a sign will be given to this generation." The phrase represents in Greek an abbreviated version of the Hebrew idiom of self-imprecation: "If such a thing should occur ... may I die!" or " ... may I be cursed!"; cf. Taylor, 136; Guelich, 415). The apodosis of the conditional clause (" ... may I die!") is missing. Thus Jesus, with deep feeling and with an oath, flatly refuses to give any sign.

As to the reason for Jesus' refusal, R. P. Martin (*Mark*, 174) cogently observes: "For Mark and Paul the answer to this wrongful insistence is the same. There is no legitimating sign—save the ambiguity of the humiliated and crucified Lord; and to see in his cross the power and wisdom of God is to be shut up to the exercise of faith, which by definition can never rest in proofs or signs, or else its character would be lost." This teaching of Jesus was doubtless what the persecuted church of Mark's day needed to hear.

13 Having so emphatically made his point, Jesus left the Pharisees, got into the boat, and, with his disciples (cf. v.14), crossed over to the eastern side of the lake.

NOTES

11 On the significance of "signs" in the OT and Judaism, see *TDNT* 7:234–36; O. Linton, "The Demand for a Sign from Heaven (Mk 8:11–12 and parallels)," *ST* 19 [1965]: 112–29; J. B. Gibson, "Jesus' Refusal to Produce a 'Sign' (Mark 8:11–13)," *JSNT* 38 (1990): 38–40.

12 R. Pesch (*Das Markusevangelium* [HTKNT; Freiburg: Herder, 1976], 1:408) asserts that the sigh indicates that what follows is a prophetic utterance. Marcus, 501, suggests that Jesus' sighing indicates, as in 7:34, a struggle with a demonic obstacle.

The "Q" parallels in Matthew 16:4; 12:39; and Luke 11:29 state that no sign shall be given "except the sign of Jonah." For Matthew, this phrase is a reference to the resurrection (12:40). For Luke, it is more ambiguous but appears to be linked to Jonah's preaching and call for repentance (see Lk 11:32).

For OT examples of the oath formula, see Genesis 14:23; Numbers 32:11; Deuteronomy 1:35; 1 Kings 3:14; Psalm 94:11 LXX (cf. Guelich, 415). The fact that the verb δοθήσεται (*dothēsetai*) is in the passive voice, indicating a circumlocution for the name of God, strengthens the statement even more. The meaning is, "Surely God will not give a sign to this generation."

L. The Yeast of the Pharisees and Herod (8:14–21)

OVERVIEW

Jesus' confrontation with the Pharisees (vv.11–13) now leads to a parallel confrontation with his disciples. Jesus uses a spiritual metaphor—leaven in bread—to warn them against the contagious nature of the Pharisees' intransigent unbelief. In turn, the disciples reveal their own spiritual dullness by failing to comprehend the significance of the metaphor. In language ominously reminiscent of ch. 4, Jesus wonders whether they, too, have eyes that cannot see and ears that cannot hear (vv.17–18; cf. 4:10–11).

This episode is the third one involving a boat in Mark. The first two instances, the calming of the sea (4:35–41) and walking on water (6:47–52), revealed Jesus' amazing power and highlighted the disciples' failure to recognize that authority. In the first episode he rebukes them for their fear and lack of faith in the face of the storm (4:40). In the second, the narrator concludes that "they had not understood about the loaves; their hearts were hardened" (6:52). This third event echoes the same theme: the disciples have failed to discern the meaning of the loaves (or better, they had failed to comprehend *the identity of Jesus and the nature of the kingdom* as revealed through the two feeding miracles). The episode sets the stage for Jesus' interaction with the disciples in chs. 8–10, where they will repeatedly fail to comprehend the suffering role of the Christ and the self-sacrificial nature of true discipleship.

14The disciples had forgotten to bring bread, except for one loaf they had with them in
the boat. 15"Be careful," Jesus warned them. "Watch out for the yeast of the Pharisees and
that of Herod."
16They discussed this with one another and said, "It is because we have no bread."
17Aware of their discussion, Jesus asked them: "Why are you talking about having no
bread? Do you still not see or understand? Are your hearts hardened? 18Do you have eyes
but fail to see, and ears but fail to hear? And don't you remember? 19When I broke the five
loaves for the five thousand, how many basketfuls of pieces did you pick up?"
"Twelve," they replied.
20"And when I broke the seven loaves for the four thousand, how many basketfuls of
pieces did you pick up?"
They answered, "Seven."
21He said to them, "Do you still not understand?"

COMMENTARY

14 Mark introduces the episode by noting that the disciples had forgotten to bring bread for the trip across the lake, except for a single loaf already present in the boat. Bread has been a consistent theme throughout this section, with both feeding miracles (6:30–44; 8:1–10), the controversy on eating with unwashed hands (7:1–23), and the reference to Gentile "dogs" eating the children's (= Israel's) bread (7:24–30). While this opening statement highlights the failure of the disciples to supply adequate provisions, Jesus will criticize them not for this error but for obsessing over such a trivial physical issue while failing to perceive true spiritual realities.

Some commentators see the "one loaf" as a symbolic reference to Jesus. The disciples failed to see that the one loaf they had with them was none other than Jesus, who himself was sufficient (so Garland, 310; J. Manek, "Mark viii. 14–21," *NovT* 7 [1964]: 10–14; Q. Quesnell, *The Mind of Mark* [AnBib 38; Rome: Pontifical Biblical Institute, 1969], 231–32). While the symbolism is possible, without clearer contextual factors such a nuanced allusion is unlikely to have been intended by Mark or picked up by his readers.

15 With the reference to only one loaf—inadequate to feed twelve disciples—the reader might expect another feeding miracle; but the episode is headed in a different direction. Jesus warns his disciples about the "yeast of the Pharisees and of Herod." The rendering of *zumē* as "yeast" (NIV, NLT, TEV, etc.) instead of "leaven" is functionally correct as a symbol of permeating power but is not historically precise. Most bread in the ancient world was baked not with yeast but leaven (*zumē*), with a small amount of the previous week's dough reserved for this purpose (cf. BDAG 429; Marcus, 506). Here, as commonly in the OT and Judaism, leaven is a symbol of sin or evil. As only a very small amount of it is necessary to leaven a loaf of bread, so does evil have a permeating power (*TDNT* 2:905–6; cf. 1Co 5:6; Gal 5:9). The background is the command to the Jews associated with the exodus and the Feast of Unleavened Bread to remove all leaven from their homes and to eat unleavened bread for seven days (Ex 12:14–20).

What, then, is the leaven of the Pharisees and the leaven of Herod? In the synoptic parallels, Luke speaks only of the leaven of the Pharisees and identifies it as hypocrisy (12:1). Matthew replaces Herod with the Sadducees and identifies the leaven as the teaching of the Pharisees and Sadducees (16:12). Contextually, for Mark the leaven of the Pharisees refers most naturally to the preceding episode and their demand for a sign (8:11). But what about Herod? While in Luke 23:8 Herod will also seek a sign, Mark does not record this tradition. The leaven, therefore, probably refers generally to persistent unbelief and opposition to Jesus and his mission. Mark has already recorded Herod's concerns about Jesus in 6:14–16, and back in 3:6 the Pharisees and the Herodians—strange bedfellows—had conspired against him. While sharing little in common politically or religiously, the Pharisees and Herod (together with his Herodian supporters) both viewed Jesus as a threat to their authority and influence. Jesus warns the disciples not to let pride and selfish ambition blind them to the purpose of God being accomplished through him. These pitfalls will be precisely their areas of weakness in the chapters that follow.

16 The disciples demonstrate that they are clueless regarding Jesus' warning. The imperfect *dielogizonto* could be taken as durative, "they continued discussing," or could be inceptive, "they began to discuss" (Guelich, 424). In the former case, the disciples are already arguing about the bread when Jesus tries to interject a spiritual metaphor. They simply ignore him and keep arguing (cf. France, 317). In the latter case, Jesus begins with a metaphorical warning, which is misunderstood as a rebuke about not bringing enough bread, thus initiating the argument (so Lane, 281). The first view seems more likely in light of Mark's introductory verse about the lack of bread (v.14). In either case, the disciples show themselves to be preoccupied with temporal concerns and inattentive to Jesus' teaching.

17–21 Jesus responds with a series of five rhetorical questions (vv.17–18), two real questions the disciples must answer (vv.19–20), and a final (exclamatory) rhetorical question: "Do you still not understand?" (v.21). The result is a strong and pressing rebuke.

17–18 After chiding them about their obsession with bread (v.17a), the next two questions in 17b ("Do you still not see or understand? Are your hearts hardened?") echo Jesus' statement about "outsiders" in 4:11–12 and Mark's narrative comment about the disciples in 6:52, following the second boat incident. Hard-heartedness indicates persistent resistance to God's purposes (cf. Pharaoh in Ex 10:1, 20, 27; 11:10; 14:8 and Israel in Eze 3:7; 11:19; see Donahue and Harrington, 252). The language of v.18a ("Do you have eyes but fail to see, and ears but fail to hear?") is very close to Jeremiah 5:21 and Ezekiel 12:2 (cf. Eze 3:7; Ps 115:5–6) but is, like Jesus' quotation in 4:12, conceptually parallel to Isaiah 6:9–10. Jesus ominously warns that the disciples are in danger of becoming like "outsiders," who have eyes but do not see and ears but do not hear. Are they succumbing to the leaven of the Pharisees?

19–20 The bread the disciples should be focusing on was not their present provisions (or lack thereof) but the two miracles of multiplication they had witnessed; so Jesus rehearses with them the meager provisions, the numbers fed, and the basketfuls left over. The disciples' ability to recall the precise number of leftovers confirms that they remembered well how abundantly Jesus had provided for them on both occasions. Jesus' questions are meant, on the one hand, to remind the disciples that it is senseless to quarrel about a lack of bread when the Great Provider is with them in the boat. But of course, there was more to the feeding miracles than the satisfying of hunger. They revealed something extraordinary about the identity of Jesus: his unique authority and his role in God's plan of salvation. It is these characteristics, especially, which the disciples have failed to comprehend (cf. 6:52).

21 Almost pleadingly Jesus asks, "Do you still not understand?" This final question repeats almost verbatim the first question of v.17b and so frames Jesus' rebuke around this point. The necessity of the disciples to understand the purpose of God in Jesus will become the controlling theme of the following two chapters.

NOTES

15 The imperfect διεστέλλετο (*diestelleto*, from διαστέλλω, *diastellō*, GK *1403*, "warn") suggests that this statement did not stand alone but was part of an extended teaching discourse.

Strictly speaking, yeast refers either to (1) the fungus (*Saccharomyces*) present in the leaven, which caused the bread to rise, or more commonly (2) a commercial product made with this fungus that is used for baking, brewing, and as a source of vitamins and protein. In the rabbinical writings leaven is often a symbol for "the evil influence" (*yēṣer haraᶜ*), or wicked ways and human dispositions (cf. *Gen. Rab.* 34:10).

16 The majority of Greek MSS read ἔχομεν (*echomen*, "we have"), but a significant minority read ἔχουσιν (*echousin*, "they have"). The former makes the statement one of direct discourse, rendered either as "They were discussing with one another, 'We have no bread'" (cf. RSV), or with the ὅτι (*hoti*) functioning causally: "They were discussing with one another, 'It is because we have no bread'" (cf. NIV, NRSV, TEV). The latter (ἔχουσιν, *echousin*) could take ὅτι, *hoti*, as indicating indirect discourse, "They were discussing with one another that they had no bread" (cf. NASB, ESV); as causal, " ... because they had no bread" (cf. NLT); or as an indirect interrogative, " ... why they had no bread." See Taylor, 366, for support of this last interpretation.

19 As already noted in 8:8, two different words are used for basket in the two stories of the feeding of the multitudes. Κόφινος (*kophinos*, "lunch basket") is used in all six references to the feeding of the five thousand (Mt 14:20; 16:9; Mk 6:43; 8:19; Lk 9:17; Jn 6:13), while σπυρίς (*spyris*, "hamper") is used in all four references to the feeding of the four thousand (Mt 15:37; 16:10; Mk 8:8, 20). This consistency argues powerfully in favor of two separate incidents.

M. Healing a Blind Man at Bethsaida (8:22–26)

OVERVIEW

The presence of a story about a blind man immediately after Jesus warns the disciples of spiritual blindness (vv.17–18) is probably not coincidental. Many commentators have suggested that the two-stage restoration of the man's sight is seen by Mark as a metaphor for the partial blindness and gradual enlightenment of the disciples concerning the identity of Jesus and the suffering role of the Messiah. Unlike the Pharisees, who are spiritually blind, the disciples are "insiders" whom Jesus has chosen to share in the secret of God's kingdom (4:11). Yet they see only dimly, like the blind man after Jesus' first touch (v.24). Although Peter will confess in the next passage that Jesus is the Messiah (v.29), he will fail to comprehend his suffering role (v.32). The disciples, though partially enlightened, will not come to full comprehension until after the resurrection.

The passage is a transitional one, a bridge between what precedes and what follows. It has conceptual links to the healing of blind Bartimaeus in 10:46–52. The two stories about blindness frame the next section of Mark's gospel, where—after Peter's confession—Jesus will predict his death three times (8:31; 9:31; 10:33–34) and the disciples will repeatedly fail to comprehend the significance of his suffering role. The present passage thus prepares for 8:31–10:45, where the focus will be on the failure of the disciples to comprehend Jesus' own suffering path and his repeated call to follow him in cross-bearing discipleship.

The passage also has structural links to what precedes. As noted earlier (see Overview, 8:1–10), this episode is the fifth in a series of six episodes in 8:1–30 that mirror the six episodes of 6:31–7:37. Both series are comprised of a feeding miracle, a sea crossing, a conflict with the Pharisees, a discussion about bread, a healing, and a confession of faith. The counterpart to this episode—the healing of the deaf and mute man in 7:31–37—has a number of significant parallels. In both (1) the man is brought to Jesus by others; (2) they beg Jesus to heal him by laying hands on him; (3) Jesus takes the man off privately for the healing; (4) Jesus touches the organs affected and uses spittle for the healing; and (5) there is a command to silence (only implied in

8:26). Matthew and Luke omit both miracles, perhaps because of the unusual use of spittle and, in the present episode, the gradual nature of the healing. Both episodes are surely intended by Mark to show that Jesus is fulfilling the signs of eschatological salvation predicted in Isaiah 35:5 (a passage alluded to already in 7:37): "Then will the eyes of the blind be opened, and the ears of the deaf unstopped."

22They came to Bethsaida, and some people brought a blind man and begged Jesus to
touch him. 23He took the blind man by the hand and led him outside the village. When he
had spit on the man's eyes and put his hands on him, Jesus asked, "Do you see anything?"
24He looked up and said, "I see people; they look like trees walking around."
25Once more Jesus put his hands on the man's eyes. Then his eyes were opened, his
sight was restored, and he saw everything clearly. 26Jesus sent him home, saying, "Don't
go into the village.'"

COMMENTARY

22 The incident takes place at Bethsaida ("house of the fisher"), located on the eastern bank of the Jordan River where it flows into the Sea of Galilee. Once before, Mark mentioned Bethsaida as the intended destination of the boat trip following the feeding of the five thousand (6:45)—though the boat lands in Gennesaret instead (6:53; see comments at 6:45; Notes, 6:32, for the geographical difficulties.) At Bethsaida "some people" (Mark does not identify them) brought a blind man to Jesus for healing. As in the case of the paralytic (2:3) and the deaf and mute man (7:32), the blind man is brought by friends, who beg Jesus to touch him. Jesus frequently heals by touch in Mark (1:31, 41; 5:23; 6:5; 7:33) and is often approached by those wishing to touch him for healing (cf. 3:10; 5:28; 6:56).

23–24 Why did Jesus lead the blind man out of the town? Was it to avoid the clamor and excitement of the people, or perhaps to make personal contact with the man apart from the distraction of the crowd? Some see Jesus' departure from the town and his command not to return after the healing (v.26) as part of a judgment motif, parallel to Jesus' oracle against Chorazin and Bethsaida in Matthew 11:21–22. This perspective seems unlikely, however, since Mark does not record the judgment oracle and makes no mention of the town's unbelief. As in 7:33, 36, the motivation here is probably both to give the man personal attention and to avoid the public excitement that the miracle could provoke. The conclusion of the story, in which Jesus tells the man not to return to the town (v.26), suggests that the latter is the primary reason and that this feature is part of the secrecy motif so common throughout Mark (1:34, 44; 3:12; 5:43, 7:36; 8:30). Jesus wants to define his messiahship on his own terms and to avoid provoking messianic zeal among the townspeople that would compromise his God-ordained mission.

Jesus performs a double action: he spits on the man's eyes and lays his hands on him. The only parallel to such a double treatment is in John 9, where the blind man has his eyes anointed with clay and then washed in the Pool of Siloam. As noted above (v.22), the laying on of hands is common in Jesus' healings. The use of saliva occurs only here, in 7:33, and in John 9:6. Jesus asks the man, "Do you see anything?"—the only time in the Gospels when Jesus inquires concerning the efficacy of a healing. Its narrative purpose is to prepare the reader for the partial nature of the cure. Mark's noting that the man "looked up" is probably a play on words, since *anablepō* can mean either "look up" or "regain sight." The man's response is essentially, "Yes, I can see, but not clearly" (v.24). He sees people, but they look like trees—mere objects moving about. It is likely that the man had not been born blind since he is able to identify trees as trees, and since *anablepō* normally carries the sense, "see again" (cf. E. S. Johnson, "Mark viii.22–26: The Blind Man from Bethsaida," *NTS* 25 [1978–1979]: 376–77).

25 The second laying on of hands is unique in the healing ministry of Jesus. The result was a complete cure. Mark's account of it graphically records that fact with three parallel clauses: "his eyes were opened, his sight was restored, and he saw everything clearly." The word translated "clearly" (*tēlaugōs*) means "clearly at a distance" and indicates the completeness of the restoration of the man's sight.

The healing method has raised questions, both because of the use of spittle for the healing and because of the gradual nature of the healing. Jesus' first treatment appears to be only partially successful, so that he has to touch the man again. We have discussed the use of saliva at 7:33. Concerning the two-part healing, it is unlikely that Mark views this as a particularly difficult healing for Jesus, since elsewhere he portrays him as performing even more spectacular deeds with a single word or a touch—deeds such as raising the dead (5:41–42) and calming the sea (4:35–41). In 10:52 Jesus will heal Bartimaeus, another blind man, with a single command. Perhaps Jesus moved here only as quickly as the man's faith would allow, since throughout Mark's gospel faith is emphasized as requisite for healing (2:5; 4:40; 5:34, 36; 6:5; 9:23–24; 10:52; 11:22–24). One thing is certain: The episode is surely authentic, since the early church would hardly have created a story in which Jesus appears to be only partially successful on his first attempt.

26 Jesus orders the man to go home directly without first going into the town of Bethsaida. If this command is part of Mark secrecy motif, it is a bit unusual, since the man's friends would inevitably learn about the healing. Perhaps Jesus gives the directive so that he and his disciples can move on to other places before word spreads about the healing and thus escape unwanted messianic publicity (see v.30).

NOTES

22 Mark refers to Bethsaida as a "village" or "town" (κώμη, *kōmē*) in v.23, but Josephus (*Ant.* 18.2.1 §28) says that when Philip renamed Bethsaida "Julia" (see comments at 6:45; Notes, 6:45), he enlarged the village (κώμη, *kōmē*) to a city (πόλις, *polis*) by adding to its residents and increasing it size. Matthew (11:20) and John (1:44) also refer to Bethsaida as a "city" (πόλις, *polis*). Too much should not be made of this difference in terminology. These terms are often used rather loosely and interchangeably (note that little Bethlehem is called a "city" [πόλις, *polis*] in Lk 2:4, 11). Guelich, 432, citing A. H. M. Jones, *The Cities of the Eastern Roman Provinces* [2d ed.; Oxford: Clarendon, 1971], 282), further notes that despite its size and new name, Bethsaida remained organizationally a "village" under Herod Philip. Perhaps we should think of Bethsaida as an intermediary "town" somewhere between a village and a city in size.

23 Lane, 284, downplays the secrecy motif here by noting that most of the miracles in Mark were done in public. Only on three occasions did Jesus withdraw from the people to heal: the raising of Jairus's daughter (5:35–43), the healing of the deaf and mute man (7:31–37), and here. While Lane is certainly correct that Jesus commonly performed his miracles in public, this factor does not negate the undeniable presence of a secrecy motif in Mark (1:34, 44; 3:12; 5:43, 7:36; 8:30), and so it seems unnecessary to reject such a motivation here.

26 The variant reading "Don't go and tell anybody in the city" is an attempt to clarify the reason why Jesus ordered the man not to go into the town. Doubtless the reading was influenced by other passages in Mark in which Jesus explicitly enjoins silence.

REFLECTIONS

The importance of this story for Mark is that it anticipates the gradual opening of the disciples' eyes of understanding. It is also the second incident in a pair of stories that only Mark records (cf. 7:24–37) and that fulfill the OT messianic expectations of Isaiah 35:5–6. Mark uses both incidents to lead up to the revelation of the messianic dignity of Jesus to the disciples (8:27–30) and to prepare for Jesus' teaching concerning the suffering role of the Messiah and the high cost of cross-bearing discipleship.

N. Recognizing Jesus as Messiah (8:27–30)

OVERVIEW

The first major section of Mark's gospel (1:1–8:30) mounts to a climax with the story of the disciples' recognition of Jesus' messiahship. Peter's confession (8:27–30) and Jesus' teaching that follows (vv.28–33) represent the hinge on which the whole of Mark's narrative turns. While Jesus' messiahship has been introduced by the narrator (1:1), affirmed by the Father (1:11), and acknowledged by demons (1:24; 3:11), here for the first time a human being publicly confesses that Jesus is the Messiah. While the people still puzzle over Jesus' identity (v.28), his mighty miracles and acts of power have confirmed for the disciples—represented here by Peter—that Jesus is indeed God's agent of redemption, the Messiah. Yet like the blind man in the previous episode (v.24), Peter sees only partially. From this point forward Jesus will begin to teach that the Son of Man must go to Jerusalem to suffer and die. Peter's confession is followed by the first of three passion predictions and Jesus' teaching concerning the true significance of servant leadership.

Structurally, the episode is sometimes connected to the first section of the gospel (1:1–8:30) and sometimes to the second (8:31–10:52). The former option is the better one, since Peter's confession represents the conclusion reached by the disciples after witnessing Jesus' teaching and miracles up to this point in the narrative. Yet the passage is also closely linked to what follows (vv.31–38), and the two passages together form a transition. As Peter's confession looks backward to the result of Jesus' ministry so far, so the passion prediction looks forward, introducing "the way" of the cross on which Jesus is about to embark.

Many commentators have noted parallels between this episode and the previous one, in which the blind man is healed in two stages (8:22–26). Yet the parallel may be understood in two different ways: (1) The partial restoration of the blind man's sight may be seen to represent the incomplete understanding of the people (see Lane, 286–87 n. 54). The people say Jesus is John the Baptist, or Elijah, or one of prophets. Peter, on the other hand, recognizes his true identity as the Messiah. This parallel may be set out as follows:

Blind Man Healed		**Peter's Confession**	
8:22	Circumstances	8:27	Circumstances
8:23–24	Partial sight restored	8:28	Partial understanding of the people
8:25	Full sight restored	8:29	True understanding by Peter
8:26	Injunction to silence	8:30	Injunction to silence

(2) While these structural parallels are significant, Peter and the other disciples still have an inadequate understanding of Jesus' messiahship, which Jesus begins to correct in the following passage (vv.31–33). Under this second option, the blind man's partial healing parallels not the inadequate views of the people but Peter's incomplete understanding of Jesus' messiahship (vv.29, 32), which Jesus will clarify in vv.31–33 and in the passion predictions (9:30–32; 10:32–34). This parallel may be set out as follows:

Blind Man Healed		**Peter's Confession**	
8:23–24	Partial sight restored	8:29, 32	Partial understanding by Peter
8:25	Full sight restored	8:31–33	Full understanding revealed by Jesus

While the former structure has close parallels, the latter better fits Mark's narrative. In the passages that follow, the disciples will repeatedly fail to comprehend the suffering role of the Messiah (8:32; 9:32; 10:35–45).

[27]Jesus and his disciples went on to the villages around Caesarea Philippi. On the way he asked them, "Who do people say I am?"

[28]They replied, "Some say John the Baptist; others say Elijah; and still others, one of the prophets."

[29]"But what about you?" he asked. "Who do you say I am?"

Peter answered, "You are the Christ.'"

[30]Jesus warned them not to tell anyone about him.

COMMENTARY

27 Caesarea Philippi was located twenty-five miles north of Bethsaida at the foot of Mount Hermon, on a shelf of land 1,150 feet above sea level and overlooking the northern end of the Jordan River valley. Originally the city was called Paneas (surviving today as Banias) in honor of the Roman god Pan, a shrine to whom was located there. Herod Philip had rebuilt the ancient city and named it in honor of Tiberias

Caesar and himself. Thus it was known as Caesarea Philippi and was distinguished from Caesarea, the Roman city on the Mediterranean coast. Mark does not say that Jesus and the disciples went to the city of Caesarea Philippi but rather to the villages (*komai*) nearby. (Jesus seldom enters cities in Mark's gospel.) The trip is presented as a time of retreat, away from the bustling crowds. It was somewhere "on the way" that Jesus put to his disciples the crucial question, "Who do people say that I am?"

The historicity of Jesus' question has sometimes been challenged since, according to Jewish custom, it was the disciple, not the rabbi, who asked the questions, and since Jesus surely would have already known what the people were saying about him. Yet Jesus was no ordinary rabbi, and he did not ask the question simply to get information. He used it as preliminary to his second question in v.29 (cf. Cranfield, 268). Jesus' purpose was to provoke a confession of faith from the disciples.

28 The answers given are the same popular opinions expressed in 6:14–15 (see comments there). All three reveal the high regard in which the people held Jesus; they identified him as an authentic prophet and spokesperson for God. Yet all the answers also reflect an inadequate view of his true identity. John the Baptist, though a great prophet, played a preparatory role. He looked for another messenger greater than himself (1:7–8). A common Jewish concept of the day was that of "Elijah redivivus" (Elijah returned or revived), based on Malachi 3:1; 4:5 (see comments at Mk 6:15). But he too was only a forerunner of the Messiah. "One of the prophets" probably signifies the return of an OT prophet (contrast 6:15, where it is "a prophet, like one of the prophets"). There could be an allusion here to Jewish expectations for "the prophet," often linked to the prophet like Moses of Deuteronomy 18:15.

It is surprising that the disciples do not report that anyone said Jesus was the Messiah, especially since the demons recognized who he was and said so publicly (1:24; 3:11; 5:7). But his messiahship was veiled from the crowd. From a narrative perspective, the absence of messianic acclamations heightens the dramatic and the climactic nature of Peter's confession that follows.

29 Jesus now directs the question at the disciples. His use of *hymeis* ("you"), the emphatic pronoun, is particularly important. The NIV catches this nuance by repeating the "you": "But what about you?... Who do you say I am?" In other words Jesus is asking, "Who do you, my most intimate and trusted friends—in contrast to the other people who neither know me nor understand me—think I am?"

Mark's narrative has been building to this point. Throughout the gospel the people have consistently expressed amazement and awe at Jesus' teaching and miracles (1:22, 27; 2:12; 5:20, 42; 7:37). The disciples themselves demonstrate astonishment as Jesus walks on water (6:51), and they ask in amazement, "Who is this?" when he calms the stormy sea (4:41). Now their own rhetorical question is about to be answered.

Peter, true to form, is the one to speak: "You are the Messiah" (TNIV). Peter speaks not only for himself but also as spokesperson for the Twelve, and in his confession is stated one of the central themes of this gospel—"the good news about Jesus the Messiah" (1:1 TNIV). Peter's confession carries climactic significance. Although the Father has implicitly identified Jesus as the Messiah at his baptism ("my Son," 1:11), as have demons ("the Holy One of God," 1:24; "the Son of God," 3:11), here we find the first identification of Jesus as "the Messiah" since the first line of the gospel (1:1).

The Greek word *christos* ("Christ") translates the Hebrew *māšîaḥ* ("Messiah") and means the "Anointed One" of God. In the OT the word is used of anyone who was anointed with the holy oil, as, for example, the priests and kings of Israel (cf. Ex 29:7, 21; 1Sa 10:1, 6; 16:13; 2Sa 1:14, 16). The word carries with it the idea of chosenness by God, consecration to his service, and endowment with his power to accomplish the task assigned.

Though the word "Messiah" never appears as a title in the OT (with the possible exception of Da 9:25–26), the messianic idea has its origin in the OT prophecies concerning an ideal king from the line of David, Israel's greatest king and the man after God's own heart. In the Davidic covenant, God promised to establish David's "house" (= dynasty) and kingdom forever (2Sa 7:14–16). Israel's prophets took up this promise and repeatedly predicted that God would one day restore the Davidic line, with David's enthroned son and heir reigning forever in justice and righteousness (Isa 9:1–7; 11:1–16; Jer 23:5–6; 33:14–26; Eze 34:22–24; 37:24–28; Mic 5:1–5; Zec 9:9–13). During the intertestamental period, the designation "Anointed One" or "Messiah" began to be used with reference to this coming ideal king who would be empowered by God to deliver his people and establish his righteous kingdom. Particularly important in the development of the concept was the pseudepigraphic *Psalms of Solomon* (chs. 17–18), in which the coming ruler is spoken of as restoring David's kingdom to its former prosperity and greatness:

> See, Lord and raise up for them their king,
> the son of David, to rule over your servant Israel
> in the time known to you, O God.
> Undergird him with the strength to destroy the unrighteous rulers,
> to purge Jerusalem from gentiles
> who trample her to destruction;
> in wisdom and in righteousness to drive out the sinners from the inheritance;
> to smash the arrogance of sinners
> like a potter's jar;
> To shatter all their substance with an iron rod;
> to destroy the unlawful nations with the word of his mouth;
> At his warning the nations will flee from his presence;
> and he will condemn sinners by the thoughts of their hearts.
> He will gather a holy people
> whom he will lead in righteousness;
> and he will judge the tribes of the people
> that have been made holy by the Lord their God.
> He will not tolerate unrighteousness (even) to pause among them,
> and any person who knows wickedness shall not live with them.
> For he shall know them
> that they are all children of their God....
> There will be no unrighteousness among them in his days,
> for all shall be holy, and their king shall be the Lord Messiah.
>
> *Pss. Sol. 17:21–27, 32, in James Charlesworth,* The Old Testament Pseudepigrapha *(New York: Doubleday, 1985), 2:667.*

While the literature of first-century Judaism reveals a variety of messianic figures and expectations, the hope for an ideal king from David's line was the most prominent, appearing not only in the *Psalms of Solomon* but also in the Dead Sea Scrolls and other first-century Jewish writings. The ideas that clustered around this "son of David" or "Messiah" tended to be political and national in nature. It is probably for that reason that Jesus seldom used the term. Of its seven occurrences in Mark, only three of them are in sayings of Jesus (9:41; 12:35; 13:21); in none of these does he use the title of himself.

Jesus' reluctance to speak of himself as the Messiah does not mean that he did not believe himself to be the Messiah. Here in this verse (v.29) and in 14:6–62, he accepted the title when others applied it to him (cf. Jn 4:25–26). Cranfield, 270–71, comments,

> This is hardly surprising; for the title, in spite of all the false and narrow hopes that had become attached to it, was peculiarly fitted to express his true relation both to the OT and to the people of God.... The title, applied to Jesus, designates him as the true meaning and fulfillment of the long succession of Israel's anointed kings and priests, the King and Priest ... ; the Prophet anointed with the spirit of God, who fulfills the long line of Israel's prophets; and the One in whom the life of the whole nation of Israel finds its fulfillment and meaning, in whom and for whose sake the people of Israel were, and the new Israel now is, the anointed people of God.

Peter's confession revealed real insight into the nature of Jesus' person and mission, but his concept of Jesus' messiahship was far from perfect. Peter still had much to learn of Messiah's suffering, rejection, and death, as the immediately following incident reveals.

30 Jesus' strong injunction of silence arose out of his knowledge of the disciples' defective view of his messiahship. They still needed instruction about it before they would be given permission to proclaim it without restraint. Jesus, in warning not only Peter but also the other disciples not to make this revelation known, indicates that Peter's confession is meant to represent the opinion of all of them. The word "warned" (*epitimaō*, GK *2203*) is a strong one—the same term used of Jesus' "rebuke" of demons (1:25; 3:12), and one that will be used in the following verses of Peter's rebuke of Jesus (v.32) and Jesus' counterrebuke (v.33). The impression given is of intense emotion provoked by the extreme gravity of the present situation.

NOTES

27 Mark will use the expression ἐν τῇ ὁδῷ (*en tē hodō*, "on the way") four more times to describe Jesus' journey to Jerusalem (9:33–34; 10:32, 52).

29 For expectations related to the Davidic Messiah, see Strauss, *Davidic Messiah*, 35–57. On the diversity of messianic expectation in first-century Judaism, see J. W. Neusner, W. S. Green, and E. S. Frerichs, eds., *Judaisms and Their Messiahs at the Turn of the Christian Era* (Cambridge: Cambridge Univ. Press, 1987). The Qumran sectarians expected two messiahs, one from the line of David and one from the line of Aaron. For royal-Davidic expectations at Qumran, see 1QS 9:11; 1QSa 2:11–21; 1QSb 5:20–29; 4QFlor 1:10–13 (=4Q174); 4QPBless 1–5 (=4Q252); 4QpIsa[a] frg. D 1–5 (=4Q161); 4Q504; 4Q285.

V. THE JOURNEY TO JERUSALEM (8:31–10:52)

OVERVIEW

As noted in the previous section, the confession of Peter (8:27–30) and the first passion prediction (vv.31–33) together form a transition between the first (1:1–8:30) and second (8:31–10:52) major sections of the gospel. This transition is the hinge on which the whole narrative turns. Although the two episodes flow seamlessly from one to the other, with both occurring at the same place and time and both representing Jesus' teaching at Caesarea Philippi, v.31 clearly marks the beginning of a new narrative section. The tone and direction of the story now changes as Jesus begins to teach about the suffering role of the Christ and heads down the path toward the cross.

The structure of this new section centers on three predictions Jesus makes of his coming death and resurrection. What had previously been only hinted at (cf. 2:20; 3:6; 6:4) is now stated openly: the Son of Man must go up to Jerusalem, suffer and die, and on the third day be raised from the dead. This future is the secret of Jesus' messiahship, and it is now revealed. Mark also stresses what it will mean for Jesus' followers. Throughout the section are sayings about the true nature of discipleship, with a stress on suffering. Indeed the three passion predictions are part of a larger pattern of three "cycles" that follow a common structure. Three times Jesus predicts his death (8:31; 9:31; 10:33–34). Each time the disciples, responding with pride and incomprehension, fail to get it (8:32; 9:33–34; 10:35–41). Three times, therefore, Jesus must teach that the true path of discipleship is one of suffering and sacrifice (8:33–38; 9:35–37; 10:42–45). The climax comes in 10:45 with what many consider to be the thematic verse of Mark's gospel: "For even the Son of Man did not come to be served, but to serve, and to give his life as a ransom for many." The verse echoes the role of Isaiah's Servant of the Lord, who suffers an atoning death for the sins of the nation (Isa 52:12–53:13). As the narrative turns toward its climax, the reader is reminded that the Messiah must first pass through suffering and sacrifice on his way to glory.

Another purpose of this middle section of Mark's gospel is to provide for Jesus' move from Galilee (where almost his entire ministry took place) to Jerusalem for the climactic events. Mark does so by means of a travel narrative. Jesus progressively moves closer and closer to the Holy City. The final event—the healing of blind Bartimaeus (10:45–52)—takes place when Jesus is coming out of Jericho with the crowds of people on the way to the Passover Feast in Jerusalem. Chapter 11 opens with the triumphal entry into the city, which begins the third and final section of Mark's gospel.

This middle section, with its emphasis on the suffering of the Messiah and of those who follow him, must have had special meaning for the persecuted Christians to whom Mark is writing. He reminds them that to follow Jesus is to follow the path of suffering and even death.

A. First Prediction of the Passion (8:31–33)

31 He then began to teach them that the Son of Man must suffer many things and be
rejected by the elders, chief priests and teachers of the law, and that he must be killed and
after three days rise again. 32 He spoke plainly about this, and Peter took him aside and
began to rebuke him.
33 But when Jesus turned and looked at his disciples, he rebuked Peter. "Get behind me,
Satan!" he said. "You do not have in mind the things of God, but the things of men."

COMMENTARY

31 Jesus now begins to teach his disciples what messiahship really means. However, he does not refer to himself as "Messiah" but as "the Son of Man." Since this title is so important theologically, extended comment is in order (see comments at 2:10). "Son of Man" is by far Jesus' favorite self-designation in the Gospels, where it occurs eighty-one times. In them, no one else, neither friend nor foe, refers to Jesus as "the Son of Man" (unless 2:10, 28 are viewed as Mark's editorial comments; see comments there).

"Son of Man" is a Hebrew (and Aramaic) phrase that occurs in the OT. In the Psalms it means simply "human being" (cf. Pss 8:4; 80:17); and in Ezekiel, where it occurs over ninety times, it is the particular name by which God addresses the prophet. These OT passages throw some light on the NT usage of the phrase. The most important text, however, is Daniel 7:13–14:

> In my vision at night I looked, and there before me was one like a son of man [i.e., a human being], coming with the clouds of heaven. He approached the Ancient of Days and was led into his presence. He was given authority, glory and sovereign power; all peoples, nations and men of every language worshiped him. His dominion is an everlasting dominion that will not pass away, and his kingdom is one that will never be destroyed.

This passage, depicting the Son of Man as a heavenly figure who at the end time brings the kingdom to the oppressed on earth, is especially reflected in the sayings of Jesus in Mark's gospel that speak of the coming of the Son of Man with glory and power (8:38; 13:26; 14:62). The title has, however, been infused with additional meaning, especially in those passages that associate the Son of Man with suffering and death (8:31; 9:9, 12, 31; 10:33, 45; 14:21, 41). The combination of eschatological glory with suffering and death characterizes the "Son of Man" idea in Mark's gospel and elsewhere in the Synoptics. It is evident that Jesus considered "Son of Man" a messianic title because immediately following Peter's confession of him as the Christ, he began to teach them that the Son of Man (equivalent to Christ in v.29) must suffer. Presumably, Jesus preferred the title "Son of Man" because, unlike "Messiah," it was not freighted with political connotations that might prove harmful to his God-appointed mission.

The Son of Man "must [*dei*, GK *1256*] suffer." Gould, 153, remarks, "The necessity arises, first, from the hostility of men; secondly, from the spiritual nature of his work, which made it impossible for him to oppose force to force; and thirdly, from the providential purpose of God, who made the death of Jesus the central thing in redemption."

If *dei* refers to God's will in Scripture, the most likely reference is to the Suffering Servant passage in Isaiah 52:13–53:12. The Targum to Isaiah shows how difficult it was for the Jews to associate suffering with the Messiah. There the sufferings refer to the people and the other statements in the passage to the Messiah (cf. Emil Schürer, *The History of the Jewish People in the Age of Jesus Christ (175 BC–AD 135)* [Edinburgh: T&T Clark, 1979], 2.547–49). It is debated among scholars whether first-century Jews had any conception of a suffering Messiah or whether expectations for the Davidic Messiah were explicitly linked to the Suffering Servant of Isaiah 53. Some argue that evidence for a suffering Messiah existed in Judaism before Jesus' day, but that later Jewish sources suppressed it because of anti-Christian polemic (see *TDNT* 5:677–717; Cranfield, 277). Others such as H. H. Rowley (*The Servant of the Lord and other Essays on the Old Testament* [London: Lutterworth, 1952], 90) claim that "there is no serious evidence ... of the bringing together of the concepts of the suffering servant and the Davidic Messiah before the Christian era." Whether or not such an absolute conclusion can be drawn, it seems safe to conclude, both from the NT and from the paucity of references in Second Temple Judaism, that there was little widespread or popular expectation that the Messiah would suffer and/or die. Jesus' affirmations, therefore, come as a shock and surprise to the disciples.

Jesus predicted that the rejection of the Messiah would be by three main groups: the elders, the chief priests, and the teachers of the law. These three groups made up the Sanhedrin, the Jewish high court. The elders were the lay members of the Sanhedrin. The chief priests included not only Caiaphas, the high priest, and Annas, the emeritus high priest, but also the members of the high priestly families. The teachers of the law were the professional scribes and experts in the Mosaic law, who served as advisers to the Sanhedrin (see comments at 1:22). One might wonder where the Pharisees are in this listing, since they are portrayed as Jesus' consistent enemies throughout the gospel of Mark. The answer is that the Pharisees (and Sadducees) comprised religio-political parties rather than offices. The elders identified here would have included both Pharisees and Sadducees, and many of the scribes would have also been Pharisees. There were indeed Pharisees on the Sanhedrin, though they were in the minority.

The death of the Son of Man would be followed by his vindication: after three days he would be raised from the dead. "After three days" (which occurs also in Mk 9:31; 10:34) at first sight seems problematic, since Jesus was raised on a Sunday after his crucifixion on a Friday. Matthew (16:21; 17:23; 20:19) and Luke (9:22; 18:33) use the expression "on the third day," which may indicate they had difficulty with the Markan expression. Several explanations present themselves. Some have noted that "after three days" could be another way of saying "after a short period of time" (Hurtado, 142; cf. Hos 6:2; Jnh 1:17). More likely, the phrase reflects the Jewish custom of counting any part of a day as a day, so that "after three days" is the same as "on the third day" or "the day after tomorrow" (cf. France, 337; Taylor, 378). At least twice Josephus (*Ant.* 7.11.6 §§280–81; 8.8.1 §§214, 218) uses the expression "after three days" to refer to an event that occurs on the third day.

Verse 31 is particularly important because it is the only explanation in Mark's gospel of "the messianic secret" (see comments at 9:9). Jesus did not want his messiahship to be disclosed, for it involved suffering, rejection, and death. Igniting popular expectations of messiahship would have hindered, if not prevented, the accomplishment of his divinely ordained (*dei*, "must") messianic mission.

32 Jesus now spoke "plainly" or "with boldness" (*parrēsia*) about his suffering role as Son of Man and Messiah. The message got through to Peter, but he refused to accept it. Peter had the greatest difficulty in conceiving of messiahship in any other than the popular theological and political categories. A suffering Messiah? Unthinkable! The Messiah was a symbol of strength, not weakness. So Peter took Jesus aside and, amazingly, rebuked him. As noted above (v.31), the word translated "rebuked" (*epitimaō*) here and in v.33 is the same one used for the silencing of the demons (1:25; 3:12).

33 Jesus' words to Peter were not only very severe but also deliberately spoken in the presence of the other disciples ("Jesus turned and looked at his disciples"). They probably shared Peter's views and needed the rebuke too. The severity of the rebuke arises from Jesus' recognition, in Peter's attempt to dissuade him from going to the cross, the same temptation he had experienced from Satan at the outset of his ministry. Satan offered him the option of using the world's means for accomplishing his mission (cf. Mt 4:8–10). On that occasion Jesus rebuked him, "Away from me, Satan! For it is written: 'Worship the Lord your God, and serve him only'" (Mt 4:10). Here, too, Jesus recognized the satanic opposition in Peter. "'Get behind me, Satan!' he said. 'You do not have in mind the concerns of God, but merely human concerns'" (TNIV). Peter was opposing the divine will and so acting as a spokesperson for the archenemy. He was looking at things from a merely human perspective (*ta tōn anthrōpōn*)—probably from the popular Jewish expectation that the Messiah would achieve victory through power and conquest. That was the way the world thought. But it was not how God had planned Jesus' ministry and mission, which would entail suffering and sacrifice.

NOTES

31 For a balanced treatment of the question of Jewish expectations of a suffering Messiah, see S. H. T. Page, "The Suffering Servant Between the Testaments" (*NTS* 31 [1985]: 481–97). Some late rabbinic traditions speak of two messiahs, a "messiah son of Ephraim [or 'Joseph']," who suffers and dies in battle, and a "messiah son of David," who then achieves the victory. Yet this tradition of a suffering messiah probably arose long after the time of Jesus as a reaction to the defeat of Simon bar Kokhba in the second Jewish revolt of AD 132–135. See J. Klausner, *The Messianic Idea in Israel* (New York: Macmillan, 1955), 483–501; S. H. Levey, *The Messiah: An Aramaic Interpretation* (Cincinnati: Hebrew Union College Press, 1974), 15–17, 127–28; *TDNT* 9:526–27.

REFLECTIONS

Some interpreters, doubting that Jesus could have predicted his own death, have questioned the authenticity of his teaching and suggested that it is a prophecy invented by the church after Jesus' passion took place. But Witherington, 242–43, notes four pieces of evidence in support of its authenticity: (1) There is no reference to the crucifixion in any of the passion predictions. If later Christians had invented this saying, they would likely have used language incorporating the cross. (2) Each of the three passion predictions speak of the "Son of Man," the title characteristic of the historical Jesus but seldom used of Jesus by the church. (3) The phrase "after three days" is unlikely to have been invented by the postresurrection church because of the difficulties it raises. (4) The passion prediction does not display the later atonement theology of the church; rather, Jesus is at most portrayed as a martyr for the cause. Again, if the church had invented the saying, they would likely have couched it in atonement language.

We could add several points to those of Witherington: (5) There is little doubt historically that Jesus faced opposition and even hatred from Israel's religious leaders. Surely he must have foreseen his own death as a likely outcome of this conflict. (6) Jesus repeatedly identified himself with the OT prophets of Israel, who suffered and died for their outspoken witness (Mk 6:4 par.; 12:1–11 par.; Mt 5:12; 23:29–39; Lk 6:23, 26; 11:47–50; 13:33–35). The early church, preferring exalted titles for Jesus such as "Christ," "Son of God," and "Lord," is unlikely to have created these "prophet" sayings.

B. Requirements of Discipleship (8:34–9:1)

OVERVIEW

After rebuking Peter for his false conception of the Messiah's mission, Jesus teaches how the Messiah's suffering relates to his followers. The purpose of the section is to encourage and strengthen believers who are facing persecution and trials. Mark is saying to them that such experiences are normal in the life of discipleship. Lane, 306, writes, "Jesus had called his own disciples to the realization that suffering is not only his destiny but theirs."

34Then he called the crowd to him along with his disciples and said:"If anyone would
come after me, he must deny himself and take up his cross and follow me. 35For whoever
wants to save his life will lose it, but whoever loses his life for me and for the gospel will
save it. 36What good is it for a man to gain the whole world, yet forfeit his soul? 37Or what
can a man give in exchange for his soul? 38If anyone is ashamed of me and my words in
this adulterous and sinful generation, the Son of Man will be ashamed of him when he
comes in his Father's glory with the holy angels."
9:1And he said to them, "I tell you the truth, some who are standing here will not taste
death before they see the kingdom of God come with power."

COMMENTARY

34 Now Jesus addresses the crowd as well as his disciples. This expansion of the audience is surprising, since the previous context has suggested a private retreat with the disciples far from the Galilean crowds. The narrative and theological significance for Mark is that the requirements for following Jesus are not just for the Twelve but also for all Christians. Jesus turns and addresses all those who would follow him. Two requirements of discipleship are (1) denial of self and (2) taking up one's cross and following Jesus. By denial of self, Jesus does not mean resisting specific material things. He means the renouncing of self—ceasing to make self the central focus of one's life and actions. Doing so involves a fundamental reorientation of the principle of life. God, not self, must be at the center of one's life.

Here is the first reference to the cross in Mark's gospel. It indicates an awareness on Jesus' part of the manner in which he would die. Cross bearing does not refer to some irritation in life; rather, it involves the path to crucifixion. The picture is of a victim, already condemned, required to carry his cross on the way to the place of execution, as Jesus was required to do (Lk 23:26; cf. Mk 15:21). Crucifixion, though not invented by the Romans, became one of their favorite methods of execution. It served not only as capital punishment but also as a means of terrorizing subject peoples. Although not generally practiced by the Jews, the method was well-known to the Jews of Jesus' day because of their Roman overlords. As to method, the main stake or *palus* generally remained at the place of execution, while the victim(s) would be forced to carry the crossbeam or *patibulum* (Lk 23:26). The condemned person would be affixed to the cross with ropes or, as in the case of Jesus, with nails (Jn 20:25). Death resulted from loss of blood, exposure, exhaustion, and/or suffocation, as the victim tried to lift himself to breathe. Victims sometimes lingered in agony for days. Crucifixion was viewed by ancient writers as the most ignoble of deaths; it was cruel, barbaric, and appropriate only for the most despicable of enemies and offenders (see Hengel, *Crucifixion in the Ancient World*). To bear the cross, therefore, meant to follow Jesus, even to the point of humiliation, extreme suffering, and death.

35–37 The meaning of these sayings depends on a wordplay with the Greek word *psychē* (GK *6034*), which can refer either to physical life ("life"), or spiritual/eschatological life ("soul"). Jesus warns that by denying him, one's physical life (*psychē*) may be saved, but one's eschatological life (*psychē*)—i.e., one's salvation—will be lost. Conversely, to lose one's physical life by remaining true to Christ—i.e., by confessing him under duress—is to be assured of eternal life and salvation. Thus it would have sounded a warning to anyone in Mark's church who might be thinking of defecting under trial. "For me" stresses the absoluteness of Jesus' claim for allegiance, and "for the gospel" is probably a reference to the preaching of the gospel for which people are to give their lives.

Verses 36–37 emphasize the incomparable worth of the *psychē*, here meaning "eschatological life" or "soul." Not even "the whole world" compares to it in value (v.36). And once a person has forfeited his or her share in eternal life (in this context, by denying Jesus), there is no way that person can get it back (v.37). Even the whole world, if they had it, could not buy back eternal life—another stern warning against recanting the Christian faith.

The language of profit and loss here echoes Psalm 49, where the psalmist warns against trusting in riches by pointing out that no ransom or redemption price is enough to purchase a life:

> No one can redeem the life of another
> or give to God a sufficient ransom—
> the ransom for a life is costly,
> no payment is ever enough—
> so that someone should live on forever
> and not see decay.
>
> *Psalm 49:7–9 TNIV*

38 Here is the climax of the warning. To be ashamed of Jesus and his words (the equivalent of saving one's life in v.35) has serious consequences. The Son of Man will be ashamed of that person when he "comes in his Father's glory with the holy angels." The Hebrew parallelism in this verse clearly identifies the "of me" (Jesus) in the first part with the Son of Man in the second part. The reference to "an adulterous and sinful generation" echoes Jesus' exasperation with the Pharisees ("this generation") and their request for a sign in 8:12. It also recalls the characterization by the OT prophets of Israel's idolatry as marital unfaithfulness to God (cf. Isa 1:4, 21; Eze 16:32; Hos 2:3; see Lane, 310). Those who are ashamed of Jesus and refuse to follow him in cross-bearing discipleship have allied themselves with the opponents of the kingdom of God and will suffer the same shame and loss on the day of judgment.

Most commentators understand the "coming" here to be the parousia, the return of the Son of Man to judge and to save. The mention of "his Father's glory with the holy angels" suggests the final judgment (cf. 1Th 4:13–5:11; 2Th 1:6–10; see Hurtado, 142; Lane, 310). France, 342–43, however, argues that the passage refers to the entrance of the Son of Man into his heavenly glory (so also at 13:26 and 14:62). Justification for this interpretation, he says, is the context of Daniel 7:13–14, where the Son of Man is presented before the throne of God and receives sovereign authority over the nations. The point is that just as Jesus' rejection on earth will lead to vindication and glory in heaven, so his followers should be prepared for a parallel experience.

9:1 Jesus prefaces his concluding remarks with his solemn *amēn* formula: "I tell you the truth" (see comments at 3:28). The saying that follows is one of the most difficult in Mark's gospel. What does it mean that "some who are standing here will not taste death before they see the kingdom of God come with power"? The metaphor "taste death" is a Hebraism that means "experience death." In the present context it suggests violent death for the sake of Jesus (see vv.34–35). But what does Jesus mean that some of those present will "see the kingdom of God come with power"? The question is further complicated by the fact that some commentators distinguish between what Jesus intended and how Mark understood the saying. For example, Taylor, 385–86, thinks that Mark viewed the saying as at least partially fulfilled in the transfiguration (9:2–8), although Jesus originally intended it to refer to "a visible manifestation of the rule of God displayed in the life of an elect community."

Whether for Jesus or Mark, the main interpretations are (1) the transfiguration, which immediately follows in 9:2–8 (so Cranfield, 287–88; Lane, 313; Witherington, 262); (2) the death and resurrection of Jesus (so Garland, 330; Edwards, 269); (3) the destruction of Jerusalem in AD 70 (so Wright, *Jesus and the Victory of God*, 365); (4) the coming of the Holy Spirit at Pentecost (so Swete, 186); (5) the parousia—the return of Jesus and the consummation of the kingdom (in which case Jesus was mistaken in predicting the end of the age before the death of his disciples; so Manson, *Teaching of Jesus*, 277–84; Nineham, 231–32); or (6) the present manifestation of the kingdom—evidenced in the powerful deeds of Jesus—which the disciples must see with eyes of faith (so Evans, 29; cf. Dodd, *Parables of the Kingdom*, 53–54).

The most widely held view—and the most likely—is that the reference is to the transfiguration that follows. Mark's placement of the saying and his explicit linking of the two ("after six days," 9:2) would seem to confirm that, for him at least, the purpose of the saying is to form a transition between the transfiguration (9:2–8)—a momentary manifestation of the power of the kingdom—and the parousia (8:38), the full manifestation of it. On this understanding the transfiguration anticipates and guarantees the parousia. The greatest difficulty with this view is the oddity in Jesus' saying that some of those present would not die until they saw the kingdom come, when the event was only a few days away. Cranfield, 500, answers this objection by noting that the "some" (*tines*) is intended to distinguish the three disciples who witnessed the transfiguration (Peter, James, and John) from the others. While these three would witness the power of the kingdom during their ordinary natural lives, the others would not see it until the final judgment.

NOTES

35–37 Another, less likely interpretation that does not depend on a wordplay is that ψυχή (*psychē*, GK *6034*) means "true spiritual self" or "soul" throughout these verses, and that the sense is that the person wishing to save his own soul will end up losing it, but the one who turns over ("loses") his whole soul/life/self to Jesus will save it. See E. Best, *Following Jesus: Discipleship in the Gospel of Mark* (JSNTSup 4; Sheffield: JSOT Press, 1988), 41–42.

9:1 For a fuller listing of the various views of the coming of the kingdom here and the supporters of them, see A. Plummer, *Luke* (ICC; Edinburgh: T&T Clark, 1900), 249; K. E. Brower, "Mark 9:1: Seeing the Kingdom in Power," *JSNT* 6 (1980): 17–41.

C. The Transfiguration (9:2–8)

OVERVIEW

The transfiguration is a revelation of the glory of the Son of God, a glory now hidden but to be manifested completely and openly at the end of the age, when the Son of Man will come in the glory of his Father to render judgment on the world (cf. Mk 8:38).

In the OT, mountains are places of divine revelation, and Jesus' transfiguration specifically recalls Moses' ascent to Mount Sinai to receive the law. Garland, 342, succinctly sets out a number of key parallels:

Jesus takes three disciples up the mountain (Mk 9:2)
Jesus is transfigured and his clothes become radiantly white (Mk 9:2–3)
God appears in veiled form in an overshadowing cloud (Mk 9:7)
A voice speaks from the cloud (Mk 9:7)
The people are astonished when they see Jesus after he descends from the mountain (Mk 9:15)

Moses goes with three named persons plus seventy of the elders up the mountain (Ex 24:1, 9)
Moses' skin shines when he descends from the mountain after talking with God (Ex 34:29)
God appears in veiled form in an overshadowing cloud (Ex 24:15–16, 18)
A voice speaks from the cloud (Ex 24:16)
The people are afraid to come near Moses after he descends from the mountain (Ex 35:30)

The introductory reference to "after six days" also recalls the six days the cloud covered Mount Sinai as Moses prepared to ascend (Ex 24:15–16). Together these allusions suggest that Mark views the transfiguration as the revelation of a new and greater Moses, whose coming supersedes that of the old covenant at Sinai.

The purpose of the transfiguration is directed toward the disciples. Notice the expressions "before them" (vv.2, 4) and "enveloped them" (v.7), and observe also that the voice from the cloud speaks to them (v.7). Mark places the transfiguration here as a confirmation of the difficult teaching Jesus had given to the disciples about his suffering and death (cf. 8:31–38). Six days had elapsed since that startling disclosure. So additional revelation of God's purpose in his Son was needed. To a select group of Jesus' disciples, this revelation comes via the transfiguration with God's voice booming out of the cloud: "This is my Son, whom I love. Listen to him!" (v.7). This was a direct order given to Peter, James, and John—and through them to the rest of the Twelve—to heed Jesus' disclosure at Caesarea Philippi.

[2]After six days Jesus took Peter, James and John with him and led them up a high
mountain, where they were all alone. There he was transfigured before them. [3]His clothes

became dazzling white, whiter than anyone in the world could bleach them. [4]And there
appeared before them Elijah and Moses, who were talking with Jesus.
[5]Peter said to Jesus, "Rabbi, it is good for us to be here. Let us put up three shelters—
one for you, one for Moses and one for Elijah." [6](He did not know what to say, they were so
frightened.)
[7]Then a cloud appeared and enveloped them, and a voice came from the cloud: "This is
my Son, whom I love. Listen to him!"
[8]Suddenly, when they looked around, they no longer saw anyone with them except
Jesus.

COMMENTARY

2 Mark rarely gives specific time references, so his reference here "after six days" is significant, pointing back to the previous event and Jesus' prediction that some standing there would experience the power of the kingdom of God. The "some" refers to Peter, James, and John, the inner circle of the disciples. The same three men were present at the raising of Jairus's daughter (5:37–43) and were with Jesus in Gethsemane (14:33).

The high mountain is not identified. The traditional site is Mount Tabor, a loaf-shaped mountain in the middle of the Plain of Jezreel. But Tabor is not a "high mountain" (1,843 feet above sea level) and so is an unlikely site. Mount Hermon, which is over 9,000 feet high, is a more probable site. It is located near Caesarea Philippi, where the event Mark has just recorded took place. The word *metamorphoō* (see *TDNT* 4:755–59) means "to change into another form" and is used only here, in the parallel in Matthew 17:2, and in Romans 12:2 and 2 Corinthians 3:18, where it describes the believer's progressive change into the moral likeness of Jesus Christ. Here the verb does not mean a change in Jesus' nature but an outward transformation of his appearance that reflects his true nature (cf. Edwards, 263).

3 Jesus' clothes became "dazzling white"—only Mark adds "whiter than anyone in the world could bleach them." If the event took place at night, its dazzling nature was enhanced. For a moment they saw the human appearance of Jesus "changed into that of a heavenly being in the transfigured world" (*TDNT* 4:758). In the NT and apocalyptic Judaism, heavenly beings are often described in shining white clothing (Mk 16:5; Mt 28:3; Lk 24:4; Jn 20:12; Ac 1:10; Da 7:9; *1 En.* 14:20; *2 En.* 2:8–9; *T. Job* 46:7–9; cf. France, 351).

4 Mark's reference to "Elijah and Moses" reverses the historical order. (Matthew and Luke have "Moses and Elijah," as does v.5.) This order is probably because of the discussion about Elijah that follows while Jesus and the disciples are descending the mountain (v.11). But why these two? If what the disciples saw was a glimpse of Jesus' final state of glory, then Moses and Elijah's function may be to announce the end. In Jewish expectation, Elijah clearly played that role (cf. vv.11–12; Mal 4:5). There was also an expectation for an eschatological "prophet like Moses" drawn from Deuteronomy 18:15 (cf. Ac 3:22; 7:37). In some Jewish traditions, Elijah and Moses appear together as a sign of the coming end of the age (*Deut. Rab.*

3:17 [on 10:1]; *4 Ezra* 6:25–26; cf. Plummer, 214; Garland, 344). Another possibility is that Elijah and Moses represent the Law and the Prophets—i.e., the OT, which was being superseded, or at least fulfilled, by Jesus. Moses well represents the Law, but one would perhaps have expected one of the great writing prophets such as Isaiah or Jeremiah, instead of Elijah, to represent the Prophets. France, 352, also notes that both Moses and Elijah were men of Mount Sinai (Ex 19; 1Ki 19):"It was on the mountain that each of them met with God and heard his voice, and now Jesus on another high mountain meets with them before God again speaks from the cloud." Each man represents divine revelation and affirmation.

How Peter, James, and John recognized them is not stated. Moule, 70, writes, "The fact that both figures were, in the OT, described as having ended their lives on earth in a mysterious way (Dt 34:6; 2Ki 2:11) adds to the appropriateness of their mysterious reappearance in this preview of the glorious climax of Jesus' ministry."

5 True to form, Peter responded impulsively. His words "Rabbi, it is good for us to be here" show that he was greatly moved by the experience yet did not understand it. His odd comment about building shelters—"one for you [Jesus], one for Moses and one for Elijah"—has been explained in various ways. Some suggest he wanted to prolong the event by providing a place of rest and hospitality for these esteemed visitors. Another possibility is that Peter is thinking of the temporary booths erected for the Feast of Tabernacles (Lev 23; Dt 16). But there is no indication in the context that the transfiguration took place during this festival. Or, since the word for "shelter" (*skenē*) is the same Greek word used in the LXX for the OT tabernacle in the wilderness, Peter may be thinking of an eschatological new exodus. Lane, 319, writes, "The desire to erect new tents of meeting where God can again communicate with men implies that Peter regards the time of the second exodus as fulfilled and the goal of the Sabbath rest achieved." If this is the case, Peter desires to see the glory of the kingdom without the suffering and death Jesus has predicted. He again stumbles at the necessity of a suffering Messiah.

6 Before we debate too much Peter's intention, we must remember that Mark immediately dismisses it as irrelevant: "He did not know what to say, they were so frightened." Notice that not only Peter but the other disciples as well were afraid and at a loss for words. However, impetuous Peter could not abide the silence, so he impulsively spoke. But what he said was not worth saying.

7–8 The OT background of v.7 lies in the passages where the cloud is "the vehicle of God's presence (Exod 16:10; 19:9; 24:15f.; 33:9; Lev 16:2; Num 11:25), the abode of His glory, from which He speaks" (Taylor, 391). The cloud "enveloped them"—i.e., Elijah, Moses, and probably Jesus. At Jesus' baptism, the voice had spoken to him (1:11); here the disciples are addressed. The transfiguration experience was for their spiritual instruction. As with the voice at the baptism (1:11), "This is my Son" echoes Psalm 2:7 (cf. 2Sa 7:14) and so presents Jesus as the messianic king from David's line. "Listen to him!" recalls Deuteronomy 18:15 ("you must listen to him") and so likely presents Jesus as the "prophet like [Moses]" predicted there. This allusion adds weight to the strong Moses/Sinai imagery of the transfiguration noted above.

To what were they to listen? While Jesus' teaching in general is certainly in view, the command goes back especially to the teaching in the previous episode concerning the suffering role of the Messiah. Although the tendency of Peter and the disciples—thinking from a merely human perspective (8:33)—is to dismiss such a role as inappropriate and offensive for the glorious Messiah (8:32), the Father now provides divine confirmation that Jesus' words are in fact true. God's purpose and will for Jesus is that he should follow the way of the cross. "Listen" must be given its full sense of *obedience*. The only true listening known in the Bible is listening that results in obedience (cf. Jas 1:22–24). Those who would "hear" Jesus must take up their cross and follow him, as Jesus has called them to do (8:34).

The divine voice also confirms the uniqueness of Jesus. Calvin, 2:314, correctly points out that when God "enjoins us to *hear him*, he appoints [Christ] to be the supreme and only teacher of his Church. It was his design to distinguish Christ from all the rest, as we truly and strictly infer from these words, that by nature he was God's *only Son*" (emphasis his). This uniqueness of Christ is highlighted by the fact that suddenly—as suddenly as they had appeared—Moses and Elijah were gone; and the three disciples "no longer saw anyone with them except Jesus" (v.8). Jesus now stands alone as the culmination and fulfillment of the OT revelation.

NOTES

2–8 Rudolf Bultmann (*History of the Synoptic Tradition*, 259) and others have argued that the transfiguration was originally a resurrection account that has been projected back into the life of Jesus (cf. T. J. Weeden, *Mark: Traditions in Conflict* [Philadelphia: Fortress, 1971], 118–26; F. Watson, "The Social Function of Mark's Secrecy Theme," *JSNT* 24 [1985]: 55). This idea is unlikely to be true, since the Gospels' resurrection appearances have little in common with the glorious appearance of Jesus on the mountain. As Gundry, 471, points out, "None of the early accounts of his appearances ... describe his garments as glistening and exceedingly white" (for more, see R. H. Stein, "Is the Transfiguration [Mark 9:2–8] a Misplaced Resurrection-Account?" *JBL* 95 [1976]: 79–96; Gundry, 471–74).

2 Another possible site for the transfiguration has been suggested by W. Liefeld ("The Transfiguration Narrative," in *New Dimensions in New Testament Study*, ed. R. N. Longenecker and M. C. Tenney [Grand Rapids: Zondervan, 1974], 167). His suggestion is Mount Meron, which rises to the height of 3,926 feet and is located to the west of the Sea of Galilee. Since the name of the mountain on which the transfiguration took place is not given in the Gospels, its certain identification is not possible.

4 Elijah's role with reference to the end times appears to have arisen because he, like Enoch (Ge 5:24), did not die (2Ki 2:11). Although Moses died and was buried by God (Dt 34:5–6), the mysterious manner of this death led to speculation in some Jewish circles that he did not die (see *TDNT* 2:939 n. 92).

D. The Coming of Elijah (9:9–13)

9As they were coming down the mountain, Jesus gave them orders not to tell anyone
what they had seen until the Son of Man had risen from the dead. 10They kept the matter
to themselves, discussing what "rising from the dead" meant.
11And they asked him, "Why do the teachers of the law say that Elijah must come first?"

[12]Jesus replied, "To be sure, Elijah does come first, and restores all things. Why then is it written that the Son of Man must suffer much and be rejected? [13]But I tell you, Elijah has come, and they have done to him everything they wished, just as it is written about him."

COMMENTARY

9 On the way down the mountain, Jesus gave the three disciples orders to keep their experience of the transfiguration secret till after the resurrection of the Son of Man. This order is the last command to silence in Mark (but see 9:30) and the first to be qualified with a time reference: the disciples should keep the secret only until the resurrection (cf. Edwards, 272). The transfiguration was a revelation of the glory of the Son of Man. To proclaim this glory before the cross would have been too much in keeping with current popular ideas of messiahship. First must come suffering and death. Then after the resurrection (in itself a manifestation of the glory of the Son of Man), divulging the transfiguration experience would be appropriate. But until that time Jesus enjoined the disciples to keep secret what they had seen.

As we have seen, on many occasions in Mark's gospel—especially after Jesus performs a miracle—he commands those involved to keep the matter quiet (cf. 1:25, 34, 43–44; 3:11–12; 5:43; 7:36; 8:26, 30; 9:9). Based on these texts, William Wrede developed his theory of a "messianic secret" (see Introduction, p. 674). He held that the tradition about Jesus was nonmessianic; that is, Jesus never actually claimed to be the Messiah, and there were no authentic traditions that affirmed him as such. It was the post-Easter church that came to believe and teach that Jesus was the Messiah. In order to resolve this contradiction, Mark, according to Wrede, created incidents in which Jesus commands that his messiahship be kept secret and thus accounted for the nonmessianic tradition. One problem with Wrede's theory is that there is little evidence that a nonmessianic tradition about Jesus ever existed. Every stratum of gospel material contains messianic implications. Another problem is that in Mark's narrative the secret is seldom kept. Although Jesus tries to calm messianic fervor, people repeatedly go out and proclaim Jesus' fame far and wide. If Mark is using this narrative device to show why Jesus' messiahship remained a secret during his ministry, he has done a very poor job of it. Instead, the impression gained is that though Jesus tried to conceal his messianic identity (for the purpose of defining it himself), there was enormous popular excitement surrounding him. In fact, it is this point that Mark is making.

10 On this occasion the disciples obeyed Jesus' injunction. But they were puzzled by his statement about the resurrection of the Son of Man. As Jews they were familiar with the idea of a general resurrection of the dead at the time of the final judgment. But this special resurrection of the Son of Man baffled them.

11 Apparently, the disciples did not feel free to ask Jesus what he meant by his "rising from the dead" (v.10). Instead they asked him about Elijah. No doubt the fact that three of them had seen Elijah at the transfiguration reminded them of what the teachers of the law said about him—that he would come before the Messiah and restore all things (Mal 4:5–6; see comments at 6:15). Restoring all things involved, among other tasks, leading the people to repentance. Now if Elijah comes first and does his preparatory work, how is it that when the Son of Man comes he finds people so unprepared for him that they completely reject him and indeed kill him? If this reconstruction correctly represents the thinking of the disciples, then behind their question lay the idea of a suffering Messiah—a stumbling by which they were still perplexed.

12 Jesus' answer is that the teachers of the law are right about Elijah. He will come first and restore all things. But whatever that involves, it does not preclude the suffering and rejection of the Son of Man. The Scriptures, Jesus says, predict it: "the Son of Man must suffer much and be rejected." This comment is probably an allusion to Isaiah 53:3, where the Suffering Servant is "despised and rejected by men." There may also be an allusion to Psalm 118:22: "The stone the builders rejected has become the capstone." Jesus will cite this latter passage in Mark 12:10 (see Notes).

13 Jesus' statement about Elijah goes beyond that of the teachers of the law: not only must Elijah come; he already has come in the person of John the Baptist. Though John is not named here, the reference to him is obvious. "They have done to him everything they wished" is a reference to his treatment by Herod, i.e., his imprisonment and death. "Just as it is written about him" probably refers to what the OT says about Elijah in his relationship to Ahab and Jezebel (cf. 1Ki 19:1–2). Herod and Herodias were foreshadowed in Ahab and Jezebel. Although there is no prediction of suffering associated with Elijah's eschatological ministry, the main thrust of Jesus' reply in vv.12–13 makes clear to the disciples that the eschatological ministry of Elijah in no way does away with the necessity for the Son of Man to suffer and die.

NOTES

10 For a detailed discussion of the resurrection hope in the OT and Judaism, see Wright, *Resurrection of the Son of God*, 85–206.

12 The verb translated "be rejected" (ἐξουδενέομαι, *exoudeneomai*) is a different verb from that used in the LXX of Psalm 118:22 and in Mark 12:10 (ἀποδοκιμάζομαι, *apodokimazomai*). However, when Psalm 118:22 is quoted in Acts 4:11, ἐξουδενέομαι (*exoudeneomai*) is used, so the allusion may still be present in Mark's mind.

12–13 Some commentators interpret these verses differently, claiming that the first sentence in v.12 should be punctuated as a question (so Marcus, *Way of the Lord*, 97–107; Garland, 347–48). In this case, Jesus asks "Is it really true that Elijah comes first and restores all things?" (v.12a). If Elijah's role was to restore all things, Jesus asks, "Why then is it written that the Son of Man must suffer much and be rejected?" (v.12b). Jesus then clarifies that Elijah has indeed come (in the person of John), but has suffered martyrdom (v.13). The fulfillment of the prophecies has taken an unexpected turn—at least from the perspective of the teachers of the law—with reference both to the coming of Elijah and the coming of the Son of Man. Both would first suffer before seeing vindication. If this interpretation is correct, the prophecy of Malachi is particularly significant (Mal 4:5–6). There it is said that if the people do not respond to Elijah's ministry of restoration and reconciliation between fathers and children, then God "will come and strike the land with a curse" (4:6). In Mark 13 Jesus predicts that in the days ahead "brother will betray brother to death, and a father his child" (13:12) and that the temple will be destroyed (cf. Garland, 347). Though the ministries of both John the Baptist ("Elijah") and Jesus (the Son of Man) will end in death and apparent failure, all these outcomes were predicted in Scripture and are part of God's plan to provide salvation.

E. Healing a Boy with an Evil Spirit (9:14–29)

OVERVIEW

This episode is one of only three healing stories in the second part of Mark's gospel (8:31–10:52). The other two are the healing of a blind man in Bethsaida (8:22–26) and the healing of blind Bartimaeus in Jericho (10:46–52). These two episodes, as we have seen, form bookends framing the whole second section (see Overview, 8:22–26). The gradual restoration of the blind man's sight in Bethsaida symbolically represents the gradual enlightenment of the slow-to-learn disciples. The reason there are so few miracles in the second section seems clear. While the purpose of Mark's first section was to demonstrate Jesus' messianic power and authority (1:1–8:30), the purpose of the second is to reveal his suffering role and to highlight the disciples' failure to understand this mission. The exorcism here fits well this purpose, for it highlights the spiritual weakness and lack of faith of the disciples.

As is often the case, Mark records a more elaborate account of this story than either Matthew or Luke. The author clearly relishes the role of storyteller, as shown in his utilizing vivid descriptions and drama more than the other Synoptics. Matthew especially tends to abbreviate Mark's colorful narrative.

14When they came to the other disciples, they saw a large crowd around them and the
teachers of the law arguing with them. 15As soon as all the people saw Jesus, they were
overwhelmed with wonder and ran to greet him.
16"What are you arguing with them about?" he asked.
17A man in the crowd answered, "Teacher, I brought you my son, who is possessed
by a spirit that has robbed him of speech. 18Whenever it seizes him, it throws him to the
ground. He foams at the mouth, gnashes his teeth and becomes rigid. I asked your disciples to drive out the spirit, but they could not."
19"O unbelieving generation," Jesus replied, "how long shall I stay with you? How long
shall I put up with you? Bring the boy to me."
20So they brought him. When the spirit saw Jesus, it immediately threw the boy into a
convulsion. He fell to the ground and rolled around, foaming at the mouth.
21Jesus asked the boy's father, "How long has he been like this?"
"From childhood," he answered. 22"It has often thrown him into fire or water to kill him.
But if you can do anything, take pity on us and help us."

[23]"'If you can'?" said Jesus."Everything is possible for him who believes."
[24]Immediately the boy's father exclaimed, "I do believe; help me overcome my unbelief!"
[25]When Jesus saw that a crowd was running to the scene, he rebuked the evil spirit. "You deaf and mute spirit," he said, "I command you, come out of him and never enter him again."
[26]The spirit shrieked, convulsed him violently and came out. The boy looked so much like a corpse that many said, "He's dead."
[27]But Jesus took him by the hand and lifted him to his feet, and he stood up.
[28]After Jesus had gone indoors, his disciples asked him privately, "Why couldn't we drive it out?"
[29]He replied, "This kind can come out only by prayer.'"

COMMENTARY

14 The episode occurs when Jesus, Peter, James, and John rejoin the other disciples after the experience of the transfiguration. The disciples were engaged in a debate with the teachers of the law while a large crowd looked on. If the transfiguration took place on Mount Hermon, the presence of the teachers of the law so far north in Palestine indicates their concern in monitoring the teaching and preaching of Jesus. As elsewhere in Mark, they stand in opposition to Jesus and his disciples and seek to discredit them (cf. 2:6, 16; 3:22; 7:1). Although the nature of the debate is not given, it likely concerned scribal accusations against the disciples' claims to authority in exorcisms—criticism exacerbated by the disciples' lack of success.

15 Why were the people "amazed" (*exethambēthēsan*; NIV, "overwhelmed with wonder") when they saw Jesus? Was it because the afterglow of the transfiguration lingered on his face? This is possible but unlikely, especially in view of his instruction for the disciples to keep the event a secret. It may have been because he arrived at an opportune time for meeting a critical need. Or perhaps Jesus' authoritative presence itself provoked wonder. A fourth possibility is that it was not Jesus' appearance but his arrival that sparked the excitement. His fame and reputation were such that his arrival, like a celebrity's today, meant that all the attention turned toward him.

16–18 Jesus' inquiry as to what the other disciples and the crowd were arguing about (v.16) prompted a reply from a man who had brought his son for healing (v.17). The man had brought his son to Jesus (*pros se*, "to you" [singular]) but, because of Jesus' absence, had approached the disciples. Doubtless the disciples had fully expected to be able to exorcise the demon. Had doing so not been a part of their commission (3:15; 6:7), and had they not already been successful at it (6:13)?

The description the father gives of his son's illness is graphic: he is possessed by a "muting spirit" (*pneuma alalon*), i.e., a demon that has caused loss of speech. He also has seizures accompanied by foaming at the mouth, grinding of the teeth, and bodily paralysis (v.18). These symptoms resemble those of epilepsy, and in his parallel account Matthew uses a verb that is often associated with epilepsy (*selēniazomai*, "have seizures," Mt 17:15). This condition does not rule out demonization, however, since demons are often described as inflicting physical symptoms, including blindness, muteness (Mt 22:22), deformity (Lk 13:11), and madness (Mk 5:1–20). In any case, the narrative repeatedly confirms that this case is one of demon-possession (vv.17–18, 25–26), whether the physical symptoms represent epilepsy or demonic torment only. The appropriate cure is an exorcism.

19 Jesus now launches into a lament against this "unbelieving generation" by using language that echoes prophetic denunciations of Israel in the OT (cf. Dt 32:5; Jer 5:21). But who is the "unbelieving generation"? The antecedent is unclear; grammatically, it could be the disciples, the crowd, the scribes, or any combination of these groups. Since the failure of the disciples to exorcise the demon is on center stage, they are almost certainly included. Their inclusion also fits thematically with this section of the gospel, in which the disciples' lack of faith and inability to discern Jesus' teaching is repeatedly emphasized. But how could Jesus' opponents, the teachers of the law, not be included, especially since the Pharisees—their close associates—are rebuked in 8:12 as "this generation" (cf. 8:38)? It seems best to see the reference as a general one directed toward all those involved in the dispute: the crowds, the scribes, and the disciples. Jesus expresses frustration that the people, "this generation"—Israel and her leadership—just don't get it yet. This conclusion also fits better the semantic range of "generation" (*genea*), which would be very odd to use with reference to the limited group of nine disciples.

Of course, such a blanket statement indicts the disciples most of all, since they have been Jesus' constant companions and by now should have learned better. Thus the cry of Jesus especially reveals his bitter disappointment with them. In the crucial moment they had failed because of their lack of faith. Van der Loos (*Miracles of Jesus*, 399) says, "It is not too bold to presume that during the absence of Jesus and His three intimates, a spirit of unbelief and laxity had overcome the disciples, perhaps partly as a result of conversations between them, leading to their impotence."

"How long shall I stay with you" may suggest Jesus' longing, in the face of unbelief, for his heavenly Father. "How long shall I put up with you" suggests his weariness with the disciples' spiritual obtuseness. But in teaching his disciples, Jesus never ran out of patience. Mark seems particularly anxious to show his persistence in instructing them (9:30–31; 14:28; 16:7).

Lane, 332, points out the high Christology implicit in this verse: "The opposition expressed between 'I' and 'you' in these statements is seen in its true character only when it is recognized that what God says of his relationship to faithless Israel (cf. Isa 63:8–10), Jesus now says of his relationship to the future community of faith."

20–22 Here Mark describes the deadly conflict between Jesus and the demonic powers. Confronted by Jesus, the demon immediately threw the boy into a convulsion and made him fall on the ground and foam at the mouth (v.20). Mark alone tells us that Jesus asked how long the boy had suffered from the disease (v.21). This detail shows Jesus' sympathetic concern but also serves to emphasize the power of the cure. This was no recent condition that might disappear on its own, but a chronic and persistent demonic presence. The boy had been possessed "since childhood" and had experienced numerous attacks in which the demon had attempted to kill him by convulsing him and throwing him into fire and water (v.22). Mark uses the plural form of water (*hydata*), which probably refers to attempts to drown the boy in pools or streams. Demons by nature are destructive creatures (cf. 5:13). The danger of injury or death adds a further sense of urgency to the situation.

Evidently the failure of the disciples to help has produced doubt and uncertainty in the man. When he left home to bring his son to Jesus, he apparently believed the boy would be healed. Now he is not certain and so says, "If you can do anything, take pity on us and help us."

23–24 Jesus immediately fixes on the first part of the father's statement by repeating his words, "If you can?" Some interpreters take these words as elliptical, meaning something like, "As to your 'if you can' ..." (so Cranfield, 302). But they are better read either as a question with the sense, "What do you mean 'if I can'?" (so NLT), or as an exclamation, "'If you can' indeed!" (so France, 367). In both renderings, Jesus is pointing out that it is not a question of whether he has the power to heal the boy—he certainly does!—but whether the father has faith to believe that Jesus can. "Everything is possible for one who believes" (TNIV). Anything—even moving mountains (Mt 17:20)—is possible when faith is placed in an all-powerful God. This is because what is impossible for human beings is possible for God (Mk 10:27).

Jesus' statement, which is really a promise, elicited faith from the father. "I do believe," he exclaimed; but he recognized that his faith was far from perfect (v.24). It was still mixed with unbelief. So in a beautiful display of honesty, he asked Jesus to help him overcome his unbelief. Calvin, 2:325, comments, "He declares that he *believes* and yet acknowledges himself to have *unbelief*. These two statements may appear to contradict each other but there is none of us that does not experience both of them in himself" (emphasis his).

25 The mention of a crowd "running to the scene" seems strange in view of v.14, which states that a crowd was already there. While no mention is made of the crowd's withdrawing, it is possible that Jesus has pulled the man and his son aside (as in 8:23). Or perhaps this picture is of a growing crowd, with many more people running to the scene. In this case, Jesus, wanting to avoid further publicity as much as possible, exorcised the demon before additional people arrived on the scene. As Hiebert, 223, puts it, "He did not want to perform miracles for gaping sightseers." The demon, referred to as an "unclean [*akathartos*] spirit" (see 1:23) and "a deaf and mute spirit," i.e., one that causes deafness and muteness, was exorcised by Jesus' direct command. He was ordered to come out and stay out for good. This latter command is unique in the Gospels and is probably included here as assurance to a father who has seen his son suffer "since childhood" (v.21).

26–27 The demon's exorcism is accompanied by cries and convulsions (see 1:23, 26 for a similar demonic response). The cry is one of both anger and frustration, revealing violent opposition but powerlessness to resist Jesus' authority. The effect on the boy was so severe that he seemed to the crowd to be dead. He was not in fact dead (*hōsei nekros*, "as one dead"), even though "many" declared him to be dead. Completely exhausted and looking like a corpse, the boy responded to the touch of Jesus (v.27). The phrase "took him by the hand" recalls Jesus' personal touch in the raising of Jairus's daughter (5:41). Lane, 334, though granting that the text does not say the boy was dead, remarks that "the accumulation of the vocabulary of death and resurrection in verses 25–27, and the parallelism with the narrative of the raising of Jairus' daughter, suggest that Mark wished to allude to a death and resurrection. The dethroning of Satan is always a reversal of death and an affirmation of life."

28–29 Why were the nine disciples powerless to act in behalf of this boy? Here Mark gives us the answer. After Jesus went indoors (lit., "in a/the house"), the disciples came to him privately and asked why they had failed. Private instruction and clarification for the disciples is a common theme in Mark (4:10, 34; 7:17; 10:10). They are the "insiders" to whom the secrets of the kingdom are revealed (4:11). The question expressed their deep concern. They had been given authority over evil spirits (6:7) and had successfully driven out many demons before this incident (6:13). Why their failure now? Jesus answered, "This kind can come out only by prayer" (v.29). Apparently, they had taken for granted the power given to them or had come to believe that it was inherent in them. So they no longer depended prayerfully on God for it, and their failure showed their lack of faith. "This kind" is probably not meant to distinguish this demon as a particularly powerful type, but rather indicates that demons in general are too powerful to respond to merely human intervention (cf. France, 370). Only in God's power can believers drive them out.

NOTES

17–18 In the ancient world epilepsy was sometimes called the "sacred disease" because of its mysterious nature (Donahue and Harrington, 281; France, 363). For a discussion of this passage from the perspective of a medical doctor, see J. Wilkinson, "The Case of the Epileptic Boy" (*ExpTim* 79 [1967]: 39–42). The verb σεληνιάζομαι (*selēniazomai*) is related to the word for "moon" (σελήνη, *selēnē*) and reflects the belief of some ancients that the moon played a role in causing seizures (cf. Galen 9.903). Lucian (*Philopseudes*, 16) refers to demon-possessed people who "fall down in the light of the moon, and roll their eyes and fill their mouths with foam" (cited in France, 363 n. 39). The KJV reflected this lunar etymology by translating the word in Matthew 17:15 as "lunatic."

23 The neuter article τό (*to*) in the Greek phrase τὸ εἰ δύνῃ (*to ei dunē*, "the if you can") may serve to make the conditional clause substantival, in which case Jesus means "now concerning your 'if you can' statement." More likely, however, it serves to introduce a quoted word (so NIV). Copyists had trouble with this cryptic phrase, and some MSS add the word πιστεῦσαι (*pisteusai*), "if you can believe."

29 After ἐν προσευχῇ (*en proseuchē*, "by prayer") most MSS add καὶ νηστείᾳ (*kai nēsteia*, "and fasting"). But among the MSS that support the omission of "and fasting" are important representatives of the Alexandrian, Western, and Caesarean types of texts. In the light of the early church's increasing stress on fasting, the words καὶ νηστείᾳ, *kai nēsteia*, are probably an early scribal gloss (see Metzger, 85).

F. Second Prediction of the Passion (9:30–32)

OVERVIEW

The second of three "cycles" begins here (cf. 8:31–38; 10:33–45). Jesus again predicts his death (9:30–31), the disciples respond with ignorance and pride (vv.32–34), and Jesus again teaches them about humility and servant leadership (vv.35–37). This pattern of teaching and response exemplifies the tone of this entire section of Mark's gospel.

[30]They left that place and passed through Galilee. Jesus did not want anyone to know where they were, [31]because he was teaching his disciples. He said to them, "The Son of Man is going to be betrayed into the hands of men. They will kill him, and after three days he will rise." [32]But they did not understand what he meant and were afraid to ask him about it.

COMMENTARY

30–31 Jesus' return to Galilee from the territory of Herod Philip was not for the purpose of pursuing another public Galilean ministry. His public ministry was finished in Galilee. Now he was on his way to Jerusalem to complete his redemptive mission. He was focusing his teaching ministry on the Twelve, and he sought seclusion to do this. The disciples needed to be away from the distractions of the crowds to concentrate on what Jesus was saying to them. Jesus continued to teach them about his passion (v.31) because they by no means had understood his first prediction of his passion. This second prediction of it included the new element of betrayal. The verb *paradidotai* ("is going to be betrayed") is a futuristic present. Although the betrayal is still in the future, it is as good as happening right now.

By translating *paradidotai* as "betrayed," the NIV opts for Judas as the implied subject of the action. This interpretation is possible, and elsewhere in Mark the verb is sometimes used with reference to Judas's actions (3:19; 14:10–11, 18, 21). But the subject of the action is not here stated, and the verb is more accurately rendered "to be delivered over" (so TNIV). As early as Origen (AD 185–254), it was interpreted as a divine passive to mean "delivered over by God." Plummer, 222, points out that if *paradidōmi* refers to Judas, "into the hands of human beings [*anthrōpoi*]" is almost superfluous. (To whom else would he betray him?) It seems better to understand the word as Origen did: God took the initiative in providing human salvation. The delivering up of Jesus was part of God's plan for the world's redemption (cf. Ro 4:25; 8:32). Nineham, 249, insightfully points out that "the play on the words *Son of man* [*anthrōpos*] ... *men* [*anthrōpoi*] is no doubt deliberate; in a fallen world men had become so hostile to God that when, as the culmination of his plans for their salvation, he sent to them the Man, their Savior and ultimate model, they regarded and treated him as their worst enemy. Men and the Son of Man stood on opposite sides in God's eschatological battle against the powers of evil." (For a discussion of Son of Man, see comments at 8:31.) The use of *paradidōmi* also recalls the language of Isaiah 53:6, 12 (LXX), where the Suffering Servant is delivered over by the Lord for the sins of others (Edwards, 284).

32 The disciples still did not understand. Mark does not downplay their shortcoming. But perhaps some light was getting through to them. Was their fear of asking Jesus about what he had said due to their fear of facing a full disclosure of the suffering that lay ahead? Or was it due to their failure to understand Jesus' answer when they had earlier asked about the coming of Elijah (9:1)? Or were they fearful of being rebuked, as Peter had been (8:33)? Whatever their reasons, they were afraid to ask Jesus for an explanation. Instead they chose to occupy themselves with arguing about who was the greatest among them (see vv.33–34).

G. A Question about Greatness (9:33–37)

[33]They came to Capernaum. When he was in the house, he asked them, "What were you arguing about on the road?" [34]But they kept quiet because on the way they had argued about who was the greatest.

[35]Sitting down, Jesus called the Twelve and said, "If anyone wants to be first, he must be the very last, and the servant of all."

[36]He took a little child and had him stand among them. Taking him in his arms, he said to them, [37]"Whoever welcomes one of these little children in my name welcomes me; and whoever welcomes me does not welcome me but the one who sent me."

COMMENTARY

33–34 Jesus returned to Capernaum, where his great Galilean ministry had begun (1:21) and where his headquarters in Galilee had been located. This time he did not linger there, since his public ministry in the region had ended. He instructed his disciples "in the house," i.e., privately (cf. 4:10, 34; 7:17; 9:28–29; 10:10). The house is probably the one belonging to Peter and Andrew (cf. 1:29). The instruction runs from v.33 to v.50.

The disciples must have been embarrassed and ashamed of their arguing among themselves about who was greatest (v.34), for Jesus' question about it elicited only silence. And well might they have been ashamed. Instead of contemplating Jesus' passion and the suffering it would involve for both him and them, they had been occupied with senseless arguing about greatness. Mark does not say what prompted their argument, but the issue of supremacy will come up again in 10:35–45, when James and John seek the chief seats in the kingdom. Perhaps here, too, they are thinking of messianic glory and arguing about who will assume the highest places beside Jesus when he establishes his messianic reign. Garland, 367, captures well the ironic tone of the passage: "The picture Mark presents has tragic-comic dimensions. Jesus walks ahead in silence on his way to his sacrificial death while his straggling disciples push and shove, trying to establish the order of the procession behind him."

The dispute of the disciples is not surprising in the light of ancient Near Eastern culture, in which honor, status, and position were of utmost importance (Malina and Rohrbaugh, 76–77, 213–14, 309–11). In both Greco-Roman and Jewish contexts, places of honor at all public events, such as banquets, were carefully assigned according to one's status (see Lk 14:7–11; Malina and Rohrbaugh, 135–36, 191–92). The rabbis even discussed the seating order in Paradise and who would be positioned closer to the throne of God. It was debated whether greatness in the kingdom would be based on righteousness (Ps 11:7), knowledge of Torah, or good deeds. It was generally agreed that martyrs would be the greatest in the kingdom (Edwards, 286 n. 7). The Dead Sea Scrolls similarly show great concern for proper order, based on one's status and rank in the community, when entering the assembly: "This is the Rule for the session of the Many. Each one by his rank: the priests will sit down first, the elders next and the remainder of all the people will sit down in order of rank" (1QS 6.8; cf. 2.20–23; 5.20–24). In this cultural context, Jesus' subsequent teaching about the last being first was radically subversive.

35 Jesus assumed the posture of a Jewish rabbi—he sat down (Mt 5:1; 13:1; Lk 5:3; Jn 8:2; cf. Mk 12:41) and called the Twelve to him. True greatness comes through service of others. To become first, you must be last—the position of a lowly servant. The term "servant" (*diakonos*) commonly referred to a table waiter or domestic servant, someone whose sole purpose was to meet the needs of others. Swete, 205, writes, "The spirit of service is the passport to eminence in the Kingdom of God, for it is the spirit of the Master Who Himself became *diakonos pantōn* ['servant of all']." This teaching is a complete reversal of worldly values. How important this principle was for Jesus can be seen by its repetition throughout the gospel tradition (Mk 10:31, 43–44; Mt 20:26–27; 23:8–11; Lk 22:24–27; cf. Php 2:1–11; *Gos. Thom.* 22). The very fact that the disciples were concerned about who was greatest underscores again their failure to understand Jesus' statements about his suffering and death. The kind of service Jesus was talking about involved radical self-sacrifice for others.

36–37 Jesus doesn't just teach this principle; he dramatically illustrates it. He takes a child, perhaps one from the family in whose house he was teaching (Peter's or Andrew's child?), and places the child by his side. (The text does not say whether the child was male or female, and the Greek word for "child," *paidion* [v.36], is neuter.) Then Jesus took the child into his arms (cf. 10:16) and said, "Whoever welcomes one of these little children in my name welcomes me." Jesus' words must not be understood as extolling the purity or innocence or honesty or trusting nature of children. These Western ideas about children are not those of the ancient Near East. Children in Jesus' day lacked social status or rights of their own. They were wholly dependent on their parents. They were at the bottom of the social ladder. Jesus' point is that true greatness means caring about even the most insignificant people—like children—because Jesus himself is concerned about them. To "receive" or "welcome" (*dechomai*) is a general term, but here it probably means to extend hospitality as though to an esteemed guest. Welcoming "in my name" indicates representing Jesus as host. When one cares about such people, one is really welcoming Jesus, and the one who welcomes Jesus is really welcoming God, who sent him (v.37b).

There are several important implications of this saying. First, Jesus radically challenges the social conventions of his day by confirming the high status of even the lowliest. Welcoming those of low social status is made equivalent to welcoming God, the one of ultimate status. Furthermore, to welcome the lowly is to adopt the mind-set of Jesus and of the Father, and so to demonstrate the eternal values of the kingdom of God. Third, the language of "sending" is unusual for Mark but characteristic of John's gospel, in which Jesus is the eternal Son sent into the world by the Father (Jn 3:17, 34; 4:34; 5:23, 24, 30, 36–37; 6:29, 38–39, 44, 57, etc.). While the language here cannot be assumed to express quite the same exalted Christology as the fourth gospel, the sense of divine representation is not much different. Jesus so faithfully represents God's nature and purpose that to welcome him is to welcome the One who sent him.

NOTES

33 France, 373 n. 63, suggests that the disciples' argument may have been sparked by their grasping from his words that his death was a real possibility, so leading to their dispute about who would take the lead when he was gone. He cites a similar passage in the *Gospel of Thomas* 12: "The disciples said to Jesus, 'We know that you will go away from us. Who is it that will then be great over us?'"

36 M. Black ("The Markan Parable of the Child in the Midst," *ExpTim* 59 [1947–1948]: 14–16) makes the suggestion that since the words "child" and "servant" are represented by one word in Aramaic, we have here a picture parable. The Twelve are to become like little children in their discipleship; and Jesus assures them that when they do so, they are his true representatives. Those who welcome them welcome Christ (v.37), and in welcoming Christ they welcome God himself. While this suggestion is attractive, it is unlikely to have been Mark's intention, since he is writing in Greek. Furthermore, Jesus does not speak here about becoming like children (contrast Mt 18:3–4) but about welcoming them. Even when in Matthew's version Jesus tells his disciples they must "become" like children to enter the kingdom of God (18:3), he does not mean innocent or pure or trusting. He means, instead, without claim to rights or authority and thus completely dependent on God.

37 Moule, 75, reminds us that "Jesus was one of the first ever to see how essentially precious any person is, particularly a young child. A concern for children was not invented by the welfare state: it goes back to the teaching of Jesus."

H. Driving Out Demons in Jesus' Name (9:38–41)

OVERVIEW

The sayings of vv.38–50 all relate to the theme of discipleship and appear to be linked around a series of catchword associations. The reference to welcoming "in my name" in v.37 is picked up in vv.38–39, 41; "to cause to stumble" from v.42 appears again in vv.43, 45, 47; "fire" in v.43 is repeated in vv.48–49; and the "salted with fire" of v.49 leads to a second "salt" saying in v.50. Whether the sayings were originally linked around these catchwords when Mark received them from the tradition, or whether he was responsible for the ordering, is uncertain.

Verses 38–41 are related to the previous episode by the theme of pride and status. The disciples, who have been arguing about who is the greatest, consider themselves to have exclusive authority to practice exorcisms in Jesus' name. Jesus responds by rejecting such exclusivity and affirming that all those who are doing God's work are on Jesus' side. The interests of the kingdom take precedence over personal ambition and status.

38"Teacher," said John, "we saw a man driving out demons in your name and we told
him to stop, because he was not one of us."
39"Do not stop him," Jesus said. "No one who does a miracle in my name can in the next
moment say anything bad about me, 40for whoever is not against us is for us. 41I tell you

the truth, anyone who gives you a cup of water in my name because you belong to Christ will certainly not lose his reward."

COMMENTARY

38 John's use of "we" shows that he is speaking for all the disciples. Perhaps John felt that as one of the "inner circle" (Peter, James, and John), he should assume leadership in protecting the interests of the Twelve. Only here in Mark is John mentioned alone. He and James will approach Jesus with an even more inappropriate request in 10:35–45. The exorcist had been driving out demons in Jesus' name, i.e., with his authority. While the NT elsewhere testifies to Jewish exorcists other than Jesus and the apostles (Mt 12:27; Lk 11:19), and even refers to an unsuccessful attempt to exorcize in Jesus' name (with disastrous results; Ac 19:13–16), it contains only this one positive reference to an outside exorcist. This individual was evidently a follower of Jesus, though not one of the Twelve, and they viewed it as their exclusive right to drive out demons in Jesus' name. What may have irked them even more was that his exorcisms were evidently successful, while they had recently failed at one of their own attempts (9:14–18). So in their pride and indignation they took it upon themselves to stop him.

39 Jesus' reply shows that his view of who could legitimately participate in his mission was less restrictive than that of his disciples. The driving out of demons was done by God's power, and the dissemination of his power was not limited to the Twelve. So Jesus tells his disciples not to stop the unknown exorcist, for he is not likely soon to speak badly of Jesus if he does a miracle in Jesus' name. The passage recalls Numbers 11:26–29, in which Joshua tried to get Moses to stop Eldad and Medad from prophesying in the camp of the Israelites. Moses responded, "Are you jealous for my sake? I wish that all the LORD's people were prophets and that the LORD would put his Spirit on them!"

40 Successfully driving out demons demonstrated that the man was not against Jesus, and "whoever is not against us is for us." The statement is a proverbial one (it appears in a similar form, e.g., in Cicero's *Pro Ligario*, 33, where the philosopher pleads with Caesar on behalf of a client by pointing out, "While we considered all who were not on our side to be our opponents, you held all those who were not against you to be your adherents"). Since the statement is proverbial, we would expect it to be a general truth rather than an absolute one, and Jesus cites the inverse statement in Matthew 12:30 (cf. Lk 11:23): "He who is not with me is against me." Cranfield, 311, sees in Jesus' statement an indication of the messianic veiledness of Jesus. Jesus did not want to force people into making a quick decision about him. He wanted to give them plenty of decision-making time, during which the principle in Mark 9:40 applies. But when the critical moment for decision arrives, the inverse principle laid down in Matthew 12:30 takes over.

41 This verse about giving a cup of water seems to go best with v.37 and the issue of welcoming "these little ones," in other words, before John's interruption in vv.38–40. However, it also serves well as a concrete example of the principle stated in v.40. In a Middle Eastern culture that highly valued hospitality, the giving of a cup of water was a very small act.

Yet if it is given to one who belongs to Christ, this act will be rewarded. Here resurfaces the Jewish idea that a representative legitimately stands in for the person represented. To give a cup of water to one of Christ's followers is the same as giving it to Christ. In the context of Mark's persecuted church, the saying may indicate small acts of kindness or tolerance provided by Gentile unbelievers in the face of social pressure to reject Christians. Such acts, Jesus says, will not go unrewarded. The imagery parallels Matthew's parable of the sheep and the goats, where eschatological reward goes to those who provide essential material aid to the followers of Jesus experiencing dire circumstances—"the least of these brothers and sisters of mine" (Mt 25:31–46 TNIV).

Jesus introduces the statement about reward with his solemn formula of affirmation: "I tell you the truth" (*amēn legō hymin*; see comments at 3:28). The NIV places the formula at the beginning of the verse, but it seems best to place it in the middle (where it occurs in the Greek), before the statement about reward. This provides additional emphasis to the reward clause, which already utilizes an emphatic negation in Greek: "I tell you the truth, he will certainly not [*ou mē*] lose his reward." The reward is not specified, though the parallels to Matthew's parable of the sheep and the goats suggest that it has eschatological significance. Statements about eschatological reward are uncommon in Mark, but another will be found in 10:28–30.

NOTES

38–50 That these verses represent independent sayings brought together by Mark (or in the tradition he received) is further indicated by their various locations in the gospel tradition: vv.38–39 have a partial parallel in Luke 9:49–50; v.41 is parallel to Matthew 10:42; vv.42–48 appear in Matthew 18:6–9 (cf. Mt 5:13; Lk 17:2); and v.49 is parallel to Matthew 5:13 and Luke 14:34–35.

41 The phrase ὅτι Χριστοῦ ἔστε (*hoti Christou este*, "because you belong to Christ") presents a problem since Jesus does not use the title "Christ" without the definite article in the Synoptics. ℵ* reads ἐμόν (*emon*, "me") instead of *Christou*. The suggestion that the original reading was ἐμοι (*emoi*, "mine") goes back to T. W. Manson in a verbal communication to Vincent Taylor. It is possible that Mark originally wrote ἐμοι, *emoi*, and that ἐμόν, *emon*, is a copyist's error. If this hypothesis is true, then the meaning of the phrase would be "because you are mine" (Taylor, 408).

I. Demanding Requirements of Discipleship (9:42–50)

42"And if anyone causes one of these little ones who believe in me to sin, it would be better for him to be thrown into the sea with a large millstone tied around his neck. 43If your hand causes you to sin, cut it off. It is better for you to enter life maimed than with two hands to go into hell, where the fire never goes out. 45And if your foot causes you to sin, cut it off. It is better for you to enter life crippled than to have two feet and be thrown into hell. [47]And if your eye causes you to sin, pluck it out. It is better for you to enter the kingdom of God with one eye than to have two eyes and be thrown into hell, [48]where

"'their worm does not die,
and the fire is not quenched.'

[49]Everyone will be salted with fire.

[50]"Salt is good, but if it loses its saltiness, how can you make it salty again? Have salt in yourselves, and be at peace with each other."

COMMENTARY

42 As noted above (see Overview, 9:38–41), the sayings in vv.37–50 are loosely connected around the theme of discipleship and appear to have been placed together on the basis of a series of catchwords. Verse 42 is linked with what follows by the catchword "cause to stumble" (*skandalizō*, GK *4997*], vv.43, 45, 47). Its connection with what precedes is less clear, but it may be seen as a warning pointing back to the disciples' attempt to prevent the unknown exorcist from doing his work in Jesus' name (v.38) or to prevent anyone from giving a cup of water in his name (v.41). "Little ones" would not then refer to children as such but to followers of Jesus, and "to stumble" means to prevent them from acting in Jesus' name. The NIV's translation "cause to sin" is too specific, and the TNIV properly corrects it to "cause to stumble." The phrase refers to anything that would compromise the faith of another believer, whether temptation that leads to sin, false teaching that distorts belief, or something else.

The offense is so serious that it is better for one to drown than to commit it. The phrase translated a "large millstone" means literally, "millstone of a donkey" (*mylos onikos*), i.e., the kind turned by donkey power rather than by hand—in other words, a big one!

43–48 In vv.43–48, the catchword "cause to stumble" is now applied not to another believer but to oneself. The main point of these verses is that it is so important to enter into life—i.e., eternal life, eschatological life—that radical means must be taken to remove what can prevent it, namely, sin. The identification of sin with physical body parts—the hand (v.43), foot (v.45), and eye (v.47)—is meant to encompass all areas of life. The hand likely signifies whatever is done, the foot wherever one goes, and the eye whatever one sees. This shocking, graphic comment is hyperbolic. Jesus is not prescribing the excision of human body parts; but he is demanding the cessation of the sinful activities associated with these members. Radical spiritual surgery is demanded. Nothing less is at stake than life—eternal life (cf. v.47, where "kingdom of God" stands in parallel to "life" in vv.43, 45).

43 The word translated "hell" is *geenna*, a Greek form of the Hebrew words *gê hinnōm* ("Valley of Hinnom"). This valley lies on the southern side of the city of Jerusalem and was used as the city's garbage dump. In the most apostate of OT times, it was the site of human sacrifice to the pagan god Molech (cf. Jer 7:31; 19:5–6; 32:35)—a dreadful practice to which King Josiah put a stop (2Ki 23:10). As the place where human excrement and rubbish, including animal carcasses, were disposed of and burned, the fires of *Gehenna* never went out, so that in the intertestamental period the name came to be used symbolically to represent the place of divine punishment. The pseudepigraphic work *1 Enoch* (27:2) reads, "This accursed valley is for those who are accursed forever; here will all those be gathered who utter unseemly words against God, and here is the place of their punishment." Compare *1 Enoch* 90:26: "A like abyss was opened in the midst of the earth, full of fire, and they were all judged and found guilty and cast into that fiery abyss, and they burned" (cf. *4 Ezra* 7:36; *TDNT* 1:657–58).

48 Verse 48, "where 'their worm does not die, and the fire is not quenched'," is an allusion to Isaiah 66:24, which speaks of the eternal punishment of those who have rebelled against God. Verses 44 and 46 (identical with v.48) are omitted by the NIV, TNIV, and most other versions. They are lacking in important early MSS and were likely added by later scribes to round out the parallelism in vv.47–48 (see Metzger, 86–87).

49 The catchword associations continue in vv.49–50. Verse 49, "Everyone will be salted with fire," picks up the catchword "fire" from v.48; then "salt" is picked up in v.50 and applied in different contexts. Both verses are among the most difficult in Mark to interpret.

Over a dozen different interpretations for v.49 are found in the commentaries. Of these interpretations, two commend themselves; and both take their cue from the insertion by a copyist of the words "and every sacrifice shall be salted with salt" (see Notes). This comment is a reference to Leviticus 2:13: "Season all your grain offerings with salt. Do not leave the salt of the covenant of your God out of your grain offerings; add salt to all your offerings."

One interpretation sees in the sacrificial salt a symbol of the covenantal relationship the children of Israel had with God. For every disciple of Jesus, the salt of the covenant is the Divine Fire (cf. Mt 3:11), "which purifies, preserves and consummates sacrifice—the alternative to the Fire that consumes" (Swete, 213). The fire in this case would refer to the Holy Spirit.

Another interpretation sees in the fire the trials and persecutions of the disciples of Jesus. The previous verses relate to the dedication to God of the various members of the body (hand, foot, eye). These must be sacrificed, if need be, to enter into the kingdom of God. Here in v.49 the total self is in mind. Every true disciple is to be a total sacrifice to God (cf. Ro 12:1); and as salt always accompanied the temple sacrifices, so fire—i.e., persecution, trials, and suffering—will accompany the true disciple's sacrifices (cf. 1Pe 1:7; 4:12). This latter interpretation would seem to be the most likely (C. Link, "Exegetical Study of Mark 9:49," *Notes* 6/4 [1992]: 21–35).

This saying, which is preserved only by Mark, must have had special meaning for Mark's persecuted church. It helped them understand that the purifying fires of persecution were not to be thought of as foreign to their vocation as Christians, for "everyone will be salted with fire."

50 In this verse, salt must be understood in a domestic setting, not in a religious or ritual one as in v.49. Salt played an important role in the ancient world. The rabbis considered it necessary for life. "The world cannot survive without salt" (*Sop.* 15.8). It was used for many purposes, including as a flavoring, a cleansing agent, and a preservative to keep food from spoiling. What does Jesus mean by salt's losing its saltiness (cf. Lk 14:34; Mt 5:13)? Sodium chloride (table salt) is a stable compound and cannot actually lose its saltiness. There are several possible explanations for Jesus' words. He may be indicating an absurdity ("If salt were able to lose its saltiness ..."). More likely, his statement refers to the kind of salt found around the Dead Sea, which is a mixture of sodium chloride and other compounds. When water evaporates from this mixture, the sodium chloride crystallizes first and may be removed. What is left are gypsum and other impurities, i.e., "salt" that has lost its saltiness (France, 385). Jesus is warning his disciples not to lose that characteristic in them that brings life to the world and prevents its decay. But what is that characteristic which, if lost, will make the disciples of Jesus worthless? It is the disciples' spirit of devotion and self-sacrifice (cf. v.49) to Jesus Christ and his gospel.

The second saying of v.50 should probably be translated "have salt *among* yourselves" rather than "have salt in yourselves" (NIV), and so it stands in synonymous parallelism with the next phrase, "and be at peace with each other." The image is one of a meal shared together in the context of true fellowship and peace (Garland, 370). The salt of self-sacrificial giving will result in a spirit of peace and unity among believers, where devotion to one another takes precedence over personal self-interest (cf. v.34).

NOTES

49 The first words of this verse have come down to us in essentially three forms: (1) as translated in the NIV—"Everyone will be salted with fire"—a reading with the best MS evidence; (2) "Every sacrifice will be salted with salt"; and (3) "Every one will be salted with fire and every sacrifice will be salted with salt." The history of these variants is probably as follows. The original reading was the first; a copyist, finding in Leviticus 2:13 a clue to the understanding of this difficult saying, noted the OT passage in the margin; subsequently, his marginal gloss was added to the original reading by another copyist and combined together with it by yet another.

J. Teaching on Divorce (10:1–12)

OVERVIEW

Jesus has completed his ministry in Galilee. He is moving closer and closer to the ancient city of Jerusalem, where the final acts of the redemptive drama were to take place. He set his face toward the accomplishment of his divine mission. Since the events of Mark 9:30 Jesus had been directing his teaching ministry toward his disciples, but now, surprisingly, he is again among the crowds and teaching them. This context of public teaching sets the stage for another challenge and test from the Pharisees. The passage therefore fits the present context in Mark by showing the continuing opposition to Jesus—opposition that will climax in his arrest in Jerusalem.

1 Jesus then left that place and went into the region of Judea and across the Jordan.
Again crowds of people came to him, and as was his custom, he taught them.

[2]Some Pharisees came and tested him by asking, "Is it lawful for a man to divorce his wife?"
[3]"What did Moses command you?" he replied.
[4]They said, "Moses permitted a man to write a certificate of divorce and send her away."
[5]"It was because your hearts were hard that Moses wrote you this law," Jesus replied.
[6]"But at the beginning of creation God 'made them male and female.' [7]'For this reason a
man will leave his father and mother and be united to his wife, [8] and the two will become
one flesh.' So they are no longer two, but one. [9]Therefore what God has joined together, let
man not separate."
[10]When they were in the house again, the disciples asked Jesus about this. [11]He answered,
"Anyone who divorces his wife and marries another woman commits adultery against her.
[12]And if she divorces her husband and marries another man, she commits adultery."

COMMENTARY

1 The textual tradition reveals that the copyists had problems with the sequence of Jesus' journey here, since he first travels southward into Judea and then eastward across the Jordan River (see Notes). The copyists smoothed this out by saying that he traveled to Judea *through* the regions beyond the Jordan. But there is no compelling reason why Jesus could not have traveled southward from Capernaum, over the mountains of Samaria into Judea, and then eastward across the Jordan into Perea.

2 The question posed by the Pharisees was not a sincere one. They were not honestly seeking information from Jesus about divorce. They were testing him, trying to catch him in some statement about a subject on which they themselves had no agreement and then use it against him. The fact that Jesus was in Perea, Herod Antipas's territory, is probably significant. Antipas had put John the Baptist to death because John had denounced Antipas's marriage to Herodias. Perhaps the Pharisees hoped that Jesus, by his statements on marriage and divorce, would get himself into trouble with Antipas and would suffer the same fate as John.

On the question of the lawfulness of divorce, there was general unanimity among the Jews: divorce was allowed. The real difference of opinion centered in the grounds for divorce. The fundamental text was Deuteronomy 24:1: "If a man marries a woman who becomes displeasing to him because he finds something indecent about her, and he writes her a certificate of divorce ..." The crucial words are "something indecent." What did that include? The school of Shammai, the stricter of the schools, understood these words to mean something morally indecent—in particular, adultery. The school of Hillel interpreted the words much more freely. Just about anything in a wife that a husband did not find to his liking was suitable grounds for divorce. Even if she burned his food! Rabbi Akiba is cited as saying that divorce was allowed even if the man "found another fairer than she" (*m. Giṭ.* 9:10). So where did Jesus stand on this issue? That was the Pharisees' question.

3–4 As often when confronted by the Jewish religious leaders, Jesus did not answer the question directly but countered with a question of his own.

Moses was their authority—what did *he command*? Jesus knew they would appeal to Moses; so he had them make the first commitment. Their response alludes to Deuteronomy 24:1–4. They acknowledge that Moses did not actually *command* divorce but rather "permitted a man to write a certificate of divorce and send her away" (v.4). The text from Deuteronomy does not explicitly sanction divorce nor does it set out grounds for it; rather, the text recognizes the reality of divorce—*that* it happens—and stipulates that a man who divorces his wife may not remarry her after she remarries and is divorced for a second time (or becomes a widow). The primary purpose of the command was to protect the wife from arbitrary divorce. A man could not divorce his wife and then accuse her of adultery or claim her back after she remarried. Nor could he remarry her for financial gain when, following a second divorce, she received her dowry back, or after she gained a widow's inheritance. S. E. Johnson (*The Gospel According to St. Mark* [HNTC; New York: Harper & Brothers, 1960], 169–70) summarizes the rabbinic perspective on divorce:

> Jewish marriage was not a contract between equals; a woman did not marry, but was "given in marriage." It is only fair, however, to add that Pharisaic rules afforded a certain protection to the more helpless party. Her husband had to give her a writ of divorce that was valid in every respect, written on durable material and with ink that did not fade, and once he had delivered the writ he could not retract it; the woman was free. While a wife could not divorce her husband, she could go before the court and force him to divorce her if he engaged in disgusting occupations such as tanning [animal hides], had certain diseases, took vows to her detriment, or forced her to take such vows. Furthermore, the rabbis bitterly condemned indiscriminate divorce even if it was legal.

5 Jesus' answer reaches back to first principles. Moses' permission to divorce (v.4) was an accommodation to human weakness (v.5). It was because their "hearts were hard" (*sklērokardia*; GK *5016*) that God allowed for divorce. Though here is the first use of this term in Mark's gospel, similar expressions have appeared with reference both to the disciples (6:52; 8:17) and the religious leaders (3:5; 4:12; 7:6; cf. 7:21). It indicates insensitivity to God's purpose resulting in disobedience or rebellion. God's allowance for divorce was an attempt to bring some sort of order in a society that had disregarded God's standards. But God did not intend for marriage to end in divorce. His design in creating man and woman was that marriage should be an unbroken, lifelong union. Cranfield, 319, points out that a distinction must be made between what is the absolute will of God and what the provisions are that take into account the sinfulness of human beings and are intended to limit and control its effects. Moses' bill of divorce falls into the second category. The rabbis mistook God's gracious provision in allowing divorce as his approval of it.

6 Since divorce is not part of God's original purpose, but rather God's condescension to human sinfulness, Jesus does not want to talk about divorce at all, let alone the "grounds" for it. He wants instead to talk about marriage as a sacred covenant established by God. Jesus therefore ignores the text from Deuteronomy cited by his opponents and takes his hearers back to the foundational text for marriage: At the beginning of creation God "made them male and female" (Ge 1:27). Man and woman, he says, were created to be equals in a lifelong partnership of mutual love and respect. John Murray (*Divorce* [Philadelphia: Presbyterian and Reformed, 1974], 29) writes, "Marriage is grounded in this male and female constitution: as to its nature it implies that the man and the woman are united in one flesh; as to its sanction, it is divine; as to its continuance it is permanent. The import of all this is that marriage from its very nature and from the divine institution by which it is constituted is ideally indissoluble."

7–8 Jesus continues his argument by quoting Genesis 2:24. The marriage is enacted when the man leaves his father and mother, is united with his wife, and the two become "one flesh." Since marriage is a lifelong union between a man and a woman, its claims take precedence over ties to father and mother. Schweizer, 203, comments, "The forsaking of the house of one's father was far more meaningful at that time, since a man would forsake the solidarity and protection of his own clan." The Semitic expression "one flesh" means "united together like one person" and emphasizes the permanence of the bond. To break this bond is like ripping a single person in two.

9 Behind the concept of the indissolubility of marriage is the authority of God himself. And what God has joined together, no human agent should separate. As Murray (*Divorce*, 33) puts it, "Divorce is contrary to the divine institution, and contrary to the nature of marriage, contrary to the divine action by which the union is effected. It is precisely here that its wickedness becomes singularly apparent—it is the sundering by man of a union God has constituted. Divorce is the breaking of a seal which has been engraven by the hand of God."

There is debate today over whether Jesus' words mean that the divinely sanctioned bond between husband and wife *should not* be broken or whether it *cannot* be broken. For those who hold the former view, while divorce is a great tragedy and is contrary to God's design for marriage, for those with sufficient "grounds" divorce effectively dissolves the marriage bond and so allows for remarriage. For those who hold the latter view, the marriage bond can never be dissolved in God's eyes, so remarriage after divorce is always forbidden.

10–12 Mark records no response of the Pharisees to Jesus' teaching about divorce but instead moves directly to Jesus' later discussion "in the house" with the Twelve. As so often in Mark, Jesus provides private instruction for his disciples away from the crowds (4:10, 34; 7:17; 9:28–29). When they ask for clarification (v.10)—no doubt because they are surprised at Jesus' radical teaching (cf. Mt 19:10)—he responds with the even more shocking statement that remarriage after divorce constitutes adultery (v.11). Jesus' teaching here is strongly countercultural. In the Judaism of Jesus' day, divorce by definition included the right to remarriage. The Mishnah says, "The essential formula in the bill of divorce is 'Lo, thou art free to marry any man'" (*m. Giṭ.* 9:10). Jesus, however, says that anyone who divorces his wife and remarries commits adultery against her. The reason is that in God's eyes the original marriage covenant is still in force, so that sexual relations with the second spouse constitute adultery.

In Matthew's parallels, an exception is introduced: "But I tell you that anyone who divorces his wife, except for marital unfaithfulness [*porneia*], causes her to become an adulteress" (Mt 5:32; cf. 19:9). Scholars debate the meaning of this exception. Some argue that Jesus would have assumed the right to remarry after a "legitimate" divorce, i.e., one caused by adultery (or desertion; see 1Co 7:15). Others claim that Matthew's exception ("except for marital unfaithfulness") does not legitimate either the divorce or remarriage but only qualifies the adultery clause. If a wife has already been sexually unfaithful, her husband can hardly be said to have *made* her commit adultery when she (in Jesus' day out of economic necessity) remarries.

In addition to challenging the cavalier attitude toward divorce, Jesus also did what the rabbis refused to do: he recognized that a man could commit adultery against his wife (v.11). In rabbinic Judaism, a woman, by sexual infidelity, could commit adultery against her husband; and a man, by having sexual relations with another man's wife, could commit adultery against the woman's husband. But a man could never commit adultery against his wife, no matter what he did. Jesus, by putting the husband under the same moral obligation as the wife, raised the status and dignity of women.

The parallel statement about the wife's divorcing her husband in v.12 may reflect a Roman origin for Mark's gospel. While Judaism generally forbade a wife to divorce her husband (see Josephus, *Ant.* 15.7.10 §259), Roman law allowed it. Matthew, writing for Jews, omits the statement; Mark includes it. Cranfield, 322, remarks, "The words in Mark may represent an adaptation of Jesus' teaching to the situation of a Gentile church (Jewish law did not allow a wife to divorce her husband), or it may be that Jesus himself was looking beyond the custom of his own people (he can hardly have been altogether unaware of Gentile practice)."

NOTES

1 The textual variants reveal the difficulty some copyists had with Mark's geography. The most substantiated reading is that in the NIV: "into the region of Judea and [καί, *kai*] across the Jordan." The Byzantine tradition is reflected in the NKJV: "the region of Judea by [διά, *dia*] the other side of the Jordan." This reading appears to reflect a copyist's attempt to "correct" Mark's geography by having Jesus travel from Galilee to Judea via the eastern side of the Jordan (bypassing Samaria). A third reading omits the καί (*kai*, "and") before the word πέραν (*peran*, "across"), so that the verse reads "into the region of Judea across the Jordan." This reading has some merit and would suggest that "Judea" is being used in a general sense of the southern part of the country, including the area east of the Jordan. But it may also represent an assimilation to the parallel in Matthew 19:1 (see Metzger, 87–88).

2 For OT and Jewish background on divorce and remarriage, see especially Craig S. Keener, *... And Marries Another: Divorce and Remarriage in the Teaching of the New Testament* (Peabody, Mass.: Hendrickson, 1991); W. A. Heth and G. J. Wenham, *Jesus and Divorce: Towards an Evangelical Understanding of New Testament Teaching* (3d ed.; Carlisle: Paternoster, 2002); David Instone-Brewer, *Divorce and Remarriage in the Bible: The Social and Literary Context* (Grand Rapids: Eerdmans, 2002).

9 The word συνέζευξεν (*synezeuxen*) means literally "yoked together" (NIV, "joined together"). It graphically stresses the importance of a husband and wife's working together as a team of oxen yoked together. The word is often used in Greek literature of the marriage relationship.

11 For various views on remarriage after divorce, see Paul Engle and Mark L. Strauss, eds., *Remarriage after Divorce in Today's Church* (Grand Rapids: Zondervan, 2006; for the view that adultery or desertion constitutes legitimate grounds for remarriage, see the chs. by Heth and Keener; for the rejection of any such "grounds," see the ch. by Wenham); see also W. A. Heth, "Jesus on Divorce: How My Mind Has Changed," *SBJT* 6/1 (Spring 2002): 4–29; and the works cited in the Notes at v.2.

12 Lane, 352, favors the reading, supported by the Western and Caesarean texts, that speaks of the woman's "separating" (ἐξέλθῃ, *exelthē*) from her husband (without divorce) and marrying another man. He argues that the textual tradition that supports this reading is particularly appropriate to the situation of Herodias and Herod Antipas. Taylor, 425, also favors this reading.

REFLECTIONS

While pastors and Christian leaders must deal with the painful reality of divorce and remarriage in our fallen society and make difficult decisions about which actions to condone and which to condemn, it is important not to parse Jesus' words in the same casuistic way that the rabbis dealt with the law. Jesus did not provide detailed instructions on the legitimacy or illegitimacy of divorce in specific cases. Instead, he affirmed the fundamental principles that divorce is wrong and is contrary to God's design, and that marriage was created to be a lifelong covenant of self-sacrificial love and mutual support between a man and a woman. First and foremost, the church should take from this passage that the preparation for and preservation of lifelong, loving marriages are the goals God desires for his people and ones that must be relentlessly pursued.

K. Blessing the Children (10:13–16)

OVERVIEW

Here we have a pronouncement story without details of time and place. Mark may have positioned it at this point because a story about children is a fitting sequel to Jesus' teaching about marriage. Matthew also places it in this context but makes a closer connection with what precedes it by the use of the word "then." (Mark uses the conjunction "and" [*kai*], untranslated in the NIV.)

Jesus has already used a child to illustrate a point in 9:36–37. There he taught that whoever welcomes a child in Jesus' name welcomes Jesus himself. To honor those of low social status is to honor Jesus, and to honor Jesus is to honor God, who sent him. Here Jesus again uses the lowly status of children to make his point, and he models the act of welcoming them that he taught in 9:37. Yet his application is not about welcoming them, per se, but about following their example by receiving the kingdom through childlike dependence on God. The passage continues three key themes of the gospel: (1) with compassion Jesus reaches out with love and grace to the lowliest members of society; (2) the disciples fail to comprehend the nature of servant leadership; (3) receiving the kingdom of God means childlike dependence on God.

13People were bringing little children to Jesus to have him touch them, but the disciples
rebuked them. 14When Jesus saw this, he was indignant. He said to them, "Let the little
children come to me, and do not hinder them, for the kingdom of God belongs to such
as these. 15I tell you the truth, anyone who will not receive the kingdom of God like a little
child will never enter it." 16And he took the children in his arms, put his hands on them and
blessed them.

COMMENTARY

13 Mark does not identify those who were bringing the children to Jesus. In Greek the subject of the verb is indefinite—"they." The NIV translates, "People were bringing ..." While these "people" are presumably the parents, Mark leaves off extraneous details to emphasize the words and actions of Jesus. The word Mark uses for children (*paidia*) is the same one used of the twelve-year-old daughter of Jairus (5:39–41). Here, however, it appears to denote small children (since Jesus took them into his arms). In the parallel passage in his gospel, Luke uses the word *brephē*, which means "babies." Among Jews, as among other peoples, it was customary to bring children to great men to have them blessed (cf. Ge 48:13–20; W. Grundmann, *Das Evangelium nach Markus* [THKNT 2; Berlin: Evangelische Verlagsanstalt, 1973], 206). Jesus often heals with touch in Mark's gospel (1:31, 41; 5:41; 6:5, 56; 7:33; 8:23–25), and people press forward to touch him (3:10; 5:23, 27; 6:56; 7:32).

Why the disciples wanted to prevent the children from coming to Jesus is not stated. While we might suppose that they were simply protecting him from needless interruptions, in context the reason is more likely their desire to exert their own authority (9:34) or to keep Jesus to themselves (9:38). Children had little status in the ancient world and were generally viewed simply as immature adults (see comments at 9:36–37). In the disciples' eyes, they were unworthy of the teacher's time or attention. Yet, as elsewhere, Jesus reaches out to the lowliest and least empowered members of society.

14 Only Mark records that Jesus was "indignant" when he realized what the disciples were doing. Mark never softens the human emotions of Jesus (cf. 1:41; 3:5), nor is he less than candid about the failings of the disciples. Jesus was indignant that his disciples continued to express exclusionary pride and self-centered indifference to the lowly and seemingly unimportant members of society. Jesus uses the same phrase "do not hinder" that he used of the man driving out demons in Jesus' name in 9:38. The disciples have not yet comprehended the open invitation to the kingdom Jesus is proclaiming.

Children should not be hindered, Jesus says, because "the kingdom of God belongs to such as these." What qualities of children does Jesus have in mind? In our Western society we might think of the purity or innocence of children, but these traits would not have occurred to a first-century audience. Instead, Jesus is likely referring to the lowly social status of children, their dependence, and the openness to receive freely. Rawlinson, 137, comments:

> The point of comparison is not so much the innocence and humility of children (for children are not invariably either innocent or humble); it is rather the fact that children are unselfconscious, receptive, and content to be dependent on others' care and bounty; it is in such a spirit that the kingdom must be "received"—it is a gift of God, and not an achievement on the part of man; it must be simply accepted, inasmuch as it can never be deserved.

Some interpreters have found in this passage a defense of infant baptism (so O. Cullmann, *Baptism in the New Testament* [London: SCM Press, 1950], 71–80) or teaching regarding the salvation of children. Yet this surely goes beyond the intent of the text. There are no indications in the context that the author has baptism in mind. Furthermore, Jesus is not speaking only about children here but about "such as these" (*toioutōn*), i.e., all those who demonstrate a childlike dependence on God and who receive salvation as a free gift.

15 The solemn pronouncement "I tell you the truth" (*amēn legō hymin*) occurs thirteen times in

Mark (see Notes, 3:28). These words always signal sayings of great importance, often promises or warnings about spiritual rewards and penalties (3:28; 9:1, 41; 10:29; cf. France, 397). Here the pronouncement reiterates and expands the point made in v.14 with a warning: those who fail to receive the kingdom of God in a childlike way will certainly not enter it. The saying confirms the multidimensional nature of the kingdom. It is both a gift to be received in the present and a realm to be entered in the future (see Hooker, 239).

16 Jesus now takes the children in his arms (as he did in 9:36), places his hands on them, and blesses them—a striking act showing his love for them. He thus reveals that he is the model disciple who "welcomes one of these little children" (9:37) and so proves to be "the first" by becoming "the servant of all" (9:35). Mark's dual reference that Jesus took them in his arms and placed his hands on them emphasizes the act of touching, which indicates acceptance, and Jesus' indifference to the boundaries of exclusion that the disciples were seeking to enforce.

The prefix *kata* on the verb *kateulogeō* ("bless") may have an intensifying force, but it would be overtranslating to say that Jesus blessed them "intensely" or "fervently." We might rather say that in strong contrast to the disciples' insensitivity and exclusivity, Jesus warmly welcomed them by bestowing love, honor, and grace on those whom society viewed as insignificant and irrelevant. Jesus again models God's grace for all people.

NOTES

15 Another, though less likely, interpretation claims that the word "child" (παιδίον, *paidion*) is in the accusative case rather than the nominative, so that the sentence does not prescribe receiving the kingdom "as a child receives it" but rather receiving the kingdom "as one receives a child" (F. A. Schilling, "What Means the Saying about Receiving the Kingdom of God as a Little Child?" *ExpTim* 77 [1965/66]: 56–58). People should receive the kingdom with the same openness and delight that Jesus welcomed children. This interpretation, though intriguing, fits the context less well—a context in which it is the quality of childlike dependence that enables one to enter the kingdom (vv.13–14, 16). This saying is found in another context in Matthew 18:3 and could be an independent saying placed here by Mark.

L. Riches and the Kingdom of God (10:17–31)

OVERVIEW

This section is made up of three parts: (1) vv.17–22, which describe Jesus' encounter with a rich man; (2) vv.23–27, a logion on the difficulty of a rich man's entering the kingdom of God; and (3) vv.28–31, Peter's statement about leaving all to follow Jesus and Jesus' reply to it. Myers (*Binding the Strong Man*, 272) suggests a concentric structure:

A Question about eternal life (v.17)
  B Rich man cannot leave possessions and follow (vv.18–22)

C Jesus' explanation, disciples' reaction (twice; vv.23–27)

B' Disciples have left possessions and followed (vv.28–29)

A' Answer to question about eternal life (v.30)

The central message of the passage comes in the middle ("C"), with Jesus' twin statements about the difficulty of the rich for entering the kingdom of God (vv.22, 24), illustrated with the striking analogy of the camel and the eye of a needle (v.25); the double statement of the disciples' amazement (vv.24, 26); and Jesus' conclusion that what is impossible for human beings to accomplish is possible for God. The passage stresses the need for both complete dependence on God and total commitment to him.

The position of this episode in Mark's narrative is significant. It follows Jesus' teaching about the importance of childlikeness and so serves as a recognition of the necessity of weakness and dependence for entrance into the kingdom (vv.13–16), and it precedes Jesus' third prediction of his passion. The impossibility of wealth as a means to gain the kingdom (v.27) looks back to the lesson from the children (v.15), and the call to commitment (vv.29–31) looks forward to the statement about his passion (vv.33–34).

17 As Jesus started on his way, a man ran up to him and fell on his knees before him.
"Good teacher," he asked, "what must I do to inherit eternal life?"
18 "Why do you call me good?" Jesus answered. "No one is good—except God alone.
19 You know the commandments: 'Do not murder, do not commit adultery, do not steal,
do not give false testimony, do not defraud, honor your father and mother.'"
20 "Teacher," he declared, "all these I have kept since I was a boy."
21 Jesus looked at him and loved him. "One thing you lack," he said. "Go, sell everything
you have and give to the poor, and you will have treasure in heaven. Then come, follow
me."
22 At this the man's face fell. He went away sad, because he had great wealth.
23 Jesus looked around and said to his disciples, "How hard it is for the rich to enter the
kingdom of God!"
24 The disciples were amazed at his words. But Jesus said again, "Children, how hard it
is to enter the kingdom of God! 25 It is easier for a camel to go through the eye of a needle
than for a rich man to enter the kingdom of God."
26 The disciples were even more amazed, and said to each other, "Who then can be
saved?"
27 Jesus looked at them and said, "With man this is impossible, but not with God; all
things are possible with God."
28 Peter said to him, "We have left everything to follow you!"
29 "I tell you the truth," Jesus replied, "no one who has left home or brothers or sisters
or mother or father or children or fields for me and the gospel 30 will fail to receive a
hundred times as much in this present age (homes, brothers, sisters, mothers, children and

fields — and with them, persecutions) and in the age to come, eternal life. 31 But many who are first will be last, and the last first."

COMMENTARY

17 This incident, unlike those in vv.2–12 and 13–17, is connected with the journey mentioned in 10:1 by the phrase, "As Jesus started on his way." The reader is reminded that Jesus is on his way to Jerusalem, where he will make the ultimate sacrifice for others. The episode is sometimes called "the rich young ruler," but Mark introduces the man only as a certain "one" and, at the conclusion, identifies him as very wealthy (v.22). Only Matthew says he was young (19:20), and Luke calls him a ruler (18:18), probably meaning that the man was a member of some official council or court.

Running is considered undignified in the Middle East, and the man's deference to Jesus in falling at his feet and his flattering address, "Good teacher," may indicate an overeagerness to please. Nineham, 270, comments: "The stranger was altogether too obsequious and effusive in his approach." Yet false motives appear to be ruled out by Mark's comment in v.21 that Jesus "looked at him and loved him." Despite his shortcomings, the man has a sincere respect for Jesus and a desire to learn from him. His question, however—"What must I do to inherit eternal life?"—indicates that he was thinking in terms of Jewish works of righteousness. He wanted to do something to merit eternal life, whereas Jesus taught that eternal life (the kingdom of God) is a gift to be received (cf. v.15).

18 Jesus does not at first answer the question; rather, he challenges the man's address. Jesus' reply may seem unnecessarily abrupt, but we must remember that he was calling attention to the man's unthinking use of language. R. P. Martin (*Mark*, 124) writes, "Jesus calls him to sober reflection. What does the epithet 'good' mean? It belongs to God who is good; and it should not be used unthinkingly or as a flippant gesture of praise."

Jesus' statement has caused concern for many in the church. Is he claiming not to be good? Is he claiming not to be God? But these questions miss Jesus' point. The man addresses Jesus' as good because he believes Jesus is a faithful teacher who has *earned* this title. Jesus responds that no human being can be called "good" because of what he or she has done. Salvation is not something that is earned by merit. Only God is truly good. In other words, Jesus' statement is not self-referential or christological; rather, it concerns the nature of fallen humanity. It prepares the audience for his subsequent teaching concerning the impossibility of earning salvation apart from complete dependence on God (vv.20, 27). Jesus is saying, "Before you address me as 'good,' you had better think soberly about what the implications are, and especially what they are for you."

19 Jesus answers by listing the second half of the Ten Commandments (the Decalogue), those commands that deal with one's relationship to others (Ex 20:13–17). He also adds the fifth commandment, concerning honoring one's parents (Ex 10:12; cf. Mk 7:8). Only Mark's account includes a command not to defraud, which seems to be a substitute for the Decalogue's prohibition of coveting (Ex 20:17). Since the other five commands that Jesus lists deal with concrete actions (murder, adultery, stealing, false testimony, and honoring parents) rather than thoughts, fraud may represent an outward result of coveting. Another possibility is that fraud here replaces coveting, since the wealthy may be less envious of others but may have gained their riches by defrauding or exploiting others (Evans, 96). It was a firm Jewish belief, based on OT teaching, that the person who kept the law would live (Dt 30:15–16). So Jesus began there.

20 The young man answered confidently. From boyhood he had kept all the commandments Jesus cited (cf. Ac 26:4). Boyhood may refer to the age of thirteen, when a Jewish boy became a "son of the commandment" and so responsible to keep the law as an adult (cf. *m. Nid.* 5:6; Lk 2:42). The man's declaration was sincere, for to him keeping the law was a matter of external conformity. Paul says something similar when he declares his "faultless" obedience to the law prior to coming to Christ (Php 3:6). Yet he, like the man in our story, did not yet comprehend that the law required inner obedience, which could not be achieved by any human effort.

21 Recognizing the young man's sincerity, Jesus responded in love. The verb *emblepō* ("gazed intently"; cf. v.27) suggests that Jesus, looking penetratingly at the man, discerned his attitude of heart. Some commentators suggest that the words "loved him" indicate an outward expression, such as a touch or a hug (so Nineham, 274–75; Anderson, 249). That Jesus did so is possible, but nothing in the text or context demands that understanding. Mark's point, rather, is that Jesus treats the man's response not as one of self-righteousness or hypocrisy but as sincere.

But sincerity isn't enough. The one thing that prevented this man from having eternal life was the security of his wealth. Jesus put his finger on the sensitive place by commanding him to go, sell all he had, and give it to the poor. These commands led up to the final and conclusive one: "Come, follow me." For this man there could be no following of Jesus before he sold everything he had and gave it away. His wealth and all it meant to him for position, status, comfort, and security prevented him from entering eternal life. Mitton, 80, writes, "The only way to 'life' is through the narrow gate of full surrender, and through that gate we may take, not what we want, but only what God allows. For this man his wealth was the hindrance."

Jesus' command here is shocking (like the analogy that follows in v.25), with the result that many Christians assume too quickly that Jesus' command was for this man only and not for all believers. Jesus' words are sometimes softened to mean that Christians must be *willing* to sell everything (at which time a sigh of relief passes through the congregation). Yet we dare not take the punch out of Jesus' teaching (see Reflections below). It is certainly true that those who followed Jesus did not always divest themselves of all their property. In Jesus' immediate ministry, Peter retained his house in Capernaum (1:29), and the women who supported Jesus from their resources obviously had retained their possessions (Lk 8:2–3). Acts shows some people as selling their possessions to meet specific needs (Ac 4:34–37), but doing so was neither universal nor mandatory (see Jesus' comment to Ananias in Ac 5:4). Many homes and possessions remained as private property.

Jesus' promise of "treasure in heaven" recalls his similar teaching in the Sermon on the Mount, in which Jesus exhorts his followers to store up treasures in heaven, where they can never be stolen or destroyed (Mt 6:19–21; cf. Lk 12:33–34). The concept of storing up spiritual treasures rather than physical ones was common in Judaism, especially with reference to almsgiving. Tobit 4:8–9 (NRSV) reads, "If you have many possessions, make your gift from them in proportion; if few, do not be afraid to give according to the little you have. So you will be laying up a good treasure for yourself against the day of necessity." *Psalms of Solomon* 9:5 reads, "He that does righteousness lays up [as a treasure] for himself life with the Lord" (cf. *2 Bar.* 24:1; Sir 29:10–12). Treasure in heaven is not some material reward in the afterlife but the joy of eternal life in relationship with God. The "treasure" received is God himself. In Jesus' teaching the sacrifice made to achieve this treasure is not almsgiving but giving up all to follow him.

22 Notice the intimate eyewitness details. When he heard Jesus' words, the young man's "face fell." The verb used here is a rare one, appearing elsewhere in the NT only in Matthew 16:3, where it refers to the darkening sky of an approaching storm. In the LXX it can have the sense of "shocked" or "appalled" (Eze 27:35; 28:19; 32:10), and its cognate adjective of "gloomy" or "dismayed" (Da 2:12). The TEV translates it here "gloom spread over his face." As Plummer, 240–41, writes, "He was gloomy and sullen with a double disappointment; no perilous exploit was required of him, but he was asked to part with what he valued most." To obey Jesus was too great a risk for him to take. So the security of wealth kept him out of the kingdom of God. "He went away sad, because he had great wealth" (v.22b). Obedience to God brings joy; disobedience brings sorrow.

23–26 In the second part of this episode, the failure of the rich man to respond to the challenge leads to one of Jesus' most striking pronouncements. Twice Jesus states how difficult it is for the rich to enter the kingdom of God (vv.23, 24b) and then backs up this statement with a shocking analogy that seems to indicate not just difficulty but impossibility (v.25). The disciples respond twice, first with shock and amazement (v.24), and then with even greater shock and amazement (v.26). Jesus brings a measure of resolution by announcing that what is humanly *im*possible *is* possible with God (v.27).

23 Jesus' initial statement, "How hard it is for the rich to enter the kingdom of God!" runs counter to traditional Jewish thought and so provokes the amazement of the disciples (v.24). Judaism generally viewed wealth as evidence of divine favor and blessing (Dt 28:1–14; Job 1:10; 42:10; Ps 128:1–2; Isa 3:10). Proverbs 10:22 reads, "The blessing of the LORD brings wealth, and he adds no trouble to it." While wealth was considered a blessing from God, its potentially destructive power was also acknowledged. Riches gained through treachery or exploiting the poor would result in God's judgment, and the rich are put on notice to be generous to the poor. These positive and negative sides of wealth appear together in the intertestamental work titled The Wisdom of Jesus son of Sirach. First the dangers:

> One who loves gold will not be justified;
> one who pursues money will be led astray by it.
> Many have come to ruin because of gold,
> and their destruction has met them face to face.
> It is a stumbling block to those who are avid for it,
> and every fool will be taken captive by it.
>
> *Sirach 31:5–7 NRSV*

While the love of riches leads to destruction, Sirach also affirms that the righteous rich are particularly blessed:

> Blessed is the rich person who is found blameless,
> and who does not go after gold.
> Who is he, that we may praise him?
> For he has done wonders among his people.

Who has been tested by it and been found perfect?
Let it be for him a ground for boasting.

Sirach 31:8–10 NRSV

Jesus does not share this positive assessment. Throughout the gospel tradition, he warns about this destructive side of riches (Mk 4:19; Mt 6:19–21, 24; Lk 12:13–34) and frequently speaks of the radical reversal of fortunes the kingdom of God will bring (Lk 6:24–25; 16:19–31; cf. Lk 1:53). Wealth distracts people from things that have eternal value and hinders them from putting their trust in God.

24 When the disciples respond with amazement, Jesus stresses a second time the difficulty of entering the kingdom of God. This time he addresses them as "children" (*tekna*) and omits any specific reference to the rich. While these features universalize Jesus' teaching, the rich are clearly still in mind, as the following illustration will show (v.25). The address of the disciples as "children" could be an intentional allusion to the previous passage (vv.13–16; cf. 9:36–37), in which Jesus stresses the need to become like children (*paidia*) to enter the kingdom of God (although here Jesus uses *tekna* instead of *paidia*).

25 Jesus supports his statement with an astonishing proverb: "It is easier for a camel to go through the eye of a needle than for a rich man to enter the kingdom of God." Attempts have been made to downplay the meaning of this proverb. A notable one identifies the "eye of the needle" with a small gate leading into the city of Jerusalem in front of which camels had to kneel and unload their burdens in order to get through. This allusion would mean that a rich man must be willing to humble himself and release his dependence on wealth in order to enter the kingdom. But the interpretation is certainly wrong. There is no early or reliable evidence for the existence of such a gate, and it appears to have been first suggested in the eleventh century by the Byzantine exegete Theophylact (see Gundry, 565). Another way to explain away Jesus' radical statement appeals to a few late MSS that read "rope" (*kamilon*) instead of "camel" (*kamēlon*). But this reading, too, certainly represents a later copyist's attempt to soften the force of Jesus' words. All such conjectures fail to recognize the intentional shock value of Jesus' words or to grasp the full force of what he is saying, namely, that "for a rich man to enter the kingdom of God" is indeed "impossible." The camel was the largest animal encountered in everyday life in ancient Israel, and a needle's eye was the smallest opening imaginable. Jesus' dramatic point may be hyperbolic, but it is also reality: no camel could ever squeeze through such an opening, and it is impossible for the rich (indeed, for anyone) to enter the kingdom by virtue of their own resources.

26 Whereas before the disciples were "amazed" (*ethambounto*, v.24), now they are "even more amazed" (*perissōs exeplēssonto*). The radical nature of the proverb was not lost on the disciples. As shown by their question to each other, "Who then can be saved?" they completely understood Jesus' meaning.

27 As Jesus "gazed intently" (*emblepō*) at the rich man to discern his heart (v.21), so now he gazes at the disciples. The dramatic pause prepares for Jesus' climactic pronouncement and the solution to human weakness and sin: "With human beings this is impossible, but not with God; all things are possible with God" (TNIV). This answer makes clear that salvation is totally the work of God. Apart from the grace of God, it is impossible for anyone—especially the rich—to enter God's kingdom. Humanly speaking, none can be saved by their own efforts. But what we can never do for ourselves, God does for us. As France, 406, puts it,

"The salvation of the rich is always a miracle, but miracles are God's specialty." Was the rich man still within hearing range, and were these words meant for him too? Mark does not say. Notice that "eternal life," "salvation," and "entrance into the kingdom" are all used synonymously here.

28 Verses 28–31 represent a new scene, but one that follows naturally from Jesus' climactic pronouncement in v.27. In contrast to the failure of the rich man to give up what he had and to follow Jesus, Peter points out that the disciples had given up everything to follow him. There is a certain ambiguity here. Although the passage positively contrasts the disciples' willingness to give up everything with the rich man's unwillingness to give up his wealth, Peter's statement also carries a slight sense of self-righteous pride: "We have done more than he was willing to do!" Jesus' response in vv.29–30 also carries ambiguity: they will receive much in return for their sacrifice, including suffering and persecution! Matthew in the parallel passage reports Peter's additional words: "What then will there be for us?" (19:27)—further evidence that the disciples (Peter being their spokesman) were still thinking of material values rather than in spiritual terms.

29–30 Instead of rebuking Peter for his pride or selfishness, Jesus makes a promise, introduced by the solemn "I tell you the truth" (*amēn legō hymin*; cf. 10:15 and comments at 3:28). The effect is to universalize the statement beyond the context of the moment for the audience of the disciples. No one who forsakes home, loved ones, or property for Jesus' sake and the gospel's will fail to receive back in this life a hundredfold what he has and to gain eternal life in the age to come. The hundredfold return in this life is to be understood in the context of the new community of faith into which the believer in Jesus comes. There he or she finds a multiplication of relationships, closer and more spiritually meaningful than blood ties. The church as an extended family ("God's household," Eph 2:19) is a common theme throughout the NT, and fellow believers are often identified as "brothers and sisters" (*adelphoi*) as well as with other familial terms (cf. 1Jn 2:12–14; 1Th 2:7, 11). Jesus' failure to repeat "fathers" when he speaks of the rewards is probably because believers ultimately have only one Father—God himself (Mt 23:9; cf. Mk 3:35). The reference to receiving "homes" and "fields" likely refers to the shared resources of the Christian community and the hospitality Christians were expected to provide for one another. The early traveling missionaries would depend on the hospitality of their brothers and sisters in Christ (cf. 6:8–11).

Though the spiritual benefits of the faith community are enormous, they do not come without cost. Jesus is also realistic about the Christian life. There will be persecutions (only Mark includes this qualification). Again, the relevance of this statement for the situation in Mark's church (likely the persecuted church in Rome) is obvious. It is through trials and persecutions that the new relationships as members of the Christian community develop and flourish. The promise is for a full, though admittedly difficult, life here and now. But not only a full life here and now; for Jesus promises eternal life in "the age to come." Everything that happens in the present is an earnest of that far richer and complete fulfillment in the future, when there will no longer be any persecutions. The characteristic Jewish language of two ages—the present age and the age to come—is unusual in Mark (cf. 4:19) but here clearly refers to the full salvation that will be achieved at the consummation of the kingdom of God.

31 This saying of Jesus also appears in other contexts (cf. Mt 20:16; Lk 13:30). Jesus probably said it more than once; it lends itself to more than one application. Here it refers to the future, when God will evaluate the lives of men and women and when human values will be reversed. Those people who have rank and position now will not have them then, and those who do not have them now will have them then. This may be a kind of summary of Jesus' teaching in vv.17–31. In eternity the rich and the powerful will have the tables turned on them. Or perhaps it is a warning to the disciples in view of what they said: "We have left everything to follow you" (v.28). They must not conceive of their discipleship in terms of rewards. Discipleship entails suffering and service; it must be entered in terms of love and commitment to Jesus, not because of what one hopes to get out of it either in this life or in the life to come. To illustrate the point, Matthew, at this juncture, inserts in his gospel the parable of the workers in the vineyard (Mt 20:1–16).

NOTES

18 For a classic theological response to the question of whether this passage challenges Jesus' sinlessness, see B. B. Warfield, "Jesus' Alleged Confession of Sin," *PTR* 12 (1914): 177–228.

19 William Lane, 366 (citing H. L. Strack and P. Billerbeck), writes, "That man possesses the ability to fulfill the commandments of God perfectly was so firmly believed by the rabbis that they spoke in all seriousness of people who had kept the whole law from A to Z."

24 The variant reading τοὺς πεποιθότας ἐπὶ [τοῖς] χρήμασιν (*tous pepoithotas epi* [*tois*] *chrēmasin*, "for those who trust in riches"), though found in the majority of Greek MSS, is probably a gloss intended to soften the force of the strong statement found in v.23.

25 There are some later rabbinic parallels to this proverb that speak of the impossibility of an elephant's passing through the eye of a needle (*b. Ber. 55b*; *b. Baba Meṣiʿa 38b*; *b. ʿErubin 53a*). The Babylonian Talmud was compiled in Mesopotamia, where the elephant (like the camel in Israel) was recognized as the largest of land animals (see Garland, 399 n. 11).

REFLECTIONS

What do Jesus' words "Go, sell everything you have and give to the poor ... Then come, follow me" (v.21) mean for believers? It is significant that Jesus says the man lacks *one* thing but then gives him *four* commands: go, sell everything, give to the poor, and follow me. The one thing necessary for eternal life is not selling property or giving to the poor—it is complete allegiance to the kingdom of God and full submission to Jesus in discipleship. For this man such allegiance was impossible without renouncing the wealth that provided his security. This principle should give no comfort to those who assume that a halfhearted commitment will suffice. Instead we must ask, "If Jesus demanded so much from this man, what is he asking from us?" While authentic discipleship and complete submission to the kingdom may take different forms in different contexts, it is no less radical or demanding. James Edwards, 309, writes, "The call to follow Jesus does not constitute an additional obligation in life, but rather judges, replaces, and subordinates all obligations and allegiances to the one who says, 'Follow me.'"

M. Third Prediction of the Passion (10:32–34)

OVERVIEW

This passion prediction initiates the third cycle of episodes, which follow a similar pattern: Jesus predicts his death (8:31–32; 9:30–31; 10:32–34), the disciples respond with ignorance and pride (8:32; 9:32–34; 10:35–41), and Jesus teaches them concerning humility, sacrifice, and servant leadership (8:33–38; 9:35–37; 10:32–45). This last triad forms the climax, concluding with the key "ransom saying," which for the first time identifies the purpose of the passion: "For even the Son of Man did not come to be served, but to serve, and to give his life as a ransom for many" (10:45). Many commentators justifiably treat this as the thematic verse of Mark's gospel, both because of its important place in the narrative and because of its profound theological content. It summarizes the theme of suffering and sacrifice, which characterizes the second part of Mark's narrative and prepares the reader for Jesus' entrance into Jerusalem (11:1–11). Jesus' ministry is about to reach its climax and denouement.

32They were on their way up to Jerusalem, with Jesus leading the way, and the disciples
were astonished, while those who followed were afraid. Again he took the Twelve aside
and told them what was going to happen to him. 33"We are going up to Jerusalem," he
said, "and the Son of Man will be betrayed to the chief priests and teachers of the law.
They will condemn him to death and will hand him over to the Gentiles, 34who will mock
him and spit on him, flog him and kill him. Three days later he will rise."

COMMENTARY

32 Mark's journey motif now continues and specifies for the first time Jerusalem as the destination (see Overview, 8:31–10:52). It is Passover season, and Jesus and his disciples would have become part of the large body of Jewish pilgrims going up to Jerusalem for the festival. Jews always went "up" to Jerusalem, not only because it is on a hill, but especially because it is the Holy City of God.

Mark notes that Jesus takes the lead, thus indicating his intensity and determination to finish the task God has given him. In his gospel, Luke catches this same sense of intensity when he notes at the beginning of the journey that "Jesus *resolutely* set out for Jerusalem" (Lk 9:51, italics added; cf. Isa 50:7). Jesus' new level of intensity catches the disciples off guard, and they are "astonished." While Mark does not explicitly state the reason for this amazement, it is likely related to the messianic expectations that have been swirling around Jesus, together with the renewed determination he now expresses to reach Jerusalem, his goal. This view would also help to explain the next statement: "those who followed were afraid." This group, which Mark appears to distinguish from the Twelve, likely represents the wider circle of Jesus' followers, or perhaps the curious "crowds" who are fascinated and amazed at Jesus' teaching and miracles (cf. 10:1). They, too, are on their way to the festival at Jerusalem. A messianic claimant entering Jerusalem during the spiritually—and nationally—charged atmosphere of Passover in Jerusalem could provoke revolution and war with Rome. Amazement and fear are natural emotions under such circumstances.

In this electrified atmosphere Jesus separates the Twelve from the crowd, as he so often does in Mark's gospel (cf. 4:34; 7:17; 9:2, 28; 13:3; 14:33), for renewed instruction about his coming passion.

33–34 Here is the third major prediction of the passion in Mark (cf. 8:31 and 9:31). In addition to these three, there is a brief reference to Jesus' death in the sequel to the transfiguration narrative (cf. 9:9–12). Here the prediction is more detailed and precise than the others. (For a helpful chart comparing these three predictions, see Taylor, 436.) The first two refer generally to Jesus' (1) suffering at the hand of the religious leaders (8:31) or his betrayal into human hands (9:31), (2) execution (8:31; 9:31), and (3) resurrection (8:31; 9:31). The third prediction contains six main points: (1) The event will occur in Jerusalem; (2) Jesus will be handed over to the chief priests and scribes (v.33), (3) who will sentence him to death and (4) hand him over to the Gentiles, (5) who will mock him, spit on him, flog him, and execute him (v.34), but (6) after three days he will rise.

Thus here we have the first explicit reference to both the Jerusalem context and the Roman role in the execution. The word "crucify" does not occur in any of the passion predictions in Mark (cf. Mt 20:19, where it is used for the first time of Jesus' death). But the statement that Jesus will be handed over to the Gentiles reveals in a veiled way his coming crucifixion. France, 413, notes that the twofold Jewish phase of the passion described here agrees with what we know historically about the authority of the Jewish leadership. While they could pronounce a prisoner guilty, the execution itself must be carried out by the Roman authorities (cf. Jn 18:31; *y. Sanh.* 1:1; 7:2).

The sequence of events here sounds like a brief summary of the passion narrative and so has led some scholars to consider vv.33–34 a prediction after the event—i.e., the verses represent postresurrection church tradition and not tradition originating with Jesus. One's Christology plays an important role in decisions on matters such as this. If Jesus was who he claimed to be—the unique Son of God—then it causes no surprise that he predicted his passion in detail. If he is less than the Son of God, admittedly there are problems. That the events did not take place historically in the precise chronological sequence in which they are given in v.34 (cf. 14:65; 15:15, 16–20) would tend to cast doubt on the prediction's having been created from the passion narrative. In any case, it was certainly within Mark's authority as an inspired author to summarize Jesus' statement in his own words and to edit them in the light of the narrative that follows. Evans, 106–7, points out that many of the elements of Jesus' prediction go back to the earliest kerygma and almost certainly to Jesus himself, so that "there is no compelling reason not to believe that the essence of the prediction derives from Jesus."

Mark does not record any response by the disciples to this startling statement. Luke (18:34), however, says, "The disciples did not understand any of this." Mark's similar statement in 9:32, together with the arrogant quest for power expressed in the following episode (10:35–45), suggests a similar response here. Mark does not feel the need to express the disciples' spiritual dullness, since the following episode will speak for itself.

NOTES

32 The phrase οἱ δὲ ἀκολουθοῦντες ἐφοβοῦντο (*hoi de akolouthountes ephobounto*, "while those who followed were afraid") created problems for the copyists because it suggests another group distinct from the disciples. The variants, none of which have strong MS support, try to eliminate this distinction. That Mark wanted to indicate two distinct groups is clear from the definite article οἱ (*hoi*, "those") and the δὲ (*de*, "and," "but"; NIV, "while") used with it, which construction regularly indicates a change of subject. Two distinct groups are implied in the NIV's "the disciples were astonished, while those who followed were afraid."

N. The Request of James and John (10:35–45)

OVERVIEW

As noted above, this passage parallels both 8:27–38 and 9:30–37. All three passages begin with passion predictions, followed by some demonstration of pride or spiritual immaturity by the disciples, and then Jesus teaches on the nature of servant leadership and true discipleship. The parallels between 9:30–37 and 10:35–45 are especially striking, since both have the disciples' vying for greatness (9:34; 10:32), followed by Jesus' teaching that to be first one must become last, and that true greatness comes from service for others (9:35; 10:43–44).

The passage may be divided into two parts: (1) the request by James and John, and Jesus' response (vv.35–40); and (2) Jesus' teaching concerning servant leadership (vv.41–45). There is no reason to doubt the authenticity of the story, since it is unlikely that the church would have created a story that cast such disrepute on the character of two of the best-known disciples.

35Then James and John, the sons of Zebedee, came to him. "Teacher," they said, "we
want you to do for us whatever we ask."
36"What do you want me to do for you?" he asked.
37They replied, "Let one of us sit at your right and the other at your left in your glory."
38"You don't know what you are asking," Jesus said. "Can you drink the cup I drink or be
baptized with the baptism I am baptized with?"
39"We can," they answered.
Jesus said to them, "You will drink the cup I drink and be baptized with the baptism I
am baptized with, 40but to sit at my right or left is not for me to grant. These places belong
to those for whom they have been prepared."
41When the ten heard about this, they became indignant with James and John. 42Jesus
called them together and said, "You know that those who are regarded as rulers of the

Gentiles lord it over them, and their high officials exercise authority over them. [43]Not so with you. Instead, whoever wants to become great among you must be your servant, [44]and whoever wants to be first must be slave of all. [45]For even the Son of Man did not come to be served, but to serve, and to give his life as a ransom for many."

COMMENTARY

35–37 James and John, sons of Zebedee and fishermen, were called by Jesus to be disciples immediately after he called Peter and Andrew, the other fishermen brothers (1:16–20). Together with Peter they form an "inner circle" of disciples who accompany Jesus at important junctures in the narrative: the raising of Jairus's daughter (5:37), the transfiguration (9:2), and the praying of Jesus in Gethsemane (14:33). Jesus had nicknamed James and John "Sons of Thunder" (see comments at 3:17), probably because of their aggressive temperaments. Perhaps this ambitious nature is what prompted them to act on this occasion. Jesus is nearing Jerusalem; there are messianic expectations in the air. Yet when Jesus is enthroned, who will be his chief advisers? The Sons of Thunder jump at the chance to seize the most honored positions beside the king.

Their initial request is remarkably audacious. They want Jesus to do for them whatever they ask (v.35)—a carte blanche request! Jesus refuses to grant such a demand and asks what they are requesting (v.36). Their answer is that they might have the positions of highest honor in the messianic kingdom (v.37). The seat to the right of the king was the most prestigious (cf. Ps 110:1–2), perhaps reserved for the son and heir. The position to the left would be for his next closest adviser. To be beside the king is to have his ear and to share in his glory and authority. Some commentators claim that "in your glory" means at the parousia (so Taylor, 440), but this view misses the narrative context. Jesus has told the disciples that "some who are standing here will not taste death before they see the kingdom of God come with power" (9:1), and James and John surely think this prophecy is about to be fulfilled in an earthly messianic kingdom.

The request reveals clearly that before the crucifixion the disciples believed Jesus to be the Messiah. Since it was now clear that he was going up to Jerusalem, they expected his messianic glory to be revealed there. In this way, the request parallels Peter's confession in 8:27–30. Peter confesses, "You are the Christ" (8:29), while James and John request the best seats in the kingdom Jesus will soon receive. Both the confession and the request, therefore, reveal a measure of faith and confidence that Jesus is indeed the Messiah. Yet both also fail to comprehend that the kingdom will be achieved not through conquest and domination but through service and sacrifice (8:32–33; 10:38). Calvin, 2:417, comments: "This narrative contains a bright mirror of human vanity for it shows that proper and holy zeal is often accompanied by ambition.... They who are not satisfied with himself alone, but seek this or the other thing apart from him and his promises, wander egregiously from the right path."

38 Jesus' answer is sharp and penetrating. The two disciples did not really know what they were asking. The way to privileged position in the messianic kingdom is not by grabbing for power but by relinquishing it through suffering and death. Jesus explains this way to them by using the analogies of the cup and baptism. The cup, symbolizing trouble and suffering, is found in the OT. "In the hand of the LORD is a cup full of foaming wine mixed with spices; he pours it out, and all the wicked of the earth drink it down to its very dregs" (Ps 75:8). "Rise up, O Jerusalem, you have drunk from the hand of the LORD the cup of his wrath, you who have drained to its dregs the goblet that makes men stagger" (Isa 51:17; cf. Jer 49:12; La 4:21; Eze 23:31–34). In his Gethsemane prayer Jesus will again use the symbolism of the cup with reference to his suffering (Mk 14:36). In the OT, the image often refers to God's judgment on the wicked and so may perhaps allude to Jesus' vicarious death as payment for sins. However, the cup can also refer to suffering in general (Jer 49:12) and when used of judgment is usually qualified as the "cup of wrath" or with some similar expression (Isa 51:17, 22; Jer 25:15; Rev 14:10; 16:19). That James and John will also drink Jesus' cup (v.39) suggests that suffering rather than judgment is the primary sense intended here.

Unlike the cup imagery, the term "baptism" does not have clear OT precedent as a symbol for suffering or death. Isaiah 21:4 (LXX) comes the closest by using the verb *baptizō* of an overwhelming flood of lawlessness: "lawlessness overwhelms [*baptizei*] me." Suffering and judgment are often described in the OT as a deluge that overtakes someone (Pss 18:16; 42:7; 69:1–2; Isa 43:2), and this is Jesus' meaning here. In Luke 12:50, he declares, "I have a baptism to undergo, and how distressed I am until it is completed!" John the Baptist spoke of the baptism "with the Holy Spirit and with fire"—a deluge of judgment and purification—which the Messiah would accomplish (Mt 3:11; Lk 3:16), but here Jesus is speaking of his own suffering and death. While it is unlikely that Jesus has Christian baptism in mind, Mark's readers would perhaps think of their own "baptism into [Christ's] death" (Ro 6:3) and the suffering that had resulted from their identification with him.

39 Jesus' question in v.38 may have been rhetorical, but James and John answer it anyway. They are evidently still thinking of a messianic war with Rome when they respond with a confident "We can." They are ready and willing to suffer through whatever trials will come to achieve the messianic kingdom. Yet they are also naive—they fail to comprehend the nature of the sacrifice Jesus will undergo.

Jesus responds that they will indeed drink his cup and experience his baptism. The reference may be to suffering in general or to martyrdom. Although James was martyred early (Ac 12:2), church tradition has John living to an old age in the environs of Ephesus (Irenaeus, *Haer.* 3.1.1–2; cf. Rev 1:9–11). In any case, Jesus' vagueness here suggests the authenticity of the statement and argues against the claim by some that this is a *vaticinium ex eventu* (a "prophecy" created after the fact by the early church; so Bultmann, *History of the Synoptic Tradition*, 24). It is unlikely that the church, knowing the different fates of James and John, would have invented a saying in which Jesus says both of them will experience the same cup and the same baptism.

40 Jesus continues with the remarkable statement that to grant them privileged positions in his kingdom was not within his authority. Jesus refused to usurp the authority of his Father. God alone will grant the places at Jesus' right and left to "those for whom they have been prepared." Again, a statement such as this points to the episode's authenticity, since the church is unlikely to have invented a saying limiting Jesus' authority. So who are the ones for whom these seats have been prepared? The text, surely intentionally, does not say. Jesus has been repeatedly teaching his disciples that in the kingdom of God the last will be first and true leaders are those who serve (9:35; cf. 10:43). To come to the

Father one must become like a little child, wholly humble and dependent (10:15). The most honored seats in the kingdom do not go to the powerful and the famous but to nameless servants. Paradoxically, to be great in the kingdom the disciples must humble themselves and outserve one another. From a narrative perspective, it is ironic that in the near future the two people on Jesus' "right and left" will be not the disciples (who will flee in terror at the first sign of trouble) but the criminals crucified beside him (15:27).

41 Although Jesus had previously rebuked the spirit of ambition and jealousy among his disciples (cf. 9:35), it was still very much alive in them. The other ten were indignant with James and John. This anger was, of course, not righteous indignation at their insensitivity to Jesus' words about his suffering, or righteous anger at their callous attempt to seize the chief seats in the kingdom. Rather, it was jealousy that these two men had beaten them to the punch. All the disciples were surely thinking about the implications of Jesus' approach to Jerusalem and the nearness of the kingdom. None had comprehended what Jesus meant when he spoke of his passion.

42 So Jesus pauses and calls them together for another lesson in true greatness. By this point in the narrative, after the repeated failures of the disciples to comprehend Jesus' mission, the summons contains a wearisome sense of "here we go again." Jesus begins by drawing a striking contrast between the kingdoms of this world and the kingdom of God. With synonymous parallelism he notes that "those who are regarded as rulers of the Gentiles lord it over them" (i.e., over their subjects), and "their high officials [*megaloi*, 'great ones'] exercise authority over them." The rulers of the ancient world were deemed "great" because of their ability to conquer and dominate others. This fact is something "you know" (*oidate*), Jesus says. It is the way things are in the present age. The disciples did not need to look far in a Palestine ruled by Rome and the Herodian dynasty to see that power, oppression, and coercion were the preferred means of leadership.

43–44 But among true followers of Jesus a very different model applies. The Greek uses a present tense here: "It is [*estin*] not so with you." As Edwards, 325, notes, "Verse 43a is thus not an admonition to behave in a certain way as much as a description of the way things actually are in the kingdom of God." Among Jesus' disciples, greatness is not achieved by asserting rank but by humble service (cf. 9:34–35). As Jesus' description of the world's standard of greatness was given in synonymous parallels (v.42), so also is the description of true greatness in the kingdom of God: "Whoever wants to become great [*megas*] among you must be your servant [*diakonos*]," and "whoever wants to be first [*prōtos*] must be slave [*doulos*] of all" (vv.43b–44). *Diakonos* commonly referred to one who waited tables, but the word could be used to designate any kind of servant or assistant. *Doulos* was a stronger term that denoted a slave, one solely committed or subject to another (BDAG, 259). The second clause, although parallel, intensifies the first. To be first exceeds mere greatness, and to be a slave is even lower than a servant. The effect is to drive home Jesus' amazing paradox and to emphasize the upside-down values of the kingdom of God.

45 The climax to the episode comes in this verse. In the kingdom of God humble service is the rule, and the Son of Man is the example par excellence, especially in his redemptive mission. Every part of this verse is important. "Son of Man" is the veiled messianic title Jesus often uses of himself. The title is sometimes contrasted with "Son of God" and assumed to refer to Jesus' humble human nature. Yet its primary background is the exalted messianic figure of Daniel 7 (see comments at 8:31), where "one like a son of man" (i.e., a human being) is presented before the Ancient of Days and given "authority, glory and sovereign power." All the nations of the earth worship him, and he receives an eternal dominion and an indestructible kingdom (Da 7:13–14). This exalted background explains why Jesus says, "*Even* [*kai*] the Son of Man"—even the glorious Messiah, who will receive all glory, power, and dominion—"did not come to be served, but to serve." This statement summarizes Jesus' incarnate life. He did not come as a potentate whose every personal whim was to be catered to by groveling servants, but he came as a servant himself. And his coming meant giving "his life as a ransom for many."

The word translated "ransom" is *lytron*, which means "the price of release" (cf. BDAG, 605). The noun occurs in the NT only here and in Matthew's parallel (Mt 20:28). In Koine Greek *lytron* was often used of payment for the release of slaves or captives. The LXX uses the term for various payments, including compensation for crimes (Nu 35:31–32) or the redemption of those who, because of poverty, had sold their tribal land or themselves into slavery (Lev 25:26, 51–52). Since every firstborn, whether human or animal, belonged to the Lord, a "ransom" was to be paid to redeem the firstborn son (Nu 18:15). The verb *lytroō* could mean "to set free by paying a ransom" but commonly meant simply "to set free, deliver, or rescue." It is used in the LXX of God's deliverance of Israel from Egypt (Ex 6:6; Dt 7:8; 9:26; etc.). Paul uses the cognate *apolytrōsis* for the redemption from sins accomplished through Christ's death (Ro 3:24; 8:23; 1Co 1:30). The sense in the present passage is that Jesus' death pays the price to set his people free.

The prepositional phrase "for many" translates *anti pollōn*. The ordinary meaning of the preposition *anti* is "in place of" or "instead of"—a clear indication of substitution. Although it can be used to mean "in behalf of," this meaning is not its usual one, and here its use with *lytron* seems to demand the sense "instead of." The expression "the many" is not to be understood as a limiting adjective, meaning "some but not all," but rather in contrast to the one: the *one* died for the *many*. A single life is given for the ransom of others (see Bratcher and Nida, 337). The entire phrase "to give his life a ransom for many" therefore emphasizes the substitutionary and atoning element in Jesus' death. The one takes the place of the many. What should have happened to them happened to him instead.

Significant debate has focused on two key issues related to the ransom saying: its background and its authenticity. While it was once widely assumed that the conceptual background to the ransom saying was to be found in Isaiah's fourth Servant Song (Isa 52:13–53:12), this conclusion was seriously challenged by C. K. Barrett ("The Background of Mark 10:45," in *New Testament Essays*, ed. A. J. B. Higgins [Manchester: Manchester Univ. Press, 1959], 1–18), and M. D. Hooker, 129–31. Both scholars argue against Isaianic Servant imagery and instead find the background in Daniel 7 and in the experience of the Maccabean martyrs, who suffered and died so that the nation might live (see 2 Macc 7:37–38; 4 Macc 6:28–29; 17:21–22). While scholars continue to debate this issue, there is good evidence that Jesus indeed has Isaiah's fourth Servant Song in view: (1) The language of service that permeates Mark 10:43–45 recalls the role of the Servant, who sacrificially gives himself for others. Although the word "servant" in Isaiah 52:13 LXX is *pais* instead of *diakonos* or *doulos*, the terms are conceptually similar, and the cognate verb *douleuō* does appear with reference to the Servant in Isaiah 53:11 LXX. (2) The phrase "give his life" in Mark 10:45 is very close to Isaiah 53:12, where the Servant "poured out his life unto death" (cf. 53:10b). (3) In Isaiah 53:10 the Lord makes the Servant's life a "sin offering," i.e., a sacrifice covering the sins of others.

Similar language appears in v.6b, where "the LORD has laid on him the iniquity of us all," in close parallel to the Son of Man's role as a "ransom" or payment price (*lytron*) for the sins of others. (4) Perhaps most significantly, the striking image of the *one* suffering for the *many* appears both in Isaiah 53:11–12 and Mark 10:45 (cf. 14:24). Though individually none of these allusions are conclusive, together they make a convincing case that behind Jesus' words lies Isaiah's image of the Suffering Servant, who offers himself as a sacrifice for others.

The second key issue related to Mark 10:45 is its authenticity and whether Jesus attributed atoning significance to his own death. A strong case may be made for the authenticity of the saying: (1) The claim that the saying was created under the influence of Pauline theology of the atonement is unlikely, given the fact that Paul never uses *lytron* to refer to the redemption Jesus has accomplished (see Cranfield, 344). (2) The saying has a strong Semitic flavor and is easily translatable back into Aramaic (see S. Kim, *The Son of Man as the Son of God* [Grand Rapids: Eerdmans, 1985], 39). (3) The idea of the suffering or death of one person's providing atonement or benefit for others was not alien to Jesus' world; the idea appeared in Maccabean and other Jewish sources (2 Macc 7:37–38; 4 Macc 6:27–29; 17:22; 18:4; 1QS 5:6; 11QtgJob 38:2–3; Pr Azar 3:38–40; *L.A.E.* 3:1; cf. Evans, 122; McKnight, *Jesus and His Death*, 168–71). (4) Evans, 124 (citing V. Taylor, "The Origin of the Markan Passion-Sayings," in *New Testament Essays*) points out that the Semitic phrase "son of man" (which is natural Hebrew and Aramaic but very awkward Greek or Latin) certainly has its origin in the ministry of Jesus rather than in the later Hellenistic church. Similarly, the description of Jesus as "servant" "would be open to serious misunderstanding, even ridicule" in the Greco-Roman world. As the gospel moved out of its Jewish and Palestinian contexts, titles such as "Lord," "Son of God," and "Savior" became preferred titles for Jesus. Both the Son of Man traditions arising from Daniel 7 and the Servant traditions of Isaiah "are better explained as originating in the teaching of Jesus, rather than in the early church" (Evans, 124).

NOTES

37 In Matthew's gospel, it is the mother of James and John, rather than the disciples themselves, who makes the request (Mt 20:20). Many commentators consider this feature to be Matthew's redactional attempt to cast the disciples in a better light. Another possibility is that Matthew has recorded the specifics, while Mark emphasizes that James and John are ultimately responsible for the request. Matthew also acknowledges that the request is ultimately theirs by switching to the plural in Jesus' response in v.22: "You [plural] do not know what you are asking. Are you [plural] able ..." (v.22).

45 For further discussion on an Isaianic background to the ransom saying, see R. T. France, *Jesus and the Old Testament* (London: Tyndale, 1971), 116–21; W. J. Moulder, "The Old Testament Background and Interpretation of Mark x. 45," *NTS* 24 (1977–1978): 120–27; Martin Hengel, *The Atonement* (Philadelphia: Fortress, 1981), 49–65; Peter Stuhlmacher, *Jesus of Nazareth—Christ of Faith* (Peabody, Mass.: Hendrickson, 1993), 49–57; Evans, 120–24; McKnight, *Jesus and His Death*, 159–339 (McKnight [p. 338] eventually reaches a negative conclusion, claiming "there is negligible evidence to suggest [Jesus] saw his life as the Servant of Isaiah").

O. Restoring Blind Bartimaeus's Sight (10:46–52)

OVERVIEW

This last of the healing miracles in Mark's gospel takes place near Jericho. Jesus has just identified himself as the Son of Man who has come to serve (10:45), and here he renders service to a poor blind beggar named Bartimaeus. But there is more to the episode than a compassionate healing. The setting in Jericho reminds the reader that Jesus is approaching Jerusalem. The blind man cries out to Jesus by calling him "son of David," a title with strong messianic implications. The episode therefore not only emphasizes Jesus' compassion for the lowly and poor but also reminds Mark's reader that the Messiah from David's line is about to enter Jerusalem. Israel's salvation is drawing near (see C. Burger, *Jesus als Davidssohn* [FRLANT 98; Göttingen: Vandenhoeck & Ruprecht, 1970], 42–46, 49–63).

Bartimaeus also serves as a model disciple in the kingdom of God. In contrast to the rich man who fails to answer Jesus' radical call to discipleship (vv.17–31), and the powerful rulers who exalt themselves and dominate others (vv.35–45), Bartimaeus comes to Jesus like a child (see v.15)—humbly and in total dependence ("have mercy on me!" v.48)—and willingly follows Jesus along the way (v.52). As noted previously, this passage also has conceptual links to the previous healing of a blind man in 8:22–26, and the two passages "frame" the entire section 8:31–10:45, a section that highlights the failure of the disciples to comprehend Jesus' mission. The faith and spiritual "sight" of the blind men thus stands in contrast to the spiritual blindness of the disciples.

46Then they came to Jericho. As Jesus and his disciples, together with a large crowd,
were leaving the city, a blind man, Bartimaeus (that is, the Son of Timaeus), was sitting by
the roadside begging. 47When he heard that it was Jesus of Nazareth, he began to shout,
"Jesus, Son of David, have mercy on me!"
48Many rebuked him and told him to be quiet, but he shouted all the more, "Son of
David, have mercy on me!"
49Jesus stopped and said, "Call him." So they called to the blind man, "Cheer up! On your
feet! He's calling you." 50Throwing his cloak aside, he jumped to his feet and came to Jesus.
51"What do you want me to do for you?" Jesus asked him.
The blind man said, "Rabbi, I want to see."
52"Go," said Jesus, "your faith has healed you." Immediately he received his sight and
followed Jesus along the road.

COMMENTARY

46 Jericho is located five miles west of the Jordan River and about fifteen miles northeast of Jerusalem. There was an old Jericho (the famous site of Joshua's conquest, Jos 5) and a new Jericho. In Jesus' time, the old city was likely still inhabited, but a new city was now located about one mile to the south. It had been originally built by the Hasmoneans and then expanded by Herod the Great, who had his winter palace there. Luke says the healing occurred on the way to Jericho (Lk 18:35), while Mark reports that it took place on the way out of the city. It is possible that the miracle was done somewhere between the old Israelite city and the new Herodian one.

As usual, Jesus is accompanied by a large crowd. While this could refer generally to the crowds of pilgrims going up to Jerusalem for Passover, the fact that they rebuke the blind man for calling out to Jesus suggests that they are there especially for Jesus. They are pilgrims accompanying *him* to the festival. Jesus' intense popularity as a healer and teacher continues to be an important theme in Mark (1:37; 2:2, 13; 3:9, 20; 4:1; 5:21, 24; 9:14–15; 10:1).

In the Middle East, a blind man sitting along the road begging is a common sight (cf. Jn 9:1, 8). The road from Jericho to Jerusalem would have been a strategic location for receiving alms both from merchants and pious pilgrims traveling to Jerusalem (Evans, 131). Mark is the only evangelist who identifies the man by name, and only here in his gospel does he refer to a healed individual in this way—according to some scholars, because Bartimaeus became a follower of Jesus and so was known to Mark's church. Mark explains the meaning of the Aramaic name for his Greek readers: "son of Timaeus."

47 Apparently Bartimaeus had heard of Jesus' reputation as a healer. When he discovered that Jesus was coming by, he seized the opportunity to approach him. By the first century, the title "son of David" was coming into its own as a messianic title referring to the eschatological king from David's line (*Pss. Sol.* 17:21; cf. Isa 11:1, 10; Jer 23:5–6; Eze 34:23–24; see Strauss, *Davidic Messiah*, 38–57). The narrative does not say how Bartimaeus recognized Jesus as the son of David or what he meant by it. Some scholars have suggested that he is drawing on traditions related to a Solomon-like (i.e., "son of David") healer and exorcist (Josephus, *Ant.* 8.2.5 §§46–49; *T. Sol.* 20; see D. C. Duling, "Solomon, Exorcism and the Son of David," *HTR* 68 [1975]: 235–52). While this case is possible, these traditions relate specifically to Solomon rather than to the Messiah, and to exorcism rather than to healing in general. More likely, Bartimaeus was motivated by the general expectation that the Messiah would deliver the poor and oppressed (cf. Isa 11:4; *Pss. Sol.* 17:40–41; *T. Jud.* 24:6). Psalm 72:12–14 says the ideal Davidic king "will deliver the needy who cry out, the afflicted who have no one to help." This expectation, together with the hope that the messianic age would be a time when the "eyes of the blind will see" (Isa 29:18–19; cf. 35:5–6; 61:1), would have been enough to prompt Bartimaeus's cry for help.

While the title "son of David" is understandable in this context, it is nevertheless surprising in Mark's narrative. It appears only here (twice) and in Jesus' enigmatic discussion of the Messiah's Davidic ancestry in 12:35. (Contrast Matthew's frequent use: 1:1; 9:27; 12:23; 15:22; 20:30–31; 21:15; 22:42.) This infrequency makes Bartimaeus's proclamation all the more significant. Up to this point, Peter is the only human being who has openly acknowledged that Jesus is the Messiah. But now, as Jesus is about to enter Jerusalem, a lowly *blind* beggar shows extraordinary spiritual (in)*sight* by recognizing Jesus' true identity.

48 The crowd did not appreciate Bartimaeus's loud shouting and tried to silence him, but he shouted all the more. Why they wanted him to keep quiet is not explained. It is possible that the title he gave to Jesus offended them. More likely they were annoyed that a person of such low social status would try to draw Jesus' attention away. In their eyes Jesus was too important to be bothered by a blind beggar.

The reader is reminded of the disciples' earlier attempt to prevent lowly children from approaching Jesus (vv.13–16). Here, as there, Jesus intervenes to meet the needs of the smallest and least significant members of society. Despite the crowd's rebuke, Bartimaeus cries out "all the more." This kind of persistence is precisely what Jesus is looking for, and throughout Mark's gospel persistent faith is rewarded with healing (2:5; 5:23, 34; 7:27–29, 32; 8:22; 9:24).

49–50 That the man's cries stopped Jesus not only reveals his compassion but also implies that he did not reject the title "son of David." Since Jesus was now close to the fulfillment of his messianic mission, it was no longer necessary to keep the secret.

Jesus first asked them to call the beggar to him. Only Mark gives us the graphic details of vv.49–50. The crowd's complete change of attitude toward the beggar is remarkable. Instead of trying to silence him, they encouraged him. The word translated "Cheer up!" is *tharsei*. It occurs only seven times in the NT (Mt 9:2, 22; 14:27; Mk 6:50; 10:49; Jn 16:33; Ac 23:11), and six of the seven are from the lips of Jesus. The exception is here. Bartimaeus's response was immediate (v.50). The cloak was his outer garment, which he had probably spread on the ground to receive the alms.

51–52 Jesus did not immediately heal the blind beggar. He first asked him a question to stimulate faith (v.51). Having done that, without any overt action or healing word on Jesus' part, he sent him away with the words "Go,... your faith has healed you" (v.52).

The cure was immediate. Mark's statement that the man "followed" Jesus could mean that he simply joined the crowd going up to the festival rather than that he followed him as a disciple. However, the man's initial confession of Jesus as "son of David," his immediate response to Jesus' call (by leaving his cloak behind [v.50]; cf. 1:16–20; 2:13–14), and the language of "following" Jesus "along the way" (v.52) all imply that Mark has something deeper in mind. In contrast to those who have rejected Jesus' proclamation and so have been blinded to the true values of the kingdom, this formerly blind man now "sees" and so follows Jesus in discipleship.

NOTES

46 That Matthew speaks of two blind men (Mt 20:30) has sometimes been explained as his creative editing, either to increase the significance of the miracle or to provide a second testimony, since Jewish law required at least two witnesses (cf. Mt 9:27–31). A similar scenario appears in Matthew 8:28–34, where Matthew identifies two demoniacs instead of Mark's one. While such editing is possible, a harmonizing solution is that Mark (followed by Luke) simply notes the more prominent of the two men.

REFLECTIONS

The close of ch. 10 sets the stage for the climax of the story. The journey to Jerusalem is ended. Jesus is about to enter the Holy City, where the last acts of the drama of redemption will take place. His opening the eyes of the blind man stands in sharp contrast to the blindness of the religious leaders he is about to encounter there.

VI. THE JERUSALEM MINISTRY (11:1–13:37)

OVERVIEW

At this point a new section in the gospel of Mark begins. Jesus arrives in Jerusalem, and the rest of his ministry takes place within the confines of the city. Traditionally, this period, beginning with the triumphal entry on Sunday and ending with the crucifixion and resurrection seven days later, has been designated as Passion Week. But if we had only Mark's gospel, it would be possible to allow for a Jerusalem ministry longer than one week. Some scholars do, in fact, argue for an entrance into Jerusalem in the fall of the year at the time of the Feast of Tabernacles, thus extending Jesus' final ministry in the city to about six months. However, in view of John 12:1 and 12:12–15, which closely associate Jesus' final visit to Jerusalem with the Passover, a weeklong ministry is more probable.

The Jerusalem ministry of 11:1–13:37 may be divided into three parts: (1) Jesus' royal entrance into Jerusalem and his challenge to the city and its religious leaders through the symbolic actions of cleansing the temple and cursing a fig tree (11:1–25); (2) a series of resulting conflicts and debates between Jesus and the religious leaders (11:27–12:44); (3) and the Olivet Discourse, where Jesus predicts the destruction of Jerusalem and the signs of the end of the age (13:1–37).

A. The Triumphal Entry (11:1–11)

OVERVIEW

The primary significance of Jesus' approach to Jerusalem with reference to both the mind-set of the historical Jesus and Mark's theological narrative is that Jesus intentionally acts out the prophecy of Zechariah 9:9–10, where the humble and righteous messianic King comes to Jerusalem riding on a donkey, proclaiming peace to the nations:

> Rejoice greatly, O Daughter of Zion!
> Shout, Daughter of Jerusalem!
> See, your king comes to you,
> righteous and having salvation,
> gentle and riding on a donkey,
> on a colt, the foal of a donkey.
> I will take away the chariots from Ephraim
> and the war-horses from Jerusalem,
> and the battle bow will be broken.
> He will proclaim peace to the nations.
> His rule will extend from sea to sea
> and from the River to the ends of the earth.

Although Mark—unlike Matthew (21:5) and John (12:15)—does not explicitly cite the OT text, he also seems to have it in view. The implications for Jesus' ministry are threefold. (1) First, this is Jesus' strongest public affirmation yet of his royal and messianic identity. The messianic secret, which Jesus has enforced throughout Mark's narrative, is coming to an end. (2) Together with this self-revelation comes a confrontation. Jesus will now openly challenge the authority of the religious leaders of Jerusalem. (3) Jesus comes to Jerusalem not as a conquering hero on a warhorse but humbly riding on a donkey, thereby indicating that his messianic victory will come not through force-of-arms but through his sacrificial death (cf. 10:45).

The traditional designation "triumphal entry" is something of a misnomer, since Jesus' royal procession concerns his approach to Jerusalem rather than his entrance to the city. Only in v.11 does Jesus briefly enter the city before returning to Bethany for the night. The primary point is that the King has arrived at his destination, Jerusalem. The stage is set for the narrative's climax.

[1]As they approached Jerusalem and came to Bethphage and Bethany at the Mount of
Olives, Jesus sent two of his disciples, [2]saying to them, "Go to the village ahead of you, and
just as you enter it, you will find a colt tied there, which no one has ever ridden. Untie it
and bring it here. [3]If anyone asks you, 'Why are you doing this?' tell him, 'The Lord needs it
and will send it back here shortly.'"

[4]They went and found a colt outside in the street, tied at a doorway. As they untied
it, [5]some people standing there asked, "What are you doing, untying that colt?" [6]They
answered as Jesus had told them to, and the people let them go. [7]When they brought the
colt to Jesus and threw their cloaks over it, he sat on it. [8]Many people spread their cloaks
on the road, while others spread branches they had cut in the fields. [9]Those who went
ahead and those who followed shouted,

"Hosanna!"

"Blessed is he who comes in the name of the Lord!"

10 "Blessed is the coming kingdom of our father David!"

"Hosanna in the highest!"

[11]Jesus entered Jerusalem and went to the temple. He looked around at everything, but
since it was already late, he went out to Bethany with the Twelve.

COMMENTARY

1 The approach to Jerusalem was through Bethany and Bethphage. Bethphage ("house of figs") was a village close to Jerusalem. Its precise location is not known. Bethany, located on the eastern slope of the Mount of Olives, lay about two miles from Jerusalem (cf. Jn 11:18). The Mount of Olives is directly east of the city and rises to an elevation of about twenty-six hundred feet. Its summit commands a magnificent view of Jerusalem and especially of the Temple Mount. Mark's mention of the mountain may be more than geographical, since the Mount of Olives carries eschatological significance in Zechariah 14:4 as the place where the Lord will stand on the day of judgment. Thus the reference here has messianic and eschatological overtones.

2 From this vicinity, Jesus sent two of his (unnamed) disciples "to the village ahead" to get a colt. The village is not identified and could have been either Bethphage or Bethany, or perhaps another nearby village. The word translated "colt" (*pōlos*) can mean the young of any animal; but here, as in the LXX's parallel (Zec 9:9), it likely means the colt of a donkey (cf. Mt 21:2; Jn 12:15). The description of the tethered colt (vv.2, 4) may indicate a secondary allusion to Genesis 49:9–11, where the Messiah from Judah's line will "tether his donkey to a vine, his colt to the choicest branch." In the LXX, the words for "colt" and "tether" are the same as those used here.

Jesus stipulated that the colt must be an unused one ("which no one has ever ridden"). Such animals were regarded as especially suitable for sacred purposes (such as sacrifices [Nu 19:2; Dt 21:3] and, formerly, pulling the ark of the covenant [1Sa 6:7]). The Mishnah says that no one else may ride on the king's animal (*m. Sanh.* 2:5). Some commentators have suggested that the background to Jesus' command is the right of "impressment," which stipulated that a king or other person of authority could borrow an animal that was needed for immediate service (cf. 1Sa 8:16; J. M. D. Derrett, "Law in the New Testament: The Palm Sunday Colt," *NovT* 13 [1971]: 243–49). If correct, this allusion would add still further royal imagery to the passage.

3 Jesus anticipated that the actions of the disciples might be questioned; so he instructed them that, when asked why they were taking the colt, they should answer, "The Lord needs it." The term "Lord" (*kyrios*) is ambiguous and could here refer to (1) Jesus himself (so Gundry, 624, 628; Nineham, 295); (2) God, in whose authority Jesus is acting (so France, 432; Evans, 143); or (3) the owner of the colt (so Taylor, 455; Cranfield, 350; Lane, 395). By capitalizing "Lord," the NIV has interpreted the passage to mean either the first or second option. But *kyrios* can mean simply "master," and some commentators favor the third. On this understanding, Jesus has made an arrangement with the owner (who may have been with Jesus at the time) to borrow the animal, and the last phrase of v.3—"and will send it back here shortly"—is an assurance by the owner that the animal would be returned promptly after he was through with it. While this interpretation is possible, it would apparently contradict Luke 19:33, which says that while the disciples were untying the colt, "its owners [*hoi kyrioi autou*] asked them, 'Why are you untying the colt?'" It seems more likely, therefore, that *ho kyrios* in Mark 11:3 refers to Jesus or to God. The former makes the most sense of the scene by explaining why the bystanders so easily relinquish the animal (v.6). Jesus was probably well-known by this time in the area around Bethany, and his authority was recognized.

Mark does not say whether Jesus had earlier arranged to borrow the colt or whether his awareness of its presence was an act of divine foreknowledge. In either case, as I. H. Marshall (*Gospel of Luke* [NIGTC; Grand Rapids: Eerdmans, 1978], 713–14) notes, "The fact that the trivial detail of obtaining the animal is told at such length ... suggests that the Evangelists saw some importance in it, and this lay in its testimony to the authority and perhaps the prescience of Jesus."

4–6 The disciples found the colt as Jesus had told them and carried out his orders to the letter. Mark makes no mention that the owners of the colt were present, but the phrase "some people standing there" (v.5) may be equivalent to Luke's "its owners" (Lk 19:33). The people (owners?) did not object to the disciples' taking the colt (v.6) either because Jesus had arranged for the procurement ahead of time or because they knew of Jesus and recognized his authority.

7–8 Jesus' act of riding is significant at several levels. First, nowhere else in the Gospels is he seen riding an animal. Second, the normal approach to Jerusalem by pilgrims was on foot, so Jesus' mounted entry again indicates that he is performing a unique and symbolic act. Third, the ride is reminiscent of the ceremony at Solomon's coronation (1Ki 1:32–40), which itself has both royal and messianic connotations. Finally, as noted in the Overview, the whole approach to Jerusalem seems to be Jesus' intentional enactment of the messianic prophecy of Zechariah 9:9–10 (which itself echoes Solomon's coronation).

The action of the crowd was evidently spontaneous. The outer garments on the back of the donkey made a kind of saddle for Jesus to ride on (v.7). When he mounted the colt (Luke 19:15 says the people put Jesus on it), other people in the crowd spread on the road before him garments, branches, and foliage (v.8). The spreading of garments recalls the greeting given to Jehu in 2 Kings 9:13—an act of royal homage. Palm branches, hymns of praise, and songs are associated with the entrance of Simon Maccabeus into Jerusalem in 1 Maccabees 13:51. The word *stibadas* (NIV, "branches") is a general term for vegetation and can mean "leaves, leafy branches, tall grass," or "stalks of grain" (MM, 589; BDAG, 945). This vegetation could easily have been cut from the fields located nearby. Like the garments, the foliage is placed before Jesus to make a path for him. Both actions signify honor for a figure of high rank and authority. Only John specifically mentions palm branches (12:13), which could have come from Jericho. They are not native to Jerusalem, though in protected places they are known to grow there.

9–10 The crowds surrounded Jesus. Some people went ahead of him, some behind. All shouted, "Hosanna." Cranfield, 351, comments,

> Perhaps the foliage that was being strewn to make a path of honor for Jesus reminded someone of the *lûlabîm* (bundles of palm, myrtle, and willow) that were carried at the Feast of Tabernacles and shaken at the occurrence in the liturgy of the word *hosiahnna* in Psalm 118:25 ... and so called to his mind and lips the passage of the psalm, which once repeated would quite naturally be taken up by the crowd of pilgrims.

"Hosanna" means "save now," but it had become simply an exclamation of praise. "Blessed is he who comes in the name of the LORD" is an accurate quotation of Psalm 118:26, one of the Hallel Psalms (Pss 113–118), which were used liturgically at the feasts of Tabernacles and Passover. This quotation was a customary religious greeting or blessing pronounced on pilgrims who had come to Jerusalem for the feast, but as Lane, 397, suggests, that use did not exhaust its meaning, since "the formulation is ambiguous and Mark may well have intended his readers to detect a deeper, messianic significance in the phrase 'he who comes in the name of the Lord' (cf. Gen 49:10)."

Verse 10 seems to support that interpretation. The blessed kingdom is the "kingdom of our father David," clearly the messianic kingdom promised to David's son (cf. 2Sa 7:14–16; Isa 9:1–7; 11:1–16; Jer 23:5–6; 33:14–16). R. P. Martin (*Mark*, 138) claims that not even this statement gives away the secret of Jesus' person, "since ... the cry of Hosanna is related to the coming kingdom and does not directly designate Jesus as Davidic King." While it is certainly true that the messianic intentions of the crowd are more explicit in the other three gospels ("Blessed is the King who comes ..." [Lk 19:38]; "Hosanna to the Son of David!" [Mt 21:9]; "Blessed is the King of Israel" [Jn 12:13]), there can be little doubt that Mark expects his readers to see the crowd's cry as messianic and centered on Jesus himself. That it is so is evident from the intensity of the homage directed toward Jesus, as well as the acclamation "son of David" by Bartimaeus in the previous episode (10:47–48). At the same time, the crowd's cry is less than explicit, and its nationalistic tone will be sharply qualified in the narrative that follows. In 12:35–37 Jesus himself will question the adequacy of the title "son of David," and the passion narrative will radically redefine the nature of messianic salvation.

11 On entering the city Jesus went to the temple. Mark uses the word *hieron*, which here means the "temple area," not the building itself (which would be *naos*). Apparently, the crowd had quickly dispersed, and only the disciples remained with Jesus. "He looked around at everything," not as a first-time tourist viewing the sacred precincts (Jesus had been to Jerusalem before), but as the sovereign Lord examining the institution to see whether it was fulfilling its divinely appointed mission. The examination prepared for the prophetic act of cleansing. But since the hour was late, Jesus delayed his action against the temple and instead withdrew with his disciples to Bethany for the night. Mark does not say with whom Jesus stayed in Bethany, but John's gospel refers to the home of his friends Lazarus, Mary, and Martha there (11:1; cf. Lk 10:38–42), and Mark will later describe Jesus' dinner at the home of Simon the Leper (14:1–11).

Rawlinson, 151, sums up well the significance of the triumphal entry:

> On the whole, it seems to be the most probable conclusion that the entry in this peculiar fashion into Jerusalem was deliberate on the part of our Lord, and was meant to suggest that, though He was indeed the Messiah and "son of David," yet the Messiahship which He claimed was to be understood in a spiritual and non-political sense, in terms of the prophecy of Zechariah, rather than in terms of the "son of David" idea as interpreted by contemporary expectation (e.g., in the Psalms of Solomon). The time had in fact come for our Lord to put forward His Messianic claims, and to make His appeal to Jerusalem in a deliberately Messianic capacity. He does so, however, in a manner that is suggestive rather than explicit, and that was so calculated as to afford the minimum of pretext for a charge of quasi-political agitation.

NOTES

2 Matthew's parallel says both the colt and his mother were brought (21:7), which many commentators have taken to be his mistaken understanding of the synonymous parallelism of the prophecy in Zechariah. Another possibility is that Matthew is recording an historical reminiscence and that the mother was brought along with the unbroken colt to keep it calm.

10 Moloney, 220, differs from the majority of commentators by interpreting Mark's presentation of the cry of the crowds and the disciples as "false messianic expectation"—a nationalistic misunderstanding of Jesus' true mission and identity. Taking the cry as a misunderstanding, however, would seem to run contrary to Jesus' apparent acceptance of the title "son of David" in 10:47–48.

11 France, 436, 442, argues that v.11 is better understood as the introduction to the next passage (vv.11–25) rather than the conclusion to this one (where it appears as something of an anticlimax). Taken as an introduction, it forms a well-structured narrative sequence focused on the temple.

A First visit to the temple (v.11)
    B Cursing of the fig tree (vv.12–14)
A Jesus takes action in the temple (vv.15–19)
    B The fig tree is found to be dead (vv.20–25)
A Jesus returns to the temple (v.27)

B. The Unfruitful Fig Tree (11:12–14)

OVERVIEW

The next three episodes—the cursing of the fig tree, the "cleansing" of the temple, and the discovery of the withered fig tree—are closely related and represent another one of Mark's intercalations or sandwiching devices. The episode in the temple interrupts the fig tree account and provides the clue to its meaning. Both represent symbolic acts of judgment against Israel's religious leaders for failing to produce spiritual fruit.

This summary helps to explain what is admittedly one of the most unusual and theologically difficult stories in the Gospels. The cursing of the fig tree is not found in Luke. (Did he have problems with it and omit it, or was it unknown to him?) Many modern commentators would just as soon that it were not here at all. Rawlinson, 154, says that it "approximates more closely than any other episode in Mark to the type of 'unreasonable' miracle characteristic of the non-canonical gospel literature." Hunter, 110, comments, "With our knowledge of Jesus from other sources, we find it frankly incredible that he could have used his power to wither a fig tree because it did not yield figs two or three months before its natural time of fruitage." While rejecting the historicity of this account, Hunter finds the kernel of history in this story in the parable of the barren fig tree found in Luke 13:6–9. What was originally a parable has been changed into a factual story. However, such appeals to nonhistoricity are unnecessary and fail to appreciate that Jesus is not arbitrarily and maliciously destroying nature but is intentionally acting out a parable for his disciples to see.

12 The next day as they were leaving Bethany, Jesus was hungry. 13 Seeing in the distance
a fig tree in leaf, he went to find out if it had any fruit. When he reached it, he found
nothing but leaves, because it was not the season for figs. 14 Then he said to the tree, "May
no one ever eat fruit from you again." And his disciples heard him say it.

COMMENTARY

12–13 The incident occurred on the way to Jerusalem from Bethany, where Jesus had spent the night. He was hungry. Noticing a fig tree, he went to see whether it had any figs on it (v.13). Fig trees around Jerusalem usually leaf out in March or April, but they do not produce figs till June. This tree was no exception. It was in full leaf; but, as Mark tells his readers, there were no figs on it "because it was not the season for figs." It is this phrase that makes the story such a problem for some commentators. Grant, 828, says Mark's explanation "only increases the problem, as it reflects on the good sense of Jesus." An easy solution is to consider the phrase a scribal gloss (so Lohmeyer, 234; Anderson, 265). But that will not do, because there is no textual evidence to support it. Also there is the fact that explanatory notes are a feature of Mark's style (cf. 1:16; 5:42; 7:3–4, 19; 13:14). It seems best to consider the phrase Mark's own insertion to explain to people unfamiliar with the characteristics of a fig tree why one fully leafed out would not have fruit on it.

14 Jesus addressed the tree directly and by his words performed a miracle of destruction. It is the only miracle of destruction attributed to Jesus in the Gospels. T. W. Manson's verdict on the action here ascribed to Jesus is well-known: "It is a tale of miraculous power wasted in the service of ill temper (for the supernatural energy employed to blast the unfortunate tree might have been more usefully expended in forcing a crop of figs out of season); and as it stands it is simply incredible" ("The Cleansing of the Temple," *BJRL* 33 [1951]: 259).

As noted above, however, a better explanation is to see the miracle as an enacted parable. Jesus' hunger provides the occasion for his use of this teaching device. The fig tree represents Israel (cf. Jer 8:13; Hos 9:10, 16–17; Mic 7:1; Na 3:12). The tree is fully leafed out, and on a tree in such a state one would normally expect to find fruit. Its lack of fruit symbolizes the hypocrisy of Israel's leaders, who have made her ripe for the judgment of God. As Cranfield, 356–57, puts it, "A people which honored God with their lips but whose heart was all the time far from him (7:6) was like a tree with abundance of leaves but no fruit. The best commentary on verses 12–14 and 20f. is to be found in the narrative which these verses enframe."

NOTES

12–14 For a detailed discussion of the background to the cursing of fig tree and the parallels with the cleansing of the temple, see W. R. Telford, *The Barren Temple and the Withered Tree* (JSNTSup 1; Sheffield: JSOT Press, 1980) and "More Fruit from the Withered Fig Tree," in *Templum Amicitiae*, ed. W. Horbury (JSNTSup 48; Sheffield: JSOT Press, 1991), 264–304.

13 W. J. Cotter ("For it was Not the Season for Figs" [*CBQ* 48 (1986): 62–66]) suggests that the clause "for it was not the season for figs" is meant to explain why Jesus "went out to find out if it had any fruit" rather than to explain why the tree did not have figs (i.e., to modify "he found nothing but leaves"). The verse would then read, "Seeing in the distance a fig tree in leaf, he went to find out if it had any fruit (for it was not the season for figs). When he reached it, he found nothing but leaves." This would remove some of the tension from the episode, since Jesus would not be approaching a tree that could not possibly fruit but is rather holding out hope that some early fruit has already appeared. The other option, of course, is that Jesus is simply acting out a parable and did not really expect to find any fruit—"because it was not the season for figs."

C. The Cleansing of the Temple (11:15–19)

OVERVIEW

The cleansing of the temple was Jesus' second action with strong messianic significance during Passion Week, the first being the triumphal entry. As noted above, Mark sandwiches ("intercalates") the episode between the beginning and end of the fig tree episode—an arrangement meant to link the accounts, with each interpreting the other. The judgment symbolized by the cursing of the fig tree is initiated by Jesus' cleansing of the temple, and the cleansing of the temple is prophetic of the destruction of Jerusalem and the eschatological judgment (cf. Mk 13).

All three synoptic writers place the cleansing of the temple at the end of Jesus' ministry. Only John has it at the beginning (2:14–22). Most commentators prefer the synoptic placement and reject the possibility of two cleansings. But why Jesus could not have cleansed the temple twice—once at the beginning and once at the end of his public ministry—is never adequately explained. The objection that the authorities would have been ready for Jesus and prevented the incident is not a strong one. The first episode—which was likely viewed by the authorities as a brief and minor disturbance—would have been long since forgotten by the time of Jesus' final Passover visit two or three years later. Jesus could have easily slipped in and caught the temple authorities off guard in the crush of the crowds at Passover time.

Almost all scholars consider Jesus' actions in the temple to be an authentic historical tradition. Most also affirm it was this event that prompted the authorities in Jerusalem to act against him. The significance of the event for Jesus, however, has been hotly debated. S. G. F. Brandon (*Jesus and the Zealots* [Manchester: Manchester Univ. Press, 1967]) claimed that Jesus was acting as a revolutionary attempting to seize control of the temple precincts. This thesis has been rejected by most scholars and falters on the fact that neither the leadership of the Jewish temple nor the Roman authorities acted immediately against Jesus. E. P. Sanders (*Judaism*, 61–76) thinks that Jesus' actions were prophetic and symbolic and that Jesus expected God would destroy the present temple and rebuild a new one "not made with hands" (Mk 14:58 TNIV). Evans, 173–82, claims that Jesus' actions likely had not only prophetic but also messianic significance. He points to the close verbal parallels between Solomon's prayer at the dedication of the temple in 1 Kings 8:41–43 and the two OT passages Jesus cites in Mark 11:17 (Isa 56:7; Jer 7:11). Solomon prays that God would answer the prayer of the foreigner who prays toward this house (temple) "so that all the peoples of the earth may know your name and fear you, as do your own people Israel, and may know that this house I have built bears your Name" (1Ki 8:43). Evans follows Robert Gundry (*Matthew: A Commentary on His Literary and Theological Art* [Grand Rapids: Eerdmans, 1982], 642) in affirming that it was Israel's kings, rather than prophets, who cleansed and restored the temple, and in the *Psalms of Solomon* the Davidic Messiah is expected to arise and "purge Jerusalem" so that the nations would "come from the ends of the earth to see his glory" (*Pss. Sol.* 17:30–31). Jesus' challenge was therefore both prophetic and messianic. As God's agent to inaugurate the kingdom, he called on the religious authorities to restore true worship to the temple or face God's judgment and destruction.

This raises the further question of whether Jesus' actions were a symbolic destruction of the temple (so Sanders) or whether he was symbolically "cleansing" or purging it—i.e., calling Israel's leaders to return to true worship (so C. A. Evans, "Jesus' Action in the Temple: Cleansing or Portent of Destruction?" *CBQ* 51 [1989]: 237–70). If the former, did Jesus expect God to replace the temple with a new one (as Sanders asserts), or was he signaling that the sacrificial system was permanently at an end? While Jesus' actions alone provide insufficient evidence to answer these questions, throughout the gospel tradition Jesus repeatedly predicts the coming judgment and destruction of Jerusalem and the temple (Mk 13:2 par.; Lk 13:34–35; 19:41–44). Furthermore, at his trial and crucifixion he is accused of claiming that *he* would destroy the temple (Mk 14:58 par.; Mk 15:29 par.; cf. Ac 6:14). This accusation may have stemmed from a distortion of his prediction in John about Jerusalem's destruction and his teaching about "the body of his temple" (Jn 2:19–21). The juxtaposition of the cursing and withering of the fig tree with Jesus' actions in the temple suggest a symbolic act of destruction rather than merely purification. It seems likely, therefore, that Jesus' actions went beyond "cleansing" to an enacted parable of the temple's destruction.

15On reaching Jerusalem, Jesus entered the temple area and began driving out those
who were buying and selling there. He overturned the tables of the money changers and
the benches of those selling doves, 16and would not allow anyone to carry merchandise
through the temple courts. 17And as he taught them, he said, "Is it not written:

"'My house will be called
a house of prayer for all nations'?

But you have made it 'a den of robbers.'"
18The chief priests and the teachers of the law heard this and began looking for a way
to kill him, for they feared him, because the whole crowd was amazed at his teaching.
19When evening came, they went out of the city.

COMMENTARY

15–16 Mark describes the events simply and with little introduction: Jesus enters the temple courts (*hieron*; see comments at v.11) and begins "driving out" (*ekballō*, the same strong word used for exorcisms) those who are buying and selling. For the convenience of pilgrims traveling to Jerusalem, the animal sellers and the money changers had set up business in the temple's outer area, the Court of the Gentiles. The animals were sold for sacrifices. It was far easier for a pilgrim to Jerusalem to purchase an animal that was guaranteed kosher than to have to bring an animal with him and have it inspected for meeting the kosher requirements. Mark mentions only doves or pigeons (*peristeras*), which were sacrificial offerings for the poor (Lev 5:7, 11; 12:8; cf. Lk 2:24). John also speaks of sheep and oxen (Jn 2:15). The Roman money the pilgrims brought to Jerusalem had to be changed into the Tyrian currency (the closest thing to the old Hebrew shekel), since the annual temple tax (Ex 30:11–16) had to be paid in that currency. According to the Mishnah, the temple tax was due in the weeks leading up to Passover (*m. Šeqal.* 1:1–3).

Both the sacrificial animals and the exchange of currency were necessary for the effective functioning of the temple, and there is no indication in

Mark that the transactions themselves were wrong. It is possible, of course, that the sellers were practicing extortion. The Mishnah speaks of an occasion on which the temple authorities were charging exorbitant prices for pigeons (*m. Ker.* 1:7), and Jesus' quotation from Jeremiah 7:11 about a "den of robbers" (v.17) could carry this implication. But the word used there normally means a bandit or insurrectionist (*lēstēs*), not a swindler or extortionist. The real problem Jesus confronts is not the selling per se, but its location in the temple and the disruption to worship it caused. The temple was meant to be "a house of prayer for all nations" (v.17; Isa 56:7).

In John's account Jesus drove the sellers out with a whip made from pieces of rope. Mark does not mention a whip. Nevertheless the words "driving out" and "overturned the tables" suggest that Jesus used force. By overturning the tables of the money changers and the benches of those selling doves, Jesus was directly challenging the authority of the high priest, because they were there by his authorization. V. Epstein ("The Historicity of the Gospel Account of the Cleansing of the Temple," *ZNW* 55 [1964]: 42–58) notes the rabbinic evidence that there were originally markets set up on the Mount of Olives for such transactions and suggests that their introduction into the temple courts was a recent innovation by the high priest Caiaphas. If this suggestion is accurate, Jesus' actions would have been a personal affront to the high priest and his associates.

The statement of v.16 that Jesus prevented the transporting of merchandise through the temple occurs only in Mark. It has been suggested that it may be Peter's own recollection of the event. Jesus not only cleansed the temple of its profanation by the merchants, but he also put a stop to its casual use as a shortcut between the city and the Mount of Olives. Using the temple area for transport is prohibited in the Mishnah (*m. Ber.* 9:5).

17 The first passage quoted by Jesus is Isaiah 56:7, a prediction that non-Jews who worship God will be allowed to worship in the temple. By allowing the Court of the Gentiles, the only place in the temple area where Gentiles were allowed to worship God, to become a public market, the Jewish religious leaders were preventing Gentiles from exercising the spiritual privilege promised to them. God's house was supposed to be "a house of prayer for all nations." The second quotation—"But you have made it 'a den of robbers'"—is from Jeremiah 7:11 and emphasizes that instead of allowing the temple to be what it was meant to be, a place of prayer, they had allowed it to become a robbers' lair. As noted above, this label is to be understood not so much in terms of the Jewish merchants' dishonest dealings with pilgrims as of their robbing the Gentiles of their rightful claim to worship Israel's God.

The significance of the cleansing of the temple, then, is that with the coming of the Messiah, "[Jesus] seeks to make available to the Gentiles the privileges which belonged to the new age and thereby he proclaims that the time of universal worship, uninhibited by Jewish restrictions, has come" (Martin, *Mark*, 225). This development would have been particularly meaningful for Mark's predominantly Gentile readers.

18–19 The Pharisees and Herodians in Galilee had decided that Jesus must be put out of the way (cf. 3:6). Now the chief priests and teachers of the law (scribes) come to the same decision. The chief priests comprised the upper echelons of Jerusalem's priesthood, especially the family of Caiaphas the high priest (see comments at 8:31). The teachers of the law, as we have seen, were professional scribes and experts in the Mosaic law (see comments at 1:22). Both groups, together with the "elders," were represented on the Sanhedrin, the Jewish high court. In his passion predictions Jesus has twice declared that he would be opposed by the chief priests and teachers of the law (8:31; 10:33). While the latter have repeatedly opposed him during his Galilean ministry (2:6, 16; 3:22; sometimes in league with the Pharisees—7:1, 5; 9:14), here is the first time in Mark's gospel that the chief priests reveal active hostility toward him. For Jesus is now on their turf—in Jerusalem and in the temple. His actions in the temple have directly challenged their authority. So they go into action against him, but not openly, because they fear the response of the people. Jesus' charismatic actions and teaching have already captivated Jerusalem's crowds.

Again Jesus and his disciples withdraw from Jerusalem for the night (v.19), presumably returning to Bethany. Do they withdraw because Jerusalem is not a safe place for Jesus at night?

D. The Withered Fig Tree and Sayings on Faith and Prayer (11:20–25[26])

OVERVIEW

The first three verses of this section form the second part of the story of the fig tree (11:12–14), which sandwiches the account of the cleansing of the temple. (For the theological significance of this "intercalation," see Overview, 11:15–19.)

20In the morning, as they went along, they saw the fig tree withered from the roots.
21Peter remembered and said to Jesus, "Rabbi, look! The fig tree you cursed has withered!"
22"Have faith in God," Jesus answered. 23"I tell you the truth, if anyone says to this
mountain, 'Go, throw yourself into the sea,' and does not doubt in his heart but believes
that what he says will happen, it will be done for him. 24Therefore I tell you, whatever you
ask for in prayer, believe that you have received it, and it will be yours. 25And when you
stand praying, if you hold anything against anyone, forgive him, so that your Father in
heaven may forgive you your sins.'"

COMMENTARY

20–21 The next morning (presumably Tuesday of Passion Week) Jesus and his disciples, on returning to Jerusalem from Bethany, again passed the fig tree. It was totally destroyed ("withered from the roots"). Jesus had predicted that no one would ever eat fruit from it again (v.14); and Peter, remembering what Jesus had said, called his attention to the withered tree (v.21). Jesus does not explicitly interpret the event, yet the meaning seems clear: Jesus' predicted judgment on the temple will come to pass as surely as did his prediction that the fig tree would wither.

22 We have noted that the cursing of the fig tree is closely related to the cleansing of the temple, with both symbolizing God's judgment against Israel. Yet oddly, Jesus does not make this connection explicit. Instead, in this verse and in the teaching that follows, he links the miracle of the fig tree's destruction to the power of faith and prayer. This feature suggests to some commentators that the sayings of vv.22–25 have no historical connection with what precedes and that Mark (or the tradition before them) has added them out of a misunderstanding of the symbolism of the fig tree's destruction. While this is possible, it is more likely that Jesus took this opportunity to draw a second application from the miracle and that Mark (and Matthew, who follows him) has retained this application. Jesus uses the incident of the fig tree to teach critical lessons on faith and prayer. The source of the power for performing the miracle is God. He must be the object of our faith.

23 As with previous pronouncements of Jesus, this one is preceded by the solemn introductory formula "I tell you the truth"—a way of indicating its importance (see comments at 3:28). Since Jesus was standing on the Mount of Olives, from which the Dead Sea can be seen on a clear day, he may have been referring specifically to that mountain. Of course, the image of throwing a mountain into the sea is figurative for something that is humanly impossible (Zec 4:7). Jesus is saying that the greatest possible difficulties can be removed when a person has faith (cf. Jas 1:6). A similar image of the power of faith to move mountains appears in the saying concerning the mustard seed in Matthew 17:20 (cf. Lk 17:6).

24 There is a close connection between the kind of faith Jesus speaks of here and prayer. E. Stauffer (*New Testament Theology* [London: SCM, 1955], 169) clearly brings out this connection: "The 'faith' of Mark 11:23f. is a faith that prays.... Prayer is the source of its power, and the means of its strength—God's omnipotence is its sole assurance, and God's sovereignty its only restriction." Jesus elsewhere affirms the unlimited power of prayer to accomplish results (Mt 7:7; 18:19; Lk 11:9).

25 Admittedly the transition between v.24 and v.25 is abrupt (with v.24 speaking of faith, v.25 of forgiveness). Still there is a connection. To be effective, prayer must be offered in faith—faith in the all-powerful God, who works miracles. But it must be offered in the spirit of forgiveness. Faith and the willingness to forgive are the two conditions of efficacious prayer. Matthew omits this verse, perhaps because of the abrupt change in subject or because he has provided a parallel saying in the Sermon on the Mount (Mt 6:14), immediately following the Lord's Prayer.

26 This verse does not occur in the NIV or most other modern versions because it is not found in the best and most ancient MSS of the NT. It represents an insertion from Matthew 6:15.

NOTES

20–21 Matthew refers to the cursing of the fig tree only after the cleansing of the temple and says the tree withered "at once" (Mt 21:19). These differences fit his tendency to abbreviate and condense episodes (cf. Mt 8:5–13; 9:18–26).

22 The variant reading that inserts εἰ (*ei*, "if") before ἔχετε (*echete*, "you have") has rather strong MS support. But it is probably not original, for (1) the solemn "I tell you the truth" is never preceded by a conditional clause, and (2) the introductory "if" probably arose by assimilation to the saying in Luke 17:6 (cf. Mt 21:21).

E. The Question about Jesus' Authority (11:27–33)

[27]They arrived again in Jerusalem, and while Jesus was walking in the temple courts, the chief priests, the teachers of the law and the elders came to him. [28]"By what authority are you doing these things?" they asked. "And who gave you authority to do this?"

[29]Jesus replied, "I will ask you one question. Answer me, and I will tell you by what authority I am doing these things. [30]John's baptism—was it from heaven, or from men? Tell me!"

[31]They discussed it among themselves and said, "If we say, 'From heaven,' he will ask, 'Then why didn't you believe him?' [32]But if we say, 'From men' ...." (They feared the people, for everyone held that John really was a prophet.)

[33]So they answered Jesus, "We don't know."

Jesus said, "Neither will I tell you by what authority I am doing these things."

COMMENTARY

27–28 After the incident of the fig tree and the lesson on faith, prayer, and forgiveness, Jesus and his disciples came to Jerusalem and entered the temple area—the focal point of his ministry while in the city (cf. 11:11, 15–18, 27; 12:35, 41; 13:1–2; 14:49; see Lane, 413). On this occasion the opposition came from three elements of the Jewish religious establishment: chief priests, teachers of the law, and elders. As noted above (vv.18–19), these groups made up the Sanhedrin, the high court of the Jews, so these men are representatives of Israel's highest leadership (cf. 8:31). Their presence demonstrates just how drastic Jesus' action in cleansing the temple was. They would have arrested Jesus on the spot, but his popularity among the people prevented their doing so—at least for the time being. Instead they direct at him two questions related to his authority (v.28): by what authority is he doing "these things," and who gave him this authority? What "these things" are is not specified, but it certainly refers to Jesus' actions in the temple and perhaps also his royal approach to Jerusalem. Their hope is evidently to arrest Jesus on a charge of blasphemy for a claim of divine authority. The scribes had earlier treated Jesus' words as blasphemous when he claimed the prerogative of God to forgive sins (2:7). Later at Jesus' trial the high priest will accuse him of blasphemy for claiming to be the Lord's Anointed and the authoritative Son of Man (14:62).

29–30 Again Jesus evasively answers a question by asking a counterquestion (cf. 10:2–3). While Jesus' actions since coming to Jerusalem have been more provocative and explicitly messianic than those done previously, the messianic secret is still not fully disclosed. The narrative purpose for Jesus' evasive question is at least threefold. First, Jesus continues to speak in enigmatic ways ("in parables"; cf. 4:11) to those whose hearts are opposed to God and his kingdom. Second, in this episode and those that follow, Jesus will repeatedly shame and confound his opponents by defeating them through his superior words and wisdom. Third, by withholding the full disclosure of his identity until the right moment (see 14:62), Jesus demonstrates that he is in control of his destiny. The Messiah is decisively moving God's plan forward to its consummation.

Hunter, 113, paraphrases Jesus' question: "Do you think God was behind John's mission or not?" The question was particularly appropriate for the situation. John had clearly testified to the divine source of Jesus' mission. If they recognized the divine authority of John's mission, they would be forced to recognize Jesus' also and his cleansing of the temple as the legitimate exercise of his authority. By "John's baptism" (v.30) Jesus meant John's ministry and teaching as evidenced by its outward expression. "From heaven" means "from God," since "heaven" was a common Jewish substitute for the divine name.

31–33 Jesus' counterquestion proved too much for them. The narrator notes that they "discussed it among themselves." Edwards, 352–53, points out that the (ostensibly neutral) Greek verb used here occurs seven times in Mark, always in contexts of people's trying to evade the force of Jesus' word or claim on them (2:6, 8; 7:21; 8:16, 17; 9:33). The leaders clearly saw that either alternative—"from heaven" or "of human origin" (TNIV)—would place them in a difficult position (vv.31–32). An admission of John's divine authority would compel them to believe in Jesus, whose way John had prepared (1:1–3, 7–8); a denial would place them in an unfavorable position with the people, who accepted John as a true prophet (cf. 11:18; 12:12). So to save face they pleaded ignorance: "We don't know" (v.33). Of course the real problem was not ignorance but unbelief. They did not believe John's ministry was from God and have rejected Jesus' divine authority. But rather than admitting so, they retreat into a claim of agnosticism. Their answer reveals not only unbelief, but also that they consider their position and authority more important than their convictions.

Jesus' reply was that he, too, would refuse to answer their question—at least directly. He had given them a veiled answer in his counterquestion (cf. v.30): both John's authority and his own came from God.

F. The Parable of the Tenants (12:1–12)

OVERVIEW

Having outmaneuvered the religious leaders on the question of his authority (11:27–33), Jesus now goes on the offensive by telling a parable that challenges their authority. The parable of the tenants represents an important narrative turn in Mark's story. Back in ch. 4, Jesus had explained to his disciples that he spoke in parables to *reveal* the secrets of the kingdom to them and to *conceal* that message from those who, because of their hard hearts (i.e., the religious leaders), were rejecting the message. He spoke to these "outsiders" in parables, so that "'they may be ever seeing but never perceiving, and ever hearing but never understanding; otherwise they might turn and be forgiven!'" (4:12, citing Isa 6:9–10). Ironically, while Jesus had previously spoken in parables to hide the truth from his opponents, he now tells one that *reveals* the truth to them and that they fully understand. And it is this parable that provokes them to plot against him (12:12). With the parable Jesus is guiding the story to its narrative climax.

The parable contains allegorical features and draws its imagery from Isaiah's Song of the Vineyard (Isa 5:1–7). Notice the parallel introductions:

I will sing for the one I love
a song about his vineyard:
My loved one had a vineyard
on a fertile hillside.
He dug it up and cleared it of stones
and planted it with the choicest vines.
He built a watchtower in it
and cut out a winepress as well.
Then he looked for a crop of good grapes,
but it yielded only bad fruit.

Isaiah 5:1–2

He then began to speak to them in parables: "A man planted a vineyard. He put a wall around it, dug a pit for the winepress and built a watchtower. Then he rented the vineyard to some farmers and went away on a journey."

Mark 12:1

In Isaiah's parable, the vineyard represents Israel, which has failed to produce fruit and so will be judged by God. The interpretation is given in Isaiah 5:7: because of the nation's injustice and unrighteousness, God will remove his wall of protection and will allow her enemies—the Assyrian invaders—to overrun her. Jesus takes Isaiah's familiar imagery and adapts it to his own circumstances. The vineyard is again Israel, and the owner is God. Yet now new players are introduced: the tenants are the Jewish religious leaders, the guardians of the nation. The point is no longer the unfruitfulness of the vineyard but the unfaithfulness of its caretakers. The servants are the many prophets whom God has sent through the centuries to call Israel's leaders to obedience and justice. The beloved son and heir is Jesus himself. In this way, the whole history of Israel, climaxing in the coming of Jesus, is played out in miniature. The rejection of the prophets culminates in the rejection of the Son. Ironically, when the religious leaders hear the parable and recognize their duplicitous role in it, they do not repent but rather fulfill that very role by plotting against Jesus (v.12).

Garland, 451, compares the parable to the clever trap Nathan set for David with the story of the ewe lamb (2Sa 12:1–14). Just as the prophet caught David by drawing out his sympathy for the man whose lamb was stolen, so the religious leaders—God's representative leaders of Israel—would at first sympathize with the offended owner of the vineyard. Like David, who is finally revealed as the culprit ("You are the man!"), they are exposed as the villains who have killed God's messengers and will now kill his son. Unlike David, they fail to repent.

Doubts have been raised about the authenticity of this parable because of its allegorical features. While it is true that most of Jesus' parables have but one point to make, with the details having no separate significance, Jesus did use allegory on occasion (cf. Mk 4:13–20). There is no compelling reason to doubt the genuineness of this parable. Its setting fits well the situation of Galilee in Jesus' day, with its great landed estates and the inevitable tension between absentee owners and the dispossessed peasantry (see Dodd, *Parables of the Kingdom*, 93–98; Jeremias, *Parables of the Kingdom*, 175–76; C. A. Evans, "Jesus' Parable of the Tenant Farmers in Light of Lease Agreements in Antiquity," *JSP* 14 [1996]: 65–83; J. D. Hester, "Socio-Rhetorical Criticism and the Parable of the Tenants," *JSNT* 45 [1992]: 34–36). The absence of any reference to the vindication or resurrection of the son suggests that the parable was not created by the early church. Only if we assume that Jesus could not have spoken about his own mission or predicted his own death must the parable be judged inauthentic. For a defense of the general historicity of the parable, see K. Snodgrass, *The Parable of the Wicked Tenants* (Tübingen: Mohr, 1983).

1He then began to speak to them in parables: "A man planted a vineyard. He put a wall
around it, dug a pit for the winepress and built a watchtower. Then he rented the vineyard
to some farmers and went away on a journey. 2At harvest time he sent a servant to the
tenants to collect from them some of the fruit of the vineyard. 3But they seized him, beat
him and sent him away empty-handed. 4Then he sent another servant to them; they struck
this man on the head and treated him shamefully. 5He sent still another, and that one they
killed. He sent many others; some of them they beat, others they killed.
6"He had one left to send, a son, whom he loved. He sent him last of all, saying, 'They will
respect my son.'
7"But the tenants said to one another, 'This is the heir. Come, let's kill him, and the inheritance will be ours.' 8So they took him and killed him, and threw him out of the vineyard.
9"What then will the owner of the vineyard do? He will come and kill those tenants and
give the vineyard to others. 10Haven't you read this scripture:

"'The stone the builders rejected
has become the capstone;
11 the Lord has done this,
and it is marvelous in our eyes'?"

12Then they looked for a way to arrest him because they knew he had spoken the
parable against them. But they were afraid of the crowd; so they left him and went away.

COMMENTARY

1 Mark does not identify who Jesus' hearers were (he simply says "them"). Among "them" were included Jesus' opponents (the chief priests, teachers of the law, and elders; cf. 11:27), as the reaction recorded in v.12 makes clear. As noted above, the description in v.1 reflects the language of Isaiah 5:1–2. Jesus has just cursed a fig tree—representing Israel—for its unfruitfulness (11:12–14, 20–21). The conceptual parallels to Isaiah's parable of the vineyard are obvious. The vineyard again symbolizes Israel (cf. Ps 80:8–16; Isa 27:2–6; Jer 2:21; 12:10; Eze 19:10–14; Hos 10:1). The details mentioned here—the wall (usually made of unmortared rocks), the pit (in which the juice of the grapes was collected), the press (usually made of solid limestone), the tower (for the protection of the vineyard and shelter for the farmer)—are all known to anyone who has traveled in Israel. No separate allegorical significance should be given to these details. They are intended to demonstrate the care the owner lavishes on his vineyard and to provide conceptual echoes of Isaiah 5.

When the vineyard had been completely prepared, its owner rented it to tenants and went on a journey. This detail reflects a condition that actually prevailed in Galilee in Jesus' time, where much of the land was in the hands of absentee landowners who contracted with tenants on a crop-sharing basis.

2–5 When harvest time came, the absentee landlord sent one of his servants to collect his due from the tenants. The payment was to be made in produce of the land according to a previously agreed-upon percentage. The landlord sent three servants in succession to collect the payment (vv.3–5), but the tenants repudiated the agreement and rejected the messengers. The tenants' treatment of the servants grows increasingly worse, from their beating the first (v.3), to their striking on the head and shaming the second (v.4), to their killing the third (v.5). The detail of v.5b—"he sent many others"—according to Lane, 418—"was intended by Jesus to force his listeners beyond the framework of the parable to the history of Israel. In the OT the prophets are frequently designated 'the servants' of God (cf. Jer 7:25; 25:4; Am 3:7; Zec 1:6) and it is natural to find a reference to their rejection in the words 'some ... they beat, others they killed.'" Jeremiah 7:25–26 is characteristic: "From the time your forefathers left Egypt until now, day after day, again and again I sent you my servants the prophets. But they did not listen to me or pay attention. They were stiff-necked and did more evil than their forefathers."

Elsewhere in the Gospels Jesus refers to the suffering fate of the prophets (Mt 5:12; 23:31–39; Lk 4:24; 11:47–51) and identifies himself with them (Lk 4:24; 13:33–34). This theme is also that of Stephen's speech in Acts 7. Israel's rejection of Jesus the Messiah culminates the nation's history of always rejecting God's messengers: "Was there ever a prophet your fathers did not persecute? They even killed those who predicted the coming of the Righteous One. And now you have betrayed and murdered him" (Ac 7:52; cf. 1Th 2:15; Heb 11:36–38).

6–8 The sending of the son underscores the serious view the owner of the vineyard took of the situation. He was a "beloved" (*agapētos*, GK *28*) son. The idiom *huios agapētos* likely carries the sense of "only son," as in the LXX of Genesis 22:2, 12, 16 (cf. Jer 6:26). Twice before in Mark's narrative—at the baptism and the transfiguration—Jesus has been identified by the Father with the same idiom (1:11; 9:7; "my Son, whom I love"). The owner of the vineyard assumes that "they will respect my son" (v.6). This statement cannot be pressed so far as to claim that God expected Jesus to be received positively and was caught off guard by his rejection. God surely knew beforehand that Jesus would be rejected. The statement is simply a part of the story and should not be allegorized. It expresses the respect a landowner (and the readers) would expect his son to be shown on the basis of his status and dignity. The owner's expectations were thwarted. The tenants' greed led to outrageous action (v.7). The phrase "Come let's kill him" is the same one spoken by Joseph's brothers when they decided to get rid of Jacob's most-loved son (Ge 37:20; see Edwards, 359). The tenants see the coming of the son as an opportunity to seize the property. They may have inferred from the son's coming that the owner had died (Jeremias, *Parables of the Kingdom*, 75–76). Perhaps they surmised that if they did away with his son (v.8), the property would be ownerless and therefore available to the first claimants.

Jeremias, 72–73, argued that Jesus' original audience would not have identified the son in the parable with the Messiah, "since no evidence is forthcoming for the application of the 'Son of God' to the Messiah in pre-Christian Palestinian Judaism." Yet subsequent research from the Dead Sea Scrolls and elsewhere in Judaism suggests that "Son of God" was beginning to be used as a messianic designation in first-century Judaism (4QFlor 1:10–14; 1QSa 2:11–12; 4QapocrDan ar (= 4Q246); see Hengel, *Son of God*, 44–45; Marshall, *Origins of New Testament Christology*, 113). In the context of Mark's narrative, there is no doubt that Jesus' hearers identified him as the son in the parable, as their reaction in v.12 makes clear.

After killing the son, the tenants "threw him out of the vineyard" (v.8). The cultural significance here is that the body is discarded as carrion rather than given a proper burial—a cause of great shame in the Mediterranean world. The tenants treat the son shamelessly. Both Matthew and Luke reverse the order and stress the rejection of the son's authority over the vineyard. He is cast out of the vineyard and then killed (cf. Mt 21:39; Lk 20:15). This detail also plays on the allegorical nature of the parable, thereby bringing it in line with the historical circumstances of Jesus' death outside the city walls of Jerusalem.

9 Jesus draws out the meaning of the parable with the question, "What then will the owner of the vineyard do," and then proceeds to answer it himself (cf. Isa 5:3–6; in Mt 21:41 the people answer the question). Doubts have been cast on the authenticity of this verse, since ordinarily Jesus does not answer his own questions (cf. Lk 17:9). But there is no inherent reason why he could not have done so in this situation. The answer underscores the seriousness of the action of the wicked tenants. Their punishment will be capital, and the vineyard will be let to other tenants, who "will give him his share of the crop at the harvest time" (Mt 21:41). Cranfield, 367–68, points out that the warning "is directed specifically to the leaders of the people and not to the people at large," because "whereas in Isaiah 5 the vineyard was at fault, here it is only the husbandmen." The killing of the tenants may be a not-so-veiled prophecy of the destruction of Jerusalem, and the "others" to whom the vineyard is given are the people who make up the new community of faith, composed of both Jews and Gentiles. Several times in Mark's gospel there have been hints that the gospel message will soon go forth to the Gentiles (Mk 7:24–8:10; 11:17).

10–11 The quotation is from Psalm 118:22–23, the same psalm the joyful cry "Hosanna" came from (11:9). The OT image of a rejected "stone" may have been drawn from the construction of Solomon's temple (Lane, 420): one of the stones was rejected but became the *kephalēn gōnias* (lit., "head of the corner," KJV, RSV; "capstone," NIV; "cornerstone,"TNIV, NRSV, NLT, ESV; "chief cornerstone," NASB). Plummer, 275, believes the reference is to "a cornerstone uniting two walls; but whether at the base or at the top is not certain." Some think it refers to a keystone that completes the building and holds it together (*TDNT* 1:792–93). Whether a cornerstone, a capstone, or a keystone, the metaphor clearly refers to the most important stone in the building. The symbolism intended in the original psalm is uncertain. It may have referred to Israel as a nation, despised by the pagan nations but after her return from exile exalted to the status of nationhood. J. D. M. Derrett ("The Stone That the Builders Rejected," *SE* 4 [1968]: 180–86) sees an originally messianic reference, with David as the rejected stone. The Targum on v.22 reads, "The *boy* which the builders abandoned was among *the sons of Jesse* and he is worthy to be appointed *king*" (cf. France, 462 n. 19).

Here Jesus applies the psalm to himself. The "stoneship" of Jesus, based on this passage (Ps 118:22–23) together with Isaiah 8:14 and 28:16, was a familiar theme in early Christianity. The psalm is cited by Jesus in Luke 20:17 and again by Peter in Acts 4:11 as he confronts the Sanhedrin with the rejection and vindication of the Messiah: "the stone you builders rejected ... has become the cornerstone." In Romans 9:33, Paul combines the image of a foundation stone from Isaiah 28:16 with the stone of stumbling in Isaiah 8:14: "See, I lay in Zion a stone that causes men to stumble and a rock that makes them fall, and the one who trusts in him will never be put to shame" (cf. Lk 2:34). First Peter 2:7–8 combines all three "stone" passages in a catena describing Jesus as the chosen and precious cornerstone (Isa 28:16) rejected by the builders but then vindicated (Ps 118:22), and now a cause of stumbling for some in Israel (Isa 8:14). The stone metaphor thus became a powerful apologetic tool for the early church in defending Jesus' crucifixion and vindication, and the subsequent failure of many in Israel to respond. Although there is no specific reference to the resurrection in Psalm 118, Jeremias (*TDNT* 1:793) remarks, "The early community found in Ps. 118:22 scriptural evidence for the death and resurrection of Jesus. The Crucified is the rejected stone which in the resurrection is made by God the chief corner-stone in the heavenly sanctuary (Ac. 4:11), to be manifested as such in the *parousia*." While the parable therefore itself speaks only of the judgment against the tenants, not the vindication of the son, Jesus' citation of the psalm confirms that following rejection there will be vindication. By continuing the psalm's citation to v.23 ("the Lord has done this, and it is marvelous in our eyes"), Jesus sets the rejection of the son in the context of God's sovereign purpose and plan. Though evil human actions will result in the death of the son, God will use this "rejected stone" to accomplish his marvelous plan of salvation (cf. Ac 2:23; 3:18; 4:28).

12 The application of the parable was obvious, but again the religious leaders did not dare harm Jesus, for they feared the crowd (cf. 11:18, 32). It was getting close to the time of the feast, and more and more pilgrims from Galilee were arriving in Jerusalem. Many of these people knew Jesus either through personal contact or by reputation. The religious leaders knew it would be unwise to make their move at the moment, "so they left him and went away." The similarity of this verse with 11:18–19 may mark the end of Jesus' third day (Tuesday) in Jerusalem during Passion Week.

NOTES

8 Rabbinic writings discuss the grounds for "usucaption"—the acquisition of land by virtue of uninterrupted possession of it. The Mishnah pronounces, however, that "tenants and guardians cannot secure title by usucaption" (*m. B. Bat.* 3:3; cf. *b. B. Bat.* 54*a*).

G. The Question about Paying Taxes to Caesar (12:13–17)

OVERVIEW

This is the third episode illustrating the growing controversy between Jesus and the religious leaders in Jerusalem. After the challenge to his authority to clear the temple (11:27–33), Jesus responded with the parable of the tenants, allegorically portraying the leaders as evil tenant farmers who stand in opposition to God's purposes for Israel (12:1–12). The controversies now continue as three groups approach Jesus in turn, with each raising questions that challenge his authority. The first question comes from a coalition of Pharisees and Herodians and concerns the legitimacy of paying taxes to Caesar (vv.13–17). The second is raised by the Sadducees and relates to marriage and the resurrection (vv.18–27); and the third is from an individual teacher of the law who asks about the greatest commandment (vv.28–34). Mark does not say when or where these incidents took place, but his chronology of Passion Week would place it on Tuesday or Wednesday, perhaps in one of the courts of the temple. The NIV's introductory adverb "later" reflects the generality of the Greek, which simply states that "they sent [historical present] some of the Pharisees and Herodians to Jesus ...." The "they" are no doubt the chief priests, the teachers of the law, and the elders, who in the previous verse (v.12) have been plotting against Jesus. As the main groups making up the Sanhedrin (see comments at 11:18–19, 27–28), they represent the official Jewish leadership in Jerusalem.

13Later they sent some of the Pharisees and Herodians to Jesus to catch him in his words. 14They came to him and said, "Teacher, we know you are a man of integrity. You aren't swayed by men, because you pay no attention to who they are; but you teach the way of God in accordance with the truth. Is it right to pay taxes to Caesar or not? 15Should we pay or shouldn't we?"

But Jesus knew their hypocrisy. "Why are you trying to trap me?" he asked. "Bring me a denarius and let me look at it." 16They brought the coin, and he asked them, "Whose portrait is this? And whose inscription?"

"Caesar's," they replied.

17Then Jesus said to them, "Give to Caesar what is Caesar's and to God what is God's." And they were amazed at him.

COMMENTARY

13 As in 3:6, Herodians and Pharisees make strange bedfellows—their association here automatically raises eyebrows. The Herodians (see comments at 3:6) were as opposed to the Pharisees on political grounds as the Sadducees were on theological grounds. While the Herodians supported the pro-Roman Herodian dynasty, the Pharisees rejected any rule apart from a theocratic kingdom under a Davidic ruler (cf. *Pss. Sol.* 17). Yet the two groups united in their opposition to Jesus. The Pharisees viewed Jesus as a threat to their religious authority, while the Herodians would have been suspicious of his political motivations. Herod Antipas had executed John the Baptist, and Jesus' ties to John's ministry were surely well-known. Together the purpose of the two groups was to trip Jesus up in his words so that he would lose the support of the people, thus leaving the way open for them to destroy him.

14–15a The question was prefaced with an obvious piece of flattery (v.14). The reference to Jesus as being "true" (*alēthēs*, GK *239*), or having "integrity" (NIV), is defined in the following clauses. They acknowledge that Jesus speaks God's truth impartially and without seeking to flatter or coerce others. Ironically, they are using this same kind of flattery in their attempt to trap Jesus. The narrator confirms their insincerity by introducing the episode as their attempt "to catch him in his words" (v.13) and then noting Jesus' discernment of their hypocrisy (v.15). With their question, "Is it right to pay taxes to Caesar?" the Pharisees and Herodians were intending "to impale [Jesus] on the horns of a dilemma" (Hunter, 116).

Judea had become a Roman province in AD 6, when Archelaus, son of Herod the Great and tetrarch of Judea, was deposed by Caesar Augustus because of misrule. The Jews of Judea, now governed by a Roman prefect under the authority of the emperor, were required to pay taxes into the *fiscus*, the emperor's treasury. The imposition of this poll tax in AD 6 sparked a revolt by Judas the Galilean, who chided his countrymen for paying tribute to the Romans rather than to God alone (Josephus, *J.W.* 2.8.1 §118; *Ant.* 18.1.6 §23; 18.1.1 §§5–7; cf. Ac 5:37). The revolt was quickly put down, but the tax remained highly unpopular among patriotic Jews. Some (e.g., the Zealots) flatly refused to pay it, because it was for them an admission of the Roman right to rule. The Pharisees disliked paying it for the reasons stated above, but they did not actively oppose it. The Herodians had no objections to it, since the Herodian dynasty ruled in Galilee under the authority of the Romans. The intent of the question posed to Jesus was to force him to identify himself either with the Zealots or with the Herodians. If he sided with the Zealots against taxation, he could be accused of rebellion against the Roman authorities. If he sided with the Herodians in support of taxation, he would lose face with the people, who hated Roman rule and suffered under its crushing tax burden.

15b–16 Jesus was not about to fall into their trap. He recognized their question for the "hypocrisy" (*hypokrisin*, GK *5694*) it was. So he asked them for a Roman denarius. There is no indication that they had to send away for the coin; one was readily available—so implying that they had already answered their own question. It was Caesar's coinage they were using (v.16); and by using it they were tacitly acknowledging Caesar's authority and thus their obligation to pay the tax. The coin they produced would have been stamped with an image of Tiberius Caesar, who ruled Rome from AD 14–37, and the words DIVI AUG. FILIUS, "son of the divine Augustus." Such a coin should have been highly offensive to pious Jews, since it bore an idolatrous image and extolled the emperor as a god and so violated both the first and second of the Ten Commandments (Ex 20:3–4; Dt 5:7–8). Even before answering, Jesus humbles his questioners by revealing their hypocrisy in dealing in the emperor's pagan coins.

17 Jesus' answer avoided the trap. On the surface, Jesus affirmed that Caesar has a legitimate claim, and so does God. Give to each his rightful claim. Hunter, 116, notes that "so long as God's rights were safeguarded ... there was no need to question the rights of Caesar. Civil obedience, attested by the payment of the tax, no more contradicted than it abolished the obedience due to God." For a more complete doctrine of the Christian's relationship to the state, this statement of Jesus must be taken with Romans 13:1–7; 1 Timothy 2:1–6; and 1 Peter 2:13–17.

However, Jesus does not say that the claims of God and those of Caesar are the same. As Cranfield, 372, points out,

> Though the obligation to pay to Caesar some of his own coinage in return for the amenities his rule provided is affirmed, the idolatrous claims expressed on the coins are rejected. God's rights are to be honored. Here Jesus is not saying that there are two quite separate independent spheres, that of Caesar and that of God (for Caesar and all that is his belongs to God); but he is indicating that there are obligations to Caesar which do not infringe the rights of God but are indeed ordained by God.

Jesus' answer was powerful, not only because it affirmed the authority of both Caesar and God, but also because of its inherent ambiguity, thereby enabling it to be heard differently by different listeners. To the Herodians, it could be seen as an affirmation of Caesar's authority and a tacit acceptance of Roman rule. To the Pharisees (as well as the Zealots, the Essenes, and other opposition groups), it could be heard as a veiled rejection of Caesar's authority. "Give to Caesar what is Caesar's" raises the fundamental question of what *truly* belongs to Caesar. And as Psalm 24:1 affirms, "The earth is the LORD's, and everything in it, the world, and all who live in it" (cf. 1Co 10:26). The universe is a theocracy under the jurisdiction of God alone. If everything is God's, nothing ultimately belongs to Caesar.

Jesus' clever response took his opponents off guard. It was simple yet profound, and "they were amazed at him." Despite this recognition, Luke will report that at Jesus' trial, he is accused of "subverting our nation, forbidding us to pay the tribute tax to Caesar and claiming that he himself is Christ, a king" (Lk 23:2 [NET]). Whether Jesus' words were misunderstood or deliberately distorted by his opponents is uncertain.

H. The Question of Marriage at the Resurrection (12:18–27)

OVERVIEW

Following the challenge to Jesus by the Herodians and the Pharisees (vv.13–17), the Sadducees take their turn. Their goal, like that of the previous challengers, is to discredit Jesus. They do it by seeking to show that his belief in the resurrection is illogical and absurd.

Reliable information about the Sadducees (mentioned here for the first time by Mark) is difficult to obtain because no documents that are clearly Sadducean have been preserved. What we know of them comes primarily from Josephus or from the views of their opponents. Their origin is uncertain, but they appear to have arisen from the priestly families of Jerusalem's aristocracy, who supported the Hasmonean dynasty. The word "Sadducee" probably comes from the Hebrew name Zadok (Gk. *Saddouk*) and is usually traced to the high priest of that name during the time of David.

In the time of Jesus, the Sadducees were numerically small but exerted significant political and religious power. They dominated the Sanhedrin (Ac 5:17—though that council included a strong dissenting voice from the Pharisees [Ac 23:6–8]) and had considerable influence among the priestly leadership. The Sadducees were not, however, popular among the masses. Josephus says they were educated men and that many of them held prominent positions (*Ant.* 18.1.4 §17). They represented the urban, wealthy, sophisticated class and were centered in Jerusalem. Because of their political power, they were the party of the status quo, more content than other groups with the order and stability brought by the Romans. When Jerusalem and the temple were destroyed in AD 70, they disappeared from history.

18Then the Sadducees, who say there is no resurrection, came to him with a question.
19"Teacher," they said, "Moses wrote for us that if a man's brother dies and leaves a wife

but no children, the man must marry the widow and have children for his brother. [20]Now
there were seven brothers. The first one married and died without leaving any children.
[21]The second one married the widow, but he also died, leaving no child. It was the same
with the third. [22]In fact, none of the seven left any children. Last of all, the woman died too.
[23]At the resurrection whose wife will she be, since the seven were married to her?"
[24]Jesus replied, "Are you not in error because you do not know the Scriptures or the
power of God? [25]When the dead rise, they will neither marry nor be given in marriage;
they will be like the angels in heaven. [26]Now about the dead rising — have you not read
in the book of Moses, in the account of the bush, how God said to him, 'I am the God of
Abraham, the God of Isaac, and the God of Jacob'? [27]He is not the God of the dead, but of
the living. You are badly mistaken!"

COMMENTARY

18 In the NT the Sadducees are mentioned only fourteen times, whereas the Pharisees are mentioned about one hundred times. Mark mentions them only in this verse and identifies them with the statement "who say there is no resurrection." Josephus similarly affirms the Sadducees' teaching "that souls die with their bodies" (Josephus, *Ant.* 18.1.4 §16; cf. 13.10.6 §§293–98; *J.W.* 2.8.14 §§162–66). The Sadducees held this position because they accepted only the Pentateuch (the Torah = Genesis through Deuteronomy) as authoritative and rejected many beliefs and practices not found there. Since they claimed to be unable to find clear teaching about the resurrection in the Torah, they rejected the doctrine. This rejection set them against the Pharisees, who considered all the Hebrew Scriptures (the Christian OT), as well as their oral traditions, to be authoritative.

Although not a prominent doctrine in the OT, the resurrection of the dead is explicitly taught in Daniel 12:1–2: "At that time ... multitudes who sleep in the dust of the earth will awake: some to everlasting life, others to shame and everlasting contempt" (cf. Isa 26:19). By Jesus' day, belief in the resurrection was widespread among the Jews; it is widely affirmed in Second Temple Jewish writings, especially in the apocalyptic literature (for a good survey, see Wright, *Resurrection of the Son of God*, 129–206). An apparent polemic against the Sadducean belief appears in the Mishnah, where, included among those who "have no share in the world to come" are those who claim that "there is no resurrection of the dead taught in the law" (i.e., the Pentateuch; *m. Sanh.* 10:1). When Paul is taken before the Sanhedrin in Acts 23, he capitalizes on the differences between the Pharisees and the Sadducees in this regard to divide the assembly and so distract them from their accusations against him (Ac 23:6–10).

19–23 Although the Sadducees addressed Jesus with the honorific title "Teacher," their purpose was not to learn from him. It was manifestly hostile. Swete, 278, writes, "The extreme case they offer for [Jesus'] opinion is clearly intended as a *reductio ad absurdum* of any view but their own." The case cited arose out of a provision in the Mosaic law (Dt 25:5–6), which required that if a man died without children, his brother had to marry his widow. The purpose of this levirate law (from the Lat. *levir*, "brother-in-law") was to protect the widow and guarantee the continuance of the family line. An entire tractate in the Mishnah deals with issue related to levirate marriage (*Yebamot*, meaning "sisters-in-law"). Using levirate marriage as a springboard for their argument, the Sadducees present a hypothetical case in which one woman marries seven brothers in turn, all of whom die childless (vv.20–22). In the resurrection, they ask, whose wife of the seven would she be (v.23)? The case may have been a well-known Sadducean joke used for poking fun at the Pharisees' doctrine of the resurrection.

24–25 In his answer Jesus accuses the Sadducees of ignorance of both the Scriptures and the power of God. He then proceeds to take up the second accusation first. In the resurrection there will be a new order of existence brought about by the power of God (v.25). Plummer, 281, comments, "The questioners did not see that God could not only grant life in another world, but also make it very different from life in this world." Marriage will not exist as it does now, but life will be "like the angels in heaven." This does not mean, as is often portrayed in the popular media, that humans *become* angels in the afterlife. Angelic and human existence are fundamentally different, with each being unique creations of God (Heb 1:5–14; 2:5–8). What Jesus means is that our glorified existence will be of a fundamentally different nature from our mortal earthly existence. The comparison with angelic life probably also means that resurrection life will be characterized especially by service for God and fellowship with him.

This passage is disturbing to Christians who would hope and expect the intimacy of their marital relationship to continue into eternity. But Jesus does *not* claim that the intimacy of earthly relationships will be discontinued in eternity. He only says that there will be no need for the institution of marriage. Since there will be no more death, the need for marriage and the propagation of the race will not exist. We may reasonably posit, however, that all relationships, including those most dear to us today, will exist on an even higher plane in eternity.

26–27 Jesus next turns to his first-mentioned cause of the Sadducees' erroneous thinking: ignorance of the teaching of the OT (cf. 2:25; 12:10). He directed them back to the story of Moses and the burning bush (Ex 3:6). His use of a text from the Pentateuch was significant because the Sadducees considered only this part of the OT as fully authoritative. The quotation—"I am the God of Abraham, the God of Isaac, and the God of Jacob"—may be understood as follows: Abraham, Isaac, and Jacob had long since died when God made the statement to Moses. Nevertheless God's covenantal relationship with these patriarchs continued into Moses' time, thus confirming that they were indeed alive (v.27); and if they were alive then, we may be sure that in the resurrection God will raise up their bodies to share in the blessedness of eternal life. It is sometimes claimed that Jesus makes his point from the tense of the verb: "I *am* the God of Abraham ..." rather than "I *was* the God of Abraham ...." This argument is not quite correct, as France, 471, correctly notes, since there is no verb in either the Hebrew or the Greek text. (The verb "to be" is only implied, so there is no present or past tense indicated.) Jesus' point is not made through the tense of the (nonexistent) verb but through his affirmation of the *continuing covenantal relationship between God and the patriarchs*. "I am the God of Abraham, the God of Isaac, and the God of Jacob" confirms the covenantal faithfulness of God, whose promises can be relied on and whose relationship with his people endures forever.

NOTES

18 On the background and beliefs of the Sadducees, see *TDNT* 7:35–54; Sanders, *Judaism*, ch. 15; A. J. Saldarini, *Pharisees, Scribes and Sadducees in Palestinian Society* (Wilmington, Del.: Michael Glazier, 1988), ch. 13; "Sadducees," in *ABD* 5:892–95. Lane, 426, questions a clear connection between the Sadducees and the temple hierarchy and points out that during the 107-year period between Herod's appointment of Ananel and the destruction of the temple in AD 70, only one high priest, Hanan ben Hanan, is explicitly identified as a Sadducee (Josephus, *Ant.* 20.9.1 §199); and he only held the office for three months. Lane observes, "The disputes between Sadducean and Pharisaic scribes show a pronounced interest in the Temple but do not warrant the assertion that the Temple hierarchy was by conviction Sadducean or was inclined to follow the traditions of the Sadducees." While Lane is certainly correct that the entire priesthood cannot be assumed to have been Sadducean in its beliefs, there seems little doubt that Sadducean views were prominent (even dominant) among the priestly hierarchy of Jerusalem.

20–23 The inspiration for this hypothetical case probably came from the apocryphal book of Tobit, where a woman named Sarah marries seven husbands one by one (all kinsmen), but each is killed by the demon Asmodeus before the marriage is consummated (Tob 3:7–8; 7:11). Sarah eventually marries Tobias, son of Tobit (and another relative), who survives the wedding night through prayer and by repelling the demon with the help of the angel Raphael (Tob 8:1–18). Though the stories in Mark and in Tobit serve very different purposes, both include the death of seven husbands in the context of levirate marriage.

24–25 The mention of angels in this context may also be significant as a correction of another theological error of the Sadducees mentioned in Acts: the denial of angels or spirits (cf. Ac 23:8). This passage, however, may not mean that the Sadducees denied the existence of angels per se (which denial seems unlikely, since angels appear in the Pentateuch), but rather their denial of the kind of angelic hierarchies described in the Jewish apocalyptic literature.

I. The Question concerning the Great Commandment (12:28–34)

OVERVIEW

Jesus has been questioned by the Pharisees and Herodians about paying taxes to Caesar (12:13–17) and by the Sadducees about the resurrection (12:18–27). Now in this third encounter, he is approached by one of the scribes, or teachers of the law (*grammateis*; see comments at 1:22). The teachers of the law have appeared regularly in Mark's gospel, often in association with the Pharisees and almost always in opposition to Jesus (1:22; 2:6, 16; 3:22; 7:1, 5; 8:31; 9:11, 14; 10:33; 11:18, 27). This passage contains one of the few positive portrayals of them in the NT (cf. Mt 23:1–2). Mark suggests that the question asked by this man, in contrast to many that had been asked by his colleagues, was a sincere one. Even the parallels to this passage in Matthew 22:34 and Luke 10:25 are less positive. There the purpose of the question is "to test him," and no commendation by Jesus appears at the end ("You are not far from the kingdom of God," Mk 12:34). The unusual positive portrayal is evidence that Mark is recording an authentic historical event, since elsewhere the scribes are portrayed as plotting Jesus' death (12:12).

28One of the teachers of the law came and heard them debating. Noticing that Jesus
had given them a good answer, he asked him, "Of all the commandments, which is the
most important?"
29"The most important one," answered Jesus, "is this: 'Hear, O Israel, the Lord our God,
the Lord is one. 30Love the Lord your God with all your heart and with all your soul and
with all your mind and with all your strength.' 31The second is this: 'Love your neighbor as
yourself.' There is no commandment greater than these."
32"Well said, teacher," the man replied. "You are right in saying that God is one and there
is no other but him. 33To love him with all your heart, with all your understanding and with
all your strength, and to love your neighbor as yourself is more important than all burnt
offerings and sacrifices."
34When Jesus saw that he had answered wisely, he said to him, "You are not far from
the kingdom of God." And from then on no one dared ask him any more questions.

COMMENTARY

28 The teacher of the law had been impressed by Jesus' answer to the previous question and so ventured one of his own. His positive assessment of Jesus may have come in part from Jesus' refutation of the Sadducees' argument, since most scribes would have affirmed belief in the resurrection. The teacher of the law asks a question of great relevance to his profession: What is the greatest of all commandments? Later rabbis counted 613 individual statutes in the law—365 that were negative and 248 positive. Attempts were made to differentiate between the "heavy," or "great," and the "light," or "little," commandments (*TDNT* 4:535–36). Some rabbis also made attempts to formulate great principles from which the rest of the law could be deduced. The most famous example comes from Hillel (ca. 40 BC–AD 10), who expressed the negative version of the Golden Rule. When challenged by a Gentile, "Make me a proselyte on condition that you teach me the whole law while I stand on one foot," Hillel replied, "What you hate for yourself, do not do to your neighbor: this is the whole law, the rest is commentary; go and learn" (*b. Šabb. 31a*; cf. Tob 4:15). Rabbi Akiba similarly summed up the law: "but you shall love your neighbor as yourself ... This is the encompassing principle of the law" (*Sifra* on Lev 19:15–20).

29–30 In answer to the question, Jesus quotes two passages from the OT (Dt 6:4–5; Lev 19:18). Deuteronomy 6:4 ("Hear O Israel ...") represents the opening words of the Shema, a confession of faith that is recited by pious Jews every morning and evening. The Shema is comprised of Deuteronomy 6:4–9; 11:13–21; and Numbers 15:37–41; it is named after the first Hebrew word of Deuteronomy 6:4, which means "Hear" (v.29). It makes two basic affirmations:

(1) the unity of God ("the LORD is one") and (2) the covenantal relationship of God to the Jewish people ("the LORD our God"). In telling this story, only Mark included Deuteronomy 6:4 here. Its relationship to the words that follow is important. God is to be loved completely and totally (v.30) because he, and he alone, is God and because he has made a covenant of love with his people. In the covenant, God gives himself totally in love to his people; therefore, he expects his people to give themselves totally to him. Deuteronomy 6:5 speaks of "heart," "soul," and "strength." Jesus adds a fourth: "mind." Both expressions indicate the same thing. A person's entire being is to be devoted to God.

31 Jesus brought Leviticus 19:18 together with Deuteronomy 6:5 to show that love of neighbor is a natural and logical outgrowth of love for God. These two commandments belong together; they cannot be separated. The Ten Commandments themselves can be divided into two "tables" of commands (Ex 20:1–17; Dt 5:6–21): those related to God (1–4) and those related to fellow human beings (5–10; cf. Mk 10:19). The former are foundational for the latter. Thus although the teacher of the law had asked for the one most important commandment, Jesus gave him two. In Leviticus 19:18 the neighbor is identified as "one of your people," i.e., a fellow Israelite. The Jews of Jesus' day interpreted "fellow Israelites" even more narrowly than the OT passage; for there (cf. Lev 19:34) it included resident aliens, whereas for Jesus' contemporaries it included only Jews and full proselytes. In his parable of the good Samaritan, Jesus redefined the term to mean anyone with whom we have dealings, even a hated enemy (Lk 10:25–37). Mitton, 99, in a most practical application of this verse, remarks:

> [Neighbor embraces] all within our home, those we meet at work, in our church, and in recreations. And more than that: our employer is our neighbor too; so are our work people, all who serve us in shops, the men who empty our dust bins and those who try to keep streets and parks clean. So too are the people of Jamaica, of West Africa, of Kenya, of Germany and of Russia. If we love our neighbors as we love ourselves, we shall want for them the treatment we should want for ourselves, were we in their place.

32–33 Only Mark records the favorable response of the teacher of the law and Jesus' statement that he was "not far from the kingdom of God" (v.34). In repeating the commandment, the teacher of the law omits the divine name "the Lord," perhaps in keeping with the practice of pious Jews of avoiding the pronunciation of God's name (v.32). The phrase "and there is no other but him" is an interpretive addition from Deuteronomy 4:35, which underscores the uniqueness of Israel's God (cf. Isa 45:21; Ex 20:3). In his repetition of what Jesus said, the teacher of the law substitutes *synesis* ("understanding") for *dianoia* ("mind") and omits *psychē* ("soul"). There is, however, no appreciable difference in the meaning.

The additional statement by the teacher of the law that love of God and neighbor are "more important than all burnt offerings and sacrifices" (v.33) has parallels in the OT prophets (1Sa 15:22; Isa 1:10–17; Jer 7:22–23; Hos 6:6); but it is an advance on the teaching of Judaism in his time. In Judaism the law and sacrifices are set side by side with love. The Mishnah quotes Rabbi Simeon the Just as saying, "By three things is the world sustained: by the law, by the [temple-]service, and by deeds of loving-kindness" (*m. ʾAbot* 1:2). The teacher of the law, by contrast, declares the supremacy of love to sacrifices (Taylor, 489). While he does not speak of the abolition of the sacrificial system, rather only of its secondary status, Mark's readers would likely have found implications that the kingdom of God inaugurated through Jesus' life, death, and resurrection would mean the abolition of the sacrificial system.

34 The reply of the teacher of the law shows that what Jesus said was getting through to him and elicits Jesus' response that he was close to the kingdom of God—a statement no doubt meant to stimulate and challenge him to further thoughtful reflection and decisive action. Whether or not he responded to this kingdom invitation is not stated.

Jesus had so forcefully demonstrated his ability to answer questions meant to trap him and to turn such questions back on his accusers that from this time on "no one dared ask him any more questions." Verse 34 points forward to the next incident recorded by Mark, in which Jesus, not the religious leaders, asks the question about the "son of David."

NOTES

28 The Greek is odd here, since the word πάντων, *pantōn* ("of all"), is neuter or masculine rather than feminine, as would be expected with the feminine noun ἐντολή, *entolē* ("commandment"). It could mean "Which commandment supersedes *everything*?" (Edwards, 370), or it could be a stereotypical idiom whose neuter form has become frozen regardless of the gender of its antecedent (BDF §164 [1] 91; France, 479).

33 While the scribe's statement about the superiority of love to sacrifices is remarkable for the Judaism of Jesus' day, it may not be unprecedented. J. M. Baumgarten ("Messianic Forgiveness of Sin in CD 14:19 [4Q266 10 I 12–13]," in *The Provo International Conference on the Dead Sea Scrolls*, ed. D.W. Parry and E. Ulrich; [STDJ 30; Leiden: Brill, 1999], 537–44) cites several fragments from the Dead Sea Scrolls (1QS 9:4; 4Q266 [= 4QD[a]]) that suggest that in the eschatological age of salvation, atonement for sins will be achieved through the perfect righteousness of God's people (the Messiah and the Qumran community) rather than through ritual sacrifice (see Evans, 266).

J. The Question about David's Son (12:35–37)

OVERVIEW

This episode forms a transition from the previous controversy stories (11:27–12:34) to the teaching episodes that follow (12:35–13:36). Mark introduces the pericope by noting that Jesus is still in the temple courts (v.35)—a link to the previous controversies (cf. 11:27)—but that he is now "teaching" rather than answering questions. He has won the previous challenges by silencing his opponents with his wise and powerful answers (12:34) and now goes on the offensive. He first challenges the scribes' inadequate view of the Messiah (vv.35–37) and then warns the people about their pride and greed (vv.39–40), while illustrating the latter with the story of the widow's offering (vv.41–44).

[35]While Jesus was teaching in the temple courts, he asked, "How is it that the teachers of the law say that the Christ is the son of David? [36]David himself, speaking by the Holy Spirit, declared:

"'The Lord said to my Lord:
"Sit at my right hand
until I put your enemies
under your feet."'

37 David himself calls him 'Lord.' How then can he be his son?"
The large crowd listened to him with delight.

COMMENTARY

35 The Messiah (see comments at 8:29), the Anointed One, the King appointed by God, was expected to be from the family of David (cf. 10:46). Davidic messianic expectation arose from the covenant made with David in 2 Samuel 7:11–16 and developed in the Latter Prophets (Isa 9:2–7; 11:1–9; Jer 23:5–6; 30:9; 33:15, 17, 22; Eze 34:23–24; 37:24; Hos 3:5; Am 9:11). "Son of David," a favorite messianic title for the later rabbis, does not appear in the OT with reference to the Messiah, but *Psalms of Solomon* 17:21 (first century BC) confirms that by the first century it was coming into use as a title for the coming king from the line of David (Strauss, *Davidic Messiah*, 40–43, 53–57). The title has already appeared in Mark in the cry of blind Bartimaeus (10:47–48). That passage, together with the cry of the crowd at the triumphal entry ("Blessed is the coming kingdom of our father David," 11:10), reveals that the restored Davidic kingdom was a popular expectation in Israel. Jesus' question is, "In what sense [cf. NIV, 'How is it?'] is the Messiah the son of David?"

36 Jesus does not wait for an answer from his listeners. He provides it himself. The quotation is from Psalm 110:1. There is considerable debate concerning the original context and meaning of this psalm. (For a good summary of the debate, see L. C. Allen, *Psalms 101–150* [WBC 21; Waco, Tex.: Word, 1983], 83–86.) It was once held by many that Psalm 110 was Maccabean in date (second century BC), but the discovery at Qumran of a complete Psalter dated to the third century BC has disproved the former view. Debate today centers especially on whether the psalm was originally "royal" or "messianic." If the former, the psalm was likely composed as an enthronement hymn at the coronation of one of the Davidic kings (perhaps David himself). The anonymous psalmist describes Yahweh's affirmation of the current king: "The LORD [*Yahweh*] said to my Lord [*adoni* = the king], 'Sit at my right hand ....'"

Royal psalms are viewed as typologically rather than uniquely fulfilled in Christ. If the psalm was originally messianic, David himself was speaking about the future Messiah by calling him "my Lord" (*adoni*) and hence regarding him as superior. Both the Hebrew and Greek texts identify this song as "a psalm of David," and Jesus (and Mark) assumes both authorship by David ("David himself ... declared ...") and his inspiration in writing it (v.36). "Speaking by the Holy Spirit" is a typical rabbinic formula to describe divinely inspired utterance.

There is no evidence that Psalm 110 was interpreted with reference to the Messiah in Judaism before the third century AD, and Gundry, 718, suggests that Jesus "exhibits exegetical brilliance by being the first to interpret the psalm in this way." Another possibility is that the psalm's messianic interpretation was suppressed by the Jews because of Christian usage and reintroduced at a later period. In any case, Jesus' introduction of the psalm in the context of his discussion about the Messiah as David's son presupposes its messianic interpretation.

37 David calls the Messiah "my Lord." How can he at the same time be David's son and David's Lord? The presupposition is that a son would normally be viewed as subordinate to a father, yet David treats his "son" (= descendant) as his superior. The answer Jesus intended to elicit was that the Messiah is indeed to be descended from David, but he has a more exalted role than that of a successor of David. Or as Moule, 99, puts it: "Because, although he is his son by descent and therefore his junior in age, he is also in some mysterious way superior to David and therefore his senior in rank." Some interpreters have claimed that Jesus' statement is a denial of the Messiah's Davidic ancestry either by Jesus himself or by the early Christian community (so Bultmann, *History of the Synoptic Tradition*, 66, 145–46). But Mark cannot intend such a denial since he portrays Jesus as accepting both Bartimaeus's calling him "son of David" (10:47–48) and the acclamation of the crowd at the triumphal entry (11:10). Jesus' descent from David stands on firm historical ground by being independently attested in the birth narratives and genealogies of Matthew and Luke, as well as in a variety of early Christian sources (Ro 1:3–4; 2Ti 2:8; Rev 5:5; 22:16; probably ironically in Jn 7:42).

The point is not that the Messiah is not David's son, but that this category is inadequate to explain his exalted person and work. Does Mark have another title in mind? His emphasis elsewhere on Jesus' divine sonship may indicate that intent here: Jesus is not just the son of David; he is the Son of God (1:1, 11; 3:11; 5:7; 9:7; 12:6; 13:32; 14:36, 61; 15:39; cf. Ro 1:3). Others have suggested that Jesus is thinking of his role as the exalted Son of Man of Daniel 7:13 (F. Neugebauer, "Die Davidssohnfrage (Mark xii. 35–37 parr.) und der Menschensohn," *NTS* 21 [1974]: 81–108; Lohmeyer, 162–63). While the former seems more likely in the light of Mark's narrative, in either case the fundamental point is that the Messiah's status and role far exceed traditional expectations.

Mark says that the crowd was delighted to listen to Jesus (v.37b). Apparently, they enjoyed seeing the so-called experts stumped! The remark also serves to show that, though the religious leaders opposed Jesus, the common people were (at least for now) supportive of him.

K. The Warning about the Teachers of the Law (12:38–40)

38As he taught, Jesus said, "Watch out for the teachers of the law. They like to walk
around in flowing robes and be greeted in the marketplaces, 39and have the most
important seats in the synagogues and the places of honor at banquets. 40They devour
widows' houses and for a show make lengthy prayers. Such men will be punished most
severely."

COMMENTARY

38–39 This paragraph is probably a continuing account of Jesus' teaching in the temple courts (v.35), though it is possible that Mark placed it here because, like the previous paragraph, it concerns the teachers of the law (v.38). Jesus had warned earlier of the leaven of the Pharisees and of Herod (8:15), a reference to their persistent unbelief and opposition to Jesus and his mission. Now he similarly warns against the scribes, this time focusing on issues of character, namely, their pride and avarice. (In Matthew, this short denunciation becomes a lengthy condemnation and series of "woes" against both the scribes and the Pharisees [Mt 23:1–36].) It is interesting that Jesus had shortly before commended a particular teacher of the law for his spiritual insight (12:34). Yet now he launches a general denunciation of the profession. The point seems to be that while there were individual exceptions, the religious establishment as a whole was characterized by widespread corruption. Moule, 100, correctly observes:

> There is no evidence that all the theologians of Jesus' day were frauds, using their position merely as a cloak for cruelty and greed.... But the most influential of them seemed to have conceived a bitter hatred of Jesus, and one can only guess that this was because they were indeed using their powers selfishly and irresponsibly and detested his exposure of their real motives.

Here Jesus condemns "their love of religious uniform ('ecclesiastical millinery') and public deference ('the raised hats of the laity'); a failing not yet wholly extinct in the clerical class" (Hunter, 120). Four areas of ostentation are mentioned: long robes, greetings in the marketplace, the best seats in the synagogue, and places of honor at banquets. Teachers of the law wore long white linen robes that were fringed and reached almost to the ground. Evans, 278, suggests that these garments imitated the robes worn by priests (cf. Josephus, *Ant.* 3.7.1 §151) and so signified religious devotion—a literal wearing of piety on one's sleeve! The "greetings" in the marketplace relate to social position. Those of lower social status were expected to greet those higher up, and religious leaders were addressed with honorific titles such as "Rabbi," "Father," and "Master" (cf. Mt 23:7). According to the Jerusalem Talmud, "a person must greet one who is greater than he in knowledge of Torah" (*y. Ber.* 2:1). In the synagogue the leading teachers of the law occupied the bench in front of the ark, which contained the sacred scrolls of the Law and the Prophets. There the teachers could be seen by all the worshipers in the synagogue (Lane, 440; Cranfield, 384). They were often invited to banquets because of their prestige and were given special places of honor. Banquets in the first century were rituals of social status at which the most honored guests were given the best seats and the best food (Malina and Rohrbaugh, 135–36, 191–92; cf. Josephus, *Ant.* 15.2.4 §21). Jesus elsewhere warns against seeking such places of honor (Lk 14:7–11).

40 Widows are viewed throughout Scripture as among the most vulnerable members of society, and the OT repeatedly warns against exploiting them (Ex 22:22; Dt 10:18; 24:17; 27:19; Ps 68:5; Isa 1:23; 10:2; Jer 22:3; Eze 22:7; Zec 7:10; Mal 3:5). Jesus joins in this prophetic warning by accusing the scribes of "devouring widows' houses." How they did so is not stated. J. Jeremias (*Jerusalem*, 111–16) notes that the Mishnah forbids scribes from receiving payment for teaching the law (*m. ʾAbot* 1:13; *m. Bek.* 4:6; cf. *b. Ned.* *37a*, *62a*) and claims that most lived off subsidies and many were poor. This passage, he concludes, refers to "the scribes' habit of sponging on the hospitality of people of limited means." Other scholars have suggested that "devouring widows' houses" refers to cheating widows out of estates over which the scribes had been entrusted as lawyers (so J. D. M. Derrett, "'Eating Up the Houses of Widows': Jesus' Comment on Lawyers," *NovT* 14 [1972]: 1–9), or, connecting this phrase with the next one, taking money for intercessory prayer. Whatever the circumstances, Jesus accuses them of preying on those who are most vulnerable and least able to defend themselves.

Jesus further condemns their hypocrisy in uttering long prayers that only masked their greed. "For a show" is a translation of the Greek word *prophasis*. It is difficult to know whether it should be taken with what precedes and be translated "and to cover it up" (i.e., to cover up their devouring of widow's houses) or with what follows (the long prayers) and translate it "and for a show," as does the NIV. In either case, there is a connection between their long prayers and their greed. Hiebert, 310–11, comments, "To rob the poor and the bereaved under the guise of personal piety doubles the guilt." Jesus promises punishment to all such hypocrites—a reference to God's judgment in the last day.

L. The Widow's Offering (12:41–44)

OVERVIEW

After this incident (the last recorded one in his public ministry), Jesus spends his time exclusively with the disciples. The placement of this story here may be to contrast the greed of the teachers of the law with the liberality of the widow. Or it may be that its teaching—that the true gift is to give everything we have (v.44)—sums up what has gone before in the gospel and makes a superb transition to the story of how Jesus gave everything for us (Nineham, 334–35).

[41]Jesus sat down opposite the place where the offerings were put and watched the crowd putting their money into the temple treasury. Many rich people threw in large amounts. [42]But a poor widow came and put in two very small copper coins, worth only a fraction of a penny.

[43]Calling his disciples to him, Jesus said, "I tell you the truth, this poor widow has put more into the treasury than all the others. [44]They all gave out of their wealth; but she, out of her poverty, put in everything—all she had to live on."

COMMENTARY

41–42 The setting is the Court of the Women, into which both men and women were allowed to come. Jesus sat down on a bench from where he could watch the people bring their offerings for the temple and put them in one of the thirteen trumpet-shaped boxes used for that purpose. It was not the rich with their large gifts who caught Jesus' attention but a poor widow. She placed in the box two copper coins (*lepta*), the smallest coins in circulation in Palestine (see Notes). Their value was only a few cents. Two *lepta* could purchase about a handful of flour, or the equivalent of one meager meal (Evans, 283).

43–44 The disciples were not sitting with Jesus; so he called them to him. The lesson he wanted to teach them was important enough for them to be there to see it for themselves as well as to hear it. Again Jesus precedes his pronouncement with the solemn "I tell you the truth" (*amēn legō hymin*; see comments at 3:28). The widow's offering counted for more than all the others because, while they gave a small fraction of their wealth, she gave 100 percent from her poverty. She put in "everything—all she had to live on" (v.44). Her gift was greater "in proportion, and also in the spirit in which she gave; it was in the latter that she was richer than all of them.... The means of the giver and the motive are the measure of true generosity" (Plummer, 290). Mark does not say how Jesus knew that what she gave constituted her entire livelihood. The statement may be hyperbolic, or Jesus may have inferred it from the woman's impoverished appearance (which probably bespoke her widowhood), or he may have discerned her state through divine insight (cf. 2:8; 3:4; 5:30; 12:15).

NOTES

41–44 While the story of the widow's offering is usually taught as an example of self-sacrificial giving, some commentators see it as more lament than praise. Jesus' primary point, it is said, is not to praise the gift but to castigate the temple's establishment for their failure to care for such widows and for "robbing" this woman of her last coins (see A. G. Wright, "The Widow's Mites: Praise or Lament—A Matter of Context," *CBQ* 44 [1982]: 256–65; Evans, 282). While this interpretation has merit, especially in the light of Jesus' criticism of the scribes for devouring widow's houses (v.40), Jesus' insistence that the widow's gift is greater than that of the rich surely constitutes a commendation for her actions. She is not being manipulated into giving to false charity but is sacrificially giving her life to God.

41 The term γαζοφυλακίον (*gazophylakion*) could refer to one of various treasury rooms that were located in the temple (Josephus, *J.W.* 6.5.2 §282; 5.5.2 §200; *Ant.* 19.6.1 §294; 1 Macc 14:49; 2 Macc 3:4–40), or it could refer to a chest or receptacle used to receive the money. The Mishnah speaks of thirteen shofar chests (trumpet-shaped receptacles) located in the temple that were used to collect various kinds of offerings (*m. Šeq.* 6:1, 5; cf. Ne 12:44.). Since people are "throwing" (βάλλω, *ballō*) money into the γαζοφυλακίον, *gazophylakion*, this latter sense seems the most likely.

42 A λέπτον (*lepton*, lit., "a tiny thing"; cf. the English word "mite"), the only Jewish coin mentioned in the NT, was worth less than one hundredth of a denarius, the daily wage of a laborer. Mark explains to his Roman readers, who would be unfamiliar with the value of the Palestinian coin, that the two λεπτά (*lepta*) were about equivalent to a κοδράντης (*kodrantēs*; Gk. transliteration of the Lat. *quadrans*), a coin worth only a few cents by today's standards. That Mark felt it necessary to explain the value of a λέπτον, *lepton*, and that he does so by the use of a Latin coin (*quadrans*) known primarily in the West, may be added to the circumstantial evidence that he is writing to the church in Rome.

44 There is a later rabbinic parallel to this story in *Leviticus Rabbah* 3:5 (on Lev 1:17), where a priest despises a woman for bringing a mere handful of flour as an offering. In a dream, however, he is told not to despise her since her gift is the equivalent of sacrificing her own life.

M. The Olivet Discourse (13:1–37)

OVERVIEW

The Olivet Discourse follows naturally from the preceding episodes in Mark's gospel. Since entering Jerusalem (11:1–11), Jesus has been in conflict with the religious leaders (11:27–33; 12:12–37), a conflict that climaxes in a series of warnings against their pride and corruption (12:38–40). Jesus has also been performing symbolic actions (11:12–14, 15–17, 20–21) and telling parables (12:1–12) that illustrate Israel's rejection of her Messiah and the judgment that will follow. Israel's leaders have failed to submit to God's rule and now face judgment. In the discourse that follows, Jesus predicts the destruction of Jerusalem, the persecution of his followers, and the events leading up to the end of the age.

Here is the longest connected discourse in Mark's gospel. It is also the most difficult. The three major questions that present themselves in the study of Mark 13 are: (1) What is the origin of the passage? (2) What is its genre and purpose? and (3) What is its meaning, and how does its structure relate to this meaning?

First, wide divergences of opinion exist as to the *origin* of the passage. Some scholars have rejected the authenticity of the discourse as a whole and claim that Jesus never used this kind of apocalyptic language to speak of the end of the age or his return in glory. Mark in fact drew his material from a Jewish, or Jewish-Christian, apocalyptic tract written in one of several possible contexts: during Pilate's placement of Roman ensigns in Jerusalem, or when the Roman emperor Caligula threatened to set up his image in the Jerusalem temple, or when the Roman armies surrounded the city of Jerusalem in AD 70. This "Little Apocalypse" theory was first popularized by T. Colani in his 1864 work *Jésus-Christ et les Croyances Messianiques de son Temps*. The theory has since been developed in a variety of directions by many scholars. Basically, however, it asserts that since the apocalyptic tract was wrongly attributed to Jesus, none of the apocalyptic material in Mark 13 may be ascribed to him. For full discussion of the Little Apocalypse theory, see G. R. Beasley-Murray, *Jesus and the Last Days* (Peabody, Mass.: Hendrickson, 1993).

Although the Little Apocalypse theory has many adherents, it does not stand up under careful scrutiny. The chief problem is that the apocalyptic element in the discourse is too integrally bound up with the exhortative to allow for an originally apocalyptic tract. The structure of the discourse evidences this problem for the theory. The apocalyptic statements are followed by exhortations, which in turn are followed by clauses beginning with *gar* ("for") that state the reason for the exhortation (cf. vv.8, 11, 19, 22, 33, 35; see Lane, 445–46; L. Gaston, *No Stone on Another* [Leiden: Brill, 1970], 52).

Other scholars seek to isolate three kinds of material in ch. 13: (1) traditional sayings, (2) apocalyptic material, and (3) redactional comments. The difficulty of classifying the material in this way—

evidenced by wide disagreement as to what falls into which category—creates skepticism as to the method. G. R. Beasley-Murray has shown that there are no compelling reasons not to accept the discourse as substantially from Jesus. Whether Jesus spoke its contents on a single occasion is another matter. Mark may have brought into the discourse material he deemed dealt with the same theme (observe that Mk 13:9b–12 is not found in Mt 24 but in the missionary discourse of Mt 10:17–21). Yet if Mark did so, he used the material within the bounds of its original intent in the context of Jesus' ministry.

Second, with regard to the *genre and purpose*, the discourse has many elements in common with apocalyptic literature. This kind of literature was well-known in first-century Judaism. Daniel in the OT and Revelation in the NT are examples of books that are apocalyptic in nature. These books, as well as the noncanonical Jewish and Christian apocalypses, are full of symbolic and sometimes bizarre imagery. All of them purport to reveal information about the end of the age. Mark's discourse has a number of features in common with this apocalyptic literature: it describes the signs of the times, the severe testing and persecution of God's people, the imminent intervention of God in human history to judge and to save, and a call to God's people to persevere and remain faithful. Yet many characteristics common to the Jewish apocalypses are missing: the revelation is not ascribed to a prophetic figure from Israel's past; there are no angelic mediators or other-worldly journeys, no symbolic beasts representing nations or persons, and no schematizations of world history. What is most distinctive about Mark's discourse, in fact, is its exhortative character. The entire chapter is filled with exhortation and admonition. There are nineteen imperatives in vv.5–37, thus making it abundantly clear that the discourse's main purpose is not to satisfy curiosity about the future but to give practical, ethical teaching. In this discourse Jesus combines eschatology with exhortation, with emphasis on the latter. He is preparing his disciples—and beyond them the church—to live and to witness in a hostile world. As R. P. Martin (*Mark*, 136) well notes, Mark desires "to present Jesus as Lord of history and as one in control of all events which may bring trouble to the church. Believers should in no way be startled or dispirited by what they see or have to endure. Their Lord has foretold these things. Better still, he will be with them in the Holy Spirit (v.11)."

Third, the question of the *structure and meaning* of the passage is closely tied in with the two major predictions in it: the destruction of the city of Jerusalem in AD 70 and the end of the age. The structure of the discourse is as follows: (1) Jesus' prophecy of the destruction of the temple, and the questions of the disciples (vv.1–4, which form an introduction to the discourse); (2) warnings against deceivers, and false signs of the end (vv.5–23); (3) the coming of the Son of Man (vv.24–27); (4) the lesson of the fig tree (vv.28–31); and (5) an exhortation to watchfulness (vv.32–37).

So which parts of the discourse concern Jerusalem's destruction and which concern the end of the age? Attempts to project the whole of the discourse into the remote future with no reference to AD 70 are unconvincing. The question of the disciples in v.4 is in response to Jesus' prediction of the temple's destruction (v.2), and various references in the discourse—especially vv.14–18—appear to allude to this event. On the opposite side, a few commentators understand the whole discourse as relating only to AD 70. This view has been ably defended in recent years by N. T. Wright (*Jesus and the Victory of God*, 339–66). Other commentators believe the passage concerns the destruction of Jerusalem and the temple until v.32, where the topic changes to the parousia and the end of the age (so France, 500–546). A third solution claims the discourse moves back and forth between the two events, taking an A-B-A-B form.

A vv.5–23	Destruction of Jerusalem and the temple
B vv.24–27	Parousia and the end of the age
A' vv.28–31	Destruction of Jerusalem and the temple
B' vv.32–37	Parousia and call to watchfulness

The difficulty with these last three views is that the mention of the worldwide preaching of the gospel (v.10) and the unequaled days of distress (v.19) seems to point to something beyond AD 70, as does the appearance of "the abomination that causes desolation" (v.14; see comments there). This problem may be partly solved by ending the first section at v.13, as Edwards, 386, does:

A vv.1–13	End of the temple and fall of Jerusalem
B vv.14–27	Tribulation and parousia
A' vv.28–31	End of the temple and fall of Jerusalem
B' vv.32–37	Parousia and watchfulness

Yet now we stumble over vv.14–18, which appear to contain clear allusions to the chaos and tumult surrounding the destruction of Jerusalem.

The best solution may be to see in the discourse an intentional prophetic merging and overlap of the two events, with the goal of viewing one as a pattern and model for the other. Edwards, 386–87, correctly observes: "Chap. 13 is thus constructed according to a twofold scheme of tension and paradox ... in which the destruction of the temple and fall of Jerusalem function as a prefigurement and paradigm for the Parousia." This merging of near and remote fulfillment is characteristic of OT prophecy, so we should not be surprised to find it in Jesus' prophetic teaching.

See comments at v.30 for discussion of the question of whether Jesus mistakenly predicted the end within his own generation.

1. Prophecy of the Destruction of the Temple (13:1–2)

[1]As he was leaving the temple, one of his disciples said to him, "Look, Teacher! What massive stones! What magnificent buildings!"

[2]"Do you see all these great buildings?" replied Jesus. "Not one stone here will be left on another; every one will be thrown down."

COMMENTARY

1 Mark introduces this section by noting Jesus' departure from the temple. While this statement sets the stage for the following narrative about the temple's destruction, it also serves as a conclusion to the controversies with the religious leaders, which began when Jesus entered the temple in 11:27. Mark's references to Jesus' entering and leaving the temple together bracket the controversies in a kind of inclusio (11:27–13:1). Jesus exits victorious in his debates with the temple authorities and religious leaders and then turns to pronounce judgment against them (v.2). He will not return to the temple in Mark's gospel. France, 495, notes the striking parallel between this departure and that described by the prophet Ezekiel, when the chariot throne of God's glory rises up from the temple, pauses at the eastern gate, and comes to rest on "the mountain east of the city" (Eze 10:18–19; 11:22–23). Similarly, Jesus withdraws from the temple and crosses over to the Mount of Olives (v.3), thereby leaving the temple to its destruction.

Jesus' prophetic words were prompted by the exclamation of one of his disciples on looking at the temple in all its grandeur. The temple area, including the temple building itself, had been rebuilt by Herod the Great. (The second temple, built by Zerubbabel, had fallen into disrepair.) The courtyard had been greatly enlarged (to about four hundred by five hundred yards) in order to accommodate the large throngs of Jews who came to Jerusalem for the festivals. To accomplish this enlargement, a huge platform had to be erected to compensate for the sharp falling off of the land to the southeast. An enormous retaining wall was built to hold the platform in place. The massive stones used in the construction of this wall may still be seen today, since part of the wall escaped the destruction of AD 70. At the southeastern corner the temple platform towered two hundred feet above the Kidron Valley. In addition to the temple building itself, on the platform stood porticoes and cloistered courts flanked by beautiful colonnades. The temple area covered approximately one-sixth of the area of the city of Jerusalem. It was an architectural wonder whose size and location dominated the ancient city.

The disciples exclaimed over the beauty of the buildings and the massiveness of the stones. A later rabbinic proverb reads, "He who has not seen the temple of Herod has never seen a beautiful building in his life" (*b. B. Bat. 4a*; *b. Sukkah 51b*). Josephus gives a detailed description of the buildings and ornaments and remarks that "the exterior of the building wanted nothing that could astound either mind or eye." The sun reflecting off the massive golden plates on the building "radiated so fiery a flash that persons straining to look at it were compelled to avert their eyes as from solar rays." Massive white stones twenty-five cubits long, eight cubits high, and twelve cubits wide were used in the construction (a cubit measured about 18 inches). These stones gave the building a brilliant white appearance so that to approaching strangers the temple looked like a snow-covered mountain (*J.W.* 5.5.6 §§222–24; *Ant.* 15.11.3–7 §§391–425; *m. Mid.* 3.4).

2 Jesus' reply was startling. Great though the temple buildings were, they would be completely destroyed. Jesus' actions in clearing the temple earlier in the week had represented a symbolic judgment against the temple (11:15–17), and his cursing of the fig tree functioned as an enacted parable of judgment against Israel and her religious institutions (11:12–14, 20–21). Now Jesus explicitly predicts the temple's destruction. The prophecy was fulfilled in AD 70, when the Roman general Titus destroyed Jerusalem and the temple.

At his trial Jesus will be accused of threatening to destroy the temple and rebuilding another "not made with hands" (14:58 TNIV); passersby at the crucifixion will mock him for threatening to destroy the temple but being unable to save himself (15:29). These accusations likely arose from Jesus' actions in clearing the temple and also the prediction of its destruction recorded here. Yet according to Mark, the accusations at Jesus' trial were "false testimony" (14:57). Jesus did not threaten personally to destroy the temple but rather predicted its coming destruction as divine judgment for Israel's unfaithfulness.

Jesus' prophecy is very specific: "Not one stone here will be left on another." Although some of the huge stones used by Herod's workmen for the great walls supporting the temple's platform were not battered down by Titus's soldiers, all of the buildings on the platform—including the temple itself, to which the prophecy refers—were utterly destroyed. So completely were they destroyed that no trace of them remains today. Even their exact location on the Temple Mount is disputed. The Western, or "Wailing," Wall that stands today was part of the retaining wall for the temple compound, not part of the temple proper. Josephus (*J.W.* 7.1.1 §§1–3) points out that the walls of Jerusalem were so thoroughly leveled by the Romans that one could hardly tell the place was ever inhabited.

NOTES

2 The word translated "do you see" (βλέπεις, *blepeis*) may carry a slight rebuke: Are you allowing your attention to be taken up with these great and beautiful buildings when you shouldn't be? Swete, 295–96, comments: "The disciples are warned that the pride which as Jews they naturally felt in this grand spectacle was doomed to complete humiliation."

There is OT prophetic precedent for predictions of the temple's destruction. In the eighth century BC, Micah (3:12) warned that because of the injustice and sin of Israel and Judah's leaders, "Jerusalem will become a heap of rubble, the temple a mound overgrown with thickets." In the years leading up to Nebuchadnezzar's siege of Jerusalem and the destruction of the first (Solomon's) temple in 586 BC, Jeremiah repeatedly predicted the city's destruction (7:12–15; 12:7; 22:5; 26:6), and the prophet Uriah was executed for the same prediction (26:20–23). More contemporary with Jesus, Josephus (*J.W.* 6.5.3 §§300–309) describes a man named Jesus son of Ananus, who for four years before the Jewish revolt and then for three years during it, wandered the city crying "Woe, woe to Jerusalem!" Though whipped first by the Jewish leadership and then by the Roman procurator Albinus, he continued his tirade. He was eventually killed during the Roman siege of Jerusalem by a stone heaved from a catapult (for other predictions of the temple's destruction in Second Temple and rabbinic literature, see Evans, 296–97).

2. The Disciples' Twofold Question (13:3–4)

3As Jesus was sitting on the Mount of Olives opposite the temple, Peter, James, John and Andrew asked him privately, 4"Tell us, when will these things happen? And what will be the sign that they are all about to be fulfilled?"

COMMENTARY

3–4 Between v.2 and v.3 the location shifts. Jesus is now on the Mount of Olives. With him are the four disciples whom he called first (1:16–20): Peter, James, John, and Andrew. From the top of the mount they could clearly see the Kidron Valley, running below the eastern wall of the city, and especially the Temple Mount. Its full grandeur was spread out below them. Private instruction for the disciples is common in Mark and usually follows perplexing statements made by Jesus in public (cf. 4:10; 7:17; 10:10).

The question the four disciples asked Jesus privately not only goes back to the statement he made as they were leaving the temple area (cf. v.2) but actually expands it. "These things" (v.4) refers to the destruction of the temple. The disciples wanted to know when that event would take place and what the sign would be that would indicate "they are all about to be fulfilled." Although from Mark's gospel it would be possible to consider these two questions as essentially one (referring only to the destruction of the temple), Matthew's report (24:3) of the questions apparently distinguishes two separate events: "'Tell us,' they said, 'when will this happen, and what will be the sign of your coming and of the end of the age?'" Ladd (*Theology of the New Testament*, 197) writes, "There can be little doubt but that the disciples thought of the destruction of the temple as one of the events accompanying the end of the age and the coming of the eschatological Kingdom of God."

The disciples wanted some sure sign by which they might know that the destruction of the temple was about to occur and that the end of the age was approaching. While certain eschatological portents are mentioned in the discourse—most notably the "abomination of desolation" (v.14) and disturbances in the heavens (vv.24–25)—the purpose of the discourse does not revolve around such signs. Indeed, the only appearance of the word "signs" (*sēmeia*, GK *4956*) here is a negative one, referring to the signs and wonders performed by false prophets and false messiahs (13:22). Instead of identifying a sign, Jesus first and foremost exhorts the disciples to spiritual preparedness in order to stand firm through the many trials coming their way.

3. Warnings against Deceivers and False Signs of the End (13:5–8)

5Jesus said to them: "Watch out that no one deceives you. 6Many will come in my name,
claiming, 'I am he,' and will deceive many. 7When you hear of wars and rumors of wars,
do not be alarmed. Such things must happen, but the end is still to come. 8Nation will
rise against nation, and kingdom against kingdom. There will be earthquakes in various
places, and famines. These are the beginning of birth pains."

COMMENTARY

5–6 The first word of the discourse proper is *blepete* ("watch"). This word recurs throughout the passage (cf. vv.9, 23, 33)—a clear indication that admonition is Jesus' main concern. He begins by warning the disciples against false claimants to messiahship. This is apparently what "in my name" and "I am he" (i.e., the Messiah) refer to (v.6). That Jesus said there would be *many* such false messiahs suggests that his statement should be understood broadly to refer to various kinds of "messianic" figures. Eschatological expectations were high in first-century Palestine, and at various times individuals claiming to be God's agent of deliverance gained prominence. In Acts 5, the rabbi Gamaliel speaks of two such messianic pretenders: Theudas, who "claimed to be somebody" (a messiah?), and Judas the Galilean, who led a tax revolt against the Romans (5:36–37). Similarly, in Acts 21:38 Paul is suspected by the commander of the Roman temple guard of being a certain Egyptian who led four thousand Jews to the Mount of Olives in a messianic action. Josephus (*J.W.* 2.13.4–6 §§258–65; cf. *J.W.* 6.5.4 §§312–13) describes some of these prophetic and messianic figures and more. In one account he relates how a group of "wicked men" deceived the people by claiming divine inspiration and leading them into the wilderness to await a sign of God's deliverance. The procurator Felix responded by sending troops to destroy and disperse them. Writing in the wake of the destruction of Jerusalem, Josephus takes a pro-Roman view and describes these messianic figures as dangerous brigands whose actions were disastrous for the Jewish nation. Beasley-Murray (*Commentary on Mark Thirteen*, 31) speaks of the situation in Palestine before AD 70 when he writes, "Whereas the popular messianism hardly ever produced a claimant to the messianic office in the strictest sense, it both fostered and was nourished by men who asserted the possession of messianic authority or who regarded themselves as forerunners of the Kingdom."

7–8 Wars and rumors of war are not to be a cause for alarm (v.7), for they have always been part of human history and will continue to be so ("Such things must happen"). When they occur, they must not be mistaken as introducing the end. Jesus clearly says the "end is still to come." The "end" Jesus is talking about here is not clear. If the entire section (vv.5–23) deals only with the destruction of Jerusalem, then "the end" refers to the end of God's judgment on the Holy City. It is more likely, however, that "end" is intentionally ambiguous and refers both to that event and the end of the age.

Cataclysmic events, whether human conflicts such as war and revolution or natural disasters such as earthquakes and famine, cause great human suffering and so naturally raise expectations for a soon end of the world. D. A. Hagner (*Matthew 14–28* [WBC 33B; Dallas: Word, 1995], 691) notes, "The horror and human suffering connected with war are bound to raise eschatological thoughts—and they have indeed throughout history." In the OT and Judaism, wars, earthquakes, and famines are often associated with God's judgment. The judgments of the day of the Lord are marked by earthquakes and other cosmic disturbances (Isa 2:19, 21; 13:13; 24:18; 29:5–6; Eze 38:19; Joel 2:10). Apocalyptic Judaism drew strongly on this imagery. In the third vision of 2 Esdras (= *4 Ezra*), Ezra asks the Lord when the signs he has been shown will take place. The Lord responds,

> Measure carefully in your mind, and when you see that some of the predicted signs have occurred, then you will know that it is the very time when the Most High is about to visit the world that he has made. So when there shall appear in the world earthquakes, tumult of peoples, intrigues of nations, wavering of leaders, confusion of princes, then you will know that it was of these that the Most High spoke from the days that were of old, from the beginning.
>
> *2 Esdras 9:1–5 NRSV (cf. Mk 13:31; 2 Bar. 27:7; 70:2–8; Josephus,* J.W. *6.5.3 §299; Rev 6:12; 8:5; 11:13, 19; 16:18)*

Jesus responds against overzealous apocalyptic fervor by pointing out that these events are typical of human history and should not be taken as marking the end. They do, however, have some eschatological significance, since they are the beginnings of "birth pains" (*ōdines*). The image of eschatological birth pains appears in Jewish apocalyptic and later rabbinic writings. The "messianic woes" or "birth pains of the Messiah" came to refer to a period of intense suffering that would immediately precede the coming of the messianic age (*TDNT* 9:670–72; Hagner, *Matthew 14–28*, 691). It is uncertain whether the term here carries this later technical sense or whether it is a general one related to intense suffering. In either case, the primary conceptual significance seems to be that the present period of suffering will give way to the joy of new birth (i.e., salvation and restoration) for those who persevere. The apostle Paul uses the birth pain image in a similar way in Romans 8:18–25. The present creation—for which salvation has been inaugurated but not consummated—"waits in eager expectation for the children of God to be revealed" (v.19). This period of waiting is metaphorically described as "groaning ... as in the pains of childbirth" (v.22). The agonizing pain (the residual effects of humanity's fall) provokes eager longing for the new birth (the consummation of the new age).

NOTES

6 Messianic and prophetic figures described by Josephus include Judas the Galilean (*Ant.* 17.10.5 §§271–72), Simon (*Ant.* 17.10.6 §§273–77), Anthronges (*Ant.* 17.10.7 §§278–81), Theudas (*Ant.* 20.5.1 §§97–99), the Egyptian (*Ant.* 20.8.6 §§169–72; *J.W.* 2.13.5 §§261–63), and a certain Samaritan (*Ant.* 18.4.1 §§85–87).

8 God's judgment is often manifested in the OT as catastrophic events, such as wars (2Ch 15:6; Isa 19:2; Jer 4:20; Joel 3:9–14; Da 11:44; Rev 6:4, 8; 11:13), earthquakes (Ps 18:7–8; Isa 5:25; 13:13; 29:6; 1Sa 14:15; Am 1:1; Hag 2:6, 21; Zec 14:4), and famines and plagues (Jer 14:12; 21:6–7; Eze 14:21).

Ladd (*Theology of the New Testament*, 202) contends that the statement of v.8 related to birth pains is perhaps the most important of the discourse:

> The Old Testament speaks of the birth of a nation through a period of woes (Isa 66:8; Jer 22:23; Hos 13:13; Mic 4:9–10) and from these verses there arose in Judaism the idea that the messianic Kingdom must emerge from a period of suffering that was called the messianic woes or "the birth pangs of the Messiah." This does not mean the woes that the Messiah must suffer, but the woes out of which the messianic age is to be born.

4. Warnings of Persecution and Strife and a Call to Steadfastness (13:9–13)

OVERVIEW

Jesus now turns from the general signs of eschatological turmoil—false messiahs, wars, earthquakes, and famine (vv.5–8)—to the specific trials the disciples themselves will face (vv.9–13). A second command is given to "watch out" (*blepete*), this time emphatically addressed to the disciples:

"*You* [*hymeis*] watch out *for yourselves* [*heautous*]" (v.9a).

The structure of vv.9–13 is especially interesting. The section includes three separate sayings of Jesus held together by the key word *paradidōmi*, translated in the NIV as "handed over" (v.9), "arrested" (v.11), and "betray" (v.12). The first occurrence speaks of being handed over to religious courts and appearing before civil authorities; the second promises the presence of the Holy Spirit when disciples are arrested and brought to trial; and the last deals with the family hostility and hatred that loyalty to Jesus Christ will bring about. Verse 10, which is concerned with the worldwide preaching of the gospel, is sandwiched between the first and second sayings; and for this reason some scholars consider it a gloss. Verses 9–13 are not, with the exception of v.10, found in the parallel account in Matthew 24. They occur in Matthew 10:17–22 in the context of the mission charged to the Twelve. Luke has them in his parallel account (21:12–17), with the exception of v.10, and in another context (12:11–12) gives a variant of v.11 as a separate logion of Jesus. All this evidence suggests that the material in Mark 13:9, 11–13 was given by Jesus on more than one occasion or that Mark has collected sayings from other contexts and put them here because of their relevance.

9"You must be on your guard. You will be handed over to the local councils and
flogged in the synagogues. On account of me you will stand before governors and kings
as witnesses to them. 10And the gospel must first be preached to all nations. 11Whenever
you are arrested and brought to trial, do not worry beforehand about what to say. Just say
whatever is given you at the time, for it is not you speaking, but the Holy Spirit.
12"Brother will betray brother to death, and a father his child. Children will rebel against
their parents and have them put to death. 13All men will hate you because of me, but he
who stands firm to the end will be saved."

COMMENTARY

9 Jesus warns his disciples to be on their guard (*blepete*), because persecutions of various kinds await them. Jesus describes persecution at the hands of both the church's Jewish religious opponents as well as secular authorities. The word translated "local councils" (*synedria*) is the plural form of "Sanhedrin" (*synedrion*) and was used of local Jewish religious courts. These bodies were made up of the elders of the synagogues assembled for the purpose of exercising disciplinary powers. Josephus (*Ant.* 4.8.14 §§214–18) describes such local courts as mandated by Moses and comprised of seven men for every city. From these courts, Jesus warns, they will be taken into the synagogues and publicly flogged. This passage will find its earliest fulfillment in Acts 5:40, when the apostles are flogged on orders of Jerusalem's Sanhedrin for proclaiming the message of Jesus. The apostle Paul also speaks of disciplinary action imposed by such courts when he writes to the Corinthians, "Five times I received from the Jews the forty lashes minus one" (2Co 11:24; cf. *TDNT* 4:516; *m. Mak.* 3:10–12). The number is drawn from Deuteronomy 25:1–3, which delimits forty lashes as the maximum punishment. The Jews chose to administer only thirty-nine in order not to violate the law inadvertently.

In addition to persecution from Jewish religious authorities, Jesus' disciples will also be brought before secular authorities ("governors and kings"). It is "on account of me"—i.e., because of their testimony about Jesus and the gospel—that they will experience such suffering. It is significant that Jesus will shortly appear before both the Jewish Sanhedrin and the Roman governor. In Acts, Paul will appear before the Roman governors Festus and Felix and before King Agrippa (Ac 24–26).

But persecution, whether by Jews or Gentiles, would be an opportunity for witness. The phrase *eis martyrion autois* may be translated "for evidence against them," i.e., the authorities (cf. 1:44; 6:11). If this meaning applies here, the assumption is that the witness of the disciples will be rejected by the authorities and on the day of judgment will be used against those authorities (cf. *TDNT* 4:502–3). In view of Luke 21:13, it seems best to follow the NIV's "as witnesses to them." This verse clearly anticipates fulfillment in the near future.

10 The Greek impersonal verb *dei* ("must") underscores the will of God, who has decreed that the gospel be preached to all the nations (or Gentiles; *ta ethnē*). This task Jesus mandates to his disciples and through them to his church (cf. Mt 28:18–20; Ac 1:8). "First" (*prōton*) may mean before the destruction of the city of Jerusalem. People who hold this view see the promise fulfilled in the proclamation of the gospel throughout the Roman world by AD 60, when Paul arrived in Rome (cf. Ac 28:31). This interpretation sees analogies to Luke's narrative purpose in Acts, where the expansion of the gospel from Jerusalem to "the ends of the earth" (Ac 1:8) is symbolized through its narrative progression from Jews to Gentiles and from Jerusalem to Rome. It seems best, however, to understand "first" in terms of the end. Certainly Matthew understood it that way. He immediately follows the statement of the universal preaching of the gospel with "and then the end will come" (Mt 24:14). Jesus seems to be saying here, "Instead of looking for signs of the end, get busy and spread the good news! All nations must hear it before the end comes."

Some missiologists see this verse as placing very specific conditions on the return of Christ. They claim that every people group (*panta ta ethnē*) must be evangelized before the end will come. Christ's followers are subsequently encouraged to hasten Christ's return by completing the task of world evangelism with reference to even the remotest of tribal groups. While such encouragement is commendable and certainly in line with Christ's command to take the gospel to all nations (Mt 28:18–20; Ac 1:8), the phrase here is not so much a specific *condition* of Christ's return as an assurance that the end will be preceded by a time of worldwide proclamation. Whether this period refers to the decades leading up to the destruction of Jerusalem (with "all nations" referring to the Roman Empire and its immediate neighbors), or to the worldwide proclamation of the gospel continuing today, depends on one's interpretation of the entire discourse (see Overview, 13:1–37). Since we have taken the discourse to refer simultaneously both to the destruction of Jerusalem and the parousia of Christ, the reference here would likely also carry a double reference. For the same kind of double reference, see Acts 1:8 and Acts 28, in which Paul's arrival in Rome marks a symbolic "ends of the earth," but the worldwide proclamation of the gospel has only begun.

11 The disciples will be hauled into court and cross-examined by the authorities. Jesus promises them strength and resources beyond their own through the Holy Spirit. Although they are "unschooled, ordinary men" (Ac 4:13), the disciples need not be intimidated by people with greater human authority and knowledge. The Spirit will reveal to them on the spot the appropriate words to speak (cf. Jer 1:9; Ac 6:10; 7:55). For the fulfillment of this promise in the preaching of the apostles, see Acts 2:4; 4:8, 31; 6:10; 13:9. (To use this verse to justify lack of careful preparation for teaching or preaching is, of course, irresponsible exegesis.)

12–13 The breaking of ties of natural affection will be another trial the disciples will have to face. Verse 12 is conceptually similar to Micah 7:6: "For a son dishonors his father, a daughter rises up against her mother, a daughter-in-law against her mother-in-law—a man's enemies are the members of his own household" (cf. Isa 19:2). While in Micah the context is the collapse of societal structures and values, here the focus is on the division of families provoked by one member's allegiance to Christ (France, 518). In Luke 12:51–53 (cf. Mt 10:35) Jesus similarly warns that families will split because of the gospel:

> Do you think I came to bring peace on earth? No, I tell you, but division. From now on there will be five in one family divided against each other, three against two and two against three. They will be divided, father against son and son against father, mother against daughter and daughter against mother, mother-in-law against daughter-in-law and daughter-in-law against mother-in-law.

Jesus' saying in the present context goes even further than division by speaking of "betrayal to death" of brothers, parents, and children. Through fear or hatred of the gospel, family members will turn other members over to the authorities, with execution as the result. We do not hear explicitly of such betrayals in the NT, but a letter by Pliny the Younger, governor of Bithynia, to the emperor Trajan in about AD 112 speaks of informers turning in the names of Christians, who are subsequently arrested, questioned, and executed (Pliny, *Epis.* 10.96).

The hatred will not be limited to relatives (v.12), but "everyone will hate you" (v.13 TNIV). The prediction recalls descriptions of the early Christians by various Roman historians and satirists. In the late first century, Tacitus (*Ann.* 15.44) refers to Christians as a class "hated for their shameful deeds" and followers of a "destructive superstition." Juvenal (*Sat.* 3.62) said they belonged to the sewage of the Orontes that had discharged itself into the Tiber, and Suetonius (*Nero* 16:2) speaks of Christians as "a race of human beings given to a new and wicked superstition." Such hatred arose because of the Christians' total devotion to Christ ("because of me," v.13) and their refusal to honor the gods of the Greco-Roman world.

Testing will be another feature of the last times. Not all will stand the test, "but those who stand firm to the end will be saved" (v.13 TNIV). The "end" (*telos*) here is not, as in v.7, the end of the age, but either a general reference to the end of the trial or more specifically to the end of a person's life. Endurance, then, means faithfulness to Christ and to the gospel throughout these trials. While "saved" in Mark normally carries the sense of physical restoration or healing, here it clearly means spiritual salvation, or eternal life (cf. 8:35). Jesus is not setting forth a doctrine of salvation by works. He is rather emphasizing that genuine faith will issue in Christian living that will endure trial and persecution. A good commentary on v.13b is 2 Timothy 2:12: "If we endure, we will also reign with him." This section (vv.9–13), with its warnings and encouragements, would have had special relevance for the life situation of the persecuted church to which Mark is writing.

NOTES

9 Whereas Josephus refers to seven-man councils, the Mishnah speaks of local Jewish courts made up of twenty-three members (*m. Sanh.* 1:6). Perhaps Josephus refers to small towns and the Mishnah to larger cities.

10 Since this verse appears to interrupt the passage's flow of thought, and for other reasons, its authenticity has been questioned. Possibly, it is an originally independent saying of Jesus inserted here by Mark to stress the missionary enterprise of the church in spite of opposition and trial.

5. The Abomination that Causes Desolation, and the Necessity of Flight (13:14–23)

OVERVIEW

Verses 14–23 turn to focus especially on the events associated with the destruction of Jerusalem, including the abomination that causes desolation (v.14a), the encouragement to flee Judea (vv.14b–16), the severity of suffering and distress during those days (vv.17–20), another warning of the deceiving influence of false messiahs and false prophets (21–22), and a renewed call to be on their guard, for Jesus has warned them ahead of time (v.23).

14"When you see 'the abomination that causes desolation' standing where it does
not belong—let the reader understand—then let those who are in Judea flee to the
mountains. 15Let no one on the roof of his house go down or enter the house to take
anything out. 16Let no one in the field go back to get his cloak. 17How dreadful it will be
in those days for pregnant women and nursing mothers! 18Pray that this will not take
place in winter, 19because those will be days of distress unequaled from the beginning,
when God created the world, until now—and never to be equaled again. 20If the Lord
had not cut short those days, no one would survive. But for the sake of the elect, whom
he has chosen, he has shortened them. 21At that time if anyone says to you, 'Look, here is
the Christ!' or, 'Look, there he is!' do not believe it. 22For false Christs and false prophets will
appear and perform signs and miracles to deceive the elect—if that were possible. 23So
be on your guard; I have told you everything ahead of time."

COMMENTARY

14a This verse is one of the most difficult in Mark's gospel, if not in the entire NT. The key phrase is "abomination that causes desolation," an expression derived from the book of Daniel (9:27; 11:31; 12:11). In Matthew's gospel (24:15) Jesus explicitly identifies its originating with that book. The first word of the phrase, *bdelygma* (GK *1007*, "abomination"), suggests something repugnant to God, while the second, *erēmōsis* (GK *2247*, "desolation"), suggests that because of the abomination the temple is left deserted and desolate. In vacating it, the holy and pious worshipers leave it to God's judgment. The initial fulfillment of Daniel's prophecy is found in the desecration of the temple by the Seleucid king Antiochus IV "Epiphanes" in 167 BC. First Maccabees recounts Antiochus's attempts to eradicate Judaism and replace it with pagan religion—events that sparked the Maccabean revolt:

> Now on the fifteenth day of Chislev, in the one hundred forty-fifth year [= 167 BC], they erected a desolating sacrilege on the altar of burnt offering. They also built altars in the surrounding towns of Judah, and offered incense at the doors of the houses and in the streets. The books of the law that they found they tore to pieces and burned with fire. Anyone found possessing the book of the covenant, or anyone who adhered to the law, was condemned to death by decree of the king. They kept using violence against Israel, against those who were found month after month in the towns. On the twenty-fifth day of the month they offered sacrifice on the altar that was on top of the altar of burnt offering. According to the decree, they put to death the women who had their children circumcised, and their families and those who circumcised them; and they hung the infants from their mothers' necks.
>
> But many in Israel stood firm and were resolved in their hearts not to eat unclean food. They chose to die rather than to be defiled by food or to profane the holy covenant; and they did die. Very great wrath came upon Israel.
>
> *1 Maccabees 1:54–64 NRSV*

The fact that Jesus uses the same expression "abomination that causes desolation" here makes it clear that its fulfillment was not restricted to the events of the time of the Maccabees. What the phrase does refer to has been hotly debated. Interpreters who hold the view that all the events described in vv.5–23 have to do with the fall of Jerusalem suggest various possibilities: (1) the entrance of the Roman army into Jerusalem at the time of the destruction, and in particular the military standards the Jews considered idolatrous and an abomination (cf. Lk 21:20); (2) the entrance of the Roman general Titus into the Most Holy Place at the climax of the destruction (Josephus, *J.W.* 6.4.7 §260; Moloney, 259); (3) a desecration by the Zealots defending Jerusalem themselves—perhaps their farcical appointment of Phannias to be high priest (Josephus, *J.W.* 4.3.6–8 §§147–57; see Lane, 469).

Others interpreters see this prophecy as fulfilled in the end time by the Antichrist. They cite the following evidence: (1) The use of the masculine participle *hestēkota* ("standing") suggests a person (cf. NLT, "When you will see the sacrilegious object that causes desecration standing where he should not be"). (2) Paul's statements in 2 Thessalonians 2:3–10 about the eschatological Antichrist seem to be derived from a similar tradition. (3) The person referred to must be associated with the end, for in Matthew's gospel his appearance is immediately followed by the coming of the Son of Man (cf. 24:29–30). None of these arguments are decisive. The masculine participle, though odd, could refer to Titus or even to a male idol set up in the temple. It need not refer to a still-future Antichrist. Paul's statement in 2 Thessalonians (written around AD 52) may itself refer to the destruction of Jerusalem rather than to a figure of the distant future. Finally, the close connection between the abomination and the coming of the Son of Man simply reflects the problem of the discourse as a whole, in which the destruction of Jerusalem and the end are closely—almost inextricably—linked throughout.

In the light of the many uncertainties, we may cautiously interpret Jesus' reference in the same way that we have interpreted the discourse as a whole. Jesus' reference to Daniel's abomination functions as an eschatological image with multiple fulfillments: (1) the Maccabean period, (2) the events of AD 66–70, and (3) the end time. Jesus uses the various desecrations of the temple in history to predict a final great catastrophic crisis that will occur in the immediate lead-up to the coming of the Son of Man and the end of the age.

The meaning of the exhortation "let the reader understand" is also disputed. (1) It may be a narrative aside, prompting the original readers of Mark's gospel to consider the present historical situation (the imminent threat of Jerusalem's destruction). If so, it would suggest that Mark's gospel was written shortly before the temple's destruction, perhaps at the beginning of hostilities around AD 66. (2) A second possibility is that the exhortation is not a narrative aside but Jesus' own comment and so part of the original discourse. In this case, "the reader" is not the ancient reader of Mark's gospel but the disciples who have read (or heard) Daniel's prophecy. Jesus would be saying, "Let the reader *of Daniel* recognize this biblical allusion to the abomination that causes desolation" (Evans, 320). (3) Ernest Best proposes a third possibility related to the oral reading of Mark's gospel in the church. In the light of the grammatical irregularity in the previous sentence—in which the participle "standing" is a masculine noun, but the noun "abomination" is neuter—the author has added a marginal note telling the person reading aloud to the church *not* to correct the irregular grammar but to read it as it is written. Best compares this device to the modern use of *sic*, which alerts the reader to a word or phrase that seems to be odd or misspelled but in fact replicates what the author actually wrote. The result would read: "But when you see that thing, the abomination of desolation, standing where he [*sic*] should not be ..." (E. Best, "The Gospel of Mark: Who Is the Reader?" *IBS* 11 [1989]: 129; Garland, 496). The first option—that Mark is telling his readers to see and recognize the events of his day—remains the most likely.

14b–18 It is difficult to consign the admonitions of these verses to the end time. No one will be able to flee from the judgment of God in that day. The warnings, however, make good sense in the context of the approaching Roman army before the fall of Jerusalem in AD 70. In times of war it was normal for people to flee *into* a walled city for protection, and they did just so during the Jerusalem siege. Yet Jesus counsels his disciples to do just the opposite: "Let those who are in Judea flee to the mountains." Josephus reports that many of Jerusalem's defenders expected God to intervene supernaturally to destroy the Roman army and deliver the city. But Jesus warns that God will not do so. Jerusalem and the temple stand under divine judgment and will be destroyed.

Two admonitions stress the urgency of the situation: (1) Anyone on the roof of the house is not, on descending the outside staircase, to go inside to get any of his belongings (v.15); and (2) anyone in the field is not to return to the house even to get an outer garment (v.16). The outer garment (or "cloak") was used at night to keep one warm; in the daytime it was taken off to allow more freedom of movement in working. Though a cloak would be especially useful when fleeing to the mountains (v.14b) where the night air is cold, the situation would be too urgent to allow one even to fetch it. A hurried flight to the mountains would be very hard for pregnant women and nursing mothers (v.17; cf. Lk 23:28–29). And if the flight took place in winter (v.18), it would be even more difficult, since both the cold and the rain-swollen wadis would present formidable hazards (see Cranfield, 403).

The early church historian Eusebius (*Hist. eccl.* 3.5.3) reports that members of the Jerusalem church received an oracle before the siege warning them to flee to the city of Pella in Perea, thereby escaping the destruction (cf. Epiphanius, *Pan.* 29.7.7–8; 30.2.7). Scholars debate whether this "oracle" was Jesus' teaching here or a separate prophecy received by the church at the time of the war. Since Pella is not in the mountains, Jesus' words do not precisely match Eusebius's reference. In either case, many Jerusalem Christians apparently escaped the horrific destruction by fleeing the city before the Romans arrived.

19–20 Here again there is great difficulty in discerning whether Jesus' language refers to the first-century destruction of Jerusalem or to the final eschatological conflict. Josephus describes in detail the horrific suffering of the people of Jerusalem during the Roman siege, including famine, disease, cannibalism, and infighting among the city's inhabitants. The Romans crucified so many Jews that they ran out of trees to construct crosses. Yet the apocalyptic description of tribulation "unequalled from the beginning" and "never to be equaled" again (v.19) may shift the referent back to the end. The language echoes Daniel's portrayal of the last days: "There will be a time of distress such as has not happened from the beginning of nations until then. But at that time your people—everyone whose name is found written in the book—will be delivered" (Da 12:1; cf. Jer 30:7; Joel 2:2). Though the prophecy was fulfilled partially in the great distress that occurred at the fall of Jerusalem in AD 70, its ultimate referent is the great tribulation that will precede the end.

This point is reinforced by the statement that "no one would survive" without the Lord's shortening of those days (v.20). While this verse may hyperbolically be applied to the inhabitants of Jerusalem, it ultimately fits better the context of the end. The "elect" (*eklektoi*) in the OT and Judaism refers to Israel as God's covenantal people (1Ch 16:13; Pss 105:6; 106:5; Wis 3:6; 4:15; Sir 46:1). Second Esdras 16:74 (NRSV) echoes the present context of eschatological deliverance: "Listen, my elect ones, says the Lord; the days of tribulation are at hand, but I will deliver you from them." Although *eklektoi* appears in Mark only in this passage (cf. vv.22, 27), other NT writers apply it to the church, made up of both Jews and Gentiles, as God's covenantal people (Ro 8:33; Col 3:12; 2Ti 2:10; Tit 1:1). Peter, especially, echoes the OT language related to Israel with reference to the church (1Pe 1:1; 2:4, 6, 9). In the context of AD 70, "the elect, for whose sake the siege was shortened, are probably the faithful members of the Church of Jerusalem ... whose intercession or whose presence secured this privilege, though it did not avail to save the city" (Swete, 309). In the context of the end, the elect would be the people of God generally.

21–22 The section (vv.5–23) ends as it began—with a warning against false Christs and false prophets. A crisis such as that of the fall of the city would be sure to produce many messianic pretenders. So would the crisis of the approaching end. They will wield supernatural power great enough to perform "signs and miracles" (v.22), but they will not be able to deceive God's people, as indicated by the force of the phrase "if that were possible." But it will not be possible. God will guard his elect. Beasley-Murray (*Commentary on Mark Thirteen*, 86) comments:

> As in all the Scriptures, the assurance of God's care for his elect (implied in εἰ δυνατόν [*ei dynaton*, "if it were possible"], v.22), is not regarded as ground for presumption. "Do on your part take care. If the temptations of false prophets are strong enough to endanger the chosen of God, you will not be exempt. I have told you all these things in order that you may be fully prepared. Remain on the alert."

23 Jesus concludes this section with the same emphatic command with which he began (vv.5, 9): "Be on your guard!" (*hymeis blepete*). Again, the hortatory purpose of the discourse is evident.

NOTES

14 Some have linked the desolating sacrilege to the order by the emperor Caligula in AD 40 to erect images of him in the Jerusalem temple as objects of worship (Josephus, *Ant.* 18.8.2–3 §§261–72). (In 2 Thessalonians 2:3–10 Paul may be thinking of this event as a kind of prototype for the coming Antichrist.) It is unlikely, however, that this episode is what Jesus is describing. Caligula's order was in fact never carried out, owing to its delay by the Syrian legate Petronius and the subsequent assassination of Caligula.

Eusebius's report concerning the Christian flight from Jerusalem has been rejected by some as a fabrication (see Gerd Lüdemann, "The Successors of Pre–70 Jerusalem Christianity: A Critical Evaluation of the Pella Tradition," in *Jewish and Christian Self-Definition*, ed. E. P. Sanders [London: SCM, 1980] 1:161–73). Many other scholars, however, defend the authenticity of the flight, though without necessarily linking it to Jesus' words here. For details, see V. Balabanski, *Eschatology in the Making: Mark, Matthew and the Didache* (SNTSMS 97; Cambridge: Cambridge Univ. Press, 1997), 101–5; Moloney, 260 n. 228. Martin Hengel (*Studies in the Gospel of Mark*, 14–20) notes the differences between Mark's description and the actual events and argues against a *vaticinium ex eventu* ("prophecy" created after the fact).

20 The idea of a divine shortening or "hastening" of days occurs occasionally in apocalyptic literature (2Es 2:13; *1 En.* 80:2; Sir 36:10; *2 Bar.* 20:1–2; 83:1; see France, 527).

21 Josephus refers to several attempts by individuals to establish themselves as king during the Jerusalem siege, including Menahem (*J.W.* 2.17.8–9 §§433–48) and Simon Bar-Giora (*J.W.* 4.9.3–8 §§503–44). Similarly, false prophets arising in the city deceived the desperate inhabitants by promising God's deliverance (*J.W.* 6.5.2–3 §§285–300; cf. *J.W.* 2.13.4–5 §§258–63).

6. The Coming of the Son of Man (13:24–27)

OVERVIEW

Verses 24–27 form a unit and relate to the parousia and the end of the age. They are set off from the previous verses by the strong adversative *alla* ("but"). Whereas the preceding verses (5–23) point ambiguously to both the destruction of Jerusalem and the end time, these verses appear to speak exclusively of the end time. Following a series of catastrophic signs in the heavens, the Son of Man, returning in the clouds, will send his angels to gather the elect from the ends of the earth, judge the wicked, and establish his eternal kingdom. The salvation achieved through the ransom-sacrifice of the Son of Man on the cross will reach its consummation with his return in glory.

With the majority of commentators, we take this section to refer to the final act of history and the establishment of the kingdom of God. For a contrary view, see Wright, *Jesus and the Victory of God*, 354–68, 510–19, who argues that the "coming" of the Son of Man refers not to the physical descent from heaven of the Messiah but to the vindication of God's people and their representative, Jesus Christ, in the destruction of Jerusalem and the temple. According to this perspective, the apocalyptic language used here was never intended to be taken literally, but instead (and characteristically for such language) stands for something else, namely, God's victory over and judgment against those who opposed his representative. Wright, 515, summarizes his perspective:

> The discourse as a whole then works as follows. Jesus has been asked about the destruction of the Temple. His reply has taken the disciples through the coming scenario: great tribulation, false messiahs arising, themselves hauled before magistrates. They need to know both that Jerusalem is to be destroyed and that they must not stand and fight, but must escape while they can. There will then occur the great cataclysmic event which will be at the same time (a) the final judgment on the city that has now come, with awful paradox, to symbolize rebellion against YHWH; (b) the great deliverance promised in the prophets; and (c) the vindication of the prophet who had predicted the downfall, and who had claimed to be embodying in himself all that Jerusalem and the Temple had previously stood for.

A similar view is espoused by France, 530–34, who claims that the disciples' question about the destruction of Jerusalem is not answered until this point in the discourse (vv.24–27). We will discuss particulars of this interpretation in the notes at the end of this section.

24"But in those days, following that distress,

"'the sun will be darkened,
and the moon will not give its light;
25 the stars will fall from the sky,
and the heavenly bodies will be shaken.'

26"At that time men will see the Son of Man coming in clouds with great power and
glory. 27And he will send his angels and gather his elect from the four winds, from the
ends of the earth to the ends of the heavens."

COMMENTARY

24–25 "In those days," a common OT expression having eschatological associations, further evidences that something beyond the destruction of Jerusalem is in view (cf. Jer 3:16, 18; 31:29; 33:15–16; Joel 3:1; Zec 8:23). In Mark, Jesus speaks of a period "following that distress" (or "tribulation"). Matthew, however, says that these cosmic events will occur "immediately" after the distress of those days (24:29), which seems to connect the destruction of Jerusalem directly to the return of the Son of Man. D. A. Carson, however, argues that the distress (*thlipsis*; GK *2568*) Matthew is referring to is the *thlipsis* of Matthew 24:9, 22, not the "great distress" of vv.15–21. "The celestial signs and the coming of the Son of Man do not immediately follow 'the abomination that causes desolation' but 'the distress of those days'—i.e., of the entire interadvent period of *thlipsis*" (see p. 567 in this volume). Like Mark, then, Matthew would be moving back and forth between references to the destruction of Jerusalem and to the end.

The coming of the Son of Man will be associated with celestial phenomena. The imagery and language derive from OT descriptions of the day of the Lord. The quotation echoes Isaiah 13:10 ("the stars of heaven and their constellations will not show their light; the rising sun will be darkened and the moon will not give its light"), but other OT passages reveal similar language (Isa 24:23; 34:4; Eze 32:7–8; Joel 2:10, 30–31; 3:4, 15, 20; Am 8:9). These celestial events are not so much portents or signs that Christ is about to return, but rather the radical transformation of creation that accompanies his return. G. R. Beasley-Murray (*Jesus and the Last Days* [Peabody, Mass.: Hendrickson, 1993], 375) writes, "The fundamental idea of signs in heaven and on earth is the reaction to the stepping forth of the awesome and terrible Creator. The elements of creation go into confusion and fear *because* he appears, not as a sign that he is about to do so (see, e.g., Jdg 5:4–5; Am 1:2; Hab 3:3–6, 10–11; Pss 77:14–16; 114:1–8)." This language is that of theophany. God is about to reveal himself through awesome power and judgment by the divine Son of Man.

It is difficult to know how much the poetic language here is to be understood literally and how much figuratively. The repeated assertion in Scripture that the end times will be accompanied by cosmic disturbances seems to imply that there will be unprecedented celestial disturbances of some sort that are literal (cf. 2Pe 3:10). This literality is not to deny that Mark may be using phenomenal language, but his language is nonetheless referring to objective events in the physical universe. These events will occur when God brings history to an end by the coming of his Son. Ladd (*Theology of the New Testament*, 203) writes, "This language does not mean necessarily the complete break-up of the universe; we know from similar language elsewhere that it designates the judgment of God upon a fallen world that has shared the fate of humanity's sin, that out of the ruins of judgment a new world may be born."

26–27 The celestial drama climaxes when the Son of Man comes in the clouds with "great power and glory." Jesus describes his coming in these verses almost entirely in the words of Scripture. The reference here is to Daniel 7:13, the first time Jesus explicitly connects the title "Son of Man" with this prophecy in Daniel (cf. Mk 14:62; for a discussion of the title "Son of Man," see comments at 8:31).

The great emphasis of these verses is on disclosure and triumph. Whereas the Son of Man has been hidden, or at least veiled, in his first coming, now he will be revealed. People "will see" him and see him for who he really is. Whereas he has been the lowly Suffering Servant, despised and rejected, the Son of Man at his parousia will come in triumph—"with great power and glory." And his chief concern at his coming will be to bring together his people so that they may be with him; so he sends forth his angels to gather the elect from all over the world (v.27). The gathering and restoration of the remnant of God's people is a common theme in the OT and Judaism (Dt 30:4; Isa 11:11–12; 43:5–6; Jer 23:3; 32:37; Eze 34:12–13; 36:24; Zec 2:10; *Pss. Sol.* 8:28; 11:1–4; 17:21–28). The fact that they are called "his angels" reflects a remarkably high Christology. Throughout the OT it is God who commands and directs the angels of heaven (Evans,

329). Here it is the Son of Man, the one who is "given authority, glory and sovereign power" and who will be worshiped by "all nations and peoples of every language" (Da 7:14 TNIV).

NOTES

24 The translators of the NIV and TNIV avoid the word "tribulation" both here and in Matthew's parallel, probably because of the word's abuse in contemporary eschatological scenarios. But "tribulation" is used in the RSV, ESV, and CSB. The NLT has "anguish," the NRSV, "suffering."

24–25 Interpreters who identify these celestial signs with the destruction of Jerusalem point out that the OT background passages often concern not the end of time but the judgment of nations (such as Babylon) within history. In this case Jesus, like the prophets, would be using hyperbolic, cosmic language to describe the awesome judgment of God against Jerusalem and the temple (see, e.g., T. R. Hatina, "The Focus of Mark 13:24–27—The Parousia, or the Destruction of the Temple?" *BBR* 6 [1996]: 43–66; Wright, *Jesus and the Victory of God*, 362, 513; France, 532–33).

27 Interpreters who relate these verses to the destruction of Jerusalem claim that this "ingathering" of the elect refers to the missionary expansion of the gospel in the first century and that the ἄγγελοι, *angeloi*, are either human "messengers" of the gospel (Wright, *Jesus and the Victory of God*, 362–63), or angels who are viewed as aiding missionaries in the task of world evangelism (cf. Heb 1:14; see France, 536–37).

7. The Lesson of the Fig Tree (13:28–31)

OVERVIEW

The last two sections of the discourse (vv.28–31; vv.32–37) continue to stress the need for watchfulness and preparation. The first (apparently) has its primary reference in the destruction of Jerusalem (vv.28–31) and the second in the return of the Son of Man (vv.32–37). Again, however, the distinction is less than obvious, and the two events blend and merge as the former serves as the prototype for the latter. Both sections contain an illustration, the first about a fig tree whose early leaves signal the onset of summer just as the "birth pains" signal the coming destruction of Jerusalem (vv.28–29). The second is about a householder who, leaving his servants in charge of the estate while he is away, expects them to be ready at any moment for his return. In the same way, Jesus' disciples must be always vigilant for the return of the Son of Man (vv.34–35).

28 "Now learn this lesson from the fig tree: As soon as its twigs get tender and its leaves
come out, you know that summer is near. 29 Even so, when you see these things happening,
you know that it is near, right at the door. 30 I tell you the truth, this generation will certainly
not pass away until all these things have happened. 31 Heaven and earth will pass away,
but my words will never pass away."

COMMENTARY

28–30 The "parable" of a fig tree is really an analogy (NIV, "lesson"; for this broad definition of the Greek term *parabolē*, see Overview, 4:1–34). In Palestine most trees retain their leaves in the winter (the olive, oak, evergreen, terebinth, etc.), but the fig tree is an exception. In the fall it loses its leaves; and when in the spring the sap rises in its branches and the tree begins to leaf out, summer cannot be far off (Lane, 479). Jesus points out that just as the new shoots on the tree reveal that summer is near, so when "these things" are seen to be happening, his disciples will know that "it" (or "he") is near (v.29).

Four closely related questions emerge: (1) What does the fig tree symbolize? (2) What are "these things" that the disciples will witness? (3) What is the thing (or person) that is "near"? and (4) What is "this generation" that will not pass away until "all these things have happened" (v.30)? The answers to these questions are closely tied to our interpretation of the discourse as a whole.

(1) Jesus had earlier cursed the fig tree (11:12–25), which was symbolic of God's judgment against Israel and the temple. It is possible, therefore, that the leafing of the fig tree in the springtime symbolizes the restoration of God's people in the new community of the Messiah (cf. T. J. Geddert, *Watchwords: Mark 13 in Markan Eschatology* [JSNTSup 26; Sheffield: Sheffield Academic Press, 1989], 251–52). Yet Jesus does not draw such a specific analogy. The fundamental point seems to be more general: the certainty of summer following the leafing of a fig tree confirms that what Jesus has predicted will certainly come to pass.

(2) So which prediction is in view that will surely come to pass—the destruction of Jerusalem, or the coming of the Son of Man at the end of the age? The simplest and least problematic solution is to take the *primary referent* as the destruction of Jerusalem (Lane, 478; France, 538; Garland, 502; Witherington, 348). Both "these things" (*tauta*) of v.29, and "all these things" (*tauta panta*) of v.30 refer to the events of vv.5–23, which climax in the "abomination of desolation" and the destruction of Jerusalem. As we have seen throughout the discourse, this cataclysmic event then serves as a prototype and model for the ultimate crisis, which will precede the final tribulation and the coming of the Son of Man.

(3) Following this interpretation consistently throughout the passage, the next phrase in v.29, *engys estin*, should not be translated "he is near" (NRSV, NET, CSB, ESV; cf. NLT)—a reference to the Son of Man—but rather "it is near" (NIV, TNIV; cf. TEV and CEB, "the time"), referring either to the "abomination that causes desolation" (cf. v.14) or the fall of the city itself. Just as summer follows the sprouting of the fig tree, so the destruction of Jerusalem will follow the preparatory signs Jesus has described.

(4) Finally, this interpretation allows the most natural and straightforward sense of the expression "this generation" (*hē genea hautē*) in v.30. A multiplicity of interpretations has been suggested for this difficult phrase, including humanity in general, the Jewish people, Christians, and unbelievers. None of these fit the context well. It seems best, therefore, to understand it to mean Jesus' own generation. This is the sense of the phrase elsewhere in Mark (8:12, 38; 9:19). A biblical generation was about forty years, which was "not coincidentally the length of time between Jesus' prediction and the destruction of Jerusalem" (Witherington, 349). "All these things" (*tauta panta*), then, refers to the signs found in vv.5–23, which are not confined to a remote future but "are to be experienced, though

not necessarily exhausted, by the contemporary generation" (A. L. Moore, *The Parousia in the New Testament* [Leiden: Brill, 1966], 133).

Since Jesus' words here are preceded by the solemn "I tell you the truth" (*amēn legō hymin*; see comments at 3:28), they are not to be taken lightly. To suggest that Jesus was mistaken in the statement he made in this verse, but that the mistake was regarding a matter of such small consequence that it makes no difference, is to fail to take seriously the solemnity of these introductory words.

31 Jesus strongly emphasizes the certainty and reliability of his predictions. "Heaven and earth" is a reference to the whole of the universe, all creation. The certitude and absolute reliability of Jesus' words are far greater than the apparent continuance of the universe. It will someday cease to exist, but Jesus' words will always have validity (Ps 102:25–27; Isa 40:6–8; 51:6).

NOTES

29 Instead of "it is near" (or "he is near"), Luke has "the kingdom of God is near" (21:31). This expansion does not solve the problem, however, since Luke's version of the Olivet Discourse focuses on the destruction of Jerusalem even more emphatically than Mark's. It is unclear, therefore, whether by "the kingdom of God" Luke means the return of Christ, the resurrection, the destruction of Jerusalem, or something else.

30 The Greek word for generation is γενεά (*genea*, GK *1155*). It "primarily denotes those descended from a single ancestor, a tribe, a race; then it comes to signify those born within the same period, a generation of contemporary men; finally a period of time occupied by a particular generation" (Beasley-Murray, *Commentary on Mark Thirteen*, 99). E. Earle Ellis, however, remarks, "In the Qumran writings the term 'last generation' (1Qp Hab 2.7; 7:2) apparently included several lifetimes. Their usage indicates that in the New Testament 'this (last) generation,' like 'last hour' (1Jn 2:18) or 'today,' means only the last phase in the history of redemption" (*The Gospel of Luke* [NCBC; Greenwood, S.C.: Attic 1966], 246). According to this interpretation, "this generation" is the final period before the end, however long that period may be.

A prominent problem raised by v.30 is the NT's insistence on the nearness of the end (cf. Ro 13:12; 1Co 7:29; Php 4:5; Heb 10:25; Jas 5:8–9; 1Pe 4:7; 1Jo 2:18; Rev 22:20). Cranfield, 408, asks:

> Are we to say (with Dodd, Glasson, Taylor, et al.) that the primitive Church read into Jesus' ideas apocalyptic teachings that were alien to it? Or (with Schweitzer, Werner, T. W. Manson, Barrett, et al.) that Jesus was himself mistaken? Or is the solution to be found in a more theological understanding of what is meant by the nearness of the End?... If we realize that the Incarnation-Crucifixion-Resurrection-Ascension, on the one hand, and the Parousia, on the other, belong essentially together, and are in a real sense one Event, one divine Act, being held apart only by the Mercy of God who desires to give men opportunity for faith and repentance, then we can see that ... the latter is always imminent now that the former has happened. It was, and still is, true to say that the Parousia is at hand—and indeed this, so far from being an embarrassing mistake on the part either of Jesus or of the early Church, is an essential part of the Church's faith. Ever since the Incarnation men have been living in the last days.

This type of thinking is difficult for modern Western people, but it seems consistent with the biblical material.

8. The Necessity of Watchfulness (13:32–37)

OVERVIEW

In this final section the primary referent shifts back again to the coming of the Son of Man and the end of the age. Evidence for this shift is the introductory phrase *peri de* ("Now concerning ..."), which indicates a change of topic. Furthermore, the term "that day" (*hēmera ekeinē*, v.32) is almost certainly a reference to the great and final day of the Lord (Joel 3:18; Am 8:3, 9, 13; 9:11; Ob 8; Mic 4:6; Zep 1:9–10; 3:11, 16; Zec 9:16; Mt 7:22; Lk 10:12; 2Ti 1:12, 18; 4:8; cf. 1Co 3:13). Finally, while the preceding section spoke of the disciples' ability to discern the approaching time (of Jerusalem's destruction, v.29), here the entire emphasis is on the need for preparation *since no one knows the time* (of the Son of Man's return). France, 531, comments, "We have moved emphatically from the known to the unknown." Jesus' call for vigilance pervades this paragraph—"Be on guard! Be alert!" (v.33); "Therefore keep watch" (v.35); "do not let him find you sleeping" (v.36); and "Watch!" (v.37).

32"No one knows about that day or hour, not even the angels in heaven, nor the Son,
but only the Father. 33Be on guard! Be alert! You do not know when that time will come.
34It's like a man going away: He leaves his house and puts his servants in charge, each with
his assigned task, and tells the one at the door to keep watch.
35"Therefore keep watch because you do not know when the owner of the house will
come back—whether in the evening, or at midnight, or when the rooster crows, or at
dawn. 36If he comes suddenly, do not let him find you sleeping. 37What I say to you, I say to
everyone: 'Watch!'"

COMMENTARY

32 Few would challenge the authenticity of this verse. The early church is unlikely to have created a logion that has resulted in such consternation and embarrassment as this one has. As noted above, "that day" clearly refers to the parousia. It is the great day, the eschatological day that will bring to an end "those days" (vv.17, 19, 24). Of "those days" certain signs have been given; but of "that day" neither the angels of heaven nor Jesus himself knows the time. Only the Father knows. And Jesus, at his ascension, clearly says that it was not for the disciples "to know the times or dates the Father has set by his own authority" (Ac 1:7). A map of the future would be a hindrance, not a help, to faith. Their responsibility and ours is to get busy and do his work without being concerned about date setting.

Jesus' ignorance of the day or hour of his return must be understood in terms of the NT's teaching concerning the incarnation. A real incarnation involved such lack of knowledge. Jesus purposely but temporarily laid aside the exercise of his omniscience as part of what was involved in becoming a human being. Though the passage has sometimes been viewed as reflecting negatively on Jesus' divine status, in fact it manifests a very high Christology. Jesus identifies himself with the absolute title "the Son," which in the context is a status higher even than the angels. In relationship with the absolute title "the Father," it carries strong implications of deity.

33–36 Vigilance is the order of the day because the time of the parousia is not known. *Blepete* ("be on guard") is the keynote of the entire discourse, and *gar* ("for," untranslated in NIV) states the reason watchfulness is necessary. Swete, 317, writes, "If the Master Himself does not know, the disciples must not only acquiesce in their ignorance, but regard it as a wholesome stimulus to exertion." The word for time here is *kairos*, meaning God's appointed time.

The parable has in it some of the features of that of the talents (Mt 25:14–30) and the ten minas (Lk 19:12–27). There is a privilege (*exousia*, "charge") and a responsibility (*ergon*, "assigned task," v.34). The parable does not develop these elements but turns attention to the doorkeeper who has a special task. Then Jesus applies it to the disciples. Like a doorkeeper who must watch because he does not know when the owner will return, they also must be on guard (v.35). Evening, midnight, rooster's crowing, and dawn designate the four watches of the night used by the Romans. The Greek adverb *exaiphnēs* ("suddenly") emphasizes the suddenness of the parousia (v.36). Beasley-Murray (*Commentary on Mark Thirteen*, 117) writes, "The element of surprise is ineradicable from the parousia expectation. Signs, like the fig tree, are an indication of promise, not a clock."

37 The discourse addressed to four of the disciples (v.3) began with the imperative "Watch." This exhortation recurs throughout the discourse. Now at the end it is repeated once more, but this time it is no longer addressed only to the four disciples but to "everyone." In this way Jesus shows his concern not only for the disciples but also for the whole community—all his followers, for whom he was about to die—and his message is "Watch!" Beasley-Murray, 118, comments, "This word the first community took seriously. When their hour came they were ready. In crises since that day it has shone as a lamp in the gloom."

VII. THE PASSION AND RESURRECTION NARRATIVE (14:1–16:8[9–20])

OVERVIEW

The conflict of Jesus with the religious leaders, which in Mark's gospel begins as early as 2:1–3:6, reaches its climax in the passion narrative and is followed by the triumph of the resurrection announcement on Easter morning. Already in 3:6, the Pharisees and Herodians had begun to plot to take Jesus' life. Now their plans come to fruition. Yet this development is no defeat for Jesus but rather the goal to which he has been heading (10:45). The importance of the passion and resurrection for the early church is evidenced by the relatively large amount of space the narrative takes in each of the gospels and especially in Mark. Out of Mark's 661 verses, 128 are devoted to the passion and resurrection account, and a total of 242 are devoted to the last week (from the triumphal entry to the resurrection) of Jesus' life. The church obviously had more than a passing historical interest in Jesus' death and resurrection. These events formed the basis of the church's witness and worship—the lifeblood of early Christianity. The witnessing church proclaimed a crucified and living Savior, and the worshiping church reflected on the meaning of these events for its inner life.

The passion narrative may be divided into two main sections: the events leading to Jesus' arrest (14:1–52), and his trials, crucifixion, and burial (14:53–15:47). The first section contains the anointing of Jesus at Bethany (14:6–9) intercalated (sandwiched) into the account of the plot against Jesus and his betrayal by Judas (14:1–2, 10–11), the Last Supper (14:17–26), Jesus' prediction of Peter's denial (14:27–31), the agony in Gethsemane (14:32–42), and the betrayal and arrest (14:43–52). The second section contains Jesus' trial before the Sanhedrin (14:53–65), the denial by Peter (14:66–72), the trial before Pilate (15:1–15), the mocking of Jesus (15:16–20), the crucifixion (15:21–32), his death (15:33–41), and his burial (15:42–47). The women's visit to the tomb and the announcement of the resurrection conclude the gospel (16:1–8).

The overarching theme is the purpose and plan of God. Although from a human perspective, events seem to be spinning out of control, yet God through his agent Jesus is accomplishing his salvation-bringing purpose. This theme, evident already in Jesus' three passion and resurrection predictions (8:31; 9:31; 10:33–34; cf. 10:45), now plays itself out in the narrative. While wicked men secretly plot Jesus' death (14:1–2, 10–11), Jesus announces that his body is being anointed for burial (vv.6–9). He knows ahead of time that he will be betrayed (vv.20–21), denied (v.30), struck down as the shepherd (v.27; Zec 13:7) and deserted (v.27). Though deeply dreading this fate, he willingly submits *since this is the will of God* (v.36).

This overarching theme of divine purpose develops through the (sub)themes of suffering and vindication. The suffering of Jesus is highlighted by: (1) his betrayal (by Judas), desertion (by all the disciples), and denial (by Peter); (2) the injustice and mockery of his trials before the Sanhedrin and Pilate; and finally, (3) the brutality and shame of crucifixion. Through it all Jesus remains faithful and thus confident of vindication by the Father. He tells the disciples, "After I have risen, I will go ahead of you into Galilee" (14:28), and he confidently announces to the high priest at his trial, "You will see the Son of Man sitting at the right hand of the Mighty One and coming on the clouds of heaven" (14:62). Though dying in agony and despair, at his death the temple curtain is torn from top to bottom, and the centurion cries out, "Surely this man was the Son of God!" (15:39). Ultimate vindication follows with the angelic announcement of the resurrection on the third day (16:6), "He has risen!" And on this note, Mark's gospel—"the good news about Jesus Christ" (1:1)—comes to a close.

Additional comments on chs. 14–15. Whereas much of Mark's gospel is made up of individual episodes (pericopes) only loosely tied to each other or to their narrative context, Mark's passion narrative is made up of a series of closely linked episodes that, apparently from the start, functioned as a connected narrative. It is likely that since these events constitute the heart of the Christian gospel (cf. 1Co 15:1–4), they were the first part of the story of Jesus to be written down and circulated as a continuous whole. Lane, 485, notes, "It is commonly recognized that for chs. 14–15 Mark had access to a primitive source, whether oral or written, embodying authentic historical remembrance, which he took over virtually intact." For extensive bibliography and summary of various source theories, see Evans, 347–53.

A. The Plot to Arrest Jesus (14:1–2)

[1]Now the Passover and the Feast of Unleavened Bread were only two days away, and
the chief priests and the teachers of the law were looking for some sly way to arrest Jesus
and kill him. [2]"But not during the Feast," they said, "or the people may riot."

COMMENTARY

1–2 These verses serve to introduce the passion and resurrection narrative. Passover is the Jewish festival commemorating the occasion when the angel of the Lord "passed over" (Heb. *pāsaḥ*) the homes of the Hebrews on the night he killed all the firstborn sons of the Egyptians (cf. Ex 12:13, 23, 27). The lambs used in the feast were slain on the fourteenth of Nisan (March/April), and the meal was eaten that evening between sundown and midnight. According to Jewish reckoning, that day would be the fifteenth of Nisan, since the Jewish day began at sundown. The Feast of Unleavened Bread followed Passover and lasted seven days (15–21 Nisan; cf. Ex 12:15–20; 23:15; 34:18; Dt 16:1–8). Since the Last Supper was probably a Passover meal and took place on Thursday night, the incident reported here likely took place on Wednesday of Passion Week. This calculation keys off the temporal phrase *meta duo hēmeras* ("after two days"). If "after three days" means "on the third day" (8:31; 9:31; 10:34), then "after two days" would mean "on the second day," i.e., "tomorrow." The NIV's "only two days away" (v.1) is ambiguous and must be understood in accordance with Jewish usage of the temporal phrase.

For a long time the religious authorities had been looking for a way to get rid of Jesus (3:6; 11:18; 12:12). Now they renewed and intensified their efforts. But it was necessary for them to proceed with the utmost caution. Passover was one of the three great pilgrim feasts that adult Jewish males were expected to attend (Tabernacles and Pentecost were the other two). So great throngs of people invaded the Holy City to celebrate. It is said that the population doubled (perhaps from twenty-five thousand to fifty thousand) during the week. The chief priests and teachers of the law (the two main bodies that made up the Sanhedrin, the Jewish high court) realized that it would be too risky to move against Jesus with such a highly excitable crowd present. The possibility of a riot was too great (v.2). It would be wiser to wait for a more opportune moment—perhaps after the pilgrims had left the city to go home. God's purposes were otherwise, and this part of their plan miscarried. Perhaps the unexpected help from one of Jesus' disciples (14:10–11) changed their minds, and they decided to go through with their scheme despite the presence of the Passover pilgrims.

NOTES

2 Population estimates for the city of Jerusalem vary widely among scholars. Jeremias (*Jerusalem*, 84) suggests twenty thousand in the city and five to ten thousand outside the city. Others claim as many as one hundred twenty thousand, increasing to up to three hundred thousand during Passover (Garland, 513–14, citing W. Reinhardt). Ancient writers are of little help in this regard, since their numbers can be wildly exaggerated. Josephus, for example, claims that three million people came to Jerusalem during Passover (*J.W.* 2.14.3 §280; 6.9.3 §§423–27).

B. The Anointing at Bethany (14:3–9)

OVERVIEW

Mark places the account of the anointing at Bethany in one of his characteristic "intercalations," or sandwichings, between the plot of the religious leaders to destroy Jesus in vv.1–2 and the opportunity to achieve that goal through the betrayal by Judas in vv.10–11 (on intercalation, see Introduction, pp. 689–90). The woman's reverent act of devotion—interpreted by Jesus as a loving anointing for his burial—stands in stark contrast to the treachery of those trying to kill him.

Though regarding this incident Matthew follows Mark's order, the chronological placement of the narrative is different in John's gospel, where it appears before Passion Week begins (cf. Jn 12:1: "six days before the Passover"). The most likely explanation is that for Mark the theological significance is more important than the chronological. His placement contrasts the hatred of the religious leaders with the love and devotion of the woman. Although Luke 7:36–50 is similar to John 12:1–8 and Mark 14:3–9, the differences are significant; thus Luke likely records a different incident (see Notes).

[3]While he was in Bethany, reclining at the table in the home of a man known as Simon
the Leper, a woman came with an alabaster jar of very expensive perfume, made of pure
nard. She broke the jar and poured the perfume on his head.
[4]Some of those present were saying indignantly to one another, "Why this waste of
perfume? [5]It could have been sold for more than a year's wages and the money given to
the poor." And they rebuked her harshly.
[6]"Leave her alone," said Jesus. "Why are you bothering her? She has done a beautiful
thing to me. [7]The poor you will always have with you, and you can help them any time you
want. But you will not always have me. [8]She did what she could. She poured perfume on
my body beforehand to prepare for my burial. [9]I tell you the truth, wherever the gospel is
preached throughout the world, what she has done will also be told, in memory of her."

COMMENTARY

3 The episode takes place at Bethany in the home of Simon "the Leper." The occasion for the dinner is not specified. Simon's name probably indicates he was a leper who had been healed—indeed he may have been healed by Jesus. Was the dinner an expression of gratitude for the healing? Mark does not identify the woman who anointed Jesus, but John (12:3) identifies her as Mary, the sister of Martha and Lazarus (if these are indeed the same events). The "alabaster jar" (*alabastros*) that contained the perfume was a "vessel with a rather long neck which was broken off when the contents were used" (BDAG, 40). The "nard" (perfume) was made from the root of a plant found chiefly in India and was very expensive. The woman took the bottle and broke the neck so that she could pour the ointment profusely over Jesus' head.

What was the significance of the anointing? Kings and priests were anointed in Israel, and some commentators have suggested that the woman's actions carry messianic significance. While they may do so, anointing was also an act of hospitality or devotion for an honored guest, and this explanation better fits the occasion here. For to describe the woman's action Mark does not use *chriō* ("anoint"), which would have echoed Jesus' status as *christos*, the "Anointed One" (cf. 1:1; 8:29); rather, he uses "poured" (*katacheō*, v.3) and "anoint with ointment" (*myrizō*, v.8). The action is not a messianic installation but an act of love and devotion.

4–5 Instead of specifying those who reacted so indignantly at the "waste" of the costly perfume, Mark refers to them generally as "some [*tines*] of those present" (v.4). Matthew points the finger at the disciples (26:8), while John names Judas Iscariot (12:4–5). John notes that Judas's comment was motivated not by love for the poor but by greed, since he was the treasurer of the Twelve and would pilfer from the money bag (12:6). No such motivation is mentioned in Mark, where the guests' indignation arises instead from the extravagant waste. This makes Jesus' reply in v.6 all the more striking and forces the reader to ponder how an act of devotion could be of greater spiritual value than a huge donation to the poor. The perfume had a value of more than three hundred denarii (one denarius was the average daily wage for a laborer—thus the NIV's "more than a year's wages"). Mark uses very strong language to describe the guests' feelings toward the woman: they "were indignant" (*aganakteō*; cf. 10:14, 41) and "rebuked her harshly" (*embrimaomai*; cf. 1:43).

6–7 Jesus rushed to the woman's defense. Instead of condemning her, the guests should have commended her. Her act was a beautiful expression of love and devotion to him, and she should not be berated. In addition, Jesus would not be with them very long (v.7). Before Jesus lay Gethsemane, his trials, crucifixion, and resurrection. Time for such expression of devotion and love while he was still here was running out. In contrast, opportunities for helping the poor would continue. In Jesus' statement there is no evidence of a lack of concern for the poor. On the contrary, there is ample evidence elsewhere that their interests and needs lay close to his heart (cf. Mt 5:3; 6:2–4; 19:21; Lk 6:20, 36–38; 21:1–4; Jn 13:29). The point, rather, is that the presence of Jesus in the world and the monumental task he is about to accomplish are of much greater significance than a single act of charity. He is about to change the course of human history by offering himself as a ransom for sins.

8 In addition to being an expression of devotion, the woman's act was interpreted by Jesus as an anointing of his body in preparation for burial. Was she aware of this aspect of what she was doing?

Mark gives no indication that she did. He represents the anointing as a simple act of love and devotion, not one of prophecy or prescience. It is, rather, Jesus who connects the episode to his coming death and so once again predicts his passion.

9 This pronouncement is preceded by the solemn "I tell you the truth" (see comments at 3:28). As in the Olivet Discourse (13:10), Jesus predicts that the gospel will be proclaimed throughout the whole world. In an indirect way Jesus is here predicting his resurrection, because the preaching of the gospel presupposes the resurrection. The central message of the good news is Jesus' defeat of sin and death through his resurrection. And anywhere in the world that this good news is preached, this woman's act of love and devotion will be remembered. The incorporation of this story in Mark's gospel confirms the fulfillment of Jesus' prediction.

NOTES

3 The incident in vv.3–9 should not be confused with that in Luke 7:36–50. The details, except the name Simon, are very different. "The Leper" may be added to Simon's name to differentiate him from the Simon in Luke 7:36–50, since Simon was a very common name. Plummer, 312, correctly comments: "The difficulty of believing in two anointings is infinitesimal.... Whereas the difficulty of believing that Mary of Bethany had ever been 'a sinner' is enormous. There is no evidence of a previous evil life, and what we know of her renders a previous evil life almost incredible."

4 According to Lane, 493, the mention of the poor is natural in this context because it was the custom for the Jews to give gifts to the poor on the evening of the Passover (*m. Pesaḥ.* 9:11–10:1; cf. Jn 13:29; see Gundry, 811). On the great importance of almsgiving in Judaism, see Jeremias, *Jerusalem*, 126–34.

C. The Betrayal by Judas (14:10–11)

10Then Judas Iscariot, one of the Twelve, went to the chief priests to betray Jesus to
them. 11They were delighted to hear this and promised to give him money. So he watched
for an opportunity to hand him over.

COMMENTARY

10–11 As noted above, these verses are related to vv.1–2, with the anointing at Bethany (vv.3–9) sandwiched between the two. The chief priests and teachers of the law were looking for "some sly way to arrest Jesus" (v.1), and Judas "watched for an opportunity to hand him over" (v.11). Judas is identified specifically as "one of the Twelve" (v.10). He had all the advantages of being in the inner circle, yet he betrayed Jesus. Spiritual privilege in itself is not enough. True discipleship requires a response of faith and love.

Judas's offer to betray Jesus was readily accepted by the chief priests and teachers of the law because Judas, being on the inside, could choose the most opportune time to hand Jesus over to them. In that way they could avoid what they feared the most—a popular riot. It was undoubtedly the offer of Judas—who took the initiative by approaching the religious leaders—that changed their minds about not arresting Jesus during the feast. It was a golden opportunity, and they were not about to lose it. Mark merely mentions that money was involved in the deal (v.11), but Matthew says that the agreed-on payment for the betrayal was thirty silver coins (26:15).

REFLECTIONS

What motivated Judas to betray Jesus? Many guesses have been made—jealousy, greed, disappointment with Jesus' mission, to name a few. None of the evangelists answer the question. There can be little doubt, however, that Judas was the betrayer. It is not likely that the church would have invented a story in which one of Jesus' closest followers turns against him.

D. The Last Supper (14:12–26)

OVERVIEW

Mark's narrative of the Last Supper is comprised of three parts: (1) the preparation of the meal (vv.12–16), (2) the announcement of the betrayal (vv.17–21), and (3) the institution of the Lord's Supper (vv.22–26). Jesus takes the traditional Jewish Passover celebration and transforms its significance for all time. What was formerly a celebration of Israel's redemption from slavery in Egypt will become a remembrance and celebration of Jesus' new-exodus deliverance of his people from the power of sin and Satan. Jesus' own blood sacrifice—symbolized by the Passover cup of wine—will replace the blood of the lamb placed over the doorpost to protect the firstborn sons of Israel. The covenant sealed with blood, which God made through Moses and Mount Sinai (Ex 24:8), will become the new covenant predicted in Jeremiah 31 and inaugurated by Jesus' death on the cross.

1. Preparation of the Meal (14:12–16)

[12]On the first day of the Feast of Unleavened Bread, when it was customary to sacrifice
the Passover lamb, Jesus' disciples asked him, "Where do you want us to go and make
preparations for you to eat the Passover?"
[13]So he sent two of his disciples, telling them, "Go into the city, and a man carrying a jar
of water will meet you. Follow him. [14]Say to the owner of the house he enters, 'The Teacher

asks: Where is my guest room, where I may eat the Passover with my disciples?' [15]He will show you a large upper room, furnished and ready. Make preparations for us there."

[16]The disciples left, went into the city and found things just as Jesus had told them. So they prepared the Passover.

COMMENTARY

12 Ordinarily "the first day of the Feast of Unleavened Bread" would mean 15 Nisan (Lev 23:6; Nu 28:17), the day following Passover. But the added description of the day—"when it was customary to sacrifice the Passover lamb"—makes it clear that 14 Nisan is meant, because Passover lambs were killed on 14 Nisan. The entire eight-day celebration, including Passover, was sometimes referred to as the Feast of Unleavened Bread (cf. Josephus, *Ant.* 2.15.1 §317); and there is some evidence that 14 Nisan was loosely referred to as the "first day of Unleavened Bread" (cf. *m. Pesaḥ.* 1:1–3; Josephus, *J.W.* 5.3.1 §99).

The day of the week was Thursday. Jesus and his disciples were probably in Bethany. It is clear from v.13 that they were outside the city of Jerusalem. Since the Passover had to be eaten within the walls of the city (*m. Pesaḥ.* 7:9), the disciples asked Jesus where in Jerusalem they were to go to make preparation. There was no time to lose, for the Passover meal had to be eaten between sundown and midnight, the first hours of 15 Nisan.

13–16 Jesus gave explicit instructions to two of his disciples. Luke identifies the two as Peter and John (Lk 22:8). The "man carrying a jar of water" would easily be identified because customarily women, not men, carried water jars. The man was to lead them to the house where the owner had a guest room (v.14). Mark seems to indicate that Jesus had made previous arrangements with the owner of the house ("Where is my guest room ...?" v.14), but it is not altogether clear from Mark's narrative whether this case was so, or whether Jesus identified the man with the water jar through divine foreknowledge. The upstairs room is described as "furnished and ready" (v.15), i.e., with what was necessary for the celebration: table, couches, cushions, etc. The disciples would have to get the food and prepare it. The meal would include unleavened bread, wine, bitter herbs, sauce, and the lamb. The two disciples went into the city as instructed by Jesus, found everything as he had said, and made the necessary preparations (v.16).

NOTES

12 The word πάσχα (*pascha*) here means "the Passover lamb" (so NIV). In 14:1 it designates the feast day and in 14:12b, 14, 16 the Passover meal. While Mark and the other Synoptics identify the Last Supper as a Passover meal (Mk 14:16 par.), some commentators have disputed this view and claimed that it was an earlier meal in Passover week (see McKnight, *Jesus and His Death*, 264–73). John seems to treat it as an ordinary meal before Passover (John 13:2; 18:28) in order to portray Jesus as the Lamb of God crucified on the eve of Passover, when the Passover lambs were sacrificed in Jerusalem (John 19:14, 31, 42).

Various solutions have been suggested. Some scholars claim the Passover was celebrated on different days by different groups of Jews (Galileans vs. Judeans; Sadducees vs. Pharisees), or that the massive crowds in Jerusalem required staggered Passover celebrations throughout the week. Others claim that the Johannine phrase παρασκευὴ τοῦπάσχα, *paraskeuē tou pascha* ("preparation for Passover"), does not mean preparation day *for the Passover meal* but preparation day *for the Sabbath* of Passover week (i.e., Friday; see Mk 15:42 for this sense of παρασκευὴ, *paraskeuē*). Both John and the Synoptics would then have Jesus eating the Passover on Thursday evening and crucified on Friday, the eve of the *Sabbath* of Passover week. While none of these options are without some difficulties, each represents a plausible solution. For further details, see Craig Blomberg, *The Historical Reliability of the Gospels* (Downers Grove, Ill.: InterVarsity, 1987), 175–78; Brooks, 224–26.

2. Announcement of the Betrayal (14:17–21)

17When evening came, Jesus arrived with the Twelve. 18While they were reclining at the table eating, he said, "I tell you the truth, one of you will betray me — one who is eating with me."

19They were saddened, and one by one they said to him, "Surely not I?"

20"It is one of the Twelve," he replied, "one who dips bread into the bowl with me. 21The Son of Man will go just as it is written about him. But woe to that man who betrays the Son of Man! It would be better for him if he had not been born."

COMMENTARY

17 Jesus and his disciples had probably spent the day in Bethany. In the evening they returned to the city. Mark says Jesus "arrived with the Twelve," thus suggesting that the two disciples, after making preparations, returned to Bethany, a distance of only a couple of miles, and then accompanied Jesus when he went into the city in the evening. The other possibility is that "the Twelve" was a designation for the close followers of Jesus, whether all twelve were present or not. Since the Jewish day began at sundown, it was now Thursday night, 15 Nisan.

18 The Passover meal was originally eaten while standing: "This is how you are to eat it: with your cloak tucked into your belt, your sandals on your feet and your staff in your hand. Eat it in haste; it is the LORD's Passover" (Ex 12:11). But in Jesus' time it had become customary to eat it in a reclining position. While Jews normally sat for meals, reclining was the posture for a more formal banquet or celebratory meal. Jesus uses the solemn formula "I tell you the truth" (cf. v.9 and comments at 3:28) to disclose the fact that one of them would betray him.

Jesus further identified the betrayer as "one who is eating with me." Meals were rituals of social status in the Mediterranean world, and to share table fellowship with someone indicated friendship and social acceptance. To betray a friend after eating with him was, and still is, regarded as the worst kind of treachery in the Middle East. Jesus may have had in mind Psalm 41:9: "Even my close friend, whom I trusted, he who shared my bread, has lifted his heel against me."

19 The response of the disciples to Jesus' startling disclosure was one of sadness and dismay. One by one they ask Jesus, "Surely not I?" (The Greek construction expects a negative answer [see Gundry, 836].) In Matthew's gospel even Judas asks the question (Mt 26:25). It was an honest question coming from the rest of the disciples and was prompted by fear and lack of confidence in their own spiritual and moral strength. With Judas it was hypocritical and an attempt to cover his intent; for him not to have asked the question with the other disciples would have made him liable to suspicion.

20 Jesus says the betrayer is one of the Twelve, i.e., one who is eating with him at that moment. The "one who dips bread in the bowl" refers to dipping a piece of unleavened bread in the sauce (*ḥarôset*) that was part of the Passover meal. Jesus' statement is not meant to specify the betrayer further (as though only one of the disciples would dip bread in the dish), but rather dramatically reinforces the point of v.18, namely, that the betrayer is one in closest relationship with Jesus. In John, Jesus specifically identifies Judas as the betrayer by dipping the bread in the dish and giving it to him (13:16–17). In Matthew, Jesus responds to Judas's question, "Is it I, Master?" with the ambiguous yet affirmative "you have said it" (26:25).

21 Behind Judas's action a divine purpose is being carried out. What happens to the Son of Man does not just happen. In this betrayal the Scriptures are being fulfilled (cf. 9:12). The reference to fulfillment could be a general statement that all Jesus is doing is in accordance with God's plan. Or Jesus may be thinking of a specific scriptural passage. If the latter, the betraying friend of Psalm 41 (alluded to in v.18) may be in view, or perhaps in view is Isaiah 53:12 LXX, in which the servant "bore the sins of many and was delivered up [*paradidōmi*] because of their iniquities." The woe pronounced on the betrayer emphasizes the personal responsibility of Judas. As Cranfield, 424, puts it, "The fact that God turns the wrath of man to his praise does not excuse the wrath of man."

3. Institution of the Lord's Supper (14:22–26)

OVERVIEW

The NT records four accounts of the Lord's Supper (Mt 26:26–30; Mk 14:22–26; Lk 22:19–20; 1Co 11:23–25). Matthew's account closely follows Mark's, while those of Luke and Paul have certain agreements. All four include the taking of the bread, the thanksgiving or blessing, the breaking of the bread, the saying "This is my body," and the taking of the cup. Only Paul (and Luke if the longer reading [22:19b–20] is adopted) identifies Jesus' body as "[given] for you." Paul alone records Jesus' command to continue to celebrate the Supper: "Do this in remembrance of me."

22While they were eating, Jesus took bread, gave thanks and broke it, and gave it to his disciples, saying, "Take it; this is my body."

23 Then he took the cup, gave thanks and offered it to them, and they all drank from it.
24 "This is my blood of the covenant, which is poured out for many," he said to them. 25 "I
tell you the truth, I will not drink again of the fruit of the vine until that day when I drink it
anew in the kingdom of God."
26 When they had sung a hymn, they went out to the Mount of Olives.

COMMENTARY

22 The bread Jesus took was presumably the unleavened bread of the Passover meal. He first gave thanks. Two different Greek verbs (*eulogeō* and *eucharistē*) are translated "give thanks" in vv.22–23. Both are equivalent to the Hebrew verb *bārak*, to "bless" or "praise" God. At Passover the blessing for the bread that immediately preceded the meal itself went thus: "Praised be Thou, O Lord, Sovereign of the World, who causes bread to come forth from the earth." After the blessing Jesus divided the bread and gave it to his disciples with the words, "This is my body." Since this saying of Jesus was separated from the cup saying by the eating of the main part of the meal, it is best to understand it as separate from that saying. The significant action of Jesus was the distribution of the bread, not its breaking. The bread represented his body, i.e., his abiding presence, promised to the disciples on the eve of his crucifixion; and the words become a pledge of the real presence of Jesus wherever and whenever his followers celebrate the Supper. Sacrificial ideas, though crucially important in the cup saying, are not of primary importance here.

That Jesus did not mean that the bread became his body is clear. There is no indication that the bread was changed—it remained ordinary bread. Furthermore, Jesus often used symbolic language to speak of himself. He spoke of himself as the true vine, the way, the door, etc., by which he meant that certain aspects of his person or work were symbolized by these objects. In the same way the bread symbolized his body, i.e., his abiding presence, and the wine symbolized his blood about to be shed.

23–24 The cup Jesus referred to is probably the third cup of the Passover meal, which was drunk after the meal was eaten. Again Jesus gave thanks. The verb is *eucharisteō*, from which "Eucharist" is derived. The meaning of the cup, unlike that of the bread, is clearly placed in a sacrificial context. The phrase "my blood of the covenant" (v.24) echoes Exodus 24:8 LXX ("Behold the blood of the covenant that the Lord has made with you") and Zechariah 9:11 ("As for you, because of the blood of my covenant with you, I will free your prisoners from the waterless pit"). The word *diathēkē* (GK *1347*) means "testament" or "will" in classical Greek, but here it translates the Hebrew *b*^{e}*rît* ("covenant"). It indicates the relationship of lordship and obedience God establishes between himself and human beings, and the "blood of the covenant" is the sign of its existence and the means by which it is effected (Taylor, 546). Although the reading "new" found in some MSS before the word "covenant" may be an assimilation to 1 Corinthians 11:25, it expresses an important truth: Jesus' death inaugurated a new era. Jeremiah had prophesied of just such a new day (31:31–33). The blood that establishes the covenant will be "poured out" (a clear reference to Jesus' death). Brooks, 230, comments, "Just as the blood of a sacrificial animal sealed the covenant God made with Israel at Sinai, so the blood of Jesus sealed the new covenant God made with his new people, the church, at the cross." Jesus' blood will be poured out "for many." The word "many" here does not mean "some but not all," but rather "the *one* in place of the *many*." The language echoes Isaiah 53:12, where the Servant (the one) "poured out his life unto death, and was numbered with the transgressors. For he bore the sin of many, and made intercession for the transgressors."

25 Jesus solemnly declared that this would be his last festal meal with his disciples till the dawn of the messianic kingdom. "The fruit of the vine" is a liturgical formula for wine used at the feast. The drinking of the cup at the Supper anticipates the perfected fellowship of the messianic age. In the OT and Judaism, God's ultimate salvation is sometimes portrayed as a great feast—the "messianic banquet" (Isa 25:6–8; 65:13–14; *1 En.* 72:14; cf. Lk 13:29; 22:29–30; Mt 8:11; see *TDNT* 4:1103). The vow of Jesus consecrated him for his sacrificial death, but it also held out the promise of victory and salvation. He will drink the festal cup anew, i.e., with a new redeemed community in the kingdom of God (cf. Lk 14:15; Rev 3:20–21; 19:6–9).

26 Assuming the meal to have been a Passover meal, it ended with the singing of the second part of the Hallel (Pss 115–118). It is significant that Jesus went to Gethsemane and its agony with such promises as follows:

> The LORD is my strength and my song;
> he has become my salvation.
> Shouts of joy and victory
> resound in the tents of the righteous:
> "The LORD's right hand has done mighty things!
> The LORD's right hand is lifted high;
> the LORD's right hand has done mighty things!"
> I will not die but live,
> and will proclaim what the LORD has done.
>
> *Psalm 118:14–17*

NOTES

25 Jesus ate and presumably drank with his disciples following his resurrection (Lk 24:30, 41–43; Jn 21:9–13), so how can he say "I will not drink again ..."? Some claim that the kingdom of God means the inauguration of the kingdom at Jesus' resurrection, and so this prophecy was fulfilled during the postresurrection appearances. But Jesus seems to be speaking here of the consummation of the kingdom, not its inauguration. More likely, Jesus did not mean that he would not eat or drink at all, but rather that he would not celebrate this festal meal until its consummation in the kingdom.

E. The Prediction of Peter's Denial (14:27–31)

27"You will all fall away," Jesus told them, "for it is written:

> "'I will strike the shepherd,
> and the sheep will be scattered.'

[28]But after I have risen, I will go ahead of you into Galilee."
[29]Peter declared, "Even if all fall away, I will not."
[30]"I tell you the truth," Jesus answered, "today — yes, tonight — before the rooster crows
twice you yourself will disown me three times."
[31]But Peter insisted emphatically, "Even if I have to die with you, I will never disown
you." And all the others said the same.

COMMENTARY

27–28 The predictions recorded here were probably spoken by Jesus as he walked with his disciples from the upper room to the Mount of Olives. The verb *skandalizō* (GK *4997*, NIV, "fall away") is difficult (cf. 4:17; 9:42–47). Notice the many renderings: NLT, "desert"; CEV, "reject"; CSB, "run away"; NAB, "have your faith shaken"; NKJV, "be made to stumble." Here it seems to be defined by the words from Zechariah that immediately follow. Thus it means not that the disciples will lose their faith in Jesus but rather that their courage will fail and they will forsake him. When the Shepherd (Jesus) is struck, the sheep (the disciples) will be scattered. The quotation is from Zechariah 13:7 and clearly indicates that the death of Jesus is the result of the action of God ("*I* will strike the shepherd") and that it results in the scattering of the sheep. The prediction was fulfilled. The disciples were filled with fear to be identified with Jesus in his trial and death, and that fear caused them to forsake him. This forsaking was especially true of Peter, whose actions are often representative of the disciples'.

After the death of the Shepherd, however, there will be a glorious resurrection and a reunion of Shepherd and sheep in Galilee (v.28). Marxsen (*Mark the Evanglist*, 86–87) sees in this verse and in the statement in Mark 16:7 a reference to the parousia. But the obvious reference is to a postresurrection appearance. The phrase "I will go ahead of you" does not necessarily mean that he will arrive before them, but rather that he will continue to be their leader and guide, as a shepherd goes before the sheep to lead and protect them (cf. Jn 10:3–4). This statement is a promise of restoration.

29–31 Jesus' prediction of failure on the part of the disciples was too much for Peter to accept. For the other disciples it may come true, but certainly not for him. Peter's words contain more than a hint of pride; and Jesus' reply emphasizes the absolute certainty of Peter's denial (v.30). Not only does Jesus use the *amēn* ("I tell you the truth") formula, but he also uses the emphatic "today — yes, tonight." The denial is not only certain — it is imminent. It was also to be a repeated denial (three times), and that in spite of the twice-repeated warning by the crowing of the rooster. The reference to a second crowing is found only in Mark and may have come from Peter's eyewitness testimony.

Cranfield, 429, correctly points out that the prediction is unlikely to be a *vaticinium ex eventu* (post-event "prophecy"): "The early Church would hardly have created a prediction which aggravated the baseness of Peter's denial, even for the sake of showing that Jesus was not surprised."

Jesus' explicit description of Peter's forthcoming denial was not convincing to him. He insisted on his willingness even to die with Jesus rather than deny him (v.31). But Peter did not know how weak he really was—nor did the rest of the disciples know their weakness, for they quickly chimed in with him to declare their allegiance (cf. vv.50, 71–72).

NOTES

27 On the significant role the prophecies of Zechariah 9–14 have for the Markan passion narrative, see Marcus, *Way of the Lord*, 157–59.

30 Some have suggested that the cock's crowing refers to the bugle call that marked the third division of the Roman night, called *gallicinium* in Latin and ἀλεκτοροφωνία, *alektorophōnia* ("cockcrow"), in Greek (so C. H. Mayo, "St. Peter's Token of the Cock Crow," *JTS* 22 [1921]: 367–70; Lane, 512 n. 69). This view is possible, but Mark's language suggests a literal rooster's crowing (cf. 14:72). See D. Brady, "The Alarm to Peter in Mark's Gospel," *JSNT* 4 (1979): 44–46.

F. The Agony of Gethsemane (14:32–42)

OVERVIEW

Gethsemane reveals a remarkable portrait of Jesus' true humanity. He is shown to be "anything but above temptation. So far from sailing serenely through his trials like some superior being unconcerned with this world, he is almost dead with distress" (Moule, 117). Yet he perseveres through it all in willing submission to God's will. As so often in Mark, the spiritual dullness of the disciples stands in stark contrast to the faithfulness of Jesus and his attentiveness to the will of God. He alone represents the true model of discipleship, trusting God despite the fear and anguish of imminent suffering and death. The passage also gives us a glimpse into the unique relationship between the Father and the Son, as Jesus addresses God with the intimate Aramaic term ʾ*abba* ("father").

The account has a strong claim to authenticity. It is unlikely the early church would have created a story that portrayed Jesus as desiring to escape the task God had given him and that presented the leading disciples in such a negative light.

32They went to a place called Gethsemane, and Jesus said to his disciples, "Sit here
while I pray." 33He took Peter, James and John along with him, and he began to be deeply
distressed and troubled. 34"My soul is overwhelmed with sorrow to the point of death," he
said to them. "Stay here and keep watch."

[35]Going a little farther, he fell to the ground and prayed that if possible the hour might
pass from him. [36]"*Abba*, Father," he said, "everything is possible for you. Take this cup from
me. Yet not what I will, but what you will."
[37]Then he returned to his disciples and found them sleeping. "Simon," he said to Peter,
"are you asleep? Could you not keep watch for one hour? [38]Watch and pray so that you
will not fall into temptation. The spirit is willing, but the body is weak."
[39]Once more he went away and prayed the same thing. [40]When he came back, he
again found them sleeping, because their eyes were heavy. They did not know what to
say to him.
[41]Returning the third time, he said to them, "Are you still sleeping and resting? Enough!
The hour has come. Look, the Son of Man is betrayed into the hands of sinners. [42]Rise! Let
us go! Here comes my betrayer!"

COMMENTARY

32–34 The name "Gethsemane" is probably from the Hebrew *gat š*^{e}*mānî* ("press of oils"). It was a garden (Jn 18:1) located somewhere on the lower slopes of the Mount of Olives, where there were olive trees and olive presses. It was one of Jesus' favorite spots in Jerusalem, no doubt often used by him and his disciples as a place to be alone (cf. Lk 22:39; Jn 18:2). Here he faced one of his most crucial tests.

Leaving the rest of the disciples behind, Jesus took with him the three men of the inner circle—Peter, James, and John (v.33; cf. 5:37; 9:2). He must have felt his need for their presence in this time of crisis. Or perhaps he brought them because they were the ones who had expressed such an emphatic willingness to suffer with him (10:38–39; 14:31). The two verbs translated "deeply distressed and troubled" together "describe an extremely acute emotion, a compound of bewilderment, fear, uncertainty and anxiety, nowhere else portrayed in such vivid terms as here" (Bratcher and Nida, 446). This deep agony Jesus shared with his disciples (v.34). The phrase "my soul is overwhelmed with sorrow" echoes the repeated refrain of the righteous sufferer of Psalms 42:5–6, 11; 43:5. As elsewhere in his passion, Jesus reaches for Israel's psalms of lament to express the intensity of his suffering (cf. Ps 22:1 in 15:34).

Why did Jesus share his sorrow with the disciples? Probably because he wanted them to know something of the depths of suffering he was about to experience for the redemption of the world. Jesus' command to them to "keep watch" meant either that they were to stay spiritually alert and so share in his agony or that they were to be on the lookout for those Jesus knew were on their way to arrest him. John 18:2 says that Judas knew the place where Jesus was accustomed to praying.

35–36 Having shared his feelings with the three disciples, Jesus withdrew to be alone with his Father. Jesus did not die serenely, as many Christian and Jewish martyrs have done. He was no mere martyr; he was the Lamb of God bearing the penalty of the sins for all humanity. The wrath of God was turned loose on him. Only this understanding can approach an adequate explanation for what happened in Gethsemane. Jesus "fell to the ground" (v.35), either because the burden and agony were so great that he could not stand up, or he did so in an act of reverent submission before God (or perhaps both). Twice before in Mark, Jesus has been identified as praying (1:35; 6:46), though only here do we hear his words. His prayer, uttered in a prone position, was addressed to "*Abba*, Father" (v.36). The word *ʾabba* is an intimate Aramaic word for "father"—a word the Jews did not normally use to address God because they thought it to be disrespectful. Jesus used it to express the intimacy of his relationship with his Father. By virtue of his unique relationship, he then invited his disciples to address God in the same way. The Greek *patēr* of the Lord's Prayer almost certainly has behind it the Aramaic *ʾabba*. This new father-son relationship with God available to believers through Jesus' death and resurrection made a profound impact on Jesus' followers, as evidenced in Paul's reproduction of the Aramaic term *ʾabba* even when writing to his Greek-speaking congregations (Ro 8:15; Gal 4:6).

Jesus believed that with God anything was possible; therefore, he prayed for the "cup" to be removed from him. This cup is the same one Jesus referred to in 10:38–39—the cup of the wrath of God. In the OT it is regularly used as a metaphor for punishment and judgment (cf. Pss 11:6; 60:3; 75:8; Isa 51:17, 21–23; Jer 25:15–29; 49:12; 51:57; La 4:21; Eze 23:31–34; Hab 2:16; Zec 12:2). Here it obviously refers to Jesus' death. Jesus' desire was for the removal of the cup. But he voluntarily submitted his will to that of his Father.

37–38 On returning to his disciples, Jesus found them sleeping. They were doubtless very tired. The hour was late, probably past midnight, and they had experienced some exciting events during the long day. Nevertheless it was a critical time, and they were expected to be awake. Jesus' rebuke in v.37 is addressed to Peter, whereas in v.38 it is addressed to all three disciples. Peter is probably singled out because he was the one who had boasted of his fidelity to Jesus. He who had said he was willing to die with Jesus (v.31), if need be, could not watch for one hour.

The verbs "watch" (*grēgoreite*) and "pray" (*proseuchesthe*) are both imperatives and are addressed to all three disciples, not just to Peter. Conquering temptation (not yielding to it, not "entering into" it) can only come through these two actions. The word for temptation (*peirasmos*, GK *4280*) can also mean "testing," and there is an element of testing here. The disciples are being tested to see whether they will remain spiritually alert. The spirit (a reference to the human spirit) might be willing to do what is right, but the human body (*sarx*, GK *4922*) is weak. Some commentators take *sarx* to mean our poor, unaided human nature ("flesh" in the Pauline sense). Here, however, it seems to mean the physical body and refers to the inability of the disciples to stay awake.

39–40 Again after having left his disciples to pray (v.39), Jesus returned to find them sleeping (v.40). Because of sheer fatigue, they were unable to stay awake. When confronted by Jesus, they "did not know what to say to him"—probably because they were so embarrassed and ashamed. Even Peter had nothing to say on this occasion (cf. 9:6).

41 A third time Jesus left them to pray (cf. Mt 26:44) and on returning again found the disciples asleep. The next words may be either ironic—"Go ahead and sleep. Have your rest" (NLT; cf. GWT, NJB)—or a question—"Are you still sleeping and resting?" (NIV, NRSV). The latter seems better in view of the situation.

The rendering of the next word (*apechei*, GK *600*) is very difficult. The Greek word can carry a variety of meanings: "to receive in full," "to suffice," "to be distant," "to abstain from" (BDAG, 102–3).

The NIV renders it "Enough!" apparently meaning "enough of sleep"; i.e., it is time for the disciples to wake up (cf. NET, "Enough of that!"). Other possibilities include an ironic question following on the previous one—"Are you still sleeping and resting? *Is it [the end] far off?*" (Taylor, 557; Evans, 417)—or a financial sense common in the papyri—"paid in full." In this case, the word could mean (1) "he has received it"; i.e., Judas has received the money for the betrayal; (2) "the account is closed," metaphorically meaning "the end has come" (cf. GWT, "It's all over"); or (3) "it is settled," meaning Jesus is accepting that it is God's will for him to go to the cross; i.e., the cup will not be taken from him. The first two possibilities would find support in Jesus' previous statement ("Are you still sleeping?"), while the latter three in the next statement, "The hour has come," i.e., the time of his betrayal and death. A decision is very difficult. The first is perhaps the simplest and least problematic.

Jesus' statement "Look, the Son of Man is betrayed" recalls the passion predictions (8:31; 9:31; 10:33–34) and the Last Supper narrative (14:18). The "sinners" into whose hands the Son of Man is to be betrayed are not specifically identified, but they would include all those acting on Satan's behalf to bring about Jesus' death: Judas, the religious leaders, and the Roman authorities. God has delivered his servant over to "sinners," who will do great evil to him, but through this apparent failure salvation will be achieved.

42 Apparently, the disciples were still lying on the ground; so when Jesus heard the approach of the arresting party, he told the disciples to get on their feet: "Rise! Let us go!" Swete, 349, writes, "The call to 'go' ends the scene in Gethsemane, but cannot be intended to suggest flight, for the Lord had always reserved Himself for this 'hour,' and had now finally embraced the Divine Will concerning it." Jesus did not go to flee from Judas but to meet him.

Rawlinson, 211, explains the significance of the experience of the disciples in Gethsemane for the persecuted Christians to whom Mark is writing:

> For the church of Mark's day the example of Jesus in the garden, as contrasted with the behavior of the three disciples, must have had special value as setting forth the spirit in which the vocation of martyrdom should be approached. The Christian witness must not presume upon the fact that his spirit is willing: he must ever be mindful also of the weakness of the flesh. It is essential therefore that he should *watch* and *pray*, that when the hour of trial comes he may not break down. [emphasis Rawlinson's]

NOTES

33 The Greek word ἐκθαμβέω (*ekthambeō*, GK *1701*) is peculiar to Mark (1:27; 9:15; 16:5–6). It is a difficult word to translate. Swete has "terrified surprise"; Rawlinson, "shuddering awe"; Taylor, "amazement amounting to consternation." The word ἀδημονέω (*adēmoneō*, GK *86*) is translated in the NIV as "troubled." Swete, 342, says it describes the "distress that follows a great shock"; the NEB has "My heart is ready to break with grief."

36 The classic study of Jesus' use of *ʾabba* is found in Joachim Jeremias's *The Prayers of Jesus* (pp. 11–65). In a famous article James Barr ("Abba Isn't 'Daddy,'" *JTS* 39 [1988]: 28–47) argued that the term does not mean "Daddy" (as many preachers have claimed), since it was used by adult children as well as by disciples for their teacher. While it is true that both adults and disciples used the term, their use of it does not *preclude* what sounds to us like a more childlike meaning (cf. the modern addressing of fathers as "Daddy" by adult children in America's South). Further, Jesus' use of the term was certainly unique and revealed a level of intimacy with the Father that was unprecedented in Judaism before his time.

41 For the many interpretations of ἀπέχει (*apechei*), see Evans, 416–17; Cranfield, 435–36. That several Western MSS (D W Φ) and a few later ones include the Greek τὸ τέλος (*to telos*, "the end") suggests some early copyists may have been reading the phrase as "Is the end far away?"

42 The word ἄγωμεν (*agōmen*) may be translated, "Let us advance to meet them."

G. The Betrayal and Arrest (14:43–52)

OVERVIEW

The arrest of Jesus marks a key turning point in the narrative as Jesus is "delivered over to human hands" (9:31 [TNIV]; cf. 8:31; 10:33; 14:18). While up to this point Jesus has been instructing the disciples and guiding events forward, from now on others will determine his fate. Yet God is still in control. Though wicked people act against Jesus with betrayal and deceit, it is God who had delivered him over to them. His purpose and plan will be accomplished, as "the Scriptures must be fulfilled" (v.49).

43Just as he was speaking, Judas, one of the Twelve, appeared. With him was a crowd
armed with swords and clubs, sent from the chief priests, the teachers of the law, and the
elders.
44Now the betrayer had arranged a signal with them: "The one I kiss is the man; arrest
him and lead him away under guard." 45Going at once to Jesus, Judas said, "Rabbi!" and
kissed him. 46The men seized Jesus and arrested him. 47Then one of those standing near
drew his sword and struck the servant of the high priest, cutting off his ear.
48"Am I leading a rebellion," said Jesus, "that you have come out with swords and clubs
to capture me? 49Every day I was with you, teaching in the temple courts, and you did not
arrest me. But the Scriptures must be fulfilled." 50Then everyone deserted him and fled.
51A young man, wearing nothing but a linen garment, was following Jesus. When they
seized him, 52he fled naked, leaving his garment behind.

COMMENTARY

43 The note that Judas was "one of the Twelve" is redundant, since Mark has just mentioned so in v.10 (cf. vv.18, 20). While the repetition may indicate Mark's use of a source (see Notes), from a narrative perspective it serves "to keep this tragic element of the situation before us" (Gould, 273). Jesus is betrayed by one of his own. Judas is accompanied by a "crowd" (*ochlos*) sent from the three constituent groups of the Sanhedrin: the chief priests, teachers of the law, and elders. John's gospel notes that the group included a detachment of soldiers (*speiran*) under a commander (*chiliarchos*) and some officials from the chief priests (18:3, 12), while Luke refers to officers of the temple guard (22:52). This group is not just a mob; it is an official police contingent dispatched for action. They came armed with swords and clubs. Apparently, they thought they would meet resistance.

44–46 The prearranged "signal" (*syssēmon*), or means of identifying Jesus, was for Judas to kiss him. The need for a signal suggests that the members of the arresting party did not know Jesus, or perhaps since it was dark they wanted to be sure not to arrest the wrong person (v.46). Customarily, disciples greeted their rabbi with a kiss, so Judas's act would not be suspected for what it really was. Judas's instructions to the crowd were designed to assure the successful accomplishment of the arrest. They were to lead Jesus away "securely" (*asphalōs*; NIV, "under guard")—with no chance of his escaping. Once Judas had become involved in this evil action, he did not want to make a fiasco of it.

47 Mark does not say who wielded the sword, but John relates that it was Peter and that the ear belonged to Malchus, a servant of the high priest (18:10). Apparently Peter aimed at his head, but Malchus sidestepped the blow, and Peter only caught his ear. Jesus' rebuke of Peter (Mt 26:52) and the restoration of the ear (Lk 22:51) are not recorded by Mark. His use of the diminutive *ōtarion* for "ear" perhaps suggests that only the lobe was cut off, thus possibly explaining Luke's statement that Jesus healed the ear instead of reconnecting it (Lk 22:51).

48–50 Jesus protested the manner of his arrest. The crowd sent from the Sanhedrin had come after him with swords and clubs, as though he were a dangerous criminal or an insurrectionist. The NIV's phrase "Am I leading a rebellion?" (cf. NLT, "Am I some dangerous revolutionary?") rendered literally is, "Have you come against me like a thief?" (cf. NRSV, NASB, ESV). The Roman authorities used the Greek *lēstēs* ("thief," "robber," "bandit") to designate rebels or insurrectionists (common thugs or criminals in the Romans' eyes). The "thieves" crucified with Jesus were probably insurrectionists like Barabbas (15:7, 27). Jesus points out that he had been teaching every day in the temple courts (v.49). The religious leaders could have arrested him there. Why, then, had they come at night? And why had they chosen to arrest him outside the city? The obvious answer is that they feared the people's reaction to Jesus' arrest. So they carefully chose both the time and the place.

The circumstances of Jesus' arrest were a fulfillment of Scripture. Mark does not say what specific passage Jesus had in mind. It may have been Isaiah 53:12: "And [he] was numbered with the transgressors." But in view of v.50—"Then everyone deserted him and fled"—he may have had in view Zechariah 13:7, which Jesus quoted in 14:27 and which is fulfilled here. The words of v.50 "drive home, as it were with hammer-blows, the failure of the disciples without exception ... and the complete forsakenness of Jesus" (Cranfield, 438).

51–52 Only Mark records this mysterious episode. The "young man" is not identified, but some speculate that it was Mark himself. Why else would the author insert such an odd and trivial detail in so solemn a story? Was this Mark's way of saying, "I was there"? The theory is sometimes embellished with the suggestion that the Last Supper took place in the home of John Mark's mother, Mary of Jerusalem (Ac 12:12). Did Mark secretly follow the group from the upper room to Gethsemane, only to be surprised by the arrival of the arresting party? While intriguing, we have no solid evidence to confirm or refute this hypothesis. Against it is the claim by Papias (AD 130) that Mark "neither heard the Lord nor followed him" (Eusebius, *Hist. eccl.* 3.39.15). This would apparently rule out such close contact with Jesus and his disciples. On the other hand, Papias may have been mistaken or may only be claiming that Mark was not one of Jesus' close disciples. As a resident of Jerusalem rather than Galilee, Mark would have had limited opportunities to hear Jesus teach.

Ordinarily men wore an undergarment called a *chitōn*. This young man had only a *sindōn*, an outer garment, so that when it was seized he fled naked (v.51). A *sindōn* was usually made of wool. This one, however, was linen, an expensive material worn only by the rich. Some see here another possible link to Mary of Jerusalem, who was presumably quite wealthy since she owned a house in Jerusalem large enough for meetings of a house church (Ac 12:12).

Perhaps the main point of the story—and the reason Mark included it—was to show that the forsakenness of Jesus was total. Even this youth forsook him.

NOTES

43 Some scholars think that the description of Judas as "one of the Twelve" (as though it were the first mention of him in the narrative) indicates that at this point Mark is inserting into his account the primitive passion narrative that contained no prior mention of Judas.

It is debated whether John's "detachment of soldiers" under a "commander" (Jn 18:3, 12) were Roman soldiers or temple police. France, 593, thinks the latter, since the temple police had well-organized military regiments (cf. Ac 4:1; 5:24–26) and since there was no reason for the Romans to be involved yet. Others posit the former, since the Greek term normally refers to a Roman cohort. Although normally stationed at Caesarea, such a Roman force would have been garrisoned in Jerusalem during the festival for crowd control and to put down any potential rebellion.

45 The verb καταφιλέω (*kataphileō*), a compounded form of φιλέω (*phileō*, "to kiss"), usually means "to kiss fervently" and here probably indicates a prolonged kiss (not just a peck on the cheek) to ensure the identification of Jesus.

H. Jesus before the Sanhedrin (14:53–65)

OVERVIEW

All four gospels affirm that the trial of Jesus took place in two stages: a religious trial followed by a civil one. Harmonizing their accounts, we find three episodes in each stage. The religious trial included (1) the preliminary hearing before Annas (reported only in Jn 18:12–14, 19–23), (2) the trial before Caiaphas and the Sanhedrin (Mk 14:53–65 par.), and (3) the trial before the same group just after daybreak (Mk 15:1 par.). The three episodes of the civil trial were (4) the trial before Pilate, (5) the trial before Herod Antipas (recorded only in Lk 23:6–12), and (6) the trial before Pilate continued and concluded. Mark does not report the hearing before Annas or Pilate's transfer of Jesus to Herod

Antipas. The trial before Pilate is recorded as a continuous and unbroken narrative (Mk 15:2–15).

Mark's account of the Jewish trial represents another of his intercalations, or narrative sandwiches. The account of the arrest and trial by the Sanhedrin is interrupted twice, first by the statement that Peter followed at a distance (14:54), and second by his threefold denial that he knew Jesus (14:66–72). The relationship between the two is one of contrast. While Jesus courageously confesses his identity and so experiences suffering and persecution, Peter cowardly denies his relationship with Jesus and so escapes suffering.

Some critics have questioned the historicity of Mark's account of Jesus' Jewish trial and claimed that it violates procedures set out in the Mishnaic tractate *Sanhedrin*. These guidelines make it illegal for the Sanhedrin to meet at night (*m. Sanh.* 4:1), on the eve of a Sabbath or festival day (4:1), or in the high priest's home (11:2; there were only three official courtrooms in Jerusalem). A second hearing would also have been necessary for a death sentence (5:5), and a charge of blasphemy could be sustained only if Jesus had uttered the divine name (7:5). None of these arguments decisively disprove the historicity of Mark's account. First, the Mishnah was not codified until the end of the second century, and its traditions do not necessarily go back to the time of Jesus. Second, even if some of these guidelines were in place in the first century, they represent an ideal situation that may have been violated in Jesus' case. The very existence of these guidelines implies past abuses, and Jesus' hearing may have constituted one of them. Third, the Mishnah represents predominantly Pharisaic traditions, but the Sadducees were dominant in the Sanhedrin of Jesus' day. Fourth, the incident in Caiaphas's house is not depicted by Mark as a formal trial but as a preliminary hearing meant to prepare charges against Jesus. The actual trial was held before Pilate, who could render a capital verdict. Finally, there is good evidence that blasphemy was sometimes used in Judaism in a broader sense than uttering the divine name, including actions such as idolatry, arrogant disrespect for God, and insulting his chosen leaders (Bock, *Blasphemy and Exaltation*, 30–112).

53They took Jesus to the high priest, and all the chief priests, elders and teachers of the
law came together. 54Peter followed him at a distance, right into the courtyard of the high
priest. There he sat with the guards and warmed himself at the fire.
55The chief priests and the whole Sanhedrin were looking for evidence against Jesus so
that they could put him to death, but they did not find any. 56Many testified falsely against
him, but their statements did not agree.
57Then some stood up and gave this false testimony against him: 58"We heard him say,
'I will destroy this man-made temple and in three days will build another, not made by
man.'" 59Yet even then their testimony did not agree.
60Then the high priest stood up before them and asked Jesus, "Are you not going to
answer? What is this testimony that these men are bringing against you?" 61But Jesus
remained silent and gave no answer.
Again the high priest asked him, "Are you the Christ, the Son of the Blessed One?"

[62]"I am," said Jesus. "And you will see the Son of Man sitting at the right hand of the Mighty One and coming on the clouds of heaven."
[63]The high priest tore his clothes. "Why do we need any more witnesses?" he asked.
[64]"You have heard the blasphemy. What do you think?"
They all condemned him as worthy of death. [65]Then some began to spit at him; they blindfolded him, struck him with their fists, and said, "Prophesy!" And the guards took him and beat him.

COMMENTARY

53 Mark reports that Jesus was taken by his captors to the high priest (identified by Matthew and John as Caiaphas, though Mark never names him), with the entire Sanhedrin present. Annas had been high priest from AD 7–14 but had been deposed by Pilate's predecessor, Valerius Gratus. Annas's son-in-law, Caiaphas, presently held the office, which he held from AD 18–37. Annas still exercised considerable influence, however; hence the initial visit to him recorded by John (Jn 18:12–14, 19–23), as well as Luke's identification of him as "high priest" together with Caiaphas (Lk 3:2; cf. Jn 18:22; Ac 4:6). The meeting evidently took place in the palace of Caiaphas in an upstairs room (cf. v.66). Those present—"the chief priests, elders and teachers of the law" (v.53)—constituted the members of the Sanhedrin, the Jewish high court (see comments at 8:31; cf. 11:27; 14:43). If all the members were present, there would have been seventy of them, though Mark's use of "all" (v.53) and "the whole Sanhedrin" (v.55) does not necessarily mean that all seventy were present; Mark may mean, rather, that there were enough members present to constitute a quorum. Since the Sanhedrin usually met in one of the market halls, the use of Caiaphas's house may have been to ensure secrecy.

54 This verse interrupts the flow of the narrative. It is inserted here to prepare for the full account of Peter's denial (vv.66–72) and to indicate that the trial and the denial were concurrent. Plummer, 335, writes, "When the first panic was over, Peter's affection reasserted itself." He followed at a distance because he was afraid, but he *did* follow. Apparently, he could not bring himself to desert Jesus completely. Eventually he arrived at the high priest's palace. John's gospel informs us that there was "another disciple" (John?) with Peter; and, since this unnamed disciple knew the high priest, he spoke to the girl on duty at the gate, and Peter was let in (Jn 18:15–16). The palace was built around an open courtyard (*aule*) that one entered through an archway (cf. v.68). Spring nights are cool in Jerusalem (which sits at an elevation of about twenty-five hundred feet); so Peter sat with the guards and warmed himself before a charcoal fire (cf. Jn 18:18). From where he was sitting, he could see the upstairs room in which the Sanhedrin was meeting to decide Jesus' fate.

55–56 In these verses Mark emphasizes just how rigged the trial of Jesus was. Though it was late at night (in fact, probably very early Friday morning), false witnesses were available (v.56). The verdict had already been decided (14:1). All that was necessary was to find appropriate charges (France, 604). But a problem developed—the witnesses could not agree with one another. According to the law

(Nu 35:30; Dt 17:6; 19:15), two witnesses were necessary to establish guilt in cases that required the death penalty. These witnesses must give consistent evidence. The smallest inconsistency was sufficient to discredit them. (Strict guidelines for cross-examination are given in *m. Sanh.* 4:5–5:4.) As is inevitable when witnesses testify falsely, their testimonies lacked consistency. Many came to witness against Jesus (the Sanhedrin has made careful preparation for the trial [v.55]), but the contradictory nature of the evidence frustrated the court's intent.

57–59 The lack of consistent evidence did not thwart Caiaphas and the Sanhedrin for long. Although the first round of testimony proved to be of no value, soon a definite charge was made. Jesus had said he would destroy this temple "made with human hands" and in three days rebuild another "not made with hands" (v.58 [TNIV]). There is no statement just like this in the Gospels. The allusion is probably to Jesus' statement in John 2:19, made two years previously: "Destroy this temple, and I will raise it again in three days." But on that occasion Jesus did not predict that *he* would destroy the temple, and the narrator clarifies that the reference was to his own body (Jn 2:21–22). Perhaps Jesus' statement in Mark 13:2, in which he predicts the destruction of the temple, was combined with John 2:19 (misunderstood by his opponents to refer to the Jerusalem temple, Jn 2:20); and out of the two the charge was formulated. The charge, however, proved invalid because, again, the "false testimony" of the witnesses was inconsistent (vv.57, 59).

60–61 The situation had become extremely tense. There were plenty of witnesses, but they could not pass the test of Deuteronomy 17:6. Finally in exasperation the high priest stood up in the Sanhedrin (a dramatic gesture) to interrogate Jesus himself. Caiaphas apparently wanted Jesus to respond to the charges made against him in the hope of provoking an incriminating answer. But Jesus refused to give him that opportunity (v.61). Hiebert, 371, comments, "In majestic silence, Jesus refused to dignify the self-refuting testimony by any explanation of His own." The attentive reader may here recognize a fulfillment of Isaiah 53:7: "As a sheep before her shearers is silent, so he did not open his mouth."

The silence of Jesus to the first questions prompted the high priest to ask him another. The question "Are you the Christ, the son of the Blessed One?" indicates that by this time the religious authorities either knew or suspected that Jesus regarded himself as the Messiah. "Son of the Blessed" stands in apposition to the title "Christ" (or "Messiah"), and "the Blessed" functions as a reverential circumlocution to avoid the pronunciation of the name of God. "Son of God" is not to be understood here as an ascription of deity but as a royal title emphasizing the Messiah's unique relationship with God. This use of the title arose from OT passages such as 2 Samuel 7:14; Psalm 2:7; and Psalm 89:26, where the coming king from David's line is ascribed a father-son relationship with God. Evidence from Qumran suggests that the title was beginning to be used of the Messiah in first-century Judaism (4QFlor 1:10–14; 1QSa 2:11–12; 4QapocrDan ar; 4Q246 2:1; cf. Hengel, *Son of God*, 44–45; Marshall, *Origins of New Testament Christology*, 113). Although Jesus had been very cautious about identifying himself as the Messiah in Mark's gospel, his actions in entering Jerusalem, clearing the temple, and challenging Israel's leaders all carried strong messianic connotations. Furthermore, the cries of demons and people seeking healing confirm that messianic speculation swirled around him (1:24; 3:11; 5:7; 10:47–48). Jesus had also referred to himself as the "son" of the vineyard owner (= God) in a parable spoken within earshot of the religious leaders (12:1–12). In this context the question of the high priest becomes intelligible. For Mark's readers, of course, the title "Son of God" would carry even greater significance, since they would recognize both its messianic and divine connotations (cf. 1:1, 11; 9:7; 15:39).

The question achieved the desired result. If the religious authorities could not fabricate an accusation by the testimony of others, Jesus' own testimony about himself would do. Had Jesus refused to answer this question, the Sanhedrin would have had to devise some other plan.

62 Jesus' reply is a straightforward "I am." This answer stands in sharp contrast to his deliberate avoidance of calling himself the "Messiah" or having others proclaim his messiahship up to this point in his ministry. It clearly was not because he had no consciousness of being the Messiah. He avoided the messianic claim because of the false concepts of messiahship that were popular in his day and with which he did not want to be identified. Also, there always lurked the danger that an open claim to messiahship would bring about a premature crisis and abort his ministry. Now, however, the time of veiledness had passed. He was ready to state his messiahship unequivocally.

Jesus' affirmation of his messiahship is followed by a Son-of-Man saying that brings together Daniel 7:13 and Psalm 110:1. The former speaks of the exalted figure of "one like a son of man" coming with the clouds of heaven and being presented before the Ancient of Days (see comments at 8:31). The latter speaks of the enthronement of the Davidic Messiah at the right hand of God. Jesus has quoted this text earlier to raise the conundrum of how the Messiah can be at the same time David's son and David's Lord (12:36). The two passages bring together the ideas of the glorious vindication and enthronement of the Son of Man, and his eschatological coming. Jesus is looking to the future, beyond the crucifixion to his resurrection and ascension, when he will take his place at the right hand of God—the place of authority—and to his parousia, when he will come in judgment. Now Caiaphas and the Sanhedrin are sitting in judgment of him. In that day Jesus will pass judgment on them. The author of Revelation points to that day: "Look, he is coming with the clouds, and every eye will see him, even those who pierced him" (1:7). Jesus' words are a solemn warning. France, 599, points out that with this episode we reach the christological climax of the gospel: "And in that climax we reach the heart of Mark's paradoxical presentation of Jesus: at the narrative level he is overpowered and cannot save himself; at the theological level he reigns supreme."

63–64 The tearing of one's clothes was originally a sign of great grief (cf. Ge 37:29, 34; 2Ki 18:37; Jdt 14:19; Ep Jer 31; 2 Macc 4:38). In the case of the high priest (v.63), it became "a formal judicial act minutely regulated by the Talmud" (Taylor, 569). The action of the high priest showed that he had just heard a blasphemous statement (v.64; cf. *m. Sanh.* 7:5, where "the judges are to stand up on their feet and rend their garments" when they hear blasphemy). As noted above, although later Mishnaic guidelines defined blasphemy narrowly as pronouncing the divine Name itself (*m. Sanh.* 7:5; cf. Lev 24:10–23), Bock, *Blasphemy and Exaltation*, 111, has shown that the term could be used much more widely of "a whole range of actions offensive to God" (cf. Mk 2:7; 3:28–29; Jn 5:18; 10:33). Jesus' claim to be the exalted Son of Man and Messiah, who would stand in judgment over the high priest and the Sanhedrin, was interpreted by Caiaphas as blasphemous in this latter sense. All the members of the Sanhedrin concurred with Caiaphas's judgment and condemned Jesus "as worthy of death." It is perhaps significant that they do not formally condemn him to death but rather as deserving it, since the Sanhedrin did not at this time have the right of execution (Jn 18:31; see Brown, *Death of the Messiah*, 363–72). If they had, they would have ordered Jesus to be stoned, since Leviticus 24:14 prescribes stoning as the punishment for blasphemy. Instead, they will take Jesus before Pilate and there seek a capital verdict. Jesus' prophecy of Mark 10:33 has come true.

65 The decision that Jesus deserved the death penalty was the signal for some members of the Sanhedrin to release their pent-up hostilities against him. Although Rawlinson's suggestion, 223, that Mark's grammar is careless ("we are to understand a change of subject at the beginning of the verse") and absolves members of the Sanhedrin of this action, it is almost certainly wrong. "Some" at the beginning of v.65 is in contrast to "all" in v.64, and both refer to members of the Sanhedrin. This interpretation is supported by the mention of the guards as a second and distinct group of participants in the barbarous acts.

Spitting and hitting were traditional means of expressing rejection and repudiation (cf. Nu 12:14; Dt 25:9; Job 30:10; Isa 50:6). The additional words in Matthew 26:88 and Luke 22:64, "Who hit you?" shed light on the significance of the covering of the face, followed by blows, and the demand that Jesus prophesy. This attempt to make a mockery of Jesus' messianic claims relates to a rabbinic interpretation of Isaiah 11:2–4 that asserts the Messiah's ability to judge by smell without the need for sight (cf. Lane, 540; *b. Sanh. 93b*). Jesus refused to respond to their vicious jests. When the Sanhedrin had its fill of brutality and mockery, they turned Jesus over to the guards, who continued the beatings.

NOTES

53–65 For discussion and bibliography related to the historicity of Jesus' trial, see Brown, *Death of the Messiah*, 357–63. For the charge of blasphemy, see the survey of literature in Bock, *Blasphemy and Exaltation*, 5–29.

57–58 The charge of destroying and rebuilding the temple may itself carry messianic implications, since some Jewish traditions, based especially on 2 Samuel 7:13 and Zechariah 6:12, claimed that the Messiah would rebuild the Jerusalem temple (*Tg. Zec.* 6:12; cf. 4QFlor 1:6–7). In other traditions God himself rebuilds the temple (11QT 29:7–10). See discussion in D. Juel, *Messiah and Temple: The Trial of Jesus in the Gospel of Mark* (SBLDS 31; Missoula, Mont.: Scholars Press, 1977), 172–96; Bock, 213 n. 69; Evans, 445–46.

62 The variant reading σὺ εἶπας ὅτι ἐγώ εἰμι (*sy eipas hoti egō eimi*), "You say that I am," has the support of the Caesarean text (Θ f^{13} *pc* Origen). Taylor considers this text the original because it is more in keeping with Jesus' reluctance in Mark's gospel to reveal his messiahship straightforwardly and because it would account for Matthew 26:64 and Luke 22:67–68. If this reading is correct, Jesus' reply is affirmative, "but it registers a difference of interpretation 'The word is yours, Yes, if you like'; as if to indicate that the Speaker has His own ideas about Messiahship" (Taylor, 568). Against this reading, however, is the MS evidence, which overwhelmingly supports the shorter reading. Further, at this point Jesus was ready to reveal clearly his identity as the Messiah.

Jesus' use of ἡ δύναμις (*hē dynamis*, "the mighty one"), like the high priest's ὁ εὐλογητός (*ho eulogētos*, "the blessed one") in the previous verse, functions as a circumlocution to avoid the divine name.

A number of commentators consider Jesus' Son-of-Man saying here to relate not to the parousia but to the destruction of Jerusalem. For a defense of this view, see France, 612–13; Morna D. Hooker, *The Son of Man in Mark* (London: SPCK, 1967), 167–71.

65 Bock, 111, points out that acts of blasphemy in rabbinic writings "seem to concentrate on idolatry, a show of arrogant disrespect toward God, or the insulting of his chosen leaders."

I. Peter's Denial of Jesus (14:66–72)

OVERVIEW

The reference to the abuse by the guards in v.65 forms a natural transition to the account of Peter's denial, since Peter was last seen in the courtyard below warming himself with (other) guards involved in Jesus' arrest (v.54). As noted in the Overview at 14:53–65, Peter's denial stands in stark contrast to Jesus' faithful confession. By intercalating Jesus' faithfulness between Peter's failures, Mark reveals contrasting models of discipleship.

66While Peter was below in the courtyard, one of the servant girls of the high priest
came by. 67When she saw Peter warming himself, she looked closely at him.
"You also were with that Nazarene, Jesus," she said.
68But he denied it. "I don't know or understand what you're talking about," he said, and
went out into the entryway.
69When the servant girl saw him there, she said again to those standing around, "This
fellow is one of them." 70Again he denied it.
After a little while, those standing near said to Peter, "Surely you are one of them, for
you are a Galilean."
71He began to call down curses on himself, and he swore to them, "I don't know this
man you're talking about."
72Immediately the rooster crowed the second time. Then Peter remembered the word
Jesus had spoken to him: "Before the rooster crows twice you will disown me three times."
And he broke down and wept.

COMMENTARY

66–68 When Jesus was being mocked, spit on, and beaten in the upstairs room of the high priest's palace, Peter was waiting below in the courtyard to see what would happen (v.66). The fact that Peter was there at all indicates that he loved Jesus and was concerned about him, but his love did not withstand the test of fear. The servant girl (probably the "girl at the door" of Jn 18:17) recognized Peter as he stood warming himself in the light of the fire (v.67). Perhaps she had seen Peter with Jesus in the temple during the immediately preceding days or remembered that she had admitted him at the request of John, another one of Jesus' disciples. Her contempt for Jesus is revealed in the order of the words she used to speak about him—"that Nazarene, Jesus." Peter denied her charge with a redundant expression in Greek that provides emphasis: "I neither know nor understand what you are talking about" (v.68 NASB). Fearful of being identified and apprehended, Peter retreated into the archway that led into the street. He was anxious for his own safety. Yet he still could not bring himself to abandon Jesus completely. So he slunk into the darkness and safety of the archway.

69–72 Peter's retreat to safety was short-lived. The servant girl saw him slip into the entryway and reiterated her contention—this time to "those standing around," presumably the guards and others in the employ of the high priest (v.69). Her words, "This fellow is one of them," seem to show that she recognized Peter as part of a group or movement whose leader was Jesus. Peter's second denial (v.70) was unconvincing. So the next time it was not the servant girl but the others who accused him. Apparently, their suspicions were aroused by the girl and by Peter's Galilean accent (cf. Mt 26:73, where Peter's accent is specifically mentioned). Peter now reacted like a cornered animal. He called down curses on himself if he was lying and swore that he did not know "this man you're talking about" (v.71). The first two times Peter had denied being associated with Jesus. The last time he denied Jesus himself.

The third denial was followed by the second crowing of the rooster (v.72). The first crow of the rooster did not awaken Peter's conscience. But at this second crowing he remembered what Jesus had said and "broke down and wept." Luke 22:61 dramatically relates that at that very moment the Lord "turned and looked straight at Peter," thus adding to Peter's sense of overwhelming shame and guilt.

NOTES

68 Lane, 542, compares Peter's denial to a formal, legal formula of denial found in rabbinic law (cf. *m. Šebu.* 8:3: "[If the owner said,] 'Where is my ox?' and he answered, 'I do not know of what thou speakest'").

The NIV omits the reading καὶ ἀλέκτωρ ἐφώνησεν (*kai alektōr ephōnēsen*, "and the rooster crowed") at the end of this verse. It is included in UBS's fourth edition of the Greek NT but is put in brackets and given a "C" rating (significant doubt). Reasons for excluding it include: (1) it was likely added by copyists to show the literal fulfillment of Jesus' prophecy in v.30 ("before the rooster crows twice"); (2) copyists thought a second crowing in v.72 was inexplicable without a first; and (3) the external MS evidence slightly favors excluding it. Reasons for including it include: (1) copyists omitted it to assimilate to Matthew (26:69–75) and Luke (22:56–62), in which only one crowing is mentioned; (2) it was omitted by copyists to make Peter's denial seem a little less shameful—if Peter heard the first crowing of the rooster, why didn't he repent (see Metzger, 97)? The decision is a difficult one, but omission with a footnote (as in the NIV) seems the best policy.

71 The Greek ἀναθεματίζω (*anathematizō*, GK *354*) is normally a transitive verb meaning to curse someone or something, and France, 622, argues the most likely meaning is that Peter is cursing Jesus. This meaning is possible, though the NIV's sense of "curse himself" appears in Acts 23:12, 14, 21, where a group of zealots "curse themselves" (ἀνεθεμάτισαν ἑαυτούς, *anathematisan heautous*), or take an oath, not to eat or drink until they have killed Paul.

72 The last words of this verse, καὶ ἐπιβαλὼν ἔκλαιεν (*kai epibalōn eklaien*), are very difficult to translate. Some of the renderings are as follows: "he began to cry"; "he set to and wept"; "he burst into tears"; "he thought on it and wept"; "he covered his head and wept"; "he threw himself on the ground"; "he dashed out." Plummer, 342, is probably correct when he says, "We must be content to share the ignorance of all the ages" as to its meaning.

REFLECTIONS

The importance and relevance of Peter's denial for the Christians to whom Mark writes is obvious. To a church under severe pressure of persecution, the denial issued a warning. If denying Jesus Christ was possible for an apostle—and a leader of the apostles at that—then they must be constantly on guard, lest they, too, deny Jesus. The story also provided assurance that if anyone did fail Jesus under the duress of persecution, there was always a way open for repentance, forgiveness, and restoration. It is no accident that at the gospel's conclusion the angel tells the women to report the resurrection to "[Jesus'] disciples and Peter" (16:7). Mark's readers are surely aware that Peter was restored and went on to provide apostolic leadership.

J. The Trial before Pilate (15:1–15)

OVERVIEW

Since the Sanhedrin did not have the right to execute Jesus (see comments at 14:64), they resolve to take him before the governor Pilate to obtain a capital sentence. The official residence of the Roman governor of Judea was at Caesarea on the Mediterranean coast. During the major festivals, however, he would set up residence in Jerusalem to provide crowd control and keep a watchful eye on the tumultuous pilgrims. In Jerusalem Pilate probably occupied the palace of Herod, a lavish residence constructed by Herod the Great and located in the northwestern section of the city. It was likely here that the trial of Jesus before Pilate took place. The traditional site of Jesus' trial shown to most visitors in Jerusalem—the ancient pavement of the Fortress of Antonia—is almost certainly erroneous. The Antonia, located adjacent to the temple area on the northwest, served primarily as a barracks for soldiers on duty in Jerusalem. It is highly doubtful that the Roman governors visiting Jerusalem preferred the spartan accommodations of the Antonia to the luxurious facilities of Herod's palace. We know from Josephus (*J.W.* 2.14.8 §301) that Gessius Florus, one of the Roman procurators, resided in Herod's palace and had his tribunal set up in the square in front of it. Mark uses the word "Praetorium" to indicate Herod's palace in v.16.

Pontius Pilate served as prefect of Judea from AD 26–36. Some scholars have claimed that the gospel writers intentionally shift the blame for the crucifixion from the Romans to the Jewish leadership, thus painting an unrealistic portrait of Pilate as a vacillating leader coerced into crucifying Jesus against his will. Yet the portrait of Pilate in the Gospels is fully compatible with what we know of him from secular history. A pragmatic ruler, Pilate had a general disdain for the Jewish population but feared antagonizing them, lest they complain to his superiors in Rome (see Philo, *Legat.* 299–305; Josephus, *Ant.* 18.3.1 §§55–59). While he was not afraid ruthlessly to suppress revolt (as shown from Josephus's several descriptions of such incidents; cf. *Ant.* 18.3.2 §§60–62), he also sought to placate the Jewish leadership when it was politically expedient to do so. Pilate's fears were not unfounded, and he was eventually recalled to Rome in AD 36 after complaints were raised against him because of a ruthless military action he conducted against a group of Samaritans (Josephus, *Ant.* 18.4.1–2 §§85–89). Mark's description of Pilate here fits this portrait well. He does not see Jesus as a significant threat and so attempts to release him by using a tradition of Passover clemency. Yet he soon realizes that there is a greater political risk in releasing Jesus than in crucifying him and so concedes to their request. From Pilate's perspective, there was much to gain and little to lose in crucifying Jesus. It not only placated the Jewish leadership but also served as a grim warning to other would-be insurrectionists.

Mark's account of Jesus' Roman trial is the briefest of the four. John includes a lengthy dialogue between Jesus and Pilate in which Jesus speaks of his kingdom as "not of this world" (18:29–38); Luke alone inserts the account of Jesus' appearance before Herod Antipas (23:6–12); and Matthew reports that Pilate's wife warned him against having anything to do with "that righteous [or 'innocent'] man" (27:19).

1 Very early in the morning, the chief priests, with the elders, the teachers of the law and
the whole Sanhedrin, reached a decision. They bound Jesus, led him away and handed
him over to Pilate.
2 "Are you the king of the Jews?" asked Pilate.
"Yes, it is as you say," Jesus replied.
3 The chief priests accused him of many things. 4 So again Pilate asked him, "Aren't you
going to answer? See how many things they are accusing you of."
5 But Jesus still made no reply, and Pilate was amazed.
6 Now it was the custom at the Feast to release a prisoner whom the people requested.
7 A man called Barabbas was in prison with the insurrectionists who had committed murder
in the uprising. 8 The crowd came up and asked Pilate to do for them what he usually did.
9 "Do you want me to release to you the king of the Jews?" asked Pilate, 10 knowing it
was out of envy that the chief priests had handed Jesus over to him. 11 But the chief priests
stirred up the crowd to have Pilate release Barabbas instead.
12 "What shall I do, then, with the one you call the king of the Jews?" Pilate asked them.
13 "Crucify him!" they shouted.
14 "Why? What crime has he committed?" asked Pilate.

But they shouted all the louder, "Crucify him!"
15Wanting to satisfy the crowd, Pilate released Barabbas to them. He had Jesus flogged, and handed him over to be crucified.

COMMENTARY

1 What seems to be spoken of here is not another gathering of the Sanhedrin but the final stages of the meeting that had begun late the night before. The phrase *symboulion poiēsantes* is difficult. The best translation seems to be not "held a council" (NAB) but rather "reached a decision" (NIV) or "made their plans" (TEV; cf. similar phrases in Mk 3:6; Mt 12:14; 22:15; 27:7; 28:12). Apparently, the resolution or decision made by the Sanhedrin in the final stages of its meeting was to accuse Jesus before the civil authority not of blasphemy but of high treason. The Roman government would not have considered blasphemy a punishable crime. It had to do with Jewish religion and so was of little or no concern to the Roman authorities. But high treason was a crime they could not overlook. Moule, 124, points out the overpowering irony of the situation: "Jesus, who is, indeed, king of the Jews in a deeply spiritual sense, has refused to lead a political uprising. Yet now, condemned for blasphemy by the Jews because of his spiritual claims, he is accused by them also before Pilate by being precisely what he had disappointed the crowds for failing to be—a political insurgent."

Having made their decision, the members of the Sanhedrin led Jesus from the palace of the high priest, located in the southwestern part of the city, through the streets of Jerusalem to Herod's palace. He was taken "early in the morning" because that is when Pilate held trials (cf. Seneca, *On Anger* 2.7). This schedule explains why the Sanhedrin held their session late at night and very early in the morning. Mark does not mention who Pilate is or why he was in Jerusalem at that time. Apparently, Mark presupposes this knowledge on the part of his readers.

2 Pilate's first question to Jesus—"Are you the king of the Jews?"—shows obliquely that the charges against Jesus had already been made known to Pilate. Mark gives us only a summary of the trial. According to Luke (23:2), the Sanhedrin brought three charges before Pilate: (1) Jesus is "subverting our nation"; (2) he "opposes payment of taxes to Caesar"; and (3) he "claims to be Christ, a king" (Lk 23:2). The three together indicate an insurrectionist claim to royal authority and so are appropriately summed up in Pilate's question, "Are you the king of the Jews?" It is difficult to tell whether Pilate is sarcastically mocking Jesus or genuinely asking whether Jesus is claiming royal authority. In either case, from this point on Jesus' kingship will be a central concern of the passion narrative (vv.2, 9, 12, 18, 26, 32). There is heavy irony here. Although the title "king" is repeatedly used to mock and deride Jesus, the informed reader knows that Jesus is indeed the Messiah and King, who will enter his royal authority through suffering.

Jesus' answer to Pilate is a qualified one: *sy legeis* (lit., "you say"). The NIV's "Yes, it is as you say" is probably too positive and would be better rendered "You have said so" (TNIV; cf. NLT), or "those are your words" (CEV). Jesus seems to be saying, "Yes,

I am the king of the Jews; but your concept of what that means and mine are poles apart."

3–5 The chief priests now take the lead in the attack against Jesus. They accuse him of "many things," which phrase recalls the additional charges mentioned by Luke (see comments at v.2). Jesus, however, refuses to answer or defend himself (vv.4–5). The reader would likely be reminded of the Servant of Yahweh, who was "oppressed and afflicted, yet he did not open his mouth" (Isa 53:7). Pilate was "amazed" (*thaumazō*, GK *2513*) at Jesus' silence in the face of these accusations (v.5). Amazement at Jesus' words and deeds is a common theme throughout Mark's gospel (1:22, 27; 2:12; 5:20; 6:2; 7:37; 11:18; see T. Dwyer, *Motif of Wonder*). The implication here is that Pilate is in awe at Jesus' composure and recognizes there is something unique or special about him. It is perhaps this recognition that prompted him to seek Jesus' release.

6 The custom of releasing a prisoner at the Passover Feast is unknown outside the Gospels (cf. Mt 27:15; Jn 18:39). It was, however, a Roman custom and could well have been a custom in Palestine (cf. R. L. Merritt, "Jesus Barabbas and the Paschal Pardon," *JBL* 104 [1985]: 57–68; J. Blinzler, *The Trial of Jesus* [Cork: Mercier, 1959], 205–8). An example of a Roman official's releasing a prisoner on the demands of the people occurs in the Papyrus Florentinus 61.59ff. There the Roman governor of Egypt, G. Septimius Vegetus, says to Phibion, the accused: "Thou hast been worthy of scourging, but I will give thee to the people" (cited in Taylor, 580). The independent attestation of the custom in the Synoptics and in John also suggests its authenticity.

7 Mark identifies Barabbas as one of the insurrectionists in prison for committing murder in the uprising. Mark speaks of this revolt as though it were well-known, but we have no specific reference to it in our sources. This lack is not surprising, however, since our sources are fragmentary and since the first century was one of frequent insurrections and rebel movements against the Roman occupation. Luke 23:19 refers to this particular event as having happened "in the city" (i.e., Jerusalem). Barabbas was probably a member of one of the insurrectionist groups that engaged in violent resistance to the Romans. It is likely that the two "thieves" crucified with Jesus were members of the same group and had been captured together with Barabbas (see comments at 14:48–50 and 15:27).

The name "Barabbas" is an Aramaic patronymic (a name identifying a person's father) and might mean "son of the teacher" (Rabban) or "son of Abba" (Brown, *Death of the Messiah*, 799–800). "Abba" means "father," but was also a common personal name. According to a variant reading of Matthew 27:16–17, Barabbas's full name was "Jesus Barabbas" (cf. TNIV). This reading was known to Origen but rejected for theological reasons. It is entirely plausible that the reading is original and that Jesus was Barabbas's personal name (i.e., "Jesus, son of Abba"). Its omission is easily explained by the reluctance of copyists to give this criminal the revered name "Jesus." But "Jesus" was actually a common name among Jews of that day. It is certainly easier to explain why copyists would remove the name than to explain why they would have introduced it.

8 The crowd seems to have come to Pilate's tribunal for the primary purpose of asking for Barabbas's release, since it was customary for a prisoner to be released at the Passover Feast. It was Pilate who deliberately faced them with the choice between Jesus and Barabbas.

9–10 This statement (v.9) implies that the crowd had asked for the release of Jesus. If Barabbas also had the name "Jesus" (see comments at v.7), it is possible that Pilate may have mistaken the crowd's request for releasing Jesus Barabbas as a request for releasing Jesus of Nazareth. Pilate, of course, used the title "king of the Jews" contemptuously, as in v.2. He was too shrewd a politician to believe that the chief priests had handed Jesus over to him out of loyalty to Caesar. He reasoned, and rightly so, that they envied Jesus' popularity and influence with the people (v.10).

11 The original purpose of the crowd was to gain the release of the insurrectionist Barabbas. Pilate had attempted to deflect that purpose and substitute the release of Jesus instead. This was a serious threat to the purpose of the chief priests. They had already condemned Jesus to death in their council; now they were not about to allow Jesus to slip through their fingers through some clemency custom associated with the Passover Feast. No other alternative was open to them but to urge the crowd to force Pilate to carry out their request—the release of Jesus Barabbas, not Jesus of Nazareth. Mark does not tell us how the chief priests stirred up the crowd.

12–14 Pilate's question is surprising. Apparently, he held out for Jesus other options than crucifixion. In Matthew's account, Pilate had just previously received his wife's warning not to have anything to do with "that innocent [or 'righteous'] man" (27:19). Perhaps his question reflects this warning. If Barabbas was to be released, what would Pilate do with Jesus? Was Pilate suggesting the possibility of releasing Jesus too? Whatever was going through his mind, it is clear from v.14 that he was reluctant to carry out a capital sentence against this apparently innocent man. His attempt to change the mind of the crowd—if doing so was, in fact, his true intention—failed. There was no dissuading them. The chief priests had stirred them into a frenzy. "Crucify him!" they shouted (v.13). And when Pilate, in a final attempt to save Jesus, asked, "Why? What crime has he committed?" the crowd, now a mob, ignored his question (v.14). They had reached a stage beyond reasoning. So they only shouted all the louder, "Crucify him!"

15 Pilate, always the ruthless pragmatist, saw that he could not change the mind of the mob. His previous handling of matters relating to the Jews' religion had not endeared him to the people. To risk alienating them in this crisis would be too dangerous for him politically. Perhaps his wife's message had made him think more deeply about Jesus than he might otherwise have done (cf. v.12). Yet he was a career Roman politician, and a great deal was at stake for him. An official complaint to Rome by the Jewish authorities might well result in his recall. So to protect his own interests and placate the priests and the people, he released the insurrectionist Barabbas and ordered Jesus flogged.

Flogging generally preceded crucifixion (cf. Hengel, *Crucifixion in the Ancient World*, 25–29), but not always. It is possible Pilate was still hoping he could dissuade the crowd from their demand for Jesus' crucifixion by administering a severe flogging. In John's account, after the flogging Pilate tried again to persuade them against crucifixion (Jn 19:1–7). In any case, flogging was no light punishment. The Romans first stripped the victim and tied his hands to a post above his head. The whip (flagellum) was made of several pieces of leather with pieces of bone and lead embedded near the ends. Two men, one on each side of the victim, usually did the flogging. The Jews mercifully limited flogging to a maximum of forty stripes; the Romans had no such limitation. The following is a medical doctor's description of the physical effects of flogging.

> The heavy whip is brought down with full force again and again across Jesus' shoulders, back, and legs. At first the heavy thongs cut through the skin only. Then, as the blows continue, they cut deeper into the subcutaneous tissues, producing first an oozing of blood from the capillaries and veins of the skin, and finally spurting arterial bleeding from vessels in the underlying muscles.... Finally

> the skin of the back is hanging in long ribbons and the entire area is an unrecognizable mass of torn, bleeding tissue.
>
> *C. Truman Davis, "The Crucifixion of Jesus,"* Arizona Medicine *22/3 (March 1965): 185*

It is not surprising that Roman floggings were often fatal.

After going through this terrible ordeal, Jesus was handed over by Pilate to be crucified. The use of the phrase "handed over" may be a deliberate attempt to identify Jesus with the Suffering Servant of Isaiah 53:6, 12 (LXX), since the same term (*paradidōmi*) is used there of the Servant. This "handing over" has been a constant theme both of Jesus' passion predictions (9:31; 10:34) and throughout the arrest and trial narrative as Jesus is "betrayed" and "handed over" from one human agent to the next (14:10–11, 18, 21, 41–42, 44; 15:1, 15). Ultimately, of course, it is God who "hands over" his Servant to serve as a ransom sacrifice for sins (see comments at 9:30–31).

NOTES

1 In 1961 at Caesarea on the Mediterranean coast, Italian archaeologists discovered a two-by-three foot footstone that has on it the following inscription in three-inch lettering:

CAESARIENS TIBERIEVM
PONTIVS PILATVS
PRAEFECTVS IVDAEAE
DEDIT
[Pontius Pilatus, Prefect of Judea, has presented the Tiberieum to the Caesareans]

What the Tiberieum was is not clear (perhaps a building or monument). What is important is that this discovery constituted the first archaeological evidence for the existence of Pontius Pilate. It also confirms that his official title was "prefect" rather than the later term "procurator" used for the governors of Judea (cf. J. Vardaman, "A New Inscription which Mentions Pilate as 'Prefect'," *JBL* 81 [1962]: 70–71).

2 Had Jesus wanted to declare his kingship openly, he could have answered ναί (*nai*, "Yes!"), or, as in 14:62, ἐγώ εἰμί (*egō eimi*, "I am"). R. P. Martin (*Mark*, 178) suggests the paraphrase "You do well to ask"—"a reply which deflects the thrust of Pilate's interrogation and makes possible a continuation of the dialogue in the Trial scenario."

3 The variant reading at the end of v.3 that is included in the KJV, αὐτὸς δὲ οὐδὲν ἀπεκρίνατο (*autos de ouden apekrinato*, "but he answered nothing"), is supported by predominantly Caesarean witnesses. Taylor thinks the reading may be original because the following verse (v.4) seems to require some such statement. The external evidence is, however, so weak that the UBS Greek text does not even list it as a variant.

6 In addition to the example of clemency cited in the commentary, there is in the Mishnah a rule that a paschal lamb may be slaughtered for one who has been promised release from prison (*m. Pesaḥ.* 8:6a).

7 Cranfield, 450, thinks "Jesus Barabbas" is likely original in Matthew 27:16–17 and, since Matthew is dependent on Mark, was originally present here in Mark as well. While this reading is possible, its complete absence from any MS of Mark renders unwise the introduction of it here.

K. The Mocking of Jesus (15:16–20)

OVERVIEW

In his third passion prediction, Jesus had said that the religious leaders would condemn him to death and hand him over to the Gentiles, who would "mock him and spit on him, flog him and kill him" (10:33–34). This prophecy is vividly fulfilled here, as Pilate's soldiers mock and abuse Jesus (cf. 14:65; 15:29–32). As throughout the trial and crucifixion narrative, the scene is heavily ironic. Jesus, the true Messiah and King of the Jews, is derisively mocked as a pretender to the throne (Brooks, 253). The informed reader knows that it is through suffering and death that Jesus will be exalted and glorified to the right hand of God. As in Jesus' predictions in 10:33–34 and the abuse of 14:65, this passage recalls the prophecies of suffering related to Yahweh's Servant in Isaiah 50:6 and 53:4–5.

[16]The soldiers led Jesus away into the palace (that is, the Praetorium) and called together the whole company of soldiers. [17]They put a purple robe on him, then twisted together a crown of thorns and set it on him. [18]And they began to call out to him, "Hail, king of the Jews!" [19]Again and again they struck him on the head with a staff and spit on him. Falling on their knees, they paid homage to him. [20]And when they had mocked him, they took off the purple robe and put his own clothes on him. Then they led him out to crucify him.

COMMENTARY

16 The scourging of Jesus likely took place in front of the palace of Herod and in the presence of all the people. Afterward Jesus was taken by the soldiers into the *aulē*, a term that commonly means "courtyard" but which the NIV translates as "palace" because of Mark's explanatory clause—"that is, the Praetorium." The term is used in 1 Maccabees 11:46 in this sense. Another possibility is that the courtyard (*aulē*), being the most public part of the Praetorium, "may well have been known by the Latin name of the whole" (Swete, 374). The NLT translates *aulē* as "the courtyard of the governor's headquarters" (cf. CEV, TEV). "Praetorium" is a Latin loanword in Greek. Used originally of a general's tent or the headquarters in a camp, here it designates the Roman governor's official residence. (For the identification of the Praetorium with Herod's palace, see comments at v.1.)

The soldiers who led Jesus into the courtyard and then mocked and abused him were a part of the auxiliary troops Pilate had brought up to Jerusalem from Caesarea. They were likely non-Jews recruited from Palestine and other parts of the empire. Mark says the whole company (*speira*) took part in their perverted humor. Since a *speira* (the tenth part of a legion) consisted of two hundred to six hundred men, the word is probably used loosely here by Mark to include only the soldiers immediately at hand.

17–18 The soldiers thought it was a great joke that this common Jewish teacher claimed to be a king.

So they took a purple robe and threw it across his shredded and bleeding back. It was probably a scarlet military cloak (cf. Mt 27:28), "a cast-off and faded rag, but with color enough left in it to suggest the royal purple" (Swete, 375). To add to the royal mockery, a crown was fashioned from thorny branches and pressed onto Jesus' scalp. Again there must have been copious bleeding, for the scalp is one of the most vascular areas of the body. The term "crown" is *stephanos*, which refers to a laurel wreath worn by victorious athletes or someone of high status. In this context it is clearly a royal symbol. The term "thorny" (*akanthinos*) is not specific and could refer to a variety of prickly plants grown in Palestine. "Hail, king of the Jews'" (v.18) is a parody of "Hail, Emperor Caesar!"

19 The mocking was followed by further physical violence. The blows that hit Jesus' head from the staff would have driven the thorns more deeply into his scalp and caused even more profuse bleeding. Matthew 27:29 says that they first forced Jesus to hold the staff as a mock scepter. They also kept spitting (Gk. imperfect tense) on him, and the climax came when they mockingly fell on their knees and paid homage to him.

20 At last, tiring of their mockery, the soldiers tore the robe from Jesus' back. The fabric had probably stuck to the clots of blood and serum in the wounds. Thus when it was callously ripped off him, it caused excruciating pain, just as when a bandage is carelessly removed. Jesus' own clothes were now put back on him. The custom was for those condemned to death by crucifixion to be led naked to the place of execution and to be flogged on the way (Josephus, *Ant.* 19.4.5 §269). Jesus, however, had already been scourged and was too weak to have survived an additional brutal beating.

NOTES

17–18 Philo (*Flacc.* 6.36–40) relates a somewhat similar episode that occurred in Alexandria in about AD 38. King Herod Agrippa I was mocked by a pagan crowd, who dressed up a demented Jew named Carabbas as "king" and pretended to pay homage to him. They supplied him with robe made of a doormat, a crown of papyrus leaf, and a scepter of papyrus stalk. Philo criticizes the Egyptian governor Flaccus Avillius for not intervening against the mockery.

20 In John's account Pilate, making one final appeal to the crowd after Jesus' scourging (19:4–16), is even more reluctant to crucify Jesus. He brings Jesus, wearing the purple robe and the crown of thorns, before the crowd and says, "Here is the man!" (v.5). John says that Pilate wanted to set Jesus free (v.12), but the Jewish leaders warned that if he let Jesus go he was no friend of Caesar. So Pilate, who felt his political future at stake, acquiesced to their cries.

L. The Crucifixion (15:21–32)

OVERVIEW

Mark's crucifixion narrative is marked especially by its simplicity and irony. Jesus is repeatedly mocked as king of the Jews. Since he claimed to save others, he should be able to come down from the cross and save himself. The irony is that Jesus is indeed the King of the Jews who has been saving others throughout his ministry. Yet it is by staying on the cross rather than coming down that he will accomplish the ultimate salvation—dying as a ransom payment for the sins of others (10:45).

21 A certain man from Cyrene, Simon, the father of Alexander and Rufus, was passing
by on his way in from the country, and they forced him to carry the cross. 22 They brought
Jesus to the place called Golgotha (which means The Place of the Skull). 23 Then they
offered him wine mixed with myrrh, but he did not take it. 24 And they crucified him.
Dividing up his clothes, they cast lots to see what each would get.
25 It was the third hour when they crucified him. 26 The written notice of the charge
against him read: THE KING OF THE JEWS. 27 They crucified two robbers with him, one on his
right and one on his left. 29 Those who passed by hurled insults at him, shaking their
heads and saying, "So! You who are going to destroy the temple and build it in three days,
30 come down from the cross and save yourself!"
31 In the same way the chief priests and the teachers of the law mocked him among
themselves. "He saved others," they said, "but he can't save himself! 32 Let this Christ,
this King of Israel, come down now from the cross, that we may see and believe." Those
crucified with him also heaped insults on him.

COMMENTARY

21 Those condemned to die by crucifixion were customarily required to carry the heavy wooden crosspiece (*patibulum*), on which they were to be nailed, to the place of execution. Jesus apparently started out carrying his cross (Jn 19:17), but it proved too much for him. The scourging and loss of blood had weakened him too much. So apparently at random they apprehended one Simon of Cyrene and forced him into service. Since Cyrene (in North Africa) had a large Jewish population, Simon was probably a Jew. He may have been a visitor coming to the city for the Passover celebration, or a resident—part of the Cyrenian community of Jews who lived there (Ac 6:9). If the latter, he was likely returning to the city from a journey or from work in the countryside. Mark probably mentions Simon's two sons Alexander and Rufus because they were known to his church. If this Rufus is the same one referred to by Paul in Romans 16:13, the fact would provide additional evidence for the claim that Mark's gospel was written in Rome.

22 Both Roman and Jewish executions were customarily performed outside the city. John says that the place where Jesus was crucified was near the city, but it was outside the city wall (19:20; cf. Heb 13:12). In the first century AD, as closely as can now be determined, the northern wall of the city ran northward from Herod's palace, turned sharply to the east past Golgotha, which was just west of it, and then continued to the Fortress of Antonia.

"Golgotha" is a slightly modified transliteration of the Aramaic word for "skull," whereas the designation "Calvary" (commonly used in English) is derived from the Vulgate's translation "*Calvariae locus*," *calva* being the Latin word for "skull." How this site came to be named "Golgotha" is unknown. The common conjecture is that the place looked like a skull. The traditional site of the crucifixion (and Jesus' nearby burial) is located inside the famous Church of the Holy Sepulchre, which is within the present walls of the city (but outside the walls of Jerusalem in Jesus' day). See Notes for further discussion.

23 Jesus was offered wine mixed with myrrh when he arrived at the place of execution. Mark does not identify who offered the drink to Jesus. Lane, 564, posits women of Jerusalem who provided a narcotic drink to condemned criminals in order to deaden the pain (cf. *b. Sanh. 43a*). W. Michaelis (*TDNT* 7:457–59) thinks Jesus, because he was weak and exhausted, was offered soldiers' wine by the executioner. In any case the drink must have been meant to deaden the pain. Jesus, refusing it, chose rather to experience the terrible sufferings of the crucifixion with his senses intact.

24 With incredible restraint, Mark states simply, "And they crucified him." Such brevity is remarkable when one considers that crucifixion was, as Cicero said, "the cruelest and most hideous punishment possible" (*Verr.* 5.64.165; cf. Hengel, *Charismatic Leader and His Followers*, 29–32). The Persians seem to have invented the practice, but it was Romans who perfected it and used it to maximum effect. Crucifixion served both as a means of execution and for "exposing" an executed body to shame and humiliation. The cruelty and public nature of the event also served as a weapon of terror, a stark warning to the populace about the dire consequences of challenging Roman authority.

The Romans practiced a variety of forms of crucifixion. The main stake, or *palus*, generally remained at the place of execution, while the victim would be forced to carry the *patibulum* there (see comments at v.21). The crossbeam was placed either on top of the *palus* (like a "T") or in the more traditional cross shape (†). The victim would be affixed to the cross with ropes or, as in the case of Jesus, with nails (Jn 20:25). Various positions were used to maximize torture and humiliation. Josephus (*J.W.* 5.11.1 §451) records the crucifixion of thousands of Jews by the Romans during the siege of Jerusalem: "So the soldiers, out of the rage and hatred they bore the prisoners, nailed those they caught, in different postures, to the crosses, by way of jest; and their number was so great that there was not enough room for the crosses, and not enough crosses for the bodies."

Death by crucifixion could come very slowly, especially if the victim was tied instead of nailed to the cross. Nailing caused loss of blood and thus hastened death. The physical condition of the victim and the severity of the scourging also affected the length of survival. Death was caused by loss of blood, exposure, and exhaustion and/or suffocation (since the hanging weight of the victim, and the pain of having to push himself up with his nail- or rope-fastened feet in order to be able to expand his lungs and rib cage with breath, made it increasingly difficult for him to inhale sufficient air). If the victim was slow in dying, his legs could be broken by a club so that he could not push himself up to breathe. According to John's gospel, Jesus had been so brutally beaten that when the soldiers came to him to see whether they would have to break his legs, he was dead already (19:31–33).

Jesus' clothes had been removed when he was nailed to the cross. They were now in the hands of the soldiers, who proceeded to while away their time by casting lots for the clothes. The passage recalls Psalm 22:18: "They divide my garments among them and cast lots for my clothing." Though this psalm of a righteous sufferer is not explicitly quoted until Jesus' words from the cross in v.34, it echoes throughout the crucifixion narrative (see comments at vv.29, 34).

25 Mark says that Jesus was crucified at the third hour, i.e., 9:00 a.m.—the first of three specific time markers mentioned by the narrator: crucifixion in the third hour (9:00 a.m., v.25); the darkness in the sixth hour (noon, v.33); and the cry of Jesus and his death in the ninth hour (3:00 p.m., v.34). Jesus' body is then taken down "as evening approached" (about 6:00 p.m.? v.42). Mark's sequence, however, apparently conflicts with John's account, which says that the trial before Pilate was not quite over by the sixth hour—i.e., noon—therefore implying that the crucifixion took place later still (Jn 19:14). A number of solutions to this difficult problem have been suggested.

(1) Some say John was using Roman time. Thus the sixth hour was 6:00 a.m., not noon; and the three-hour interval was taken up with the scourging, mocking, and preparations for the crucifixion. This explanation, however, seems a desperate attempt at harmonization, since there is no evidence for it.

(2) The discrepancy is a scribal error. The whole of v.25 may be a gloss (i.e., added by later copyists), since both Matthew and Luke do not include it, and they ordinarily follow Mark's indications of time in the passion narrative. Another possibility is that an early copyist has confused a Greek Γ (*gamma*)—the letter that stands for the number 3—with a Ϝ (*digamma*)—the letter that stands for 6. This latter suggestion was made by the church historian Eusebius in the fourth century AD. The problem is that in the MSS we possess Mark uses the word "third" (*tritē*) instead of the *gamma* (Γ).

(3) The scribal error could be in John 19:14 rather than in Mark 15:25. In this case a scribe has introduced the prominent time reference, which appears in all three Synoptics ("the sixth hour"; Mk 15:33; Mt 27:45; Lk 23:44), into John's account, but introduced it in the wrong place—at the end of the trial scene instead of at the time of darkness (France, 645).

(4) John has altered the chronology for theological reasons, namely, to place Jesus' death as closely as possible to the time of the Passover sacrifices (Cranfield, 455–56; Gundry, 957; Evans, 503).

(5) Mark has altered the chronology for the structural reason of providing a well-ordered account.

Of these suggestions, either a scribal alteration—solution 2 or 3—or a Johannine theological emphasis (4) seems the most likely. But all remain speculative.

26 A wooden board (*titulus*) stating the specific charge against the condemned man was commonly tied around his neck or carried before him to the execution. Mark does not state where the *titulus* was placed, but Matthew says it was "above his head" (27:37), and John confirms that it was fastened to the cross (19:19). In Mark's account the inscription reads "THE KING OF THE JEWS." John relates that it was written in Hebrew, Latin, and Greek (19:20). The precise wording varies among the four gospels, but all assert that Jesus was crucified on the charge of claiming to be the king of the Jews. For the Romans, that claim was high treason.

27 The two criminals crucified on either side of Jesus are called *lēstas*, a word normally meaning "robbers." As noted earlier, however, here it likely means "insurrectionists" (see comments at 11:17 and 14:48–50). They had probably been a part of the same insurrection Barabbas was involved in (cf. 15:7) and had been sentenced at the same time as Jesus (cf. *TDNT* 4:262). They seemed to know that the charges against him were false (cf. Lk 23:41). His placement in the middle, between the two criminals, was probably to mock him as the insurrectionist par excellence—the "king of the Jews." The wording "one on his right and one on his left" recalls the request of James and John for the chief seats when Jesus entered his "glory" (10:37; see Brooks, 259), thus reminding the reader that status in God's kingdom comes not through power and domination but through service and sacrifice.

28 This verse (see NIV text note) does not appear in the most ancient MSS of the NT. Most textual critics consider it an interpolation from Luke 22:37 (quoting Isa 53:12), where it is authentic. Mark does not usually point out OT fulfillment.

29–30 It is evident from these verses that the crucifixion took place in a public area, perhaps beside a thoroughfare where people were coming and going. The Romans intentionally made crucifixions a public spectacle in order to "advertise" as widely as possible the consequences of revolt. As some people passed by, they took the opportunity to vent their hostility on Jesus (v.29). The phrase "shaking their heads"—a gesture of derision—echoes Psalm 22:7 (cf. La 2:15), once again identifying Jesus as the righteous sufferer of that psalm (see comments at v.24). They particularly remembered the charge made against him of destroying and rebuilding the temple (cf. 14:58). Surely if he could destroy and rebuild the temple, he could save himself now (v.30).

31–32 The chief priests and teachers of the law were also there to add their mockery to that of the passersby. This must have been especially difficult for Jesus to bear. As the spiritual leaders of the people, they should have championed Jesus' cause; instead, they had condemned him and demanded his crucifixion. They "mocked him among themselves," no doubt within the hearing of Jesus. Yet as they did so, they unconsciously bore witness to his miraculous powers: "He saved others"—a reference to his healing miracles. Their statement "he can't save himself" is both false and true. In the sense they meant it—he lacks the power—it is false. But in a profound sense, if Jesus was to fulfill his messianic mission, he could not save himself. His death was necessary for humanity's redemption.

The epithet "This Christ, this King of Israel" is full of derision (v.32). The phrase brings together the two phases of Jesus' trial. The claim before the Sanhedrin to be Israel's Messiah was brought before Pilate as a claim to royal authority—a king in opposition to Caesar. Pilate had placed over Jesus the title "THE KING OF THE JEWS," a phrase more naturally used by a Gentile. The Jewish leaders use terminology more appropriate to their status, "King of Israel," so mocking his claim to be the king of the people of God. And they tauntingly demanded a demonstration of his power—"come down now from the cross, that we may see and believe." Like the Pharisees in 8:11–12, they want to see a sign—proof of Jesus' messianic authority.

Jesus also had to bear the insults of the criminals who were crucified on either side of him. Mark adds this note to show the utter degradation and humiliation of the cross. Even the lowliest of criminals view Jesus with derision.

NOTES

22 Archaeological excavations tend to support the historicity of the traditional site. For example, Kathleen Kenyon's excavations in 1967 discovered a rock quarry on the southern side of the church, and just west of the Church of the Holy Sepulchre tombs have been discovered. That rock quarries were seldom found inside the walls of cities, simply because the crowded conditions made it impossible to work them, and that burials were not allowed within the city walls give supporting evidence to the tradition that the Church of the Holy Sepulchre was the site of Jesus' crucifixion and burial. Gordon's Calvary (located on a skull-shaped knoll outside the present walls of the city between and north of the Damascus and Herod gates), and the nearby Garden Tomb, though major tourist attractions, have little historical support as the site of Jesus' crucifixion and burial.

25 For various harmonizing solutions to the time of Jesus' death, see J.V. Miller, "The Time of the Crucifixion," *JETS* 26 (1983): 157–66.

32 The imagery here is similar to the taunts of oppressors against the righteous man of Wisdom of Solomon 2:17–18: "Let us see whether his words be true; let us find out what will happen to him. For if the just one be the son of God, he will defend him and deliver him from the hand of his foes." Compare Matthew 27:42–43, which has even stronger conceptual echoes to this passage.

M. The Death of Jesus (15:33–41)

33At the sixth hour darkness came over the whole land until the ninth hour. 34And at the
ninth hour Jesus cried out in a loud voice, *"Eloi, Eloi, lama sabachthani?"*—which means,
"My God, my God, why have you forsaken me?"
35When some of those standing near heard this, they said, "Listen, he's calling Elijah."
36One man ran, filled a sponge with wine vinegar, put it on a stick, and offered it to
Jesus to drink. "Now leave him alone. Let's see if Elijah comes to take him down," he said.
37With a loud cry, Jesus breathed his last.
38The curtain of the temple was torn in two from top to bottom. 39And when the centurion, who stood there in front of Jesus, heard his cry and saw how he died, he said, "Surely
this man was the Son of God!"
40Some women were watching from a distance. Among them were Mary Magdalene,
Mary the mother of James the younger and of Joses, and Salome. 41In Galilee these
women had followed him and cared for his needs. Many other women who had come
up with him to Jerusalem were also there.

COMMENTARY

33 All three of the Synoptics report the darkness; none say what caused it. It could hardly have been an eclipse of the sun at the time of the Passover full moon. Perhaps the darkness was caused by dark clouds that obscured the sun, or by a black sirocco—a wind that comes in from the desert, not uncommon in Jerusalem in the month of April. Whatever its immediate cause, Mark and his readers clearly understood it to result from a supernatural act of God and probably interpreted it as a sign of judgment. In the OT, darkness is one of the ten plagues God sent against Egypt in the account of events leading to the exodus (Ex 10:21–23), and darkness is identified with the eschatological judgments of the day of the Lord (Isa 13:10; 34:4; Joel 2:10; 3:15; Am 5:18, 20; 8:9). Jesus alluded to this latter imagery in his Olivet Discourse (13:24–25). The darkness lasted for three hours (noon–3:00 p.m.) and fell "over the whole land," i.e., Judea, not the whole earth.

34 In the four gospels Jesus makes seven statements from the cross (the "seven last words"). Yet

Mark records only one of them: *Eloi, Eloi, lama sabachthani?*—an Aramaic version of Psalm 22:1, meaning, "My God, my God, why have you forsaken me?" It is significant that Mark, the evangelist who most stresses the suffering role of the Messiah, records only Jesus' cry of forsakenness. The narrative of the crucifixion paints a dark and foreboding scene.

The saying is surely authentic, since it is unlikely that the church would have invented a saying in which Jesus expresses utter forsakenness by God. Some commentators have tried to soften its meaning by claiming that Jesus has in mind the entire context of Psalm 22, and so contemplates not only his suffering but also his vindication and restoration to fellowship with God (cf. Ps 22:22–31). This interpretation is unlikely. While it is true that Mark uses this and other allusions to Psalm 22 to portray Jesus as the righteous sufferer par excellence (cf. vv.24, 29), nothing in the context indicates that Jesus' words express confidence or trust in God. Although Jesus does not abandon or reject God (whom he still refers to as "*my* God"), the cry is certainly one of true anguish and despair. While we should be cautious about reading a developed theology of atonement into the episode, the best explanation from Mark's narrative perspective is that Jesus is experiencing God's cup of judgment (14:36), suffering as a ransom payment for the sins of "the many" (10:45; 14:24). This view is not far from Paul's affirmations that "God made him who had no sin to be sin for us" (2Co 5:21) and that "Christ redeemed us from the curse of the law by becoming a curse for us" (Gal 3:13). God cannot look on sin and so turns his back on his own Son, thus allowing him to suffer its judgment alone. Taylor, 549, remarks: "The depths of the saying are too deep to be plumbed, but the least inadequate interpretations are those which find in it a sense of desolation in which Jesus felt the horror of sin so deeply that for a time the closeness of His communion with the Father was obscured."

35 Some of the bystanders mistook the first words of Jesus' cry "*Eloi, Eloi*" ("My God, my God") to be a cry for Elijah, so they say, "Listen, he's calling Elijah." Whether this comment reflects a true misunderstanding or a mocking distortion of Jesus' words is unclear. There was a common Jewish belief that Elijah would return before the eschatological day of God's judgment (Mal 3:1; 4:5; Sir 48:9–10), a belief that has surfaced elsewhere in Mark's gospel (6:15; 8:28; and esp. 9:11–13). Elijah was also regarded as a deliverer of those in trouble (cf. *TDNT* 2:930).

36 Mark does not identify the person who went to get the wine vinegar (or "sour wine," *oxos*). This drink "relieved thirst more effectively than water and, being cheaper than regular wine, was a favorite beverage of the lower ranks of society and of those in moderate circumstances ... especially of soldiers" (BDAG, 715). The sour wine was probably present for the soldiers, but the fact that this individual speaks of Elijah may indicate that he was one of the Jewish bystanders. In any case, a sponge was filled with the drink, placed around the tip of a stick (of hyssop, according to Jn 19:29), and held up to Jesus' lips so that he could suck the liquid from it. The NIV translates *aphete* as "Now leave him alone." But the equally valid rendering "Let me alone" seems more in keeping with the context. Apparently, some of the bystanders wanted to prevent the soldier from giving the wine vinegar to Jesus. The soldier insisted on doing it, however, and then added his own taunt: "Let's see if Elijah comes to take him down." Gould's paraphrase, 295, of the last part of this verse catches its meaning: "Let me give him this, and so prolong his life, and then we shall get an opportunity to see whether Elijah comes to help him or not." The offer of wine echoes Psalm 69:21, where the tormenters of a righteous sufferer give him gall in his food and "vinegar for my thirst."

37 After six hours of torture, Jesus cried out and died. Usually those who were crucified took a long time to die (cf. v.44, where Pilate expresses surprise on hearing that Jesus had already died). The "loud cry" of Jesus is unusual, for crucifixion sapped the strength of its victims, especially when they were near death. Mark does not specify Jesus' words, and it is difficult to tell whether his cry continues the tone of despair in the previous cry (v.34) or whether it was a more positive one. If it was the same as that recorded by either Luke ("Father, into your hands I commit my spirit!" 23:46) or John ("It is finished!" 19:30), then it would indicate either trust or triumph (France, 655). But Mark does not say. Our only clue is the positive reaction of the centurion in v.39 (see comments there), which would suggest something more profound than the last gasp of an anguished soul. Perhaps it was a shout of victory in anticipation of the triumph of the resurrection.

38 All the synoptic writers record this event. The curtain mentioned here could be either the one that separated the Holy Place from the inner courtyard or the curtain between the Holy Place and the Holy of Holies (Ex 26:33–37; 27:16). Josephus (*J.W.* 5.5.4 §212) describes the former as a magnificent Babylonian curtain of blue, scarlet, and purple symbolically representing the universe. Mark's assertion that the curtain was ripped in two "from top to bottom" confirms that it was a supernatural act of God. But Mark does not identify its spiritual significance. It may refer to (1) God's judgment against the temple and its corrupt leadership (a common theme in Mark), (2) the cessation of the temple sacrifices, or (3) new access into God's presence available through Jesus' death. Hebrews 10:19–22 identifies Jesus' body as the curtain that opens up "a new and living way" into the presence of God. One or more of these ideas may have been in Mark's mind.

How this event became public knowledge is not known. If the inner curtain was torn, only the priests permitted entrance into the Holy Place would have seen it. Perhaps the event became part of Christian tradition through the report of priests who subsequently converted to Christianity (cf. Ac 6:7).

39 The Roman centurion in command of the detachment of soldiers at the cross had witnessed the scourging, mocking, spitting, crucifixion, wagging of heads, and darkness, and now he heard Jesus' last cry and watched him die. The soldier was deeply impressed. He had never seen anything like this before! The statement "Surely this man was the Son of God!" is difficult to translate, since it seems unlikely that a pagan Roman centurion would have understood the full theological significance of the title "Son of God." The Greek has no definite article *ho* ("the") before *huios* ("son"), and it could possibly be rendered "a son of God" or "a son of a god." The centurion in this case may have recognized something divine in the behavior of this crucified Jew. Yet whatever the centurion's original intent, this ambiguity cannot characterize the way in which Mark and his readers understood the title. Jesus as *the* Son of God is a central theme in Mark's Christology, a theme that reaches its climax here in the centurion's words. If the phrase "the Son of God" in 1:1 is an original part of the gospel (see comments there), then the centurion's confession here forms its twin, the matching "bookend" that completes the frame around the whole gospel. Even if the phrase in 1:1 is not original, the Father's declaration in 1:11, "You are my Son," has the same profound effect. The one whom the Father declared to be his Son at the beginning of the gospel is now confirmed to be the Son of God by a Gentile centurion. And this recognition comes not because Jesus is a conquering warrior king but because he has died as a "ransom" for sins (10:45). Whether or not the centurion realized the full import of his words, they were for Mark and his readers a profoundly true statement of the identity of the man on the cross. It is equally significant that the man who recognizes this truth is not one of the Jewish religious leaders (who rejected Jesus' claim, 14:62–63), nor even one of the disciples (Peter's having proclaimed Jesus to be the Messiah but being unable to comprehend his suffering role, 8:27–33), but a Gentile—those to whom the gospel message will soon go forth. If Mark is writing to the church in Rome, then this confession by a Gentile Roman soldier is even more significant.

40–41 Although Jesus' male followers had deserted him, his women disciples did not, and some observed the crucifixion from afar. Surprisingly, here is the first mention in Mark of the "many" women who supported Jesus' ministry. They will prove to be important witnesses to the crucifixion, burial, and resurrection. Out of the many who had come up to Jerusalem with Jesus from Galilee, Mark identifies three who were "watching from a distance"—Mary Magdalene; Mary the mother of James the younger and of Joses; and Salome, the wife of Zebedee and mother of James and John.

Mary Magdalene (i.e., Mary of Magdala, a fishing village on the western shore of the Sea of Galilee) is mentioned only here in Mark. From Luke 8:2, however, we know that Jesus had cast seven demons out of her, and from John 20:11–18 we learn that she was the first to see the risen Lord. The second Mary is designated as the "mother of James the younger and of Joses." Although little is known about her, her sons were apparently well-known in the early church. She is referred to as the "mother of Joses" in 15:47 and the "mother of James" in 16:1. In the NIV James is described as "the younger." The Greek adjective *mikros* can also mean "the less," i.e., "the smaller, less important," or "less known." It is difficult to decide which meaning applies here. This Mary may have been the wife of Clopas, mentioned in John 19:25. The third woman Mark mentions is Salome, Zebedee's wife and the mother of James and John (cf. Mt 27:56).

These women had been with Jesus in Galilee (v.41) and had served him there. They had come up to Jerusalem, along with many other women, especially to be with him and to serve him.

NOTES

33 In addition to apocalyptic judgment, darkness is also associated with the death of great men in both Greco-Roman and Jewish traditions. It is reported with reference to the deaths of Alexander the Great, Caesar, Aeschylus, and others (see BDAG, 931; *TDNT* 7:439).

34 The seven last words are (in probable chronological order): (1) "Father, forgive them, for they do not know what they are doing" (Lk 23:34); (2) to his mother, "Dear woman, here is your son," and to the beloved disciple, "Here is your mother" (Jn 19:26–27); (3) to the thief, "I tell you the truth, today you will be with me in paradise" (Lk 23:43); (4) "I am thirsty!" (Jn 19:28); (5) "My God, my God, why have you forsaken me!" (Mk 15:34; Mt 27:46); (6) "Father, into your hands I commit my spirit!" (Lk 23:46); and (7) "It is finished" (Jn 19:30).

Matthew records the same "My God, my God" saying as Mark but begins with the Hebrew *Eli, Eli*, and then finishes with the Aramaic *lema sabachthani* (TNIV). Either the Hebrew or Aramaic version could be original. Jesus may have recited the psalm in Hebrew and the Aramaic-speaking church rendered it into Aramaic. Or he may have originally spoken in Aramaic and Matthew introduced the familiar Hebrew *Eli, Eli*.

35 Some commentators claim that Jesus probably originally said *Eli, Eli* instead of *Eloi, Eloi*, since the former would more likely have been mistaken for a cry for Elijah. This is possible, but the anguished cry of a man near death is unlikely to have been enunciated clearly, and either cry could have been mistaken for Elijah.

39 Mark does not specifically say what impressed the man—only that it resulted from seeing "how he died." Some MSS, however, add that he "*heard his cry* and saw how he died" (so NIV text; TNIV text note), thus indicating that it was, in part at least, what Jesus said in his last cry that made such a profound impact. The textual evidence, however, favors the shorter reading.

Although there is no definite article ὁ (*ho*, "the") before υἱός (*huios*, "son") in the centurion's confession, the NIV appropriately translates, "Surely this man was *the* Son of God" (emphasis mine), since a definite predicate noun that precedes the verb usually does not have the article (cf. Jn 1:1).

N. The Burial of Jesus (15:42–47)

OVERVIEW

The account of Jesus' burial is an important part of the gospel's story. The fact that Jesus was buried confirms that he was truly dead and sets the place and stage for the resurrection narrative. When Paul summarizes the essential gospel message in 1 Corinthians, he gives the burial a prominent place: "For what I received I passed on to you as of first importance: that Christ died for our sins according to the Scriptures, that he was buried, that he was raised on the third day ..." (1Co 15:3–4).

The Romans did not generally allow crucified victims to be buried. Part of the humiliation of crucifixion was to allow the body to decompose on the cross or to be left unburied for scavengers to eat. Yet the Romans were also aware of Jewish religious concerns, and OT law required the bodies of executed victims to be buried before nightfall so as not to desecrate the land (Dt 21:22–23; cf. Jn 19:31). Josephus (*J.W.* 4.5.2 §317) confirms that, contrary to Roman practice, the Jews tended to bury crucified victims. In this context, the release of the body of Jesus by Pilate is entirely plausible.

[42]It was Preparation Day (that is, the day before the Sabbath). So as evening approached,
[43]Joseph of Arimathea, a prominent member of the Council, who was himself waiting for
the kingdom of God, went boldly to Pilate and asked for Jesus' body. [44]Pilate was surprised
to hear that he was already dead. Summoning the centurion, he asked him if Jesus had
already died. [45]When he learned from the centurion that it was so, he gave the body to
Joseph. [46]So Joseph bought some linen cloth, took down the body, wrapped it in the linen,
and placed it in a tomb cut out of rock. Then he rolled a stone against the entrance of the
tomb. [47]Mary Magdalene and Mary the mother of Joses saw where he was laid.

COMMENTARY

42–43 "Preparation Day" was the name given to the day before a festival or a Sabbath (v.42). Here it refers to the day before the Sabbath, as Mark explains for the benefit of his Gentile readers. Since the Jewish Sabbath began at sundown, and it was now late in the afternoon (probably around 4:00 or 5:00 p.m.), there was not much time to take Jesus' body down from the cross. Apparently, temporal urgency spurred Joseph of Arimathea to action.

Joseph's request for the body of Jesus (v.43) is described by Mark as a bold act, as indeed it was, because it would inevitably have identified Joseph with Jesus and his followers. For a man in Joseph's position ("a prominent member of the Council," i.e., the Sanhedrin), such an act could have serious consequences. But he was a pious man who "was himself waiting for the kingdom of God." Though Mark does not give us any more information about Joseph, Matthew says he was a "disciple" (27:57), and John clarifies that he held this discipleship "secretly" and that Nicodemus assisted him in the burial (19:38–39). Luke describes him as "a good and upright man who had not consented to their [the Sanhedrin's] decision and action" (23:50–51). Whether Joseph was absent during the Sanhedrin's deliberations or had abstained from the vote is unknown.

Ordinarily, a relative or close friend would have requested the body, but apparently the mother of Jesus was too distraught; and Jesus' disciples had fled. There is no evidence that Jesus' brothers and sisters were in Jerusalem at the time of the crucifixion.

The burial of Jesus by Joseph of Arimathea has a very strong claim to authenticity, since it is unlikely that the church would have invented a story in which a member of the council that so vehemently condemned Jesus now steps forward to give him an honorable burial.

44–45 Pilate was surprised to hear that Jesus had already died, since death usually came much more slowly to crucified victims than it had to Jesus. Only after he received confirmation of Jesus' death from the centurion was Pilate willing to turn Jesus' body over to Joseph (v.45). Had it not been for Joseph's actions, Jesus' body would likely have been buried in a common criminal's grave. For Pilate to release the body of a condemned criminal—especially one condemned of high treason—to someone other than a relative was highly unusual. It suggests that Pilate did not take seriously the charge of high treason against Jesus and had only pronounced sentence against him because of political expediency. This action of Pilate is consistent with Mark's account of Jesus' trial before Pilate (vv.1–15).

46 Mark does not mention that anyone assisted Joseph in the actions described here. He must, however, have had help in removing the body from the cross, preparing it for burial, and carrying it to the place of burial. Matthew 27:57 describes Joseph as being rich (cf. Isa 53:9), so he doubtless had servants to help him. Moreover, John says that Nicodemus, who had previously come to Jesus at night, helped Joseph and supplied some of the spices used in the preparation of the body for burial (Jn 19:39). Although no specific mention is made of washing the blood-soaked body, this important Jewish rite must have been performed before the body was wrapped for burial in the linen cloths. After being properly prepared for burial (cf. Jn 19:40), the body was placed in "a tomb cut out of rock." Such tombs were generally meant to be family tombs, with multiple shelves for bodies carved into the interior walls of the cave. This use and design explain Matthew's statement that the tomb belonged to Joseph and that it was new—i.e., none of Joseph's family had yet been placed in it (Mt 27:60; cf. Jn 19:41).

The tomb was located in a garden near the site of the crucifixion (Jn 19:41). Archaeological excavation has shown that the traditional site of Jesus' burial (the Church of the Holy Sepulchre in Jerusalem) served as a cemetery during the first century AD (see comments at v.22). Tombs cut out of the rock were closed by rolling a stone against the entrance—either a flat stone disc that rolled side to side in a sloped channel, or simply a large rock that could be rolled in front of the opening. (For an interesting discussion of what kind of stone is meant, see Dalman, *Sacred Sites and Ways*, 374ff.)

47 The two Marys mentioned in 15:40 as being witnesses of the crucifixion were also present at Jesus' burial. Mark mentions their presence in anticipation of 16:1 and particularly 16:5. The two women could identify the tomb on Sunday morning because they had been present at the burial.

NOTES

42–47 The bones of a crucified man named Jehohanan were discovered in 1968 at *Giv'at ha Mivtar* in the Kidron Valley northeast of the Old City of Jerusalem and have been dated between AD 7 and 70. For details, see J. Zias and J. H. Charlesworth, "Crucifixion: Archaeology, Jesus, and the Dead Sea Scrolls," in *Jesus and the Dead Sea Scrolls*, ed. J. H. Charlesworth (New York: Doubleday, 1992), 273–89.

43 Arimathea, the birthplace of Samuel (1Sa 1:1), is probably to be identified with Ramathaim-Zophim, a village in the hill country of Ephraim about twenty miles north of Jerusalem.

44 At the end of v.44, some MSS have Pilate inquiring whether Jesus had "already" (ἤδη, *ēdē*) died (cf. NET, TEV, CEV, NKJV), while in others he asks whether Jesus has been dead "for a long time" (πάλαι, *palai*; cf. NIV, NASB). The MS evidence for the latter is slightly stronger.

45 The Greek word translated here as "body" (πτῶμα, *ptōma*) means "corpse," thus confirming that Jesus is indeed dead (cf. ESV, CSB). Some later MSS use the more common word for "body," σῶμα (*sōma*), which, of course, can also mean "corpse." Since "body" represents more natural English in this context, it is uncertain whether versions such as NLT, NIV, TEV, NET, etc. are following the reading σῶμα (*sōma*) or whether they are simply translating πτῶμα, *ptōma*, as "body."

46 Matthew alone narrates the sealing of the tomb and the posting of a guard at the instigation of the chief priests and Pharisees (27:62–66).

O. The Resurrection Announced (16:1–8)

OVERVIEW

The climax to Mark's gospel is the resurrection. Without it, the life and death of Jesus, though noble and admirable, are nonetheless overwhelmingly tragic events. With it, Jesus is declared to be the Son of God with power (Ro 1:4), and the disciples are transformed from lethargic and defeated followers into the fiery witnesses of the book of Acts. The good news about Jesus Christ is that God, through the resurrection of Jesus, defeated sin, death, and hell. It was this message that lay at the heart of the apostolic preaching.

All four gospels tell the story of the resurrection and do so with the same dignity and restraint they use in telling the story of the crucifixion. As the crucifixion was a historical event—something that actually happened at a specific time and place—so the tomb in which Jesus had been placed on Friday afternoon was actually found to be empty on the following Sunday morning. To this fact all four evangelists bear witness. The explanation of the historical event, unavailable to people apart from divine revelation, is given by the young man (whose white robe identifies him as an angelic being): "He has risen!" This word of revelation, the truth of the resurrection of Jesus, is the focal point in all four gospel accounts. Any claim that the resurrection was a fabrication (of Mt 27:62–65) or a delusion is implicitly denied.

That all four gospels also agree that a group of women discovered the empty tomb is significant, for women were not generally treated as reliable witnesses in first-century Judaism (cf. *m. Šebu.* 4:1; Josephus, *Ant.* 4.8.15 §219; Philo, *QG* 4:15). The gospels' agreement, therefore, is strong evidence for the historicity of this event. If the disciples had invented this story, they are unlikely to have made women the primary witnesses to the empty tomb.

1When the Sabbath was over, Mary Magdalene, Mary the mother of James, and Salome
bought spices so that they might go to anoint Jesus' body. 2Very early on the first day
of the week, just after sunrise, they were on their way to the tomb 3and they asked each
other, "Who will roll the stone away from the entrance of the tomb?"
4But when they looked up, they saw that the stone, which was very large, had been
rolled away. 5As they entered the tomb, they saw a young man dressed in a white robe sitting on the right side, and they were alarmed.
6"Don't be alarmed," he said. "You are looking for Jesus the Nazarene, who was crucified.
He has risen! He is not here. See the place where they laid him. 7But go, tell his disciples and
Peter, 'He is going ahead of you into Galilee. There you will see him, just as he told you.'"
8Trembling and bewildered, the women went out and fled from the tomb. They said
nothing to anyone, because they were afraid.

COMMENTARY

1 When the Sabbath was over (at about 6:00 p.m. on Saturday), the three women mentioned at the crucifixion (15:40), two of whom were also present at Jesus' burial (15:47), bought aromatic oils to anoint the body of Jesus. These oils were apparently additions to the spices and perfumes that were prepared before the Sabbath began (cf. Lk 23:56). The anointing was not for the purpose of preserving the body (as the Jews did not practice embalming) but was an act of love and devotion probably meant to reduce the stench of the decomposing body.

2 Since it would have been too dark to go to the tomb on Saturday night after the end of the Sabbath, the women waited until Sunday morning (the "first day of the week"). The expressions *lian prōi* ("very early") and *anateilantos tou hēliou* ("just after sunrise") present a problem, evidenced by the variation of readings that appear in the MS tradition. Ordinarily, "very early" would refer to the period before 6:00 a.m., when it would still be dark (cf. Jn 20:1); but used here with the expression "just after sunrise" it must mean the period of time immediately after the sun rose on Sunday morning.

3 As the women walked to the tomb, their chief concern was with the heavy stone they knew had been rolled in front of the opening of the tomb (cf. 15:46–47). Their concern was significant, for no matter what kind of stone it was, it would have been difficult to move. A circular stone disc, though relatively easy to put in place since usually it was set in a sloped track, once positioned was very difficult to remove. It would either have to be rolled back up the incline or lifted out of the groove and then removed. Any other kind of stone placed in front of the tomb's entrance would be as difficult or even more difficult to remove.

4–5 Mark makes no attempt to explain how the stone was removed. He only notes that it was very large and that it "had been rolled away" (v.4). The passive here may be a divine passive, indicating that God did it. Matthew gives more details by describing a great earthquake and an angel's descending from heaven to roll back the stone (28:2). Notice that the removal of the stone was not to allow the resurrection to take place—it had already occurred!—but to provide evidence that the tomb was now empty. Once inside the tomb, the women saw a young man (*neaniskos*) dressed in a white robe (v.5). His dress suggests he was an angel (cf. Ac 1:10; Rev 4:4), and though Mark does not explicitly identify him as such, Matthew 28:2 does. Cranfield's note, 465–66, on angels is worth repeating:

> It may be suggested that the purpose of the angel's presence at the tomb was to be the link between the actual event of the Resurrection and the women. Human eyes were not permitted to see the event of the Resurrection itself. But the angels as the constant witnesses of God's action saw it. So the angel's word to the women, 'He is risen,' is, as it were, the mirror in which men were allowed to see the reflection of this eschatological event.

The reaction of the women to the angel was what one would expect: "They were dumbfounded" (NEB, REB; NIV, "alarmed")—*ekthambeō*, a strong verb used only by Mark in the NT (9:15; 14:33).

6 The women's fright was calmed by words of reassurance: "Don't be alarmed." The angel knew whom they were seeking. These were Galilean women, and the mention of Jesus "the Nazarene" struck a familiar note in their memories (cf. 1:9, 24; 14:67). The angel then spoke the revelatory word "He has risen!" and invited them to see the evidence of the empty tomb. An empty tomb, however, only invites the question, What happened to the body of Jesus? There needed to be a word from God to interpret the meaning of the empty tomb, and the angel was God's gracious provision. The explanation is *resurrection*! Across the centuries many explanations have been proposed: the body of Jesus was stolen; the women came to the wrong tomb; Jesus did not actually die on the cross so he walked out of the tomb still alive; etc. Some of these proposals have enjoyed success with skeptics, yet none adequately reconcile the facts surrounding the event. The only reasonable explanation is still what the angel said to the women at the tomb on the first Easter morning: "He has risen!"

7 "Go, tell his disciples and Peter" reveals God's gracious provision for Peter. He is singled out because he had denied Jesus (14:66–72) and now needed reassurance that he was not excluded from the company of the disciples. Jesus had forgiven and restored him. Jesus had predicted not only the scattering of the sheep (14:27) but also their regathering in Galilee (14:28). What was the purpose of the meeting in Galilee? Jesus had done a large part of his work there. Perhaps he wanted to meet not only with the disciples but also with the community of believers in Galilee to give them his last instructions before his ascension.

Galilee was a fitting place for the launching of a Gentile mission. The contention of some scholars (e.g., Lohmeyer, Marxsen) that the reference to Galilee in 14:28 and here is to the parousia (the second coming) and not to a postresurrection appearance of Jesus has little to support it and has been largely rejected.

8 The confrontation with the angel proved to be too much for the women. They fled "trembling and bewildered." This reaction is understandable in the light of the empty tomb, the sudden angelic appearance, and the astonishing announcement. But Mark's next (and final) statement is surprising and disturbing for many readers: "They said nothing to anyone, because they were afraid." Here the gospel ends—at least in our earliest MSS. But did the women proclaim their message to the disciples (as in Matthew 28:8 and Luke 24:9)? Did the resurrected Lord appear to the women and to the other disciples? What about the restoration of Peter and the rest of Jesus' disciples who had deserted him?

One of the most perplexing and difficult issues concerning Mark's gospel is the abrupt and unusual nature of its ending. Two questions must be dealt with here. First, is the longer ending to Mark's gospel (vv.9–20, preserved in some MSS) authentic, i.e., did Mark himself write it, or was it added by a later hand? Second, if the longer ending is *not* original, did Mark intend to end his gospel at v.8, or was his original ending lost?

The first question is actually the easier one to answer. There is overwhelming evidence—both internal and external—that vv.9–20 were not composed by Mark. Their style and vocabulary are non-Markan, and their content is clearly secondary. This evidence, together with a discussion of two other spurious endings, is detailed in the Appendix (pp. 986–88).

The more difficult question is whether Mark intended to end his gospel at this point, or whether the original ending was somehow lost.

(1) Some commentators argue that the abrupt ending is intentional and fits well Mark's narrative purpose. Throughout the gospel, a sense of mystery and awe surrounds Jesus' identity, as characters in the story repeatedly ask, "Who is this?" and respond with wonder and amazement at Jesus' words and deeds. This same mystery surrounds the report of the resurrection. The women are not granted appearances by the resurrected Jesus but only the *announcement* that he is risen. The omission does not mean, of course, that the author doubts the resurrection. Jesus—always a reliable character in Mark's narrative—has repeatedly predicted his death *and resurrection* (8:31; 9:9; 9:31; 10:34) and has assured the disciples that after his resurrection he will meet them in Galilee (14:28). He has also affirmed that the gospel message will be proclaimed to all nations (13:10; 14:9). Mark is surely aware that Jesus' disciples saw him in Galilee, were restored in their leadership roles, and proclaimed the good news far and wide. So why does Mark not narrate resurrection appearances? According to this view, he intentionally leaves the readers in *the same position as the women at the tomb*—with the proclamation of the resurrection and a call to decision. Will Mark's readers respond with faith and action, or with fear and unbelief? Will they, like Jesus, stay faithful to God in the face of suffering and trials, or will they flee and deny him like the disciples? The abrupt ending of the gospel calls the reader to decision.

(2) Although there are staunch supporters of the view that it was Mark's intention to end his gospel at v.8, other commentators claim that the difficulties related to the present ending are too great. First, the early church clearly felt strongly that this ending was inadequate, as evidenced by the insertion of

both the shorter and longer endings (see Appendix, pp. 986–88). Second, it is surprising that a book that purports to be the "good news about Jesus Christ" should end portraying women stricken with fear (even allowing for Mark's emphasis on the awesomeness and mystery of Christ's person). Third, Mark repeatedly stresses the fulfillment of Jesus' predictions, so one would expect him to narrate the fulfillment of the predicted resurrection (8:31; 9:9, 31; 10:34), as well as the fulfillment of his promise to appear to Peter and the other disciples in Galilee (14:28; 16:7). Fourth, it is highly unusual (though not impossible) to end a sentence with *gar* ("for"), as v.8 ends in the Greek text. Fifth and finally, the claim that Mark intended to end his gospel as an implicit call to decision has been deemed too subtle and (post)modern for an ancient author such as Mark and for an audience more accustomed to a straightforward narrative presentation.

Although a decision on this issue is very difficult, with excellent scholars on both sides, the scale would seem to tip in favor of the second option, namely, that Mark did not intend to end his gospel at 16:8.

So what happened to the original ending? While it is possible that Mark was unable to complete his work—perhaps because of persecution or martyrdom—it seems more likely that the ending was lost before it was reproduced by copyists. A single page of papyrus could have come loose from the binding of the original codex, perhaps while the document was in transport.

What did the original ending contain? Gundry, 1021, suggests that it may have looked something like Matthew 28:9–10, 16–20 and Luke 24:9b–12 and included the women's report to the disciples, a resurrection appearance to the women, a visit to the tomb by Peter, an appearance to the eleven disciples in Galilee, and the Great Commission. This suggestion is plausible but remains speculative.

The uncertainties concerning the ending of this powerful and dramatic gospel can be disturbing to some Christians today. But this need not be so. It must be recognized that for Mark and his readers, the resurrection of Jesus was in no way in doubt; rather, it was an indisputable historical fact. Jesus himself—the hero of Mark's story and an absolutely trustworthy character throughout the narrative—has four times referred explicitly to his own resurrection (8:31; 9:31; 10:33; 14:28). Now, at the end of the gospel, an angel from God—an equally trustworthy character in Mark's drama—announces that this prediction has come true. Jesus is risen! (16:6); and his disciples will shortly see him in Galilee (16:7). From Mark's historical perspective, writing in the latter half of the first century AD, these resurrection appearances to the disciples in Galilee were not rumors or speculation but indisputable facts of history. Mark's faith, like the faith of his fellow believers, was based on the certain testimony of the apostles and many others who had seen Jesus alive (1Co 15:3–8). A missing page from a codex (if indeed it is missing) cannot silence the testimony of the multitude of eyewitnesses who went on to proclaim this message of hope and salvation throughout the whole world: "He is risen indeed!"

NOTES

2 In Codex D ἀνατέλλοντος (*anatellontos*, "while [the sun] was rising") in place of ἀνατείλαντος (*anateilantos*, "after [the sun] rose") solves the temporal problem but is obviously a copyist's emendation.

8 Among commentators who believe Mark intended to end his gospel at 16:8 are E. Lohmeyer, R. H. Lightfoot, William L. Lane, Morna D. Hooker, David E. Garland, and Ernest Best. For a detailed defense of this view on literary grounds, see J. L. Magness, *Sense and Absence: Structure and Suspension in the Ending of Mark's Gospel* (Atlanta: Scholars Press, 1986). Among those who think the ending was lost are C. E. B. Cranfield, Eduard Schweizer, Robert H. Gundry, R. T. France, Ben Witherington, and Craig Evans.

APPENDIX: THE LONGER ENDING (16:9–20)

9When Jesus rose early on the first day of the week, he appeared first to Mary
Magdalene, out of whom he had driven seven demons. 10She went and told those who
had been with him and who were mourning and weeping. 11When they heard that Jesus
was alive and that she had seen him, they did not believe it.
12Afterward Jesus appeared in a different form to two of them while they were walking
in the country. 13These returned and reported it to the rest; but they did not believe them
either.
14Later Jesus appeared to the Eleven as they were eating; he rebuked them for their
lack of faith and their stubborn refusal to believe those who had seen him after he had
risen.
15He said to them, "Go into all the world and preach the good news to all creation.
16Whoever believes and is baptized will be saved, but whoever does not believe will be
condemned. 17And these signs will accompany those who believe: In my name they will
drive out demons; they will speak in new tongues; 18they will pick up snakes with their
hands; and when they drink deadly poison, it will not hurt them at all; they will place their
hands on sick people, and they will get well."
19After the Lord Jesus had spoken to them, he was taken up into heaven and he sat at
the right hand of God. 20Then the disciples went out and preached everywhere, and the
Lord worked with them and confirmed his word by the signs that accompanied it.

COMMENTARY

9–20 The gospel of Mark actually has four different endings in the MS tradition (see Notes), but only two have any significant claim to authenticity: (1) the ending that concludes the gospel with v.8, and (2) the so-called longer ending (vv.9–20). Both the external and internal evidence weigh against the longer ending.

External Evidence. The two oldest Greek uncial MSS, ℵ and B, do not contain these verses. They are also absent from the Old Latin codex Bobiensis, the Sinaitic Syrian MS, about one hundred Armenian MSS, and the two oldest Georgian MSS (AD 897 and AD 913). Neither Clement of Alexandria nor Origen shows any knowledge of the existence of vv.9–20. Almost all the Greek copies of Mark known to Eusebius and Jerome did not contain these verses. The original form of the Eusebian sections makes no provision for numbering sections beyond 16:8. Some MSS that include the verses have scribal notes stating that they are absent in older Greek copies, and in other Greek MSS the verses are marked with obeli or asterisks to indicate they are spurious (see Metzger, 102–6).

In addition there are MSS and versions in which the shorter ending (followed by the longer ending) is found. B. B. Warfield (*An Introduction to the Textual Criticism of the New Testament* [New York: Whittaker, 1890], 200) correctly says, "The existence of the shorter conclusion ... is *a fortiori* evidence against the longer one. For no one doubts that this shorter conclusion is a spurious invention of the scribes; but it would not have been invented, save to fill the blank."

The great majority of MSS contain the longer ending. They include A C D K X W Δ Θ Π Ψ 099 0112 *f*[13] 28 33 et al. Irenaeus and Tatian's Diatessaron are the earliest patristic witnesses for the inclusion. Justin Martyr is uncertain. The external evidence seems to indicate that the longer ending was in circulation by the middle of the second century and was probably composed in the first half of the same century. Its inclusion in the TR and so in the KJV made this reading the "standard" in English Bibles until textual advances in the nineteenth and twentieth centuries. (For a scholarly defense of the longer ending, see W. R. Farmer, *The Last Twelve Verses of Mark* [Cambridge: Cambridge Univ. Press, 1974].)

Internal Evidence: Vocabulary. Many of the words in this section are non-Markan; i.e., they do not appear elsewhere in the gospel or they are used differently from the way Mark uses them elsewhere. In the Greek text there are 101 different words in vv.9–16 (167 words total). After disregarding unimportant words such as the definite article, connectives, proper names, etc., there remain 75 different significant words. Of these, 15 do not appear to this point in Mark, and 11 others are used in a sense different from typical Markan usage. These features mean that slightly over one-third of the words are "non-Markan." After due allowance is made for different subject matter requiring different vocabulary, it would seem that the marked difference in vocabulary between vv.9–20 and the rest of Mark's gospel makes it difficult to believe that they both came from the same author (see Metzger, 104; Bratcher and Nida, 519ff.).

Internal Evidence: Style. Here the argument against Markan authorship of vv.9–20 is even stronger. The connection between v.8 and vv.9–20 is abrupt and awkward. Verse 9 begins with the masculine nominative participle *anastas*, which demands for its antecedent "he," i.e., Jesus; but the subject of the last sentence of v.8 is the women, not Jesus. Mary Magdalene is referred to as though she had never been mentioned before; yet she appears three times in the crucifixion, burial, and resurrection narratives that immediately precede (15:40, 47; 16:1). It is also strange that the detail "out of whom he had driven seven demons" is for the first time mentioned here. Also, the women who were commissioned in v.7 to "go, tell his disciples and Peter" of Jesus' resurrection are not mentioned with Mary Magdalene in the longer ending. The angel at the tomb spoke of a postresurrection appearance to the disciples in Galilee, but in the longer ending Jesus' appearances are confined to Jerusalem and its immediate vicinity. All of these factors weigh heavily against the authenticity of these verses. To this evidence should be added the words of Bratcher and Nida, 520: "The narrative is concise and barren, lacking the vivid and lifelike details so characteristic of Markan historical narrative."

Internal Evidence: Content. Finally, the content of vv.9–20 appears to be a summary of postresurrection appearances from the other gospels. For example, Jesus' appearance to Mary Magdalene alone (vv.9–11) likely comes from John 20:11–18. The fact that Mary had been possessed by seven demons (v.9) is reported elsewhere only in Luke 8:2. The reluctance of the disciples to believe Mary's report (v.11) echoes Luke 24:11, and the appearance to two disciples on a journey (vv.12–13) is an abbreviated version of Luke's account of the disciples on the road to Emmaus (Lk 24:13–35). The ascension (v.19) is narrated briefly in Luke 24:51 and in more detail in Acts 1:9, but not in the other gospels.

There are also other content issues that suggest the material is non-Markan. The rebuke Jesus gives his disciples in v.14 is particularly severe—more severe than any he gives elsewhere in the gospel. Neither of the words used here—*apistia* ("without faith") and *sklērokardia* ("stubborn refusal to believe," "obtuseness")—is elsewhere used by Jesus of his disciples. Speaking in tongues (v.17) is not mentioned elsewhere in the gospels and seems to reflect the post-Pentecost situation of Acts (cf. Ac 2:3–4; 10:46; 19:6). The same may be said of the confirmation of the gospel through signs (vv.17, 20; cf. Ac 2:43; 4:30; 5:12; Heb 2:4). Until this passage, confirmatory "signs" (*sēmeia*) have been referred to only negatively in Mark's gospel—they are demanded by those without faith (Mk 8:11–12; 13:4, 22). Luke 10:19 speaks of trampling on snakes but not of picking them up with one's hands (v.18; cf. Ac 28:3–6). The drinking of poison without harm is unknown in the NT. (Superstitious use of this verse has given rise to the snake-handling and poison-drinking sects of, most notably, Appalachia.) Anointing the sick with oil is mentioned in 6:13, but no laying on of hands by the apostles occurs in the gospels. Paul, however, lays hands on Publius's sick father (cf. Ac 28:8). There is nothing like v.20 in any of the gospels. It sounds more like a summary of the activities of the apostles from the book of Acts.

In sum, it seems highly unlikely that vv.9–20 were an original part of the gospel. The vast majority of scholars reject their authenticity.

NOTES

9–20 In addition to MSS ending at 16:8 and those that include vv.9–20, there are two others endings in the MS tradition, although neither have any realistic claim to authenticity:

(1) A shorter ending, which reads: "But they reported briefly to Peter and those with him all that they had been told. And after this Jesus himself sent out by means of them, from east to west, the sacred and imperishable proclamation of eternal salvation." This reading appears in four uncial MSS of the seventh, eighth, and ninth centuries (L Ψ 099 0112), Old Latin k, the margin of the Harclean Syriac, several Sahidic and Bohairic MSS, and a good number of Ethiopian MSS. All of them, except k, then continue with vv.9–20. Both the external and internal evidence are clearly against the authenticity of this ending. It seems to be either an attempt to provide an ending in itself or to provide a smoother transition between v.8 and v.9.

(2) An interpolation that occurs after v.14 of the longer ending in one Greek MS, Washingtonianus (also called Freer addition, designated W), which reads:

And they excused themselves, saying, "This age of lawlessness and unbelief is under Satan, who does not allow the truth and power of God to prevail over the unclean things of the spirits. Therefore, reveal thy righteousness now"—thus they spoke to Christ. And Christ replied to them, "The term of years of Satan's power has been fulfilled, but other terrible things draw near. And for those who have sinned I was delivered over to death, that they may return to the truth and sin no more, in order that they may inherit the spiritual and incorruptible glory of righteousness which is in heaven."

Appearing in only one Greek MS, this ending is clearly not a part of Mark's gospel; it was probably inserted at this point to tone down the severe condemnation of the disciples in v.14 and to provide a smoother transition to v.15.